Book Number _____

Enter information in spaces below as instructed.

THIS BOOK IS THE PROPERTY OF:

State _____

Province _____

County _____

Parish _____

School District _____

Other _____

Issued To	Year Used	Condition	
		Issued	Returned
_____	_____	_____	
_____	_____	_____	
_____	_____	_____	
_____	_____	_____	
_____	_____	_____	
_____	_____	_____	
_____	_____	_____	
_____	_____	_____	
_____	_____	_____	

◊ **Follett**

Follett School Solutions, Inc.
1433 Internationale Parkway
Woodridge, IL 60517-4941
Phone (800) 621-4272
www.fes.follett.com

16e

Managing Human Resources

Scott Snell

Professor of Business Administration,
University of Virginia

George Bohlander

Professor Emeritus of Management,
Arizona State University

SOUTH-WESTERN
CENGAGE Learning·

Australia • Brazil • Japan • Korea • Mexico • Singapore • Spain • United Kingdom • United States

SOUTH-WESTERN
CENGAGE Learning·

Managing Human Resources, Sixteenth Edition
Scott Snell and George Bohlander

Vice President of Editorial, Business:
Jack W. Calhoun

Senior Acquisitions Editor: Michele Rhoades

Developmental Editor: Jennifer King

Editorial Assistant: Tamera Grega

Marketing Manager: Gretchen Swann

Marketing Coordinator: Leigh Smith

Senior Marketing Communications
Manager: Jim Overly

Senior Art Director: Tippy McIntosh

Rights Acquisitions Specialist:
Sam A. Marshall

Rights Acquisitions Director:
Audrey Pettengill

Manufacturing Planner:
Ron Montgomery

Production Manager: Kim Kusnerak

Media Editor: John Rich

Interior Design, Production Management,
and Composition: PreMediaGlobal

Cover Designer:
Grannan Graphic Design, Ltd.

Cover Image: ©Diana Ong, Fotosearch

For product information and technology assistance, contact us at
Cengage Learning Customer & Sales Support, 1-800-354-9706

For permission to use material from this text or product,
submit all requests online at **www.cengage.com/permissions**
Further permissions questions can be emailed to
permissionrequest@cengage.com

Library of Congress Control Number: 2011939722

Student Edition ISBN 13: 978-1-111-53282-6

Student Edition ISBN 10: 1-111-53282-6

South-Western
5191 Natorp Boulevard
Mason, OH 45040
USA

Cengage Learning is a leading provider of customized learning solutions with office locations around the globe, including Singapore, the United Kingdom, Australia, Mexico, Brazil, and Japan. Locate your local office at: **international.cengage.com/region**

Cengage Learning products are represented in Canada by Nelson Education, Ltd.

For your course and learning solutions, visit **www.cengage.com**

Purchase any of our products at your local college store or at our preferred online store **www.cengagebrain.com**

Printed in Canada
1 2 3 4 5 6 7 15 14 13 12 11

Brief Contents

Contents

©Diana Ong, Fotosearch

Part 2   Meeting Human Resources Requirements

Part 3   Developing Effectiveness in Human Resources

Part 4   Implementing Compensation and Security

Part 5   Enhancing Employee-Management Relations

Part 6 Expanding Human Resources Management Horizons

Preface

©Diana Ong. Fotosearch

The 16th edition of *Managing Human Resources* will place your students at the forefront of understanding how organizations can gain a sustainable competitive advantage through people. The role of HR managers is no longer limited to service functions such as recruiting, payroll, and benefits. Today, HR managers assume an active role in the strategic planning and decision making within their organizations. Those managers who are good at it can have a major impact on the success of their firms while elevating the practice of human resources in terms of its importance in the C-suites of their organizations. And human resource management is not limited to the HR staff. The best organizations recognize that managing people is the job of every manager, working in partnership with HR.

Each edition of the book highlights the ways in which the environment for managing human resources is changing somewhat, but reveals that the goal of utilizing an organization's talent in the best way possible never changes. Consequently, the purpose of this book is always two-fold: (1) To equip students with the tools and practices of human resources management and an appreciation for the changes they can effect by understanding how best to manage people, and (2) to present the most current challenges and opportunities graduating students will face when it comes to today's human resource management environment. These challenges exist both for those who will become HR managers and those who will go on to become other types of managers.

Toward that end, the first chapter of the book lays out in broad terms the key challenges in HRM today. It includes a discussion of the HR strategies pursued by firms in the face of the latest economic downturn and the importance of retaining and motivating employees in the process. Other aspects broached include healthcare reform laws and some of the strategies companies are using to continue attempting to control healthcare costs; how social media is affecting human resources management and employees' privacy rights in this regard; and a new discussion on how good human resources practices can help a firm achieve its corporate social responsibility and sustainability goals, making it an "employer of choice." The chapter also discusses the important partnership with line managers and the competencies required of HR management. The textbook continues with the introduction, explanation, and discussion of the individual practices and policies that make up HRM. We recognize the manager's changing role, and emphasize current issues and real-world problems and the policies and practices of HRM used to meet them.

Strategy and talent have become such central concerns of HR today that we continue to emphasize the topic in this edition of the book in Chapter 2. Chapter 5 focuses on expanding and managing the talent pool in organizations. The detailed coverage of these topics solidifies *Managing Human Resources* as perhaps the premier text for thought leadership, especially the global talent pool. Employee diversity and how firms can leverage all types of differences among their workers to their strategic advantage are examined.

Organizations in today's competitive world are discovering that it is *how* the individual HR topics are combined that makes all the difference. Managers typically don't focus on HR issues such as staffing, training, and compensation in isolation from one another. Each of these HR practices should be combined into an overall system—one that enhances employee involvement and productivity. *Managing Human Resources* ends with a final chapter that focuses on the development of high-performance work systems (HPWS). We outline the various components of the systems, including workflow design, HR practices, management processes, and supporting technologies. We also discuss the strategic processes used to implement high-performance work systems and the outcomes that benefit both the employee and the organization as a whole.

What's New in the 16th Edition

A great deal of new information is provided in this revision to accurately reflect HRM in today's business world and help the reader understand today's HRM issues more effectively.

Perhaps the most significant new feature in this edition is the new "Small Business Application" boxes. These boxes are designed to help entrepreneurs and small business owners and managers think about how to organize, implement, and leverage talent, and draws attention to resources designed especially for them to do so. We felt this was important because many students today are very interested in entrepreneurship and will go on to found their own businesses. Moreover, small businesses provide most of America's jobs to workers.

Global and international HR concerns, in particular, are covered in more detail in this edition. Today these issues are increasingly seen as "front and center" in many organizations. They include the issues surrounding multinationals, joint ventures, and the World Trade Organization; low-wage, high-growth countries such as China and India; the talent shortage and work-visa challenges facing U.S. firms since 9/11; and global rights issues such as data protection, intellectual and property rights, and the International Labor Organization's decent work agenda and efforts to promote fairness among countries as they globalize.

Of course, the 16th edition also includes a complete update of all laws, administrative rulings and guidelines, and court decisions governing HRM . There are also 14 new end-of-chapter case studies highlighting chapter content, and four new extended cases are included at the end of the book. The cases have been carefully selected to reflect current issues in managing human resources, and explore the important topics of HRM. Among the topics included are ethics and virtual HR practices; global and cultural issues; employee diversity and workforce mobility; hiring, training, onboarding, and downsizing; wrongful discharge issues; performance appraisals; and the arbitration of employee complaints.

Lastly, in addition to the changes we have already mentioned, to help instructors incorporate the new material discussed into their courses, the following is a list of major chapter-by-chapter additions:

Chapter 1

- A new discussion on retaining and motivating employees in the face of downsizings and economic downturns and better workforce planning so layoffs can be avoided in the first place.

- A new discussion on nearshoring, which is the process of moving jobs closer to one's home country.

- A new discussion on U.S. visa restrictions and immigration backlash and how firms are coping with the tightening supply of talented foreign workers.

Chapter 2

- A new discussion on the quality-of-fill metric, which attempts to measure how well new hires are performing so the company will have enough top performers to propel it towards its strategic objectives.

- A new discussion on how HR managers can significantly enhance their worth to their organizations if by effectively gathering informal information, or "intelligence," about the strategic and HRM practices of their competitors.

Chapter 3

- An expanded discussion of religious expression in the workplace and reasonable accommodation.

- An expanded discussion of the Older Workers' Benefit Protection Act

- The addition of two new acts: The Lily Ledbetter Fair Pay Act and Don't Ask Don't Tell Repeal Act.

- Additional discussion of the federal E-Verify citizenship verification systems and the companies that must use it.

- The addition of the EEOC's position on caregivers and discrimination.

- A discussion of the Supreme Court ruling in *Ricci vs. DeStafano* and its effect on promotion policies and affirmative action programs.

Chapter 4

- The addition of workflow redesign as it relates to job analysis.

- The addition of a job analysis questionnaire.

- A new discussion of dejobbing, which refers to a process of structuring organizations not around jobs but around projects that are constantly changing.

Chapter 5

- A new discussion on employee profiling, which involves surveying a firm's top performers about what they like to do, what events they attend, and how they like to be contacted and recruited. Similar candidates can then be recruited using this information.

- A new section on the strategic aspects of recruiting—how the recruiting should reflect a firm's competitive priorities, who should do the recruiting, where and how.

- A new section on employer branding and recruiting and using social networks, blogs, and philanthropic activities to improve a company's HR brand.

- New information on mobile recruiting, the process of recruiting candidates via their mobile devices using text messages and applications for Linked In, Twitter, and so forth.

- New info on job fairs and virtual job fairs.

- New information on employee referral software, which makes it easier for current employees to recommend applicants.

- New info on re-recruiting and "alumni networks." Re-recruiting is the process of keeping track of and maintaining relationships with former employees to see if they would be willing to return to the firm.

- A section on improving the effectiveness of internships.

Chapter 6

- A new section on initial screening resumes and applications and checklist for doing so.

- A new discussion on video resumes.

- New discussions on sequential interviews and phone interviews.

- The addition of a candidate evaluation form.

- A new discussion on making job offers and rejecting candidates.

Chapter 7

- New sections on employer-provided tuition assistance and corporate universities.

- A new section on onboarding.

Chapter 8

- A new section on providing ongoing performance feedback as a management tool.

- New information on focal performance appraisals and its pros and cons.

Chapter 9

- New section on compensation scorecards.

- Discussion of the financial crisis of 2008–2010 and how it has changed the landscape for compensation.

- New laws regarding compensation.

- Updated text to address issues related more to service workers and professionals.

- Increased ease and steps introduced to using job evaluations for compensation decisions.

Chapter 10

- Do's and don'ts for different types of performance-based incentives.

- New research on pay for star employees.

- How companies should proceed with caution to use pay-for-performance.

- Discussion of bonuses based on new research by the RAND corporation.

- CEO and executive pay concerns in the media and in companies.

Chapter 11

- A new section on the strategic benefits planning and gathering competitive benefit information.

- A new section on the benefits mandated by the passage of the Patient Protection and Affordable Care Act (PPACA).

- An expanded discussion on containing medical benefits costs and value-based health initiatives, which involve looking at the medical care their employees most use and need and target benefits and health programs toward them.

- A new section on the rise in the popularity of sabbaticals as a benefit.

- A new discussion of phased retirement.

- An updated discussion on domestic partner benefits.

- Expanded information on educational assistance and new information on employer-provided 529 programs.

Chapter 12

- A new section on the practice of interviewing applicants for safety.

- A new discussion on employee engagement and safety.

- New sections on employee fatigue and distracted driving.

- The addition of a sample HR policy on distracted driving.

- A new section on workplace emergencies and emergency action plans.

- The addition of an emergency-readiness checklist for firms.

Chapter 13

- New information on text messages and employees' privacy rights. and updated information on court rulings related to employees' e-mail privacy, the use of social networks, Internet postings, and computer use.

- The addition of a sample electronic communications privacy policy.

- An expanded section on HR's responsibility for safeguarding employee information and the best practices for doing so.

Chapter 14

- New collective bargaining agreements.

- Address issues faced by collective bargaining for public employees.

- Highlight on a timeline of government involvement in American labor relations.

- New section on union avoidance practices.
- New section on recent trends in union membership.

Chapter 15

- Reorganized chapter starting with a new discussion of the global environment and the similarities and differences across countries.
- New section of business services vs. manufacturing from an HR perspective.
- New discussion of integrated technology platforms as a tool for global HR.
- New section of employee selection practices in emerging markets.
- Discussion of new research on expatriate management and the importance of cultural understanding.
- Discussion of the role of civil society in improving employment conditions in emerging markets.

Chapter 16

- A new section on providing ongoing performance feedback as a management tool.
- New information on focal performance appraisals and its pros and cons.

Features of the Book

Designed to facilitate understanding and retention of the material presented, each chapter contains the following pedagogical features:

- **Learning Outcomes** listed at the beginning of each chapter provide the basis for the Integrated Learning System. Each Outcome is also listed in the margin of the chapter in which it appears, along with a thought-provoking question designed to get students thinking about how the related content applies to them personally. The outcomes are revisited in the chapter summary and discussion questions and in all of the book's ancillaries.

- **Highlights in HRM.** This popular boxed feature provides real-world examples of how organizations perform HR functions. The Highlights are introduced in the text discussion and include topics such as small businesses and international issues.

- **Key Terms** appear in boldface and are defined in margin notes next to the text discussion. The Key Terms are also listed at the end of the chapter and appear in the glossary at the end of the text.

- **Figures.** An abundance of graphic materials and flowcharts provides a visual, dynamic presentation of concepts and HR activities. All figures are systematically referenced in the text discussion.

- **Summary.** A paragraph or two for each Learning Outcome provides a brief and focused review of the chapter.

- **Discussion questions** following the chapter summary offer an opportunity to focus on each of the Learning Outcomes in the chapter and stimulate critical thinking. Many of these questions allow for group analysis and class discussion.

- **HRM Experience.** An experiential activity (described earlier) is included in each chapter.

- **End-of-chapter cases.** Two or more case studies per chapter present current HRM issues in real-life settings that allow for student consideration and critical analysis.

- **Extended cases.** Eleven extended cases are provided at the end of the main text. These cases use material covered in more than one text chapter and provide capstone opportunities.

Ancillary Teaching and Learning Materials
For Students

- **Study Guide to Accompany *Managing Human Resources*.** John Bowen of Ohio State University, Newark, and Columbus State Community College has revised the Study Guide. His years of HRM teaching experience allow him to bring a special insight to this popular student supplement. It includes review questions that can be used to check understanding and prepare for examinations on each chapter in this textbook. Using the Integrated Learning System, *Study Guide* questions are arranged by chapter learning objective so the student can quickly refer to the textbook if further review is needed.

- **CourseMate.** Complement your text and course content with study and practice materials. Management CourseMate brings course concepts to life with a wealth of interactive learning, study, and exam preparation tools including flashcards, interactive exercises, learning games, internet activities, audio PowerPoint lectures, and quizzes. Watch your comprehension soar as you work with the printed textbook and the textbook-specific website.

For Instructors
The following instructor support materials are available to adopters from your South-Western Cengage Representative, from the Academic Resource Center at 800-423-0563, or through http://www.cengagebrain.com. All printed ancillary materials were prepared by or under the direction of the text authors to guarantee full integration with the text. Multimedia supplements were prepared by experts in those fields.

- **Instructor's Resource CD.** The *Instructor's Resource Guide* contains all of your core teaching resources in one easy-to-use location:
  - *Instructor's Resource Guide.* Prepared by the text authors and updated by John Bowen of Ohio State University, Newark, and Columbus State Community College for each chapter in the textbook, the *Instructor's Resource Guide* contains a chapter synopsis and learning objectives; a very detailed lecture outline; answers to the end-of-chapter discussion questions and case studies; solutions to the extended cases in the textbook; and suggested answers for the chapter video exercises.

- ⁺ *Teaching Assistance Manual.* New to this edition, and also updated by John Bowen, the Teaching Assistance Manual provides additional teaching aids such as *Generating Interest* discussion topics, *Dealing With Trouble Spots* features that provide resources to address challenges, and *Involving Students* sections that suggest activities and resources.
- ⁺ **Test Bank.** The test bank has been updated by Dr. Robert McDonald of Franciscan University. Each test bank chapter provides more than 100 questions, all tagged bylearning objective, AACSB standards, and Bloom's taxonomy. There are true/false, multiple-choice, and essay items for each chapter. **ExamView**^{TM} **Test Bank.** ExamViewTM testing software contains all the questions from the test bank and allows the instructor to edit, add, delete, or randomly mix questions for customized tests.
- ⁺ **PowerPoint**^{TM} **Presentation Slides.** Completely revised and updated by Larry Flick, these presentation slides will add color and interest to lectures.

- ■ **On the Job Video Cases DVD.** This video collection features both small and large companies with innovative HR practices, many of which have been recognized for their excellence in HR practices.

- ■ **JoinIn**^{TM} on **TurningPoint**®. Combined with your choice of several leading keypad systems, JoinIn turns your ordinary PowerPoint® application into powerful audience response software. With just a click on a handheld device, your students can respond to multiple-choice questions, short polls, interactive exercises, and peer review questions. You can take attendance, check student comprehension of difficult concepts, collect student demographics to better assess student needs, and even administer quizzes without collecting papers or grading. In addition, we provide interactive text-specific slide sets that you can modify and merge with any existing PowerPoint lecture slides for a seamless classroom presentation.

- ■ **CourseMate.** Snell/Bohlander *Managing Human Resource 16e* includes Management CourseMate, which helps you make the grade by providing study and practice materials. Management CourseMate brings course concepts to life with a wealth of interactive learning, study, and exam preparation tools including an interactive eBook with note taking and search capabilities, flashcards, interactive exercises, learning games, internet activities, audio PowerPoint lectures, and quizzes. Watch student comprehension soar as your class works with the printed textbook and the textbook-specific website.

- ■ **CengageNOW.** CengageNOW is an online teaching and learning resource that gives you more control in less time & delivers better outcomes – NOW. Designed by instructors for instructors, this easy-to-use online resource saves you time with resources that mirror the way you teach. Easily prepare lectures, create assignments and quizzes, grade, and tracking student progress with CenageNOW^{TM}. This premium engagement tool also includes videos, Personalized Study Plans, and assignable visual learning outcome summaries **WebTutor**^{TM}. WebTutor is used by an entire class under the direction of the instructor and is particularly convenient for distance learning courses. It provides students with Web-based learning resources, such as flashcards, interactive exercises, learning games, internet activities, audio PowerPoint lectures, and quizzes, well as powerful communication and other course management tools, including course calendar, chat, and e-mail for instructors. WebTutor is available on WebCT and Blackboard.

- **Aplia.** Engage, prepare, and educate your students with this ideal online learning solution. **Aplia's**™ management solution ensures that students stay on top of their coursework with regularly scheduled homework assignments and automatic grading with detailed, immediate feedback on every question. Interactive teaching tools and content further increase engagement and understanding. **Aplia** assignments match the language, style, and structure of *Managing Human Resources*, 16e, allowing your students to apply what they learn in the text directly to their homework. For more information, visit HYPERLINK "http://www .cengage.com/aplia"www.cengage.com/aplia.

- *Managing Human Resources, 16e* **Support Web Site.** The www.cengagebrain.com website provides learning and teaching resources and support for instructors.

Acknowledgments

Because preparation of manuscript for a project as large as *Managing Human Resources* is a continuing process, we would like to acknowledge the work of those colleagues who provided thoughtful feedback for this and the previous editions of the text. We were fortunate to have the results of an extensive survey whose participants offered suggestions based on their actual use of this and other texts in their courses, as well as the careful evaluations of our colleagues. Our appreciation and thanks go to:

Steve Ash, University of Akron
Michael Bedell, California State University, Bakersfield
Brad Bell, Cornell University
Mary Connerley, Virginia Tech University
Susie Cox, McNeese State University
Paula S. Daly, James Madison University
Sharon Davis, Central Texas College
Douglas Dierking, University of Texas, Austin
Suzanne Dyer-Gear, Carroll Community College
Joe J. Eassa, Jr., Palm Beach Atlantic University
Robert E. Ettl, SUNY Stony Brook
Diane Fagan, Webster University
Angela L. Farrar, University of Nevada, Las Vegas
Lou Firenze, Northwood University
Olene L. Fuller, San Jacinto College
Judith Gordon, Boston College
Mike Griffith, Cascade College
Daniel Grundmann, Indiana University
Xuguang Guo, University of Wisconsin, Whitewater
Sally Hackman, Central Methodist College
Rich Havranek, SUNY Institute of Technology
Kim Hester, Arkansas State University

Stephen Hiatt, Catawba College
Alyce Hochhalter, St. Mary Woods College
Madison Holloway, Metropolitan State College of Denver
David J. Hudson, Spalding University
Barbara Luck, Jackson Community College
Avan Jassawalla, SUNY at Geneseo
Pravin Kamdar, Cardinal Stritch University
Cheryl L. Kane, University of North Carolina Charlotte
Jordan J. Kaplan, Long Island University
Steve Karau, Southern Illinois University at Carbondale
Joseph Kavanaugh, Sam Houston State University
John Kelley, Villanova University
Dennis Lee Kovach, Community College of Allegheny County
Kenneth Kovach, University of Maryland
Chalmer E. Labig, Jr., Oklahoma State University
Alecia N. Lawrence, Williamsburg Technical College
Scott W. Lester, University of Wisconsin, Eau Claire
J. Jonathan Lewis, Texas Southern University
Beverly Loach, Central Piedmont Community College
L. M. Lockhart, Penn State Greater Allegheny
Gloria Lopez, New Mexico Highlands University
Larry Maes, Davenport University
Jennifer Malfitano, Delaware County Community College
Michael Matukonis, SUNY Oneonta
Doug McCabe, Georgetown University
Lee McCain, Seminole Community College
Marjorie L. McInerney, Marshall University
Veronica Meyers, San Diego State University
Robert T. Mooney, Texas State University
Julia Morrison, Bloomfield College
Harold Nolan, Georgian Court University
David Nye, Kennedy-Western University
Paul Olsen, Saint Michael's College
Donald Otto, Lindenwood University
Charles Parsons, Georgia Institute of Technology
Dane Partridge, University of Southern Indiana
Bryan J. Pesta, Cleveland State University
David Pitts, Delaware Technical and Community College
Alex Pomnichowski, Ferris State University
Victor Prosper, University of the Incarnate Word
Michael Raphael, Central Connecticut State University
Charles Rarick, Barry University
June Roux, Salem Community College
Robert Rustic, University of Findlay
Laura L. Sankovich, Capella University
Kelli Schutte, Calvin College

Mike Sciarini, Michigan State University
Tom Sedwick, Indiana University of Pennsylvania
Jim Sethi, University of Montana Western
Patricia Setlik, William Rainey Harper College
William L. Smith, Emporia State University
Emeric Solymossy, Western Illinois University
Howard Stanger, Canisius College
Scott L. Stevens, Detroit College of Business
Michael Sturman, Cornell University
Nanette Swarthout, Fontbonne College
Michael T. Korns, Indiana University of PA
Karen Ann Tarnoff, East Tennessee State University
Thomas Taveggia, University of Arizona
Donna Testa, Herkimer County Community College
Alan Tillquist, West Virginia State College
Sue Toombs, Weatherford College
Richard Trotter, University of Baltimore
William Turnley, Kansas State University
Catherine L. Tyler, Oakland University
Harvell Walker, Texas Tech University
Barbara Warschawski, Schenectady County Community College
Steve Werner, University of Houston
Liesl Wesson, Texas A&M University
JoAnn Wiggins, Walla Walla University
Jim Wilkinson, Stark State College
L. A. Witt, University of New Orleans
Evelyn Zent, University of Washington, Tacoma
Ryan Zimmerman, Texas A&M University

In the manuscript for this edition, we have drawn not only on the current literature but also on the current practices of organizations that furnished information and illustrations relating to their HR programs. We are indebted to the leaders in the field who have developed the available heritage of information and practices of HRM and who have influenced us through their writings and personal associations. We have also been aided by students in our classes, by former students, by the participants in the management development programs with whom we have been associated, by HR managers, and by our colleagues. In particular, we would like to express our appreciation to Shad Morris at The Ohio State University, Dorothy Galvez and Amy Ray for their helpful insights and support for this edition of the text. We appreciate the efforts of everyone at Cengage who helped to develop and produce this text and its supplements. They include Michele Rhoades, Senior Acquisitions Editor; Jennifer King, Developmental Editor; Gretchen Swann, Marketing Manager; Leigh T. Smith, Marketing Coordinator; Jim Overly, Senior Marketing Communications Manager; Joseph Malcolm, Project Manager; Tippy McIntosh, Senior Art Director; John Rich, Media Editor; and Tamara Grega, Editorial Assistant.

Our greatest indebtedness is to our wives—Ronnie Bohlander and Marybeth Snell—who have contributed in so many ways to this book over the years. They are always sources of invaluable guidance and assistance. Furthermore, by their continued enthusiasm and support, they have made the process a more pleasant and rewarding experience. We are most grateful to them for their many contributions to this publication, to our lives, and to our families.

Scott A. Snell
University of Virginia

George W. Bohlander
Arizona State University

About the Authors

Scott Snell

Scott Snell is the E. Thayer Bigelow Professor of Business Administration at the University of Virginia's Darden Graduate School of Business. He teaches courses in Leadership, Strategic Management, and Developing Organizational Capability. His research focuses on strategic human resource management, and he was recently listed among the top 150 most-cited authors in the field of management. He is co-author of four books: *Management: Leading and Collaborating in a Competitive World*, *M: Management*, *Managing Human Resources*, and *Managing People and Knowledge in Professional Service Firms*. His research has been published in number of journals such as the *Academy of Management Journal*, *Academy of Management Review*, *Strategic Management Journal*, *Journal of Management*, *Journal of Management Studies*, and *Human Resource Management*, and he has served on the boards of the Society for Human Resource Management Foundation, the Academy of Management's Human Resource Division, the *Human Resource Management Journal*, *the Academy of Management Journal* and the *Academy of Management Review*. Scott has worked with companies such as AstraZeneca, Deutsche Telekom, Shell, and United Technologies to align investments in talent and strategic capability. Prior to joining the Darden faculty in 2007, Scott was professor and director of executive education at Cornell University's Center for Advanced Human Resource Studies and a professor of management in the Smeal College of Business at Pennsylvania State University. He received a B.A. in psychology from Miami University, as well as M.B.A. and Ph.D. degrees in business administration from Michigan State University.

George Bohlander

George Bohlander is Professor Emeritus of Management at Arizona State University (ASU). He received his MBA from the University of Southern California and his PhD from the University of California at Los Angeles. His areas of expertise include employment law, Compensation work teams, public policy, and labor relations. He has received the Outstanding Undergraduate Teaching Excellence Award presented by the College of Business at ASU and also received the prestigious ASU Parents Association Professorship for his contributions to students and teaching.

Dr. Bohlander is an active researcher and author. He has published over 50 articles and monographs in professional and practitioner journals such as *National Productivity Review*, *HR Magazine*, *Labor Law Journal*, *The Journal of Collective Bargaining in the Public Sector*, and others. Dr. Bohlander continues to be a consultant to public and private organizations including the U.S. Postal Service, BFGoodrich, McDonnell Douglas, Banner Health Services, and Del Webb. He is also an active labor arbitrator.

1

The Challenge of Human Resources Management

After studying this chapter, you should be able to

LEARNING OUTCOME 1 Explain how human resources managers can help their firms gain a sustainable competitive advantage through the strategic utilization of people.

LEARNING OUTCOME 2 Explain how globalization affects human resources management.

LEARNING OUTCOME 3 Explain how good human resources practices can help a firm achieve its corporate social responsibility and sustainability goals.

LEARNING OUTCOME 4 Describe how technology can improve how people perform and are managed.

LEARNING OUTCOME 5 Discuss how cost pressures affect human resources management policies.

LEARNING OUTCOME 6 Discuss how firms can leverage employee differences to their strategic advantage.

LEARNING OUTCOME 7 Explain how educational and cultural changes in the workforce are affecting human resources management.

LEARNING OUTCOME 8 Provide examples of the roles and competencies of today's HR managers.

We use a lot of words to describe how important people are to organizations. The terms *human resources, human capital, intellectual assets,* and *talent management* imply that it is people who drive the performance of their organizations (along with other resources such as money, materials, and information). Successful organizations are particularly adept at bringing together different kinds of people to achieve a common purpose. This is the essence of human resources management (HRM). Human resources management involves a wide variety of activities, including analyzing a company's competitive environment and designing jobs so a firm's strategy can be successfully implemented to beat the competition. This, in turn, requires identifying, recruiting, and selecting the right people for those jobs; training, motivating, and appraising these people; developing competitive compensation policies to retain them, and grooming them to lead the organization in the future—and the list goes on.

human resources management (HRM)

The process of managing human talent to achieve an organization's objectives

Why Study Human Resources Management?

Why should you study human resources management? You might be wondering how the topic relates to your interests and career aspirations. Suppose you want the opportunity to manage people, either for another a firm or one you start yourself. Having a good understanding of human resources management is important for managers and entrepreneurs of all types—not just human resources (HR) personnel. All managers are responsible for at least some of the activities that fall into the category of human resources management. Managers play a key role in selecting employees, training and motivating them, appraising them, promoting them, and so forth.

What if you do a poor job of these activities? Believe it or not, many businesspeople with great business strategies, business plans, and products and services fail because they do not fully grasp the importance of human resources management. Laments one entrepreneur: "My first year after investing in a small business that was failing, I tripled the amount of business that company did, and made a lot of money. But I didn't pay my personnel enough or motivate them. They eventually abandoned me, and a larger competitor muscled me out of the marketplace. I now understand the important role personnel play in a business. They can make or break it."

In addition, great business plans and products and services can easily be copied by your competitors. Great personnel cannot. Their knowledge and abilities are among the most distinctive and renewable resources upon which a company can draw. As Thomas J. Watson, the founder of IBM, said, "You can get capital and erect buildings, but it takes people to build a business."[1]

Human Capital and HRM

human capital

The knowledge, skills, and capabilities of individuals that have economic value to an organization

The idea that organizations "compete through people" highlights the fact that achieving success increasingly depends on an organization's ability to manage talent, or human capital. The term *human capital* describes the economic value of employees' knowledge, skills, and capabilities. Although the value of these assets might not show up directly on a company's balance sheet, it nevertheless has tremendous impact on an organization's performance. The following quotations from notable CEOs and former CEOs illustrate this point:[2]

- "If you look at our semiconductors and melt them down for silicon, that's a tiny fraction of the costs. The rest is intellect and mistakes." (Gordon Moore, Intel)

- "An organization's ability to learn, and translate that learning into action rapidly, is the ultimate competitive business advantage." (Jack Welch, General Electric)

- "Successful companies of the twenty-first century will be those who do the best jobs of capturing, storing, and leveraging what their employees know." (Lew Platt, Hewlett-Packard)

Human capital is intangible and cannot be managed the way organizations manage jobs, products, and technologies. One reason why is because employees, *not* the organization, own their own human capital. If valued employees leave a company, they take their human capital with them, and any investment the company has made in training and developing these people is lost.

To build human capital in organizations, managers must continue to develop superior knowledge, skills, and experience within their workforces and retain and promote top performers.[3] Beyond the need to invest in employee development, organizations have to find ways to better utilize the knowledge of their workers. Too often employees have knowledge that goes unused. As Dave Ulrich, a professor of business at the University of Michigan, notes: "Learning capability is *g* times *g*—a business's ability to *generate* new ideas multiplied by its adeptness at *generalizing* them throughout the company."[4]

Human resources management and programs are often the conduit through which knowledge is developed and transferred among employees. A survey by the Human Resource Planning Society revealed that 65 percent of responding companies believed that their HR groups play a key role in developing human capital. Arvinder Dhesi, the head of talent for the insurance company Aviva, explains that his firm's goal is to treat *everyone* as talent and not just focus on a few. "We talk about the sum of people's

Staffing programs focus on identifying, recruiting, and hiring the best and the brightest talent available. A jobs fair is one resource, and often brings in many applicants for few positions.

Frances Roberts/Alamy

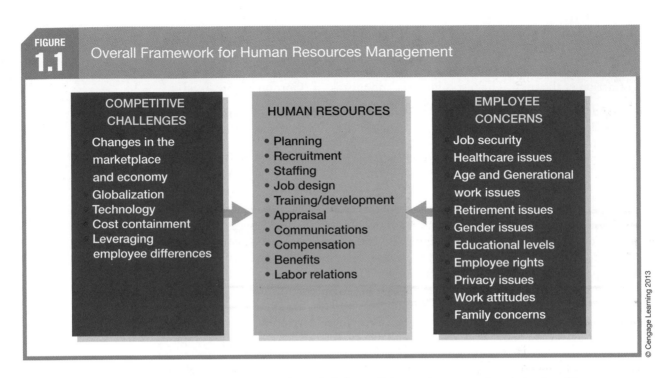

FIGURE 1.1   Overall Framework for Human Resources Management

COMPETITIVE CHALLENGES

Changes in the marketplace and economy

Globalization

Technology

Cost containment

Leveraging employee differences

HUMAN RESOURCES

- Planning
- Recruitment
- Staffing
- Job design
- Training/development
- Appraisal
- Communications
- Compensation
- Benefits
- Labor relations

EMPLOYEE CONCERNS

Job security

Healthcare issues

Age and Generational work issues

Retirement issues

Gender issues

Educational levels

Employee rights

Privacy issues

Work attitudes

Family concerns

© Cengage Learning 2013

experiences as well as their skills," says Dhesi, who notes that Aviva is rolling out new software that will create "talent profile" of each of the firm's employees worldwide.

Although "competing through people" is a major theme of human resources management, on a day-to-day basis, managers of all types have to carry out the specific activities for a company to effectively do so. Figure 1.1 provides an overall framework of these activities. From this figure, we can see that managers have to help blend many aspects of management; at this point, we will simply classify them as either "competitive challenges" or "employee concerns." We will use Figure 1.1 as a basis for our discussion throughout the rest of this chapter.

 # Competitive Challenges and Human Resources Management

Professional organizations such as the Society for Human Resource Management (SHRM) and the Human Resource Planning Society (HRPS) conduct ongoing studies of the most pressing competitive issues facing firms. By seeking the input of chief executives and HR managers, these organizations keep a finger on the pulse of major trends. The top trends, or challenges, they name today include those outlined in the sections that follow.

Challenge 1: Responding Strategically to Changes in the Marketplace

Given the pace of commerce, organizations can rarely stand still for long. In today's highly competitive environments in which competition is global and innovation is continuous, being able to adapt has become the key to capturing Opportunities and Overcome Obstacles as well as the very survival of organizations. As one pundit put it, "No change means chance." Successful companies, says Harvard Business School professor Rosabeth Moss Kanter, develop a culture that just keeps moving all the time.[5]

Consider what happened to the parts suppliers for U.S. automakers when the bankruptcy of General Motors, Chrysler, and Ford looked imminent in 2008–2009. Most of the suppliers sold exclusively to the three automakers. As a result, they had to rapidly find other markets, products to make for those markets, and ways to sell them—all of which required significant human resources changes and challenges.

Human Resources Managers and Business Strategy

Ten or 20 years ago, human resources personnel were often relegated to conducting administrative tasks. But that has changed. Executives know that human resource professionals can help them improve not only a company's bottom line by streamlining employment costs but the top line by forecasting labor trends, designing new ways to acquire and utilize employees, measuring their effectiveness, and helping managers enter new markets. Says Robin Lissak with the HR consulting arm of Deloitte, "Most business leaders say they want [HR] to focus on the new types of services companies need and want. They include driving mergers and acquisitions and helping companies enter new markets, like expanding to China." Executives at these companies expect their HR personnel to be able to answer questions such as, "What is our entry strategy? Who should we send first? Where should we locate our sales, production, and other personnel, and how do we keep them safe abroad? How do we manage a crisis should it occur?[6]

To answer questions such as these, human resources managers need an intimate understanding of their firms' competitive business operations and strategies, whatever they may be. During what is being called the "Great Recession," which began in 2008, many companies pursued cost-cutting strategies, often in part by trimming workers' benefits. Other companies took a different strategy: They beefed up their benefit programs to attract top talent from other companies and expanded in order to be ready when the economy began growing again.

Total quality improvements (TQM), reengineering, downsizing, outsourcing, and the like are also examples of the means organizations use to modify the way they operate in order to be more successful. Six Sigma quality is a set of principles and practices whose core ideas include understanding customer needs, doing things right the first time, and striving for continuous improvement. Reengineering has been described as "the fundamental rethinking and radical redesign of business processes to achieve dramatic improvements in cost, quality, service, and speed."[7] Downsizing is the planned elimination of jobs, and outsourcing simply means hiring someone outside the company to perform business processes that were previously done within the firm.

A common denominator of all these strategies is that they require companies to engage in change management. Change management is a systematic way of bringing about and managing both organizational changes and changes on the individual level. According to a survey by the research institute Roffey Park, two-thirds of firms believe that managing change is their biggest challenge. Although most employees understand that change is continuous—responsibilities, job assignments, and work processes change—people often resist it because it requires them to modify or

LEARNING OUTCOME 1

Think of a firm you do business with that is facing dramatic changes in order to survive. (Blockbuster is an example.) How do you think the firm's personnel can help it adapt? What role will the company's HR staff play in helping with that goal?

Six Sigma quality
A set of principles and practices whose core ideas include understanding customer needs, doing things right the first time, and striving for continuous improvement

reengineering
Fundamental rethinking and radical redesign of business processes to achieve dramatic improvements in cost, quality, service, and speed

downsizing
Planned elimination of jobs

outsourcing
Contracting outside the organization to have work done that formerly was done by internal employees

change management
Change management is a systematic way of bringing about and managing both organizational changes and changes on the individual level

abandon ways of working that have been successful or at least familiar to them. Successful change rarely occurs naturally or easily.

To manage change, executives and managers, including those in HR, have to envision the future, communicate this vision to employees, set clear expectations for performance, and develop the capability to execute by reorganizing people and reallocating assets. Organizations that have been successful in engineering change:

- Link the change to the business strategy.

- Show how the change creates quantifiable benefits.

- Engage key employees, customers, and their suppliers early when making a change.

- Make an investment in implementing and sustaining change.[8]

Some of the strategic changes companies pursue are reactive changes that result when external forces, such as a the competition, a recession, law change, or a crisis (such as BP's offshore oil spill in the Gulf of Mexico in 2010) have already affected an organization's performance. Other strategies are proactive change, initiated by managers to take advantage of targeted opportunities, particularly in fast-changing industries in which followers are not successful.

Good HR managers know that they can be key players when it comes to driving the business strategies of their organizations in order to make changes. That is why forward-looking CEOs such as Gary Kelly of Southwest Airlines, Howard Schultz at Starbucks, and Jeff Immelt at GE make certain that their top HR executives report directly to them and help them address key issues.

A rapidly growing number of companies, including Ford, Intel, and United Technologies, are assigning HR representatives to their core business teams to make certain they are knowledgeable about core business issues. Companies are increasingly rotating non-HR managers *into* HR positions and vice versa to give them exposure to different areas of the organization. Rather than emphasizing the administrative aspects of HR, forward-thinking companies develop and promote their HR personnel and provide them with key business statistics and numbers they can use to measure the effectiveness of the workforce. We will discuss more about competitive HR strategies and HR in Chapter 2. Meanwhile, keep in mind that HR's role is not all about providing advice to CEOs and supervisors. In addition to serving as a strategic partner to management, HR managers are also responsible for listening to and advocating on behalf of employees to make sure their interests are aligned with those of the firm and vice versa. A good deal of evidence suggests that this is one of the toughest parts of an HR manager's job. We will discuss more about this aspect of the job later in the chapter.

Challenge 2: Competing, Recruiting, and Staffing Globally

The strategies companies are pursing today increasingly involve one or more elements of globalization. The integration of world economies and markets has sent businesses abroad to look for opportunities as well as fend off foreign competitors domestically. Consumers around the world want to be able to buy "anything, anytime, anywhere," and companies are making it possible for them to do so. Want to buy a Coke in Pakistan? No problem. Coca-Cola has an elaborate delivery system designed to transport its products to some of the remotest places on the planet. In fact, the company

---

reactive change
Change that occurs after external forces have already affected performance.

proactive change
Change initiated to take advantage of targeted opportunities

Six Sigma
A process used to translate customer needs into a set of optimal tasks that are performed in concert with one another

globalization
The trend toward opening up foreign markets to international trade and investment

LEARNING OUTCOME 2

Why do firms that sell their products only domestically have to be concerned about globalization and its HRM implications?

has long generated more of its revenues abroad than it does in the U.S. But globalization is not of interest only to large firms like Coca-Cola. While estimates vary widely, approximately 70 to 85 percent of the U.S. economy today is affected by international competition, including small companies.

About 10 percent of what Americans produce every year dollar-wise is sold abroad. According to the Small Business Administration, nearly 97 percent of all U.S. exporters are small companies. These firms employ about half of all the private sector employees in the nation. On the flip side, since the 1970s, every year, American citizens and businesses have purchased more goods and services abroad—including labor—than they have sold.

Thanks to today's global economy in which many companies, large and small, market their products in their home countries and abroad, it is possible to find familiar products for sale virtually anywhere in the world.

John Coletti/Jon Arnold Images Ltd/Alamy

Partnerships and mergers are two other ways companies both large and small are globalizing. Coca-Cola has tried to expand in China by partnering with that nation's largest juice maker. Spring Hill Greenhouses, a small firm in Lodi, Ohio, partners with florists through associations such as FTD and Teleflora to work with lily and tulip growers in the Netherlands and rose growers in Colombia to serve customers around the world.

As a result of globalization, the national identities of products are blurring too. BMW has traditionally been a German brand, but now the automaker builds cars in the United States, China, and elsewhere. Likewise, you probably think of Budweiser as an American beer, but would it surprise you to know that the maker of Budweiser (Anheuser-Busch) is owned by a Belgian company called InBev? Like many other companies, Anheuser-Busch InBev is now looking for factories and brands in China to purchase in order to expand its sales.[9]

Numerous free-trade agreements forged between nations in the last half century have helped quicken the pace of globalization. The first major trade agreement of the twentieth century was made in 1948, following World War II. Called the General Agreement on Tariffs and Trade (GATT), it established rules and guidelines for global commerce between nations and groups of nations. Although the Great Recession temporarily caused a sharp drop in the amount of world trade, since GATT began world trade has literally exploded, increasing nearly thirty times the dollar volume of what it once was. This is three times faster than the world's overall output has grown during the same period. GATT paved the way for the formation of many major trade agreements and institutions, including the European Union in 1986 and the North American Free Trade Agreement (NAFTA) in 1994, encompassing the United States, Canada, and Mexico. The World Trade Organization (WTO), headquartered in Lausanne, Switzerland, now has more than 150 member countries, and new free-trade agreements seem to be forged annually.[10]

How Globalization Affects HRM

For all of the opportunities afforded by international business, when managers talk about "going global," they have to balance a complicated set of issues related to different geographies, including different cultures, employment laws, and business practices, and the safety of employees and facilities abroad. Human resources issues underlie each of these concerns. They include such things as dealing with employees today who, via the Internet and social media, are better informed about global job opportunities and are willing to pursue them, even if it means working for competing companies or foreign companies. Gauging the knowledge and skill base of workers worldwide and figuring out how best to hire and train them (sometimes with materials that must be translated into a number of different languages) is also an issue for firms. Relocating managers and training foreign managers abroad to direct the efforts of an international workforce is a challenge as well. In Chapter 15, we will explain how these challenges are tackled.

Challenge 3: Setting and Achieving Corporate Social Responsibility and Sustainability Goals

LEARNING OUTCOME 3

Does a company's HRM function need to be an integral part of its sustainability and corporate social responsibility efforts? Why or why not?

Globalization has led to an improvement in people's living standards in the last half century. As a result of free trade, Americans are able to buy products made abroad more cheaply. Conversely people in low-wage countries that make those goods and services are becoming wealthier and are beginning to buy American-made products. Nonetheless, globalization stirs fierce debate—especially when it comes to jobs. Since the turn of the century, millions of U.S. jobs—both white and blue collar—have been exported to low-wage nations all around the world. Some people worry that free trade is creating a "have/have not" world economy, in which the people in developing economies and the world's environment are being exploited by companies in richer, more developed countries. This has sparked anti-free-trade protests in many nations.

Concerns such as these, coupled with corporate scandals over the years, including the use of sweatshop labor in third-world countries, risky lending tactics that fueled a worldwide banking crisis, and a class action lawsuit alleging Walmart discriminated against hundreds of thousands of female employees over the years, have led to a new focus on corporate social responsibility, or good citizenship. In a recent survey, the Chronicle of Philanthropy found that 16 percent of companies were making more donations of products and services and that 54 percent of companies were encouraging more employees to volunteer their time.[11] Companies are learning (sometimes the hard way) that being socially responsible both domestically and abroad can not only help them avoid lawsuits but also improve their earnings. For example, researchers at the Boston College's Center for Corporate Citizenship found that as a company's reputation improved, so did the percentage increase in the number of people who would recommend that firm. Nearly two-thirds of the members of the 80-million strong millennial generation (people born in the 1980s and 1990s) consider a company's social reputation when deciding where to shop, and 9 out of 10 of them say they would switch brands based on their perceptions of a company's commitment to social responsibility.[12] Moreover, prospective workers are saying corporate responsibility is now more important to their job selection.

Sustainability is closely related to corporate social responsibility. Sustainability refers to a company's ability to produce a good or service without damaging the environment or depleting a resource. Achieving complete sustainability is nearly impossible, but companies are making strides to reduce their "carbon footprints." Those that are not are finding themselves under pressure from consumers and groups determined that they do. Consider what happened to Hewlett-Packard (HP). After HP broke

corporate social responsibility

The responsibility of the firm to act in the best interests of the people and communities affected by its activities

KAREN BLEIER/AFP/Getty Images

After the 2010 Deepwater Horizon oil spill in the Gulf of Mexico—one of several accidents in BP Oil's history that have harmed both people and the environment—many people, including these demonstrators, demanded that BP change its approach to corporate social responsibility

a promise to eliminate toxic materials in its computers by 2009, Greenpeace activists painted the words "Hazardous Products" on the roof of the company's headquarters in Palo Alto, California. Meanwhile, a voicemail message from *Star Trek* actor William Shatner was delivered to all of the phones in the building. "Please ask your leader [HP CEO Mark Hurd] to make computers that are toxin free like Apple has done," Shatner said in the recording. The stunt and publicity it generated worked. HP got the message and later delivered on its promise.[13]

One of HR's leadership roles is to spearhead the development and implementation of corporate citizenship throughout their organizations, especially the fair treatment of workers.[14] Highlights in HRM 1 lists a number of Internet sites of organizations that have developed different conduct codes used by firms around the world. Also listed are a number of general websites useful to HR professionals.

Challenge 4: Advancing HRM with Technology

Advancements in information technology have enabled organizations to take advantage of the information explosion. Computer networks and "cloud computing" (Internet computer services and data storage) have made it possible for nearly unlimited amounts of data to be stored, retrieved, and used in a wide variety of ways. Collaborative software that allows workers anywhere anytime to interface and share information with one another electronically—wikis, document-sharing platforms such as Google Docs, online chat and instant messaging, web and video conferencing, and electronic calendar systems—have changed how and where people and companies do business. For example, Boeing Satellite Systems has a "lessons learned" site on its intranet where people from all areas of the company can store the knowledge they have and others can access it. Executives at Boeing estimate the measure has reduced the cost of developing a satellite by as much as $25 million.[15]

LEARNING OUTCOME 4

In what ways can the HR managers and employees of small firms facilitate their competitiveness relative to firms with superior technology? Why are employees still key?

collaborative software

Software that allows workers to interface and share information with one another electronically

HIGHLIGHTS IN HRM
A Guide to HR Internet Sites

HR professionals can access the following websites for current information related to human resources.

Codes of Conduct

- Global Business Initiative on Human Rights' Guiding Principles (www.global-business-initiative.org)
- APEC Course of Action on Fighting Corruption and Ensuring Transparency (http://www.apec.org)
- Caux Round Table Principles for Business (http://www.cauxroundtable.org)
- Fair Labor Association Workplace Code of Conduct (http://www.fairlabor.org)
- Global Sullivan Principles of Social Responsibility (http://www.thesullivanfoundation.org)
- ILO Tripartite Declaration of Principles Concerning Multinational Enterprises and Social Policy (http://www.ilo.org)
- OECD Guidelines for Multinational Enterprises (www.oecd.org)
- OECD, Corporate Governance Principles (http://www.oecd.org)
- Rules of Conduct to Combat Extortion and Bribery in International Business Transactions (International Chamber of Commerce, http://www.iccwbo.org)
- United Nations Universal Declaration of Human Rights (http://www.un.org)

General

- AFL-CIO (http://www.aflcio.org)—union news, issue papers, press releases, links to labor sites
- American Management Association (http://www.amanet.org)—AMA membership, programs, training, and so on
- U.S. Department of Commerce's FedWorld (http://www.fedworld.gov)—a gateway to many government websites
- HR Professional's Gateway to the Internet (http://www.hrprosgateway.com)—links to HR-related web pages
- Occupational Safety and Health Resources (http://www.osh.net)—OSHA-related sites, government pages, resources, and so on
- Society for Human Resource Management (http://www.shrm.org)—current events, information, connections, and articles
- Telecommuting, Telework, and Alternative Officing (http://www.gilgordon.com)—telecommuting and flexible hours
- Training, Learning, and Development Resource Center (http://www.thetrainingworld.com)—job mart, training links, and electronic mailing list links
- U.S. Department of Labor (http://www.dol.gov)—job bank, labor statistics, press releases, grants, and contract information

The Internet and social media are also having an impact. Social media networking has become the new way to find employees and check them out to see if they are acceptable candidates. Companies are hiring firms such as Social Intelligence, which combs through Facebook, LinkedIn, Twitter, Flickr, YouTube and "thousands of other sources" to create reports about the "real you"—not the "you" you have presented in your resume.[16] (Care to change your Facebook page, anyone?) HR managers are also grappling with whether or not to develop blogging and social media policies, and whether or not to establish rules about the amount of time employees can spend online or install software that cuts them off after a certain amount of time.

From Touch Labor to Knowledge Workers

Advanced technology tends to reduce the number of jobs that require little skill and to increase the number of jobs that require considerable skill. In general, this transformation has been referred to as a shift from "touch labor" to knowledge workers, in which employee responsibilities expand to include a richer array of activities such as planning, decision-making, and problem-solving.[17]

Technology, transportation, communications, and utilities industries tend to spend the most on training. Knowledge-based training has become so important that Manpower Inc., the largest employment agency in the United States, offers free information technology training through its Manpower Training and Development Center (http://www.manpowertdc.com), an online university for its employees in its 4,000 offices worldwide. The Manpower site features thousands of hours of online instruction in technology applications, along with professional development, business skills, and telecommunications courses. In fact, Manpower is so focused on developing technical skills in potential employees that it has set up the system so that some training and career planning information is available to those who simply send the company a resume. "Just-in-time" learning delivered via the Internet to employees' desktops when and where they need training has become commonplace. "Virtual" learning is taking place as well. IBM, Cisco, Kelly Services, and Manpower are among the companies that have built training facilities, offices, and meeting rooms inside the online reality game Second Life. The spaces these companies build online enable them to do certain things more easily and cheaply than they can in the real world—for example, bringing people from several continents into one room for training.[18]

Influence of Technology on HRM

Perhaps the most central use of technology in HRM is an organization's human resources information system (HRIS). Because HR affects the entire workforce—everyone who works for the company must be hired, trained, paid, and promoted, usually through HR—the impact of HRIS has been dramatic. It has become a potent weapon for lowering administrative costs, increasing productivity, speeding up response times, improving decision-making, and tracking a company's talent.

The most obvious impact has been *operational*—that is, automating routine activities, alleviating administrative burdens, reducing costs, and improving productivity internal to the HR function itself. The most frequent uses include automating payroll processing, maintaining employee records, and administering benefits programs. "Self-service"—setting up systems, usually on an intranet, allows managers to access employee records themselves for administrative purposes and allows employees to access and change their own benefits and other personal information.

The second way in which information technology is affecting human resources management is *relational* in nature—connecting people with each other and with HR data they need. For example, companies are using software to recruit, screen, and pretest applicants online before hiring them as well as to train, track, and promote employees once they have been hired. The drugmaker Merck's HRIS captures information from job recruiting sites, scans applicants resumes, and makes the information immediately accessible to managers so they can search systematically for the people whose skills they want. Managers can search online for internal and external talent by running searches of candidates who have been categorized by skill set.[19]

knowledge workers
Workers whose responsibilities extend beyond the physical execution of work to include planning, decision-making, and problem-solving

human resources information system (HRIS)
A computerized system that provides current and accurate data for purposes of control and decision-making

The third effect of human resources information systems is *transformational* in nature—changing the way HR processes are designed and executed. Corning, Inc. uses HR software, among other things, to set the developmental goals of its employees once they have been hired and to gauge how well they are meeting them. Employees can look online to see their own goals and mark their progress as well as see everyone else's goals in the command chain, from the CEO down to their immediate supervisors. This "cascading" of goals has helped Corning's employees align their personal goals with the organization's overall objectives in order to reach higher levels. "Like any large company, we tended to get 'silo-ed' and fragmented the more we grew," said one vice president at a company using a system similar to Corning's. "We needed a better way to pull our global team together and get people focused on what the priorities are for our business."[20]

So what sort of system should HR professionals choose among the many options available to them? Prepackaged, or "canned," HR web-based solutions are as commonly used as custom-designed systems. Generally, companies also have the choice of hosting the applications on their own servers or having software vendors such as IBM or PeopleSoft do it for them. Experts say the first step in choosing a HRIS is for HR personnel to evaluate the biggest "headaches" they experience, or most time-consuming tasks, and then choose the applications that can have the strongest impact on the firm's financial measures—that is, the ones that get the "biggest bang for the buck." These applications are more likely to get "buy-in" from the firm's top managers. HR managers should then calculate the costs based on average salaries, or HR hours, that could be saved by using a human resources information system, along with the hours of increased productivity that would occur as a result. Highlights in HRM 2 shows the other factors that need to be evaluated.

When an effective HRIS is implemented, perhaps the biggest advantage gained is that HR personnel can concentrate more effectively on the firm's strategic direction instead of on routine tasks. This can include forecasting personnel needs (especially for firms planning to expand, contract, or merge), planning for career and employee promotions, and evaluating the impact of the firm's policies—both those related to HR functions and other functions—to help improve the firm's earnings and strategic direction. "We wanted our HR teams to focus on people issues instead of data problems," explains Sandra Hoffman, CIO-in-residence at the Advanced Technology Development Center, which is part of the Enterprise Innovation Institute at Georgia Tech.

Although the initial drive to adopt human resources information systems was related to cutting HR costs, HR managers have since discovered that the systems have allowed them to share information with departmental managers, who, by having access to it, have been able to come up with better production practices and cost control solutions. As a result, HR managers are now requiring their application providers to provide them with software to meet certain goals, including lowering a company's total spending on employee health care and improving its customer service.[22]

However, companies simply cannot turn over their strategic talent issues to a human resources information system. Researchers Douglas Ready and Jay Conger found that despite such systems—electronic or otherwise—most of the firms they examined lacked high-potential employees to fill strategic management roles. Although companies had talent management processes in place, they were no longer in sync with the company's strategic direction. In addition, managers often get sidetracked by priorities other than identifying talent.[23]

HIGHLIGHTS IN **HRM**
2
Factors to Consider When Evaluating a Human Resources Information System

The following factors are key considerations HR managers need to consider when their firms are evaluating a human resources information system (HRIS).

- *Fit of the application to the firm's employee base.* If many of the firm's employees work on a factory floor, is the system appropriate, or does HR need to install kiosks in employee areas? How will the information be secured? Will employees need to be assigned passwords? Can they access the information from off-site, for example, from their homes?

- *Ability to upgrade or customize the software.* What sorts of costs will be involved to upgrade the software in the coming years?

- *Compatibility with current systems.* Does the HRIS link into existing, or planned, information systems easily and inexpensively?

- *User friendliness.* Does the software provide additional features such as links to learning resources or help for managers who might need it?

- *Availability of technical support.* Should the HRIS system be supported internally, or should the vendor host it? What are the vendor's technical support capabilities?

- *Time required to implement and train staff members to use the HRIS, including HR and payroll personnel, managers, and employees.* Who is responsible for training employees, and how will it be done?

- *Initial costs and annual maintenance costs.* Is a "suite" of applications needed or just a few key applications? Experts advise HR managers to price each application separately and then ask vendors for a "bundled" price.[21]

Procter & Gamble (P&G) is an exception, noted Ready and Conger. P&G's HRIS system makes good internal candidates visible to managers instead of the managers having to scour the company to find them. The system contains information about its 135,000 employee worldwide for promotion purposes at the country, business category, and regional levels. It contains employees' career histories and capabilities, as well as education and community affiliations, their development needs, and tracks the diversity of candidates. Perhaps most importantly, managers are evaluated and compensated on their ability to find and groom talented employees. Procter & Gamble's results are consistent with Ready and Conger's findings that firms do a better job of fostering talent when there is commitment, involvement, and accountability by a company's supervisors to do so rather than when the task is "owned" by the HR department.[24]

LEARNING OUTCOME 5

If you were an HR manager, do you think it would be possible to maintain the morale of your firm's employees in the face of shrinking budgets and benefits? How might you do so?

Challenge 5: Containing Costs While Retaining Top Talent and Maximizing Productivity

For years, most human resources managers have been under pressure to cut labor costs. When the Great Recession hit, stretching a company's labor dollars while gaining productivity from workers became an even bigger priority. Organizations take many approaches to lowering labor-related costs, including carefully managing employees' benefits, downsizing, outsourcing, offshoring, furloughing employees, and engaging in employee leasing in an attempt to enhance productivity.

Few jobs come with lifetime guarantees and benefits that will never change. Nonetheless, employees want to work for employers that can provide them with a certain amount of economic security. Layoffs and cuts in employee benefits have heightened these concerns. Some companies, such as Google, are able hire talented employees by offering them a great deal of job security and fantastic benefits. However, most companies, especially small ones or ones that are struggling, find it hard to compete with bigger firms like Google with deluxe benefit packages. What can they do? This is where an HR manager's expertise and creativity comes in. Read on to see how firms are handling this challenge.

Managing Benefits

Labor costs are one of the largest expenditures of any organization, particularly in service- and knowledge-intensive companies. As a result, most firms closely monitor employee pay and benefit programs. One casualty of cost cuts has been employee pensions. In 1980, a little under 40 percent of private-sector workers had pension plans, guaranteeing them a certain amount of money in retirement. Today, only 15 percent do.[25] In difficult economic times, some companies temporarily suspend contributing to employees' 401(k) plans and lower or cut their bonus plans.

The biggest HR concern presently has, when it comes to benefits, is skyrocketing health care costs and complying with the nation's new health care reform laws. In many industries health care costs are now approaching 30 percent of total compensation.[26] One trend is for firms to shift employees to high-deductible plans. Employees pay lower premiums, but they have to pay a certain amount of money, even for basic care, before their insurance will begin picking up the tab. Another approach is to offer employees incentives to get healthy—for example, by quitting smoking, losing weight, or exercising. According to research by the University of Pennsylvania's Center for Health Centers, at least one-third of companies offer or plan to offer their employees incentives for activities such as these. Some companies offer money, prizes, vacation trips, lower health premiums, or refund the cost of weight loss programs. OhioHealth, a hospital chain whose employees are mostly overweight, went so far as to outfit them with pedometers and pay them up to $500 a year depending upon how far they walk.[27] Rather than cutting its health care benefits, Cerner Corp., a medium-sized Kansas-City based technology company, looked at statistics and other data to find out which diseases its workers were most likely to suffer from and adjusted its employee health-and-wellness programs accordingly. The company has been able to lower its health care costs as a result. Cerner employees benefit too. Those who get screened for health issues get points that lower their insurance premiums.

Downsizing

As you probably know, downsizing was used extensively by firms during the Great Recession, causing the U.S. unemployment rate to jump up to about 10 percent. (In some states it was higher: 15 percent in Nevada and over 12 in percent California and Michigan. By contrast, in North Dakota, it was a little over 4 percent.)[28] Downsizing does not just take a toll on those who lose their jobs. Employees who are "lucky" enough to keep their jobs often feel guilty they have been retained, mourn the loss of their coworkers, and worry that they will be the next to go. These people, who are generally the firm's best performers, also usually end up picking up the work their former coworkers used to do for the same salary. When the economy improves or they see a chance, they tend to head for the door.

How do firms continue to encourage employees to work hard for the company in the face of such insecurity? More than one executive has concluded that you do not get dedicated and productive employees if, at the first sign of trouble, you show them that you think they are expendable. To approach downsizing more intelligently, companies such as Continental Airlines and Dial Corporation have made special efforts to reassign and retrain employees for new positions when their jobs are eliminated. When L. L. Bean realized the company needed to eliminate some jobs, instead of simply laying off people, it offered early retirement and "sweetened" voluntary separation programs as well as sabbaticals to employees for continuing their education.[29]

Downsizing is no longer just a short-term fix when times are tough, though. It has now become a tool continually used by companies to adjust to changes in technology, globalization, and the firm's business direction. For example, in a study that surveyed 450 senior HR executives at companies that had downsized, only 21 percent said that financial difficulties had spurred the cutbacks. Thirty-four percent of the executives said that the downsizing was done to strengthen their companies' future positions, 21 percent said it was done to achieve fundamental staff realignment, and 17 percent said it was due to a merger or acquisition.

Whatever the reason, while some firms improve efficiency (and lower costs) with layoffs, many others do not. Some hidden costs of downsizing include the following:

- Severance and rehiring costs

- Accrued vacation and sick day payouts

- Pension and benefit payouts

- Potential lawsuits from aggrieved workers

- The loss of institutional memory and trust in management

- A lack of staffers when the economy rebounds

- Survivors who are risk averse, paranoid, and focused on corporate politics

Concerns such as these have led some firms to establish a policy of "no layoffs." Nucor Steel is one company with a no-layoff policy. Companies like Nucor say they get some important benefits from such policies:

- A fiercely loyal, more productive workforce

- Higher customer satisfaction

- Readiness to snap back with the economy

- A recruiting edge

- Workers who, knowing their jobs are safe, are not afraid to innovate.[30]

The results of working hard to retain an organization's talent are measurable as well. A Watson Wyatt study showed that companies with excellent recruiting and retention policies provide a 1.4 percent higher return to shareholders compared to those that do not.

Furloughing

furloughing

A situation in which an organization asks or requires employees to take time off for either no pay or reduced pay

An alternative to downsizing is furloughing. When a company furloughs employees, it asks them to take time off for either no pay or reduced pay. Some companies are utilizing creative furlough strategies to avoid downsizing and losing talent to competitors. Instead of laying off people, the consulting firm Accenture instituted a voluntary sabbatical program known as "Flexleave." Employees got 20 percent of their salaries and continued benefits for 6–12 months, and their stock options remained in place. The workers could take other jobs during their sabbaticals, as long as they did not work for a competitor. Cisco Systems offered 8,500 employees an unusual deal as well. Instead of a severance package, they received a third of their salaries, all benefits, and stock-option awards while working for one year at a not-for-profit group already associated with the company. Likewise, when Texas Instruments (TI) had to lay off some of its employees, it did not just send them out the door. It found them jobs with its suppliers with the agreement that the employees would return to TI when business picked up.[31]

Although furloughs might sound preferable to downsizing, they have their drawbacks, too, say some human resources experts. Costs are not cut as significantly as they would be with downsizing because employees generally retain their benefits while they are furloughed. Employees who are not furloughed often end up with more work and feel resentful, and product and service quality as well as innovation suffer as a result of the higher workloads. And, as with downsizing, furloughing employees can hurt a company's recruiting efforts when the public discovers it has resorted to such a measure.[32]

More diligent workforce planning is a better solution, says John Sullivan, an HR expert and consultant. Business revenues seldom fall off overnight. Sullivan says the best managers look for warning signs and develop a process that pinpoints skills the company no longer needs, low-impact jobs, and poor performers in advance of a crisis. Instead, part-time or contract employees can be hired and their hours of service adjusted as needed.[33]

Outsourcing

Over the past twenty-five years, the employment relationship between companies and employees has shifted from relationship based to transaction based. Fewer people are working for one employer over the course of their lifetimes, and as we have explained, the Internet has created a workforce that is constantly scanning for new opportunities. In addition, more people are choosing to work on a freelance, or contract, basis or to work part-time, especially women and senior citizens. Outsourcing is evidence of this trend.[34] Companies hire accounting firms to take care of their financial services. They hire advertising firms to handle promotions, software firms to develop data-processing systems, and law firms to handle their legal issues. Maintenance, security, catering, payroll (and in small companies, sometimes entire HR departments) are outsourced to increase the organization's flexibility and lower its overhead costs.

The interest in outsourcing has been spurred on by executives who want to focus their organization's activities on what they do best. In fact, some management experts predict companies will one day strip away every function not regarded as crucial. Even now, many firms are outsourcing what would seem to be their core functions. Drug companies such as GlaxoSmithKline are outsourcing their research and development functions to smaller firms that can more cheaply and nimbly create new products for them. Procter & Gamble outsources a major portion of its product development.

Outsourcing has been one of the most prominent HR trends of the last ten years and will continue to be.[35]

Offshoring

Offshoring, also referred to as "global sourcing," involves shifting work to locations abroad. Cost reductions are among the key motivators for offshoring. Dramatically reduced labor costs can be achieved by reallocating work to countries such as India, where highly educated workers can perform the same jobs as U.S. workers at half the price. Other labor markets include the Philippines, Russia, China, Mexico, Brazil, Hungary, and Bosnia, where workers are paid only a small fraction of what American workers make.

In some cases, offshoring is done to allocate work across the various countries in which a company does business. In other cases, managers are finding that if they save money by offshoring, they can rescue failing businesses, make better use of their skilled U.S. labor, and deliver products more cheaply and quickly because they have people across the globe working 24-7 on them.[36]

But as with downsizing, hidden costs can sometimes chew up much of the financial gains from offshoring, including the costs associated with finding foreign vendors, productivity lost during the transition, domestic layoff costs, language difficulties, international regulatory challenges, and political and economic instability that can threaten operations and even employees. (French workers, for example, have, on occasion, been known to take a CEO or two captive to get what they want in terms of their labor demands.) Drawbacks such as these have led some companies to bring jobs back to their domestic markets. Delta Air Lines is among the firms that returned their call-center operations to the United States after customers complained about the service they received from personnel in foreign companies.

Another new trend is "nearshoring." Nearshoring is the process of moving jobs closer to one's home country. For example, rising labor costs in China are now making it attractive for U.S. firms to offshore work to Mexico and Central America. Shipping the finished goods made there is also cheaper, and the products get to sellers (and ultimately the buyers who want them) more quickly, which can provide a firm with a competitive advantage. Yet another new way companies are both economizing and bringing jobs back to their domestic markets is by "homeshoring." Call-center jobs are a notable example. When a company homeshores call-center jobs, it outsources the work to domestic independent contractors who work out of their homes.

Offshoring, nearshoring, and homeshoring are going to continue to be key employment strategies as global economies continue to shift. The key is for top managers, finance departments, and the offshoring consulting firms they hire to begin working in conjunction with their companies' HR departments prior to these activities occurring. "Companies can minimize hidden costs and maximize their returns by enabling HR to have a seat at the table early so they can carefully address issues such as the types of jobs that should and should not be outsourced, skill and language

Offshoring work to countries that offer a highly educated yet lower paid work force has become a common cost-cutting strategy for American firms.

© Andrew Holbrooke/Corbis

offshoring
The business practice of sending jobs to other countries

requirements, labor costs by market, alternative talent pools, workforce training, re-training, and change management," says Mark Arian, a corporate restructuring executive for the HR consulting group Hewitt. To minimize problems, HR managers have to work together with the firm's other functional groups to define and communicate transition plans, minimize the number of unknowns, and help employees identify their employment options.[37]

Employee Leasing

employee leasing

The process of dismissing employees who are then hired by a leasing company (which handles all HR-related activities) and contracting with that company to lease back the employees

As an alternative to downsizing, outsourcing, offshoring, and furloughing, many companies, especially small ones, have decided to sign employee leasing agreements with professional employer organizations (PEOs). A PEO—typically a larger company—takes over the management of a smaller company's HR tasks and becomes a coemployer to its employees. The PEO performs all the HR duties of an employer—hiring, payroll, and performance appraisal. Because PEOs can coemploy a large number of people working at many different companies, they can provide employees with benefits that small companies cannot afford, such as 401(k) and health care plans, workers' compensation, and even adoption assistance. In addition, many PEOs offer their employees flextime, job sharing, part-time employment, consulting arrangements, seasonal work, and on-call work. The value of employee leasing lies in the fact that an organization can essentially maintain its working relationships with its employees but shift some employment costs to the PEO, in return for a fee. More details on employee leasing will be discussed in Chapter 5.[38]

Productivity Enhancements

The results of pure cost-cutting efforts such as downsizing, furloughing, outsourcing, and employee leasing can be disappointing, however, if managers use them as simple solutions to complex performance problems. Overemphasizing labor costs misses the broader issue of improving a firm's productivity. Employee productivity is the result of a combination of employees' abilities, motivation, and work environment and the technology they use to work. Since productivity can be defined as "the output gained from a fixed amount of inputs," organizations can increase their productivity either by reducing their inputs (the cost approach) or by increasing the amount that employees produce by adding more human and/or physical capital to the process. Companies such as Southwest Airlines, Nucor, and the manufacturing and technology firm Danaher achieve low costs in their industries not because they scrimp on employees but because they are the most productive.

In absolute terms, the United States remains the world's most productive nation, even when it comes to manufacturing. Apparel and textile manufacturing have dried up in the nation, but they have been replaced by industries that rely more on technological precision and brainpower than on low-skilled labor—industries for aircraft, sophisticated machinery, medical devices, and so on.[39] However, the growth in output per worker is now climbing fast in less-developed countries such as China that have lacked expertise and technology in the past but are making strides to close the gap. When the investment in faster computers and more efficient machine tools levels off, this limits how much assistance technology can offer employees in terms of their productivity. Any additional productivity will have to come from the enhanced ability of employees, their motivation, and their work environment, which makes the job of the HR manager in the coming years all the more crucial.[40]

Many companies are finding that providing work flexibility is a good way to improve the productivity and motivation of valuable employees, especially when giving them

Small Business Application

A Small Business Built on Helping Small Businesses

As experienced and highly respected HR professionals, Delise West and Tonya Rochette could have easily furthered their careers by pursuing positions in large corporations or academia. Instead, they chose to forge a new path for themselves by founding Human Resource Partners, a small human resources consulting firm in Concord, New Hampshire. Friends and family thought they were both a little crazy to enter the "risky" world of owning a small business, but since joining forces twelve years ago, they have been very successful at serving other small, entrepreneurial businesses just like theirs.

West and Rochette both recognized early on that small businesses need to address HR issues just as much as larger businesses, yet small-business owners usually do not have the time or expertise to devote to these issues themselves and often do not have the financial resources to hire a full-time, knowledgeable HR manager. This pair of entrepreneurs saw that reality as an opportunity to provide a full spectrum of HR services to companies in need.

"There are so many companies who don't have the right HR infrastructure in place," said West, whose firm works mostly with companies under 70 employees. "Oftentimes, an owner of a growing business will come to me and simply say, 'I can't do it anymore' because it has become too time consuming." Some of the companies that have turned to West and Rochette for help with HR functions and strategy include a major car dealership, a regional construction company, and a local nursery.

Work with a new client typically begins with an evaluation of the firm's level of HR compliance and best practices, such as job description documentation, payroll systems, and legal interviewing practices. From there, Human Resource Partners develops strategies for the client to implement in the areas of recruiting, screening, interviewing, and hiring new staff; evaluating and recognizing current employee performance; and improving employee relations and developing supervisory skills.

By giving small firms the tools, services, and training they need, West and Rochette allow their clients to focus on their core business. Said West, Human Resource Partners lets small firms "realize the return on their investments in their greatest assets: their people."

Sources: Michael McCord, "Outsourcing Frees Owners from Time Consuming Tasks," *SeaCoastonline.com* (January 10, 2011), http://www.seacoastonline.com; company website: h-rpartners.com.

larger benefit packages is not an option. For example, when gasoline prices skyrocketed in 2008, most companies could not afford to automatically increase employees' pay because they were facing higher transportation costs themselves for the goods and services they had to buy. But some companies let employees either telecommute or, or like the state of Utah did, let employees work ten hours per day, four days a week.

Challenge 6: Responding to the Demographic and Diversity Challenges of the Workforce

Almost half of organizations reported that the biggest investment challenge facing organizations over the next ten years is obtaining human capital and optimizing their human capital investments.[41] Why is this so? Changes in the demographic makeup of employees, such as their ages, education levels, and ethnicities, is part of the reason why.

LEARNING OUTCOME 6

Think about some of
the teams you have
been a member of.
Which of them per-
formed better—those
that were diverse or
those that were not?
What challenges and
opportunities did the
more diverse teams
present? How do you
think they translate
to human resources
management?

To forecast trends to support the strategies of their organizations, HR managers frequently analyze the capabilities of different demographic groups and how well each is represented in both fast-growing and slow-growing occupations. Women, for example, are fairly well represented in fast-growing occupations such as health services but are also represented in some slow-growth occupations such as administrative jobs and computer and financial records processing jobs. Blacks and Hispanics have been heavily concentrated in several of the slow-growth and declining occupations. The U.S. labor force also grew more slowly in the last decade than it did in the previous one, a trend that is projected to continue.

To accommodate shifts such as these, find qualified talent, and broaden their customer bases, businesses know it is absolutely vital to increase their efforts to recruit and train a more diverse workforce. And with a more diverse workforce comes more diverse expectations on the part of employees for their employers to meet.

Ethnic and Racial Diversity in the Workforce

Figure 1.2 shows the current composition of the U.S. population and what it is expected to be in 2050. As you can see, minorities in the United States are increasing relative to the total population. U.S. workers are becoming more diverse as well. Much of the growth of the minority workforce has been due to not only the arrival of immigrants but also high birthrates among some minority groups, such as Hispanics. By 2050, the percentage of Hispanics in the United States is expected to double, and the percentage of people of Asian descent is expected to nearly double.[42]

Firms have long been criticized for hiring immigrant workers—both legal and illegal—because people believe they prevent U.S. citizens from getting jobs. Following 9/11, the backlash increased, and the number of work visas issued to foreigners by the U.S. government fell. This is a problem because, despite high unemployment rates in the nation, many American employers lack the highly qualified workers they need for key positions. To bring in the talent it needs from abroad, Microsoft has opened a facility in Vancouver, B.C., across from its Redmond, Washington, headquarters. In years past, the United States was able to attract the best and brightest of the world's talent, which fueled the country's success. But as you will learn in Chapter 15, that is changing.[43]

It is not just the most highly educated who are in demand either. Some businesses, including those in agricultural business, face labor shortages that would be even more severe without less-skilled immigrants willing to work for low pay and few or no benefits. The jobs these people do are often labor intensive and must be done in bad weather or in agricultural facilities in less-than-pleasant conditions. Throngs of

FIGURE 1.2	Composition of the U.S. Population	
	2010	**2050**
White	64.7%	46.3%
Hispanic/Latino (of any race)	16.0	30.2
African American	12.9	13.0
Asian Americans	4.6	7.8

Source: U.S. Census Bureau.

people are not lining up for these jobs. Moreover, state governments and the federal governments are beginning, to a greater extent, to crack down on firms that hire illegal immigrants, something they have been more reluctant to do in the past. Later in the book we will discuss in more detail what companies are doing in response to minority and immigration challenges and opportunities.[44]

Age Distribution of the Workforce

A significant proportion of American workers—79 million baby boomers, who constitute 26 percent of the population—are hitting retirement age. According to the Pew Research Center, 10,000 U.S. workers will turn 65 each and every day over the course of the next 19 years.[45] As a result of the retirements, the Bureau of Labor Statistics projects a shortfall of 10 million workers in the United States by 2012.

Not all baby boomers are retiring, though. Due to advances in medicine, people are staying healthier as they age and remaining in the labor force longer. A variety of factors—including an increase in the official retirement age in the United States from 65 to 67 are also keeping baby boomers working. So are economic factors: Many baby boomers' 401(k) retirement accounts have not grown as well as expected. Other boomers have not saved enough, or they have borrowed heavily to buy homes they hoped would increase in value but have not. Consequently, the number of people in the labor force aged 65 and older is expected to grow about ten times faster than the total labor force. Figure 1.3 shows the projected changes in the number of workers in the labor force by their age groups between now and 2018.

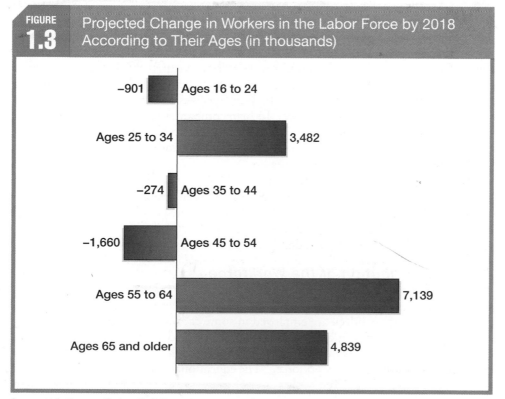

FIGURE 1.3   Projected Change in Workers in the Labor Force by 2018 According to Their Ages (in thousands)

−901	Ages 16 to 24
Ages 25 to 34	3,482
−274	Ages 35 to 44
−1,660	Ages 45 to 54
Ages 55 to 64	7,139
Ages 65 and older	4,839

Source: U.S. Bureau of Labor Statistics.

Hiring older workers can be a win-win situation for both older employers and the firms that hire them. Many firms find that older workers are generally mature, dependable, and remain on the job longer than younger workers who operate more like free agents. Older workers are also often willing to work flexible hours. Websites that try to connect older Americans with employers include retirementjobs.com, seniors4hire.org, seniorjobbank.com, and yourencore.com. Home Depot, AT&T, and Pitney Bowes are among the companies that have participated in a program sponsored by the American Association of Retired Persons (AARP) in an effort to attract older workers.

The millennial generation, of which you may be a member, is also having an effect on the labor market in the United States. Also known as Generation Y, millennials are generally regarded as having good technological know-how and initiative, especially when it comes to starting their own businesses. (Facebook founder Mark Zuckerberg is a notable example.) They are particularly interested in meaningful work that will improve the world around them. As we indicated earlier in the chapter, the group is also 80 million people strong, making it the largest generation ever. Similar to the trends with baby boomers, those who constitute this new population bulge are experiencing greater competition for advancement from others of approximately the same age.

The other major generation in the workforce is Generation X, people born between 1964 and 1979. Many members of Generation X watched their baby-boomer parents get downsized at some point in their lives. Consequently, now that they are raising children themselves, Generation X-ers value job security. However, they are less likely to think of themselves as being wed to one employer as their parents were. The members of Generation X are also independent. They like challenging work rather than repetitive work, and dislike supervisors who look over their shoulders.

Managers can find themselves challenged in terms of getting the three generations to work well together. Baby boomers sometimes categorize younger workers as having a poorer work ethic. Some younger workers have the perception that older workers are set in their ways and are technologically challenged. The situation can also create supervisory issues. How will a fifty-five-year-old react to being managed by someone in their twenties or thirties? To help companies overcome these obstacles, HR departments and experts are developing programs to help the generations understand one another better so they can capitalize on one another's strengths rather than preying upon one another's weaknesses.

Keep in mind that the three generations of workers we have described here are generalizations. Individual employees are vastly different from one another and motivated by different factors, even if they belong to the same generation. It is up to managers to figure out what drives each person so as to best utilize his or her talents and to meet the person's employment demands and career aspirations.

Gender Distribution of the Workforce

Women now constitute a little under half of the U.S. workforce. About 60 percent of women age 16 and older are in the labor force, and approximately 71 percent of mothers with school-age children are employed in some capacity. As Figure 1.4 shows, although the number of women joining the U.S. labor force has leveled off, the Bureau of Labor Statistics projects that the number of women will continue to increase relative to the number of men in the workforce.[46] The educational attainment of women is also increasing relative to men. Today, three out of every five college graduates are women.

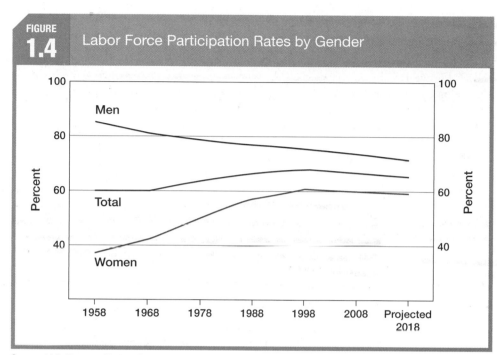

FIGURE 1.4 Labor Force Participation Rates by Gender

Source: U.S. Bureau of Labor Statistics.

Women's wages have increased too. In 1979, on average, women made 62 percent of what men made. Although the gap has not closed, it has narrowed. Women who are employed full time today make about 80 percent of what men employed full time make.[47] Unfortunately, the closing of the wage gap between the sexes has slowed since the 1990s, as has the march of women into top executive positions, despite some studies that show female CEOs frequently outperform their male counterparts.[48]

Employers wanting to attract the talent that women have to offer are taking measures to ensure they are treated equally in the workplace in terms of their advancement opportunities and compensation. In addition, more companies are accommodating working parents by offering them parental leave, part-time employment, flexible work schedules, job sharing, telecommuting, child and elder care assistance, and adoption assistance.

As we have suggested, harnessing a company's talent means being aware of characteristics *common* to employees while also managing these employees as *individuals*. It means not just tolerating or accommodating all sorts of differences but supporting, nurturing, and utilizing these differences to the organization's advantage—in other words, strategically leveraging them rather than simply managing them so that people are treated equitably and "everyone gets along."[49] HR managers have to ask themselves the following questions: What is it about the experiences, mindsets, and talents of different groups of people that can be utilized in a strategic way? After all, despite our similarities, *all* of us are different in one way or another, aside from the obvious differences we have outlined in this section. These differences, too, can be the source of organizational strength. Later in the book, we will discuss more about the steps firms can take to leverage employee differences.

Education of the Workforce

Some people say the United States is losing its edge when it comes to the education of its workforce. Other people say the problem is exaggerated because the American culture encourages innovation and risk taking. Which group do you fall into? How might changing societal norms affect innovation and risk taking in an HRM context?

Challenge 7: Adapting to Educational and Cultural Shifts Affecting the Workforce

Over the years, the educational attainment of the U.S. labor force has risen dramatically.[50] Figure 1.5 shows that it clearly pays to get a college education. An education also helps a person stay out of the ranks of the unemployed. For example, in 2010, the unemployment rate of people ages twenty to twenty-four hit 17 percent. But those in the same age range with college degrees fared better. The unemployment rate for them was a little over 9 percent.[51]

Despite the fact the educational attainment of the labor force has risen in general, American students' math and science test scores lag behind those of students in China, Japan, Singapore, Finland, and several other nations. The U.S. Department of Education has found that less than half of all high school seniors can handle mathematics problems involving fractions, decimals, percentages, elementary geometry, and simple algebra. And between 45 and 50 percent of adults in the United States have only the limited reading and writing abilities needed to handle the minimal demands of daily living or job performance.

Businesses now spend billions of dollars on basic skills training for their employees. As David Kearns, the renowned former CEO of Xerox Corporation and ardent

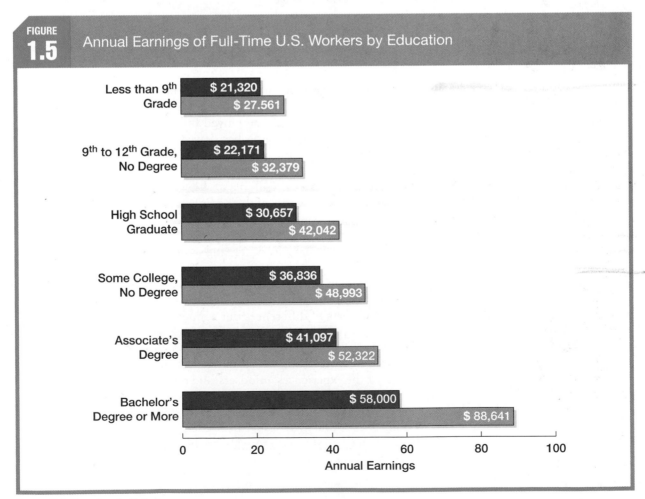

FIGURE 1.5   Annual Earnings of Full-Time U.S. Workers by Education

Source: U.S. Department of Labor.

education advocate, said, "The American workforce is in grave jeopardy. We are running out of qualified people. If current demographic and economic trends continue, American business will have to hire a million new workers a year who can't read, write, or count."[52] As the baby boomers retire, the problem will likely worsen. HR departments may have to offer higher compensation packages to attract qualified candidates, and recruiting and selection systems will have to function much more competitively.

Using the INTERNET

The U.S. Department of Labor website provides more information about employment. Go to

www.cengagebrain.com

Cultural and Societal Changes Affecting the Workforce

The attitudes, beliefs, values, and customs of people in a society are an integral part of their culture. Naturally, their culture and society affect their behavior on the job and the environment within the organization, influencing their reactions to work assignments, leadership styles, and reward systems. Cultural and societal changes are ongoing. HR policies and procedures therefore must be adjusted to cope with these changes.

Employee Rights

Laws affecting employee rights are continually changing. In this book we will discuss the major laws affecting companies today. Among them are laws granting employees the right to equal employment opportunities (Chapter 3); union representation if they desire it (Chapter 14); a safe and healthful work environment (Chapter 12); unemployment and health care benefits as required by law, and the regulation of pension plans by the government (Chapter 11); equal pay for equal work (Chapter 9); and so on. An expanded discussion of the specific areas in which rights and responsibilities are of concern to employers and employees will be presented in Chapter 13.

Privacy Concerns of Employees

HR managers and their staff members, as well as line managers in positions of responsibility, generally recognize the importance of discretion in handling all types of information about employees. Since the passage of the federal Privacy Act of 1974, increased attention to privacy has been evident, heightened by the increase in identity theft in recent years. While the act applies almost exclusively to records maintained by federal agencies, it has drawn attention to the importance of privacy and has led to the passage of additional privacy legislation, including the Health Insurance Portability and Accountability Act of 1996 (HIPAA) and the associated privacy rule issued by the U.S. Department of Health and Human Services, which protects the use and disclosure of personal medical information.

In addition to implementing privacy policies, most companies try to limit the use of Social Security numbers on time sheets, log-in sheets, and other employment forms. Companies also restrict access to employee files, conduct background checks on employees who have access to others' files, and contract with outside firms specializing in identity theft to prevent the abuse of employee information. Globalization has added another twist to privacy compliance. For example, EU countries prohibit the transfer of personal data to countries with inadequate data protection laws.[53]

Although the Electronic Communications Privacy Act of 1986 protects people's electronic communications such as their e-mail, the rules are different when it comes to the privacy that employees can expect with regard to their electronic communications at work. Workers are learning the hard way that their employers have a right to monitor their e-mail and Internet use, for example. The information employees post on the web—either on social networking sites or on job-hunting sites such as Monster—has also become subject to scrutiny by employers.

Because there is always a potential for litigation, firms have to tread lightly when it comes to employee privacy, though. Companies that have disciplined or fired employees for making disparaging remarks about their organizations on Internet sites such as Facebook have found themselves sued by the employees and labor organizations claiming that doing so violates the right of workers to communicate and congregate freely. Similarly, the U.S. Equal Opportunity Employment Commission has indicated it is willing to sue organizations if the background checks they conduct on candidates (to uncover their criminal backgrounds, credit histories, and so forth) have a discriminatory effect on minority groups.[54]

Camera surveillance in the workplace is also an issue, as is the use of Global Positioning Systems (GPS). The nonprofit organization Workplace Fairness reports that employers are using GPS in company cars to track where workers are, how fast they are driving, and the length of their breaks by monitoring how long their vehicles have not moved. Tracking chips in cell phones have also been used to trace the movements of employees.[55]

Is it legal to do these things? Legislators have not addressed all of these situations, but some of them are being decided in courts. However, most employers do not want to find themselves there. In Chapter 13, we will discuss employer-implemented privacy programs and guidelines along with the privacy employees can expect while on the job.

Changing Attitudes toward Work

Employees today are less likely to define their personal success only in terms of financial gains. Many employees, especially younger ones, believe satisfaction in life is more likely to result from balancing their work challenges and rewards with those in their personal lives. Though most people still enjoy work and want to excel at it, they tend to be focused on finding interesting work and are more inclined to pursue multiple careers. In fact, in a survey of more than 3,000 workers, 86 percent said work fulfillment and work-life balance were their top priorities. Only 35 percent said being successful at work and moving up the ladder were their top priorities. People also appear to be seeking ways of living that are less complicated but more meaningful. These new lifestyles cannot help having an impact on the way employees must be motivated and managed. Consequently, HRM has become more complex than it was when employees were concerned primarily with economic survival.

Balancing Work and Family

Even though new Census Bureau figures show couples postponing marriage and parenthood, balancing work and family continues to be a major concern for firms and their employees. Employees are already working more hours than they have at any time since 1973, and increasingly employees are tethered to their companies around the clock via communication technologies. Complicating the task is the fact that today's families are also more diverse. They can consist of two-wage-earner families, single-parent families, families headed by same-sex couples, and families in which multiple generations of adults are living under one roof. Competitive organizations are finding it advantageous to provide employees with more family-friendly options. Those options include telecommuting, flexible work hours, day care, elder care, part-time work, job sharing, parental leave, adoption assistance, spousal involvement in career planning, and assistance with family problems. About 57 percent of Fortune 500 companies, for example, provide same-sex partner health insurance benefits, as do some states for their employees.[56]

Companies with programs such as these calculate that accommodating their employees' individual needs and circumstances is a powerful way to attract and retain top-caliber people. Aetna Life and Casualty, for example, cut its turnover by 50 percent after it began offering six-month parental leaves, coupled with an option for part-time work when employees return to the job. Bank of America encourages all its employees to visit their children's schools or volunteer at any school—on company time.[57] Family-friendly companies have to balance the benefits they provide to families versus their single employees, though. The majority of employees have no children under 18. A Conference Board survey of companies with family-friendly programs found that companies acknowledge that childless employees sometimes harbor resentment against employees with children who are able to take advantage of these programs when they cannot.[58]

HRM 3 outlines some of the issues resources managers face as a result of demographic changes and changes in employees' expectations due to societal shifts.

HIGHLIGHTS IN **HRM**
3 Demographic and Cultural Issues Changing HRM

Changing Demographics: The coming decades will bring a more diverse and aging workforce to developed countries such as the United States. This has major implications for all aspects of HRM because it alters traditional experience and expectations regarding the labor pool. Among the issues in this area are:

- Globalization
- Shrinking pool of skilled entry-level workers
- Rising health care costs for employees
- Outsourcing, offshoring, furloughing, and the use of temporary, contract, and part-time employees
- Strategies designed to leverage people's differences
- Social Security and retirement issues
- Continual skills development and retraining

Employer/Employee Rights: This area reflects the shift toward organizations and individuals attempting to define rights, obligations, and responsibilities. Among the issues here are:

- Relationship employment versus transactional-based employment
- Concern for the privacy of employees
- Employer-employee ethics
- Equal pay for equal work
- Whistle-blowing
- Legal compliance
- Mandated benefits

Attitudes toward Work and Family: Employees are working more hours per week than they have since 1973, which has created demand for family-friendly options in the workplace. The Family Leave Act, which allows workers to take up to 12 unpaid weeks off to deal with family matters, is also affecting people's attitudes toward work and family. Among the issues are:

- Day care and elder care
- Job sharing
- Job rotation
- Parental leave
- Flextime
- Alternative work schedules
- Telecommuting
- Adoption assistance
- Same-sex benefits

The Partnership of Line Managers and HR Departments

line managers

Non-HR managers who are responsible for overseeing the work of other employees

We have taken a good deal of time up front in this book to outline today's competitive and social challenges to reinforce the idea that managing people is not something that occurs in a back room called the HR department. As we explained at the outset of the chapter, managing people is every manager's business. Successful organizations combine the experience of line managers with the expertise of HR managers to develop and utilize the talents of employees to their greatest potential. Line managers are non-HR managers who are responsible for overseeing the work of other employees. CEOs and line managers work with different HR managers at different times, depending upon the type of personnel situation being dealt with.

Just as there are different types of line managers who specialize in different functions—operations, accounting, marketing, and so forth—there are different types of human resources managers who specialize in different HR functions. Some of these workers specialize in employee training and development, recruitment, or compensation. Other HR employees specialize in studying the effects of industry and occupational trends, or concentrate on labor relations and prepare information for managers to use during negotiations with labor unions. By contrast, a human resources generalist can be responsible handle all aspects of human resources work depending on his or her employer's needs.[59] Figure 1.6 shows salary information for some of the HR positions we have discussed.

The Bureau of Labor Statistics forecasts that the number of positions needed in the HR field will grow much faster than average between now and 2018. Nonetheless, we understand that most readers of this book will be line managers and supervisors, rather than HR specialists. The text is, therefore, oriented to *helping people manage people more effectively,* whether they become first-line supervisors or chief executive officers. Students now preparing for careers in organizations will find that the study of HRM provides a background that will be valuable in managerial and supervisory positions. Becoming familiar with the role HR managers play should help facilitate closer cooperation between the different departments of firms and enable line and executive-level managers to fully utilize the assistance and services offered by their HR groups.

FIGURE 1.6   Positions in HR and Their Median Annual Wages

Position	Annual Wage
Training and development managers	$87,700
Benefits managers	$86,500
Human resources managers (all other)	$96,130
Compensation, benefits, and job analysis specialists	$53,860
Employment recruitment, and placement specialists	$45,470
Training and development specialists	$51,450

Source: U.S. Bureau of Labor Statistics.

Responsibilities of Human Resources Managers

The major activities for which a HR manager is typically responsible are as follows:

1. *Strategic advice and counsel.* The HR manager often serves as an in-house consultant to supervisors, managers, and executives. Given their knowledge of internal employment information and productivity metrics as well as their awareness of external trends such as economic and unemployment data and new legal and regulatory issues, HR managers can be an invaluable resource for making decisions. In some companies, generally larger ones, chief compliance or ethics officers help employees wade through gray areas when it comes to right and wrong and ensure personnel comply with the laws and regulations that affect their industries. The firm's top HR manager is in a good position for this job. HR managers are also being relied on more heavily to advise compensation committees, which are more closely scrutinizing executives' pay than they have in years past.

2. *Service.* HR managers perform a host of service activities such as recruiting, selecting, testing, and planning and conducting training programs. Technical expertise in these areas is essential for HR managers as they design and implement talent-management programs.

3. *Policy formulation and implementation.* HR managers generally propose and draft new policies or policy revisions to cover recurring problems or to prevent anticipated problems. Ordinarily, the policies are proposed to the senior executives of the organization, who actually issue them. HR managers also monitor the firm's managers and employees to ensure they follow established HR policies, procedures, and practices. Perhaps more important, they are a resource to whom managers can turn for policy interpretation.

4. *Employee advocacy.* One of the enduring roles of HR managers is to serve as an employee advocate—listening to employees' concerns and representing their needs to managers—to make certain that the interests of employees and the interests of the organization are aligned with one another.

Competencies Human Resources Managers Require

As top executives expect HR managers to assume a broader role in overall organizational strategy, many of these managers will need to acquire a complementary set of competencies. These competencies are summarized here and shown graphically in Figure 1.7.

- *Business mastery.* As we have explained, HR professionals need to know the businesses of their organizations and their strategies thoroughly. This requires an understanding of an organization's customers and economic and financial capabilities to help a firm achieve its strategic direction and adjust it as needed. Human resource managers who have good problem-solving skills and are also innovative and creative are a strategic asset to their firms.

- *HR mastery.* HR professionals are the organization's behavioral science experts. HR professionals should develop expert knowledge in the areas of staffing, development, appraisals, rewards, team building, performance measurement, and communication. Good interpersonal skills are essential.

- *Personal credibility.* Like other management professionals, HR professionals must establish personal credibility in the eyes of people internal and external to the firm. Credibility and trust are earned by developing good relationships with people both

LEARNING OUTCOME 8

Explain the dual role HR managers play in terms of serving both management and staff. Have you ever found yourself in a similar situation at work or school? Were you able to keep both groups happy? How were the challenges you faced similar to those faced by HR managers?

internal and external to the firm, demonstrating the values of the firm, standing up for one's own beliefs, and dealing with all parties equitably. Highlights in HRM 4 outlines the code of ethics HR professionals should follow, according to the Society for Human Resource Management.

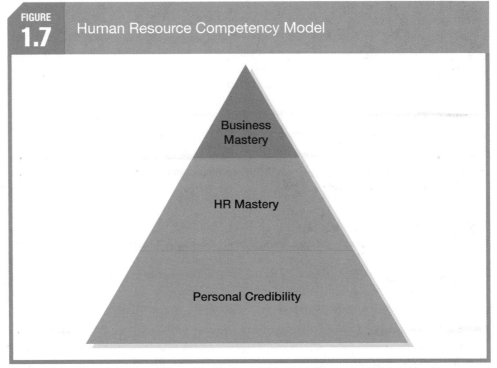

FIGURE 1.7   Human Resource Competency Model

Source: Adapted from Arthur Yeung, Wayne Brockbank, and Dave Ulrich, "Lower Cost, Higher Value: Human Resource Function in Transformation," reprinted with permission from *Human Resource Planning*, vol. 17, no. 3 (1994). Copyright 1994 by The Human Resource Planning Society, 317 Madison Avenue, Suite 1509, New York, NY 10017, (212) 490-6387.

HIGHLIGHTS IN HRM
4
SHRM Code of Ethical and Professional Standards in Human Resource Management

Society for Human Resource Management
CODE PROVISIONS

Professional Responsibility
Core Principle

As HR professionals, we are responsible for adding value to the organizations we serve and contributing to the ethical success of those organizations. We accept professional responsibility for our individual decisions and actions. We are also advocates for the profession by engaging in activities that enhance its credibility and value.

SHRM Code of Ethical and Professional Standards in Human Resource Management (continued)

Intent

- To build respect, credibility, and strategic importance for the HR profession within our organizations, the business community, and the communities in which we work.
- To assist the organizatiotns we serve in achieving their objectives and goals.
- To inform and educate current and future practitioners, the organizations we serve, and the general public about principles and practices that help the profession.
- To positively influence workplace and recruitment practices.
- To encourage professional decision-making and responsibility.
- To encourage social responsibility.

Guidelines

1. Adhere to the highest standards of ethical and professional behavior.
2. Measure the effectiveness of HR in contributing to or achieving organizational goals.
3. Comply with the law.
4. Work consistent with the values of the profession.
5. Strive to achieve the highest levels of service, performance, and social responsibility.
6. Advocate for the appropriate use and appreciation of human beings as employees.
7. Advocate openly and within the established forums for debate in order to influence decision-making and results.

Professional Development

Core Principle

As professionals we must strive to meet the highest standards of competence and commit to strengthen our competencies on a continuous basis.

Intent

- To expand our knowledge of human resource management to further our understanding of how our organizations function.
- To advance our understanding of how organizations work ("the business of the business").

Guidelines

1. Pursue formal academic opportunities.
2. Commit to continuous learning, skills development, and application of new knowledge related to both human resource management and the organizations we serve.
3. Contribute to the body of knowledge, the evolution of the profession, and the growth of individuals through teaching, research, and dissemination of knowledge.
4. Pursue certification such as CCP, CEBS, PHR, SPHR, etc. where available, or comparable measures of competencies and knowledge.

(continued)

SHRM Code of Ethical and Professional Standards in Human Resource Management (continued)

Ethical Leadership
Core Principle
HR professionals are expected to exhibit individual leadership as a role model for maintaining the highest standards of ethical conduct.

Intent
- To set the standard and be an example for others.
- To earn individual respect and increase our credibility with those we serve.

Guidelines
1. Be ethical; act ethically in every professional interaction.
2. Question pending individual and group actions when necessary to ensure that decisions are ethical and are implemented in an ethical manner.
3. Seek expert guidance if ever in doubt about the ethical propriety of a situation.
4. Through teaching and mentoring, champion the development of others as ethical leaders in the profession and in organizations.

Fairness and Justice
Core Principle
As human resource professionals, we are ethically responsible for promoting and fostering fairness and justice for all employees and their organizations.

Intent
To create and sustain an environment that encourages all individuals and the organization to reach their fullest potential in a positive and productive manner.

Guidelines
1. Respect the uniqueness and intrinsic worth of every individual.
2. Treat people with dignity, respect, and compassion to foster a trusting work environment free of harassment, intimidation, and unlawful discrimination.
3. Ensure that everyone has the opportunity to develop their skills and new competencies.
4. Assure an environment of inclusiveness and a commitment to diversity in the organizations we serve.
5. Develop, administer, and advocate policies and procedures that foster fair, consistent, and equitable treatment for all.
6. Regardless of personal interests, support decisions made by our organizations that are both ethical and legal.
7. Act in a responsible manner and practice sound management in the country(ies) in which the organizations we serve operate.

SHRM Code of Ethical and Professional Standards in Human Resource Management (continued)

Conflicts of Interest

Core Principle

As HR professionals, we must maintain a high level of trust with our stakeholders. We must protect the interests of our stakeholders as well as our professional integrity and should not engage in activities that create actual, apparent, or potential conflicts of interest.

Intent

To avoid activities that are in conflict or may appear to be in conflict with any of the provisions of this Code of Ethical and Professional Standards in Human Resource Management or with one's responsibilities and duties as a member of the human resource profession and/or as an employee of any organization.

Guidelines

1. Adhere to and advocate the use of published policies on conflicts of interest within your organization.
2. Refrain from using your position for personal, material, or financial gain or the appearance of such.
3. Refrain from giving or seeking preferential treatment in the human resources processes.
4. Prioritize your obligations to identify conflicts of interest or the appearance thereof; when conflicts arise, disclose them to relevant stakeholders.

Use of Information

Core Principle

HR professionals consider and protect the rights of individuals, especially in the acquisition and dissemination of information while ensuring truthful communications and facilitating informed decision-making.

Intent

To build trust among all organization constituents by maximizing the open exchange of information, while eliminating anxieties about inappropriate and/or inaccurate acquisition and sharing of information

Guidelines

1. Acquire and disseminate information through ethical and responsible means.
2. Ensure only appropriate information is used in decisions affecting the employment relationship.
3. Investigate the accuracy and source of information before allowing it to be used in employment related decisions.
4. Maintain current and accurate HR information.
5. Safeguard restricted or confidential information.
6. Take appropriate steps to ensure the accuracy and completeness of all communicated information about HR policies and practices.
7. Take appropriate steps to ensure the accuracy and completeness of all communicated information used in HR-related training.

Source: Reprinted by permission of SHRM

Summary

LEARNING OUTCOME 1   HR managers who have a good understanding of their firm's business can help it achieve its strategies—whatever they may be—through the effective utilization of people and their talents. An organization's success increasingly depends on the knowledge, skills, and abilities of its employees. To "compete through people," organizations have to do a good job of managing human capital: the knowledge, skills, and capabilities that have value to organizations. Managers must develop strategies for identifying, recruiting, and hiring the best talent available; developing these employees in ways that are firm-specific; helping them to generate new ideas and generalize them throughout the company; encouraging information sharing; and rewarding collaboration and teamwork among employees.

LEARNING OUTCOME 2   Globalization has become pervasive in the marketplace. It influences the number and kinds of jobs that are available and requires that organizations balance a complicated set of issues related to managing people working under different business conditions in different geographies, cultures, and legal environments. HR strategies and functions have to be adjusted to take into account these differences.

LEARNING OUTCOME 3   The fast pace of globalization along with corporate scandals over the years have led to a new focus on corporate social responsibility (good citizenship) and sustainability (a company's ability to produce a good or service for without damaging the environment or depleting a resource). Companies are finding out that having a good reputation for pursuing these efforts can enhance their revenues and improve the caliber of talent they are able to attract. One of HR's leadership roles is to spearhead the development and implementation of corporate citizenship throughout their organizations, especially the fair treatment of workers.

LEARNING OUTCOME 4   Technology has tended to reduce the number of jobs that require little skill and to increase the number of jobs that require considerable skill, a shift we refer to as moving from touch labor to knowledge work. This displaces some employees and requires that others be retrained. In addition, information technology has influenced HRM through human resources information systems (HRIS) that streamline HR processes, make information more readily available to managers and employees, and enable HR departments to focus on the firm's strategies. The Internet and social media are also affecting how employees are hired, work, and are managed.

LEARNING OUTCOME 5   To contain costs, organizations have been downsizing, outsourcing, offshoring, furloughing, and leasing employees, as well as enhancing productivity. HR's role is to not only implement these programs but consider the pros and cons of programs such as these and how they might affect a company's ability to compete, especially if they lead to the loss of talented staff members.

LEARNING OUTCOME 6   The workforce is becoming increasingly diverse, and organizations are doing more to address employee concerns and to maximize the benefit of different kinds of employees. But to benefit from those differences managers need to look past the obvious differences between employees and see not so obvious differences such as how they think, learn, work, solve problems, manage their time, and deal with other people. By first seeing the differences, exploring them, and then discovering how they can provide value to the organization, HR managers can leverage those differences.

LEARNING OUTCOME 7   HR managers have to keep abreast of the educational abilities of the talent available to their organization. Despite the fact the educational attainment of the labor force has risen in general, many firms are finding it difficult to find workers with the basic skills they need. As the baby boomers retire, HR departments may have to offer higher compensation packages to attract qualified candidates, and recruiting and selection systems will have to function much more competitively. Employee rights, privacy concerns, attitudes toward work, and efforts to balance work and family are becoming more important to workers as the cultural dynamics in the labor force shift. Companies are finding that accommodating employees' individual needs as a result of these shifts is a powerful way to attract and retain top-caliber people.

LEARNING OUTCOME 8 In working with line managers to address their organization's challenges, HR managers play a number of important roles; they are called on for strategic advice and ethics counsel, various service activities, policy formulation and implementation, and employee advocacy. To perform these roles effectively, HR managers must have a deep understanding of their firm's operational, financial and personnel capabilities. HR managers who do and are creative and innovative can help shape a firm's strategies so as to respond successfully to changes in the marketplace. Ultimately, managing people is rarely the exclusive responsibility of the HR function. Every manager's job involves managing people. Consequently, successful companies combine the expertise of HR specialists with the experience of line managers and executives to develop and use the talents of employees to their greatest potential.

Key Terms

change management
collaborative software
corporate social responsibility
downsizing
employee leasing
globalization
human capital
human resources information system (HRIS)

human resources management (HRM)
knowledge workers
line managers
managing diversity
offshoring
outsourcing

furloughing
proactive change
reactive change
reengineering
Six Sigma
total quality management (TQM)

Discussion Questions

LEARNING OUTCOME 1 Are people always an organization's most valuable asset? Why or why not?

LEARNING OUTCOME 2 Suppose your boss asked you to summarize the major people-related concerns related to opening an office in China. What issues would be on your list?

LEARNING OUTCOME 3 Name a company you hope to work for someday. What is its track record in terms of corporate social responsibility and sustainability? Are these factors important to you? Why or why not?

LEARNING OUTCOME 4 Will technology eliminate the need for human resources managers?

LEARNING OUTCOME 5 Do cost-containment pressures work against the effective management of people? Why or why not?

LEARNING OUTCOME 6 What are the pros and cons of having a more diverse workforce? Is the United States in a better position to compete globally because of its diverse population?

LEARNING OUTCOME 7 Why do HR managers need to stay abreast of the educational levels and work expectations of people in the workforce?

LEARNING OUTCOME 8 In your opinion, what is the most important role HR managers play?

On the Job: Video Cases

Fruit Guys: Responding Strategically to the Marketplace

Executives at the firm discuss the strategic challenges when it comes to operating a profitable business. Specific challenges including entering new markets are discussed, as well as some setbacks and some successes. The importance of hiring the right talent is also discussed, as is the importance of trying to balance profitability with the nimbleness to take advantage of new opportunities.

What to Watch for and Ask Yourself

- The Fruit Guys' CEO describes one poorly planned attempt to expand into Chicago. How did the organization change its strategy to successfully expand into other geographic markets?

- What are some possible legal/political influences the Fruit Guys face? (b) What are some possible demographic changes the Fruit Guys face?

- How do you think the company's HR strategy affects its success when it comes to expanding the firm's operations and growing its profits.

Case Study 1

New HR Strategy Makes Lloyd's A "Best Company"

After a mere 320 years in business, the iconic global insurer Lloyd's of London finally set out to establish its first true HR strategy, starting with the hiring of HR Director Suzy Black in 2009. "I was brought in to transform the HR function from one modeled on an old-style personnel office to a function that is more cutting edge, business focused, and value adding," says Black.

Black's first order of business was to evaluate the current state of affairs, particularly how the corporation's senior managers perceived the HR role. With this information in hand, Black and her team began to develop an overarching strategic agenda as well as specific tactics, addressing everything from recruitment to performance management to basic policies to rewards and compensation. Early on, Black admits, her main priority was simply "getting the basics right," an objective that was made more challenging by the global reach of the company that demanded flexibility and variation to meet the needs of all Lloyd's employees while still benefitting the company.

Changing long-time employees' perception of HR then took a bit of convincing, but employees quickly began to recognize the value of Black's actions. Through repeated presentations, employees worldwide grew to appreciate Black's insistence on transparency regarding the nature of the employer/employee relationship. Gradually, they could see how the HR strategies were effectively creating conditions in which they could develop in their careers, be successful, and find meaning and value in their work. Today, Lloyd's employees list the company's challenging work environment, healthy incentive programs, and meaningful community outreach programs among the key reasons they enjoy working for the insurance giant.

And Black's efforts are now gaining recognition outside the firm, positioning the company as a desirable place to work. In 2011, Lloyd's landed on the *sunday Times* Top 100 Best Companies to Work For (in the UK) list and was hailed as one of the

UK's Top 40 Business Brands by an independent researcher. Black emphasizes that the transformation was a companywide effort, and Lloyd's CEO Richard Ward adds, "I believe Lloyd's to be an inspiring and rewarding place to work and am pleased that our staff agree. I am extremely proud of the achievements of the corporation over the last 12 months and thank all Lloyd's employees for their continuing dedication, commitment, and professionalism."

Ironically, this leadership position is the first HR position Black has ever held, having risen through the ranks in other arenas in business. But her experience has given her a clear definition of the ideal characteristics of the HR professionals of the future. Black says they must be commercial, challenging, and focused on delivery and excellence. "They must understand change and transformation, excel at operations, and balance tactical and strategic thinking and acting." She adds, "They will have to be able to manage and navigate organizational complexity and ambiguities and not be afraid to say no occasionally in order to establish appropriate boundaries with the business."

Questions

1. What skills does Black think employees need to work successfully in the area of HR?
2. What are some of the outcomes of the company's new HR strategy?
3. What do you think might be some of the challenges of establishing HR policies for a global company?
4. What types of situations do you think might require an HR manager to say "no"?

Sources: Helen William, "City Slicker" *Personnel Today* (August 11, 2009): 10–11; *Digby Morgan Human Resourcefulness Newsletter*, February 2010, http://www.digbymorgannewsletter.com/story04_HR_02_10.htm; company website: www.lloyds.com.

Case Study 2

Shell's Top Recruiter Takes His Cues from Marketing

When Navjot Singh joined Royal Dutch Shell in 2003, the company was facing an extraordinary challenge: The rate at which Shell's engineers were retiring meant the global firm needed to double the number of new recruits it hired from 2,697 in 2005 to 5,440 by 2006 and to nearly 8,000 in 2008. Yet at the time, Shell was not considered an employer of choice. The global oil and gas company needed to project a new image—fast! Says Singh, "In the same way marketers know they need to advertise to be a market leader, HR had to know how to create an employer brand. Marketing is the only way to ensure customers buy products. It was also the only way to ensure Shell got the best people coming to us first."

Wait! Why is Shell's HR guy talking about marketing? As both an HR and marketing expert, Singh sees a powerful synergy between the two. "I'm 50% a marketer—the rest is HR, communications, and recruitment," says Singh. "But I'm an HR person, really." Singh's official job title, however, is Global Marketing Manager, Recruitment and Global HR Communications Manager, Shell (UK), a title and position like no other. Having come to Shell from DaimlerChrysler, where he served as the marketing director, Singh initially started out as VP of customer relationship management, but quickly joined the HR team when he recognized Shell's emerging need for new talent and the immense potential for him to use classic marketing techniques to help the company achieve its objectives. His vision, skill sets, and experience were a perfect match for the company's situation.

So in Singh's mind, addressing the company's need for new talent meant building a brand as an employer, which in turn meant creating a cohesive message. But Shell's global recruiting approach was anything but cohesive. "At the time we had 1,200 recruitment systems, 35 recruitment companies, and 400 executive search companies working for us," he recalls. "I attended a careers event at Cambridge University where there were three Shell stands beside each other—one from the UK, one from Malaysia, and another from Nigeria. This was a fragmented approach and tough for candidates to understand." Shell needed to create a unified outreach program if it was going to meet its need for numbers while fulfilling its desire for a global talent pool. The company recruits from among 90 different nationalities each year because it recognizes the benefits of cultural diversity.

Singh and his team set about applying various marketing techniques to the recruitment process, which have since resulted in an 80 percent cut in recruitment costs, a 20 percent reduction in the time to hire new staff, and a very real claim to being the top employer in its market segment. In fact, Shell has won 80 awards for its unique HR strategy. "I think it's important to make sure that employer branding activities are efficient and effective and that you have the right tools and processes, but also that it's competitively positioned from a cost perspective," notes Singh. "I also think you need to look at it in terms of satisfaction, with the employer value proposition which you create. You need to ensure that there is a high satisfaction level amongst your staff, that they are motivated and have pride in working for your company."

Having come so close to putting itself in danger of not attracting enough skilled candidates, Shell intends to continue running its recruitment program just like any other branding effort, thus ensuring it has the right human resources to deliver on its promises and achieve worldwide success. Singh believes Shell is typical of many firms, noting, "In the future, companies will have to apply for skilled people to work for them rather than candidates applying to work at an organization. HR must still realize the strategic value it can bring."

Questions

1. What functions of HRM are similar to marketing functions? How can thinking about "marketing" a company's jobs improve the strategic focus of human resources personnel?
2. If you were planning to use marketing strategies to "brand" a company as an employer of choice, what are some of the factors you'd consider?
3. Do you agree with Singh's statement that in the future, companies will have to apply for skilled people to work for them, rather than candidates applying to work at an organization? Why or why not?

Sources: Excerpted from Don Wood, "Lateral Thinking," Human Resources (January 2010): 12–13; Christopher Van Mossevelde, "Views from the Top," Employer Branding Today (April 16, 2009), http://www.employerbrandingtoday.com; Peter Crush, "Shell UK Combines HR and Marketing to Sell the Brand," HR Magazine (August 25, 2009), http://www.hrmagazine.co.uk.

Notes and References

1. T. J. Watson, Jr. *A Business and Its Beliefs: The Ideas That Helped Build IBM* (New York: McGraw-Hill, 1963).

2. Donald C. Busi, "Assignment Reviews (ARs): Moving toward Measuring Your Most Valuable Asset," *Supervision* 66, no. 1 (January 2005): 3–7.

3. David Lepak and Scott Snell. 2003. "Managing the human resource architecture for knowledge-based competition." In S. Jackson, M. Hitt, and A. DeNisi (eds.), *Managing knowledge for sustained competitive advantage: Designing strategies for Effective Human Resource Management.* (SIOP Scientific Frontiers Series, 127–154); David Lepak and Scott Snell, "Examining the Human Resource Architecture: The Relationship among Human Capital, Employment, and Human Resource Configurations," *Journal of Management* 28, no. 4 (2002): 517–543; Steve Bates, "Study Links HR Practices with the Bottom Line," *HRMagazine* 46, no. 12 (December 2001): 14; Ann Pomeroy, "Cooking Up Innovation: When It Comes to Helping Employees Create New Products and Services, HR's Efforts Are a Key Ingredient," *HRMagazine* 49, no. 11 (November 2004): 46–54.

4. Dave Ulrich, Steve Kerr, and Ron Ashkenas, *The GE Work-Out: How to Implement GE's Revolutionary Method for Busting Bureaucracy & Attacking Organizational Problems* (New York: McGraw-Hill Professional Publishing, 2002).

5. John P. Kotter, "Ten Observations," *Executive Excellence* 16, no. 8 (1999): 15–16.

6. "HR Success Increasingly Tied to Showing of Strong Business Acumen," *HRFocus* (December 2010): 1–5.

7. M. Hammer and J. Champy, *Reengineering the Corporation* (New York: HarperCollins, 1994). See also Michael Hammer, *Beyond Reengineering: How the Process-Centered Organization Is Changing Our Work and Our Lives* (New York: HarperBusiness, 1996); William M. James, "Best HR Practices for Today's Innovation Management," *Research-Technology Management* 45, no. 1 (January–February 2002): 57–61.

8. Lee G. Bolman and Terry E. Deal, "Four Steps to Keeping Change Efforts Heading in the Right Direction," *Journal of Quality and Participation* 22, no. 3 (May/June 1999): 6–11; "Coaching Employees through the Six Stages of Change," *HRFocus* 79, no. 5 (May 2002): 9; Stefan Stern, "Forever Changing," *Management Today* (February 7, 2005): 40; Dennis Smillie, "Managing Change, Maximizing Technology," *Multi-Housing News* 40, no. 1 (January 2005): 4.

9. "Beermaker Eyes Chinese Factories," *Fort Worth Star-Telegram* (December 28, 2010): 3C; Susan Meisinger, "Going Global: A Smart Move for HR Professionals," *HRMagazine* 49, no. 3 (March 2004): 6.

10. World Trade Organization, *World Trade Report, 2010* (Geneva: WTO Publications): 20; "One Ninth of All U.S. Production Is for Export," *PPI Trade Fact of the Week* (March 19, 2008).

11. Laura McKnight, "For Companies, Doing Good Is Good Business," *Kansas City Star* (December 26, 2010), http://www.kansascity.com.

12. Ibid.

13. Jeff Tanner and Mary Anne Raymond, *Principles of Marketing* (Nyack, NY: FlatWorld Knowledge, 2010): Chapter 10.

14. Nancy R. Lockwood, "Corporate Social Responsibility: HR's Leadership Role," *HRMagazine* 49, no. 2 (December 2004): S1–11.

15. Benoit Guay, "Knowledge Management Is a Team Sport," *Computing Canada* 27, no. 3 (July 13, 2001): 23; Pimm Fox, "Making Support Pay," *Computerworld* 36, no. 11 (March 11, 2002): 28; "Visions of the Future," *Human Resources* (January 2008): 22.

16. Carol Carter, *Keys to Business Communication* (Upper Saddle River, NJ: Pearson), 2012: 414.

17. "China Engineers Next Great Leap with Wave of 'Knowledge Workers,'" *Milwaukee Journal Sentinel* (via Knight-Ridder/Tribune News Service), December 31, 2003; "Edward Yourdon's New Book Helps 'Knowledge Workers' Put Emotion Aside to Look at the Facts of the New Economic Reality," *PR Newswire* (October 4, 2004); Marshall Goldsmith, "Supervisors of the Smart," *BRW* 30, no. 20 (May 22, 2008): 57–57.

18. Ben Worthen, "Measuring the ROI of Training," *CIO* 14, no. 9 (February 15, 2001): 128–36; Hashi Syedain, "Out of this World," *People Management* 14, no. 8 (April 17, 2008): 20–24.

19. Scott A. Snell, Donna Stueber, and David P. Lepak, "Virtual HR Departments: Getting Out of the Middle," in R. L. Heneman and D. B. Greenberger (eds.), *Human Resource Management in Virtual Organizations* (Columbus, OH: Information Age Publishing, 2002); Samuel Greengard, "How to Fulfill Technology's Promise," *Workforce* (February 1999): *HR Software Insights* supplement, 10–18.

20. Drew Robb, "Building a Better Workforce: Performance Management Software Can Help You Identify and Develop High-Performing Workers," *HRMagazine* 49, no. 10 (October 2004): 86–92.

21. Robb, "Building a Better Workforce," 86–92; "How to Implement an Effective Process for a New HR Management System," *HRFocus* (January 2005): 3–4; "New Study Finds HRIS Key to Reducing Costs," *Payroll Managers Report* 7, no. 5 (May 2007): 13.

22. Bruce Shutan, "HRMS Flexibility Unlocks Secret to Success," *Employee Benefits* (August 1, 2004); "New Study Finds HRIS Key to Reducing Costs," *Payroll Managers Report* 7, no. 5 (May 2007): 13.

23. Douglas A. Ready and Jay A Conger, "Make Your Company a Talent Factory," *Harvard Business Review* (June 2007): 1.

24. Douglas A. Ready and Jay A Conger, "Make Your Company a Talent Factory," *Harvard Business Review* (June 2007): 1, 8.

25. Dave Carpenter, "Is Your Retirement in Jeopardy?" *Fort Worth Star-Telegram* (January 1, 2010): 5B.

26. "Shared HR Releases List of Top Five SMB Trends for 2011," *PRWeb* (October 7, 2010), http://www.prweb.com.

27. "Mike Stobbe, "Dieting Like It's Your Job: Does Paying for Healthy Habits Work?" *USA Today* (June 1, 2010), http://www.usatoday.com.

28. "Geographic Profile of Employment and Unemployment," *U.S. Bureau of Labor Statistics*, accessed December 29, 2010 at http://www.bls.gov.

29. "Up to Speed: L. L. Bean Moves Employees as Workloads Shift," *Chief Executive* (July–August 1996): 15; Darrell Rigby, "Look before You Lay Off," *Harvard Business Review* 80, no. 4 (April 2002): 20–21.

30. Stephanie Armour, "Some Companies Choose No-Layoff Policy," *USA Today*, December 17, 2001, B-1; Gene Koretz, "Hire Math: Fire 3, Add 5," *Business Week Online* (March 13, 2000); Michelle Conlin, "Where Layoffs Are a Last Resort," *Business Week Online* (October 8, 2001); Lynn Miller, "Downsizing Trend Brings New Change to HR Directors," *HRMagazine* 45, no. 1 (January 2001); Norman E. Amundson, William A. Borgen, Sharalyn Jordan, and Anne C. Erlebach, "Survivors of Downsizing: Helpful and Hindering Experiences," *Career Development Quarterly* 52, no. 3 (March 2004): 256–72.

31. Ruth Morss, "Creative Approaches to Layoffs," *Salary.com*, accessed December 29, 2010, at http://www.salary.com.

32. Ibid.

33. John Sullivan, "Employee Furloughs Can Be a Bad Alternative to Layoffs," *ere.net* (February 9, 2009). http://www.ere.net/.

34. Gubman, "HR Strategy and Planning," 13–21.

35. Gubman, "HR Strategy and Planning," 13–21; Thomas W. Gainey, Brian S. Klaas, and Darla Moore, "Outsourcing the Training Function: Results from the Field," *Human Resource Planning* 25, no. 1 (2002): 16–23, 873, 881; Denise Pelham, "Is It Time to Outsource HR?" *Training* 39, no. 4 (April 2002): 50–52; Tom Anderson, "HR Outsourcing Expected to Surge this Year," *Employee Benefit News* (February 1, 2005); Jessica Marquez, "More Piecemeal Approach to HRO Emerging," *Workforce Management*, 87, no. 8 (May 5, 2008): 10.

36. Pete Engardio, Michael Arndt, and Dean Foust, "The Future of Outsourcing," *BusinessWeek* (January 30, 2006).

37. Pam Babcock, "America's Newest Export: White-Collar Jobs," *HRMagazine* 49, no. 4 (April 2004): 50–54.

38. Elliot Spagat, "Procter & Gamble to Outsource about 80% of Back-Office Work," *The*

Wall Street Journal Online* (June 14, 2002); "Outsourcing HR," *Industry Week* 249, no. 10 (May 15, 2000): 71; Carolyn Hirschman, "For PEOs, Business Is Booming," *HRMagazine* 45, no. 2 (February 2000): 42–47; Brian Klaas, "Trust and the Role of Professional Employer Organizations: Managing HR in Small and Medium Enterprises," *Journal of Managerial Issues* 14, no. 1 (Spring 2002): 31–49; Chris Pentilla, "Got It Covered: If You Can't Afford to Offer Employee Benefits on Your Own, Why Not Join Forces with a PEO?" *Entrepreneur* 32, no. 2 (February 2004): 66–68; Milan Yager, "Outsource to Gain Human Resources Expertise," *Hotel & Motel Management* 223, no. 7 (April 21, 2008): 14.

39. Bruce Stokes, Is There a Future for "Made in America," *The Atlantic* (December 9, 2010).

40. Patrick Barta and Andrew Caffrey, "Productivity Leap Shows Potential of U.S. Economy—Rise at 8.6 Percent Pace, Positive for Profits, Doesn't Bode Very Well for Employment," *The Wall Street Journal*, May 8, 2002, A1; Jon E. Hilsenrath, "The Economy: Big U.S. Service Sectors Boosted Late 1990s Surge in Productivity," *The Wall Street Journal*, April 22, 2002, A2; Karen Lowry Miller, "Economy: Out of Steam—A Dip in U.S. Productivity Provokes Anxious Questions," *Newsweek International* (February 21, 2005): 34; Milan Yager, "Outsource to Gain Human Resources Expertise," *Hotel & Motel Management* 223, no. 7 (April 21, 2008): 14.

41. "Poll Identifies Top Challenges For HR During Next 10 Years," *HRMagazine*. 55, no. 11 (November 2010): 80.

42. "Table 4. Projections of the Population by Sex, Race, and Hispanic Origin for the United States: 2010 to 2050," U.S. Census Bureau, accessed January 1, 2011 at http://www.census.gov.

43. Kim L. Hunter, "A Changing Work Force: Why Business—and the PR Profession—Needs More Diversity in Its Ranks," *Public Relations Tactics* 14, no. 7 (July 2007): 13.

44. Irwin Speizer, "Diversity on the Menu: Rachelle Hood, Denny's Chief Diversity Officer, Has Boosted the Company's Image. But That Hasn't Sold More Breakfasts," *Workforce Management* 83, no. 12 (November 1, 2004): 41; Patrick Purcell, "Older Workers: Employment and Retirement Trends," *Journal*

of Pension Planning & Compliance* 34, no. 1 (Spring 2008): 32–48.

45. Dan Barry, "For Those Who Seemed Forever Young, Old Age is Arriving," *Fort Worth Star-Telegram* (January 1, 2011): 5A The U.S. Department of Labor's Bureau of Labor Statistics also maintains projections and percentages in these categories. Interested readers can access this information at http://www.bls.gov.

46. U.S. Bureau of Labor Statistics, *Occupational Outlook Quarterly Online* (Winter 2009–2010): http://www.bls.gov.

47. Institute for Women's Policy Research, *The Gender Wage Gap, 2009* (Updated September 2010): 1.

48. Cindy Krischer Goodman, "Women's Rise to Top Job Stagnates, Study Finds," *Fort Worth Star-Telegram* (December 27, 2010): 10B–11B.

49. Kathleen Iverson, "Managing for Effective Workforce Diversity," *Cornell Hotel and Restaurant Administration Quarterly* 41, no. 2 (April 2000): 31–38; Gail Johnson, "Time to Broaden Diversity Training," *Training* 41, no. 9 (September 2004): 16.

50. The U.S. Department of Labor's Bureau of Labor Statistics keeps up-to-date projections and percentages on educational requirements for different kinds of jobs. Interested readers can access this information at http://www.bls.gov; Louis Uchitelle, "College Degree Still Pays, but It's Leveling Off," *The New York Times*, January 13, 2005, C1.

51. Don Lee, "Young Workers Careers to Carry Lifelong Scars of Recession," *Fort Worth Star-Telegram* (December 30, 2010), http://www.star-telegram.com.

52 ."Corporate America Can't Write," *Work & Family Newsbrief* (January 2005): 4; J. R. Labbe, "Future of an Illiterate Citizenry Is Dim," *Fort Worth Star-Telegram*, August 26, 2007, C1, C8.

53. "Avoiding Identity Theft," *Aftermarket Business* 114, no. 12 (December 2004): 10.

54. Steve Greenhouse, "EEOC Sues Kaplan," *New York Times* (December 21, 2010), http://www.nytimes.com.

55. "Your Rights: Surveillance at Work," *Workplace Fairness* (December 2010), http://www.workplacefairness.org/.

56. Ashley Surdin, "Benefits for Same-Sex Couples Expanding," *Washington Post*

(November 27, 2009), http://www.washington post.com.

57. Todd Raphael, "The Drive to Down-shifting," *Workforce* 80, no. 10 (October 2001): 23; Jim Olsztynski, "Flexible Work Schedules May Make More Sense: One in Six Americans Qualifies as a Caregiver Who May Benefit from Flextime," *National Driller* 26, no. 2 (February 2005): 16–19; Karen Springen, "Cutting Back Your Hours," *Newsweek*, 151, no. 19 (May 12, 2008): 60.

58. Leah Carlson, "Flextime Elevated to National Issue," *Employee Benefit News* (September 15, 2004).

59. U.S. Bureau of Labor Statistics, "Human Resources, Training, and Labor Relations Managers and Specialists, *Occupational Outlook Handbook, 2010–11*, accessed January 20, 2011 at http://www.bls.gov/.

2 Strategy and Human Resources Planning

After studying this chapter, you should be able to

LEARNING OUTCOME 1 Identify the advantages of integrating human resources planning and strategic planning.

LEARNING OUTCOME 2 Understand how an organization's competitive environment influences its strategic planning.

LEARNING OUTCOME 3 Understand why it is important for an organization to do an internal resource analysis.

LEARNING OUTCOME 4 Describe the basic tools used for human resources forecasting.

LEARNING OUTCOME 5 Explain the linkages between competitive strategies and HR.

LEARNING OUTCOME 6 Understand what is required for a firm to successfully implement a strategy.

LEARNING OUTCOME 7 Recognize the methods for assessing and measuring the effectiveness of a firm's strategy.

One of the clichés about the annual reports of companies is that they often claim that "people are our most important asset." Although we might believe this to be true, the fact is that historically managers often have not acted as though they themselves really believed it. Too often the focus has been on minimizing the number of a firm's employees rather than strategically utilizing their talents. In the past, executives often tried to remove human capital from the strategy equation by substituting capital for labor where possible or by creating hierarchical structures that separated those who think from those who actually do the work. But for many firms, this is changing.

Surveys show that 92 percent of chief financial officers now believe human capital affects an organization's customer service, 82 percent believe it affects profitability, and 72 percent believe it affects innovation.[1] And in a survey by the consulting firm Deloitte, nearly 80 percent of corporate executives said the importance of HRM in their firms has grown substantially over the years, and two-thirds said that HR expenditures are now viewed as a strategic investment rather than simply a cost to be minimized. Indeed, research shows that strategically designed and implemented HR systems increase the value of firms, something executives are keenly interested in accomplishing. They are also demanding their human resources groups push past short-term projections and provide detailed forecasts for needs and the associated costs over a two- to three-year horizon. Even small companies are realizing that their employees are the key to ensuring their ability to compete and survive. As General Electric's legendary ex-CEO Jack Welch puts it: "We live in a global economy. To have a fighting chance, every company needs to get every employee, with every idea in their heads and every morsel of energy in their bodies, into the game."[2]

Strategic Planning and Human Resources

LEARNING OUTCOME 1

Why is HR planning integral to a firm's strategic planning? As an HR professional, what do you think you could do to tie the two functions together?

strategic planning

Procedures for making decisions about the organization's long-term goals and strategies

human resources planning (HRP)

The process of anticipating and providing for the movement of people into, within, and out of an organization

As we explained in Chapter 1, "competing through people" is the theme for this book. But the idea remains only a premise for action until we put it into practice. To deliver on this promise, we need to understand some of the systems and processes in organizations that link human resources management and strategic management. A few definitions may be helpful up front.

First of all, strategic planning involves a set of procedures for making decisions about the organization's long-term goals and strategies. In this chapter, we discuss strategic plans as having a strong external orientation that covers major portions of the organization. The plans especially focus on how the organization will position itself relative to its competitors in order to ensure its long-term survival, create value, and grow. Human resources planning (HRP), by comparison, is the process of anticipating and providing for the movement of people into, within, and out of an organization. Overall, its purpose is to help managers deploy their human resources as effectively as possible, where and when they are needed, to accomplish the organization's goals. Strategic human resources management combines strategic planning and HR planning. It can be thought of as the pattern of human resources deployments and activities that enable an organization to achieve its strategic goals.

HR planning is an essential activity of organizations. Consider CNA Financial Corp., a Chicago-based insurance company, for example. CNA Financial discovered via HR planning that it would run short of underwriters—a key skill pool in the company—in just two years' time if their turnover rates continued at their current pace. The global strategies firms are increasingly pursuing, such as mergers, joint ventures, offshoring, the relocation of plants, product innovation plans, and downsizing, are also making HR planning more critical and more complex for managers. According to Walt Cleaver, an HR strategist and president of the Cleaver Consulting Group, increased global competitiveness in many industries has led to the commoditization of products based on price, which is making talent the "great differentiator" among firms. As we explained in Chapter 1, it is relatively easy for a competitor to copy your product and make it more cheaply. But duplicating the talents of your employees will prove much more difficult.[3] Globalization and shifts in the composition of the labor force that are occurring also require that HR managers become more involved in planning because these changes affect the full range of a company's HR practices (such as employee recruitment, selection, training, compensation, and motivation).

strategic human resources management (SHRM)

The pattern of human resources deployments and activities that enable an organization to achieve its strategic goals

Strategic Planning and HR Planning: Linking the Processes

Good HR managers "marry" human resources planning to the strategic planning for their organizations as a whole. Human resources planning relates to strategic planning in several ways, but at a fundamental level, we can focus on two issues: strategy formulation and strategy implementation. Human resources planning provides a set of inputs into the strategic *formulation* process in terms of what is possible, that is, whether a firm has the types and numbers of people available to pursue a given strategy. For example, when Barnes & Noble executives contemplated the move into web-based commerce to compete with Amazon.com, one of the issues they had to address was whether they had the talent needed to succeed in that arena.

In addition to strategy formulation, HRP is important in terms of strategy *implementation*. In other words, once the firm has devised its strategy, the company's executives must make resource allocation decisions to implement that strategy, including decisions related to the firm's structure, processes, and human capital.[4] Companies such as GE, IBM, and CIGNA have taken strides to combine these two aspects of strategic management.[5] 3M's managers have the two aspects down to a science. Not only does the company engage in elaborate workforce planning, it has figured out how to utilize its employees to expand into markets worldwide. Once primarily a domestic company, today 70 percent of its products are sold abroad. According to Brian Ronningen, 3M's manager of human capital management, the company is able to project "the demand for any workforce category, in any business, in any part of the world."[6]

Figure 2.1 shows how companies align their HRP and strategic planning in this way. When this occurs, a firm's board of directors and top managers recognize that strategic planning decisions affect—and are affected by—HR concerns. As James Walker, a noted HRP expert, puts it, "Today, virtually *all* business issues have people implications; *all* human resource issues have business implications."

Step One: Mission, Vision, and Values

mission

The basic purpose of the organization as well as its scope of operations

The first step in strategic planning is establishing a mission, vision, and values for the organization. The mission is the basic purpose of the organization, as well as its scope of operations. It is a statement of the organization's reason for existing. The

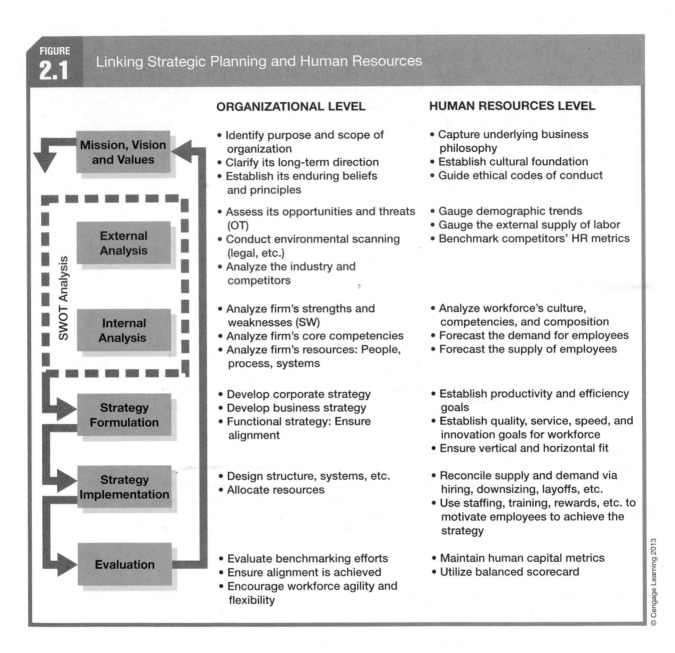

FIGURE 2.1 Linking Strategic Planning and Human Resources

SWOT Analysis

	ORGANIZATIONAL LEVEL	**HUMAN RESOURCES LEVEL**
Mission, Vision and Values	• Identify purpose and scope of organization • Clarify its long-term direction • Establish its enduring beliefs and principles	• Capture underlying business philosophy • Establish cultural foundation • Guide ethical codes of conduct
External Analysis	• Assess its opportunities and threats (OT) • Conduct environmental scanning (legal, etc.) • Analyze the industry and competitors	• Gauge demographic trends • Gauge the external supply of labor • Benchmark competitors' HR metrics
Internal Analysis	• Analyze firm's strengths and weaknesses (SW) • Analyze firm's core competencies • Analyze firm's resources: People, process, systems	• Analyze workforce's culture, competencies, and composition • Forecast the demand for employees • Forecast the supply of employees
Strategy Formulation	• Develop corporate strategy • Develop business strategy • Functional strategy: Ensure alignment	• Establish productivity and efficiency goals • Establish quality, service, speed, and innovation goals for workforce • Ensure vertical and horizontal fit
Strategy Implementation	• Design structure, systems, etc. • Allocate resources	• Reconcile supply and demand via hiring, downsizing, layoffs, etc. • Use staffing, training, rewards, etc. to motivate employees to achieve the strategy
Evaluation	• Evaluate benchmarking efforts • Ensure alignment is achieved • Encourage workforce agility and flexibility	• Maintain human capital metrics • Utilize balanced scorecard

© Cengage Learning 2013

strategic vision

A statement about where the company is going and what it can become in the future; clarifies the long-term direction of the company and its strategic intent

core values

The strong and enduring beliefs and principles that the company uses as a foundation for its decisions

mission often is written in terms of general clients it services. Depending on the scope of the organization, the mission may be broad or narrow. For example, the mission of Google is "to organize the world's information and make it universally accessible and useful."[7] The strategic vision of the organization moves beyond the mission statement to provide a perspective on where the company is headed and what the organization can become in the future. Although the terms *mission* and *vision* often are used interchangeably, the vision statement ideally clarifies the long-term direction of the company and its strategic intent.

Organizational core values are the strong enduring beliefs and principles that the company uses as a foundation for its decisions. They are the essence of its corporate culture and an expression of its personality.[8] The core values for the organic grocery chain Whole Foods are as follows:

- Selling the highest quality natural and organic products available
- Satisfying and delighting our customers
- Supporting team member happiness and excellence
- Creating wealth through profits and growth
- Caring about our communities and our environment
- Creating ongoing win-win partnerships with our suppliers
- Promoting the health of our stakeholders through healthy eating education

Core values such as these are the underlying parameters for how a company intends to act toward its customers, employees, and the public in general.

Step Two: Environmental Analysis

The mission, vision, and values drive the second component of the strategic management process: an ongoing analysis of external opportunities and threats. Changes in the external environment have a direct impact on the way organizations are run and people are managed. Some of these changes represent opportunities, and some of them represent real threats to the organization. Because of this, successful strategic management depends on an accurate and thorough evaluation of the environment. Environmental scanning is the systematic monitoring of the major external forces influencing the organization.[9] Managers attend to a variety of external issues; however, the following six are monitored most frequently:

1. Economic factors and development information, including general, regional, and global conditions
2. Industry and competitive trends, including new processes, services, and innovations
3. Technological changes, including information technology, innovations, and automation
4. Government and legislative issues, including laws and administrative rulings
5. Social concerns, including child care, elder care, the environment, and educational priorities
6. Demographic and labor market trends, including the age, composition, and literacy of the labor market, and immigration

By continuously scanning the environment for changes that will likely affect an organization, managers can anticipate their impact and make adjustments early.

Competitive Environment

Many factors in the general environment—factors a firm cannot directly control— can affect its strategic decisions. This is why analyzing the firm's competitive environment is central to strategic planning. The competitive environment includes the

LEARNING OUTCOME 2

What external factors in the environment do you think firms are most likely to overlook when formulating their business strategies? How can an HR manager help its executive team get a fuller picture of the competitive environment in which it operates?

environmental scanning

Systematic monitoring of the major external forces influencing the organization

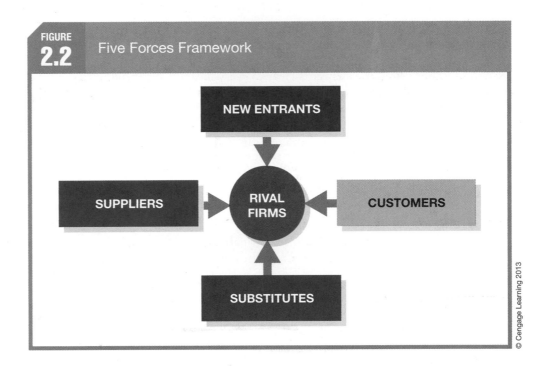

FIGURE 2.2   Five Forces Framework

NEW ENTRANTS

SUPPLIERS

RIVAL FIRMS

CUSTOMERS

SUBSTITUTES

© Cengage Learning 2013

specific organizations with which the firm interacts. As Figure 2.2 shows, the competitive environment includes the firm's customers, rival firms, new entrants, substitutes, and suppliers. Firms analyze the competitive environment in order to adapt to or influence the nature of competition. A general rule of thumb about this analysis is: The more power each of these forces has, the less profitable (and therefore attractive) the industry will be. Let us look at each of the five forces.

Customers

One of the most important assessments a firm can make is identifying the needs of its customers. At a fundamental level, a firm's strategy should focus on creating customer value—and different customers often want different things. For example, in the hotel industry, business travelers may want convenient locations with meeting facilities. Vacationers may want resort locations with swimming pools, golf courses, and luxury spas. Other travelers may just want an inexpensive room next to the highway. The point is that increasingly "one size does not fit all," so organizations need to know how they are going to provide value to customers. That is the foundation for strategy, and it influences the kinds of skills and behaviors needed from employees. For example, actions and attitudes that lead to excellent customer service can include the following:

- Speed of delivering normal orders

- Willingness to meet extraordinary needs

- Merchandise delivered in good condition

- Readiness to take back defective goods and resupply new goods quickly

- Availability of installation and repair services and parts

Rival Firms

In addition to customer analysis, perhaps the most obvious element of industry analysis is examining the nature of competition. The first question to consider is: Who *is* the competition? Often the answer is clear to everyone, but sometimes it is not. For example, for many years, Toys "R" Us viewed its main competitors to be other toy stores such as FAO Schwarz or KB Toys. However, other retailers such as Target and Walmart soon moved into this space very successfully. This had a direct effect on human resources planning for Toys "R" Us. While in the past, Toys "R" Us had been successful with a volume-based approach (that is, "stack it high, and let it fly"), bigger retailers soon gained an advantage—who can beat Walmart's volume and cost advantage? As a consequence, Toys "R" Us had to modify its strategy to compete more on customer service and the expertise of its employees. But did Toys "R" Us have the number and kind of employees required to compete in this way? Were its staffing, training, performance management, and compensation practices aligned with this strategy?

New Entrants

As we suggested previously, new companies can sometimes enter an industry and compete well against established firms, and sometimes they cannot. To protect their positions, companies often try to establish entry barriers to keep new firms out of their industries. However, when new firms do enter an industry it is often because they have a different—and perhaps better—way to provide value to customers. When Virgin America took flight in August 2007, the airline's goal was not just to sell cheap tickets. It promised to make "flying good again" by offering, among other perks, in-flight live concerts, Wi-Fi, MP3 players, mood lighting, music in the bathrooms, and top-notch customer service.[10] When we look at the challenges faced by traditional airlines because of the threat of carriers such as Virgin America, JetBlue, and Southwest Airlines, we can clearly see that new entrants can change the "rules of the game" in an industry. The impact on labor costs, productivity, skills required, and work design are important considerations in both strategic planning and human resources planning.

Virgin America, a new entrant in the airline industry, adds value to its product by selling "the experience" of flying. Do you think the company will change the rules of the game for its competitors?

REUTERS/John Decker Virgin America/Pool/Landov

Substitutes

At times, the biggest opportunity or threat in an industry does not come from direct competition but from substitution. In the telephone industry, for example, people are increasingly disconnecting their landline phones and instead using their mobile phones and VoIP (Voice-Over-the-Internet Protocol) services such as Skype. That implies that firms may need to adjust their employee skill bases to support different technologies, or they may need to think about how they will compete in different ways. As an example, think about how the travel business has changed over the years. Travel agents used to be the key resource people used to search for flights, hotels, rental cars, and the like. However, with the advent of online reservation systems, travel agents have had to adapt their approach. Today, they are as likely to compete based on the service they provide and the expertise they have about particular locations.

Suppliers

Organizations rarely create everything on their own, but instead have suppliers that provide them with key inputs. These inputs can include raw materials for production, money (from banks and stockholders), information, and people. This last factor—people, or labor as it is historically called—has direct implications for strategic planning and human resources planning.

Many factors influence the labor supply, including demographic changes in the population, national and regional economics, the educational level of the workforce, demand for specific employee skills, population mobility, and governmental policies. Consider these U.S. Census Bureau projections about how the U.S. workforce will change between 2012 and 2018:

- Employment growth will continue to be concentrated in the service-providing sector of the economy.

- About 26 percent of all new jobs created in the U.S. economy will be in the health care and social assistance industry. This industry—which includes public and private hospitals, nursing and residential care facilities, and individual and family services—is expected to grow by 24 percent, or the equivalent of 4 million new jobs.

- Within the goods-producing sector, construction is the only sector projected to grow. Employment in manufacturing industries will decline by 1.2 million jobs.

- The number of workers in the 55-and-older group is projected to grow by nearly 30 percent, more than any other age group.

- Minorities and immigrants are expected to constitute a larger share of the U.S. population and the labor force in 2018.

Of the twenty fastest growing occupations, twelve will require an associate's degree or higher. These labor force trends illustrate the importance of monitoring demographic changes as a part of environmental scanning. Fortunately, labor market analysis is aided by various published documents. Unemployment rates, labor force projection figures, and population characteristics are reported by the U.S. Department of Labor.[11] The *Monthly Labor Review* and *Occupational Outlook Handbook*, both published by the Bureau of Labor Statistics (BLS) of the U.S. Department of Labor, contain information on jobholder characteristics and predicted changes in the workforce. In addition, local chambers of commerce and individual state development and planning agencies can assist both large organizations and new business ventures by providing them with a labor market analysis of their areas. Offshore consulting firms such as IBM and Accenture can be a good source for information about labor trends in other countries. 3M's HR team regularly consults with outside recruiters to learn about the talent supplies in various countries in which it does or wants to do business.

Sources of information about the changes in the external supply of labor are invaluable for both operational and strategic reasons. HRP has to focus on both. At an operational level, labor-supply changes directly affect hiring plans that must take into account the demographic composition of the population in the area where the organization is located or plans to locate. Similarly, with a "maturing" workforce, HRP must consider the implications for recruitment and replacement policies.

From a strategic standpoint, changes in the labor supply can limit the strategies available to firms. High-growth companies in particular may find it difficult to find the talent they need to expand their businesses. While unemployment rates vary by sector, the shortage of talent in high-skill jobs continues to create real challenges for firms.

Step Three: Internal Analysis

As organizations conduct external analyses of environmental opportunities and threats, they also analyze their internal strengths and weaknesses. Conducting an internal analysis provides strategic decision makers with an inventory of organizational skills and resources as well as their performance levels.

To be sure, many resources combine to give organizations a competitive advantage. But in contrast to the past, the advantages due to physical assets are being supplanted by intangible assets, including people. As the professor and author James Brian Quinn noted, "With rare exceptions, the economic and producing power of a firm lies more in its intellectual and service capabilities than in its hard assets—land, plant, and equipment."[12]

The Three Cs: Capabilities, Composition, and Culture

In the context of human resource planning, internal analysis focuses especially on "the three Cs": capabilities, composition, and culture.

Capabilities: People as a Strategic Resource

A growing number of experts now argue that the key to a firm's success is based on establishing a set of core capabilities—bundles of people, processes, and systems that distinguish an organization from its competitors and deliver value to customers. McDonald's, for example, has developed core capabilities in management efficiency and training. Federal Express has core capabilities in package routing, delivery, and employee relations. Royal Dutch Shell has core capabilities in oil exploration and production.[13] Core capabilities tend to be limited in number, but they provide a long-term basis for technology innovation, product development, and service delivery.

In many cases, people are a key resource that underlies a firm's core capabilities. Particularly in knowledge-based industries such as the software and information services industries, success depends on "people-embodied know-how." This includes the knowledge, skills, and abilities of employees. As a result, a number of companies that previously relied on standard plans for recruiting and managing their employees are designing more tailored plans for them. These personalized plans are designed to address the individual needs of employees so they will be in a better position to help implement their firms' strategies. Microsoft goes so far as to ask certain types of employees to design their own career paths. For example, the company offers software

LEARNING OUTCOME 3

Think back to the discussion in Chapter 1 about the auto-parts makers that had to look for new business lines when GM, Ford, ad Chrysler sales plummeted in the last recession. How do you think the auto-parts makers assessed their ability to enter their new markets? Do you think they looked first at new markets and then the capabilities of their employees and external partners or vice versa?

core capabilities
Integrated knowledge sets within an organization that distinguish it from its competitors and deliver value to customers

These workers support their employer's core capabilities, which helps the company stand out from its competitors and enables it to deliver added value to its customers.

Bloomberg/Getty Images

engineers both a management-focused and technical specialist career track and allows them to move back and forth between the two.

Organizations can achieve a sustained competitive advantage through people if they are able to meet the following criteria:[14]

1. *The resources must be valuable.* People are a source of competitive advantage when they improve the efficiency or effectiveness of the company. Value is increased when employees find ways to decrease costs, provide something unique to customers, or some combination of the two. To improve the bottom line, Nordstrom and UPS are among the companies that utilize employee empowerment programs, total quality and continuous improvement efforts, and flexible work arrangements to motivate and spark the creativity of their workers.

2. *The resources must be rare.* People are a source of competitive advantage when their knowledge, skills, and abilities are not equally available to competitors. Companies such as Microsoft, Four Seasons Hotels, and Virgin America therefore invest a great deal to hire and train the best and the brightest employees in order to gain an advantage over their competitors.

3. *The resources must be difficult to imitate.* People are a source of competitive advantage when the capabilities and contributions of a firm's employees cannot be copied by others. Disney, Southwest Airlines, and Starbucks are each known for creating unique cultures that get the most from employees (through teamwork) and are difficult to imitate.

4. *The resources must be organized.* People are a source of competitive advantage when their talents can be combined and deployed to work on new assignments at a moment's notice. Companies such as IBM, GE, and, as you learned in Chapter 1, Procter & Gamble closely "track" employees and their talents. As a result, these firms are able to quickly reassign talent to different areas of their companies and the world as needed.

These four criteria highlight the importance of people and show the closeness of HRM to strategic management.

Composition: The Human Capital Architecture

A related element of internal analysis for organizations that compete on capabilities is determining the composition of the workforce. As we have indicated, managers need to determine whether people are available, internally or externally, to execute an organization's strategy. Managers have to make tough decisions about whom to employ internally, whom to contract externally, and how to manage different types of employees with different skills who contribute in different ways to the organization.

Figure 2.3 shows that different skill groups in any given organization can be classified according to the degree to which they create strategic value and are unique to

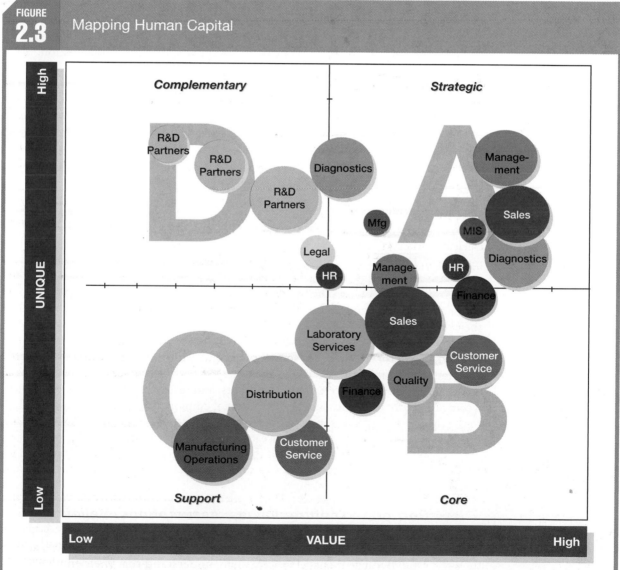

| FIGURE 2.3 | Mapping Human Capital |

the organization. This figure shows the departments for an Australian biotechnology firm and the quadrants those groups fall into as well as their gradual migration given a strategic organizational shift to one that focuses on customer service. As a general rule, managers often consider contracting externally (or outsourcing) skill areas that are not central to the firm's core competence. HRP plays an important role in helping managers weigh the costs and benefits of using one approach to employment versus another.

Evidence from research suggests that employment relationships and HR practices for different employees vary according to which segment they occupy in this matrix. Here are some general trends:

Strategic Knowledge Workers. This group of employees tends to have unique skills that are directly linked to the company's strategy and difficult to replace (such as research and development scientists in a pharmaceuticals company or computer scientists in a software development company). These employees typically are engaged in knowledge work that involves considerable autonomy. Companies tend to make long-term commitments to these employees, investing in their continuous training and development, and perhaps giving them an equity stake in the organization.

Core Employees. This group of employees has skills that are quite valuable to a company, but not particularly unique or difficult to replace (such as salespeople in a department store or truck drivers for a courier service). These employees tend to be employed in traditional types of jobs. Because their skills are transferable, it is quite possible that they could leave to go to another firm. As a consequence, managers frequently make less investment in training and development and tend to focus more on paying for short-term performance achievements.

Supporting Workers. This group of workers typically has skills that are less central to creating customer value and generally available in the labor market (such as clerical workers, maintenance workers, and staff workers in accounting and human resources). Individuals in these jobs are often hired from external agencies on a contract basis to support the strategic knowledge workers and core employees. The scope of their duties tends to be limited, and their employment relationships tend to be transaction-based, focused on rules and procedures, and less investment is made in their development.

Partners and Complementary Skills. This group of individuals has skills that are unique and specialized, but frequently not directly related to a company's core strategy (such as attorneys on retainer, consultants, and research lab scientists). Although a company perhaps cannot justify their internal employment given their indirect link to the firm's strategy, these individuals have skills that are specialized and not readily available to all firms. As a consequence, companies tend to establish longer-term alliances and partnerships with them and nurture an ongoing relationship focused on mutual learning. Considerable investment is made in the exchange of information and knowledge.[15]

Corporate Culture: Values, Assumptions, Beliefs, and Expectations (VABEs)

Think about our initial discussion of mission, vision, and values back at Step One. Because managers increasingly understand that their employees are

Using the INTERNET

For more information about contract employees and the Beacon Hill Staffing Group, go to **www.cengagebrain.com**

critical to their success, they often conduct cultural audits to examine their values, attitudes, beliefs, and expectations (VABEs). Cultural audits can consist of surveys and interviews to measure how employees feel on a number of critical issues.

According to author James Clawson, leaders who target employees' values, attitudes, beliefs, and expectations are more effective than those who simply focus on workers' behaviors or thought processes.[16] This makes sense. Recall from Chapter 1 the story about the entrepreneur who tripled his sales but, because he took his staff for granted, was then muscled out of the market by a competitor. If a firm lacks a clear idea of how employees view the organization, no matter how great the organization's plans are, those plans might never be successfully executed and sustained.

The cultural audit conducted by SAS, a business-analytics corporation that often ranks No. 1 on *Fortune* magazine's "Best Companies to Work For" list, includes detailed questions about the company's pay and benefit programs and a series of open-ended questions about the company's hiring practices, internal communications, training and recognition programs, and diversity efforts.[17] Via cultural audits, SYSCO, Sears, and Continental Airlines are among the companies that have found ways to get the most from their employees by linking their values and ideas to profits.[18] To prevent legal and ethical breaches, some firms conduct cultural audits that ask employees questions about the degree of fear associated with meeting their firms' revenue goals and incentive plans that could encourage unethical or illegal behavior.[19] Cultural audits can also be used to determine whether there are different groups, or subcultures, within the organization that have distinctly different views about the nature of the work and how it should be done.

Knowing that a company's corporate culture is a source of competitive advantage, firms are also beginning to engage in what is called values-based hiring, which involves outlining the behaviors that exemplify a firm's corporate culture and then hiring people who are a fit for them. The computer network provider Juniper Networks has identified four to six behaviors that exemplify each of its core values in action. "We are upping our game to be much more explicit about what the best talent for Juniper looks like," says Greg Pryor, vice president of leadership and organization for Juniper.[20]

cultural audits
Audits of the culture and quality of work life in an organization

values-based hiring
The process of outlining the behaviors that exemplify a firm's corporate culture and then hiring people who are a fit for them.

Forecasting: A Critical Element of Planning

An internal analysis of the three Cs (capabilities, composition, and culture) of an organization can reveal a great deal about where it stands today. However, things change. In an important sense, strategic planning is about managing that change. Managers must continually forecast both the needs and the capabilities of the firm for the future in order to do an effective job at strategic planning. As shown in Figure 2.4, managers focus on (at least) three key elements: (a) forecasting the demand for labor, (b) forecasting the supply of labor, and (c) balancing supply and demand considerations. Careful attention to each factor helps top managers meet their human resources requirements.

Consider for a moment the high costs of not forecasting—or forecasting poorly. If job vacancies are left unfilled, the resulting loss in efficiency can be very costly, particularly when you consider the amount of time it takes to hire and train replacement employees. As pointless as it may sound, we have seen situations in which employees are laid off in one department while applicants are hired for similar jobs in another department. Poor forecasting that leads to unnecessary layoffs also makes it

LEARNING OUTCOME 4

If you are currently employed, ask your manager how your firm goes about forecasting its supply and demand for employees, and then link that activity to techniques used in this section. In what ways do you think your employer could improve its forecasting?

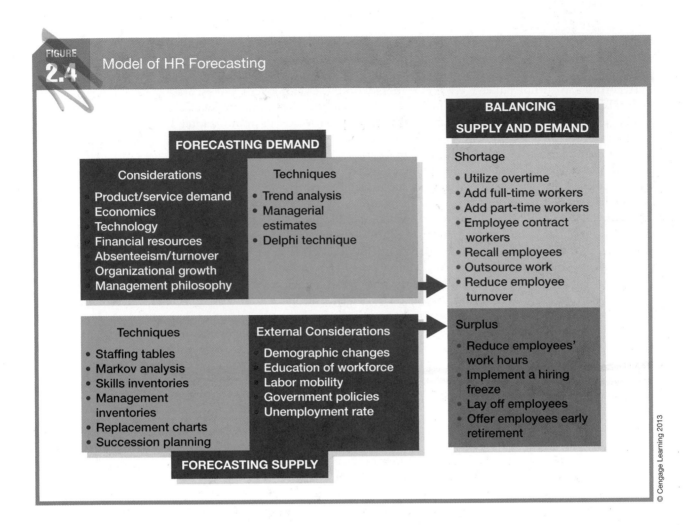

FIGURE 2.4   Model of HR Forecasting

difficult for employees to accurately assess their own career prospects and development. When this happens, some of a firm's more competent and ambitious workers will be inclined to seek other employment where they feel they will have better career opportunities.[21]

On the plus side, accurate forecasting provides the kind of information managers need to make sound decisions. It can help them ensure that they have the right number and right kinds of people in the right places at the right times, doing things that provide value to both the organization and the employees.

Forecasting a Firm's Demand for Employees

If a key component of forecasting is predicting the number and types of people an organization needs to meet its objectives, the question remains: "How can this be done?" A variety of factors, including a firm's competitive strategy, technology, structure, and productivity, can affect the demand for labor. External factors such as business cycles—economic and seasonal trends—can also play a role. For example, retailers such as The Gap, Bath & Body Works, and Marks & Spencer rely heavily on temporary employees between November and January, during the holiday season. There are two approaches to

HR forecasting—quantitative and qualitative—which we discuss next. An organization's demands will ultimately determine which technique is used. Regardless of the method, however, forecasting should not be neglected, even in relatively small organizations.

Quantitative Approaches. Quantitative approaches to forecasting involve the use of statistical or mathematical techniques. One example is trend analysis, whereby a firm's employment requirements are forecasted on the basis of some organizational index. Trend analysis is one of the most commonly used approaches for projecting HR demand and is typically done in several stages: First, select an appropriate business factor. This should be the best available predictor of human resources needs. Frequently, sales or value added (the selling price of the firm's products minus the costs of the materials and supplies used to make them) is used as a predictor in trend analysis. Second, plot a historical trend of the business factor in relation to the number of employees. The ratio of employees to the business factor will provide a labor productivity ratio (for example, sales per employee). Third, compute the productivity ratio for at least the past five years. Fourth, calculate human resources demand by multiplying the business factor by the productivity ratio. Finally, project the firm's human resources demand out to the target year. This procedure is illustrated in Figure 2.5 for a hypothetical building contractor.

Other, more sophisticated statistical planning methods include modeling or multiple predictive techniques. Whereas trend analysis relies on a single factor (such as sales) to predict employment needs, the more advanced methods combine several factors, such as interest rates, gross national product, disposable income, and sales, to predict employment levels. Forecasting methods such as these are usually used by larger companies with the help of analysts and statisticians. However, advances in data collection technology and computer software are making it easier and more affordable for smaller businesses to use more sophisticated forecasting techniques.

trend analysis

A quantitative approach to forecasting labor demand based on an organizational index such as sales

---

FIGURE 2.5 Example of a Trend Analysis Forecasting Employee Demand

YEAR	BUSINESS FACTOR (SALES IN THOUSANDS)	÷	LABOR PRODUCTIVITY (SALES/EMPLOYEE)	=	HUMAN RESOURCES DEMAND (NUMBER OF EMPLOYEES)
2007	$2,351		14.33		164
2008	$2,613		11.12		235
2009	$2,935		8.34		352
2010	$3,306		10.02		330
2011	$3,613		11.12		325
2012	$3,748		11.12		337
2013*	$3,880		12.52		310
2014*	$4,095		12.52		327
2015*	$4,283		12.52		342
2016*	$4,446		12.52		355

*Projected figures

© Cengage Learning 2013

Qualitative Approaches. Admittedly, forecasting is frequently more of an art than a science, providing inexact approximations rather than absolute results. The ever-changing environment in which an organization operates contributes to this situation. For example, estimating changes in the demand for a firm's products or services is a basic forecasting concern, as is anticipating changes in national or regional economics. A firm's internal changes are critical, too. For example, a community hospital anticipating internal changes in its technology or how the facility is organized or managed must consider these factors when it forecasts its staffing needs. Also, the forecasted staffing needs must be in line with the organization's financial resources.

In contrast to quantitative approaches, qualitative approaches to forecasting are less statistical. Management forecasts are the opinions (judgments) of supervisors, department managers, experts, or others knowledgeable about the organization's future employment needs. For example, at Souplantation and Sweet Tomatoes, a dining chain based in California, each restaurant manager is responsible for his or her store's employment forecasts. Another qualitative forecasting method, the Delphi technique, attempts to decrease the subjectivity of forecasts by soliciting and summarizing the judgments of a preselected group of individuals. HR personnel can do this by developing a list of questions to ask the managers in their companies. Highlights in HRM 1 contains a list of good questions to ask. The final forecast thus becomes a collective, or group, judgment.

Ideally, forecasting should include the use of both quantitative and qualitative approaches. Numbers without context—including the context supplied by skilled HR professionals who understand the business and can analyze and interpret the data—are less useful. "The most important software is the one running between your ears," explains one HR director about the qualitative nature of strategic human resources planning.[22]

Sun Microsystems gathers workforce data about international markets from a wide range of external sources such as the World Bank, European Union statistics, and business publications. However, the company then integrates that information with internal data as well as observations gathered by HR professionals in the field, which helps Sun's executives make decisions.[23]

Forecasting the Supply of Employees

Just as an organization must forecast its future requirements for employees, it must also determine whether sufficient numbers and types of employees are available to staff the openings it anticipates having. As with demand forecasts, the process involves both tracking current employee levels and making future projections about those levels.

Staffing Tables and Markov Analysis. An internal supply analysis can begin with the preparation of staffing tables. Staffing tables are graphic representations of all organizational jobs, along with the numbers of employees currently occupying those jobs (and perhaps also future employment requirements derived from demand forecasts). Another technique, called a Markov analysis, shows the percentage (and actual number) of employees who remain in each of a firm's jobs from one year to the next, as well as the proportions of those who are promoted, demoted, or transferred, or who exit the organization. As Figure 2.6 shows, a Markov analysis can be used to track the pattern of employee movements through various jobs and to develop a transition matrix for forecasting labor supply.

---

management forecasts

The opinions (judgments) of supervisors, department managers, experts, or others knowledgeable about the organization's future employment needs

staffing tables

Graphic representations of all organizational jobs, along with the numbers of employees currently occupying those jobs and future (monthly or yearly) employment requirements

Markov analysis

A method for tracking the pattern of employee movements through various jobs

1 HR Planning and Strategy Questions to Ask Business Managers

Workforce planning requires that HR leaders periodically interview their managers to gauge an organization's future workforce needs. Here are some sample questions to ask.

- What are your mission, vision, and values?
- What are your current pressing business issues?
- What are our organizational strengths?
- What are our competitors' organizational strengths? How do we compare?
- What core capabilities do we need to win in our markets?
- What are the required knowledge, skills, and abilities we need to execute the winning strategy?
- What are the barriers to optimally achieving the strategy?
- What types of skills and positions will be required or no longer required?
- Which skills should we have internally versus contract with outside providers?
- What actions need to be taken to align our resources with our strategy priorities?
- What recognition and rewards are needed to attract, motivate, and retain the employees we need?
- How will we know if we are effectively executing our workforce plan and staying on track?

Sources: Adapted from Agilent Technologies for The Conference Board and the Society for Human Resource Management.

FIGURE 2.6 Hypothetical Markov Analysis for a Retail Company

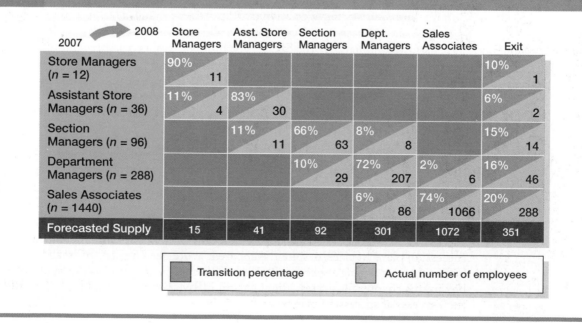

2007 → 2008	Store Managers	Asst. Store Managers	Section Managers	Dept. Managers	Sales Associates	Exit
Store Managers (n = 12)	90% 11					10% 1
Assistant Store Managers (n = 36)	11% 4	83% 30				6% 2
Section Managers (n = 96)		11% 11	66% 63	8% 8		15% 14
Department Managers (n = 288)			10% 29	72% 207	2% 6	16% 46
Sales Associates (n = 1440)				6% 86	74% 1066	20% 288
Forecasted Supply	15	41	92	301	1072	351

■ Transition percentage   ■ Actual number of employees

Forecasting the supply of human resources available to a firm requires that its managers have a good understanding of employee turnover and absenteeism. We have included formulas for computing turnover and absenteeism rates in an appendix to this chapter. Also included in the appendix is a formula for calculating a new metric called quality of fill. It was developed because managers understand that simply having "bodies" in place is not enough. The quality-of-fill metric attempts to measure how well new hires are performing so the company will have enough top performers to propel it towards its strategic objectives. We will show you how it is calculated in Chapter 5 when we discuss recruiting metrics.

Skill Inventories and Management Inventories. Staffing tables, a Markov analysis, turnover rates, and the like tend to focus on the *number* of employees in particular jobs. Other techniques are more oriented toward the *types* of employees and their skills, knowledge, and experiences. Skill inventories can also be prepared that list each employee's education, past work experience, vocational interests, specific abilities and skills, compensation history, and job tenure. Of course, confidentiality is a vital concern in setting up any such inventory. Nevertheless, well-prepared and up-to-date skill inventories allow an organization to quickly match forthcoming job openings with employee backgrounds. When data are gathered on managers, these inventories are called *management inventories*. All of this analysis is made simpler these days through the use of HR information systems that allows companies to create talent profiles of their employees.

Replacement Charts and Succession Planning. Both skill and management inventories—broadly referred to as talent inventories—can be used to develop employee replacement charts, which list current jobholders and identify possible replacements should openings occur. Figure 2.7 shows an example of how an organization might develop a replacement chart for the managers in one of its divisions. Note that this chart provides information on the current job performance and promotability of possible replacements. As such, it can be used side by side with other pieces of information for succession planning—the process of identifying, developing, and tracking talented individuals so that they can eventually assume top-level positions.

In a study conducted by the Society for Human Resources, three out of four chief executives said succession planning was their most significant challenge for the future. The software developer Taleo, for example, offers an application based on a firm's organizational chart and baseball-card-like representations of its employees. Clicking on the cards flips them over to show statistics about the employees such as their individual performance review data, career information, and succession data. Similarly, the consulting firm Accenture developed a Facebook-like application listing its employees, where they are based, and their individual areas of expertise. The application helps managers with deployment decisions and also makes it easier for Accenture's employees who do not necessarily know each other or work together to collaborate with one another.

With or without software, however, more companies are going to need to engage in succession planning. One study found that only 50 percent of U.S. companies have succession plans in place, despite the apparent acute need for it.[24] In small and family businesses, not having a succession plan can often imperil a firm, as the small business box in this chapter illustrates. Highlights in HRM 2 shows a checklist for evaluating the "success" of succession planning.

---

quality of fill
A metric designed to measure how well new hires that fill positions are performing on the job.

skill inventories
Files of personnel education, experience, interests, skills, and so on that allow managers to quickly match job openings with employee backgrounds

replacement charts
Listings of current jobholders and people who are potential replacements if an opening occurs

succession planning
The process of identifying, developing, and tracking key individuals for executive positions

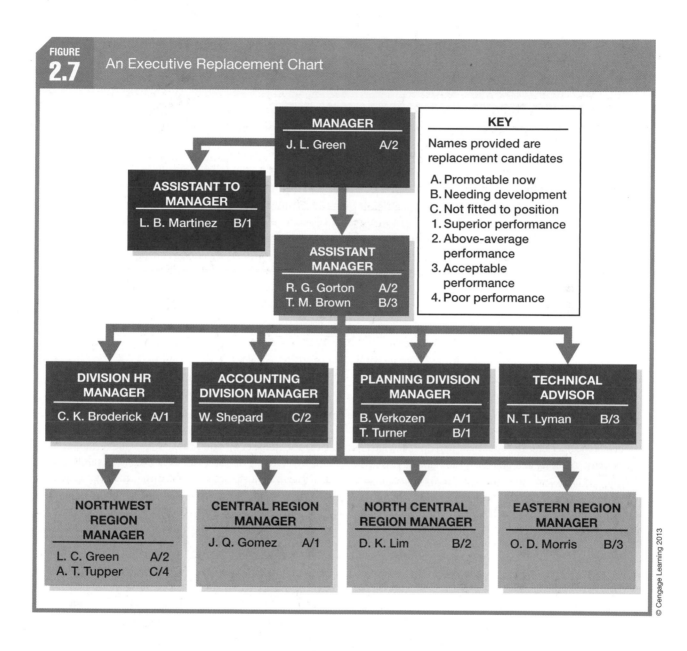

FIGURE 2.7 An Executive Replacement Chart

MANAGER
J. L. Green   A/2

ASSISTANT TO MANAGER
L. B. Martinez   B/1

ASSISTANT MANAGER
R. G. Gorton   A/2
T. M. Brown   B/3

KEY

Names provided are replacement candidates

A. Promotable now
B. Needing development
C. Not fitted to position
1. Superior performance
2. Above-average performance
3. Acceptable performance
4. Poor performance

DIVISION HR MANAGER
C. K. Broderick   A/1

ACCOUNTING DIVISION MANAGER
W. Shepard   C/2

PLANNING DIVISION MANAGER
B. Verkozen   A/1
T. Turner   B/1

TECHNICAL ADVISOR
N. T. Lyman   B/3

NORTHWEST REGION MANAGER
L. C. Green   A/2
A. T. Tupper   C/4

CENTRAL REGION MANAGER
J. Q. Gomez   A/1

NORTH CENTRAL REGION MANAGER
D. K. Lim   B/2

EASTERN REGION MANAGER
O. D. Morris   B/3

© Cengage Learning 2013

Assessing a Firm's Human Capital Readiness: Gap Analysis

Once a company has assessed both the supply and demand for employee skills, talent, and know-how, it can begin to understand its **human capital readiness.** Any difference between the quantity and quality of employees required versus the quantity and quality of employees available represents a gap that needs to be remedied.

Figure 2.8 shows how Chemico Systems, a specialty chemical manufacturing company, approaches its assessment of human capital readiness. Similar to our discussion in the preceding sections, managers begin by identifying a company's core capabilities

human capital readiness

The process of evaluating the availability of critical talent in a company and comparing it to the firm's supply

Small Business Application

Lack of Succession Planning Threatens Family Businesses

Sisters Craigie and Debbie Zildjian are the fourteenth-generation leaders of Zildjian Cymbal Company, brothers Mark and Massimo Brooke are the fifteenth-generation leaders of John Brooke & Sons, and father-and-son team Toshitaka and Masakzu Kongo are the fiftieth- and fifty-first-generation leaders of Kongo Gumi of Japan. A certain mystique exists about family businesses being carried on for generations, yet the reality revealed in PriceWaterhouseCoopers' Family Business Worldwide Survey is that many family businesses fail because they lack a succession plan. In fact, more than half of the firms surveyed still do not have proper succession plans in place.

One potential cause behind the lack of succession planning is business owners themselves. "Business owners may be reluctant to face the issue because they do not want to relinquish control, feel their successor is not ready, have few interests outside the business, or wish to maintain the sense of identity work provides," explains Dr. Al Agamy, an executive director with the Family Business Center at IMD, an international business school based in Switzerland.

In some cases, however, there is no clear successor. Dr. Ashraf Mahate, the head of export market intelligence at Dubai Exports, an agency within Dubai's Department of Economic Development, notes: "All businesses need to appreciate that the entrepreneurial spirit does not lie within one person or a generation—it lies in the motivation that a person has to search, select, implement and grow opportunities. If the rewards for such activities diminish with time or from one generation to another, so will the entrepreneurial spirit. The rewards are not only financial—although they are very important—but can stretch to non-financial aspects such as the level of control, position, etc." Sometimes the next generation just is not enthusiastic about joining the family business. Consequently, it is not advisable to force a family member into the situation. Rather, family businesses must seek ways of bringing the new generation in.

Thus, choosing and grooming the right successor is key. J. Davis, speaking on successor development at the International Family Enterprise Institute, recommends looking for a successor with the following qualities: One who knows and loves the nature of the business; one who knows his or her own strengths and weaknesses, having learned them through education and prior experience; one who wants to lead and serve; one who has earned the respect of other stakeholders; one who knows when to turn to trusted, knowledgeable advisors for guidance; and one whose skills and abilities fit the strategic needs of the business.

Even with a business owner willing to relinquish the reins and a well-chosen successor waiting in the wings, an actual transition plan—transparent and known to all involved in advance—is still required. "[Any transition] needs to be carried out without causing any alarm to the other stakeholders—that is, financiers who may be worried that such a change may increase firm-specific risk," says Mahate. "Suppliers may be concerned about providing future credit facilities or even doing business with the company. Customers may be fearful of long-term relationships with the company. Therefore, it is in everyone's interest to have an orderly change to the new structure."

Sources: Manoj Nair, "Succession Planning is the Key," *gulfnews.com* (January 19, 2011), http://gulfnews.com; Ernesto J. Poza, *Family Business*, South-Western/Cengage Learning, (2010), 85–89; Don Schwerzler, "Family Succession Plan First," http://www.family-business-experts.com/family-succession-plan.html.

and the key people and processes that are critical to those capabilities. Chemico's executive team identified eight key job "families" that comprise about 100 employees of the firm's 1,500 member staff (in other words, less than 10 percent of its workforce). For each of these critical job families, managers identified the critical knowledge, skills, and

2 HIGHLIGHTS IN **HRM**
Succession-Planning Checklist

RATE THE SUCCESS OF YOUR SUCCESSION PLANNING

For each characteristic of a best-practice succession-planning and management program appearing in the left column below, enter a number to the right to indicate how well you believe your organization manages that characteristic. Ask other decision makers in your organization to complete this form individually. Then compile the scores and compare notes.

Characteristics of a Best-Practice Succession-Planning and Management Program	How Would You Rate Your Organization's Succession Planning and Management Program on the Characteristic?				
Your organization has successfully...	Very Poor (1)	Poor (2)	Neither Poor Nor Good (3)	Good (4)	Very Good (5)
1 Clarified the purpose and desired results of the succession-planning and management program.					
2 Determined what performance is required now for all job categories in the organization by establishing competency models.					
3 Established a means to measure individual performance that is aligned with the competencies currently demonstrated by successful performers.					
4 Determined what performance is needed in the future by establishing future competency models for all job categories.					
5 Created an ongoing means by which to assess individual potential against future competency models.					
6 Established a means by which to narrow gaps through the use of individual development plans (IDPs).					
7 Created a means to follow up and hold people accountable.					
8 Created a means by which to document competence and find organizational talent quickly when needed.					
9 Created and sustained rewards for developing people.					
10 Established a means by which to evaluate the results of the succession planning and management program.					

Total (add up the scores for items 1–10 and place in the box on the right)

SCORES

50–40 Congratulations. The succession-planning and management program in your organization conforms with best practices.

29–20 Okay. While your organization could make improvements, you appear to have some of the major pieces in place for a succession-planning and management program.

39–30 Pretty good. Your organization is on the way toward establishing a first-rate succession-planning and management program.

19–10 Not good at all. Your organization is probably filling positions on an as-needed basis.

9–0 Give yourself a failing grade. You need to take steps immediately to improve the succession-planning and management practices of your organization.

Source: From William J. Rothwell, "Putting Success into Your Succession Planning," *The Journal of Business Strategy* 23, no. 3 (May/June 2002): 32–37. Republished with permission—Thomson Media, One State Street, 26th Floor, New York, NY 10004.

FIGURE 2.8 Assessing a Firm's Human Capital

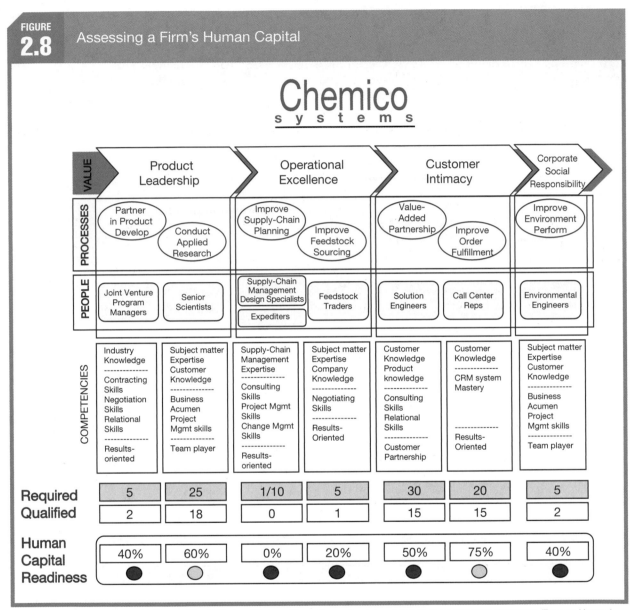

Source: Reprinted from Robert Kaplan and David Norton, *Strategy Maps: Converting Intangible Assets into Tangible Outcomes* (Boston: Harvard Business School Press, 2006), Chapter 8.

behaviors necessary to build the core capabilities. They then determined the number of people required for these positions, as well as the number who are currently qualified. As the lower portion of the figure shows, the company's human readiness ranged between 0 percent for supply chain management design specialists and 75 percent for call center representatives.

Once the assessment of the firm's human capital readiness is complete, managers have a much better foundation for establishing their strategy going forward and the specific requirements for developing the talent needed to implement the strategy.[25]

Step Four: Formulating Strategy

LEARNING OUTCOME 5

Think about a firm you enjoy doing business with or one you don't. What competitive strategy does it pursue? Do you think its employees have the right skills given the strategy? Do you detect any mismatches?

The forecasting techniques discussed previously provide critical information for strategic planning. Recall that we noted at the beginning of the chapter that HR analysis is an input to strategy formulation. However, a word of caution is needed here. Because HR forecasting techniques take us deep into the specifics of labor supply and demand, we need to be careful not to lose sight of the larger strategic picture. One of the biggest concerns among executives is that (at times) HR managers cannot "see the forest for the trees" because they become mired in the administrative details of their planning models. SWOT analysis, discussed shortly, helps managers combine various sources of information into a broader framework for analysis.

After managers have analyzed the internal strengths and weaknesses of the firm, as well as external opportunities and threats, they have the information they need to formulate corporate, business, and HR strategies for the organization. A comparison of *strengths, weaknesses, opportunities,* and *threats* normally is referred to as a SWOT analysis. A SWOT analysis helps executives summarize the major facts and forecasts derived from external and internal analyses. Strategy formulation builds on SWOT analysis to use the strengths of the organization to capitalize on opportunities, counteract threats, and alleviate internal weaknesses. In short, strategy formulation moves from simple analysis to devising a coherent course of action. Figure 2.9 is an example of a SWOT analysis done for the online digital music service Napster.

SWOT analysis

A comparison of strengths, weaknesses, opportunities, and threats for strategy formulation purposes

Corporate Strategy

A firm's corporate strategy includes the markets in which it will compete, against whom, and how. Some firms choose a concentration strategy that focuses on only a limited portion of the industry. For example, Visteon Corporation specializes in electronics, climate, and power train technologies for the automotive industry. In contrast, Henry

---

FIGURE 2.9 An Example of a SWOT Analysis for Napster

STRENGTHS	WEAKNESSES
• Installed base	• Lack of critical complementary assets
• Strong contagion effects	• File selection greatly reduced
• High market profile	• Antagonistic relationship with record labels
• Powerful design features	• Consumer-to-consumer computing
	• Transition from a free to a pay model

OPPORTUNITIES	THREATS
• Best Buy acquisition	• Large number of competitors
• Online entertainment trends	• Entry of record labels
• Potential for alliances with record labels	• Ad-Based Models
• No focused strategy for record labels	• Laws/regulation

Source: "E-Commerce: Napster SWOT Analysis," *WikiSWOT,* http://www.wikiswot.com.

Ford at one time had fully integrated his company from the ore mines needed to make steel all the way to the showrooms where his cars were sold.

Growth and Diversification

Emerging and growing companies execute their strategies differently than mature companies or those in decline. As companies grow, their strategic choices tend to focus on geographic, volume, and product expansion. HR planning is a vital input to these decisions. Growth hinges on three related elements: (a) increased employee productivity, (b) a greater number of employees, and (c) employees developing or acquiring new skills. Thus, a firm's staffing, training, employee motivation efforts, and the like can either enable the company to grow or limit its potential.

As companies diversify into new businesses, managers inevitably are faced with a "make or buy" decision. That is, should they develop the capabilities in-house or contract externally? For example, when IBM entered the personal computer market in the early 1980s, it contracted with (start-up companies) Intel and Microsoft to make the hardware and operating systems for its PC. The decision did not rest solely on human resources issues, but they were an important part of the equation. Interestingly, IBM got out of the PC business altogether in 2005, by selling its PC product lineup to the Chinese computer manufacturer Lenovo. Today IBM develops custom technology services for businesses, which it believes will be more profitable in the long run and a harder product for competitors to imitate. To help accomplish this new strategy, the company spent the first part of the decade buying up dozens of business service related companies and their talent.

Some companies diversify far beyond their core businesses. At one time GE, for example, mostly produced electrical and home appliance products. Today its products include those in the health, finance, insurance, truck and air transportation, and even the media industry following the firm's investment in NBC. To manage such a diverse portfolio, GE has invested heavily in the development of general management skills and leadership ability. CEO Jeffrey Immelt has stated that GE's future depends on pursuing businesses that leverage human capital (in contrast to its traditional focus on manufacturing, much of which it has outsourced). This new strategy is strongly linked to human resources. In fact, the strategy is viable only because the company has done such an enviable job developing talent over the years.

Mergers and Acquisitions

In addition to strategies of growth and diversification, corporate America has seen a host of mergers and acquisitions in recent years. They include such firms as Kraft Foods and the British candy maker Cadbury, Continental and United Airlines, Tata Motors and Jaguar/Land Rover, Walt Comcast and NBC, Exxon and Mobil, and Procter & Gamble and Gillette. When companies merge, they can often streamline their costs by eliminating duplicate functions, such as duplicate accounting, finance, and HR departments, for example. However, despite some of the savings realized as a result of acquisitions and mergers, many of them do not go well (measured by return on investment, shareholder value, and the like). Often the failure is due to cultural inconsistencies, as well as conflicts among the managers of each firm. The failure of the merger between the German firm Daimler-Benz (the manufacturer of Mercedes Benz vehicles) and Chrysler is an example. Although the German portion of the firm had superior technology, reportedly it was less than eager to share its know-how with its American counterparts. Problems like this one point directly to the importance of effective HR planning prior to—and during—the merger process. Highlights in HRM 3 shows key HR activities associated with different phases of a merger or acquisition.

Strategic Alliances and Joint Ventures

Sometimes firms do not acquire or merge with another firm but instead pursue cooperative strategies such as a strategic alliance or joint venture. Especially when firms enter into international joint ventures, the issues of culture (both company culture and national culture) become paramount. On the front end, HR plays a vital role in assessing the compatibility of cultures and potential problems. As the alliance is formed, HR helps select key executives and develops teamwork across the respective workforces. In addition, HR is typically involved in the design of performance assessment and mutual incentives for the alliance.

Business Strategy

While we think about corporate strategy as domain selection, business strategy is viewed in terms of domain navigation. It is more focused on how the company will compete against rival firms in order to create value for customers. We can think of value creation in a cost/benefit scenario (value = benefits − costs). Companies can increase the value they offer customers by decreasing the costs of their goods and services or by increasing the benefits their products provide (or some combination of the two). Their business strategies reflect these choices.

value creation
What the firm adds to a product or service by virtue of making it; the amount of benefits provided by the product or service once the costs of making it are subtracted

Low-Cost Strategy: Compete on Productivity and Efficiency

A low-cost strategy means keeping your costs low enough so that you can offer an attractive price to customers relative to your competitors. Organizations such as Dell, Walmart, and Southwest Airlines have been very successful competing based on a low-cost strategy. Critical success factors for this strategy focus on efficiency, productivity, and minimizing waste. These types of companies often are large and try to take advantage of economies of scale in the production and distribution of goods and services so they can sell them at lower prices, which leads to higher market shares, volumes, and (hopefully) profits. However, even a low-cost leader must offer a product or service that customers find valuable. As Gordon Bethune, the former CEO of Continental Airlines, put it, "You can make a pizza so cheap that no one will buy it."[26] Ultimately organizations need to use a cost strategy to increase value to customers, rather than take it away.

A low-cost strategy is linked to HR planning in several ways. The first has to do with productivity. A common misconception about low-cost strategies is that they inevitably require cutting labor costs. On the contrary, there are several good examples of companies that pay their employees "top dollar," but gain back cost advantages because of excellent productivity. That is, they get a terrific "bang for the buck." Either they produce more from the workforce they have, or they can produce the same amount with a smaller workforce. According to Peter Cappelli, who heads the Center for Human Resources at the Wharton School at the University of Pennsylvania, the productivity of the best-performing staffs can be five to twenty *times* higher than the productivity of the worst-performing staffs, depending upon the industry. Billy Beane, the general manager of the Oakland A's, became famous for making the most of the A's small payroll. Beane did so by carefully choosing and developing players and using them more strategically than other major league teams with bigger payroll budgets.

Oakland A's General Manager Billy Beane has made great strides by using statistics and other analytics to manage his players and make the most of his team's small payroll. Although the A's haven't won a playoff recently, Beane defends his tactics by comparing himself to a stockbroker: "Thirty years ago, stockbrokers used to buy stock strictly by feel. Let's put it this way: Anyone in the game with a 401(k) has a choice. They can choose a fund manager who manages their retirement by gut instinct, or one who chooses by research and analysis. I know which way I'd choose."

Justin Sullivan/AP Photos

The second way that low-cost strategies are linked to HR pertains to outsourcing. Companies consider contracting with an external partner that can perform particular activities or services equally well (or better) at a lower cost. Decisions such as these often result in layoffs, transfers, and the like. As noted before, organizations need to have a clear understanding of their core processes and skills in order to make these decisions. Too often, a firm approaches outsourcing decisions based on costs alone, but this can lead to detrimental effects in the long run if the skills base of its employees suffer and its core capabilities erode.

Differentiation Strategy: Compete on Unique Value Added

While decreasing costs is one important way to enhance customer value, another involves providing something unique and distinctive to customers. A differentiation strategy is often based on delivering a high-quality product, innovative features, speed to market, or superior service. Ritz-Carlton's commitment to quality and luxury, FedEx's focus on speed and flexible delivery, Neiman Marcus's commitment to fashion and customer service, and Apple's emphasis on innovation and product development are all easily identifiable examples of differentiation strategies.

Each of these strategies is rooted in the management of human resources. Companies that focus on service, for example, need to identify and support ways to empower employees to serve customers better. Relative to companies that emphasize low cost and efficiencies, differentiating companies will bend the rules a bit more and customize products and services around a customer's particular needs to let the customer "have it their way." In place of rigid rules, a service-oriented company often tries to instill its employees with the cultural values of the organization. For example, one quality Starbucks looks for in prospective employees is the ability to make good decisions on their own. Similarly, Nordstrom's employee handbook consists of just a single five- by eight-inch card that reads: "Welcome to Nordstrom. Rule #1. Use your good judgment in all situations. There will be no additional rules."

Functional Strategy: Ensuring Alignment

In addition to formulating corporate- and business-level strategies, managers also need to "translate" strategic priorities into functional areas of the organization (such as marketing, manufacturing, human resources, and the like). This involves all aspects of the business, but in particular there needs to be a clear alignment between HR and the requirements of an organization's strategy. In this regard, HR policies and practices need to achieve two types of fit: vertical and horizontal.[27]

HIGHLIGHTS IN **HRM**
3 Key HR Activities Associated with Merger or Acquisition Phases

HR Issues	Key HR Activities

Stage 1—Prior to Combining Firms

- Identifying the reasons for the action
- Forming the team/leader for the action
- Searching for potential partners
- Selecting a partner
- Planning for managing the process
- Planning to learn from the process
- Participate in the preselection assessment of the target firm

- Assist in conducting thorough due diligence assessment
- Participate in planning for the combination
- Assist in developing HR practices that support rapid learning and knowledge transfer

Stage 2—Combination

- Selecting the integration manager(s)
- Designing/implementing transition teams
- Creating the new structure/strategies/leadership
- Retaining key employees
- Managing the change process
- Communicating to and involving stakeholders
- Developing new policies and practices
- Assisting in recruiting and selecting integration manager(s)

- Assist with the transition team design and staffing
- Develop retention strategies and communicate them to top talent
- Assist in deciding who goes
- Facilitate the establishment of a new culture
- Provide assistance to ensure the implementation of HR policies and practices

Stage 3—Solidification and Assessment

- Solidifying the leadership and staffing
- Assessing the new strategies and structures
- Assessing the new culture
- Assessing the concerns of stakeholders
- Revising as needed
- Learning from the process
- Participate in establishing criteria and procedures for assessing staff effectiveness

- Monitor the new culture and recommend approaches to strengthen it
- Participate in stakeholder satisfaction
- Assist in developing and implementing plans for continuous adjustment and learning

Source: Based on Susan E. Jackson and Randall S. Schuler, *Managing Human Resources through Strategic Partnerships,* 9th ed. (Mason, OH: Thomson/South-Western, 2006), 50.

Vertical Fit/Alignment

Vertical Fit (or *vertical alignment*) focuses on the connection between the business's objectives and the major initiatives undertaken by HR. For example, as we noted earlier, if a company's strategy focuses on achieving low cost, its HR policies and practices need to reinforce this idea by reinforcing efficient and reliable behavior on the part of employees, enhanced productivity, and so on. On the other hand, if the organization competes through innovation and new product development, then its HR policies and practices would be more aligned with the notion of fostering creativity and flexibility.

Horizontal Fit/Alignment

In addition to vertical alignment, or fit, managers need to ensure that their HR practices are all aligned with one another internally to establish a configuration that is mutually reinforcing. The entire range of the firm's HR practices—from its job design, staffing, training, performance appraisal, and compensation—need to focus on the *same* objectives. Too often, one HR practice will emphasize one objective, whereas another HR practice will emphasize another. Charles Schwab & Co. faced this situation. The company has a reputation in the financial services industry for developing a culture of teamwork that has been important to its strategy. However, when it changed its compensation strategy to provide more rewards to its high-performing brokers, the firm sent mixed signals to its employees. Which is more important: teamwork or individual high flyers?[28]

Step Five: Strategy Implementation

LEARNING OUTCOME 6

Why is it difficult to translate a firm's strategy into HR deliverables that actually get the job done? What part of this endeavor do you think HR managers struggle with the most?

As the old saying goes, "well begun is half done"—but only half. Like any plan, formulating the appropriate strategy is not enough. The new plans also have to be implemented effectively. This is easier said than done. Half of managers in one survey said there is a gap between their organization's ability to develop a vision and strategy and actually execute it. Recently organizations have been paying more attention to implementation and execution.[29]

Figure 2.10 shows the now classic 7-S framework and reveals that human resources management is instrumental to almost every aspect of strategy implementation, whether it pertains to the organization's structure, systems, style, skills, staff, or shared values. In the "Hard S" category are the *strategy*, which lays out the route that the organization will take in the future; the organizational *structure* is the framework in which the activities of the organization members are coordinated. If the strategy requires employees to be reorganized or redeployed, HR will be intimately involved.

Also in the "Hard S" category are *systems* and processes. These include formal and informal procedures that govern the everyday activities of a firm. As organizations redesign their processes to implement their strategies, HR managers need to help ensure that the best workflow models are in place and that employees share their advice about the changes, too. As with strategy development, employees can be the source of valuable ideas about how work processes should be structured.

In the "Soft S" category are *shared values*, or core values, which were discussed earlier in the chapter as a guiding parameter for strategic planning. They relate to implementation as well. Strategic change often requires employees and managers to modify, or abandon, their old ways of doing things. HR managers play a central role as guardians

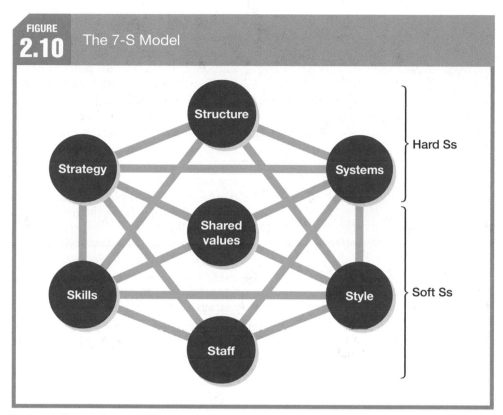

FIGURE 2.10 The 7-S Model

Source: McKinsey & Company.

of the corporate culture—the principles on which the company is founded and the fundamental ideas around which the business is built. This is tightly connected to the issue of *style*, which refers not only to the leadership approach of top managers, but also the way in which employees present themselves to the outside world (to suppliers, customers, and so on). *Skills* and *staff* relate directly to human resources management because at its most basic level, HR's role in the strategy implementation process is to reconcile (1) human resources demanded and (2) human resources available.

Taking Action: Reconciling Supply and Demand

Through HRP, organizations strive for a proper balance between demand considerations and supply considerations. Demand considerations are based on forecasted trends in business activity. Supply considerations involve determining where and how candidates with the required qualifications can be found to fill a firm's vacancies.

In an effort to meet their human resources demands, organizations have many staffing options, including recruiting and hiring full-time employees as well as reducing their turnover, having employees work overtime, recalling laid-off workers, using temporary or contract employees, and outsourcing or offshoring some of their business processes. Some of the ways firms say they are, or will, attract and retain baby boomers to avoid future labor shortages include offering employees flexible scheduling, and health care and long-term care benefits as they eventually retire.[30]

Union agreements often protect long-term employees with seniority, but these workers are not always protected in nonunion work environments.

If its labor shortages are acute, a company might go so far as to develop talent from the ground up. For example, knowing that about 40 percent of its aging workforce would be eligible for retirement in five years, Saudi Aramco, a Saudi-owned oil company, developed a system of hiring top high school graduates in the country, sponsoring their college educations, and providing them with job training. The company employs 400 planners to analyze its workforce needs for the next decade and beyond.[31]

When forecasts show a surplus of employees, organizations often restrict their hiring, reduce their employees' work hours or furlough them, and consider layoffs. Across-the-board pay cuts are sometimes utilized in lieu of or in addition to layoffs. Some organizations try to reduce their workforces by relying on attrition, which is a gradual reduction of employees that occurs due to employee resignations, retirements, and deaths. Programs in which employees are offered "sweetened" retirement benefits to leave a firm earlier than planned are common in large companies.

As we have discussed, organizations have to be constantly prepared to exit and enter new lines of business, restructure, outsource, offshore, and sometimes downsize either because they have too many employees or employees with the wrong skill sets.[32] Decisions about employee layoffs are usually based on seniority and/or performance. In some organizations, especially in Japanese firms, seniority is more likely to be the primary consideration. In other organizations, factors such as an employee's ability and productivity take precedence over seniority. In the case of unionized organizations, the criteria for determining who will be laid off are typically set forth in union agreements and based on seniority. Unions recognize seniority because they feel that their members deserve certain rights proportionate to the years they have invested in their jobs.

Employers often recognize the seniority of employees who are *not* unionized, though. But one disadvantage of doing so is that the less-competent employees can end up receiving the same rewards and security as the more-competent employees. Also, the practice of using seniority as the basis for deciding which workers to lay off can inadvertently have a disparate impact on women and minority workers, who often have less seniority than other groups of workers.[33] When firms are downsizing, HR managers must ensure no laws are violated in the process, of which there are many. They range from laws designed to protect minorities and older employees from being unfairly targeted to laws requiring companies of a certain size laying off a certain number employees to give them between sixty days to six months warning. Firms must also comply with government provisions giving some workers who have been laid off and their families the right to temporary health care coverage at group rates. We will talk more about these laws in Chapter 13.

Step Six: Evaluation and Assessment

At one level, it might seem that assessing a firm's effectiveness is the final step in the planning process. But it is also the first step. Planning is cyclical, of course, and while we have somewhat conveniently placed evaluation at the end of this chapter, the information it provides actually provides firms with inputs they need for the next cycle in the planning process.

Evaluation and Assessment Issues

To evaluate their performance, firms need to establish a set of "desired" outcomes as well as the metrics they will use to monitor how well their organizations delivered against those outcomes. The outcomes can include achieving a certain levels of productivity, revenues, profits, market share, market penetration, customer satisfaction, and so forth. Because strategic management is ultimately aimed at creating a competitive advantage, many firms also evaluate their performance against other firms. Benchmarking is the process of identifying "best practices" in a given area and then comparing your practices and performance to those of other companies. To accomplish this, a benchmarking team would collect metrics on its own company's performance and those of other firms to uncover any gaps. The gaps help determine the causes of performance differences, and ultimately the team would map out a set of best practices that lead to world-class performance. For its clients, PriceWaterhouseCoopers publishes monthly and annual human capital benchmarking information, which includes metrics from almost 900 companies.

Interestingly, the target company for benchmarking does not need to be a competitor. For example, when Xerox wanted to learn about excellent customer service, it benchmarked L.L. Bean. By working with noncompeting companies, Xerox was able to get access to information a competitor would not divulge.

The HR metrics a firm collects fall into two basic categories: human capital metrics and HR metrics. Human capital metrics assess aspects of the workforce, whereas HR metrics assess the performance of the HR function itself. Highlights in HRM 4 shows some of the basic HR metrics companies use. Most larger companies use software to track their HR metrics over time. Figure 2.11 shows an example of an HR "dashboard," which is software that tracks and graphically displays HR statistics so they can be viewed by managers at a glance (as you do your dashboard readings when you are driving).

Smart HR managers can significantly enhance their worth to their organizations if they go a step further by gathering informal information, or "intelligence," about the strategic and HRM practices of their competitors. This can be done by legal means, such as by reading industry blogs, checking competitors' press releases, and signing up for their news feeds, if they provide them, as well as signing up for Google e-mail alerts that are triggered when competing firms' names appear in the news. Attending industry conventions and talking to your company's suppliers about business and employment trends are other good ways of gathering competitive intelligence. So are interviews with job candidates. Simply asking candidates who turned down job offers at other companies why they did so can yield a great deal of information.

LEARNING OUTCOME 7

Why do some organizations rely more on some HR metrics than others? Think about the businesses on or near your campus. Which metrics do you think they are most likely to track?

benchmarking

The process of comparing the organization's processes and practices with those of other companies

Using the INTERNET

For more information on HR benchmarking, go to
www.cengagebrain.com

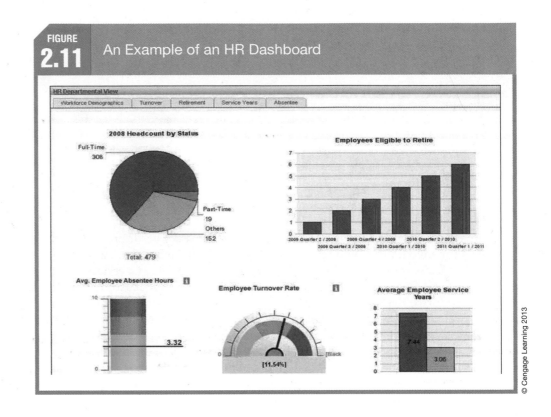

FIGURE 2.11 An Example of an HR Dashboard

© Cengage Learning 2013

Gathering competitive intelligence and benchmarking alone will not give a firm a competitive advantage, though. According to author and HRM consultant Mark Huselid, a competitive advantage is based on the unique combination of a company's human capital, strategy, and core capabilities—which differ from firm to firm. This means that HR managers cannot simply rely on the benchmarks and strategies of other firms. Instead, they must develop their own. If they can successfully do so and implement them, they can achieve a sustained competitive advantage.[34]

Measuring a Firm's Strategic Alignment

Earlier in the chapter, we discussed the importance of strategic alignment and fit as an element of strategy formulation and implementation. As an element of evaluation, some very useful techniques help managers assess the extent to which they have achieved these objectives.

Strategy Mapping and the Balanced Scorecard

One of the tools for mapping a firm's strategy to ensure strategic alignment is the Balanced Scorecard (BSC). Developed by Harvard professors Robert Kaplan and David Norton, the BSC is a framework that helps managers translate their firms' strategic goals into operational objectives. The model has four related cells: (1) financial, (2) customer, (3) processes, and (4) learning. The logic of the BSC is firmly rooted in human resources management. People management and learning help organizations improve their internal processes and provide excellent customer service. Internal processes—product development, service, and the like—are critical for creating customer satisfaction and loyalty, and they are also important for ensuring

Balanced Scorecard (BSC)

A measurement framework that helps managers translate strategic goals into operational objectives

4 HIGHLIGHTS IN **HRM**

Different companies rely on different HRM metrics, depending upon their strategic objectives. The following are some of the metrics mostly commonly used:

General

Total payroll and benefits costs
Payroll and benefits costs per employee
Revenue earned per employee
Average salary per employee
Total employee hours worked
Hours worked per employee
Employees per department
Average employee age
Employee absenteeism rate

Training and Development

Total training costs
Training costs per employee
Average training hours provided existing employees
Average training hours provided new hires

Hiring and Turnover

Total separation costs (severance, etc.)
Separation costs per employee
Average time to fill (a position)
Quality of fill
Cost per fill
Percentage of positions filled internally
Percentage of new hires retained for 90 days
Employee turnover rate
    Voluntary turnover rate
    Involuntary turnover rate

HR Metrics

Number of employees per HR professional
Total HR expenses
HR expenses per employee
Percentage of HR expenses spent on outsourced functions

productivity to contain costs for better financial performance. Customer value creation, in turn, drives up revenues, which enhances profitability.

Figure 2.12 shows how this might work at Starbucks. In each cell, Starbucks would identify the key metrics that help translate strategic goals to operational imperatives. For example, under customer metrics, Starbucks might look at percentage of repeat customers, number of new customers, growth rate, and so forth. Under people metrics, managers might measure the numbers of suggestions provided by employees, participation in Starbucks' stock sharing program, employee turnover, training hours spent, and the like. Each of these cells links vertically. People management issues such as rewards, training, and suggestions can be linked to efficient processes (brewing the perfect cup, delivering top-notch customer service, etc.). These processes then lead to better customer loyalty and growth. Growth and customer loyalty in turn lead to higher profitability and market value.

Measuring Horizontal Fit

Recall that horizontal fit means that HR practices are all aligned with one another to establish a configuration that is mutually reinforcing. Figure 2.13 shows an example

FIGURE 2.12 Building the Metrics Model

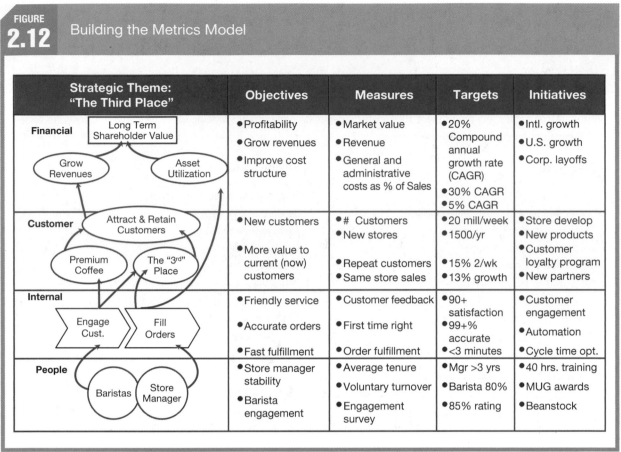

Strategic Theme: "The Third Place"		Objectives	Measures	Targets	Initiatives
Financial	Long Term Shareholder Value; Grow Revenues; Asset Utilization	• Profitability • Grow revenues • Improve cost structure	• Market value • Revenue • General and administrative costs as % of Sales	• 20% Compound annual growth rate (CAGR) • 30% CAGR • 5% CAGR	• Intl. growth • U.S. growth • Corp. layoffs
Customer	Attract & Retain Customers; Premium Coffee; The "3rd" Place	• New customers • More value to current (now) customers	• # Customers • New stores • Repeat customers • Same store sales	• 20 mill/week • 1500/yr • 15% 2/wk • 13% growth	• Store develop • New products • Customer loyalty program • New partners
Internal	Engage Cust.; Fill Orders	• Friendly service • Accurate orders • Fast fulfillment	• Customer feedback • First time right • Order fulfillment	• 90+ satisfaction • 99+% accurate • <3 minutes	• Customer engagement • Automation • Cycle time opt.
People	Baristas; Store Manager	• Store manager stability • Barista engagement	• Average tenure • Voluntary turnover • Engagement survey	• Mgr >3 yrs • Barista 80% • 85% rating	• 40 hrs. training • MUG awards • Beanstock

of how organizations can assess the horizontal fit of their HR practices. There are essentially three steps. First, managers need to identify the key workforce objectives they hope to achieve. Often this information can come from the people/learning cell of the Balanced Scorecard and might include loyalty, customer service, productivity, and creativity. Second, managers would identify each of the HR practices used to elicit or reinforce those workforce objectives (job design, staffing, training, appraisal, compensation, and so on). Third, managers would evaluate each HR practice on a scale of −5 (not supportive) to 5 (supportive). By tallying up the ratings across managers, organizations can get a very clear idea of which HR practices are working together to achieve the workforce objectives and which are not.

An important caveat to this analysis is that horizontal fit is a necessary, but insufficient, cause of strategic alignment. A company could have nearly perfect alignment among its HR practices, and they still might not be aligned with the competitive strategy. For that reason, it is important for managers to assess both vertical and horizontal fit.

Ensuring Strategic Flexibility for the Future

Apart from the need to establish and measure fit between HR and strategy, HR is also focused on ensuring flexibility and agility when the environment changes.

FIGURE 2.13 Assessing Horizontal Fit

WORKFORCE OBJECTIVES

	SALES PRODUCTIVITY	CUSTOMER SERVICE	MERCHANDISE INFORMATION	STOCK MAINTENANCE	TOTAL
Structure/Workflow					
• Cross-functional teams	3	2	0	−1	4
• Rotation (Depts.)	3	3	−1	−1	4
Staffing					
• Test battery	2	2	1	1	6
• Select for experience	5	3	2	2	12
Training					
• Retail selling skills	4	5	1	1	11
Rewards					
• Results appraisal	5	−4	−2	−5	−6
• Individual incentives	5	−5	−3	−5	−8
Leadership					
• Corporate	3	3	1	0	7
• Store manager	4	2	2	2	10
Technologies					
• Merchandise IS	5	2	5	1	13
• Daily postings	4	−3	4	−1	4
	43/55	10/55	10/55	26/55	57/220

ORGANIZATION (left axis) *FUNCTIONAL COHESION* (right axis)

SYSTEM COHERENCE   26%

5 = Strongly supports the priority
0 = Neutral
−5 = Strongly counterproductive

Ultimately, successful HRP helps increase organizational capability—the capacity of the organization to continuously act and change in pursuit of sustainable competitive advantage.[35]

Flexibility can be achieved in two primary ways: coordination flexibility and resource flexibility. *Coordination flexibility* is the ability to rapidly reallocate resources to new or changing needs. Through HRP, managers can anticipate upcoming events, keep abreast of changes in legal regulations, forecast economic trends, spot competitors' moves, and the like. With advance notice, managers can move people into and out of jobs, retrain them for new skill requirements, and modify the kinds of incentives they use. The use of a contingency workforce composed of part-timers, temporary employees, and external partners also helps achieve coordination flexibility.[36] *Resource flexibility*, on the other hand, results from having resources that can be used different ways and people who can perform different functions in different ways.

organizational capability

The capacity of the organization to act and change in pursuit of sustainable competitive advantage

Cross-training employees, rotating them into different jobs, and using teams are all efforts that focus on building a flexible workforce.

We will draw on these ideas throughout the text. But at this point we want to close the chapter by emphasizing that strategic planning is a process designed to ensure superior performance today, as well as establishing the capability and agility to respond tomorrow. As the great hockey player Wayne Gretsky used to say, "I don't skate to where the puck is. I skate to where the puck is going to be."

Summary

LEARNING OUTCOME 1 Strategic human resources management (SHRM) integrates strategic planning and HR planning. It can be thought of as the pattern of human resources deployments and activities that enable an organization to achieve its strategic goals. HR planning and strategies need to be continually monitored and assessed, especially when organizations consider global strategies, outsourcing, mergers, joint ventures, offshoring, the relocation of plants, product innovations, and downsizing, or when dramatic shifts in the composition of the labor force are occurring.

LEARNING OUTCOME 2 Analyzing the firm's competitive environment is central to strategic planning. The competitive environment includes the specific organizations with which the firm interacts. Firms analyze the competitive environment in order to adapt to or influence the nature of competition.

LEARNING OUTCOME 3 Conducting an internal analysis to gauge the firm's strengths and weaknesses involves looking at a firm's "three Cs"—its capabilities, composition, and culture. An internal analysis enables strategic decision makers to assess the organization's workforce—its skills, cultural beliefs, and values.

An organization's success increasingly depends on the knowledge, skills, and abilities of employees, particularly as they help establish a set of core capabilities that distinguish an organization from its competitors. When employees' talents are valuable, rare, difficult to imitate, and organized, a firm can achieve a sustained competitive advantage through its people.

LEARNING OUTCOME 4 HRP is a systematic process that involves forecasting demand for labor, performing supply analysis, and balancing supply and demand considerations. Forecasting demand requires using either quantitative or qualitative methods to identify the number and type of people needed to meet organizational objectives. Supply analysis involves determining whether sufficient employees are available within the organization to meet demand and also whether potential employees are available on the job market.

LEARNING OUTCOME 5 As organizations plan for their future, top management and strategic planners must recognize that strategic planning decisions affect—and are affected by—HR functions. Via HRP, human resources managers can proactively identify and initiate programs needed to develop organizational capabilities on which future strategies can be built. HRP and strategic planning tend to be most effective when there is a reciprocal relationship between the two processes.

LEARNING OUTCOME 6 Formulating an HR strategy is only half of the HR battle. The strategy must also be implemented. Employment forecasts must be reconciled against the internal and the external supplies of labor the firm faces. This can include having current employees work overtime; hiring full-time, part-time, or contract employees; downsizing employees; furloughing them; and outsourcing or offshoring. If there is a labor shortage, the firm might have to reformulate its long-term and short-term strategic plans or find ways to develop employees "from the ground up."

LEARNING OUTCOME 7 Firms need to establish a set of parameters that focus on the "desired outcomes" of strategic planning, as well as the metrics they will use to monitor how well the firm delivers against those outcomes. Issues of measurement, benchmarking, alignment, fit, and flexibility are central to the evaluation process. Firms use benchmarking, strategy mapping, and the Balanced Scorecard (BSC) as tools to gauge their outcomes.

Key Terms

Balanced Scorecard (BSC)
benchmarking
core capabilities
core values
cultural audits
environmental scanning
human capital readiness
human resources planning (HRP)

management forecasts
Markov analysis
mission
organizational capability
quality of fill
replacement charts
skill inventories
staffing tables

strategic planning
strategic vision
succession planning
SWOT analysis
trend analysis
value creation
values-based hiring

Discussion Questions

LEARNING OUTCOME 1 Identify the three key elements of the human resources planning model and discuss the relationships among them.

LEARNING OUTCOME 2 What competitive environmental forces influence a firm's strategy?

LEARNING OUTCOME 3 What criteria must be met if firms are to achieve a competitive advantage through their employees?

LEARNING OUTCOME 4 Which approach do you think should be relied on more heavily for strategy formulation—the quantitative or qualitative approach?

LEARNING OUTCOME 5 Explain the difference between a firm's corporate strategy and business strategy. Why do firms need to look at both aspects?

LEARNING OUTCOME 6 What steps does the firm need to take to reconcile labor supply and labor demand?

LEARNING OUTCOME 7 Why is organizational capability important to a firm and how can HR managers enhance it?

HRM EXPERIENCE
Customizing HR for Different Types of Human Capital

Part of strategic planning is mapping an organization's human capital. When we look at the strategic value of a person's skills as well as their uniqueness, we soon discover that organizations are comprised of different kinds of workers who have very different kinds of skills. Some are core knowledge workers; some are more traditional job-based employees; some are contract workers; and some are external partners. It is unlikely a firm would manage all of these employees the same way. There are differences in HR practices for different groups. That is not bad, but it makes the job of HR managers more difficult.

Assignment

The following are descriptions of three different employees. How would you characterize each worker? What role does each play when it comes to the organization's strategy?

Andrea Bascomb is a highly talented computer programmer for MiniFluff, Inc. She is among an elite set of engineers in the computer industry doing leading-edge work on advanced computer modeling. CEO Bill Ding believes that the future of the company rests on the innovative work that Andrea and her team are doing. He worries that someone might lure Andrea away to work for them. So he wants to give her all the room she needs to grow and stay committed to MiniFluff.

Calvin Duff is a salesperson on the retail side of MiniFluff. He has daily contact with customers and is responsible for making sales and communicating with service personnel. Make no mistake: To many customers, Calvin and his coworkers are the "face" of MiniFluff. Always on the lookout for a better position, Calvin has thought about working for PeachTree Computing, MiniFluff's main competitor. Other salespeople have found that they can leave MiniFluff and get "up to speed" easily at other firms. Their skills are very transferable, and the transition is not difficult. Bill Ding and other managers at MiniFluff recognize this fact, so they try to keep salespeople loyal and productive, recognizing that many of them do eventually leave.

Evelyn Frank is a part-time administrative assistant for MiniFluff. She handles routine typing and filing work for the company, particularly in peak periods in the summer and around the holidays. She usually works for a few weeks at a time and then takes time off. The executives at MiniFluff have considered either outsourcing her job to an agency or automating it through a new computer system. But for now things are steady.

On the Job: Video Cases

Strategic HR Planning at Focus HR Consulting

Andrea Herran of Focus HR Consulting reflects on some causes of employee turnover and performance problems and discusses some ways to address these problems. Retaining employees is addressed mainly as a function of cultural fit between the employee and the organization and the employee's skill set match to the position. The importance of clearly communicating performance expectations is highlighted.

What to Watch for and Ask Yourself

1. Herran gives the example of an organization with a rigid and strict culture, characterized by strictly enforced rules. The organization provided no leeway or creativity in how work processes were carried out. She then pointed out that "California-style, laid-back" employees would never work out there regardless of their skill sets because the culture was too uncomfortable. Do you agree with her? Why or why not?

2. Which drivers of retention does Ms. Herran address in the video?

Case Study 1

Joining Gratterpalm as HR manager five years ago was a challenging proposition—both for the company and for myself. An award-winning independent retail marketing agency based in Leeds, Gratterpalm creates advertising, point of sale, and design for major clients including the United Kingdom grocery giant ASDA and the sofa retailer DFS.

When I joined the agency in January 2003, Gratterpalm had no HR function whatsoever. Originally a family-run business, it had grown, over twenty-five years, to a team of seventy and had just undergone a management buyout.

The key to introducing HR to Gratterpalm was to introduce a performance review tool that allowed us to benchmark the success of a people-centered culture and allowed every employee the opportunity to have their say. We therefore launched "Gratter chatter," an employee survey that has become the bedrock of the agency's HR function. The initial survey highlighted several issues within the agency that clearly needed to be addressed:

- Team structures were unclear; people did not know who their line manager was and reporting lines were blurred in some departments.

- Work/life balance was poor.

- There was a lack of understanding of company values.

- Only 66 percent stated they enjoyed working at Gratterpalm.

- There was a low commitment to training and development.

- Employees did not believe the survey was confidential or anonymous, so there was an initial lack of trust and only 70 percent completion.

Small Company Uses HR as a Strategic Tool for Growth

Many initiatives have been taken to address the issues thrown up by the first and subsequent surveys. These include:

- Clearly defined role profiles, so everyone understands their role.

- Biannual people asset reviews to ensure that we are aware of all employee development needs and are able to take relevant action.

- To help address the work/life balance we introduced a "justification to recruit" procedure to ensure that there was a rigorous thought process before recruitment took place.

- An increase in flexible working opportunities—10 percent of employees now enjoy flexible working.

- The introduction of child care vouchers as a part of our range of benefits.

- Management huddles that take place on a weekly basis as a valuable communication tool—we also have an annual company meeting focusing on our three-year business plan and there is regular communication and reminders of our values.

- Introduction of an in-house training schedule that is rolled out twice a year and the establishment of a course evaluation process.

- Exit interviews that take place for all leavers.

Another important development has been the introduction of a structured appraisal procedure, "Let's Talk," which ensures that employees are given feedback on their performance and set objectives for the forthcoming year. We also put into place a clear career structure so that employees were aware of how they could progress to the next level. An internal vacancies notice board and procedure were introduced, and as a result of these initiatives 10 percent of employees were promoted internally last year. Some of the company's stars today are those who were, in the past, not thought to be strong performers, but they have managed to turn their careers around with the help of effective people management. Clients have played an active role in the recruitment process.

Some of the challenges for HR have been aligning it to the wider business as Gratterpalm grows and develops in line with its business plan. One of these areas was developing the company's corporate social responsibility (CSR) credentials. Initiatives include employees reading to children on a weekly basis at our local primary school, and the introduction of plastic, metal, and glass recycling bins into the business to encourage employees to recycle. We are establishing links with two charities, and we are currently planning an "empty car park" day to encourage car sharing, cycling, and the use of public transport.

The key results achieved by HR at Gratterpalm in the five years from 2003 to 2008 are highlighted as follows:

- Employee turnover reduced from 30 percent to 15 percent.

- Attendance rates increased from 90 percent to 98 percent through successful attendance management including welcome back meetings after all absences.

- Gratter chatter (the employee survey) response rates increased from 70 percent to 100 percent.

- Those that believe Gratterpalm is a "very good place to work" reached its highest score of 85 percent this year.

- Of new recruits taken on in the last 12 months, 60 percent have been through direct means (web or recommended through contacts/employees).

- Gratterpalm is becoming an employer of choice and our name is becoming more known within the industry.

Questions

1. How are Gratterpalm's new HR activities driving business growth for the company?
2. Why are "basic" HR functions sometimes difficult for small firms to execute? How can they improve their capacity to successfully implement HR programs?
3. Why does it takes time to see the results of HR activities?

Source: Excerpted from Helen Sauders, "Gratterpalm Uses HR as a Strategic Tool for Growth," *Strategic HR Review* 8, no. 1 (2009): 22–27.

Case Study 2

Staffing, Down to a Science at Capital One

When the financial services industry tumbled into crisis in June 2007, Capital One chairman and CEO Richard Fairbank issued a mandate to strip $700 million out of the company's operating costs by 2009. The cost reduction plan includes consolidating and streamlining functions, reducing layers of management, and eliminating approximately 2,000 jobs. The mandate did not set off a mad scramble in workforce planning, however. Instead, the planning staff simply added new defined variables to their simulations and modified their projections for the company's talent needs.

"The key to workforce planning is to start with the long-term vision of the organization and its future business goals and work back from there," says Matthew Schuyler, chief human resources officer for Capital One and its 27,000 employees. "We anticipate the strategic needs of the business and make sure that we have the workforce required to meet those needs. The $700 million mandate gives us goals and boundaries that we didn't have before. We made the adjustments."

Capital One and other leading companies are developing a set of best practices for workforce planning that reach into the future for each business unit and evolve with corporate strategic planning. In an increasingly unstable global business environment, the value of a long-term vision is clear, but effective workforce planning requires dedicated resources, heavy analytics, and, perhaps most important, the full engagement of business unit leaders and line managers.

Working Backward

The workforce planning at Capital One stems from a process executed by a metrics and analytics group of 20 people, plus hundreds of executives, managers, and analysts pulled from all the business lines and corporate functions. Leaders and analysts from the business lines work in blended teams with human resources generalists and members of the metrics group to build models for each line and the entire world force.

The models flow to Schuyler, who reports directly to the CEO. "You have to garner your long-term vision of the organization from your seat at the table and from the time you spend with business leaders, immersed in places where you can get data," Schuyler says. "You have to probe the business leaders and know the business leaders and know what their endgame looks like." Planning varies by business line. Some lines are stable, while others are restructuring or moving through rapid growth.

Part of Schuyler's job is to ensure that senior business line leaders are engaged in the process. "Their door is open," he notes. "Your ticket through the door is to show business leaders the bundles of money they can save if their workforce is the right size with the right mix and the right skills. Once you're inside, you have to act on the promise." The potential cost savings come from minimizing the inherent costs associated with the size of the workforce, plus savings from lower recruiting and severance costs and avoiding the costs of a disengaged workforce. "The cost of disengagement is difficult to quantify, but business leaders intuitively understand the cost," Schuyler says. "There is a toll paid when a workforce is disempowered, disengaged, and not sufficiently busy."

Workforce planning at Capital One forecasts not only the head count required to meet future business needs, but also the staffing mix—the ratio of internal to external resources—and the skills mix, including any changes in that mix that are required as the business moves forward. Schuyler also looks at any changes in "spans of control," which determine the number of organizational layers, optimal methods for staffing managerial positions, and the related costs. The planners also document both rational and emotional employee engagement, which affect current and future productivity and recruiting, training, and turnover costs.

The responsibility for workforce planning at Capital One resides in human resources, but the hard work takes place inside the business units, where the blended teams operate. This grounding in the business units keeps workforce planning focused on corporate goals. Workforce planning really gets traction when it is linked to the line managers who understand business needs and can project their business growth and productivity changes. The time frames for workforce planning at Capital One vary by unit and function. The legal function, for example, is very stable and can easily plan out two to four years. The credit card division, however, is rapidly evolving, so its forecasts stretch out two to four years but are reviewed every quarter. Likewise, the demand for some jobs follows the business cycle. Collections and recoveries work at Capital One was stable and predictable several years ago, for example. "But because of the current economic conditions, this work is now more important, and we had to ramp up very quickly," Schuyler explains.

Managing Demand and Supply

Schuyler refuses to choose between overshooting and undershooting staffing. "The beauty of workforce planning is that it allows the flexibility to be right on target," he says. "We don't have to wait for the next budget cycle to get it right."

That flexibility derives from a more sophisticated approach to planning that looks at a range of possible scenarios about business conditions and then calculates the labor needed to match them. Capital One's workforce planning models allow business leaders to anticipate the talent requirements for each business option and the human resources and labor cost consequences of the choices they make. Especially for companies that are just beginning to implement a workforce planning process, the best approach is to focus first on the critical roles in the organization and then expand out to cover more positions in greater detail. Avoid the tendency to drown managers in data by breaking the data down on a critical-jobs basis. At Capital One, the workforce planning process reaches down through the entire executive structure for each business unit—five or six levels of leadership plus groups of managers. Business leaders see the talent management costs and consequences of the business options at hand. Each option carries its own implications for internal and external staffing levels, recruiting, training, promotions, engagement, attrition, and total compensation costs over time. More important, workforce planning allows business leaders and line managers to see how different approaches to talent management can actually expand their business options and boost performance. "If workforce planning is done right, human resources can help business leaders think about what their endgame can be," Schuyler says.

Questions

1. Why do you think it's important for Capital One to calculate the "disengagement" factor of its employees when it comes to workforce planning?
2. What merits do you see to breaking down the planning process by business units through multiple layers of leaders? Do you see any drawbacks of doing so?

Source: Excerpted from Fay Hansen, "The Long View," *Workforce Management* 87, no. 7 (April 21, 2008): 1, 19.

Notes and References

1. Chistopher Rees, Hasanah Johari, "Senior Managers' Perceptions of the *HRM* Function during Times of Strategic Organizational Change," *Journal of Organizational Change Management* 23, no 2. (2010): 517.
2. "The Importance of HR," *HRFocus* 73, no. 3 (March 1996): 14; "Retiring Workforce, Widening Skills Gap, Exodus of 'Critical Talent' Threaten Companies: Deloitte Survey," *Canadian Corporate News* (February 15, 2005); Brian E. Becker and Mark A. Huselid, "Strategic Human Resources Management: Where Do We Go From Here?" *Journal of Management* 32, no. 6 (January 2006): 898–925; Jack Welch, "The 'But' Economy," *Wall Street Journal* (October 30, 2003).
3. Scott A. Snell, Mark Shadur, and Patrick M. Wright, "Human Resources Strategy: The Era of Our Ways," in M. A. Hitt, R. E. Freeman, and J. S. Harrison (eds.), *Handbook of Strategic Management* (Oxford, UK: Blackwell, 2002), 627–49; Patrick M. Wright, Benjamin Dunford, and Scott A. Snell, "Human Resources and the Resource-Based View of the Firm," *Journal of Management* 27, no. 6 (2002): 701–21; "What's Affecting HR Operations? Globalization, Sustainability, and Talent," *HR Focus* 84, no. 8 (August 2007): 8; Doris Sims, "Do You Know Where Your Talent Is?" *Training* 45, no. 1 (January 2008): 46–46.
4. "The Importance of HR," *HRFocus* 73, no. 3 (March 1996): 14. David Brown, "HR's Role in Business Strategy: Still a Lot of Work to Be Done," *Canadian HR Reporter* 14, no. 19 (November 5, 2001): 1–20; "How Should the HR Dept. of 2004 Be Structured?" *Human Resource Department Management Report*, no. 3 (November 2003): 1.
5. T. J. Watson, Jr., *A Business and Its Beliefs: The Ideas That Helped Build IBM* (New York: McGraw-Hill, 1963), 5; James W. Walker, "Integrating the Human Resource Function with the Business," *Human Resource Planning* 14, no. 2 (1996): 59–77; James W. Walker, "Perspectives," *Human Resource Planning* 25, no. 1 (2002): 12–14.
6. Patrick Kiger, "Serious Progress in Strategic Workforce Planning," *Workforce Management* (July 1, 2010), http:// workforce.com.
7. Bala Iyer, "Deconstructing Google," *Computerworld* 42, no. 15 (April 7, 2008): 32–33.
8. "Core Values and the Companies that Do Them Well, Grapper," *Grasslands: The Entrepreneurial Blog* (April 4, 2010), http://grasshopper.com.
9. Jay J. Jamrog and Miles H. Overholt, "Building a Strategic HR Function: Continuing the Evolution," *Human Resource Planning* 27, no. 1 (March 2004): 51; Gary L. Nielson, Karla L. Martin, and Elizabeth Powers, "The Secrets to Successful Strategy Execution," *Harvard Business Review* 86, no. 6 (June 2008): 60–70.
10. Jan Alexander, "Virgin America's Guide to Not Screwing Up Customer Service," (February 22, 2010), http://bnet.com.
11. For example, see U.S. Department of Labor, Bureau of Labor Statistics, *Geographic Profiles of Employment and Unemployment*. The data and information are accessible via the Office of Employment Projections home page at http://www.bls.gov/emp.
12. J. B. Quinn, "The Intelligent Enterprise: A New Paradigm," *Academy of Management Executive* 6, no. 4 (2002): 48–63.
13. For more information on methods to identify a firm's core capabilities, see Khalid

Hafeez, YanBing Zhang, and Naila Malak, "Core Competence for Sustainable Competitive Advantage: A Structured Methodology for Identifying Core Competence," *IEEE Transactions on Engineering Management* 49, no. 1 (February 2002): 28–35; Quinn, "The Intelligent Enterprise," 48–63; Jane Wollman Rusoff, "Outsourced Solutions: Brokerage Firms Looking to Focus on Their Core Competencies Find the Most Value in a Resource-Rich Clearing Partner," *Research* 27, no. 11 (November 2004): 37–40.

14. Snell, Shadur, and Wright, "Human Resources Strategy," 627–49; Wright, Dunford, and Snell, "Human Resources and the Resource-Based View of the Firm," 701–21; David Collis and Cynthia Montgomery, "Competing on Resources," *Harvard Business Review* 86, no. 7/8 (July–August 2008): 140–150; Susan Cantrell, "The Work Force of One," *Wall Street Journal* 249, no. 140 (June 16, 2007): R10.

15. D. P. Lepak and S. A. Snell, "The Human Resource Architecture: Toward a Theory of Human Capital Development and Allocation," *Academy of Management Review* 24, no. 1 (1999): 31–48; David Lepak and Scott Snell, "Examining the Human Resource Architecture: The Relationship among Human Capital, Employment, and Human Resource Configurations," *Journal of Management* 24, no. 1 (January 1999): 31; Brian E. Becker and Mark A. Huselid, "A Players or A Positions? The Strategic Logic of Workforce Management," *Harvard Business Review* 83, no. 12 (December 2005): 110–117; Sung-Choon Kang and S.A. Snell, "Intellectual Capital Architectures and Ambidextrous Learning: A Framework for Human Resource Management," *Journal of Management Studies* 46, no. 1 (January 2009): 65–92.

16. James Clawson, *Level Three Leadership: Getting Below the Surface*, 4th ed. (Upper Saddle River, NJ: Prentice-Hall, 2008.)

17. "SAS Again Ranks No. 1 on FORTUNE Best Companies to Work For" List in America," *SAS.com* (January 20, 2011), http://www.sas.com.

18. Ken Carrig and Patrick Wright, *Building Profit through Building People: Making Your Workforce the Strongest Link in the Value-Profit Chain* (Alexandria, VA: Society for Human Resources Management.)

19. Joseph F. Castellan and Susan S. Lightle, "Using Cultural Audits to Assess Tone at the Top," *CPA Journal* 75, no. 2 (February 2005), 6–11.

20. Jennifer J. Salpeck, "Firms Tally the Value in Values-Based Recruiting," *Workforce Management* (January 2011), http://www.workforce.com.

21. Stephenie Overman, "Gearing Up for Tomorrow's Workforce," *HRFocus* 76, no. 2 (February 1999): 1, 15; Kathryn Tyler, "Evaluate Your Next Move," *HRMagazine* 46, no. 11 (November 2001): 66–71; Bill Leonard, "Turnover at the Top," *HRMagazine* 46, no. 5 (May 2001): 46–52.

22. Carolyn Hirschman, "Putting Forecasting in Focus," *HRMagazine* 52, no. 3 (March 2007): 44–49.

23. Patrick Kiger, "Serious Progress Workforce Planning," *Workforce Management* (July 1, 2010), http://workforce.com.

24. "Talent Management: Now It's the Top Priority for CEOs and Their Organizations," *HR Focus* 85, no. 2 (February 2008): 8–9; "Finding Top Talent," *Community Banker* 17, no. 4 (April 2008): 15; Paul Bernthal and Richard Wellins, "Trends in Leader Development and Succession," *Human Resource Planning* 29, no. 2 (2006): 31–40; Sarah Needleman, "Demand Rises for Talent-Management Software," *Wall Street Journal* 251, no. 12 (January 15, 2008): B8.

25. Robert Kaplan and David Norton, *Strategy Maps: Converting Intangible Assets into Tangible Outcomes* (Boston: Harvard Business School Press, 2006), Chapter 8.

26. John Huey, "Outlaw Flyboy CEOs," *Fortune* 142, no. 11 (November 13, 2000): 237–50; "Visions of the Future," *Human Resources* (January 2008): special section, 22.

27. Brian Becker, Mark Huselid, and Dave Ulrich, *The HR Scorecard: Linking People, Strategy, and Performance* (Cambridge, MA: Harvard Business School Press, 2001). See also Shari Caudron, "How HR Drives Profits," *Workforce* 80, no. 12 (December 2001): 26–31.

28. "A Singular Sensation for Schwab Brokers," *Business Week Online* (January 24, 2002).

29. Larry Bossidy, Ram Charan, and Charles Burck, *Execution: The Art of Getting Things Done* (New York: Crown Business, 2002); Stacey L. Kaplan, "Business Strategy, People

Strategy and Total Rewards—Connecting the Dots," *Benefits & Compensation Digest* 44, no. 9 (September 2007): 1–19; Gary L. Neilson, Karla L Martin, and Elizabeth Power, "The Secrets to Successful Strategy, *Harvard Business Review* 86, no. 6 (June 2008): 60–70; Mark Vickers, "HR Growing Pains: Getting from Awkward to Accomplished," *Human Resource Planning* 30, no. 4 (2007): 20–24.

30. "Poll Shows Concern about Aging Workforce," *Credit Union Management* 34, no. 1 (January 2011): 36.

31. Patrick Kiger, "Serious Progress in Strategic Workforce Planning," *Workforce Management* (July 1, 2010), http://workforce.com.

32. Jesse Drucker, "Motorola to Cut 7,000 More Jobs and Take $3.5 Billion in Charges," *The Wall Street Journal* (June 28, 2002): B6; Dennis K. Berman, "Planning to Outsource," *HRFocus* 81, no. 5 (May 2004): 1; David Koenig, "American Airlines Workers Brace for Job Cuts," *Associated Press* (July 3, 2008).

33. Lisa Bransten, "U.S. Examining Sun Microsystems over Complaint," *The Wall Street Journal* (June 25, 2002): B6; Matthew Miklave and A. Jonathan Trafimow, "Expecting Problems from This Dismissal," *Workforce* 80, no. 12 (December 2001): 81–83.

34. Ray Brillinger, "Best Practices: Human Resources Benchmarking," *Canadian HR Reporter* 14, no. 12 (June 18, 2001): 12; Chris Mahoney, "Benchmarking Your Way to Smarter Decisions," *Workforce* 79, no. 10 (October 2000): 100–103; Brian E. Becker and Mark A. Huselid, "Strategic Human Resources Management: Where Do We Go from Here?" *Journal of Management* 32 no. 6 (January 2006): 898–925.

35. P. M. Wright and S. A. Snell, "Toward a Unifying Framework for Exploring Fit and Flexibility in Strategic Human Resource Management," *Academy of Management Review* 22, no. 4 (1998): 756–72; Snell, Shadur, and Wright, "Human Resources Strategy," 627–49; Wright, Dunford, and Snell, "Human Resources and the Resource-Based View of the Firm," 701–21.

36. R. Sanchez, "Strategic Flexibility in Product Competition," *Strategic Management Journal* 16 (1995): 135–59; Wright and Snell, "Toward a Unifying Framework." 756–72.

Appendix

©Diana Ong, Fotosearch

Calculating Employee Turnover and Absenteeism

Throughout this chapter we have emphasized that HRP depends on having an accurate picture of both the supply of and the demand for employees. Two factors, employee turnover and absenteeism, have a direct impact on HR planning strategy and recruitment processes. In this Appendix, we provide a detailed discussion of turnover and absenteeism, methods for measuring them, and suggestions for managing their impact.

Employee Turnover Rates

Employee turnover refers simply to the movement of employees out of an organization. It is often cited as one of the factors behind the failure of U.S. employee productivity rates to keep pace with those of foreign competitors. It is also one of the chief determinants of labor supply. Even if everything else about an organization stays the same, as employees turn over, its supply of labor goes down. This involves both direct and indirect costs to the organization.

Computing the Turnover Rate

The U.S. Department of Labor suggests the following formula for computing turnover rates:

$$\frac{\text{Number of separations during the month}}{\text{Total number of employees at mid month}} \times 100$$

Thus, if there were 25 separations during a month and the total number of employees at mid month was 500, the turnover rate would be:

$$\frac{25}{500} \times 100 = 5 \text{ percent}$$

Turnover rates are computed on a regular basis to compare specific units such as departments, divisions, and work groups. In many cases, comparisons are made with data provided by other organizations. The *Bureau of National Affairs Quarterly Report on Job Absence and Turnover* is a very good source of comparative turnover data.[1]

Another method of computing the turnover rate is one that reflects only the avoidable separations (S). This rate is computed by subtracting unavoidable separations

(US)—for example, due to pregnancy, return to school, death, or marriage—from all separations. The formula for this method is as follows:

$$\frac{S - US}{M} \times 100 = T \text{ (turnover rate)}$$

where M represents the total number of employees at mid-month. For example, if there were 25 separations during a month, 5 of which were US, and the total number of employees at mid month (M) was 500, the turnover rate would be:

$$\frac{25 - 5}{500} \times 100 = 4 \text{ percent}$$

Determining the Costs of Turnover

Replacing an employee is time-consuming and expensive. Costs can generally be broken down into three categories: separation costs for the departing employee, replacement costs, and training costs for the new employee. These costs are conservatively estimated at two to three times the monthly salary of the departing employee, and they do not include indirect costs such as low productivity prior to quitting and lower morale and overtime for other employees because of the vacated job. Consequently, reducing turnover could result in significant savings to an organization. Highlights in HRM 5 details one organization's costs associated with the turnover of a single computer programmer. Note that the major expense is the cost involved in training a replacement.

Employee Absenteeism Rates

How frequently employees are absent from their work—the absenteeism rate—is also directly related to HR planning and recruitment. When employees miss work, the organization incurs direct costs of lost wages and decreased productivity. It is not uncommon for organizations to hire extra workers just to make up for the number of absences totaled across all employees. In addition to these direct costs, indirect costs may underlie excessive absenteeism. A certain amount of absenteeism is, of course, unavoidable. There will always be some who must be absent from work because of sickness, accidents, serious family problems, or other legitimate reasons. However, chronic absenteeism may signal deeper problems in the work environment.

Computing Absenteeism Rates

Managers should determine the extent of the absenteeism problem, if any, by maintaining individual and departmental attendance records and by computing absenteeism rates. Although there is no universally accepted definition of "absence" or a standard formula for computing absenteeism rates, the method most frequently used is that recommended by the U.S. Department of Labor.

$$\frac{\text{Number of worker-days lost through job absence during period}}{\text{Average number of employees} \times \text{number of workdays}} \times 100$$

HIGHLIGHTS IN **HRM**

5 Costs Associated with the Turnover of One Computer Programmer

Turnover costs = Separation costs + Replacement costs + Training costs

Separation costs

1. Exit interview = cost for salary and benefits of both interviewer and departing employee during the exit interview = $30 + $30 = $60
2. Administrative and record-keeping action = $30 Separation costs = $60 + $30 = $90

Replacement costs

1. Advertising for job opening = $2,500
2. Preemployment administrative functions and record-keeping action = $100
3. Selection interview = $250
4. Employment tests = $40
5. Meetings to discuss candidates (salary and benefits of managers while participating in meetings) = $250
   Replacement costs = $2,500 + $100 + $250 + $40 + $250 = $3,140

Training costs

1. Booklets, manuals, and reports = $50
2. Education = $240/day for new employee's salary and benefits x 10 days of workshops, seminars, or courses = $2,400
3. One-to-one coaching = ($240/day per new employee + $240/day per staff coach or job expert) $\times$ 20 days of one-to-one coaching = $9,600
4. Salary and benefits of new employee until he or she gets "up to par" = $240/day for salary and benefits $\times$ 20 days = $4,800
   Training costs = $50 + $2,400 + $9,600 + $4,800 = $16,850

Total turnover costs = $90 + $3,140 + $16,850 = $20,080

Source: Adapted from the book *Turning Your Human Resources Department into a Profit Center* by Michael Mercer, PhD (Barrington, IL: Castlegate Publishers, Inc.). Copyright 2002 Michael Mercer. Reproduced with permission from Michael Mercer, PhD, http://www.DrMercer.com.

If 300 worker-days are lost through job absence during a month having 25 scheduled working days at an organization that employs 500 workers, the absenteeism rate for that month is:

$$\frac{300}{300 \times 25} \times 100 = 2.4 \text{ percent}$$

The U.S. Department of Labor defines job absence as the failure of employees to report to work when their schedules require it, whether or not such failure to report is excused. Scheduled vacations, holidays, and prearranged leaves of absence are not counted as job absence.

Comparing Absenteeism Data

The Bureau of Labor Statistics of the U.S. Department of Labor receives data on job absences from the Current Population Survey of Households conducted by the Bureau of the Census, and analyses of these data are published periodically. These analyses permit the identification of problem areas—industries, occupations, or groups of workers with the highest incidence of absence or with rapidly increasing rates of absence. Comparison with other organizations may be made by referring to Bureau of Labor Statistics data reported in the *Monthly Labor Review* or by consulting such reporting services as the Bureau of National Affairs or CCH. Both these organizations and the data they provide can be found on the web.

Costs of Absenteeism

The cost of each person hour lost to absenteeism is based on the hourly weighted average salary, costs of employee benefits, supervisory costs, and incidental costs. For example, XYZ Company, with 1,200 employees, has 78,000 person hours lost to absenteeism; the total absence cost is $560,886. When this figure is divided by 1,200 employees, the cost per employee is $467.41. (In this example, we are assuming the absent workers are paid. If absent workers are not paid, their salary figures are omitted from the computation.)

Absenteeism and HR Planning

While an employer may find that the overall absenteeism rate and costs are within an acceptable range, it is still advisable to study the statistics to determine whether there are patterns in the data. Rarely does absenteeism spread itself evenly across an organization. It is very likely that employees in one area (or occupational group) may have nearly perfect attendance records, while others in a different area may be absent frequently. By monitoring these differential attendance records, managers can assess where problems might exist and, more important, begin planning ways to resolve or improve the underlying causes. For example, incentives could be provided for perfect attendance. Alternatively, progressive discipline procedures might be used with employees having a record of recurring absenteeism.

By establishing a comprehensive absenteeism policy, Allen-Bradley (which is now a part of Rockwell Automation) cut absenteeism 83.5 percent in a twenty-five-month period. This reduced the strain on labor costs and increased productivity.

Notes and References

1. This quarterly report is part of the BNA *Bulletin to Management*. For an excellent review of the relationship between performance and voluntary turnover, see Charles R. Williams and Linda Parrack Livingstone, "Another Look at the Relationship between Performance and Voluntary Turnover," *Academy of Management Journal* 37, no. 2 (April 1994): 269–98.

3

Equal Employment Opportunity and Human Resources Management

After studying this chapter, you should be able to

LEARNING OUTCOME 1 Explain the reasons behind passage of equal employment opportunity (EEO) legislation.

LEARNING OUTCOME 2 Prepare an outline describing the major EEO laws and the employment practices they prohibit. Describe what a bona fide occupational qualification is.

LEARNING OUTCOME 3 Understand why sexual harassment, immigration reform, and other practices such as discrimination based on a person's weight, appearance, and sexual orientation have become equal employment opportunity issues.

LEARNING OUTCOME 4 Explain how the *Uniform Guidelines on Employee Selection Procedures* were developed and how firms use them to ensure they are abiding by the law.

LEARNING OUTCOME 5 Understand the concepts of adverse impact and disparate treatment.

LEARNING OUTCOME 6 Understand EEOC record-keeping and posting requirements.

LEARNING OUTCOME 7 Describe how discrimination charges are processed by the EEOC.

LEARNING OUTCOME 8 Explain what affirmative action is and how companies today are seeing the value of voluntarily having diverse workforces.

equal employment opportunity (EEO)

The treatment of individuals in all aspects of employment—hiring, promotion, training, etc.—in a fair and nonbiased manner

One of the most important topics that must be discussed in any human resources management textbook is **equal employment opportunity (EEO).** Equal employment opportunity, or the employment of individuals in a fair and nonbiased manner, commands the attention of the media, courts, legislators, HR managers, and their firms alike. In 2010, a record 99,922 private-sector workplace discrimination charges were filed with the U.S. Equal Employment Opportunity Commission (EEOC), the federal agency that enforces the nation's fair employment laws.[1] Some of the increase in the charges is believed to have occurred as a result of poor economic conditions and a sense of desperation on the part of employees who have lost their jobs. A more diverse and multicultural workforce has also made it increasingly important for managers to know and comply with a myriad of EEO laws.

When managers ignore or are unaware of fair employment laws, they and their firms run the risk of costly and time-consuming litigation, negative public attention, and potentially lower sales, lower employee morale, and even damage to their own individual careers.[2] Because even unintentional discrimination can be illegal, supervisors need to be aware of their personal biases and how they can affect their dealings with their subordinates.[3] Currently, Walmart is facing the biggest employment discrimination case in the nation's history—a sex discrimination suit that could amount to billions of dollars in back pay for hundreds of thousands of female employees.[4]

Discrimination lawsuits are not limited to just large companies such as Walmart, though. Even small businesses can face charges of discrimination. Small businesses are also vulnerable to discrimination charges because they often do not have the resources to fight them, or due to a lack of time or resources, have not diligently studied EEO laws and prepared for the EEO issues related to them that can arise. To see how firms can avoid these problems, read the small business feature in this chapter.

Employment discrimination is not only a legal issue but an emotional one. It concerns all individuals, regardless of their sex, race, religion, age, national origin, color, physical condition, or position in an organization. Fortunately, it is a problem that can be minimized with good HR practices. This chapter will help you better understand how to do that. We will also discuss the diversity efforts companies are actively pursuing, not because they have to for legal reasons but as a way to gain a strategic edge. HR professionals agree that when all functions of HRM comply with the law, the organization becomes a fairer place to work and a more effective competitor.

LEARNING OUTCOME 1

People's attitudes towards discrimination have evolved over time in the United States. What do you think will be the prevailing attitude of people towards discrimination 20 years from now? Will there be more or less discrimination in the workplace? Why?

Historical Perspective of EEO Legislation

Equal employment opportunity as a national priority has emerged slowly in the United States. Not until the mid-1950s and early 1960s did nondiscriminatory employment practices receive a great deal of attention by the public. Three factors seem to have influenced the growth of EEO legislation: (1) changing attitudes toward employment discrimination; (2) published reports highlighting the economic problems and injustices experienced by minority workers; and (3) a growing body of disparate discrimination laws and regulations at different levels of government that legislators felt should be standardized.

Small Business Application

The Perils of Non-Compliance

Starting up a new business is an exciting prospect filled with both rewards and concerns. Ironically, the kind of success that leads to growth and additional staff can also open up a small business to a new type of risk: hefty fines and penalties that result from failing to comply with federal and state employment regulations. Few entrepreneurs are equipped with the knowledge or time to deal with these issues, yet they put themselves in danger if they ignore the complex and ever-evolving laws.

That is why owners and managers of growing small businesses should consider conducting routine HR compliance assessments, either annually or perhaps each time the company reaches another significant increase in employees, for example, from less than five to closer to fifteen employees.

And there are other occasions when a small firm should check its compliance as well. Eric A. Marks, a partner in charge of the Human Resources Consulting Practice at the New York accounting firm Marks Paneth & Shron explains, "Significant changes to the business, such as mergers; the retirement of senior managers; newly hired or promoted supervisors or managers who may lack HR experience; creation or revision of an employee handbook; changes in employee morale, turnover, attendance, or disciplinary problems; taking on government contracts where compliance requirements are often stricter; and major changes in state or federal regulations—any of these are danger signs. They signal that the business has a fresh need to address compliance and make sure its house is in order."

In short, an HR compliance assessment reviews how well an employer is following employment, benefits, and safety laws. Specifically, an assessment evaluates the fairness, adequacy, and legality of a company's procedures and policies, such as its ability to keep thorough and confidential records, recruiting and selection processes, interviewing techniques, education on harassment and discrimination, performance evaluation process, compensation program, disciplinary and termination processes, health and safety provisions, and employee handbook.

Fortunately, small business owners do not have to remain in the danger zone. There are numerous HR consulting firms that can not only conduct a compliance assessment, they can assist the owner with rectifying any noncompliant systems and procedures and train the company's managers and supervisors to maintain them. There are even HR compliance self-assessment forms available online. Help is only a mouse-click away.

Source: "New Risks to Small Businesses" *Marketwire*," (February 28, 2011), http://www2.marketwire.com; "HR Compliance Assessment Overview," http://www.the-arnold-group.com/hr-assessment.cfm; "HR Challenges: Compliance," http://www.strategic-workplace-solutions.com/services/compliance.

Changing National Values

The United States was founded on the principles of individual merit, hard work, and equality. The Constitution grants to all citizens the right to life, liberty, and the pursuit of happiness. In spite of these constitutional guarantees, employment discrimination has a long history in the United States. Organizations that claim to offer fair treatment to employees have intentionally or unintentionally engaged in discriminatory practices. Well-known organizations such as Dow Chemical, Starbucks, Mitsubishi Motor Manufacturing of America, the U.S. Army, Lockheed Martin, Boeing, Home Depot, Morgan Stanley, and American Airlines have violated equal employment laws.

Public attitudes towards discrimination changed dramatically with the beginning of the civil rights movement during the late 1950s and early 1960s. Minorities—especially blacks—drew attention to their low economic and occupational positions by conducting marches, sit-ins, rallies, and clashes with public authorities.[5] The low employment status of women also gained recognition during this period. Supported by concerned individuals and church and civic leaders, the civil rights and women's movements received wide media coverage. The movements also led to a pronounced change in the attitudes of society. No longer was blatant discrimination acceptable.

Nonetheless, economic disparities still persist. As you learned in Chapter 1, women, on average, make less than men, and nonwhite employees are likely to make less than white employees. Discrimination claims today are not limited to those involving just race and gender, though. Companies can find themselves sued for discriminating against people in many ways, including because of their age, religion, health, military status, the way they dress, and even their attractiveness.

Early Legal Developments

Since as early as the nineteenth century, the public has been aware of discriminatory employment practices in the United States. In 1866, Congress passed the Civil Rights Act, which extended to all people the right to enjoy full and equal benefits of all laws, regardless of their race. Beginning in the 1930s and 1940s, more specific federal policies covering nondiscrimination began to emerge. In 1933, Congress enacted the Unemployment Relief Act, which prohibited employment discrimination on account of race, color, or creed (religious beliefs). Then in 1941, President Franklin D. Roosevelt issued Executive Order 8802, which was to ensure that every American citizen, "regardless of race, creed, color, or national origin," would be guaranteed equal employment opportunities for workers employed by firms awarded World War II defense contracts. Over the next twenty years a variety of other legislative efforts were promoted to resolve inequities in employment practices.

Unfortunately, these early efforts did little to correct employment discrimination. First, at both the state and federal levels, nondiscrimination laws often failed to give any enforcement powers to the agency charged with upholding the law. Second, the laws that were passed frequently neglected to list specific discriminatory practices or methods that needed to be corrected. Third, employers covered by the acts were required only to comply voluntarily with the equal employment opportunity legislation. Without a compulsory requirement, they often violated discrimination laws without being penalized.

Government Regulation of Equal Employment Opportunity

LEARNING OUTCOME 2
How have EEO laws changed over time? What do you think HR managers and first-line supervisors need to do to stay up to date on the changes in the laws?

Despite their shortcomings, the laws and executive orders discussed in the previous section laid the groundwork for a significant number of laws that have since been passed barring employment discrimination. Today it is illegal to discriminate against either an applicant or an employee because of that person's race, color, religion, sex (including pregnancy status), national origin, age, disabilities, or genetic information. It is also illegal to retaliate against a person because he or she complained about discrimination, filed a charge of discrimination, or participated in an employment discrimination investigation or lawsuit.[6] This is important to note because retaliation has become the most frequent EEO complaint. We will talk more about retaliation later in the chapter.[7]

Part of the reason why it's so critical for managers and supervisors to understand and apply EEO laws is that employees act as "agents" of their employers. In other words, they act on the legal behalf of their employers.[8] So, for example, if a manager or supervisor violates the law *both* she and her organization can face legal consequences. The organization cannot claim that it is not legally responsible for what the manager or supervisor did.

Figure 3.1 shows the various prohibited HR activities related to hiring, promoting, compensating employees, and so forth covered by EEO laws. If you think you already know what constitutes a legal or illegal employment practice, you might be surprised. Highlights in HRM 1 will test your current understanding of how equal employment opportunity laws are applied in the workplace. By the time you have finished reading this chapter, you will have a much better understanding of the topic and how to use this information to be a better manager.

FIGURE 3.1   Prohibited Discriminatory Employment Practices

It is illegal to discriminate in any aspect of employment, including:

- hiring and firing;
- compensation, assignment, or classification of employees;
- transfer, promotion, layoff, or recall;
- job advertisements;
- recruitment;
- testing;
- use of company facilities;
- training and apprenticeship programs;
- fringe benefits;
- pay, retirement plans, and disability leave; or
- other terms and conditions of employment.

Discriminatory practices under these laws also include:

- harassment on the basis of race, color, religion, sex, national origin, disability, genetic information, or age;
- retaliation against an individual for filing a charge of discrimination, participating in an investigation, or opposing discriminatory practices;
- employment decisions based on stereotypes or assumptions about the abilities, traits, or performance of individuals of a certain sex, race, age, religion, or ethnic group, or individuals with disabilities, or based on myths or assumptions about an individual's genetic information; and
- denying employment opportunities to a person because of marriage to, or association with, an individual of a particular race, religion, national origin, or an individual with a disability. Title VII also prohibits discrimination because of participation in schools or places of worship associated with a particular racial, ethnic, or religious group.

Source: U.S. Equal Employment Opportunity Commission.

Major Federal Laws

Major federal EEO laws have been enacted to prevent discrimination against groups of workers most often affected by unfair employment practices. These groups are referred to as protected classes.[9] Defined broadly, the classes include employees of a particular race, color, religion, national origin, sex, age, and those with physical or mental disabilities. Separate federal laws cover each of these classes. Figure 3.2 lists the major federal laws and their provisions governing equal employment opportunity. Next, we will discuss each of them.

protected classes

Individuals of a minority race, women, older people, and those with disabilities who are covered by federal laws on equal employment opportunity

Equal Pay Act of 1963

The Equal Pay Act makes it illegal to discriminate against people in terms of the pay, employee benefits, and pension they earn based on their gender when they do equal work.[10] Jobs are considered "equal" when they require substantially the same skill, effort, and responsibility under similar working conditions and in the

---

FIGURE 3.2   Major Laws Affecting Equal Employment Opportunity

LAW	PROVISIONS
Equal Pay Act of 1963	Requires all employers covered by the Fair Labor Standards Act and others to provide equal pay for equal work, regardless of sex.
Title VII of Civil Rights Act of 1964 (amended in 1972, 1991, 1994, and 2009)	Prohibits discrimination in employment on the basis of race, color, religion, sex, or national origin; created the Equal Employment Opportunity Commission (EEOC) to enforce the provisions of Title VII.
Age Discrimination in Employment Act of 1967 (amended in 1986 and 1990)	Prohibits private and public employers from discriminating against people age forty or older in any area of employment because of age; exceptions are permitted when age is a bona fide occupational qualification.
Equal Employment Opportunity Act of 1972	Amended Title VII of Civil Rights Act of 1964; strengthens the EEOC's enforcement powers and extends coverage of Title VII to government employees, employees in higher education, and other employers and employees.
Pregnancy Discrimination Act of 1978	Broadens the definition of sex discrimination to include pregnancy, childbirth, or related medical conditions; prohibits employers from discriminating against pregnant women in employment benefits if they are capable of performing their job duties.
Americans with Disabilities Act of 1990 (amended in 2008)	Prohibits discrimination in employment against people with physical or mental disabilities or the chronically ill; enjoins employers to make reasonable accommodation to the employment needs of the disabled; covers employers with fifteen or more employees.
Civil Rights Act of 1991	Provides for compensatory and punitive damages and jury trials in cases involving intentional discrimination; requires employers to demonstrate that job practices are job-related and consistent with business necessity; extends coverage to U.S. citizens working for U.S. companies overseas.
Uniformed Services Employment and Reemployment Rights Act of 1994 (amended in 1998, 2004, and 2008)	Protects the employment rights of individuals who enter the military for short periods of service.
Don't Ask, Don't Tell Repeal Act of 2010	Bars discrimination against military personnel based on their sexual orientations.

same establishment. For example, male and female plastic molders working for Medical Plastics Laboratory, a company based in Texas, must not be paid differently simply because of their gender. However, a company does not violate the Equal Pay Act when the differences in the wages it pays to men and women for equal work are based on seniority systems, merit considerations, or the workers' quantity or quality of production. Also, if a pay disparity between the sexes exists, employers cannot legally lower the wages of one gender to comply with the law; rather, they must raise the wages of the gender being underpaid. The Equal Pay Act was passed as an amendment to the Fair Labor Standards Act (FLSA), and it covers employers engaged in interstate commerce and most government employees.

Civil Rights Act of 1964

The Civil Rights Act of 1964 is a landmark law that addresses discrimination in society in general in the United States. It is the broadest and most significant of the antidiscrimination statutes. Title VII of the act specifically bars employment discrimination in all HR activities, including hiring, training, promotion, transfers, pay, employee benefits, and other conditions of employment. Discrimination is prohibited on the basis of race, color, religion, sex, or national origin. Along with prohibiting employment discrimination, Title VII of the Civil Rights Act created the Equal Employment Opportunity Commission.

In response to the growing number of immigrant workers and workplace cultural and ethnic awareness, the EEOC has issued important guidelines on national origin discrimination.[11] A "national origin group" is defined as a group of people sharing a common language, culture, ancestry, and/or similar social characteristics. This definition includes people born in the United States who are not racial or ethnic minorities. Therefore, whether the ancestry of an employee or job applicant is Mexican, Ukrainian, Filipino, Arab, Native American, or any other nationality, he or she is entitled to the same employment opportunities as anyone else.[12] Also prohibited under the act is discrimination based on pregnancy or a medical condition related to it or childbirth. The law protects hourly employees, supervisors, professional employees, managers, and executives from discriminatory practices.

Although the provisions of Title VII are extensive, the law does permit various exemptions. For example, as with the Equal Pay Act, managers are permitted to apply employment conditions differently if those differences are based on such objective factors as merit, seniority, or incentive payments. For example, the law would permit the promotion of a male office worker over a female office worker if the promotion was based on the superior skills and abilities of the male. Nowhere does the law require employers to hire, promote, or retain workers who are not qualified to perform their job duties. And managers may still reward employees differently, provided these differences are not predicated on the employees' race, color, sex, religion, or national origin.

The Civil Rights Act of 1964 covers a broad range of organizations. The law includes under its jurisdiction the following:

1. All private employers in interstate commerce who employ fifteen or more employees for twenty or more weeks per year

2. State and local governments

3. Private and public employment agencies

HIGHLIGHTS IN **HRM**

1

Test Your Knowledge of Equal Employment Opportunity Law

The following questions have been used as "icebreakers" by employers and consultants when training supervisors and managers in EEO legislation. What is your knowledge of EEO laws? Answers are found at the end of this chapter.

1. Two male employees tell a sexually explicit joke. The joke is overheard by a female employee who complains to her supervisor that this is sexual harassment. Is her complaint legitimate?

   _____ Yes _____ No

2. To be covered by Title VII of the Civil Rights Act, an employer must be engaged in interstate commerce and employ twenty-five or more employees.

   _____ True _____ False

3. People addicted to illegal drugs are classified as disabled under the Americans with Disabilities Act of 1990.

   _____ Yes _____ No

4. The Equal Pay Act of 1963 allows employers to pay different wages to men and women who are performing substantially similar work. What are the three defenses for paying a different wage?

   1. _____

   2. _____

   3. _____

5. A person applies for a job as a janitor at your company. During his interview with you, the person mentions that since birth he has sometimes experienced short periods of memory loss. Must you consider this individual a disabled person under the Americans with Disabilities Act of 1990?

   _____ Yes _____ No

6. On Friday afternoon, you tell Nancy Penley, a computer analyst, that she must work overtime the next day. She refuses, saying that Saturday is her regular religious holiday and she can't work. Do you have the legal right to order her to work on Saturday?

   _____ Yes _____ No

7. You have just told an applicant that she will not receive the job for which she applied. She claims that you denied her employment because of her age (she's 52). You claim she is not protected under the age discrimination law. Is your reasoning correct?

   _____ Yes _____ No

8. As an employer, you can select those applicants who are the most qualified in terms of education and experience.

   _____ Yes _____ No

9. As a manager, you have the legal right to mandate dates for pregnancy leaves.

   _____ True _____ False

10. State and local fair employment practice laws cover smaller employers not covered by federal legislation.

    _____ True _____ False

4. Joint labor-management committees that govern apprenticeship or training programs

5. Labor unions having fifteen or more members or employees

6. Public and private educational institutions

7. Foreign subsidiaries of U.S. organizations employing U.S. citizens

Certain employers are excluded from coverage of the Civil Rights Act. Broadly defined, these are (1) U.S. government–owned corporations, (2) bona fide, tax-exempt private clubs, (3) religious organizations employing people of a specific religion, and (4) organizations hiring Native Americans on or near a reservation. The Civil Rights Act of 1964 established the Equal Employment Opportunity Commission to administer the law in order to promote equal employment opportunity. The commission's structure and operations will be reviewed later in this chapter.

Bona Fide Occupational Qualification. Under Title VII of the Civil Rights Act, employers are permitted limited exemptions from antidiscrimination regulations if the employment preferences are based on a bona fide occupational qualification. A bona fide occupational qualification (BFOQ) permits discrimination when employer hiring preferences are a reasonable necessity for the normal operation of the business. Courts have ruled that a business necessity is a practice that is necessary for the safe and efficient operation of the organization.

However, a BFOQ is a suitable defense against a discrimination charge only when *age, religion, sex,* or *national origin* is an actual qualification for performing the job. For example, an older person could legitimately be excluded from consideration for employment as a model for teenage designer jeans. It is also reasonable to expect the Chicago Bears of the National Football League to hire male locker-room attendants or for Abercrombie and Fitch Clothing Store to employ females as models for women's fashions. Religion is a BFOQ in organizations that require employees to share a particular religious doctrine. National origin can also be a BFOQ if it is an actual qualification for a job. For example, to ensure the "authenticity" of the dining experience, an Asian restaurant could use the business-necessity defense to support its preference for hiring Asian American servers. Likewise, a filmmaker could legally advertise an acting role seeking a Native American to play a Native American character.

The BFOQ exception does *not* apply to discrimination based on race or color, though. The EEOC also does not favor BFOQs, and both the EEOC and the courts have construed the concept narrowly. When an organization claims a BFOQ, it must be able to prove that hiring on the basis of sex, religion, age, or national origin is a business necessity.

Religious Preference. Title VII of the Civil Rights Act prohibits employment discrimination based on a person's religion. Title VII does not require employers to grant complete religious freedom in employment situations, however. Employers need only make a reasonable accommodation for a current employee's or job applicant's religious observance or practice without incurring undue hardship in the conduct of the business. Managers or supervisors may have to accommodate an employee's religion in the specific areas of (1) holidays and observances (scheduling), (2) personal appearance (wearing beards, veils, or turbans), and (3) religious conduct on the job (missionary work among other employees).

What constitutes "reasonable accommodation" can be difficult to define. For example, when a library employee was fired for violating a dress code by wearing a cross, she sued under the First Amendment of the United States Constitution. The court

bona fide occupational qualification (BFOQ)
Suitable defense against a discrimination charge only when age, religion, sex, or national origin is an actual qualification for performing the job

business necessity
A work-related practice that is necessary to the safe and efficient operation of an organization

Title VII of the Civil Rights Act requires employers to make reasonable accommodations for an employee's religious practices and observances.

Zurijeta/Shutterstock.com

found that the library's interest in enforcing its dress code did not outweigh the employee's right to free speech or the free exercise of her religion. By contrast, when an office worker sued her employer for failing to accommodate her religious practice of ending some conversations with, "Have a blessed day," an appeals court ruled against her. The court said that use of the phrase is not a requirement of her religion and held that the employer did not have to satisfy an employee's every desire.[13]

The Supreme Court tried to clarify the issue of religion in *TWA v. Hardison* by ruling that employers had only to bear a minimum cost to show accommodation. The department in which Hardison, the plaintiff, worked at TWA was a twenty-four-hours-a-day operation. Hardison's religious beliefs prevented him from a working a certain shift on the Sabbath. The problem was that TWA could not accommodate him without violating a seniority provision that gave other employees with more seniority their shift preferences. To cover Hardison's shift, TWA would have had to hire an extra employee or pay current employees overtime to work it. The *Hardison* case is important because it supported union management seniority systems in which the employer had made a reasonable attempt to adjust an employee's work schedule without undue hardship.

Employer-employee cooperation and flexibility are often the key when it comes to employment accommodations, including those for religious reasons. Following 9/11, the Pentagon opened a chapel in its facility where anyone of any faith can go to pray, and an Imam conducts a service for Muslim personnel in the chapel on Fridays. Likewise, instead of mandating all employees take Christian holidays such as Christmas and Easter off, some firms let employees substitute different days to observe their own beliefs or trade days off with other employees. The EEOC's position is not that firms need to quash religious expression in the workplace but to make a reasonable effort to accommodate people with different belief systems.

Using the INTERNET

To view the EEOC's guidelines about religious discrimination (as well as other laws and regulations), go to

www.cengagebrain.com

Amendments to the Civil Rights Act of 1964

Equal Employment Opportunity Act of 1972. In 1972 the Civil Rights Act of 1964 was amended by the Equal Employment Opportunity Act. Two important changes were made. First, the coverage of the act was broadened to include state and local governments and public and private educational institutions. Second, the law strengthened the enforcement powers of the EEOC by allowing the agency itself to sue employers in court to enforce the provisions of the act.

Civil Rights Act of 1991. The Civil Rights Act of 1991 was enacted in response to a series of Supreme Court decisions limiting the rights of employees who had sued their employers for discrimination. One of the major elements of the law is that employees who can prove they were intentionally discriminated against can seek compensatory monetary damages. Compensatory damages include money for emotional pain, suffering, mental anguish, and so forth. Additional money can be awarded to employees in the form of "punitive" damages if it can be shown that the employer engaged in discrimination with malice or reckless indifference to the law.

The Civil Rights Act of 1991 also states that employees who are sent abroad to work for U.S.-based companies are protected by U.S. antidiscrimination legislation governing age and disability and Title VII of the Civil Rights Act of 1964. Thus employees can sue their U.S. employers for claims of discriminatory treatment while employed in a foreign country.

Glass Ceiling Act of 1991. The Glass Ceiling Act of 1991 was passed jointly with the Civil Rights Act of 1991. The "glass ceiling" represents an invisible barrier that prohibits protected class members from reaching top organizational positions. The act created the Glass Ceiling Commission to study and report on the status of and obstacles faced by minorities as they strive for top-level management jobs. The Commission's most recent report can be found on the EEOC's website. Additional discussion of the glass ceiling can be found in Chapter 5.

Lily Ledbetter Fair Pay Act (2009). The Lily Ledbetter Fair Pay Act states that the 180-day statute of limitations for filing an equal-pay lawsuit with EEOC resets with each new discriminatory paycheck an employee receives—not the date the employee received his or her first discriminatory paycheck as the U.S. Supreme Court had ruled. What this means is that employees can claim discrimination after years of getting unfair pay and demand to be compensated for the lost wages. Organizations therefore need to diligently and regularly examine their pay systems carefully to be sure they are equitable.

Age Discrimination in Employment Act of 1967

The Age Discrimination in Employment Act (ADEA) prohibits specific employers from discriminating against employees and applicants age forty or older in any employment area. Employers affected are those with twenty or more employees; unions with twenty-five or more members; employment agencies; and federal, state, and local governments. In recent years the number of age discrimination complaints filed with the EEOC has been steadily trending upward. Considering the fact that the U.S. workforce is aging, this perhaps should come as no surprise.[14] Managers or supervisors discriminate against older employees if they:

- Exclude older workers from important work activities.

- Make negative changes in the performance evaluations of older employees.

- Deny older employees job-related education, career development, or promotional opportunities.

- Select younger job applicants over older, better-qualified candidates.

- Pressure older employees into taking early retirement or terminate them.

- Reduce the job duties and responsibilities of older employees.[15]

Exceptions to the law are permitted when age is a bona fide occupational qualification. A BFOQ may exist when an employer can show that advanced age may affect public safety or organizational efficiency. For example, such a condition might exist for bus or truck drivers or for locomotive engineers.

In 2009 the U.S. Supreme Court raised the bar for employees trying to prove discrimination claims by ruling that employers are not violating the law if "reasonable factors other than age" affect how the employees were treated.

Amendments to the ADEA

Older Workers Benefit Protection Act of 1990. The Older Workers Benefit Protection Act of 1990 specifically prohibits employers from denying benefits to older employees except in limited circumstances. The law also allows employers to ask older employees to waive their legal rights under the ADEA in exchange for compensation such as severance packages or court settlements. As a result of the act, many firms that have downsized have been able to legally offer older employees early-retirement severance packages. However, to be valid, an ADEA waiver must be in writing, clear, and understandable, and the recipients need to be given a certain amount of time to consider the offer in the waiver.

Pregnancy Discrimination Act of 1978

Before the passage of the Pregnancy Discrimination Act, pregnant women could be forced to resign or take a leave of absence because of their condition. In addition, employers did not have to provide disability or medical coverage for pregnancy. The Pregnancy Discrimination Act amended the Civil Rights Act of 1964 by stating that pregnancy is a disability and that pregnant employees in covered organizations must be treated on an equal basis with employees having other medical conditions. So, for example, it is illegal for employers to deny sick leave for morning sickness or related pregnancy illness if sick leave is permitted for other medical conditions such as flu or surgical operations. Specifically, the Pregnancy Discrimination Act affects employee benefit programs including (1) hospitalization and major medical insurance, (2) temporary disability and salary continuation plans, and (3) sick leave policies.[16] The law also prohibits discrimination in the hiring, promotion, transfer, or termination of women because of pregnancy. Women must be evaluated on their ability to perform the job, and employers may not set arbitrary dates for mandatory pregnancy leaves. Leave dates are to be based on the individual pregnant employee's ability to work.

Americans with Disabilities Act of 1990

Discrimination against the disabled was first prohibited in federally funded activities by the Vocational Rehabilitation Act of 1973 (to be discussed later). However, the disabled were not among the protected classes covered by the Civil Rights Act of 1964. To remedy this shortcoming, Congress in 1990 passed the Americans with Disabilities Act (ADA), which prohibits employers from discriminating against individuals with physical and mental disabilities and the chronically ill.[17]

Using the INTERNET

AARP offers a number of resources to employers who want to maximize their use of older workers. Go to

www.cengagebrain.com

The law defines a disability as "(a) a physical or mental impairment that substantially limits one or more of the major activities; (b) a record of such impairment; or (c) being regarded as having such an impairment." Note that the law also protects people "regarded" as having a disability—for example, individuals with disfiguring burns.

Managers and supervisors remark that the ADA is difficult to administer because of the ambiguous definition of a disability, particularly mental impairment. The issue is what is a disability? It sounds like a simple question, yet it is not. Not every mental or physical impairment is considered a disability under the law. For example, significant personality disorders are covered under the EEOC's "Enforcement Guidance on the Americans with Disabilities Act and Psychiatric Disabilities."[18] Covered personality disorders include schizophrenia, bipolar disorders, major affective disorders, personality disorders, and anxiety disorders. These impairments are characterized by aberrant behavior, self-defeating behavior, manipulation of others, and troublesome manners of behavior. However, mental impairments described as "adjustment disorders" or attributed to stress have generally not been subject to ADA coverage. Therefore, employees who claim to be "stressed" over marital problems, financial hardships, demands of the work environment, job duties, or harsh and unreasonable treatment from a supervisor would not be classified as disabled under the ADA.

The act requires employers to make a reasonable accommodation for disabled people who are otherwise qualified to work, unless doing so would cause undue hardship to the employer.[19] "Undue hardship" refers to unusual work modifications or excessive expenses that might be incurred by an employer in providing an accommodation. **Reasonable accommodation** "includes making facilities accessible and usable to disabled persons, restructuring jobs, permitting part-time or modified work schedules, reassigning to a vacant position, changing equipment, and/or expense." "Reasonable" is to be determined according to (1) the nature and cost of the accommodation and (2) the financial resources, size, and profitability of the facility and parent organization.

Furthermore, employers cannot use selection procedures that screen out or tend to screen out disabled people, unless the selection procedure "is shown to be job-related for the position in question and is consistent with business necessity" and acceptable job performance cannot be achieved through reasonable accommodation. ("Essential functions," a pivotal issue for ensuring reasonable accommodation, will be discussed in Chapter 4.) Information and forms related to the health of employees must be kept confidential and separate from their regular personnel files.

The act prohibits covered employers from discriminating against a qualified individual regarding application for employment, hiring, advancement, discharge, compensation, training, or other employment conditions. The law incorporates the procedures and remedies found in Title VII of the Civil Rights Act, allowing job applicants or employees initial employment, reinstatement, back pay, and other injunctive relief against employers who violate the statute. The act covers employers with fifteen or more employees. The EEOC enforces the law in the same manner that Title VII of the Civil Rights Act is enforced.

reasonable accommodation
An attempt by employers to adjust, without undue hardship, the working conditions or schedules of employees with disabilities or religious preferences

The ADA prohibits employers from discriminating against individuals regarded as having physical or mental disabilities.

Jupiterimages/Workbook Stock/Getty Images

Hiring disabled individuals is not only a legal mandate, it is also good business. Employers subject to the ADA and those who value the varied skills and abilities of the disabled approach the law as a proactive business requirement. Hiring the disabled emphasizes what these individuals *can* do rather than what they *cannot* do. Two of the most comprehensive studies conducted on the ADA show that the law has had a positive effect on both business outcomes and disabled employees. Conducted by the National Council on Disability (NCD), the studies reported positive gains regarding the ADA's four major goals: equal opportunity, full participation, independent living, and economic self-sufficiency for people with disabilities.[20]

Can employers place disabled people in jobs without carefully considering their disabilities? No. Nor is it always possible for employers to make reasonable accommodations for the disabled. However, it *is* good business to hire qualified disabled people who can work safely and productively. Fortunately, there exist today manual and electronic devices to aid hearing-impaired, visually impaired, and mobility-impaired employees. In many cases, the simple restructuring of jobs permits disabled persons to qualify for employment. Figure 3.3 identifies specific ways to make the workplace more accessible to the disabled.

Amendments to the ADA

Americans with Disabilities Act Amendments Act. In response to court rulings that had weakened the ADA, in 2008, the *Americans with Disabilities Act Amendments Act* (ADAAA) was enacted. The ADAAA broadened the definition of what constitutes a disability. Previously, the Supreme Court had ruled that the language in the ADA defining a disability as "a physical or mental impairment that substantially limits one or more of the major activities" had to be interpreted strictly and a demanding standard applied for a person to qualify. The new act, which indicated that it was not Congress's intent for the law to be so restrictive, makes it less likely a person will be denied protection because his or her condition does not seem severe enough or because it is improved by drugs, prosthetic devices, and so forth.

FIGURE 3.3   ADA Suggestions for an Accessible Workplace

- Install easy-to-reach switches.
- Provide sloping sidewalks and entrances.
- Install wheelchair ramps.
- Reposition shelves for the easy reach of materials.
- Rearrange tables, chairs, vending machines, dispensers, and other furniture and fixtures.
- Widen doors and hallways.
- Add raised markings on control buttons.
- Provide designated accessible parking spaces.
- Install hand controls or manipulation devices.
- Provide flashing alarm lights.
- Remove turnstiles and revolving doors or provide alternative accessible paths.
- Install holding bars in toilet areas.
- Redesign toilet partitions to increase access space.
- Add paper cup dispensers at water fountains.
- Replace high-pile, low-density carpeting.
- Reposition telephones, water fountains, and other needed equipment.
- Add raised toilet seats.
- Provide a full-length bathroom mirror.

After the passage of the law, the EEOC filed a number of suits against companies including one that alleged that a longtime cashier with severe arthritis was denied a reasonable accommodation—a stool. The woman had used the stool for seven years, but a new manager did not like the fact and had terminated her.[21]

Genetic Information Nondiscrimination Act of 2008

Employers have been known to discriminate against employees based on genetic information. In 2002, BNSF Railway paid millions of dollars to settle an EEOC suit alleging the firm genetically tested employees without their knowledge or consent. The test was part of a medical examination given to employees who had filed claims or internal reports related to on-the-job carpal tunnel syndrome injuries. The case, which was the first ever of its type filed by the EEOC, got the attention of the public. People began to worry their employers would be legally allowed to review their genetic information and discriminate against them if it showed they had a propensity to get sick.

The Genetic Information Nondiscrimination Act (GINA) enacted in 2008 was passed to alleviate people's fears that their genetic information would be misused. Under Title II of the act, employers are prohibited from requesting, requiring, or purchasing the genetic information of workers or their family members. Employers that happen to possess genetic information as a result of health insurance records must keep the information confidential and separate from an employee's personnel files.[22]

Uniformed Services Employment and Reemployment Rights Act of 1994 (USERRA)

The Uniformed Services Employment and Reemployment Rights Act of 1994 (USERRA) covers all military personnel, including National Guard members, reservists, and active-duty military personnel, who enlist either voluntarily or involuntarily during peace or wartime. Under this act, people who enter the military for a total of five years can return to their private sector jobs without risk of loss of seniority or benefits.[23] The act protects against discrimination on the basis of military obligation in the areas of hiring, job retention, and advancement. Other provisions under the act require employers to make reasonable efforts to retrain or upgrade the skills of employees to qualify them for reemployment. Employers must also continue to let employees and their dependents participate in their health care plans, and the workers' pension plans must continue as if they had been continuously employed. The law does not require employers to pay the workers' wages while they are enlisted. However, some companies do offer enlisted personnel partial wages.

Amendments to the USERRA

Veterans Benefits Improvement Act. In 2004, the USERRA was amended by the Veterans Benefits Improvement Act requiring employers to provide a notice of rights, benefits, and obligations of both employees and employers under USERRA.[24] For their part, service members must provide their employers advance notice of their military obligations in order to be protected by the reemployment rights statute. The Labor Department's Veterans Employment and Training Service is responsible for enforcing the law.

Other Federal Laws and Executive Orders

Because the major laws affecting equal employment opportunity do not cover agencies of the federal government and because state laws do not apply to federal employees, it has at times been necessary for the president to issue executive orders to protect federal employees. Executive orders are also used to provide equal employment opportunity to individuals employed by government contractors. Since many large employers—such as General Dynamics, Intel, Dell Computer, and Motorola—and numerous small companies have contracts with the federal government, managers are expected to know and comply with the provisions of executive orders and other laws. The federal laws and executive orders that apply to government agencies and government contractors are summarized in Figure 3.4.

It is not just the government that is interested in ensuring minorities have equal opportunities, though. Many firms today are making it a point to search for diverse suppliers to contract with, as this chapter's small business box shows.

Vocational Rehabilitation Act of 1973

People with disabilities experience discrimination both because of negative attitudes regarding their ability to perform work and because of physical barriers imposed by organizational facilities. The Vocational Rehabilitation Act was passed in 1973 to correct these problems by requiring private employers with federal contracts over $2,500 to take action to hire individuals with a mental or physical disability. Recipients of federal financial assistance, such as public and private colleges and universities, are also covered. Employers must make a reasonable accommodation to hire disabled individuals but are not required to employ unqualified people. In applying the safeguards of this law, the term **disabled individual** means "any person who (1) has a physical or mental impairment which substantially limits one or more of such person's major life activities, (2) has a record of such an impairment, or (3) is regarded as having such an impairment." This definition closely parallels the definition of disabled individual provided in the Americans with Disabilities Act previously discussed.

A frequently asked question is: "Are employees affected with contagious diseases subject to the act's coverage?" The courts have said yes.[25] In cases when people with contagious diseases are "otherwise qualified" to do their jobs, the law requires employers to make a reasonable accommodation to allow the disabled to perform their jobs.[26] Individuals with AIDS or HIV are also disabled within the meaning of the

disabled individual
Any person who (1) has a physical or mental impairment that substantially limits one or more of the person's major life activities, (2) has a record of such impairment, or (3) is regarded as having such an impairment

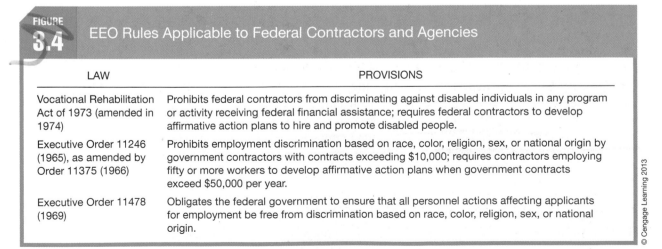

FIGURE 3.4	**EEO Rules Applicable to Federal Contractors and Agencies**

LAW	PROVISIONS
Vocational Rehabilitation Act of 1973 (amended in 1974)	Prohibits federal contractors from discriminating against disabled individuals in any program or activity receiving federal financial assistance; requires federal contractors to develop affirmative action plans to hire and promote disabled people.
Executive Order 11246 (1965), as amended by Order 11375 (1966)	Prohibits employment discrimination based on race, color, religion, sex, or national origin by government contractors with contracts exceeding $10,000; requires contractors employing fifty or more workers to develop affirmative action plans when government contracts exceed $50,000 per year.
Executive Order 11478 (1969)	Obligates the federal government to ensure that all personnel actions affecting applicants for employment be free from discrimination based on race, color, religion, sex, or national origin.

© Cengage Learning 2013

Rehabilitation Act. Therefore, discrimination on the basis of AIDS/HIV violates the law, and employers must accommodate the employment needs of people with these conditions. However, the Rehabilitation Act does not require employers to hire or retain a disabled person if he or she has a contagious disease that poses a direct threat to the health or safety of others and the individual cannot be accommodated. Also, employment is not required when some aspect of the employee's disability prevents that person from carrying out essential parts of the job, nor is it required if the disabled person is not otherwise qualified.

Executive Order 11246

Federal agencies and government contractors with contracts of $10,000 or more must comply with the antidiscrimination provisions of Executive Order 11246. The order prohibits discrimination based on race, color, religion, sex, or national origin in all employment activities. Furthermore, it requires that government contractors or subcontractors having fifty or more employees with contracts in excess of $50,000 develop affirmative action plans; such plans will be discussed later in the chapter.

Executive Order 11246 created the Office of Federal Contract Compliance Programs (OFCCP) to ensure equal employment opportunity in the federal procurement area. The agency issues nondiscriminatory guidelines and regulations similar to those issued by the EEOC. Noncompliance with OFCCP policies can result in the cancellation or suspension of government contracts. The OFCCP is further charged with requiring that contractors provide job opportunities to the disabled, disabled veterans, and veterans of the Vietnam War.

Don't Ask, Don't Tell Repeal Act of 2010. In 2010, the Don't Ask, Don't Tell Repeal Act was enacted to end the ban on gay or bisexual persons openly serving in the U.S. military—The ban was established as a compromise between the Clinton Administration and Congress in the mid-1990s to prevent members of the military from being dishonorably discharged for being gay, so long as they did not openly reveal their sexual orientation. The act repealing the ban outlines reforms that will be gradually implemented by the armed forces.

Fair Employment Practice Laws

Federal laws and executive orders provide the major regulations governing equal employment opportunity. But, in addition, almost all states and many local governments have passed laws barring employment discrimination. Referred to as **fair employment practices (FEPs),** these statutes are often more comprehensive than the federal laws. Although these laws are too numerous to review here, managers should be aware of them and how they affect HRM in their organizations.

State and local FEPs are patterned after federal legislation but often extend antidiscrimination laws to employers with one or more workers. Managers and entrepreneurs operating small businesses must pay close attention to these laws because they can be quite restrictive. They can bar discrimination based on any number of factors, including a person's sexual orientation, physical appearance, marital status, arrest records, color blindness, or political affiliation. State and local agencies that enforce antidiscrimination laws are called Fair Employment Practices Agencies (FEPAs). The Ohio Civil Rights Commission and the Massachusetts Commission against Discrimination are examples. FEPAs work together with the EEOC to resolve discrimination complaints.[27]

fair employment practices (FEPs)
State and local laws governing equal employment opportunity that are often more comprehensive than federal laws and apply to small employers

Other Equal Employment Opportunity Issues

Which types of discrimination do you think managers are most likely to have to deal with on a regular basis and why?

Federal laws, executive orders, court cases, and state and local statutes provide the broad legal framework for equal employment opportunity. Within these major laws, specific issues are of particular interest to supervisors and managers. The situations discussed in this section occur in the day-to-day supervision of employees.

Sexual Harassment

sexual harassment

Unwelcome advances, requests for sexual favors, and other verbal or physical conduct of a sexual nature in the working environment

Sexual harassment refers to unwelcome sexual advances, requests for sexual favors, and other verbal or physical harassment of a sexual nature. However, according to the EEOC, it can also include offensive remarks about a person's sex. Both the victim and the harasser can be either a woman or a man, and the victim and the harasser can be the same sex. The harasser can be the victim's supervisor, a supervisor in another area, a coworker, or someone who is not an employee of the employer, such as a client or customer.[28]

The EEOC recognizes two forms of sexual harassment as being illegal under Title VII. The first, *quid pro quo harassment*, occurs when "submission to or rejection of sexual conduct is used as a basis for employment decisions."[29] This type of harassment involves a tangible or economic consequence, such as a demotion or loss of pay. If a supervisor promotes an employee only after the person agrees to an after-work date, the conduct is clearly illegal.

The second type of harassment, *hostile environment*, can occur when unwelcome sexual conduct "has the purpose or effect of unreasonably interfering with job performance or creating an intimidating, hostile, or offensive working environment."[30] Furthermore, according to the EEOC, if favoritism based upon the granting of sexual favors is widespread in a workplace, workers who do not welcome the conduct can establish a hostile work environment, regardless of whether any objectionable conduct is directed at them.

Sexual harassment includes any type of behavior, comments, gestures, and actions of a sexual nature that create a hostile work environment for an employee.

Adam Gault/Photodisc/Getty Images

Dirty jokes, vulgar slang, nude pictures, swearing, and personal ridicule and insult create a hostile environment when an employee finds them offensive. E-mail, instant and text messages, and posts on social-networking sites have become convenient ways for employees to sexually harass their coworkers electronically.

Nationwide, 11,717 sexual harassment complaints were filed in 2010 with the EEOC and state fair employment practice agencies by employees of both small and large employers.[31] About 16 percent of these charges were filed by males. However, the number of charges filed has actually been steadily dropping over the years as people become more familiar with what constitutes sexual harassment under the law. Via a questionnaire, it is possible to test the understanding of your employees about what is and what is not sexual harassment. Highlights in HRM 2 shows some sample questions firms can ask their employees to gauge their knowledge of the topic.

Confusion about sexual harassment nonetheless persists. *Quid pro quo* harassment is becoming less common, says David Bowman, a Philadelphia labor attorney. Today employees are more likely to complain they are being sexually harassed when a coworker does not get the message that they are not receptive to their advances and the problem is hindering their ability to work. (See Case Study 2 at the end of this chapter for an example.) For this reason, some HR consultants recommend their corporate clients institute strict nonfraternization policies in their workplaces.

The EEOC considers an employer guilty of sexual harassment when the employer knew or should have known about the unlawful conduct and failed to remedy it or to take corrective action. Employers are also guilty of sexual harassment when they allow nonemployees (customers or salespeople) to sexually harass employees.[32] When charges of sexual harassment have been proved, victims forced out of their jobs can be awarded back pay, lost benefits, attorney's fees, and interest charges, and they may be reinstated in their jobs. Sexual harassment involving physical conduct can invite criminal charges, and punitive damages can be assessed against both the employer and the individual offender.[33]

Sexual Orientation

Nearly half of U.S. states and some cities also have passed laws prohibiting sexual orientation discrimination in workplaces.[34] But although Title VII of the Civil Rights Act of 1964 lists "sex" as a protected class, currently no federal law bars discrimination based on one's sexual orientation. In 1998, President Clinton signed Executive Order 13087 barring discrimination against civilian employees of the federal government based on their sexual orientation. An exception was made for military personnel, who were subject to the "don't ask don't tell" policy at the time. According to the EEOC, Executive Order 13087 did not create any new rights. However, it did set the stage for all units of the federal government to make certain that the workplace is one free from harassment and discrimination. Many cabinet-level agencies have also issued policy statements prohibiting discrimination based on sexual orientation. Some of the agencies have developed parallel EEO complaint procedures allowing federal employees to file EEO complaints based on sexual orientation within their agencies. In addition, it helped pave the way for the repeal of the military's "don't ask, don't tell" policy.[35]

For homosexual employees who do not work for the federal government, protection from discrimination largely comes from fair employment practice laws passed at state and local levels. The laws vary regarding the protection afforded homosexuals and who is covered under the laws. For example, in some states, public—but not

HIGHLIGHTS IN **HRM**

2 Questions Used to Audit Sexual Harassment in the Workplace

ACTIVITY	IS THIS SEXUAL HARASSMENT?			AWARE OF THIS BEHAVIOR IN THE ORGANIZATION?	
Employees post cartoons on bulletin boards containing sexually related material.	Yes	No	Uncertain	Yes	No
A male employee says to a female employee that she has beautiful eyes and hair.	Yes	No	Uncertain	Yes	No
A male manager habitually calls all female employees "sweetie" or "darling."	Yes	No	Uncertain	Yes	No
A manager fails to promote a female (male) employee for not granting sexual favors.	Yes	No	Uncertain	Yes	No
Male employees use vulgar language and tell sexual jokes that are overheard by, but not directed at, female employees.	Yes	No	Uncertain	Yes	No
A male employee leans and peers over the back of a female employee when she wears a low-cut dress.	Yes	No	Uncertain	Yes	No
A supervisor gives a female (male) subordinate a nice gift on her (his) birthday.	Yes	No	Uncertain	Yes	No
Two male employees share a sexually explicit magazine while observed by a female employee.	Yes	No	Uncertain	Yes	No
Female office workers are "rated" by male employees as they pass the men's desks.	Yes	No	Uncertain	Yes	No
Revealing female clothing is given as a gift at an office birthday party.	Yes	No	Uncertain	Yes	No
A sales representative from a supplier makes "suggestive" sexual remarks to a receptionist.	Yes	No	Uncertain	Yes	No

private—sector employees are protected from discrimination based on their sexual orientation. Therefore, it becomes important for managers and supervisors to know and follow the legal rights of homosexuals in their geographic area.[36]

Organizations such as S. C. Johnson, Eastman Kodak, Lucent Technologies, and Microsoft hold training sessions aimed at overcoming the stereotypes affecting gay and lesbian workers. Defense contractors Raytheon and Lockheed Martin sponsor homosexual support groups, and Walmart has adopted a nondiscrimination policy toward homosexuals. Most companies in the Fortune 500 now offer health benefits to same-sex couples.

Immigration Reform and Control

Good employment is the magnet that attracts many people to the United States. However, illegal immigration is an issue of national concern at the federal, state, and local legislative levels and among employers, unions, civil rights groups, and the general public.[37] The issue of illegal immigration is emotional, economic, and fraught with legal regulations.

To preserve our tradition of legal immigration while closing the door to illegal entry, employers must comply with the requirements of the Immigration Reform and Control Act (IRCA). The law has two employer mandates. First, all employers covered by the law are prohibited from knowingly hiring or retaining unauthorized aliens on the job.[38] Second, employers with four or more employees are prohibited from discriminating in hiring or termination decisions on the basis of national origin or citizenship.[39]

Employers must comply with the law by verifying and maintaining records on the legal rights of applicants to work in the United States. The *Handbook for Employers*, published by the U.S. Department of Justice, lists five actions that employers must take to comply with the law:

1. Have employees fill out their part of Form I-9.

2. Check documents establishing an employee's identity and eligibility to work.

3. Complete the employer's section of Form I-9.

4. Retain Form I-9 for at least three years.

5. Present Form I-9 for inspection to an Immigration and Naturalization Service officer or to a Department of Labor officer upon request.[40]

Employers with sizable contracts with the federal government must also use its E-Verification system. E-Verify is a system that provides an automated link to federal databases to help employers determine the legal eligibility of workers and the validity of their Social Security numbers. Employers that do not do business with the government can also use E-Verify. Some states require certain organizations to use it. Arizona requires all employers in the state to use E-Verify.[41]

Employers found to have violated the discrimination provisions of the Immigration Reform and Control Act will be ordered to cease the discriminatory practice. They may also be directed to hire, with or without back pay, individuals harmed by the discrimination and to pay a fine of up to $1,000 for each person discriminated against. Charges of discrimination based on national origin or citizenship are filed with the Office of Special Counsel in the Department of Justice.

Emerging Employment Discrimination Issues

Weight Discrimination

Some studies show that weight discrimination, especially against women, is not only increasing but has become almost as common as racial discrimination.[42] According to the advocacy group, the Council on Size & Weight Discrimination, workers who are heavier than average are paid $1.25 less an hour. Over a forty-year career, they will earn up to $100,000 less before taxes than their thinner counterparts.

No federal laws prohibit weight discrimination, although the EEOC has said that morbid obesity is a protected disability under the ADA. However, some cities, including Washington, DC, San Francisco, and Madison, Wisconsin, have banned discrimination based on a person's weight. The state of Michigan bars discrimination based on both height and weight. In that state, at least two waitresses have sued the Hooter's restaurant for discrimination. One of the waitresses, who was 145 lbs. at the time, claims she was advised in her performance review to join a gym in order to fit into an extra small-sized uniform: "The official uniform for Hooters waitresses, comes in 3 sizes: extra extra small, extra small, or small," stated the review.[43] The good news for employees bearing a few extra pounds is that weight seems to be gaining traction as far as becoming protected by employment laws. At some point it is not out of the realm of possibility that it could become a protected class.[44]

Attractiveness and Discrimination

A few locales, including Santa Cruz, California, and the District of Columbia, prohibit discrimination based on "physical characteristics" or "personal appearance" as a protected category. However, there are no federal laws prohibiting discrimination in the workplace based on people's attractiveness, although it undoubtedly occurs. In a survey of hiring managers conducted by *Newsweek*, 57 percent of them said that qualified but unattractive job candidates would have a harder time landing a job.

Part of the problem of implementing a law making it legal to discriminate based on a person's appearance would be deciding who is unattractive enough to be protected by the law. Moreover, in some instances, good looks can be a BFOQ. The modeling business is one example.[45]

However, like Hooter's, companies that treat people differently based on their looks are prone to legal problems. The retailer Abercrombie & Fitch is an example. In 2005 it settled a $40 million class-action lawsuit filed by the EEOC. Employees claimed the retailer hired and promoted attractive, Caucasian-looking, skinny male employees. "All-American doesn't mean all-white," says Jennifer Lu, a former Abercrombie & Fitch salesperson who says she was fired because her look was not consistent with the retailer's look.[46] (The EEOC filed the suit based on race discrimination.)

Caregivers and Discrimination

In 2007 the EEOC issued new enforcement guidelines to help prevent discrimination against workers with caregiving responsibilities. There are no federal statutes that prohibit discrimination based "solely" on a person being a caregiver. However, disparate treatment arises when an employee with caregiving responsibilities is subjected to discrimination based on a protected characteristic under equal opportunity laws (such as sex, race, age, and so forth).[47] The EEOC has outlined numerous scenarios it says could constitute discrimination against a caregiver. Denying women with young children an employment opportunity available to men with young children is an example. So is refusing to hire a worker who is a single parent of a

To avoid discriminating against employees with caregiving responsibilities, employers can follow EEOC guidelines, such as establishing more flexible workplace policies.

Picture Partners/Alamy

child with a disability based on the assumption that caregiving responsibilities will make the worker unreliable. The EEOC has developed "Best Practices" to help companies avoid discriminating against caregivers. It also cites studies that show that flexible workplace policies enhance employee productivity, reduce absenteeism and costs, aid with recruitment and retention, and provide employers with more alternatives when dealing with workforce reductions.

Uniform Guidelines on Employee Selection Procedures

Employers are often uncertain about the appropriateness of specific selection procedures, especially those related to testing and selection. To remedy this concern, the Equal Employment Opportunity Commission, along with three other government agencies, adopted the current *Uniform Guidelines on Employee Selection Procedures*.[48] The *Uniform Guidelines* is a very important procedural document for managers because it applies to employee selection procedures in the areas of hiring, retention, promotion, transfer, demotion, dismissal, and referral. It is designed to help employers, labor organizations, employment agencies, and licensing and certification boards comply with the requirements of federal laws prohibiting employment discrimination.

Validity

When using a test or other selection instrument to choose individuals for employment, employers must be able to prove that the selection instrument bears a direct relationship to success on the job. This proof is established through validation studies that show how related the test is to the job. The *Uniform Guidelines* provides strict standards for employers to follow as they validate selection procedures. The different methods of testing validity are reviewed in detail in Chapter 6.

Adverse Impact and Disparate Treatment

For an applicant or employee to pursue a discrimination case successfully, the individual must establish that the employer's selection procedures resulted in an adverse impact on a protected class. Adverse impact refers to the unintentional rejection for employment, placement, or promotion of a significantly higher percentage of members of a protected class when compared with members of nonprotected classes.[49] The *Uniform Guidelines* does not require an employer to conduct validity studies of its selection procedures when they have not resulted in adverse impact on a protected class. However, the guidelines do encourage employers to use selection procedures that are valid. Organizations that validate their selection procedures on a regular basis and use interviews, tests, and other procedures in such a manner as to avoid adverse impact will generally be in compliance with the principles of equal employment legislation.

There are two basic ways to show that adverse impact exists:

Adverse Rejection Rate, or Four-Fifths Rule.   According to the *Uniform Guidelines*, a selection program has an adverse impact when the selection rate for any racial, thnic, or sex class is less than four-fifths (or 80 percent) of the rate of the

LEARNING OUTCOME 4

As a manager, how would the *Uniform Guidelines on Employee Selection Procedures* affect how you deal with employees and applicants?

Uniform Guidelines on Employee Selection Procedures

A procedural document published in the Federal Register to help employers comply with federal regulations against discriminatory actions

LEARNING OUTCOME 5

Have you ever been the victim of adverse impact or disparate treatment? If so, in what context? Discuss your experience with your classmates.

adverse impact

A concept that refers to the rejection of a significantly higher percentage of a protected class for employment, placement, or promotion when compared with the successful, nonprotected class

class with the highest selection rate. The Equal Employment Opportunity Commission has adopted the four-fifths rule as a rule of thumb to determine adverse impact in enforcement proceedings. The four-fifths rule is not a legal definition of discrimination; rather, it is a method by which the EEOC or any other enforcement agency monitors serious discrepancies in hiring, promotion, or other employment decisions. The Appendix at the end of this chapter explains how adverse impact is determined and gives a realistic example of how the four-fifths rule is computed.

An alternative to the four-fifths rule, and one frequently used in discrimination lawsuits, is to conduct a standard deviation analysis of a firm's applicant data. The Supreme Court, in *Hazelwood School District v. United States*, set forth a standard deviation analysis that determines whether the difference between the expected selection rates for protected groups and the actual selection rates could be attributed to chance. If chance is eliminated for the lower selection rates of the protected class, it is assumed that the employer's selection technique has an adverse impact on the employment opportunities of that group.

Restricted Policy. Any evidence that an employer has a selection procedure that excludes members of a protected class, whether intentional or not, constitutes adverse impact. For example, hiring individuals who must meet a minimum height or appearance standard (at the expense of protected class members) is evidence of a restricted policy. In one case known to the authors, an organization when downsizing discharged employees primarily age 40 or older. These employees filed a class action suit claiming adverse impact under the Age Discrimination in Employment Act.

The benchmark case in employment selection procedures is *Griggs v. Duke Power Company* (1971). Willie Griggs, who was black, had applied for the position of coal handler with the Duke Power Company. His request for the position was denied because he was not a high school graduate, a requirement for the position. Griggs claimed the job standard was discriminatory because it did not relate to job success and because the standard had an adverse impact on a protected class.

In the *Griggs* decision, the Court ruled that employer discrimination need not be overt or intentional to be present. Second, under *Griggs*, employment practices must be job-related. When discrimination charges arise, employers have the burden of proving that employment requirements are job-related or constitute a business necessity. When employers use educational, physical, or intelligence standards as a basis for hiring or promotion, these must be absolutely necessary for job success. Under Title VII, good intent, or absence of intent to discriminate, is not a sufficient defense.

In EEO cases, it is important to distinguish between adverse impact and disparate treatment discrimination. Adverse impact cases deal with unintentional discrimination; disparate treatment cases involve instances of purposeful discrimination. For example, disparate treatment would arise when an employer hires men, but no women with school-aged children. Allowing men to apply for craft jobs, such as carpentry or electrical work, but denying this opportunity to women would also show disparate treatment. To win a disparate treatment case, the plaintiff must prove that the employer's actions intended to discriminate, which is often difficult.

Workforce Utilization Analysis

As you have learned, employers must be aware of the impact their selection procedures have on protected class members. Part of this process involves analyzing the composition of their internal workforce when compared with their external labor market. The EEOC refers to this comparison as workforce utilization analysis. This concept simply compares an employer's workforce by race and sex for specific job categories against the surrounding labor market. The employer's relevant labor market is that area from which employees are drawn who have the skills needed to successfully perform the job. For example, if the Vision Track Golf Corporation is hiring computer technicians from a labor market composed of 10 percent black workers, 8 percent Hispanic workers, and 2 percent Native American workers, all of whom possess the qualifications for the job, the employer's internal workforce should reflect this racial composition. When this occurs, the employer's workforce is said to be *at parity* with the relevant labor market. If the employer's racial workforce composition is below external figures, then the protected class is said to be *underutilized*, and the employer should take steps to correct the imbalance.

workforce utilization analysis
A process of classifying protected-class members by number and by the type of job they hold within the organization

Enforcing Equal Employment Opportunity Legislation

As you learned earlier in the chapter, along with prohibiting employment discrimination, Title VII of the Civil Rights Act created the Equal Employment Opportunity Commission. As the federal government's leading civil rights agency, the EEOC is responsible for ensuring that covered employers comply with the intent of this act. The commission accomplishes this goal primarily by (1) issuing various employment guidelines and monitoring the employment practices of organizations and (2) protecting employee rights through the investigation and prosecution of discrimination charges.[50] Figure 3.5 illustrates the caseload of the EEOC for recent years.

It is important to remember that the EEOC's guidelines are not federal law but administrative rules and regulations published in the *Federal Register*. However, the different guidelines have been given weight by the courts as they interpret the law and therefore should not be taken lightly.

The Equal Employment Opportunity Commission

The EEOC's work consists of formulating EEO policy and approving all litigation involved in maintaining equal employment opportunity. The day-to-day operation of the commission is performed through administrative headquarters in Washington, DC, and more than fifty district, field, area, and local offices around the country handle discrimination charges and all compliance and litigation enforcement functions. Employees filing a claim are encouraged to call the EEOC on its toll-free number or fill out a questionnaire online so the commission can begin the process of evaluating whether or not the complaint is covered by the laws it enforces. Employers, and in particular small businesses, that have questions about the laws enforced by EEOC or specific workplace situations can contact for guidance one of the EEOC's small business liaisons listed on its website.

FIGURE
3.5

U.S. Equal Employment Opportunity Commission Case Figures,
Fiscal Years 2005–2010

	2005	2006	2007	2008	2009	2010
Total Charges	75,428	75,768	82,792	95,402	93,277	99,922
Race	26,740	27,238	30,510	33,937	33,579	35,890
	35.5%	35.9%	37.0%	35.6%	36.0%	35.9%
Sex	23,094	23,247	24,826	28,372	28,028	29,029
	30.6%	30.7%	30.1%	29.7%	30.0%	29.1%
National Origin	8,035	8,327	9,396	10,601	11,134	11,304
	10.7%	11.0%	11.4%	11.1%	11.9%	11.3%
Religion	2,340	2,541	2,880	3,273	3,386	3,790
	3.1%	3.4%	3.5%	3.4%	3.6%	3.8%
Retaliation - All Statutes	22,278	22,555	26,663	32,690	33,613	36,258
	29.5%	29.8%	32.3%	34.3%	36.0%	36.3%
Retaliation - Title VII only	19,429	19,560	23,371	28,698	28,948	30,948
	25.8%	25.8%	28.3%	30.1%	31.0%	31.0%
Age	16,585	16,548	19,103	24,582	22,778	23,264
	22.0%	21.8%	23.2%	25.8%	24.4%	23.3%
Disability	14,893	15,575	17,734	19,453	21,451	25,165
	19.7%	20.6%	21.4%	20.4%	23.0%	25.2%
Equal Pay Act	970	861	818	954	942	1,044
	1.3%	1.1%	1.0%	1.0%	1.0%	1.0%
Genetic Information						201
						0.2%

Source: Data compiled by the Office of Research, Information and Planning from EEOC's Charge Data System's national database,
http://www.eeoc.gov/eeoc/statistics/enforcement/charges.cfm.

Record-Keeping and Posting Requirements

Organizations subject to Title VII are required by law to maintain specific employment records and reports. Federal contractors and subcontractors have special EEO reporting requirements. Those failing to comply with record-keeping and posting requirements or willfully falsifying records can incur penalties, including fines and imprisonment.

When a charge has been filed, employers have additional recordkeeping obligations. The EEOC also collects workforce data from some employers, regardless of whether a charge has been filed against the company.

The record-keeping requirements are both detailed and comprehensive. For example, managers must generate and retain for specific time periods different employment data. When federal contractors are required to have written affirmative action programs, the records related to the programs must be retained along with supporting documents (such as names of job applicants, rejection ratios, and seniority lists).

Employers of 100 or more employees (except state and local government employees) and government contractors and subcontractors subject to Executive Order 11286 must file annually an EEO-1 report (Employer Information Report). The report collects data about gender and race/ethnicity by ten different job categories.[51] This comprehensive report is the EEOC's basic document for determining an employer's workforce composition, investigating charges of discrimination, providing information about the employment status of minorities and women, and analyzing employment patterns, such as the representation of female and minority workers within companies, industries, and regions. Employers can submit the EEO-1 report through the agency's web-based filing system. Title VII requires retention of all the personnel or employment records, including application forms, for at least six months or until resolution of any HR action, whichever occurs later.

Posters explaining to individuals what their employment rights are and how to file complaints of discrimination have been developed by the EEOC and other administrative agencies. (See Highlights in HRM 3.) The law requires that employers display these posters and other federally required posters related to HRM in prominent places easily accessible to employees. HR employment offices, cafeterias, centrally located bulletin boards, and time clocks are popular locations. Posting requirements should not be taken lightly. For example, EEO posters show the time limits for filing a charge of discrimination. If a company fails to post these notices, the EEOC could allow an employee to file a discrimination charge late (past the 180-day filing deadline).

Processing Discrimination Charges

Figure 3.6 summarizes the process of filing a discrimination charge with the EEOC.[52] (Note that the process is slightly different for federal employees and job applicants.) Employees or job applicants who believe they have been discriminated against first file a discrimination complaint, or charge form, with the EEOC. The charge must be filed within 180 days of the alleged unlawful practice occurring.[53] The processing of a charge includes notifying the employer that a charge of employment discrimination has been filed. Employers will receive a copy of the charge within ten days of it being filed. Both parties, the plaintiff (employee) and the defendant (organization), must be prepared to support their beliefs or actions.

LEARNING OUTCOME 6

Why do you think the federal government treats small businesses differently than large businesses in terms of the employment records and statistics they must keep? Should a small business keep detailed records voluntarily? If so, why?

EEO-1 report

An employer information report that must be filed annually by employers of 100 or more employees (except state and local government employers) and government contractors and subcontractors to determine an employer's workforce composition

charge form

A discrimination complaint filed with the EEOC by employees or job applicants

LEARNING OUTCOME 7

In what ways do you think HR managers can help other managers deal with discrimination complaints so there is less of a chance employees will feel compelled to report them to the EEOC?

Equal Employment Opportunity is

THE LAW

Private Employers, State and Local Governments, Educational Institutions, Employment Agencies and Labor Organizations

Applicants to and employees of most private employers, state and local governments, educational institutions, employment agencies and labor organizations are protected under Federal law from discrimination on the following bases:

RACE, COLOR, RELIGION, SEX, NATIONAL ORIGIN

Title VII of the Civil Rights Act of 1964, as amended, protects applicants and employees from discrimination in hiring, promotion, discharge, pay, fringe benefits, job training, classification, referral, and other aspects of employment, on the basis of race, color, religion, sex (including pregnancy), or national origin. Religious discrimination includes failing to reasonably accommodate an employee's religious practices where the accommodation does not impose undue hardship.

DISABILITY

Title I and Title V of the Americans with Disabilities Act of 1990, as amended, protect qualified individuals from discrimination on the basis of disability in hiring, promotion, discharge, pay, fringe benefits, job training, classification, referral, and other aspects of employment. Disability discrimination includes not making reasonable accommodation to the known physical or mental limitations of an otherwise qualified individual with a disability who is an applicant or employee, barring undue hardship.

AGE

The Age Discrimination in Employment Act of 1967, as amended, protects applicants and employees 40 years of age or older from discrimination based on age in hiring, promotion, discharge, pay, fringe benefits, job training, classification, referral, and other aspects of employment.

SEX (WAGES)

In addition to sex discrimination prohibited by Title VII of the Civil Rights Act, as amended, the Equal Pay Act of 1963, as amended, prohibits sex discrimination in the payment of wages to women and men performing substantially equal work, in jobs that require equal skill, effort, and responsibility, under similar working conditions, in the same establishment.

GENETICS

Title II of the Genetic Information Nondiscrimination Act of 2008 protects applicants and employees from discrimination based on genetic information in hiring, promotion, discharge, pay, fringe benefits, job training, classification, referral, and other aspects of employment. GINA also restricts employers' acquisition of genetic information and strictly limits disclosure of genetic information. Genetic information includes information about genetic tests of applicants, employees, or their family members; the manifestation of diseases or disorders in family members (family medical history); and requests for or receipt of genetic services by applicants, employees, or their family members.

RETALIATION

All of these Federal laws prohibit covered entities from retaliating against a person who files a charge of discrimination, participates in a discrimination proceeding, or otherwise opposes an unlawful employment practice.

WHAT TO DO IF YOU BELIEVE DISCRIMINATION HAS OCCURRED

There are strict time limits for filing charges of employment discrimination. To preserve the ability of EEOC to act on your behalf and to protect your right to file a private lawsuit, should you ultimately need to, you should contact EEOC promptly when discrimination is suspected:

The U.S. Equal Employment Opportunity Commission (EEOC), 1-800-669-4000 (toll-free) or 1-800-669-6820 (toll-free TTY number for individuals with hearing impairments). EEOC field office information is available at www.eeoc.gov or in most telephone directories in the U.S. Government or Federal Government section. Additional information about EEOC, including information about charge filing, is available at www.eeoc.gov.

In states that have FEP laws with appropriate enforcement machinery, the discrimination charge is deferred to the state agency for resolution before action is taken by the EEOC. Conversely, if federal laws apply, cases filed initially with an FEPA will automatically be "dual-filed" with the EEOC. If the state agency fails to resolve the complaint or if the sixty-day deferral period lapses, the case is given back to the EEOC.

EEOC Poster (continued)

Employers Holding Federal Contracts or Subcontracts

Applicants to and employees of companies with a Federal government contract or subcontract
are protected under Federal law from discrimination on the following bases:

RACE, COLOR, RELIGION, SEX, NATIONAL ORIGIN
Executive Order 11246, as amended, prohibits job discrimination on the basis
of race, color, religion, sex or national origin, and requires affirmative action to
ensure equality of opportunity in all aspects of employment.

INDIVIDUALS WITH DISABILITIES
Section 503 of the Rehabilitation Act of 1973, as amended, protects qualified
individuals from discrimination on the basis of disability in hiring, promotion,
discharge, pay, fringe benefits, job training, classification, referral, and
other aspects of employment. Disability discrimination includes not making
reasonable accommodation to the known physical or mental limitations of an
otherwise qualified individual with a disability who is an applicant or employee,
barring undue hardship. Section 503 also requires that Federal contractors take
affirmative action to employ and advance in employment qualified individuals
with disabilities at all levels of employment, including the executive level.

**DISABLED, RECENTLY SEPARATED, OTHER PROTECTED,
AND ARMED FORCES SERVICE MEDAL VETERANS**
The Vietnam Era Veterans' Readjustment Assistance Act of 1974, as amended, 38
U.S.C. 4212, prohibits job discrimination and requires affirmative action to employ
and advance in employment disabled veterans, recently separated veterans (within

three years of discharge or release from active duty), other protected veterans
(veterans who served during a war or in a campaign or expedition for which a
campaign badge has been authorized), and Armed Forces service medal veterans
(veterans who, while on active duty, participated in a U.S. military operation for
which an Armed Forces service medal was awarded).

RETALIATION
Retaliation is prohibited against a person who files a complaint of discrimination,
participates in an OFCCP proceeding, or otherwise opposes discrimination
under these Federal laws.

Any person who believes a contractor has violated its nondiscrimination or
affirmative action obligations under the authorities above should contact
immediately:

The Office of Federal Contract Compliance Programs (OFCCP), U.S.
Department of Labor, 200 Constitution Avenue, N.W., Washington, D.C.
20210, 1-800-397-6251 (toll-free) or (202) 693-1337 (TTY). OFCCP may also be
contacted by e-mail at OFCCP-Public@dol.gov, or by calling an OFCCP regional
or district office, listed in most telephone directories under U.S. Government,
Department of Labor.

Programs or Activities Receiving Federal Financial Assistance

RACE, COLOR, NATIONAL ORIGIN, SEX
In addition to the protections of Title VII of the Civil Rights Act of 1964, as
amended, Title VI of the Civil Rights Act of 1964, as amended, prohibits
discrimination on the basis of race, color or national origin in programs or
activities receiving Federal financial assistance. Employment discrimination
is covered by Title VI if the primary objective of the financial assistance is
provision of employment, or where employment discrimination causes or may
cause discrimination in providing services under such programs. Title IX of the
Education Amendments of 1972 prohibits employment discrimination on the
basis of sex in educational programs or activities which receive Federal financial
assistance.

INDIVIDUALS WITH DISABILITIES
Section 504 of the Rehabilitation Act of 1973, as amended, prohibits employment
discrimination on the basis of disability in any program or activity which receives
Federal financial assistance. Discrimination is prohibited in all aspects of
employment against persons with disabilities who, with or without reasonable
accommodation, can perform the essential functions of the job.

If you believe you have been discriminated against in a program of any
institution which receives Federal financial assistance, you should immediately
contact the Federal agency providing such assistance.

EEOC 9/02 and OFCCP 8/08 Versions Useable With 11/09 Supplement

EEOC-P/E-1 (Revised 11/09)

EEOC investigations are conducted by fully trained equal opportunity specialists
(EOSs) who have extensive experience in investigative procedures, theories of discrimination, and relief and remedy techniques. The EOS will gather facts from both
sides through telephone calls, e-mails, letters and questionnaires, field visits, or jointly
arranged meetings.

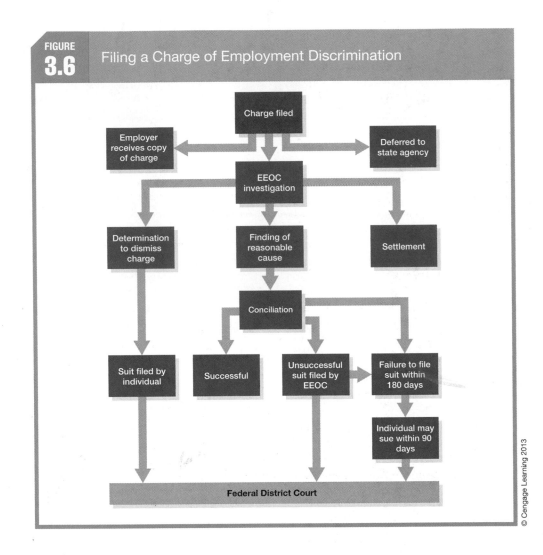

FIGURE 3.6   Filing a Charge of Employment Discrimination

© Cengage Learning 2013

Once the investigation is under way or completed, several decision points occur. First, the employer may offer a settlement to resolve the case without further investigation. If the offer is accepted, the case is closed. Second, the EEOC may find no violation of law and dismiss the charge. In this case, the charging party is sent a *right-to-sue notice*, which permits the individual to start private litigation, if he or she so desires, in federal court within ninety days. Third, if the EEOC finds "reasonable cause" of discrimination, the commission will attempt to conciliate (settle) the matter between the charging party and the employer. The conciliation process is a voluntary procedure and will not always lead to a settlement. If the employer and the EEOC cannot reach a negotiated settlement, the commission has the power to take the organization to court. However, this decision is made on a case-by-case basis depending upon how important the issue is to the commission.

Retaliation

Managers and supervisors must not retaliate against individuals who invoke their legal rights to file charges or to support other employees during EEOC proceedings.[54] Title VII of the Civil Rights Act states that an employer may not discriminate against any of his employees because the employee has opposed any unlawful employment practice, or because the employee has made a charge, testified, assisted, or participated in any manner in an investigation, proceedings, or hearing under this Act. In one case, a female dispatcher at Pepsi-Cola General Bottlers, Inc., a Chicago soft drink distributor, was awarded $400,000 in damages when she complained about sexual harassment and was retaliated against in violation of Title VII of the Civil Rights Act of 1964.[55] Retaliation can include any punitive action taken against employees who elect to exercise their legal rights before any EEO agency.[56] These actions can include terminating employees, giving them unjustified negative appraisals, subjecting them to more supervision, demoting them, and reducing their salaries and work responsibilities, and transferring to a less desirable job.[57] Of course, employees are not excused from continuing to perform their jobs or follow their company's legitimate workplace rules just because they have filed a complaint with the EEOC or opposed discrimination. Nor will the EEOC's retaliation provisions protect them if they engage in unlawful activity or threaten violence.

Preventing Discrimination Charges

Both large and small employers understand that the foundation to preventing any form of discrimination is having a comprehensive EEO policy. The Supreme Court's emphasis on the prevention and correction of discrimination means that the employers that do not have an EEO policy are legally vulnerable. Antidiscrimination policy statements must be inclusive; they must cover all applicable laws and EEOC guidelines and contain practical illustrations of specific inappropriate behavior. For the policy to have value, it must be widely disseminated to managers, supervisors, and all nonmanagerial employees. A complete policy will include specific sanctions for those found guilty of discriminatory behavior.[58]

Since managers and supervisors are key to preventing and correcting discrimination, they, in particular, must be trained to understand employee rights and managerial obligations.[59] A comprehensive training program will include (1) the prohibitions covered in the various EEO statutes and executive orders, (2) guidance on how to respond to complaints of discrimination, (3) procedures for investigating complaints (see Chapter 13), and (4) suggestions for remedying inappropriate behavior. Perhaps the ultimate key to preventing employment discrimination is for managers and supervisors to create an organizational climate in which the principles of dignity, respect, and the acceptance of a diverse workforce are the norm and therefore expected.

Affirmative Action and Diversity Management

Equal employment opportunity legislation requires managers to provide the same opportunities to all job applicants and employees regardless of race, color, religion, sex, national origin, or age. Affirmative action goes beyond not discriminating among employees. Affirmative action occurs when employers take proactive steps to help

LEARNING OUTCOME 8

What effect, if any, do you think ending affirmative action programs in the United States have on the diversity and competitiveness of U.S. businesses?

affirmative action
A policy that goes beyond equal employment opportunity by requiring organizations to comply with the law and correct any past discriminatory practices by increasing the numbers of minorities and women in specific positions

reverse the impact of past discrimination against minorities. Employers with voluntary affirmative action programs actively encourage employment diversity, post job opportunities with minority agencies, remove unnecessary barriers to employment, and offer comprehensive training and mentoring to protected class members.

Employers establish affirmative action programs for several reasons. Affirmative action programs are required by the OFCCP for employers with federal contracts greater than $50,000. The OFCCP provides regulations and suggestions for establishing affirmative action plans. Specifically, employers must (1) provide an organizational profile that graphically illustrates their workforce demographics (see workforce utilization analysis previously discussed), (2) establish goals and timetables for employment of underutilized protected classes, (3) develop actions and plans to reduce underutilization, including initiating proactive recruitment and selection methods, and (4) monitor progress of the entire affirmative action program.

Courts will sometimes mandate employers that have been found guilty of past discrimination to establish affirmative action programs, particularly when the discrimination has been pervasive and a long-held organizational practice. For example, an employer practice of denying promotional opportunities to women or persons of color could be corrected through an affirmative action court order. A court-ordered program, often implemented through a *consent decree* between the court and employer, will require the setting of hiring and promotional goals along with stated timetables for compliance. When the requirements of the consent decree are met, the employer is no longer bound by the court order.

Sometimes employers voluntarily develop their own affirmative action programs to ensure that protected class members receive fair treatment in all aspects of employment. Intel, Levi Strauss, the City of Portland, and Hilton Hotels have used these programs to monitor the progress of employees while demonstrating their equal-employment efforts. In addition, some companies employ chief diversity officers. A **chief diversity officer (CDO)** is a top executive responsible for the implementation of a firm's diversity efforts. However, as HR professionals readily note, the success of any voluntary affirmative action program or diversity effort largely depends on the support given it by senior managers and supervisors at all organization levels.[60] The EEOC recommends that organizations developing affirmative action programs follow specific steps, as shown in Highlights in HRM 4.

One of the drawbacks of implementing an affirmative action program is that an employer can be accused of **reverse discrimination,** or giving preference to members of protected classes to the extent that unprotected individuals believe they are suffering from discrimination. When these charges occur, organizations are caught between attempting to correct past discriminatory practices and handling present complaints from unprotected members alleging that HR policies are unfair. It is exactly this "catch-22" that has made affirmative action one of the most controversial issues of the past fifty years. Critics of affirmative action programs claim that they have not consistently resulted in the improvement of the employment status of protected groups, and that individuals hired as a result of them are often viewed as less capable, even if they are not.

chief diversity officers

A top executives responsible for implementing a firm's diversity efforts.

reverse discrimination

The act of giving preference to members of protected classes to the extent that unprotected individuals believe they are suffering discrimination

Court Decisions

In the 1970s, regarding two leading cases of reverse discrimination, *University of California Regents v. Bakke* and *United States Steelworkers of America v. Weber*,[61] the Supreme Court ruled that applicants must be evaluated on an individual basis and

HIGHLIGHTS IN **HRM**
4   Basic Steps in Developing an Effective Affirmative Action Program

1. Issue a written equal employment opportunity policy and an affirmative action commitment statement.
2. Publicize the policy and the organization's affirmative action commitment.
3. Appoint a top official within the organization to direct and implement the program.
4. Survey minority and female employment by department and job classification.
5. Develop goals and timetables to improve utilization of minorities and women in each area in which underutilization has been identified.
6. Develop and implement specific programs to achieve goals.
7. Establish an internal audit and reporting system to monitor and evaluate progress in each aspect of the program.
8. Develop supportive in-house and community programs.

Source: U.S. Equal Employment Opportunity Commission.

race can be one factor used in the evaluation process as long as other competitive factors are considered. The court stated that affirmative action programs were not illegal per se as long as rigid quota systems were not specified for different protected classes. Also, voluntary affirmative action programs are permissible where they attempt to eliminate racial imbalances in traditionally segregated job categories. The Supreme Court did not endorse all voluntary affirmative action programs, but it did give an important push to programs voluntarily implemented and designed to correct past racial or gender imbalances.

The judicial support for affirmative action programs has eroded over the decades, however. During the mid-1990s, federal courts increasingly restricted the use of race and ethnicity in awarding scholarships, determining college admissions, making layoff decisions, selecting employees, promoting employees, and awarding government contracts. Then in 2009, the Supreme Court heard *Ricci vs. DeStafano*, a lawsuit brought against the city of New Haven, Connecticut, by nineteen city firefighters. The firefighters alleged that the city discriminated against them by invalidating a test for a promotion because no black firefighters had passed it with a score high enough to warrant promotion. The firefighters, seventeen of whom are white and two of whom are Hispanic, claimed they were denied the promotions because of their race.

In a split decision, the court ruled in the firefighters' favor. The ruling didn't question the fire department's efforts to ensure minorities were fairly promoted. However, it said throwing out the test midstream (which, incidentally, had been designed by an outside consulting firm to be nondiscriminatory) was unfair to those who had passed it. In its ruling, the court said: ". . . once that process has been established and employers have made clear their selection criteria, they may not then invalidate the test results, thus upsetting an employee's legitimate expectation not to be judged on the basis of race."

The ruling underscores the importance of designing careful selection procedures as well as following them once they are designed. It also shows how tricky it can be to implement an affirmative action program.[62]

Perhaps the greatest current challenge to affirmative action has been laws enacted by states to prohibit preferences in racial or gender hiring. California, Washington, Michigan, and Nebraska have such laws, and other states have launched anti-affirmative action initiatives too.[63] Opponents argue that affirmative action laws greatly restrict or prohibit hiring preferences, thereby denying protected class members of important employment opportunities granted under affirmative action programs. For example, in California, the law ended long-standing state affirmative action programs in education, public employment, and government contracting.[64] Supporters of affirmative action programs point out that repealing affirmative action programs has led to a large drop in minority student enrollments at California universities, and that a similar phenomenon is occurring in Michigan.[65] Clearly, the debate over affirmative action, and its alleged benefits and drawbacks, will continue as a legal and societal issue.

Beyond Affirmative Action: Leveraging Diversity

The future of affirmative action might not rest in judicial decisions or laws, but in managers' attitudes and voluntary actions to make the workplace fairer and more competitive. Managers who embrace a diverse workforce know individual employee differences and the contributions made by people of varied abilities are one way to develop a competitive advantage. For example, some studies have found that companies with more progressive nondiscrimination policies outperform competing firms that lack them.[66] Other studies cited by the EEOC show that employers that adopt flexible workplace policies that caregivers can utilize have also been able to add to their customer bases and profits. Likewise, many firms have found it advantageous to hire older workers because they are knowledgeable, dependable, and frequently more willing to work flexible hours. And as more companies expand around the globe either physically or on the web, they are recognizing that they need to employ diverse people with different talents to better understand and compete in various markets abroad.

One of the ways companies can foster diversity within their organizations is by getting employees to talk about their differences. For example, the Mallon Group Training and Management has developed a series of Know Me games that enable participants of different cultures, races, sexual orientations, and so forth to explore issues of diversity together.

In addition, having a diverse workforce enables a company to keep up with the tumultuous changes occurring in today's competitive environment. Smart companies know that hiring the same types of employees with the same backgrounds and skills can result in a distinct disadvantage as markets change. Lastly employers with diverse workforces demonstrate to their communities that they are serious about corporate social responsibility.

According to Martin Davidson, a professor and researcher at the Darden School of Business at the University of Virginia, strategically leveraging employee's differences means seeing not only the more obvious differences between people, such as their ethnic backgrounds, sexes, ages, religions, and so forth, but how they think, learn, work, and interact with each other. How do they use their time? How do they solve problems? Why do some people "think outside of the box," whereas others do not? What is it about the experiences, mindsets, and talents of different groups of people that can be utilized in a strategic way?

Perhaps most importantly, Davidson points out, that despite our similarities, *all* of us are different from one another. Differences of all sorts among people are ubiquitous in the workforce. These differences, too, should be leveraged because they can be the source of organizational strength if we do not "gloss over" them. Conflicts among people of all different types should be tolerated because they can unearth real business problems and various employees' ideas about how to solve them. [67]

The steps toward leveraging people's differences involves seeing, understanding, and valuing them, as shown in the model in Figure 3.7. Highlights in HRM 5 shows the actual activities individuals and organizations can take to facilitate each of these steps. We will discuss more about diversity in Chapter 5 and throughout this textbook.

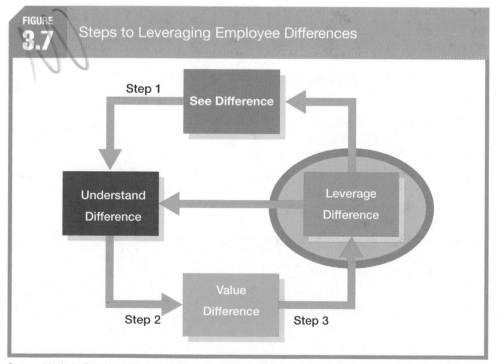

FIGURE 3.7 Steps to Leveraging Employee Differences

Step 1 — See Difference
Step 2 — Understand Difference / Value Difference
Step 3 — Leverage Difference

Source: Martin N. Davidson, *The End of Diversity as We Know It: Why Diversity Efforts Fail and How Leveraging Difference Can Succeed* (San Francisco: Berrett-Kohler Press, forthcoming, 2011).

HIGHLIGHTS IN HRM

5 Embracing Diversity and Leveraging Employee Differences

Practices for Individuals

Seeing
Openly acknowledge that relevant differences are common.
Address points of conflict.
Observe while remaining silent.

Understanding
Seek sources of information that bring understanding about the differences.
Acquire data through listening, asking questions, and sharing your story.
Involve people who are different from you in your network.

Valuing
Avoid being overly careful in dealing with differences.
Accept that there will be conflict and discomfort that require perseverance.
Use data to develop a new perspective.

Practices for Organizations

Seeing
Openly address tension among members.
Encourage members to avoid secrecy.

Understanding
Seek sources of information that bring understanding about the differences.
Gather data through surveys and other techniques.
Establish inclusive structures.

Valuing
Reward members for engaging in activities that address and diminish differences.
Hold employees accountable for employing new behaviors.
Actively seek diversity when recruiting.

Source: Adapted from Martin N. Davidson, *The End of Diversity as We Know It: Why Diversity Efforts Fail and How Leveraging Difference Can Succeed*. (San Francisco: Berrett-Kohler Press, forthcoming, 2011).

Summary

LEARNING OUTCOME 1 Employment discrimination against blacks, Hispanics, women, and other groups has long been practiced by U.S. employers. Prejudice against minority groups is a major cause in their lack of employment gains. Government reports show that the wages and job opportunities of minorities typically lag behind those for whites.

LEARNING OUTCOME 2 Effective management requires knowing the legal aspects of the employment relationship, including the laws and various executive orders mentioned in this chapter. Employers are permitted to discriminate against protected classes when doing so constitutes a reasonable business necessity or would impose an undue hardship, or when a bona fide occupational qualification for normal business operation exists.

LEARNING OUTCOME 3 Sexual harassment is an area of particular importance to managers and supervisors. Extensive efforts should be made to ensure that both male and female employees are free from all forms of sexually harassing conduct. The Immigration Reform and Control Act was passed to control unauthorized immigration into the United States. The law requires managers to maintain various employment records, and they must not discriminate against job applicants or employees because of their national origin or citizenship status. Other areas of discrimination that are or could become a concern for the EEOC in the future are discrimination based on people's weight, their appearance, or their status as a caregiver.

LEARNING OUTCOME 4 The *Uniform Guidelines on Employee Selection Procedures* is designed to help employers comply with federal bans against employment practices that discriminate on the basis of race, color, religion, gender, or national origin. The *Uniform Guidelines* provides employers with a framework for making legally enforceable employment decisions. Employers must be able to show that their selection procedures are valid when it comes to predicting a person's job performance.

LEARNING OUTCOME 5 Adverse impact plays an important role in proving employment discrimination. Adverse impact means that an employer's employment practices unintentionally resulted in the rejection of a significantly higher percentage of members of minority and other protected groups. By contrast, disparate treatment is intentional discrimination against a protected group. Refusing to hire individuals of a particular religion or denying males, but not females, clerical jobs are examples of disparate treatment discrimination.

LEARNING OUTCOME 6 To ensure that organizations comply with antidiscrimination legislation, the EEOC was established to monitor employers' actions. Employers subject to federal laws must maintain certain records and report certain employment statistics where mandated. Employers with 100 or more employees must file an EEO-1 report annually. This comprehensive document identifies employees by race/ethnicity and gender for ten job categories. Companies with government contracts of $50,000 or more must file an affirmative action plan with the OFCCP. Employers are required to collect employment data and file reports under various federal and state laws. Employers are also required to post in prominent locations EEO- related posters.

LEARNING OUTCOME 7 Employees or applicants for employment who believe they have been discriminated against may file a discrimination complaint (a charge form) with the EEOC. The employer receives a copy of the charge form that initiates an EEOC investigation of the alleged discrimination. Individuals claiming discrimination must file the complaint within 180 days of the alleged offense. After the investigation, if the Commission dismisses the charge, the plaintiff will receive a right-to-sue notice that allows the individual to start private litigation. If the EEOC finds reasonable cause for the charge, it will attempt to mediate a settlement between the parties. If an agreement is not reached, the EEOC may elect to sue the employer in federal court. Figure 3.6 illustrates the steps in filing a discrimination charge.

LEARNING OUTCOME 8 Affirmative action goes beyond providing equal employment opportunities to employees. Firms with federal contracts and firms that have been found guilty of past discrimination can be required to utilize affirmative action programs. This is accomplished by employing protected classes for jobs in which they are underrepresented. The employer's goal is to have a balanced internal workforce representative of the employer's relevant labor market. The future of affirmative action might not rest in judicial decisions or laws but in the efforts of managers to voluntary embrace and foster diversity. Differences of all sorts among people are ubiquitous in the workforce. Managers need to leverage these differences because they can be the source of organizational strength.

Key Terms

adverse impact

affirmative action

bona fide occupational qualification (BFOQ)

business necessity

charge form

chief diversity officer

disabled individual

disparate treatment

EEO-1 report

equal employment opportunity

fair employment practices (FEPs)

four-fifths rule

protected classes

reasonable accommodation

reverse discrimination

sexual harassment

Uniform Guidelines on Employee Selection Procedures

workforce utilization analysis

Discussion Questions

LEARNING OUTCOME 1 EEO legislation was prompted by significant social events. List those events and describe how they influenced the passage of various EEO laws.

LEARNING OUTCOME 2 Cite and describe the major federal laws and court decisions that affect the employment process of both large and small organizations.

LEARNING OUTCOME 3 After receiving several complaints of sexual harassment, the HR department of a city library decided to establish a sexual harassment policy. What should be included in the policy? How should it be implemented?

LEARNING OUTCOME 4 What is the *Uniform Guidelines on Employee Selection Procedures?* To whom do the guidelines apply? What do they cover?

LEARNING OUTCOME 5 Joe Alverez has filed a complaint with the EEO alleging that his employer, Universal Mortgage Company, promotes more whites than Hispanics into managerial positions. Explain the statistical methods used by the EEOC to investigate this adverse impact claim.

LEARNING OUTCOME 6 What is the EEO-1 report? Who does it apply to, and how often must the report be filed? How does the EEOC use the data collected?

LEARNING OUTCOME 7 As a marketing manager, you have recently turned down Nancy Conrad for a position as sales supervisor. Nancy believes the denial was due to her gender, and she has filed a sex discrimination charge with the EEOC. Explain the steps the EEOC will use to process the charge; include Nancy's options during the process.

LEARNING OUTCOME 8 Affirmative action is both a legal and emotional issue affecting employees and employers. Develop as many arguments as you can both supporting and opposing affirmative action as an employer policy. If you were asked to implement such a program, what steps would you follow?

On the Job: Video Cases

Diversity at Gold + Williams

This high-end furniture manufacturer and retailer is a diversity trendsetter. Mitchell Gold (Chairman and cofounder) and Bob Williams (President of Design and cofounder) started their business together, as an openly gay couple, in 1989. For more than six consecutive years, the North Carolina company has scored 100 percent on the Human Rights Campaign's Corporate Equity Index (CEI), which rates businesses' efforts to establish and maintain inclusive workplaces for lesbian, gay, bisexual, and transgender (LGBT) employees. The video describes the importance of a diverse workforce and including all types of differences in a definition of diversity.

What to Watch for and Ask Yourself

- How does a diverse workforce better serve Gold + Williams' customers?

- What are the two main forms of backlash against diversity training? Do you think these are issues that Gold + Williams' managers need to be concerned about? Why or why not?

- The Chairman of Gold + Williams states that he does not believe that LBGT is the final frontier in diversity. He thinks immigrants in American will be the next frontier. What do you think will be the next frontier of diversity in American in the next five to ten years? Why?

HRM EXPERIENCE
Sexual Harassment: A Frank Discussion

Over the past decade, the problem of sexual harassment has captured the attention of all managers and employees. While it is widely known that sexual harassment is both unethical and illegal, the incidents of sexual harassment continue to plague business. Unfortunately, when these cases arise, they cause morale problems among employees, embarrassment to the organization, and costly legal damages. Consequently, all managers and supervisors play a central role in preventing sexual harassment complaints. It is important that managers understand the definition of sexual harassment, who is covered by sexual harassment guidelines, and how to prevent its occurrence. This skill-building exercise will provide you with knowledge in each of these areas.

Assignment

1. Working in teams of female and male members, develop a list of behaviors that could be classified as quid pro quo harassment or hostile environment. Explore the possibility that some sexual harassing behaviors might be viewed differently by female and male employees. Give examples.

2. Many sexual harassment incidents go unreported. Fully discuss why this can occur and what might be done to reduce this problem.

3. The cornerstone to addressing sexual harassment is achieving organizational awareness through training. Develop a sexual harassment training program for a company of 250 employees that covers, at a minimum, the following: (1) who should attend the training sessions, (2) the content outline for the training program (the list of materials your team wants to teach), (3) specific examples to illustrate the training materials, and (4) how to investigate sexual harassment complaints.

4. This chapter will assist you with this assignment. You can obtain additional materials from EEOC offices and from various HR magazines.

5. Be prepared to present your training outline to other class members.

Case Study 1

Going to the Dogs

Let's admit it: With very few exceptions, we all love dogs. We love to be with our dogs, and our dogs love to be with us. So it is only natural, then, to want to keep our dogs with us as much as possible, even when we go to work. Pet Sitters International thinks this is such a good idea that they have instituted "Take Your Dog to Work Day," a once-a-year event designed to raise awareness of the benefits of dog ownership and to encourage pet adoption.

But maybe you would like something a bit more regular, like having the option to bring Fido to work every day? According to a 2006 survey by the American Pet Products Manufacturers Association, it should not be too hard to find an opportunity since nearly one in five companies already allows pets in the workplace. You can even find a list of employers that allow canines at work on DogFriendly.com. Fans of the dogs-at-the-office policy say it increases employee morale and decreases stress.

Before we go too far with this idea, however, perhaps we should take note of some arguments against bringing dogs to work. First, some HR experts like Ethan Winning have cautioned that dogs can be messy, placing an unfair burden on employers to clean up afterwards. Dogs can also be a distraction, and other employees may be allergic or otherwise disturbed by them. And what happens when two or more employees bring their dogs to work on the same day, and Fido and Fifi don't want to play nice?

Of course, some people actually need to bring their dogs to work, which is why the Americans with Disabilities Act permits the use of "service animals" to assist those with disabilities. For example, seeing-eye dogs are allowed to accompany blind individuals at work. The EEOC guideline is reasonable since guide dogs are necessary to blind individuals, and furthermore, guide dogs are trained not to be a nuisance.

It can be challenging, however, for employers to know where to draw the line. Take the case of Elizabeth Booth, a quadriplegic hired by Case Services Corporation as an accountant in the billing department. Booth, who uses a wheelchair for mobility, has trained her small, well-behaved dog to pick up small items that Booth has dropped. Along with a formal request to be allowed to bring her dog to work to assist her, Booth submitted to her employer a letter from her doctor stating that the dog would also help relieve Booth's stress. When Case Services's HR director denied the request, Booth immediately filed a discrimination charge with the EEOC, claiming the company did not provide a reasonable accommodation to her disability or her health needs.

When it comes to establishing a pet policy, as is so often the case, balancing the employer's needs and responsibilities with the employees' needs and wants presents something of a dilemma.

Questions

1. What is your position on this issue? Provide two or three reasons to support your argument.
2. If you were an HR manager of a company, what pet policy would you set and how would you implement it?

3. How would you decide the case of Elizabeth Booth, and which laws would you base your decision on? Explain.

Sources: James J. McDonald, Jr., "Take Your Dog To Work Every Day," *Employee Relations* Law Journal 32, no. 3 (Winter 2006): 86; "Has Your Organization Gone to the Dogs?," http://www.hrwebcafe.com/2007/06/has_your_organization_gone_to.html; Ethan A. Winning, "Pets at the Corporate Zoo," http://www.ewin.com/arch/pets.htm; "About Take Your Dog to Work Day," http://www.takeyourdog.com/About/; "Take Your Dog to Work Every Day," http://www.dogfriendly.com/server/general/workplace/.

Case Study 2

Misplaced Affections: Discharge for Sexual Harassment

Peter Lewiston was terminated on July 15, 2008, by the governing board of the Pine Circle Unified School District (PCUSD) for violation of the district's sexual harassment policy. Prior to Lewiston's termination he was a senior maintenance employee with an above-average work record who had worked for the PCUSD for eleven years. He had been a widower since 2003 and was described by his coworkers as a friendly, outgoing, but lonely individual. Beverly Gilbury was a fifth-grade teacher working in the district's Advanced Learning Program. She was twenty-eight years old and married and had worked for PCUSD for six years. At the time of the incidents, Lewiston and Gilbury both worked at the Simpson Elementary School, where their relationship was described as "cooperative." The following sequence of events was reported separately by Lewiston and Gilbury during the district's investigation of this sexual harassment case.

Gilbury reported that her relationship with Lewiston began to change during the last month of the 2007–2008 school year. She believed that Lewiston was paying her more attention and that his behavior was "out of the ordinary" and "sometimes weird." He began spending more time in her classroom talking with the children and with her. At the time she did not say anything to Lewiston because "I didn't want to hurt his feelings since he is a nice, lonely, older man." However, on May 25, when Lewiston told Gilbury that he was "very fond" of her and that she had "very beautiful eyes," she replied, "Remember, Peter, we're just friends." For the remainder of the school year, there was little contact between them; however, when they did see each other, Lewiston seemed "overly friendly" to her.

June 7, 2008. On the first day of summer school, Gilbury returned to school to find a dozen roses and a card from Lewiston. The card read, "Please forgive me for thinking you could like me. I played the big fool. Yours always, P.L." Later in the day Lewiston asked Gilbury to lunch. She replied, "It's been a long time since anyone sent me roses, but I can't go to lunch. We need to remain just friends." Gilbury told another teacher that she was uncomfortable about receiving the roses and card and that Lewiston would not leave her alone. She expressed concern that Lewiston might get "more romantic" with her.

June 8, 2008. Gilbury arrived at school to find another card from Lewiston. Inside was a handwritten note that read, "I hope you can someday return my affections for you. I need you so much." Later in the day, Lewiston again asked her to lunch, and she declined saying, "I'm a happily married woman." At the close of the school day, when Gilbury went to her car, Lewiston suddenly appeared. He asked to explain himself but Gilbury became agitated and shouted, "I have to leave right now." Lewiston reached inside the car, supposedly to pat her shoulder, but touched her head instead. She believed he meant to stroke her hair. He stated that he was only trying to calm her down. She drove away, very upset.

June 9, 2008. Gilbury received another card and a lengthy letter from Lewiston, stating that he was wrong in trying to develop a relationship with her and he hoped they could still remain friends. He wished her all happiness with her family and job.

June 11, 2008. Gilbury obtained from the Western Justice Court an injunction prohibiting sexual harassment by Lewiston. Shortly thereafter Lewiston appealed the injunction. A notice was mailed to Gilbury giving the dates of the appeal hearing. The notice stated in part, "If you fail to appear, the injunction may be vacated and the petition dismissed." Gilbury failed to appear at the hearing, and the injunction was set aside. Additionally, on June 11 she had filed with the district's EEOC officer a sexual harassment complaint against Lewiston. After the investigation, the district concluded that Lewiston's actions created an "extremely sexually hostile" environment for Gilbury. The investigative report recommended dismissal based upon the grievous conduct of Lewiston and the initial injunction granted by the Justice Court.

Questions

1. Evaluate the conduct of Peter Lewiston against the EEOC's definition of sexual harassment.
2. Should the intent or motive behind Lewiston's conduct be considered when deciding sexual harassment activities? Explain.
3. If you were the district's EEOC officer, what would you conclude? What disciplinary action, if any, would you take?

Source: This case is adapted from an actual arbitration hearing conducted by George Bohlander. The background information is factual. All names are fictitious.

Appendix

Determining Adverse Impact:
The Four-Fifths Rule

Employers can determine adverse impact by using the method outlined in the interpretive manual for the *Uniform Guidelines on Employee Selection Procedures.*

A. Calculate the rate of selection for each group (divide the number of people selected from a group by the number of total applicants from that group).
B. Observe which group has the highest selection.
C. Calculate the impact ratios by comparing the selection rate for each group with that of the highest group (divide the selection rate for a group by the selection rate for the highest group).
D. Observe whether the selection rate for any group is substantially less (usually less than four-fifths, or 80 percent) than the selection rate for the highest group. If it is, adverse impact is indicated in most circumstances.

Example

	JOB APPLICANTS	NUMBER HIRED	SELECTION RATE PERCENT HIRED
Step A	Whites 100	52	52/100 = 52%
	Blacks 50	14	14/50 = 28%
Step B	The group with the highest selection rate is whites, 52%.		
Step C	Divide the black selection rate (28%) by the white selection rate (52%). The black rate is 53.8% of the white rate.		
Step D	Since 53.8% is less than four-fifths, or 8%, adverse impact is indicated.		

Source: Adoption of Questions and Answers to Clarify and Provide a Common Interpretation of the *Uniform Guidelines on Employee Selection Procedures, Federal Register* 44, no. 43 (March 2, 1979): 11998.

ANSWERS TO HIGHLIGHTS IN HRM 1

1. Yes

2. False

3. No

4. Merit, seniority, incentive pay plans

5. Yes

6. Yes, if no reasonable accommodation can be made

7. No

8. Yes, except if under a court order

9. False

10. True

Notes and References

1. Judy Greenwald, "Workplace Discrimination Charges Set Record ," *Business Insurance* (January 12, 2011), http://www.business insurance.com.

2. Darla Marcado, "Morgan Stanley Settles $46 Million Discrimination Suit," *Investment News* (October 16, 2007), http://www. investmentnews.com.

3. Michael Orey, "White Men Can't Help It," *Business Week* (May 15, 2006), 54.

4. Adam Liptak and Steven Greenhouse, "Supreme Court Agrees to Hear Wal-Mart Appeal, *New York Times* (December 6, 2010), http://www.nytimes.com.

5. There are excellent books on the civil rights movement. See for example, Henry Hampton arid Steve Fayer, *Voices of Freedom* (New York, NY: Bantam Dell Publishing Group, 1991).

6. U.S. Equal Employment Commission, "Prohibited Employment Policies/Practices," accessed February 12, 2010, http://www.eeoc. gov/laws/practices/index.cfm.

7. Judy Greenwald, "Workplace Discrimination Charges Set Record," *Business Insurance* (January 12, 2011), http://www.business insurance.com.

8. Donald J. Peterson and Harvey R. Boiler, "Seeking a Definition of 'Supervisor': A Critical Issue in Sexual Harassment Cases,"

Employee Relations Law Journal 32, no. 4 (Spring 2007): 87. See also, "Supervisor May Be Broadly Defined in Employer Liability," *HR Focus* 48, no. 9 (September 2003): 149–155.

9. For a practical overview of EEO law, see David J. Walsh, *Employment Law for Human Resource Practice*, 3rd ed. (Mason, OH: South-Western, 2010).

10. As we explained in Chapter 1, women "on average" earn about 79–80 percent of male earnings, a gap that has not narrowed greatly in recent years. However, in 2010, women's earnings edged above 80 percent primarily because men, who are more likely to have been employed in the hard-hit industries such as manufacturing and construction, lost jobs at a faster rate than women during the last economic downturn. See Dennis Cauchon, "Gender Pay Is Smallest on Record," *USA TODAY* (September 14, 2010), http://www.usatoday.com.

11. For information on national origin discrimination, go to http://www.justice.gov and search for *Brochure: Federal Protection against National Origin Discrimination*.

12. Information on national origin guidelines is available on the EEOC's website at http:// www.eeoc.gov.

13. U.S. Equal Employment Opportunity Commission, "Library Fires Employee for Wearing

Cross," *EEOC News*, accessed February 15, 2010, http://www.eeonews.com; U.S. Equal Employment Opportunity Commission, "Have a Blessed Day," *EEOC News*, accessed February 15, 2010 , http://www. eeonews.com.

14. "Keep Young and Beautiful—Especially at Work," *Newsweek*, accessed at February 20, 2011, http://www.newsweek.com.

15. Lynn D. Lieber, "As Average Age of Workforce Increases, Age Discrimination Verdicts Rise," *Employment Relations Today* 34, no. 1 (Spring 2007): 105.

16. Maria Greco Danaher, "Include Pregnancy Leave in Pension Credit," *HR Magazine* 52, no. 11 (November 2007): 98.

17. *The Americans with Disabilities Act: A Primer for Small Business* contains examples, tips, and do's and don'ts. Published by the EEOC and available on the Internet, the handbook explains who is protected, how to avoid mistakes during interviews, when employers may ask questions about a medical condition, how to address safety issues, reasonable accommodation obligations, and tax incentives for businesses that hire and retain individuals with disabilities.

18. According to the ADA, an employer is not required to retain an employee who presents a "direct threat," implying a significant risk

of substantial harm to the health and safety of the individual or others that cannot be eliminated or reduced by reasonable accommodation. Also, some court cases have held that an employee with a psychiatric disability is not a qualified individual because he or she cannot perform the essential functions of the job.

19. Jonathan R. Mook, "Accommodation Paradigm Shifts," *HR Magazine* 52, no. 1 (January 2007): 115. See also, James J. McDonald, Jr., "Take Your Dog to Work Everyday," *Employee Relations Law Journal* 32, no. 3 (Winter 2006): 86.

20. Bill Leonard, "Studies: ADA Makes Business Better," *HR Magazine* 52, no. 10 (October 2007): 22.

21. "Broadening the Coverage of the ADA: The 2008 Amendments to the Americans with Disabilities Act," *INSIGHT into Diversity* (November 2010), 32–35.

22. "Genetic Information Nondiscrimination Act: A Primer on Title II," *Venulex Legal Summaries* (Winter 2010), Special section, 1.

23. Gary L. Tidwell, Daniel A. Rice, and Gary Kropkowski, "Employer and Employee Obligations and Rights under the Uniformed Services Employment and Reemployment Rights Act," *Business Horizons* 52, no. 3, (May 2009): 243–250, DOI: 10.1016/j.bushor.2009.01.003. Find additional information on the law at the USERRA Advisor at the Department of Labor's website, http://www.dol.gov/elaws.

24. Veterans Benefits Improvement Act of 2004, Public Law 108-454 (December 20, 2004).

25. The significant Supreme Court decision in this area is *Nassau Count, Florida v. Arline*, 480 U.S. 273, 43 FEP 81(1987).

26. As currently defined, an "otherwise qualified" employee is one who can perform the "essential functions" of the job under consideration.

27. To learn more about fair employment practice agencies, go to http://www.eeoc.gov and type "State and Local Agencies" into the search bar.

28. *Oncale v. Sundowner Offshore Services, Inc.* 72 PED 45, 175; WL 88039 (U.S. l998). http://www.eeoc.gov/laws/types/sexual_harassment.cfm.

29. *Guidelines on Discrimination Because of Sex*, 29 C.F.R. Sec. 1604.11(a) (1955).

30. *Guidelines on Discrimination*, Sec. 1605.11(a).

31. EEOC charge statistics can be found at http://www.eeoc.gov. The figures do not include the thousands of sexual harassment incidents not reported to governmental agencies or complaints reported to employers and settled internally through in-house complaint procedures.

32. John Hoft and Neal F. Thompson, "Employer Liability for Non-Employee Sexual Harassment," *Journal of the International Academy for Case Studies* 13, no. 6 (2007): 87.

33. Margaret Bryant "Harassment Lawsuits and Lessons," *Security Management* 60, no. 4 (April 2006): 50.

34. Laura G. Barron, "Sexual Orientation Employment: Anti-Discrimination Legislation and Hiring Discrimination and Prejudice," *Academy of Management Annual Meeting Proceedings* (2009): 1.

35. U.S. Equal Employment Opportunity Commission, "Facts about Discrimination Based on Sexual Orientation, Status as a Parent, Marital Status and Political Affiliation," *EEOC.gov*, accessed February 18, 2011, http://www.eeoc.gov.

36. The EEOC has ruled that transgender and transsexual individuals are not covered by Title VII of the Civil Rights Act. According to the EEOC, gender only applies to one's sex at the time of birth and not to one's sexual orientation. See Jon D. Bible, "In a Class by Themselves: The Legal Status of Employee Appearance Policies Under Title VII after Jespersen v. Harrah's Operating Co.," *Employee Relations Law Journal* 32, no. 4 (Spring 2007): 3. See also, "Stan Malos, Appearance-Based Sex Discrimination and Stereotyping in the Workplace: Whose Conduct Should We Regulate?" *Employee Responsibilities and Rights Journal* 19, no. 2 (June 2007): 95.

37. Mark Schoeff, "DHS Rule Rankles Employer Groups," *Workforce Management* 86, no. 14 (August 20, 2007): 1.

38. 8 U.S.C.A. § 1324a (a) (1), (2) (2005).

39. 8 U.S.C.A. § 1324B (1) (2005).

40. U.S. Department of Justice, Immigration and Naturalization Service, *Handbook for Employers: Instructions for Completing Form I* (Washington, DC: U.S. Government Printing Office, 2005).

41. Lindsay L. Chichester and Gregory P. Adams, "The State of E-Verify: What Every Employer Should Know," *Computer & Internet Lawyer* 26, no. 12 (December 2009): 12–17.

42. Svetlana Shkolnikova, "Weight Discrimination Could Be as Common as Racial Discrimination," *USA Today*, (May 28, 2008), http://www.usatoday.com.

43. Nathan Koppel, "Hooters Sued for Weight Discrimination," *Wall Street Journal*, (May 24, 2010), http://blogs.wsj.com.

44. "Weight Discrimination: Could It Be the Next Big Protected Category?" *HR Specialist* 8, no. 10 (October 2010): 3

45. Rebecca Leung, "The Look of Abercrombie & Fitch, *CBS News* (November 24, 2004), http://www.cbsnews.com; "Court Approves Abercrombie & Fitch Settlement of Federal Employment Discrimination Class Action," *Venulex Legal Summaries* (Winter 2005): 1.

46. Dan-Olof Rooth, "Obesity, Attractiveness, and Differential Treatment in Hiring," *Journal of Human Resources* 44, no. 3 (Summer2009): 710.

47. Gerald E. Calvasina, Richard V. Calvasina, and Eugene J. Calvasina, "Caregiver Responsibility Discrimination and EEOC Guidelines," *Journal of Legal, Ethical & Regulatory Issues* 13, no. 2 (June 2010): 1–2.

48. The guidelines themselves and examples of their application can be found at www.uniformguidelines.com.

49. *Uniform Guidelines*, Sec. 40. Adverse impact need not be considered for groups that constitute less than 2 percent of the relevant labor force.

50. The primary website for the EEOC is http://www.eeogov. This website contains a wealth of information about the EEOC, including the agency's history and administration, how discrimination charges are filed and processed, training and outreach programs, litigation statistics, and various pamphlets and posters offered free of charge to interested parties.

51. The EEOC's instruction manual for filling out the EEO-1 report can be found at http://www. eeoc.nov/eeol/index.html.

52. Howard S. Lavin and Elizabeth E. DiMichele, "The Time for Filing Charges of Discrimination: The Supreme Court's Decision and Its Aftermath," *Employee Relations*

Law Journal 33, no. 3 (Winter 2007): 113. See also, Reynolds Holding, "Stumble on the Bench," *Time* (June 18, 2007), 56.

53. The time period is 300 days in states in which the charge is deferred to a state agency.

54. David Sherwyn, Zev Eigen, and Gregg Gilman, "Retaliation: The Fastest Growing Discrimination Claim," *Cornell Hotel and Restaurant Administration Quarterly* 47, no. 4 (November2006): 350.

55. *EEOC v. Pepsi-Cola General Bottlers, Inc.,* No. 03 C 6576 (ND, IL, January 18, 2006).

56. Rebecca M. Archer and Stephen T. Lanctot, "Are Your Hands Tied? A Practical Look at Employee Claims of Retaliation," *Employee Relations Law Journal* 33, no. 1 (Summer 2007): 53. See also, Mary Price Birk, "Waking on Eggshells—Avoiding Retaliation Claims When the Employee Does Not Leave," *Employee Relations Law Journal* 32, no. 3 (Winter 2006): 10 and Martin K. LaPointe, "The Supreme Court Sets the Standard for Title VII Retaliation Claims: Burlington Northern and Santa Fe Railway v.

White," *Labor Law Journal* 57, no. 4 (Winter 2006): 205.

57. Jathan Janove, "Retaliation Nation," *HR Magazine* 51, no. 10 (October 1006): 62.

58. Heather J. Broadwater, "Preventing Workplace Sexual Harassment," *Rural Telecommunications* 25, no. 5 (September/October 2006): 34.

59. Michael W. Johnson, "Harassment and Discrimination Prevention Training," *Labor Law Journal* 55, no. 2 (Summer 2004): 119.

60. "Voluntary Diversity Plans Can Lead to Risk," *HR Focus* 84, no. 6 (June 2007): 2.

61. *University of California Regents v. Bakke,* 438 U.S. 265 (1978) and *United Steelworkers of America v. Weber,* 443, U.S. 193 (1979).

62. Daniel A Biddle and Richard E. Biddle, "Ricci v Destefano: New Opportunities for Employers to Correct Disparate Impact," *Labor Law Journal* 61, no. 3 (Fall 2010): 123–41.

63. Anne Ryman and Matthew Benson, "Affirmative Action under Fire," *The Arizona Republic* (November 6, 2007), A-1.

64. Caitlin Knowles Myers, "A Cure for Discrimination? Affirmative Action and the Case of California's Proposition 209," *Industrial and Labor Relations Review* 60, no. 3 (April 2007): 379. See also Robert K. Robinson, Geralyn McClure, and Karen Epermanis, "The Supreme Court Rulings in *Grutter v. Bollinger* and *Gratz v. Bollinger*: The Brave New World of Affirmative Action in the 21st Century," *Public Personnel Management* 36, no. 1 (Spring 2007): 33.

65. "Affirmative Action," *Diversity Inc.,* accessed February 22, 2011, http://www.diversityinc. com/department/35/Affirmative-Action/.

66. Peng Wang and Joshua L. Schwarz, "Stock Price Reactions to GLBT Nondiscrimination Policies," *Human Resource Management* 49, no. 2 (March–April 2010): 195.

67. Martin N. Davidson, *The End of Diversity as We Know It: Why Diversity Efforts Fail and How Leveraging Difference Can Succeed* (San Francisco: Berrett-Kohler Press, forthcoming, 2011).

4 Job Analysis and Job Design

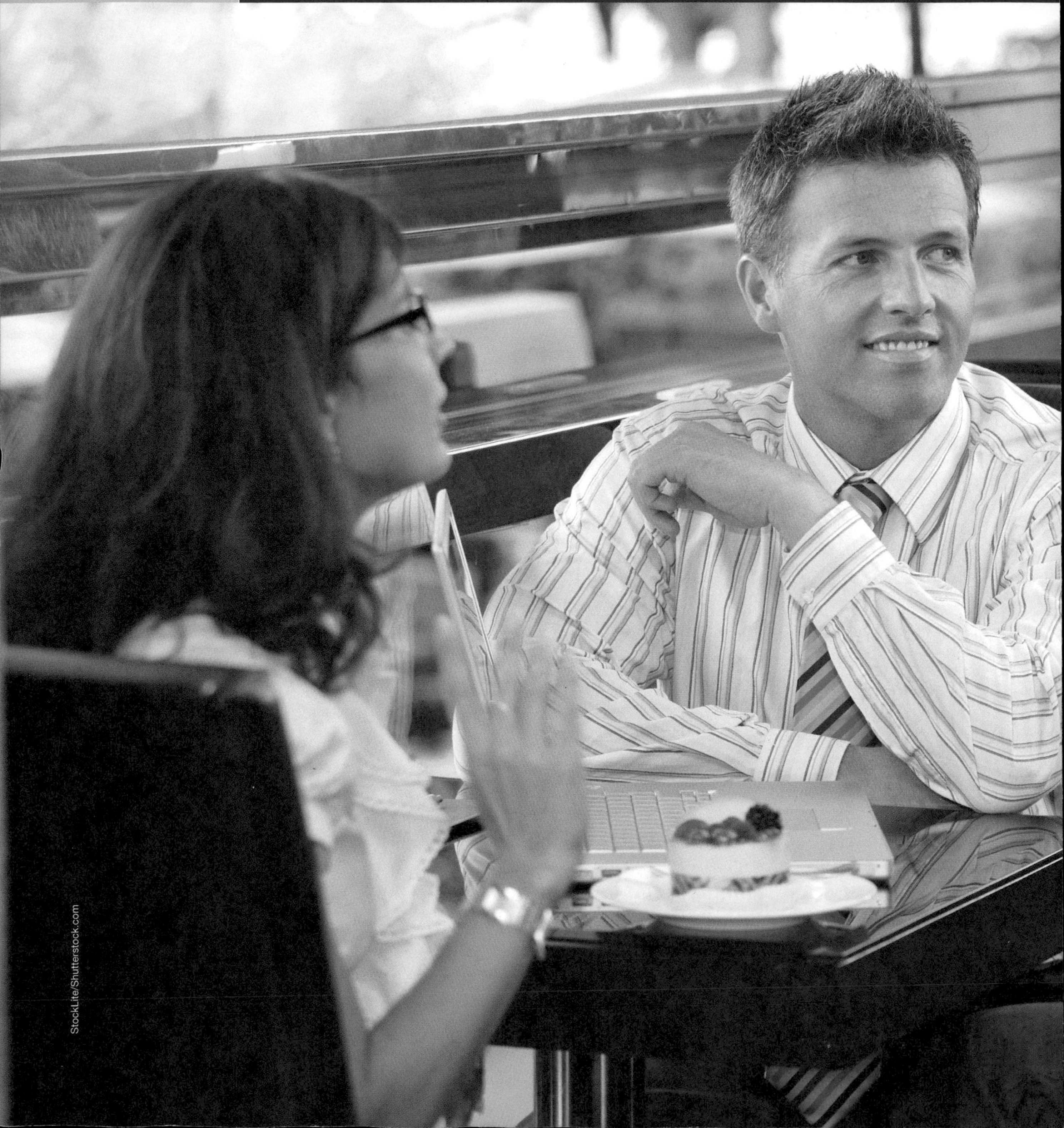

After studying this chapter, you should be able to

LEARNING OUTCOME 1 Explain what a job analysis is, the parts that comprise it and how the information it generates is used in conjunction with a firm's HRM functions.

LEARNING OUTCOME 2 Explain how the data for a job analysis typically is collected.

LEARNING OUTCOME 3 Identify and explain the various sections of job descriptions.

LEARNING OUTCOME 4 Provide examples illustrating the various factors that must be taken into account when designing a job.

LEARNING OUTCOME 5 Discuss the various job characteristics that motivate employees.

LEARNING OUTCOME 6 Describe the different group techniques used to broaden a firm's job functions and maximize the contributions of employees.

LEARNING OUTCOME 7 Identify the different types of work schedules organizations are using today to motivate their employees.

Organizations exist because people can accomplish more together than they can on their own. However, the actions of an organization need to be coordinated, and each person within it needs to do those things he or she does best. The division of labor allows for efficiency and specialization and potentially greater organizational effectiveness. The question is, how should the work be divided, and which people should do which tasks? It is a question businesspeople such as Henry Ford and scientific management researchers such as Frederick Winslow Taylor sought to answer at least a century ago, and one that managers still deal with today.

In this chapter, we will discuss how jobs can be designed to best contribute to the objectives of the organization as well as satisfy and motivate the employees who do them.[1] We will discuss why firms need to outline a job's requirements for legal reasons such as the Americans with Disabilities Act. The chapter concludes by explaining how firms are redesigning jobs and using teams to motivate employees, respond strategically to dynamic changes in the global marketplace, and ultimately improve the performance of their organizations.

What Is Job Analysis and How Does It Affect Human Resources Management?

LEARNING OUTCOME 1

Are there any HR functions that are not affected by the job analysis process? If so, what are they?

job analysis
The process of obtaining information about jobs by determining their duties, tasks, or activities

job description
A statement of the tasks, duties, and responsibilities of a job to be performed

job specification
A statement of the specific knowledge, skills, and abilities of a person who is to perform a job needs

A job analysis is the systematic process of collecting information about all of the parameters of a job—its basic responsibilities, the behaviors, skills, and the physical and mental requirements of the people who do it. A job analysis should also outline the tools needed to do the job, the environment and times at which it needs to done, with whom it needs to be done, and the outcome or performance level it should produce.[2] Studies have positively linked the job analysis process with improved performance on the part of employees and their organizations.[3] Normally, a manager or an HR manager such as a job analyst is responsible for collecting the information for a job analysis. These people rely on the cooperation of employees and their supervisors to gather the information needed for the analysis of jobs.

A job analysis generates information vital to the human resources management process. One major piece of information that comes out of job analysis is a job description. A job description is a written statement about the overall tasks, duties, and responsibilities of a job. It consists of various parts, including basic information such as where the job is located, to whom the jobholder reports, the type of wages he or she receives, and so forth.

A job specification section is often also included with a job description. A job specification outlines in detail the specific knowledge, skills, abilities, and other attributes (often referred to as KSAOs) required of the person performing the job. In the HR department for the City of Mesa, Arizona, the job specification for senior HR analyst includes the following:

1. Graduation from a four-year college with major course work (minimum fifteen hours) in human resources management

2. Three to five years experience in employee classification and compensation or selection or recruitment

3. Two years experience in developing/improving job-related compensation and testing instruments and procedures[4]

We will discuss job descriptions and job specifications in greater detail later in the chapter. However, to get a sneak peek at what a complete job description looks like with the specifications of the job incorporated, see Highlights in HRM 2. Sometimes employees are asked to write rough drafts of their job descriptions as a starting point for the person doing the job analysis to use and modify.

HRM Functions Affected by a Job Analysis

Because the information it collects serves so many HRM functions, a job analysis is sometimes called the cornerstone of HRM. These functions are discussed next and outlined in Figure 4.1.

Strategic HR Planning

A job analysis is used to examine a company's organizational structure and strategically position it for the future. Does the firm have the right numbers and types of jobs needed to cover the scope of its activities? What jobs need to be created? What skills do they require? Are those skills different than the skills required by the company's current jobs?

Workflow Analysis and Job Design

The information generated by a job analysis can also be used to analyze a company's work processes—that is, how inputs move through the company, value is added to

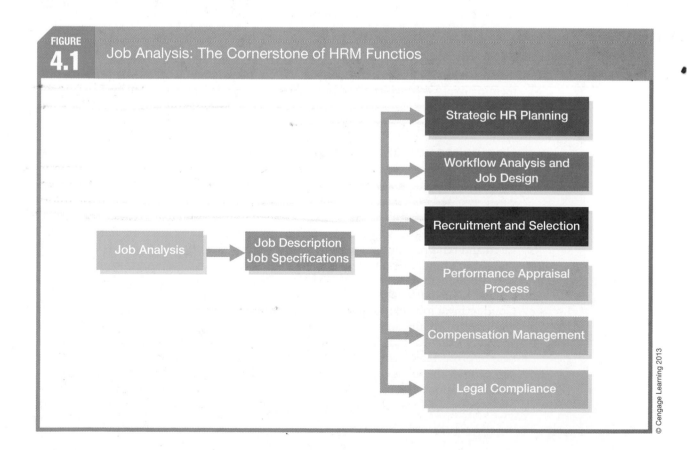

FIGURE 4.1   Job Analysis: The Cornerstone of HRM Functios

Job Analysis → Job Description Job Specifications →

- Strategic HR Planning
- Workflow Analysis and Job Design
- Recruitment and Selection
- Performance Appraisal Process
- Compensation Management
- Legal Compliance

© Cengage Learning 2013

them, and they become outputs. Would rearranging an organization's workflow or jobs help a company better compete? What about outsourcing jobs? Can the nature of the jobs be redesigned to improve the firm's performance?

These are questions that depend upon a firm's strategy. Consider Apple. Apple does not outsource its major functions and the jobs associated with them. The design of its products, operating systems, hardware, and software—even its sales—are all done at Apple by Apple employees. The company is able to manage all of the workflows associated with these activities because it focuses on far fewer products than conventional consumer electronics companies.[5]

Recruitment and Selection

The information provided via a job analysis plays an essential role in the recruiting function. The basic information and qualifications are contained in job advertisements, whether they are posted on organizational bulletin boards, Internet sites, the help-wanted sections of publications, or employment-agency listings. The information provides a basis for attracting qualified applicants and discouraging unqualified ones.

Training and Development

Any discrepancies between the knowledge, skills, and abilities demonstrated by jobholders and the requirements contained in the descriptions and specifications for their jobs provide clues to the training these jobholders need. The information also can serve as a guide to help with the career development of employees by indicating the type of training and development they need and what is required for them to advance to different jobs within the organization.

Performance Appraisal Process

Because a job analysis includes information about the requirements of someone performing a job, it provides the criteria for evaluating the people who do the work. By identifying what constitutes a good performance versus a poor performance, the firm can then take steps to improve the latter.

Compensation Management

Conducting a job analysis is important because it helps HR managers figure out the relative worth of a position so the compensation for it is fair and equitable. A job's worth is based on what the job demands of employees in terms of their skills, effort, and responsibilities, as well as the conditions and hazards under which the work is performed. Employees who are not being compensated fairly often are not fully motivated and tend to look for better positions outside the organization. We will discuss more about how to evaluate jobs and pay in Chapter 9.

Legal Compliance

Conducting a job analysis ensures that a job's duties match its job description. If the criteria used to hire and evaluate employees are vague and not job-related, employers are more likely to find themselves being accused of discriminating against the members of protected classes. In fact, before firms recognized the importance of regularly engaging in the job analysis process, examples of nonjob-related criteria were prevalent: Job applicants for laborer positions were required to have high school diplomas; applicants for skilled craft positions—plumbers, electricians, machinists—were sometimes required to be male. As you learned in Chapter 3, these kinds of job specifications are discriminatory.

Sources of Job Analysis Data

LEARNING OUTCOME 2
Answer the questions in Highlights in HRM 1 based on the job you currently hold or most recently held. Do the answers give you enough information to create a job analysis?

Job analysis data can be obtained in several ways. The more common methods of collecting the data needed to analyze jobs are interviews, questionnaires, observation, and diaries.

- *Interviews.* A job analyst or supervisor interviews individual employees and managers about the parameters of the job. Highlights in HRM 1 shows the types of questions asked as part of job-analysis interviews.

- *Questionnaires.* The job analyst or supervisor circulates questionnaires to be filled out individually by jobholders. The forms contain questions similar to those asked in an interview but employees complete the forms unassisted.

- *Observation.* The job analyst or supervisor learns about the job by observing and recording the activities associated with it on a standardized form.

- *Diaries.* Jobholders are asked to keep diaries of their work activities for an entire work cycle. The diaries are normally filled out at specific times of the work shift (such as every half hour or hour) and maintained for a two- to four-week period.

Figure 4.2 shows the job analysis process, including how data to be analyzed is collected and feeds back into the HRM functions we discussed in Figure 4.1.

Controlling the Accuracy of the Job Data Collected

When interviewing employees or reviewing their questionnaires, a job analyst should look for any responses that do not agree with other facts or impressions he or she has received about the job. Sometimes employees exaggerate the difficulty of their positions in order to inflate their egos and their paychecks.[6] Inflating a job's responsibilities can also occur unintentionally. For example, people who have been in their jobs for a long time and are good at them sometimes mistakenly believe that the skills needed for their jobs are higher than they really are.

As one job analyst noted, "When in doubt about the accuracy of employee responses, always double-check the data with others."[7] In other words, collect information from a representative sample of individuals doing the same job, not just one or two jobholders. Also, once a job analysis is done, it should be checked for accuracy by the jobholders and their managers.[8]

Methods Used to Collect Job Analysis Data and Analyze It

Do managers and job analysts have to start from scratch when it comes to designing questionnaires to gather job data and analyzing it? No, not necessarily, even if a position is a new one. Several different quantitative job analysis approaches already exist. Each has its own advantages and disadvantages.[9] Five of the more popular methods are the functional job analysis, the Position Analysis system, the critical incident method, a task inventory analysis, and a competency-based job analysis.

FIGURE
4.2   The Job Analysis Process

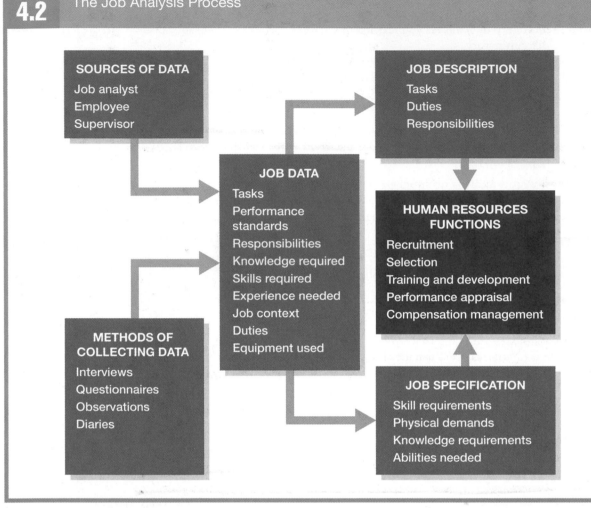

Source: U.S. Bureau of Labor Statistics.

1

HIGHLIGHTS IN **HRM**
The Job Analysis Interview

The following are examples of typical interview questions HR professionals might use to gather information for a job analysis.

1. Job purpose

- What is the essence of work in your position? What is the job's overall purpose?
- How do you see your work contributing to the overall mission/purpose of the organization, now and in the future?

2. Job duties

- Describe your duties in terms of what they are, how you do them, how often you perform them, and how long they each take.

- Does the job have to be done in the way you were trained to do it, or do you see ways to improve it?
- Are you performing duties not presently included in your job description? Describe.
- Are the instructions you receive from your supervisor clear and consistent with your job description?

3. Job criteria/results

- Have work standards been established (errors allowed, time taken for a particular task, etc.)? If so, what are they?
- Describe the successful completion and/or end results of the job.

4. Background/Knowledge

- What personal attributes are needed to be successful in this position?
- Describe the level, degree, and breadth of knowledge required for this position.
- Indicate the education, certification, and/or license requirements for the job.

5. Training

- Describe the orientation you received when you first started in this job, and evaluate its efficacy.
- What sort of on-the-job training and length of training period are needed for this position?
- What sort of tools, equipment, or other resources are needed for sufficient training (not performance) for this position?
- What assessment tests are needed to establish competency in this position?

6. Abilities required

- What are the manual skills that are required to operate machines, vehicles, equipment, or to use tools?
- Do you use special tools, equipment, or other sources of aid? If so, list the names of the principal tools, equipment, or sources of aid you use.
- What reasoning or problem solving ability must you have?
- Are any supervisory or managing abilities required?
- What physical abilities such as strength, coordination, or visual acuity must you have?

7. Working conditions

- Describe your working conditions.
- Describe the frequency and degree to which you encounter working conditions such as these: contact with hazardous materials, strenuous physical labor, cramped quarters, moving objects, vibration, inadequate ventilation.

8. Authority

- What is the level of accountability, and to whom are you accountable?
- What kinds of independent action are you allowed to take?

9. Responsibilities

- Are you responsible for any confidential material? If so, describe how you handle it.
- Are you responsible for any money or things of monetary value? If so, describe how you handle it.

10. Evaluation/Compensation

- In what ways and how often is your performance evaluated and feedback provided?
- What criteria do you think should be used in the evaluation process?
- Considering your level of productivity and the skill level required to fulfill your responsibilities, do you think you are compensated adequately?
- Describe the criteria you think should be used to determine adequate compensation for the position: responsibilities, skills, experience, knowledge, work environment, safety hazards, etc.

Sources: David Ngo, "Job Analysis Questions" *hrvinet.com*, accessed March 3, 2011, http://www.humanresources.hrvinet.com; "Job Analysis: Overview," HR Guide to the Internet, http://www.job-analysis.net/G000.htm; "Job Analysis: Asking Questions," Department for Business Innovation & Skills, http://www.bis.gov.uk.

Functional Job Analysis System

functional job
analysis (FJA)

A job-analysis approach
that utilizes an inventory of
the various types of work
activities that can constitute
any job.

Developed by the U.S. Training and Employment Service, the functional job analysis (FJA) approach utilizes an inventory of the various types of work activities that can constitute any job. Basic activities called worker functions are used to describe what workers do with regard to "data, people, and things" as part of this system.[10] For example, when it comes to people, the basic functions of a job might include coordinating and supervising them. Each job function is assigned a percentage in terms of its importance to the job. (For example, supervising might be 75 percent of the job.)

The Department of Labor's Occupational Information Network (O*Net) System

The U.S. Department of Labor's Occupational Information Network Online System (O*Net) replaced the department's *Dictionary of Occupational Titles*, which contained about 12,000 job descriptions. The new online database classifies jobs into broader functional areas, from entry level to advanced, and across various specialties. So, for example, the jobs for police, fire, and ambulance dispatchers now fall into one category instead of three. Consequently, there are fewer individual jobs listed on the site than in the *Dictionary of Occupational Titles*.

The upside of O*NET is that it contains comprehensive information about the tasks, tools and technology, KSAs, education, interests, works styles, wages, and the employment outlook associated with jobs. As a result, it is a good tool for matching the interests and abilities of job seekers with occupations and can serve as a starting point for a person doing a job analysis. It is also a free resource, unlike the *Dictionary*. Free job-analysis questionnaires can also be downloaded from the O*NET website. Although they are generic, they can be customized and used as a starting point to collect occupational data from jobholders and their managers.

Using the INTERNET

To explore the Department of Labor' O*NET database, go to

www.cengagebrain.com

The Position Analysis Questionnaire System

position analysis
questionnaire
(PAQ)

A questionnaire indentifying
approximately 200 different
tasks that, by means of a
five-point scale, seeks to determine the degree to which
different tasks are involved
in performing a job

The Position Analysis Questionnaire (PAQ), which identifies approximately 200 different worker tasks, has been used to collect and analyze job data since the 1970s. Using a five-point scale, the PAQ seeks to determine the degree, if any, to which the different tasks, or job elements, are involved in performing a particular job. The results obtained with the PAQ are quantitative and can be subjected to statistical analysis. The PAQ also permits dimensions of behavior to be compared across a number of jobs and permits jobs to be grouped on the basis of common characteristics. Although a PAQ tends to be accurate, it requires a person to have a high level of reading ability.[11] To obtain the best results, it should be administered to employees by a job analyst rather than having the employees complete the questionnaire alone. Also, the questionnaire isn't free. Firms must pay for it.

The Critical Incident Method

critical incident
method

A job analysis method by
which important job tasks
are identified for job success

The objective of the critical incident method is to identify critical job tasks. Critical job tasks are important duties, responsibilities, and behaviors performed by the jobholder that lead to job success. The approach can be used to identify both positive and negative behaviors, the combination of which shows the path to effectiveness. Information about critical incidents can be collected through interviews with employees or managers or through self-report statements written by employees.

Suppose, for example, that the job analyst is studying the job of reference librarian. The interviewer will ask the employee to describe the job on the basis of what is done, how the job is performed, and what tools and equipment are used. The reference librarian may describe the job as follows:

> I assist patrons by answering their questions related to finding books, periodicals, or other library materials. I also give them directions to help them find materials within the building. To perform my job, I may have to look up materials myself or refer patrons to someone who can directly assist them. Some individuals may need training in how to use reference materials or special library facilities. I also give library tours to new patrons. I use computers and a variety of reference books to carry out my job.

After the job data are collected, the analyst then writes separate task statements that represent important job activities. For the reference librarian, one task statement might be: "Listens to patrons and answers their questions related to locating library materials." Typically, the job analyst writes five to ten important task statements for each job under study. The final product is written task statements that are clear, complete, and easily understood by those unfamiliar with the job. The critical incident method is an important job analysis method because it teaches the analyst to focus on employee behaviors critical to job success.

A task inventory analysis uses employee input to develop lists of job tasks and descriptions common to all jobs.

JHDT Stock Images LLC/Shutterstock.com

Task Inventory Analysis

The task inventory analysis method was pioneered by the U.S. Air Force. Unlike the PAQ, which uses a standardized form to analyze jobs in different organizations, a task inventory questionnaire can be tailored for a specific organization. With the help of employees and their managers, a list of tasks and their descriptions for different jobs are developed and then rated based on how important they are. The goal is to produce a comprehensive list of task statements applicable to all jobs. Task statements then are listed on a task inventory survey form to be completed by the person analyzing the job under review. A task statement might be: "Monitors current supplies to maintain stock levels." The job analysis would also note the importance of the task, frequency of occurrence, and time spent on the task to the successful completion of the job.

Competency-Based Analysis

The approaches to job analysis we have discussed so far focus on the tasks employees do, but not what they are capable of doing. The following statement by two HR professionals highlights this concern: "Typically, job analysis looks at how a job is currently done. But the ever-changing business market makes it difficult to keep a job analysis up-to-date. Also, companies are asking employees to do more, so there is a question of whether 'jobs' as we know them are obsolete." The risk is that in a dynamic environment where job demands rapidly change, obsolete job analysis information will hinder an organization's ability to adapt to change.

When organizations operate in a fast-moving environment, managers often adopt a competency-based approach to job analysis.[12] This job analysis method relies on building job profiles that look at not only the responsibilities and activities of jobs a worker a does currently, but the competencies or capabilities he or she needs to do them well and to adapt to new job challenges. *How* the work is done (and therefore can be improved) becomes more of the focus than just *what* work is done.[13]

The objective is to identify "key" competencies for the organization's success. Competencies can be identified through focus groups, surveys, or interviews and might include such things as interpersonal communication skills, decision-making ability, conflict resolution skills, adaptability, or self-motivation. Figure 4.3 shows a form used to gather information for a competency-based job analysis.

Human-Resources-Information and Web-Based Job Analysis Systems

Software programs have greatly facilitated the job analysis process. The programs normally contain generalized task statements that can apply to many different jobs. Managers and employees select those statements that best describe the job under review, indicating the importance of the task to the total job where appropriate. The software can also combine the job analysis process with the job evaluation process to help determine the appropriate compensation of jobholders. Publications such as *HRMagazine* and *Workforce* contain advertisements from numerous software companies offering HRIS job analysis packages. Similar Internet-based packages that allow employees to access and complete questionnaires via web links are also are available.

4.3 Form Used to Gather Information for a Competency-Based Job Analysis

Part B: Skill Matrix in a Dejobbed Organisation

Job Title: XYZ

8	8	8	8	8	8
7	7	7	7	7	7
6	6	6	6	6	6
5	5	5	5	5	5
4	4	4	4	4	4
3	3	3	3	3	3
2	2	2	2	2	2
1	1	1	1	1	1
Technical Expertise	Communication & Interpersonal Ability	Business Acumen & Decision Making	Leadership & Guidance	Planning & Organising	Initiative & Problem Solving

➤ 1, 2, 3 etc. are descriptors for each level of the skill e.g. in case of technical expertise (1) might read: basic knowledge of handling machine while (8) might read: conducts and supervises complex tasks requiring advanced knowledge of a range of skills.

➤ Dark boxes indicate minimum level of skill required in each skill category for the position XYZ.

➤ Incumbent is required to move from minimum level to higher levels. The appraisal and rewards are tied to this movement to higher levels.

Source: Feza Tabassum Azmi, "Job Descriptions to Job Fluidity: Treading the Dejobbing Path," EBS Review no. 23 (2007): 8. Reprinted by permission.

Parts of a Job Description

Most job descriptions contain at least three parts: (1) the job's title and location; (2) a job "identification" section, which contains administration information such a numerical code for the job, to whom the jobholder reports, and wage information; and (3) a job duties section. The other important outcome of the job analysis is the job specification, or the description of knowledge, skills, abilities, and other attributes (KSAOs). If the job specification is not prepared as a separate document, it is usually stated in the concluding section of the job description, as Highlights in HRM 2 shows. Next, let's look at these sections.

Job Title

Selecting a job's title serves several purposes. First, the job title is psychologically important because it provides status to the employee. For instance, "sanitation engineer" is a more appealing title than "garbage collector." Second, if possible, the title provides an indication of what the duties of the job entail. Titles such as *meat inspector, electronics assembler, salesperson,* and *engineer* obviously hint at the nature of the duties of these jobs. The job title also should indicate the relative level occupied by its holder in the organizational hierarchy. For example, the title *junior engineer* implies that this job occupies a lower level than that of *senior engineer.*

LEARNING OUTCOME 3

Using your answers to the questions asked in Highlights in HRM 1, write a job description for your job or the job you most recently held. Are there elements of the job that are not reflected in the job description?

2

HIGHLIGHTS IN **HRM**
Job Description for an Employment Assistant

Job Identification

JOB TITLE: Employment Assistant

Division:	Southern Area
Department:	Human Resources Management
Job Analyst:	Virginia Sasaki
Date Analyzed:	12/3/11
Wage Category:	Exempt
Report to:	HR Manager
Job Code:	11-17
Date Verified:	12/17/11

Brief Listing of Major Job Duties

JOB STATEMENT

Performs professional human resources work in the areas of employee recruitment and selection, testing, orientation, transfers, and maintenance of employee human resources files. May handle special assignments and projects related to EEO/affirmative action, employee grievances, training, or classification and compensation. Works under general supervision. Incumbent exercises initiative and independent judgment in the performance of assigned tasks.

Essential Functions and Responsibilities

ESSENTIAL FUNCTIONS

1. Prepares recruitment literature and job advertisements.
2. Schedules and conducts personal interviews to determine applicants' suitability for employment. Includes reviewing applications and resumes mailed and submitted electronically. Supervises the administration of the applicant testing program. Responsible for developing or improving testing instruments and procedures.
3. Presents orientation program to all new employees. Reviews and develops all materials and procedures for the orientation program.
4. Coordinates the division job posting and transfer program. Establishes job posting procedures. Responsible for reviewing transfer applications, arranging transfer interviews, and determining effective transfer dates.
5. Maintains a daily working relationship with division managers on human resources matters, including recruitment concerns, retention or release of probationary employees, and discipline or discharge of permanent employees.
6. Distributes new or revised human resources policies and procedures to all employees and managers through via e-mail, the company's intranet, meetings, memorandums, and/or personal contact.
7. Performs related duties as assigned by the human resources manager.

Job Description for an Employment Assistant (continued)

Job Specifications and Requirements

JOB SPECIFICATIONS

1. Four-year college or university degree with major course work in human resources management, business administration, or industrial psychology; OR a combination of experience, education, and training equivalent to a four-year college degree in human resources management.
2. Detailed knowledge of the principles of employee selection and assignment of personnel.
3. Ability to express ideas clearly in both written and oral communications.
4. Ability to independently plan and organize one's own activities.
5. Knowledge of HRIS applications desirable.

Job Identification Section

The job identification section of a job description usually follows the job title. It includes such items as the departmental location of the job, the person to whom the jobholder reports, and the date the job description was last revised. Sometimes it also contains a payroll or code number, the number of employees performing the job, the number of employees in the department where the job is located, and the code assigned to the job using the O*NET system. A "Statement of the Job" usually appears at the bottom of this section and distinguishes the job from other jobs in the organization—something the job title might fail to do.

Job Duties, or Essential Functions, Section

Statements covering job duties are typically arranged in their order of importance. These statements should indicate the weight, or value, of each duty. Usually, but not always, the weight of a duty can be gauged by the percentage of time devoted. As a result of the Civil Rights Act of 1991, the American with Disabilities Act (ADA), and landmark court rulings, employers need to be able to show that the job criteria they use to select employees for a particular position relate specifically to the duties for that job. Moreover, the duties must be *essential functions* for success on the job. For example, if the job requires the jobholder to read extremely fine print, to climb ladders, or to memorize stock codes, these physical and mental requirements should be stated within the job description. Remember, too, that once the essential functions for a job are defined, the organization is legally required to make a reasonable accommodation for disabled individuals who would be able to do the functions if they were accommodated.

Job Specifications Section

Typically, a job specification section covers two areas: (1) the skill required to perform the job and (2) the physical demands the job places on the employee doing it. Skills relevant to a job include the education, experience, and specialized training it requires, and the personal traits or abilities and manual dexterities it requires. To comply with EEOC requirements, the physical demands of a job should refer to how

It's essential for companies to clearly define the duties associated with any job, and to demonstrate the criteria used in selecting an employee to perform the duties of that job.

Levent Konuk/Shutterstock.com

much walking, standing, reaching, lifting, bending, or talking must be done on the job. The condition of the physical work environment and the hazards an employee might encounter in the position are also among the physical demands of a job.

The job specifications section should also include interpersonal skills if a competency-based job analysis approach is used. For example, behavioral competencies might include the ability to make decisions based on incomplete information, the ability to handle multiple tasks, and resolve conflicts.

Problems with Job Descriptions

Several problems are frequently associated with job descriptions, including the following:

1. If they are poorly written, using vague rather than specific terms, they provide little guidance to the jobholder.
2. They are sometimes not updated as job duties or specifications change.
3. They may violate the law by containing specifications not related to job success.
4. They can limit the scope of activities of the jobholder, reducing an organization's flexibility.

Writing Clear and Specific Job Descriptions

When writing a job description, use statements that are terse, direct, and simply worded. Unnecessary words or phrases should be eliminated. The term "occasionally" is used to describe duties that are performed once in a while. The term "may" is used in connection with duties performed only by some workers on the job.

Even when set forth in writing, job descriptions and specifications can still be vague. To the consternation of many employers, however, today's legal environment has created what might be called an "age of specifics." Federal guidelines and court decisions now require that the specific performance requirements of a job be based on *valid* job-related criteria.[14] Personnel decisions that involve either job applicants or employees and are based on criteria that are vague or not job-related are increasingly successfully challenged. Managers of small businesses, in which employees may perform many different job tasks, must be particularly concerned about writing specific job descriptions. To help alleviate the problem of employees claiming that a task "is not my job," organizations often include language in their job descriptions stating that the jobholder will perform "other duties" as needed. Notice that the job-duties section in Highlights in HRM 2 contains the following language: *Performs related duties as assigned by the human resources manager.*

Job Design

LEARNING OUTCOME 4

Explain how industrial engineering and ergonomics can both clash with and complement each other in the design of jobs.

Industrial engineering is the study of work cycles to determine which, if any, elements of work can be modified, combined, rearranged, or eliminated to reduce the time needed to complete the work cycle. Time standards are then established by recording the time required to complete each element in the work cycle, using a stopwatch or work-sampling technique. Industrial engineering dramatically changed how people worked around the beginning of the twentieth century and for decades to come.

However, like organizations themselves, the job analysis process has evolved as people think about ways to restructure firms to better compete as the marketplace changes. Job design is part of this process. Job design, which is an outgrowth of job analysis, focuses on restructuring jobs to capture the talents of employees, improve their work satisfaction, and enhance an organization's performance.[15] Companies such as Harley-Davidson and Banner Health are among the many firms that have revamped their jobs to eliminate unnecessary job tasks and find better ways of doing work.

As Figure 4.4 illustrates, the four elements examined as a part of job design are:

1. Organizational objectives a job should fulfill;

2. Industrial engineering considerations, including ways to make the job technologically efficient;

3. Ergonomic concerns. Ergonomics is the process of studying and designing equipment and systems that are easy and efficient for employees to use so that their physical well-being isn't compromised. Ergonomics will be discussed in greater detail later in the book when we cover employee safety and health.

4. Behavioral concerns that influence an employee's job satisfaction.[16]

We have already discussed the basic organizational and strategic concerns firms try to meet as part of the job analysis process as well as how industrial engineers such as Henry Ford and Frederick Winslow Taylor improved the efficiency of work done in organizations. What we have not yet discussed in much detail are the behavioral concerns that affect the motivation of employees and their job satisfaction. This is especially important when you consider the fact that people—not machines—are the most strategic asset companies have today.

industrial engineering

A field of study concerned with analyzing work methods and establishing time standards

job design

An outgrowth of job analysis that improves jobs through technological and human considerations in order to enhance organization efficiency and employee job satisfaction

ergonomics

The process of studying and designing equipment and systems that are easy and efficient for people to use and that ensure their physical well-being.

Using the **INTERNET**

To learn more about ergonomics, go to

www.cengagebrain.com

FIGURE 4.4 Basis of Job Design

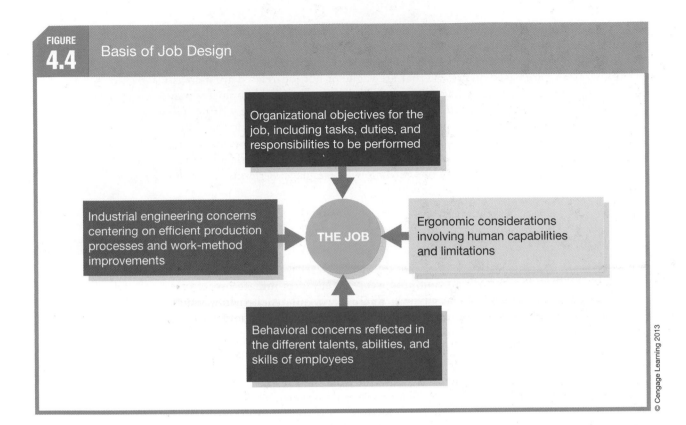

Organizational objectives for the job, including tasks, duties, and responsibilities to be performed

Industrial engineering concerns centering on efficient production processes and work-method improvements

THE JOB

Ergonomic considerations involving human capabilities and limitations

Behavioral concerns reflected in the different talents, abilities, and skills of employees

Many companies willingly invest in ergonomically designed work stations because they protect the health and productivity of employees.

Job Characteristics Model: Designing Jobs to Motivate Employees

LEARNING OUTCOME 5

Can a firm's managers control the process of job crafting? What challenges does it present for them?

Would you like it if your supervisor timed down to the minute each of the tasks associated with your job and then asked you to adhere to those times? Would you find this motivating? Probably not. In an effort to counter the motivational problems that occur when workers do standardized, repetitive tasks, researchers began proposing theories they believed could improve simultaneously the efficiency of organizations and the job satisfaction of employees.[17] Perhaps the theory that best exemplifies this research is the one advanced by Richard Hackman and Greg Oldham.[18] Hackman and Oldham's job characteristics model proposes that three *psychological states* of a jobholder result in improved work performance, internal motivation, and lower absenteeism and turnover.[19] A motivated, satisfied, and productive employee (1) experiences *meaningfulness* of the work performed, (2) experiences *responsibility* for work outcomes, and (3) has *knowledge of the results* of the work performed. Hackman and Oldham believe that five core job dimensions produce the three psychological states. The five job characteristics are as follows:

Job characteristics model

A job design theory that purports that three psychological states (experiencing meaningfulness of the work performed, responsibility for work outcomes, and knowledge of the results of the work performed) of a jobholder result in improved work performance, internal motivation, and lower absenteeism and turnover

1. *Skill variety:* The degree to which a job entails a variety of different activities, which demand the use of a number of different skills and talents by the jobholder

2. *Task identity:* The degree to which the job requires completion of a whole and identifiable piece of work, that is, doing a job from beginning to end with a visible outcome

3. *Task significance:* The degree to which the job has a substantial impact on the lives or work of other people, whether in the immediate organization or in the external environment

4. *Autonomy:* The degree to which the job provides substantial freedom, independence, and discretion to the individual in scheduling the work and in determining the procedures to be used in carrying it out

5. *Feedback:* The degree to which carrying out the work activities required by the job results in the individual being given direct and clear information about the effectiveness of his or her performance

A number of job design techniques are being used today in an effort to remake jobs as Hackman and Oldham envisioned they could be. The techniques include job enlargement, job rotation, and job enrichment. Job enlargement is the process of adding a greater variety of tasks to a job. Maytag, IBM, and AT&T are some of the firms that have used job enlargement to motivate their employees.[20] Job rotation is a process whereby employees rotate in and out of different jobs. Both job enlargement and job rotation help alleviate the boredom people experience where they perform narrow, specialized jobs. Rotating people in and out of different jobs can also help employees who do repetitive physical tasks avoid health problems and on-the-job injuries. For instance, after a number of hours on his feet, a drugstore cashier might move to the store's photo department and process photos while sitting down. Job rotation is also often used in work teams so members can trade off doing different tasks as needed.

Any effort that makes work more rewarding or satisfying by adding more meaningful tasks to an employee's job is called job enrichment. Originally popularized by Frederick Herzberg in the 1960s, job enrichment programs are designed to

Job enlargement

The process of adding a greater variety of tasks to a job.

Job rotation

The process whereby employees rotate in and out of different jobs.

job enrichment

Enhancing a job by adding more meaningful tasks and duties to make the work more rewarding or satisfying fulfill the high motivational needs of employees, such as self-fulfillment and self-esteem, while achieving long-term job satisfaction and performance goals.[21] Job enrichment can be accomplished by increasing the autonomy and responsibility of employees. Herzberg discusses five factors for enriching jobs and thereby motivating employees: achievement, recognition, growth, responsibility, and performance of the whole job versus only parts of the job. For example, managers can use these five factors to enrich the jobs of employees by increasing the level of difficulty and responsibility of their jobs and allowing them to become more involved in planning, organizing, directing, and controlling their own work. Job enrichment can also be accomplished by organizing workers into teams and giving these teams greater authority for self-management.

Job enrichment programs are not a panacea that can solve all workflow and personnel problems, such as the dissatisfaction of employees with their pay, benefits, or job security, however. Moreover, not all employees object to the mechanical pacing of an assembly line, nor do all employees seek additional responsibilities or challenges. Some people prefer routine jobs because they are predictable.

The techniques we have described so far are ones in which managers or supervisors formally change the jobs of employees. A less-structured method is to allow employees to initiate their own job changes through the concept of empowerment. Employee empowerment is a technique of involving employees in their work through the process of inclusion. Empowerment encourages workers to become innovators and managers of their own work, and it involves them in their jobs in ways that give them more control and autonomous decision-making capabilities. MetLife, AT&T, and Sports Authority are among the companies that have decentralized their work units and allowed decisions to be made by the employees who are directly involved in the production of the products or services being delivered.[22] These employees have the autonomy and flexibility to meet the demands of customers.[23] The objective is to develop jobs and basic work units that are adaptable enough to thrive in a world of high-velocity change. The cosmetics maker Avon empowered its minority managers to improve the sales and service the company offers in inner-city markets. Grounded in the belief that minority managers better understand the culture of inner-city residents, Avon turned unprofitable markets into highly profitable ones. See Highlights in HRM 3 for more examples of employee empowerment.

employee empowerment

Granting employees power to initiate change, thereby encouraging them to take charge of what they do

Employee empowerment succeeds when the culture of an organization is open and receptive to change.[24] An organization's senior managers set the tone of the organization. If they are honest, confident, trusting, receptive to new ideas, and respect employees as partners in the organization's success, it's more likely the firm will truly be able to empower its employees. The following are additional tips for managers who want to empower their employees:

- *Participation*. Employees should be encouraged to take control of their work tasks. Employees, in turn, must care to improve their work process and interpersonal work relationships.

- *Innovation*. The work environment should be receptive to people with innovative ideas and encourage people to explore new paths and to take reasonable risks at reasonable costs. An empowered environment is created when curiosity is as highly regarded as technical expertise.

3 HIGHLIGHTS IN **HRM**
Empowered Employees Achieve Results

Employers as diverse as Home Depot, Walmart, Cigna HealthCare, Costco, AutoZone, Disney, and Applebee's have turned to their employees to gain a competitive edge. As a result, employees are improving the quality of products and services, reducing costs, and successfully modifying products as well as creating new ones.

- At Kraft Foods, employees at the company's Sussex, Wisconsin, food plant participated in work redesign changes and team building that increased the plant's productivity, reduced its overhead, and cut assembly time.
- At Ford's factory in Wayne, Michigan, one group of employees made a suggestion saving $115,000 per year on the purchase of gloves used to protect workers who handle sheet metal and glass. The group figured out how to have the gloves washed so they could be used more than once.
- Home Depot's Special Project Support Teams (SPST) work to improve the organization's business and information services. Employees with a wide range of backgrounds and skills collaborate to address a variety of strategic and tactical business needs.
- American Airlines' "Rainbow Team" of gay employees brought in $192 million in annual revenue by targeting the gay community.

■ *Access to information.* Employees must have access to a wide range of information. Involved individuals decide what kind of information they need for performing their jobs.

■ *Accountability.* Empowered employees should be held accountable for producing agreed-upon results. Empowerment does not mean being able to do whatever you want.

Two new job design techniques getting attention today are job crafting and dejobbing. According to Amy Wrzesniewski at the Yale School of Management job crafting is a *naturally* occurring phenomenon whereby employees mold their tasks to fit their individual strengths, passions, and motives better.[25] Dorothy Galvez, an administrative assistant at the W. P. Carey School of Business at Arizona State University is an example. Galvez found a way to make her job more meaningful by doing a lot more than traditional administrative work. She expanded her role by planning college activities and events, preparing special college reports, and serving as the dean's representative at college and business events. Wrzesniewski says employees often reshape their jobs whether managers want them to or not, and that in many cases, job crafting results in significantly more employee engagement. Employee engagement refers to a situation in which workers are enthusiastic and immersed in their work to the degree that it improves the performance of their companies.

Dejobbing refers to a process of structuring organizations not around jobs but around projects that are constantly changing. In a dejobbed organization, a skills matrix like the one shown in Figure 4.3 is likely to be used instead of a traditional job description that defines specific work. Hackman and Oldham predict that this type of organizational structure will be the norm in the future.[26] To be sure, it is hard

job crafting
A naturally occurring phenomenon whereby employees mold their tasks to fit their individual strengths, passions, and motives better

employee engagement
A situation in which workers are enthusiastic and immersed in their work to the degree that it improves the performance of their companies

Dejobbing
refers to a process of structuring organizations not around jobs but around projects that are constantly changing.

to imagine a world without jobs. However, the idea might not be as far-fetched as you think. Consider W.L. Gore & Associates, which makes Gore-Tex fabric, surgical, aerospace, and other products. There are no bosses at W.L. Gore or traditional jobs *per se*. All employees are hired as "associates" and assigned to "sponsors" in the functional groups in which they work. The structure has helped create a culture of innovation within the company that has repeatedly landed it on *Fortune* magazine's annual list of the United States' "100 Best Companies to Work For."

Designing Work for Employee Teams

LEARNING OUTCOME 6

Describe the types of teams you have worked in. Were some more successful than others? If so, why? How might what you have learned from being a team member be applied in an HR context?

employee teams

An employee contributions technique whereby work functions are structured for groups rather than for individuals and team members are given discretion in matters traditionally considered management prerogatives, such as process improvements, product or service development, and individual work assignments

Teamwork has already become a common structure in the workplace. Says Jim Barksdale, the chairman and president of Barksdale Management Corporation, a private investment management corporation "These days it seems as if every time a task needs to be accomplished within an organization, a team is formed to do it." Organizations of all types—Federal Express, Hewlett-Packard, Trek Bicycles, Calvin Klein, and LucasFilm, producer of the *Star Wars* and *Indiana Jones* films—are using employee teams to solve unique and complex problems and improve the collaboration among workers and their morale.[27] Via teamwork, employees are reducing the costs of their organizations, creating better goods and services, and speeding up their delivery to the marketplace.

An employee team can be defined as a group of individuals working together toward a common purpose, in which members have complementary skills, members' work is mutually dependent, and the group has discretion over tasks performed. Furthermore, teams seek to make members of the work group share responsibility and accountability for their group's performance. Part of the reason why employee teams exist is that employees, not managers, are closest to the work that's actually being done in an organization. Thus, they are often in a better position to see how the work can be done better. As this chapter's small-business feature clearly explains, teams that operate effectively are especially important to small businesses and firms coping during an economic downturn as they try to survive.

Teamwork also embraces the concept of *synergy*. Synergy occurs when the interaction and outcome of team members is greater than the sum of their individual efforts.[28] Synergy in teams does not automatically happen, though. Rather, it must be nurtured within the team environment.[29] Figure 4.5 lists the behaviors that can help a team develop synergy.

Teams can operate in a variety of structures, each with different strategic purposes or functional activities. Figure 4.6 describes common team forms. They include cross-functional teams, project teams, self-directed teams, task-force teams, process-improvement teams, and virtual teams. Self-directed teams are often championed as being the highest form of teams. Also called *autonomous work groups, self-managed teams,* or *high-performance teams,* they consist of groups of employees who are accountable for an entire work process or segment that delivers a product or service to an internal or external customer. For example, in a manufacturing environment, a team might be responsible for a whole product such as a computer screen or a clearly defined segment of the production process, such as the building of an engine for a passenger car. Similarly, in a service environment, a team is usually responsible for an entire group of products and services. Or a team might be responsible for serving clients in one particular geographical area. Typical team functions include setting work schedules, dealing directly with external customers, training team members, setting

---

FIGURE 4.5 Synergistic Team Characteristics

Team synergy is heightened when team members engage in the following behaviors.

- *Support.* The team exhibits an atmosphere of inclusion. All team members speak up and feel free to offer constructive comments.

- *Listening and Clarification.* Active listening is practiced. Members honestly listen to others and seek clarification on discussion points. The team members summarize discussions held.

- *Disagreement.* Disagreements are seen as natural and are expected. The members' comments are nonjudgmental and focus on factual issues rather than personality differences.

- *Consensus.* The team's members reach agreements through consensus. Proposals that are acceptable to all team members are adopted, even if they not the first choice of some of the individual members. Common ground among ideas is sought.

- *Acceptance.* The team members value one another as individuals. They recognize that each person brings a valuable mix of skills and abilities to the team.

- *Quality.* Each team member is committed to excellence. There is emphasis on continuous improvement and attention to detail.

© Cengage Learning 2013

FIGURE 4.6 Forms of Employee Teams

Cross-Functional Teams. A group staffed with a mix of employees from an organization's marketing, production, engineering departments, and so forth and is formed to accomplish a specific objective.

Project Teams. A group formed specifically to design a new product or service. The members are assigned by their managers on the basis of their ability to contribute to the team's success. The group normally disbands after the task is completed.

Self-Directed Teams. Groups of highly trained individuals performing a set of interdependent job tasks within a natural work unit. The team members rely on consensus-type decision-making to perform their work duties, solve problems, or deal with internal or external customers.

Task Force Teams. A task force is formed by management to immediately resolve a major problem.

Process-Improvement Teams. A group made up of experienced people from different departments or functions. The group is charged with improving quality, decreasing waste, or enhancing the productivity of processes that affect all departments or functions. The members are normally appointed by management.

© Cengage Learning 2013

---

performance targets, budgeting, inventory management, and purchasing equipment or services. To operate efficiently, team members generally acquire multiple skills so that they are able to perform a variety of tasks as part of the team.

Companies are recognizing that the best people for projects are often in different locations. As a result, firms are increasingly using virtual teams. Virtual teams utilize telecommunications technology to link team members who are geographically dispersed—often worldwide across cultures and across time zones. The technology virtual teams use includes wikis, document-sharing platforms such as Google Docs, online

virtual team

A team that utilizes telecommunications technology to link team members who are geographically dispersed—often worldwide across cultures and across time zones.

Online services such as Skype and iMeet allow virtual workers to get better acquainted with one another and have face-to-face conversations across any distance.

Bernhard Lang/Photodisc/Getty Images

chat and instant messaging, web and video conferencing, and electronic calendar systems, to name a few. For a major U.S. telecommunication client, IBM used a global team to develop a web-based tool for launching new services. The team included members from Japan, Brazil, and Britain and delivered a finished product in two months, a considerable reduction in product delivery time.[30] The software company My SQL is perhaps the ultimate virtual team. MY SQL has a worldwide workforce but no offices. Employees work virtually in self-directed work teams.[31] Virtual teams do not have to work for just one organization, though. Many virtual teams consist of members from different organizations. For example, to improve workflows in supply chains, it is not uncommon for manufacturers to have their employees team up with the employees of their suppliers and the employees of the retailers who buy the manufacturers' products.

Although virtual teams have many benefits, they are not without their problems.[32] Paulette Tichenor, president of Organizational Renaissance, a team training organization, notes these concerns with virtual teams: language and cultural barriers, unclear objectives, time conflicts due to diverse geographical locations, and members' ability to work in a collaborative setting.[33] NASA encountered an extreme problem of this type in 1999 when it lost a $125 million space probe as a result of its team members around the world using different units of measurement—the English system versus the metric system.[34]

Navi Radjou, an expert in network innovations, notes, "One problem with distributing work is that you lose the intimacy of talking things through at the local café." To help virtual teams "gel," more companies are beginning to use online collaborative meeting spaces that allow the members of a team to share photos of themselves, their bios, links to the social media sites they frequent, and engage with one another via private chat. Go-To-Meeting and iMeet are examples of online meeting spaces designed to create more intimacy among team members. At Nokia, team members are encouraged to network online and to share their pictures and personal biographies.

Regardless of the structure or purpose of the team, the following characteristics have been identified with successful teams:

- A commitment to shared goals and objectives

- Motivated and energetic team members

- Open and honest communication

- Shared leadership

- Clear role assignments

- A climate of cooperation, collaboration, trust, and accountability

- The recognition of conflict and its positive resolution

Unfortunately, not all teams succeed or operate at their full potential. Power struggles, uncertainty about the roles members should play, a lack of resources, conflicts of interest, and personality differences are common team problems. Another difficulty with work teams is that they alter the traditional manager-employee relationship. Managers sometimes feel threatened by the growing power of the team and the reduced power of management.

Organizations can help prevent some of the problems a team experiences by determining how to compensate the team's members individually and jointly for its achievements and by having the members undergo team training. Complete training for the team would cover the importance of skills in (1) team leadership, (2) mission/goal setting, (3) conduct of meetings, (4) team decision-making, (5) conflict resolution, (6) effective communication, and (7) diversity awareness.[35] In addition, research shows that teams are more effective when they initially establish "ground rules" for how they should operate and their members should behave. HRM Experience, at the end of the chapter, presents an exercise to set team ground rules.

Flexible Work Schedules

Flexible work schedules alter the normal workweek of five eight-hour days in which all employees begin and end their workday at the same time. Flexible work schedules can be implemented by the organization or requested by individual employees. (See Highlights in HRM 4 for how to go about requesting a flexible work schedule from your employer.) Employers sometimes depart from the traditional workday or workweek to improve their productivity and the morale of their employees by giving them more control over the hours they work.[36] As we explained earlier in the book, flexible work schedules can be used to attract and retain employees when a company is facing tough times or is unable to offer the benefits or pay a competitor would. In one survey, 42 percent of employers who were unable to provide raises to their employees said they were willing to offer them flexible hours instead.[37] The more common flexible work schedules are the compressed workweek, flextime, job sharing, and telecommuting.

The major disadvantage of the compressed workweek involves federal laws regarding overtime. The Fair Labor Standards Act has stringent rules requiring the payment of overtime to nonsupervisory employees who work more than forty hours a week. (See Chapter 9.) Another disadvantage of the compressed workweek is that it can increase the stress managers and employees experience because long workdays can be exhausting.

Flextime

Flextime, or flexible working hours, give employees the option of choosing daily starting and quitting times, provided they work a certain number of hours per day or week. With flextime, employees are given considerable latitude in scheduling their work. However, there is a "core period" during the morning and afternoon when *all* employees are required to be on the job. Flexible working hours are most common in service-type organizations—financial institutions, government agencies, and other organizations with large clerical operations. Sentry Insurance's Scottsdale, Arizona, office has found that flextime provides many advantages for employees working in claims, underwriting, and HR areas. At Sentry Insurance, employees work a core period from 9 A.M. to 3 P.M. Flexible start times range from 6 A.M. to 9 A.M. and end times from 3 P.M. to 7 P.M.

LEARNING OUTCOME 7

Name some of the jobs people do at your school. Which of the jobs do you think could effectively incorporate flexible work schedules? Which could not?

flextime

Flexible working hours that permit employees the option of choosing daily starting and quitting times, provided that they work a set number of hours per day or week

Small Business Application

Building Teams in the Small Business Environment

Specialization and employees solely dedicated to well-defined tasks may work well in large corporations, but small businesses can't really afford that luxury. In an entrepreneurial business setting, the few employees typically wear multiple hats. They need to understand what their coworkers do and how they do it so that the business can always continue to function, regardless of circumstances. That's why a team environment—where a small number of employees are cross-trained to perform a variety of roles—is an ideal strategy for the small business owner.

Debra Bolin, business development manager for HR Connects in Evansville, Indiana, describes how a team environment has benefitted her company of two: "We are a small company that is a full-service HR company, so it's important we understand teamwork. We have to be able to work well together and to exchange ideas collectively. Otherwise, we can wind up with two people doing the same job over and over."

In some ways, establishing a team environment within a small business may be easier because it's so obvious how individuals are contributing to the whole—a key component of success in team building. Adds human resources and management development consultant Susan M. Heathfield, "Fostering teamwork is creating a work culture that values collaboration. In a teamwork environment, people understand and believe that thinking, planning, decisions, and actions are better when done cooperatively." To nurture this kind of environment, Heathfield recommends holding regular discussions about collaboration and its purpose, recognizing and rewarding teamwork both publicly and privately, and finding ways to build some fun into team activities in addition to doing the hard work.

Of course, a successful team starts with an effective leader. Some teams have a single leader while others are structured so that members take turns leading. In either case, however, all team leaders need to have the right skills for the job. Business strategist Rick Johnson says that team managers need to know how to communicate expectations clearly, how to avoid micromanaging, and how to build confidence in team members, which empowers them to perform well. This means team leaders will need to learn how to act as facilitators. "Coaching is a skill set that should be required training for all managers to improve team management," adds Johnson.

Craig Wagganer, a speaker and trainer who specializes in team building, has developed an easy-to-remember method for effectively leading teams, which he calls the CARE method. He suggests that team leaders:

- Consider each team member's strengths, goals, and relationship to the team. A good leader will not only capitalize on what the team member has to offer, the leader will help the member realize his or her potential.
- Appreciate each team member's gifts and contributions, and express that appreciation often.
- Respect differences among team members so that conflicts can be resolved fairly and impersonally and mistakes can be handled with grace, not blame.
- Encourage team members, individually and as a group, in their efforts.

Wagganer goes on to describe the ripple effect of a healthy team environment under expert leadership: "When the heart of each team member is encouraged first by the team leader, then the team will be poised to cheer on each other. It starts at the top. And when a person feels encouraged, their outlook changes and becomes one of enthusiasm for the cause and excitement for the team making a positive difference and being successful in its endeavors." That kind of optimism goes a long way in the small business environment.

Sources: Chuck Stinnett, *Evansville Courier Press*, February 26, 2011, http://www.courierpress.com; Rick Johnson, "The Six Principles of Effective Team Management," www.teambuildingtips.com; Susan M. Heathfield, "How to Build a Teamwork Culture," http://humanresources.about.com; Craig Wagganer, "Team Building Starts with Team Member Building," www.leadershipinstitute.com.

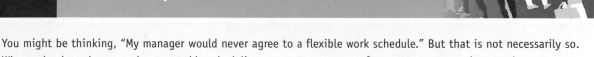

HIGHLIGHTS IN HRM
How to Request a Flexible Work Schedule

You might be thinking, "My manager would never agree to a flexible work schedule." But that is not necessarily so. When valued employees make reasonable scheduling requests, managers often try to accommodate employee proposals. Here are some proven strategies for securing different types of flexible work hour arrangements.

- *Investigate.* Look into similar arrangements others have made within your company or industry. Research your company's policy on flexible schedules. Be realistic by providing a schedule that will fit the demands of your organization.
- *Be Professional.* Treat your request as a business proposal. Be positive and assume a "can-do" attitude. Be serious and present the proposal as a benefit to both you and your company. Present your idea as a "win-win" arrangement.
- *Write It Out.* Submit your request for a flexible work hour arrangement in a well-organized, detailed written proposal.
- *Promote Yourself.* Explain your value to your organization. Have others speak to your abilities—especially those in authority. Ask to be evaluated based on your quantity and quality of work rather than on the hours you actually spend on the job.
- *Anticipate Questions.* Be prepared for potential problems and have specific answers on how to deal with these issues. For example, how you will communicate or coordinate with other employees.
- *Propose a Review.* Propose review dates to evaluate your new flexible schedule. Continually assess how you work with others and your manager.

Source: Adapted from Julie Shields, "Showing How to Flex It," *Incentive* 178, no. 3 (March 2004): 47.

Flextime provides both employees and employers with several advantages. By allowing employees greater flexibility in work scheduling, employers can reduce some of the traditional causes of tardiness and absenteeism.[38] Employees can adjust their work to accommodate their particular lifestyles and, in doing so, gain greater job satisfaction. Employees can also schedule their working hours for the time of day when they are most productive. In addition, variations in arrival and departure times can help reduce traffic congestion at the peak commuting hours, so employees spend less time on the road.

Besides being a good employee recruiting tool, flextime allows organizations that want to improve their service to customers or clients to extend their operating hours. Qwest, a telecommunications company, uses flextime to keep its business offices open for customers who cannot get there during the day. Research demonstrates that flextime can have a positive impact on the performance measures of reliability, quality, and quantity of employee work.

There are, of course, several disadvantages to flextime. First, it is not suited to some jobs. It is not feasible, for example, when specific workstations must be staffed at all times. Second, it can create problems for managers in communicating with and instructing employees. There can be drawbacks for employees too. In some organizations in which executives are expected to show up at the office early in the morning

Flextime is a popular policy among workers because it gives them greater control over how they spend their time on and off the job.

Flashon Studio, 2010/Used under license from Shutterstock.com

and not leave until after the sun has set, employees who work flexible schedules might have a harder time advancing to top positions.

Compressed Workweek

Under the compressed workweek, the number of days in the workweek is shortened by lengthening the number of hours worked per day. This schedule is best illustrated by the four-day, forty-hour week, generally referred to as 4/10 or 4/40. Employees working a four-day workweek might work ten hours a day, Monday through Thursday. Although the 4/10 schedule is probably the best known, other compressed arrangements include reducing weekly hours to thirty-eight or thirty-six hours or scheduling eighty hours over nine days (9/80), taking one day off every other week.

Several examples illustrate this popular work arrangement. At AVT, a software company in Tucson, Arizona, all general workers work four ten-hour days, with workers choosing the day they would like off. The organization's information technology employees, working swing and midnight shifts, work four nine-hour days. Working one less hour is comparable to offering a pay differential. In comparison, employees at Nahan Printing, in St. Cloud, Minnesota, work three twelve-hour shifts, while employees at the publishing company Marcel Dekker in New York City are employed on a Monday-through-Thursday office schedule with employees working a total of thirty-eight hours. At Marcel Dekker, employees are given the option of starting their workdays between 7:30 A.M. and 9:30 A.M.

Managers cite the following reasons for implementing compressed workweek schedules:

- Recruitment and retention of employees[39]

- Coordinating employee work schedules with production schedules

- Accommodating the leisure time activities of employees while facilitating employee personal appointments—medical, dental, financial

- Improvements in employee job satisfaction and morale[40]

Job Sharing

The arrangement whereby two part-time employees perform a job that otherwise would be held by one full-time employee is called *job sharing*. Job sharers usually work three days a week, "creating an overlap day for extended face-to-face conferencing." Their pay is three-fifths of a regular salary. Employers note that without job sharing two good employees might otherwise be lost. Notable companies with job sharing programs include Sprint, American Express, Lotus Development Company, Carter Howley Hale Stores, and Kaiser Permanente, one of the nation's largest health maintenance organizations.

Job sharing is suited to the needs of families in which one or both spouses desire to work only part-time.[41] It is suited also to the needs of older workers who want to phase into retirement by shortening their workweek. For the employer, the work of part-time employees can be scheduled to conform to peaks in the daily workload. Job sharing can also limit layoffs in hard economic times. A final benefit is that employees engaged in job sharing have time off during the week to accommodate personal needs, so they are less likely to be absent.

Job sharing does have several problems, however. Employers may not want to employ two people to do the work of one because the time required to orient and train a second employee constitutes an added burden. Additionally, managers may find it more difficult to supervise two employees, particularly when one job sharer is not dependable, job sharers cannot effectively work together, or they simply distrust one another.[42] The key to making job sharing work is good communications between partners, who can use a number of ways to stay in contact—phone calls, written updates, e-mail, and voice mail.

Telecommuting

Globalization and technology are drastically changing the "Future of Work," that is, how we do our jobs and the offices we do them in. Telecommuting is the use of smart phones, personal computers, and other communications technology to do work traditionally done in the workplace.[43] Telecommuting is increasing in the United States. Many people work at home on some days and in the office on other days. The practice is fairly common in California, where commute times are long. A survey by the Hudson Group, a global consulting firm, found that most workers believe that telecommuting at least some of the time is the ideal work situation.

Both managers and HR professionals note the following advantages of telecommuting.[44]

telecommuting
Use of personal computers, networks, and other communications technology such as fax machines to do work in the home that is traditionally done in the workplace

- Increased flexibility for employees—a better work/life balance

- Reduced absenteeism

- Retention of valued employees who might otherwise quit

- Reduced "carbon footprints" through minimizing daily commuting

- Increased productivity, i.e., reduced wasted office time

- Lower overhead costs and reduced office space

Telecommuting might also reduce stress. According to a research study conducted by the University of Wisconsin-Milwaukee, employees who telecommute for most of the week were more satisfied with their jobs because they experienced fewer interruptions and less office politics.[45]

FIGURE 4.7   Keys for Successful Telecommuting

- *Identify the jobs best suited to telecommuting.* Those involving sales, customer service, and auditing are logical choices.

- *Select responsible employees.* Employees who are self-starters, motivated, and trustworthy and who can work independently are ideal candidates. Establish employee feedback procedures and performance review methods for evaluating employees.

- *Establish formalized telecommuting guidelines.* The guidelines could cover hours of availability, office reporting periods, performance expectations, and weekly progress reports or e-mail updates.

- *Begin a formal training program.* The training for both telecommuters and managers should include any technical aspects of the equipment or software used to facilitate telecommuting and relationship factors such as how and when to contact the office or the availability and location of support facilities.

- *Keep telecommuters informed.* Physical separation can make telecommuters feel isolated and invisible. Department and staff updates, including telecommuters on project teams, requiring their attendance at meetings, and "chat room" discussions can keep telecommuters "in the loop."

- *Recognize when telecommuting is not working.* State in telecommunicating policies that the arrangement can be terminated when it no longer serves the company' needs or if the employee's performance declines.

Source: Adapted from Barbara Hemphill, "Telecommuting Productivity," *Occupational Health and Safety* 73, no. 3 (March 2004): 16.

There are potential drawbacks related to telecommuting, however. Some employees lack the self-discipline to work alone at home. In addition, collaboration and communication within an organization can suffer because employees are not interacting face to face with one another on a regular basis.[46] Traditional line managers accustomed to managing by observation may find supervising distributed employees stressful.

Employers wishing to have their employees telecommute must comply with wage and hour laws, liability and workers' compensation regulations, equipment purchase or rental agreements with employees, and all federal EEO regulations (see Chapter 3). Employees who are denied the opportunity to work from home may feel discriminated against and resent telecommuters. Figure 4.7 presents suggestions for establishing a successful telecommuting program.

Summary

LEARNING OUTCOME 1 A job analysis is the systematic process of collecting information about all of the parameters of a job—its basic responsibilities, the behaviors, skills, and the physical and mental requirements of the people who do it. A job analysis should also outline the tools needed to do the job, the environment and times at which it needs to done, with whom it needs to be done, and the outcome or performance level it should produce. The information a job analysis collects serves many HRM functions, including a firm's workflow and design of jobs, its legal compliance efforts, and the recruitment, selection, training and development, performance appraisal, and compensation of employees. To comply with the law, human resources decisions must be based on criteria objectively collected by analyzing the requirements of each job.

LEARNING OUTCOME 2 Job analysis data can be gathered in several ways—via interviews, questionnaires, observations, and diaries. Other more quantitative approaches include the U.S. Department of Labor's job analysis system, the Position Analysis Questionnaire system, the critical incident method, a task inventory analysis, and a competency-based analysis.

LEARNING OUTCOME 3 The format of job descriptions varies widely, often reflecting the needs of the organization and the expertise of the writer. At a minimum, job descriptions should contain a job title, a job identification section, and an essential functions section. A job specification section might also be included. Job descriptions should be written in clear and specific terms with consideration given to their legal implications.

LEARNING OUTCOME 4 Job design, which is an outgrowth of job analysis, focuses on restructuring jobs in order to capture the talents of employees, improve their work satisfaction, and an organization's performance. Four basic factors need to be taken into account when a job is designed: the organization's objectives; industrial engineering concerns of analyzing work methods and establishing time standards; ergonomic considerations; and behavioral aspects such as the motivation of employees.

LEARNING OUTCOME 5 In the job characteristics model, five job factors affect employees' satisfaction: job skill variety, task identity, task significance, autonomy, and feedback. All factors should be built into jobs, since each factor affects the psychological state of employees. Job enlargement, job enrichment, job rotation, employee empowerment, and job crafting are techniques that have been developed to address the motivation of employees.

LEARNING OUTCOME 6 Increasingly, firms are using employee teams to solve unique and complex problems, enhance the collaboration among workers, improve their morale and performance, and make the most of a firm's scarce resources. An employee team is a group of individuals working together toward a common purpose, in which members have complementary skills, members' work is mutually dependent, and the group has discretion over the tasks it performs. The types of teams commonly used are cross-functional teams, project teams, self-directed teams, task-force teams, process-improvement teams, and virtual teams.

LEARNING OUTCOME 7 Flexible work schedules can be implemented by the organization or requested by individual employees. Employers sometimes depart from the traditional workday or workweek to improve their productivity and the morale of their employees by giving them more control over the hours they work. Compressed workweeks, flextime, job sharing, and telecommuting allow employees to adjust their work periods to accommodate their particular lifestyles.

Key Terms

critical incident method
dejobbing
employee empowerment
employee teams
ergonomics
flextime
industrial engineering
job

job analysis
job characteristics model
job crafting
job description
job design
job enlargement
job enrichment
job rotation

job specification
position analysis questionnaire
 (PAQ)
task inventory analysis
telecommuting
virtual team

Discussion Questions 💬

LEARNING OUTCOME 1 Place yourself in the position of general manager of a service department. How might formally written job requirements help you manage your work unit?

LEARNING OUTCOME 2 Discuss the various methods by which job analysis can be completed. Compare and contrast these methods, noting the pros or cons of each.

LEARNING OUTCOME 3 Working with a group of three or four students, collect at least five different job descriptions from organizations in your area. Compare the descriptions, highlighting similarities and differences.

LEARNING OUTCOME 4 Why is accounting for employee motivation such an important aspects of designing today's jobs?

LEARNING OUTCOME 5 The job characteristics model has five components that enhance employee jobs—skill variety, task identity, task significance, autonomy, and feedback. Give an example illustrating how each component can be used to improve the organization and the job of the employee. (Suggestion: Consider your present or a recent job to answer this question.)

LEARNING OUTCOME 6 Figure 4.6 shows the different forms of employee teams. Provide an example of where each type of team can be used. How do teams create synergy?

LEARNING OUTCOME 7 As a small business employer, explain how nontraditional work schedules might make it easier for you to recruit employees.

On the Job: Video Cases 🎞

Analyzing the Workflow and Jobs at Zappos.com

Zappos executives discuss the focus of the company on customer service and the need for employees to internalize this corporate culture and reflect it in their work behaviors. The stress on employee input into solving problems and making suggestions is emphasized. The necessity for shift work to cover the twenty-four-hour customer service aspects of an Internet business is covered.

What to Watch for and Ask Yourself

- The 24-hour nature of the Zappos Internet business and Zappos' commitment to rapid customer service requires that the call center and warehouse be staffed twenty-four hours a day, seven days a week. If you were the HR director at Zappos, what issues would you expect to encounter because of this twenty-four-hour schedule?

- What argument might Zappos executives make for not allowing the company's call center employees to work from home? After all, this would be technologically feasible, and Zappos makes use of technological potential.

- In the video you can see that Zappos has a diverse workforce. What would be the specific issues that would be part of the business case for diversity at Zappos?

HRM EXPERIENCE
Establishing Ground Rules for a Team's Success

Professional trainers understand that setting ground rules for teams helps them operate successfully. Ground rules—or team norms—are agreed-on formal rules that guide the behavior of a group's member. Ground rules simply state how members want to be treated and how members agree to treat others. Ground rules help teams maintain order, promote positive behavior, and can be used to correct undesirable actions.

Assignment

1. Divide your class into teams. Working within your team, select what you believe are the ten most important norms for team behavior.
2. From the following Behavior List, have each team member *silently* select two lists of ten items each of the behaviors they believe most critical for a team success. The first list of ten items (your A list) is considered the most important for group conduct. The second list (the B list) consists of behaviors that are desirable.
3. Have the members of your team select a final list of ten items from both lists. These will become your team's final norms. During your discussion, items can be modified or combined to meet your team's specific needs.

Behavior List

While working in our team, individuals should:

1. Do their fair share of the work.
2. Check to ensure that everyone clearly understands what is to be done.
3. Encourage planning, including short-range agendas as well as long-range goals.
4. Encourage open and candid opinions about issues.
5. Listen willingly and carefully to other people's ideas, even if those people have a different viewpoint.
6. Prepare thoroughly before meetings.
7. Make team members feel at ease during discussions.
8. Encourage members to ask questions when they do not clearly understand tasks or procedures.
9. Outline the pros and cons of decisions faced by the team.
10. Follow through on task assignments.
11. Help other members when they need assistance.
12. Treat all team members as equals.
13. Paraphrase or restate what someone else says in order to check its meaning.
14. Openly voice opinions and share ideas.
15. Be flexible in arranging meeting schedules.
16. Compliment others for things they have said or done.
17. Be willing to meet whenever it is necessary to discuss a problem.
18. Bring conflicts to the attention of the team and deal with them directly.
19. Express enthusiasm about what the team is doing.
20. Encourage budgeting of the team's time.
21. At the end of a meeting, have members restate their own responsibilities to check for agreement.
22. Be serious about the team's work.
23. Arrive on time for regularly scheduled meetings.
24. Be willing to listen to other team members' ideas.
25. Get the team's approval on important matters before proceeding.

Case Study **1**

Companies Learning to Be Flexible

After Bangalore-based Chitra Iyengar decided to adopt a child, she became serious about a adopting a flexible work schedule after an encounter with her manager at IBM India who said: "I do not care whether you sit in the park or at home. I am concerned with your deliverables." For Iyengar, it was eye-opening to realize that work did not mean a place she went to, but something that she did.

In recent years, many firms like IBM India have taken to offering a flexible work schedule alternative to many of their employees, a benefit that offers positive outcomes to employees and employers alike. Flex-time allows workers to choose their own start and end times, as long as they put in the required number of hours following any limits placed by the employer. Susan M. Heathfield, a human resources and management development consultant, writes that flex-time enables employees to achieve a better work-life balance and to work when they're at their optimal best, which reduces stress and burnout. For employers, flex-time typically reduces absenteeism and turnover, and helps employers attract the best candidates for job openings.

Of course, individual managers may struggle with the logistics of flex-time, which is why Dawn Rosenberg McKay, a career planning expert, says that managers and employees must work together to devise a realistic plan that balances the company's objectives with individuals' needs. Done well, flex-time can ensure that all employees are available at peak times and that the office is manned during all operating hours and days of the week. Thus, it is probably useful to document the details of a flex-time program and to evaluate how well the program is working from time to time.

For Iyengar, a career-oriented person who loves to work, it took a lot of effort initially to adjust to the program, but now she is quite happy with the benefits, noting, "Flexi-work is a definite enabler in my life."

Questions

1. What are the pros and cons of flexible schedules from an employee's perspective?
2. What considerations should an employer take into account when designing a flex-time work schedule?
3. What can HR managers do to help facilitate flexible work schedules in their organizations?

Source: Saumya Bhattacharya, "Look Ma, No Clock," *Business Today*, (February 24, 2011), http://businesstoday.in; Susan M. Heathfield, Advantages and Disadvantages of Flexible Work Schedules, http://humanresources.about.com; Dawn Rosenberg McKay, "Flextime: An Alternative Work Arrangement," http://careerplanning.about.com.

Case Study **2**

Virtual Teams in Action: Building the F-35 Fighter

The F-35 Lighting II Program, also known as the Joint Fighter Program, is the U.S. Department of Defense's next generation stealth fighter aircraft. The Department of Defense named Lockheed Martin Aeronautics of Fort Worth, Texas, to design and build the fighter with Northrop Grumman and BAE Systems as major partners.

Countries, including Italy, Australia, Canada, Turkey, India, and Israel, have contributed toward development costs of the program.

The success of the mega project hinges greatly on intricate teamwork and the cooperation of countless individuals. For example, more than 80 suppliers worked at 187 locations worldwide to build components for the fighter. A seventy-five member technology group at Lockheed's aeronautics division linked the suppliers along with the U.S. Air Force, Navy, and Marines to Britain's Defense Ministry to track progress and make midstream design and production changes. Individuals working at more than 40,000 computer stations collaborated to get the first plane airborne in just four years. Speaking of the teamwork involved, Mark Peden, vice president for information systems at Lockheed Aeronautics, said, "It's the true virtual connection."

Teams working both nationally and internationally were connected as if team members were working in the same room. Teams communicated via their computers while looking at shared documents, carried on e-mail chats, and used electronic whiteboards on which geographically separated team members could draw pictures or charts, in real time, as others watched and responded. The Internet was designed to allow people from different companies with incompatible computing systems to interface on websites that speak a common language.

Questions

1. What advantages did Lockheed Martin gain by using virtual teams? Explain.
2. Identify and discuss potential problems with using virtual teams—for example, interpersonal, technical, or geographical concerns.
3. Discuss the characteristics that virtual team members should possess.
4. What specific training should virtual teams receive?

Notes and References

1. Arnold B. Bakker, Evangelia Demeroob, and Willem Verbeke, "Using the Job Demands Resources Model to Predict Burnout and Performance," *Human Resources Management* 43, no. 1 (Spring 2004): 83.

2. "Job Description: HR Glossary," *Times Ascent HR Hub*, accessed March 1, 2011, http://timesascent.in.

3. Rehman Safdar, Ajmal Waheed, and Khattak Hamid Rafiq, "Impact of Job Analysis on Job Performance: Analysis of A Hypothesized Model," *Journal of Diversity Management*, 5 no. 2 (Summer 2010): 17–36.

4. Adapted from job description for "Senior HR Analyst," City of Mesa, Arizona.

5. Steve Tobak, "Ten Ways to Think Different: Inside Apple's Cult-Like Culture," *BNET*, (March 2, 2011), http://www.bnet.com.

6. Fredenick P. Morgeson, Kelly Delaney-Klinger, Melinda S. Mayfield, Philip Ferrara, and Michael A. Campion, "Self-Presentation Processes in Job Analysis: A Field Experiment Investigating Inflation in Abilities, Tasks, and Competencies," *Journal of Applied Psychology* 89, no. 4 (August 2004): 674.

7. Interview with job analyst Carol Tucker, Mesa, Arizona, (May 10, 2006).

8. Angela R. Connell, and Satris S. Culbertons, "Eye of the Beholder: Does What Is Important About a Job Depend on Who Is Asked?" *Academy of Management Perspectives*, 24, no. 2 (May 2010): 83.

9. A detailed description of different job analysis techniques is beyond the scope of this text. For those interested in more comprehensive information or job analysis tools, see Michael T. Bannick, Edward L. Levine, and Frederick P. Morgeson, *Job and Work Analysis: Methods, Research, and Applications for Human Resource Management*, 2nd ed. (Thousand Oaks, CA: Sage, 2007).

10. V. S. Rama Rao, "Quantitative Job Analysis Techniques," *The Cite Man Network*, accessed March 4, 2011, http://www.citeman.com.

11. Piers Steel and John Kammeyer-Mueller, "Using a Meta-Analytic Perspective to Enhance Job Component Validation," *Personnel Psychology*, 62 no. 3 (2009): 533.

12. Jessica Marquez, "A Talent Strategy Overhaul at Pfizer," *Workforce Management* 86, no. 3 (February 12, 2007): 1.

13. Eric Klas, et al. "From Task-Based to Competency-Based," *Personnel Review*, 39, no. 3 (2010): 325–346, DOI: 10.1108/0048348101103052.

14. Chapter 3 discusses the *Uniform Guidelines on Employee Section Procedures* and the necessity for performance standards to be based on valid job-related criteria.

15. Gensheng Liu, Rachna Shah, and Roger G. Schroeder, "Linking Work Design to Mass

Customization: A Socio-technical Systems Perspective," *Decision Sciences* 37, no. 4 (November 2006): 519; Nicolai J. Foss, Dana B. Minbaeva, Torben Pedersen, and Mia Reinholt, "Encouraging Knowledge Sharing Among Employees: How Job Design Matters," *Human Resource Management*, 48, no. 5 (2009): 871.

16. Pooja Garg and Renu Rastogi, "New Models of Job Design: Motivating Employees' Performance," *The Journal of Management Development* 25, no. 6 (2006): 572.

17. Narasimhaiah Gorla, Ravi Chinta, and Tam Wai Chu, "An Enhanced Business Process Re-engineering Model for Supply Chain Management and a Case Study," *Journal of Information Technology Case and Application Research* 9, no. 2 (2007): 5.

18. For the original article on the job characteristics model, see J. Richard Hackman and Greg R. Oldham, "Motivation through the Design of Work: Test of a Theory," *Organizational Behavior and Human Performance* 16, no. 2 (August 1976): 250–79.

19. Jed DeVaro, Robert Li, and Dana Brookshire, "Analyzing the Job Characteristics Model: New Support from a Cross-Section of Establishments," *The International Journal of Human Resource Management* 18, no. 6 (June 2007): 986.

20. O.C. Ferrell, Geoffrey Hirt, and Linda Ferrell, *Introduction to Business* (Burr Ridge, Ill: McGraw-Hill, 2008): 309.

21. For Herzberg's important article on job enrichment, see Frederick Herzberg, "One More Time: How Do You Motivate Employees?" *Harvard Business Review* 46, no. 2 (January-February 1968): 53–62.

22. Peter Coy, "COG or Co-worker?; The Organization Man Isn't Extinct or Even Endangered—but the Role Has Been Refined Over the Past 100 Years," *Business Week*, Issue 4047 (August 2007): 58.

23. Michael Hammer, "The Process Audit," *Harvard Business Review* 85, no. 4 (April 2007): 111.

24. Richard E. Wilmot and Robert Galford, "A Commitment to Trust," *Communication World* 24, no. 2 (March/April 2007): 34.

25. Nick Tasler, Help Your Employees Do a Better Job," *BusinessWeek*, March 26, 2010, http://www.businessweek.com/.

26. Feza Tabassum Azmi, "Job Descriptions to Job Fluidity: Treading the Dejobbing Path," *EBS Review* no. 23 (2007): 8.

27. Brian Hindo, "The Empire Strikes at Silos," *Business Week*, (August 20, 2007), 63.

28. Vojko Potocan and Bostjan Kuralt, "Synergy in Business: Some New Suggestions," *Journal of American Academy of Business* 12, no. 1 (September 2007): 199.

29. Leigh Thompson, "Improving the Creativity of Organizational Work Groups," *The Academy of Management Executive* 17, no. 1 (February 2003): 96.

30. Michael Mandel, "Which Way to the Future," *Business Week* (August 20, 2007), 45.

31. O.C. Ferrell, Geoffrey Hirt, and Linda Ferrell, *Introduction to Business* (Burr Ridge, Ill: McGraw-Hill, 2008): 310.

32. Laura A. Hambley, Thomas A. O'Neil, and Theresa J. B. Klien, "Virtual Team Leadership: The Effects of Leadership Style and Communication Medium on Team Interaction Styles and Outcomes," *Organizational Behavior and Human Decision Processes* 103, no. 1 (May 2007): 1.

33. Interview with Paulette Tichenor, Arizona State University, Tempe, Arizona, (January 18, 2007).

34. Jay F. Nunamaker Jr., Bruce A. Reinig, and Robert O. Briggs, "Principles for Effective Virtual Teamwork," *Communications of the ACM* 52, no. 4 (2009): 113.

35. Stephen B. Knouse, "Building Task Cohesion to Bring Teams Together," *Quality Progress* 40, no. 3 (March 2007): 49.

36. Michelle Conlin, "Smashing the Clock," *Business Week* (December 11, 2006): 60. See also Susan Meisinger, "Flexible Schedules Make Powerful Perks," *HR Magazine* 52, no. 4 (April 2007): 12.

37. "Employers Willing to Negotiate Salary," *OfficePro* 7, no.1 (2011): 4.

38. Rita Zeidner, "Bending with the Times," *HR Magazine* 53, no. 7 (July 2008): 10.

39. Kathy Gurchiek, "Good News for Moms Reconsidering Work," *HR Magazine* 51, no. 7 (August 2006): 39.

40. James A. Breaugh and N. Kathleen Frye, "An Examination of the Antecedents and Consequences of the Use of Family-friendly Benefits," *Journal of Management Issues* 19, no. 1 (Spring 2007): 35.

41. "Have You Considered Job Sharing as a Retention Tool?" *HR Focus* 83, no. 9 (September 2006): 10.

42. Susan Berfield, "Two for the Cubicle," *Business Week*, (July 24, 2006): 88.

43. Mandel, 45.

44. http://www.wikipedip.org/wiki/telecommuting.

45. Tony Bradley, "Another Good Reason to Work from Home," *Globe and Mail* (February 11, 2011), http://www.theglobeandmail.com.

46. Wendell Joice, "Implementing Telework: The Technology Issue," *Public Manager* 36, no. 2 (Summer 2007): 64.

5

Expanding the Talent Pool: Recruitment and Careers

After studying this chapter, you should be able to

LEARNING OUTCOME 1 Describe how a firm's strategy affects its recruiting efforts.

LEARNING OUTCOME 2 Outline the methods by which firms recruit internally.

LEARNING OUTCOME 3 Outline the methods by which firms recruit externally.

LEARNING OUTCOME 4 Explain the techniques organizations can use to improve their recruiting efforts.

LEARNING OUTCOME 5 Explain how career management programs integrate the needs of individual employees and their organizations.

LEARNING OUTCOME 6 Explain why diverse recruitment and career development activities are important to companies.

In the past, recruiting was often a reactive process firms engaged in periodically when a position needed to be filled. Today, however, more companies see the recruiting function as a strategic imperative and, therefore, an ongoing process. Instead of waiting for a job opening, HR managers are studying their firms' strategies in conjunction with their organizational charts, job analysis information, and external factors such as the labor market and the competition, and then recruiting proactively and continually. The greater competition for talent means that recruiting has become more important for managers. Recruiting not only involves looking for talented pools of employees, but making an effort to figure out what they want and establishing the firm as an employer of choice so people will want to work for it.

The Container Store, which regularly tops Fortune's "100 Best Companies to Work For," is a good example of a company that makes recruiting an ongoing process. Individual managers spend two to three hours a week on recruiting activities to locate good candidates, regardless of whether there are job openings at their stores or not. Employees are also encouraged to focus their efforts on recruiting. "Basically we have mini human resources departments in each of our stores. We challenge each of our 4,000 employees to be recruiters and refer us to great people," says the Container Store's Director of Recruiting Karyn Maynard.[1]

In this chapter, we will discuss the many strategies and techniques organizations use both internally and externally to recruit the talent they need. For example, to find ways to reach out to and recruit the right kinds of candidates, some companies develop employee profiles by surveying their top performers about what they like to do, what events they attend, and how they like to be contacted and recruited. They then pursue candidates using this information. We will also discuss the approaches that organizations take toward career management over time. This is important because, unlike physical assets, human assets (employees) can decide to leave the firm of their own accord. The Internet has helped make workers better informed about opportunities and allowed them to telecommute or work off-site. As a result, rival firms are in a better position to lure good employees away. Finally, at the end of the chapter, we devote special attention to the recruitment and career development of minorities and women.

employee profile
A profile of a worker developed by studying an organization's top performers in order to recruit similar types of people

Strategic Aspects of Recruiting

LEARNING OUTCOME 1

This section describes some of the major factors that can affect a firm's recruiting. What other factors might play a role? Hint: Refer to Chapter 1.

Decisions about talent—regardless of whether they pertain to recruiting, transferring, promoting, developing, or deploying people—need to be considered within the context of a business's strategies and priorities. Consider the decision to outsource and offshore work: Most American clothing makers have outsourced or offshored work because labor costs are cheaper outside the United States. (Nearly all of the clothing purchased in the United States today is imported. Just check your clothing labels.) But that's not the strategy Round House Workwear, based in Oklahoma, and All American Clothing, based in Ohio, have pursued. These companies have managed to carve out a niche by selling products with the "Made in America" label to foreigners who see that label as a sign of prestige and Americans who do not want to buy foreign products. The point of this story is that recruiters always have to consider the firm's strategy.

The broad factors that can affect a firm's recruiting strategy include a firm's recruiting abilities, whether to recruit externally versus internally, the labor market for the types of positions it is recruiting for, including global labor markets, and the strength of a firm's employment "brand." We will talk about each of these factors next. Note that at any given time a firm might need to use multiple recruiting strategies. Moreover, a strategy that works for one firm or one job might not work for another firm (or job). For example, an engineering firm might place a premium on finding highly qualified applicants, whereas an amusement park ramping up for a new season might place a premium on hiring quickly. Recruiting strategies and their effectiveness can change over time as well. As a result, firms need to continuously examine their recruiting efforts and refine them. So, for example, if the engineering firm landed a huge construction contract, being able to hire engineers quickly could become a priority.

Who Should Do the Recruiting?

The size of an organization often affects who performs the recruitment function. Most large firms have full-time, in-house HR recruiters. In smaller organizations, the recruiting might be done by an HR generalist. If the organization has no HR function, managers and/or supervisors recruit their own employees. At companies such as Macy's and Williams-Sonoma, the members of work teams help select new employees for their groups.

Organizations that want to focus on their core functions, including small businesses that lack time or HR personnel, sometimes outsource their recruiting functions to outside firms. This practice is known as recruiting process outsourcing (RPO). Organizations also sometimes use RPO providers when they need to hire a lot of employees or hire employees quickly. RPO providers can also be useful when a firm has had trouble finding suitable candidates in the past or needs a different way to tap different talent pools, perhaps to find more diverse candidates.

recruiting process outsourcing (RPO)
The practice of outsourcing an organization's recruiting function to an outside firm.

Many companies use their own internal intranet websites as well as their public-facing websites and other job posting websites to recruit candidates.

Rido/Shutterstock.com

Regardless of who does the recruiting, it is imperative that these individuals have a good understanding of the knowledge, skills, abilities, experiences, and other characteristics required for the job and be personable, enthusiastic, and competent. Recruiters can often enhance the perceived attractiveness of a job and an organization—or detract from it. They are often a main reason why applicants select one organization over another.

Should a Firm Recruit Internally or Externally?

Most managers try to follow a policy of filling job vacancies above the entry-level position through promotions and transfers. By filling vacancies in this way, an organization can capitalize on the investment it has made in recruiting, selecting, training, and developing its current employees, who might look for jobs elsewhere if they lack promotion opportunities.

Promoting employees rewards them for past performance and encourages them to continue their efforts. It also gives other employees a reason to believe that if they perform similarly, they will be promoted too. This can improve morale within the organization and support a culture of employee engagement. Furthermore, the employee's familiarity with the organization and its operations can eliminate the orientation and training costs that recruitment from the outside would entail. Most important, the transferee's performance record is likely to be a more accurate predictor of the candidate's success than the data gained about outside applicants. Promotion-from-within policies at Marriott, Nordstrom's, Nucor Steel, and Whole Foods have contributed to the companies' overall growth and success.[2]

Managers need to be aware of potential limitations of recruiting internally as well, though. For example, jobs that require specialized training and experience cannot always be easily filled from within the organization and may need to be filled from the outside. This is especially common in small organizations where the existing talent pool is limited. Potential candidates from the outside should also be considered in order to prevent the "inbreeding" of ideas and attitudes. CEOs are often hired externally. Applicants hired from the outside, particularly for certain technical and managerial positions, can be a source of creativity and innovation, and may bring with them the latest knowledge acquired from their previous employers. It is not uncommon for firms to attempt to gain secrets from their competitors by hiring away their employees. Procter & Gamble sued a rival papermaker when it hired former employees who had a great deal of knowledge about the making of Charmin toilet paper and Bounty paper towels—both P&G products. Amazon.com was sued by Walmart, which accused Amazon of hiring away employees who had in-depth knowledge about Walmart's sophisticated inventory systems.[3]

Some applicants bring more than knowledge to their new employers. They bring revenue. Talented salespeople, doctors, accountants, lawyers, and hairdressers are examples. When these people leave their organizations, their clients often go with them. Recruiting externally in this case makes sense. Reaching an employer's diversity goals is another factor that can lead a firm to recruit externally.

Labor Markets

internal labor market

Labor markets in which workers are hired into entry level jobs and higher levels are filled from within

The condition of the labor can have a big effect on a firm's recruiting plans. During periods of high unemployment in the economy, organizations might be able to maintain an adequate supply of qualified applicants from unsolicited résumés and from their internal labor markets. Internal labor markets are those where workers are hired into entry-level jobs and higher levels are filled from within.[4] A tight labor market, one with low unemployment, might force the employer to advertise heavily and/or seek assistance from local employment agencies. Keep in mind that the actual labor market a company faces depends upon the industry in which the firm operates and the types of position it is seeking to fill. In one industry, the supply of qualified individuals might be plentiful for a particular position. Other jobs are chronically hard to fill, such as the jobs for machinists, engineers, and IT professionals.

Regional and Global Labor Markets

Have you ever noticed that competing firms are often located in the same areas? Oil and gas companies are plentiful in the Houston area. Film and television companies are clustered around Los Angeles. This is not a coincidence. The clustering occurs because the resources these firms need—both human and natural—are located in some areas and not others. Many manufacturers have located to the South because lower-cost labor is plentiful there and unions are less prevalent than they are in the north. Likewise, because nearby Stanford University is one of the top computer-science schools in the country, high-tech companies have flocked to Silicon Valley in California.[5] You could open a high-tech firm in Bismarck, North Dakota, but you might have a hard time getting talent to relocate there.

In addition to locating near their talent, to stay apace of their competitors and expand their operations around the world, companies are also looking globally for goods and services, including labor. This practice is referred to as global sourcing. As we explained earlier in the book, companies are no longer simply offshoring work to save labor costs. They are also looking abroad to develop better products around the clock via a global workforce and to attract the best talent wherever it may be. For example, after the fall of the Soviet Union in the 1990s, firms abroad began recruiting talented Soviet scientists who had worked for the government and no longer had jobs. Emerging countries such as China and India are also heating up the competition for talent as firms there attempt to staff the burgeoning high-tech industries in these nations.

It is not just technical positions firms are trying to fill either. It is lower-skilled positions, too. Resorts and vacation areas are among the businesses having trouble finding employees to staff their operations. "There are not enough American teenagers or twenty-somethings to fill those service jobs," says Rebecca Wolever of Signature Worldwide, a company that offers employees customer service and sales training.

Recruiting abroad can be very complicated, however. In addition to having to deal with a myriad of local, national, and international laws, employers also have to take into account the different labor costs, preemployment and compensation practices, and cultural differences associated with the countries in which they are recruiting. In volatile areas of the world, security is a concern.

To help them navigate challenges such as these, many companies utilize firms such as Genpact and Robert Half International, which specialize in global recruiting. These firms help companies address the numerous legal complications associated with obtaining various types of visas and work permits for the foreign workers they are trying to hire. A good starting point for human resources managers looking to hire outside of the United States is *Employees: Handbook on Global Recruiting, Screening, Testing and Interviewing Criteria* by Salvador del Rey and Robert J. Mignin (editors). One chapter is devoted to each of fifty-five nations covered in the reference book and legal guide.

Using the INTERNET

All types of media releases, including weekly unemployment figures and special reports, are available at the Department of Labor's website. Go to

www.cengagebrain.com

global sourcing
The business practice of searching for and utilizing goods sources from around the world.

Branding

branding

A company's efforts to help existing and prospective workers understand why it is a desirable place work

Whomever and wherever a firm is recruiting, it wants to be *the* employer of choice to attract and hire top candidates before its competitors do. Branding can help organizations do this. Branding refers to a company's efforts to help existing and prospective workers understand why it is a desirable place to work.

So how does a company "burnish" its employment brand? One way is to think of applicants as consumers and focus on what they want in terms of jobs and careers as opposed to what an organization has to "sell" them, says Diane Delich, with the Kansas City, Missouri–based recruiting company Executive Pursuits. Delich advises companies to listen to and reach out to applicants just like they do consumers. In fact, some firms make their customers their employers. A high percentage of the people the Container Store recruits are customers who like doing business with the storage-solution company.

Some of the newer ways firms are building their employer brands is by reaching out to people via social networks. Instead of just posting jobs on the Internet, firms are creating Facebook pages to promote the careers they have to offer, striking up conversations with potential applicants on those pages, and giving them a preview of what it is like to work for their firms. Writing blogs and articles for industry publications is another way. (We will talk more about social networks as a recruiting tool later in the chapter.)

Philanthropic activities are another avenue for reaching out to prospective employees, especially Generation Y applicants who are looking for more than just a paycheck and promotions in their careers. For example, to establish relationships with promising young employees, the accounting and consulting firm Deloitte has teamed up with United Way Worldwide and Teach For America Inc. to sponsor alternative spring-break programs for undergraduate students who work alongside employees to help communities in need.

In the global arena, branding can be enormously helpful because locals are often unfamiliar with foreign firms. In India, the firms people work for are very important to applicants and their families. Genpact has set up "storefronts" in major Indian cities to promote the employment brands of its corporate clients. Candidates can walk in and chat with company representatives about what these firms do and the kinds of opportunities they offer.

Firms need to be sure the brand they promote to prospective employees truly reflects their internal cultures, however. Painting a rosier picture of your organization can backfire because it can leave applicants disillusioned after they have been hired. (To help prevent this from occurring, some firms use realistic job previews, which are discussed later in this chapter.) Highlights in HRM 1 shows how the hotel chain Marriott has been able to establish its brand as an employer of choice by actually engaging in good recruiting practices. The brand actually reflects Marriott's culture.

Recruiting Internally

LEARNING OUTCOME 2

Sometimes firms do not post internal openings for which anyone may apply. Instead, they select someone to promote. Why might a firm do this and what drawbacks could result?

It is only natural for a firm to look internally first when it needs talent. Internal candidates are readily available, get up to speed faster, and there is less uncertainty about how they will perform. You also do not have to run advertisements to find them, which can be costly. Next, let's look at the ways internal candidates are commonly identified for job openings.

Internal Job Postings

Internal job postings are a quick way to find qualified employees interested in a position. A small business might simply post a notice on a bulletin board in its

HIGHLIGHTS IN **HRM**
Marriott's Recruitment Principles: Living Up to the Employment Brand

1. **Build the Employment Brand.** Marriott attracts employees the same way it attracts customers. Just as consumers buy experiences, not just products, potential employees are looking for a great work experience when they shop for jobs. Communicating the promise of a great work experience is what employment branding is all about. It is basically a value proposition. According to CEO J. W. Marriott, "For more than 70 years, we've lived by a simple motto: If we take care of our associates, they'll take care of our guests. That isn't just a sentiment. It is a strategy—one all businesses must adopt to remain competitive in an environment where our most valuable resource, human capital, drives economic value for our company."

2. **Get It Right the First Time.** Marriott "hires friendly" and "trains technical." It is better to hire people with "the spirit to serve" and train them to work than hire people who know business and try to teach them to enjoy serving guests. Marriott hires cooks who love to cook and housekeepers who love to clean. They have learned that this approach works both for delivering excellent service and for retaining their employees.

3. **Money Is a Big Thing, But . . .** The top concern of Marriott associates is total compensation. But intangible factors taken together, such as work-life balance, leadership quality, opportunity for advancement, work environment, and training, far outweigh money in their decisions to stay or leave. Pay matters less, and the other factors matter more the longer someone works for Marriott. From flexible schedules to tailored benefit packages and development opportunities, Marriott has built systems to address these nonmonetary factors.

4. **A Caring Workplace Is a Bottom-Line Issue.** When employees come to work, they feel safe, secure, and welcome. Committed associates are less likely to leave, and associate work commitment is one of the key drivers of guest satisfaction. Managers are accountable for associate satisfaction ratings and for turnover rates. Every day, associates in each of Marriott's full-service hotels participate in a fifteen-minute meeting to review basic values such as respect. Managers also encourage associates to raise their personal concerns. They take the time to celebrate birthdays and anniversaries. Marriott calls this the loyalty program because it builds loyalty among associates and repeat business from customers. The result is that everyone has a stake in making the hotel a success.

5. **Promote from Within.** More than 50 percent of Marriott's current managers have been promoted from within. All associates are given the opportunity to advance as far as their abilities will carry them. Elevating veterans to positions of leadership helps Marriott pass on the soul of its business—its corporate culture—from one generation to the next. In addition, promoting from within is a powerful tool for recruitment and retention. Associates cite "opportunity for advancement" as a key factor in their decisions to stay with Marriott. (Accompanying that is a $100-million-a-year commitment to training.)

Source: J. W. Marriott, "Competitive Strength," *Executive Excellence* 18, no. 4 (April 2001): 3–4; J. W. Marriott, "Our Competitive Strength: Human Capital," *Executive Speeches* 15, no. 5 (April/May 2001): 18–21.

break room. Larger companies generally post their openings on their intranet sites. The intranets of some companies alert employees about jobs in which they may be interested. As a position becomes available, a list of employees interested in that position is retrieved, and the records of these employees are reviewed to select possible candidates for interviews. The employees can be electronically notified about interview schedules and track their progress electronically through the various hiring stages.[6]

Identifying Talent through Performance Appraisals

Successful performers are often good candidates for a promotion. Identifying and developing all employees is a role that all managers should take seriously. A tool called a 9-box grid is helping firms such as General Electric, Novartis and others do this. The grid helps managers assess appraisal and assessment data to be compiled into a single visual reference so they can see both an employee's actual performance as well as potential performance. This can then help managers determine what the developmental needs of the employee are and what the person's next steps within the organization might be. Figure 5.1 is an example of a 9-box grid.

Skills Inventories and Replacement Charts

As we discussed in Chapter 2, firms use skills inventories to help track an employee's education, past work experience, vocational interests, specific abilities and skills, compensation history, and job tenure to see how it can best be used. Procter & Gamble and HSBC are among the firms that track their employees this way in order to locate capable employees who can be recruited to fill open positions. Along with skill inventories, replacement charts are an important tool for succession planning. At GE, for every position at or above a director level, two or three people are usually identified who can easily step in when the current jobholder moves on.[7]

As we also discussed in Chapter 2, more firms are electronically capturing the qualifications of each of their employees. Companies such as PeopleSoft and SAP have developing automated staffing and skills management software. These information systems allow an organization to rapidly screen its entire workforce to locate suitable

9-box grid
A comparative diagram that includes appraisal and assessment data to allow managers to easily see an employee's actual and potential performance

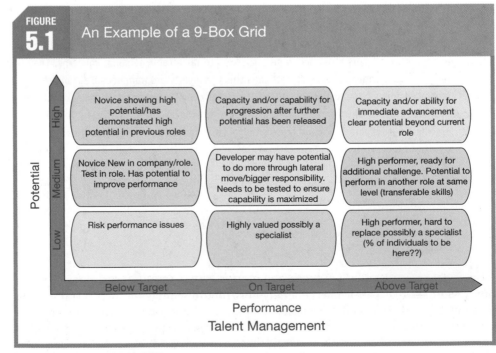

FIGURE 5.1 An Example of a 9-Box Grid

Source: © RapidBI.com 2000–2008

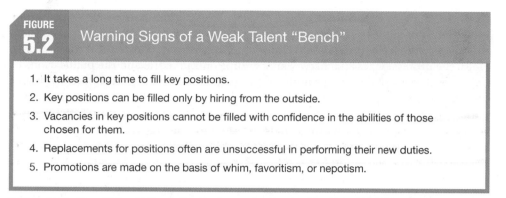

FIGURE 5.2   Warning Signs of a Weak Talent "Bench"

1. It takes a long time to fill key positions.
2. Key positions can be filled only by hiring from the outside.
3. Vacancies in key positions cannot be filled with confidence in the abilities of those chosen for them.
4. Replacements for positions often are unsuccessful in performing their new duties.
5. Promotions are made on the basis of whim, favoritism, or nepotism.

Source: Adapted from William Rothwell, *Effective Succession Planning* (New York: AMACOM, 2000).

candidates to fill an internal opening. The data can also be used to predict the career paths of employees and to anticipate when and where promotion opportunities might arise.[8]

At least one research study has found that managers often hire external candidates rather than promote their current employees because they have a tendency to overvalue unfamiliar candidates and undervalue known ones.[9] This tendency can leave a firm's current employees disillusioned to the point where they begin looking elsewhere for jobs, even when the external candidates hired end up being very qualified for their positions. When experienced employees leave an organization they take with them years of corporate know-how that is hard to replace. Some signs that the firm needs to work harder at grooming internal talent are shown in Figure 5.2. To lessen the chances of losing top performers, some managers actively identify high potential "at risk" employees and take steps to retain these people.

Recruiting Externally

The sources from which employers recruit externally will vary with the type of position to be filled. A computer programmer, for example, is not likely to be recruited from the same source as a machine operator. Trade schools can be a good source of applicants for entry-level positions, though these recruitment sources are not as useful when highly skilled employees are needed. Some firms keep detailed statistics by job type on the sources from which their employees are hired. This helps human resources managers make better decisions about the places to begin recruiting when different job openings arise. We will talk more about recruiting statistics later in the chapter.

Advertisements

Advertising job openings on websites and in newspapers and trade journals is a common way to attract candidates. But help-wanted signs, billboards, and even Craigslist are sometimes used. In countries in which literacy rates are low, radio and television ads can be more effective. Ads and pages on social networking sites, e-mail campaigns, Twitter, and text-messages are new ways recruiters are getting the word out about job openings.

LEARNING OUTCOME 3

If you were a small business owner, how would you go about attracting top external candidates to your firm?

Advertising has the advantage of reaching a large audience of possible applicants. However, some degree of selectivity can be achieved by using newspapers and journals directed toward a particular group of readers. Professional and trade journals, blogs, the professional social networking groups on LinkedIn, and the publications of unions and various fraternal or nonprofit organizations will attract different types of candidates than help wanted signs, for example.

Preparing recruiting advertisements not only is time-consuming, it requires creativity in terms of developing their design and message content. Well-written advertisements highlight the major assets of the position while showing the responsiveness of the organization to the job, career, and lifestyle needs of applicants. Also, there appears to be a correlation between the accuracy and completeness of information provided in job advertisements and an organization's recruitment success. The more information disclosed, the better. Among the information typically included in advertisements is that the recruiting organization is an equal opportunity employer.

However, even when a job opening is described thoroughly in an advertisement, many unqualified applicants will still apply. HR personnel often have to sift through stacks of inquiries and résumés to locate qualified candidates. In fact, for each vacant position, HR staff and managers typically review 20 to 100 résumés. Fortunately, software developers are designing new tools companies can use to prescreen applicants online, digitize their résumés, distribute the data into company databases, and automate the process of candidate referrals from in-house personnel.[10]

Walk-Ins and Unsolicited Applications and Résumés

Walk-in job seekers seeking jobs that pay hourly wages are common in smaller organizations. Employers also receive unsolicited applications and résumés. Walk-in applicants and individuals who send unsolicited résumés to firms may or may not be good prospects for employment. However, it is a source that cannot be ignored. In fact, it is often believed that individuals who contact employers on their own initiative will be better employees than those recruited through college placement services or newspaper advertisements.

Good public relations dictate that any person contacting an organization for a job be treated with courtesy and respect. Not treating applicants with respect will harm a company's employer brand. If there is no present or future possibility of employment in the organization, the applicant should be tactfully and frankly informed. Research has shown that a candidate who has been treated well by a potential employer will, on average, tell one other person. On the other hand, a candidate who has been treated poorly—perhaps receiving a tardy rejection letter or no letter all—will, on average, tell eleven other people.[11]

The Internet, Social Networking, and Mobile Recruiting

Looking on the Internet is the most commonly used search tactic by job seekers and recruiters to get the word out about new positions. Both companies and applicants find the approach cheaper, faster, and potentially more effective. There are tens of thousands of independent job boards on the web. The top three—Monster, Career-Builder, and Yahoo's Hot Jobs—make up about half of the people recruited from independent job boards. Specialty Internet recruiting sites such as AttorneyJobs.com, Medzilla (for the pharmaceutical industry), AMFMJobs.com (for radio personnel), Vets4Hire.com, and 6FigureJobs.com (for executives) are

In some market segments, such as retail stores and restaurants, it is quite common for employers to find excellent prospective employees through walk-in applications.

© Melanie Stetson Freeman/Christian Science Monitor/The Image Works

common too. Recruiters can place ads on these sites, or they search for résumés based on keywords. Monster has a premium service that narrows down applicants, ranks candidates, and compares them side by side. Staffing experts say it is also a good idea to post your firm's jobs at free association and trade group sites, where your specific talent pool is most likely to congregate.[12] Of course, most large companies post job openings on their own corporate websites, usually under a link titled "Careers." Some companies are now posting podcasts that profile the working lives of their different employees.

As we indicated earlier in the chapter, to help establish their employer brands as well as recruit talent, many companies are making use of social networking tools to recruit employees. Recruiters are joining groups on LinkedIn that target certain types of professionals. And, of course, companies are flocking to Facebook, for example, to create free recruiting sites where recruiters post job information, showcase their company's attractive features, offer job advice, and post company news. The organizations then buy advertisements on Facebook directing potential candidates to their sites.

Software developers have created talent search software, which can be customized to search the web for valuable but passive job candidates, based on information they post on industry blogs, social networking sites, and so forth. Passive job seekers are people who are not looking for jobs but could be persuaded to take new ones given the right opportunity. Zoominfo.com is one such tool.

Mobile recruiting has given creative recruiters another new tool to use in the war for talent. Mobile recruiting is the process of recruiting candidates via their mobile devices. It is no secret that people are glued to their mobile phones these days. For this reason, whatever social networking or Internet platform an organization uses should have a mobile application tied to it, recruiting experts advise. On the three-block walk

passive job seekers
People who are not looking for jobs but could be persuaded to take new ones given the right opportunity

between his office and parking spot, Owen Williams, Macy's executive recruiting director, uses a mobile application of LinkedIn and Twitter to post job openings and extend invitations to connect to potential candidates and to keep up with what is happening in his industry. Williams says that mobile recruiting has the advantage of speed, which is important in competitive labor markets and when a firm needs to recruit talent fast. "You never know how long a great candidate will be on the market, so you have to capitalize on the moment," says Williams.[13]

Text messages are also being used to send prospective employees information about jobs. Some surveys show it is the most popular type of e-recruiting, perhaps because people know how to use it the best. Text messages work well because they are inexpensive, easy to send, fast, and work with any cell phone. Plus, because most people have their mobile devices on all of the time, they get the messages immediately instead of having to launch applications on their phones to get to a site such as Facebook or LinkedIn.

Using social networks is an inexpensive way to recruit people as compared to print ads, which can cost hundreds of dollars to run. But there can still be costs involved a recruiter might not necessarily think about. Patrice Rice, the president of Patrice and Associates Inc., a Dunkirk, Maryland, hospitality industry recruiter, figures in one year alone she spent $60,000 on branding, a Facebook campaign, and employing a part-time social media manager to maintain the company's online presence, partly so recruiters do not have to, but also to be quicker to respond to queries from potential candidates.[14]

Another potential drawback of using social media, such as Facebook, Twitter, and the Internet in general, is that some groups of people are less likely to be "wired." The disabled are an example. A 2010 study by the Kessler Foundation and National Organization on Disability (NOD) found that whereas 85 percent of adults without disabilities access the Internet, only 54 percent of adults with disabilities do. As a result, relying too heavily on electronic recruiting could hurt a company's diversity efforts. And despite the fact that social media is a burgeoning way to recruit employees, some surveys show that the number of employees actually hired via social media recruiting is still relatively small compared to other methods.

Job Fairs

Job fairs can be a good way to cast a wide net for diverse applicants in a certain region. At a job fair companies and their recruiters set up booths, meet with prospective applicants, and exchange employment information. Often the fairs are industry specific.

One drawback of job fairs is that although they attract a lot of applicants, many of them might not be qualified. Another problem is that they only attract applicants in the regional area in which they are held. One way to get around the latter problem is to hold a "virtual job fair" that anyone, anywhere can attend. During a virtual job fair, recruiters man "virtual booths" online, where they provide links to their career resources, collect résumés, and talk with candidates via online chat functions. Companies can also administer screening questionnaires and, if a web cam feature is incorporated, see the candidates. Unicruit.com is a company that hosts virtual job fairs. Holding a virtual job fair can also be cost effective for both recruiters and attendees because they do not have to pay travel costs.

Employee Referrals

The recruitment efforts of an organization can be greatly aided by employee referrals, or recommendations from the firm's current employees about potential candidates. In fact, word-of-mouth recommendations are the way most job positions are filled. (Apparently there is truth to the phrase, "It is not what you know, but who you know.") Managers have found that the quality of employee-referred applicants is normally quite high, since employees are generally hesitant to recommend individuals who might not perform well. In general, applicants who are referred by a current employee, if hired, tend to remain with the organization longer as well.[15]

Some firms have created referral pages on their intranets to make it easier for employees to refer candidates as well as track their progress through the hiring process.[16] Accenture is a company that has such a site. See Case Study 1 to learn how computer widgets are being used to facilitate employee referrals as well. Highlights in HRM 2 shows some additional ways firms can encourage employee referrals.

HIGHLIGHTS IN **HRM**
2 Employee Referral Programs That Work

A company's current employees just may be its greatest source of future employees, too, thanks to a well-designed and well-promoted Employee Referral Program. Here are several suggestions for creating an effective program:

- *Make the ERP part of the company culture.* Companies typically need more of certain types of skills than others, and they often have a general profile of background, education, values, and ethics in mind for their candidates. So a big part of building an effective referral program is educating employees about the kinds of people the organization wants to hire—and continuing to keep that profile in the forefront. Helping employees see how finding the right types of candidates will enhance the overall team also adds to their enthusiasm for the program.

- *Be responsive.* Failing to acknowledge referrals promptly makes employees feel as if their efforts have disappeared into a black hole, which is demotivating. Instead, let the candidate and the referring employee know right away when a referral has entered the system. Then give the referred candidate priority processing in terms of screening and interviewing to demonstrate how much good referrals are valued.

- *Up the ante.* Consider creating two tiers of financial incentives for referrals: small rewards for candidates that meet the company's requirements but are not selected, and larger rewards for successful matches.

- *Provide rewards that employees value.* Some companies offer healthy bonuses, all-expense paid weekend trips, donations to the referring employee's favorite charity, or free insurance as incentives for successful referrals, but there are plenty of other options available, too. Many experts agree that public recognition, perhaps at a company meeting or department luncheon, can be equally rewarding.

- *Give employees the right tools.* Consider supplying employees with special "we're recruiting" business cards to hand out when meeting people face-to-face. And make it easy for employees to post or tweet information about job openings to their online network of associates.

- *Measure results.* It should go without saying that after the program is implemented, managers need to study the results in terms of the volume of referrals, qualifications of candidates, and success of new hires on the job. These results can then be used to fine-tune the program.

Source: "How a Talent Management Plan Can Anchor Your Company's Future," *HR Focus* 81, no. 10 (October 2004): 7–10; Susan M. Heathfield, "You Can Inspire Great Employee Referrals," http://humanresources.about.com; John Sullivan, "Advanced Employee Referral Programs—Best Practices You Need to Copy," www.drjohnsullivan.com.

There are some negative factors associated with employee referrals and profiles, though. They include the possibility of corporate "inbreeding." Since employees and their referrals tend to have similar backgrounds, employers who rely heavily on employee referrals to fill job openings may intentionally or unintentionally screen out, and thereby discriminate against, protected classes. Some researchers have found that inbreeding occurs gradually as part of a three-stage trend: According to the Attraction-Selection-Attrition (ASA) model, in the first stage (Attraction) people with values similar to an organization are attracted to it and become employees. In the second stage (Selection), these employees then choose applicants similar to themselves. In the final stage (Attrition) employees who do not fit in leave. The result is an ultra-homogenized organization.[17]

nepotism

A preference for hiring relatives of current employees

The practice of hiring relatives, referred to as nepotism, can invite charges of favoritism, especially in appointments to desirable positions. HR personnel hiring globally, however, need to realize that in other cultures, including Asia and the Middle East, nepotism is the norm. Even in the United States, nepotism gets mixed reviews, in part because family members are in an ideal position to pass job knowledge and skills on to one another. Many corporate dynasties (Ford Motor Company and the Rockefeller Foundation among them) have been built on nepotism. Labor unions would not have flourished without it. In recent years, a number of law firms and universities have dropped restrictions against hiring spouses on the basis that they are prejudicial.[18]

Rerecruiting

rerecruiting

The process of keeping track of and maintaining relationships with former employees to see if they would be willing to return to the firm

Rerecruiting is the process of keeping track of and maintaining relationships with former employees to see if they would be willing to return to the firm. Rerecruiting is not uncommon. At the accounting and consulting firm Deloitte, over 75,000 former employees are kept track of via an "alumni network." Other organizations that have alumni networks include Microsoft, Oshkosh, and Ernst & Young.[19]

Executive Search Firms

In contrast to public and private employment agencies, which help job seekers find the right job, executive search firms (often called "headhunters") help employers find the right person for a job. Firms such as Korn/Ferry International, Heidrick & Struggles, and Mercer & Associates are top recruiting firms for executives. Executive search firms do not advertise in the media for job candidates, nor do they accept a fee from the individual being placed.

The fees charged by search firms can range anywhere from 25 to 40 percent of the annual salary for the position to be filled. For the recruitment of senior executives, this fee is paid by the client firm, whether or not the recruiting effort results in a hire. It is for this practice that search firms receive the greatest criticism.

Nevertheless, as we noted earlier, hiring new chief executive officers (CEOs) from outside the organization has become commonplace. A large number of these new CEOs are placed in those positions through the services of an executive search firm. However, newer data suggest that CEOs who are promoted from within their organizations actually outperform those hired from the outside. Moreover, due to high-profile CEO-related scandals and bankruptcies that have occurred in recent times, human resources personnel are increasingly being called on to demand more from executive search firms and to assist boards of directors in the careful selection of top executives. In some instances, executive search firms have been criticized for selling the "Superman" qualities of outside CEOs—for which firms pay a premium.

Educational Institutions

Educational institutions typically are a source of young applicants with formal training but relatively little full-time work experience. High schools are usually a source of employees for clerical and blue-collar jobs. Community colleges, with their various types of specialized training, can provide candidates for technical jobs. These institutions can also be a source of applicants for a variety of white-collar jobs, including those in the sales and retail fields. Some management trainee jobs are also staffed from this source.

For technical and managerial positions, colleges and universities are generally the primary source. Given these numbers and the strong demand for highly skilled employees, colleges are likely to remain a good recruiting source. In addition, many U.S. universities are setting up campuses overseas. As a result, HR professionals in the coming years will have a new source from which to recruit employees abroad.[20]

Not using campus placement offices effectively and trying to visit too many campuses instead of concentrating on select institutions are common mistakes firms make when recruiting on campus. Rather than recruiting students from dozens of schools as they have done in the past, companies such as Nestle are targeting fewer colleges and forming closer partnerships with them. Employees guest lecture at the schools and develop relationships with instructors, who then recommend students for jobs. (Yes, it pays to be nice to your teacher.) Another mistake recruiting firms make is not continuing the college-recruiting effort on a long-term basis once it is begun.

Furthermore, some recruiters sent to college campuses are not sufficiently trained or prepared to talk to interested candidates about career opportunities or the requirements of specific openings or do not follow up with them. This is a grave mistake because research shows that students' perceptions of recruiters have a big impact on which jobs and companies they choose to pursue. "It is all about how [students] are treated in the campus recruiting process and the feeling that they get from the people they interact with," says Mary Scott, the founder of a college recruitment consulting firm in West Hartford, Connecticut. Figure 5.3 shows some of the steps firms can take to strengthen their on-campus recruiting relationships.

FIGURE 5.3   Steps for Strengthening a Firm's On-Campus Recruiting Relationships

- Invite professors and advisers to visit your office and take them to lunch.
- Invite them to bring a student group to the office.
- Send press releases and newsletters by mail or e-mail to bring them up to date on the firm's latest news and innovations.
- Provide guest speakers for classes.
- Conduct mock interviews, especially in years when not interviewing for full-time or internship positions.
- Provide scholarships to students.
- Attend the campus career fair, even when the firm is not going to be hiring, so that its name becomes known by the faculty and students.
- Offer job-shadowing programs for students.

Sources: Bruce Busta, D'Arcy Becker, and Jane P. Saly, "Effective Campus Recruiting: The Faculty Perspective," *CPA Journal* 77, no. 7 (July 2007): 62–65; Deborah J. Sessions, "Recruiting Made Easy," *Journal of Accountancy* 201, no. 5 (May 2006): 31–34.

To attract high-demand graduates, in addition to offering higher pay, firms sometimes employ innovative recruitment techniques such as work-study programs, low-interest loans for promising recruits, scholarships, and internships. Internships can be a great way for firms to "try out" college students who want to work in their fields and for students to decide if they want to work for an organization long term. However, many internships are not as successful as they should be because the sponsoring firms haven't thought through how to effectively utilize their interns. This can lead to bored interns who can, in turn, become disillusioned about their fields. Highlights in HRM 3 shows steps companies can take to ensure their internships are truly successful.

Professional Associations

Many professional associations and societies offer a placement service to members as one of their benefits. Lists of members seeking employment may be advertised in their journals or publicized at their national meetings. For the mutual benefit of employers and job seekers, placement centers are usually included at the national meetings of professional associations. The Society for Human Resource Management

HIGHLIGHTS IN HRM
3 Making Your Internship Program a Success

Let's assume your company's management has realized that internships benefit both your firm and the students they employ. And let's assume management understands that statistically interns usually make the best future full-fledged employees. So now let's look at how to make your internship program a success. Experts agree you should:

- Reach out to colleges and universities to begin building relationships with them. Let the career advisors at these schools know what you are looking for and what you have to offer the interns, and continue to promote your program on an ongoing basis.
- Clearly define what you are looking for in a candidate in terms of: current enrollment, GPA, preferred or required major, specific skills, attributes, and other experience.
- Devise a budget for intern recruiting, selection, compensation, relocation, housing, and travel.
- For each intern position, develop a work plan—a list of responsibilities and tasks that will be performed by this person. Since the intern will probably be assigned to a supervisor who will serve as the intern's mentor, it might be useful to get input from the supervisor regarding the position.
- Write an internship handbook that includes information on intern orientation, mentoring, executive engagement, project work, and cross-functional activity opportunities. Provide this to all of the supervisor/mentors in the program as well as the interns.
- Set up a system for providing interns with feedback on their performance, preferably at the midpoint of their internship and again at the conclusion. Make the experience a teachable moment.

Source: Getting the Most from Internship Programs," *Supply Chain Management Review* 13, no. 8 (2009): 34; Audrey Watters, "5 Tips for Creating an Internship Program for Your Startup," www.readwriteweb.com; Jean Scheid, "Designing Internship Programs," www.brighthub.com; Penny Loretto, "Developing an Internship Program," http://internships.about.com.

(SHRM), for example, helps employers and prospective HR employees come together.

Labor Unions

Labor unions have been a principal source of applicants for blue-collar and some professional jobs. Some unions, such as those in the maritime, printing, and construction industries, maintain hiring halls that can provide a supply of applicants, particularly for short-term needs. Employers wishing to use this recruitment source should contact the local union under consideration for employer eligibility requirements and applicant availability.

Public Employment Agencies

Each of the fifty U.S. states maintains an employment agency that administers its unemployment insurance program. Many of the state agencies bear such titles as Department of Employment or Department of Human Resources. They are subject to certain regulations and controls administered by the U.S. Employment and Training Administration (ETA).

State agencies maintain local public employment offices in most communities of any size. Individuals who become unemployed must register at one of these offices and be available for "suitable employment" in order to receive their weekly unemployment checks. As a result, the agencies are able to refer to employers with job openings those applicants with the required skills who are available for employment. Most of the local employment offices have a local job bank book published as a daily computer printout. Many of the jobs can also be found on the web at America's Job Exchange and America's Career InfoNet (ACINet). Employer openings are listed along with other pertinent information, such as number of openings, pay rates, and job specifications. Employment interviewers in an agency can access a list of all job openings in the geographic area for which applicants assigned to them might qualify. Furthermore, applicants looking for a specific job can review the lists and apply directly to organizations with openings.

In addition to matching unemployed applicants with job openings, public employment agencies sometimes assist employers with apprenticeship programs, employment testing, job analysis, evaluation programs, and community wage surveys.

Private Employment and Temporary Agencies

Charging a fee enables private employment agencies to tailor their services to the specific needs of their clients. Snelling Staffing Services, Manpower, Kelly Services, and Olsten are among the largest private employment agencies. However, it is common for agencies to specialize in serving a specific occupational area or geographic area. When recruiting abroad, companies frequently use local employment agencies because they understand a country's culture, labor market, and better how to recruit workers there.

Depending on who is receiving the most service, the fee may be paid by the employer, the job seeker, or both. It is not uncommon for private employment agencies to charge an employer a 25 to 30 percent fee, based on the position's annual salary, if the employer hires an applicant found by the agency.

Private employment agencies differ in the services they offer, their professionalism, and the caliber of their counselors. If counselors are paid on a commission basis, their desire to do a professional job may be offset by their desire to earn a commission.

Thus, they may encourage job seekers to accept jobs for which they are not suited. Because of this, job seekers would be wise to take the time to find a recruiter who is knowledgeable, experienced, and professional. When talking with potential recruiters, individuals should discuss openly their philosophies and practices with regard to recruiting strategies, including advertising, in-house recruiting, screening procedures, and costs for these efforts. They should try to find a recruiter who is flexible and who will consider their needs and wants.

In addition to placing permanent workers, many private agencies hire and place workers in temporary positions. "Temps" are typically used for short-term assignments or to help when managers cannot justify hiring a full-time employee, such as for vacation fill-ins, for peak work periods, or during an employee's pregnancy leave or sick leave. Increasingly, temps have been employed to fill positions once staffed by permanent employees. Figure 5.4 shows the major temporary agencies in the United States and the types of employees in which they specialize.

Temps give organizations added flexibility because they can be hired and laid off as needed. Also, the employment costs of temporaries are often lower than those of permanent employees because temps are not provided with benefits and can be let go without the need to file unemployment insurance claims. To keep their costs down as well as gain flexibility, some companies use a just-in-time staffing approach in which a core staff of employees is augmented by a trained and highly skilled supplementary workforce. Some of these temps are retirees who once worked for the firm but do not want to work full time. Others are part-time workers who already have health insurance via their spouses. According to the Bureau of Labor Statistics, amid the worst part of the last economic recession, the number of temporary employees increased 29 percent.

FIGURE 5.4   Major Temporary Help Agencies in the United States

ALLEGIS GROUP
www.allegisgroup.com
Technical, industrial, IT, accounting, finance, human resources, sales, legal

EXPRESS PERSONNEL SERVICES
www.expresspros.com/
Clerical, accounting, customer service, warehousing, industrial

HUDSON
www.hudson.com
Legal, IT, finance, engineering

KELLY SERVICES
www.kellyservices.com
Office services, accounting, engineering,
IT, law, science, marketing, creative

services, light industrial, education, health care

MANPOWER
www.manpower.com
Administrative, industrial, IT, engineering, finance, accounting, contact center, skilled trades

RANDSTAD
www.randstad.com
Office, executive office, industrial, technical, call center, finance, accounting

ROBERT HALF INTERNATIONAL
www.rhi.com
Accounting, finance, technical, legal, design/creative, clerical, administrative

TRUEBLUE
www.trueblueinc.com
General labor, light industrial, skilled trades

VEDIOR
www.vedior.com
IT, engineering, accounting, finance, health care, human resources, legal, commercial

VOLT WORKFORCE SOLUTIONS
www.volt.com
Accounting, finance, administrative, call center, creative/design, legal, light industrial, sales, marketing, technical, engineering, IT

Source: "Temporary Staffing Firms," *Workforce Management* 87, no. 2 (February 4, 2008): 14. Copyright of *Workforce Management* is the property of Crain Communications Inc. (MI), and its content may not be copied or e-mailed to multiple sites or posted to a listserv without the copyright holder's express written permission. However, users may print, download, or e-mail articles for individual use.

Many temporary employees are eventually hired full-time. Temping allows them and the firms they contract with to try one another out before a permanent commitment is made. However, numerous companies, including Microsoft and FedEx, have encountered legal problems by categorizing permanent workers as "temps" or "independent contractors" in an effort to cut employment costs. To prevent such abuses Congress, the courts, and the U.S. Department of Labor have established criteria that must be followed when it comes to hiring temps. Another concern related to using temps is that they have less of an incentive to be loyal to an employer and its clients or to go the extra mile to help a company achieve success.

For reasons such as these, some organizations are scaling back their use of temporary help. Instead of hiring temps, the Hilton hotel chain sends full-time employees from one hotel to another to address temporary spikes in demand. This strategy not only makes efficient use of the hotel chain's staff but also helps develop an agile workforce.[21]

Employee Leasing

Employee leasing by professional employer organizations (PEOs) has grown rapidly since the passage of the Tax Equity and Fiscal Responsibility Act of 1982. As we explained in Chapter 1, today about 700 PEOs oversee two to three million U.S. workers, according to the National Association of Professional Employer Organizations (NAPEO) in Alexandria, Virginia. Basically, a PEO—typically a larger company—takes over the management of a smaller company's HR tasks and becomes a coemployer to its employees. The PEO performs all the HR duties of an employer—recruiting, background checks, hiring, payroll, performance appraisal, benefits administration, and other day-to-day HR activities—and in return is paid a placement fee of normally 4 to 8 percent of payroll cost plus 9 to 20 percent of gross wages. Because PEOs can coemploy a large number of people working at many different companies, they can provide employees with benefits such as 401(k) and health plans that small companies cannot afford. (The average client of a PEO is a business with nineteen employees.) Employees who work for large PEOs are also eligible for COBRA, which gives them the option of purchasing healthcare benefits through their employers' group plans for a certain period of time should they lose their jobs. Unlike temporary agencies, which supply workers only for limited periods, employee leasing companies place their employees with subscribers on a permanent basis. The Society for Human Resource Management reports that companies with fewer than fifty employees can save anywhere from $5,000 to $50,000 in time and labor costs annually by hiring a PEO.[22]

employee leasing
The process of dismissing employees who are then hired by a leasing company (which handles all HR-related activities) and contracting with that company to lease back the employees

Improving the Effectiveness of Recruiting

How well is a company doing when it comes to recruiting talent from all sources? Have the firm's recruiters been able to hire enough employees to meet the company's needs, including key personnel? Are the recruiters slow or fast when it comes to filling positions? Are line managers happy with the process and the quality of the people hired? Are the people who have been hired happy with their jobs and likely to remain with the firm and advance in the organization? HR managers have many tools available to them to gauge their efforts and improve their recruiting. Let's now look at a few of them.

LEARNING OUTCOME 4

If you're employed, ask your boss what methods he or she has most successfully used to recruit employees. Compare your findings with your classmates. Does the recruiting source seem to depend upon the type of job?

Using Realistic Job Previews

realistic job preview (RJP)

Informing applicants about all aspects of the job, including both its desirable and undesirable facets

One way organizations may be able to increase the effectiveness of their recruitment efforts is to provide job applicants with a realistic job preview (RJP). An RJP informs applicants about all aspects of the job, including both its desirable and undesirable facets. In contrast, a typical job preview presents the job in only positive terms. The RJP might also include a tour of the working area, combined with a discussion of any negative health or safety considerations. Proponents of RJPs believe that applicants who are given realistic information regarding a position are more likely to remain on the job and be successful because there will be fewer unpleasant surprises. In fact, a number of research studies on RJPs report that they can yield results such as realistic job expectations on the part of employees, better job satisfaction, and lower turnover.

Some companies are taking their realistic job previews online. The bank SunTrust reports cutting its teller recruitment costs in half and upping its retention of tellers by at least 10 percent by doing so. At their own convenience on the Web, SunTrust candidates answer questions and perform various simulated teller tasks, such as looking up account information and entering customer data. Online job previews can help candidates get a better feel for the work than can a written description. They can also help employers screen potentially good candidates.[23]

Surveys

Another way to improve a company's recruiting is to survey managers about how satisfied they are with the process. Are managers happy with the time it takes to hire new employees, the degree to which they need to be involved in the process, and ultimately the overall quality of the people recruited? Why or why not? New hires can also be surveyed to see how satisfied they are. Lastly, candidates who turned down jobs often can provide valuable information about why they did not accept the firm's offer.

Recruiting Metrics

As we explained earlier in the chapter, recruiters should keep statistics on the sources from which candidates are recruited and hired as well as the costs of each source. The time it takes to recruit various employees from various sources as well as the quality of employees are other statistics recruiters collect and study. Doing so helps them understand which recruiting sources work best for different employees, which allows them to find better employees faster and at a lower cost.

Quality of Fill Statistics

As we indicated in the appendix to Chapter 2, hiring quality employees is a primary concern of recruiters. Firms have attempted to develop a quality-of-fill statistic they can use to improve their recruiting processes. The following is one suggested way of calculating an annual quality-of-fill metric for an organization.

$$\text{Quality of Hire} = (PR + HP + HR) / N$$

PR = Average job performance rating of new hires
HP = % of new hires reaching acceptable productivity with acceptable time frame

HR = % of new hires retained after one year

N = number of indicators

Example:

PR = Average 3.5 on a 5.0 scale = 70%

HP = Of 100 hires made one year ago, 75 are meeting acceptable productivity levels = 75%

HR = 20% turnover = 80% HR

N = 3

Quality of Hire = (70 + 75 + 80) / 3 = 75

The result is a quality level of 75 percent for new employees hired during the year.

Time to Fill

The **time-to-fill** metric refers to the number of days from when a job opening is approved to the date the person ultimately chosen for the job is selected. Figure 5.5 shows an example of how the time-to-fill metric is calculated. Generally speaking, lower time-to-fill statistics are better. However, a trade-off has to be made between the time to fill a position and the quality of the candidates needed for the position.

Yield Ratios

Yield ratios help indicate which recruitment sources are most effective at producing qualified job candidates. Quite simply, a yield ratio is the percentage of applicants from a particular source that make it to the next stage in the selection process. For example, if 100 résumés were obtained from an employment agency and seventeen of the applicants submitting those résumés were invited for an on-site interview, the yield ratio for that agency would be 17 percent (17/100). This yield ratio could then be recalculated for each subsequent stage in the selection process (for example, after the interview and again after the final offer), which would result in a cumulative yield ratio. By calculating and comparing yield ratios for each recruitment source, it is possible to find out which sources produce qualified applicants.

yield ratio

The percentage of applicants from a recruitment source that make it to the next stage of the selection process

FIGURE 5.5   Time-to-Fill Calculations

Position	Date Position Approved	Date Offer Accepted	Date Started Work	Selection Time	Time to Start
Engineer	10/10/11	11/30/11	12/15/11	51	15
Marketing Manager	10/11/11	11/24/11	12/16/11	44	22
Salesperson	10/12/11	11/13/11	11/20/11	32	7
Administrative Assistant	10/13/11	11/7/11	11/14/11	25	7
Clerk	10/13/11	10/30/11	11/14/11	17	15
Averages				**33.8**	**13.2**

© Cengage Learning 2013

Costs of Recruitment

The cost of various recruiting procedures can be computed using a fairly simple set of calculations. For example, the average source cost per hire (SC/H) can be determined by the following formula:

$$\frac{SC}{H} = \frac{AC + AF + RB + NC}{H}$$

where

AC = advertising costs, total monthly expenditure (example: $32,000)
AF = agency fees, total for the month (example: $21,000)
RB = referral bonuses, total paid (example: $2,600)
NC = no-cost hires, walk-ins, nonprofit agencies, etc. (example: $0)
 H = total hires (example: 119)

Substituting the example numbers into the formula gives:

$$\frac{SC}{H} = \frac{\$32,000 + \$21,000 + \$2,600 + \$0}{119}$$

$$= \frac{\$55,600}{119}$$

$$= \$467.23 \text{ (source cost of recruits per hire)}$$

When combined with information about yield ratios, these calculations can provide invaluable information to managers about the utility of different approaches to and sources of recruitment. In that way, they can make more informed decisions about both controlling the costs of recruitment and increasing its effectiveness. For example, although advertisements and employee referrals may both yield qualified applicants, managers may find that referral bonuses are a more economical alternative.

An applicant tracking system (ATS) can help a firm automatically track and calculate the statistics we've discussed. An ATS is a software application recruiters use to post job openings, screen résumés, contact via e-mail potential candidates for interviews, and track the time and costs related to hiring people. About 50 percent of all mid-sized companies and almost all large corporations use some type of applicant tracking system.[24]

applicant tracking system (ATS)
A software application recruiters use to post job openings, screen résumés, and contact via e-mail potential candidates for interviews, and track the time and costs related to hiring people

Career Management: Developing Talent over Time

LEARNING OUTCOME 5

Why should both employees and their employers be concerned about career management programs?

Regardless of the source from which employees are recruited—internally or externally—managers play a key role in expanding the talent pools of the firms. Good managers listen to their employees' aspirations, act as coaches, identify their strengths and areas for improvement, and offer them continual feedback about their performance. They also ensure employees receive training and are provided with self-assessment tools and information about the organization and possible career paths within it. Compared to recruiting, helping employees grow and working to develop their skills is a more proactive—and strategic—approach to systematically expanding the talent pool relative to bringing people in from the outside and banking on them being right for the job.

Integrating career development with other HR programs creates synergies in which all aspects of HR reinforce one another. Figure 5.6 illustrates how HR structures relate to some of the essential aspects of the career management process. For example, to plan their careers, employees need organizational information—information that strategic planning, forecasting, succession planning, and skills inventories can provide. Similarly as they obtain information themselves and use it to plan their careers, employees need to know what the career paths within their organizations are and how management views their performance.

The Goal: Matching Individual and Organizational Needs

A career development program should be viewed as a dynamic process that matches the needs of the organization with the needs of employees. Each party has a distinctive role to play.

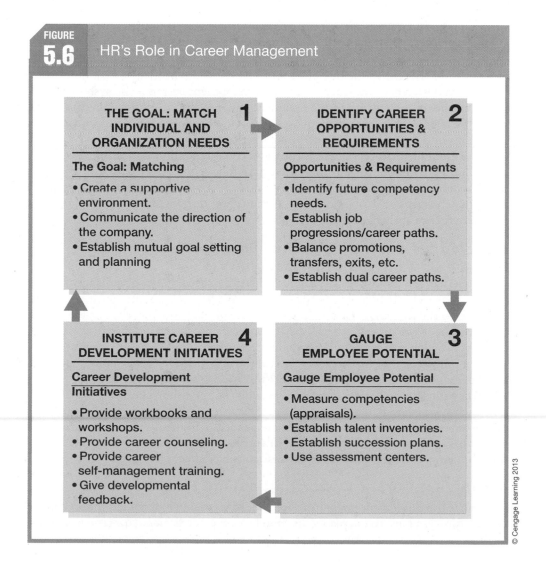

FIGURE 5.6   HR's Role in Career Management

THE GOAL: MATCH INDIVIDUAL AND ORGANIZATION NEEDS   1

The Goal: Matching

- Create a supportive environment.
- Communicate the direction of the company.
- Establish mutual goal setting and planning

IDENTIFY CAREER OPPORTUNITIES & REQUIREMENTS   2

Opportunities & Requirements

- Identify future competency needs.
- Establish job progressions/career paths.
- Balance promotions, transfers, exits, etc.
- Establish dual career paths.

INSTITUTE CAREER DEVELOPMENT INITIATIVES   4

Career Development Initiatives

- Provide workbooks and workshops.
- Provide career counseling.
- Provide career self-management training.
- Give developmental feedback.

GAUGE EMPLOYEE POTENTIAL   3

Gauge Employee Potential

- Measure competencies (appraisals).
- Establish talent inventories.
- Establish succession plans.
- Use assessment centers.

© Cengage Learning 2013

The Employee's Role

Changes in the workplace are occurring so rapidly that employees need to take an active role in planning their careers. What new technological skills will they need to be successful in the workforce in the future? What careers utilize those skills? What career options would a person be able to pursue if he or she were downsized? At some point in their careers, most employees will face this situation.

Because having a successful career involves creating your own career path—not just following a path that has been established by the organization—employees need to identify their knowledge, skills, abilities, interests, and values and to seek out information about career options in conjunction with their managers. Managers can help with the process by offering their subordinates continual feedback about their performance and provide them with self-assessment tools, training, and information about the organization and possible career paths within it. General Motors, for example, has prepared a career development guide that groups jobs by fields of work such as engineering, manufacturing, communications, data processing, financial, HR, and scientific. These categories give employees an understanding of the career possibilities in the various fields.

The Organization's Role: Establishing a Favorable Career Development Climate

If career development is to succeed, it must receive the complete support of top management. Ideally, senior line managers and HR department managers should work together to design and implement a career development system. The system should reflect the goals and culture of the organization, and the HR philosophy should be woven throughout. An HR philosophy can provide employees with a clear set of expectations and directions for their own career development. Says Karyn Maynard with the Container Store: "There is constant, consistent communication with management on growth opportunities. Rather than follow one career path, the company works to leverage employees' talents for new and different roles, as well as giving them as much exposure as possible to other positions and responsibilities in the company to ensure they're challenged."[25]

Blending the Goals of Individual Employees with the Goals of the Organization

Of course, a career development program should be based on the organization's goals and needs as well. As Figure 5.7 shows, the organization's goals and needs should be linked with the individual career needs of its employees in a way that improves the effectiveness of workers and their satisfaction as well as achieving the firm's strategic objectives. Before a firm's employees can engage in meaningful career planning, however, not only must they have an awareness of the organization's philosophy, they must also have a good understanding of the organization's more immediate goals. Otherwise, they might plan for personal change and growth without knowing whether or how their own goals match those of the organization. For example, if the technology of a business is changing and new skills are needed, will the organization retrain its employees to meet this need or hire new talent? Is there growth, stability, or decline in the number of employees needed? How will turnover affect this need?

Identifying Career Opportunities and Requirements

While talent management integrates a number of related HR activities, those who direct the process have to keep a steady watch on the needs and requirements of the

FIGURE 5.7 Blending the Needs of Individual Employees and with the Needs of Their Organizations

ORGANIZATION'S NEEDS

Strategic
- Current competencies
- Future competencies
- Market changes
- Mergers, etc.
- Innovation
- Growth
- Downsizing
- Restructuring

Operational
- Employee turnover
- Absenteeism
- Recruiting
- Outsourcing
- Productivity

INDIVIDUAL'S NEEDS

Personal
- Age/tenure
- Family concerns
- Spouse's employment
- Ability to relocate
- Outside interests

Professional
- Career stage
- Education & training
- Promotion aspirations
- Performance
- Current career path

CAREER MANAGEMENT

© Cengage Learning 2013

organization. This involves an analysis of the competencies required for jobs, progression among related jobs, and supply of ready (and potential) talent available to fill those jobs. A variety of approaches can be used to do this, including surveys, informal group discussions, and interviews. The process should involve personnel from different groups, such as new employees, managers, longtime employees, minority employees, and technical and professional employees. Identifying the needs and problems of these groups provides the starting point for the organization's career development efforts.

Begin with a Competency Analysis

It is important for an organization to study its jobs carefully to identify and assign weights to the knowledge and skills that each one requires. This can be achieved with job analysis and evaluation systems such as those used in compensation programs. The system used at Sears measures three basic competencies for each job: know-how, problem-solving, and accountability. Know-how is broken down into three types of job knowledge: technical, managerial, and human relations. Problem-solving and accountability also have several dimensions. Scores for each of these three major competencies are assigned to each job, and a total value is computed for each job. For any planned job transfer, the amount of increase (or decrease) the next job represents in each of the skill areas, as well as in the total point values, can be computed. This information is then used to make certain that a transfer to a different job is a move that requires growth on the part of the employee.

Sears designs career development paths to provide the following experiences: (1) an increase in at least one skill area on each new assignment, (2) an increase of at least 10 percent in total points on each new assignment, and (3) assignments in several different functional areas.[26]

Identify Job Progressions and Career Paths

job progressions

The hierarchy of jobs a new employee might experience, ranging from a starting job to jobs that successively require more knowledge and/or skill

career paths

Lines of advancement in an occupational field within an organization

Once the skill demands of jobs are identified and weighted according to their importance, it is then possible to plan job progressions. A new employee with no experience is typically assigned to a "starting job." After a period of time in that job, the employee can be promoted to one that requires more knowledge and/or skill. While most organizations concentrate on developing job progressions for managerial, professional, and technical jobs, progressions can be developed for all categories of jobs. Job progressions then can serve as a basis for developing career paths—the lines of advancement within an organization—for individuals. Figure 5.8 illustrates a typical line of advancement in the human resources area of a large multinational corporation. As you can see from the figure, in this firm, a person has to be prepared to move geographically to advance very far in the human resources department. This might also be true of other career fields within the organization.

Although these analyses can be quite helpful to employees—and are perhaps essential for organizations—a word of caution is appropriate here. Even with the best career planning, it is almost impossible for people to have perfect certainty about where their careers are going. People change over time, and because of that, their needs and interests change. Moreover, successful career paths often do not proceed in a lockstep manner. Many successful individuals readily admit that their career paths are idiosyncratic to their circumstances. See Amazon.com founder Jeff Bezos's career path in Highlights in HRM 4. (Before founding the worldwide retailer, Bezos spent a number of years in the financial industry.) These people often note that they were either "in the right place at the right time" or carved out entirely new career paths for themselves. Other people's careers progress quite predictably and linearly.

FIGURE 5.8　Typical Line of Advancement in HR Management

				Vice president, HR
			Corporate HR director	
		Corporate HR manager	Division HR director	
		Asst. division HR director		
	Regional HR manager	Plant HR manager		
	Asst. plant HR manager			
Regional HR associate	HR supervisor			
HR associate				

© Cengage Learning 2013

HIGHLIGHTS IN **HRM**

4 Career Path of Jeff Bezos, Founder of Amazon.com

1986—Graduated from Princeton University with a B.S. in electrical engineering and computer science

1986—Hired by Fitel, a telecommunications and information technology firm that created software for tracking international stock trades

1988—Hired by Bankers Trust, Co., a financial firm that specialized in risk management utilizing new sophisticated computer systems

1990—Promoted to vice president

1990—Hired by D.E. Shaw, an investment and hedge fund company

1992—Promoted to senior vice president

1995—Founded Amazon.com

Track Career Stages

A person's knowledge, skills, abilities, and attitudes as well as career aspirations change with age and maturity. The challenges and frustrations people face at the same stages in their careers are remarkably similar. A model describing these stages is shown in Figure 5.9. The stages are: (1) preparation for work, (2) organizational entry, (3) early career, (4) midcareer, and (5) late career. The typical age range and the major tasks of each stage are also presented in the figure.

The first stage—preparation for work—encompasses the period prior to entering an organization, often extending until age twenty-five. It is a period in which individuals must acquire the knowledge, abilities, and skills they will need to compete in the marketplace. It is a time when careful planning, based on sound information, should be the focus. The second stage, typically from ages eighteen to twenty-five, is devoted to soliciting job offers and selecting an appropriate job. During this period, a person might also be involved in preparing for work. The next three stages entail fitting into a chosen occupation and organization(s), modifying one's goals, remaining productive, and finally, preparing for retirement. In the remainder of the chapter we will look at the challenges faced by students, many of whom are likely to be in the early stages of their careers. Retirement planning will be discussed in Chapter 11.

Recognize Different Career Paths

Career development and planning systems were once primarily focused on promotions. However, in today's flatter organizations and more dynamic work environment, an individual's career advancement can move along several different paths via promotions, transfers, demotions, and even exits. A **promotion** is a change of assignment to a job at a higher level in the organization. The new job normally provides an increase in pay and status and demands more skill or carries more responsibility. The three principal criteria for determining promotions are merit, seniority, and potential. Often the problem is to determine how much consideration to give each factor. A common problem in organizations that promote primarily on past performance and

promotion
A change of assignment to a job at a higher level in the organization

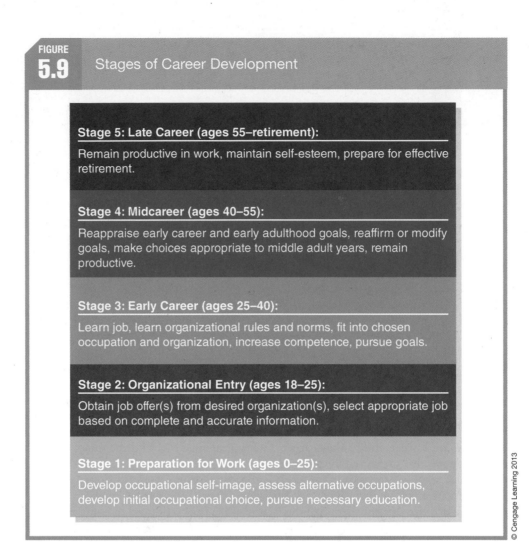

FIGURE 5.9   Stages of Career Development

Stage 5: Late Career (ages 55–retirement):

Remain productive in work, maintain self-esteem, prepare for effective retirement.

Stage 4: Midcareer (ages 40–55):

Reappraise early career and early adulthood goals, reaffirm or modify goals, make choices appropriate to middle adult years, remain productive.

Stage 3: Early Career (ages 25–40):

Learn job, learn organizational rules and norms, fit into chosen occupation and organization, increase competence, pursue goals.

Stage 2: Organizational Entry (ages 18–25):

Obtain job offer(s) from desired organization(s), select appropriate job based on complete and accurate information.

Stage 1: Preparation for Work (ages 0–25):

Develop occupational self-image, assess alternative occupations, develop initial occupational choice, pursue necessary education.

© Cengage Learning 2013

seniority is called the Peter Principle. This refers to the situation in which individuals are promoted as long as they have done a good job in their previous jobs. The situation continues until someone does poorly in his or her new job. Then he or she is no longer promoted. This results in people being promoted to their level of incompetence. There are other intrafirm challenges related to promotions. Sometimes extremely good employees are prevented from being promoted to other departments because their current managers are reluctant to lose them. And as we pointed out earlier in the chapter, some managers favor external candidates versus internal candidates because they are not familiar yet with the external candidates' flaws. This helps explain why companies so often look outside of their firms in an effort to hire "savior" CEOs.[27]

In flatter organizations, there are fewer promotional opportunities, so many individuals find career advancement through lateral moves. A **transfer** is the placement of an employee in another job for which the duties, responsibilities, status, and pay and benefits are approximately equal to those of the previous job he or she held (although as an incentive to make a transfer, organizations sometimes offer transferred

transfer
Placement of an individual in another job for which the duties, responsibilities, status, and remuneration are approximately equal to those of the previous job

employees small pay increases). Individuals who look forward to change or want a chance to learn more about their organizations and obtain different skills often seek out transfers. Frequently these employees do so with an effort to augment their skills so they will be more promotable in the future.

A transfer sometimes requires the employee to change work group, workplace, work shift, or organizational unit; it may even necessitate moving to another geographic area. Thus, transfers make it possible for an organization to place its employees in jobs where there is a greater need for their services and where they can acquire new knowledge and skills.

A downward transfer, or *demotion*, moves an individual into a lower-level job that can provide developmental opportunities. Although such a move is ordinarily considered unfavorable, some individuals actually may request it to return to their "technical roots." It is not uncommon, for example, for organizations to appoint temporary leaders (especially in team environments) to positions with the understanding that they will eventually return to their former jobs.

Transfers, promotions, and demotions require individuals to adjust to new job demands and usually to a different work environment. A transfer that involves moving to a new location within the United States or abroad places greater demands on an employee because it requires the person to adapt to a new work environment and new living conditions. The employee with a family has the added responsibility of helping family members adjust to the new living arrangements. Even though some employers provide all types of relocation services—including covering moving expenses, helping to sell a home, and providing cultural orientation and language training—there is always some loss in the employee's productivity during the relocation process. Pre-transfer training, whether related to job skills or to lifestyle, has been suggested as one of the most effective ways to reduce lost productivity.

Of course, many employees choose to exit their organizations as part of their career development. When a person's career opportunities within a firm are limited and his or her skills are in demand externally, the best career options could be for the individual to switch companies or to work as freelancers, consultants, or entrepreneurs. Although some employees leave voluntarily, other employees are forced to leave. Larger organizations often provide outplacement services to help terminated employees find jobs elsewhere. Jack Welch, the former chairman of General Electric, was one of the first executives to make a commitment to employees to try to ensure *employability* when the company could no longer guarantee lifetime employment. That is, GE has committed to providing employees with the skills and support they would need to find a job in another organization.[28]

The Workforce Investment Act of 1998 set up "one-stop" service centers in co-operation among businesses and local governments to provide unemployed and underemployed people with a variety of services, including career counseling, skill assessments, training, job search assistance, and referrals to related programs and services. For example, the Northside Workforce Center, based in Fort Worth, Texas, is one of hundreds of nonprofit career centers across the country where people can apply for unemployment and training benefits, meet with career counselors and veterans' reps, mail and fax résumés to prospective employers free of charge, and gain access to child care. In addition, the American Society for Training and Development (ASTD) publishes a federal training assistance guide that has information on more than 200 federal grants and other assistance programs that can be used for workforce training and development.[29]

relocation services
Services provided to an employee who is transferred to a new location, which might include help in moving, selling a home, orienting to a new culture, and/or learning a new language

outplacement services
Services provided by organizations to help terminated employees find a new job

Small Business Application

Small Companies Often Offer Big Rewards

Once upon a time, it seemed all young professionals dreamed of working their way up the corporate ladder to success in a large company and retaining those well-paid, perk-laden positions until the employees were ready to fade into the sunset. Yet evolving trends over the last twenty years have turned that rosy view of corporate life into a myth, and no one seems to be the worse for it. Quite the contrary. Many new grads and seasoned professionals alike are choosing to work for less-than-500-employee firms because of the many advantages they offer, and smaller firms are welcoming these knowledge workers with open arms.

For the midterm and advanced career professionals, transitioning from a large corporation to a smaller one often means jumping straight into the limelight. The change is rejuvenating, as they find themselves taking on more diverse responsibilities, getting involved in new arenas, and seeing more clearly how their own efforts impact the company's results. And with all of that comes greater recognition. "Your work and contributions will be noticed," says Lindsey Pollak, a management expert of next-generation career trends. "You are more likely to be listened to, and to feel that you are an important part of the company and that your ideas really matter."

Even those with fewer years of experience under their belts are likely to be energized by working in smaller firms. Job descriptions tend to be less defined in these environments, giving employees the chance to push themselves in new directions beyond the confines of their jobs. They also often find themselves working with the highest-level managers, learning directly from experts.

Small-firm employees of all types often cite another benefit: Working in a small company means enjoying a big-picture view of the business and industry, rather than getting pigeonholed into one small aspect of the work at hand. "You get divorced from the nuts and bolts of operating a business when you work for large companies," says Mike Barnes, a newly hired logistics executive at Halton Co., a provider of construction equipment in Portland, Oregon. Like many people in his situation, Barnes says this closer connection to the mission of the business gives him a level of job satisfaction he has not felt in a long time.

However, employees who opt for working in a small firm cannot expect to find everything they might get in a larger corporation. Tighter budgets mean smaller companies sometimes cannot afford to pay salaries equal to those of big firms, and they often cannot provide the support systems or perks, like generous expense accounts, hefty bonuses, and company-paid smart phones. But many small employers provide alluring trade-offs such as shorter work weeks, less travel, and work-life balance incentives, including telecommuting and flex-time.

Where people decide to work really comes down to determining how they are going to meet their career and life goals. Notes management author and analyst Tony Jacowski, "Your choice of organization should be based on the quality of work experience you will gain rather than the size of the organization. If you have the talent and the expertise, you will quickly climb the corporate ladder irrespective of the size of the company."

Source: Sarah E. Needleman, "Moving to a Small Company Can Lead to Big Rewards," *Wall Street Journal,* March 5, 2008, http://online.wsj.com/article/; Lindsey Pollak, "The Advantages of Working for a Small Company," www.lindseypollak.com; Tony Jacowski, "Benefits of Working in a Small Company vs a Corporation, http://ezinearticles.com; Jacqueline Parks, "The Benefits of Working for a Small Business," www.associatedcontent.com.

Consider Dual Career Paths for Employees

One of the most obvious places where career paths have been changing is in technical and professional areas. One of the ironies of organizations in the past has been that the most successful engineers, scientists, and professionals were often promoted right out of their area of specialization into management. Instead of doing what they were good at, they were promoted into a job they often did not understand or enjoy.

It has become apparent that there must be another way to compensate these types of professionals without putting them in management positions. The solution has been to develop dual career paths, or tracks, that provide for progression in special areas such as information technology, finance, marketing, and engineering, with compensation that is comparable to that received by managers at different levels. As we explained in Chapter 2, Microsoft offers software engineers both a management-focused and technical-specialist career track and allows them to move back and forth between the two.

Consider the Boundaryless Career

A generation ago, career success was synonymous with ascending a corporate hierarchy over the course of a lifetime spent in a single firm. Today, however, individuals pursuing *boundaryless careers* prefer to see themselves as self-directed "free agents" who develop a portfolio of employment opportunities by proactively moving from employer to employer, simultaneously developing and utilizing their marketable skills. As shown in Figure 5.10, it is possible to map the different career profiles.

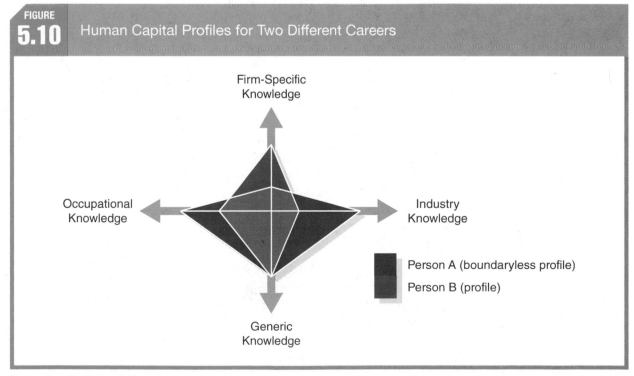

FIGURE 5.10   Human Capital Profiles for Two Different Careers

Source: Scott Snell, Cornell University.

Employees pursuing boundaryless careers develop their human capital along dimensions of industry and occupational knowledge. That is, they may be experts in computer programming or have great insights into trends in the banking industry. In contrast, individuals pursuing more traditional careers develop their knowledge in ways specific to a given firm.

Both approaches can be beneficial, but they are not the same. Under the boundaryless career model, success depends on continually learning new skills, developing new relationships, and capitalizing on existing skills and relationships. These individuals place a premium on flexibility and the capacity to do several different types of tasks, learn new jobs, adjust quickly to different group settings and organizational cultures, and move from one firm, occupation, or industry to another. Their employment security depends on their marketable skills rather than their dedication to one organization over time. A number of studies have shown that people with boundaryless careers find them very satisfying. Organizations can also benefit from boundaryless careers because it allows them to attract top talent from all over the world on a project-by-project basis.[30]

Help Employees Progress beyond Career Plateaus

career plateau

A situation in which for either organizational or personal reasons the probability of moving up the career ladder is low

Career plateaus are common obstacles in the career development of employees. A career plateau is a situation in which, for either organizational or personal reasons, the probability of moving up the career ladder is low. There are three types of plateaus: structural, content, and life. A *structural plateau* marks the end of promotions. A *content plateau* occurs when a person has learned a job too well and is bored with day-to-day activities. A *life plateau* is more profound and may feel like a midlife crisis. People who experience life plateaus often have allowed work or some other major factor to become the most significant aspect of their lives, and they experience a loss of identity and self-esteem when they are no longer advancing in their careers. Figure 5.11 lists some probing questions employees can ask themselves if they find themselves in, or trying to overcome, a career plateau.

sabbatical

An extended period of time in which an employee leaves an organization to pursue other activities and later returns to his or her job

Organizations can help individuals cope with plateaus by providing them with opportunities for lateral growth or allowing them to choose their own assignments when opportunities for advancement do not exist. Companies with international divisions can encourage employees to take assignments abroad to expand their horizons, lead philanthropic and volunteer activities for their firms, or take sabbaticals. A sabbatical is an extended period of time during which an employee leaves an organization to pursue other activities before returning to the firm. Career enrichment programs can help people learn more about what gives them satisfaction within a company, as well as what kinds of opportunities will make them happiest if they go elsewhere.

Career Development Initiatives

In a study undertaken by the human resources consulting firm Drake Beam Morin, the six most successful career management practices used within organizations are as follows:

- Placing clear expectations on employees so they know what is expected of them throughout their careers with the organization.

- Giving employees the opportunity to transfer to other office locations, both domestically and internationally.

- Providing a clear and thorough succession plan to employees.

- Encouraging performance through rewards and recognition.

- Giving employees the time and resources they need to consider short- and long-term career goals.

- Encouraging employees to continually assess their skills and career direction.

In contrast, organizations also need to be mindful of the internal barriers that inhibit employees' career advancement. Generally, these barriers can include such things as the following:

- Lack of time, budgets, and resources for employees to plan their careers and to undertake training and development.

- Rigid job specifications, lack of leadership support for career management, and a short-term focus.

- Lack of career opportunities and pathways within the organization for employees.[31]

A variety of tools are available to help employees further their careers within an organization. Informal counseling by HR staff and supervisors is used widely. Career planning workbooks and workshops are also popular tools for helping employees identify their potential and the strength of their interests.

Career Planning Workbooks and Workshops

Several organizations have prepared workbooks to guide their employees individually through systematic self-assessment of values, interests, abilities, goals, and personal development plans. General Motors' *Career Development Guide* contains a section

FIGURE 5.11   Career Plateau Questions

1. Do I accept high visibility assignments?
2. Do I continue to advance my education, both formal and vocational?
3. Am I recognized by other leaders in my organization?
4. Am I routinely promoted?
5. Am I known as a versatile employee?
6. Do I continue to get larger-than-normal raises?
7. Do I rate at the high end of the performance ratings?
8. Do I have a plan with measurable objectives, and have I updated it recently?

Source: John Rosche, "Who's Managing Your Career?" *Contract Management* 44, no. 2 (February 2004): 20–22.

called "What Do You Want Your Future to Be?" in which the employee makes a personal evaluation. General Electric has developed an extensive set of career development programs, including workbooks to help employees explore life issues that affect career decisions.

Some organizations prefer to use workbooks written for the general public. Popular ones include Richard N. Bolles's *What Color Is Your Parachute?* and Dan Zadra and Kristel Wills' book, *Where Will You Be Five Years from Today?* These same books are recommended to students for help in planning their careers.

Like workbooks, career planning workshops help employees seek career planning information, make career decisions, set goals, and at the same time build confidence and self-esteem.[32] However, workshops give employees the opportunity to compare and discuss their concerns and plans with other people in similar situations and the professionals who conduct the workshops. Some workshops focus on current job performance and development plans. Others deal with broader life and career plans and values.

career counseling

The process of discussing with employees their current job activities and performance, personal and career interests and goals, personal skills, and suitable career development objectives

Career Counseling

Career counseling is the process of talking with employees about their current job activities and performance, personal and career interests and goals, personal skills, and suitable career development objectives. Career counseling can be provided by HR staff members, managers and supervisors, specialized staff counselors, or outside consultants. To truly expand an organization's talent pool, managers should make career counseling part of the performance appraisals. They can do so by simply asking employees what their career aspirations are. Once the conversation has begun, how those goals can be achieved and fit in with the organization's goals can be discussed and a career "action" plan for the employees established. Several techniques for career counseling are outlined at the end of this chapter. (See the chapter Appendix titled Personal Career Development.) As employees approach retirement, they may be encouraged to participate in preretirement programs, which often include counseling. Preretirement programs will be discussed in Chapter 11.

In helping individuals plan their careers, it is important for organizations to recognize that younger employees today seek meaningful training assignments

Gordon Miller has truly had a boundaryless career. Miller increased his salary by more than $100,000 in five years by changing employers every year. He subsequently wrote a best seller called *Quit Your Job Often* to teach other people how to do it. Today he provides career coaching for executives and continues to author books.

Courtesy of Gordon Miller

that are interesting and involve challenge, responsibility, and a sense of empowerment. They also have a greater concern for the contribution that their work in the organization will make to society. Unfortunately, they are frequently given responsibilities they view as rudimentary, boring, and composed of too many "busy-work" activities. Some organizations are attempting to retain young managers with high potential by offering a **fast-track program** that enables them to advance more rapidly than those with less potential. A fast-track program can provide for a relatively rapid progression—lateral transfers or promotions—through a number of managerial positions designed to expose the employee to different functions within the organization.

Mentoring

It is common to hear people mention individuals at work who influenced them. They frequently refer to their immediate managers who were especially helpful as career developers. But they also mention others at higher levels in the organization who provided them with guidance and support in the development of their careers. Executives and managers who coach, advise, and encourage employees are called mentors.

A mentoring relationship need not be formal. In reality, informal mentoring goes on daily within every type of organization. Generally, the mentor initiates the relationship, but sometimes an employee will approach a potential mentor for advice. Most mentoring relationships develop over time on an informal basis. They frequently end that way, too. However, proactive organizations emphasize formal mentoring plans that assign a mentor to employees considered for upward movement in the organization. GE, for example, selects the top 20 percent of its performers and allows these people to choose their own mentors from a list of top executives. Under a good mentor, learning focuses on goals, opportunities, expectations, standards, and assistance in fulfilling one's potential. Microsoft, Boeing, Hewlett-Packard, Intel, Southwest Airlines, and State Farm Insurance are among the many companies with mentoring programs.[33]

The top ten myths about mentors are shown in Figure 5.12. Figure 5.13 shows a list of the most effective features of mentors as well as partners. To form an effective mentoring relationship, an employee seeking a mentor should follow a few general guidelines.

> **mentors**
> Individuals who coach, advise, and encourage individuals of lesser rank

1. *Research the person's background.* Do your homework. The more you know about your potential mentor, the easier it will be to approach him or her and establish a relationship that will work for both of you.

2. *Make contact with the person.* Have a mutual friend or acquaintance introduce you, or get involved with your potential mentor in business settings. That will help the mentor see your skills in action.

3. *Request help on a particular matter.* Let the mentor know that you admire him or her, and ask for help in that arena. For example, you might say, "You're good at dealing with customers. Would it be OK if I came to you for advice on my customers?" Keep your request simple and specific.

4. *Consider what you can offer in exchange.* Mentoring is a two-way street. If you can do something for your potential mentor then, by all means, tell him or her.

5. *Arrange a meeting.* Once your specific request has been accepted, you are ready to meet with your potential mentor. Never go into this meeting cold. Set goals, iden-

tify your desired outcomes, and prepare a list of questions. Listen attentively. Then ask your prepared questions and request specific suggestions.

6. *Follow up.* After the meeting, try some of your potential mentor's suggestions and share the results. Express appreciation by identifying something in particular that was significant to you.

7. *Ask to meet on an ongoing basis.* After your potential mentor has had a chance not only to meet and interact with you, but also to see the value of what he or she can provide, you are in a good position to request an ongoing relationship. Suggest that you meet with him or her regularly, or ask permission to get help on an ad hoc basis.[34]

When done well, the mentoring process is beneficial for both the pupil and the mentor. One survey found, for example, that 77 percent of companies with successful mentoring programs reported that they effectively increased employee retention.[35] Firms can help facilitate mentoring by rewarding mentors in their performance appraisals.

FIGURE 5.12   Top Ten Myths about Mentors

Myth 1: *Mentors exist only for career development.* Sometimes the mentor focuses on formal career development. Sometimes the mentor is teacher, counselor, and friend. Some mentors assume all these roles. This enhances both personal and professional development.

Myth 2: *You need only one mentor.* We can have multiple mentors in our lives. Different mentors provide different things and tap different facets of our lives.

Myth 3: *Mentoring is a one-way process.* Learning flows both ways. The mentor often learns from the protégé, so the growth is reciprocal.

Myth 4: *A mentor has to be older than the protégé.* Age does not matter. Experience and wisdom matter. Do not deprive yourself of learning opportunities from others who have rich experiences.

Myth 5: *A mentor has to be the same gender and race as the protégé.* The purpose of mentoring is to learn. Do not deprive yourself. Seek mentors who are different from you.

Myth 6: *Mentor relationships just happen.* Being in the right place at the right time can help, but the key to selecting a good mentor is what (not whom) you need. Do not be afraid to actively seek a mentor.

Myth 7: *Highly profiled people make the best mentors.* Prestige and success can be good, but good advice, leadership styles, work ethics, and the like vary by individuals. Good mentors are people who challenge you according to your needs, readiness, and aspirations.

Myth 8: *Once a mentor, always a mentor.* Over time, the mentor should pull back and let the protégé go his or her own way. Although the two may maintain contact, the relationship changes over time.

Myth 9: *Mentoring is a complicated process.* The most complicated part is getting out of a bad mentor relationship. If the relationship is not productive, find a tactful way to disengage.

Myth 10: *Mentor-protégé expectations are the same for everyone.* Individuals seek mentors for the same reasons: resources, visibility, enhanced skills, and counsel. But each individual brings different expectations. The key is understanding where the protégé is now, not where he or she should be.

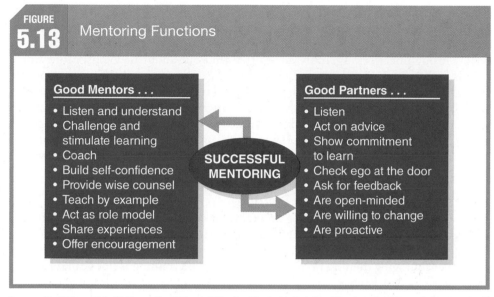

FIGURE 5.13   Mentoring Functions

Good Mentors . . .
- Listen and understand
- Challenge and stimulate learning
- Coach
- Build self-confidence
- Provide wise counsel
- Teach by example
- Act as role model
- Share experiences
- Offer encouragement

SUCCESSFUL MENTORING

Good Partners . . .
- Listen
- Act on advice
- Show commitment to learn
- Check ego at the door
- Ask for feedback
- Are open-minded
- Are willing to change
- Are proactive

Source: Matt Starcevich, PhD and Fred Friend, "Effective Mentoring Relationships from the Mentee's Perspective," *Workforce*, supplement (July 1999): 2–3. Used with permission of the Center for Coaching and Mentoring, Inc., http://coachingandmentoring.com.

Not surprisingly, mentoring is also being done via e-mail or using software or online programs, a type of mentoring that has become known as *e-mentoring*. E-mentoring is commonplace at IBM. "A lot of our people work virtually, and mentoring can erase geographic and business-unit borders," explained one IBM manager.[36] At Rockwell Collins, a communication and aviation electronics company, nearly 6,000 employees utilize an e-mentoring software solution developed by Triple Creek. The software can connect to a firm's existing talent management software, gauge competency gaps, and match mentors and mentees based upon their knowledge and learning needs.[37]

Networking

As the number of contacts grows, mentoring broadens into a process of **career networking**. As a complement to mentoring, in which relationships are more selective, networking relationships tend to be more varied and temporary. The networks can be internal to a particular organization or connected across many different organizations.

According to the Monster Career Advice Center, there are many ways to identify networking contacts. Some of the best places to consider are the following:

- Your college alumni association or career office networking lists

- Your own extended family

- Your friends' parents and other family members

- Your professors, advisors, coaches, tutors, and clergy

- Your former bosses and your friends' and family members' bosses

- Members of clubs, religious groups, and other organizations to which you belong

- All of the organizations near where you live or go to school

career networking
The process of establishing mutually beneficial relationships with other businesspeople, including potential clients and customers

Monster also has a networking feature that allows job seekers to meet up with other people who have similar career interests. Social networking sites such as LinkedIn.com and Tribe.net have begun connecting professionals in formal and informal ways as well. Through networking, individuals often find out about new jobs, professional trends, and other opportunities. In a survey of executives by the human resources firm DBM, 61 percent said that they had found new positions in the previous year through networking. Another study of fifteen high-ranking executive women found that although many of them lacked formal mentors, they had successfully engaged in a kind of "360-degree" networking: The women made it a point to form and maintain relationships with people above, below, and at the same level as themselves, which helped advance their careers.[38]

Career Self-Management Training

Many organizations are establishing programs for employees on how they can engage in *career self-management*. The training focuses on two major objectives: (1) helping employees learn to continuously gather feedback and information about their careers and (2) encouraging them to prepare for mobility. The training is not geared to skills and behaviors associated with a specific job, but rather toward long-term personal effectiveness. Essentially, career self-management is not a process but an event. Employees typically undertake self-assessments to increase their awareness of their own career attitudes and values. In addition, they are encouraged to widen their viewpoint beyond the next company promotion to broader opportunities in the marketplace, attend conferences, and develop good long-term relationships with their bosses or other mentors. Participants might be encouraged to engage in career networking or to identify other means to prepare for job mobility, such as hearing reports from employees who made transitions to new job opportunities both within and outside the organization.[39]

 # Developing a Diverse Talent Pool

LEARNING OUTCOME 6

How are the career challenges of minorities both similar to and different from those of women in your opinion?

To meet their legal obligations to provide equal employment opportunities, employers often develop formal EEO/affirmative action policies to recruit and promote members of protected classes so that their representation at all levels within the organization approximates their proportionate numbers in the labor market. But the reasons to develop a diverse talent pool are not merely legal ones—not by a long shot. Today, ethnic groups represent approximately 30 percent of the total U.S. population. In the next ten years, however, the number is expected to grow to 50 percent. By 2060, the U.S. Census Bureau estimates that ethnic minorities will account for an astounding 90 percent of the population. These groups have a huge amount of buying power, and that power is growing. Some researchers predict that companies that fail to diversify their talent pools will have a hard time identifying with their target customers and competing with firms that do. But perhaps most importantly, as companies face tougher competition in the United States and abroad, they will need all the leadership, productivity, innovation, and creativity the talent pool has to offer. Put simply, a diverse talent pool increases the range of human capital available to the firm.

Recruiting and Developing Women

Making up a little under half of the total U.S. labor force, women constitute the largest of the protected classes. A major employment obstacle for women, both skilled and unskilled, is the stereotyped thinking that persists within our society. Women traditionally have been at a disadvantage because they have not been part of the so-called "good old boys' network." The good old boys' network is an informal network of interpersonal relationships that has traditionally provided a way for senior (male) members of the organization to pass along news of advancement opportunities and other career tips to junior (male) members as well as to recommend them.

Still another barrier has been that women in the past had fewer years of experience in the workforce and were not as likely as men to have professional training and preparation for entrance or advancement into management positions. This situation is changing, however. Today, three out of five college graduates are women, and there have been significant increases in the enrollment of women in programs leading to degrees in management and other professional fields. As a consequence of these changes, an increasing number of women enter the labor force in managerial positions. At IBM, scores of women run $100 million-plus divisions.

Still, the entire picture is not necessarily a rosy one. A 2008 Catalyst survey of more than 4,000 full-time employed men and women who graduated from top MBA programs worldwide found that the women are paid $4,600 less in their first post-MBA jobs, occupy lower-level management positions, and have significantly less career satisfaction than their male counterparts with the same education.[40] And the proportion of women in top echelons of management, although growing, still remains extremely low. In 2011, only fifteen of the companies in the Fortune 500 were run by women. But that is twelve more than there were in 2000. Although these data suggest that there has been some progress, there is much left to do to break the "glass ceiling."

Eliminating Women's Barriers to Advancement

Glass ceiling audits, also known as "corporate reviews," are conducted by the Department of Labor to identify practices that appear to hinder the upward mobility of both qualified women and minorities. Black women in particular are at risk of not being promoted relative to other groups, say labor economists. The Department of Labor looks for such things as equal access to the following:

- Upper-level management and executive training

- Rotational assignments

- International assignments

- Opportunities for promotion

- Opportunities for executive development programs at universities

- Desirable compensation packages

- Opportunities to participate on high-profile project teams

- Upper-level special assignments

Organizations are increasingly conducting their own glass ceiling audits prior to government review to avoid fines and externally imposed corrective action. These audits can document any ceilings and the reasons they exist. Self-audits are one step toward tapping the potential of a diversified workforce. Following the largest class-action suit ever brought in the United States, Walmart began conducting self-audits. The company now has certain promotion goals for women and minorities. For example, if 40 percent of the qualified people who apply for assistant store manager positions are women, 40 percent of those hired should be women.

To combat their difficulty in advancing to management positions, female employees have developed their own women's networks. At Burlington Northern Santa Fe Railway, a women's network serves as a system for encouraging and fostering women's career development and for sharing information, experiences, and insights. Women in lower levels of the company are mentored by women at higher levels. Corporate officers are invited to regularly scheduled network meetings to discuss such matters as planning, development, and company performance. Network members view these sessions as an opportunity to let corporate officers know of women who are interested in and capable of furthering their careers.[41] Minorities and women are also breaking through the glass ceiling by starting their own businesses. As one entrepreneur put it, "It's not hard to break through the glass ceiling when you own it."

Advancing Women to Management

In addition to breaking down the barriers to advancement, the development of women managers demands a better understanding of women's needs and the requirements of the management world. Many employers now offer special training to women who are on a management career path. They may use their own staff or outside firms to conduct this training. Opportunities are also available for women to participate in seminars and workshops that provide instruction and experiences in a wide variety of management topics.

Accommodating Families

One of the major problems women have faced is balancing their careers with their families. Women whose children are at an age requiring close parental attention often experience conflict between their responsibility to the children and their duty to the employer. If the conflict becomes too painful, they may decide to forgo their careers, at least temporarily, and leave their jobs.

In recent years, many employers, including AFLAC, SunTrust Banks, Quaker Oats Company, Abbott Labs, Bristol-Myers Squibb, IBM, and the accounting firm KPMG, have launched programs that are mutually advantageous to the career-oriented woman and the employer. The programs, which include alternative career paths, extended leave, flextime, job sharing, and telecommuting, provide new ways to balance career and family. AFLAC, for example, offers families hot take-home meals at their on-site cafeterias to ease the burden of employees' having to prepare dinner after leaving the office for the day. The company also subsidizes babysitting for parents on Saturday nights so they can spend some free time together.[42] These efforts are paying off. Both IBM and KPMG, for example, report that their programs have helped them retain and increase their numbers of women workers.

Nonetheless, maintaining a balance between work and family still appears difficult for employees. After reaching a high in 1998, the number of working women with children under age one has dropped off slightly. A survey by the Pew Research Center found that 60 percent of employed mothers see part-time work as the ideal scenario, a 12 percent jump up from a survey taken in 1997. "Women are about to quit their jobs because of this," says Cary Funk with the center. "It's more an expression of the difficulties in combining work and child-raising responsibilities in today's world."

It is now not just mothers who are feeling the tug-of-war between work and family. In the last decade, the number of stay-at-home dads has tripled.[43]

Recruiting and Developing Minorities

Since the passage of the Civil Rights Act of 1964, many members of minority groups have been able to realize a substantial improvement in their social and economic well-being. Increasing numbers of blacks and Hispanics are now in the upper income tax brackets by virtue of their entrance into professional, engineering, and managerial positions. However, the proportion of minorities in these areas is still substantially below their proportions in the total population. Moreover, unemployment among minorities, particularly youth, continues to be critically high. The rates climb even higher during economic downturns when employment opportunities become harder to find.

For many minorities, employment opportunities still remain exceedingly limited because of educational and societal disadvantages. Also, mainstream, traditional recruitment methods may prove ineffective in reaching them. Community action agencies, civil rights organizations, and church groups within communities can provide a means for recruiters to reach inner-city residents. Special media advertising targeted to this group can also be effective. Highlights in HRM 5 shows how to design a tailored approach to diversity planning.

Providing Minority Internships

Internships are one way in which organizations are building ongoing relationships with prospective minority employees. For example, in the media industry, ABC, NBC, CBS, Fox, and a host of cable companies have made substantial contributions to the Emma L. Bowen Foundation, which provides internships, college scholarships, and postgraduate employment for minorities. *The Chicago Tribune* offers a newsroom training program for aspiring minority journalists who want to work as news reporters. In another effort, Lockheed Martin teamed up with Operation Enterprise, the

Businesswoman Indra Nooyi has broken through many barriers on her rise to the role of CEO of PepsiCo.

NATALIA KOLESNIKOVA/AFP/Getty Images

American Management Association's summer program for high school and college students, to offer ten-week paid internships to students of America's historically black colleges and universities.[44]

Since 1973, Inroads, Inc., an internship organization, has arranged for minority college students to get tutoring, counseling, and summer internships with large corporations. Inroads has twenty-five offices serving more than 2,000 interns at over 200 companies. Participants report that Inroads has raised their aspirations and has taught them how to adjust to the corporate world, and more than three-quarters of them end up taking permanent jobs with companies where they have interned. Benefits for the corporation include early access to talented minorities, opportunities to hire college graduates who understand the company's business and its culture, and a greater number of minorities pursuing careers in the traditionally underrepresented fields of engineering and business.[45]

Advancing Minorities to Management

The area of employment that has been the slowest to respond to affirmative action appeals is the advancement of minorities to middle- and top-management positions. That will likely change as the demographics of the United States changes and the percentage of people with minority backgrounds increases. Abbott Laboratories and Sara Lee are among a growing number of companies that are committed to increasing their ranks of minority managers. These companies believe that increasing the number of the minorities they hire and promote today is critical to their future success.[46] The Society of Human Resources Management offers annual conferences, which offer a training and networking opportunity for HR professionals responsible for recruiting diverse workforces. General Electric provides much-needed access to mentors and actively fosters leadership along the way through minority networks. Its African-American Forum (AAF) began informally but has grown into a major initiative.[47]

In recent years, black women have been rising more rapidly than black men in corporate America. Over the past decade, this group has grown dramatically. The reasons black women are overtaking black men are many and complex. However, in spite of their progress, both black women and black men need continued support in their development and advancement.

While minority managers do play a part in creating a better climate for groups that are discriminated against in advancement opportunities, top managers and the HR department have the primary responsibility for creating conditions within their organizations that are favorable for recognizing and rewarding performance on the basis of objective, nondiscriminatory criteria.

Other Important Talent Concerns

Recruiting the Disabled

If someone told HR managers where they could find six million working-age people who are proven problem-solvers, provide a tax benefit for their companies, and have higher retention rates than average employees, they likely would ask: "What's the catch?" Not only is there no catch, but such a group of potential employees also currently exists. They are disabled people.[48]

According to the U. S. Census Bureau, about 49.7 million Americans, including people of all ages, have a disability. About two-thirds of these individuals have a severe disability. Currently, however, only about 21 percent of disabled Americans

HIGHLIGHTS IN **HRM**
Recruiting for Diversity

5

With increasingly higher levels of globalization, it is clear that organizations must actively pursue workforce diversity in order to reach new markets and develop greater intellectual capital. To create a program that taps into and retains a diverse pool of top talent, an organization's HR professionals must:

- Ascertain whether diversity is adequately represented in the firm's workforce by comparing company data to the statistics on diversity within the general workforce in the region. Diversity data within a firm should be broken down and measured across various specific categories, such as management, customer service, accounting, and so forth.
- Clearly define the goals of the diversity recruitment and retention program, and ensure that managers of all levels understand its significance and support its motives.
- Understand demographic changes in the workforce.
- Build long-term relationships with minority organizations, colleges, and other strategic resources.
- Become the employer of choice for a diverse workforce by developing a diversity-friendly corporate culture and fostering a culturally sensitive work environment.
- Establish a presence among minority communities by participating in job fairs, targeting recruitment advertising to minority publications such as *Diversity Inc.*, and monitoring all known websites where résumés of diverse individuals can be found.
- Use internal employee resource groups. Demonstrate the organization's commitment to diversity by making it a formal part of the Employee Referral Program.
- Train hiring managers to ensure that diverse applicants are not discounted in the interviewing process because they are different.
- Measure the efficacy of these recruitment efforts, and use the results to improve the program.

Source: Condensed from Patricia Digh, "Getting People in the Pool: Diversity Recruitment That Works," *HRMagazine* 44, no. 10 (October 1999): 94–98; John Sullivan and Sally Baack, "Diversity Recruiting Is a Failure: It's Time to Raise the Bar," www.multiculturaladvantage.com; Aaron Green, "Diversity Recruiting: Getting It Right," www.boston.com.

between ages twenty-one and sixty-four are working.[49] The greatest numbers have impairments that are hearing-, vision-, or back-related.

Of those who do not work, the majority would like to. These individuals have often been rejected for employment because of the mistaken belief that there were no jobs within an organization that they might be able to perform effectively. Fears that the disabled might have more accidents or that they might aggravate existing disabilities have also deterred their employment. The lack of special facilities for physically impaired people, particularly those who use wheelchairs, has been a further employment restriction. However, physical obstructions are being eliminated as employers are making federally legislated improvements to accommodate disabled workers.

As you learned in Chapter 3, the Americans with Disabilities Act of 1990 and the amendments to it require employers to provide "reasonable accommodations" to people with disabilities, including people with serious chronic ailments such as diabetes, epilepsy, intellectual disabilities, multiple sclerosis, muscular dystrophy, cancer, and many other impairments. Many managers are unaware of how little these accommodations cost. According to data from the U.S. Department of Labor's Office of Disability Employment, 15 percent of accommodations cost nothing; 51 percent cost between $1 and $500; 12 percent cost between $501 and $1,000; and 22 percent cost more than $1,000. For example, an employee in a wheelchair who might not be able to perform duties that involve certain physical activities may be quite capable of working at a bench or a desk. The fact that disabled people are dependable, achieve superior attendance, and experience lower turnover offsets the costs of accommodating them in most cases.

IBM hired its first disabled employee in 1914. This is not surprising, since the company makes software and other products that help eliminate workplace barriers for the disabled. IBM's viewpoint is that no employee should be overlooked because of a disability because he or she might be the person to develop the next generation of hardware or software from which the company will profit. Indeed, several of the company's deaf researchers are doing world-class work with new technologies, including voice recognition technology.

IBM also participates in mentoring and internships for the disabled. The Workforce Recruitment Program for College Students with Disabilities (WRP) is one internship organization. WRP puts together profiles of thousands of college students and recent graduates seeking summer internships or permanent employment nationwide with federal agencies. These profiles are then made available free of charge to business owners. The candidates are skilled in a wide variety of fields, and each has a disability. This effort to help employers find workers and help the disabled find jobs is cosponsored by the U.S. Department of Labor and the Office of Disability Employment Policy. Similarly, the American Association for the Advancement of Science has a program called Entry Point, which has placed more than hundreds of science and engineering students with disabilities in internships in the public and private sectors. The vast majority of these students have gone on to graduate schools or jobs in science and technology. Highlights in HRM 6 lists tips from employers that have been successful in hiring and retaining talented employees with disabilities along with various sources for their recruitment.

Finally, there is the illiteracy handicap. Between 45 and 50 percent of adults in the United States have only limited reading and writing abilities needed to handle the minimal demands of daily living or job performance. One in seven are considered illiterate. Employers are encountering increasing numbers of employees, including college graduates, whose deficient reading and writing skills limit their performance on the job. The U.S. Department of Labor estimates that illiteracy costs U.S. businesses upward of $60 billion a year in lost productivity. To address literacy problems, organizations such as Smith & Wesson, Hewlett-Packard, Motorola, and the City of Phoenix instituted basic skill assessment programs to teach reading, math, and communication skills to employees who show some level of deficiency. America's Literacy Directory (ALD), sponsored by the National Institute for Literacy, connects employers, learners, volunteers, social service providers, and others with literacy programs in all fifty states and U.S. territories. Employees and employers need only go to ALD's online directory and type in their locations to find the literacy help centers nearest them.

Employing the Older Workforce

Today there is a definite trend by organizations to hire older people. In addition, many workers are expressing an interest in postponing their retirements or working

HIGHLIGHTS IN **HRM**
6
Hiring and Retaining Employees with Disabilities

Here are seven tips for organizations that want to successfully recruit, hire, and retain employees with disabilities:

1. *Dispel any myths with real data.* When it comes to hiring people with disabilities, there are many preconceived ideas that present barriers to employment. For example, some employers mistakenly believe their workers' compensation insurance will increase if they hire someone with a disability. This is a myth. Insurance rates are based on the hazards of the operation and the organization's accident experience, not on the physical conditions of the workers. Another common assumption is that people with disabilities do not have training or education, yet many of these candidates are well qualified due to college degrees and/or extensive experience.

2. *Know the laws.* Hiring managers in all sizes and types of organizations should familiarize themselves with the required legal provisions for employees with disabilities, especially those spelled out in the Americans with Disabilities Act (ADA). It is essential for employers to know both their rights and their obligations under the law so they can be prepared to comply with all regulations.

3. *Make sure your company is physically safe and accessible.* Some employers are reluctant to hire people with disabilities because they fear the costs associated with making their workplace accessible and safe. For example, they know they may need to widen doors, provide wheelchair ramps, and install a wheelchair-accessible restroom facility. However, the President's Committee on Job Accommodation Networks (JAN) often assesses employers of people with disabilities, and it has found that access and safety accommodations can often be made easily and relatively inexpensively.

4. *Define and analyze all jobs within the company and their requirements, then put them in writing.* Written job descriptions identify essential job functions and help applicants identify which jobs he or she would be qualified for and enjoy. This is the best means of ensuring a good match between job and candidate.

5. *Maintain the organization's standards and expectations.* Some people believe that individuals with disabilities receive special treatment and unfair advantages, but the purpose of "accommodations" as defined by law is to enhance an individual's ability to accomplish work tasks, not to lower the organization's expectations. Employers need to be fair and responsible, but should not go overboard on accommodating an employee with a disability.

6. *Make a companywide commitment.* Time and again, success stories are always found in companies in which the organization's leadership is committed to hiring people with disabilities and this commitment is assimilated into the company culture.

7. *Connect with similar businesses that have hired employees with disabilities.* If an organization is just starting to explore the possibility of hiring employees with disabilities, it might be useful to discover other organizations that have successfully achieved this goal. Chambers of commerce, local business associations, and online forums all offer valuable resources for learning how other firms have integrated employees with disabilities into their workforces.

Sources: Ed Holen and Penny Jo Haney, "Consider Employing People with Disabilities," Wenatchee Business Journal 17, no. 10 (October 2003): A19; Kelly Butler, "Ten Million Ways to Fill the Talent Gap," Employee Benefit News 21, no. 3 (March 2007): 22–24; Oce Harrison, "Employing People with Disabilities: Small Business Concerns and Recommendations," www.foremployers.com.

part-time in their retirement years.[50] The move has come both as a result of changing workforce demographics, rising health care costs, and the shrinking retirement savings account of workers as a result of the last recession. Organizations realize that older workers have proven employment experience, have job "savvy," and are reliable employees. They are also an excellent recruitment source to staff part-time and full-time positions that are otherwise hard to fill.

As we have indicated, retirees often return or stay in the workforce at the behest of their employers, who cannot afford to lose the knowledge accumulated by longtime employees or their reliable work habits that have a positive effect on the entire work group. To prevent an exodus of talent, employers will need to implement human resources strategies to help retain and attract the talent older workers have to offer. Moreover, as the workforce ages, employers will need to make workplace adaptations to help older workers cope with the physical problems they will experience, such as poorer vision, hearing, and mobility.

For some firms, especially in jobs for which it is difficult to attract and retain skilled, reliable employees, older workers can be the permanent solution to an intractable problem. Many older workers gravitate to non-full-time forms of work, especially independent contracting or consulting, on-call work (such as substitute nursing or teaching), and temporary work in administrative or IT roles. Employers are coming through for them.

The AARP, the advocacy group for retired people, has a "National Employer Team" page on its website with links to firms that recruit older workers by offering them flexible work schedules and health benefits. The Home Depot, Staples, and Toys "R" US are some of the firms featured on the site.

Employing Dual Career Couples

As discussed throughout this book, the employment of both members of a couple has become a way of life in North America. Economic necessity and social forces have encouraged this trend to the point that over 80 percent of all marriages are now **dual career partnerships** in which both members follow their own careers and actively support each other's career development. As with most lifestyles, the dual career arrangement has its positive and negative sides. A significant number of organizations are concerned with the problems facing dual career couples and offer assistance to them. Flexible working schedules are the most frequent organizational accommodation to these couples. Other arrangements include extended leave policies under which either parent may stay home with a newborn, policies that allow work to be performed at home, daycare on an organization's premises, and job sharing.

The difficulties that dual career couples face include the need for quality child care, time demands, and emotional stress. However, the main problem these couples face is the threat of relocation, which is why gaining the support of a spouse or significant other is crucial for employees. Many large organizations now offer some kind of job-finding assistance for spouses of employees who are relocated, including payment of fees charged by employment agencies, job counseling firms, and executive search firms.

Organizations are also developing networking relationships with other employers to find jobs for the spouses of their relocating employees. These networks can provide a way to "share the wealth and talent" in a community while simultaneously assisting in the recruitment efforts of the participating organizations.[51]

Relocating dual career couples to foreign facilities is a major issue that international employers face. Fewer employees are willing to relocate without assistance for their spouses. Many employers have developed effective approaches for integrating the various allowances typically paid for overseas assignments when husband and wife work

dual career partnerships

Couples in which both members follow their own careers and actively support each other's career development

for the same employer. Far more complex are the problems that arise when couples work for two different employers. The problems associated with overseas assignments of dual career couples will be examined in greater detail in Chapter 15.

Summary

LEARNING OUTCOME 1 To expand the talent pool of organizations—the number and kind of people available for employment—organizations must focus on multiple approaches to recruitment and career management. Which internal and outside sources and methods are used in recruiting will depend on the strategy and goals of the organization, conditions of the labor market, and specifications of the jobs to be filled.

LEARNING OUTCOME 2 Employers usually find it advantageous to use internal promotions and transfers to fill as many openings as possible above the entry level. By recruiting from within, an organization can capitalize on the previous investments they have made in recruiting, selecting, training, and developing its current employees and rewarding them. Internal job postings, performance appraisals, skills inventories, replacement charts, and assessment centers are ways in which firms identify internal talent.

LEARNING OUTCOME 3 Outside candidates are recruited when internal talent is lacking or a firm wants to hire employees with expertise from other organizations for competitive reasons and to prevent the inbreeding of ideas within their organization. To help meet a firm's EEO requirement and diversify its talent pools, firms also look externally for candidates. Advertisements, the Internet, social networks, mobile recruiting, employment agencies, tapping educational institutions and professional associations, and rerecruiting are among the many ways firms recruit external candidates.

LEARNING OUTCOME 4 HR managers have many tools available to them to gauge their efforts and improve their recruiting. Using realistic job reviews, surveying managers and applicants about the process, and examining metrics such as the cost per hire, time to fill a position, and yield ratios are some of the ways

in which firms evaluate their recruiting efforts. An applicant tracking system (ATS) can help a firm automatically track and calculate many of these statistics.

LEARNING OUTCOME 5 Identifying and developing talent is a responsibility of all managers. A career development program is a dynamic process that should integrate the career goals of employees with the goals of the organization. Job opportunities can be identified by studying jobs and determining the knowledge and skills each one requires. Once that is accomplished, key jobs can be identified, and job progressions can be planned. These progressions can then serve as a basis for developing the career paths of employees. Employees need to be made aware of the organization's philosophy and its goals; otherwise they will not know how their goals match those of the organization. Mentoring has been found to be valuable for providing guidance and support to employees and potential managers.

LEARNING OUTCOME 6 The first step toward facilitating the career development of women is to eliminate barriers to their advancement. Creating women's networks, providing special training for women, accepting women as valued members of the organization, providing mentors for them, and accommodating families have been found to be effective ways to facilitate women's career development.

A diversified workforce is composed of many different groups, an important segment of which is minority groups. Many organizations have special programs such as internships that provide minority groups with hands-on experience as well as special training opportunities. Other groups that require the attention of management are the disabled, older workers, and dual career couples, who often need flexible working options.

Key Terms

applicant tracking system
branding
career counseling
career networking
career paths
career plateau
dual career partnerships
employee leasing
employee profile

fast-track program
global sourcing
internal labor market
job progressions
mentors
nepotism
9-box grid
outplacement services
passive job seekers

promotion
recruiting process outsourcing
  (RPO)
realistic job preview (RJP)
relocation services
rerecruiting
sabbatical
transfer
yield ratio

Discussion Questions 💬

LEARNING OUTCOME 1 Name some companies with whom you have done business. Then discuss how you view their employer brands. Would you want to work for them or not? How might these firms improve their employer brands?

LEARNING OUTCOME 2 More than 50 percent of all MBAs leave their first employer within five years. Although the change may mean career growth for these individuals, it represents a loss to the employers. What are some of the probable reasons a MBA would leave his or her first employer?

LEARNING OUTCOME 3 In what ways do executive search firms differ from traditional employment agencies?

LEARNING OUTCOME 4 Explain how realistic job previews (RJPs) operate. Why do they appear to be an effective recruitment technique?

LEARNING OUTCOME 5 What contributions can a career management program make to an organization that is forced to downsize its operations?

LEARNING OUTCOME 6 What are some of the barriers to advancement opportunities for women and minorities in many organizations?

On the Job: Video Cases 🎬

Career Development at Metropolitan Bakery

The two co-owners of Metropolitan Bakery plus a store manager and a warehouse employee talk about how talent is managed and developed. Special issues for a small business are described as well as a description about how the organization has evolved from the beginning. The organization has a culture of developing talent, and the video describes the various approaches including apprenticeships, coaching, adding responsibilities as employees learn, pairing new employees with excellent seasoned workers, and providing continuous performance feedback to encourage growth.

What to Watch for and Ask Yourself

- Would Metropolitan Bakery's approach to employee development reflect an organization-centered approach to career planning or an individual-centered approach to career planning? Explain your answer.

- The video introduces an employee that works in packaging and a store manager. What career stages would apply to these two specific employees? Explain your answer. Is Metropolitan Bakery providing development for each of these employees that is appropriate to their career stage?

HRM EXPERIENCE
Career Management

We often think that successful people plan their careers out in advance and then work toward their goals in a very logical, sequential manner. Although some successes are designed and implemented this way, others are created through insight, preparedness, and taking advantages of opportunities as they arise.

Assignment

1. Form teams of four to six members. Identify three different people to interview about their careers. One person should be in the early stages of his or her career; one should be in midcareer; and one should be in the final stages of his or her career.

2. Ask each person to identify his or her career goals and how they have changed or are expected to change over time.

3. Ask each person to describe the sequence of events that led to where he or she is. How well does that story align with the traditional model of careers?

4. Ask each person what (if anything) he or she would do differently. Ask what advice he or she has for you about how to approach your career.

Case Study   1

Employee referrals and social recruiting, which already began melding through Job-vite, and other tools are growing even closer as new vendors enter the field and corporations test how well their jobs spread on Facebook and other sites. A New York startup called Referrio is quietly entering this niche. On the Referrio site, Cisco, for example, lists eleven jobs and is offering about $2,500 per job for people who fill the openings by spreading the word through social media sites or email.

Meanwhile, Virginia Mason Medical Center has set up a "grab this widget" tool for employees to share the organization's jobs. The Seattle-area nonprofit needs to fill a director of nursing informatics job, IT jobs for people with Cerner experience, and more. At Enterprise Rent-A-Car, employees are adding widgets about company jobs to their personal Facebook pages, and getting paid if the widgets result in a hire.

Grab a Widget and Get Paid for an Employee Referral

At Banner Health, the Phoenix and Western U.S. nonprofit, experienced nurses and occupational/speech/physical therapists are among the highest in demand. Michael Seaver, sourcing program manager, said there was "unreal" interest when the 36,000-employee organization moved to an electronic employee referral system two months ago. About 1,500 people referred candidates in about a month. This was not a social media campaign per se, but that is likely coming soon.

One sign of the employee-referral times is that Select Minds, a company mainly known for its work on alumni networks for corporations, is moving deeper into the referral world. What happens with SelectMinds is that an automated e-mail goes out to people who might be able to help fill a job. Let's say hypothetically we are talking about a software job at Nationwide, and that the job is in Dayton, Ohio. An automated email about the job opening might go out to (1) Nationwide employees in any region who are in IT jobs, and (2) all Nationwide employees in Dayton. The Select Minds e-mail allows employees to either e-mail selected contacts on LinkedIn, Facebook, and Twitter to tell them about the job, or update their LinkedIn and Facebook statuses with info on the job. The chain of link-forwarding gets tracked as it moves around online, and the employee either gets the whole referral kitty, or can share part of it with a second person, depending on how the company sets it all up.

The employee who is doing the referring can tell their company, via a short form, how well they know their friend, and what they think of them. The referring employee also gets e-mails notifying them if their contact has expressed interest in the job. Meanwhile, recruiters view a dashboard listing how many times a job was referred, and how many applications came in for it. A recruiter can drill down and see who is referring whom.

This smart marriage of referrals and social sites is where we are headed.

Questions

1. How does automating the employee referral process encourage referrals?
2. What do you think some of the drawbacks of getting referrals from social network sites might be?

Source: Excerpted from Todd Raphael, Employee Referral Programs Using More Social Media, *ere.net*, (June 22, 2010), http://www.ere.net.

Case Study 2

Preparing a Career Development Plan

Sue Ann Scott was a receptionist at the headquarters of a large corporation. A high school graduate, she had no particular skills other than an ability to organize her job duties and a pleasant personality. Unfortunately, she did not have any particular plan for career development; nevertheless, she wanted very much to improve her economic position. Recognizing her educational limitations, she began taking accounting courses on a random basis in an evening adult education program.

Scott also took advantage of the corporation's job bidding system by applying for openings that were posted, even though in many instances she did not meet the specifications listed for them. After being rejected several times, she became discouraged. Her depressed spirits were observed by Elizabeth Burroughs, one of the department managers in the corporation. Burroughs invited Scott to come to her office for a talk about the problems she was having. Scott took full advantage of this opportunity to express her frustrations and disappointments. As she unburdened herself, it became apparent both to her and to Burroughs that during interviews she repeatedly apologized for having "only a high school education," an attitude that had probably made it difficult for the interviewers to select her over other candidates who were more positive about their backgrounds and skills. Burroughs suggested that Scott might try taking a more positive approach during her interviews. For example, she could stress her self-improvement efforts at night school and the fact that she was a dependable and cooperative person who was willing to work hard to succeed in the job for which she was applying.

Following Burroughs's advice, Scott applied for a position as invoice clerk, a job for which she felt she was qualified. She made a very forceful and positive presentation during her interview, stressing the favorable qualities she possessed. As a result of this approach, she got the job. While the pay for an invoice clerk was not much more than that for a receptionist, the position did offer an avenue for possible advancement into the accounting field, in which the accounting courses she was taking would be of value.

Questions

1. What are some of the possible reasons Scott did not seek or receive advice from her immediate supervisor?
2. After reviewing the chapter, suggest all possible ways that Scott can prepare herself for career advancement.

Notes and References

1. Blake Landau, "The Uncontained Culture of the Container Store," *Human Resources IQ* (March 6, 2008), http://www.humanresourcesiq.com.
2. J. W. Marriott, "Our Competitive Strength: Human Capital," *Executive Speeches* 15, no. 5 (April–May 2001): 18–21.
3. Debbie Mack, "P&G Fights to Protect Its Bounty," *Corporate Legal Times* 13, no. 135 (February 2003): 64.
4. Edward P. Lazear, Paul Oyer, Internal and External Labor Markets: A Personnel Economics Approach, *NBER* (working paper, 2003), accessed at http://www.nber.org/papers/w10192.
5. Jeff Tanner and Mary Anne Raymond, *Principles of Marketing* (Nyack, NY: FlatWorld Knowledge, 2010): 77.
6. "The Pros and Cons of Online Recruiting," *HR Focus* 81 (April 2004 Supplement): S2.
7. Robert Rodriguez, "Filling the HR Pipeline," *HRMagazine* 49, no. 9 (September 2004): 78–84; James W. Walker, "Perspectives," *Human Resource Planning* 25, no. 1 (2002): 12–14; Stanely Ragalevsky, "CEO Succession: Five Best Practices for Internal Candidates," *Community Banker* 17, no. 2 (February 2008): 24–25.
8. "How to Implement an Effective Process for a New HR Management System," *HRFocus* 82, no. 1 (January 2005): 3–4.
9. "Heading for the Fast Track: New Studies Examine Who Gets Promoted and Why," *Knowledge@Wharton* (August 10, 2005), http//knowledge.wharton.upenn.edu.
10. Rob Yeung, "Finders Keepers," *Accountancy Magazine* 134, no. 1335 (November 2004): 42–44; Joe Dysart, "New Directions in Internet Recruiting," *Contractor Magazine* 53, no. 7 (July 2006): 33–36.
11. Ibid.
12. Jennifer Taylor Arnold, "Employee Referrals at a Keystroke," *HRMagazine* 51, no. 10 (October 2006): 82–88; Victoria Furnes, "The New Frontier," *Personnel Today* (January 22, 2008): 13–16.
13. Michelle V. Rafter, "Goin' Mobile," *Workforce Management* (February 2011): 26.
14. Ibid.
15. Douglas P. Shuit, "Monster Board Games," *Workforce Management* 82, no. 2 (November 2003): 37–42; Joe Dysart, "New Directions in Internet Recruiting," *Contractor Magazine* 53, no. 7 (July 2006): 33–36.
16. Jennifer Salopek, "Employee Referrals Remain a Recruiter's Best Friend," *Workforce Management* (December 2010), http://www.workforce.com.
17. Greg Patrick Haudek, "A Longitudinal Test of the Attraction-Selection-Attrition Model," *ETD Collection for Wayne State University* (January 1, 2001), Paper AAI3010091, http://digitalcommons.wayne.edu.
18. "In Praise of Nepotism?" *Business Ethics Quarterly* 15, no. 1 (January 2005): 153–161; Richard Reeve and Gavin Sheridan, "Nepotism: Is It Back?" *New Statesman* 135 (September 29, 2003): 22–25.
19. Madeline Laurano, "Best Practices in Re-Recruiting Top Talent," Bersin & Associates (blog), (August 06, 2009), http://www.bersin.com.
20. Leslie Stevens-Huffman, "Commitment, Consistency Are Key to College Recruiting," *Workforce Management* 85, no. 6 (March 27, 2006): 42–43.
21. Ed Frauenheim, "Companies Focus Their Attention on Flexibility," *Workforce Management* (February 2011): 3–4.

22. Chris Pentilla, "Got It Covered: If You Can't Afford to Offer Employee Benefits on Your Own, Why Not Join Forces with a PEO?" *Entrepreneur* 32, no. 2 (February 2004): 66–68; Bill Leonard, "Small Firms Prepare for Aging Workforce," *HR Magazine* 53, no. 5 (May 2008): 32.

23. Connie Winkler, "Job Tryouts Go Virtual," *HR Magazine* 51, no. 9 (September 2006): 131–134.

24. "Applicant Tracking System," *SearchCIO. com*, accessed March 18, 2011 at http://searchcio.techtarget.com.

25. Blake Landau, "The Uncontained Culture of the Container Store," *Human Resources IQ* (March 6, 2008), http://www.humanresourcesiq.com.

26. Peg O'Herron and Peggy Simonsen, "Career Development Gets a Charge at Sears Credit," *Personnel Journal* 74, no. 5 (May 1995): 103–106. See also Jules Abend, "Behind the Scenes at: Sears," *Bobbin* 39, no. 11 (June 1998): 22–26; Shari Caudron, "The De-Jobbing of America," *Industry Week* 243, no. 16 (September 5, 1994): 30–36; Edward E. Lawler III, "From Job-Based to Competency-Based Organizations," *Journal of Organizational Behavior* 15, no. 1 (January 1994): 3–15; Douglas T. Hall, "Accelerate Executive Development—At Your Peril!" *Career Development International* 4, no. 4 (1999): 237–39.

27. "How a Talent Management Plan Can Anchor Your Company's Future," *HR Focus* 81, no. 10 (October 2004): 7–10, "Heading for the Fast Track? New Studies Examine Who Gets Promoted and Why," *Knowledge@Wharton* (August 10, 2005), http://knowledge.wharton.upenn.edu.

28. Elizabeth Craig, John Kimberly, and Hamid Bouchikhhi, "Can Loyalty Be Leased?" *Harvard Business Review* 80, no. 9 (September 2002): 24–34; Edward Potter, "Improving Skills and Employability in the 21st Century," *Industrial and Labor Relations Review* 55, no. 4 (July 2002): 739–45.

29. Bonnie Rothman Morris, "New Skills, and Paying for Them," *The New York Times* (October 29, 2002), G6.

30. Suzanne C. de Janasz, Shery E. Sullivan, and Vicki Whiting, "Mentor Networks and Career Success: Lessons for Turbulent Times," *Academy of Management Executive* 17, no. 4 (November 2003): 78–92; Kate Walsh and Judith Gordon, "Creating an Individual Work Identity," *Human Resource Management Review* 18, no. 1 (March 2008): 46–61.

31. Larry Cambron, "Career Development Pays," *Far Eastern Economic Review* 164, no. 42 (October 25, 2001): 83.

32. Susan Wells, "Smoothing the Way," *HRMagazine* 46, no. 6 (June 2001): 52–58; Heath Row, "Market Yourself," *Fast Company* 58 (May 2002): 24.

33. de Janasz, Sullivan, and Whiting, "Mentor Networks and Career Success," 78–92; Carole Gaskell, "Reward Coaching Behavior to Encourage Its Use," *People Management* 14, no. 4 (February 21, 2008): 70.

34. Jeff Barbian, "The Road Best Traveled," *Training* 39, no. 5 (May 2002): 38–42; Kathleen Barton, "Will You Mentor Me?" *Training and Development* 56, no. 5 (May 2002): 90–92.

35. Elaine Biech, "Executive Commentary," *Academy of Management Executive* 17, no. 4 (November 2003): 92–94.

36. Jennifer Alsever, "How to Start a Mentorship Program," *BNET* (June 24, 2008), http://www.bnet.com.

37. Laura M. Francis, "The Shifting Shape of Mentoring," *Training & Development* (September 2009), http://www.astd.org/.

38. de Janasz, Sullivan, and Whiting, "Mentor Networks and Career Success," 78–92; Jill Rachline Marabix, "Job Search 2. Oh!" *U.S. News & World Report* 136, no. 8 (March 8, 2004): 60–63.

39. Thomas A. Stewart, "What's in It for Me?" *Harvard Business Review* 83, no. 1 (January 2005): 8; Marilyn Clarke and Margaret Patrickson, "The New Covenant of Employability," *Employee Relations* 30, no. 2 (2008): 121–141.

40. Louann Brizendine, "One Reason Women Don't Make It to the C-Suite," *Harvard Business Review* 86, no. 6 (June 2008): 36; Christine Larsen, "NAFE Top 30 Companies for Executive Women," *NAFE Magazine* 30, no. 1 (Spring 2007): 8–16; Yoji Cole, "Why Are So Few CEOs People of Color and Women?" *Diversity, Inc.* (November 7, 2007); Herminia Ibarra, Nancy M. Carter, and Christine Silva, "Why Mean Still Get More Promotions Than Women," *Harvard Business Review* (September 2010), http://hbr.org.

41. Anne M. Walsh and Susan C. Borkowski, "Cross-Gender Mentoring and Career Development in the Health Care Industry," *Health Care Management Review* 24, no. 3 (Summer 1999): 7–17.

42. Alison Stein Wellner, "Welcoming Back Mom," *HRM Magazine* 49, no. 6 (June 2004): 76–83.

43. "Mothers' Labor Force Participation," *Monthly Labor Review* 137, no. 5 (May 2004): 2; Brian Braiker and Anna Kuchment, "Just Do not Call Me Mr. Mom," *Newsweek* 150, no. 15 (October 8, 2007): 52–55; Melissa Fletcher, "Working Moms Fully in Favor of Going Part-Time," *Fort Worth Star-Telegram* (August 30, 2007): E1, 9.

44. "Recruiting Minorities," *Black Enterprise* 35, no. 6 (January 2005): 53; Debbie Smith, "Building a New Diversity Road Map," *Multichannel News* 25, no. 38 (September 20, 2004): 82.

45. "IFD, INROADS Partner for Summer Enrichment Program Internships," *AHA News* 40, no. 18 (September 6, 2004): 8; Michelle Neal, "Get Real with Diversity," *Oregon Business Magazine*, 29, no. 7 (July 2006): 9.

46. Miles White, "Paying More Than Lip Service to Diversity," *Chief Executive* 242, no. 16 (October 2002): 20–22.

47. Yeung, "Finders Keepers," 42–44; Janny Scott, "Nearly Half of Black Men Found Jobless," *The New York Times* (February 28, 2004), B1; Sylvia Ann Hewlett, Carolyn Buck Luce, and Cornel West, "Leadership in Your Midst," *Harvard Business Review* 83, no. 11 (November 2005): 74–82.

48. Joe Mullich, "Hiring without Limits," *Workforce Management* 83, no. 6 (June 1, 2004): 53–60; Julie Hotchkiss, "Growing Part-Time Employment among Workers with Disabilities," *Economic Review* 89, no. 3 (July 2004): 25–42; "Entry Point Interns Top 400 in Seventh Year," *Science* 301, no. 5637 (August 29, 2003): 1195; Kelly Butler, "Ten Million Ways to Fill the Talent Gap, *Employee Benefit News* 21, no. 3 (March 2007): 22–24.

49. "As ADA Turns 20, Harris Interactive Survey Finds Lifestyle and Economic Gaps Still Remain between Americans with and without Disabilities," Kessler Foundation and National Organization on Disability (press release), July 26, 2010.

50. Christopher Reynolds, "Boomers, Act II," *American Demographics* 27, no. 8 (October 2004): 10–12; Theresa Minton-Eversole, "Senate Forum Explores Ways to Keep Aging Workforce Working," *HR Magazine* 48, no. 10 (October 2003): 30; Carly Foster, "Rehiring Retirees among 2008's Top Recruiting Trends," *Employee Benefit News* (January 8, 2008): 5.

51. Janice Rosenberg, "Dual Career Couples Face Expensive Choices," *Bankrate.com* (July 2, 2007); Erin White, "Help Increases for Partners of Relocated Workers," *Wall Street Journal* 251, no. 70 (Marcy 25, 2008): D4.

Appendix

Personal Career Development

Because you are likely to spend more time working during your life than doing anything else, it makes sense to plan your career. There are numerous ways for an employer to contribute to an individual employee's career development and at the same time meet the organization's HR needs. Although organizations can certainly be a positive force in the development process, the primary responsibility for personal career growth still rests with the individual. After all, your career is likely to begin before and often continue after a period of employment with a particular organization. To help you, as students and prospective employees, achieve your career objectives, this Appendix is included to provide some background for your personal development and decisions.

Developing Personal Skills and Competencies

Planning for a career involves more than simply acquiring specific job knowledge and skills. Job know-how is clearly essential, but you must also develop other skills to be successful as an employee. To succeed as a manager, you must achieve still higher-level skills in the areas of communication, time management, self-motivation, interpersonal relationships, and leadership.

Hundreds of self-help books, professional journals, and magazines have been written on these topics or contain articles about them, and myriad opportunities to participate in workshops are available, often sponsored by employers.[1] For example, the pointers on the basic skills of successful career management listed in Highlights in HRM 7 shows the competencies candidates "must have" to embark on a career in any field.

Choosing a Career

Many years ago, when the management expert Peter Drucker was asked about career choices, he said, "The probability that the first job choice you make is the right one for you is roughly one in a million. If you decide your first choice is the right one, chances are that you are just plain lazy."[2] The implications of this statement are just as true today. You often have to do a lot of searching and changing to find a career path that is psychologically and financially satisfying. According to the U.S. Bureau of Labor Statistics (BLS), education, health services, and professional and business services represent the industry divisions with the strongest projected employment from now until 2016. These industries are projected to grow twice as fast as the overall economy. Information technology, leisure and hospitality, and transportation and warehousing are also projected to grow faster than average.

7 HIGHLIGHTS IN **HRM**
The Seven Career Competencies

The following are "must haves" according to a broad range of employers surveyed by Capital Workforce Partners, a Connecticut organization established by the Workforce Reinvestment Act of 1998. The organization coordinates private and public programs critical to developing a skilled, educated and vital workforce.

1. Basic Skills:
- Comprehend, explain, and analyze information
- Interpret the meaning of written material
- Perform all basic math functions with whole numbers, decimals, and fractions
- Interpret and solve algebraic equations, use math in business, i.e., calculating discounts and percentages
- Create and use tables and graphs and integrate information from multiple sources
- Employ basic and business writing skills, including accuracy in spelling, punctuation, and grammar and the ability to create business letters, e-mails, and other written communications
- Have effective oral communication skills including the ability to speak professionally and speak so others can understand

2. Computer Literacy
- Keyboarding skills
- General data entry skills
- Ability to navigate in Microsoft Windows
- Understand and use computer terminology appropriately
- Connect to the Internet or an online service
- Use e-mail (compose, retrieve, read, respond in a professional manner)

3. Customer Service
- Appropriately address customers, either in person, by telephone, e-mail, or other means
- Identify customer needs by gathering information, assessing customer's knowledge of products/services
- Provide accurate, courteous and timely information, including responding to customer comments and questions
- Work calmly with "difficult" or upset customers
- Work in a team environment
- Solve customer problems and know when to escalate a problem to a manager

4. Problem Solving and Decision Making Skills
- Read and follow multistep directions
- Learn, reason, and think creatively
- Make appropriate and reasonable decisions
- Prioritize workload
- Ask pertinent questions

5. Interpersonal Skills
Individuals meeting this competency can
- Work without supervision
- Work well with people from culturally diverse backgrounds

The Seven Career Competenciest (continued)

- Develop and maintain productive group relations
- Cooperate with others and accept supervision

6. Personal Qualities

- Has a positive, "can do" attitude
- Is a self-starter
- Habitually arrives on time and does not leave early
- Understands and can adapt to workplace culture
- Can control emotional outbursts
- Shows flexibility and adaptability
- Demonstrates self-management and dependability
- Comes to work appropriately dressed
- Demonstrates honesty and integrity
- Has addressed barriers to employment, such as substance abuse, the need for child care or related services, transportation, or criminal justice involvement

7. Job Seeking Skills

- An up-to-date, accurate résumé customized for each job using key words from advertisement and listing accomplishments; résumé should include accurate spelling and grammar, action words, appropriate white space, bullets, not paragraphs, and appropriate e-mail name and phone voice message
- Cover letter
- List of up-to-date professional references
- "Dress for Success" interview clothing
- Proof of education attainment (diploma, etc.) and any certificates earned
- At least one work-based learning experience obtained through internship (paid or unpaid); a job; work experience provided by the program with a skill rating from the supervisor in addition to letters of reference

Source: Capital Workforce Partners.

Use of Available Resources

A variety of resources are available to aid in the process of choosing a satisfying career path. Counselors at colleges and universities, as well as those in private practice, are equipped to assist individuals in evaluating their aptitudes, abilities, interests, and values as they relate to career selection. Placement offices and continuing education centers offer some type of career planning assistance. In addition to career exploration, most of them offer résumé writing help, interview preparation, and job placement assistance. Looking on the Internet is also a great way to jump-start your career planning. For example, About.com's career planning website contains a wealth of information that will help get you started. Most job-posting websites, including Monster and CareerBuilder, contain free career information as well.

Accuracy of Self-Evaluation

Successful career development depends in part on an individual's ability to conduct an accurate self-evaluation. When you are doing a self-evaluation, you need to consider factors that are personally significant to you. The most important internal factors are your interests, academic aptitude and achievement, occupational aptitudes and skills, social skills, communication skills, and leadership abilities. What activities do you like to do? Do you like working alone or with other people? Do you like technical work or creative work? Do you think you would like working in an office or would you prefer another setting? What have you always dreamed of doing?

You also need to consider the salary level, status, opportunities for advancement, and growth for the job you seek. External factors that should be assessed include your family values and expectations, economic conditions, employment trends, and job market information.

Interest Inventories

Psychologists who specialize in career counseling typically administer a battery of tests. The *Strong Vocational Interest Bank* (SVIB), developed by E. K. Strong, Jr., was among the first of the interest tests.[3] Strong found substantial differences in interests that vary from occupation to occupation and that a person's interest pattern, especially after age twenty-one, tends to become quite stable. By taking his test, now known as the *Strong Interest Inventory*, you can learn the degree to which your interests correspond with those of successful people in a wide range of occupations. Your personality type can also be obtained by using a special scoring key on the *Strong Interest Inventory* answer sheet. This key, developed by John Holland, provides scores on six personality types: (1) realistic, (2) investigative, (3) artistic, (4) social, (5) enterprising, and (6) conventional. These categories characterize not only a type of personality, but also the type of working environment that a person would find most satisfying. The *Strong Interest Inventory* must be administered by someone certified by the product's distributor CPP.[4]

Another inventory that measures both interests and skills is the *Campbell Interest and Skill Survey* (CISS), which can be taken online at a number of sites for a fee, as can the *Strong Interest Inventory*.[5] People report their levels of interest and skill using a six-point response scale on 200 interest items and 120 skill items. This information is then translated into seven orientations—influencing, organizing, helping, creating, analyzing, producing, and adventuring—and further categorized into twenty-nine basic scales such as leadership and supervision to identify occupations with advice about whether each of the occupations should be "pursued," "explored," or "avoided" by the person who took the test. Figure 5A.1 shows a portion of a profile for one individual.

Profiles such as these help individuals see how their interests and skills compare with those of a sample of people happily employed in a wide range of occupations. The About.com website includes a number of free self-assessments as do other sites such as MyPlan.com, CareerPath, LiveCareer, and JobDiagnosis. Note, however, that people have taken interest and skills inventories that dissuaded them from their chosen careers, pursued them anyway, and have become extremely successful. If you find yourself in such a situation do not be discouraged about your career choice. Consider exploring the career further via internships, informational interviews, and job shadowing (discussed next). Also, keep in mind that most people change careers multiple times during the lives. If your first choice of a career is not what you hoped it would be, you are always free to pursue another.

FIGURE 5A.1 Campbell Interest and Skill Survey

Influencing Orientation Occupational Scales

	Standard Scores	Orientation Scale					Interest/ Skill Pattern
		Very Low (30 35)	Low (40 45)	Mid-Range (50 55)	High (60)	Very High (65 70)	
Influencing	I 74						Pursue
	S 73						

	Orientation Code	Standard Scores	Influencing Occupational Scales					Interest/ Skill Pattern
			Very Low (25 30 35)	Low (40 45)	Mid-Range (50 55)	High (60 65)	Very High (70 75)	
Attorney	I	I 52						Explore
		S 84						
Financial Planner	IO	I 73						Pursue
		S 89						
Hotel Manager	IO	I 75						Pursue
		S 81						
Manufacturer's Representative	IO	I 49						Explore
		S 98						
Marketing Director	IO	I 74						Pursue
		S 87						
Realtor	IO	I 75						Pursue
		S 91						
CEO/President	IOA	I 72						Pursue
		S 90						
Human Resources Director	IOH	I 52						Explore
		S 83						
School Superintendent	IOH	I 88						Pursue
		S 87						
Advertising Account Executive	IC	I 45						Explore
		S 87						
Media Executive	IC	I 52						Explore
		S 85						
Public Relations Director	IC	I 57						Pursue
		S 84						
Corporate Trainer	ICH	I 48						Explore
		S 76						
			Very Low	Low	Mid-Range	High	Very High	

Scores: I (▬▬) = Interests; S (▬▬) = Skills
Range of middle 50% of people in the occupation: ▬ = Interests; ▬ = Skills
Orientation Code: I=Influencing; O=Organizing; H=Helping; C=Creating; N=aNalyzing; P=Producing; A=Adventuring

Source: Campbell™ Interest and Skill Survey (CISS®). Copyright © 1992 David Campbell, Ph.D. Reproduced with permission of the publisher NCS Pearson, Inc. All rights reserved. "Campbell" and "CISS" are trademarks of David P. Campbell, Ph.D.

Informational Interviews, Job Shadowing, and Internships

An **informational interview** is a conversation you have with someone in an occupation that you are interested in. You invite the person to lunch or for coffee and ask him or her what the job is really like—the good and the bad, qualifications needed, the outlook for the career, and so forth. Most people are flattered to be asked to provide career information and like to talk about what they do. However, make it clear that you are not soliciting the person for a job—just seeking information.

Job shadowing is the process of observing someone in his or her own work environment to better understand what he or she does. Generally this is done in for a few hours to a half a day. The Internet is giving people a virtual way to shadow professionals. Virtualjobshadow.com, for example, is a website where you can watch professionals in about 100 different careers explain their jobs. The site also contains information about the earnings, and outlook of the profession, its educational requirements, and search function that show the colleges that offer degrees appropriate for the profession. People that sign up for the site can also ask professional questions they might have. As we explained earlier in this chapter, internships can be a great way "tries out" a particular field of work, as is volunteering. Check with your college advisor and career placement center to find opportunities such as these.

Evaluating Long-Term Employment Opportunities

When choosing a career, you should attempt to determine the probable long-term opportunities in the occupational fields you are considering. The Department of Labor's O*Net, which we discussed in Chapter 4, contains comprehensive information about hundreds of jobs, the education they require, the types of people who enjoy doing them, the types of working conditions job holders experience, the wages they earn, and the employment outlook associated with jobs. The information is free and should be a first research step for anyone considering a particular career. Many libraries also have publications that provide details about jobs and career fields. Other online sources include America's Career Info Net, sponsored by the U.S. government. The site offers demographic and labor market information at the local, state, and national levels. Most job boards offer similar information.

Choosing an Employer

Once an individual has made a career choice, even if only tentatively, the next major step is deciding where to work. The choice of employer may be based primarily on location, the immediate availability of a position, starting salary, or other basic considerations. Douglas Hall proposes that people frequently choose an organization on the basis of its climate and how it appears to fit their needs. According to Hall, people with high needs for achievement are more likely to choose aggressive, achievement-oriented organizations. Power-oriented people are more likely to choose influential, prestigious, power-oriented organizations. Affiliative people are more likely to choose warm, friendly, supportive organizations. We know that people whose needs fit with the climate of an organization are rewarded more and are more satisfied than those who fit in less well, so it is natural to reason that fit would also be a factor in a person's choice of an organization.[6]

Knowing something about an employer and industry can give you a competitive edge both in terms of getting an interview, landing a job, and negotiating a good salary. Numerous company directories containing information about privately and publicly held companies are available. Hoovers.com is one online source. Corporate websites are another source. Often under the "Investors" or "Media" tabs you can find press releases issued by the companies in which you are interested. The releases often highlight the initiatives companies are pursuing and the directions in which they are taking their businesses. Business, industry, and professional publications are a good source, too. Simply "googling" a company can turn up a great deal of information.

Once you have landed an interview, you have the opportunity to learn more about an employer, including the type of people who work there, its corporate culture, benefits, and so forth. If you are offered a job with the firm, a website such as salary.com can help you determine whether the firm's offer is appropriate. CNNMoney.com's cost of living calculator titled "How far will my salary go in another city?" can help you figure out whether it is monetarily feasible to relocate for a job. Highlights in HRM 8 shows the questions you should ask yourself before you accept a job offer with a particular company.

Becoming an Entrepreneur

At the opening of the century, no discussion of careers would be complete if entrepreneurship opportunities were not mentioned. Being an entrepreneur—someone who starts, organizes, manages, and assumes responsibility for a business or other enterprise—offers a personal challenge that many individuals prefer over being an employee. Small businesses are typically run by entrepreneurs who accept the personal financial risks that go with owning a business but who also benefit directly from the success of the business.[7]

Small businesses are actually big employers. They employ half of all private sector employees and account for a little less than half of the total U.S. private payrolls. They also generate 60 to 80 percent of new jobs annually.[8] Someone considering starting a small business can obtain assistance from the Small Business Administration (SBA),

entrepreneur
One who starts, organizes, manages, and assumes responsibility for a business or other enterprise

8	**HIGHLIGHTS IN HRM** **Questions to Ask Yourself Before** **You Accept a Job Offer**

- Have I been offered a fair salary? Is it comparable to what other people in the same position are making?
- Have I met my potential boss? Does he or she seem like someone with whom I can have a good working relationship?
- What do I know about my potential coworkers?
- Will I be comfortable in this office environment?
- Is the corporate culture in line with my own values, attitudes, and goals?
- Can I handle the commute to this job?

FIGURE
5.A2   Twelve Steps for Starting a New Business

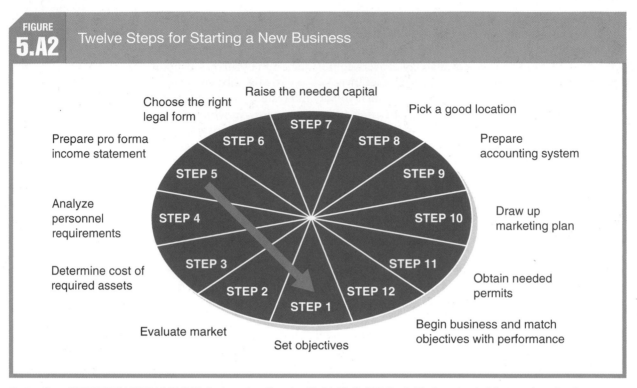

Source: From CUNNINGHAM/ALDAG/BLOCK. Business in a Changing World, 3E. © 1993 South-Western, a part of Cengage Learning, Inc. Reproduced by permission. www.cengage.com/permissions.

Using the **INTERNET**

Information about starting a business can also be found at the Small Business Administration's website. Material concerning SCORE (as a small business resource or a retirement activity) is also available on the Internet. Go to

www.cengagebrain.com

which advises and assists millions of small businesses in the United States. It is essential for one considering a small business to obtain as much information as possible from the SBA, libraries, and organizations and individuals who are knowledgeable about the type of business one is considering. For instance, valuable assistance may be obtained from members of the Service Corps of Retired Executives (SCORE), who offer advisory services under the auspices of the SBA.

Since the details of organizing a business are beyond the scope of this book, Figure 5.A1 is presented to provide an overview of the basic steps in starting a new business.[9]

Keeping a Career in Perspective

For most people, work is a primary factor in the overall quality of their lives. It provides a setting for satisfying practically the whole range of human needs and is thus of considerable value to the individual. Nevertheless, it is advisable to keep one's career in perspective so that other important areas of life are not neglected.

Developing Off-the-Job Interests

Satisfaction with one's life is a product of many forces. Unfortunately, when people complain about not having a good work-life balance, often the problem is not too much work, but too little "life," according to Randall Craig of Pinetree Advisors, a human resources strategy consulting firm.[10] Some of the more important ingredients of "life" are physical health, emotional well-being, financial security, harmonious interpersonal relationships, freedom from too much stress, and achievement of one's goals. While a career can provide some of the satisfaction that one needs, most people find it necessary to turn to interests and activities outside their career. Off-the-job activities not only provide a respite from daily work responsibilities, but also offer satisfaction in areas unrelated to work. With that said, it is up to you to decide what is important to you and how to spend your work and off-the-job time. Your life is yours to live, and it is shorter than you think.

Balancing Marital and/or Family Life

As we have said, the one event that often poses the greatest threat to family needs is relocation. Families often experience conflicts between the desire to advance the careers of different parents and the desire to stay in one place and put down family roots. Many employers now provide assistance in this area, including relocation counseling, in an effort to reduce the severity of the pain that can accompany relocations.

Although relocation is a serious threat to employees with families, there are also other sources of conflict. Some work-related sources of conflict include the number of hours a person must work per week, frequency of the overtime they work, and frequency and irregularity of shift work. If an employee is experiencing ambiguity and/or conflict with his or her work role, a low level of supervisory support, or disappointment due to unfulfilled work expectations, this can affect his or her family life as well. Other sources of conflict include the need to spend an unusually large amount of time with a person's family members, either to care for children, aging elders, or a spouse. The different employment patterns in a family and dissimilarity in a couple's career orientations are also commonplace and can take a toll on employees.

A number of employers are doing more today to help their employees cope with these problems via alternative work options. Many employees are also actively looking for companies that have family-friendly policies. *Working Mother* magazine annually publishes a survey of the 100 top companies in the United States for working parents. Understand that "to be a success in the business world takes hard work, long hours, persistent effort, and constant attention. To be a success in marriage takes hard work, long hours, persistent effort, and constant attention. . . . The problem is giving each its due and not shortchanging the other."[11]

Planning for Retirement

Although you might be many years from retirement, it is never too early to plan for it. In your twenties, you will want to begin a savings plan and perhaps pay off your student loans. As you get older, your goals will probably change. Perhaps you will want to buy a home, and you will need money for a downpayment. Regardless of what stage of your life you are in, you should never neglect saving for your retirement throughout your working years. This is because a small sum of money saved early, compounded with interest over years, can amount to millions of dollars. But if you wait until later, you will have to save a lot of money for it to amount to as much.

Your employer can help you with some aspects of retirement planning by providing you with information about tax-advantaged employer and individual savings plans. But although employer-sponsored preretirement programs can be helpful (as we will see in Chapter 11), planning for your own retirement is up to you. Do you want to travel or live in another state or country? What kind of retirement does your spouse envision? How much money will all of this require? Your employer will not be able to answer these questions. However, by reading about the subject of retirement and taking it seriously while you are young, you will be able to answer these questions yourself. Planning early will help you set the stage for a healthy and satisfying retirement as free as possible from worries—especially worries that could have been avoided or minimized had you taken a few easy steps earlier in life.

Key Terms

entrepreneur

informational interview

job shadowing

Notes and References

1. A selection of self-help publications on a variety of topics may be found in any bookstore. College and university bookstores typically have a wide selection in their trade or general books department. One such book is Paul D. Tieger's *Do What You Are: Discover the Perfect Career for You through the Secrets of Personality Type.*

2. Mary Harrington Hall, "A Conversation with Peter Drucker," *Psychology Today* (March 1968): 22.

3. E. K. Strong, Jr., of Stanford University, was active in the measurement of interests from the early 1920s until his death in 1963. Since then his work has been carried on by the staff of the Measurement Research Center, University of Minnesota. The Strong Interest Inventory is distributed by Consulting Psychologists Press, Inc., to qualified people under an exclusive license from the publisher, Stanford University Press.

4. Gary D. Gottfredson and John L. Holland, *Dictionary of Holland Occupational Codes* (Lutz, FL: Psychological Assessment Resources, December 1996); Derek Parker, "The Skills Shortage: Making Headway, but No Easy Answers," *Manufacturers' Monthly* (September 2007).

5. David Lubinski, Camilla P. Benbow, and Jennifer Ryan, "Stability of Vocational Interests among the Intellectually Gifted from Adolescence to Adulthood: A 15-Year Longitudinal Study," *Journal of Applied Psychology* 80, no. 1 (February 1995): 196–200; Hope Samborn, "Left Click, Left Law," *ABA Journal* 92, no. 7 (July 2006): 58.

6. Douglas T. Hall and Jonathan E. Moss, "The New Protean Career Contract: Helping Organizations and Employees Adapt," *Organizational Dynamics* 26, no. 3 (Winter 1998): 22–37. See also Douglas T. Hall, *The Career Is Dead, Long Live the Career: A Relational Approach to Careers* (San Francisco: Jossey-Bass, 1996); Douglas T. Hall, "Protean Careers of the 21st Century," *Academy of Management Executive* 10, no. 4 (1996): 8–16; Douglas T. Hall and Associates, *Career Development in Organizations* (San Francisco: Jossey-Bass, 1986); Yue-Wah Chay and Samuel Aryee, "The Moderating Influence of Career Growth Opportunities on Careerist Orientation and Work Attitudes: Evidence of the Protean Career Era in Singapore," *Journal of Organizational Behavior* 20, no. 5 (September 1999): 613–23.

7. Julie Rose, "The New Risk Takers," *Fortune Small Business* 12, no. 2 (March 2002): 28–34; Jack Howard, "Balancing Conflicts of Interest When Employing Spouses," *Employee Responsibilities & Rights* 20, no. 1 (March 2008): 29–43.

8. U.S. Bureau of the Census; Advocacy-funded research by Joel Popkin and Company (Research Summary #211); U.S. Department of Labor, Bureau of Labor Statistics, Current Population Survey; U.S. Department of Commerce, International Trade Administration.

9. For information on starting a business, the interested reader might look into Bob Adams, *Adams Streetwise Small Business Startup* (Holbrook, MA: Adams Media Corporation, 1996); Linda Pinson and Jerry Jinnett, *Anatomy of a Business Plan: Starting Smart, Building a Business and Securing Your Company's Future* (Chicago: Upstart, 1996); Kenneth Cook, *AMA Complete Guide to Strategic Planning for Small Business* (Lincolnwood, IL: NTC Business Books, 1995); Priscilla Y. Huff, *101 Best Small Businesses for Women* (Rocklin, CA: Prima, 1996); Constance Jones, *The 220 Best Franchises to Buy: The Sourcebook for Evaluating the Best Franchise Opportunities* (New York: Bantam Doubleday Dell, 1993).

10. Jamie Eckle, "Randall Craig," *Computerworld* 42, no. 26 (June 23, 2008): 36.

11. Christopher Caggiano, "Married ... with Companies," *Inc.* 17, no. 6 (May 1995): 68–76; Sue Shellenbarger, "Sustaining a Marriage When Job Demands Seem to Be Endless," *The Wall Street Journal* (December 8, 1999), B1; Johan A. Turner, "Work Options for Older Americans: Employee Benefits for the Era of Living Longer," *Benefits Quarterly* 24, no. 3, (2008): 20–25.

Employee Selection

After studying this chapter, you should be able to

LEARNING OUTCOME 1 Explain the objectives of the personnel selection process.

LEARNING OUTCOME 2 Explain what it is required for an employee selection tool to be reliable and valid.

LEARNING OUTCOME 3 Illustrate the different approaches to conducting an employment interview.

LEARNING OUTCOME 4 Compare the value of different types of employment tests.

LEARNING OUTCOME 5 Describe the various decision strategies for selection.

Regardless of whether the company is large or small, hiring the best and the brightest employees lays a strong foundation for excellence. But how should this be done? And what happens if it is not done right? A recent study by the Society for HR Management found that the cost of hiring someone for a wrong intermediate position is approximately $20,000, and the cost of hiring the wrong person for a senior manager's position is $100,000. In addition, equal employment opportunity legislation, court decisions, and the *Uniform Guidelines* (discussed in Chapter 3) have also provided an impetus for making sure that the selection process is done well. The bottom line is good selection decisions make a difference. So do bad ones.

Overview of the Selection Process

selection

The process of choosing individuals who have relevant qualifications to fill existing or projected job openings

Selection is the process of choosing individuals who have relevant qualifications to fill existing or projected job openings. Figure 6.1 shows in broad terms that the overall goal of selection is to maximize "hits" and avoid "misses." Hits are accurate predictions, and misses are inaccurate ones. The cost of one type of miss would be the direct and indirect expense of hiring an employee who turns out to be unsuccessful. The cost of the other type of miss is an opportunity cost—someone who could have been successful did not get a chance to contribute to the organization. Although the

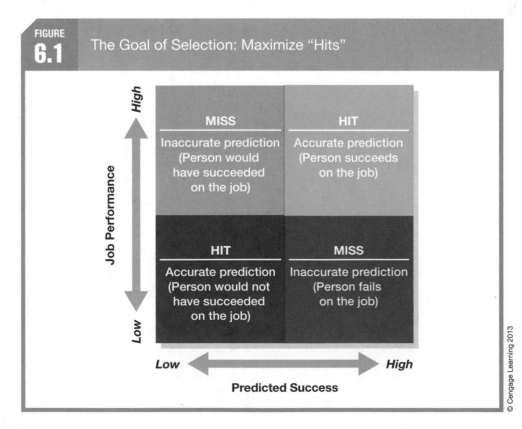

FIGURE 6.1 The Goal of Selection: Maximize "Hits"

Job Performance (High / Low) vs. Predicted Success (Low / High)

MISS — Inaccurate prediction (Person would have succeeded on the job)

HIT — Accurate prediction (Person succeeds on the job)

HIT — Accurate prediction (Person would not have succeeded on the job)

MISS — Inaccurate prediction (Person fails on the job)

© Cengage Learning 2013

design of a firm's overall selection program is often the formal responsibility of the organization's HR department, line managers typically make the final decisions about the people hired into their units.

Begin with a Job Analysis

In Chapter 4, we discussed the process of analyzing jobs. Job specifications help identify the *individual competencies* employees need for success—the knowledge, skills, abilities, and other factors (KSAOs) that lead to superior performance. Managers then use selection methods such as interviews, references, preemployment tests, and the like to measure applicants' KSAOs against the competencies required for the job. Complete and clear job specifications help interviewers differentiate between qualified and unqualified applicants and reduce the effect of an interviewer's biases and prejudices. Applicants whose KSAOs are well matched to the jobs they are hired for are also found to perform better and be more satisfied.[1]

Ordinarily, line managers are well acquainted with the requirements pertaining to the skills, physical demands, and other characteristics of the jobs in their organizations. Interviewers and members of the HR department who participate in the selection process should become thoroughly familiar with the jobs and competencies needed to perform them as well. In addition to the requirements of the job, many organizations, including Morgan Stanley, Merck, Southwest Airlines, and Starbucks, also try to hire individuals who match their values and cultures. Recall from Chapter 2 that this process is referred to as values-based hiring. The drawback of values-based recruiting is that it can result in a lack of diversity, so firms need to be cautious about hiring too many of the same types of people.

Steps in the Selection Process

The number of steps in the selection process and their sequence will vary, not only with the organization, but also with the type and level of jobs to be filled. Each step should be evaluated in terms of its contribution to the process. The steps that typically make up the selection process are shown in Figure 6.2. Not all applicants will go through all of these steps. Some will be rejected after the preliminary interview, others after taking tests, and so on.

As Figure 6.2 shows, organizations use several different means to obtain information about applicants. These methods include gathering résumés and applications, and conducting interviews, tests, medical examinations, and investigations. For internal candidate not all of the steps may be required. For example, a company is likely to require the candidate to submit a résumé and go through an interview, but not necessarily a background investigation. Because more steps are generally required when filling positions externally, companies often try to hire within and advertise externally only as a last result. According to the executive search firm Heidrick & Struggles, internal promotions accounted for more than half of all positions filled in 2009–2010—up from 34 percent in 2007.[2]

However, some experts say it is a good idea to treat internal and external candidates the same way because it helps both managers and a firm's employees feel confident that the process was fair, no special treatment was given to any one candidate, and the best person for the job was chosen.

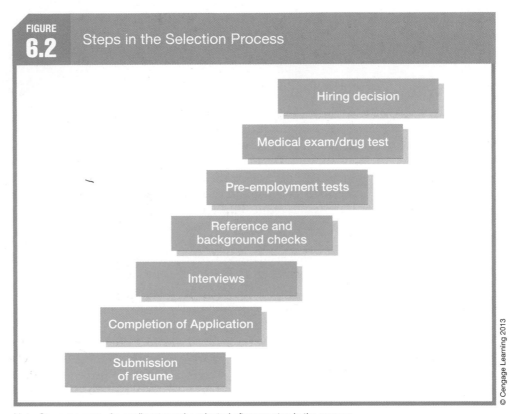

FIGURE 6.2   Steps in the Selection Process

- Hiring decision
- Medical exam/drug test
- Pre-employment tests
- Reference and background checks
- Interviews
- Completion of Application
- Submission of resume

© Cengage Learning 2013

Note: Steps may vary. An applicant may be rejected after any step in the process.

Obtaining Reliable and Valid Information

LEARNING OUTCOME 2

Many employers do Internet searches to turn up information on job candidates. Can you see any problem related to doing so?

reliability
The degree to which interviews, tests, and other selection procedures yield comparable data over time and alternative measures

validity
The degree to which a test or selection procedure measures a person's attributes

Regardless of whether a position is filled internally or externally, it is essential that the information gathered about candidates be reliable and valid, gathered legally, and the privacy of applicants safeguarded. The degree to which interviews, tests, and other selection procedures yield comparable data over a period of time is known as reliability. For example, unless interviewers judge the capabilities of a group of applicants to be the same today as they did yesterday, their judgments are unreliable (that is, unstable). Likewise, a test that gives widely different scores when it is administered to the same individual a few days apart is unreliable. Reliability also refers to the extent to which two or more methods (interviews and tests, for example) yield similar results or are consistent. Interrater reliability—agreement among two or more raters—is one measure of a method's consistency.

In addition to the information about a person's suitability for a job being reliable, it must be valid. Validity refers to what a test or other selection procedure measures and how well it measures it. In other words, the selection process should be able to predict how well a person performs on the job. Like a new medicine, a selection procedure must be validated before it is used. There are two reasons for validating a procedure. First, validity is directly related to increases in employee productivity, as we will demonstrate later. Second, EEO regulations require selection procedures to be valid.[3]

Initial Screening

Employers use many different pieces of information to try to determine if an applicant will be successful on the job. The initial pieces of information for screening candidates include résumés, cover letters, and applications, and often the Internet.

Cover Letters and Résumés

Résumés and cover letters have been used for decades to assess the suitability of applicants, especially for salaried positions. Generally, these documents are reviewed first with an eye towards who can be eliminated because they do not have the skills, abilities, education, or experience outlined in the job description for the application. Did the applicant submit a thoughtful cover letter? Or is he or she simply "spamming" companies with résumés? A lack of a cover letter could be one way of eliminating applicants. Was the cover letter well written? Well-written cover letters are important if a requirement of the job is having good written communication skills, which is the case for many jobs. So, for example, if a person who applied for an online customer service job that includes writing chat messages to customers submitted a cover letter with numerous typos, this could be grounds for passing over the person. Good writing skills might be less important for a person who works as a Walmart greeter. Good verbal or interpersonal skills might suffice for this position.

Evaluating résumés can be a subjective process. Evaluators often have a difficult time applying a set of consistent standards across multiple candidates or they consistently apply standards that are irrelevant to success on the job. The fact that there is no "set" format for writing résumés—that they vary from person to person—can make them difficult for people to screen. Bias can also enter the process. For example, one research study found that qualified applicants with black-sounding names had to send out fifteen résumés to get an interview, whereas candidates with white-sounding names only had to send out ten.[4]

Developing explicit evaluation criteria and a structured way to review résumés can help make the process less subjective. Once applicants who clearly are not qualified are eliminated, a company might use an assessment grid like the one shown in Figure 6.3 to take some of the guesswork out of the process. Job description criteria are placed in the left-hand column of the grid, and candidates are then ranked based on a scale as to whether the skills outlined in their résumés and cover letters match the job. The totals for the candidates are then compared.

The downside of manually screening and assessing cover letters is that it is not uncommon for a firm to get hundreds of résumés for a single position. To speed up the evaluation process, many firms are now using software to scan résumés to find qualified applications. For example, a hiring manager or human resources representative will specify the educational and experience levels a job requires and keywords indicative of that experience. The software then scans the résumés collected for that position, pulls a list of qualified candidates, and ranks them according to how closely they match the job criteria. Applicant tracking systems generally include a résumé screening feature. Some of the systems also prescreen people who submit résumés by first asking them to take a short questionnaire to determine how qualified they are.

Not all HR professionals are fans of résumé screening software, however. There is concern that capable people are routinely being rejected by machines, even before a human lays eyes upon their credentials. Also, applicants have learned to "pepper"

FIGURE 6.3   Application/Résumé Assessment Grid

Rate each candidate on a scale of 1–5, with 5 being the highest rating.

Quantitative requirements	Applicant A	Applicant B	Applicant C	Applicant D
Business degree and/or MBA	5			
Two years' managerial experience	5			
Ability to develop strategies	2			
Ability to manage budgets	2			
Qualitative requirements				
Demonstrated interpersonal skills	4			
Demonstrated coaching and development skills	4			
Ability to manage diverse teams and work with other departments	4			
Flexibility	3			
Writing and verbal skills	4			
Presentation skills	4			
Level of integrity	4			
Totals	**41**			

© Cengage Learning 2013

Many HR professionals use computer software to make the process of screening résumés faster and easier. Yet some practitioners fear this may inadvertently screen out qualified applicants.

EDHAR/www.shutterstock.com

their résumés with a job's keywords to get past résumé-screening software. Considering the volume of résumés firms can get, however, the practice is probably here to stay. Many companies, including TGI Fridays, say that résumé screening software works well for them.[5] Case Study 2 at the end of the chapter takes a closer look at résumé screening.

Internet Checks and Phone Screening

As you learned in Chapter 1, HR professionals and hiring managers will often "Google" applicants' names and check online social networking sites before deciding whether or not to invite them for an actual face-to-face interview. The downsides of conducting Internet searches relates to the privacy of applicants. In Finland, the practice is illegal. It is also difficult to verify the authenticity of information posted online (did the candidate really post the information, or did someone else?) and easy to confuse an applicant with someone else who has the same name.

Short phone interviews, or screening interviews, are also often conducted, many times by HR personnel, to narrow down the field and save managers time by eliminating candidates who are not likely to be hired. Video is being used to prescreen applicants as well.

iCandidateScreener is a product that allows candidates to interview themselves with their webcams. Managers can quickly screen through the candidates when they have time before bringing applicants in for a face-to-face interview. To give employers a "preview" of themselves, candidates are also posting video résumés on YouTube, Jobster, and sites such as HireVue.[6] Video résumés are short video clips that highlight applicants' qualifications beyond what they can communicate via their résumés and cover letters. The videos allow employers to see how well they present themselves and decide whether they should be called in for an interview. However, there is some concern that video résumés will cause employers to screen people based on their looks rather than their qualifications.

video résumés
Short video clips that highlight applicants' qualifications beyond what they can communicate on their résumés

Application Forms

Application forms provide a fairly quick and systematic means of obtaining a variety of information about the applicant, such as whether the applicant meets the minimum requirements for experience, education, and so on. For example, McDonald's uses a form that is quite brief but asks for information that is highly relevant to job performance. The form also provides information regarding the employer's conformity with various laws and regulations. For scientific, professional, and managerial jobs, a more extended form is likely to be used.

Even when applicants come armed with elaborate résumés, it is important that they complete an application form because it is a way to gather consistent information about candidates. People, even those in high positions, frequently exaggerate their qualifications on their résumés and omit unflattering information. For example, George O'Leary had to resign as head football coach at Notre Dame after admitting to falsely claiming he had played football at New Hampshire and had a master's degree from New York University. Similarly, Radio Shack CEO David Edmondson was forced to resign after claiming on his résumé that he had earned college degrees in theology and psychology. Not only had he not graduated, but the college he attended did not even offer a psychology degree.[7]

The EEOC and the courts have found that many questions asked on application forms disproportionately discriminate against females and minorities and often are not job-related. Application forms should therefore be developed with great care and revised as often as necessary. Because of differences in state laws on fair employment practices (FEPs) (see Chapter 3), organizations operating in more than one state will find it difficult to develop one form that can be used nationally.

Asking applicants to transcribe specific résumé material onto a standardized application form can help alleviate this problem. Far fewer people lie on application forms relative to their résumés, a survey by CareerBuilder found. The applicant is then asked to sign a statement that the information

Using the INTERNET

You can learn more about lawful interview and application questions online. Go to **www.cengagebrain.com**

contained on the form is true and that he or she accepts the employer's right to terminate the candidate's employment if any of the information is subsequently found to be false.[8]

Many managers remain unclear about the questions they can ask on an application form. While most know they should steer clear of issues such as age, race, marital status, and sexual orientation, other issues are less clear. In addition to consulting their state's employment laws, some of which are more restrictive than others, the following are some suggestions for putting together an application form:

- *Application date.* The applicant should date the application. This helps managers know when the form was completed and gives them an idea of the time limit (for example, one year) that the form should be on file.

- *Educational background.* The form should contain blanks for grade school, high school, college, and postcollege attendance—but not the dates attended, since that can be connected with age.

- *Experience.* Virtually any questions that focus on work experience related to the job are permissible.

- *Arrests and criminal convictions.* Traditionally application forms have included questions about convictions and arrests. Questions about arrests are not permissible, and questions about convictions and guilty pleadings can be problematic if they are not related to the job. Some states have made these questions illegal, and the EEOC has indicated that they can have a disparate impact on African-American and Hispanic workers.

- *National origin.* Such questions are not permitted. However, it is allowable to ask whether the person is legally prevented from working in the United States. This is important because before beginning work, all employees, including U.S. citizens, must complete an I-9 form for their employers to submit to the government verifying that they are eligible to work in the United States. They must also provide supporting documents proving as much.

- *References.* Most applications include blanks for the names, addresses, and phone numbers of references provided by applicants. (We will cover this in more detail later.)

- *Disabilities.* This is a potentially tricky area. The Americans with Disabilities Act prohibits discriminating against a person with a disability who, with or without reasonable accommodation, can perform essential job functions. But employers are not allowed to ask applicants questions designed to elicit information about the existence, nature, or severity of a disability. Inquiries about the ability of the person to perform job functions, however, are acceptable. Under the most recent guidelines issued by the EEOC, employers can ask whether an applicant needs reasonable accommodation—*if* the disability is obvious or *if* the applicant has voluntarily disclosed the disability.

Disclaimers

- *EEOC and at-will statements.* It is a good idea to state on the application form that the firm does not discriminate and is an EEOC employer. If your state allows it, the form should state that all employees are hired *at will*. This gives both the employer and employee the right to end the employment relationship at any time without reason. (How the employment-at-will principle works will be discussed in greater detail in Chapter 13.)

- *Reference checks.* Included on the application form should be language that gives the hiring firm the right to contact the applicants' previous employers listed on the form and their résumés.

- *Employment testing.* Any tests the applicant may have to take should be listed on the form.

- *Information falsification.* This section should disclose to applicants that any falsification of the information they provide could result in their disqualification or termination should they be hired.

Many of these issues will be addressed again, particularly in the section on employment interviews.

Some organizations use what is referred to as a *weighted application blank (WAB)*. The WAB, which is also sometimes called a *scored application form*, is an application that is designed to distinguish between successful and unsuccessful employees. If managers can identify application items that have predicted employee success in the past, they may use that information to screen new applicants. Some evidence suggests that use of the WAB has been especially helpful for reducing turnover costs in the hospitality industry.

Online Applications

Most large companies accept applications online, and some conduct preapplication screening tests online. One of the key advantages of accepting applications online is that companies can recruit candidates and fill their job openings much faster. The discount stock broker Charles Schwab claims that by using the Internet, it can now fill a job opening in just one week.

As with résumés accepted online, companies report that the downside of accepting online applications is that it can lead to a large volume of them being submitted—many of which fail to meet minimum qualifications. The upside, however, is that generating a larger number of applicants tends to promote greater employee diversity. Home Depot, for example, successfully implemented an online application system called the Job Preference Program to get a broader pool of applicants than it previously had been getting. It ultimately enabled the company to hire more women.

Employment Interviews

The next step after screening résumés, cover letters, and applications for qualified candidates is oftentimes interviewing them. Traditionally, the employment interview has played a central role in the selection process—so much so that it is rare to find an instance in which an employee is hired without some sort of interview. Depending on the type of job, applicants might be interviewed by one person, members of a work team, or other individuals in the organization. Although researchers have raised some doubts about its validity, the interview remains a mainstay of selection because (1) it is especially practical when there are only a small number of applicants; (2) it serves

LEARNING OUTCOME 3

If you a know a candidate, in addition to interviewing the person, do you still need to check his or her job references and do a background check? Can any of these steps be skipped?

other purposes, such as public relations; and (3) interviewers maintain great faith and confidence in their judgments. Nevertheless, the interview can be plagued by problems of subjectivity and personal bias. In this section, we review the characteristics, advantages, and disadvantages of various types of employment interviews. We highlight the fact that the structure of the interview and the training of interviewers strongly influence the success of the hiring process.[9]

Interview methods differ in several ways, most significantly in terms of the amount of structure, or control, exercised by the interviewer. In highly structured interviews, the interviewer determines the course that the interview will follow as each question is asked. In the less structured interview, the applicant plays a larger role in determining the course the discussion will take. Next, let's look at the different types of interviews from the least structured to the most structured. Note that different types of interview styles and questions they utilize can be mixed and matched to yield a more complete picture of candidates.

The Nondirective Interview

nondirective interview

An interview in which the applicant is allowed the maximum amount of freedom in determining the course of the discussion, while the interviewer carefully refrains from influencing the applicant's remarks

In a nondirective interview, the interviewer carefully refrains from influencing the applicant's remarks. The applicant is allowed the maximum amount of freedom in determining the course of the discussion. The interviewer asks broad, open-ended questions—such as "Tell me more about your experiences on your last job"—and permits the applicant to talk freely with a minimum of interruption. Generally, the nondirective interviewer listens carefully and does not argue, interrupt, or change the subject abruptly. The interviewer also uses follow-up questions to allow the applicant to elaborate, makes only brief responses, and allows pauses in the conversation; the pausing technique is the most difficult for the beginning interviewer to master.

The greater freedom afforded to the applicant in the nondirective interview helps bring to the interviewer's attention any information, attitudes, or feelings a candidate might not disclose during more structured questioning. However, because the applicant determines the course of the interview and no set procedure is followed, little information that comes from these interviews enables interviewers to cross-check agreement with other interviewers. Thus the reliability and validity of these interviews are not likely to be as great. This method is most likely to be used in interviewing candidates for high-level positions and in counseling, which we will discuss in Chapter 13.

The Structured Interview

structured interview

An interview in which a set of standardized questions having an established set of answers is used

Because a structured interview has a set of standardized questions (based on job analysis) and an established set of answers against which applicant responses can be rated, it provides a more consistent basis for evaluating job candidates. For example, staff members of Weyerhaeuser Company's HR department have developed a structured interviewing process used for all candidates:

1. The interview process is based exclusively on the duties and requirements critical to a person's job performance.

2. There are sample (benchmark) answers, determined in advance, to each question. Candidates' responses are rated on a five-point scale relative to those answers.

3. Candidates are interviewed by multiple people who rate the responses.

4. The interviewers take notes for future reference and in case of a legal challenge.

A structured interview is more likely to provide the type of information needed for making sound decisions. According to a report by the U.S. Merit Systems Protection Board, a quasijudicial agency that serves as the guardian of federal merit systems, structured interviews are twice as likely as nondirective interviews to predict on-the-job performance. Structured interviews are also less likely than nondirective interviews to be attacked in court.[10]

The Situational Interview

One variation of the structured interview is called the situational interview. With this approach, an applicant is given a *hypothetical* incident and asked how he or she would respond to it. The applicant's response is then evaluated relative to pre-established benchmark standards. Interestingly, many organizations are using the situational interview to select new college graduates. Highlights in HRM 1 shows a sample question from a situational interview used to select systems analysts at a chemical plant. Highlights in HRM 2 lists some of the biggest blunders made by job applicants.

The Behavioral Description Interview

In contrast to a situational interview, which focuses on hypothetical situations, a behavioral description interview (BDI) focuses on *actual* work incidents in the interviewee's past. The BDI format asks the job applicant what he or she actually did in

situational interview

An interview in which an applicant is given a hypothetical incident and asked how he or she would respond to it

behavioral description interview (BDI)

An interview in which an applicant is asked questions about what he or she actually did in a given situation

1 HIGHLIGHTS IN **HRM**
Sample Situational Interview Question

Question:

It is the night before your scheduled vacation. You are all packed and ready to go. Just before you get into bed, you receive a phone call from the plant. A problem has arisen that only you can handle. You are asked to come in to take care of things. What would you do in this situation?

Record Answer:

_____

_____

_____

Scoring Guide:

Good: "I would go in to work and make certain that everything is OK. Then I would go on vacation."

Good: "There are no problems that *only* I can handle. I would make certain that someone qualified was there to handle things."

Fair: "I would try to find someone else to deal with the problem."

Fair: "I would go on vacation."

a given situation. For example, to assess a potential manager's ability to handle a problem employee, an interviewer might ask, "Tell me about the last time you disciplined an employee." Such an approach to interviewing, based on a critical incidents job analysis, assumes that past performance is the best predictor of future performance. It also may be somewhat less susceptible to applicant faking. In addition, recent research indicates that the behavioral description interview is more effective than the situational interview for hiring higher-level positions such as general managers and executives.[11]

Panel and Sequential Interviews

panel interview

An interview in which a board of interviewers questions and observes a single candidate

Another type of interview involves a panel of interviewers who question and observe a single candidate. In a typical panel interview, the candidate meets with three to five interviewers who take turns asking questions. After the interview, the interviewers pool their observations and their rating scores if the interview is structured to reach a consensus about the suitability of the candidate. HRM specialists using this method at Philip Morris USA and Dominion Virginia Power report that panel interviews provide several significant advantages over traditional one-to-one interviews, including higher reliability because they involve multiple inputs. They can also result in a shorter decision-making period, and applicants are more likely to accept the decisions made. Studies also suggest that if the panels are composed of a diverse group of

HIGHLIGHTS IN **HRM**
2 Hiring Managers Reveal Mistakes Candidates Make during Job Interviews

Hiring managers often share the most memorable blunders that caused them to pass on a particular candidate. Below is a sample of some of them.

- "The candidate spoke no English, so he brought his mother to translate for him during the interview. It was for a customer-service position."
- "She kept telling me about her marital problems."
- "The candidate knew nothing about the job being offered or our organization."
- "One guy ate a sandwich."
- "The candidate asked me to hurry up because she left her child in the car."
- "He told me the only reason he was here was because his mother wanted him to get a job. He was 37."
- "One candidate did not wear shoes to the interview."
- "Body odor so bad I had to excuse myself midinterview and put lip gloss in my nose in order to get through the rest."
- "One guy mentioned his arrest during the interview after stating on his application that he had never been arrested."
- "One guy asked if we drug-tested and if we gave advance notice (we are a drug treatment facility)."

Sources: CareerBuilder.com, *Reader's Digest.*

interviewers, hiring discrimination is minimized.[12] A sequential interview is one in which a candidate is interviewed by multiple people, one right after another. Sequential interviews are very common. They allow different interviewers who have a vested interest in the candidate's success to meet and evaluate the person one-on-one. The interviewers later get together and compare their assessments of the candidates.

sequential interview

A format in which a candidate is interviewed by multiple people, one right after another

Phone Interviews

Most interviews take place in person. However, under certain circumstances, phone interviews can be effective and actually help expand a company's pool of talent. Via phone, Pacific Islands Club, a resort in Guam, is able to recruit people from around the world who want to work for the resort. Rebecca Cummings, a young woman living in the United States, went to work for the Pacific Islands Club as an activities director after successfully interviewing via phone. A face-to-face interview would have been cost prohibitive.[13]

Automated phone interviews are also used, albeit as an initial screening device. A few years ago, Pic 'n Pay Shoe Stores created an interview that could be conducted over the phone using an 800 number. The interview focused on honesty, work attitudes, candor, dependability, and self-motivation. After implementing the system, the company cut turnover by 50 percent and reduced employee theft by almost 40 percent. In addition to the benefits of objectivity, some research evidence suggests that applicants may be less likely to engage in "impression management" in computerized interviews than in face-to-face interviews.[14]

Computer Interviews

With advances in information technology, more and more organizations are using computers and the Internet to help with the interviewing process. Nike, Cigna

Many employers use telephone interviews for both initial, prescreening interviews and for interviews that occur later in the process.

Elena Elisseeva/Shutterstock.com

Insurance, and Pinkerton Security have all developed expert systems to gather information as well as compare candidates. Typically, a computer interview requires candidates to answer a series (75 to 125) of multiple-choice questions tailored to the job. These answers are compared either with an ideal profile or with profiles developed on the basis of other candidates' responses.

The computer interview can also be used as a screening device to help filter out unqualified applicants applying online who do not merit a personal interview. Depending on the vendor and the software used, a computer interview conducted in conjunction with online tests can measure everything from contradictory responses and latent responses (time delays related to answering a question) to the applicant's typing speed and ability to use different kinds of software. CareerBuilder.com, for example, offers a service called IntelligentHire that screens out the ten most qualified and interested applicants posting for a job on CareerBuilder's site. IntelligentHire then generates a report for the employer that includes the applicants' résumés, answers to questions, background check results, and their overall rankings against one another.[15] So far, organizations have used computer and phone interviews mainly as a complement to, rather than as a replacement for, conventional interviews.[16]

Video Interviews

Companies such as AT&T, Dell Computer, and Nike are using videoconference technologies to evaluate job candidates. Some utilize technologies such as webcams and Skype; others use outside service partners. FedEx Kinko's, for example, rents video-conferencing rooms at 120 of its stores for about $225 per hour.

Called virtual interviews, they have several potential advantages related to flexibility, speed, and cost. As we explained earlier in the chapter, employers can also use them as a prescreening tool to make preliminary assessments about applicants before incurring the costs of a face-to-face meeting. The goal is to enable faster, higher-quality decisions at lower cost.

In addition to offering a broad range of candidate assessment services, a number of recruiting companies, including BioPharma Worldwide, digitally record job applicants and post their interviews to their websites. Corporations log onto the sites and check out candidates free of charge or for a small fee, depending on the vendor. By recording and playing back the interviews to several companies' executives, firms can eliminate complications involved in setting up many more interviews.[17]

virtual interviews

Interviews conducted via videoconferencing or over the web

Guidelines for Employment Interviewers

Organizations should be cautious in selecting employment interviewers. The qualities of a good interviewer include humility, the ability to think objectively, maturity, and poise. Given the importance of diversity in the workforce, experience in associating with people from a variety of backgrounds is also desirable. Qualities to avoid in interviewers include over-talkativeness, extreme opinions, and biases.

Figure 6.4 summarizes the variables and processes involved in the employment interview. The figure shows that a number of applicant characteristics and situational factors can influence the perceptions of the interviewer and thus the hiring decision. For example, the race and sex of an applicant can shape the expectations, biases, and behaviors of an interviewer, which in turn can affect the interview outcome. Even a limited understanding of the variables shown in Figure 6.4 can help increase the interviewing effectiveness of managers and supervisors.

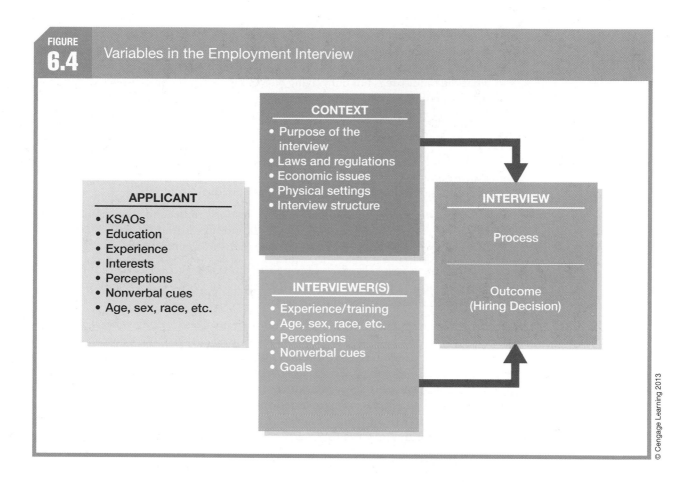

FIGURE 6.4   Variables in the Employment Interview

Interviewer Training

Training has been shown to dramatically improve the competence of interviewers. If not done on a continuing basis, training should at least be done periodically for managers, supervisors, and HR representatives who conduct interviews. Interviewer training programs should include practice interviews conducted under guidance. Practice interviews can be recorded and evaluated later in a group training session. Some variation in technique is only natural. However, the following list presents ten ground rules for employment interviews that are commonly accepted and supported by research findings.

1. *Understand the job.* Perhaps the most critical step to ensuring interviewers do a good job is to be sure they understand the job and its requirements. Research studies have shown that interviewers who understand the parameters of a job are better at interviewing people and evaluating their responses.

2. *Establish an interview plan.* Examine the purposes of the interview and determine the areas and specific questions to be covered. Review the job requirements, application form data, test scores, and other available information before seeing the applicant.

3. *Establish and maintain rapport and listen actively.* This is accomplished by greeting the applicant pleasantly, explaining the purpose of the interview, displaying sincere interest in what the person has to say, and listening carefully. Try to understand what the candidate is not only saying but implying. Keep non-job-related conversation to a minimum to prevent from coming into play any biases you might have.

4. *Pay attention to nonverbal cues.* An applicant's facial expressions, gestures, body position, and movements often provide clues to that person's attitudes and feelings. Interviewers should be aware of what they themselves are communicating nonverbally.

5. *Provide information as freely and honestly as possible.* Answer fully and frankly the applicant's questions. Present a realistic picture of the job.

6. *Use questions effectively.* Ask open-ended questions rather than questions that can be answered with a simple "yes" or "no." Do not ask questions that "lead" candidates to the "right" answer. Phrase the questions in a neutral way.

7. *Separate facts from inferences.* During the interview, record factual information. Later, record your inferences or interpretations of the facts. Compare your inferences with those of other interviewers.

8. *Recognize stereotypes and biases.* Stereotyping involves forming generalized opinions about people of a given gender, race, ethnic background, or appearance. As we have mentioned, one typical bias is for interviewers to consider candidates who have interests, experiences, and backgrounds similar to their own to be more acceptable. Another bias occurs when interviewers "fall into like" with applicants, especially if a candidate is extroverted and charming. If extroversion is an important characteristic of the job (such as a sales job), choosing an extroverted candidate might be appropriate. However, a less-extroverted candidate who is more conscientious might be better for a job that is detail oriented or requires a person to work alone. In other words, evaluate candidates based on the characteristics of the job and not, for example, the fact that they went to the same college you did.

9. *Avoid the "halo error," or judging an individual favorably or unfavorably overall on the basis of only one strong point (or weak point) on which you place high value.* Also avoid the influence of "beautyism." Discrimination against unattractive but talented people is a persistent and pervasive form of employment discrimination. (If you are a candidate, remember that it can be difficult for interviewers to control their biases, so first impressions count. The degree to which employers are influenced by a candidate's appearance are shown in Figure 6.5.)

10. *Control the course of the interview.* Establish an interview plan and stick to it. Provide the applicant with ample opportunity to talk, but maintain control of the situation in order to reach the interview objectives.

11. *Standardize the questions asked.* To increase the reliability of the interview and avoid discrimination, ask the same questions of all applicants for a particular job. Keep careful notes; record facts, impressions, and any relevant information, including what was told to the applicant.

Diversity Management: Are Your Questions Legal?

The entire subject of what is legal or illegal in an employment interview gets pretty complicated. There are differing and sometimes contradictory interpretations by the courts, the EEOC, and the Office of Federal Contract Compliance Program about

FIGURE 6.5 How Candidates' Physical Attributes Influence Employers

	NO INFLUENCE	SLIGHT INFLUENCE	STRONG INFLUENCE
Grooming	6%	21%	73%
Nontraditional interview attire	13	38	49
Handshake	22	45	33
Body piercing	26	43	31
Obvious tattoos	25	46	29
Nontraditional hair color	26	46	28
Unusual hairstyle	30	49	21
Earring (male)	54	34	12
Beard	73	22	5
Mustache	83	16	1

Source: *Occupational Outlook Quarterly.*

what you can ask in an interview. Under federal laws no questions are expressly prohibited. However, the EEOC looks with disfavor on direct or indirect questions related to race, color, age, religion, sex, national origin, caregiver status, and other factors we talked about in Chapter 3. Some questions that interviewers once felt free to ask are now potentially hazardous. Federal courts have severely limited the areas of questioning. An interviewer, for example, can ask about physical disabilities if the job involves manual labor, but not otherwise. It is inappropriate, for example, to ask women (or men) if they are married or have children. Several states have fair employment practice laws that are more restrictive than federal legislation. In general, if a question is job-related, is asked of everyone, and does not discriminate against a certain class of applicants, it is likely to be acceptable to government authorities.

Employers often provide their interviewers with instructions on how to avoid potentially discriminatory questions in their interviews. The examples of appropriate and inappropriate questions shown in Highlights in HRM 3 can serve as guidelines for application forms as well as preemployment interviews. Complete guidelines can be developed from current information available from district and regional EEOC offices and from state fair employment practices offices.

Post-Interview Screening

When the interviewer is satisfied that the applicant is potentially qualified, information about previous employment as well as other information provided by the applicant is investigated.

Reference Checks

Organizations check the references of employees in a number of ways. Generally, telephone checks are preferable because they save time and provide for greater candor.

3 | HIGHLIGHTS IN **HRM**
Appropriate and Inappropriate Interview Questions

	APPROPRIATE QUESTIONS	INAPPROPRIATE QUESTIONS
National origin	What is your name? Have you ever worked under a different name? Do you speak any foreign languages that may be pertinent to this job?	What is the origin of your name? What is your ancestry?
Age	Are you over 18? If hired, can you prove your age?	How old are you? What is your date of birth?
Gender	(Say nothing unless it involves a bona fide occupational qualification.)	Are you a man or a woman?
Race	(Say nothing.)	What is your race?
Disabilities	Do you have any disabilities that may inhibit your job performance? Are you willing to take a physical exam if the job requires it?	Do you have any physical defects? When was your last physical? What color are your eyes, hair, etc.?
Height and weight	(Not appropriate unless it is a bona fide occupational qualification.)	How tall are you? How much do you weigh?
Residence	What is your address? How long have you lived there?	What are the names/relationships of those with whom you live?
Religion	(You may inform a person of the required work schedule.)	Do you have any religious affiliation?
Military record	Did you have any military education/experience pertinent to this job?	What type of discharge did you receive?
Education and experience	Where did you go to school? What is your prior work experience? Why did you leave? What is your salary history?	Is that a church-affiliated school? When did you graduate?
Criminal record	Have you ever been convicted of a crime? (May not be appropriate unless *not* being convicted is a bona fide occupational qualification.)	Have you ever been arrested?
Citizenship	Do you have a legal right to work in the United States?	Are you a U.S. citizen?
Marital/family status	What is the name, address, and telephone number of a person we may contact in case of an emergency?	Are you married, divorced, single? Do you prefer Miss, Mrs., or Ms.? Do you have any children? How old are they?

But references via faxes, mail, and e-mail are also used. Prescient InfoTech, a computer systems managing company in Fairfax, Virginia, first calls references to establish contact and then faxes or e-mails them a two-page questionnaire, asking them to numerically rank the applicant's various job-related attributes. There is room at the end of the questionnaire for comments and recommendations.

The most reliable information usually comes from supervisors, who are in the best position to report on an applicant's work habits and performance. Written verification of information relating to job titles, duties, and pay levels from a former employer's HR office is also very helpful. Highlights in HRM 4 includes a list of helpful questions to ask about applicants when checking their references.[18]

Based on the Privacy Act of 1974, individuals have a legal right to examine letters of reference about them (unless they waive the right to do so). Although the Privacy Act applies only to the records maintained by federal government agencies, other forms of privacy legislation in most states have influenced employers to "clean up" their personnel files and open them up to review and challenge by the employees concerned.[19]

It is important to ask the applicant to fill out forms permitting information to be solicited from former employers and other reference sources. Even with these safeguards, many organizations are reluctant to put into writing an evaluation of a former employee for fear of being sued by the person. Many employers will only verify former employees' employment dates and positions. Nonetheless, even firms that have failed to give an employee a recommendation have found themselves sued. Other firms have found themselves sued for negligent hiring—knowing a former employee posed a danger to others but failing to disclose the fact. Recognizing this predicament, a number of states have enacted statutes offering protection from liability for employers who give references in good faith.[20]

HIGHLIGHTS IN **HRM**
Sample Reference-Checking Questions

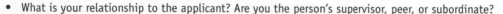

- What is your relationship to the applicant? Are you the person's supervisor, peer, or subordinate?
- What were the start and end dates of the applicant's employment?
- What were the applicant's title and responsibilities?
- In what areas did the applicant excel?
- In what areas did the applicant need improvement?
- What was the applicant's biggest accomplishment at your organization?
- How well does the applicant communicate with and get along with others?
- How does the applicant deal with conflicts and stress?
- To what extent is the applicant driven to succeed?
- Did the applicant miss a lot of work?
- Was the applicant punctual?
- For what reason did the applicant leave your organization?
- Would you rehire the applicant?
- Are there any serious problems with the applicant we should know about?
- Is there any additional information about the applicant you would like to share with me?

Sources: Alison Doyle, "Reference Check Questions," About.com, accessed March 24, 2011, http://www.about.com; Carolyn Hirschman, "The Whole Truth," *HRMagazine* 45, no. 6 (June 2000): 86–72.

Background Checks

Following 9/11 and a rash of corporate scandals at companies such as the now defunct energy firm Enron, background investigations have become standard procedure for many companies to prevent a variety of problems ranging from embezzlement and theft of merchandise to workplace violence. Moreover, state courts have ruled that companies can be held liable for negligent hiring if they fail to do adequate background checks. Federal law requires comprehensive background checks for all child care providers, for example. It also prohibits convicted felons from engaging in financial and security-oriented transactions.

negligent hiring
The failure of an organization to discover, via due diligence, that an employee it hired had the propensity to do harm to others

Among the checks are Social Security verification, past employment, education, and certification and license verification. A number of other checks can be conducted if they pertain to the job for which one is being hired. They include a driving-record check (for jobs involving driving), a credit check (for money-handling jobs), and a military records check. Checks for criminal convictions have become a standard part of background checks. According to the Society of Human Resources Management, 73 percent of major firms check candidates' backgrounds for criminal records. However, as we have indicated, the EEOC has found that they can have a disparate impact on black and Hispanic workers, who, relative to other groups of people have higher conviction and incarceration rates. If criminal histories *are* taken into account employers must also consider the nature the job, the seriousness of the offense, and how long ago it occurred, the EEOC has stated. For example, it may make sense to disqualify an applicant convicted of embezzlement for a bookkeeper's position, but not if he or she was convicted of drunk driving.[21]

Credit Checks

Credit checks have been widely used by employers to screen applicants. They are conducted more often and are cheaper in the United States today than in other countries because the United States has a national credit reporting system. But the Fair and Accurate Credit Transactions Act of 2003 (which was designed, among other things, to make identity theft more difficult), along with the Consumer Reporting Employment Clarification Act of 1998, and the Consumer Credit Reporting Reform Act of 1996 now restrict the sharing of some credit information. To rely on a report such as this in making employment decisions, organizations must follow five important steps.

First, the organization must check state laws to see if credit reports can legally be used. Too often credit checks are used when they are not really needed. Credit checks can also adversely affect qualified applicants who have been unemployed for long periods of time or faced bankruptcies or home foreclosures—problems that became more common among workers during the last recession. Recognizing this problem and the fact that credit checks can lead to identify theft, some states have begun limiting their use. For example, the state of Washington prohibits their use for employment purposes altogether. The EEOC also recently warned employers that they can have an adverse impact on some protected groups.

Organizations must advise and receive written consent from applicants if such a report will be requested. If the organization decides not to hire the applicant based on the report, it must provide an adverse action notice to that person. Although the notice can be provided verbally, in writing, or electronically, it must contain the name, address, and phone number of the agency that provided the report. The employer must also provide a statement that the reporting agency did not make the hiring decision, that the applicant has a right to obtain an additional free copy of the report, and that the applicant has a right to dispute the accuracy of information with the reporting agency.[22]

Like the application process, many checks that were once done manually are now being done online using existing computer databases. However, this frequently requires checking many different databases on a county-by-county basis. Information on international applicants is even harder to obtain. Additionally, delving into areas of an applicant's background irrelevant to the job requirements he or she is applying for can leave the firms exposed to violation-of-privacy claims.

To comply with different state laws regarding privacy and treat all applicants fairly and consistently, many firms use the Department of Homeland Security's free e-Verify system to conduct their background checks. e-Verify is being more widely used because employers are under increasing pressure by the federal and state governments to verify that the people they hire are legally able to work in the United States. Other companies outsource some or all of the checks to third-party screeners, which should be certified by the National Association of Professional Background Screeners.

Some job boards now have online screening tools allowing an applicant to conduct his or her own self-background check and post it online prior to any sort of interview. The idea is to demonstrate up front to prospective employers that the applicant has a clean criminal record, a good job history, and would make a good employee.[23] And as we have explained, an increasing number of companies are simply using Internet searches to uncover background information on a potential candidate.

Preemployment Tests

A **preemployment test** is an objective and standardized measure of a sample of behavior that is used to gauge a person's knowledge, skills, abilities, and other characteristics (KSAOs) relative to other individuals.[24] As the United States mobilized for World War I in the summer of 1917, some of the most talented psychologists in the country worked together to develop what later became known as the Army Alpha and Beta Tests of intelligence. (The Alpha exam was written for the general population, and the Beta was designed for internationals and those with poor reading skills.) The tests were used to help identify potential officer candidates as well as select and place other potential recruits. Since that time, preemployment tests have played an important part in the HR programs of both public and private organizations.[25] Not all companies conduct preemployment tests, but many more are doing so. An American Management Association study found that 44 percent of the group's members use tests to select employees.

One of the drawbacks of preemployment testing is that it creates the potential for legal challenges. A small but growing number of companies are being taken to court by candidates claiming that the tests they took were discriminatory. There is also some evidence that the more tests that are required, the higher the likelihood of a lawsuit, and the more important it is for companies to demonstrate their reliability and validity in their procedures. The relative frequency of discrimination suits also

LEARNING OUTCOME 4

Personality tests, like other tests used in employee selection, have been under attack for several decades. Why do you think some applicants find personality tests objectionable? On what basis could their use for selection purposes be justified?

preemployment test

An objective and standardized measure of a sample of behavior that is used to gauge a person's knowledge, skills, abilities, and other characteristics (KSAOs) relative to other individuals

Small Business Application

Adding Structure to the Employee Selection Process in Small Businesses

How do small businesses go about selecting employees to work at their firms? Not very systematically, some human resources professionals and researchers say. "Unfortunately, I have found that small businesses typically do a very poor job at selecting their employees ... all too often, employees are relatives or friends that lack the basic skills to augment the organization's ability to be profitable/successful," says one executive and blogger who coaches other businesspeople in an effort to help them achieve superior results.

Sometimes a small firm will make poor selections because they are anxious to get someone hired when the firm is short staffed. But if the wrong person is hired, that only compounds the problem. Another pitfall is being too confident about the right "type" of person for the job, which can cause hiring managers to make snap judgments about candidates based on casual conversations before mapping out the candidates' qualifications for the job.

Properly vetting candidates not only can lead to better employees, it can help a company defend itself should it be accused of discriminatory practices. A business owner who can show he or she hired employees based on a systematic process is less likely to find himself or herself with legal woes in this area. In addition, at least one research study has found that the use of formal recruitment and selection techniques gives employees a positive perception of their firms and their bosses, and results in greater loyalty to their organizations.

Hiring experts offer the following advice to small business managers: Adding structure to the selection process doesn't have to be difficult. You can map out the qualifications for the job on a form similar to the one shown in Figure 6.3. Then develop a series of open-ended and situational questions designed to elicit information about the candidate's job knowledge, conscientiousness, interest in the work, and how well his or her personality squares with the job. Once you have the questions drafted, ask the same questions of all candidates. Providing the job has not changed, the same form and questions can then be reused when subsequent job openings arise so you do not have to reinvent the wheel over and over again. Lastly, embezzlement and theft can be particularly devastating to small businesses, so *do* run background checks on employees and check their references, even if you know the candidates. You might be surprised by what you find.

Sources: "Selecting the Best," *elitefts*, November 9, 2010, http://www.elitefts.com/; Barbara Reda and Linda Dyer, "Finding Employees and Keeping Them: Predicting Loyalty in the Small Business," *Journal of Small Business & Entrepreneurship* 23, no. 3 (2010): 445.

appears to vary by industry and job type. Police, firefighting, and teaching areas—which generally require applicants to pass more tests—appear to be more prone to discrimination litigation.[26]

Nonetheless, tests have played a more important part in government HR programs in which hiring on the basis of merit is required by law. Government agencies experienced the same types of problems with their testing programs as did organizations in the private sector. However, their staffs were forced to improve their testing programs rather than to abandon them.

Many organizations use professional test consultants such as Wonderlic Inc. in Libertyville, Illinois, to improve their testing programs and to meet EEO requirements. It is a test developer's responsibility to ensure it meets accepted standards of validity and reliability.[27] The data about a test's reliability are ordinarily presented in the manual for the test. However, a firm should not just take a developer's word that its tests are reliable and valid. One source of information about commercially available tests—the *Mental Measurements Yearbook (MMY)*—is available in most libraries. Published periodically, the *MMY* contains descriptive information plus critical reviews by experts in the various types of tests. The reviews are useful in evaluating a particular test for tryout in employment situations. The firm should also check to be sure the test was professionally validated in compliance with the Uniform Guidelines on Employee Selection Procedures, that it has been vetted for disparate impact, and has not been contested in court or by the EEOC.

Keep in mind that even if a test is reliable and valid for positions in other organizations, it might not be reliable and valid for the positions in your organization because they may be somewhat different. Managers therefore need to do a thorough job analysis to determine the skills that candidates actually need to be tested for and eliminate any unnecessary or duplicate tests. For example, FedEx used to administer a basic skills test for the purposes of promoting employees but it dropped the test following a lawsuit that alleged it was discriminatory. Other considerations are the cost, time, and ease of administering and scoring the tests. For some jobs, the costs of testing may outweigh the benefits.

Types of Tests

We will talk more about what the EEOC demands as far as the validity of preemployment tests goes later in this section. First let's look at the different types of preemployment tests.

Job Knowledge Tests

Government agencies and licensing boards usually develop job knowledge tests, a type of achievement test designed to measure a person's level of understanding about a particular job. The Uniform CPA Examination used to license certified public accountants is one such test. Most civil service examinations, for example, are used to determine whether an applicant possesses the information and understanding that will permit placement on the job without further training.[28] Job knowledge tests are also used by the U.S. Army, Navy, Air Force, and Marines. Anyone who wants to become a pilot in the armed services and fly multimillion-dollar jets, for example, must undergo extensive job knowledge testing.

Work Sample Tests

Work sample tests, or job sample tests, require the applicant to perform tasks that are actually a part of the work required on the job. Like job knowledge tests, work sample tests are constructed from a carefully developed outline that experts agree includes the major job functions; the tests are thus considered content valid. Organizations that are interested in moving toward *competency-based selection*—that is, hiring based on observation of behaviors previously shown to distinguish successful employees—increasingly use work samples to see potential employees "in action."[29]

Work samples have been devised for many diverse jobs: a map reading test for traffic control officers, a lathe test for machine operators, a complex coordination test for pilots, an in-basket test for managers, a group discussion test for supervisors, and a judgment and decision-making test for administrators, to name a few. The city of

With jobs like this one that require specific skills, it is quite common for employers to ask candidates to demonstrate their abilities through work sample tests.

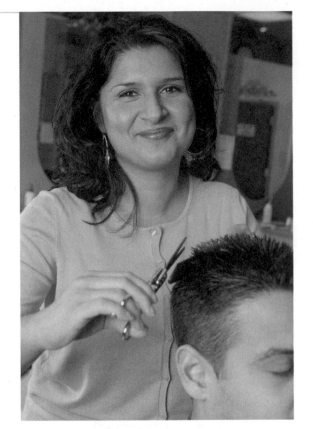

Miami Beach has used work sample tests for jobs as diverse as plumbers, planners, and assistant chief accountants. The U.S. Air Force has used work samples for enlisted personnel in eight different specialty areas. In an increasing number of cases, work sample tests are aided by computer simulations, particularly when testing a candidate might prove dangerous. The reports are that this type of test is cost-effective, reliable, valid, fair, and acceptable to applicants.[30]

Assessment Center Tests

An **assessment center** is a process (not a place) used to evaluate candidates as they participate in a series of situations that resemble what they might be called on to handle on the job. Candidates engage in the following types of activities at assessment centers.

assessment center
A process by which individuals are evaluated as they participate in a series of situations that resemble what they might need to handle on the job.

- *In-basket exercises.* This method is used to simulate a problem situation. The participants are given several documents, each describing some problem or situation requiring an immediate response. They are thus forced to make decisions under the pressure of time and also to determine what priority to give each problem.

- *Leaderless group discussions.* With this activity, trainees are gathered in a conference setting to discuss an assigned topic, either with or without designated group roles. The participants are given little or no instruction in how to approach the topic, nor are they told what decision to reach. Leaderless group trainees are evaluated on their initiative, leadership skills, and ability to work effectively in a group setting.

- *Role-playing.* The exercise might involve preparing for and engaging in a customer meeting or a team leader meeting with one's subordinates. A trained assessor then assesses the participant using a structured rating scale.

- *Behavioral interviews.* The interviewer asks the participant a series of questions about what he or she would do in particular work circumstances. Sometimes behavioral interviews are combined with videos showing work simulations, and participants are asked at intervals to make choices about what they would do in the situations shown.

At the end of the assessment center period, the assessors' observations are combined to develop an overall picture of the strengths and needs of the participants. A report is normally submitted to the organization that commissioned the tests, and feedback is given to the participants. Because of the costs involved, assessment centers are usually used to select managers.

Cognitive Ability Tests

Cognitive ability tests measure mental capabilities such as general intelligence, verbal fluency, numerical ability, and reasoning ability. A host of paper-and-pencil tests measure cognitive abilities, including the General Aptitude Test Battery (GATB), Scholastic Aptitude Test (SAT), Graduate Management Aptitude Test (GMAT), and Bennett Mechanical Comprehension Test. Figure 6.6 shows some items that could be used to measure different cognitive abilities.

Although cognitive ability tests can be developed to measure very specialized areas such as reading comprehension and spatial relations, many experts believe that the validity of cognitive ability tests simply reflects their connection to general intelligence. However, measures of general intelligence (such as IQ) have been shown to be good predictors of performance across a wide variety of jobs.[31]

FIGURE 6.6   Examples of Questions on a Cognitive Ability Test

Verbal

1. What is the meaning of the word "surreptitious"?
   - a. covert
   - b. winding
   - c. lively
   - d. sweet

2. How is the noun clause used in the following sentence? "I hope that I can learn this game."
   - a. Subject
   - b. predicate nominative
   - c. direct object
   - d. object of the preposition

Quantitative

3. Divide 50 by 0.5 and add 5. What is the result?
   - a. 25
   - b. 30
   - c. 95
   - d. 105

4. What is the value of 1442?
   - a. 12
   - b. 72
   - c. 95
   - d. 20736

Reasoning

5. _____ is to *boat* as *snow* is to _____.
   - a. Sail, ski
   - b. Water, winter
   - c. Water, ski
   - d. Engine, water

6. Two women played 5 games of chess. Each woman won the same number of games, yet there were no ties. How can this be?
   - a. There was a forfeit.
   - b. One player cheated.
   - c. They played different people.
   - d. One game is still in progress.

Mechanical

7. If gear A and gear C are both turning counterclockwise, what is happening to gear B?
   - a. It is turning counterclockwise.
   - b. It is turning clockwise.
   - c. It remains stationary.
   - d. The whole system will jam.

Answers: 1. a, 2. c, 3. d, 4. d, 5. c, 6. c, 7. b

Biodata Tests

Biodata tests collect biographical information about candidates that has shown to correlate with on-the-job success. Candidates are questioned about events and behaviors that reflect attitudes, experiences, interests, skills, and abilities. Typically the questions relate to events that have occurred in a person's life and ask what the person typically did in those situations. The idea is that past behavior is the best predictor of future behavior. For example, a question on a biodata test might ask, "How many books have you read in the last 6 months?" or "How often have you put aside tasks to complete another, more difficult assignment?" Test takers choose one of several predetermined alternatives to best match their past behavior and experiences.

A response to a single biodata question is of little value. Rather, it is the pattern of responses across several different situations that give biographical data the power to predict future behavior on the job. Although biodata tests have been found to be good predictors of on-the-job success, they are sophisticated and must be professionally developed and validated. Another drawback is that the questions might not appear to be clearly related to the job being tested for, so applicants might question the test's validity and believe the test invades their privacy.[32]

Personality and Interest Inventories

Whereas cognitive ability tests measure a person's mental capacity, personality tests measure disposition and temperament. During the 1990s, for example, testing by the U.S. Army found that cognitive ability tests were the best predictors of how well soldiers were able to acquire job knowledge and, ultimately, of their technical proficiencies. But personality tests were the better predictors of their motivation, such as their leadership efforts and propensity to adhere to rules. Years of research show that five dimensions can summarize personality traits. The "Big Five" factors are the following:

1. *Extroversion*—the degree to which someone is talkative, sociable, active, aggressive, and excitable

2. *Agreeableness*—the degree to which someone is trusting, amiable, generous, tolerant, honest, cooperative, and flexible

3. *Conscientiousness*—the degree to which someone is dependable and organized and perseveres in tasks

4. *Neuroticism*—the degree to which someone is secure, calm, independent, and autonomous

5. *Openness to experience*—the degree to which someone is intellectual, philosophical, insightful, creative, artistic, and curious[33]

Well-known personality tests include the California Psychological Inventory (CPI), the Myers-Briggs Type Indicator (MBTI), and the 180-question Caliper test, whose users range from FedEx to the Chicago Cubs.

Using the INTERNET

Find additional information about the administration and interpretation of the Kuder Inventory. Go to

www.cengagebrain.com

Although there is some evidence to show that when used in combination with cognitive ability tests measures of personality traits (such as conscientiousness) can help predict how well a person will perform on the job, historically the connection between the two has been quite low.[34] Personality tests can also be problematic if they inadvertently discriminate against individuals who would otherwise perform effectively,[35] which is why several states severely restrict their usage. In addition, personality tests that reveal anything about a person's mental impairment or a psychological condition, even inadvertently, violate the Americans with Disabilities Act. Rather than being used to make hiring decisions, personality and interest inventories may be most useful for helping people with their occupational selection and career planning.

Honesty and Integrity Tests

In response to the Employee Polygraph Protection Act, many employers have dramatically increased their use of pencil-and-paper honesty and integrity tests. These tests have commonly been used in settings such as retail stores where employees have access to cash or merchandise. For example, Payless ShoeSource, based in Topeka, Kansas, has used a paper-and-pencil honesty test to reduce employee theft. When the company began its program, losses totaled nearly $21 million per year among its 4,700 stores. Within only one year of implementing its screening program, inventory shrinkage fell by 20 percent to less than 1 percent of sales.[36] Questions that might appear on an integrity test include the following:

- How likely would you be to report a coworker you discovered was stealing office supplies?

- Should an employee who lied on his application be fired if the falsification is uncovered?

Although some studies have shown that honesty tests are valid for predicting job performance as well as a wide range of disruptive behaviors such as theft, disciplinary problems, and absenteeism, other studies have questioned their validity.[37] It is possible that the tests "work" not because they predict behavior but because they deter less-than-honest applicants from joining a company. Lastly, applicants sometimes view the tests as an invasion of their privacy. Given these issues, HRM specialists should consider the use of honesty tests very cautiously and most certainly in conjunction with other sources of information.[38]

Polygraph Tests

The polygraph, or lie detector, is a device that measures the changes in breathing, blood pressure, and pulse of a person who is being questioned. It consists of a rubber tube around the chest, a cuff around the arm, and sensors attached to the fingers that record the physiological changes in the examinee as the examiner asks questions that call for an answer of yes or no. Questions typically cover such items as whether a person uses drugs, has stolen from an employer, or has committed a serious undetected crime.

The growing swell of objections to the use of polygraphs in employment situations culminated in the passage of the federal Employee Polygraph Protection Act of 1988. The Act generally prohibits using lie detectors for prehire screening and random testing of a firm's current employees and applies to all private employers except pharmaceutical companies and companies that supply security guards for health and safety operations as well as government agencies.[39] It defines the term *lie detector* to include the polygraph, deceptograph, voice stress analyzer, psychological stress evaluator, and any similar mechanical or electrical device used to render a diagnostic opinion about the honesty or dishonesty of an individual.

Other provisions of the act set qualification standards for polygraph examiners, conditions for examinations, and disclosure of information when the use of the polygraph is authorized. Because of the law, employers have had to resort to such alternatives as written tests of honesty and background checks of applicants. Among the organizations most affected are Wall Street firms, banks, and retail companies, which used to rely heavily on polygraphs. Polygraphs are used by only a small percentage of firms in the general population, although their use is prevalent among law enforcement agencies.[40]

Physical Ability Tests

In addition to learning about a job candidate's mental capabilities, employers frequently need to assess a person's physical abilities. Particularly for demanding and potentially dangerous jobs such as those held by firefighters and police officers, physical abilities such as strength and endurance tend to be good predictors not only of performance, but also of accidents and injuries.[41]

Physical ability tests must be used cautiously as well. In the past, requirements for physical characteristics such as strength, agility, height, and weight were often determined by an employer's unvalidated notion of what should be required. This often put women and disabled job applicants at a disadvantage, a situation that can lead to lawsuits. After a Dial Corp. plant in Fort Madison, Iowa, began using a strength test in 2000, the company found itself subject to such a suit. Prior to the test's use, nearly 50 percent of the people hired at the plant were women. Once the test was implemented, the percentage dropped dramatically. An appeals court subsequently ruled the test had a disparate impact on women because, although injuries at the plant fell, they actually began doing so after the company instituted new safety rules, which happened years before the strength test was implemented.[42]

Because of situations such as these, requirements that tend to discriminate against women have consequently been questioned and modified so as to represent typical job demands. In addition, the evidence suggests that although the average man is stronger, faster, and more powerful than the average woman, women tend to have better balance, manual dexterity, flexibility, and coordination than men. For these reasons, it is clear that (as with other methods for screening potential employees) the use of physical ability tests should be carefully validated on the basis of the essential functions of the job.

Medical Examinations

The medical examination is one of the later steps in the selection process because the law prohibits it being administered to an applicant before he or she has been made a conditional employment offer. A medical examination is generally given to ensure that the health of an applicant is adequate to meet the job requirements. It also provides a baseline against which subsequent medical examinations can be compared and interpreted. The latter objective is particularly important in determinations of work-caused disabilities under workers' compensation laws.[43]

The Americans with Disabilities Act severely limits the types of medical inquiries and examinations that employers may use. Walmart, for example, paid $6 million to settle one lawsuit involving an ADA claim. According to the EEOC, Walmart's hiring questionnaire violated an ADA provision restricting the kinds of medical information companies can request from prospective employees. The law explicitly states that all exams must be directly related to the requirements of the job. In addition, the examinations must be required of all candidates offered the job. Furthermore, the ADA prohibits companies from screening out a prospective employee because he or she has an elevated risk of on-the-job injury or a medical condition that could be aggravated because of job demands.

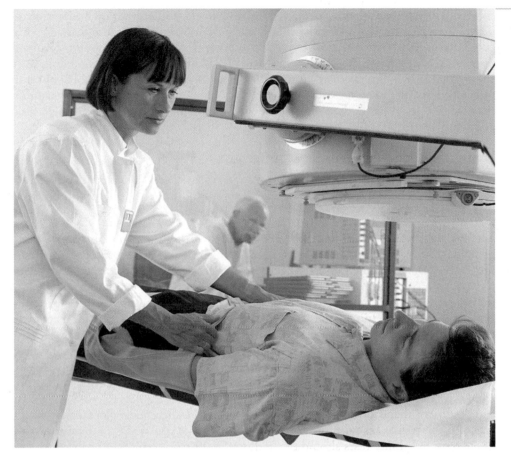

Because medical examinations are costly, they are usually reserved for final candidates.

Drug Tests

Like medical examinations, drug tests can only be given to candidates after they have been extended job offers. Since passage of the Drug-Free Workplace Act of 1988, applicants and employees of federal contractors, Department of Defense contractors, and those under Department of Transportation regulations are subject to testing for illegal drug use. Approximately 40 percent of private firms test their employees. (See Chapter 13 for an extended discussion of this topic, including a sample policy statement for a drug-free workplace.) Urine, hair, saliva, and sweat testing are most common. Hair testing, for example, can show drug use going back months. Saliva, or oral fluid, testing works well at accident scenes involving drug use by current employees when urine testing is inconvenient. Sweat testing is efficient for workers returning to duty after testing positive because it captures drug use within a specific window of weeks or days.

Some recent studies have failed to show that drug testing makes the workplace safer or leads to improvements in the performance of workers, however. Moreover, relatively few applicants test positive for drugs (less than 5 percent). Alcohol use, in fact, appears to create more problems than illegal drugs in the workplace.[44] Different countries also have different standards. Canada, for example, severely limits preemployment drug and alcohol tests (as well as random drug and alcohol tests of one's current employees). For reasons such as these, some companies no longer conduct drug tests. Sun Microsystems is one of them. Dell Computer, on the other hand, routinely tests its employees. In addition, federal courts have ruled that public, but not private, companies must have a special need for conducting drug tests. The weight of the evidence suggests that testing is most appropriate for staff members in high-risk and safety-critical positions.

Determining the Validity of Tests

The *Uniform Guidelines* (see Chapter 3) recognizes and accepts different approaches to validating tests: criterion-related validity, content validity, and construct validity.

Criterion-Related Validity

The extent to which a test significantly correlates with important elements of work behavior is known as criterion-related validity. How well a person performs on a test, for example, is compared with his or her actual production records, supervisor's ratings, training outcomes, and other measures of on-the-job success. In a sales job, for example, it is common to use sales figures as a basis for comparison. In production jobs, the quantity and quality of output are likely to be the best indicators of job success.

There are two types of criterion-related validity: concurrent and predictive. Concurrent validity involves obtaining criterion data from *current employees* at about the same time that test scores (or other predictor information) are obtained. For example, a supervisor will be asked to rate a group of clerical employees on the quantity and quality of their performance. These employees are then given a clerical aptitude test, and the test scores are compared with the supervisor's ratings to determine the degree of relationship between them. Predictive validity, on the other hand, involves testing *applicants* and obtaining criterion data *after* those applicants have been hired and have been on the job for a certain period of time. For example, applicants are given clerical aptitude tests, which are then filed away for later study. After the individuals have been on the job for several months, supervisors, who should not know the employees' test scores, are asked to rate them on the quality and quantity of their performance. The test scores are then compared with the supervisors' ratings.

Regardless of the method used, cross-validation is essential. Cross-validation is a process in which a test or battery of tests is administered to a different sample of people (drawn from the same population) for the purpose of verifying the results obtained from the original validation study. One way to measure a test's validity is to administer it to an organization's current employees and create a benchmark score to which applicants' scores can be compared. This is what FedEx has agreed to do before administering any new tests.

Correlation methods are generally used to determine the relationship between predictor information such as test scores and criterion data. The correlation scatterplots in Figure 6.7 illustrate the difference between a selection test with zero validity (A) and one with high validity (B). Each dot represents a person. Note that in scatterplot A, there is no relationship between test scores and success on the job; in other words, the validity is zero. In scatterplot B, those who score low on the test tend to have low success on the job, whereas those who score high on the test tend to have high success on the job, indicating high validity. In actual practice we would apply a statistical

criterion-related validity
The extent to which a selection tool predicts, or significantly correlates with, important elements of work behavior

concurrent validity
extent to which the test scores of current employees correlate with job performance

predictive validity
The extent to which applicants' test scores match criterion data obtained from those applicants/employees after they have been on the job for some indefinite period

cross-validation
Verifying the results obtained from a validation study by administering a test or test battery to a different sample (drawn from the same population)

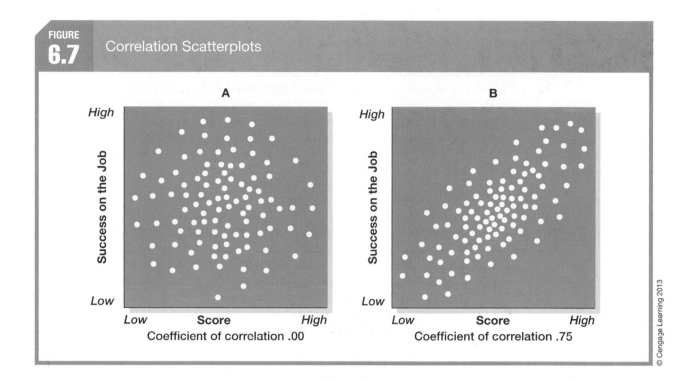

FIGURE 6.7 Correlation Scatterplots

formula to the data to obtain a coefficient of correlation referred to as a *validity coefficient*. Correlation coefficients range from 0.00, denoting a complete absence of relationship, to +1.00 and to −1.00, indicating a perfect positive and perfect negative relationship, respectively. Combining two or more procedures such as an interview or a test can improve the validity of a firm's selection process. The higher the overall validity is, the greater the chances are of hiring individuals who will be the better performers.

Content Validity

When it is not feasible to use the criterion-related approach, often because of limited samples of individuals, the content method is used. Content validity is assumed to exist when a test adequately samples the knowledge and skills a person needs to do a particular job. The closer the content of the selection instrument is to actual work samples or behaviors, the greater its content validity. For example, a civil service examination for accountants has high content validity when it requires applicants to solve accounting problems representative of those found on the job. Asking an accountant to lift a sixty-pound box, however, is a selection procedure that has content validity only if the job description indicates that accountants must be able to meet this requirement.

Content validity is the most direct and least complicated type of validity to assess. It is generally used to evaluate job knowledge and skill tests, to be described later. Unlike the criterion-related method, content validity is not expressed as a correlation. Instead, an index is computed (from evaluations of an expert panel) that indicates the relationship between the content of the test items and a person's performance on the job.[45] While content validity does have its limitations, it has made a positive

content validity

The extent to which a selection instrument, such as a test, adequately samples the knowledge and skills needed to perform a particular job

contribution to job analysis procedures and to the role of expert judgment in sampling and scoring procedures.

Construct Validity

construct validity

The extent to which a selection tool measures a theoretical construct or trait

The extent to which a test measures a theoretical construct, or trait, is known as **construct validity.** Typical constructs are intelligence, mechanical comprehension, and anxiety. They are in effect broad, general categories of human functions that are based on the measurement of many discrete behaviors. For example, the Bennett Mechanical Comprehension Test consists of a wide variety of tasks that measure the construct of mechanical comprehension.

Measuring construct validity requires showing that the psychological trait is related to satisfactory job performance and that the test accurately measures the psychological trait. There is a lack of literature covering this concept as it relates to employment practices, probably because it is difficult and expensive to validate a construct and to show how it is job-related.[46]

As you can tell from this discussion, developing valid selection procedures, especially selection tests, can be complicated and require expertise. Because valid custom tests are more defensible in court if applicants challenge them, many large organizations that subject applicants to multiple tests hire outside vendors with industrial-organizational psychologists on staff to help them develop selection procedures. Highlights in HRM 5 contains some "best practice" preemployment testing suggestions offered by the EEOC.

HIGHLIGHTS IN HRM

5 Best Practices for Employee Testing and Selection

- Employers should administer tests and other selection procedures without regard to race, color, national origin, sex, religion, age (forty or older), or disability.
- Employers should ensure that employment tests and other selection procedures are properly validated for the positions and purposes for which they are used. The test or selection procedure must be job-related and its results appropriate for the employer's purpose. While a test vendor's documentation supporting the validity of a test may be helpful, the employer is still responsible for ensuring that its tests are valid under UGESP.
- If a selection procedure screens out a protected group, the employer should determine whether there is an equally effective alternative selection procedure that has less adverse impact and, if so, adopt the alternative procedure. For example, if the selection procedure is a test, the employer should determine whether another test would predict job performance but not disproportionately exclude the protected group.
- To ensure that a test or selection procedure remains predictive of success in a job, employers should keep abreast of changes in job requirements and should update the test specifications or selection procedures accordingly.
- Employers should ensure that tests and selection procedures are not adopted casually by managers who know little about these processes. A test or selection procedure can be an effective management tool, but no test or selection procedure should be implemented without an understanding of its effectiveness and limitations for the organization, its appropriateness for a specific job, and whether it can be appropriately administered and scored.

Reaching a Selection Decision

The most critical step is the decision to accept or reject applicants. Thus it requires systematic consideration of all the relevant information about applicants. It is common to use summary forms and checklists such as the one shown in Figure 6.8 to ensure that all of the pertinent information has been included in the evaluation of applicants.

LEARNING OUTCOME 5

How have your skills, knowledge, aptitudes, and motivation affected the types of jobs you have applied for in the past or how well you did a particular job?

FIGURE 6.8 Candidate Evaluation Form

Position:
Candidate Name:
Interviewer Name:
Interview Date:

Complete the comments section as you interview the candidate. After the interview, circle your ratings for each section, and then add them together for a final score. The ratings scale is as follows:

RATINGS SCALE
1. Negligible or doesn't meet requirements
2. More needed
3. Adequate
4. Exceeds requirements

Education
Comments:
Rating: _____

Experience
Comments:
Rating: _____

Job Knowledge
Comments:
Rating: _____

Job Skills
Comments:
Rating: _____

Interest in Position
Comments:
Rating: _____

Problem Solving Ability
Comments:
Rating: _____

Communication Skills
Comments:
Rating: _____

Leadership Skills
Comments:
Rating: _____

_____ TOTAL POINTS

Rater's Recommendation:

Summarizing Information about Applicants

Fundamentally, an employer is interested in what an applicant can do and will do. Evaluating candidates on the basis of information you have assembled should focus on these two factors, as Figure 6.9 shows. The "can-do" factors include a candidate's knowledge and skills, as well as the aptitude (the potential) for acquiring new knowledge and skills. The "will-do" factors include the candidate's motivation, interests, and other personality characteristics. Both factors are essential to successful performance on the job. The employee who has the ability (can do) but is not motivated to use it (will not do) is little better than the employee who lacks the necessary ability.

It is much easier to measure what individuals can do than what they will do. The can-do factors are readily evident from test scores and verified information. What the individual will do can only be inferred. Employers can use the responses to interview and application form questions and references to obtain information for making inferences about what an individual will do.

Decision-Making Strategy

The strategy used for making personnel decisions for one category of jobs might differ from that used for another category. The strategy used to select managerial and executive personnel, for example, will be different than the strategy used to select clerical and technical personnel. Although many factors have to be considered in terms of making hiring decisions, the following are some of the questions that managers must consider:

1. Should the individuals be hired according to their highest potential or according to the needs of the organization?

2. At what grade or wage level should the individual be hired?

3. Should the selection be concerned primarily with finding an ideal employee to match the job currently open, or should a candidate's potential for advancement in the organization be considered?

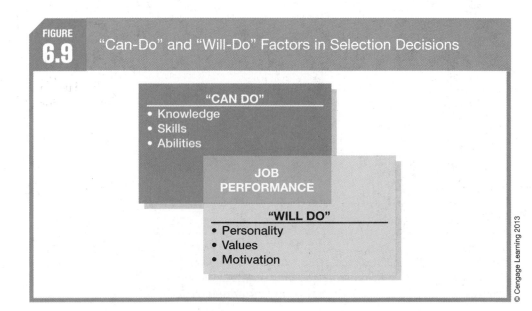

FIGURE 6.9 "Can-Do" and "Will-Do" Factors in Selection Decisions

"CAN DO"
- Knowledge
- Skills
- Abilities

JOB PERFORMANCE

"WILL DO"
- Personality
- Values
- Motivation

© Cengage Learning 2013

4. To what extent should those who are not qualified but are qualifiable be considered?

5. Should overqualified individuals be considered?

6. What effect will a decision have on the firm meeting its affirmative action plans and diversity considerations?

In addition to these types of factors, managers must also consider which approach they will use in making hiring decisions. Two basic approaches to selection exist: clinical (personal judgment) and statistical.

Clinical Approach

In the clinical approach to decision making, those making the selection decision review all the data on the applicants. Then, on the basis of their understanding of the job and the individuals who have been successful in that job, they make a decision. Different individuals often arrive at different decisions about an applicant when they use this approach because each evaluator assigns different weights to the applicant's strengths and weaknesses. Unfortunately, personal biases and stereotypes are frequently covered up by what appear to be rational reasons for either accepting or rejecting a candidate. Plus, it can lead to a homogenous workforce because, as you learned in Chapter 5, according to the attraction-selection-attrition (ASA) model, people are often tempted to hire applicants like themselves.

Statistical Approach

In contrast to the clinical approach, the statistical approach to decision making is more objective. It involves identifying the most valid predictors and weighting them using statistical methods such as multiple regression.[47] Quantified data such as scores or ratings from interviews, tests, and other procedures are then combined according to their weighted value. Individuals with the highest combined scores are selected. A comparison of the clinical approach with the statistical approach in a wide variety of situations has shown that the statistical approach is superior. Although this superiority has been recognized for many decades, the clinical approach continues to be the one most commonly used.

With a strictly statistical approach, a candidate's high score on one predictor (such as a cognitive ability test) will make up for a low score on another predictor (such as the interview). For this reason, this model is a **compensatory model**. However, it is frequently important that applicants achieve some minimum level of proficiency on all selection dimensions. When this is the case, a **multiple cutoff model** can be used in which only those candidates who score above the minimum cutoff on all dimensions are considered. The selection decision is made from that subset of candidates.[48]

A variation of the multiple cutoff model is referred to as the **multiple hurdle model**. This decision strategy is sequential in that after candidates go through an initial evaluation stage, those who score well are provisionally accepted and are assessed further at each successive stage. The process continues through several stages (hurdles) before a final decision is made. This approach is especially useful when either the testing or training procedures are lengthy and expensive.

Each of the statistical approaches requires that a decision be made about where the cutoff lies—that point in the distribution of scores above which a person should be considered and below which the person should be rejected. The score that the applicant must achieve is the cutoff score. Depending on the labor supply and diversity and anti-discrimination considerations, it may be necessary to lower or raise the cutoff score.

compensatory model

A selection decision model in which a high score in one area can make up for a low score in another area

multiple cutoff model

A selection decision model that requires an applicant to achieve some minimum level of proficiency on all selection dimensions

multiple hurdle model

A sequential strategy in which only the applicants with the highest scores at an initial test stage go on to subsequent stages

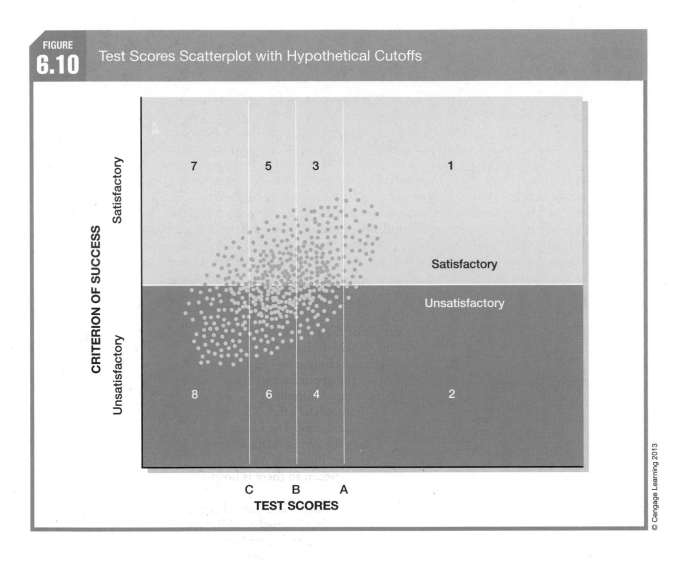

FIGURE 6.10 Test Scores Scatterplot with Hypothetical Cutoffs

© Cengage Learning 2013

The effects of raising and lowering the cutoff score are illustrated in Figure 6.10. Each dot in the center of the figure represents the relationship between the test score (or a weighted combination of test scores) and the criterion of success for one individual. In this instance, the test has a fairly high validity, as represented by the elliptical pattern of the dots. Note that the high-scoring individuals are concentrated in the satisfactory job success category, whereas the low-scoring individuals are concentrated in the unsatisfactory category.

If the cutoff score is set at A, only the individuals represented by areas 1 and 2 will be accepted. Nearly all of them will be successful. If more employees are needed, the cutoff score can be lowered to point B. In this case, a larger number of potential failures will be accepted, as shown in quadrants 2 and 4. Even if the cutoff is lowered to C, the total number of satisfactory individuals selected (represented by the dots in areas 1, 3, and 5) exceeds the total number selected who are unsatisfactory (areas 2, 4, and 6). Thus, the test serves to maximize the selection of probable successes and to minimize the selection of probable failures. This is all we can hope for in terms of predicting on-the-job success: the probability of selecting a greater proportion of individuals who will be successful rather than unsuccessful.

A related factor helps ensure the best qualified people are selected: having an adequate number of candidates from which to make a selection. This factor is typically expressed in terms of a selection ratio, which is the ratio of the number of applicants to be selected to the total number of applicants. A ratio of 0.10, for example, means that 10 percent of the applicants will be selected. A ratio of 0.90 means that 90 percent will be selected. If the selection ratio is low, only the most promising applicants will be hired. When the ratio is high, very little selectivity will be possible because even applicants with mediocre abilities will have to be hired if the firm's vacancies are to be filled. When this is the situation, a firm's managers can fall prey to what some experts call the "desperation bias"—choosing someone because you are in a pinch. It is a common problem among managers because of the many time and operating constraints they face.

selection ratio
The number of applicants compared with the number of people to be hired

Final Decision

In large organizations, managers or supervisors usually make the final decision about whom to hire and communicate it to the human resources department. HR personnel then notify external applicants about the decision and make job offers to candidates. The HR department should confirm the details of the job, working arrangements, hours, wages, and so on and specify a deadline by which the applicant must reach a decision. If, at this point, findings from the medical examination or drug test are not yet available, an offer is often made contingent on the applicant's passing the examination. This information can be verbally communicated initially. It is commonplace to first contact candidates by phone to inform them of the offer. The offer should then be put in writing, generally in a letter to the candidate. The process of notifying internal candidates is slightly different. Generally the hiring manager contacts the candidates personally and informs them of the decision. However, it is still important to put the offer in writing if an internal candidate is chosen so there is no ambiguity or dispute about its terms.

Rejecting both internal candidates and external candidates is a difficult task, but rejecting internal candidates can be particularly tricky. Most internal candidates seeking a promotion are valuable employees their firms would rather not lose. According to the Bridgespan Group, a nonprofit that helps other philanthropic nonprofits achieve success, the manager delivering the bad news should explain to the employee that the person who got the job has skills that more closely aligned with the firm's needs but that the process has given the organization a better understanding of her or his background when future job openings arise. Also emphasize that the decision was made in a systematic way based on objective criteria but that it was nonetheless a hard one to make.[49]

Lastly, organizations should not fail to notify candidates who are not chosen for the position. This happens too often with both internal candidates and external candidates. It is not uncommon for external candidates to be customers of the firms to which they apply. Not letting them know about the employment decision can jeopardize that relationship. The same is true for internal candidates. One employee lamented that after applying internally for a job, no one contacted him or the other candidates to tell them they did not get the job. They only learned about it after a manager sent out an e-mail about the new hire. "After 10-plus years of working for the company, I felt I deserved better treatment than that," says the employee.

Summary

LEARNING OUTCOME 1 Selection is the process of choosing individuals who have relevant qualifications to fill existing or projected job openings. The selection process should start with a job analysis. Research shows that complete and clear job specifications help interviewers differentiate between qualified and unqualified applicants and reduces the effect of an interviewer's biases and prejudices. The number of steps in the selection process and their sequence will vary, not only with the organization, but also with the type and level of jobs to be filled.

LEARNING OUTCOME 2 The employee selection process should provide as much reliable and valid information as possible about applicants so that their qualifications can be carefully matched with the job's specifications. The information that is obtained should be clearly job-related or predict success on the job and free from potential discrimination. Reliability refers to the consistency of test scores over time and across measures. Validity refers to the accuracy of the measurements taken. Validity can be assessed in terms of whether the measurement is based on a job specification (content validity), whether test scores correlate with performance criteria (predictive validity), and whether the test accurately measures what it purports to measure (construct validity).

LEARNING OUTCOME 3 Interviews are customarily used in conjunction with résumés, application forms, biographical information blanks, references, background investigations, and various types of preemployment tests. Despite problems with its validity, the employment interview remains central to the selection process. Depending on the type of job, applicants could be interviewed by one person, members of a work team, or other individuals in the organization. Structured interviews have been found to be better predictors of the performance of job applicants than nonstructured interviews. Some interviews are situational and can focus on hypothetical situations or actual behavioral descriptions of a candidate's previous work experiences. Regardless of the technique chosen, those who conduct interviews should receive special training to acquaint them with interviewing methods and EEO considerations. The training should also make them more aware of the nature of the job and its requirements.

LEARNING OUTCOME 4 Preemployment tests are more objective than interviews and can give managers a fuller sense of the capabilities of different candidates. A wide range of tests exists. Cognitive ability tests are especially valuable for assessing verbal, quantitative, and reasoning abilities. Personality and interest tests are perhaps best used for placement or career development. Job knowledge and work sample tests are achievement tests that are useful for determining whether a candidate can perform the duties of the job without further training. Physical ability tests can be used to prevent accidents and injuries, particularly for physically demanding work. However, they must not be used if they have a disparate impact on candidates in protected classes. Medical examinations and drug tests can only be legally administered after a conditional offer of employment has been made.

LEARNING OUTCOME 5 In the process of making decisions, all "can-do" and "will-do" factors should be assembled and weighted systematically so that the final decision can be based on a composite of the most reliable and valid information. Although the clinical approach to decision-making is used more than the statistical approach, the former lacks the accuracy of the latter. Compensatory models allow a candidate's high score on one predictor to make up for a low score on another. When the multiple cutoff model is used, only those candidates who score above a minimum cutoff level remain in the running. A variation of the multiple cutoff is the multiple hurdle model, which involves several stages and cutoff levels. Whichever of these approaches is used, the goal is to select a greater proportion of individuals who will be successful on the job.

Key Terms

assessment center
behavioral description interview
  (BDI)
compensatory model
concurrent validity
construct validity
content validity
criterion-related validity
cross-validation

multiple cutoff model
multiple hurdle model
negligent hiring
nondirective interview
panel interview
predictive validity
preemployment test
reliability
selection

selection ratio
sequential interview
situational interview
structured interview
validity
virtual interviews
video résumés

Discussion Questions

LEARNING OUTCOME 1 Is there a "best" employment process stepwise? What steps must come first and last?

LEARNING OUTCOME 2 What is meant by the term *criterion* as it is used in personnel selection? Give some examples of criteria used for jobs with which you are familiar.

LEARNING OUTCOME 3 Compare briefly the major types of employment interviews described in this chapter. Which type would you prefer to conduct? Why?

LEARNING OUTCOME 4 What characteristics do job knowledge and job sample tests have that often make them more acceptable to the examinees than other types of tests?

LEARNING OUTCOME 5 In what ways does the clinical approach to selection differ from the statistical approach? How do you account for the fact that one approach is superior to the other?

HRM EXPERIENCE
Designing Selection Criteria and Methods

Making hiring decisions is one of the most important—and difficult—decisions a manager makes. Without good information, managers have almost no chance of making the right choice. They might as well be using a Ouija board. The process begins with a sound understanding of the job: the tasks, duties, and responsibilities associated with it and the knowledge, skills, and abilities needed to do it. A job analysis should be done to make certain that all managers have assembled all of the information they need to ensure a good person-job fit. However, this information may not be enough. Other information about the company's values and philosophy are likely to be required to ensure that a good person-organization fit results.

Assignment

1. Working in teams of four to six individuals, choose a job with which you are familiar and identify the most important knowledge, skills, abilities, and other characteristics needed for someone doing the job to perform well.

2. Next, identify which methods you would use to find candidates with these qualities. Would you use applications, interviews, cognitive or ability tests, work samples, or what? Explain why you would use these methods you identified and justify the cost and time required to conduct each.

3. After you have identified your selection criteria and methods, do a "reality check" in a real organization. Interview a manager who employs someone in that job. For example, if the job you selected is salesperson, go to a local business to learn how they select individuals for sales jobs. Compare what you thought would be a good selection approach with what you learned from the company you visited.

4. Identify the reasons for any discrepancies between your approach and theirs. Are the reasons justified and sound?

On the Job: Video Cases

Scripps Hospital La Jolla

In this video, the personnel at Scripps Hospital La Jolla in San Diego discuss their philosophy about selecting employees that match the hospital's organizational culture. Behavioral based interviews, realistic job previews, hiring for "attitude," and multiple types of interviews are mentioned as tools for selecting the right candidate. The video also mentions the importance of forecasting workforce supply and demand to help predict staffing needs.

What to Watch for and Ask Yourself

1. Scripps Hospital La Jolla stresses "culture fit" and "hiring for attitude" as critical criteria for applicant selection. Discuss this in terms of (a) validity and reliability and (b) legal requirements for nondiscrimination.

2. Describe the selection process at Scripps Hospital La Jolla.

3. Scripps Hospital La Jolla appears to rely heavily on the selection interview to make hiring decisions. (a) What does this mean as far as reliability and validity? (b) What are some possible problems or common interviewing mistakes that should be watched for in interviewing?

Case Study 1

When it comes to preemployment tests, companies are not necessarily just handing candidates a pen and a pencil or having them answer multiple-choice questions via a computer or phone anymore. A small but growing number of assessments have gone virtual. The assessments, which often conducted via the computer or the web, simulate a job's functions. You can liken them to video games but within a work setting. Toyota, Starbucks, the paint maker Sherwin Williams, and numerous financial firms such as SunTrust Bank, KeyBank, and National City Bank have successfully used virtual job simulations to assess applicants.

At Toyota, applicants participating in simulations read dials and gauges, spot safety problems, and use their ability to solve problems as well as their general ability to learn as assessed. The candidates can see and hear about the job they're applying for from current Toyota employees. National City Bank has used virtual assessments to test call-center candidates and branch manager candidates. Call center candidates are given customer-service problems to solve, and branch manager candidates go through a simulation that assesses their ability to foster relationships with clients and make personnel decisions.

The virtual assessments tools, which are produced by companies such as Shaker Group Consulting, Profiles International, and others do not come cheap. But although they can cost tens of thousands of dollars, larger companies that can afford them are saying they are worth it. The benefits? Better qualified candidates, faster recruiting, and lower turnover among employees hired. KeyBank says that by using virtual testing tools, it realized savings of more than $1.75 million per year due to lower turnover. Toyota began using computer-based assessments in the early 2000s, which have been so successful the company has since rolled them out to its other plants around the world.

Candidates also seem to like the assessments because they provide a more realistic job preview and make them feel like they are being chosen for jobs on more than just their personalities or how they performed during an interview. "It was a very insightful experience that made you think about what exactly you like and dislike in the workplace and if you really enjoy helping customers and have patience to do so," says one candidate tested for a customer service job. It is not just Gen X or Y candidates who have played a lot of video games who like them either. "We haven't seen any adverse impact," says Ken Troyan, SunTrust Bank's chief staffing officer. "There's some mythology—if you will—about older people not being computer-savvy, and that's just not so." One study found that the simulations also tend to result in less of a gap between minority and white candidates than when paper-and-pencil tests are used.

HR experts warn that companies need to be sure they are not simply buying glitzy simulations that do not translate well to the jobs for which they are hiring. Also, the screening tools could potentially eliminate candidates who have trouble with simulations or computers but might make good employees. You should still use the U.S. Department of Labor's "whole person approach" to hiring, says one HR professional. The "whole person approach" factors in the results of a variety of accepted tests along with prior actual performance and interview results to get the most complete picture of an employee or candidate.

Questions

1. What do you think are the prime advantages and disadvantages of "virtual tryouts"?
2. Do you think there would be any EEO concerns regarding this system?
3. Do you think virtual job tryouts might be better suited for some jobs than others? If so, which ones?

Sources: Karen Vilardo, "KeyBank's Success With the 'Virtual_Job_Tryout," *Journal of Corporate Recruiting Leadership* 5, no. 4 (May 2010): 24; Ira S. Wolfe and "Success Performance Solutions," *The Total View Newsletter* (May12, 2010); Connie Winkle, "HR Technology: Job Tryouts Go Virtual" *HR Magazine* (September 1, 2006), http://www.shrm.org/; Gina Ruiz, "Job Candidate Assessment Tests Go Virtual," *Workforce Management Online* (January 2008), http://www.workforce.com; "Clients and Case Studies," Shaker Consulting Group, accessed March 27, 2011, http://www.shakercg.com.

Case Study 2

Cleaning Up the "Resu-mess"

Electronic submission systems and a tough job market have left HR and hiring managers drowning in a sea of résumés and applications. Some large retailers can get a million or more résumés a year. Even small businesses can find themselves flooded with them. For example, when Raising Cain, a Louisiana-based fast-food chain, opened an office in Dallas, the firm needed to hire 35 people. It received 10,000 résumés and had to hire an outside firm to help sort through them.

Given this trend, it is not surprising harried HR personnel, managers, and business owners are rushing to install software that promises to do the screening and sifting of résumés for them. In fact, recruiters say the percentage of online applications viewed by an actual human being today ranges from just 5 to 25 percent. Résumé screening software built into applicant tracking systems used to be expensive—something that only large firms could afford. Today, however, many are web-based, easy to use, and relatively inexpensive.

For example, when Southern Company, an energy company based in Atlanta, posts jobs on its site, applicants click on the links and are taken to Hire.com, where the screening is done. The applicants do not even realize that they have left the firm's corporate website. Hire.com also has a feature that allows companies to ask applicants screening questions related to their education, job knowledge, experience using certain work equipment, and so forth. PreVisor and Kenexa are two firms that offer close to a thousand online assessments, with prices ranging from a couple of bucks to $50 a test.

Many job boards now feature prescreening questions as well and have algorithms to the recommend candidates similar to the way Amazon.com recommends products based on what a person has purchased in the past. The boards also let employers send automated responses to applicants when their résumés are received and their prescreening tests have been taken. The messages help let candidates know where they stand in the selection process and what the next steps are.

Some recruiters have found ways to avoid the "resu-mess" altogether. Instead of posting job ads, they use social networking sites to get the word out for the types of employees they are looking to hire. Kevin Mercuri, president of Propheta Communications, a public relations firm in New York City is one of them. Mercuri got tired of being swamped by résumés generated by ads he posted on Craigslist. Now when he needs to recruit personnel, Mercuri posts a message about job openings on his LinkedIn page. "I get people vouching for each applicant, so I don't have to spend hours sorting through resumes," he says.

Questions

1. What impact do you think résumé screening tools are having on HR departments?
2. What competitive advantages do you see in using résumé screening tools?
3. Do you see any drawbacks associated with them, and, if so, how might they be addressed?

Sources: Darren, Dahl, "Tapping the Talent Pool... without Drowning in Resumés" *Inc.* 31 no. 3 (April 2009): 122; Anne Kadet, "Did You Get My Résumé?" *Smart Money* (February 27, 2009), http://www.smartmoney.com; Drew Robb, "Screening for Speedier Selection," *HRMagazine* 49, no. 9 (September 2004): 143–147.

Notes and References

1. Misty L. Loughry, Matthew W. Ohland, and D. Dewayne Moore, "Development of a Theory-Based Assessment of Team Member Effectiveness," *Educational & Psychological Measurement* 67, no. 3 (June 2007): 505–524; Patrick D. Converse, Fredrick L. Oswald, Michael A. Gillespie, Kevin A. Field, and Elizabeth B. Bizot, "Matching Individual to Occupations Using Abilities and the O*NET," *Personnel Psychology* 57, no. 2 (Summer 2004): 451–488.

2. Joe Williams, "Bringing the Human Touch to Recruitment," *Bloomberg Businessweek* (January 24, 2011), http://bx.businessweek.com.

3. Mary-Kathryn Zachary, "Discrimination without Intent," *Supervision* 64, no. 5 (May 2003): 23–29; Neal Schmitt, William Rogers, David Chan, Lori Sheppard, and Danielle Jennings, "Adverse Impact and Predictive Efficiency of Various Predictor Combinations," *Journal of Applied Psychology* 82, no. 5 (October 1997): 719–30.

4. Michael Luo, "'Whitening' the Resume," *New York Times* (December 5, 2009), http://www.nytimes.com.

5. Joe Williams, "Bringing the Human Touch to Recruitment," *Bloomberg Businessweek* (January 24, 2011), http://bx.businessweek.com.

6. Lisa Takeuchi Cullen, "It's a Wrap: You're Hired," *Time* (February 22, 2007), http://www.time.com.

7. "A New Assistant at Georgia Tech Made False Claims," *The New York Times* (January 29, 2002), D7; Stephanie Armour, "Security Checks Worry Workers; Padded Resumes Could Be Exposed," *USA Today* (June 19, 2002), B1.

8. "Busted," *Training Development* 60, no. 12 (December 2006): 19; Pamela Babock, "Spotting Lies," *HRMagazine* 48, no. 10 (October 2003): 46–51; Tammy Prater and Sara Bliss Kiser, "Lies, Lies, and More Lies," *A.A.M. Advance Management Journal* 67, no. 2 (Spring 2002): 9–14.

9. Amy Maingault, John Sweeney, and Naomi Cossack, "Interviewing, Management Training, Strikes," *HRMagazine* 52, no. 6 (June 2007): 43; James Bassett, "Stop, Thief!" *Gifts & Decorative Accessories* 104, no. 1 (January 2003): 130–34; Richard A. Posthuma,

Frederick Morgeson, and Michael Campion, "Beyond Employment Interview Validity: A Comprehensive Narrative Review of Recent Research and Trends over Time," *Personnel Psychology* 55, no. 1 (Spring 2002): 1–8.

10. Yen-Chun Chen, Wei-Chi Tsai, and Changya Hu, "The Influences of Interviewer-Related and Situational Factors on Interviewer Reactions to High Structured Job Interviews," *International Journal of Human Resource Management* 19, no. 6 (June 2008): 1056–1071. For an excellent review of research on the structured interview, see Michael A. Campion, David K. Palmer, and James E. Campion, "A Review of Structure in the Selection Interview," *Personnel Psychology* 50, no. 3 (Autumn 1997): 655–702; see also Karen van der Zee, Arnold Bakker, and Paulien Bakker, "Why Are Structured Interviews So Rarely Used in Personnel Selection?" *Journal of Applied Psychology* 87, no. 1 (February 2002): 176–84.

11. Jesus F. Salgado and Silvia Moscoso, "Comprehensive Meta-Analysis of the Construct Validity of the Employment Interview," *European Journal of Work and Organizational*

Psychology 11, no. 3 (September 2002): 299–325; Allen Huffcutt, Jeff Weekley, Willi Wiesner, Timothy Degroot, and Casey Jones, "Comparison of Situational and Behavior Description Interview Questions for Higher-Level Positions," *Personnel Psychology* 54, no. 3 (Autumn 2001): 619–44.

12. Peter Herriot, "Assessment by Groups: Can Value Be Added?" *European Journal of Work & Organizational Psychology* 12, no. 2 (June 2003): 131–46; Salgado and Moscoso, "Comprehensive Meta-Analysis"; Amelia J. Prewett-Livingston, John G. Veres III, Hubert S. Field, and Philip M. Lewis, "Effects of Race on Interview Ratings in a Situational Panel Interview," *Journal of Applied Psychology* 81, no. 2 (April 1996): 178–86; see also Damodar Y. Golhar and Satish P. Deshpande, "HRM Practices of Large and Small Canadian Manufacturing Firms," *Journal of Small Business Management* 35, no. 3 (July 1997): 30–38.

13. Carol Carter, *Keys to Business Communication* (Upper Saddle River, NJ: Pearson, 2012): Chapter 15.

14. Darren, Dahl, "Tapping the Talent Pool... without Drowning in Resumés. Darren. Inc., 31 no. 3 (April 2009): 122.

15. Jack Welch and Suzy Welch, "Hiring Is Hard Work," *Business Week Online*, no. 4091 (July 7, 2008): na; Michele V. Rafter, "Candidates for Jobs in High Places Sit for Tests That Size Up Their Mettle," *Workforce Management* 83, no. 5 (May 2004): 70–73; Patricia Buhler, "Computer Interview: Managing in the New Millennium," *Supervision* 63, no. 10 (October 2002): 20–23.

16. Victoria Reitz, "Interview without Leaving Home," *Machine Design* 76, no. 7 (April 1, 2004): 66; Jessica Clark Newman et al., "The Differential Effects of Face-to-Face and Computer Interview Modes," *American Journal of Public Health* 92, no. 2 (February 2002): 294; David Mitchell, "ijob.com Recruiting Online," *Strategic Finance* 80, no. 11 (May 1999): 48–51.

17. Dan Hanover, "Hiring Gets Cheaper and Faster," *Sales and Marketing Management* 152, no. 3 (March 2000): 87.

18. Kira Vermond, "References Done Right," *Profit* 26, no. 2 (May 2007): 101; Kathleen Samey, "A Not-So-Perfect Fit," *Adweek* 44, no. 47 (December 1, 2003): 34; Ann Fisher, "How Can We Be Sure We're Not Hiring a Bunch of Shady Liars?" *Fortune* 147, no. 10 (May 26, 2003).

19. "Legal Issues Raised by Giving Bad References," *Fair Employment Practice Guidelines*, no. 594 (November 2004): 1–3; Robert L. Brady, "Employee Loses Defamation Suit over Bad Reference," *HRFocus* 73, no. 7 (July 1996): 20; Glenn Withiam, "Complexities of Employee References," *Cornell Hotel and Restaurant Administration Quarterly* 37, no. 3 (June 1996): 10; Mimi Moon, "Justices Consider FERPA in Student's Privacy Claim," *News Media and the Law* 26, no. 2 (Spring 2002): 37–38.

20. Mary-Kathryn, "Labor Law for Supervisors, *Supervision* 67, no. 2 (February 2006): 22–23; Diane Cadrian, "HR Professionals Stymied by Vanishing Job References," *HRMagazine* 49, no. 11 (November 2004): 31–32.

21. Sam Hananel, "Some Job-Screening Tactics May Be Illegal," *Fort Worth Star-Telegram* (August 12, 2010): 5A.

22. "New Employee Privacy Rights in Oregon and Washington," *Venulex Legal Summaries* (2007 Q3): 1–4; Barry J. Nadell, "The Cut of His Jib Doesn't Jibe," *Security Management* 48, no. 9 (September 2004): 108–114; William Atkinson, "Who Goes There?" *LP/Gas* 64, no. 9 (September 2004): 16–24; Amelia Deligiannis, "Fair Credit Reporting Act Pre-Emption Debate Heats Up," *Corporate Legal Times* 13, no. 139 (June 2003): 22–24.

23. Doug Eisenschenk and Elaine Davis, "Background Checks in Hiring and Compensation: The Next Generation," *Benefits & Compensation Digest* 41, no. 10 (October 2004): 1–4; "What's New," *HR Magazine* 49, no. 4 (April 2004): 153–156; "Why You Should Update Your Background Checks," *HRFocus* (February 2004): 12–13; Merry Mayer, "Background Checks in Focus," *HRMagazine* 47, no. 1 (January 2002): 59–62. In addition, organizations use other resources, such as the following: *The Guide to Background Investigations: A Comprehensive Source Directory for Employee Screening and Background Investigations*, 8th ed. (TISI, 2000).

24. Elizabeth D. MacGillivray, Juanita H. Beecher, and Diedre M. Golden, "Employment Testing: The New Hot Button Issue for Federal Agencies—and Other Legal Developments," *Global Business & Organizational Excellence* 27, no. 3, (March–April 2008): 68–78.

25. Judy Greenwald "EEOC Move May Signal More Scrutiny of Employment Tests," *Business Insurance* 41, no. 52 (December 24, 2007): 4–20; Rod Kurtz, "Testing, Testing …," *Inc.* 26, no. 6 (June 2004): 35–38; Gillian Flynn, "A Legal Examination of Testing," *Workforce* 81, no. 6 (June 2002): 92–94.

26. Ely A. Leightling and Pamela M. Ploor, "When Applicants Apply through the Internet," *Employee Relations Law Journal* 30, no. 2 (Autumn 2004): 3–13; "EEOC Clarifies the Definition of Who Is an 'Applicant' in the Context of Internet Recruiting and Hiring," *Fair Employment Practices Guidelines*, no. 587 (April 1, 2004): 3–13; Kathryn Tyler, "Put Applicants' Skills to the Test," *HRMagazine* 45, no. 1 (January 2000): 74–80.

27. Standards that testing programs should meet are described in *Standards for Educational and Psychological Tests* (Washington, DC: American Psychological Association, 1999). HR managers who want to examine paper-and-pencil tests should obtain specimen sets that include a test manual, copy of the test, answer sheet, and scoring key. The test manual provides the essential information about the construction of the test; its recommended use; and instructions for administering, scoring, and interpreting the test.

28. John Bret Becton, Hubert S. Feild, William F. Giles, and Allison Jones-Farmer, "Racial differences in promotion candidate performance and reactions to selection procedures: a field study in a diverse top-management context," *Journal of Organizational Behavior* 29, no. 3 (April 2008): 265–285.

29. Rachel Suff, "Testing the Water: Using Work Sampling for Selection," *IRS Employment Review*, no. 802 (June 18, 2004): 44–49; Leonard D. Goodstein and Alan D. Davidson, "Hiring the Right Stuff: Using Competency-Based Selection," *Compensation & Benefits Management* 14, no. 3 (Summer 1998): 1–10.

30. Noelle Murphy, "Testing the Waters: Employers' Use of Selection Assessments," *IRS Employment Review* 852 (August 4, 2006): 42–48; Florence Berger and Ajay Ghei,

"Employment Tests: A Facet of Hospitality Hiring," *Cornell Hotel and Restaurant Administration Quarterly* 36, no. 6 (December 1995): 28–31; Malcolm James Ree, Thomas R. Carretta, and Mark S. Teachout, "Role of Ability and Prior Job Knowledge in Complex Training Performance," *Journal of Applied Psychology* 80, no. 6 (December 1995): 721–30.

31. Justin Menkes, "Interviewing for Executive Intelligence," *HR Professional* 25, no. 3 (April–May 2008): 54; Chris Piotrowski and Terry Armstrong, "Current Recruitment and Selection Practices: A National Survey of Fortune 1000 Firms," *North American Journal of Psychology* 8, no. 3 (2006): 489–496; Sara Rynes, Amy Colbert, and Kenneth Brown, "HR Professionals' Beliefs about Effective Human Resource Practices: Correspondence between Research and Practice," *Human Resource Management* 41, no. 2 (Summer 2002): 149–74.

32. "Biographical Data (Biodata) Tests," *Personnel Selection and Resource Center* (Washington DC: U.S. Office of Personnel Management), accessed April 17, 2011, http://apps.opm.gov.

33. Kris Frieswick, "Casting to Type," *CFO* 20, no. 9 (July 2004): 71–73; Timothy Judge and Joyce Bono, "Five-Factor Model of Personality and Transformational Leadership," *Journal of Applied Psychology* 85, no. 5 (October 2000): 751–65; J. Michael Crant, and Thomas S. Bateman, "Charismatic Leadership Viewed from Above: The Impact of Proactive Personality," *Journal of Organizational Behavior* 21, no. 1 (February 2000): 63–75.

34. Frederick P. Morgeson, Michael A. Campion, Robert L. Dipboye, John R. Hollenbeck, Kevin Murphy, and Neal Schmitt, "Reconsidering the Use of Personality Tests in Personnel Selection Contexts," *Personnel Psychology* 60, no. 3 (Autumn 2007): 683–729; Arielle Emmett, "Snake Oil or Science? The Raging Debate on Personality Testing," *Workforce Management* 83, no. 10 (October 2004): 90–93; Gregory Hurtz and John Donovan, "Personality and Job Performance: The Big Five Revisited," *Journal of Applied Psychology* 85, no. 6 (December 2000): 869–79.

35. George B. Yancey, "The Predictive Power of Hiring Tools," *Credit Union Executive Journal*

40, no. 4 (July–August 2000): 12–18; Jeffrey A. Mello, "Personality Tests and Privacy Rights," *HRFocus* 73, no. 3 (March 1996): 22–23.

36. Constance L. Hays, "Tests Are Becoming Common in Hiring," *The New York Times* (November 28), 1997, D1. See also Gregory M. Lousig-Nont, "Avoid Common Hiring Mistakes with Honesty Tests," *Nation's Restaurant News* 31, no. 11 (March 17, 1997): 30; "If the Shoe Fits," *Security Management* 40, no. 2 (February 1996): 11; Michelle Cottle, "Job Testing: Multiple Choices," *The New York Times* (September 5, 1999), 3: 10.

37. Thomas J. Ryan, "Nerves of Steal," *SGB* 37, no. 6 (June 2004): 8–10; D. S. Ones, C. Viswesvaran, and F. L. Schmidt, "Comprehensive Meta-Analysis of Integrity Test Validities: Findings and Implications for Personnel Selection and Theories of Job Performance," *Journal of Applied Psychology* 78 (August 1993): 679–703. See also Deniz S. Ones and Chockalingam Viswesvaran, "Gender, Age and Race Differences on Overt Integrity Tests: Results across Four Large-Scale Job Applicant Data Sets," *Journal of Applied Psychology* 83, no. 1 (February 1998): 35–42.

38. James Krohe Jr., "Are Workplace Tests Worth Taking?" *Across the Board* 43, no. 4 (July–August 2006): 16–23; "Honesty Tests Flawed," *People Management* 3, no. 2 (January 23, 1997): 15; Hays, "Tests Are Becoming Common in Hiring"; Stephen A. Dwight and George M. Alliger, "Reactions to Overt Integrity Test Items," *Educational and Psychological Measurement* 57, no. 6 (December 1997): 937–48.

39. Lawrence Peikes and Meghan D. Burns, "Polygraph Test Request Unlawful," *HRMagazine* 50, no. 7 (July 2005): 110; "Pretext for Discrimination: How to Avoid Looking Like a Liar," *Fair Employment Practices Guidelines*, no. 592 (September 1, 2004): 1–3; Gillian Flynn, Diane D. Hatch, and James E. Hall, "Know the Background of Background Checks," *Workforce* 81, no. 9 (September 2002): 96–98.

40. Paul Zielbauer, "Small Changes Could Improve Police Hiring, Panel Says," *The New York Times* (January 7, 1999), 8; Lynn McFarland and Ann Marie Ryan, "Variance in Faking across Noncognitive Measures,"

Journal of Applied Psychology 85, no. 5 (October 2000): 812–21; David Arnold and John Jones, "Who the Devil's Applying Now?" *Security Management* 46, no. 3 (March 2002): 85–88; "Polygraph Testing Considered Personnel Tool," *Crime Control Digest* 33, no. 14 (April 9, 1999): 4.

41. Walter C. Borman, Mary Ann Hanson, and Jerry W. Hedge, "Personnel Selection," *Annual Review of Psychology* 48 (1997): 299–337; Charles Sproule and Stephen Berkley, "The Selection of Entry-Level Corrections Officers: Pennsylvania Research," *Public Personnel Management* 30, no. 3 (Fall 2001): 377–418.

42. M. S. Sothmann, D. L. Gebhardt, T. A. Baker, G. M. Kastello, and V. A. Sheppard, "Performance Requirements of Physically Strenuous Occupations: Validating Minimum Standards for Muscular Strength," *Ergonomics* 47, no. 8 (June 22, 2004): 864–76; T. L. Stanley, "The Wisdom of Employment Testing," *Supervision* 65, no. 2 (February 2004): 11–14; Maria Greco Danaher, "Strength Test Falls," *HRMagazine* 52, no. 2 (February 2007): 115–116.

43. Michael Adams, Ben Van Houten, Robert Klara, and Elizabeth Bernstein, "Access Denied?" *Restaurant Business* 98, no. 2 (January 15, 1999): 36–48; "Medical Screening: Are Employers Going Too Far?" *Employee Benefit Plan Review* 53, no. 11 (May 1999): 42–43.

44. "Constitution Limits Pre-employment Drug Testing by Public Employers," *Venulex Legal Summaries* (2008 Q1): 1; "Drug Testing Is Common and Codified at Many Workplaces," *HRFocus* 83, no. 6 (June 2006): 9; "New Developments Question the Use of Drug Tests in the Workplace," *Safety Director's Report* 4, no. 9 (September 2004): 3–6; Sandy Smith, "What Every Employer Should Know about Drug Testing in the Workplace," *Occupational Hazards* 66, no. 8 (August 2004): 45–48.

45. Philip Bobko, Philip L. Roth, and Maury A. Buster, "The Usefulness of Unit Weights in Creating Composite Scores: A Literature Review, Application to Content Validity, and Meta-Analysis," *Organizational Research Methods* 10, no. 4 (October 2007): 689–709; Kobi Dayan, Ronen Kasten, and Shaul Fox, "Entry-Level Police Candidate Assessment Center: An Efficient Tool or a Hammer to

Kill a Fly?" *Personnel Psychology* 55, no. 4 (Winter 2002).

46. Deniz S. Ones, Chockalingam Viswesvaran, and Frank L Schmidt, "No New Terrain: Reliability and Construct Validity of Job Performance Ratings," *Industrial & Organizational Psychology* 1, no. 2 (June 2008): 174–179; D. Brent Smith and Lill Ellingson, "Substance versus Style: A New Look at Social Desirability in Motivating Contexts," *Journal of Applied Psychology* 87, no. 2 (April 2002): 211–19; Ken Craik, et al., "Explorations of Construct Validity in a Combined Managerial and Personality Assessment

Programme," *Journal of Occupational and Organizational Psychology* 75, no. 2 (June 2002): 171–93.

47. Multiple regression is a statistical method for evaluating the magnitude of effects of more than one independent variable (e.g., selection predictors) on a dependent variable (e.g., job performance) using principles of correlation and regression.

48. Patricia M. Buhler, "Managing in the New Millennium," *Supervision* 68, no. 11 (November 2007): 17–20; David E. Bowen and Cheri Ostroff, "Understanding HRM—Firm Performance Linkages: The Role of the

Strengths of the HRM System," *Academy of Management Review* 29, no. 2 (April 2004): 203–22; Ann Marie Ryan, Joshua Sacco, Lynn McFarland, and David Kriska, "Applicant Self-Selection: Correlates of Withdrawal from a Multiple Hurdle Process," *Journal of Applied Psychology* 85, no. 2 (April 2000): 163–79.

49. "Considering and Evaluating Internal Candidates for Senior-Level Nonprofit Positions," *Bridgestar,* accessed March 27, 2011, http://www.bridgestar.org.

7 Training and Development

After studying this chapter, you should be able to

LEARNING OUTCOME 1 Discuss the strategic approach to training and development.

LEARNING OUTCOME 2 Describe the components of a training needs assessment.

LEARNING OUTCOME 3 Identify the principles of learning and describe how they facilitate training.

LEARNING OUTCOME 4 Identify the types of training methods used for managers and nonmanagers.

LEARNING OUTCOME 5 Discuss the advantages and disadvantages of various evaluation criteria.

LEARNING OUTCOME 6 Describe additional training programs often conducted firms.

Workplace training used to be rather boxlike. It focused on teaching employees to do particular activities—operate machines, process work, and so forth. However, as the workplace has shifted from "touch labor" to "knowledge workers" (see Chapter 1), the focus of training has shifted as well. Companies are realizing that workers need not only operational know-how but superior job expertise; knowledge about competitive, industry, and technological trends; and the ability to continually learn and utilize new information. These characteristics better help an organization adapt and innovate to compete far more effectively in today's fast-paced global business world. Because training plays a central role in nurturing, strengthening, and expanding the capabilities of a firm in this way, it has become part of the backbone of strategic management.

The Scope of Training

Many new employees come equipped with most of the KSAs needed to start work. Others require extensive training before they are ready to make much of a contribution to the organization. The term *training* is often used casually to describe almost any effort initiated by an organization to foster learning among its members. However, many experts distinguish between *training*, which tends to be more narrowly focused and oriented toward short-term performance concerns, and *development*, which, as you learned in Chapter 5, tends to be oriented more toward broadening an individual's skills for future responsibilities. The two terms tend to be combined into a single phrase—*training and development*—to recognize the combination of activities organizations use to increase the knowledge and skills of employees.

Investments in Training

Research shows that an organization's revenues and overall profitability are positively correlated to the amount of training it gives its employees. According to *Training* magazine's ongoing industry report, U.S. businesses spend about $50 billion annually to provide each of their employees with about 40 hours of training annually.[1] By contrast, the 100 best U.S. companies to work for, as cited by *Fortune* magazine, provide their employees with approximately double that amount of training and sometimes even more. New employees hired by the Ritz Carlton hotel chain get over 300 hours of training. The greatest proportion of training is spent on rank-and-file employees and supervisors (see Figure 7.1). However, the amount of money spent on developing and training managers has been increasing, perhaps as more companies try to recruit and retain strong leaders amid tough economic times.[1] Technology, transportation, communications, and utilities industries tend to spend the most on training.

In addition to the billions of dollars spent by U.S. businesses each year on formal training, nearly *four times* that amount is spent on informal instruction. The types of training given employees range from simple, on-the-job instruction to sophisticated skills training conducted on multimillion dollar simulators. Other types of training include regular training given to new hires, customer service and communication-skills training, and compliance training—training employees must receive as a result of various legal mandates, such as EEO requirements or OSHA requirements. Airline attendants must undergo mandatory safety training designated by the Federal Aviation Administration. Train crews must annually undergo training mandated by the Federal Railroad Administration. Managers should also undergo training to avoid

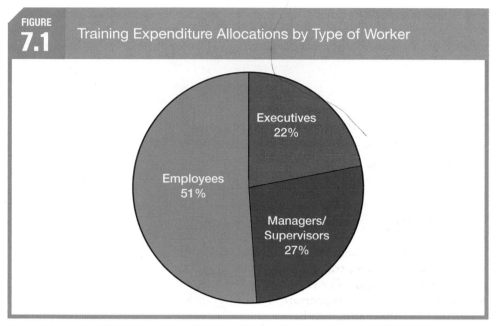

FIGURE 7.1   Training Expenditure Allocations by Type of Worker

Executives
22%

Managers/
Supervisors
27%

Employees
51%

Source: Adapted from "2011 Industry Report," *Training* 47, no. 6 (November–December) 2010: 18–31.

wage-and-hour violations, such as asking employees to work off-the-clock without paying them overtime. Walmart has agreed to pay as much as $640 million to resolve 63 class-action lawsuits involving wage-and-hour violations across the nation.[2] And although it is not mandatory, many companies are seeing the value of training programs designed to prevent violence in the workplace.

A Strategic Approach to Training

From the broadest perspective, the goal of training is to contribute to the organization's overall goals. Training programs should be developed with this in mind. Managers should keep a close eye on their firm's goals and strategies and orient their training accordingly. For example, is it the firm's goal to develop new product lines? If so, how should this goal affects its training initiatives? Is the firm trying to lower its costs of production so it can utilize a low-cost strategy to capture new business? If so, are there training initiatives that can be undertaken to deliver on this strategy?

Unfortunately, some organizations fail to make the connection between training and an organization's goals. Instead, fads, fashions, or "whatever the competition is doing" can sometimes be the main drivers of an organization's training agenda. As a result, training programs are often misdirected, poorly designed, and inadequately evaluated—not to mention a waste of money. One, not all of a firm's strategic initiatives can be accomplished with training. Two, not all training programs—no matter how widely they are adopted by other organizations—will be a strategic imperative for your firm.

To ensure that a firm's training and development investment has the maximum impact possible, a strategic and systematic approach should be used that involves four phases: (1) needs assessment based on the firm's competitive objectives, (2) program design, (3) implementation, and (4) evaluation. A model that is useful to designers of

LEARNING OUTCOME 1

What aspects of training plans do you think are strategic, and how are these plans similar or dissimilar to the college and career plans you have created for yourself?

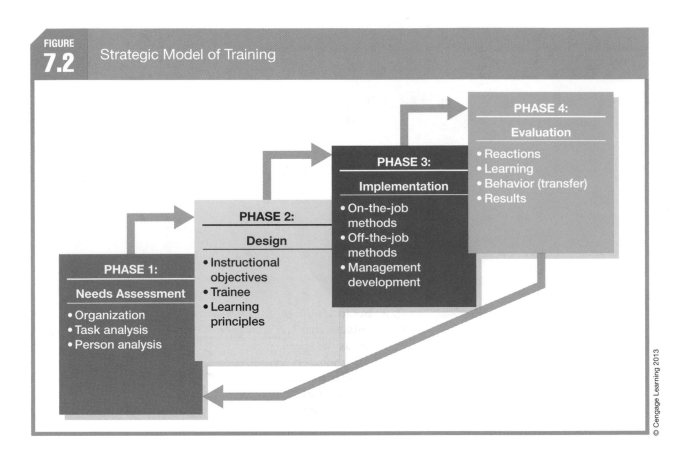

FIGURE 7.2   Strategic Model of Training

PHASE 1:

Needs Assessment

• Organization
• Task analysis
• Person analysis

PHASE 2:

Design

• Instructional objectives
• Trainee
• Learning principles

PHASE 3:

Implementation

• On-the-job methods
• Off-the-job methods
• Management development

PHASE 4:

Evaluation

• Reactions
• Learning
• Behavior (transfer)
• Results

© Cengage Learning 2013

training programs is presented in Figure 7.2. We will use this model as a framework for organizing the material throughout this chapter.

Phase 1: Conducting the Needs Assessment

If you were launching a new business, what factors would you look at to do a training-needs assessment for the organization?

chief learning officer

A high-ranking manager directly responsible for fostering employee learning and development within the firm

Because business conditions change rapidly, as does technology, keeping abreast of the types of training a firm's employees need to remain competitive can be a challenge. If employees consistently fail to achieve their productivity objectives, this might be a signal that training is needed. Likewise, if organizations receive an excessive number of customer complaints, this, too, might suggest a firm's training is inadequate. About 30 percent of larger firms, including GE, Walmart, and IBM, have what are called chief learning officers. These people are top executives within their firms who are responsible for making certain that a company's training is timely and focused on the firm's top strategic issues. However, regardless of who does the needs assessment within an organization, it should be conducted systematically by utilizing the three different types of analysis shown in Figure 7.3: organization analysis, task analysis, and person analysis. Each of these is discussed next.

Unfortunately, because of the costs, expertise, and time required, a study conducted a few years ago by the American Society for Training and Development found that organizations conduct needs assessment less than 50 percent of the time. However,

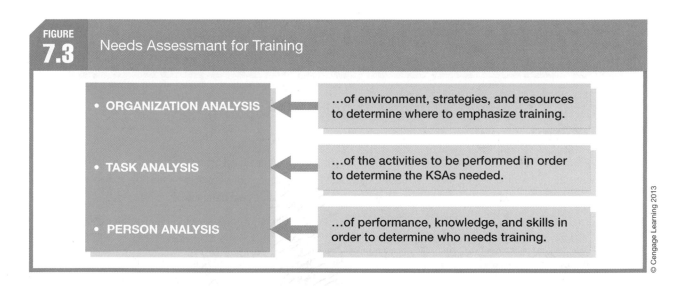

FIGURE 7.3   Needs Assessmant for Training

- ORGANIZATION ANALYSIS — ...of environment, strategies, and resources to determine where to emphasize training.

- TASK ANALYSIS — ...of the activities to be performed in order to determine the KSAs needed.

- PERSON ANALYSIS — ...of performance, knowledge, and skills in order to determine who needs training.

© Cengage Learning 2013

this situation has improved somewhat, in part because tighter training budgets as the result of the recession have forced firms to ensure that the training they conduct is well aligned with their objectives. Moreover, as the speed of change increases, managers are realizing that good needs assessments conducted regularly are essential. Being able to quickly assess the training your employees need is especially important for small businesses that may not have the time or resources to do lengthy needs assessment analyses. Doing a needs assessment does not need to be a laborious task, as this chapter's small business feature shows.[3]

Organization Analysis

The first step in a needs assessment is identifying the broad forces that can influence a firm's training needs. An organization analysis is an examination of the environment, strategies, and resources the firm faces so as to determine what training it should emphasize. As we have explained, a firm's training should revolve around the strategic initiatives of the organization. Mergers and acquisitions, for example, frequently require that employees take on new roles and responsibilities and adjust to new cultures and ways of conducting business. Nowhere is this more prevalent than in grooming new leaders within organizations. Other issues such as technological change, globalization, and quality improvements all influence the way work is done and the types of skills needed to do it. Still other concerns may be more tactical, but no less important in terms of their impact on training. If an organization is restructuring, downsizing, or undertaking new employee-empowerment or teamwork initiatives, these efforts will impact the firm's training requirements.

Economic and public policy issues influence corporate training needs as well. For example, since the September 11 terrorist attacks on the United States, the training of airport security personnel has increased substantially. It has also increased for flight crews of airlines, employees in the transportation industry, workers in nuclear power plants, and even security staff at theme parks.[4] Finally, trends in the workforce itself affect a firm's training needs. As older workers near retirement, younger workers need to focus on gaining the skills and knowledge needed to take their place.

organization analysis

Examination of the environment, strategies, and resources of the organization to determine where training emphasis should be placed

Small Business Application ılılı

A Small Business's Guide to Quickly Assessing Its Training Needs

Do environmental scanning. Continually look at what is going on in your industry and organization in order to anticipate upcoming training needs. Enlist the help of employees and managers in the process. Question managers about their strategic goals, their impact on the organization, and gear your analysis accordingly.

Do internal scanning. Determine what skills are most important to acquire in terms of your organization's current and future needs. Which ones will provide the biggest payback?

Gather organizational data. Performance data for your firm (such as errors, sales, and customer complaints) and staffing data (such as turnover and absenteeism) can be very helpful as a starting point.

Develop a Plan

Once the training need has been identified, identify various ways to deliver it and consider the costs and benefits of each. Determine what kind of growth or other measure is a reasonable result of the training.

Utilize state and local government programs. Many state and local governments have programs to help small businesses train their employees. For example, the Texas Workforce Commission will pay small businesses in Texas up to $1,450 for each new full-time employee hired and trained at a local college. (The amount is $725 for each current employee trained.)

Make the needs-assessment process ongoing. Repeat these activities as your business needs change.

Sources: "TWC Launches Small Business Employee Training Program," *Your Houston News* (November 20, 2010), http://www.yourhoustonnews.com; "Employee Training Tips," *D&B.com*, http://smallbusiness.dnb.com; Ron Zemke, "How to Do a Needs Assessment When You Think You Don't Have Time," *Training* 35, no. 3 (March 1998): 38–44.

Conducting an organization analysis also involves closely examining a firm's resources—technological, financial, and human—available to meet the company's training objectives. HR personnel typically collect data such as information on their companies' direct and indirect labor costs, quality of goods or services, absenteeism, turnover, and number of accidents. The availability of potential replacements and the time required to train them are other important factors in organization analysis.

To cope with budget constraints yet continue to meet their strategic imperatives, firms have become more focused on efficiently using their training budgets. Companies such as Motorola, Ford, and Merck have found that by using information technology wisely, they significantly cut their training budgets. To "do more with less," managers have to plan carefully where they will spend their training dollars, and this means doing a rigorous organization analysis. Other companies outsource their training programs, or at least part of them, to external partners to cut costs or to take advantage of expertise the firm lacks. Other organizations purchase "off the shelf" course materials developed by training companies rather than develop their own. A new trend is for companies to partner with other firms in their supply chains so as to jointly train their employees more cost effectively.[5]

Task Analysis

The second step in training-needs assessment is task analysis. Task analysis involves reviewing the job description and specifications to identify the activities performed in a particular job and the KSAs needed to perform them. The first step in task analysis is to list all the tasks or duties included in the job. The second step is to list the steps performed by the employee to complete each task. The type of performance for each task (such as manipulation, speech, and discrimination), along with the skills and knowledge necessary to do it, can then be identified. For example, in the task of taking a chest X-ray, a radiologist correctly positions the patient

Noel Hendrickson/Digital Vision/Getty Images

As older workers near retirement, younger workers must be trained to develop the skills and knowledge needed to take their place. The availability of potential replacements and the time required to train them are two factors that must be considered in organization analysis.

(manipulation), gives special instructions (speech), and checks the proper distance of the X-ray tube from the patient (discrimination). The types of skills and knowledge that trainees need can be determined by observing and questioning skilled jobholders and/or by reviewing job descriptions. This information helps trainers select program content and choose the most effective training methods.

Instead of focusing on a fixed sequence of tasks, more firms are finding that their employees need more flexible sets of competencies in order to perform in a superior way. Competency assessment focuses on the sets of skills and knowledge employees need to be successful, particularly for decision-oriented and knowledge-intensive jobs. But competency assessment goes beyond simply describing the traits an employee must have to successfully perform the work. It also captures elements of how those traits should be used within an organization's context and culture. That might include an employee's motivation level, personality traits, interpersonal skills, and so on. "It's easy for top performers to become experts in a certain niche, but 'talent factories' focus on creating generalists. To get the most from talented employees, they should know how to handle a wide range of functions," explains one HR consultant.[6]

Competency assessments have been adopted extensively in the health care industry.[7] Instead of offering a laundry list of training plans as it used to, Amway has established job competencies for all 17,000 of its employees around the world. The competencies denote the particular skills each employee needs for his or her job and a training "road map" to get them. The company also got rid of off-the-shelf training courseware that did not align with business goals.[8] Highlights in HRM 1 shows an example of a partial competency assessment tool used for evaluating a manager.

task analysis

The process of determining what the content of a training program should be on the basis of a study of the tasks and duties involved in the job

competency assessment

Analysis of the sets of skills and knowledge needed for decision-oriented and knowledge-intensive jobs

HIGHLIGHTS IN HRM

1 A Competency Assessment for a Managerial Position

For each item, circle the number that best describes the manager's characteristics. For items that do not apply, circle **NA** (not applicable). For other items for which you lack sufficient observations or documentary evidence, circle **DK** (don't know).

4 – Exemplary

3 – Proficient

2 – Progressing

1 – Needs Assistance

NA – Not Applicable

DK – Don't Know

Competency 1: Behaves professionally and encourages other staff members to do likewise.

4 3 2 1 NA DK

Evidence: _____

_____

_____

_____

_____

Competency 2: Behaves ethically and encourages staff members to do likewise.

4 3 2 1 NA DK

Evidence: _____

_____

_____

_____

_____

Competency 3: Uses a variety of modes of communication and conveys information fully and clearly.

4 3 2 1 NA DK

Evidence: _____

_____

_____

_____

_____

Competency 4: Seeks input from all levels and demonstrates fairness and consistency.

4 3 2 1 NA DK

Evidence: _____

_____

| A Competency Assessment for a
Managerial Position (continued) |
| :--- |

_____
_____
_____

Competency 5: Engages in an open style of management and is open to criticism from supervisors and subordinates.

4   3   2   1   NA   DK

Evidence: _____
_____
_____
_____
_____

Competency 6: Searches for and embraces innovative solutions to improve department's programs and products.

4   3   2   1   NA   DK

Evidence: _____
_____
_____
_____
_____

Person Analysis

Along with organization and task analyses, it is necessary to perform a person analysis. A **person analysis** involves determining which employees require training and, equally important, which do not. In this regard, conducting a person analysis is important for several reasons. First, a thorough analysis helps organizations avoid the mistake of sending all employees into training when some do not need it. In addition, a person analysis helps managers determine what prospective trainees are able to do when they enter training so that the programs can be designed to emphasize the areas in which they are deficient.

Performance appraisal information can be used for the purposes of conducting a person analysis. Companies such as Teradyne and HP are among the many firms that do so. However, although performance appraisals might reveal which employees are not meeting the firm's expectations, they typically do not reveal why. If the performance deficiencies are due to ability problems, training is likely to be a good solution. However, if the performance deficiencies are due to poor motivation or factors outside an employee's control, training might not be the answer. Conducting a deeper performance diagnosis is discussed in Chapter 8 on performance appraisal. Ultimately, managers have to sit down with employees to talk about areas for improvement so that they can jointly determine the developmental approaches that will have maximum benefit.[9]

person analysis
Determination of the specific individuals who need training

Phase 2: Designing the Training Program

Once the training needs have been determined, the next step is to design the training program. Experts believe that the design of training programs should focus on at least four related issues: (1) the training's instructional objectives, (2) "readiness" of trainees and their motivation, (3) principles of learning, and (4) characteristics of instructors.

Instructional Objectives

instructional objectives

Desired outcomes of a training program

After conducting organization, task, and person analyses, managers should have a more complete picture of their firms' training needs. On the basis of this information, they can more formally state the desired outcomes of training through written instructional objectives. Generally, instructional objectives describe the skills or knowledge to be acquired and/or the attitudes to be changed. One type of instructional objective, the performance-centered objective, is widely used because it lends itself to an unbiased evaluation of the results. For example, the stated objective for one training program might be that: "Employees trained in team methods will be able to perform the different jobs of their team members within six months." Performance-centered objectives typically include precise terms, such as "to calculate," "to repair," "to adjust," "to construct," "to assemble," and "to classify."[10]

Trainee Readiness and Motivation

Two preconditions for learning affect the success of those who are to receive training: readiness and motivation. *Trainee readiness* refers to whether or not the experience of trainees has made them receptive to the training they will receive. Prospective trainees should be screened to ensure that they have the background knowledge and the skills necessary to absorb what will be presented to them. Recognizing the individual differences of trainees in terms of their readiness is as important in organizational training as it is in any other teaching situation. Consequently, it is often desirable to group individuals according to their capacity to learn, as determined by test scores or other assessment information, and to provide alternative types of instruction for those who need it.

The receptiveness and readiness of participants in training programs can be increased by having them complete questionnaires about why they are attending training and what they hope to accomplish as a result of it. Participants can also be asked to give copies of their completed questionnaires to their managers.

The other precondition for learning is *trainee motivation*. The organization needs to help employees understand the link between the effort they put into training and the payoff. Why is the training important? What will happen if it does not occur? Moreover, what is in it for the individual employee? By focusing on the trainees themselves, managers can create a training environment that is conducive to learning.

Most employees are motivated by training opportunities that allow them to develop their skills and advance their careers. However, employees differ from one another in the relative importance of these needs at any given time. For example, new college graduates often have a high desire for advancement, and they have established specific goals for career progression. The training's objectives should therefore be clearly related to trainees' individual needs to succeed.[11] Allowing employees to undergo training in areas that they want to pursue rather than merely assigning them certain training activities can also be very motivating. So can enlisting employees to train other employees with the information they learn. Who in an organization does not want to be called upon for their expertise?

Principles of Learning

As we move from assessing an organization's needs and instructional objectives to employee readiness and motivation, we obviously shift our focus from the organization to employees. Ultimately, however, training has to build a bridge between employees and the organization. One important step in this transition is giving full consideration to the psychological principles of learning—that is, the characteristics of training programs that help employees grasp new material, make sense of it in their own lives, and transfer it back to their jobs. All things considered, training programs are likely to be more effective if they incorporate the principles of learning shown in Figure 7.4.

LEARNING OUTCOME 3

What has your college experience taught you about how people learn that can be applied to the workplace?

Goal Setting

The value of goal setting for focusing and motivating behavior extends into training. When trainers take the time to explain the training's goals and objectives to

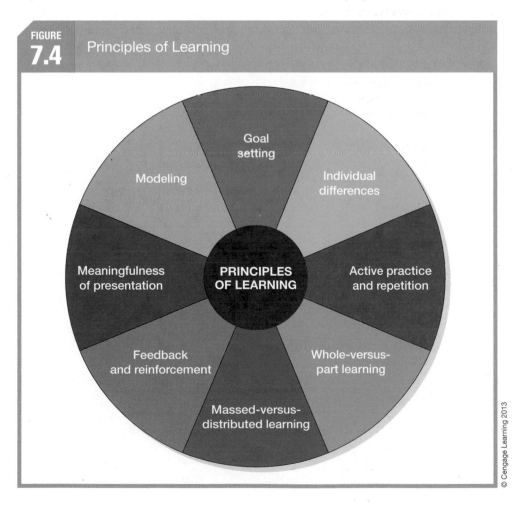

FIGURE 7.4   Principles of Learning

© Cengage Learning 2013

trainees—or when trainees are encouraged to set goals on their own—the level of interest, understanding, and effort directed toward the training is likely to increase. In some cases, goal setting can simply take the form of a "road map" of the course/program, its objectives, and its learning points.[12]

Meaningfulness of Presentation

One principle of learning is that the material to be learned should be presented in as meaningful a manner as possible. Quite simply, trainees will be better able to learn new information if it is presented using terminology they can understand, and the training is connected with things already familiar to them. This is the reason why trainers frequently use colorful examples to which trainees can relate. The examples make the material meaningful. In addition, material should be arranged so that each experience builds on preceding ones. In this way, trainees are able to integrate the experiences into a usable pattern of knowledge and skills.

Modeling

The old saying "a picture is worth a thousand words" applies to training. Just as examples increase the meaningfulness of factual material or new knowledge in a training environment, modeling increases the salience of behavioral training. Quite simply, we learn by watching. For example, if you were learning to ride a horse, it would be much easier to watch someone do it—and then try it yourself—than to read a book or listen to a lecture and hope you can do it right.[13]

Modeling can take many forms. Real-life demonstrations and demonstrations on DVDs are often helpful; visual aids, pictures, and drawings can get the message across. In some cases, modeling the wrong behavior can even be helpful if it shows trainees what not to do and then clarifies the appropriate behavior.

Individual Differences

People learn at different rates and in different ways. Visual learners absorb information best through pictures, diagrams, and demonstrations. Verbal learners absorb information best through spoken or written words. Similarly, some students who do horribly in large lecture settings will excel in small discussion classes. Trainers can help accommodate different learning styles in a variety of ways. The key is to avoid delivering the material in only one way. So, for example, instead of delivering a monologue, trainers should incorporate variety into their presentations. They should use visualize aids, encourage the participation of learners by including them in demonstrations, and ask them questions about their own experiences. Hands-on activities and breaking large groups into smaller groups for specific activities can also help trainers accommodate different learning styles.[14]

Active Practice and Repetition

Those things we do daily become a part of our repertoire of skills. Trainees should be given frequent opportunities to practice their job tasks in the way they will ultimately be expected to perform them. The individual who is being taught how to operate a machine should have an opportunity to practice on it. The manager who is being taught how to train should be given supervised practice in training.

In some cases, the value of practice is that it causes behaviors to become second nature. For example, when you first learned to drive a car, you focused a great deal on the mechanics: "Where are my hands, where are my feet, and how fast am I going?" As you practiced driving, you began to think less about the mechanics and more about the road, the weather, and the traffic. Other forms of learning are no different—by practicing, a trainee can forget about distinct behaviors and concentrate on the subtleties of how they are used.

Whole-versus-Part Learning

Most jobs and tasks can be broken down into parts that lend themselves to further analysis. Determining the most effective manner for completing each part then provides a basis for giving specific instruction. Learning to sell a product, for example, is made up of several skills that are part of the total process. Although the process sounds daunting, it can essentially be broken down into a few discrete steps: finding customer opportunities; eliciting a prospective customer's needs by learning the proper questions to ask him or her; presenting the firm's product in a way that meets those needs; and finally, learning how and when to ask the customer to buy the product (closing the deal). In evaluating whole-versus-part learning, it is necessary to consider the nature of the task to be learned. If the task can be broken down successfully, it probably should be broken down to facilitate learning; otherwise, it should probably be taught as a unit.

Massed-versus-Distributed Learning

Another factor that determines the effectiveness of training is the amount of time devoted to practice in one session. Should trainees be given training in five two-hour periods or in ten one-hour periods? It has been found in most cases that spacing out the training will result in faster learning and longer retention. This is the principle of *distributed learning*.

Feedback and Reinforcement

Can any learning occur without feedback? Some feedback comes from trainees themselves via self-monitoring, whereas other feedback comes from trainers, fellow trainees, and the like. Feedback can help individuals focus on what they are doing right and what they are doing wrong. Think about when you first learned how to throw a baseball, ride a bicycle, or swim. Someone, perhaps a parent, told you what you were doing right and what things to correct. As you corrected those things, you perhaps got better.

In addition to providing participants with information about their performance, feedback also plays an important motivational role. For example, a person's training progress, measured in terms of either mistakes or successes, can be plotted on a chart commonly referred to as a "learning curve." Figure 7.5 presents an example of a learning curve common in the acquisition of many job skills. In many learning situations, there are times when progress does not occur. Such periods show up on the curve as a fairly straight horizontal line called a *plateau*. A plateau can occur because of reduced motivation or because a person gets discouraged when he or she does not always perform a new task as well as hoped. It is a natural phenomenon, and learners usually experience a spontaneous recovery later, as Figure 7.5 shows.

Over the years organizations have used **behavior modification,** a technique that operates on the principle that behavior that is rewarded, or positively reinforced, will be exhibited more frequently in the future, whereas behavior that is penalized or unrewarded will decrease in frequency. For example, in safety training it is possible to identify "safe" behavioral profiles—that is, actions that ensure fewer accidents—as well as unsafe profiles. As a follow-up to training or as part of the training itself, managers can use relatively simple rewards to discourage undesired behaviors and

behavior modification

A technique that operates on the principle that behavior that is rewarded, or positively reinforced, will be exhibited more frequently in the future, whereas behavior that is penalized or unrewarded will decrease in frequency

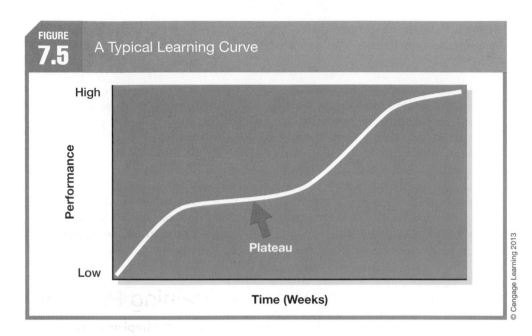

FIGURE 7.5   A Typical Learning Curve

encourage and maintain desired behaviors. Companies such as Monsanto, Target, and Bowater (the largest newsprint maker in America) have found that nothing more than words of encouragement and feedback are needed to strengthen employee behaviors. However, more tangible rewards such as prizes, awards, and ceremonies can help reinforce desirable behaviors over time as well as help employees get over plateaus they might experience. Encouragement is most effective when it is given immediately after a trainee successfully accomplishes a certain task. This is why some employers have instituted **spot rewards** programs. Spot rewards programs award employees "on the spot" when they do something particularly well during training or on the job. The awards can consist of cash, gift cards, time off, or anything else employees value.

spot rewards

Programs that award employees "on the spot" when they do something particularly well during training or on the job

Characteristics of Instructors

The success of any training effort will depend in large part on the teaching skills and personal characteristics of those responsible for conducting the training. What separates good trainers from mediocre ones? Often a good trainer is one who shows a little more effort or demonstrates more instructional preparation. However, training is also influenced by the trainer's personal manner and characteristics. Here is a short list of desirable traits:

1. *Knowledge of subject.* Employees expect trainers to know their job or subject thoroughly. Furthermore, they are expected to demonstrate that knowledge.

2. *Adaptability.* Because some individuals learn faster or slower than others, the instructor should be able to adapt to the learning ability of trainees.

3. *Sincerity.* Trainees appreciate sincerity in trainers. Along with this, trainers need to be patient with trainees and tactfully address their concerns.

4. *Sense of humor.* Learning can be fun; very often a point can be made with a story or anecdote.

5. *Interest.* Good trainers have a keen interest in the subject they are teaching; this interest is readily conveyed to trainees.

6. *Clear instructions.* Naturally, training is accomplished more quickly and retained longer when trainers give clear instructions.

7. *Individual assistance.* When training more than one employee, successful trainers always provide individual assistance.

8. *Enthusiasm.* A dynamic presentation and a vibrant personality show trainees that the trainer enjoys training; employees tend to respond positively to an enthusiastic atmosphere.[15]

For training programs to be most successful, organizations should reward managers who are excellent trainers. Too often managers are not recognized for their contributions to this important aspect of HRM. Likewise, good training specialists in the HR function should be recognized for their efforts.

Phase 3: Implementing the Training Program

Instructional methods are where "the rubber meets the road" in implementing a training program. A major consideration in choosing among various training methods is determining which ones are appropriate for the KSAs to be learned. For example, if the material is mostly factual, methods such as lecture, classroom, or programmed instruction may be fine. However, if the training involves a large behavioral component, other methods such as on-the-job training, simulation, or web or computer-based training (CBT) might work better.[16]

To organize our discussion of various training methods, we will break them down into two primary groups: those used for nonmanagerial employees and those used for managers. Keep in mind that many of the methods are used to train both types of employees.

Training Methods for Nonmanagerial Employees

A wide variety of methods are available for training employees at all levels. Some methods, such as classroom instruction, have long been used. Newer methods have emerged over the years out of a greater understanding of human behavior, particularly in the areas of learning, motivation, and interpersonal relationships. More recently, technological advances, computer hardware and software, the Internet, mobile devices, and so forth have resulted in training methods that in many instances are more effective and economical than the traditional training methods.

LEARNING OUTCOME 4

What training methods have you personally experienced? Which were most effective in your opinion, and why?

On-the-Job Training

By far the most common method used for training nonmanagerial employees is on-the-job training (OJT). By some estimates, 80–90 percent of employee learning occurs via OJT. OJT has the advantage of providing hands-on experience under normal working conditions and an opportunity for the trainer—a manager or senior employee—to build good relationships with new employees. OJT is viewed by some to be potentially the most effective means of facilitating learning in the workplace.[17]

on-the-job training (OJT)

A method by which employees are given hands-on experience with instructions from their supervisor or other trainer

Although it is used by all types of organizations, OJT is often one of the most poorly implemented training methods. Three common drawbacks are (1) the lack of a well-structured training environment, (2) poor training skills on the part of managers, and (3) the absence of well-defined job performance criteria. To overcome these problems, training experts suggest the following:

1. Develop realistic goals and/or measures for each OJT area.

2. Plan a specific training schedule for each trainee, including set periods for evaluation and feedback.

3. Help managers establish a nonthreatening atmosphere conducive to learning.

4. Conduct periodic evaluations after training is completed to ensure employees have not forgotten what they have learned.[18]

Figure 7.6 shows the basic steps of an OJT program. KLM Royal Dutch Airlines uses on-the-job training to train its cabin attendants. The airline started a program that places cabin attendant trainees in the classroom for a certain period and then gives them additional training during an evaluation flight. On these flights, experienced cabin attendants provide the trainees with on-the-job training, based on a list of identified job tasks. Some tasks, such as serving meals and snacks, are demonstrated

FIGURE 7.6 The PROPER Way to Do On-the-Job Training

P **Prepare.** Decide what employees need to be taught. Identify the best sequence or steps of the training. Decide how best to demonstrate these steps. Have materials, resources, and equipment ready.

R **Reassure.** Put each employee at ease. Learn about his or her prior experience, and adjust accordingly. Try to get the employee interested, relaxed, and motivated to learn.

O **Orient.** Show the employee the correct way to do the job. Explain why it is done this way. Discuss how it relates to other jobs. Let him or her ask lots of questions.

P **Perform.** When employees are ready, let them try the job themselves. Give them an opportunity to practice the job and guide them through rough spots. Provide help and assistance at first, then less as they continue.

E **Evaluate.** Check the employees' performance, and question them on how, why, when, and where they should do something. Correct errors; repeat instructions.

R **Reinforce and Review.** Provide praise and encouragement, and give feedback about how the employee is doing. Continue the conversation and express confidence in his or her doing the job.

Source: Scott Snell, University of Virginia.

during the actual delivery of services to passengers. Other tasks are presented to trainees away from passengers between meal service.[19]

Apprenticeship Training

An extension of OJT is apprenticeship training. With this method, individuals entering an industry, particularly in the skilled trades such as machinist, laboratory technician, and electrician, are given thorough instruction and experience, both on and off the job. For example, Bonneville Power Administration and General Physics Corporation developed an apprenticeship program for substation operators to give employees both a strong technical foundation in the fundamentals of electricity and a hands-on ability to operate equipment within power substations. Ultimately, the program was also designed to help future electrical operators respond to emergencies.[20]

Apprenticeship programs originated in Europe centuries ago as part of its guild system and are still used extensively there. Germany alone has more than 350 kinds of accredited apprenticeships. College students generally become apprentices too, dividing their time between studying and gaining on-the-job experience.[21] Typically, the programs involve cooperation between organizations and their labor unions, between industry and government, or between organizations and local school systems.

In the United States, tens of thousands of organizations have registered their programs with the U.S. Department of Labor's Bureau of Apprenticeship and Training (BAT) and state agencies. Approximately two-thirds of apprenticeships are in the construction and manufacturing industries. However, there are apprenticeships available in a wide range of other industries, including the telecommunications, arts, and health fields. One apprenticeship program, which is based in Detroit and called Focus: HOPE, provides young, low-income, unemployed adults apprenticeship opportunities to learn advanced manufacturing skills for high-tech jobs. The program's six-year curriculum integrates study in applied engineering and computer-integrated manufacturing along with on the-job training with the Computer Technology Industry Association and companies such as Cisco and Microsoft.[22]

Generally, an apprentice is paid 50 percent of a skilled journey worker's wage to start with, but the wage increases at regular intervals as the apprentice's job skills increase. When the apprentice successfully completes the apprenticeship, he or she becomes a certified journey-level worker earning full pay. According to BAT, many journey workers earn as much as college graduates, and some earn more.[23]

Cooperative Training, Internships, and Governmental Training

Similar to apprenticeships, cooperative training programs combine practical on-the-job experience with formal classes. However, the term *cooperative training* is typically used in connection with high school and college programs that incorporate part- or full-time experiences. In recent years, there has been an increased effort to expand opportunities that combine on-the-job skill training with regular classroom training so that students can pursue either technical work or a college degree program. Many organizations, including Fannie Mae, Burger King, Champion International, Cray, Inc., and the insurance company UNUM have invested millions of dollars in educational cooperative training programs in conjunction with public schools.

apprenticeship training

A system of training in which a worker entering the skilled trades is given thorough instruction and experience, both on and off the job, in the practical and theoretical aspects of the work

cooperative training

A training program that combines practical on-the-job experience with formal educational classes

Apprenticeships are a good way to recruit and train employees.

runzelkorn/Shutterstock.com

Internship programs, which we discussed in Chapter 5, are jointly sponsored by colleges, universities, and a variety of organizations. The programs offer students the chance to get real-world experience while finding out how they will perform in work organizations. Organizations benefit by getting student-employees with new ideas, energy, and eagerness to accomplish their assignments. Many universities and community colleges allow students to earn college credits on the basis of successful job performance and fulfillment of established program requirements.

The federal government and various state governments have begun working together with private employers to sponsor a multitude of training programs for new and current employees at career centers nationwide. These One Stop career centers (sometimes called "Job Service" or "Workforce Development" centers) have enabled thousands of organizations to help local citizens get jobs and job training assistance. The One Stop centers were modeled on Minnesota's successful program to help workers find jobs, help employers find qualified workers, and provide job training and other employment services all under one roof (hence the name One Stop). 3M, Northwest Airlines, Honeywell, and General Mills are just a few of the companies involved in the One Stop program.[24]

internship programs
Programs jointly sponsored by colleges, universities, and other organizations that offer students the opportunity to gain real-life experience while allowing them to find out how they will perform in work organizations

Classroom Instruction

When most people think about training, they think about classrooms. Some of the advantages of classroom instruction relate to motivation and attendance. Have you ever taken a self-directed course that lacked a classroom setting? If so, you might have had a hard time completing it. As one professor put it, "When it comes to learning, just getting to class is half the battle." In addition, if a trainee experiences problems, a live instructor is generally in the best position to help the trainee. The classroom training method also lends itself particularly well to what is called **blended learning,** in which lectures and demonstrations are combined with other audiovisual material such as films, DVDs, videotapes, or computer and online instruction. Despite the rise of many other types of learning—electronic and otherwise—classroom instruction is still the number one training method, as Figure 7.7 shows.[25]

blended learning
The use of multiple training methods to achieve optimal learning on the part of trainees

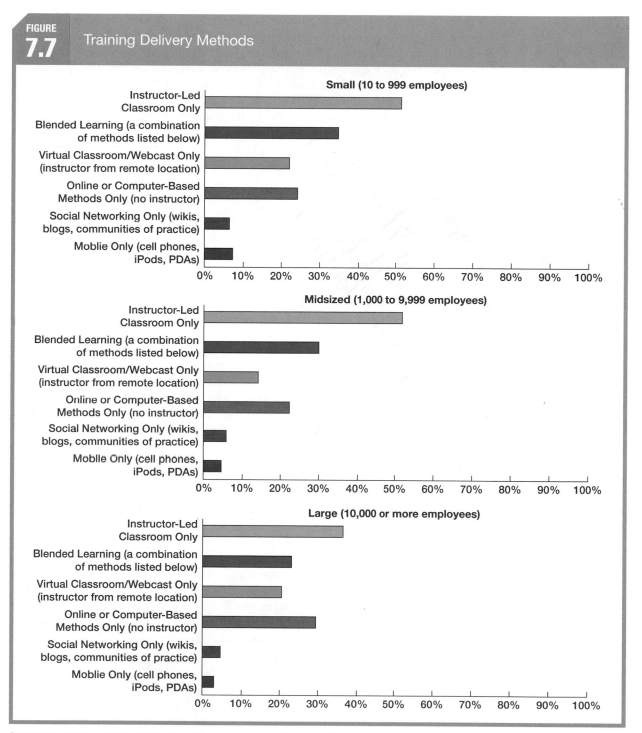

FIGURE 7.7 Training Delivery Methods

Source: Adapted from "2011 Industry Report," *Training* 47, no. 6 (November–December 2010): 18–31.

Programmed Instruction

Programmed instruction, which is also referred to as *self-directed learning*, utilizes books, manuals, or computers to break down content into sequences for employees to learn at their own pace. After being presented with a small segment of information, the trainee is required to answer a question, either by writing in a response or selecting one on a computer. If the response is correct, the trainee is told so and is presented with the next step (or screen) in the material. If the response is incorrect, further explanatory information is given, and the trainee is told to try again. Trainees are actively involved in the instructional process, and the feedback and reinforcement provided them are immediate.

Audiovisual Methods

To teach skills and procedures for many production jobs, audiovisual devices can be used. For example, video recordings are often used to illustrate the steps in a procedure such as assembling electronic equipment or working with a problem employee. Trainers and trainees can view an on-the-spot recording and get immediate feedback. Golf and tennis coaches frequently record their students to let them see their mistakes. CDs and DVDs allow trainees to access any segment of the instructional program, which is especially useful for individualized instruction when employees have different levels of knowledge and ability.[26]

When it is not possible to obtain video, audio recordings can be very valuable. For example, to instruct flight crew trainees, airlines might play actual cockpit tapes recorded on airplanes involved in accidents. After listening to the recordings, the trainees discuss the behavior of the crew during the crisis. By listening to the recorded statements of others and observing their failure to operate as a team, pilot trainees better understand how to balance their sense of self-reliance with an ability to listen to their superiors and subordinates.

Teleconferencing and videoconferencing allow an instructional program to be transmitted to many locations simultaneously and permit trainees to interact with one another. Electronic Data Systems has used teleconferencing to train its employees wherever they are in the world rather than having them travel to one location. The company conducted a "coaching skills for leaders" program that was disseminated to 1,500 managers in 41 countries via teleconferencing.

Web conferencing is used to conduct live meetings or presentations over the Internet. During a web conference, trainees sit at their own computers and are connected to other participants via the web. To attend the conference, they simply enter a website address and also dial in to a 1-800 number to talk to one another and the trainer via phone. A webinar is a one-way conference, from the speaker to the audience with limited audience interaction. A number of organizations are also using podcasts to provide their employees, such as sales reps, with information on the go. Podcasts allow reps to learn about new products while they are in the field rather than having to take time off to travel to corporate headquarters to get the information.

Simulation Method

Sometimes it is either impractical or unwise to train employees on the actual equipment used on the job. An obvious example is training employees to operate aircraft, spacecraft, and other highly technical and expensive equipment. The simulation method emphasizes realism in equipment and its operation at minimum cost and maximum safety.

Southwest Airlines boasts perhaps the most technologically advanced flight simulator in the airline industry: a $10.8 million full-motion Boeing 737-700 unit housed in an 110,000-square-foot flight operations training center adjacent to Southwest's headquarters at Dallas's Love Field. The facility can house up to six 737 simulators and can train up to 300 pilots at one time. Facing a serious worker shortage, the Federal Aviation Administration developed a sophisticated simulator to dramatically speed up the training of air traffic controllers, a process that used to take as long as five years. Variables such as wind speed, precipitation, and the number of airplanes to be guided can be adjusted on the simulator to test the ability of trainees. Trainees who do poorly in certain situations are then targeted for additional training in those areas. Simulators that represent human patients are being integrated into medical training as well.[27]

The distinction between simulation and computer-based training has blurred. For example, a simulation developed by Wicat in partnership with Airbus and Singapore Airlines runs on a PC and replicates a cockpit with control displays and throttle/flap controls. Even though the PC-based simulation is relatively inexpensive, it is powerful. Pilots are taken through a self-paced program that simulates "taxi, takeoff, climb, cruise, descent, approach, landing, and go-around." To train its forklift operators, the aluminum company Alcoa uses a computer simulation called Safedock, developed by Etcetera Edutainment. In the simulation, trainees perform common tasks such as moving loads from one end of a loading area to the other. If a trainee makes a wrong move, he or she instantly sees the consequences: the forklift might end up driving off the dock or crashing into another forklift.[28] These types of technologies are making it easier to offer training in new and different ways.

E-Learning

The training methods we just discussed are evolving into what trainers today refer to as e-learning. E-learning covers a wide variety of applications such as web and computer-based training (CBT), and social networks. It includes the delivery of content via the Internet, intranets and extranets, mobile devices, DVDs, CD-ROMs, MP3 players, and even "virtual classrooms" found in the gaming platform Second Life. Today one of every three hours of training is delivered via some form of technology, and companies are reporting that they are saving anywhere from 30 to 70 percent on their training costs by doing so.[29]

E-learning transforms the learning process in several ways. First, as we have said, it allows the firm to bring the training to employees rather than vice versa, which is generally more efficient and cost-effective. The nuclear power plant industry is a case in point: Nuclear power plant training is frequent and time-consuming. For workers just to remove their protective gear and commute to a separate training venue can take an hour or more. One nuclear power company that switched to e-learning reported that it saved nearly $1 million and 10,000 employee hours in just one year by doing so.

E-learning also allows companies to offer individual training components to employees when and where they need them. This type of training, which is referred to as just-in-time training, helps alleviate the boredom trainees experience during full-blown training courses, and employees are

e-learning
Learning that takes place via electronic media

just-in-time training
Training delivered to trainees when and where they need it to do their jobs, usually via computer or the Internet

Using the INTERNET

Read how Caterpillar University extends its training worldwide by using e-learning methods. Go to **www.cengagebrain.com**

more likely to retain the information when they can immediately put it to use. Cisco has thousands of online training videos employees can download off the company's intranet as needed.[30] Microsoft's product experts have created hundreds of short audio and video podcasts the company's sales professionals can download on their mobile devices as they need them. The company realized that full-blown training courses pulled people away from making sales, and that with so many products continually being launched, it was difficult for them to keep up to date if they had to take frequent training sessions. Also, employees didn't remember the training if they could not put it to use immediately.[31]

Communities of practice is a new but growing type of training that allows people to share knowledge and collaborate with one another via social networking tools. Blogs and wikis—sites where people can post information as they can on Wikipedia—are examples of the tools used to facilitate learning via the communities of practice method. The U.S. Army has a communities of practice site. When soldiers were having problems using a grenade launcher, a unit commander posted a question on the site. Shortly thereafter, someone who had experienced a similar problem posted a simple solution. The Cheesecake Factory restaurant chain trains employees by letting them upload and share video snippets on job-related topics, including how to prepare certain foods and provide good customer service. The consulting firm Accenture has a communities of practice site that allows employees to vote for the best answers.[32]

E-learning systems need not be overly expensive. Many e-learning training programs use existing applications employees are familiar with such as PowerPoint, Word, Adobe Acrobat, and audio and video files that can be easily uploaded and viewed or listened to online with any web browser.

Learning Management Systems

learning management system (LMS)
Online system that provides a variety of assessment, communication, teaching, and learning opportunities

Organizations combining their e-learning, employee assessment tools, and other training functions into electronic **learning management systems (LMS),** custom built for them by software vendors. Using the software, managers can assess the skills of employees, register them for courses, deliver interactive learning modules directly to employees' desktops when they need or want them, evaluate and track their progress, and determine when they are ready to be promoted. Purchasing a learning management system does not alleviate HR personnel and a firm's managers from conducting a thorough needs assessment, however—especially because the systems are costly. After conducting a thorough needs analysis, managers have to then research vendors, ask them to conduct demonstrations, get bids from them, and ultimately choose the type of systems that will work best.

Methods for Management Development

Many of the methods used to train front-line employees are also used to train supervisors and first-level managers. But other methods are used primarily to improve the preparation and development of mid- to senior-level managers. Over the past decade, the importance of management development has grown because so many experienced baby boomer managers have begun retiring and firms are having a hard time replacing the expertise they provided. In one study cited in an American Society of Training and Development paper, 70 percent of companies reported moderate to major leadership shortages, and many expected the problem to get worse.[33]

On-the-Job Experiences

Some skills and knowledge can be acquired just by listening and observing or by reading. But others must be acquired through actual practice and experience. Because they present managers with opportunities to perform under pressure and to learn from their mistakes, on-the-job development experiences are some of the most powerful and commonly used techniques. The following are methods for providing on-the-job experiences.

1. *Coaching* involves a continuing flow of instructions, comments, and suggestions from the manager to the subordinate. (*Mentoring*, discussed in Chapter 5, is a similar approach to personal and informal management development.)

2. *Understudy assignments* groom an individual to take over a managerial job by giving trainees experience in handling important functions of the job.

3. *Job rotation and lateral transfers* provide trainees with a variety of work experiences and broaden the understanding they need to manage people more effectively.

4. *Special projects* and *junior boards* give trainees an opportunity to study an organization's challenges, make decisions, and plan and work on new initiatives.

5. *Action learning* is a training method whereby trainees work full-time on projects with others in the organization and then discuss with them the aspects that went right and wrong. In some cases, action learning is combined with classroom instruction, conferences, and other types of blended learning opportunities.

6. *Managerial staff meetings* enable participants to become more familiar with the problems and events occurring outside their immediate areas by exposing them to the ideas and thinking of other managers.

7. *Planned career progressions* (discussed in Chapter 5) utilize all these different methods to provide employees with the training and development necessary to progress through a series of jobs requiring higher and higher levels of knowledge and/or skills.[34]

Although these methods are used most often to develop managers for higher-level positions, they also provide valuable experiences for those who are being groomed for other types of positions in the organization. While on-the-job experiences constitute the core of management training and development, other off-the-job methods of development can be used to supplement these experiences.

Seminars and Conferences

Seminars and conferences, like classroom instruction, are useful for bringing groups of people together for training and development. In terms of developing managers, seminars and conferences can be used to communicate ideas, policies, or procedures, but they are also good for raising points of debate or discussing issues (usually with the help of a qualified leader) that have no set answers or resolutions. For this reason, seminars and conferences are often used when attitude change is a goal.

Outside seminars and conferences are often conducted jointly with universities and consulting firms. The construction and mining equipment manufacturer Caterpillar is one company that, in conjunction with an outside consulting firm, has developed a training program to groom new managers. The challenge for Caterpillar is to get enough leaders and managers in place to effectively run the company by 2020. To meet this challenge, Caterpillar launched a leadership development initiative through its Caterpillar University of Leadership. The effort began with a series of high-level meetings and strategy sessions. Out of those meetings eleven characteristics were identified that the company seeks in its managers and leaders. So far, thousands of managers and executives have gone through the program, which is designed to help them become more self-aware as managers and develop their financial management skills and abilities to better formulate strategies to increase Caterpillar's global competitiveness. Associations and third-party organizations, such as the American Management Association, the Conference Board, and the Center for Creative Leadership, also offer many different types of management seminars.[35]

Case Studies

A particularly useful method used in classroom learning situations is the case study. The FBI's Integrated Case Scenario method is used as part of a 16-week training program for all new FBI agents. Using documented examples, case-study participants learn how to analyze (take apart) and synthesize (put together) facts, become conscious of the many variables on which management decisions are based, and, in general, improve their decision-making skills. Experienced educators and trainers generally point out that the case study is most appropriate when:

1. Analytic, problem-solving, and critical thinking skills are most important.

2. The KSAs are complex, and participants need time to master them.

3. Active participation is desired.

4. The process of learning (questioning, interpreting, and so on) is as important as the content.

5. Team problem-solving and interaction are possible.[36]

Figure 7.8 provides a set of guidelines for when and how to conduct case studies.

Management Games and Simulations

Games are now being widely used as a management development method. Generally, player-managers are faced with the task of making a series of management decisions affecting a hypothetical organization. The effects that every decision has on each area within the organization can be simulated with a computer program. IBM has developed a video game called Innov8 that trains managers in hypothetical situations. The company developed the game after its research showed that employees who play online multiplayer games were better at assessing risks, gathering information, and making decisions.[37] At Marriott International, a computer program called Business Acumen has been used to train its non-U.S. property-level managers on the finer points of hotel operation. The program simulates hotel operations scenarios such as budgetary decisions.[38]

FIGURE
7.8   Case Studies

When Using Case Studies ...

- Decide which goals can best be achieved by using case studies.

- Identify available cases that might work or consider writing your own.

- Set up the activity—including the case material, the room, and the schedule.

- Give all participants a chance to take part in the discussions and activities and try to keep the groups small.

- Bridge the gap between the theories presented in case studies and how they can actually be put into practice in your organization.

Source: Adapted from Albert A. Einsiedel, Jr., "Case Studies: Indispensable Tools for Trainers," *Training and Development* (August 1995): 50–53.

Simulations do not always require a computer, however. Motorola developed a noncomputer-based game called "Equal Employment Opportunity: It's Your Job" to teach the basic principles of equal employment opportunity. The players get caught up in the competitive spirit of a game and at the same time absorb and remember government regulations. They also become aware of how their own daily decisions affect their employer's compliance with these regulations.[39]

In addition, games and simulations are being used to help the managers of government agencies such as the Federal Emergency Management Agency better respond to crises. The company Presagis, for example, has developed computer software that simulates a chemical cloud over a replication of an actual city. During the training, the cloud can move and grow, challenging emergency response officials to dynamically change their emergency responses.[40]

Role-Playing

Role-playing consists of playing the roles of others, often a supervisor and a subordinate who are facing a particular problem, such as a disagreement or a performance problem. By acting out another's position, participants in the role-playing can improve their ability to understand and cope with others. Role-playing is used not only for managers, but also to train salespeople to question customers to understand their needs for goods and services. Health care professionals also engage in role-playing to learn to be empathetic and sensitive to the concerns of patients. At Virgin America, via role-playing exercises, new employees lean how to keep their cool when dealing with irate or unruly passengers. "We push our role-playing to the limits," says Patrick Cournoyer, Virgin America's manager of in-flight training

At times, participants may be hesitant to engage in role-play exercises. Successful role-playing takes planning. Instructors should do the following:

1. First ensure that members of the group have gotten to know one another. In other words, do not make a role-play the first activity in a training session.

2. Prepare the role-players by introducing a specific situation.

3. Realize that volunteers make better role-players.

4. Prepare the observers by giving them specific tasks, such as evaluating the role-play and offering feedback once it is over.

5. Guide the role-play enactment through its bumps (because it is not scripted).

6. Keep it short.

7. Discuss the enactment and prepare bulleted points of what was learned.[41]

Role-playing is a versatile teaching model, applicable to a variety of training experiences. Planned and implemented correctly, role-playing can bring realism and insight into dilemmas and experiences that otherwise might not be shared. Computer programs that simulate role-playing have also been developed. Virtual Leader, a product by SimuLearn, is one such program: Management trainees interact with animated "employees"—some of whom are more cooperative than others. The trainees are then given feedback as to how well they applied their managerial skills to each situation.

Behavior Modeling

behavior modeling

An approach that demonstrates desired behavior and gives trainees the chance to practice and role-play those behaviors and receive feedback

One technique that combines several different training methods, and therefore multiple principles of learning, is the behavior modeling technique. Behavior modeling consists of four basic components:

1. *Learning points.* At the beginning of instruction, the goals of the program are outlined. In some cases, the learning points are a sequence of behaviors that are to be taught. For example, the learning points might describe the recommended steps for giving employees feedback.

2. *Modeling.* Participants view videos in which a model manager is portrayed dealing with an employee in an effort to improve his or her performance. The model shows specifically how to deal with the situation and demonstrates the learning points.

3. *Practice and role-play.* Trainees then rehearse the behaviors demonstrated by the models. The greatest percentage of training time is spent in these skill practice sessions.

4. *Feedback and reinforcement.* As the trainee's behavior increasingly resembles that of the model, the trainer and other trainees reinforce the behavior with praise, approval, encouragement, and attention. Digitally recording the sessions can also be very instructive.

Behavior modeling seems to work, according to various studies. The training can help managers better interact with employees, administer discipline, introduce changes, and increase their productivity. Military training is a classic example of how behavior modeling can work. Drill sergeants model the behavior expected of new recruits, who, in turn, by emulating them, develop discipline and confidence.[42]

Tuition Assistance Programs

About half of all large corporations offer their employees tuition assistance if they take courses related to the firms' businesses. For example, managers or would-be managers might be reimbursed for taking post-graduate classes such as MBA courses or other courses related to their professional development. Tuition assistance programs, which are generally administered through a company's HR department, offer employees the opportunity to further integrate their educational credentials with their career plans. A study conducted by Motorola showed that for every $1 invested in learning (education and/or training), about $10 came back in productivity for the corporation.[43] The terms of the programs vary as do the amounts employees are reimbursed annually. Sometimes the amount of reimbursement depends on the grade an employee earns in class. Also, companies often require employees who are reimbursed for courses to remain with their firms for a certain amount of time after completing the courses.

Corporate Universities

It's not unusual for large corporations to have their own "universities" where they train their employees and future managers. We mentioned earlier in the chapter that Caterpillar has its own leadership university. Hamburger University operated by McDonald's Corporation in a suburb of Chicago is probably the best known corporate university. General Electric is renowned worldwide for its training programs. The company has a 53-acre training campus 35 miles north of New York City, where about 10,000 people attend classes each year. Most are GE employees, but about 7 to 10 percent are customers. The Campbell's Soup Company operates Campbell University, which features a two-year program focused on personal leadership development for both aspiring and seasoned managers. Candidates are nominated by their business unit presidents or functional leaders.

Tens of thousands of managers and owner/operators of McDonald's franchises have been trained at Hamburger University outside of Chicago.

Tannen Maury/Bloomberg/Getty Images

Phase 4: Evaluating the Training Program

Training, like any other HRM function, has to be evaluated to determine its effectiveness. A variety of methods are available to assess the extent to which a firm's training programs improve learning, affect behavior on the job, and impact the bottom-line performance of an organization. Unfortunately, many organizations do not adequately evaluate their training programs. But this is changing. Today, human resources departments are under pressure to calculate the return on their firms' training investment dollars. We will explain how this is done later in this section.

Figure 7.9 shows that four basic criteria are available to evaluate training: (1) reactions, (2) learning, (3) behavior, and (4) results. Some of these criteria are easier to measure than others, but each is important in that it provides different information about the success of the programs. The combination of these criteria can give a total picture of the training program in order to help managers decide where problem areas lie, what to change about the program, and whether to continue with a program.[44]

Criterion 1: Reactions

One of the simplest and most common approaches to evaluating a training program is assessing participants' reactions. Happy trainees will be more likely to want to focus on training principles and to utilize the information on the job. Trainees can do more than tell you whether they liked a training program. They can give insights into the content and techniques they found most useful. They can critique the instructors or make suggestions about participant interactions, feedback, and the like. Potential questions might include the following:

- What were your learning goals for this program?

- Did you achieve them?

- Did you like this program?

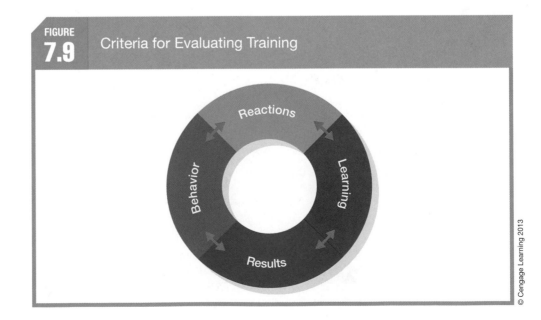

FIGURE 7.9 Criteria for Evaluating Training

© Cengage Learning 2013

- Would you recommend it to others who have similar learning goals?

- What suggestions do you have for improving the program?

- Should the organization continue to offer it?

While evaluation methods based on reactions are improving, too many conclusions about training effectiveness are still based on broad satisfaction measures that lack specific feedback. Furthermore, it should be noted that positive reactions are no guarantee that the training has been successful. It may be easy to collect glowing comments from trainees, but as gratifying as this information is, it may not be useful to the organization unless it translates into tangible, improved on-the-job performance based on the firm's strategic goals. In the final analysis, reaction measures should not stop with assessing the training's entertainment value.[45]

Criterion 2: Learning

Beyond what participants *think* about the training, it might be a good idea to see whether they actually learned anything. Testing the knowledge and skills of trainees before and after a training program will help determine their improvement. The skill and knowledge levels of employees who have undergone a training program can also be compared to employees who have not. Federal Express took this approach by studying twenty van drivers who attended a weeklong new hire training program. The company then compared the performance of these drivers with a control group of twenty drivers who had received only on-the-job training. FedEx found that the drivers who had been formally trained made fewer package processing errors, saving the company about $500 per trained driver.[46]

Criterion 3: Behavior

You might be surprised to learn that much of what is learned in a training program never gets used back on the job. It is not that the training was necessarily ineffective. But for several reasons, trainees do not demonstrate behavior change back on the job. The **transfer of training** refers to how well employees apply what they have learned to their jobs. To maximize the transfer of training, managers and trainers can take several approaches:

transfer of training
Effective application of principles learned to what is required on the job

1. *Feature identical elements.* Transferring the training to the job can be facilitated by having conditions in the training program come as close as possible to those on the job. For example, instead of verbally explaining a manufacturing process, it is better to demonstrate it on a factory floor.

2. *Focus on general principles, if necessary.* When jobs change or the work environment cannot be matched exactly, trainers often stress the general principles behind the training rather than focusing on rote behavior. This approach helps trainees learn how to apply the main learning points to varying conditions on the job.

3. *Establish a climate for transfer.* In some cases, trained behavior is not implemented because old approaches and routines are still reinforced by other managers, peers, and employees. To prevent this kind of problem, managers need to support, reinforce, and reward trainees for applying the new skills or knowledge. Oftentimes this requires firms to train their managers to actively embrace the strategic changes their organizations are seeking to implement.

4. *Give employees transfer strategies.* Particularly in settings that are not conducive to transfer, managers should also provide trainees with strategies and tactics for dealing with their transfer environment. One approach, called *relapse prevention (RP)*, teaches individuals how to anticipate and cope with the inevitable setbacks they will encounter back on the job—that is, a relapse into former behaviors. By identifying high-risk situations that jeopardize transfer and developing coping strategies, relapse prevention can help employees gain better control over maintaining learned behaviors.[47]

There are several methods for assessing transfer of learned skills back to the job. At Xerox, for example, trainers observe trainees once they return to their regular positions, interview the trainees' managers about their progress later on, and examine their posttraining performance appraisals.

Criterion 4: Results, or Return on Investment (ROI)

As we have indicated, human resource managers are under pressure to show that their training programs produce "bottom-line" results.[48] Most organizations today measure their training in terms of its return on investment (ROI), which is also sometimes referred to as the *utility* the firm gets for its training dollars. A company's ROI refers to the benefits it derives from training its employees relative to the costs it incurs. HR managers are responsible for calculating and presenting these benefits to the company's top managers. The benefits can include higher revenues generated, increased productivity, improved quality, lower costs, more satisfied customers, higher job satisfaction, and lower employee turnover.

The following are the types of questions HR managers should try to answer as they calculate a training program's benefits:

- How much did quality improve because of the training program?

- How much has it contributed to profits?

- What reduction in turnover and wasted materials did the company get after training?

- How much has productivity increased, and by how much have costs been reduced?

To answer these questions, HR managers use various types of data such as sales data, human resources and financial data, and employee survey and control group data gathered from various sources within the organization. Of course, the costs of the training program need to be measured, too. The ROI formula can then be calculated fairly simply:

$$ROI = Results/Training\ Costs$$

A firm's training costs include the various expenses it incurs related to the training, including the direct costs of the programs (materials, employee travel and meals, meeting site costs, equipment, trainers' salaries or fees, and so on) as well as the indirect costs of the programs (participants' salaries and the productivity they lose while they are attending the training). So, for example, if the ROI ratio of the training is >1, its benefits exceeds its cost; if the ROI ratio is <1, the costs of the training exceed the benefits. Highlights in HRM 2 shows some simple examples of ROI calculations. A firm's training ROI can also be measured in terms of how long it takes before the

2 HIGHLIGHTS IN **HRM**
Calculating Training ROI: Examples

ROI = Results/Training Costs

If the ROI ratio is >1, the benefits of the training program are greater than its costs. By contrast, the training program's costs outweigh the benefits if the ratio is <1.

Example 1: A program to train dental hygienists on a new process costs $15,000 to develop and implement. If the average number of patients processed each year increased by 350 following the training, and the profit earned from each patient is $30, this results in an extra $10,500 as a result of the training.

ROI = $10,500/$5,250 = 2

Since the ROI is greater than 1, the training's benefits outweigh its costs.

Example 2: A program to train call-center representatives to better help customers troubleshoot their Internet connectivity problem costs a cable company $225,000. One year later, the number of customers who dropped their service due to connectivity problems fell by 1,250. The average profit earned from each customer per year is $150. This results in an additional $187,500 for the firm.

ROI = $187,500/$225,000 = 0.83

Since the ROI of the training was only .83, the costs of the program are greater than the benefits.

Source: Adapted from Richard J. Wagner and Robert J. Weigand, "Can the Value of Training Be Measured? A Simplified Approach to Evaluating Training," *The Health Care Manager* 23, no. 1 (January–March 2004): 71–78; Ron Drew Stone, "ROI Is Like a Box of Chocolates," *Chief Learning Officer* (January 2011): 36; Howard Prager and Susan Vece, "Simplified ROI: Measuring What Matters Most," *Chief Learning Officer* (November 2009): 28.

benefits of the training pay off. This analysis is done by adding the costs and dividing the benefits realized in a single month. The result will indicate the overall time required for the training to pay for itself.[49]

Despite the emphasis on ROI today, some human resources experts think managers can get overly preoccupied with ROI calculations. Why? Because often the benefits of training can be intangible or take a long time to appear. Measuring participants' reactions can be done immediately, of course. However, measuring improved employee skills, customer satisfaction, and so forth can take somewhat longer, and factors other than training can also affect these measures. Finally, the development of groundbreaking new products or processes can also be sparked by training but take years to develop, making them hard to attribute to training. Developments such as these nonetheless can transform organizations.

Benchmarking

Closely related to calculating the firm's training ROI is the process of benchmarking developmental services and practices against those of recognized leaders in industry. While no single model for exact benchmarking exists, the simplest

benchmarking

The process of measuring one's own services and practices against the recognized leaders in order to identify areas for improvement

models are based on the late W. Edwards Deming's classic four-step process. The four-step process advocates that managers:

1. **Plan.** Conduct a self-audit to define internal processes and measurements; decide on areas to be benchmarked, and choose the comparison organization.

2. **Do.** Collect data through surveys, interviews, site visits, and/or historical records.

3. **Check.** Analyze data to discover performance gaps and communicate findings and suggested improvements to management.

4. **Act.** Establish goals, implement specific changes, monitor progress, and redefine benchmarks as a continuous improvement process.

The American Society of Training has developed training benchmarks from hundreds of different companies to which other firms can compare the data on their training costs, staffing, administration, design, development, and delivery of training programs. Benchmarks such as these can help organizations evaluate their current and future training programs.[50] Highlights in HRM 3 shows several aspects of training that can be benchmarked against organizations considered superior in the training function and how those aspects are calculated.

As e-learning continues to change training, the benchmarks for it are also likely to change as well. For example, the extent to which learning content has been accessed, downloaded, and the ratings given it by users are likely to become new measures of how well a firm's training programs are working.[51] Nonetheless, the key to improving a training program's effectiveness is continually evaluating it. The information

HIGHLIGHTS IN **HRM**
Benchmarking HR Training

MEASUREMENT	HOW TO CALCULATE
Percent of payroll spent on training	Total training expenditures ÷ total payroll
Training dollars spent per employee	Total training expenditures ÷ total employees served
Average training hours per employee	Total number of training hours (hours 3 participants) 4 total employees served
Percent of employees trained per year	Total number of employees receiving training ÷ total employee population
HRD staff per 1,000 employees	Number of human resource development staff ÷ total employee population 3 1,000
Cost savings as a ratio of training	Total savings in scrap or waste ÷ dollars invested expenses in training
Profits per employee per year	Total yearly gross profits ÷ total number of employees
Training costs per student hour	Total costs of training ÷ total number of hours of training

generated by the evaluations then feeds back into Phase 1 of the training process as shown in Figure 7.2. By tying the training closely to key performance metrics and then measuring the training's impact against them, a firm will be in a better position to improve its programs over time.[52]

Additional Training and Development Programs

In addition to training that addresses the KSAs reflecting the demands of a particular job, many employers develop training programs to meet the special needs of employees. In this final section, we summarize some of these programs, including orientation training and onboarding, basic skills training, team training and cross-training, ethics training, and diversity training. International training will be covered in Chapter 15.

Orientation Training

To get new employees off to a good start, organizations generally offer a formal orientation program. Orientation is the formal process of familiarizing new employees with the organization, their jobs, and their work units. Like training, which emphasizes the *what* and the *how*, orientation often stresses the *why*. It is designed to influence employee attitudes about the work they will be doing and their role in the organization. It defines the philosophy behind the organization's rules and provides a framework for job-related tasks.

An organization's HR department ordinarily is responsible for coordinating orientation activities and for providing new employees with information about conditions of employment, pay, benefits, and other areas not directly under a supervisor's direction. However, the supervisor has the most important role in the orientation program. New employees are interested primarily in what the supervisor says and does and what their new coworkers are like.

Given the immediate and lasting impact of orientation programs, careful planning—with emphasis on program goals, topics to be covered, and methods of organizing and presenting them—is essential. In many cases, organizations devise checklists for use by those responsible for conducting the orientation so that no item of importance to employees is overlooked. The checklist would include such things as (1) an introduction to other employees, (2) an outline of training, (3) expectations for attendance, conduct, and appearance, (4) the conditions of employment, such as hours and pay periods, (5) an explanation of job duties, standards, and appraisal criteria, (6) safety regulations, (7) a list of the chain of command, and (8) an explanation of the organization's purpose and strategic goals. Highlights in HRM 4 shows the types of materials new hires can be given and the various steps that can ease their transition into the workplace.[53] To be sure no materials are forgotten, companies often post orientation materials on their intranets and then provide new hires with passwords to access the sites.

Some organizations combine orientation programs with computer-based training. Macy's cut its orientation training time in half this way, orienting 2,500 new employees in just six weeks. New hires at SumTotal Systems, an e-learning company based in Bellevue, Washington, go online for virtual tours of the company's various departments, with introductions to company leaders sprinkled throughout. Of course, these types of programs *supplement*—but do not replace—the value of face-to-face orientation.[54]

LEARNING OUTCOME 6

To what extent do firms need to utilize additional training programs? Does it depend upon the type of firm or the types of employees who need training?

orientation

The formal process of familiarizing new employees with the organization, their jobs, and their work units

4 | HIGHLIGHTS IN **HRM**
Checklist for Orienting New Employees

Orientation Items

- Welcome information outlining the company background's, corporate vision, and mission statement
- Map of the facility, including parking information
- Computer passwords, security cards, and parking decals
- Current organizational chart
- Information about where to find the firm's corporate news, intranet sites, and bulletin boards
- Telephone numbers, e-mail addresses, and locations of key personnel and help desk personnel
- A copy of the employee's specific job goals and job description
- Lists of unique terms in the industry, company, and job
- Training class schedules
- Safety and emergency procedures
- The organization's policy handbook, including the firm's EEOC policies, office hours, dress code, vacation, and e-mail and Internet-use rules
- List of employee benefits, including insurance plans
- Holiday schedule

Follow-Up Activities

- Ensure that employee has completed the required paperwork, including benefit enrollment forms
- Revisit the employee's performance standards
- Schedule the first performance appraisal meeting

Onboarding

onboarding

The process of systematically socializing new employees to help them get "on board" with an organization.

Onboarding is the process of systematically socializing new employees to help them get "on board" with an organization. Onboarding goes beyond just orienting new employees to their new environments. It brings them into the organization's fold so that they truly feel as if they are a part of it. This is important because new hires are at a high risk of quitting.

Many new hires quit their jobs not because they cannot handle the tasks related to them but because they are going through culture shock within their new organizations. When new hires quickly quit, companies often have to begin recruiting, interviewing, and screening candidates all over again. The best recruiting and selection processes are therefore of little value if a firm is not able to retain the people it hires. The more time and effort spent in helping new employees feel welcome, the more likely they are to identify with the organization and become valuable members of it.

To help new hires avoid culture shock, some companies make video and podcasts available to new hires before they even begin work. The mission and goals of an organization, a mini-tour of its facilities, and interviews with current employees talking about what they like about the organization are featured. Executives are often featured as well, which helps new hires develop an early understanding of who's who in the organization.

It is also common practice for supervisors or other managerial personnel to recruit coworkers to serve as volunteer "sponsors," or mentors, for incoming employees. In addition to providing practical help to newcomers, experienced colleagues represent an important source of information about the norms and nuances of the work group, the culture of the organization, and what it expects from its employees. These relationships are vital to the socialization of new employees and contribute significantly to their long-term success within the organization.

Southwest Airlines approaches onboarding as a welcoming party. "It was so much fun and so informative. [The company] stresses that we are a family, so when I speak of Southwest Airlines, I will only speak in terms of *we* and not *they*," remarked one eager new employee after Southwest's onboarding process.[55] New employees always start on Fridays at CityMax.com, a build-your-own-website service in Vancouver, British Columbia. On Fridays, the work is less hectic, people are in a better mood and more relaxed, and everyone has time to introduce him- or herself.[56]

Basic Skills Training

Remedial training for adults has grown to be a full-blown educational industry on which businesses now spend billions of dollars annually. A report by the National Endowment for the Arts recently concluded that employers ranked the lack of reading and writing skills as the top deficiencies in new hires. Although literacy levels today are similar to what they were in 1970, the economy has changed drastically since then. Most U.S. workers today need to be able to read and analyze complex, often very technical material to succeed. "Jobs that don't have much in the way of skills have moved out of the United States or are not living-wage jobs," says Timothy Shanahan, the past president of the International Reading Association and a professor of urban education and reading at the University of Illinois at Chicago. Companies are also saying their employees need help with emotional skills such as persistence, self-discipline, and self-awareness.[57]

As the baby boom generation retires, the situation will only be exacerbated. Businesses report that they are already having a harder time finding workers with the basic skills they seek. Many businesses say it is their top problem. A list of typical basic skills employees need includes the following:

- Reading
- Writing
- Computing
- Speaking
- Listening

- Problem-solving
- Managing oneself/self-discipline
- Knowing how to learn
- Working as part of a team
- Leading others

Ford, Polaroid, United Technologies, and AT&T are among the many companies who now offer remedial courses to their employees, many of which are conducted in-house. A number of states offer businesses tax credits for conducting remedial training (and other types of training) for their employees.[58] Recognizing that the skills gap is increasing, colleges and companies have begun teaming up to bridge the gap.

For example, Pierce College, a two-year college in California (which had previously concentrated on preparing students for four-year colleges), now provides remedial instruction to employees at the offices of more than thirty companies in the San Fernando Valley area, where the college is located.[59] To implement a successful program in basic and remedial skills, managers should do the following:

1. Explain to employees why and how the training will help them in their jobs.

2. Relate the training to the employees' goals.

3. Respect and consider participants' experiences, and use these as a resource.

4. Use a task-centered or problem-centered approach so that participants "learn by doing."

5. Give employees feedback on their progress toward meeting their learning objectives.

The key to developing a successful basic skills program is *flexibility*, reinforcing the principle of individual differences while acknowledging the reality of work and family constraints.

Team Training and Cross-Training

As we discussed earlier in the book, organizations rely on teams to help them attain their strategic and operational goals. Whether the team is an aircrew, a research team, or a manufacturing or service unit, the contributions of the individual members of the team are not only a function of the KSAs of each individual, but also of the interaction of the team members. The teamwork behaviors of effective teams are shown in Figure 7.10.

Coca-Cola's Fountain Manufacturing Operation (which makes the syrup for Coke and Diet Coke) developed team training for its manufacturing employees. The program focused on three skill categories: (1) technical, (2) interpersonal, and (3) team action. The technical component, called Four-Deep Training, meant that each individual should learn four different jobs to allow for team flexibility. The interpersonal skills component, called Adventures in Attitudes, focused on listening, conflict resolution, influence, and negotiation. Team action training focused on team leadership, management of meetings, team roles, group dynamics, and problem-solving—all skills needed to function effectively as a team. The training not only increased quality and customer satisfaction, but has also helped decrease costs and set up a model for preparing employees for the future.[60]

cross-training

The process of training employees to do multiple jobs within an organization

Closely related to team training is **cross-training**. Cross-trained employees learn how to do different jobs within an organization as well as their own. Part of the motivation for cross-training is that it gives firms flexible capacity. Workers can be dynamically shifted when and where they are needed, unlike specialized workers and equipment, which cannot. Moreover, by keeping workers interested and motivated, cross-training can cut turnover, increase productivity, pare down labor costs, and lay the foundation for careers rather than dead-end jobs. For example, at Boston's The Gourmet Pizza, employees begin cross-training their first day on the job. Staffers run through every function in the back and front of the restaurant and then plot their own course of cross-training. If they are interested in the bar, they have the opportunity to work there in various positions; those who want to become managers or franchise owners learn the entire operation, a process that takes eight to twelve months.[61]

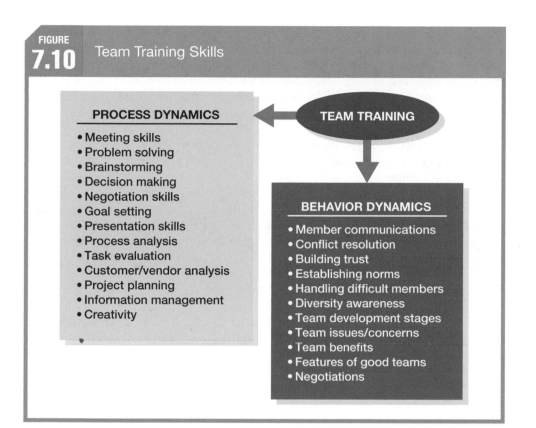

FIGURE 7.10 Team Training Skills

PROCESS DYNAMICS

- Meeting skills
- Problem solving
- Brainstorming
- Decision making
- Negotiation skills
- Goal setting
- Presentation skills
- Process analysis
- Task evaluation
- Customer/vendor analysis
- Project planning
- Information management
- Creativity

TEAM TRAINING

BEHAVIOR DYNAMICS

- Member communications
- Conflict resolution
- Building trust
- Establishing norms
- Handling difficult members
- Diversity awareness
- Team development stages
- Team issues/concerns
- Team benefits
- Features of good teams
- Negotiations

Source: George Bohlander and Kathy McCarthy, "How to Get the Most from Team Training," National Productivity Review (Autumn 1996): 25–35

Cross-training represents a shift from Henry Ford's assembly line production to flexible production. Some companies are using cross-training to keep their workers and plants in the United States versus offshoring them. Pace Worldwide, a Maryland-based company that sells soldering equipment, watched all of its competitors move offshore. To keep up with the productivity of its low-cost rivals abroad, Pace grouped workers into teams and trained each team to build an entire product as well as different products. "Some of the people could only do certain things, and if they had no work, they would just sit and wait," said one Pace manager. "Now they have ownership of it all." Employees have an incentive to learn because their hourly wages get bumped up as they master more skills. Now Pace builds products to meet actual customer demand, rather than storing inventory, which is more costly, and it has been able to shorten its production times and move its operations into one building versus two. In addition to making them more productive, research shows that cross-training gives employees the "big picture," making them more creative and better problem-solvers.[62]

Ethics Training

Ethics training became more prevalent in companies following the high-profile corporate scandals such as those that occurred at Enron in 2001. Corporate scandals are, of course, not new to the twenty-first century. What is new is a recent increase in the funding for the Department of Justice, the Department of Labor, the EEOC, and other agencies to investigate wrongdoing by employers. The most common forms of ethics violations, such as harassment, health and safety, and wage-and-hour violations, are related to employment laws. One study found that the problem gets worse in difficult economic times as companies try to cut costs.

Government contractors and subcontractors with contracts that last for 120 days or more and are more than $5 million are required by law to have business ethics codes and compliance policies and procedures. Other organizations are not legally required to. However, in the event of a violation, those that have "effective programs to prevent and detect violations of law" will face reduced penalties under U.S. federal sentencing guidelines.

Top managers play a key role in terms of ethics training because employees take their cues from them and mirror their behavior. Thus, a firm's top executives and managers should behave in accordance with their companies' values. If this does not happen, no ethics training program within a company can be effective. Senior managers should also broach the topic of ethics often in their speeches and presentations, and a company's ethics training should be a part of the new employee orientation. In addition, a firm's current employees need to undergo ethics training at regular intervals.

Workers who are responsible for areas that expose them to ethical lapses are likely to require special training. Employees who do the purchasing for their firms are one example. Likewise, some firms offer special training to their overseas personnel who work in countries in which corruption and bribery are prevalent. (We will talk more about bribery in Chapter 15, which covers international topics.) Bringing in an outside expert trained in ethics or values-based management can be helpful as can surveying employees, managers, and sometimes even customers about what they believe the ethical state of their companies are and where improvements could be made.

Other efforts a firm can take to ensure employees at all levels are behaving ethically and legally include establishing toll-free ethics hotlines and secure e-mail addresses where employees can confidentially report violations they have noticed.[63] Some firms go so far as to appoint chief ethics officers—high-ranking managers directly responsible for fostering the ethical climate within their firm. Highlights in HRM 5 contains some additional sources human resource managers can turn to in order to develop ethics training programs.

chief ethics officer
A high-ranking manager directly responsible for fostering the ethical climate within the firm

Diversity Training

Two out of three U.S. companies have broadened their diversity programs because of increasing globalization, according to a survey of 1,780 human resources and training executives by the Boston-based consulting firm Novations/J. Howard & Associates. Of those that have not done so, most expect to update diversity efforts in the near future. In addition to globalization, the increased emphasis on diversity training has been sparked by an awareness of the varied demographics of the workforce, challenges of affirmative action, dynamics of stereotyping, changing values of the workforce, and potential competitive payoffs from bringing different people together for a common purpose. There are basically three types of diversity training: (1) awareness building, which helps employees appreciate the benefits of diversity, and (2) training to prevent discrimination and harassment, and (3) skill building, which provides employees with the KSAs necessary for working with people who are different from them. For example, a skill-building diversity program might teach managers how to conduct performance appraisals with people from different cultures or teach male supervisors how to coach female employees toward better career opportunities. All of the diverse dimensions—race, gender, age, disabilities, lifestyles, culture, education, ideas, and backgrounds—should be considered in the design of a diversity training program.[64] Diversity issues related to age are becoming more commonplace. According to a 2011 survey by the Society of Human Resources, nearly 60 percent of firms are saying they are now training managers to respond to generational differences in the workplace.

Likewise, following a couple of highly publicized incidents of intolerance, the San Francisco 49ers football team underwent diversity training. In 2002, 49ers running back Garrison Hearst said in a newspaper interview that he would never accept a gay teammate. Lindsey McLean, a

Using the INTERNET

The focus of GE's commitment to leadership development is the John F. Welch Leadership Center at Crotonville, New York, the world's first major corporate business school. To find information about the development programs offered at the center, go to

www.cengagebrain.com

5

HIGHLIGHTS IN HRM
Additional Ethics Training Resources

The following organizations and links are good resources relevant to ethics codes and ethics training.

Business Roundtable Institute for Corporate Ethics

www.corporate-ethics.org

The Darden Graduate School of Business Administration

The Business Roundtable Institute for Corporate Ethics is an independent entity established in partnership with the Business Roundtable—an association of chief executive officers of leading U.S. companies. Says Dean Krehmeyer, the executive director of the organization, "The Institute brings together leaders from business and academia to fulfill its mission to renew and enhance the link between ethical behavior and business practice through executive education programs, practitioner-focused research, and outreach."

Ethics Resource Center

www.ethics.org

The Ethics Resource Center conducts and facilitates independent research to advance the ethical standards and practices in public and private institutions. It is the oldest nonprofit in the United States devoted to organizational ethics. ERC researchers analyze current and emerging issues and produce new ideas and benchmarks that enhance the public's trust. The ERC also sponsors character development programs for educational institutions and a Fellows Program in which chief ethics and compliance officers from business and government meet twice yearly to address ethics issues in the workplace and form working groups for further exploration and discussion.

Ethics & Compliance Officer Association

www.theecoa.org

The Ethics & Compliance Officer Association (ECOA) is a member-driven association for individuals responsible for their organization's ethics, compliance, and business conduct programs. Its members represent the largest group of ethics and compliance practitioners in the world. The ECOA is credited with formally "founding" the ethics and compliance field in 1991.

retired gay trainer with the team, admitted publicly that he was gay and that he had endured taunts and humiliation from players at times during his twenty-four years with the 49ers. "We're trying to create an environment where we can talk about these things and eliminate the problems and violence that can take place and help them understand that they can create an environment that people can work in, even if they are different," said one 49ers manager.[65]

Increasingly, diversity training is being combined with other training programs, an occurrence that some believe represents the "mainstreaming" of diversity with other strategic issues, such as ethics, facing organizations. Honeywell, for example, subsumes diversity training within a weeklong advanced management program and as part of its sales training programs. General Electric trains mentors and protégés in a program that is not explicitly a diversity initiative but nevertheless clearly helps women and ethnic minorities.

To achieve a good outcome in terms of diversity training, managers will want to do the following:

1. *Forge a strategic link.* Begin by establishing the reasons for diversity training. Clarify the links between diversity and a firm's business goals in order to provide a context for training. Affirmative action and valuing diversity are not the same thing. Ultimately, diversity enhances differences and unites those differences toward a common goal.

2. *Do not settle for "off the shelf" programs.* Each company has somewhat different goals, and its training should reflect this.

3. *Choose your training methods carefully.* Most diversity training is really education (awareness building). Managers may hope they are developing skills, but this requires more in-depth training. Employees may benefit from either awareness or skill building, but they are not the same.

4. *Document the individual and organizational benefits of the training.* Diversity training, when done well, can enhance communications, improve a firm's responsiveness to social issues, reduce its lawsuits, create a climate of fairness, improve employee productivity, and increase the company's revenues, profits, and competitiveness.

The last point—documenting the benefits of diversity training—is particularly important. Oftentimes, companies fail to do this, so the training ends up merely being a "feel good" exercise. Diversity training needs to be held to the same rigorous standards as other training programs. If the training is truly working, it should show up eventually in a company's employee demographics and strategy. According to Alexandra Kalev, a doctor of philosophy at Princeton University who has studied diversity training, having an affirmative action plan that is annually evaluated, checking the numbers in your company vis-à-vis the labor market you recruit from, and having an active diversity committee and a full-time staff person dedicated to diversity can make a firm's diversity training programs more effective.[66]

Summary

LEARNING OUTCOME 1 The types of training given employees range from simple, on-the-job instruction to sophisticated skills training conducted on multimillion dollar simulators. Training programs cover a broad range of subjects and involve personnel at all levels. The goal of training is to contribute to an organization's overall strategic goals. To be effective, training programs need to be developed systematically. This approach consists of four phases: (1) needs assessment, (2) program design, (3) implementation, and (4) evaluation.

LEARNING OUTCOME 2 The needs assessment phase begins with an organization analysis. Managers must establish a context for training by deciding where training is needed, how it connects with their firms' strategic goals, and how their companies' resources can best be used in terms of training. A task analysis is used to identify the knowledge, skills, and abilities employees need. A person analysis is used to identify which people need training.

LEARNING OUTCOME 3 When designing a training program, managers must consider the two fundamental preconditions for learning: readiness and motivation of trainees. In addition, the principles of learning should be considered to create an environment that is conducive to learning. These principles include goal setting, the meaningfulness of presentation, modeling, individual differences, active practice and repetition, whole-versus-part learning, massed-versus-distributed learning, and feedback and reinforcement.

LEARNING OUTCOME 4 A wide variety of methods are available to train nonmanagerial personnel. On-the-job training is one of the most commonly used methods because it provides trainees with hands-on experience and an opportunity to build a relationship with their supervisor and coworkers. Apprenticeship training and internships are especially effective. Classroom training is still the most popular way to train employees. However, programmed instruction, computer-based training, simulations, and interactive e-learning utilizing teleconferencing, video conferencing, webinars, the communities of practice method, and other means are becoming more popular. Using multiple methods, or what is called blended learning, has been found to be most effective.

The training and development of managers is becoming increasingly critical for firms because they are facing increasing competition from across the globe and the baby boomer generation in the United States is retiring. A wide variety of training methods are used for developing managers. On-the-job experiences include coaching, understudy assignment, job rotation, lateral transfers, project and committee assignments, and staff meetings. Off-the-job experiences include analysis of case studies, management games and simulations, role-playing, and behavior modeling. Tuition assistance programs and corporate universities are other tools organizations utilize to help train employees for leadership positions.

LEARNING OUTCOME 5 The evaluation of a training program should focus on several criteria: participants' reactions, the amount of learning they have acquired, their behavioral changes on the job, and bottom-line results such as the program's return on investment. The transfer of training is measured via examination of the degree to which trained skills are demonstrated back on the job. Benchmarking and utility analysis help evaluate the impact of training and provide the information for further needs assessment.

LEARNING OUTCOME 6 In addition to training that addresses the KSAs of a particular job, many employers develop additional training programs for various purposes. Orientation training allows new hires to more quickly acquire the knowledge, skills, and attitudes that increase the probabilities of their success within the organization. Onboarding programs go beyond orientation by bringing new hires into an organization's fold so that they truly feel like they are a part of it. This is important because new hires are at a high risk of quitting. Basic skills training, team and cross-training, ethics training, and diversity training are other programs commonly conducted by organizations.

Key Terms

apprenticeship training
behavior modeling
behavior modification
benchmarking
blended learning
chief ethics officer
chief learning officer
competency assessment

cooperative training
cross-training
e-learning
instructional objectives
just-in-time training
learning management
    system (LMS)
on-the-job training (OJT)

onboarding
organization analysis
orientation
person analysis
spot rewards
task analysis
transfer of training

Discussion Questions

LEARNING OUTCOME 1   What economic, social, and political forces have made employee training even more important today than it was in the past?

LEARNING OUTCOME 2   What analyses should be done to determine the training needs of an organization? After the needs are determined, what is the next step?

LEARNING OUTCOME 3   Which principles of learning do you see demonstrated in your own classes? In what ways might you bring other principles into them?

LEARNING OUTCOME 4   Suppose that you are the manager of an accounts receivable unit in a large company. You are switching to a new system of billing and record-keeping and need to train your three supervisors and twenty-eight employees in the new procedures. What training method(s) would you use? Why?

LEARNING OUTCOME 5   Participants in a training course are often asked to evaluate the course by means of a questionnaire. What are the pros and cons of this approach? Are there better ways of evaluating a course?

LEARNING OUTCOME 6   A new employee is likely to be anxious the first few days on the job.
a. What are some possible causes of this anxiety?
b. How may the anxiety be reduced?

On the Job: Video Cases

Training at Scripps Hospital La Jolla

Hospital executives discuss the training initiatives at Scripps Hospital La Jolla in San Diego. They discuss the training needs related to all employees and specifically the training needs associated with new graduate nurses and new, more experienced nurses and medical staff. The video emphasizes learning principles and blended learning methods. The importance of an extensive orientation program and an ongoing commitment to professional development opportunities is also discussed. Both mandatory and optional training are mentioned as well as a needs assessment to determine training needs.

What to Watch for and Ask Yourself

- Scripps Hospital La Jolla conducts an annual needs assessment to determine what type of training is needed. The video does not go into detail about the sources for this assessment but gives specific examples that could be used for analysis of the training needs for medical staff.

- The video mentions various types of training delivery or "different learning experiences" that are used at Scripps Hospital La Jolla. Identify at least three types of internal delivery options of training that are mentioned in the video.

- The evaluation of the hospital's training programs are not detailed specifically in the video; however, what type(s) of training evaluation do you think might be used at Scripps Hospital La Jolla for its new graduate nurses training program that is mentioned in the video?

HRM EXPERIENCE
Training and Learning Principles

Even though it is not difficult to do so, a surprising number of training programs do not explicitly incorporate the principles of learning (goal setting, modeling, individual differences, and feedback) discussed in the chapter. To prove incorporating them is not difficult to do, complete the following assignment for building a paper airplane.

Assignment

1. Form teams of four to six members. Identify someone on the team who knows how to make a paper airplane. That person will be the trainer.

2. Identify someone who will be the observer/recorder. That person will not participate in the training but will write down how many (and how effectively) principles of learning are used in the instruction:
   a. Goal setting
   b. Modeling
   c. Meaningfulness
   d. Individual differences
   e. Whole-versus-part learning
   f. Mass-versus-distributed learning
   g. Active practice
   h. Feedback

3. Give the trainer ten to fifteen minutes to train the group in making a paper airplane. The observer/recorder will keep notes of effective and ineffective training techniques (demonstrated learning principles).

4. Have someone from each team—not the trainer—volunteer to come before the class for a friendly competition. The instructor will give each team member two minutes to make a paper airplane. Then just for fun, they can compete by seeing which one flies the farthest. (No wagering, please.)

5. To finish the exercise, the observers/recorders will lead a discussion of the learning principles that were demonstrated. If the principles were incorporated for this activity, discuss why they might not be incorporated in other training settings.

Case Study   1

Loews Hotels: Training for Four Diamond Service AND MORE

Most people expect to receive great service at four-diamond hotels. But that's not good enough for Loews. The New-York based hotel chain, which has properties in sixteen cities across the United States and Canada, tries to "wow" every one of its guests with high-quality accommodations, impressive surroundings, personalized service, and thoughtful amenities for a luxurious experience. Loews refers to the effort as its "Four Diamond AND MORE" service. And apparently it is working. The chain was selected number one in customer satisfaction among all luxury hotel companies in the second quarter 2010 Market Metrix Hospitality Index.

A key element of the Loews' success is the extensive training it provides its employees. Between 2006–2011, it spent over 264,000 hours training its employees, and it has been the only hotel chain to be ranked in consecutive years as a Top 75 Company by *Training* magazine. Employees at all levels undergo training. Whether they work at the front desk, as housekeepers, accountants, or marketing managers, they learn about the big-picture goals of the company and how the quality of service differentiates one company from another in the hotel business. "The key is to train *all* departments of your organization to be customer-centric," says Jon Tisch, the company's CEO. "Thinking about customers can't be left to marketing and sales alone. Manufacturing, R&D, strategy, management, all have to be focused on the needs and desires of the customer."

Customer-facing employees at Loews undergo classroom training, including role playing and simulations to learn how to deal with customers. "Living Loews," a two-day training program teaches employees not only the finer points of etiquette but how to really sell the Loews experience—even when things go wrong. "Part of this training deals with how to handle pressure, which is something employees in any industry are bound to face. We're all human, so mistakes can happen," Tisch explains. "But when they do, we train our coworkers to impress our guests with an extraordinary recovery that we hope they'll remember even more."

Training sessions such as "Green" Training, "Loews Meeting Experience," "Loews Pool Concierge" program, "Spa 101," and the "YouFirst" guest loyalty program ensure that customers of all types who use the hotel's various services get top-notch service. The training does not end with the sessions, though. Once it is over, training managers go out on the front lines to do spot checks and offer feedback to employees to make sure the training really "sticks." A train-the-trainer program and other managerial workshops such as "Communicating Loews" help managers promote the hotel brand and inspire their employees to do so as well. A comprehensive executive training program covers topics ranging from communication and salesmanship to public speaking and presentation skills.

Loews also tries to "grow" its own talent. Its high-potential program offers additional training, development planning, and extra opportunities to employees who show promise. Most training managers, for example, are promoted from line-level jobs or from operations, so they know the company's processes and culture firsthand. The company also has a tuition assistance program.

To recruit undergraduates, Loews offers paid summer internships that allow students to work in a variety of areas such as the rooms division, food and beverage department, sales and marketing, and human resources. Each intern is assigned a mentor and given opportunities to network by attending operational meetings. At the conclusion of their internships they complete a report on their experience. Successive year internships give them exposure to additional functional areas, project work, supervisory experience and ultimately the opportunity to join the company's management training program.

So successful is the training at Loews that even trainers are impressed. Douglas Kennedy, the founder and president of the Kennedy Training Network, which specializes in hospitality training, says he was knocked out by his experience while conducting training at Loews' various properties. "I have never received more genuine, authentic welcome notes with my amenities, which were always a welcome treat after a long day of training and an evening of travel. Each note was personally written, and not just the standard 'welcome to our hotel, hope you enjoy your stay' messages. I also got to indulge in the supremely comfortable guest rooms and enjoy uniquely local dining options, décor, and overall hotel ambiance," Kennedy says. "I have to say I've become a bit spoiled now by all this, and I'm sure it will be a rude awakening next month when I return to staying in more typical upscale hotels."

Questions

1. How do Loews' training programs relate to the company's business strategy?
2. Why does the company encourage its employees to focus on the customers' needs versus other metrics?

Sources: Jill Busch "Training Reveals Rankings for 2011 Top 125," *Training Magazine*, February 8, 2011, http://www.trainingmag.com; Ann LaGreca, "Loews Hotels CEO Jonathan Tisch on the Essence of Customer Service: Experience, Service and Quality," *Knowledge@Emory*, July 11, 2007, http://knowledge. emory.edu; "Loews Hotels Named Among 'Top 125' by Training Magazine," *Hotel and Motel Management*, March 9, 2009, at http://www.hospitalityworldnetwork.com; http://www.trainingmag.com; Holly Dolezalek, "We Train to Please" *Training* 45, no. 3 (March–April 2008): 34–35.

Case Study 2

Kodak Gets the Picture in Executive Education

Eastman Kodak has changed dramatically to compete in a world of new technologies, emerging markets, and global customers. As a result, Kodak's efforts in executive education have pushed the limits to create innovative "learning events" for senior management, which are designed to be as dynamic and future-oriented as the company's business environment.

For years, Kodak was the dominant player in its market. It enjoyed worldwide brand recognition, extraordinary customer loyalty, and enviable profits. Understandably, few employees (or managers) wanted to do anything to upset the status quo as most of them looked forward to a lifetime of employment and security.

Then things changed. The company restructured in order to go head-to-head with competitors in a much tougher digital marketplace, and in the process, there has been a one-third reduction in executive positions. These events drove complacency far from the environs of Rochester, New York, Kodak's headquarters city. Agility has replaced *stability* as the watchword of the future.

As a consequence of Kodak's transformation—not to mention the personnel changes—the majority of senior managers have been in their positions for far fewer years. Executive education is viewed as a critical tool for improving Kodak's managerial ranks. But Kodak believed that the development programs needed to be as active, innovative, and future-oriented as the company. Off-the-shelf materials were out, as were case studies, lectures, and other passive learning approaches. A new approach meant inventing from scratch, letting go of control, and taking monumental risks. Skills in anticipating the business, pushing the culture, and networking were demanded. These objectives led to the creation of three new programs for the senior management team:

- *The Kodak Prosperity Game.* This game teamed fifty Kodak executives with twenty-five peer executives from other companies. These "reality-based" teams worked on meaningful, implementable strategies, alliances, and deals.

- *The Digital Executive.* This program consisted of a "scavenger hunt" exploring Kodak's digital present and future. Using digital products and the Internet, small teams researched digital competitors and interacted with a consumer focus group via videoconferencing. One innovative feature of this program was the upward mentoring of the participants by technology "whiz kids."

- *The Future of the Company.* This was a two-part program, developed in partnership with the Global Business Network and focused on learning about possible futures for the industry and the company. Part I was a two-day "conversation" about Kodak and its environment in the coming years. Industry scenarios for growth were developed in small team discussions involving Kodak executives and customers, alliance partners, and futurists. The resulting scenarios launched Part II, in which additional outsiders and provocative thinkers mixed ideas with the participants. The outcomes were a set of new ideas and potential strategies for the Kodak businesses.

After Kodak's executives committed to an all-out digital strategy, the company's revenues climbed. In 2004, Kodak surpassed Sony, the market leader, in the number of digital cameras shipped in the United States. The firm's executives say Kodak is well-positioned in the consumer digital imaging and graphic communications markets. For example, during 2010, it grew its share of the pocket video camera market by 10 percentage points and today is the number two player. However, it still faces a very tough competitive environment. Profits in 2010 were negative, and a New Jersey investment-management firm is pushing the company's top shareholders to take the lead in either turning around or selling it.

Questions

1. What can you tell about how Kodak did needs assessment for executive education? What recommendations would you give Kodak for improving this analysis, and what type of training do you think should be done now?
2. How would you go about evaluating the effectiveness of these educational experiences? Do you believe that company profitability should be used as a criterion? Can more training save Kodak?

Sources: William G. Stopper, "Agility in Action: Picturing the Lessons Learned from Kodak and 23 Other Companies." Adapted with permission from *Human Resource Planning*, vol. 21, no. 1 (1998). Copyright 1998 by The Human Resource Planning Society, 317 Madison Avenue, Suite 1509, New York, NY 10017, Phone: (212) 490-6387, Fax: (212) 682-6851; "Kodak Overtakes Sony in U.S. Digital Camera Shipments," *Kyodo News International* (Tokyo, Japan) (via *Knight-Ridder/Tribune Business News*) (February 3, 2005); "NJ Investor Group Seeks Sale or Turnaround At Kodak," *Wall Street Journal* (March 2, 2011), http://online.wsj.com.

Notes and References

1. (2011 Industry Report) *Training* 47, no. 6 (November–December 2010): 18–31.

2. Margaret Cronin Fisk, "Wal-Mart Wins Final Approval of Workers' Wage Suit Settlement," *Bloomberg* (November 9, 2009), http://www.bloomberg.com

3. Lori Freifeld, "Best of the Best," *Training* 45, no. 2 (February 2008): 8.

4. David Dubois and William Rothwell, "Competency-Based or a Traditional Approach to Training?" *Training and Development* 58, no. 4 (April 2004): 46–59; See also Irwin L. Goldstein and J. Kevin Ford, *Training in Organizations: Needs Assessment, Development and Evaluation*, 4th ed. (Belmont, CA: Wadsworth, 2002). For the classic citation on needs assessment, see William McGehee and Paul W. Thayer, *Training in Business and Industry* (New York: John Wiley and Sons, 1961).

5. Laurie Bassi and Daniel McMurrer, "How's Your Return on People?" *Harvard Business Review* 8, no. 3 (March 2004): 18; Tracy Mauro, "Helping Organizations Build Community," *Training and Development* 56, no. 2 (February 2002): 25–29; Liam Lahey, "RFIDs Touted as Standard for Airport Security," *Computing Canada* 28, no. 13 (June 21, 2002): 21; Caroline Wilson, "Ensuring a Smooth Ride," *Security Management* 46, no. 8 (August 2002): 92.

6. Brad Long, "Strategic Human Resource Management and the Worker's Experience," *Journal of Individual Employment Rights* 12, no. 3 (2007): 265–282; "E-Learning and Teleconferencing Join Needs Assessment to Control Training Costs," *Managing Training & Development*, no. 3 (December 2003): 1; Thomas Gainey, Brian Klaas, and Darla Moore, "Outsourcing the Training Function: Results from the Field," *Human Resource Planning* 25, no. 1 (2002): 16; Sarah Fister Gale, "Creative Training: Doing More with Less," *Workforce* 80, no. 10 (October 2001): 82–88.

7. Rieva Lesonsky, "Want to Keep Key Employees?" *Small Business Trends* (January 19, 20100), http://smallbiztrends.com.

8. Scott A. Yorkovich, Gregory S. Waddell, and Robert K. Gerwig, "Competency-based Assessment Systems: Encouragement Toward a More Holistic Approach," *Proceedings of the Northeast Business & Economics Association* (2007): 77–81; Patty Davis, Jennifer Naughton, and William Rothwell, "New Roles and New Competencies for the Profession: Are You Ready for the Next Generation," *Training and Development* 58, no. 4 (April 2004): 26–38; David Dubois and William Rothwell, "Competency-Based or a Traditional Approach to Training?" *Training and Development* 58, no. 4 (April 2004): 46–59.

9. Gary Kranz, "Special Report: More To Learn," *Workforce Management* (January 2011), http://www.workforce.com/

10. Thomas Hoffman, "Motivation: These IT Leaders Keep Staffers Upbeat during Lean Times by Targeting What Drives Them: Technology and Training," *Computerworld* 38, no. 1 (January 5, 2004): 39; Elwood Holton, Reid Bates, and Sharon Naquin, "Large-Scale Performance-Driven Training Needs Assessment: A Case Study," *Public Personnel Management* 29, no. 2 (Summer 2000): 249–67.

11. Gail Johnson, "The Development Framework: Booz Allen Hamilton's Holistic Method of Employee Development Gives Its Employee a Roadmap to Success—Both Professionally and Personally," *Training* 40, no. 2 (February 2003): 32–34; Robert Mager, "Contract Training Tips," *Security Management* 45, no. 6 (June 2001): 30.

12. Debbie Schachter, "How to Set Performance Goals: Employee Reviews Are More Than Annual Critiques," *Information Outlook* 8, no. 9 (September 2004): 26–30; "Burger Olympics," *Training* 41, no. 7 (July 2004): 20; Jason A. Colquitt and Marcia J. Simmering, "Conscientiousness, Goal Orientation, and Motivation to Learn during the Learning Process: A Longitudinal Study," *Journal of Applied Psychology* 83, no. 4 (August 1998): 654–65.

13. Annette Towler and Robert Dipboye, "Effects of Trainer Expressiveness, Organization, and Trainee Goal Orientation on Training Outcomes," *Journal of Applied Psychology* 86, no. 4 (August 2001): 664–73; Steve Kozlowski, Stanley Gully, Kenneth Brown, and Eduardo Salas, "Effects of Training Goals and Goal Orientation Traits on Multidimensional Training Outcomes and Performance Adaptability," *Organizational Behavior and Human Decision Processes* 85, no. 1 (May 2001): 1–31.

14. The classics by Albert Bandura include *Social Foundations of Thought and Action: A Social Cognitive Theory* (Englewood Cliffs, NJ: Prentice Hall, 1986) and *A Social Learning Theory* (Englewood Cliffs, NJ: Prentice Hall, 1977); See also Melesa Altizer Bolt, Larry Killough, and Hian Chye Koh, "Testing the Interaction Effects of Task Complexity in Computer Training Using the Social Cognitive Model," *Decision Sciences* 32, no. 1 (Winter 2001): 1–20; Susan Pedersen and Min Liu, "The Transfer of Problem-Solving Skills from a Problem-Based Learning Environment: The Effect of Modeling an Expert's Cognitive Processes," *Journal of Research on Technology in Education* 35, no. 2 (Winter 2002): 303–21.

15. Stanley Gully, Stephanie Payn, K. Lee Kiechel Koles, and John-Andrew Whiteman, "The Impact of Error Training and Individual Differences on Training Outcomes: An Attribute-Treatment Interaction Perspective," *Journal of Applied Psychology* 87, no. 1 (February 2002): 143–55; Steven John Simon, "The Relationship of Learning Style and Training Method to End-User Computer Satisfaction and Computer Use: A Structural Equation Model," *Information Technology, Learning, and Performance Journal* 18, no. 1 (Spring 2000): 41–59.

16. Joe M. Ricks, Jacqueline A. Williams, and William A. Weeks, "Sales Trainer Roles, Competencies, Skills, and Behaviors: A Case Study," *Industrial Marketing Management* 37, no. 5 (July 2008): 593–609; John L. Bennett, "Trainers as Leaders of Learning," *Training and Development* 55, no. 3 (March 2001): 42–45; Ruth Palombo Weiss, "Deconstructing Trainers' Self-Image," *Training and Development* 55, no. 12 (December 2001): 34–39.

17. Eduardo Salas and Janis Cannon-Bowers, "The Science of Training: A Decade of Progress," *Annual Review of Psychology* 52 (2001): 471–99.

18. Cohn Terry, "Enabling Staff to Access the Knowledge They Need, When They Need It," *Industrial & Commercial Training* 39, no. 7 (2007): 368–371; Diane Walter, *Training on the Job* (Alexandria, VA: American Society for Training and Development, 2001); Toni Hodges, *Linking Learning and Performance: A Practical Guide to Measuring Learning and On-the-Job Application* (Burlington, MA: Butterworth-Heinemann, 2001); Gary Sisson, *Hands-On Training: A Simple and Effective Method for On-the-Job Training* (San Francisco: Barrett-Koehler, 2001).

19. Teresa M. McAleavy, "U.S. Schools Fail to Provide Job Training," *Knight-Ridder/Tribune Business News* (June 9, 2004); "Eight Steps to Better On-the-Job Training," *HRFocus* 80, no. 7 (July 2003): 11; Alison Booth, Yu-Fu Chen, and Gylfi Zoega, "Hiring and Firing: A Tale of Two Thresholds," *Journal of Labor Economics* 20, no. 2 (April 2002): 217–48.

20. Ronald L. Jacobs and Michael J. Jones, "Teaching Tools: When to Use On-the-Job Training," *Security Management* 41, no. 9 (September 1997): 35–39.

21. Information found on the Apprenticeship page, Spokane Community College website (February 9, 2005), http://www.scc.spokane.edu/tech/apprent.

22. Jack Ewing, "The Apprentice: Germany's Answer to Jobless Youth," *Bloomberg Businessweek* (October 27, 2009) http://www.businessweek.com.

23. "Project Focuses on Placing Women, Minorities into IT," *Certification Magazine* 9, no. 4 (April 2007): 9; "Agilisys Automotive Helps to Build Tomorrow's Leaders through Focus: HOPE Sponsorship at Important Auto Industry Event," *PR Newswire* (August 4, 2003).

24. For more information about the Bureau of Apprenticeship and Training, see the Bureau's website at http://oa.doleta.gov.

25. "Workforce Investment Act: One-Stop Centers Implemented Strategies to Strengthen Services and Partnerships, but More Research and Information Sharing Is Needed," *General Accounting Office Reports & Testimony* 2003, no. 7 (July 2003).

26. Phil Britt, "E-Learning on the Rise in the Classroom: Companies Move Content Online: Cisco Systems' Employees and Partners Routinely Watch Videos on the Internet," *EContent* 27, no. 11 (November 2004): 36–41; Heather Johnson, "The Whole Picture: When It Comes to Finding Out How Employees Feel about Training, Many Companies Fail to Get a Clear Picture," *Training* 47, no. 7 (July 2004): 30–35.

27. Laura Chubb, "EDS Uses Teleconferencing to Train Leaders in Coaching Skills," *People Management* 13, no. 23 (November 15, 2007): 13; "What Does Teleconferencing Cost?" *T+D* 61, no. 10 (October 2007): 96.

28. Ericka Johnson, "Surgical Simulators and Simulated Surgeons: Reconstituting Medical Practice and Practitioners in Simulations," *Social Studies of Science* 37, no. 4 (August 2007): 585–608; "Soup to Nuts: Simulator Manufacturing Is a Lucrative but Risky Business, Which Is Why Market Leader CAE Has Tapped into the More Stable World of Flight Training," *Air Transport World* 40, no. 5 (May 2003): 69–71; "SimsSir: Modeling and Simulation Are Leading the Assault on New Learning Technologies That Are Winning Favor with the U.S. Military," *Training and Development* 57, no. 10 (October 2003): 46–52.

29. Sarah Fister Gale, "Virtual Training with Real Results," *Workforce Management* (December 2008), http://www.workforce.com.

30. "What to Do Now That Training Is Becoming a Major HR Force," *HRFocus* (February 2005): 5–6; Tammy Galvin, "The Delivery," *Training* 38, no. 10 (October 2001): 66–72; Kenneth G. Brown, "Using Computers to Deliver Training: Which Employees Learn and Why?" *Personnel Psychology* 54, no. 2 (Summer 2001): 271–96; Bill Roberts, "E-Learning New Twist on CBT," *HRMagazine* 46, no. 4 (April 2001): 99–106.

31. Scott A. Snell, Donna Stueber, and David P. Lepak, "Virtual HR Departments: Getting Out of the Middle," in R. L. Heneman and D. B. Greenberger (eds.), *Human Resource Management in Virtual Organizations* (Greenwich, CT: Information Age Publishing, 2002).

32. "Learning 2.0: Improving Workforce Productivity," *Workforce Management* (April 2010), http://www.workforce.com.

33. Ibid.

34. Garry Kranz, "E-learning Hits Its Stride," *Workforce Management Online* (February 2008); Martin Delahoussaye, Kristine Ellis, and Matt Bolch, "Measuring Corporate Smarts," *Training* 39, no. 8 (August 2002): 20–35; Daniel Crepin, "From Design to Action: Developing a Corporate Strategy," *Quality Progress* 35, no. 2 (February 2002): 49–56; Brad Miller, "Making Managers More Effective Agents of Change," *Quality Progress* 34, no. 5 (May 2001): 53–57.

35. Yabome Gilpin-Jackson and Gervase R. Bushe, "Leadership Development Training Transfer: A Case Study of Post-Training Determinants," *Journal of Management Development* 26, no. 10 (2007): 980–1004; Joseph Alutto, "Just-in-Time Management Education in the 21st Century," *HRMagazine* 44, no. 11 (1999): 56–57; Gordon Dehler, M. Ann Welsh, and Marianne W. Lewis, "Critical Pedagogy in the 'New Paradigm,'" *Management Learning* 493, no. 4 (December 2001): 493–511.

36. "Caterpillar University College of Leadership," *Leadership Development Strategy: Caterpillar* (2007): 47–51.

37. Chris Whitcomb, "Scenario-Based Training to the F.B.I.," *Training and Development* 53, no. 6 (June 1999): 42–46; Anne Hoag, Dale Brickley, and Joanne Cawley, "Media Management Education and the Case Method," *Journalism and Mass Communication Educator* 55, no. 4 (Winter 2001): 49–59.

38. Aili McConnon, "The Games Managers Play," *BusinessWeek* (June 25, 2007): 12.

39. Ibid.

40. Adam Kirby "Guest Service Is Fun and Games," *Hotels* 42, no. 5 (May 2008): 71–72; Dan Heilman, "Putting Games to Work: Game-Based Training Is Shaping Up to Be One of This Generation's Primary Teaching Tools, in Business and Elsewhere," *Computer User* 22, no. 2 (February 2004): 14–16.

41. Rick Markley, "Virtual Training," *Fire Chief* 52, no. 6 (June 2008): 66–70.

42. Patricia Robinson, "In Practice: Western Companies Show Asian Counterparts That It Pays to Play," *Chief Learning Officer* 6, no. 12 (December 2007): 30; Christopher Hosford, "Serious Fun: Computer Training Finds a Niche," *Meeting News* 28, no. 7 (December 2004): 16; Rick Sullivan, "Lessons in Smallness," *Training and Development* 56, no. 3 (March 2002): 21–23; James W. Walker, "Perspectives," *Human Resource Planning* 23, no. 3 (2000): 5–7.

43. T. L. Stanley, "Be a Good Role Model for Your Employees," *Supervision* 65, no. 5 (January 2004): 5–8; Gary May and William Kahnweiler, "The Effect of a Mastery Practice Design on Learning and Transfer in Behavior Modeling Training," *Personnel Psychology* 53, no. 2 (Summer 2000): 353–73.

44. E. Faith Ivery, "Corporate Tuition Assistance Plans Fund Lifelong Education," *WD Communications*, http://www.back2college.

45. Wendy Larlee, "Training Programs: Key to Collections: Companies in the Collections Business Face Significant Challenges: Putting Solid Training Program in Place Can Help," *Collections & Credit Risk* 9, no. 2 (December 2004): 42–44; Heather Johnson, "The Whole Picture: When It Comes to Finding Out How Employees Feel about Training, Many Companies Fail to Get a Clear Picture," *Training* 47, no. 7 (July 2004): 30–35; Martin Delahoussaye, "Show Me the Results," *Training* 39, no. 3 (March 2002): 28–29; Reinout van Brakel, "Why ROI Isn't Enough," *Training and Development* 56, no. 6 (June 2002): 72–74.

46. "Dissatisfaction with Job Training Contributes to Low Job Satisfaction," *Managing Training & Development* (November 2003): 8; James Pershing and Jana Pershing, "Ineffective Reaction Evaluation," *Human Resource Development Quarterly* 12, no. 1 (Spring 2001): 73–90.

47. Andreas Putra, "Evaluating Training Programs: An Exploratory Study of Transfer of Learning onto the Job at Hotel A and Hotel B, Sydney, Australia," *Journal of Hospitality and Tourism Management* 11, no. 1 (April 2004): 77–78; Thomas Hoffman, "Simulations Revitalize e-Learning," *Computerworld* 37, no. 31 (August 4, 2003): 26–28.

48. Jathan Janove, "Use It or Lose It," *HRMagazine* 47, no. 4 (April 2002): 99–104; Max Montesino, "Strategic Alignment of Training, Transfer-Enhancing Behaviors, and Training Usage: A Posttraining Study," *Human Resource Development Quarterly* 13, no. 1 (Spring 2002): 89–108; Siriporn Yamnill and Gary McLean, "Theories Supporting Transfer of Training," *Human Resource Development Quarterly* 12, no. 2 (Summer 2001): 195–208.

49. Delahoussaye, "Show Me the Results," 28–29; van Brakel, "Why ROI Isn't Enough," 72–74.

50. Richard J. Wagner and Robert J. Weigand, "Can the Value of Training Be Measured? A Simplified Approach to Evaluating Training," *The Health Care Manager* 23, no. 1 (January–March 2004): 71–79; van Brakel, "Why ROI Isn't Enough," 72–74; Sarah Fister Gale, "Measuring the ROI of E-Learning," *Workforce* 81, no. 8 (August 2002): 74–77; Earl Honeycutt, Kiran Karande, Ashraf Attia, and Steven Maurer, "A Utility-Based Framework for Evaluating the Financial Impact of Sales Force Training Programs," *Journal of Personal Selling and Sales Management* 21, no. 3 (Summer 2001): 229–38.

51. "Three Quick and Easy Ways to Gauge Your Training Outcomes," *IOMA's Report on Managing Training & Development* (January 2005): 4–5; "Use This Eight-Step Process to Predict the ROI of Your Training Programs," *IOMA's Human Resource Department Management Report* (December 2004): 4–5; Ellen Drost, Colette Frayne, Keven Lowe, and J. Michael Geringer, "Benchmarking Training and Development Practices: A Multi-Country Comparative Analysis," *Human Resource Management* 41, no. 1 (Spring 2002): 67–86; Daniel McMurrer, Mark Van Buren, and William Woodwell, "Making the Commitment," *Training and Development* 54, no. 1 (January 2000): 41–48.

52. Doug Harward, "Ten Predictions for 2011: Trends that Will Shape the Training Industry," TrainingIndustry.com (December 17, 201), http://www.trainingindustry.com.

53. Jenny Cermak and Monica McGurk, "The Boys & Girls Clubs of America Put a Value on Training," *McKinsey Quarterly*, no. 4 (2010): 111.

54. Mike Frost, "Creative New Employee Orientation Programs," *HRMagazine* 47, no. 8 (August 2002): 120–21; Marilyn Moats Kennedy, "Setting the Right Tone, Right Away," *Across the Board* 36, no. 4 (April 1999): 51–52.

55. Emmanuella Plakoyiannaki, Nikolaos Tzokas, Pavlos Dimitratos, and Michael Saren, "How Critical Is Employee Orientation for Customer Relationship Management? Insights from a Case Study," *Journal of Management Studies* 45, no. 2 (March 2008): 268–293.

56. Kathryn Tyler, "Take New Employee Orientation off the Back Burner," *HRMagazine* 43, no. 6 (May 1998): 49–57; Noel Tichy, "No Ordinary Boot Camp," *Harvard Business Review* 79, no. 4 (April 2001): 63–70.

57. Leigh Buchanan, "How to Make New Hires Feel at Home," *Inc.* (June 8, 2010), http://www.inc.com.

58. Anne C. Lewis, "Necessary Basic Skills," *Tech Directions* 66, no. 4 (November 2006): 6–8; "How to Prepare for Training's Critical Role in the Labor Force of the Future," *IOMA's Report on Managing Training & Development* (September 2004): 2–3; Steve Hook, "Basic Skills Training on Target," *Times Educational Supplement* 4444 (August 31, 2001): 39.

59. "Corporate America Can't Write," *Work & Family Newsbrief* (January 2005): 4; Matt Bolch, "School at Work," *Training* 39, no. 2 (February 2002); Slav Kanyba, "Community Colleges React to Job-Training Request," *San Fernando Valley Business Journal* 9, no. 2 (June 7, 2004): 1–2.

60. Michael A. Verespej, "The Education Difference," *Industry Week* 245, no. 9 (May 6, 1996): 11–14; Richard D. Zalman, "The Basics of In-House Skills Training," *HRMagazine* 34, no. 2 (February 1990): 74–78; Ron Zemke, "Workplace Illiteracy—Shall We Overcome?" *Training* 26, no. 6 (June 1989): 33–39.

61. "Behavior-Based Sales Team Training Produces a 56% Increase in Revenues," *Managing Training & Development* (April 2004): 1.

62. J. K. Winch, X Cai, and G.L. Vairaktarakis, "Cyclic Job Scheduling in Paced Assembly Lines with Cross-Trained Workers," *International Journal of Production Research* 45, no. 4 (February 2, 2007): 803–828; Lisa Bertagnoli, "The Ten-Minute Manager's Guide to …Cross-Training Staff," *Restaurants & Institutions* 114, no. 18 (August 15, 2004): 26–28; Wallace J. Hopp and Mark P. Van Oyen, "Agile Workforce Evaluation: A Framework for Cross-Training and Coordination," *IIE Transactions* 36, no. 10 (October 2004): 919–41.

63. Lorraine Mirabella, "Productivity Gains in Maryland Mean Less Hiring But More Job Cross-Training," *The Baltimore Sun (via

Knight-Ridder/Tribune Business News) (April 17, 2004).

64. Gary Stern, "Small Slights Bring Big Problems," *Workforce* 81, no. 8 (August 2002): 17; Bill Leonard, "Ways to Tell If a Diversity Program Is Measuring Up," *HRMagazine* 47, no. 7 (July 2002): 21.

65. "49ers Decide to Add Diversity to Training Camp," *The New York Times* (July 8, 2004), D3; Irwin Speizer, "Diversity on the Menu: Rachelle Hood, Denny's Chief Diversity Officer, Has Boosted the Company's Image. But That Hasn't Sold More Breakfasts," *Workforce Management* 83, no. 12 (November 1, 2004): 41.

66. Matthew Budman, "What Works—and What Doesn't," *Conference Board Review* 44, no. 4 (July–August 2007): 22–23.

8

Performance Management and the Employee Appraisal Process

After studying this chapter, you should be able to

LEARNING OUTCOME 1 Explain what performance management is and how the establishment of goals, ongoing performance feedback, and the appraisal process are part of it.

LEARNING OUTCOME 2 Explain the purposes of performance appraisals and the reasons they sometimes fail.

LEARNING OUTCOME 3 Describe the different sources of appraisal information.

LEARNING OUTCOME 4 Explain the various methods used to evaluate the performance of employees.

LEARNING OUTCOME 5 Outline the characteristics of an effective performance appraisal interview.

Performance Management Systems

Does your school have a performance management system in place to help students succeed? If so, how do you think the system might be similar or different to performance management systems in the workplace?

performance management

The process of creating a work environment in which people can perform to the best of their abilities

performance appraisal

The result of an annual or biannual process in which a manager evaluates an employee's performance relative to the requirements of his or her job and uses the information to show the person where improvements are needed and why

We have discussed some of the ways managers can acquire and develop top-notch employees, and train and develop them. But how do managers know if their efforts are really paying off in terms of what their employees are contributing once they are on the job?

Performance management is the process of creating a work environment in which people can perform to the best of their abilities in order to meet a company's goals. It is an entire work system that emanates from a company's goals. Figure 8.1 shows the elements of a performance management process.

Performance appraisals, which are an important part of performance management systems, are the result of an annual or biannual process in which a manager evaluates an employee's performance relative to the requirements of his or her job and uses the information to show the person where improvements are needed and why. Appraisals are therefore a tool organizations can use to maintain and enhance their productivity and facilitate progress toward their strategic goals. But as you can see from Figure 8.1, appraisals are just part of the performance management process. Aligning the goals of employees with that of the firm, providing workers with continual on-the-job feedback, and rewarding them are critical as well.

You might compare a performance appraisal to taking a test in college. Do tests motivate you? Do they make you want to truly excel, or do you just want to get through them? Now compare your test-taking experience with an experience in which your instructor talked to you about your career plans, complimented you on your performance, and offered you suggestions for improving it. That probably had a greater motivating effect on you.

We hope you can see the analogy we are making. Employers have to appraise you, just as your university has to test you to be sure you graduate with the qualifications people in society expect. But your performance in either scenario consists of so much more than that. That is why organizations need to look at the performance management system as a whole, rather than just appraisals. Appraisals are simply a logical extension of the day-to-day performance management process.[1]

Ongoing Performance Feedback

Because feedback is most useful when it is immediate and specific to a particular situation, it should be a regularly occurring activity. For example, if you are a sales manager, should you wait to appraise your employees once or twice a year? Probably not. Most likely you would want to monitor their sales on a weekly and monthly basis. Has a particular salesperson met his or her customer-contact numbers this week? Why or why not? Is the salesperson closing deals with the people he or she does contact? If at the six-month mark, the salesperson isn't making his or her goals, how can you help the person if you haven't provided the individual with ongoing feedback? The lack of sales will be hard to make up at this point.

It's not just salespeople who need continual feedback. All types of employees can benefit from ongoing performance conversations with their managers. Managers need to constantly engage in a dialogue with their subordinates. Once the manager and employees have a series of discussions, there is an ebb and flow of ideas, some with the potential to serve as catalysts for improvement within the company.[2] The ultimate purpose is to better both parties.

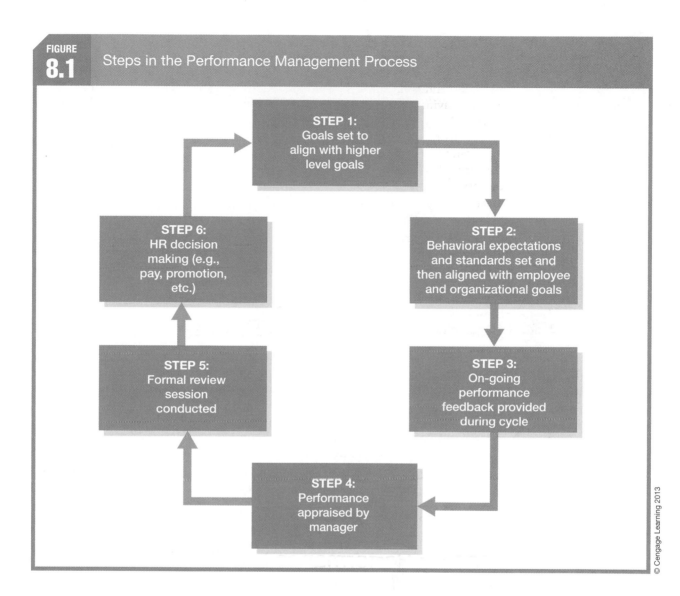

FIGURE 8.1 Steps in the Performance Management Process

STEP 1: Goals set to align with higher level goals

STEP 2: Behavioral expectations and standards set and then aligned with employee and organizational goals

STEP 3: On-going performance feedback provided during cycle

STEP 4: Performance appraised by manager

STEP 5: Formal review session conducted

STEP 6: HR decision making (e.g., pay, promotion, etc.)

© Cengage Learning 2013

The University of Indiana's "University HR Services" function provides training and development in the area of employee feedback for its managers and leaders. In that training, the university identifies eight key points to address during feedback sessions:

- Give specific examples of desirable and undesirable behaviors. Without specific examples of real life situations, the employee will only be confused by the vagueness of the feedback.

- Focused feedback on behavior, not the person. This will help the employee to "hear" the message and will defuse what could be a confrontational conversation.

- Frame the feedback in turns of helping the employee be successful. Let the employee know that you are trying to help him or her be a successful employee within the organization.

- Direct the feedback towards behavior the employee can control. Employees cannot do much about things over which they have no control.

- The feedback should be timely. When an event takes place, it is important to provide feedback within a reasonable amount of time.

- Limit feedback to the amount the employee can process. Most employees are able to handle feedback on one or two issues at a time.

- Use active communication skills and confirm the employee is engaged in the conversation.

Providing employees with feedback on a continual basis also helps them know where they stand when they receive their formal appraisals. As a result, the anxiety they experience during formal appraisals is often alleviated, and a more meaningful conversation with them and their supervisors can take place. If employees are surprised by their reviews, it is probably safe to say that their supervisors have not been providing them much ongoing feedback.

Performance Appraisal Programs

LEARNING OUTCOME 2

Have ever been given a formal performance appraisal? If you have not, what do you think your employer's rationale was for not appraising you or other employees?

focal performance appraisal

An appraisal system in which all of an organization's employees are reviewed at the same time of year rather than on the anniversaries of their individual hire dates

The federal government began evaluating employees in 1842, when Congress passed a law mandating yearly performance reviews for department clerks. From this early beginning, performance appraisal programs have spread to large and small organizations in both the public and private sectors. Typically the appraisals are delivered annually, biannually, or sometimes quarterly by a supervisor to a subordinate. New employees are often put on probationary status for a period of time and evaluated thirty, sixty, or ninety days after being hired, with their continued employment contingent upon their performing satisfactorily. In many organizations, performance appraisals are conducted only once a year. However, an increasing number of organizations are finding value in conducting them on a semiannual and even quarterly basis.

A focal performance appraisal is one in which all employees of a company are reviewed at the same time of year rather than on the anniversary dates they were hired. This appraisal strategy can be very helpful if a company is experiencing change and must quickly alter its strategy. After the new strategic goals of the firm are established, they can then be translated into individual goals employees receive all at the same time. That way, all employees can begin working toward those goals immediately. A focal performance appraisal also enables managers to compare the performance of different employees simultaneously, which can result in appraisals that are more accurate and fair. The review of an employee is also less likely to be overlooked if all of an organization's managers review employees at the same time.

The Purposes of Performance Appraisal

It has been said that "what gets measured gets done." Performance appraisals are part of an organization's measurement process. Good appraisal systems have the capability to influence employee behavior and improve an organization's performance. One study showed that organizations with strong performance management systems are 40 to 50 percent more likely to outperform their competitors in the areas of revenue growth, productivity, profitability, and market value.[3] This is why experts advise companies to continue to appraise their employees during an economic downturn, even if they cannot afford to give them raises.

Formal appraisal processes also ensure employees get at least *some* feedback from their supervisors. A recent poll by the research company Gallup found that employees who receive no feedback from their supervisors exhibit the least amount of engagement. Jim Harter, a Gallup research scientist and coauthor of the report, says even negative feedback is better than none. Negative feedback, he says, "at least lets people know that they matter."[4]

In addition to improving a firm's overall performance and profitability, Figure 8.2 shows the other two most common purposes of performance appraisals, which are *administrative* and *developmental*.

Administrative Purposes

Appraisal programs provide input that can be used for the entire range of HRM activities, such as promotions, transfers, layoffs, and pay decisions. The practice of "pay-for-performance"—basing employees' pay on their achievements—is found in all types of organizations. Studies have shown employees who earn performance-based pay are more satisfied.[5] Performance appraisal data can also be used for HR planning, to determine the relative worth of jobs, and as criteria for recruiting particular types of employees and validating selection tests. Yet another purpose of conducting performance appraisals is to document HRM actions that can result in legal action. Because of the government's equal employment opportunity and affirmative action directives, employers need to maintain accurate, objective employee performance records in order to defend themselves against possible charges of discrimination when it comes to promotions, salaries, and terminations. Finally, it is important to recognize that the success of the entire HR program depends on knowing how the performance of employees compares with the goals established for them. This knowledge is best derived from a carefully planned and administered HR appraisal program.

FIGURE 8.2	Purposes of a Performance Appraisal

DEVELOPMENTAL	ADMINISTRATIVE
• Provide performance feedback • Identify individual strengths and weaknesses • Recognize individual performance achievements • Help employees identify goals • Evaluate goal achievement of employees • Identify individual training needs • Determine organizational training needs • Reinforce authority structure • Allow employees to discuss concerns • Improve communication • Provide a forum for leaders to help employees	• Document personnel decisions • Promote employees • Determine transfers and assignments • Identify performance problems and develop ways to correct them • Make retention, termination, and layoff decisions • Validate selection criteria • Meet legal requirements • Evaluate training programs/progress • Assist with human resources planning • Make reward and compensation decisions

Developmental Purposes

From the standpoint of individual development, appraisal provides the feedback essential for discussing an employee's goals and how they align with the organization's. As with ongoing feedback, the appraisal process provides managers and employees the opportunity to discuss ways to build on their strengths, eliminate potential weaknesses, identify problems, and set new goals for achieving high performance. Performance appraisals are also used to develop training and development plans for employees. By taking a developmental approach to appraisals, managers help employees understand that the appraisals are being conducted to improve their future competencies and further their careers and are not being conducted simply to judge them based on their past performance.

Companies such as Best Buy and EDS, a business unit of Hewlett-Packard, redesigned their performance appraisal systems to focus more on employee development and learning. EDS, for example, integrated its performance appraisal system to work in concert with the company's learning and career management objectives. The new system, called the Career Resource System, includes a detailed job description, performance review, and career planner to track employees' long-term goals, as well as access to the company's automated career library. The system is ultimately linked to the company's succession policies. By creating this overall system, EDS hopes to shift the role of manager from that of "judge" to one of "coach."[6]

Why Appraisal Programs Sometimes Fail

Performance appraisals often fall short of their potential. In an ongoing survey of employee attitudes by the HR consulting firm Watson Wyatt, only 30 percent of employees said they thought their company's performance management process actually improved employee performance; only one in five thought it helped poorly performing employees do better.[7] Some people believe performance appraisals discourage teamwork because it frequently focuses on the individual achievements of workers versus what their teams or firms accomplish. (Who gets the best rating and the biggest raise? Who does not?) Others contend that appraisals are useful only at the extremes—for highly effective or highly ineffective employees—and are not as useful for the majority of employees in the middle. Still others point out that appraisals often focus on short-term achievements rather than long-term improvement and learning. For reasons such as these, organizations such as SAS, Del Taco, and others do not perform formal evaluations and use coaching, individual development plans, or other feedback systems instead. Other organizations, including Xerox, Motorola, and Procter & Gamble, have modified their performance appraisals to try to improve them.[8]

Figure 8.3 shows the primary reasons why the performance appraisal process often ends up being less effective than it could be. Many managers are as nervous about administering appraisals as employees are about receiving them. Oftentimes they just want them to be over. When this happens managers do not engage employees in much of a conversation during the appraisals, which is a major drawback. Even when appraising an outstanding employee, managers often are reluctant to evaluate an employee's performance. Sometimes it is as simple as the manager lacks the skills to execute an effective performance review session; sometimes there is never enough money to recognize even the top performer. So reviews are postponed or handled poorly, and the result is that the organization's best performers are left frustrated, angry, disillusioned, and demotivated. In addition, those top performers are looking at the organization's competitor.

FIGURE

8.3   Let Me Count the Ways . . .

There are many reasons why performance appraisal systems might not be effective. Some of the most common problems include the following:

- Inadequate preparation on the part of the manager.
- Employee is not given clear objectives at the beginning of performance period.
- Manager may not be able to observe performance or have all the information.
- Performance standards may not be clear.
- Inconsistency in ratings among supervisors or other raters.
- Manager rating personality rather than performance.
- The halo effect, contrast effect, or some other perceptual bias.
- Inappropriate time span for evaluation (either too short or too long).
- Overemphasis on uncharacteristic performance.
- Inflated ratings because managers do not want to deal with "bad news."
- Subjective or vague language in written appraisals.
- Organizational politics or personal relationships cloud judgments.
- No thorough discussion of causes of performance problems.
- Manager may not be trained at evaluation or giving feedback.
- No follow up and coaching after the evaluation.

Sources: Patricia Evres, "Problems to Avoid during Performance Evaluations," *Air Conditioning, Heating & Refrigeration News* 216, no. 16 (August 19, 2002): 24–26; Clinton Longnecker and Dennis Gioia, "The Politics of Executive Appraisals," *Journal of Compensation and Benefits* 10, no. 2 (1994): 5–11; "Seven Deadly Sins of Performance Appraisals," *Supervisory Management* 39, no. 1 (1994): 7–8.

Employee performance avoidance often starts on day one of the new job. Rather than clearly outline the expectations, many managers show the new employees to their workstations and dump them off, leaving the new hires to their own means. Job assignments may be delivered and retrieved on a routine basis with little or no feedback or comments from the manager.

Unclear performance standards, biased ratings because managers lack training, too many time-consuming forms to complete, and use of the program for conflicting purposes can also hamper the effectiveness of performance appraisals. For example, if an appraisal program is used to determine an employee's future pay and at the same time to motivate the person to perform better, the two purposes can end up conflicting with one another. Often when salary decisions are discussed during a performance appraisal, they tend to become the dominant topic of conversation, and managers spend a lot of time justifying their pay decisions. As a result, ways to improve the employee's future job performance get less discussion.

One of the main concerns employees have about appraisals relates to the fairness of the performance appraisal systems of their firms. Organizational politics, a firm's culture, the orientation of its managers, history, and current competitive conditions can all affect how managers conduct and rate their employees.[9] For example, managers sometimes inflate evaluations because they want to obtain higher salaries for their employees or because higher ratings for their subordinates make them look good as supervisors. Alternatively, managers might want to get rid of troublesome employees by inflating their ratings and passing them off to another department. Even when appraisals are supposed to be confidential, employees often have a keen sense about whether the process is fair or not, or at least they think they do. Employees who believe the system is unfair are likely to consider the appraisal interview a waste of time and leave the interview feeling frustrated and cynical. Also, they may view compliance with the appraisal system as perfunctory and thus play only a passive role during the interview process. By addressing these employee concerns during the planning stage of the appraisal process and reassuring them that they can meet the requirements and will be rewarded accordingly, an appraisal program is more likely to be successful.[10]

Small Business Application

Does a Small Business Formally Appraise Its Employees?

So now you have your own business. That means you can dispense with those pesky, time-consuming performance reviews everyone dreads, right? You never liked them as an employee. In fact, maybe they helped solidify your desire to work for yourself. Why would you like them any more as a manager, entrepreneur, or small business owner?

Do not be so fast to dump performance appraisals. Without them, you might end up "flying blind" when it comes to some important performance metrics. "In a small business in particular, the performance review is like a dashboard—it gives you all kinds of gauges about quality, job knowledge, customer service," says Robert Chanin, the director of human resources for The Alcott Group, a PEO that provides HR and other services. "If there isn't any gauge, you don't know if your business is doing well or not."

By contrast, put a good performance appraisal system in place and the sky is the limit, says Barrie Gross, a human resources expert and employment law attorney. "They're one of the tools businesses can use to get employees more involved, increase their motivation, and help them achieve success," Gross explains. Evaluating your employees also lets them know they are not just human cogs in the production process—that you care about them, their involvement in the firm, and their personal goals. This can help a small business retain its top employees rather than losing them to big companies where they are often treated more impersonally. The feedback can be verbal, if the reviews are for development purposes only. However, if the evaluations are used in conjunction with raises and promotions, they should be written. Legal experts counsel employers to maintain written records in order to provide themselves with greater legal protections.

Small businesses with few employees or that are just launching their performance appraisal systems can utilize off-the-shelf appraisal systems consisting of either printed forms or software. Popular software brands include Success-Factors' Performance Management system, Appraisal Smart, and Halogen's eAppraisal product, the latter two of which are web-based. Generally, a manager can customize appraisal forms in software packages by selecting elements from a list of attributes and behaviors that describe on-the-job success for a position.

Keep in mind that performance reviews are not about the forms, though. They are a two-way discussion designed to benefit both parties. In addition to your employees learning about how they can improve their performance, the appraisals can help you learn how to improve yours as well.

Sources: Amy Linn, "Boost Performance with Performance Reviews," *Small Business Review*, http://smallbusinessreview.com; David Javitch, "How to Survive Employee Appraisals," *Entreprenur.com*, http://www.entrepreneur.com.

As with all HR practices, if the support of a firm's top managers is lacking, the appraisal program will not be successful. Even the best-conceived program will not work in an environment where appraisers are not encouraged by their superiors to take the program seriously. To underscore the importance of this responsibility, top management should make the effectiveness of appraising and developing subordinates a standard by which the appraisers themselves will be evaluated.

Developing an Effective Appraisal Program

The HR department ordinarily has the primary responsibility for overseeing and coordinating a firm's appraisal program. However, managers from the company's operating departments must also be actively involved, particularly when it comes to helping establish the objectives for the program. Furthermore, employees are more likely to accept and be satisfied with the performance appraisal program when they have the chance to participate in its development. Their concerns about the fairness and accuracy of the program insofar as it determines their raises, promotions, and the like tend to be alleviated somewhat when they have been involved at the planning stage and have helped develop the performance standards themselves. It also helps ensure that the appraisal takes into account all of the tasks that need to be done in an organization, especially when major changes in the firm and its jobs are taking place.[11]

What Are the Performance Standards?

Before any appraisal is conducted, the standards by which performance is to be evaluated should be clearly defined and communicated to the employee. As we discussed in Chapter 4, these standards should be based on job-related requirements derived from a job analysis and reflected in an employee's job description and job specifications. When performance standards are properly established, they help translate an organization's goals and objectives into job requirements that communicate to employees the definitions of acceptable and unacceptable performance levels.

As shown in Figure 8.4, there are four basic elements that must be considered when establishing performance standards: strategic relevance, criterion deficiency, criterion contamination, and reliability.

Strategic Relevance

Strategic relevance refers to the extent to which the standards of an appraisal relate to the strategic objectives of the organization in which they are applied. For example, if an organization has established a standard that "95 percent of all customer complaints are to be resolved in one day," then it is relevant for the customer service representatives to be held to this standard when they are evaluated. Companies such as 3M and Buckman Laboratories have strategic objectives to the effect that a certain percent of their sales are to be generated from products developed within the past five years. These objectives are then translated into performance standards for their employees. General Motors and Whirlpool's strategic objectives include cost, quality, and speed, and the two companies have developed metrics to identify and compare their performance around the world on these measures. A strategy-driven performance appraisal process also provides the documentation HR managers need to justify various training expenses in order to close any gaps between employees' current skills and those they will need in the future to execute the firm's strategy. Moreover, because

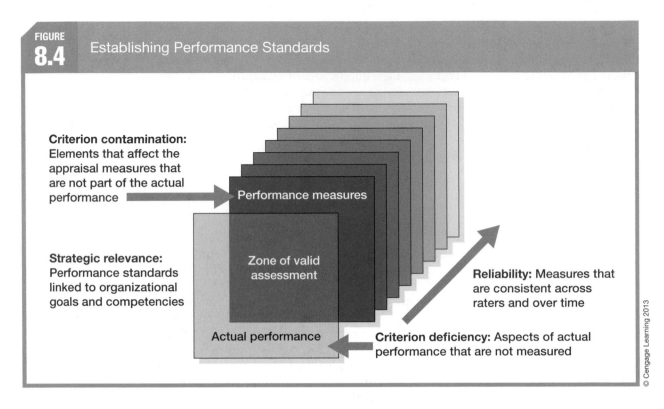

FIGURE 8.4   Establishing Performance Standards

Criterion contamination: Elements that affect the appraisal measures that are not part of the actual performance

Performance measures

Strategic relevance: Performance standards linked to organizational goals and competencies

Zone of valid assessment

Reliability: Measures that are consistent across raters and over time

Actual performance

Criterion deficiency: Aspects of actual performance that are not measured

© Cengage Learning 2013

they provide evidence of a person's performance, appraisal metrics based on a firm's strategy are more defensible in court.[12]

Criterion Deficiency

A second consideration in establishing performance standards is the extent to which the standards capture the entire range of an employee's responsibilities. When performance standards focus on a single criterion (such as sales revenues) to the exclusion of other important but less quantifiable performance dimensions (such as customer service), then the appraisal system is said to suffer from criterion deficiency.[13]

Criterion Contamination

Just as performance criteria can be deficient, they can also be contaminated. There are factors outside an employee's control that can influence his or her performance. A comparison of performance of production workers, for example, should not be contaminated by the fact that some work with newer machines than others do. A comparison of the performance of traveling salespeople should not be contaminated by the fact that territories differ in terms of their sales potential.[14]

Reliability

As we discussed in Chapter 6, reliability refers to the stability or consistency of a standard, or the extent to which individuals tend to maintain a certain level of performance over time. In terms of appraisal ratings, reliability can be measured by correlating two sets of ratings made by a single rater or by two different raters. For example, two managers would rate the same individual and estimate his or her suitability for a promotion. Their ratings would then be compared to determine inter-rater reliability.

To make sure managers are rating employees consistently, some companies use a process called calibration. During calibration meetings, a group of supervisors, led by their managers and facilitated by an HR professional, discuss the performance of individual employees to ensure all managers apply similar standards to all of the firm's employees. The supervisors begin the process by rating employees whose performances are especially good or especially poor. They then attempt to rate employees who lie more in the middle and try to achieve a consensus on their performance. Initially, the ratings are likely to vary considerably simply because some managers are hard raters and others are not. Over subsequent evaluation periods and calibration meetings, however, the ratings should begin to converge, or become more similar. Calibration meetings can be particularly helpful after a merger or acquisition— especially one that is global. Why? Because differences in the corporate cultures and the appraisal standards of the formerly separate companies can cause the same employees to be rated quite differently. For example, when Lawson Software, a Minnesota-headquartered firm, grew from 1,400 employees in three countries to 4,000 employees in thirty countries, it successfully used calibration to be sure its managers across the globe were assessing employees accurately.[15]

Performance standards also permit managers to specify and communicate precise information to employees regarding quality and quantity of output. This is why the standards should be defined in quantifiable and measurable terms and written down. For example, "the ability and willingness to handle customer orders" is not as good a performance standard as "all customer orders will be filled in four hours with a 98 percent accuracy rate." When the standard is expressed in specific, measurable terms, comparing an employee's performance against the standard results in a more accurate and justifiable appraisal.

calibration

A process whereby managers meet to discuss the performance of individual employees to ensure their employee appraisals are in line with one another

Are You Complying with the Law?

Because performance appraisals are used as one basis for HRM actions, they must meet certain legal requirements. In *Brito v. Zia*, for example, the Supreme Court ruled that performance appraisals were subject to the same validity criteria as selection procedures.[16] As the courts have made clear, a central issue is to have carefully defined and measurable performance standards. In one landmark case involving test validation, *Albemarle Paper Company v. Moody* (discussed in Chapter 3), the U.S. Supreme Court found that employees had been ranked against a vague standard, open to each supervisor's own interpretation. The Court stated that "there is no way of knowing precisely what criteria of job performance the supervisors were considering, whether each supervisor was considering the same criteria, or whether, indeed, any of the supervisors actually applied a focused and stable body of criteria of any kind."[17] This decision has prompted organizations to try to eliminate vagueness in descriptions of traits such as attitude, cooperation, dependability, initiative, and leadership. For example, the trait "dependability" can be made much less vague if it is spelled out in terms of employee tardiness and/or unexcused absences. In general, reducing the room for subjective judgments will improve the entire appraisal process.

Furthermore, other court decisions show that employers might face legal challenges to their appraisal systems when appraisals indicate an employee's performance is acceptable or above average, but then the person is later passed over for promotion, disciplined for poor performance, discharged, or laid off from the organization. In these cases, the performance appraisals can undermine the legitimacy of the subsequent personnel decision. Intel, for example, was taken to court by a group of former employees on grounds that the performance appraisal system (used for layoff decisions) was unreliable and invalid. Other companies such as Goodyear and Ford have also faced legal battles because their performance appraisals were viewed as discriminatory against older workers.[18] In light of court cases such as these, performance appraisals should meet the following legal guidelines:

- Performance ratings must be job-related, with performance standards developed through a job analysis. Only evaluate those areas that are necessary for effective job performance.

- Employees must be provided with clear, written job standards in advance of their appraisals so they understand what they need to do to get top ratings.

- Managers who conduct the appraisals must be able to observe the behavior they are rating. This implies having measurable standards with which to compare employee behavior.

- Do not allow performance problems to continue unchecked. Document problems when they occur and refer to them in employeesí appraisals.

- Supervisors should be trained to use the appraisal form correctly. They should be instructed as to how to apply the appraisal standards when making judgments.

- The appraisals should be discussed openly with employees and counseling or corrective guidance offered to help poor performers improve their performance. Be open to the possibility that employees could be transferred to other positions that better suit their abilities.

- An appeals procedure should be established to enable employees to express their disagreement with the appraisals.[19]

To comply with the legal requirements of performance appraisals, employers must ensure that managers and supervisors document appraisals and reasons for subsequent HRM actions. This information may prove decisive should an employee take legal action. An employer's credibility is strengthened when it can support performance appraisal ratings by documenting instances of poor performance. In addition, HR professionals should review the appraisal comments made by supervisors for comments that could indicate the firm is not complying with the law. Consider the following comments: "Ted was absent for several weeks in 2011, which adversely affected operations." If some of Ted's absences were taken in conjunction with the Family Medical Leave Act, the comment could be used in court to show Ted was deprived of his right to take

Specific, measurable job standards help remove vagueness and subjectivity from performance appraisals.

© Bill Varie/CorbisSyndicate

leave under the act without being retaliated against.[20] Having appraisals reviewed by a supervisor's superior can also reduce the chance of biased evaluations and evaluations that could be legally problematic.

Who Should Appraise an Employee's Performance?

Just as there are multiple standards by which to evaluate performance, there are also multiple candidates for appraising performance. Given the complexity of today's jobs, it is often unrealistic to presume that one person can fully observe and evaluate an employee's performance. At IBM, employees with high potential are regularly reviewed by a broad cross-section of the company's leaders, not just their immediate bosses. As shown in Figure 8.5, the raters can include supervisors, peers, team members, themselves, subordinates, customers, vendors, and suppliers. Each may be more or less useful for the administrative and developmental purposes we discussed earlier. Companies such as Cigna, Morgan Stanley, and Disney are among the many organizations that have used a multiple-rater approach—or 360-degree appraisal— to evaluate employee performance.[21] We will talk more about 360-degree appraisal at the end of this section.

Manager/Supervisor Appraisal

Manager and/or supervisor appraisal has been the traditional approach to evaluating an employee's performance. In most instances, supervisors are in the best position to perform this function, although it may not always be possible for them to do so. Managers with many subordinates often complain that they do not have the time to fully observe the performance of each of them. These managers must then rely on performance records to evaluate an employee's performance. If reliable and valid measures

LEARNING OUTCOME 3

Do you think as an employee you would be in a good position to appraise your boss? What aspects of his or her performance might you be in a good position to appraise?

manager and/or supervisor appraisal
A performance appraisal done by an employee's manager and often reviewed by a manager one level higher

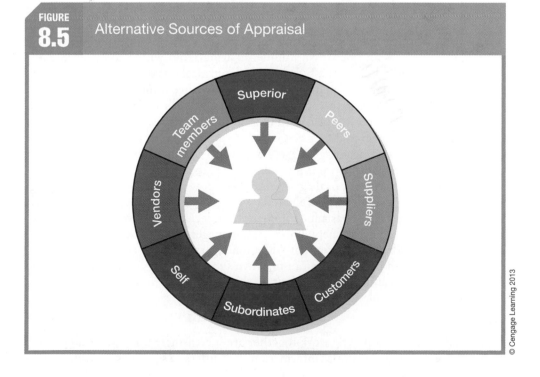

FIGURE 8.5 Alternative Sources of Appraisal

© Cengage Learning 2013

are not available, the appraisal is likely to be less than accurate. (Recall our earlier discussion of criterion deficiency and criterion contamination.) In addition, research has shown that the ratings managers give employees they have known for less than one year are less reliable, which can be a drawback when an organization uses focal performance appraisals.[22]

Self-Appraisal

self-appraisal

A performance appraisal done by the employee being evaluated, generally on an appraisal form completed by the employee prior to the performance interview

Sometimes employees are asked to evaluate themselves on a self-appraisal form. The self-appraisal is beneficial when managers seek to increase an employee's involvement in the review process. A self-appraisal system requires an employee to complete the appraisal form prior to the performance interview. At a minimum, this gets the employee thinking about his or her strengths and weaknesses and may lead to discussions about barriers to effective performance. During the performance appraisal, the manager and the employee discuss the employee's job performance and agree on a final appraisal. This approach also works well when the manager and the employee jointly establish future performance goals or employee development plans.

Critics of self-appraisal argue that self-raters are more lenient than managers in their assessments and tend to present themselves in a highly favorable light. There is also evidence that self-appraisals can lead employees to believe that they will have more influence over the appraisal's outcome. If that expectation is not met, the employee can become frustrated. For this reason, self-appraisals are often best used for developmental purposes rather than for administrative decisions. However, used in conjunction with other methods, self-appraisals can be a valuable source of appraisal information. They at least serve as a catalyst for discussion during the appraisal.[23]

Subordinate Appraisal

subordinate appraisal

A performance appraisal of a superior by an employee, which is more appropriate for developmental than for administrative purposes

Subordinate appraisals have been used by both large and small organizations to give managers feedback on how their subordinates view them.[19] Subordinates are in a good position to evaluate their managers because they are in frequent contact with their superiors and occupy a unique position from which to observe many performance-related behaviors. Subordinate appraisals have also been shown to improve the performance of managers. The performance dimensions judged most appropriate for subordinates to appraise include a manager's leadership, oral communication, delegation of authority, coordination of team efforts, and interest in his or her subordinates. However, dimensions related to managers' specific job tasks, such as planning and organizing, budgeting, creativity, and analytical ability, are not usually considered appropriate dimensions for subordinates to appraise.

Because subordinate appraisals give employees power over their bosses, managers are sometimes hesitant to be evaluated by the people they supervise, particularly when it might be used as a basis for compensation decisions. However, when the information is used for developmental purposes, managers tend to be more open to the idea. Available evidence suggests that when managers heed the advice of their subordinates, their own performance can improve substantially. Nevertheless, to avoid potential problems, subordinate appraisals should be submitted anonymously and combined across several individual raters.[24]

Peer Appraisal

peer appraisal

A performance appraisal done by one's fellow employees, generally on forms that are compiled into a single profile for use in the performance interview conducted by the employee's manager

Individuals of equal rank who work together are increasingly asked to evaluate each other. A peer appraisal provides information that differs to some degree from ratings by a superior, since an employee's peers often see different dimensions of his or her performance. Peers can readily identify leadership and interpersonal skills along with other strengths and weaknesses of their coworkers. For example, a superior asked to rate a patrol officer on a dimension such as "dealing with the public" might not have had much opportunity to observe it. Fellow officers, on the other hand, likely would have.

One advantage of peer appraisals is the belief that they furnish more accurate and valid information than appraisals by superiors. The supervisor often sees employees putting their best foot forward, while those who work with their fellow employees on a regular basis may see a more realistic picture. With peer appraisals, coworkers complete an evaluation on the employee. The forms are then usually compiled into a single profile, which is given to the supervisor for use in the final appraisal. For employees who have trouble confronting their coworkers about problems, the reviews provide a forum in which to address issues and resolve conflicts. They also provide an opportunity to hand out praise.[25] Despite the evidence that peer appraisals are possibly the most accurate method of judging employee behavior, they often are not solicited.[26] Managers are sometimes reluctant to give up control of the process or worry that the ratings are simply a popularity contest.

Peer appraisals alone should not be used to make administrative decisions related to salaries, bonuses, promotions, and other major decisions about an employee. Employers using peer appraisals must also be sure to safeguard confidentiality in handling the review forms. Any breach of confidentiality can create interpersonal rivalries or hurt feelings and foster hostility among fellow employees.

team appraisal

A performance appraisal, based on TQM concepts, that recognizes team accomplishment rather than individual performance

Team Appraisal

An extension of the peer appraisal is the team appraisal. In a team setting, it may be nearly impossible to separate out an individual's contribution. Advocates of team appraisals argue that, when this is the case, individual appraisals can be dysfunctional and distract a team from focusing on critical issues. To address this issue, organizations ranging from Boeing and Texas Instruments to Jostens and Ralston Foods have used team appraisals to evaluate the performance of their teams as a whole.[27] These companies believe that team appraisals can help break down barriers between individual employees and encourage a joint effort on their part.

Much of the interest in team appraisals grew out of company commitments to total quality management (TQM) in the 1980s. But the principles and practices are no less relevant today. At its root, TQM is a control system that involves setting standards (based on customer requirements), measuring a firm's performance against those standards,

Some managers give their teams autonomy but hold them accountable for results.

© The Image Bank/Getty Images

and identifying opportunities for continuous improvement. In this regard, TQM and performance appraisals complement one another. However, a basic tenet of TQM is that a firm's performance is best understood at the level of the system as a whole, whereas performance appraisals traditionally focus on individual performance.[28] Frequently, the system is complemented by the use of team incentives or group variable pay. (See Chapters 10 and 16.)

Customer Appraisal

customer appraisal

A performance appraisal that, like team appraisal, is based on TQM concepts and includes evaluation from both a firm's external and internal customers

Also driven by TQM concerns, an increasing number of organizations use internal and external customer appraisals as a source of performance appraisal information. External customers' evaluations, of course, have been used for some time to appraise restaurant personnel. However, companies such as Federal Express, Best Buy, and Isuzu are among the companies that have utilized external customers as well. Poor customer appraisals undoubtedly explain why some firms, including Dell and others, have reconsidered offshoring their customer service functions. Other companies survey their vendors and suppliers as part of the appraisal process. By including the firm's business partners in the performance reviews, managers hope to produce more objective evaluations, more effective employees, more satisfied customers, and better business performance.[29]

In contrast to external customers, internal customers include anyone inside the organization who depends on an employee's work output. For example, managers who rely on the HR department for selection and training services would be candidates for conducting internal customer evaluations of that department. For both developmental and administrative purposes, internal customers can provide extremely useful feedback about the value added by an employee or team of employees.

Putting It All Together: 360-Degree Appraisal

As mentioned previously, companies such as Intel and Morgan Stanley combine various sources of performance appraisal information to create multirater—or 360-degree—appraisal and feedback systems. Jobs are multifaceted, and different people see different things. As the name implies, 360-degree feedback is intended to provide employees with as accurate a view of their performance as possible by getting input from all angles: supervisors, peers, subordinates, customers, and the like. Although in the beginning, 360-degree systems were purely developmental and were restricted mainly to management and career development, they have migrated to performance appraisal and other administrative applications.

Because the system combines more information than a typical performance appraisal, it can become administratively complex. For that reason, organizations have recently begun using performance management software to compile and aggregate the information.[30] For example, Workstream 7.0, developed by Workstream, Inc., a Florida company, gives managers a single view of all their talent management information: performance reviews, 360-degree assessments, compensation planning, development data, and succession planning, all unified in one application.[31] Figure 8.6 shows a list of pros and cons of 360-degree appraisal. When Intel established a 360-degree system, the company observed the following safeguards to ensure its maximum quality and acceptance:

FIGURE 8.6 Pros and Cons of 360-Degree Appraisal

PROS

- The system is more comprehensive in that responses are gathered from multiple perspectives.
- Quality of information is better. (Quality of respondents is more important than quantity.)
- It complements TQM initiatives by emphasizing internal/external customers and teams.
- It may lessen bias/prejudice since feedback comes from more people, not one individual.
- Feedback from peers and others may increase employee self-development.

CONS

- The system is complex in combining all the responses.
- Feedback can be intimidating and cause resentment if employee feels the respondents have "ganged up."
- There may be conflicting opinions, though they may all be accurate from the respective standpoints.
- The system requires training to work effectively.
- Employees may collude or "game" the system by giving invalid evaluations to one another.
- Appraisers may not be accountable if their evaluations are anonymous.

Sources: Compiled from David A. Waldman, Leanne E. Atwater, and David Antonioni, "Has 360-Degree Feedback Gone Amok?" *Academy of Management Executive* 12, no. 2 (May 1998): 86–94; Bruce Pfau, Ira Kay, Kenneth Nowak, and Jai Ghorpade, "Does 360-Degree Feedback Negatively Affect Company Performance?" *HRMagazine* 47, no. 6 (June 2002): 54–59; Maury Peiperl, "Getting 360-Degree Feedback Right," *Harvard Business Review* 79, no. 1 (January 2001): 142–47; Joyce E. Bono and Amy E. Colbert, "Understanding Responses to Multi-Source Feedback: The Role of Core Self-Evaluations," *Personnel Psychology* 58, no. 1 (Spring 2005): 171–205.

- *Assure anonymity.* Make certain that no employee ever knows how any evaluation team member responded. (The supervisor's rating is an exception to this rule.)

- *Make respondents accountable.* Supervisors should discuss each evaluation team member's input, letting each member know whether he or she used the rating scales appropriately, whether his or her responses were reliable, and how other participants rated the employee.

- *Prevent "gaming" of the system.* Some individuals may try to help or hurt an employee by giving either too high or too low an evaluation. Team members may try to collude with one another by agreeing to give each other uniformly high ratings. Supervisors should check for obviously invalid responses.

- *Use statistical procedures.* Use weighted averages or other quantitative approaches to combine evaluations. Supervisors should be careful about using subjective combinations of data, which could undermine the system.

- *Identify and quantify biases.* Check for prejudices or preferences related to age, gender, ethnicity, or other group factors.[32]

Training Appraisers

A weakness of many performance appraisal programs is that managers and supervisors are not adequately trained for the appraisal task, and so the feedback they provide their subordinates is not as useful as it might be and can often be meaningless, if not destructive. This is perhaps one reason why some experts believe firms should no longer conduct performance appraisals of their employees. However, training appraisers can vastly improve the performance appraisal process. According to one HR manager: "What's not important is the (appraisal) form or the (measuring) scale. What's important is that managers can objectively observe people's performance and objectively give feedback on that performance." Nonetheless, in a survey of fifty-five HR managers from medium and large companies, more than half said their companies did either little or no evaluation of how well their managers do appraisals.[33]

Establishing an Appraisal Plan

A training program for raters is most effective when it follows a systematic process that begins with an explanation of the objectives of the firm's performance appraisal system. It is also important for the rater to know the purpose for which the appraisal is to be used. For example, using the appraisal for compensation decisions rather than development purposes can affect how the rater evaluates the employee, and it may change the rater's opinion of how the appraisal form should be completed. The mechanics of the rating system should also be explained, including how frequently the appraisals are to be conducted, who will conduct them, and what the standards of performance are. In addition, appraisal training should alert raters to the weaknesses and problems of appraisal systems so that they can be avoided.

Performance appraisal programs are most effective when managers have been properly trained to adequately observe and give feedback to their employees.

© Thomas Barwick/The Image Bank/Getty Images

Eliminating Rater Error

Appraisal training should focus on eliminating the subjective errors made by managers in the rating process. Gary Latham and Kenneth Wexley stress the importance of performance appraisal training by noting that

> [R]egardless of whether evaluations are obtained from multiple appraisers or from only the employee's immediate superior, all appraisers should be trained to reduce errors of judgment that occur when one person evaluates another. This training is necessary because to the degree to which a performance appraisal is biased, distorted, or inaccurate, the probability of increasing the productivity of the employee is greatly decreased. Moreover, wrong decisions could be made regarding whom to promote, retain, or replace, which in turn will penalize the organization's bottom line. In addition, when a performance appraisal is affected by rating errors, the employee may be justified in filing a discrimination charge.[34]

With any rating method, certain types of errors can arise that should be considered. The "halo error" we discussed in Chapter 6 when we looked at selecting employees can occur during the appraisal process if raters do not have carefully developed descriptions of the employee behaviors being rated. The "horn error" is the opposite of the halo effect. It occurs when a manager focuses on one negative aspect about an employee and generalizes it into an overall poor appraisal rating. A personality conflict between a manager and his or her employees increases the probability of the horn effect, which can lead to a high level of frustration on the employee's part if it is not corrected.[35]

Some types of rating errors are *distributional errors* in that they involve a group of ratings given across various employees. For example, raters who are reluctant to assign either extremely high or extremely low ratings commit the error of central tendency. In this case, all employees are rated about average. It is a good idea to explain to raters that among large numbers of employees, one should expect to find significant differences in their behavior, productivity, and other characteristics.

In contrast to central tendency errors, it is also common for some raters to give unusually high or low ratings. For example, a manager might erroneously assert, "All my employees are excellent" or "None of my people are good enough." These beliefs give rise to what is called leniency or strictness error.[36] One way to reduce this error is to clearly define the characteristics or dimensions of performance and to provide meaningful descriptions of behavior, known as "anchors," on the scale. Another approach is to require ratings to conform to a forced distribution, which is also sometimes referred to as *forced ranking*. Managers appraising employees under a forced distribution system are required to place a certain percentage of employees into various performance categories. For example, it may be required that 10 percent of ratings be poor (or excellent). This is similar to the requirement in some schools that instructors grade on a curve. GE, Ford Motor Company, and UBS are some of the companies that have utilized forced distributions in their appraisal processes. (GE refers to the distribution as a "vitality curve."[37]) A variation of this is *peer ranking*, a system whereby employees in a work group are ranked against one another from best to worst.

Although forced distribution and peer ranking may solve leniency and strictness errors, they can create other rating errors—particularly if most employees are performing above standard. Moreover, if the system has a disparate impact on a legally

---

error of central tendency

A performance rating error in which all employees are rated about average

leniency or strictness error

A performance rating error in which the appraiser tends to give employees either unusually high or unusually low ratings

forced distribution

A performance appraisal ranking system whereby raters are required to place a certain percentage of employees into various performance categories

protected group, such as a minority or older employers, it can result, and has resulted, in discrimination lawsuits, which GE, among other companies, has experienced firsthand. Other companies, including Ford and Goodyear, abandoned their forced ranking systems after lawsuits, lower morale, decreased teamwork, and destructive employee competition ensued following their use. In addition, not all corporate cultures are conducive to forced ranking systems. For example, at Starbucks, which fosters a corporate climate based on teamwork, using a forced ranking system would probably be counterproductive. Because of the legal issues related to forced ranking, companies that use these methods obviously need to carefully train their appraisers.[38]

Some rating errors are *temporal* in that the performance review is biased either favorably or unfavorably, depending on the way performance information is selected, evaluated, and organized by the rater over time. For example, when the appraisal is based largely on the employee's recent behavior, good or bad, the rater has committed the **recency error.** Managers who give higher ratings because they believe an employee is "showing improvement" may unwittingly be committing recency error. Without work record documentation for the entire appraisal period, the rater is forced to recall recent employee behavior to establish the rating. Having the rater routinely document employee accomplishments and failures throughout the whole appraisal period can minimize the recency error. One way for managers to do this is by keeping a diary or a log. Rater training also will help reduce this error.

Contrast error occurs when an employee's evaluation is biased either upward or downward because of another employee's performance, evaluated just previously. For example, an average employee may appear especially productive when compared with a poor performer. However, that same employee could appear unproductive when compared with a star performer. Contrast errors are most likely when raters are required to rank employees in order from the best to the poorest. Employees are evaluated against one another, usually on the basis of some organizational standard or guideline. For example, they may be compared on the basis of their ability to meet production standards or their "overall" ability to perform their job. As with other types of rating errors, contrast error can be reduced through training that focuses on using objective standards and behavioral anchors to appraise performance.[39]

The **similar-to-me error** occurs when appraisers inflate the evaluations of people with whom they have something in common. For example, if both the manager and the employee are from the same state or went to the same schools, the manager may unwittingly have a more favorable impression of the employee. The effects of a similar-to-me error can be powerful, and when the similarity is based on race, religion, gender, or some other protected category, it can result in discrimination.

Furthermore, raters should be aware of any stereotypes they may hold toward particular groups. For example, one study found that men who experience conflicts between family and work received lower overall performance ratings and lower reward recommendations than men who did not experience such conflicts. Women, on the other hand, were judged no differently, whether they experienced family-work conflicts or not. A host of organizations such as Sears and Weyerhaeuser have developed formal training programs to reduce the subjective errors commonly made during the rating process. This training can pay off, particularly when participants have the opportunity to (1) observe other managers making errors, (2) actively participate in

recency error

A performance rating error in which the appraisal is based largely on the employee's most recent behavior rather than on behavior throughout the appraisal period

contrast error

A performance rating error in which an employee's evaluation is biased either upward or downward because of comparison with another employee just previously evaluated

similar-to-me error

A performance rating error in which an appraiser inflates the evaluation of an employee because of a mutual personal connection

discovering their own errors, and (3) practice job-related tasks to reduce the errors they tend to make.[40]

Feedback Training

Finally, a training program for raters should provide some general points to consider for planning and providing feedback on an ongoing basis and during the appraisal interview. Managers need to understand that employees want feedback—that is, they want to know how they are doing and how they can improve. They are less eager to be appraised or judged. This is why it is important for their managers to provide them with ongoing feedback and not just "dump on them" during a formal appraisal. Feedback training should cover at least three basic areas: (1) communicating effectively, (2) diagnosing the root causes of performance problems, and (3) setting goals and objectives. A checklist like the one in Highlights in HRM 1 can be used to help supervisors prepare for the appraisal interview.[41]

HIGHLIGHTS IN **HRM**
1 Supervisor's Checklist for the Performance Appraisal

Scheduling

1. Schedule the review and notify the employee ten days to two weeks in advance.
2. Ask the employee to prepare for the session by reviewing his or her performance, job objectives, and development goals.
3. Clearly state that this will be the formal annual performance appraisal.

Preparation

1. Review the performance documentation collected throughout the year. Concentrate on work patterns that have developed.
2. Be prepared to give specific examples of above- or below-average performance.
3. When performance falls short of expectations, determine what changes need to be made. If the performance meets or exceeds expectations, discuss this and plan how to reinforce it.
4. After the appraisal is written, set it aside for a few days and then review it again.
5. Follow whatever steps are required by your organization's performance appraisal system.

Conducting the Review

1. Select a location that is comfortable and free of distractions.
2. Discuss each topic in the appraisal one at a time and address both the employee's strengths and shortcomings in that area.
3. Be specific and descriptive, not general and judgmental. Report occurrences rather than evaluating them.
4. Discuss your differences and resolve them. Solicit agreement with the evaluation.
5. Jointly discuss and design plans for taking corrective action for growth and development.
6. Maintain a professional and supportive approach to the appraisal discussion.

Performance Appraisal Methods

LEARNING OUTCOME 4

As an employee, would you rather be evaluated on your personal traits or characteristics, your on-the-job behaviors, or the results you get? Would it depend upon the job you were doing?

Since the early years of their use by the federal government, methods of evaluating personnel have evolved considerably. Old systems have been replaced by new methods that reflect technical improvements and legal requirements and are more consistent with the purposes of appraisal. Likewise, paper appraisals are being replaced by electronic appraisals built into firms' performance management systems. In the discussion that follows, we will examine in some detail the methods that have found widespread use, and we will briefly touch on other methods that are used less frequently. Performance appraisal methods can be broadly classified as measuring traits, behaviors, or results. Trait approaches continue to be used despite their subjectivity. Behavioral approaches provide more action-oriented information to employees and therefore may be best for development. The results-oriented approach has become more popular because it focuses on the measurable contributions that employees make to the organization.

Trait Methods

Trait approaches to performance appraisal are designed to measure the extent to which an employee possesses certain characteristics—such as dependability, creativity, initiative, and leadership—that are viewed as important for the job and the organization in general. Trait methods became popular because they are easy to develop. However, if not designed carefully on the basis of job analysis, trait appraisals can be notoriously biased and subjective.

Graphic Rating Scales

graphic rating scale method

A trait approach to performance appraisal whereby each employee is rated according to a scale of characteristics

In the graphic rating scale method, each trait or characteristic to be rated is represented by a scale on which a rater indicates the degree to which an employee possesses that trait or characteristic. An example of this type of scale is shown in Highlights in HRM 2. There are many variations of the graphic rating scale. The differences are to be found in (1) the characteristics or dimensions on which individuals are rated, (2) the degree to which the performance dimension is defined for the rater, and (3) how clearly the points on the scale are defined. In Highlights in HRM 2, the dimensions are defined briefly, and some attempt is made to define the points on the scale. Subjectivity bias is reduced somewhat when the dimensions on the scale and the scale points are defined as precisely as possible. This can be achieved by training raters and by including descriptive appraisal guidelines in a performance appraisal reference packet.[42]

Also, the rating form should provide sufficient space for comments on the behavior associated with each scale. These comments improve the accuracy of the appraisal because they require the rater to think in terms of observable employee behaviors while providing specific examples to discuss with the employee during the appraisal interview.

Mixed-Standard Scales

mixed-standard scale method

A trait approach to performance appraisal similar to other scale methods but based on comparison with (better than, equal to, or worse than) a standard

The mixed-standard scale method is a modification of the basic rating scale method. Rather than evaluating traits according to a single scale, the rater is given three specific descriptions of each trait. These descriptions reflect three levels of performance: superior, average, and inferior. After the three descriptions for each trait are written, they are randomly sequenced to form the mixed-standard scale. As shown in Highlights in HRM 3, supervisors evaluate employees by indicating whether their performance is better than, equal to, or worse than the standard for each behavior.

Forced-Choice Method

The forced-choice method requires the rater to choose from statements, often in pairs, that appear equally favorable or equally unfavorable. The statements, however, are designed to distinguish between successful and unsuccessful performance. The rater selects one statement from the pair without knowing which statement correctly

forced-choice method

A trait approach to performance appraisal that requires the rater to choose from statements designed to distinguish between successful and unsuccessful performance

2 HIGHLIGHTS IN **HRM**
Graphic Rating Scale with Provision for Comments

Appraise employee's performance in PRESENT ASSIGNMENT. Check (✔) most appropriate square. Appraisers are *urged to freely use* the "Remarks" sections for significant comments descriptive of the individual.

1. KNOWLEDGE OF WORK: Understanding of all phases of his/her work and related matters	Needs instruction or guidance ☐	☐	Has required knowledge of own and related work ☐	Has exceptional knowledge of own and related work ☑	☐
	Remarks: *Is particularly good on gas engines.*				
2. INITIATIVE: Ability to originate or develop ideas and to get things started	Lacks imagination ☐	Meets necessary requirements ☑	☐	Unusually resourceful ☐	☐
	Remarks: *Has good ideas when asked for an opinion, but otherwise will not offer them. Somewhat lacking in self-confidence.*				
3. APPLICATION: Attention and application to his/her work	Wastes time Needs close supervision ☐	☐	Steady and willing worker ☑	Exceptionally industrious ☐	☐
	Remarks: *Accepts new jobs when assigned.*				
4. QUALITY OF WORK: Thoroughness, neatness, and accuracy of work	Needs improvement ☐	☐	Regularly meets recognized standards ☐	Consistently maintains highest quality ☑	
	Remarks: *The work he turns out is always of the highest possible quality.*				
5. VOLUME OF WORK: Quantity of acceptable work	Should be increased ☐	☐	Regularly meets recognized standards ☑	Unusually high output ☐	☐
	Remarks: *Would be higher if he did not spend so much time checking and rechecking his work.*				

describes successful job behavior. For example, forced-choice pairs might include the following:

1. _____ a) Works hard   _____ b) Works quickly
2. _____ a) Shows initiative   _____ b) Is responsive to customers
3. _____ a) Produces poor quality _____ b) Lacks good work habits

The forced-choice method is not without limitations, the primary one being the cost of establishing and maintaining its validity. The fact that it has been a source of frustration to many raters has sometimes caused the method to be eliminated from appraisal programs. In addition, it cannot be used as effectively as some of the other methods as a tool for developing employees.

essay method

A trait approach to performance appraisal that requires the rater to compose a statement describing employee behavior

Essay Method

Unlike rating scales, which provide a structured form of appraisal, the essay method requires the appraiser to compose a statement that best describes the employee being appraised. The appraiser is usually instructed to describe the employee's strengths

3 HIGHLIGHTS IN HRM
Example of a Mixed-Standard Scale

DIRECTIONS: Please indicate whether the individual's performance is above (+), equal to (0), or lower than (−) each of the following standards.

1. _____ Employee uses good judgment when addressing problems and provides workable alternatives; however, at times does not take actions to prevent problems. (*medium PROBLEM-SOLVING*)

2. _____ Employee lacks supervisory skills; frequently handles employees poorly and is at times argumentative. (*low LEADERSHIP*)

3. _____ Employee is extremely cooperative; can be expected to take the lead in developing cooperation among employees; completes job tasks with a positive attitude. (*high COOPERATION*)

4. _____ Employee has effective supervision skills; encourages productivity, quality, and employee development. (*medium LEADERSHIP*)

5. _____ Employee normally displays an argumentative or defensive attitude toward fellow employees and job assignments. (*low COOPERATION*)

6. _____ Employee is generally agreeable but becomes argumentative at times when given job assignments; cooperates with other employees as expected. (*medium COOPERATION*)

7. _____ Employee is not good at solving problems; uses poor judgment and does not anticipate potential difficulties. (*low PROBLEM-SOLVING*)

8. _____ Employee anticipates potential problems and provides creative, proactive alternative solutions; has good attention to follow-up. (*high PROBLEM-SOLVING*)

9. _____ Employee displays skilled direction, effectively coordinates unit activities, is generally a dynamic leader, and motivates employees to high performance. (*high LEADERSHIP*)

and weaknesses and to make recommendations for his or her development. Often the essay method is combined with other rating methods because it provides additional descriptive information about an employee's performance that cannot be generated with a structured rating scale. Essays also provide an excellent opportunity for supervisors to point out the unique characteristics of the employee being appraised, including specific points about the employee's promotability, special talents, skills, strengths, and weaknesses.

A major limitation of the essay method is that composing an essay that attempts to cover all of an employee's essential characteristics is a very time-consuming task (though when combined with other methods, this method does not require a lengthy statement). Another disadvantage of the essay method is that the quality of the performance appraisal could be affected by the supervisor's writing skills and composition style. Good writers may simply be able to produce more favorable appraisals. A final drawback of this appraisal method is that it tends to be subjective and might not focus on the relevant aspects of a person's job performance.

Behavioral Methods

As we mentioned, one of the potential drawbacks of a trait-oriented performance appraisal is that traits tend to be vague and subjective. We discussed earlier that one way to improve a rating scale is to have descriptions of behavior along a scale, or continuum. These descriptions permit the rater to readily identify the point where a particular employee falls on the scale. Behavioral methods have been developed to specifically describe which actions should (or should not) be exhibited on the job. They are also often used to provide employees with developmental feedback.

Critical Incident Method

The critical incident method, described in Chapter 4 in connection with job analysis, is also used as a method of appraisal. Recall that a critical incident occurs when employee behavior results in unusual success or unusual failure in some part of the job. An example of a favorable critical incident occurs when a janitor observes that a file cabinet containing classified documents has been left unlocked at the close of business and calls the firm's security officer to correct the problem. An example of an unfavorable incident occurs when a mail clerk fails to deliver an Express Mail package immediately, instead putting it in with regular mail to be routed two hours later. The manager keeps a log or diary for each employee throughout the appraisal period and notes specific critical incidents related to how well they perform.

When completing the appraisal form, the manager refers to the critical incident log and uses this information to substantiate an employee's rating of outstanding, satisfactory, or unsatisfactory in specific performance areas and overall. This method can also help a manager counsel employees when they are having performance problems while the problem is still minor. It also increases the objectivity of the appraisal by requiring the rater to use job performance criteria to justify the ratings.[43]

critical incident

An unusual event that denotes superior or inferior employee performance in some part of the job

Behavioral Checklist Method

One of the oldest appraisal techniques is the behavioral checklist method. It consists of having the rater check the statements on a list that the rater believes are characteristic of the employee's performance or behavior. A checklist developed for computer salespeople might include a number of statements such as the following:

_____ Is able to explain equipment clearly
_____ Keeps abreast of new developments in technology
_____ Tends to be a steady worker
_____ Reacts quickly to customers' needs
_____ Processes orders correctly

Behaviorally Anchored Rating Scale (BARS)

behaviorally anchored rating scale (BARS)
A behavioral approach to performance appraisal that consists of a series of vertical scales, one for each important dimension of job performance

A behaviorally anchored rating scale (BARS) consists of a series of five to ten vertical scales—one for each important dimension of performance identified through job analysis. These dimensions are anchored by behaviors identified through a critical incident job analysis. The critical incidents are placed along the scale and are assigned point values according to the opinions of experts. A BARS for the job of firefighter is shown in the upper portion of Highlights in HRM 4. Note that this particular scale is for the dimension described as "Firefighting Strategy: Knowledge of Fire Characteristics."

A BARS is typically developed by a committee that includes both subordinates and managers. The committee's task is to identify all the relevant characteristics or dimensions of the job. Behavioral anchors in the form of statements are then established for each of the job dimensions. Several participants are asked to review the anchor statements and indicate which job dimension each anchor illustrates. The only anchors retained are those that at least 70 percent of the group agrees belong with a particular dimension. Finally, the anchors are attached to their job dimensions and are placed on the appropriate scales according to values that the group assigns to them.

At present there is no strong evidence that a BARS reduces all of the rating errors mentioned previously. However, some studies have shown that scales of this type can yield more accurate ratings. One major advantage of a BARS is that personnel outside the HR department participate with HR staff in its development. Employee participation can lead to greater acceptance of the performance appraisal process and of the performance measures that it uses.

The procedures followed in developing a BARS also result in scales that have a high degree of content validity. The main disadvantage of a BARS is that it requires considerable time and effort to develop. In addition, because the scales are specific to particular jobs, a scale designed for one job might not apply to another.

Using the INTERNET

Find more information about how the U.S. Army Research Institute uses BARS by going to

www.cengagebrain.com

Behavior Observation Scale (BOS)

behavior observation scale (BOS)
A behavioral approach to performance appraisal that measures the frequency of observed behavior

A behavior observation scale (BOS) is similar to a BARS in that they are both based on critical incidents. However, the lower portion of Highlights in HRM 4 shows that rather than asking the evaluator to choose the most representative behavioral anchor, a BOS is designed to measure how frequently each of the behaviors has been observed.

The value of a BOS is that this approach allows the appraiser to play the role of observer rather than of judge. In this way, he or she can more easily provide constructive feedback to the employee, who will be more willing to accept it. Companies such as AT&T and Weyerhaeuser have used the BOS, and research shows that users of the system frequently prefer it over the BARS or trait scales for (1) maintaining

4 HIGHLIGHTS IN **HRM**
BARS and BOS Examples

Example of a BARS for Municipal Fire Companies

FIREFIGHTING STRATEGY: Knowledge of Fire Characteristics. This area of performance concerns the ability of a firefighter to understand fire characteristics to develop the best strategy for fighting a fire.

HIGH	7	—Finds the fire when no one else can
	6	—Correctly assesses best point of entry for fighting fire
	5	—Uses type of smoke as indicator of type of fire
AVERAGE	4	—Understands basic hydraulics
	3	—Cannot tell the type of fire by observing the color of flame
	2	—Cannot identify location of the fire
LOW	1	—Will not change firefighting strategy in spite of flashbacks and other signs that accelerants are present

Source: Adapted from Landy, Jacobs, and Associates. Reprinted with permission.

Sample Items from Behavior Observation Scales

For each behavior observed, use the following scale:

5 represents *almost always*	95–100% of the time
4 represents *frequently*	85–94% of the time
3 represents *sometimes*	75–84% of the time
2 represents *seldom*	65–74% of the time
1 represents *almost never*	0–64% of the time

SALES PRODUCTIVITY	NEVER				ALWAYS
1. Reviews individual productivity results with manager	1	2	3	4	5
2. Suggests to peers ways of building sales	1	2	3	4	5
3. Uncovers specific needs for each contact	1	2	3	4	5
4. Keeps account plans updated	1	2	3	4	5
5. Follows up on customer leads	1	2	3	4	5

objectivity, (2) distinguishing good performers from poor performers, (3) providing feedback, and (4) identifying training needs.[44]

Results Methods

Rather than looking at the traits of employees or the behaviors they exhibit on the job, many organizations evaluate employees' accomplishments—the results they achieve through their work. Advocates of results appraisals argue that they are more objective and empowering for employees. Looking at results such as sales figures and production output involves less subjectivity and therefore may be less open to bias. Furthermore, results appraisals often give employees responsibility for their outcomes while giving them discretion over the methods they use to accomplish them (within limits). This is employee empowerment and engagement in action.

Productivity Measures

A number of results measures are available to evaluate performance. Salespeople are evaluated on the basis of their sales volume (both the number of units sold and the dollar amount in revenues). Production workers are evaluated on the basis of the number of units they produce and perhaps the scrap rate or number of defects that are detected. Executives are frequently evaluated on the basis of company profits or growth rate. Each of these measures directly links what employees accomplish to results that benefit the organization. In this way, results appraisals can directly align employee and organizational goals.

But there are some problems with results appraisals. First, recall our earlier discussion of criteria contamination. Results appraisals can be contaminated by external factors that employees cannot influence. Sales representatives who have extremely bad markets or production employees who cannot get materials will not be able to perform up to their abilities. In this case, it is unfair to hold these employees accountable for results that are contaminated by circumstances beyond their control.

Furthermore, results appraisals can inadvertently encourage employees to "look good" on a short-term basis, while ignoring the long-term ramifications. Line supervisors, for example, might let their equipment suffer to reduce maintenance costs. For jobs that are more service oriented, for example, it is not enough to simply look at production or sales figures. Factors such as cooperation, adaptability, initiative, and concern for human relations are important to the job success of employees, too. If these factors are important job standards, they should be added to the appraisal review. Thus, to be realistic, both the results and the methods or processes used to achieve them should be considered.[45]

Management by Objectives

management by objectives (MBO)

A philosophy of management that rates performance on the basis of employee achievement of goals set by mutual agreement of employee and manager

One method that attempts to overcome some of the limitations of results appraisals is management by objectives (MBO). MBO is a philosophy of management that has employees establish objectives (such as production costs, sales per product, quality standards, and profits) by consulting with their superiors. Employees are then evaluated based on these objectives.[46] An MBO system (see Figure 8.7) consists of a cycle that begins with setting the organization's common goals and objectives and ultimately returns to that step. The system acts as a goal-setting process whereby objectives are established for the organization (Step 1), departments (Step 2), and individual managers and employees (Step 3).

As Figure 8.7 illustrates, a significant feature of the cycle is the establishment of specific goals by the employee, but those goals are based on a broad statement of the employee's responsibilities prepared by the person's supervisor. Employee-established goals are discussed with the supervisor and jointly reviewed and modified until both parties are satisfied with them (Step 4). The goal statements are accompanied by a detailed account of the actions the employee proposes to take to reach the goals. During periodic reviews, as objective data are made available, the progress that the employee is making toward the goals is then assessed (Step 5). The goals may be changed at this time as new or additional data are received. At the conclusion of

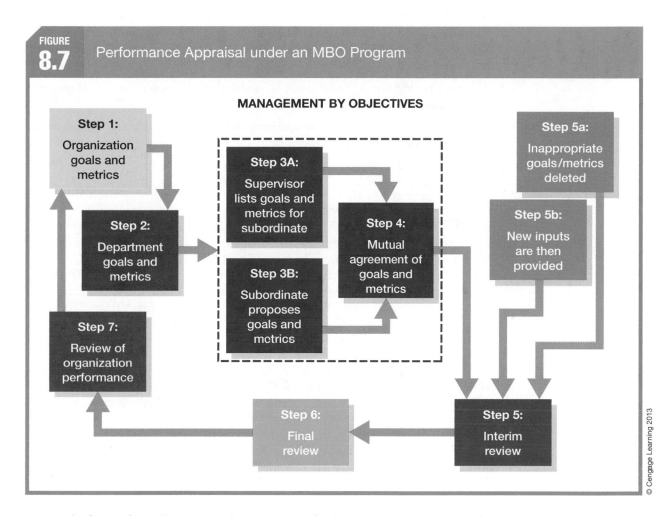

FIGURE 8.7 Performance Appraisal under an MBO Program

a period of time (usually six months or one year), the employee makes a self-appraisal of what he or she has accomplished, substantiating the self-appraisal with factual data wherever possible. The "interview" is an examination of the employee's self-appraisal by the supervisor and the employee together (Step 6). The final step (Step 7) is reviewing the connection between the employees' performance and the organization's. Notice how the steps in an MBO program are similar to the steps in Figure 8.1 at the beginning of the chapter but are more specific. MBO programs should be viewed as part of a total system for managing, not as merely an addition to the manager's job. Managers must be willing to empower employees to accomplish their objectives on their own, giving them discretion over the methods they use (but holding them accountable for outcomes). The following guidelines can help an MBO program succeed:

1. Managers and employees must be willing to establish goals and objectives together. Goal setting has been shown to improve employee performance, typically ranging from 10 to 25 percent. Goal setting works because it helps employees focus on important tasks and makes them accountable for completing these tasks. It also establishes an automatic feedback system that aids learning because employees can regularly evaluate their performance against their goals.[47]

2. The objectives should be quantifiable and measurable for the long and short terms. The goal statements should be accompanied by a description of how the goals will be accomplished.

3. The results that are expected must be under the employee's control. Recall our early discussion of criterion contamination.

4. The goals and objectives must be consistent for each employee level (top executive, manager, and employee).

5. Managers and employees must establish specific times when the goals are to be reviewed and evaluated.

The Balanced Scorecard

The Balanced Scorecard (BSC), which we first discussed in Chapter 2, can be used to appraise individual-employees, teams, business units, and the corporation itself. A BSC appraisal takes into account four related categories: (1) financial, (2) customer, (3) processes, and (4) learning. These internal processes—product development, service, and the like—are critical for creating customer satisfaction and loyalty. In turn, creating value for customers is what drives a firm's financial performance and profitability.

Highlights in HRM 5 shows how a balanced scorecard in the financial category translates to a personal scorecard for an employee. As you can see, the corporation's financial objectives have already been spelled out on the scorecard. Then the various business unit targets are added, followed by the target objectives of the firm's teams and individual employees. The value of this is that each individual can see more clearly how his or her performance ties into the overall performance of the firm. Target objectives for the customer category of the scorecard (not shown) might include customer satisfaction and retention rates, delivery performance to customers, and so forth.

Similar in some ways to an MBO system, a BSC appraisal enables managers to translate broad corporate goals into divisional, departmental, and team goals in a cascading way. Some recommendations for ensuring the method's success include the following:

■ *Translate the strategy into a scorecard of clear objectives.* Because the BSC process begins with strategic objectives, unless these are clear, the rest of the system is doomed to ambiguity and potential failure. Translating a strategy into objectives provides managers and frontline employees with goals that are more understandable and attainable. Typically, having fewer goals adds clarity and focus.

■ *Attach measures to each objective.* For managers and employees to know if and when the objectives are achieved, clear measures must be attached to each goal. Each objective should be given at least one metric that can be measured either by a preexisting system or manually within an organization.

■ *Cascade scorecards to the front line.* It is often said that the real strategic work happens at the front line. For all employees to understand how their roles and job duties are aligned with the firm's higher-level goals, the scorecards should be cascaded to the individual level. Cascading scorecards ensures that strategy then becomes "everyone's" job.

■ *Provide performance feedback based on measures.* As with other performance management systems, unless managers provide employees with solid feedback on how they are doing, the system is likely to be ineffective. As part of this process, employees must know that they are accountable for achieving their objectives and for providing an explanation when they do not hit their targets.

- *Empower employees to make performance improvements.* Individuals, on their own or working in teams, may understand ways of achieving higher performance. One of the benefits of a results-based system such as the BSC is that it gives employees the latitude to continuously improve their work methods.

- *Reassess the strategy.* One of the key benefits of the BSC is that it is a continuous loop process. Managers should monitor performance and use this information to reassess the strategy and make continuous adjustments. Those who have had the best success with the BSC argue that the system helps improve communication and learning rather than fixing in place a mechanical set of controls.[48]

HIGHLIGHTS IN HRM

5 Personal Scorecard

CORPORATE OBJECTIVES

- Double our corporate value in seven years.
- Increase our earnings by an average of 20% per year.
- Achieve an internal rate of return 2% above the cost of capital.
- Increase both production by 20% in the next decade.

☑ Corporate
☐ Business Unit
☐ Team/Individual

Corporate Targets and Business-Unit Targets									Team/Individual Objectives
2011	2012	2013	2014		2011	2012	2013	2014	1.
Financial (millions of dollars)									
100	120	160	180	Earnings					
35	55	85	100	Net profits					
15	35	65	75	Net cash flow					2.
Operating (millions of dollars)									
35	35	40	50	Production and development costs					
30	30	35	30	Overhead and operating costs					
100	105	108	110	Total annual production (million units)					3.

Team/Individual Measures		Targets			
1.					
2.					4.
3.					
4.					

Source: Adapted from Robert Kaplan and David Norton, "Using the Balanced Scorecard as a Strategic Management System," *Harvard Business Review* (January–February 1996): 75–85.

FIGURE 8.8   Summary of Various Appraisal Methods

	ADVANTAGES	DISADVANTAGES
Trait Methods	1. Are inexpensive to develop 2. Use meaningful dimensions 3. Are easy to use	1. Have high potential for rating errors 2. Are not useful for employee counseling 3. Are not useful for allocating rewards 4. Are not useful for promotion decisions
Behavioral Methods	1. Use specific performance dimensions 2. Are acceptable to employees and superiors 3. Are useful for providing feedback 4. Are fair for reward and promotion decisions	1. Can be time-consuming to develop/use 2. Can be costly to develop 3. Have some potential for rating error
Results Methods	1. Have less subjectivity bias 2. Are acceptable to employees and superiors 3. Link individual performance to organizational performance 4. Encourage mutual goal setting 5. Are good for reward and promotion decisions	1. Are time-consuming to develop/use 2. May encourage a short-term perspective 3. May use contaminated criteria 4. May use deficient criteria

Which Performance Appraisal Method to Use?

The method chosen should be based largely on the purpose of the appraisal. Figure 8.8 lists some of the strengths and weaknesses of trait, behavior, and results approaches to appraising employees. Although researchers and HR managers generally believe that the more sophisticated and time-consuming methods offer more useful information, this may not always be the case. Ronald Gross, an industrial psychologist and human resources consultant, states: "I can't judge a performance appraisal system just by looking at the paperwork. The back of an envelope can work just fine. I've seen many systems fail miserably because they're too complex, too time-consuming, and too burdensome. I've never seen a system fail because it was too simple."[49] One way to assess whether an organization's appraisal system is effective is by doing an annual, or at least periodic, audit of the process using a survey instrument that both managers and employees complete on a periodic basis. This should give HR a better sense of whether the appraisal process is improving.

Of course, having a first-rate appraisal method does no good if the manager simply "shoves the information in a drawer." Even a rudimentary system, when used properly, can initiate a discussion between managers and employees that genuinely leads to better performance on the part of individual workers. In addition, as we have explained, performance appraisals should not be just for middle managers and rank-and-file employees. If the organization's goals are to cascade downward, the firm's top executives need to be involved in the appraisal process as well.

LEARNING OUTCOME 5

As a manager, how might you get an employee who is reluctant to talk during an appraisal to share his or her thoughts?

Appraisal Interviews

The appraisal interview is perhaps the most important part of the entire performance appraisal process. The appraisal interview gives a manager the opportunity to discuss a subordinate's performance record and to explore areas of possible improvement and growth. The format for the appraisal interview will be determined in large part by the purpose of the interview, type of appraisal system used, and organization of the interview form. Most appraisal interviews attempt to give feedback to employees on how well they are doing their jobs and on planning for their future development. Interviews should be scheduled far enough in advance to allow the interviewee, as well as the interviewer, to prepare for the discussion. Usually ten days to two weeks is a sufficient amount of lead time.

Sometimes discussing an employee's past performance and future development goals can make for an appraisal interview that is too long. It can also be difficult for a supervisor to perform the role of both evaluator and counselor in the same review period. Dividing the appraisal interview into two sessions, one for the performance review and the other for the employee's growth plans, can be helpful. Moreover, by separating the interview into two sessions, the interviewer can give each session the proper attention it deserves. Dividing the sessions can also improve the communication and cooperation between the parties, thereby reducing any stress and defensiveness that might arise.

Three Types of Appraisal Interviews

The individual who has probably studied different approaches to performance appraisal interviews most thoroughly is Norman R. F. Maier. In his classic book *The Appraisal Interview*, he analyzes the cause-and-effect relationships in three types of appraisal interviews: tell-and-sell, tell-and-listen, and problem-solving.

- **Tell-and-Sell Interview.** The skills required in the tell-and-sell interview include the ability to persuade an employee to change in a prescribed manner. This may require the development of new behaviors on the part of the employee and skillful use of motivational incentives on the part of the appraiser/supervisor.

- **Tell-and-Listen Interview.** In the tell-and-listen interview, the appraiser/supervisor communicates the strong and weak points of an employee's job performance during the first part of the interview. During the second part of the interview, the employee's feelings about the appraisal are thoroughly explored. The tell-and-listen method gives both managers and employees the opportunity to release and iron out any frustrating feelings they might have.

- **Problem-Solving Interview.** Listening, accepting, and responding to feelings are essential elements of the problem-solving interview. However, this method goes beyond an interest in the employee's feelings. It seeks to stimulate the growth and development of an employee by discussing his or her problems, needs, and on-the-job satisfaction and dissatisfaction.

Managers should not assume that only one type of appraisal interview is appropriate for every review session. Rather, they should be able to use one or more of the interview types, depending on the topic being discussed or on the behavior of the employee being appraised. The interview should be seen as requiring a flexible approach.

Conducting the Appraisal Interview

There are probably no hard-and-fast rules for how to conduct an appraisal interview, but some guidelines can increase an employee's willingness to discuss his or her performance and improve it, accept feedback from his or her supervisors, and increase the person's overall satisfaction with the interview. Many of the principles of effective interviewing discussed in Chapter 6 apply to performance appraisal interviews as well. Here are some other guidelines that should also be considered:

Ask for a Self-Assessment

As we noted earlier in the chapter, it is useful to have employees evaluate their own performance prior to the appraisal interview. Even if this information is not used to determine the final rating on the review, the self-appraisal starts the employee thinking about his or her accomplishments. Self-appraisal also ensures that the employee knows against what criteria he or she is being evaluated, thus eliminating any potential surprises.

Recent research suggests that employees are more satisfied and view the appraisal system as providing more *procedural justice* when they have input into the process. When the employee has evaluated his or her own performance, the interview can be used to discuss areas in which the manager and the employee have reached different conclusions—not so much to resolve the "truth," but to work toward the resolution of problems.

Invite Participation

Most experts advise supervisors to encourage their employees to speak freely and listen closely to what they have to say during appraisal interviews. These experts emphasize that the communication during performance appraisals should be a two-way street. To the extent that an employee is an active participant in that discussion, the more likely it is that the root causes and obstacles to his or her performance will be uncovered and that constructive ideas for improvement will be developed. In addition, research suggests that an employee's participation is

The purpose of a performance appraisal interview is to initiate a dialogue that will help an employee improve his or her performance, making the employee an active participant in the discussion. Such participation is strongly related to an employee's satisfaction with appraisal feedback.

strongly related to the person's satisfaction with the appraisal feedback delivered, the extent to which the person believes it is fair and useful, and the desire to improve his or her performance. As a rule of thumb, supervisors should spend only about 30 to 35 percent of the time talking during the interview. They should spend the rest of the time listening to the information their employees volunteer and their responses to questions.

Express Appreciation

Praise is a powerful motivator, and in an appraisal interview, particularly, employees are seeking positive feedback. It is frequently beneficial to start the appraisal interview by expressing appreciation for what the employee has done well. In this way, he or she may be less defensive and more likely to talk about aspects of the job that are not going so well. However, supervisors should try to avoid the obvious use of the "sandwich technique" in which positive statements are followed by negative ones, which are then followed by positive statements. This approach may not work for several reasons. Praise often alerts the employee that criticism will be coming. If managers follow an appraisal form, the problem of the sandwich technique will often be avoided. Furthermore, if employees are kept informed of their behavior on a regular basis, there will be no need to use this appraisal technique.

Minimize Criticism

Even the most stoic employees can absorb only so much criticism before they start to get defensive. If an employee has many areas in need of improvement, managers should focus on the issues that are most problematic or most important to the job. In other words, criticism should be given in small doses.

Some tips for using criticism constructively include the following:

- *Consider whether it is really necessary.* Sometimes a manager's frustration with a performance problem sometimes leads to his is or her doing little more than "letting off steam" during an appraisal interview. Make certain that the criticism focuses on a recurrent problem or a consistent pattern of behavior over which the employee has control.

- *Consider the person.* Everyone handles criticism differently. Some people are able to handle it well. Others react very negatively to even the lightest criticism.

- *Be specific and do not exaggerate.* Even managers who dislike criticizing may find that, once they get started, they tend to overdo it. Sometimes we overstate problems in order to be convincing or to demonstrate our concern. Try to keep criticism simple, factual, and to the point. Avoid using terms such as always, completely, and never.

- *Watch your timing.* Properly timed criticism can often mean the difference between success and failure. Even good criticism given late in the day, for example, can touch a raw nerve if the employee is tired. If the interview gets emotional or heated, take a break, even if it means finishing the appraisal the following day.

- *Make improvement your goal.* Frankly, it is hard to change a person's behavior with a single conversation, so "laying it on the line" is not probably a good idea. Moreover, any criticism needs to be complemented with managerial support. This point is elaborated on next.[50]

Change the Behavior, Not the Person

Managers frequently try to play psychologist, to "figure out" why an employee has acted a certain way. Empathizing with employees in order to understand their point of view can be very helpful. However, when dealing with a problem area, in particular, remember that it is not the person who is bad, but the actions exhibited on the job. Avoid making suggestions to employees about personal traits they should change; instead suggest more acceptable ways of performing. For example, instead of focusing on a person's "unreliability," a manager might focus on the fact that the employee "has been late to work seven times this month." It is difficult for employees to change who they are; it is usually much easier for them to change how they act.

Focus on Solving Problems

When addressing performance issues, it is also frequently tempting to get into the "blame game" in which both manager and employee enter into a potentially endless discussion of why a situation has arisen. Frequently, solving problems requires an analysis of the causes, but ultimately the appraisal interview should be directed at devising a solution to the problem.

Be Supportive

One of the better techniques for engaging an employee in the problem-solving process is for the manager to ask: "What can I do to help?" Employees frequently attribute performance problems to either real or perceived obstacles (such as bureaucratic procedures or inadequate resources). By being open and supportive, the manager conveys to the employee that he or she will try to eliminate roadblocks and will work with the employee to achieve a higher standard of performance.

Establish Goals

Because one of the major purposes of the appraisal interview is to improve an employee's future performance, his or her manager should focus the person's attention on the future rather than the past:

- Emphasize strengths on which the employee can build rather than weaknesses to overcome and how the employee's efforts will contribute to the organization during the coming year.

- Concentrate on opportunities for growth that exist within the framework of the employee's present position and drop unproductive tasks.

- Limit plans for growth to a few important items that can be accomplished within a reasonable period of time.

- Establish specific action plans that spell out how each goal will be achieved. The plans might also include a list of resources, contacts of people who can help the employee achieve the goals, and timetables for following up to ensure they are met.

- End the review on a positive note by highlighting how both the employee and firm will excel if the goals are achieved.

Follow Up Day to Day

As you have learned, feedback is most useful when it is immediate and specific to a particular situation. Unfortunately, both managers and employees are frequently happy to finish the interview and file away the appraisal form. A better approach is to have informal talks periodically, perhaps quarterly, to follow up on the issues raised in the appraisal interview. Levi Strauss, for example, offers employees informal feedback and coaching sessions on an ongoing basis. This puts managers in more of a coaching role versus that of a judge.

Improving Performance

In many instances, the appraisal interview will provide the basis for noting deficiencies in employee performance and for making plans for improvement. Unless these deficiencies are brought to the employee's attention, they are likely to continue until they become quite serious. Sometimes underperformers do not understand exactly what is expected of them. However, once their responsibilities are clarified, they are in a position to take the corrective action needed to improve their performance.

Identifying Sources of Ineffective Performance

A person's performance is a function of several factors, but perhaps it can be boiled down to three primary concerns: ability, motivation, and environment. Each individual has a unique pattern of strengths and weaknesses that play a part. But talented employees with low motivation are not likely to succeed. In addition, other factors in the work environment—or even in the external environment, which includes personal, family, and community concerns—can affect a person's performance either positively or negatively. Figure 8.9 provides a better picture of how these three factors (ability, motivation, and environment) can influence people's performance.

It is recommended that a diagnosis of poor employee performance focus on these three interactive elements. As Figure 8.10 shows, if an employee's performance is not up to standards, the cause could be a skill problem (knowledge, abilities, technical competencies), an effort problem (motivation to get the job done), and/or some problem in the external conditions of work (poor economic conditions, worker shortages due to downsizing, difficult sales territories).[51] Any one of these problem areas could cause performance to suffer.

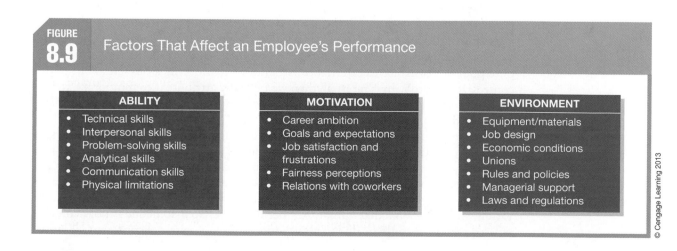

FIGURE 8.9 Factors That Affect an Employee's Performance

ABILITY	MOTIVATION	ENVIRONMENT
• Technical skills	• Career ambition	• Equipment/materials
• Interpersonal skills	• Goals and expectations	• Job design
• Problem-solving skills	• Job satisfaction and	• Economic conditions
• Analytical skills	frustrations	• Unions
• Communication skills	• Fairness perceptions	• Rules and policies
• Physical limitations	• Relations with coworkers	• Managerial support
		• Laws and regulations

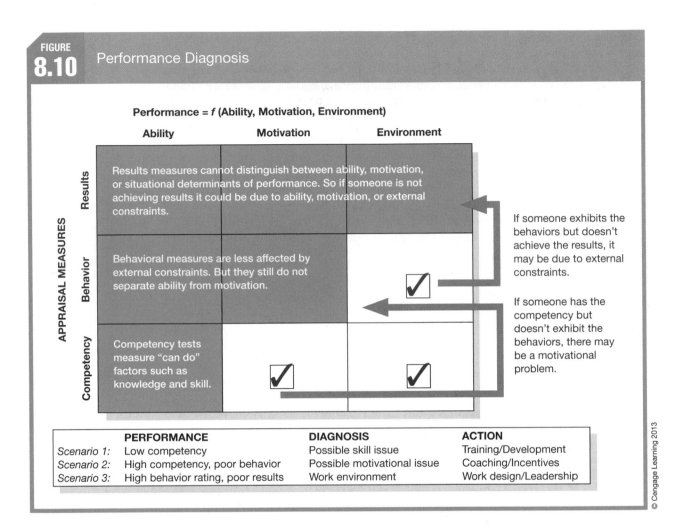

FIGURE 8.10 Performance Diagnosis

Performance = *f* (Ability, Motivation, Environment)

	Ability	Motivation	Environment
Results	Results measures cannot distinguish between ability, motivation, or situational determinants of performance. So if someone is not achieving results it could be due to ability, motivation, or external constraints.		
Behavior	Behavioral measures are less affected by external constraints. But they still do not separate ability from motivation.		✓
Competency	Competency tests measure "can do" factors such as knowledge and skill.	✓	✓

APPRAISAL MEASURES

If someone exhibits the behaviors but doesn't achieve the results, it may be due to external constraints.

If someone has the competency but doesn't exhibit the behaviors, there may be a motivational problem.

	PERFORMANCE	DIAGNOSIS	ACTION
Scenario 1:	Low competency	Possible skill issue	Training/Development
Scenario 2:	High competency, poor behavior	Possible motivational issue	Coaching/Incentives
Scenario 3:	High behavior rating, poor results	Work environment	Work design/Leadership

© Cengage Learning 2013

Performance Diagnosis

Although performance appraisal systems can often tell us who is not performing well, they typically cannot reveal why. Unfortunately, managers often assume that poor performance is first due to lack of ability, second to poor motivation, and then to external conditions an employee faces. Ironically, research also suggests that we tend to make just the opposite attributions about our own performance. We first attribute poor performance to external constraints such as bad luck or factors out of our control. If the problem is internal, then we typically attribute it to temporary factors such as motivation or energy ("I had a bad day") and only as a last resort admit that it might be due to our abilities or lack of them.

So what can be done to diagnose the real reasons for poor performance? More specifically, how can managers identify the root causes and get to work on a solution that improves performance? By comparing different performance measures, managers can begin to get an idea of the underlying causes of performance problems. For example, as shown in Figure 8.10, results measures cannot distinguish between ability, motivation, and situational determinants of performance. So if someone is not achieving desired results, it could be due to ability, motivation, or external constraints. On the other hand, behavioral measures are less affected by external constraints. So if some-one is demonstrating all the desired behaviors but is not achieving the desired results, logic suggests that it might be due to factors beyond his or her control.

Other kinds of diagnoses are possible by comparing different measures of per-formance. Only by correctly diagnosing the causes of performance problems can managers—and employees—hope to improve them.

Managing Ineffective Performance

Once the sources of performance problems are known, a course of action can be planned. The action might involve providing training in areas that would increase the knowledge and/or skills the employee needs to perform effectively. A transfer to another job or department might give an employee a chance to become a more effec-tive member of the organization. In other instances, different ways to motivate the individual might have to be found.

If the ineffective performance persists, it may be necessary to transfer the employee, take disciplinary action, or discharge the person from the organization. Not only is the ineffective behavior likely affecting the manager and the organization as a whole, but it is also probably affecting the person's coworkers. Whatever action is taken, however, should be done objectively, fairly, and with an understanding of the feelings of the individual involved. A new manager is likely to need training in this area be-cause it is one of the most difficult aspects of being a manager.

A final word of caution when it comes to managing performance problems: Be-cause research consistently shows that managers often attribute poor performance to characteristics of the individuals (their abilities or motivation), while employees themselves typically blame external factors for their miscues, this can establish a neg-ative cycle if not handled properly. Managers who assume that employees are not mo-tivated or not capable may begin to treat them differently (perhaps supervising them too closely or watching for their next mistake). This can actually decrease an em-ployee's motivation and cause him or her to withdraw. Seeing this might confirm the manager's initial belief that the employee does not "measure up." As you can probably tell, this "set-up-to-fail" syndrome can be self-fulfilling and self-reinforcing. We hope the ideas and suggestions in this chapter will help managers accurately identify who is performing well (and why) and give them some focus for improving the productivity of their employees.[52]

Summary

LEARNING OUTCOME 1   Performance management is the process of creating a work environment in which people can perform to the best of their abilities to meet a company's goals. Performance appraisals are the result of an annual, biannual, or quarterly pro-cess in which a manager evaluates an employee's per-formance relative to the requirements of his or her job and uses the information to show the person where improvements are needed and why. Apprais-als are just part of the performance management process, however. Aligning the goals of employees with that of the firm, providing employees with con-tinual on-the-job feedback, and rewarding them are critical as well.

LEARNING OUTCOME 2 Performance appraisal programs serve many purposes, but in general, those purposes can be clustered into two categories: administrative and developmental. The administrative purposes include decisions about who will be promoted, transferred, or laid off. Appraisals are also conducted to make compensation decisions. Developmental decisions include those related to improving and enhancing an individual's capabilities. These include identifying a person's strengths and weaknesses, eliminating external performance obstacles, and establishing training needs.

Some human resource experts and firms believe performance appraisals are ineffective. Managers frequently avoid conducting appraisals because they dislike passing judgment on people. Furthermore, if managers are not adequately trained, subjectivity and organizational politics can distort employee reviews. They do not develop good feedback skills and are often not prepared to conduct an appraisal. As a consequence, the appraisal is done begrudgingly once a year and then forgotten. The ultimate success or failure of a performance appraisal program depends on the philosophy underlying it, its connection with the firm's business goals, and the attitudes and skills of those responsible for its administration.

LEARNING OUTCOME 3 Appraisal information can be derived from a variety of sources, including an employee's supervisor, peers, customers, suppliers, subordinates as well as the employee being appraised. However, the raters need training so the appraisals are reliable, strategically relevant, and free from either criterion deficiency or criterion contamination. Appraisal systems must also comply with the law and, like selections tests, be valid and reliable. For example, ratings must be job-related, employees must understand their performance standards in advance, appraisers must be able to observe job performance, appraisers must be trained, feedback must be given, and an appeals procedure must be established. Some companies now hold calibration meetings to ensure their

managers are accurately rating employees. Using multiple raters is frequently a good idea because different individuals see different facets of an employee's performance. An increasing number of organizations are using 360-degree appraisals to get a more comprehensive picture of how well their employees are performing. Regardless of the source of appraisal information, appraisers should be thoroughly trained in the particular methods they will use in evaluating their subordinates.

LEARNING OUTCOME 4 Several methods can be used for performance appraisals. These include trait approaches (such as graphic rating scales, mixed-standard scales, forced-choice forms, and essays), behavioral methods (such as critical incident ratings, checklists, BARS, and BOS), and results methods (MBO). The choice of method depends on the purpose of the appraisal. Trait appraisals are simple to develop and complete, but they have problems in terms of their subjectivity and are not useful for feedback. Behavioral methods provide more specific information for giving feedback but can be time-consuming and costly to develop. Results appraisals are more objective and can link individual performance to the organization as a whole, but they may encourage a short-term perspective (such as annual goals) and may not include subtle yet important aspects of performance.

LEARNING OUTCOME 5 The degree to which a performance appraisal program benefits an organization and its members is directly related to the quality of the appraisal interviews that are conducted. Interviewing skills are best developed through instruction and supervised practice. Although there are various approaches to the interview, research suggests that employee participation and goal setting lead to higher satisfaction and improved performance. Discussing problems with employees, showing support for them, minimizing criticism, and rewarding them when they perform well are also beneficial practices. During the interview, performance deficiencies can be discussed and plans for improvement can be made.

Key Terms

behavior observation scale (BOS)

behaviorally anchored rating scale (BARS)

calibration

contrast error

critical incident

customer appraisal

error of central tendency

essay method

focal performance appraisal

forced-choice method

forced distribution

graphic rating scale method

leniency or strictness error

management by objectives (MBO)

manager and/or supervisor appraisal

mixed-standard scale method

peer appraisal

performance appraisal

performance management

recency error

self-appraisal

similar-to-me error

subordinate appraisal

team appraisal

360 degree appraisal

Discussion Questions

LEARNING OUTCOME 1   Describe how the performance management process is linked to employee selection, training, and development.

LEARNING OUTCOME 2   Discuss the guidelines that performance appraisals should meet to be legally defensible.

LEARNING OUTCOME 3   What sources could be used to evaluate the performance of people working in the following jobs?

a. Sales representative
b. TV repairer
c. Director of nursing in a hospital
d. HR manager
e. Air traffic controller

LEARNING OUTCOME 4   Three types of appraisal interviews are described in this chapter.

a. What different skills are required for each type of appraisal interview? What reactions can one expect from using these different skills?
b. How can a manager develop the skills needed to conduct a problem-solving type of interview?
c. Which method do you feel is the least desirable? Why?

LEARNING OUTCOME 5   Discuss how you would go about diagnosing poor performance problems. List several factors to consider.

On the Job: Video Cases

Metropolitan Bakery

The two co-owners of Metropolitan Bakery talk about how performance is managed and evaluated. Special issues for a small business with many short-term employees are described. Certain performance standards related to attendance and customer service are absolute in an organization where relationships and customer satisfaction are critical to success. The organization is committed to providing continuous performance feedback to encourage growth.

What to Watch for and Ask Yourself

- The video discusses some performance management linkages between organizational strategies and employee performance. Describe at least one example where an organizational strategy of Metropolitan Bakery is reflected in performance management and leads to organizational outcomes.

- What type(s) of performance information (trait-based, behavior-based, or results-based) tends to be used at Metropolitan Bakery?

- Who appears to conduct the performance appraisals at Metropolitan Bakery? What are other possible rating sources that might be used at Metropolitan Bakery? Do you think adding additional ratings from different groups is a good idea for Metropolitan Bakery? Why or why not?

- Which method of performance appraisal do you think makes the most sense for Metropolitan Bakeryís employees? Explain your rationale. Would you recommend a different method for supervisory employees than nonsupervisory employees? Why or why not?

HRM EXPERIENCE
Performance Diagnosis

Managing the performance is an important—yet delicate—process for managers to undertake. They need to make tough calls at times regarding who is performing well or not. Also, they need to play the role of coach to help each employee improve his or her performance. One of the toughest aspects of performance management is assessing why someone is not performing well. Although it may be easy to spot who is not performing well, it is not always easy to diagnose the underlying causes of poor performance (such as motivation, ability, and external constraints). But without a correct diagnosis, it is nearly impossible to cure the problem.

Assignment

The following are descriptions of three different employees. Describe the potential causes of poor performance in each case. For each potential cause, identify appropriate solutions to enhance performance.

1. *Carl Spackler* is the assistant greenskeeper at Bushwood Country Club. Over the past few months, members have been complaining that gophers are destroying the course and digging holes in the greens. Although Carl has been working evenings and weekends to address the situation, the problem persists. Unfortunately, his boss is interested only in results, and because the gophers are still there, he contends that Carl is not doing his job. He has accused Carl of "slacking off" and threatened his job.

2. *Clark Griswold* works in research and development for a chemical company that makes nonnutritive food additives. His most recent assignment has been the development of a non-nutritive aerosol cooking spray, but the project is way behind schedule and seems to be going nowhere. CEO Frank Shirley is decidedly upset and has threatened that if things do not improve, he will suspend bonuses again this year, as he did last year. Clark feels dejected because without the bonus he will not be able to make a down payment on the family's swimming pool.

3. Tommy Callahan Jr. recently graduated from college after seven years and returned home to Sandusky, Ohio. His father, Big Tom Callahan, owner of Callahan Motors, offers Tommy a job in the auto parts factory that makes brake pads. Through a twist of fate, the factory is in severe danger of going under unless sales of the new brake pads increase dramatically. Tommy must go on the road with Richard (Big Tom's right-hand man) in a last-ditch effort to save the company. But Tommy proves to be unfocused, inexperienced, and lacking in confidence. Sales call after sales call he meets with rejection, even when the prospect looks promising. Customers express some concern about a warranty on the brake pads, but Richard believes that Tommy's inexperience and awkward approach are the big problems.

Case Study 1

Performance Management System Helps Freeport-McMoRan Switch Strategic Gears

What do you do when your organization needs to completely turn around its strategy due to a changing marketplace or for competitive reasons? Situations such as these are common in today's fast-paced business environment. Suppliers to the U.S. automotive industry found themselves in such a position during the last recession. They had to quickly find new markets and prepare to retool their businesses when GM, Ford, and Chrysler were looking like they would fail. How does a firm manage drastic changes like this? A good performance management system can help.

Freeport-McMoRan Copper & Gold is a case in point. The company, which is based in Phoenix, is the second largest copper mining company in the world. It employs near 30,000 workers and has mining operations that span four different continents. But it wasn't a poor market condition that caused Freeport-McMoRan to shift gears. It was a booming one. During much of the 1990s and 2000s, the price of copper was low—only about 75 cents per pound, making mining less profitable than it had been in the past. Mining a large amount of copper therefore became less of a priority than keeping costs low for Freeport-McMoRan.

However, in 2006 the price of copper jumped sharply upward, eventually hitting as much as $4.50 a pound. As a result, Freeport-McMoRan realized it needed to change its strategy—and fast. It needed to ramp up production and invest in new people and equipment in order to mine as much copper as possible while its price was high. The question became how to implement the change. Compounding the task was the fact that each mine was run separately. The firm's top managers did not even know how its employees were organized at the separate mines, let alone what their goals were or the metrics they were expected to achieve. The company had also acquired a rival mining company twice its size—Phelps Dodge—which made coordinating the performance of its people and operations even more difficult.

To align the goals of everyone in the company and get all of its various mines performing at top capacity, Freeport-McMoRan decided it would need a new performance management system. The system would hopefully enable the company to quickly implement and monitor the changes needed, while giving it the agility to change strategies again if or when the price of copper dropped.

Many of the employees who work in its mines do not use computers regularly on the job, so Freeport-McMoRan needed a system that was easy to use. For this reason, the company adopted a web-based performance management system by the software developer Taleo that employees could use at home. Initially, the firm rolled out the system to 500 employees as a pilot program. When it proved to be successful, the entire company began to use the system.

Apparently the system is working well. The company has been reporting very strong earnings that have surprised even Wall Street analysts. Its performance measures and strong management also earned it a spot in *Newsweek's* rankings of the top "greenest" 500 companies in the United States.

Meanwhile, Taleo and other performance management software developers are prospering, too, as they report big increases in the sales of their products. Why are these companies doing so well? For one, as the Freeport-McMoRan example shows, the software keeps everyone in an organization focused on a company's most important goals, which can have a strong impact on the firm's financial performance. It also helps organizations measure the contributions of its employees and to nurture, motivate, and reward employees based on their achievements. "Managers need reliable real-time data and pragmatic e-tools to measure, identify, analyze, and understand their organization's people capability—and what capability is needed to compete in the future," explains Jonathon Hogg, with PA Consulting Group, an IT and management consulting firm.

Questions

1. Why did Freeport-McMoRan need a performance management system? How will it help the company if it has to adjust its strategy in the future?
2. Do you think a pen-and-paper performance management system could have been as effective as the electronic system Freeport-McMoRan adopted? Why or why not?

Sources: Josh Bersin, "Performance Management Creates Agility in Copper Mining," Bersin & Associates [blog] (February 24, 2008), http://www.bersin.com; Jessica Twentyman, "Talent Management: Software Highlights Stars and Slackers," *Financial Times* (April 20, 2011), http://www.ft.com; David Lee Smith, "You Can't Afford to Pass Up Freeport-McMoRan," *Motley Fool* (April 5, 2011); http://www.fool.com.

Case Study 2

Appraising Employees at the San Diego Zoo

More than 3,000 people work for the Zoological Society of San Diego, a nonprofit organization that operates the San Diego Zoo, the San Diego Zoo's Wild Animal Park, and San Diego Zoo's Institute for Conservation Research. The people who work for the society are not quite as varied as the 800 species of animals the society deals with, but they do represent a wide cross section of all sorts of employees. They include everyone from veterinarians and scientists to food service personnel and security staff.

For years the society had used a paper-and-pen system to evaluate employees. However, there were no consequences if a supervisor did not bother to complete his or her reviews and submit them to HR. Enter Tim Mulligan, the society's new HR director. "The old review process was spotty at best," says Mulligan. "There were managers within the organization who had not received reviews in ten years," says Mulligan. There was simply no way to monitor whether the reviews were getting done and more importantly, there was no understanding by employees or managers of the need for them, says Mulligan.

Mulligan wanted to change the situation. He wanted the society and its managers to set some goals for themselves and their workers and for people to be to be paid based upon those goals. "It's hard to insist on accountability if there are no goals to hold anyone to," he says.

Consequently, Mulligan put together a team to explore the possibility of adopting a performance management system. After some research, the team determined that the zoo needed a system that would:

■ Be easy to use, even for those with limited computer skills; many people in the company were leery of having to learn how to operate a piece of software, so this was a top priority;

■ Effectively link employee goals with the Zoological Society's objectives;

- Objectively measure employee performance so that it could be linked with compensation;

- Better manage the process of tracking the review process; and

- Contain a journal feature so employees could record their achievements on a year-round basis.

Eventually the society decided to adopt Halogen Software's eAppraisal system. The software has built-in prompts that guide managers through the review process, and it frees HR professionals from the task of reminding managers that appraisals are due. The appraisal process can also be tailored to include multiple raters.

There was just one problem, the society had no goals. So, a second team of more than 200 managers was formed to establish goals and determine the key competencies that lead to a manager's success in the organization. At the beginning of the year, each manager chooses five goals, at least three of which must be linked to the organization's overall objectives. Those goals are based on everything from guest satisfaction to revenue. "The solution was not shoved down their throats by HR," said Mulligan. "No matter what department you worked in, you had a vote on the competencies that were going to be included."

Since implementing the eAppraisal systems, the appraisal completion rate has gone from about 50 percent to a full 100 percent. "At first, I think our employees found it hard to believe this was all really happening," says Mulligan, "Seeing managers being held accountable for customer satisfaction, employee satisfaction, budgets, and training and development is helping to strengthen our organization's employee accountability and to boost overall morale." Nor is the human touch lost when it comes to appraisals. Performance appraisals must be delivered in person, and supervisors and their employees discuss the results as they review the appraisals together. An employee cannot just pull up his appraisal on the web and read it.

"People come to work at the Zoo and the Wild Animal Park because they believe in our efforts to conserve endangered species," said Douglas Myers, executive director and CEO for the Zoological Society. "Tim has worked to ensure that this dedication is recognized and rewarded."

Questions

1. Why do nonprofits such as the San Diego Zoological Society need an appraisal system if their goal is not to maximize their profits?
2. What do you think are the pros and cons of using a web-based appraisal system?
3. How do you the new appraisal system will affect employees and the types of employees who work at the zoo?

Source: "The Zoological Society of San Diego Redefined Its Corporate Culture with Its New Employee Performance Management System," Halogen Software [case study], accessed April 23, 2011; Todd Henneman, "Employee Performance Management: What's Gnu at the Zoo," *Workforce Management*, September 2006; "San Diego Zoo Human Resources Director Honored," *Imperial Valley New* (July 16, 2008), http://www.ivpressonline.com.

Notes and References

1. Susan Scherreik, "Your Performance Review: Make It Perform," *Business Week*, no. 3762 (December 17, 2001): 139; Dick Grote, "Performance Evaluations: Is It Time for a Makeover?" *HRFocus* 77, no. 11 (November 2000): 6–7; "Employers Need to Do a Better Job of Performance Management," *Managing Training & Development* (April 2003): 8; Christopher D. Lee, "Feedback, Not Appraisal," *HRMagazine* 51, no. 11 (November 2006): 111–114. Cardy, R. L. and Leonard, B. 2011. Performance management: concepts, skills, and exercises. M. E. Sharpe, Inc.

2. Dana Jarvis, "Why Should We Continue Performance Appraisals if We Can't Give Raises, *Workforce Management* (September 2010) http://www.workforce.com.

3. David Allen and Rodger Griffeth, "Test of a Mediated Performance-Turnover Relationship Highlighting the Moderating Roles of Visibility and Reward Contingency," *Journal of Applied Psychology* 86, no. 5 (October 2001): 1014–21; Charles Pettijohn, Linda Pettijohn, and Michael D'Amico, "Characteristics of Performance Appraisals and Their Impact on Sales Force Satisfaction," *Human Resource Development Quarterly* 12, no. 2 (Summer 2001): 127–46; Scott and Einstein, "Strategic Performance Appraisal in Team-Based Organizations," 107–16; "Organizations Seek Stronger Performance Management—and PFP," *Pay for Performance Report* 4, no. 6 (June 2004): 2–4.

4. Garry Kranz, "Employees Want Feedback Even If It's Negative," *Workforce Management* (February 17, 2010), http://www.workforce.com.

5. Janet Wiscombe, "Can Pay for Performance Really Work?" *Workforce* 80, no. 8 (August 2001): 28–34; Charlotte Garvey, "Meaningful Tokens of Appreciation: Cash Awards Aren't the Only Way to Motivate Your Workforce," *HRMagazine* 49, no. 8 (August 2004): 101–106; Lisa D. Sprenkle, "Forced Ranking: A Good Thing for Business?" *Workforce.com*.

6. Donna Doldwasser, "Me a Trainer?" *Training* 38, no. 4 (April 2001): 60–66; Rebecca Ganzel, "Mike Carter," *Training* 38, no. 7 (July 2001): 28–30; Carla Joinson, "Making Sure Employees Measure Up," *HRMagazine* 46, no. 3 (March 2001): 36–41; Morton D. Rosenbaum, "Gratitude Adjustment: When a Pat on the Back Isn't Enough," *Meetings & Conventions* 39, no. 7 (June 2004): 20; James W. Smither, Manuel London, and Richard R. Reilly, "Does Performance Improve Following Multisource Feedback?" *Personnel Psychology* 58, no. 1 (Spring 2005): 33–67.

7. Matthew Boyle, "Performance Reviews: Perilous Curves Ahead," *Fortune* 143, no. 11 (May 28, 2001): 187–88; Susanne Scott and Walter Einstein, "Strategic Performance Appraisal in Team-Based Organizations: One Size Does Not Fit All," *Academy of Management Executive* 15, no. 2 (May 2001): 107–16; "Study Questions Performance Appraisal," *Australasian Business Intelligence* (May 1, 2003); Drew Robb, "Building a Better Workforce: Performance Management Software Can Help You Identify and Develop High-Performing Workers," *HRMagazine* 49, no. 10 (October 2004): 86–93.

8. Jonathan A. Segal, "86 Your Appraisal Process?" *HRMagazine* 45, no. 10 (October 2000): 199–206; Barry Witcher and Rosie Butterworth, "Honshin Kanri: How Xerox Manages," *Long-Range Planning* 32, no. 3 (June 1999): 323–32.

9. Kathryn Bartol, Cathy Durham, and June Poon, "Influence of Performance Evaluation Rating Segmentation on Motivation and Fairness Perceptions," *Journal of Applied Psychology* 86, no. 6 (December 2001): 1106–19; Anne P. Hubbell, "Motivating Factors: Perceptions of Justice and Their Relationship with Managerial and Organizational Trust," *Communication Studies* 56, no. 1 (March 2005): 47; Rebecca M. Chory-Assad, "Room for Improvement," *Training* 40, no. 11 (December 2003): 18–20; Deanna M. Merritt, "Appraising the Performance Appraisal," *Supervision* 68, no 4 (April 2007): 3–5.

10. John Newman, J. Mack Robinson, Larry Tyler, David Dunbar, and Joseph Zager, "CEO Performance Appraisal: Review and Recommendations/Practitioner Application," *Journal of Healthcare Management* 46, no. 1 (January/February 2001): 21–38; Bob Losyk, "How to Conduct a Performance Appraisal," *Public Management* 84, no. 3 (April 2002): 8–12; Arup Varma and Shaun Pichler, "Interpersonal Affect: Does It Really Bias Performance Appraisals?" *Journal of Labor Research* 28, no. 2 (Spring 2007): 397–412.

11. David Javitch, "How to Survive Employee Appraisals," *Entreprenur.com*, accessed April 23, 2011 at http://www.entrepreneur.com.

12. Doug Cederblom, "From Performance Appraisal to Performance Management: One Agency's Experience," *Public Personnel Management* 31, no. 2 (Summer 2002): 131–40; "Anonymous 360-Feedback Drives Vauxhall Strategy," *Personnel Today* (August 19, 2003): 16; Cindy Romaine, "Staying Relevant: Competencies and Employee Reviews," *Information Outlook* 8, no. 7 (April 2004): 21–25; Jerry K. Palmer and James M. Loveland, "The Influence of Group Discussion on Performance Judgments: Rating Accuracy, Contrast Effects, and Halo," *Journal of Psychology* 142, no. 2 (March 2008): 117–130; "When Promotions Are on the Line, Follow Your Criteria and Beware Supervisor Bias," *HR Specialist: Ohio Employment Law* 3, no. 12 (December 2009): 2.

13. Jason D. Shaw and Nina Gupta, "Job Complexity, Performance, and Well-Being: When Does Supplies-Values Fit Matter?" *Personnel Psychology* 57, no. 4 (Winter 2004): 847–80.

14. Joel Lefkowitz, "The Role of Interpersonal Affective Regard in Supervisory Performance Ratings: A Literature Review and Proposed Causal Model," *Journal of Occupational and Organizational Psychology* 73, no. 1 (March 2000): 67–85; Scott Highhouse, "Assessing the Candidate as a Whole: A Historical and Critical Analysis of Individual Psychological Assessment for Personnel Decision Making," *Personnel Psychology* 55, no. 2 (Summer 2002): 363–397.

15. Joanne Sammer, "Calibrating Consistency," *HRMagazine* 53, no. 1 (January 2008): 73–75.

16. *Brito v. Zia Company*, 478 F.2d 1200 (10th Cir. 1973); Treena L. Gillespie and Richard O. Parry, "Fuel for Litigation? Links

between Procedural Justice and Multisource Feedback," *Journal of Managerial Issues* 18, no. 4 (Winter 2006): 530–546.

17. *Albemarle Paper Company v. Moody*, 422 U.S. 405 (1975); Terry Gillen, "Appraisal: When Best Practice Is Bad Practice," *People Management* 11, no. 19 (September 29, 2005): 58.

18. Timothy Aeppel, "Goodyear Ends Ratings System ahead of Lawsuit," *The Wall Street Journal* (September 12, 2002), B8; "How to Stay 'Legal' with Performance Evaluation and Testing," *Managing Training & Development*, no. 4 (February 2004): 9.

19. Gillian Flynn, "Getting Performance Reviews Right," *Workforce* 80, no. 5 (May 2001): 76–78; David C. Martin, Kathryn M. Bartol, and Patrick E. Kehoe, "The Legal Ramifications of Performance Appraisal: The Growing Significance," *Public Personnel Management* 29, no. 3 (Fall 2000): 381; Deanna M Merritt, "Appraising the Performance Appraisal," *Supervision* 68, no 4 (April 2007): 3–5; Kevin R. Murphy, "Perspectives on the Relationship between Job Performance and Ratings of Job Performance," *Industrial & Organizational Psychology* (June 2008): 197–205; Cindy Miller, "Performance Appraisals in a Legal Context," *HR Info* (July 8, 2008), http://cindymiller.wordpress.com/.

20. "Loose Lips Lose Lawsuits: Screen Performance Reviews for FMLA comments," *Business Management Daily* (August 31, 2010), http://www.businessmanagementdaily.com.

21. Joan Brett and Leanne Atwater, "360-Degree Feedback: Accuracy, Reactions, and Perceptions of Usefulness," *Journal of Applied Psychology* 86, no. 5 (October 2001): 930–42; Bruce Pfau, Ira Kay, Kenneth Nowak, and Jai Ghorpade, "Does 360-Degree Feedback Negatively Affect Company Performance?" *HRMagazine* 47, no. 6 (June 2002): 54–59; Maury Peiperl, "Getting 360-Degree Feedback Right," *Harvard Business Review* 79, no. 1 (January 2001): 142–47; Robert Gandossy and Tina Kao, "Talent Wars: Out of Mind, Out of Practice," *Human Resource Planning* 27, no. 4 (December 2004): 15–20.

22. Corey E. Miller and Carl L. Thornton, "How Accurate Are Your Performance Appraisals?" *Public Personnel Management* (Summer 2006): 153–162; Edward J. Inderrieden, Robert E. Allen, and Timothy J. Keaveny, "Managerial Discretion in the Use of Self-Ratings in an Appraisal System: The Antecedents and Consequences," *Journal of Managerial Issues* 16, no. 4 (Winter 2004): 460–484.

23. Jeffrey Seglin, "Reviewing Your Boss," *Fortune* 143, no. 12 (June 11, 2001): 248; Ann Harrington, "Workers of the World, Rate Your Boss!" *Fortune* 142, no. 6 (September 18, 2000): 340–42; Robert Thompson, "Management Lite: Less Control, More Innovation," *HRMagazine* 44, no. 8 (August 1999): 10.

24. Ibid.

25. Brett and Atwater, "360-Degree Feedback," 930–42; Paula Silva and Henry L. Tosi, "Determinants of the Anonymity of the CEO Evaluation Process," *Journal of Managerial Issues* 16, no. 1 (Spring 2004): 87–103.

26. Ann Pomeroy, "Great Places, Inspired Employees: The Nation's Best Employers Show That Inspiring Employee Involvement through Good HR Practices Makes Good Business Sense," *HRMagazine* 49, no. 7 (July 2004): 44–64; Sue Browness, "Full-Circle Feedback," *Profit* 25, no. 2 (May 2006): 77.

27. John Drexler, Jr., Terry Beehr, and Thomas Stetz, "Peer Appraisals: Differentiation of Individual Performance on Group Tasks," *Human Resource Management* 40, no. 4 (Winter 2001): 333–45.

28. Scott and Einstein, "Strategic Performance Appraisal in Team-Based Organizations," 107–16; Debbie Kibbe and Jill Casner-Lotto, "Ralston Foods: From Greenfield to Maturity in a Team-Based Plant," *Journal of Organizational Excellence* 21, no. 3 (Summer 2002): 57–67; Simon Taggar and Mitchell Neubert, "The Impact of Poor Performers on Team Outcomes: An Empirical Examination of Attribution Theory," *Personnel Psychology* 57, no. 4 (Winter 2004): 935–69.

29. Bradley Kirkman and Benson Rosen, "Powering Up Teams," *Organizational Dynamics* 28, no. 3 (Winter 2000): 48–66; Matthew Valle and Kirk Davis, "Teams and Performance Appraisal: Using Metrics to Increase Reliability and Validity," *Team Performance Management* 5, no. 8 (1999): 238–43; Ebrahim Soltani, Robert Van der Meer, Terry M. Williams, and Pei-chun Lai, "The Compatibility of Performance Appraisal Systems with TQM Principles: Evidence from Current Practice," *International Journal of Operations & Production Management* 26, no. 1 (2006): 92–112.

30. Michael Cohn, "Best Buy Beefs Up Customer Value at the Call Center," *Internet World* 8, no. 6 (June 2002): 42–43; Joe Kohn, "Isuzu Has IDEA for Boosting Sales," *Automotive News* 76, no. 5973 (March 4, 2002): 41; D. L. Radcliff, "A New Paradigm of Feedback," *Executive Excellence* 19, no. 4 (April 2002): 20; Neeraj Bharadwaj and Anne Roggeveen, "The Impact of Offshored and Outsourced Call Service Centers on Customer Appraisals," *Marketing Letters* 19, no.1 (January 2008): 13–23.

31. Pfau, Kay, Nowak, and Ghorpade, "Does 360-Degree Feedback Negatively Affect Company Performance?" 54–59; Peiperl, "Getting 360-Degree Feedback Right," 142–47; Jack Kondrasuk, and Matt Graybill, "From Paper to Computer," *The Human Resource Professional* 13, no. 6 (November/December 2000): 18–19.

32. Gary Meyer, "Performance Reviews Made Easy, Paperless," *HRMagazine* 45, no. 10 (October 2000): 181–84; Douglas P. Shuit, "Huddling with the Coach—Part 2," *Workforce Management* 84, no. 2 (February 1, 2005): 5; "Ceridian and Softscape Announce an Agreement to Deliver Employee Performance and Development Solutions," *Payroll Manager's Report* (May 2004): 13; K. Sanwong, "The Development of a 360-Degree Performance Appraisal System: A University Case Study," *International Journal of Management* 25, no. 1 (March 2008): 16–22.

33. "Performance Appraisal," *HRMagazine* 47, no. 10 (October 2002): 146; Frank E. Kuzmits, Arthur J. Adams, Lyle Sussman, and Louis E. Raho, "360-Feedback in Health Care Management: A Field Study," *The Health Care Manager* 23, no. 321 (October–December 2004): 321–29; Jerry K. Palmer and James M. Loveland, "The Influence of Group Discussion on Performance Judgments: Rating Accuracy, Contrast Effects, and Halo. Preview," *Journal of Psychology* 142, no 2 (March 2008): 117–130; S. Bartholomew Craig and Kelly Hannum, "Research Update: 360-Degree Performance Assessment," *Consulting Psychology Journal: Practice & Research* 58, no. 2 (Spring 2006): 117–124;

G.N. Salunke "Colleagues, Managers, Customers, and Competitors Keys to Development: 360 Degree Approach to Development," *Advances in Management* 3, no. 8 (August 2010): 32.

34. Gary E. Roberts, "Perspectives on Enduring and Emerging Issues in Performance Appraisal," *Public Personnel Management* 27, no. 3 (Fall 1998): 301–20; William Hubbartt, "Bring Performance Appraisal Training to Life," *HRMagazine* 40, no. 5 (May 1995): 166, 168; Filip Lievens, "Assessor Training Strategies and Their Effects on Accuracy, Interrater Reliability, and Discriminant Validity," *Journal of Applied Psychology* 86, no. 2 (April 2001): 255–64; Dick Grote, "Performance Appraisals: Solving Tough Challenges," *HRMagazine* 45, no. 7 (July 2000): 145–50; Leslie A. Weatherly, "Performance Management: Getting It Right from the Start," *HRMagazine* 49, no. 3 (March 2004): S1–S12.

35. Gary P. Latham and Kenneth N. Wexley, *Increasing Productivity through Performance Appraisal*, 2nd ed. (Reading, MA: Addison-Wesley, 1994), 137.

36. Lefkowitz, "The Role of Interpersonal Affective Regard in Supervisory Performance Ratings," 67–85; Edwin Arnold and Marcia Pulich, "Personality Conflicts and Objectivity in Appraising Performance," *The Health Care Manager* 22, no. 3 (July–September 2003): 227; Krista Uggersly and Lorne M. Suksy, "Using Frame-of-Reference Training to Understand the Implications of Rater Idiosyncrasy for Rating Accuracy," *Journal of Applied Psychology*, 93, no. 3 (May 2008): 711–719.

37. Deidra J. Schleicher and David V. Day, "A Cognitive Evaluation of Frame-of-Reference Rater Training: Content and Process Issues," *Organizational Behavior and Human Decision Processes* 73, no. 1 (January 1998): 76–101; Wanda Smith, K. Vernard Harrington, and Jeffery Houghton, "Predictors of Performance Appraisal Discomfort: A Preliminary Examination," *Public Personnel Management* 29, no. 1 (Spring 2000): 21–32; Krista L. Uggerslev and Lorne M. Sulsky, "Using Frame-of-Reference Training to Understand the Implications of Rater Idiosyncrasy for Rating Accuracy," *Journal*

of Applied Psychology 93, no. 3 (May 2008): 711–719.

38. Christopher Bartlett and Andrew McLean, "GE's Talent Machine," *Harvard Business School* (2006), Case # 9-304-049.

39. Gail Johnson, "Forced Ranking: The Good, the Bad, and the Alternative," *Training* 41, no. 5 (May 2004): 24–31; Christine A. Amalfe and Eileen Quinn Steiner, "Forced Ranking Systems: Yesterday's Legal Target?" *New Jersey Law Journal* (March 28, 2005); Jessica Marquez, "Is GE'S Ranking System Broken?" *Workforce Management* 86, no. 12 (June 25, 2007): 1–3.

40. Lisa Keeping and Paul Levy, "Performance Appraisal Reaction: Measurement, Modeling, and Method Bias," *Journal of Applied Psychology* 85, no. 5 (October 2000): 708–23.

41. Adam B. Butler and Amie Skattebo, "What Is Acceptable for Women May Not Be for Men: The Effect of Family Conflicts with Work on Job-Performance Ratings," *Journal of Occupational and Organizational Psychology* 77, no. 4 (December 2004): 553–64; Cheri Ostroff, Leanne E. Atwater, and Barbara J. Feinberg, "Understanding Self-Other Agreement: A Look at Rater and Ratee Characteristics, Context, and Outcomes," *Personnel Psychology* 57, no. 1 (Summer 2004): 333–37; Mike Schraeder and Jim Simpson, "How Similarity and Liking Affect Performance Appraisals," *Journal for Quality & Participation* 29, no. 1 (Spring 2006): 34–40.

42. Kristina E. Chirico, M. Ronald Buckley, Anthony R. Wheeler, Jeffrey D. Facteau, H. John Bernardin, and Danielle S. Beu, "A Note on the Need for True Scores in Frame-of-Reference (FOR) Training Research," *Journal of Managerial Issues* 16, no. 3 (Fall 2004): 382–98; Christopher D. Lee, "Feedback, Not Appraisal," *HRMagazine* 51, no. 11 (November 2006): 111–114.

43. Stephen C. Behrenbrinker, "Conducting Productive Performance Evaluations in the Assessor's Office," *Assessment Journal* 2, no. 5 (September/October 1995): 48–54; Aharon Tziner, Christine Joanis, and Kevin Murphy, "A Comparison of Three Methods of Performance Appraisal with Regard to Goal Properties, Goal Perception, and Ratee Satisfaction," *Group & Organization Management* 25, no. 2 (June 2000): 175–90.

44. Elaine Pulakos, Sharon Arad, Michelle Donovan, and Kevin Plamondon, "Adaptability in the Workplace: Development of a Taxonomy of Adaptive Performance," *Journal of Applied Psychology* 85, no. 4 (August 2000): 612–24; Leslie A. Weatherly, "Performance Management: Getting It Right from the Start," *HRMagazine* 49, no. 3 (March 2004): S1–S12; Edwin Arnold and Marcia Pulich, "Personality Conflicts and Objectivity in Appraising Performance," *The Health Care Manager* 22, no. 3 (July–September 2003): 227.

45. Latham and Wexley, *Increasing Productivity*; Tziner, Joanis, and Murphy, "A Comparison of Three Methods of Performance Appraisal," 175–90; Simon Taggar and Travor Brown, "Problem-Solving Team Behaviors: Development and Validation of BOS and a Hierarchical Factor Structure," *Small Group Research* 32, no. 6 (December 2001): 698–726; Paul Falcone, "Big-Picture Performance Appraisal," *HR Focus* 84, no. 9 (September 2007): 1–15.

46. Daniel Bachrach, Elliot Bendoly, and Philip Podsakoff, "Attributions of the 'Causes' of Group Performance as an Alternative Explanation of the Relationship between Organizational Citizenship Behavior and Organizational Performance," *Journal of Applied Psychology* 86, no. 6 (December 2001): 1285–93; Susan Leandri, "Measures That Matter: How to Fine-Tune Your Performance Measures," *Journal for Quality and Participation* 24, no. 1 (Spring 2001): 39–41.

47. Peter F. Drucker, *The Practice of Management* (New York: Harper & Brothers, 1954); reissued by HarperCollins in 1993); Janice S. Miller, "High Tech and High Performance: Managing Appraisal in the Information Age," *Journal of Labor Research* 24, no. 3 (Summer 2003): 409–425.

48. E. Locke and G. Latham, *A Theory of Goal Setting and Task Performance* (Englewood Cliffs, NJ: Prentice Hall, 1990). See also John J. Donovan and David J. Radosevich, "The Moderating Role of Goal Commitment on the Goal Difficulty-Performance Relationship: A Meta-Analytic Review and Critical Reanalysis," *Journal of Applied Psychology* 83, no. 2 (April 1998): 308–15; Cindy Romaine, "Staying Relevant: Competencies and Employee Reviews," *Information*

Outlook 8, no. 4 (April 2004): 21–25; Gail Johnson, "Room for Improvement," *Training* 40, no. 11 (December 2003): 18–20.

49. Jack Steele, "Transforming the Balanced Scorecard into Your Strategy Execution System," *Manage* 53, no. 1 (September/October 2001): 22–23. See also Robert Kaplan and David Norton, "Strategic Learning and the Balanced Scorecard," *Strategy & Leadership* 24, no. 5 (September/October 1996): 18–24; Robert Kaplan and David Norton, "Using the Balanced Scorecard as a Strategic Management System," *Harvard Business Review* (January–February 1996): 75–85; Joe Mullich, "Get in Line: People Talk about Aligning Corporate, Departmental and Employee Goals, But Not Many Actually Do It," *Workforce Management* 82, no. 13 (December 2003): 43; "Good Appraisal Is Simple, Happens Often, Experts Say," *The Orlando Sentinel* (via *Knight-Ridder/Tribune News Service*), December 3, 2003; Li-cheng Chang, "The NHS Performance Assessment Framework as a Balanced Scorecard Approach," *International Journal of Public Sector Management* 20, no 2 (2007): 101–117.

50. Deloris McGee Wanguri, "A Review, an Integration, and a Critique of Cross-Disciplinary Research on Performance Appraisals, Evaluations, and Feedback," *Journal of Business Communications* 32, no. 3 (July 1995): 267–93; Tziner, Joanis, and Murphy, "A Comparison of Three Methods of Performance Appraisal," 175–90; "Good Appraisal Is Simple, Happens Often, Experts Say"; Joanna Haworth, "Measuring Performance," *Nursing Management—UK* 15, no. 3 (June 2008): 22–28.

51. Kwok Leung, Steven Su, and Michael Morris, "When Is Criticism Not Constructive? The Roles of Fairness Perceptions and Dispositional Attributions in Employee Acceptance of Critical Supervisory Feedback," *Human Relations* 54, no. 9 (September 2001): 1155–87; Ted Pollock, "Make Your Criticism Pay Off," *Electric Light & Power* 81, no. 1 (January 2003): 31; "Five Ways to Tackle Poor Performers," *Law Office Management & Administration Report* 6, no. 12 (December 2006): 9.

52. "Focus on Success," *Aftermarket Business* 115, no. 2 (February 2005): 1.

53. Helen Wilkie, "The Tricky Art of Criticism," *HRMagazine* 49, no. 12 (December 2004): 77–83.

After studying this chapter, you should be able to

LEARNING OUTCOME 1 Explain how to formulate a strategic compensation program.

LEARNING OUTCOME 2 Indicate how pay is determined.

LEARNING OUTCOME 3 Know how to effectively perform a job evaluation.

LEARNING OUTCOME 4 Explain the purpose of a wage survey.

LEARNING OUTCOME 5 Define the wage curve, pay grades, and rate ranges as parts of the compensation structure.

LEARNING OUTCOME 6 Understand the importance of using a compensation scorecard.

LEARNING OUTCOME 7 Identify the major provisions of the federal laws affecting compensation.

In 2011, Google gave all its employees a 10 percent raise. The companywide pay boost, spread across 20,300 employees, probably cost the company $1 billion a year. In an e-mail to employees, former Google CEO Eric Schmidt explained that they have received feedback that salary is more important than other sources of pay (i.e., bonuses and stock in the company).[1] Schmidt explained that even in a slowed-down economy they are in a "war for talent" and that employees had expressed concerns "dealing with sky-high property prices, mortgages, and those kinds of things." But ultimately, Schmidt stated that the primary reason for the raise was that "we just thought it was good for the whole company!"[2]

Compensation is a way to increase employee loyalty. In Google's case, it is seen as a way to decrease the likelihood that its employees will be hired away by competitors like Facebook.[3] It reflects a strategic move on the part of the company to show that its employees are the most important component for Google's success. So why focus on compensation? Why not better select employees who will be more loyal? Why not improve the training programs or evaluation systems? The answer is simple. Compensation is directly linked to an employee's livelihood. Employees can receive stellar training, copious growth opportunities, and be completely satisfied with their work and the environment, but they will not show up to work if there is no paycheck in return.

What is Compensation?

Compensation consists of three main components. *Direct compensation* encompasses employee wages and salaries, incentives, bonuses, and commissions. *Indirect compensation* comprises the many benefits supplied by employers, and *nonfinancial compensation* includes employee recognition programs, rewarding jobs, organizational support, work environment, and flexible work hours to accommodate personal needs. See Figure 9.1.

The way these three components of compensation are allocated sends a message to the employees about what management believes is important and the types of activities it encourages.[4] Furthermore, for an employer, compensation constitutes a sizable operating cost. In certain manufacturing environments, compensation is as high as 60 percent of total costs and even higher for many service organizations.[5] Ravin Jesuthasan, compensation specialist at Towers Perrin, notes, "Labor costs are a significant portion of expenses for any organization and a very substantial portion for some, but companies continue to spend on pay programs without any evidence of business relevance."[6] This means that compensation should be managed strategically to ensure that costs are kept down while employee motivation and performance are kept up. Achieving such a balance is no easy task.

In this chapter we will help you learn how to strategically align the three aspects of compensation with an organization's objectives, design a pay mix based on the compensation strategy, implement the mix using a series of pay tools, and assess the compensation system using a scorecard. We will also discuss how government regulation might influence these decisions about compensation. See Figure 9.2 for details. In Chapter 10 we will review financial incentive plans for employees. Employee benefits that are part of the total compensation package are discussed in Chapter 11.

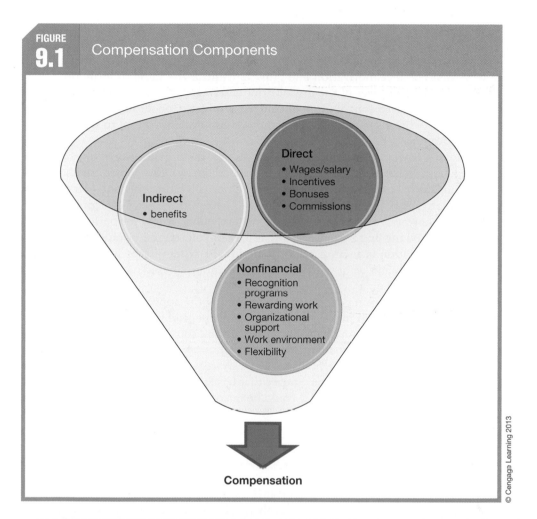

FIGURE 9.1 Compensation Components

Indirect
• benefits

Direct
• Wages/salary
• Incentives
• Bonuses
• Commissions

Nonfinancial
• Recognition programs
• Rewarding work
• Organizational support
• Work environment
• Flexibility

Compensation

© Cengage Learning 2013

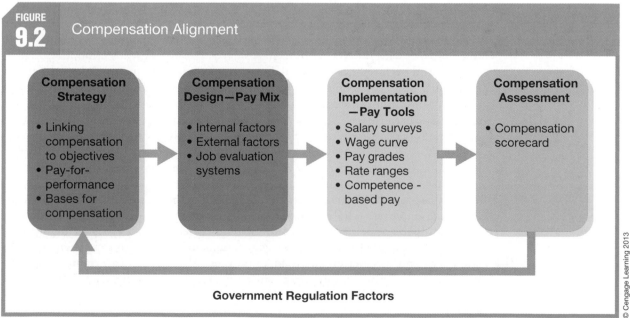

FIGURE 9.2 Compensation Alignment

Compensation Strategy
• Linking compensation to objectives
• Pay-for-performance
• Bases for compensation

Compensation Design—Pay Mix
• Internal factors
• External factors
• Job evaluation systems

Compensation Implementation—Pay Tools
• Salary surveys
• Wage curve
• Pay grades
• Rate ranges
• Competence-based pay

Compensation Assessment
• Compensation scorecard

Government Regulation Factors

© Cengage Learning 2013

Strategic Compensation

LEARNING OUTCOME 1

Facebook has over 2,000 employees and offices in over a dozen countries. How would you develop a compensation strategy to match Facebook's business objectives of continual innovation and growth?

What is strategic compensation? Simply stated, it is the compensation of employees in ways that enhance motivation and growth, while at the same time aligning their efforts with the objectives of the organization. Strategic compensation has redefined the role and perceived contribution of compensation. No longer merely a "cost of doing business," when used strategically compensation becomes a tool to secure a competitive advantage.

Developing a compensation strategy requires that the organizational objectives are first analyzed. What does the company want to be known for? What are its growth projections? What are its core competencies? Once you figure this out, you can then decide what types of behaviors and skills will be rewarded. By rewarding specific skills and behaviors, you demonstrate that you are willing to pay for performance and not just for showing up to work. Finally, as part of your strategy you need to decide on the compensation base most appropriate for the types of jobs in your company. For example, you might want to pay a sales representative based more on commission and a manager more on a yearly salary.

Strategic compensation goes beyond determining the appropriate market rates to pay employees, although market rates are one element of compensation planning. Strategic compensation should also purposefully link compensation to the organization's mission and general business objectives. For example, while Google's decision to increase base pay for all its employees was a strategic move to be more competitive with market rates, Google also recognizes that base pay is not everything. One product development manager stated, "I could be making much more than I'm getting at Google, but I chose Google because of the flexibility to grow and work on exciting new products . . . plus, where else can you get a chef making you breakfast, lunch, and dinner anytime you want?"[7] In this regard, Google has not only aligned its compensation strategy with the external market, it has also aligned it with its desire to be a flexible and innovative company whose core competency is found in the creativity of its people. Commenting on the importance of strategic compensation to organizational success, Gerald Ledford and Elizabeth Hawk, two compensation specialists, note, "Companies throughout the economy have begun to rethink their compensation systems in search for competitive advantage."

Additionally, strategic compensation serves to mesh the monetary payments made to employees with other HR initiatives, such as recruitment, selection, training, retention, and performance appraisal. For example, starting pay can make a difference in whether or not someone will apply for the job. A compensation specialist speaking to one of the authors noted, "The linkage of pay levels to labor markets is a strategic policy issue because it serves to attract or retain valued employees while affecting the organization's relative payroll budget." For example, colleges such as Idaho State University; Mesa Community College in Mesa, Arizona; and the University of Georgia know that they cannot attract or retain qualified professors unless their pay strategy is linked to competitive market rates.

Many fast-food restaurants, such as Burger King, Taco Bell, and Blimpie's—traditionally low-wage employers—have needed to raise their starting wages to attract a sufficient number of job applicants to meet staffing requirements. If pay rates are high, which creates a large applicant pool, then organizations may choose to raise their selection standards and hire better-qualified employees. This in turn can reduce employer training costs. When employees perform at exceptional levels, their performance appraisals may justify an increased pay rate. For these reasons and others, an organization should develop a formal program to manage employee compensation. Step one of this program is to develop a compensation strategy that is linked to the organization's objectives.

Linking Compensation to Organizational Objectives

The financial crisis of 2007–2010 changed the landscape for compensation. Now companies are more heavily scrutinized by shareholders, government, and the public for how much they pay their people. For example, due to complaints of bloated federal government salaries, exorbitant Wall Street banker bonuses, and overly generous autoworker benefits, managers are trying to ensure that their compensation plans are in strict alignment with the organization's objectives.

In particular, a Bloomberg National Poll showed that more than 70 percent of Americans thought big bonuses should be banned for Wall Street companies that took taxpayer bailouts. A law aimed at giving shareholders more of a say in the compensation of bankers was passed in July, 2010.[8] Wall Street banks are now much more careful to reward employees only when they perform in line with organizational objectives. Furthermore, American President Obama enacted a two-year (2011–2012) freeze on federal salaries to help the government achieve its objectives of reducing the deficit. President Obama stated that "[the freeze] would save . . . $28 billion in cumulative savings over the next five years."[9] Finally, due in part to poor strategic decisions, General Motors (GM) experienced high pension, wage, and benefit costs that the company could not sustain in the financial crisis. As a result, GM ended up laying off more than 107,000 employees during the financial crisis.[10] While the United Autoworker Union (UAW) was partly to blame for its lack of flexibility in adjusting salary and benefit plans, GM managers were also guilty for not aligning compensation with organizational objectives to compete with foreign automakers.[11]

The new compensation landscape requires that managers be more strategic about their compensation decisions. Managers must first and foremost understand the strategic objectives of the organization in relation to the industry in which it operates. Next, they need to move away from paying for a specific position or job title to rewarding employees on the basis of their individual competencies or work contributions to these organizational objectives. In fact, a sample of Fortune 500 companies headquartered in America, Europe, and Asia showed that pay for performance that is linked to organizational objectives is a primary component of most compensation systems.[12] Another study showed that 91 percent

GM's failure to align compensation with the company's objectives is partly to blame for its massive layoffs in recent years.

Jim West / Alamy

of participating companies link their pay strategy with organizational performance. The study found that a written compensation plan indicates that senior management understands and is committed to aligning their business strategy with pay, suggesting the alignment of pay with organizational objectives can positively impact company performance.[13]

Increasingly, compensation specialists are asking which components of the compensation package (benefits, base pay, incentives, and so on), both separately and in combination, create value for the organization and its employees. Managers are asking questions such as: "How will this pay program help to retain and motivate valued employees?" and "Does the benefit or pay practice affect the administrative cost?" Payments that fail to advance either the employee or the organization are removed from the compensation program.[14]

It is not uncommon for organizations to establish very specific goals for linking their organizational objectives to their compensation program.[15] Formalized compensation goals serve as guidelines for managers to ensure that wage and benefit policies achieve their intended purpose. The more common goals of a strategic compensation policy include the following:

1. To reward employees' past performance[16]

2. To remain competitive in the labor market

3. To maintain salary equity among employees

4. To mesh employees' future performance with organizational goals

5. To control the compensation budget

6. To attract new employees

7. To reduce unnecessary turnover[17]

To achieve these goals, policies must be established to guide management in making decisions. Formal statements of compensation policies typically include the following:

1. The rate of pay within the organization and whether it is to be above, below, or at the prevailing market rate

2. The ability of the pay program to gain employee acceptance while motivating employees to perform to the best of their abilities

3. The pay level at which employees may be recruited and the pay differential between new and more senior employees

4. The intervals at which pay raises are to be granted and the extent to which merit and/or seniority will influence the raises

5. The pay levels needed to facilitate the achievement of a sound financial position in relation to the products or services offered

The Pay-for-Performance Standard

"Companies are looking for ways to pay for performance, and segmenting their workforce helps them identify their most valuable contributors. Rewarding top performers is essential for the ongoing success of the company," states Stephen E. Gross, global leader for Mercer Consulting, a Manhattan human-resource consulting company.[18] Why is this statement significant? A pay-for-performance standard, as discussed in Chapter 11, serves to raise productivity and lower labor costs in today's competitive economic environment. It is agreed that managers must tie at least some reward to employee effort and performance. Without this standard, motivation to perform with greater effort will be low, resulting in higher wage costs to the organization. Additionally, most employees believe that their compensation should be directly linked to their relative performance.

The term "pay for performance" refers to a wide range of compensation options, including merit-based pay, bonuses, salary commissions, job and pay banding, team/group incentives, and various gainsharing programs. (Gainsharing plans are discussed in Chapter 10.) Each of these compensation systems seeks to differentiate between the pay of average performers and that of outstanding performers. When Plum Creek Timber Company, the largest timberland owner in the United States, merged with The Timber Company, it emphasized a pay-for-performance philosophy by forming new salary ranges based on each job's impact on the business and incentive rewards linked more directly to individual and company performance.

Unfortunately, designing a sound pay-for-performance system is not easy. You need to consider how employee performance will be measured. For example, measuring an employee's output may be relatively easy and objective on an assembly line but more difficult (and subjective) when the employee works in a service environment. Other concerns include the monies to be allocated for compensation increases, which employees to cover, the payout method, and the periods when payments will be made.

A critical concern for a successful pay-for-performance system is the perceived fairness of the pay decision. The decision to freeze federal government employee salaries for 2011 and 2012 may make sense in decreasing the deficit, but at the same time, may seem unfair to many federal workers. A survey by Mercer, found that more than 98 percent of private-sector companies nationwide were awarding pay increases in 2011.[19] Media reports showed that many federal employees were discouraged by this decision because they see many of their peers in the private sector receiving substantial performance raises. For example, one worker snidely remarked, "as a federal worker, I'm certainly looking forward to bearing a share of the bonuses and raises that private-sector workers will no doubt enjoy during the next economic boom."[20]

Motivating Employees through Compensation

Pay constitutes a quantitative measure of an employee's relative worth. For most employees, pay has a direct bearing not only on perceived fairness, but also on the status and recognition they may be able to achieve both on and off the job. Because pay represents a reward received in exchange for an employee's contributions, it is essential, according to the equity theory, that the pay be equitable in terms of those contributions. It is essential also that an employee's pay be equitable in terms of what other employees are receiving for their contributions.

Pay Equity

Simply defined, equity embraces the concept of fairness. Equity theory, also referred to as *distributive fairness*, is a motivation theory that explains how people respond to situations in which they feel they have received less (or more) than they deserve.[21]

pay-for-performance standard

A standard by which managers tie compensation to employee effort and performance

A central point the theory makes is that individuals make comparisons with people both inside and outside their organization, and that these comparisons influence their motivation.[22] In a work setting, individuals form a ratio of their inputs (abilities, skills, experiences) to their outputs (salary, benefits). They then compare the value of that ratio with the value of the input/output ratio for other individuals in a similar class of jobs either internal or external to the organization. If the value of their ratio equals the value of another's, they perceive the situation as equitable and no tension exists. However, if they perceive their input/output ratio as inequitable relative to others', this creates tension and motivates them to eliminate or reduce the inequity. The strength of their motivation is proportional to the magnitude of the perceived inequity. Figure 9.3 illustrates pay equity and feelings of being fairly paid.

pay equity

An employee's perception that compensation received is equal to the value of the work performed

For employees, pay equity is achieved when the compensation received is equal to the value of the work performed. There are three kinds of pay equity:

1. external equity—people in similar jobs compare themselves to what others are making in different organizations,

2. internal equity—people compare themselves to peers in different jobs in the same organization,

3. individual equity—people compare themselves to others in their organization with the same job.

Research clearly demonstrates that employees' perceptions of pay equity, or inequity, can have dramatic effects on their motivation for both work behavior and productivity. Managers must therefore develop strategic pay practices that are both internally and externally equitable.

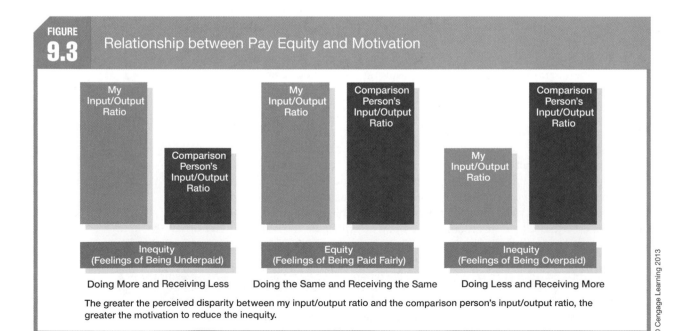

FIGURE 9.3   Relationship between Pay Equity and Motivation

My Input/Output Ratio	Comparison Person's Input/Output Ratio
Inequity (Feelings of Being Underpaid)	
Doing More and Receiving Less	

My Input/Output Ratio	Comparison Person's Input/Output Ratio
Equity (Feelings of Being Paid Fairly)	
Doing the Same and Receiving the Same	

My Input/Output Ratio	Comparison Person's Input/Output Ratio
Inequity (Feelings of Being Overpaid)	
Doing Less and Receiving More	

The greater the perceived disparity between my input/output ratio and the comparison person's input/output ratio, the greater the motivation to reduce the inequity.

Expectancy Theory and Pay

Another tool to help determine your compensation strategy is expectancy theory. The expectancy theory of motivation predicts that one's level of motivation depends on the attractiveness of the rewards sought and the probability of obtaining those rewards.[23] The theory has developed from the work of psychologists who consider humans as thinking, reasoning people who have beliefs and anticipations concerning future life events. Expectancy theory therefore holds that employees should exert greater work effort if they have reason to expect that it will result in a reward that is valued.[24] To motivate this effort, the value of any monetary reward should be attractive. Employees also must believe that good performance is valued by their employer and will result in their receiving the expected reward.

Figure 9.4 shows the relationship between pay-for-performance and the expectancy theory of motivation. The model predicts, first, that high effort will lead to high performance (expectancy). For example, if an employee believes she has the skills and abilities to perform her job and if she works hard (effort), then her performance will improve or be high. Second, high performance should result in rewards that are appreciated by the employee (valued). Elements of the compensation package are said to have *instrumentality* when an employee's high performance leads to monetary rewards that are valued. As previously stated, pay-for-performance leads to a feeling of pay satisfaction, and this feeling should reinforce one's high level of effort.

Thus, how employees view compensation can be an important factor in determining the motivational value of compensation. Furthermore, the effective communication of pay information together with an organizational environment that elicits employee trust in management can contribute to employees' having more accurate perceptions of their pay. The perceptions employees develop concerning their pay are influenced by the accuracy of their knowledge and understanding of the compensation program's strategic objectives.

Pay Secrecy

Misperceptions by employees concerning the equity of their pay and its relationship to performance can be created by secrecy about the pay that others receive. There is

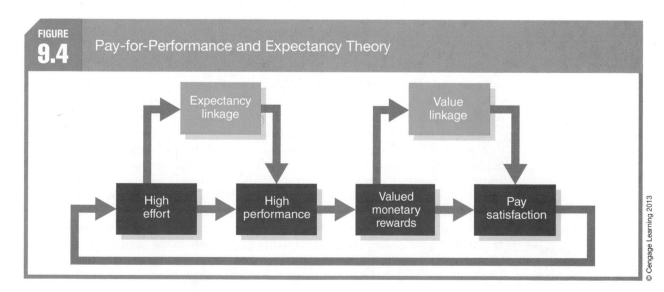

FIGURE 9.4   Pay-for-Performance and Expectancy Theory

© Cengage Learning 2013

reason to believe that secrecy can generate distrust in the compensation system, reduce employee motivation, and inhibit organizational effectiveness. Yet pay secrecy seems to be an accepted practice in many organizations. Employers may have overt or implicit prohibitions on sharing pay information, and some even put the policies in writing.[25] A U.S. survey found that 19 percent of employees say they work in a place where discussions of pay are "formally prohibited and/or employees caught discussing wages could be punished." Another 31 percent said that discussions of pay were discouraged, while only 16 percent said that pay could be discussed among employees.[26]

Managers may justify secrecy on the grounds that most employees prefer to have their own pay kept secret. Probably one of the reasons for pay secrecy that managers may be unwilling to admit is that it gives them greater freedom in compensation management. If pay decisions are not disclosed, there is no need to justify or defend them.[27] Employees who are not supposed to know what others are being paid have no objective base for pursuing complaints about their own pay. Secrecy also serves to cover up inequities existing within the internal pay structure. For example, Lilly Ledbetter, the plaintiff in the epic employment discrimination case "Ledbetter v. Goodyear Tire & Rubber Co." may have found out that she was being paid less than men doing the same job and remedied the problem much earlier if she had been allowed to ask about other workers' pay. Furthermore, secrecy surrounding compensation decisions may lead employees to believe that there is no direct relationship between pay and performance.

Managers wishing to maintain pay secrecy among employees may encounter problems with Internet salary survey data. Ready access to free online salary surveys gives employees an approximate idea of how their salary compares to others nationally or locally. This information could put managers "on the spot" should employees discover that their salaries are lower than those of other employees at comparable organizations.

The Bases for Compensation

hourly work

Work paid on an hourly basis

piecework

Work paid according to the number of units produced

Work performed in most private, public, and not-for-profit organizations has traditionally been compensated on an hourly basis. It is referred to as hourly work, in contrast to piecework, in which employees are paid according to the number of units they produce. Hourly work, however, is far more prevalent than piecework as a basis for compensating employees.

Employees compensated on an hourly basis are classified as *hourly employees*, or wage earners. Those whose compensation is computed on the basis of weekly, biweekly, or monthly pay periods are classified as *salaried employees*. Hourly employees are normally paid only for the time they work. Salaried employees, by contrast, are generally paid the same for each pay period, even though they occasionally may work more hours or fewer than the regular number of hours in a period. They also usually receive certain benefits not provided to hourly employees.

nonexempt employees

Employees covered by the overtime provisions of the Fair Labor Standards Act

exempt employees

Employees not covered by the overtime provisions of the Fair Labor Standards Act

Another basis for compensation centers on whether employees are classified as *nonexempt* or *exempt* under the Fair Labor Standards Act (FLSA).[28] Nonexempt employees are covered by the act and must be paid at a rate of one and a half times their *regular* pay rate for time worked in excess of forty hours in their workweek. Most hourly workers employed in interstate commerce are considered nonexempt workers under the FLSA. Employees not covered by the overtime provision of the FLSA are classified as exempt employees. Managers and supervisors as well as a large number of white-collar employees are in the exempt category. The U.S. Department of Labor (DOL) imposes a narrow definition of exempt status, and employers wishing to classify employees as exempt must convince the DOL that the job is exempt on the basis of the independent judgment of the jobholder and other criteria. Therefore employers should check the exact terms and conditions of exemption before classifying employees as either exempt or nonexempt. (See "Exemption from Overtime Provisions" later in this chapter.)

To help in these types of decisions, larger companies will often use compensation consultants. A study showed that about 86 percent of large U.S. companies use a compensation consultant to help them with their compensation strategy and pay mix. The four largest providers of compensation consulting are Towers Perrin, Mercer Consulting, Frederic W. Cook & Co., and Hewitt Associates.[29]

Compensation Design—The Pay Mix

An employee may ask: "How is my pay determined?" In practice, a combination of *internal* and *external* factors can influence, directly or indirectly, the rates at which employees are paid. Through their interaction these factors constitute the pay mix, as shown in Figure 9.5. For example, the area pay rate for administrative assistants might be $11.50 per hour. However, one employer may elect to pay its administrative assistants $14.25 per hour because of their excellent performance. The influence of government legislation on the pay mix will be discussed later in the chapter.

LEARNING OUTCOME 2

Google's decision to increase pay by 10 percent was based on many internal and external factors. What specific factors would you say led to Google's compensation redesign?

Internal Factors

The internal factors that influence pay rates are the organization's compensation strategy, the worth of a job, an employee's relative worth in meeting job requirements, and an employer's ability to pay.

Compensation Strategy

Highlights in HRM 1 illustrates the compensation strategies of two organizations, Tri Star Performance and Preventive Health Care. The pay strategy of Preventive

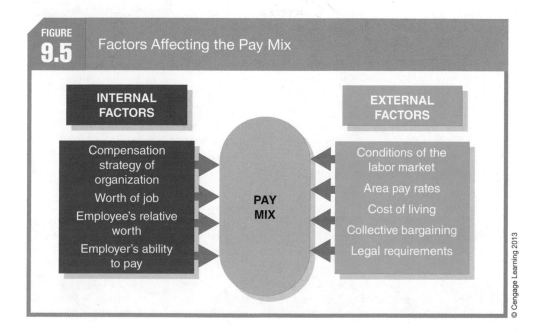

FIGURE 9.5   Factors Affecting the Pay Mix

INTERNAL FACTORS
- Compensation strategy of organization
- Worth of job
- Employee's relative worth
- Employer's ability to pay

PAY MIX

EXTERNAL FACTORS
- Conditions of the labor market
- Area pay rates
- Cost of living
- Collective bargaining
- Legal requirements

© Cengage Learning 2013

Health Care is to be an industry pay leader, while Tri Star Performance seeks to be pay competitive. Both employers strive to promote a compensation policy that is internally fair.

Tri Star Performance and Preventive Health Care, like other employers, will establish numerous compensation objectives that affect the pay employees receive. At a minimum, both large and small employers should set pay policies reflecting (1) the internal wage relationship among jobs and skill levels, (2) the external competition, or an employer's pay position relative to what competitors are paying, (3) a policy of rewarding employee performance, and (4) administrative decisions concerning elements of the pay system such as overtime premiums, payment periods, and short-term or long-term incentives.

Worth of a Job

Organizations without a formal compensation program generally base the worth of jobs on the subjective opinions of people familiar with the jobs. In such instances, pay rates may be influenced heavily by the labor market or, in the case of unionized employers, by collective bargaining. Organizations with formal compensation programs, however, are more likely to rely on a system of *job evaluation* to aid in rate determination. (Note that this topic will be covered later in the chapter under pay structure.) Even when rates are subject to collective bargaining, job evaluation can assist the organization in maintaining some degree of control over its pay structure.

The use of job evaluation is widespread in both the public and the private sector. The cities of Chicago and Miami use job evaluation in establishing pay structures, as do Google, Goldman Sachs, and GM. The jobs covered most frequently by job evaluation are clerical, technical, and various blue-collar groups. Other jobs covered are managerial and top executive positions.

Several factors should be taken into consideration when determining how much a worker like this one should be paid

© Frances Roberts / Alamy

In today's competitive environment, compensation professionals believe that the worth of a job should be based on more than market prices or using only an internally driven job evaluation program. Rather, a job's value should be based on *the total value* delivered to the organization. That is, some jobs may simply be more important to organizational success than others regardless of how they are internally evaluated.[30] Valuing work not only properly enables organizations to price "important" jobs effectively, but also provides insight into how a job relates to the organization's objectives. Additionally, valuing work properly serves to attract and retain the right talent to drive organizational performance.[31]

Employee's Relative Worth

In both hourly and salary jobs, employee performance can be recognized and rewarded through promotion and with various incentive systems. (The incentive systems used most often will be discussed in Chapter 10.) Superior performance can also be rewarded by granting merit raises on the basis of steps within a rate range established for a job class. If merit raises are to have their intended value, however, they must be determined by an effective performance appraisal system that differentiates between employees who deserve the raises and those who do not. This system, moreover, must provide a visible and credible relationship between performance and any raises received. Unfortunately, too many so-called merit systems provide for raises to be granted automatically. As a result, employees tend to be rewarded more for merely

HIGHLIGHTS IN **HRM**
Comparison of Compensation Strategies

Compensation strategies and objectives can differ widely across large and small employers as well as across employers in the private and public sectors. Here are the compensation strategies at Tri Star Performance and Preventive Health Care.

Tri Star Performance

- Promote pay-for-performance practices
- Pay market-competitive compensation
- Achieve internal and external pay equity
- Achieve simplicity in compensation programs
- Strive for employee commitment and a collaborative work environment
- Promote gender fairness in pay and benefits
- Comply with all governmental compensation regulations
- Minimize increased fixed costs

Preventive Health Care

- Be a pay leader in the health care industry
- Promote open and understandable pay practices
- Ensure fair employee treatment
- Offer benefits promoting individual employee needs
- Offer compensation rewarding employee creativity and achievements
- Offer compensation to foster the strategic mission of the organization
- Obtain employee input when developing compensation practices
- Emphasize performance through variable pay and stock options

being present than for being productive on the job. Also, as previously noted, most increases may lack motivational value to employees when organizational salary budgets are low.[32]

Employer's Ability to Pay

Pay levels are limited by earned profits and other financial resources available to employers. This is clearly illustrated by financially burdened companies that ask their employees for pay cuts. For example, small businesses are often most burdened by financial downturns and find that their access to capital to pay employees is much more limited than their larger competitors. Furthermore, an organization's ability to pay is determined in part by the productivity of its employees. This productivity is a result not only of their performance, but of the amount of capital the organization has invested in labor-saving equipment. Generally, increases in capital investment reduce the number of employees required to perform the work and increase an employer's ability to provide higher pay for those it employs.

Economic conditions and competition faced by employers can also significantly affect the rates they are able to pay. Competition and recessions can force prices down and reduce the income from which compensation payments are derived. In such situations, employers have little choice but to reduce wages and/or lay off employees or, even worse, to go out of business. This is especially the case for small businesses. In a 2010 survey of more than 1,000 entrepreneurs, 35 percent of all small businesses in the United States had to make pay cuts and 23 percent had to make valuable staff cuts.[33]

External Factors

The major external factors that influence pay rates include labor market conditions, area pay rates, cost of living, collective bargaining if the employer is unionized, and legal requirements. The legal requirements of compensation will be discussed later in the chapter.

Labor Market Conditions

The labor market reflects the forces of supply and demand for qualified labor within an area. These forces help influence the pay rates required to recruit or retain competent employees. It must be recognized, however, that counterforces can reduce the full impact of supply and demand on the labor market. The economic power of unions, for example, may prevent employers from lowering pay rates even when unemployment is high among union members. Government regulations also may prevent an employer from paying at a market rate less than an established minimum.

Area Pay Rates

A formal pay structure should provide rates that are in line with those being paid by other employers for comparable jobs within the area. Data pertaining to area pay rates may be obtained from local wage surveys. For example, the Arizona Department of Economic Security conducts an annual wage survey for both large and small employers in various cities throughout the state. Wage survey data also may be obtained from a variety of sources, including the American Management Association, Administrative Management Society, U.S. Department of Labor, and Federal Reserve Banks. Smaller employers such as the Woodsmith Corporation and Golden State Container use government surveys to establish rates of pay for new and senior employees. Many organizations, such as the City of Atlanta, Northwest Airlines, and Progress Energy, conduct their own surveys. Others engage in a cooperative exchange

Small Business Application

Compensation for Small Businesses

As compensation is one of the biggest costs for small businesses, employees are often first to be short-changed. At the same time, the old adage, "you get what you pay for," holds true. The ability to attract and retain talented employees depends largely on a company's ability to offer suitable compensation. For small businesses, what is considered suitable differs from that of larger businesses.

Big business can woo job candidates by offering comprehensive compensation packages that include stock options, consistent pay raises, security, and sometimes even a Starbucks in the lobby. While small businesses cannot offer these things, they can offer more customized pay packages to deal with employees' individual needs.[34] For example, not having a complex and bureaucratic compensation system means a small company can more readily adjust its employees' wages to match those of the external market. Furthermore, small companies offer more opportunity for upward growth and the chance to more rapidly increase one's pay.

If the small business is private, there are many opportunities to attract and retain top talent by padding lower salaries with stock in the company. By offering shares of a private company as a form of compensation, small, private companies can offer the possibility for its employees to make larger sums of money in the future. Offering shares or options to buy shares as a form of compensation can be extremely attractive, as employees can make a lot of money when their young company finally goes public and is sold on the stock market. In fact, this form of compensation is enough to make employees leave secure, hefty salaries in a big company for lower salary and shares of a private company. For example, when Google became a public company on August 18, 2004, it sold shares of its company for $85 per share. Some of the employees who were with the company early on were awarded shares that were worth as little as $.30 per share. As you can imagine, someone who had just 10,000 Google shares at this rate was quickly made a millionaire. And, in fact, hundreds of employees did become millionaires at this time.

Of course, what comes around goes around. Now Google is a big company and is losing people to other companies that are not necessarily offering higher salaries. Large public companies like Yahoo and Google are losing their people because private companies, such as Facebook, are offering stock and stock options that may exponentially increase in value when and if the company goes public.[35] As a result, a smart manager in a small business can enhance compensation packages that consist of lower salaries through greater opportunities to increase wealth in the future by issuing stock and stock options as part of the pay mix.

Below is a list of specific things small businesses can do to compete with the compensation packages of big business:[36]

1. **Tailor the pay mix to individual employee needs and wants.** For example, one employee may value greater bonus opportunities than base pay, while another may want the money the company would spend on health insurance to be paid in salary.

2. **Provide stock options in high-growth environments.** Potential employees will find the opportunity to be part of a high-growth company as an exciting and potentially lucrative risk.

3. **Provide faster promotions.** Express how the smallness of your company allows people to move into new and exciting positions quickly, without the bureaucratic red tape found in big business.

4. **Provide frequent contact to top management.** Not being able to interact with and receive mentoring from top management is a major concern for young talent. Smaller companies are able to offer more of these types of growth opportunities than larger competitors.

5. **Provide a greater sense of personal involvement.** One of the advantages of a small company is that they can treat their employees like family. In an age of depersonalized billion-dollar companies, a sense of belongingness, where you know the company cares about you, can go a long way in compensating for lower pay.

of wage information or rely on various professional associations for these data. A high percentage of wage data surveys are inexpensive—less than $100—and are therefore available to all employers, regardless of size.

Wage surveys (discussed fully later in the chapter) serve the important function of providing external pay equity between the surveying organization and other organizations competing for labor in the surrounding labor market. Importantly, data from area wage surveys can be used to prevent the rates for jobs from drifting too far above or below those of other employers in the region. When rates rise above existing area levels, an employer's labor costs may become excessive. Conversely, if they drop too far below area levels, it may be difficult to recruit and retain competent personnel. Wage survey data must also take into account indirect wages paid in the form of benefits.

Cost of Living

consumer price index (CPI)

A measure of the average change in prices over time in a fixed "market basket" of goods and services

Because of inflation, compensation rates have had to be adjusted upward periodically to help employees maintain their purchasing power. Employers make these changes with the help of the consumer price index (CPI). The CPI is a measure of the average change in prices over time in a fixed "market basket" of goods and services. The consumer price index is based on prices of food, clothing, shelter, and fuels; transportation fares; charges for medical services; and prices of other goods and services that people buy for day-to-day living. The Bureau of Labor Statistics collects price information on a monthly basis and calculates the CPI for the nation as a whole and various U.S. city averages. Separate indexes are also published by size of city and by region of the country. Employers in a number of communities monitor changes in the CPI as a basis for compensation decisions.

CPI figures can have important consequences for organizational morale and productivity. Granting wages based largely on "cost-of-living" figures will not inspire

Employee wages may be based in part on how much money people in that area need for day-to-day living

Jan Tadeusz / Alamy

higher employee performance and may cause valued employees to leave the organization. Cost-of-living payments, when traditionally given, may be seen by employees as "entitlements" unrelated to individual performance. Furthermore, should cost-of-living increases be discontinued, managers can expect disgruntled employees, particularly those not likely to receive merit raises.

Employees who work under a union contract may receive wage increases through escalator clauses found in their labor agreement. These clauses provide for cost-of-living adjustments (COLA) in wages based on changes in the CPI. The most common adjustments are 1 cent per hour for each 0.3- or 0.4-point change in the CPI. COLAs are favored by unions during particularly high periods of inflation.

Collective Bargaining

One of the primary functions of a labor union, as emphasized in Chapter 14, is to bargain collectively over conditions of employment, the most important of which is compensation.[37] The union's goal in each new agreement is to achieve increases in real wages—wage increases larger than the increase in the CPI—thereby improving the purchasing power and standard of living of its members. This goal includes gaining wage settlements that equal or exceed the pattern established by other unions within the area.

The agreements negotiated by unions tend to establish rate patterns within the labor market. As a result, wages are generally higher in areas where organized labor is strong. To recruit and retain competent personnel and avoid unionization, nonunion employers must either meet or exceed these rates. The "union scale" also becomes the prevailing rate that all employers must pay for work performed under government contract. The impact of collective bargaining therefore extends beyond the segment of the labor force that is unionized. However, if these negotiations lead to pay that is unbearable by the company and by the external market, then it threatens the long-term viability of those companies being able to provide continued employment. This will result in companies sending more of their jobs to areas with less union pressure.

Job Evaluation Systems

As we discussed earlier, one important component of the pay mix is the worth of the job. Organizations formally determine the value of jobs through the process of job evaluation. Job evaluation is the systematic process of determining the *relative* worth of jobs to establish which jobs should be paid more than others within the organization. Job evaluation helps establish internal equity between various jobs. The relative worth of a job may be determined by comparing it with others within the organization or by comparing it with a scale that has been constructed for this purpose. Each method of comparison, furthermore, may be made on the basis of the jobs as a whole or on the basis of the parts that constitute the jobs.[38]

Three traditional methods of comparison provide the basis for the principal systems of job evaluation:

1. Rank the value of jobs from highest to lowest

2. Classify jobs so they can be benchmarked internally and externally

3. Award points to each job based on how much they are linked to organizational objectives

escalator clauses

Clauses in labor agreements that provide for quarterly cost-of-living adjustments in wages, basing the adjustments on changes in the consumer price index

real wages

Wage increases larger than rises in the consumer price index, that is, the real earning power of wages

LEARNING OUTCOME 3

During the financial crisis of 2008–2010, companies had to reassess the value of specific jobs—leading to some unfortunate cuts in salary and benefits. How would you determine the worth of someone's job to ensure equity?

job evaluation

A systematic process of determining the relative worth of jobs in order to establish which jobs should be paid more than others within an organization

Such a job valuation system can prove effective not only in designing employee compensation but in determining whether a job can be contracted to a local or off-shore company—a major decision that should always take into account the value of the job. For example, in 2009 Delta Airlines brought back more than 4,500 customer service jobs from overseas to the United States. They reported that "customers weren't happy with the service they got from operators based [overseas]."[39] Perhaps this decision to offshore these jobs could have been avoided in the first place had Delta determined the value of their customer service representatives more accurately.

We will begin by discussing the simpler nonquantitative approaches and conclude by reviewing the more popular quantitative system. Also discussed is a newer method of job evaluation—work evaluation. Regardless of the methodology used, it is important to remember that all job evaluation methods require varying degrees of managerial judgment. Also, those involved in evaluating jobs must consider the impact of the Americans with Disabilities Act on the process. (See Chapter 3.)

Job Ranking System

job ranking system

The simplest and oldest system of job evaluation by which jobs are arrayed on the basis of their relative worth

The simplest and oldest system of job evaluation is the job ranking system, which arrays jobs on the basis of their relative worth. One technique used to rank jobs consists of having the raters arrange cards listing the duties and responsibilities of each job in order of the importance of the jobs. Job ranking can be done by a single individual knowledgeable about all jobs or by a committee comprised of management and employee representatives.

The basic disadvantage of the job ranking system is that it does not provide a very precise measure of each job's worth. Another weakness is that the final ranking of jobs indicates the relative importance of the job, not the differences in the degree of importance that may exist between jobs. A final limitation of the job ranking method is that it can be used only with a small number of jobs, probably no more than fifteen. Its simplicity, however, makes it ideal for use by small businesses.

Job Classification System

job classification system

A system of job evaluation in which jobs are classified and grouped according to a series of predetermined wage grades

In the job classification system, jobs are classified and grouped according to a series of predetermined grades. Successive grades require increasing amounts of job responsibility, skill, knowledge, ability, or other factors selected to compare jobs. For example, Grade GS-1 from the federal government grade descriptions reads as follows:

> GS-1 includes those classes of positions the duties of which are to perform, under immediate supervision, with little or no latitude for the exercise of independent judgment (A) the simplest routine work in office, business, or fiscal operations; or (B) elementary work of a subordinate technical character in a professional, scientific, or technical field.

The descriptions of each of the job classes constitute the scale against which the specifications for the various jobs are compared. Managers then evaluate jobs by comparing job descriptions with the different wage grades in order to "slot" the job into the appropriate grade. While this system has the advantage of simplicity, it is less precise than the point system because the job is evaluated as a whole. The federal civil service job classification system is probably the best-known system of this type. The job classification system is widely used by municipal and state governments.[40]

Point System

The point system is a quantitative job evaluation procedure that determines a job's relative value by calculating the total points assigned to it.[41] It has been successfully used by high-visibility organizations such as Digital Equipment Company, Met Life, Johnson Wax, Prudential Financial, TransAmerica, and many other public and private organizations, both large and small. Although point systems are rather complicated to establish, once in place they are relatively simple to understand and use. The principal advantage of the point system is that it provides a more refined basis for making judgments than either the ranking or classification systems and thereby can produce results that are more valid and less easy to manipulate.

The point system permits jobs to be evaluated quantitatively on the basis of factors or elements—commonly called *compensable factors*—that constitute the job.[42] The skills, efforts, responsibilities, and working conditions that a job usually entails are the more common major compensable factors that serve to rank one job as more or less important than another. More contemporary factors might include fiscal accountability, leadership, teamwork, and project accountability. The number of compensable factors an organization uses depends on the nature of the organization and the jobs to be evaluated. Once selected, compensable factors will be assigned weights according to their relative importance to the organization. For example, if responsibility is considered extremely important to the organization's objectives, it could be assigned a weight of 40 percent. Next, each factor will be divided into a number of degrees. Degrees represent different levels of difficulty associated with each factor.

point system
A quantitative job evaluation procedure that determines the relative value of a job by the total points assigned to it

The Point Manual

The point system requires the use of a *point manual*. The point manual is, in effect, a handbook that contains a description of the compensable factors and the degrees to which these factors may exist within the jobs. A manual also will indicate—usually by means of a table—the number of points allocated to each factor and to each of the degrees into which these factors are divided. The point value assigned to a job represents the sum of the numerical degree values of each compensable factor that the job possesses.

Using the Point Manual

Job evaluation under the point system is accomplished by comparing the job descriptions and job specifications, factor by factor, against the various factor-degree descriptions contained in the manual. Each factor within the job being evaluated is then assigned the number of points specified in the manual. When the points for each factor have been determined from the manual, the total point value for the job as a whole can be calculated. The relative worth of the job is then determined from the total points that have been assigned to that job.

Work Valuation

Work valuation is a relatively new job evaluation system championed to meet the demands of a dynamic business environment. The cornerstone for work valuation is that work should be valued relative to the business goals of the organization rather

work valuation
A job evaluation system that seeks to measure a job's worth through its value to the organization

than by an internally applied point-factor job evaluation system.[43] As noted by one compensation specialist, "Valuing work properly enables organizations to not only price individual jobs effectively, but provides insight into how jobs relate to overall organizational goals and objectives and how roles ultimately contribute to organizational success."[44] Additionally, work valuation serves to direct compensation dollars to the type of work pivotal to organizational goals.

With work valuations, work is measured through standards that come directly from business goals. For example, jobs might be valued relative to financial, operational, or customer service objectives. All forms of work, employee roles, and ways of organizing work (such as teams) are valued. The work evaluation process ends with a work hierarchy that is an array of work by value to the organization. The work hierarchy is eventually priced through wage surveys to determine individual pay rates.

Job Evaluation for Management Positions

Because management positions are more difficult to evaluate and involve certain demands not found in jobs at the lower levels, some organizations do not attempt to include them in their job evaluation programs for hourly employees. Rather, they employ either a standardized (purchased) program or customize a point method to fit their particular jobs. However, regardless of the approach adopted, point plans for executive and managerial employees operate similarly to those for other groups of employees.

One of the better-known standardized job evaluation programs for evaluating executive, managerial, and professional positions is the Hay profile method, developed by Edward N. Hay. The three broad factors that constitute the evaluation in the "profile" are knowledge (or know-how), mental activity (or problem-solving), and accountability. The Hay method uses only three factors because it is assumed that these factors represent the most important aspects of all executive and managerial positions. The profile for each position is developed by determining the percentage value to be assigned to each of the three factors. Jobs are then ranked on the basis of each factor, and point values that make up the profile are assigned to each job on the basis of the percentage-value level at which the job is ranked.

Hay profile method

A job evaluation technique using three factors—knowledge, mental activity, and accountability—to evaluate executive and managerial positions

 # Compensation Implementation—Pay Tools

Compensation design systems, such as job evaluations, provide for internal equity and serve as the basis for pay rate determination. They do not in themselves determine the pay rate. The evaluated worth of each job in terms of its rank, class, points, or monetary worth must be implemented into an hourly, daily, weekly, or monthly pay rate. To appropriately implement compensation, specific tools must be incorporated. The primary compensation tool used to set pay is the wage and salary survey.

Wage and Salary Surveys

The wage and salary survey is a survey of the wages paid by employers in an organization's relevant labor market—local, regional, or national, depending on the job. The labor market is frequently defined as the area from which

LEARNING OUTCOME 4

Imagine you have been assigned by Delta to decide if the pay being offered to new customer service representatives is consistent with what competitors are paying. What tools would you use to help in your assessment?

employers obtain certain types of workers. The labor market for office personnel would be local, whereas the labor market for engineers would be national and even global. It is the wage and salary survey that permits an organization to maintain external equity—that is, to pay its employees wages equivalent to the wages similar employees earn in other establishments.

When job evaluation and wage survey data are used jointly, they link the likelihood of both internal and external equity. Although surveys are conducted primarily to gather competitive wage data, they can also collect information on employee benefits or organizational pay practices (such as overtime rates or shift differentials).

wage and salary survey

A survey of the wages paid to employees of other employers in the surveying organization's relevant labor market

Collecting Survey Data

While many organizations conduct their own wage and salary surveys, a variety of "preconducted" pay surveys are available to satisfy the requirements of most public and not-for-profit or private employers. The Bureau of Labor Statistics (BLS) is the major publisher of wage and salary data. The BLS publishes the National Compensation Survey (NCS), a statistically valid and comprehensive compensation program of wage, salary, and benefit information. (See Highlights in HRM 2.) As described on the BLS website, "The National Compensation Survey is the umbrella program that combines several BLS compensation programs into a single vehicle that can produce local, regional, and national statistics on levels, trends, and characteristics of pay and benefits."[45]

Many states conduct surveys on either a municipal or county basis and make them available to employers. Besides these government surveys, trade groups such as the Dallas Personnel Association, Administrative Management Society, Society for Human Resource Management, American Management Association, National Society of Professional Engineers, and Financial Executive Institute conduct special surveys tailored to their members' needs.[46] Employers with global operations can purchase international surveys through large consulting firms. The overseas compensation survey offered by *TPF&C* reports on payment practices in twenty countries. While all of these third-party surveys provide certain benefits to their users, they also have various limitations. Two problems with all published surveys are that (1) they are not always compatible with the user's jobs, and (2) the user cannot specify what specific data to collect. To overcome these problems, organizations may collect their own compensation data.

HRIS and Salary Surveys

Wage and benefits survey data can be found on numerous websites. The previously mentioned National Compensation Survey is an example. Also readily available are commercial products such as those offered at http://www.salary.com: the Salary Wizard, Comp Analyst, and Survey Finder surveys. Survey Finder has a database of hundreds of compensation surveys offered by more than fifty independent vendors. Managers and compensation specialists can search for applicable surveys for either purchase or participation.[47]

Employer-Initiated Surveys

Employers wishing to conduct their own wage and salary survey must first select the jobs to be used in the survey and identify the organizations with whom they actually compete for employees. Since it is not feasible to survey all the jobs in an organization, normally only key jobs, also called benchmark jobs, are used.

The survey of key jobs will usually be sent to ten or fifteen organizations that represent a valid sample of other employers likely to compete for the employees of the surveying organization. Precisely defining the compensation data needed will greatly increase the accuracy of the information received and the number of purposes for which it can be used.[48] Once the survey data are tabulated, the compensation structure can be completed.

HIGHLIGHTS IN HRM

2

Bureau of Labor Statistics National Compensation Survey

NCS data are used by managers and compensation specialists in large and small organizations to answer such questions as the following:

- How much must I pay accountants in Atlanta, Georgia?
- Is a 3 percent benefits increase comparable to that of other employers in the manufacturing industry?
- Is vision coverage a prevalent benefit among large employers in the Northeast?
- How have wage costs changed over the past year?

How the NCS Survey Works

The National Compensation Survey is an area-based survey. Wage and benefit data are collected from a predetermined set of 154 metropolitan and nonmetropolitan areas through the fifty states and the District of Columbia to represent the United States. Compensation information is collected from such diverse locations as Knoxville, Tennessee; Pittsburgh, Pennsylvania; Reno, Nevada; and Richland-Kennewick-Pasco, Washington. All areas are selected to produce regional estimates for nine broad geographic divisions and four broad regions.

Within each area, a scientific sample of establishments represents all area establishments. An "establishment" is a single physical location, such as a plant, warehouse, corporate office, or retail outlet. State and local government offices are also included in the survey.

Once an establishment has been chosen for inclusion in the survey, a BLS economist selects occupations within that establishment to represent all occupations in the establishment. The BLS limits the selection to a small number of occupations to reduce the survey burden for employers. Data are collected for all incumbents in a selected occupation.

The selected occupations are then classified based on the Census Bureau's occupation classification system. The census classification categorizes approximately 450 individual occupations into ten major groupings such as sales, professional specialty, and technical, and machine operators, assemblers, and inspectors. For the occupations selected, wage and benefit data are collected. Items included in the collection of wages are time-based payments, piece rates, commissions, hazard pay, and other items directly related to the work being performed. A variety of benefit data are collected, including paid vacations, paid holidays, paid sick leave, shift differentials, and nonproduction bonuses.

The Wage Curve

The relationship between the relative worth of jobs and their pay rates can be represented by means of a **wage curve**. This curve may indicate the rates currently paid for jobs within an organization, new rates resulting from job evaluation, or rates for similar jobs currently being paid by other organizations within the labor market. A curve may be constructed graphically by preparing a scattergram consisting of a series of dots that represent the current pay rates. As shown in Figure 9.6, a freehand curve is then drawn through the cluster of dots in such a manner as to leave approximately an equal number of dots above and below the curve. The wage curve can be relatively straight or curved. This curve can then be used to determine the relationship between the value of a job and its pay rate at any given point on the line.

Pay Grades

From an administrative standpoint, it is generally preferable to group jobs into **pay grades** and to pay all jobs within a particular grade the same rate or rate range. When the classification system of job evaluation is used, jobs are grouped into grades as part of the evaluation process. When the point system is used, however, pay grades must be established at selected intervals that represent either the point or the evaluated monetary value of these jobs. The graph in Figure 9.5 illustrates a series of pay grades designated along the horizontal axis at fifty-point intervals.

One of the objections to Google granting wage increases on a percentage basis is that the lowest-paid employees, who are having the most trouble "dealing with sky-high property prices, mortgages, and those kinds of things," get the smallest increase, while the highest-paid employees get the largest increase. Is this objection a valid one?

wage curve

A curve in a scattergram representing the relationship between relative worth of jobs and pay rates

pay grades

Groups of jobs within a particular class that are paid the same rate

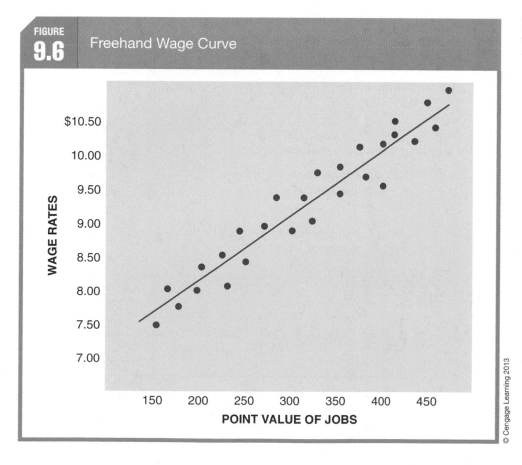

FIGURE 9.6   Freehand Wage Curve

© Cengage Learning 2013

The grades within a pay structure may vary in number.[49] The number is determined by such factors as the slope of the wage curve, the number and distribution of the jobs within the structure, and the organization's wage administration and promotion policies. The number utilized should be sufficient to permit difficulty levels to be distinguished, but not so great as to make the distinction between two adjoining grades insignificant.

Rate Ranges

Although a single rate may be created for each pay grade, as shown in Figure 9.7, it is more common to provide a range of rates for each pay grade. The rate ranges may be the same for each grade or proportionately greater for each successive grade, as shown in Figure 9.8. Rate ranges constructed on the latter basis provide a greater incentive for employees to accept a promotion to a job in a higher grade.

Rate ranges generally are divided into a series of steps that permit employees to receive increases up to the maximum rate for the range on the basis of merit or seniority or a combination of the two. Most salary structures provide for the ranges of adjoining pay grades to overlap. The purpose of the overlap is to permit an employee

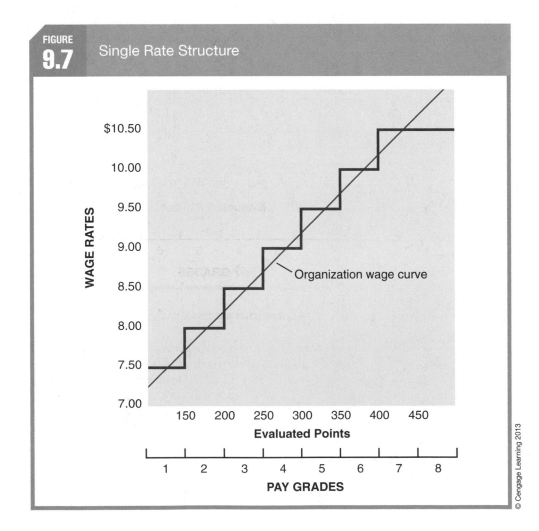

FIGURE 9.7   Single Rate Structure

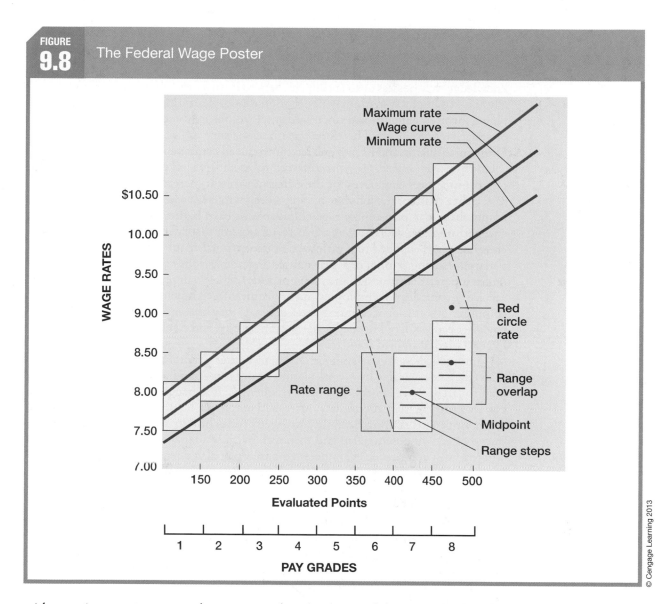

FIGURE 9.8 The Federal Wage Poster

with experience to earn as much as or more than a person with less experience in the next higher job classification.

The final step in setting up a wage structure is to determine the appropriate pay grade into which each job should be placed on the basis of its evaluated worth. Traditionally, this worth is determined on the basis of job requirements without regard to the performance of the person in that job. Under this system, the performance of those who exceed the requirements of a job may be acknowledged by merit increases within the grade range or by promotion to a job in the next higher pay grade.[50]

Organizations may pay individuals above the maximum of the pay range when employees have high seniority or promotional opportunities are scarce. Wages paid above the range maximum are called **red circle rates**. Because these rates are exceptions to the pay structure, employers often "freeze" these rates until all ranges are shifted upward through market wage adjustments.

red circle rates
Payment rates above the maximum of the pay range

Competence-Based Pay

The predominant approach to employee compensation is still the job-based system. Unfortunately, such a system often fails to reward employees for their skills or the knowledge they possess or to encourage them to learn a new job-related skill. Additionally, job-based pay systems may not reinforce an organizational culture stressing employee involvement or provide increased employee flexibility to meet overall production or service requirements. Therefore, organizations such as Frito-Lay, Nortel Networks, Sherwin-Williams, and Honeywell have introduced competence-based pay plans.

competence-based pay

Pay based on an employee's skill level, variety of skills possessed, or increased job knowledge

Competence-based pay, also referred to as skill-based pay or knowledge-based pay, compensates employees for the different skills or increased knowledge they possess rather than for the job they hold in a designated job category.[51] Regardless of the name, these pay plans encourage employees to earn higher base wages by learning and performing a wider variety of skills (or jobs) or displaying an array of competencies that can be applied to a variety of organizational requirements. For example, in a manufacturing setting, new tasks might include various assembly activities carried out in a particular production system or a variety of maintenance functions. Within service organizations, employees might acquire new knowledge related to advanced computer systems or accounting procedures. Organizations will grant an increase in pay after each skill or knowledge has been mastered and can be demonstrated according to a predetermined standard.

Competence-based pay systems represent a fundamental change in the attitude of management regarding how work should be organized and how employees should be paid for their work efforts. The most frequently cited benefits of competence-based pay include greater productivity, increased employee learning and commitment to work, improved staffing flexibility to meet production or service demands, and reduced effects of absenteeism and turnover, because managers can assign employees where and when needed. Competence-based pay also encourages employees to acquire training when new or updated skills are needed by an organization.

Unfortunately, competence-based plans bring some long-term difficulties. Some plans limit the amount of compensation employees can earn, regardless of the new skills or competencies they acquire. Thus, after achieving the top wage, employees may be reluctant to continue their educational training. Perhaps the greatest challenge in paying individuals for their skills, knowledge, and competencies is developing appropriate measures. It is difficult to write specific knowledge and skill descriptions for jobs that employees perform and then establish accurate measures of acquired skills or knowledge.

Broadbanding

Organizations that adopt a competency-based or skill-based pay system frequently use *broadbanding* to structure their compensation payments to employees. Broadbanding simply collapses many traditional salary grades into a few wide salary bands. Broadbands may have midpoints and quartiles, or they may have extremely wide salary ranges or no ranges at all. Banding encourages lateral skill building while addressing the need to pay employees performing multiple jobs with different skill level requirements. Additionally, broadbands help eliminate the obsession with grades and, instead, encourage employees to move to jobs in which they can develop in their careers and add value to the organization. Paying employees through broadbands enables organizations to consider job responsibilities, individual skills and competencies, and career mobility patterns in assigning employees to bands.[52] In all, such pay tools help to more effectively implement a compensation strategy.

Compensation Assessment

Getting your compensation system up and running is not the end of your task as a manager. Once it has been implemented, assessing the effectiveness of your compensation system is vitally important to linking compensation with strategy. With the right measures, you can (1) help the company detect potential compensation problems, (2) make compensation decisions more transparent, and (3) improve the alignment of compensation decisions with organizational objectives. The **compensation scorecard** collects and displays the results for all the measures that a company uses to monitor and compare compensation among internal departments or units. While different companies will use different measures of compensation, the scorecard creates a comparative tool within the organization that can reinforce desired outcomes that are unique to the company's strategy.

Managers in companies without compensation scorecards often struggle to know if the promotions, raises, bonuses, and pay adjustments they make are in line with the rest of the organization and its strategy. A scorecard improves transparency of how people are rewarded and makes managers responsible for how they spend company money. Most compensation scorecards are completed once a year by HR.

For example, Figure 9.9 represents an example of a compensation scorecard. Each functional department in the company reports the average performance rating received by its employees on a scale of 1 (low) to 5 (high). This measure helps to show managers where they are in terms of evaluating their employees. Average merit increases are also gathered. The company had budgeted enough money for a 4 percent increase, on average. If the average merit increase you give your employees is above this 4 percent level, then the additional money needed to compensate employees in your function will need to be drawn from elsewhere in the company. Grade inflation is the growth or decline of the average salary grade distribution. It shows whether or not you vary in pay raises on a year to year basis. Compa ratio is a measure of the appropriateness of the salaries given by a function. In essence it is an internal benchmark of salaries.

LEARNING OUTCOME 6

How do you know if a company's compensation system is helping to reach its objectives?

FIGURE 9.9 Sample Compensation Scorecard

Function	Average Performance Rating (1–5)	Average Merit Increase (4% Budget)	Grade Inflation	Compa Ratio	Annual Incentive (% of Target)
Marketing	3.4	4.3%	–3%	101%	100%
R&D	3.2	4.4%	0%	98%	102%
Production	4.0	4.2%	12%	96%	105%
Sales	4.1	3.4%	8%	99%	100%
Customer Service	3.6	3.6%	17%	88%	110%

* **Grade inflation** is determined by calculating the percentage change in the number of employees in each grade in comparison to the year before.
** **Compa ratio** is actual salary divided by the midpoint of the salary range. It is a gauge of the appropriateness of the organization's salary ranges.
*** **The direct correlation** between profit growth over a three-year period relative to LTI expense.

Functions with a compa ratio below 100 percent are considered to be paying their employees below the company norm. Finally, a measure of the percent of annual incentives in relation to organizational targets helps to assess whether a function is meeting its targets and paying its employees in accordance with those objectives.[53]

Government Regulation of Compensation

LEARNING OUTCOME 7

Federal laws governing compensation raise important issues for both employers and employees. How do regulations influence compensation decisions? How do they protect employees from discrimination?

Compensation management, like the other areas of HRM, is subject to state and federal regulations. A majority of states have minimum wage laws or wage boards that fix minimum wage rates on an industry-by-industry basis. When an employee is subject to both the state and federal minimum wage laws, the employee is entitled to the higher of the two minimum wages. (See Highlights in HRM 3 for state minimum wage laws.) Most states also regulate hours of work and overtime payments.

The three principal federal laws affecting wages are the Davis-Bacon Act, Walsh-Healy Act, and Fair Labor Standards Act. These laws were enacted during the 1930s to prevent the payment of abnormally low wage rates and to encourage the spreading of work among a greater number of workers. The latter objective was accomplished by forcing organizations to pay a premium rate for overtime work (all hours worked in excess of a prescribed number).

Davis-Bacon Act of 1931

The Davis-Bacon Act, also referred to as the Prevailing Wage Law, was passed in 1931 and is the oldest of the three federal wage laws. It requires that the minimum wage rates paid to people employed on federal public works projects worth more than $2,000 be at least equal to the prevailing rates and that overtime be paid at one and one-half times this rate. The act is criticized because the prevailing rates are often the union rates for jobs in the area and are often higher than the average (nonunion) rates.

Walsh-Healy Act of 1936

The Walsh-Healy Act, which is officially called the Public Contracts Act, was passed in 1936 and covers workers employed on government contract work for supplies, equipment, and materials worth in excess of $10,000. The act requires contractors to pay employees at least the prevailing wage rates established for the area by the Secretary of Labor and overtime of one and one-half times the regular rate for all work performed in excess of eight hours in one day or forty hours in one week, depending on which basis provides the larger premium.

Fair Labor Standards Act of 1938 (as Amended)

The Fair Labor Standards Act (FLSA), commonly referred to as the Wage and Hour Act, was passed in 1938 and since then has been amended many times. It covers employees who are engaged in the production of goods for interstate and foreign commerce, including those whose work is closely related to or essential to such production. The act also covers agricultural workers, as well as employees of certain retail and service establishments whose sales volume exceeds a prescribed amount. The major provisions of the FLSA are concerned with minimum wage rates and overtime payments, child labor, and equal rights.[54]

HIGHLIGHTS IN **HRM**
Minimum Wage Laws in the States

Note: Where Federal and state law have different minimum wage rates, the higher standard applies.

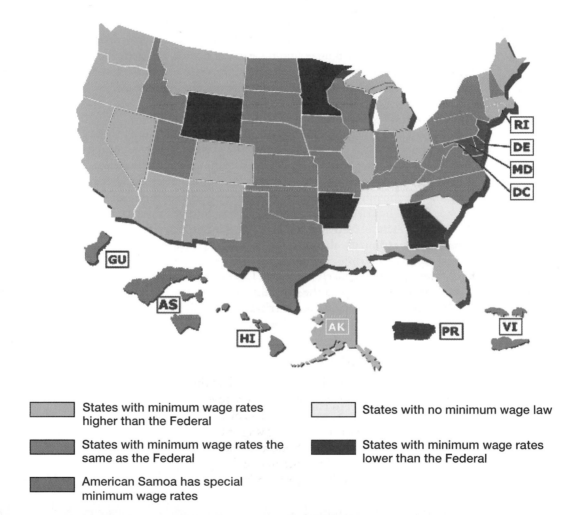

States with minimum wage rates higher than the Federal	States with no minimum wage law
States with minimum wage rates the same as the Federal	States with minimum wage rates lower than the Federal
American Samoa has special minimum wage rates	

Wage and Hour Provisions

The minimum wage prescribed by federal law has been raised many times, from an original figure of 25 cents per hour to $7.25 per hour on July 24, 2009. (See Highlights in HRM 4 for the federal minimum wage poster that employers are required to display.) The minimum wage is assessed every few years to ensure it is adjusted for cost-of-living factors (e.g., Consumer Price Index). This minimum rate applies to the actual earning rate before any overtime premiums have been added. An overtime rate of one and one-half times the base rate must be paid for all hours worked in excess of forty during a given week. The base wage rate from which the overtime rate is computed must include incentive payments or bonuses that are received during the period. When employees are given time off in return for overtime work (referred to as *compensatory time off* or *comp time*), it must be granted at one and one-half times the number of hours that were worked as overtime. Employees who are paid on a piece-rate base must receive a premium for overtime work. The FLSA does not, however, require severance pay, sick leave, vacation, or holidays.

Furthermore, under the FLSA, an employer must pay an employee for whatever work the employer "suffers or permits" the employee to perform, even if the work is done away from the workplace and even if it is not specifically expected or requested. This condition could likely occur when employees work away from headquarters and are unsupervised or when they telecommute on a frequent basis.

Minimum Wage and Pay Compression

pay rate compression

Compression of pay between new and experienced employees caused by the higher starting salaries of new employees; also the differential between hourly workers and their managers

Some argue that increases in the minimum wage may lead to pay compression. Pay rate compression means that differences between low- and high-paying jobs decrease. It occurs when less experienced, often junior employees, earn as much or more than experienced employees due to high starting salaries for new employees. It also occurs when the minimum wage requirements push up salaries for lower tier salaries but not for higher tier. For example, if starting hourly wages for preschool teachers is $8.19 and preschool teacher aides is $7.25, a minimum wage increase to $8.00 would bring both to essentially the same starting wage (the U.S. median salary for preschool teachers is $10.50, while the bottom 10 percent make $8.19).

Not only are lower paid jobs at risk of pay compression, higher paid jobs also experience pay compression. The reasons are usually more market based than government based. For example, the scarcity of qualified applicants in computers, engineering, and other professional and technical fields has forced starting salaries for these occupations to be at or near the salaries paid employees with considerable experience and seniority. Pay compression can also occur when hourly employees, at the top of their pay grades, earn only slightly less than managers at the low end of their pay grades.

Identifying pay rate compression and its causes is far simpler than implementing organizational policies to alleviate its effect. Organizations wishing to minimize the problem may incorporate the following ideas into their pay policies:

- Reward high performance and merit-worthy employees with large pay increases.

- Design the pay structure to allow a wide spread between hourly and supervisory employees.

- Prepare high-performing employees for promotions to jobs with higher salary levels.

- Provide equity adjustments for selected employees hardest hit by pay compression.[55]

Since pay rate compression is largely an internal pay equity concern, if not addressed fairly, it can cause low employee morale, leading to issues of reduced employee performance, hard feelings between employees, higher absenteeism and turnover, and even delinquent behavior such as employee theft.

4 HIGHLIGHTS IN HRM
The Federal Wage Poster

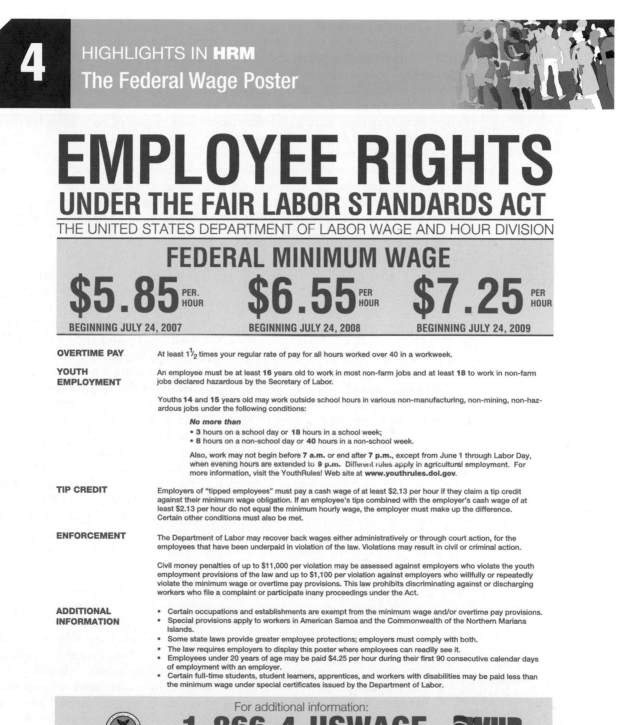

EMPLOYEE RIGHTS
UNDER THE FAIR LABOR STANDARDS ACT
THE UNITED STATES DEPARTMENT OF LABOR WAGE AND HOUR DIVISION

FEDERAL MINIMUM WAGE

$5.85 PER. HOUR	$6.55 PER HOUR	$7.25 PER HOUR
BEGINNING JULY 24, 2007	BEGINNING JULY 24, 2008	BEGINNING JULY 24, 2009

OVERTIME PAY At least 1½ times your regular rate of pay for all hours worked over 40 in a workweek.

YOUTH EMPLOYMENT An employee must be at least **16** years old to work in most non-farm jobs and at least **18** to work in non-farm jobs declared hazardous by the Secretary of Labor.

Youths **14** and **15** years old may work outside school hours in various non-manufacturing, non-mining, non-hazardous jobs under the following conditions:

No more than
- **3** hours on a school day or **18** hours in a school week;
- **8** hours on a non-school day or **40** hours in a non-school week.

Also, work may not begin before **7 a.m.** or end after **7 p.m.**, except from June 1 through Labor Day, when evening hours are extended to **9 p.m.** Different rules apply in agricultural employment. For more information, visit the YouthRules! Web site at **www.youthrules.dol.gov**.

TIP CREDIT Employers of "tipped employees" must pay a cash wage of at least $2.13 per hour if they claim a tip credit against their minimum wage obligation. If an employee's tips combined with the employer's cash wage of at least $2.13 per hour do not equal the minimum hourly wage, the employer must make up the difference. Certain other conditions must also be met.

ENFORCEMENT The Department of Labor may recover back wages either administratively or through court action, for the employees that have been underpaid in violation of the law. Violations may result in civil or criminal action.

Civil money penalties of up to $11,000 per violation may be assessed against employers who violate the youth employment provisions of the law and up to $1,100 per violation against employers who willfully or repeatedly violate the minimum wage or overtime pay provisions. This law prohibits discriminating against or discharging workers who file a complaint or participate in any proceedings under the Act.

ADDITIONAL INFORMATION
- Certain occupations and establishments are exempt from the minimum wage and/or overtime pay provisions.
- Special provisions apply to workers in American Samoa and the Commonwealth of the Northern Mariana Islands.
- Some state laws provide greater employee protections; employers must comply with both.
- The law requires employers to display this poster where employees can readily see it.
- Employees under 20 years of age may be paid $4.25 per hour during their first 90 consecutive calendar days of employment with an employer.
- Certain full-time students, student learners, apprentices, and workers with disabilities may be paid less than the minimum wage under special certificates issued by the Department of Labor.

For additional information:
1-866-4-USWAGE
(1-866-487-9243) TTY: 1-877-889-5627

WHD U.S. Wage and Hour Division

WWW.WAGEHOUR.DOL.GOV

U.S. Department of Labor | Employment Standards Administration | Wage and Hour Division

WHD Publication 1088 (Revised June 2007)

Child Labor Provisions

Another concern with the minimum wage is that the "floor" it imposes makes it more difficult for high school students and young adults to find jobs. Many employers who might otherwise be willing to hire these individuals are unwilling to pay them the same rate as adults because of their lack of experience. For unskilled workers, the FLSA permits employers to pay a "training wage" of $6.16 per hour for employees younger than age twenty during their first ninety days of employment, provided their employment does not displace other workers.

The FLSA forbids the employment of minors between ages sixteen and eighteen in hazardous occupations such as mining, logging, woodworking, meatpacking, and certain types of manufacturing. Minors under sixteen cannot be employed in any work destined for interstate commerce except that which is performed in a nonhazardous occupation for a parent or guardian or for an employer under a temporary work permit issued by the Department of Labor.

Exemption from Overtime Provisions

The feature of the FLSA that perhaps creates the most confusion is the exemption from overtime requirements for certain groups of employees or from coverage by certain of the act's provisions. In fact, the Department of Labor itself has struggled to classify its own employees—the very employees trying to clarify exemption requirements for others. In a twist of fate, employees from the DOL filed a complaint against the DOL, saying that over 1,900 employees were misclassified as being exempt. The violations involved unpaid overtime and working off-the-clock, including the use of electronic communication devices away from home.[56] "This case shows the difficulty that any employer has when it comes to classifying workers as either exempt or nonexempt under the Fair Labor Standards Act," said D. Mark Wilson, principal of Applied Economic Strategies in Washington. "It really does illustrate that even the agency charged with enforcing the law has a very difficult time making these determinations."[57]

As exemplified in Figure 9.10, six employee groups—executive, administrative, learned, creative, computer, and outside salespeople—are specifically excluded from overtime provisions provided they meet defined job requirements as stated under the law. Importantly, job titles do not determine exempt status. Employees are also exempt from overtime pay if their weekly or annual earnings exceed certain limits.

The DOL provides an online seminar that describes the new Fair Pay Rules.[58]

Pay Equity Provisions

There are three laws that protect employees against pay discrimination. The Equal Pay Act of 1963 prohibits unequal pay for equal or "substantially equal" work performed by men and women (See Chapter 2.) Title VII of the Civil Rights Act of 1964 prohibits wage discrimination on the basis of race, color, sex, religion, or national origin. And the Federal Age Discrimination Act of 1967, as amended, extends the equal rights provisions by forbidding wage discrimination based on age for employees age forty and older. None of these acts, however, prohibits wage differentials based on factors other than age, race, color, religion, national origin, or sex. Seniority, merit, and individual incentive plans, for instance, are not affected.

In spite of these acts, pay discrimination is still found in many companies today. For example, in 2010 B&H Foto Electronics Corp. had to pay out $4.3 million in wages and benefits to 149 employees who were paid less than

Using the **INTERNET**

Get more information from the National Committee on Pay Equity by going to

www.cengagebrain.com

FIGURE 9.10 Six Excluded Employee Groups

Category	Job Duties Required
Executive	Primary duty must be managing the enterprise, or managing a customarily recognized department or subdivision of the enterprise; must customarily and regularly direct the work of at least two or more other full-time employees or their equivalent; and must have the authority to hire or fire other employees, or the employee's suggestions and recommendations as to the hiring, firing, advancement, promotion or any other change of status of other employees must be given particular weight.
Administrative	Primary duty must be the performance of office or non-manual work directly related to the management or general business operations of the employer or the employer's customers; and includes the exercise of discretion and independent judgment with respect to matters of significance.
Learned	Primary duty must be the performance of work requiring advanced knowledge, defined as work which is predominantly intellectual in character and which includes work requiring the consistent exercise of discretion and judgment; the advanced knowledge must be in a field of science or learning; and the advanced knowledge must be customarily acquired by a prolonged course of specialized intellectual instruction.
Creative	Primary duty must be the performance of work requiring invention, imagination, originality or talent in a recognized field of artistic or creative endeavor.
Computer	Must be employed as a computer systems analyst, computer programmer, software engineer or other similarly skilled worker in the computer field. The primary duty must consist of: 1) the application of systems analysis techniques and procedures, including consulting with users, to determine hardware, software or system functional specifications; 2) the design, development, documentation, analysis, creation, testing or modification of computer systems or programs, including prototypes, based on and related to user or system design specifications; 3) the design, documentation, testing, creation or modification of computer programs related to machine operating systems; or 4) a combination of the aforementioned duties, the performance of which requires the same level of skills.
Outside Sales	Primary duty must be making sales (as defined in the FLSA), or obtaining orders or contracts for services or for the use of facilities for which a consideration will be paid by the client or customer; and must be customarily and regularly engaged away from the employer's place or places of business.
Highly Compensated	The regulations contain a special rule for "highly-compensated" workers who are paid total annual compensation of $100,000 or more. A highly compensated employee is deemed exempt under Section 13(a)(1) if: the employee earns total annual compensation of $100,000 or more, which includes at least $455 per week paid on a salary basis; the employee's primary duty includes performing office or non-manual work; and the employee customarily and regularly performs at least one of the exempt duties or responsibilities of an exempt executive, administrative or professional employee.
Other	Teachers are exempt if their primary duty is teaching, tutoring, instructing or lecturing in the activity of imparting knowledge, and if they are employed and engaged in this activity as a teacher in an educational establishment. Practice of Law or Medicine: An employee holding a valid license or certificate permitting the practice of law or medicine is exempt if the employee is actually engaged in such a practice. An employee who holds the requisite academic degree for the general practice of medicine is also exempt if he or she is engaged in an internship or resident program for the profession.

Adapted from Vicki M. Lambert, "The top three FLSA violations and how to avoid them", ADP, 2008.

their non-Hispanic coworkers with the same responsibilities. The company was also accused of failing to provide health benefits and promote them due to their national origin. As part of the settlement, B&H also agreed to equalize the Hispanic employees' wages with their peers and maintain a written nondiscriminatory policy.[59] Furthermore, progress in closing the gender earnings gap has slowed considerably since the early 1990s. While the gender earnings ratio for full-time employees increased by 12.9 percent from 1980 to 1993, it grew by only 3.1 percent from 1993 to 2009. As of 2009, women in full-time jobs received only 77 percent of what men made.[60] Figure 9.11 further examines pay inequality based on race and gender.

FIGURE 9.11   Race and Gender Pay Inequality

Race and Ethnicity	Male	Female	Women's Earnings as % of White Male Earnings*
All Races	47,127	36,278	77.00%
White Alone, not Hispanic	51,405	38,533	75.00%
Black or African American only	37,496	31,824	61.90%
Asian only	51,760	42,331	82.30%
Hispanic or Latino (any race)	31,393	27,181	52.90%

*The ratio for All Races is for Male and Females of All Races

Source: Institute for Women's Policy Research Compilation of Current Population Survey Labor Force Statistics, 2009 http://www.census.gov/hhes/www/cpstables/032010/perinc/new05_001.htm

Summary

LEARNING OUTCOME 1 Establishing strategic compensation programs requires an assessment of organizational objectives in relation to specific employment goals—employee retention for continued growth, compensation distribution to ensure employees feel treated fairly, communication of compensation methods to increase employee understanding of organizational objectives, and adherence to a budget for cost efficiencies, for instance. Compensation must reward employees for past efforts (pay-for-performance) while motivating employees' future performance. Internal and external equity of the pay program affects employees' concepts of fairness. Organizations must

balance each of these concerns while still remaining competitive. The ability to attract and retain qualified employees while controlling labor costs is a major factor in allowing organizations to remain viable in the domestic or international markets.

LEARNING OUTCOME 2 The basis on which compensation payments are determined and the way they are administered can significantly affect employee productivity and the achievement of organizational goals. Internal influences include the employer's compensation policy, worth of the job, performance of the employee, and employer's ability to pay. External factors influencing pay rates include labor market conditions, area pay rates, cost of living, outcomes of collective bargaining, and legal requirements.

LEARNING OUTCOME 3 Organizations use one of four basic job evaluation techniques to determine the relative worth of jobs. The job ranking system arranges jobs in numerical order on the basis of the importance of the job's duties and responsibilities to the organization. The job classification system slots jobs into preestablished grades. Higher-rated grades will require more responsibilities, working conditions, and job duties. The point system of job evaluation uses a point scheme based on the compensable job factors of skill, effort, responsibility, and working conditions. The more compensable factors a job possesses, the more points are assigned to it. Jobs with higher accumulated points are considered more valuable to the organization. The work valuation system evaluates jobs based on their value relative to organizational goals—financial, customer service, and so on—and the job's contribution to organization success.

LEARNING OUTCOME 4 Wage surveys determine the external equity of jobs. Data obtained from surveys will facilitate establishing the organization's wage policy while ensuring that the employer does not pay more, or less, than needed for jobs in the relevant labor market.

LEARNING OUTCOME 5 The wage structure is composed of the wage curve, pay grades, and rate ranges. The wage curve depicts graphically the pay rates assigned to jobs within each pay grade. Pay grades represent the grouping of similar jobs on the basis of their relative worth. Each pay grade will include a rate range. Rate ranges will have a midpoint and minimum and maximum pay rates for all jobs in the pay grade.

LEARNING OUTCOME 6 The effectiveness of a compensation system can be assessed by using a compensation scorecard. The scorecard collects and displays where all departments and/or functions sit in terms of their relative compensation. It increases the transparency of compensation systems, the accountability of managers, and helps companies align their compensation decisions with organizational objectives.

LEARNING OUTCOME 7 Both the Davis-Bacon Act and the Walsh-Healy Act are prevailing wage statutes. These laws require government contractors to pay wages normally based on the union scale in the employer's operating area. The Walsh-Healy Act also requires payment of one and one-half times the regular pay for hours over eight per day or forty per week. The Fair Labor Standards Act contains provisions covering the federal minimum wage, hours worked, and child labor. Pay rate compression is the narrowing of pay between new, less experienced employees and experienced senior employees. The primary cause of the problem is the high salaries paid to new employees and minimum wage increases. Hourly employees and their managers may experience pay compression when the salary spread between the two groups is low.

Key Terms

broadbanding	job evaluation	real wages
competence-based pay	job ranking system	red circle rates
consumer price index (CPI)	nonexempt employees	wage and salary survey
escalator clauses	pay equity	wage curve
exempt employees	pay-for-performance standard	pay rate compression
Hay profile method	pay grades	work valuation
hourly work	piecework	
job classification system	point system	

Discussion Questions

LEARNING OUTCOME 1   Tomax Corporation has 400 employees and wishes to develop a compensation policy to correspond to its dynamic business strategy. The company wishes to employ a high-quality workforce capable of responding to a competitive business environment. Suggest different compensation objectives to match Tomax's business goals.

LEARNING OUTCOME 2   Since employees may differ in terms of their job performance, would it not be more feasible to determine the wage rate for each employee on the basis of his or her relative worth to the organization? Explain.

LEARNING OUTCOME 3   What is job evaluation? Explain the differences between the major job evaluation systems, noting the advantages and disadvantages of each.

LEARNING OUTCOME 4   Describe the basic steps in conducting a wage and salary survey. What are some factors to consider?

LEARNING OUTCOME 5   One of the objections to granting wage increases on a percentage basis is that the lowest-paid employees, who are having the most trouble making ends meet, get the smallest increase, while the highest-paid employees get the largest increase. Is this objection a valid one? Explain.

LEARNING OUTCOME 6   What is a compensation scorecard and how does it help align a company's strategy with its compensation system?

LEARNING OUTCOME 7   Federal laws governing compensation raise important issues for both employers and employees. Discuss the following:
a. The effect of paying a prevailing wage as required by the Davis-Bacon Act
b. The effects of raising the minimum wage

HRM EXPERIENCE
Why This Salary?

A question frequently asked is, "Why is that person paid more than I am when we both perform the same job?" The answer to this question lies in understanding the components of the pay mix as discussed in this chapter. While we may disapprove of the idea that someone is paid more or less than we are for similar work; nevertheless, factors both internal and external to the organization influence the final salary paid to a job or a specific person. Often we have little control over the pay mix factors. However, at other times, we can improve our wage by gaining additional job experience or seniority or by obtaining increases in job knowledge or skills. This project is designed to give you experience in understanding why jobs are paid different salaries.

Assignment
Shown here are the annual median salaries paid to selected occupations listed in the 2010–2011 edition of the *Occupational Outlook Handbook*. Study the salaries paid to these occupations and then answer the questions that follow as to why the differences in salaries exist. Relate these reasons to the internal and external factors of the pay mix that are discussed in the text.

Why This Salary? (continued)

Occupation	Median Annual Salary
• Flight attendant	$40,010
• Librarian	$53,710
• Construction laborer	$29,150
• Computer systems analyst	$77,080
• Police officer	$53,210
• Truck driver, heavy	$37,730
• Lawyer	$113,240

1. What factors may account for the wide differences among salaries for different occupations?
2. What factors may account for the differences among salaries for the identical occupation in the same organization?
3. What factors may account for the differences among salaries for the identical occupation in different organizations?

You may work individually or in teams to complete this skill-building exercise. The *Occupational Outlook Handbook* published by the U.S. Bureau of Labor Statistics can be found at http://www.bls.gov.

On the Job: Video Cases

Bright Horizons: Total Compensation

Bright Horizons was founded in 1986 by a husband-and-wife team interested in improving early childhood education. Today, Bright Horizons Family Solutions is the world's leading provider of employer-sponsored child care, early education, and work/life solutions. Conducting business in the United States, Europe, and Canada, they have serviced more than 700 client companies, including more than 90 of the Fortune 500.

Known for excellence and innovation in child care and education, Bright Horizons is also a great place to work. They have consistently been the only child care organization named to the "100 Best Companies to Work for in America" list by *Fortune* magazine.

What to Watch for and Ask Yourself

- Why is turnover so high for the child care industry?

- What kinds of incentives and benefits are considered valuable for child care workers?

- What motivates people at Bright Horizons?

- What is the HR manager at Bright Horizons doing to make sure employees stay motivated?

Case Study 1

Pay Decisions at Performance Sports

Katie Perkins's career objective while attending Rockford State College was to obtain a degree in small business management and to start her own business after graduation. Her ultimate desire was to combine her love of sports and a strong interest in marketing to start a mail-order golf equipment business aimed specifically at beginning golfers.

In February 2003, after extensive development of a strategic business plan and a loan in the amount of $75,000 from the Small Business Administration, Performance Sports was begun. Based on a marketing plan that stressed fast delivery, error-free customer service, and large discount pricing, Performance Sports grew rapidly. At present the company employs sixteen people: eight customer service representatives earning between $11.25 and $13.50 per hour; four shipping and receiving associates paid between $8.50 and $9.50 per hour; two clerical employees each earning $8.25 per hour; an assistant manager earning $15.25 per hour; and a general manager with a wage of $16.75 per hour. Both the manager and assistant manager are former customer service representatives.

Perkins intends to create a new managerial position, purchasing agent, to handle the complex duties of purchasing golf equipment from the company's numerous equipment manufacturers. Also, the mail-order catalog will be expanded to handle a complete line of tennis equipment. Since the position of purchasing agent is new, Perkins is not sure how much to pay this person. She wants to employ an individual with five to eight years of experience in sports equipment purchasing.

While attending an equipment manufacturers' convention in Las Vegas, Nevada, Perkins learns that a competitor, East Valley Sports, pays its customer service representatives on a pay-for-performance basis. Intrigued by this compensation philosophy, Perkins asks her assistant manager, George Balkin, to research the pros and cons of this payment strategy. This request has become a priority because only last week two customer service representatives expressed dissatisfaction with their hourly wage. Both complained that they felt underpaid relative to the large amount of sales revenue each generates for the company.

Questions

1. What factors should Perkins and Balkin consider when setting the wage for the purchasing agent position? What resources are available for them to consult when establishing this wage?
2. Suggest advantages and disadvantages of a pay-for-performance policy for Performance Sports.
3. Suggest a new payment plan for the customer service representatives.

Case Study 2

For many businesses in today's belt-tightening economy, decisions on pay need to be strategic to ensure that employees are treated fairly and to ensure that businesses can remain viable. This requires knowing what your competitors pay their employees and knowing your own salary budget. But knowing what your competitors are paying can be both valuable and painful.

As CEO of Costa Vida, a fast growing chain of fresh Mexican restaurants, Nathan Gardner knew he was competing against some restaurant chains with competitive compensation systems. Costa Vida is a fresh Mexican grill featuring Baja-inspired foods that are made from scratch daily. Following a trip to Cabo San Lucas on the Baja Coast in Mexico, Costa Vida founders JD and Sarah Gardner were inspired with a vision. Bring the freshly made local cuisine with the vibrant lifestyle to the United States. They started their first restaurant in 2001 and after just 10 years Costa Vida has more than 50 franchises in Arizona, California, Colorado, Idaho, New Mexico, Texas, Washington and Utah. One of the main challenges Costa Vida faces is the fierce competition for customers as well as employees. "You'd be surprised how much of a difference having good employees in all areas of the business makes," commented the CEO.

"For the fast-casual food industry," remarked Nathan, "you are dependent upon your people. If you don't treat your people well, they won't treat your customers well. If your customers aren't treated well, you have no business." For months, Nathan agonized over how he could develop a competitive compensation plan that matched the objectives of the organization, but that fell in line with the tight budget of each individually owned franchise unit. He stated, "We, of course, leave the final compensation decision to the franchise owner, but we do all we can to educate and persuade our franchisees to be competitive and fair. In the long run, this is how they can maintain a superior level of customer satisfaction."

Nathan pointed out that a strong benchmark for them is In-N-Out Burger. In-N-Out started in California and is known for its great compensation package. As of 2011, they start out all their new "associates" (aka employees) at a minimum of $10 an hour. They also offer flexible schedules to accommodate school and other activities, paid vacation, free meals, and a 401k retirement plan. For full-time associates they provide medical, dental, vision, life, and travel insurance coverage. Their reason for paying so high is based on a strategy that lower turnover and more committed workers will lead to better service. "What In-N-Out does for their employees is truly amazing," commented Nathan. "We often see employees moving from one fast-food chain to another, but we rarely see employees coming from In-N-Out."

Nathan had a tough challenge ahead in trying to convince his franchise owners and managers to think more strategically about their pay systems. He needed to help them realize that paying wages and offering other compensation benefits that were better than their competitors may mean lower profit margins up front, but that the returns would be greater in the long run. He also needed to offer evidence to show that this was not just about being fair, but it was about being strategic. The restaurant business is a fast and fierce industry and companies come and go all the time. What was it going to take for Costa Vida to stay for the long haul?

Questions

1. Why is it important for pay to be externally fair?
2. Why is it important for pay to be internally fair?
3. What should Costa Vida's compensation strategy look like? Hint: what are the company objectives and how can employee pay help to achieve those objectives?
4. What should the pay structure look like? What pay mix would you recommend?
5. How should Nathan communicate a new compensation strategy to his franchisee owners and managers?
6. What effect will paying higher wages have on Costa Vida in the short term? What effect will it have in the long term? Explain.

Notes and References

1. Henry Blodget, "Google gives all employees surprise $1000 cash bonus and 10% raise." *Business Insider SAI* (November 9, 2010).

2. O'Reilly Media. Web 2.0 Summit 2010: Eric Schmidt, "A Conversation with Eric Schmidt". http://www.youtube.com/watch?feature=player_embedded&v=AKOWK2dR4Dg#!.

3. John Dorian, "Google's 10% salary increase, $1000 cash bonus part of company's competitive compensation plan," *International Business Times* (November 10, 2010).

4. Debra L. Nelson and James Campbell Quick, *Understanding Organizational Behavior*, 3rd ed. (Mason, OH: South-Western, 2008), Chapter 5.

5. Zingheim, P.K. and Schuster, J.R. Revisiting effective incentive design. *Worldatwork Journal*, (2005, first quarter): 50–58.

6. For a frequently referenced book on strategic compensation planning, see Edward E. Lawler III, *Strategic Pay: Aligning Organizational Strategies and Pay Systems* (San Francisco: Jossey-Bass, 1990). See also Susan E. Jackson and Randall S. Schuler, *Managing Human Resources: Through Strategic Partnerships*, 9th ed. (Mason, OH: South-Western, 2006): Chapter 9.

7. Personal interview with Product Development Manager at Google. (December 11, 2010).

8. Catherine Dodge, "Banning big Wall Street bonuses favored by 70% of Americans," *Bloomberg Businessweek* (December 13, 2010).

9. Joe Davidson, "President's salary freeze for federal workers gets a cold reception," *The Washington Post* (November 30, 2010).

10. Douglas Mcintyre, "The layoff kings: The 25 companies responsible for 700,000 lost jobs," *Daily Finance, AOL Money and Finance* (August 18, 2010).

11. Sanford Jacoby, "GM: What led to the downfall of a corporate giant," *UCLAToday* (October 15, 2008); Chris Bury, "Autoworker pay clip," http://www.youtube.com/watch?v=27PNuaDAeVk;ABC World News.

12. Jonathon Trevor, "Can pay be strategic: A critical exploration of strategic pay in practice," (Palgrave Macmillan, 2011).

13. Fay Hansen, "Control and Customization," *Workforce Management* 86, no. 19 (November 2007): 42.

14. Hai-Ming Chen and Yi-Hua Hsien, "Key Trends in the Total Reward System of the 21st Century," *Compensation and Benefits Review* 38, no. 6 (November/December 2006): 64.

15. George T. Milkovich, Jerry M. Newman & Barry Gerhart, *Compensation*, 10th ed. (Boston: McGraw-Hill Irwin, 2010).

16. Patricia K. Zingheim and Jay R. Schuster, "What Are Key Issues Right Now?" *Compensation and Benefits Review* 39, no. 3. (June 2007): 51. See also "Reward 'Stars' and Pay for Performance Lead in Pay Control Strategies," *HR Focus* 84, no. 11 (November 2007): 3.

17. Valerie L. Myers and Janice L. Dreachslin, "Recruitment and Retention of a Diverse Workforce: Challenges and Opportunities," *Journal of Healthcare Management* 52, no. 5 (September/October 2007): 290.

18. Stephen Miller, "2008 Pay: More Ties to Performance," *HR Magazine* 52, no. 10 (October 2007): 26. See also Jay Schuster, Paul Weatherhead, and Patricia Zingheim, "Pay for Performance Works: The United States Postal Service Presents a Powerful Business Case," *WorldatWork Journal* 15, no. 1 (First Quarter 2006): 24.

19. Carrie Mason-Draffen and Bill Bleyer, "Cool response on LI to federal salary freeze," Newsday.com, (Nov. 30, 2010), http://www.newsday.com/long-island/cool-response-on-li-to-federal-salary-freeze-1.2503160.

20. Letters to the Editor, December 4, 2010. "The Fairness of a federal pay freeze", *Washington Post*.

21. For one of the classic articles on equity theory, see J. Stacey Adams, "Integrity in Social Exchange," in L. Berkowitz (ed.), *Advances in Experimental Social Psychology* (New York: Academic Press, 1965): 276–99.

22. Andrew J. DuBrin, *Fundamentals of Organization Behavior*, 4th ed. (Mason, OH: South-Western, 2007), Chapter 6.

23. Victor H. Vroom, *Work and Motivation* (San Francisco: Jossey-Bass, 1994). This landmark book, originally published in 1964, integrates the work of hundreds of researchers seeking to explain choice of work, job satisfaction, and job performance.

24. Joseph Champoux, *Organizational Behavior: Integrating Individuals, Groups, and*

Organizations, 3rd ed. (Mason, OH: South-Western, 2006), Chapter 8.

25. "Supreme Court Decision Touches on Employees Sharing Pay Data," *HR Focus* 84, no. 10 (October 2007): 12.

26. Press Release by Caroline Dobuzinskis, "Pay secrecy and paycheck fairness: New data shows pay transparency needed," Institute for Women's Policy Research (November 16, 2010).

27. Brian Hindo, "Mind If I Peek at Your Paycheck?" *Business Week* (June 18, 2007): 40.

28. Detailed discussion of exempt and nonexempt rules under the Fair Labor Standards Act can be found at http://www.dol.gov.

29. Martin J. Conyon, "Compensation consultants and executive pay", in Kent Baker and Ronald Anderson (eds.), Corporate Governance: A synthesis of theory, research, and practice, (New Jersey: John Wiley and Sons, 2010).

30. David Lepak and Scott Snell, "The human resource architecture: Toward a theory of human capital allocation and development," *Academy of Management Review* (1999) Vol. 24, No. 1: 31–48.

31. James R. Bowers, "Valuing Work: An Integrated Approach," *WorldatWork* 12, no. 2 (Second Quarter 2003): 28–39. See also Robert L. Heneman, Peter V. LeBlanc, and Tim L. Reynolds, "Using Work Valuation to Identify and Protect the Talent Pool," *WorldatWork* 11, no. 2 (Third Quarter 2002): 31–41.

32. Kathryn Cohen and Alison Avalos, "Salary Budget Increases: Slow but Steady," *Workspan* (September 2007): 29.

33. "The state of small business report: June 2010 Survey of Small Business Success", Network Solutions, LLC and University of Maryland, (July 2010).

34. "How to attract talent to a small company," *The Wall Street Journal* (November 18, 2010), http://guides.wsj.com/small-business/hiring-and-managing-employees/how-to-attract-talent-to-a-small-company/print/.

35. Miguel Helft, "Mark Zuckerberg's most valuable friend," *New York Times* (October 2, 2010).

36. Adapted from SME Toolkit. Build Your Business. "Compensation Management from Buzgate.org," http://us.smetoolkit.org/us/en/content/en/2188/Compensation-Management.

37. William H. Holley, Jr., Kenneth H. Jennings, and Rogert W. Wolters, *The Labor Relations Process* 9th ed. (Mason, OH: South-Western, 2009), Chapter 6.

38. Robert L. Heneman, "Job and Work Evaluation," *Public Personnel Management* 32, no. 1 (Spring 2003): 1–25.

39. Bruce Einhorn, "India's outsourcers should worry about Delta's move," *Bloomberg Businessweek*, (April, 20, 2009).

40. For information on the federal job classification system, go to http//www.opm.gov.

41. Emin Kahya, "Revising the Metal Industry Job Evaluation System for Blue-Collar Jobs," *Compensation and Benefits Review* 38, no. 6 (November/December 2006): 49.

42. Lance A. Berger and Dorothy R. Berger, *The Compensation Handbook*, 5th ed. (Boston: McGraw-Hill, 2008).

43. Robert L. Heneman, Peter V. LeBlanc, and Howard Risher, "Work Valuation Addresses Shortcomings of Both Job Evaluation and Market Pricing," *Compensation and Benefits Review* 35, no. 1 (January–February 2003): 7–11.

44. James R. Bowers, "Valuing Work," *WorldatWork* 12, no. 1 (Second Quarter 2003): 28.

45. The Bureau of Labor Web site is at http://www.bls.gov.

46. Robert P. Parker, "New Monthly Hours and Earnings Measures from the Bureau of Labor Statistics' Current Employment Statistics Program," *Business Economics* 42, no. 2 (April 2007): 69.

47. Nona Tobin, "Can Technology Ease the Pain of Salary Surveys?" *Public Personnel Management* 31, no. 1 (Spring 2002): 65–76.

48. John H. Davis, "Statistics for compensation: A practical guide to compensation analysis" (Wiley, 2011); Charles H. Fey and Madhura Tare, "Market Pricing Concerns," *WorldatWork* 16, no. 2 (Second Quarter 2007): 61.

49. Curt Finch, "How to Create an Effective Pay Structure," *Employee Benefit Plan Review* 61, no. 10 (April 2007): 26. See also Gregory A.

Stoskopf, "Choosing the Best Salary Structure for Your Organization," *WorldatWork* 11, no. 4 (Fourth Quarter 2004): 28–36.

50. Organizations may have a compensation program that pays a differential based on geographic location. See Thomas J. Atchison, "Branch Office Salary Structure," *Compensation and Benefits Review* 39, no. 3 (June 2007): 35.

51. Mirta Diaz-Fernandez, Alvaro Lopez-Cabrales, and Ramon Valle-Cabrera, "What companies pay for: The strategic role of employee competencies," *European Journal of International Management* Vol. 3, No. 4 (2009): 439–456.

52. Howard Risher, "Second-Generation Banded Salary Systems," *WorldatWork* 16, no. 1 (First Quarter 2007): 20.

53. Jim Kochanski and David Insler, "The compensation scorecard: What gets measured gets done," *WorldatWork Journal*, (June, 28, 2010).

54. Because the FLSA is always subject to amendment, an employer should consult the appropriate publications of one of the labor services previously mentioned or the Wage and Hour Division of the U.S. Department of Labor to obtain the latest information regarding its current provisions, particularly the minimum wage rate. Changes to the FLSA can also be found at the DOL website, http://www.dol.gov.

55. Susan Ladika, "Decompression Pay," *HR Magazine* 50, no. 10 (December 2005): 79.

56. HR Policy Association, "DOL embroiled in its own FLSA overtime dispute...," (December 2, 2010), http://www.hrpolicy.org/issues_story.aspx?gid=384&sid=3955&miid=8.

57. David Shadovitz, "DOL gets taste of its own medicine," Human Resource Executive Online (December 16, 2010).

58. The online seminar can be viewed at the DOL website, http://www.dol.gov.esa.

59. Christian Schappel, "Cost of noncompliance: Company pays $4.3m in suit," HR Morning.com, (February 4, 2010).

60. Fact Sheet, "The gender wage gap: 2009," Institute for Women's Policy Research (September 2010).

After studying this chapter, you should be able to

LEARNING OUTCOME 1 Know how to implement incentive programs.

LEARNING OUTCOME 2 Identify the different types of incentive programs and why they work.

LEARNING OUTCOME 3 Explain why merit raises may fail to motivate employees and discuss ways to increase their motivational value.

LEARNING OUTCOME 4 Indicate specific ways to compensate salespeople.

LEARNING OUTCOME 5 Differentiate how gains may be shared with employees under the Scanlon and Improshare gainsharing systems.

LEARNING OUTCOME 6 Differentiate between profit sharing plans and explain advantages and disadvantages of these programs.

LEARNING OUTCOME 7 Describe the main types of ESOP plans and discuss the advantages of ESOPs to employers and employees.

The recent economic downturn did much to change the outlook of pay-for-performance. Companies are now likely to tie compensation more closely to performance.[1] Whether you are a heavily scrutinized big bank on Wall Street or a belt-tightening small store in Wisconsin, you want the biggest bang for your buck. For many, this means aligning the interests of the employees with the interests of the company. One of the best ways to do this is to reward people for their performance. But this is no small task. The process of (1) choosing the right incentive plans based on organizational objectives, (2) setting up performance measures, and (3) administering those incentive plans may seem a bit daunting—especially since so much can go wrong if not done right.

One company that has done this right is Lincoln Electric (www.lincolnelectric.com), a leading manufacturer of welding products. Based in Cleveland, Ohio, Lincoln Electric has used pay-for-performance as a vital component of its strategy for more than 175 years. Lincoln's pay strategy is to handsomely reward people for their productivity, high quality, cost reduction ideas, and contribution to the company. Year-end bonuses sometimes double a person's regular pay. Regular pay is based entirely on how much they produce. In essence, the pay-for-performance system consists of three main components.

The first is that you get paid based on how many welding products you produce. The more pieces you produce, the more you get paid. The second is based on the quality of your products, cost reduction ideas, and contribution to the company. This is assessed and paid out at the end of each year as a bonus. And the third is based on how well the entire company does. In this way you share in the profits made by the company.[2]

According to the *WorldatWork* 2010–2011 salary budget survey, most companies are taking a lesson from companies like Lincoln Electric and ramping up their pay-for-performance programs. In fact, in 2011 low performers were expected to receive no pay increase. Average performers could expect roughly a 2.4 percent increase and the highest performers a 3.7 percent increase. In other words, companies are seeing more of a need to differentiate their employees based on performance.[3]

In this chapter, we will discuss incentive plans in terms of the objectives they hope to achieve and the various factors that may affect their success. Because many organizations have implemented broad-based incentive programs to differentiate employees and their performance, for discussion purposes we have grouped incentive plans into three broad categories: individual incentive plans, group incentive plans, and enterprise incentive plans, as shown in Figure 10.1.[4] At the end of the chapter, we also discuss some special incentive plans for professional employees and executives.

Strategic Reasons for Incentive Plans

variable pay

Tying pay to some measure of individual, group, or organizational performance

A major element of strategic compensation management is the use of incentive plans, also called **variable pay** programs. Variable pay programs consist of bonuses, incentives, or recognition for good work. They allow organizations to reward employees for continued contributions. More than 80 percent of companies globally are offering variable pay programs. As head of global compensation consulting at Hewitt Associates, Shekhar Purohit said, "Over the past decade, and increasingly in the past year,

FIGURE 10.1	Types of Incentive Plans		

INDIVIDUAL	GROUP	ENTERPRISE
Piecework	Team compensation	Profit sharing
Standard hour plan	Scanlon Plan	Stock options
Bonuses Merit pay	Improshare	Employee stock ownership plans (ESOPs)
Lump sum merit pay		
Incentive awards		
Sales incentives		
Professional employee incentive plans		
Executive incentive plans		

variable pay has become the standard as companies reward strong performance and lower overhead costs. We expect this trend to continue in the coming years."[5] Variable pay is more flexible than fixed pay (salaries, hourly wages), as variable pay is attached to fixed costs that allow flexibility to increase, decrease, or maintain future payments to employees as business conditions warrant.[6] Most HR managers see variable pay as strategic because it allows the organization to align its employees' interests and outcomes with those of the organization.

However, an additional strategic component that HR managers seem to forget is that variable pay can be used to exercise fairness and equity within the organization. As a result, variable pay not only motivates employees to do what the organization wants them to do. It ensures that employees feel the organization is fair and responsive to their individual contributions.

For example, it has been said that "no good deed goes unpunished." For employees who make valuable contributions, this is sometimes not far from the truth. A study of 20,000 employees found that 27 percent of "high potential" employees planned to leave their company by the end of 2010.[7] The reason? Feelings of pay inequity. In the recent aftermath of the economic recession, many high-performing employees felt they were asked to take on additional work without additional pay. As a result, challenges meant to be energizing can feel like punishment for success if they are not attached to additional rewards.[8]

One of the difficulties faced by companies during difficult times is that they ask everyone to tighten their belts, yet high performers know their market worth and like to be rewarded for it. Furthermore, even employees who are not high performers work harder (and seem happier) when they work for a company that rewards people who deserve it.[9] Shell Corporation is one company that has gone through great effort to demonstrate equity and fairness by making sure managers differentiate between the performance of their employees and reward them appropriately. Overall, employees argue that high performers expect to receive higher levels of pay. In fact, the better an employee performs, the more they are concerned with incentive rewards based on performance.[10]

Incentive rewards are based entirely upon a pay-for-performance philosophy (see Chapter 9). Incentive pay plans establish a performance "threshold" (a baseline performance level) that an employee or group of employees must achieve to qualify for incentive payments. According to one compensation manager, "The performance threshold is the minimum level an employee must reach in order to qualify for variable pay." Additionally, incentive plans emphasize a shared focus on organizational objectives by broadening the opportunities for incentives to employees throughout the organization. Incentive plans create an operating environment that champions a philosophy of shared commitment through the belief that every individual contributes to organizational performance and success.

Incentive Plans as Links to Organizational Objectives

Contemporary arguments for incentive plans focus on linking compensation rewards, both individual and group, to organizational goals. Specific company goals or objectives might be to lower labor costs, improve customer satisfaction, expand product markets, or maintain high levels of productivity and quality, which in turn improve the market for U.S. goods and services in a global economy. By meshing compensation and organizational objectives, managers believe that employees will assume "ownership" of their jobs, thereby improving their effort and overall job performance. Incentives are designed to encourage employees to put out more effort to complete their job tasks—effort they might not be motivated to expend under hourly and/or seniority-based compensation systems. Also, incentive pay is highly valued as a compensation strategy to attract and retain top-performing employees.[11] Figure 10.2 summarizes the major advantages of incentive pay programs as noted by researchers and HR professionals.

Do incentive plans work? The answer is both yes and no. Various studies, along with reports from individual organizations, show a measurable relationship between incentive plans and improved organizational performance.[12] However, the degree of success obtained depends on several factors including (1) identifying important organizational metrics by which to measure employee performance, and (2) a customized incentive plan which effectively measures employee output and rewards exceptional

FIGURE 10.2   Advantages of Incentive Pay Programs

- Incentives focus employee efforts on specific performance targets. They provide real motivation that produces important employee and organizational gains.
- Incentive payouts are variable costs linked to the achievement of results. Base salaries are fixed costs largely unrelated to output.
- Incentive compensation is directly related to operating performance. If performance objectives (quantity and/or quality) are met, incentives are paid. If objectives are not achieved, incentives are withheld.
- Incentives foster teamwork and unit cohesiveness when payments to individuals are based on team results.
- Incentives are a way to distribute success among those responsible for producing that success.
- Incentives are a way to increase equity and justice in an organization.
- Incentives are a means to reward or attract top performers when salary budgets are low.

employee performance.[13] For example, ranked as the #1 hospital for cancer in 2010–2011, the University of Texas M. D. Anderson Cancer Center's health care employees are eligible for up to a 10 percent merit raise, depending on whether they meet or exceed important hospital performance expectations. Importantly, in a survey designed to assess the hospital's incentive pay program, employee responses showed a high relationship between hospital goals and the linkage between pay and performance.[14] At AFLAC Insurance, sales people who achieve sales targets receive significant bonuses, merchandise awards, and recognition through the company's Web site and in-house publications.[15] Because of practices such as these, AFLAC has consistently been rated as one of the 100 Best Companies to Work For by *Fortune* magazine.[16]

Unfortunately, studies also show that variable pay plans may not achieve their proposed objectives or lead to organizational improvements. First, incentive plans sometimes fail to satisfy employee expectations for pay gains. Second, management may have failed to give adequate attention to the design and implementation of the plan, leaving employees confused about how incentive payments are calculated. Third, employees may have little ability to affect performance standards. Furthermore, the success of an incentive plan will depend on the environment that exists within an organization. A plan is more likely to work in an organization where morale is high, employees believe they are being treated fairly, and there is harmony between employees and management.[17]

Requirements for a Successful Incentive Plan

For an incentive plan to succeed, employees must believe in it. This belief can be influenced in part by how successful management is in introducing the plan and convincing employees of its benefits. Encouraging employees to participate in developing and administering the plan is likely to increase their willingness to accept it.

Employees must be able to see a clear connection between the incentive payments they receive and their job performance. This connection is more visible if there are objective quality or quantity standards by which they can judge their performance. Commitment by employees to meet these standards is also essential for incentive plans to succeed. This requires mutual trust and understanding between employees and their supervisors, which can best be achieved through open, two-way channels of communication. Management should guard against incentive payments being seen as an *entitlement*. Instead, these payments should be viewed as a reward that must be earned through effort. This perception can be strengthened if the incentive money is distributed to employees in a separate check. Compensation specialist Joanne Sammer notes the following as characteristics of a successful incentive plan:[18]

- Identify important organizational metrics that encourage employee behavior.

- Involve employees. Incentive programs should seem fair to employees.

- Find the right incentive payout. Payout formulas should be simple and understandable.

- Establish a clear link between performance and payout.

Furthermore, the best-managed incentive pay programs are clearly and continuously communicated to employees. This is true during both good and bad economic periods. According to Roisin Woolnough, compensation consultant, "Communicate

LEARNING OUTCOME 1

As a direct competitor of Lincoln Electric, Illinois Tool Works Inc. has decided to develop more performance-based incentives. As an HR manager for Illinois Tool Works, how would you successfully implement an incentive program similar to Lincoln Electric's?

what you are doing and why it is critical to success. Everyone needs to know what the goals are and what the rewards are for achieving those goals."[19] Proactive organizations find it advisable to continually evaluate the operation and administration of their variable pay programs.

 # Setting Performance Measures

As we discussed in Chapter 7 on "Appraising and Managing Performance," measuring and differentiating performance among employees is one of the most difficult tasks you will face as a manager. This is especially the case when your assessments are used to distribute rewards.[20] You will need to be able to distinguish between individual contributions and those made by a group. You will need to be able to avoid biases based on who you like and dislike, different personalities, and political agendas. At the group level, you will need to distinguish how much one group contributed over another group, even if the work they do is highly interdependent.[21] In sum, measuring individual, group, and enterprise level contributions can be extremely complex. Measuring in a way that makes employees feel they are being treated unfairly can lead to serious problems. See Figure 10.3 for details on the do's and don'ts of measuring performance for incentives.

Problems with incentive plans can often be traced to the choice of performance measures.[22] Therefore, measures that are quantitative, simple, and structured to show a clear relationship to improved performance are best. Overly quantitative, complex measures should be avoided. Also, when selecting a performance

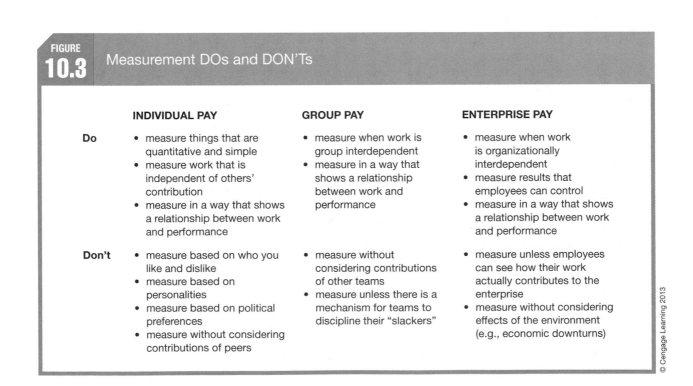

FIGURE 10.3 Measurement DOs and DON'Ts

	INDIVIDUAL PAY	GROUP PAY	ENTERPRISE PAY
Do	• measure things that are quantitative and simple • measure work that is independent of others' contribution • measure in a way that shows a relationship between work and performance	• measure when work is group interdependent • measure in a way that shows a relationship between work and performance	• measure when work is organizationally interdependent • measure results that employees can control • measure in a way that shows a relationship between work and performance
Don't	• measure based on who you like and dislike • measure based on personalities • measure based on political preferences • measure without considering contributions of peers	• measure without considering contributions of other teams • measure unless there is a mechanism for teams to discipline their "slackers"	• measure unless employees can see how their work actually contributes to the enterprise • measure without considering effects of the environment (e.g., economic downturns)

© Cengage Learning 2013

measure, you need to evaluate the extent to which the employees involved can actually influence the measurement. Finally, you must guard against "ratcheting up" performance goals by continually trying to exceed previous results. This eventually leads to employee frustration and employee perception that the standards are unattainable. The result will be a mistrust of management and a backlash against the entire incentive program.

If done correctly, however, measurement can communicate the importance of established organizational goals. For example, if the organization desires to be a leader in quality, then performance indexes may focus on customer satisfaction, timeliness, or being error free. If being a low-priced producer is the goal, then emphasis should be on cost reduction or increased productivity with lower acceptable levels of quality. While a variety of performance options are available, most focus on quality, cost control, or productivity. Highlights in HRM 1 provides five proven guidelines on how to establish and maintain an effective performance measurement program.

HIGHLIGHTS IN **HRM**
1 Setting Performance Measures—The Keys

Companies have established performance measures to improve operational success while rewarding employees for their performance outcomes. Establishing meaningful performance measures is one of the important and difficult challenges facing management today. Before managers or supervisors develop and implement organizational measures, they should consider the following guidelines.

- *Performance measures—at all organizational levels—must be consistent with the strategic goals of the organization.* Avoid nonrelevant measures or metrics that are not closely linked to the business or what employees do in their work.

- *Define the intent of performance measures and champion the cause relentlessly.* Demonstrate that performance measures are, in fact, good business management and hold managers and employees accountable for their success.

- *Involve employees.* A critical step in any measurement program is the development of an employee involvement strategy outlining the nature of employee participation, implementation, and ongoing management of the performance management program. Segment the workforce based on the nature of the work and the potential for impact. Consider which metrics require customization. Acceptance of a performance measurement program is heightened when employees "buy into" the process.

- *Consider the organization's culture and workforce demographics when designing performance measures.* For example, organizations with a more traditional hierarchical structure may need more time to introduce performance metrics compared to flatter organizations, which are more fluid and less steeped in control and command characteristics.

- *Widely communicate the importance of performance measures.* Performance messages are the principles and guidelines that communicate to employees what the required performance levels are and why the organization needs to achieve those levels of success.

Administering Incentive Plans

While incentive plans based on productivity can reduce direct labor costs, to achieve their full benefit they must be carefully thought out, implemented, and maintained. A cardinal rule is that thorough planning must be combined with a "proceed with caution" approach. In fact, for small businesses, this "proceed with caution" approach can even be conveyed as a "work in process" approach. (See Small Business Box on Administering Incentive Plans for Small Businesses for further information.) Compensation

---

Small Business Application

Administering Incentive Plans for Small Businesses

A number of incentives exist that work particularly well with small businesses. For example, annual bonus plans if targets are met, stock options or membership interest options, and restricted ownership rights. Such incentive plans can be both a blessing and a curse. They provide a great way to align the interests of the employees directly with those of the owner, but managing them can also be time consuming and lead to feelings of inequity. Many small businesses do not possess pay-for-performance plans because they think they are too complicated and potentially more harmful than helpful.

While the potential pitfalls of incentive systems in smalls businesses are great, the potential benefits are worth the risk. The key is to understand these risks and then to manage them. Below are some things small businesses can do to help administer incentive plans:

1. Keep incentive plans simple. The easier it is for employees to know how they can be rewarded, the more likely they will buy into the incentive system.

2. Treat the plan as a "work in process." Small business owners need to be open with their employees by communicating that they are trying to reward employees in a fair and equitable manner. Being open to feedback is key to continually improving the plan.

3. Set a minimum requirement around what constitutes average performance. Employees need to know that it is only after the employee exceeds general expectations that the additional rewards begin to kick in. This first ensures that the employees will feel less concerned about being able to maintain a baseline wage. Second, it shows that general performance only brings profits needed to sustain the company. It is above and beyond this subsistence level where the owner can say, "Now we share in the profits." Finally, this also shows that high performance is highly rewarded and that if you do well for the company, then you do well for yourself.

4. Decide when the rewards will be provided to the employee. The closer you can tie incentives to performance, the more likely you will be able to sustain that behavior.

5. Separate rewards from employees' regular pay. When employees can see that they are actually being given something extra based on their performance, they make a clearer distinction between showing up for work and actually contributing. It is also important to make sure that these bonuses are known by others in the organization, as doing so acts as a reward in and of itself.

6. Refine your measures and make sure employees are happy with them. Communicating with your employees is key to making sure incentive plans do not end up being scrapped the month after they are administered.

managers repeatedly stress a number of points related to the effective administration of incentive plans. Three of the more important points are :

1. Incentive systems are effective only when managers are willing to grant incentives based on differences in individual, team, or organizational performance. Allowing incentive payments to become pay guarantees defeats the motivational intent of the incentive. The primary purpose of an incentive compensation plan is not to pay off under almost all circumstances, but rather to motivate performance. Thus, if the plan is to succeed, poor performance must go unrewarded.

2. Annual salary budgets must be large enough to reward and reinforce exceptional performance. When compensation budgets are set to ensure that pay increases do not exceed certain limits (often established as a percentage of payroll or sales), these constraints may prohibit rewarding outstanding individual or group performance.

3. The overhead costs associated with plan implementation and administration must be determined. These may include the cost of establishing performance standards and the added cost of record-keeping. The time consumed in communicating the plan to employees, answering questions, and resolving any complaints about it must also be included in these costs.

Individual Incentive Plans

One word, *flexibility*, describes the design of individual incentive plans.[23] For example, technology, job tasks and duties, and/or organizational goals (such as being a low-cost producer) impact the organization's choice of incentive pay programs. Incentive payments may be determined by the number of units produced, achievement of specific performance goals, or productivity improvements in the organization as a whole. In addition, in highly competitive industries such as food and retailing, low profit margins will affect the availability of monies for incentive payouts. All of these considerations suggest that tradition and philosophy, as well as economics and technology, help govern the design of individual incentive systems.

Piecework

One of the oldest incentive plans is based on piecework. Under straight piecework, employees receive a certain rate for each unit produced. Their compensation is determined by the number of units they produce during a pay period. At Steelcase, an office furniture maker, employees can earn more than their base pay, often as much as 35 percent more, through piecework for each slab of metal they cut or chair they upholster. Under a differential piece rate, employees whose production exceeds the standard output receive a higher rate for all of their work than the rate paid to those who do not exceed the standard.

Employers include piecework in their compensation strategy for several reasons. The wage payment for each employee is simple to compute, and the plan permits an organization to predict its labor costs with considerable accuracy, since these costs are the same for each unit of output. The piecework system is more likely to succeed when units of output can be measured readily, the quality of the product is less critical, the job is fairly standardized, and a constant flow of work can be maintained.

LEARNING OUTCOME 2

If Google paid its programmers based on how many programs they wrote per day, what do you think would happen? If Lincoln Electric paid people only a standard hourly rate, would their productivity stay the same? If enlisted soldiers received an additional bonus if they reenlisted in the military, how much more likely would they be to reenlist?

straight piecework

An incentive plan under which employees receive a certain rate for each unit produced

differential piece rate

A compensation rate under which employees whose production exceeds the standard amount of output receive a higher rate for all of their work than the rate paid to those who do not exceed the standard amount

Computing the Piece Rate

Although time standards establish the time required to perform a given amount of work, they do not by themselves determine what the incentive rate should be. The incentive rates must be based on hourly wage rates that would otherwise be paid for the type of work being performed. For example, the standard time for producing one unit of work in a job paying $12.75 per hour was set at twelve minutes. The piece rate would be $2.55 per unit, computed as follows:

$$\frac{60 \text{ (minutes per hour)}}{12 \text{ (standard time per hour)}} = 5 \text{ units per hour}$$

$$\frac{\$12.75 \text{ (hourly rate)}}{5 \text{ (units per hour)}} = 2.55 \text{ per unit}$$

Piecework: The Drawbacks

Despite their obvious advantages—including their direct tie to a pay-for-performance philosophy—piecework systems have a number of disadvantages that offset their usefulness. One of the most significant weaknesses of piecework, as well as of other incentive plans based on individual effort, is that it may not always be an effective motivator. If employees believe that an increase in their output will provoke disapproval from fellow workers (often referred to as "rate busting"), they may avoid exerting maximum effort because their desire for peer approval outweighs their desire for more money. Also, jobs in which individual contributions are difficult to distinguish or measure or in which the work is mechanized to the point that the employee exercises very little control over output may be unsuited to piecework. Piecework may also be inappropriate in the following situations:

- When quality is more important than quantity

- When technology changes are frequent

- When productivity standards on which piecework must be based are difficult to develop

Importantly, piecework incentive systems can work against an organizational culture promoting workforce cooperation, creativity, or problem-solving because each of these goals can infringe on an employee's time and productivity and, therefore, total pay earned.

Standard Hour Plan

standard hour plan

An incentive plan that sets rates based on the completion of a job in a predetermined standard time

Another common incentive technique is the standard hour plan, which sets incentive rates on the basis of a predetermined "standard time" for completing a job. If employees finish the work in less than the expected time, their pay is still based on the standard time for the job multiplied by their hourly rate. Standard hour plans are popular in service departments in automobile dealerships. For example, if the standard time to install an engine in a truck is five hours and the mechanic completes the job in four and a half hours, the payment would be the mechanic's hourly rate times five hours. Standard hour plans are particularly suited to long-cycle operations or jobs or tasks that are nonrepetitive and require a variety of skills. However, while standard hour plans can motivate employees to produce more, employers must ensure that equipment maintenance and product quality do not suffer as employees strive to do their work faster to earn additional income.

Bonuses

A bonus is an incentive payment given to employees beyond their normal base wage. It is frequently given at the end of the year and does not become part of base pay. Bonuses have the advantage of providing employees with more pay for exerting greater effort, while at the same time the employees still have the security of a basic wage. Bonus payments are common among managerial and executive employees, but recent trends show that they are increasingly given to employees throughout the organization.[24] For example, a study by RAND, a nonprofit research organization, showed that increased use of cash bonuses by the U.S. Department of Defense has increased enlistment of military personnel by roughly 20 percent.[25] This increase in retention through bonuses has saved the U.S. Department of Defense money as well as helped to overcome attitudes toward the adverse effects of frequent and long deployments.

Bonuses can be a powerful tool to increase future performance. For instance, if the link between pay and performance is clearly established, bonuses can be one of the most effective tools to increase future performance. For example, a study on bonuses vs. actual pay raises showed that improving one's pay through merit increases by 1 percent would increase future performance by 2 percent. However, if the same money was applied to pay-for-performance bonuses, the employee's performance increases by 15 percent. Indeed, providing a strong pay-for-performance link for bonuses can dramatically improve employee productivity.[26]

Depending on who is to receive the bonus, the incentive payment may be determined on the basis of cost reduction, quality improvement, or performance criteria established by the organization. At the executive level, for example, performance criteria might include earnings growth or enterprise-specific, agreed-on objectives.

When some special employee contribution is to be rewarded, a spot bonus is used. A spot bonus, as the name implies, is given "on the spot," normally for some employee effort not directly tied to an established performance standard. For example, a customer service representative might receive a spot bonus for working long hours to fill a new customer's large order. Spot bonuses are championed as useful retention and motivational tools for overburdened employees, especially during lean financial times. Lauren Sejen, compensation expert with Watson Wyatt Worldwide, notes, "I think spot bonuses are one of the most underutilized forms of rewards, given how well employees respond to them. These plans make perfect sense."[27]

Merit Pay

A merit pay program (merit raise) links an increase in base pay to how successfully an employee performs his or her job. Unlike bonuses, once merit increases are given they become part of base pay, regardless of future performance. Merit increases are normally given when an employee achieves some objective performance standard (although a superior's subjective evaluation of subordinate performance may play a large role in the increase given). Merit raises can serve to motivate if employees perceive the raise to be related to the performance required to earn it.[28]

bonus
An incentive payment that is supplemental to the base wage

spot bonus
An unplanned bonus given for employee effort unrelated to an established performance measure

Theories of motivation, in addition to behavioral science research, provide justification for merit pay plans as well as other pay-for-performance programs.[29] However, research shows that a merit increase in the range of 7 to 9 percent is necessary to serve as a pay motivator.[30] Employees may welcome lower percentage amounts, but low salary increases may not lead to significantly greater effort on the part of employees to drive business results. Consequently, with low salary budgets (see Chapter 9), organizations wishing to reward top performers will be required to distribute a large portion of the compensation budget to these individuals.[31] A meaningful merit increase will catch the attention of top performers while sending a signal to poor-performing employees. A strategic compensation policy *must differentiate* between outstanding and good or average performance. Furthermore, increases granted on the basis of merit should be distinguishable from cost-of-living or other general increases.

Problems with Merit Raises

LEARNING OUTCOME 3

If you perform well, you most likely want to be rewarded for this. But what is the best model for rewarding employees who do well? Is it better to offer merit bonuses, merit pay raises, or just recognize them for their work? Whatever reward you choose, how do you make sure it motivates your employees?

Merit raises may not always achieve their intended purpose. Unlike a bonus, a merit raise may be perpetuated year after year even when performance declines. When this happens, employees come to expect the increase and see it as an entitlement, unrelated to their performance. Furthermore, what are referred to as merit raises often turn out to be increases based on seniority or favoritism. A superior's biased evaluation of subordinate performance may play a large role in the increase given. Even when merit raises are determined by performance, the employee's gains may be offset by inflation and higher income taxes. Compensation specialists also recognize the following problems with merit pay plans:

1. Money available for merit increases may be inadequate to satisfactorily raise all employees' base pay.

2. Managers may have no guidance in how to define and measure performance; there may be vagueness regarding merit award criteria.

3. Employees may not believe that their compensation is tied to effort and performance; they may be unable to differentiate between merit pay and other types of pay increases.

4. Employees and their managers may hold different views of the factors that contribute to job success.

5. Merit pay plans may create feelings of pay inequity.[32]

merit guidelines

Guidelines for awarding merit raises that are tied to performance objectives

While there are no easy solutions to these problems, organizations using a true merit pay plan often base the percentage pay raise on merit guidelines tied to performance appraisals. For example, a certain pay increase, such as "3 percent," will be tied to a certain performance evaluation, such as "above average." The percentages may change each year, depending on various internal or external concerns such as profit levels or national economic conditions as indicated by changes in the consumer price index. To prevent all employees from being rated outstanding or above average, managers may be required to distribute the performance rating according to some preestablished formula (such as only 10 percent can be rated outstanding). Additionally, when setting merit percentage guidelines, organizations should consider individual performance along with such factors as training, experience, and current earnings.

Incentive Awards and Recognition

Incentive awards and employee recognition are an important part of an employer's pay-for-performance compensation strategy. In 2011, a study by the American Psychological Association found that 43 percent of employees feel they receive inadequate nonmonetary awards and recognition for their contributions at work. In fact, almost a third (32 percent) of employees indicated that they intended to seek employment elsewhere within the next year.[33]

Many companies recognized this trend and have put considerable effort into ramping up their awards and recognition programs. Over 40 percent of companies showed an increase in their incentive awards and recognitions for 2011.[34] For example, Nordstrom offers a Pacesetters award and an All-Star award for service. Pacesetter is the title given to the top 10 percent of salespeople whose net sales meet or exceed an annual sales goal for their department. The individuals are recognized in company meetings and receive a cash prize, Nordstrom stock, and a higher merchandise discount for the year. One sales All-Star is recognized each month and one customer service All-Star is recognized each quarter. The award is presented at the company recognition meeting. The families of the employees are invited. Winners receive a higher merchandise discount of 33 percent (up from 20 percent), a cash award of $100, special business cards, and displayed photos of the employees.

Awards are used to recognize productivity gains, special contributions or achievements, and service to the organization. Popular noncash incentive awards include merchandise, personalized gifts, theater or sports tickets, vacations, dining out, gift certificates or gift cards, and personalized clothing. Tangible awards presented with

Nonmonetary rewards let employees know they are valued, which is why more and more companies are using incentives like these to recognize high performance.

gosphotodesign/Shutterstock.com

the right message and style can make employees feel appreciated while at the same time underscoring a company value.

Research clearly shows that noncash incentive awards are most effective as motivators when the award is combined with a meaningful employee recognition program. Tyler Gentry, employee recognition specialist, notes this about the importance of noncash incentive awards, "Recognition and rewards aren't so much about recognizing someone for going 'above and beyond' and giving gifts as they are about letting employees know that they are *valued* and *appreciated*. Recognition is a conduit that shows employees that the company appreciates their efforts, their unique gifts, and their contributions."[35] Employers should take care to tie awards to performance and deliver awards in a timely, sincere, and specific way. Generally, the more public the recognition, the more powerful the effect.[36]

Importantly, noncash incentive awards should support business goals and objectives. Greg Boswell, managing director of client solutions at O. C. Tanner, notes, "Employers are now thinking of awards and employee recognition more strategically with programs closely aligned to their business goals."[37] For example, if quality improvement is a business goal, then recognition needs to be tied to those behaviors that further the achievement of quality. Additionally, incentive awards work best when awards are appreciated and valued by employees. At one advertising agency, the employee-of-the-month is allowed to drive the president's car for one month—the car is a Maserati. Highlights in HRM 2 provides suggestions for noncash incentive awards based on the generational grouping of employees.

Sales Incentives

LEARNING OUTCOME 4

Siemens is one of the largest electronics and engineering companies in the world. While they produce many consumer products such as cell phones and household electronics, many of their products are sold to other companies. As a result, Siemens is very dependent upon their salespeople. What are the different payment methods you would use to increase sales at Siemens?

The enthusiasm and drive required in most types of sales work demand that sales employees be highly motivated. This fact, as well as the competitive nature of selling, explains why financial incentives for salespeople are widely used. These incentive plans must provide a source of motivation that will elicit cooperation and trust. For example, Nordstrom salespeople are paid on commission. The average salesperson's salary is $38,900 per year, and the average department manager salary is $49,500 per year, yet there are salespeople who make more than $100,000 per year. This means that, on average, Nordstrom salespeople make more than $18 an hour.[38] Motivation is particularly important for employees away from the office who cannot be supervised closely and who, as a result, must exercise a high degree of self-discipline.

Unique Needs of Sales Incentive Plans

Incentive systems for salespeople are complicated by the wide differences in the types of sales jobs. These range from department store clerks who ring up customer purchases to industrial salespeople at McGraw-Edison who provide consultation and other highly technical services. Salespeople's performance may be measured by the dollar volume of their sales and by their ability to establish new accounts. Other measures are the ability to promote new products or services and to provide various forms of customer service and assistance that do not produce immediate sales revenues.[39]

Performance standards for sales employees are difficult to develop, however, because their performance is often affected by external factors beyond their control. Economic and seasonal fluctuations, sales competition, changes in demand, and the nature of the sales territory can all affect an individual's sales record.[40] Sales volume alone therefore may not be an accurate indicator of the effort salespeople have expended.

In developing incentive plans for salespeople, managers are also confronted with the problem of how to reward extra sales effort and at the same time compensate for activities that do not contribute directly or immediately to sales. Furthermore, sales employees must be able to enjoy some degree of income stability.[41]

Types of Sales Incentive Plans

Compensation plans for sales employees may consist of a straight salary plan, a straight commission plan, a combination salary and commission plan, or a sales plus bonus plan.[42] A **straight salary plan** permits salespeople to be paid for performing various duties not reflected immediately in their sales volume. It enables them to devote more time to providing services and building up the goodwill of customers without jeopardizing their income. The principal limitation of the straight salary plan is that it may not motivate salespeople to exert sufficient effort in maximizing their sales volume.

On the other hand, the **straight commission plan**, based on a percentage of sales, provides maximum incentive and is easy to compute and understand. For example, total cash compensation might equal total sales volume times some percentage of total sales, perhaps 2 percent. Straight commission plans encourage aggressive selling, which might be needed in highly competitive industries. Under a straight commission plan, salespeople may be allowed a salary draw. A *draw* is a cash advance that must be paid back as commissions are earned.

straight salary plan

A compensation plan that permits salespeople to be paid for performing various duties that are not reflected immediately in their sales volume

straight commission plan

A compensation plan based on a percentage of sales

HIGHLIGHTS IN **HRM**
2 Customize Your Noncash Incentive Awards

Compensation specialists recognize that a successful noncash incentive program will offer employees a wide selection of awards—awards that appeal to a diverse workforce and the uniqueness of individual employees. "One-size-fits-all" is not the approach to take. What appeals to younger employees may not be attractive to older employees. For example, one marketing firm characterizes recognition and rewards based on generations as follows:

- Traditionalists (61+). These individuals are less likely to spend money on themselves. Attractive awards include entertainment venues, vacations, and technology items. They also appreciate health and wellness opportunities.
- Boomers (41–60). Personal recognition is important. These individuals want to feel appreciated for their work contributions and are likely to change jobs if they feel under-valued or unrecognized. Boomers favor incentive rewards in the areas of travel, luxury gifts, health and wellness options, and personalized plaques and awards.
- Generation X (25–41). This group values a balanced lifestyle of work and play. Generation X employees value gadgets and high-tech items along with flexible schedules and discretionary time off. A flexible "day-off-work" would appeal to this group.
- Generation Y (14–25). These employees desire immediate performance feedback. Employee-of-the-month programs appeal to these employees as do "spot" recognition plans. Gift cards, gift certificates to "trendy" stores, and movie tickets are appropriate as rewards for the immediate recognition of performance.

Source: Adapted from Alison Avalos, "Recognition: A Critical Component of the Total Reward Mix," *Workspan* (July 2007): 33.

However, the straight commission plan is limited by the following disadvantages:

1. Salespeople will stress high-priced products.

2. Customer service after the sale is likely to be neglected.

3. Earnings tend to fluctuate widely between good and poor periods of business, and turnover of trained sales employees tends to increase in poor periods.

4. Salespeople are tempted to grant price concessions.

combined salary and commission plan
A compensation plan that includes a straight salary and a commission

The **combined salary and commission plan** is the most widely used sales incentive program. For example, the most common pay mix (see "pay mix" in Chapter 9) for salespersons responsible for *new* accounts is 50 percent base pay and 50 percent variable pay. For salespersons servicing *existing* accounts, the pay distribution will lean more toward base pay and less toward commission. The ratio of base salary to commission can be set to fit organizational objectives.

For example, Siemens' Building Technologies division expects its salespeople to nearly double their base salary through commission after they have been with the company for a number of years. In fact, high performing sales agents can sometimes triple their base pay, making them some of the highest paid people in the company. As one salesperson stated, "I was identified as a high potential a number of years back. They wanted me to move into a management role. However, if I did that I would knock my salary down by almost 30 percent. Sales is where the money is . . . if you're good." The following advantages indicate why the combination salary-and-commission-plan is so widely used:

1. The right kind of incentive compensation, if linked to salary in the right proportion, has most of the advantages of both the straight salary and the straight commission forms of compensation.

2. A salary-plus-incentive compensation plan offers greater design flexibility and can therefore be more readily set up to help maximize company profits.

3. The plan can develop the most favorable ratio of selling expense to sales.

4. The field sales force can be motivated to achieve specific company marketing objectives in addition to sales volume.

salary plus bonus plan
A compensation plan that pays a salary plus a bonus achieved by reaching targeted sales goals

Sales representatives at Glaxo Pharmaceuticals are paid on a salary plus bonus program. Under **salary plus bonus plans**, the payout can be paid on a monthly, quarterly, or yearly schedule contingent upon the salesperson achieving targeted sales goals such as number of sales calls made, account servicing, or quality of sales.

 # Group Incentive Plans

The emphasis on cost reduction and productivity has led many organizations to implement a variety of group incentive plans. Group plans enable employees to share in the benefits of improved efficiency realized by major organizational units or various individual work teams. These plans encourage a cooperative—rather than individualistic—spirit among all employees and reward them for their total contribution to the organization. Such features are particularly desirable when working conditions make individual performance difficult, if not impossible, to measure.

Team Compensation

Team incentive plans reward team members with an incentive reward when agreed-on performance standards are met or exceeded. Team incentives seek to establish a psychological climate that fosters team member cooperation and a collective desire to fulfill organizational goals and objectives. While team incentive plans promote a pay-for-performance philosophy, establishing an effective incentive team plan is not easy.

One catch with setting team compensation is that not all teams are alike (see Chapter 4). For example, cross-functional teams, self-directed teams, and task-force teams make it impossible to develop one consistent type of team incentive plan. With a variety of teams, managers find it difficult to adopt uniform measurement standards or payout formulas for team pay.[43] According to Steven Gross, Hay manager, "Each type of team requires a specific pay structure to function at its peak." Highlights in HRM 3 lists important considerations when designing a team incentive plan.

When team compensation is decided upon, organizations typically use the three-step approach to establishing team incentive payments. First, they set performance measures upon which incentive payments are based. Improvements in efficiency, product quality, or reduction in materials or labor costs are common benchmark criteria. For example, if labor costs for a team represent 30 percent of the organization's sales dollars and the organization pays a bonus for labor cost savings, then whenever team labor costs are less than 30 percent of sales dollars, those savings are paid as an incentive bonus to team members. Information on the size of the incentive bonus is reported to employees on a weekly or monthly basis, explaining why incentive pay was or was not earned. Second, the size of the incentive bonus must be determined. At Thrivent Financial for Lutherans, health insurance underwriters can receive team incentive bonuses of up to 10 percent of base salary. However, the exact level of incentive pay depends on overall team performance and the company's performance over one year. Team incentives at Thrivent are paid annually. Third, a payout formula is established and fully explained to employees. The team bonus may be distributed to employees equally, in proportion to their base pay or on the basis of their relative contribution to the team. With discretionary formulas, managers, or in some cases team members themselves, agree on the payouts to individual team members.

Team incentive programs are not without their problems. The following are some noted problems associated with team compensation.

- Individual team members may perceive that "their" efforts contribute little to team success or to the attainment of the incentive reward.

- Intergroup social problems. Team members may be afraid that one individual may make the others look bad, or that one individual may put in less effort than others but share equally in team rewards—the "free-rider" effect.

- Complex payout formulas or insufficient payout rewards.

Gainsharing Incentive Plans

Gainsharing plans are organizational programs designed to increase productivity or decrease labor costs and share monetary gains with employees. These plans are based on a mathematical formula that compares a baseline of performance with actual productivity during a given period. When productivity exceeds the baseline, an agreed-upon amount of savings is shared with employees. Inherent in gainsharing is

team incentive plan
A compensation plan in which all team members receive an incentive bonus payment when production or service standards are met or exceeded

gainsharing plans
Programs under which both employees and the organization share financial gains according to a predetermined formula that reflects improved productivity and profitability

the idea that involved employees will improve productivity through more effective use of organizational resources.

Although productivity can be measured in various ways, it is usually calculated as a ratio of outputs to inputs. Sales, pieces produced, pounds, total standard costs, direct labor dollars earned, and customer orders are common output measures. Inputs frequently measured include materials, labor, energy, inventory, purchased goods or services, and total costs. An increase in productivity is normally gained when:

- Greater output is obtained with less or equal input.

- Equal production output is obtained with less input.

There are many variations of gainsharing plans, such as the Scanlon Plan and Improshare. The Scanlon Plan emphasizes participative management and encourages

HIGHLIGHTS IN **HRM**
3   Lessons Learned: Designing Effective Team Incentives

Will your team incentive program be successful? While there are no exact keys to success, team compensation specialists cite the following as important components of a meaningful team incentive plan.

- Are organizational members—employees and managers—predisposed to a team incentive reward system? Is there a "cultural readiness" for team compensation? If change is indicated, what information needs to be given to all organizational employees?

- Enlist total employee and managerial support for the incentive effort. While top management support is critical, without the encouragement of employees and middle- and lower-level managers (those directly involved in the program implementation), team incentive programs invariably fail.

- When developing new programs, include representatives from all groups affected by the incentive effort—labor, management, employees. Inclusion, not exclusion, serves to build trust and understanding of the program's intent and its overall importance to organizational success.

- Establish effective, fair, and precise measurement standards. Selected performance measures should be key indicators of organizational success. Do not attempt to measure everything. Employees should be able to directly influence the performance measures selected. Furthermore, performance measures should be challenging but realistic and obtainable. Standards must encourage increased effort without becoming entitlements.

- Incentive payout formulas must be seen as fair, be easy for employees to calculate, offer payouts on a frequent basis, and be large enough to encourage future employee effort. The goal is to create a pay-for-performance environment. When standards are not met, explain why the reward was not earned.

- Determine how incentive rewards will be distributed. Will team members receive equal dollar awards, or will team members receive differential payments based on such factors as seniority, skill levels, rates of pay, member contributions, and so forth?

- Communicate, communicate, communicate. Constantly champion the benefits of the incentive awards to employees and their contribution to organizational success.

cost reductions by sharing with employees any savings resulting from those reductions. Improshare is based on the number of finished goods that the employee work teams complete in an established period.

The Scanlon Plan

The Scanlon Plan is a specific type of gainsharing plan. The philosophy behind the Scanlon Plan is that employees should offer ideas and suggestions to improve productivity and, in turn, be rewarded for their constructive efforts. According to Scanlon's proponents, effective employee participation, which includes the use of committees on which employees are represented, is the most significant feature of the Scanlon Plan. Improvement or gains largely come from "working smarter, not harder." Figure 10.4 illustrates the Scanlon Plan suggestion process, including the duties and responsibilities of two important groups—the *shop* and *screening* committees.

Financial incentives under the Scanlon Plan are ordinarily offered to all employees (a significant feature of the plan) on the basis of an established formula. This formula is based on increases in employee productivity as determined by a norm that has been established for labor costs. The Scanlon Plan has become a fundamental way of managing, if not a way of life, in organizations such as American Value Company, TRW, Weyerhaeuser, and Watermark Credit Union.[44] Specific information on the Scanlon Plan can be obtained at the Scanlon Leadership Network.[45] The network has

LEARNING OUTCOME 5

With the new economic realities and globalization, are gainsharing plans such as Scanlon and Improshare an expensive thing of the past? Do the benefits of these team incentives outweigh the costs?

Scanlon Plan

A bonus incentive plan using employee and management committees to gain cost-reduction improvements

---

FIGURE 10.4   Types of Long-Term Incentive Plans

Stock options	Rights granted to executives to purchase shares of their organization's stock at an established price for a fixed period of time. Stock price is usually set at market value at the time the option is granted.
Stock appreciation rights (SARs)	Cash or stock award determined by increase in stock price during any time chosen by the executive in the option period; does not require executive financing.
Stock purchase	Opportunities for executives to purchase shares of their organization's stock valued at full market or a discount price, often with the organization providing financial assistance.
Phantom stock	Grant of units equal in value to the fair market value or book value of a share of stock; on a specified date the executive will be paid the appreciation in the value of the units up to that time.
Restricted stock	Grant of stock or stock units at a reduced price with the condition that the stock not be transferred or sold (by risk of forfeiture) before a specified employment date.
Performance units	Grants analogous to annual bonuses except that the measurement period exceeds one year. The value of the grant can be expressed as a flat dollar amount or converted to a number of "units" of equivalent aggregate value.
Performance shares	Grants of actual stock or phantom stock units. Value is contingent on both predetermined performance objectives over a specified period of time and the stock market.

helped organizations in manufacturing, transportation, health care, communications, warehousing, and other industries establish Scanlon Plans.

Improshare

Improshare—improved productivity through sharing—is another gainsharing program. Individual production bonuses are typically based on how much an employee produces above some standard amount, but Improshare bonuses are based on the overall productivity of the *work team*. Improshare output is measured by the number of finished products that a work team produces in a given period. Both production (direct) employees and nonproduction (indirect) employees are included in the determination of the bonus.[46]

The bonus is based on productivity gains that result from reducing the time it takes to produce a finished product. The employees and the company each receive payment for 50 percent of the improvement. Since a cooperative environment benefits all, Improshare promotes increased interaction and support between employees and management. Companies such as Hinderliter Energy Equipment pay the bonus as a separate check to emphasize that it is extra income.

Lessons from the Scanlon Plan and Improshare

Perhaps the most important lesson to be learned from the Scanlon Plan and Improshare—or any gainsharing program—is that management expecting to gain the cooperation of its employees in improving efficiency must permit them to become involved psychologically as well as financially in the organization. In fact, psychological ownership (perceptions of having sufficient information and control to do one's job) can play a stronger role in employee performance than financial ownership (opportunities to share in company gains).[47] If employees are to contribute maximum effort, they must have a feeling of involvement and identification with their organization, which does not come out of the traditional manager-subordinate relationship.

Consequently, it is important for organizations to realize that while employee cooperation is essential to the successful administration of gainsharing plans, the plans themselves do not necessarily stimulate this cooperation. Furthermore, the attitude of management is of paramount importance to the success of gainsharing plans. For example, when managers show little confidence and trust in their employees, the plans tend to fail. However, when a trusting relationship is established, gainsharing programs like Scanlon and Improshare lead to higher returns on a company's investment.

Enterprise Incentive Plans

Enterprise incentive plans differ from individual and group incentive plans in that all organizational members participate in the plan's compensation payout. Enterprise incentive plans reward employees on the basis of the success of the organization over an extended time period—normally one year, but the period can be longer. Enterprise incentive plans seek to create a "culture of ownership" by fostering a philosophy of cooperation and teamwork among all organizational members. Common enterprise incentive plans include profit sharing, stock options, and employee stock ownership plans (ESOPs).

Profit Sharing Plans

Profit sharing is any procedure by which an employer pays, or makes available to all regular employees, special current or deferred sums based on the organization's profits. As defined here, profit sharing represents cash payments made to eligible employees at designated time periods, as distinct from profit sharing in the form of contributions to employee pension funds.

Profit sharing plans are intended to give employees the opportunity to increase their earnings by contributing to the growth of their organization's profits. These contributions may be directed toward improving product quality, reducing operating costs, improving work methods, and building goodwill rather than just increasing rates of production. Profit sharing can help stimulate employees to think and feel more like partners in the enterprise and thus to concern themselves with the welfare of the organization as a whole. Its purpose therefore is to motivate a total commitment from employees rather than simply to have them contribute in specific areas.

A popular example of a highly successful profit sharing plan is the one in use at Lincoln Electric. This plan was started in 1934 by J. F. Lincoln, president of the company. Each year the company distributes a large percentage of its profits to employees in accordance with their salary level and merit ratings. It is not uncommon for employees' annual bonuses to exceed 50 percent of annual wages. The success of Lincoln Electric's incentive system depends on a high level of contribution by each employee. Unquestionably there is a high degree of respect among employees and management for Lincoln's organizational goals and for the profit sharing program.

profit sharing
Any procedure by which an employer pays, or makes available to all regular employees, in addition to base pay, special current or deferred sums based on the profits of the enterprise

Using the **INTERNET**

Lincoln Electric's website provides a description of its incentive management system. It also presents information concerning career opportunities with the company. Go to

www.cengagebrain.com

Variations in Profit Sharing Plans

Profit sharing plans differ in the proportion of profits shared with employees and in the distribution and form of payment. The amount shared with employees may range from 5 to 50 percent of the net profit. In most plans, however, about 20 to 25 percent of the net profit is shared. Profit distributions may be made to all employees on an equal basis, or they may be based on regular salaries or some formula that takes into account seniority and/or merit. The payments may be disbursed in cash, deferred, or made on the basis of combining the two forms of payments.

Weaknesses of Profit Sharing Plans

In spite of their potential advantages, profit sharing plans are also prone to

Lincoln Electric is known for its incentive program—a profit sharing plan that has made the company an employer of choice.

Bob Leavitt/Pix Inc./Time Life Pictures/Getty Images

certain weaknesses. The profits shared with employees may be the result of inventory speculation, climatic factors, economic conditions, national emergencies, or other factors over which employees have no control. As one HR manager noted, "Since there is little linkage between what employees do and their profit bonus, there is an absence of any employee involvement initiatives." Conversely, losses may occur during years when employee contributions have been at a maximum. The fact that profit sharing payments are made only once a year or deferred until retirement may reduce their motivational value. If a plan fails to pay off for several years in a row, this can have an adverse effect on productivity and employee morale.

Stock Options

What do the following companies—Apple, Google, Coca-Cola, Starbucks, Nike, Quaker Oats, and Sara Lee—have in common? The answer: Each of these diverse organizations offers a stock option program to its employees. The use of stock options is a very prevalent method of motivating and compensating hourly employees, as well as salaried and executive personnel. This appears true regardless of the industry surveyed or the organization's size.[48]

Stock option programs are sometimes implemented as part of an employee benefit plan or as part of a corporate culture linking employee effort to stock performance. However, organizations that offer stock option programs to employees do so with the belief that there is some incentive value to the systems. By allowing employees to purchase stock, the organization hopes they will increase their productivity, assume a partnership role in the organization, and thus cause the stock price to rise.[49] Furthermore, stock option programs have become a popular way to boost morale of disenfranchised employees caught in budget cuts and downsizing.

Stock option plans grant to employees the right to purchase a specific number of shares of the company's stock at a guaranteed price (the option price) during a designated time period. Although there are many types of options, most options are granted at the stock's fair market value. Not uncommon are plans for purchasing stock through payroll deductions. Highlights in HRM 4 explain employee stock option plans in greater detail.

Unfortunately, in the wake of various corporate scandals, employee stock option plans have come under attack from stockholder groups, government officials, and the general public. Criticism largely focuses on the extravagance of executive stock option plans and dubious corporate accounting procedures.[50] Nevertheless, despite these faults, stock options continue to be a popular and efficient way to pay for the performance of employees and managers. When stock prices rise, employee stock plans can be financially rewarding to employees.

Employee Stock Ownership Plans (ESOPs)

According to the National Center for Employee Ownership, in 2010 approximately 10,500 organizations have employee stock ownership plans (ESOPs) for their employees.[51] Columbia Forest Products, Hy-Vee, Publix Super Markets, Herff Jones, The Tribune Co., U.S. Sugar, The Bureau of National Affairs, and Scheels All Sports are organizations with established ESOPs. W. L. Gore and Associates also decided

LEARNING OUTCOME 7

Consider your favorite grocery store. Is it owned by its employees? Why would your local grocery store implement such a plan? What potential problems might be involved?

4   HIGHLIGHTS IN **HRM**
Employee Stock Option Plans

As of 2007, the National Center for Employee Ownership estimates that up to 10 million employees participate in broad-based stock option plans. Broad-based plans grant stock options to 50 percent or more of full-time employees.

Traditionally, stock option plans have been used as a way to reward company executives or "key" employees and to link their interests with those of the company and their shareholders. Today companies use employee stock option plans to reward, retain, and attract all levels of employees. Stock options are an effective way to share ownership with employees and to gain commitment to organizational goals.

What Is a Stock Option?

A stock option gives an employee the right to buy a certain number of shares in the company at a fixed price for a certain number of years. The price at which the option is provided is called the "grant" price and is usually the market price at the time the options are granted. Employees who have been granted stock options hope that the share price will go up and that they will be able to "cash in" by exercising (purchasing) the stock at the lower grant price and then selling the stock at the current market price.

How Stock Option Plans Work

Here is an example of a typical employee stock option plan. An employee is granted the option to purchase 1,000 shares of the company's stock at the current market price of $5 per share (the "grant" price). The employee can exercise the option at $5 per share—typically the exercise price will be equal to the price when the options are granted. Plans allow employees to exercise their options after a certain number of years or when the company's stock reaches a certain price. If the price of the stock increases to $20 per share, for example, the employee may exercise his or her options to buy 1,000 shares at $5 per share and then sell the stock at the current market price of $20 per share.

Companies sometimes revalue the price at which the options can be exercised. This may happen, for example, when a company's stock price has fallen below the original exercise price. Companies revalue the exercise price as a way to retain their employees.

Source: Adapted from "Employee Stock Options Fact Sheet, National Center for Employee Ownership, http://www.nceo.org/.

that employee stock ownership was an effective and innovative way to give employees a share of the company's success.

An **employee stock ownership plan (ESOP)** is an employer established trust that qualifies as a tax-exempt employee trust under Section 401(a) of the Internal Revenue Code. Under an employee stock ownership plan, employees do not actually buy shares in an ESOP. Instead, the company contributes its own shares to the plan, contributes cash to buy its own stock (often from an existing owner), or, most commonly, has the plan borrow money to buy stock, with the company repaying the

employee stock ownership plans (ESOPs)

Stock plans in which an organization contributes shares of its stock to an established trust for the purpose of stock purchases by its employees

loan. All of these uses have significant tax benefits for the company, the employees, and the sellers. The ESOP holds the stock for employees, and they are routinely informed of the value of their accounts. Stock allocations can be based on employee wages or seniority. When employees leave the organization or retire, they can sell their stock back to the organization, or they can sell it on the open market if it is traded publicly.

Advantages of ESOPs

Encouraged by favorable federal income tax provisions, employers use ESOPs to provide retirement benefits for their employees. Favorable tax incentives permit a portion of earnings to be excluded from taxation if that portion is assigned to employees in the form of shares of stock. Employers can therefore provide retirement benefits for their employees at relatively low cost because stock contributions are in effect subsidized by the federal government. ESOPs can also increase employees' pride of ownership in the organization, providing an incentive for them to increase productivity and help the organization prosper and grow.

Problems with ESOPs

Generally, ESOPs are more likely to serve their intended purposes in publicly held companies than in privately held ones. A major problem with the privately held company is its potential inability to pay back the stock of employees when they retire. These employees do not have the alternative of disposing of their stock on the open market. Thus, when large organizations suffer financial difficulties and the value of the companies' stocks falls, so does the value of the employees' retirement plan.

Other problems with ESOPs include the following:

- The more retirement income comes from these plans, the more dependent a pensioner becomes on the price of company stock. Future retirees are vulnerable to stock market fluctuations as well as to management mistakes.

- Unlike traditional pension plans, ESOP contributions are not guaranteed by the federally established Pension Benefit Guaranty Corporation (see Chapter 11), a major drawback to employees should their employer face serious financial setbacks or closure.

Using the **INTERNET**

Woodward Communication's website provides a description of its ESOP. Go to

www.cengagebrain.com

Incentives for Professional Employees

When it comes to individual, team, and enterprise incentives, professional employees—engineers, scientists, and attorneys, for example—are no different than anyone else. As professionals become increasingly productive, typical organizations move them into management positions. Yet in some organizations professional employees cannot advance beyond a certain point in the salary structure unless they are willing to take an administrative assignment. When they are promoted, their professional talents are no longer utilized fully. In the process, the organization may lose a good professional employee and gain a poor administrator. To avoid this situation, some organizations have extended the salary range for professional positions to equal or nearly equal that for administrative positions. The extension of this range provides a double-track wage system, as illustrated in Chapter 7, whereby professionals who do not aspire to become administrators still have an opportunity to earn comparable salaries.

For many professions, the primary incentive system is based on an "up or out" model. This means that junior professionals are hired by the organization and given a set amount of time, maybe three to six years, to make valuable enough contributions to the firm to become a partner (part owner of the company). Within this amount of time, if they have not made these contributions their employment is terminated. For many years, this has been a valuable incentive system for professional employees. However, the up or out model is seeing less results in terms of motivation as junior professionals are increasingly questioning whether the game is worth the prize. For example, one senior manager at Ernst & Young (a large accounting firm) said that "the closer I become to going up for partner, the more I realize I don't want to become one. The quality of life they live is not worth the additional pay they bring in." Shortly after his statement, this senior manager left the organization for a high-tech firm, which he says is his "dream job."

Motivation of professional employees is also influenced by their increased mobility across companies. Because professional employees are tied more to a profession than an organization, their skills can be valuable across the profession.[52] For example, a physician's skills depend on standardized training that can be applied to any hospital in the United States. In fact, it is no longer considered unethical, or even unusual, for professionals to move across competing firms to advance their careers. As a result, employee mobility has been steadily increasing since the 1980s.[53] In addition to promising partnership after so many years, managers of professionals are considering other incentive systems to keep their employees happy.

Professional employees can receive compensation beyond base pay. For example, scientists and engineers employed by high-tech firms are included in performance-based incentive programs such as profit sharing or stock ownership. These plans encourage greater levels of individual performance. Cash bonuses can be awarded to those who complete projects on or before deadline dates. Payments may also be given to individuals elected to professional societies, granted patents, or meeting professional licensing standards. In addition, some simple rules for maintaining motivation among professionals are below.

1. Provide clear goals

2. Give prompt feedback

3. Reward performance quickly

4. Involve in decision making

5. Seek their opinions often

6. Provide autonomy in work

7. Hold accountable for results

8. Tolerate impatience

9. Provide varied work opportunities

10. Keep them aware of upcoming challenging goals[54]

Today's HR managers need to be creative in finding ways to motivate and retain their professional employees.

LUCARELLI TEMISTOCLE/Shutterstock.Com

 Incentives for Executives

The Executive Pay Package

Executive compensation plans consist of five basic components: (1) base salary, (2) short-term incentives or bonuses, (3) long-term incentives or stock plans, (4) benefits, and (5) perks.[55] Each of these elements may receive different emphasis in the executive's compensation package depending on various organizational goals and executive needs.[56]

Executive Base Salaries

Executive base salaries represent between 30 and 40 percent of total annual compensation.[57] An analysis of executive salaries shows that the largest portion of executive pay is received in long-term incentive rewards and bonuses. Regardless, executives of Fortune 500 firms routinely earn an annual base salary in excess of $500,000, with executives in very large corporations earning considerably more. The levels of competitive salaries in the job market exert perhaps the greatest influence on executive base salaries. An organization's compensation committee—normally members of the board of directors—will order a salary survey to find out what executives earn in comparable enterprises.[58] For example, by one estimate, 96 percent of companies in the Standard & Poor's 500 stock index use a technique called *competitive benchmarking* when setting executive pay or to remain competitive for executive talent. As noted in *Business Week*, company boards reason that a CEO who does not earn as much as his or her peers is likely to "take a hike." Comparisons may be based on organization size, sales volume, or industry groupings. Thus, by analyzing the data from published studies, along with self-generated salary surveys, the compensation committee can determine the equity of the compensation package outside the organization.

Executive Short-Term Incentives

Annual bonuses represent the main element of executive short-term incentives.[59] A bonus payment may take the form of cash or stock and may be paid immediately (which is frequently the case), deferred for a short time, or deferred until retirement. Most organizations pay their short-term incentive bonuses in cash (in the form of a supplemental check), in keeping with their pay-for-performance strategy. By providing a reward soon after the performance and thus linking it to the effort on which it is based, they can use cash bonuses as a significant motivator. Deferred bonuses are used to provide a source of retirement benefits or to supplement a regular pension plan.

Incentive bonuses for executives should be based on the contribution the individual makes to the organization. A variety of formulas have been developed for this purpose. Incentive bonuses may be based on a percentage of a company's total profits or a percentage of profits in excess of a specific return on stockholders' investments. In other instances, the payments may be tied to an annual profit plan whereby the amount is determined by the extent to which an agreed-upon profit level is exceeded. Payments may also be based on performance ratings or the achievement of specific objectives established with the agreement of executives and the board of directors.

In a continuing effort to monitor the pulse of the marketplace, more organizations are tying operational yardsticks to the traditional financial gauges when computing executive pay. Called *balanced scorecards*, these yardsticks may measure things such as customer satisfaction, the ability to innovate, or product or service leadership.[60] Notes David Cates, a compensation principal with Towers Perrin, a balanced scorecard "allows companies to focus on building future economic value, rather than be driven solely by short-term financial results." Mobil Oil uses a balanced scorecard that better indicates exactly where the company is successful and where improvement is needed.

Executive Long-Term Incentives

Stock options are the primary long-term incentive offered to executives.[61] The principal reason driving executive stock ownership is the desire of both the company and outside investors for senior managers to have a significant stake in the success of the business—to have their fortunes rise and fall with the value they create for shareholders. Stock options can also be extremely lavish for executives. Consider these examples. For 2006, Edward E. Whitacre, Jr., CEO of AT&T, received long-term compensation totaling $38.4 million; Patrick Hassey, CEO of Allegheny Technologies, received $35.3 million; and James J. Mulva, CEO of Conoco Phillips, received $30.4 million.[62] Not surprisingly, the creativity in designing a stock option program seems almost limitless. Figure 10.5 highlights several common forms of long-term incentives.

Short-term incentive bonuses are criticized for causing top executives to focus on quarterly profit goals to the detriment of long-term survival and growth objectives. Therefore, corporations such as Sears, Combustion Engineering, Borden, and Enhart have adopted compensation strategies that tie executive pay to long-term performance measures. Each of these organizations recognizes that compensation strategies must also take into account the performance of the organization as a whole. Important to stockholders are such performance results as growth in earnings per share, return on stockholders' equity, and, ultimately, stock price appreciation. A variety of incentive plans, therefore, have been developed to tie rewards to these performance results, particularly over the long term. Additionally, stock options can serve to retain key executive personnel when exercising the options is linked to a specified vesting period, perhaps two to four years (this type of incentive is called "golden handcuffs").

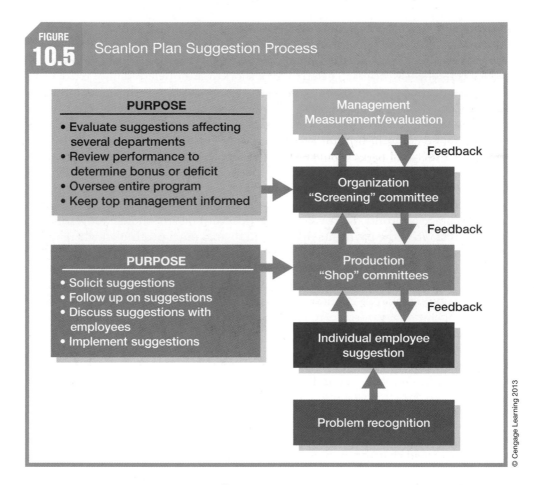

FIGURE 10.5   Scanlon Plan Suggestion Process

PURPOSE
- Evaluate suggestions affecting several departments
- Review performance to determine bonus or deficit
- Oversee entire program
- Keep top management informed

PURPOSE
- Solicit suggestions
- Follow up on suggestions
- Discuss suggestions with employees
- Implement suggestions

Management Measurement/evaluation

Feedback

Organization "Screening" committee

Feedback

Production "Shop" committees

Feedback

Individual employee suggestion

Problem recognition

© Cengage Learning 2013

Stock options are under attack.[63] Some object to the sheer magnitude of these incentive rewards. The link between pay and performance that options are championed to provide can also be undermined when compensation committees grant additional options to executives even when company stock prices fall or performance indexes decline. Peter Clapman, chief counsel for TIAA-CREF, the world's largest pension system, notes, "It's sort of heads you win, tails let's flip again." Even worse for shareholders is the dilution problem. Every option granted to executives makes the shares of other stockholders less valuable.

Executive Benefits

The benefits package offered executives may parallel one offered to other groups of employees. Various programs for health insurance, life insurance, retirement plans, and vacations are common. However, unlike other employee groups, the benefits offered executives are likely to be broader in coverage and free of charge. Additionally, executives may be given financial assistance in the form of trusts for estate planning, payment of mortgage interest, and legal help.[64]

Executive Perks

perquisites
Special nonmonetary benefits given to executives; often referred to as *perks*

Perks (or *perquisites*) are nonmonetary rewards given to executives. Perks are a means of demonstrating the executive's importance to the organization. The status that comes with perks—both inside and outside the organization—shows a pecking order and conveys authority. Corporate executives may simply consider perks a "badge of merit." Perks can also provide tax savings to executives because some are not taxed as income.

The dark side of perks is that they are viewed as wasteful spending and overly lavish. A recent study, however, shows that perks can facilitate company productivity by saving executive time (for example, private planes and chauffeur service) or improve or maintain executive health (for example, spas, health clubs, and company cabins). Therefore, the cost of perks should be weighed against the added efficiency and managerial effectiveness they generate.[65] Highlights in HRM 5 shows the more common perks offered to executives.

Executive Compensation: Ethics and Accountability

From 2007 to 2010, CEO salaries of the top 500 companies dropped. On average, pay cuts ranged from 11 to 30 percent. Yet compensation packages for CEOs are still off-the-chart amazing. Consider the total compensation drawn in 2009 by the following executives.[66]

Gregory B. Maffei, Liberty Media Corp.	$87,493,565
Fred Hassan, Merck & Co.	$49,653,063
Carol Bartz, Yahoo Inc.	$47,229,273
Michael S. Jeffries, Abercrombie & Fitch	$36,335,644

Interestingly, respected management expert Peter F. Drucker argued in a 1984 essay that CEO pay had rocketed out of control and implored compensation committees to hold CEO compensation to no more than 20 times what rank-and-file employees made. He warned that the growing pay gap between CEOs and employees would threaten the very credibility of leadership, particularly when CEOs fire thousands of their workers and their companies underperform.[67]

Given the large amount of various compensation packages, the question asked by many is: "Are top executives worth the salaries and bonuses they receive?" The answer may depend on whom you ask. Corporate compensation committees justify big bonuses in the following ways:[68]

1. Large financial incentives are a way to reward superior performance.

2. Business competition is pressure-filled and demanding.

3. Good executive talent is in great demand.

4. Effective executives create shareholder value.

Others justify high compensation as a fact of business life, reflecting market compensation trends.

Nevertheless, in an era of massive downsizing, low wage increases, and increased workloads for layoff survivors, strong criticism is voiced regarding the high monetary awards given to senior executives. Furthermore, with the large compensation packages awarded to senior managers and top-level executives, cries for performance accountability and openness abound. While not all executive pay is exorbitant and not all executive performance is poor, nevertheless angry employees, union groups, government officials, and stockholders argue for change.

5 HIGHLIGHTS IN **HRM**
The "Sweetness" of Executive Perks

Compensation consulting firms such as Coopers and Lybrand LLP, WorldatWork, and Hewitt Associates regularly survey companies nationwide to identify the perks they provide for executives and other top managers. The following are popular executive perks.

- Company car
- Company plane
- Executive eating facilities
- Financial consulting
- Company-paid parking
- Personal liability insurance
- Estate planning
- First-class air travel
- Home computers
- Chauffeur service
- Children's education

- Spouse travel
- Physical exams
- Mobile phones
- Large insurance policies
- Income tax preparation
- Country club membership
- Luncheon club membership
- Personal home repairs
- Loans
- Legal counseling
- Vacation cabins

Executive Compensation Reform

Several important changes will impact future executive compensation. First, the Internal Revenue Service (IRS) always looks for tax code violations in connection with hefty executive pay packages. The IRS makes executive pay a part of every corporate audit.[69] Second, in July 2007, the Securities and Exchange Commission issued pay disclosure rules that requires companies listed on the New York Stock Exchange and NASDAQ to disclose the true size of their top executive pay packages. Companies must reveal details on accumulated pension benefits, deferred compensation, and perks that exceed more than $10,000 in total value. Also, companies must provide a plain-English table that summarizes executives' various forms of compensation.[70] Third, the Financial Accounting Standards Board (FASB) requires that stock options be recognized as an expense on income statements. Companies and compensation committees must now weigh the benefits provided by stock option programs against the potential charge to earnings.[71] Finally, on July 21, 2010, the Dodd-Frank Wall Street Reform and Consumer Protection Act (Pub. L. 111-203) was signed into effect. Among other things, the law gives shareholders of a company "say on pay." This means that voting shareholders of a company must ultimately approve of its executive salaries.

Summary

LEARNING OUTCOME 1 The success of an incentive pay plan depends on the organizational climate in which it must operate, employee confidence in it, and its suitability to employee and organizational needs. Importantly, employees must view their incentive pay as being equitable and related to their performance. Performance measures should be quantifiable, be easily understood, and bear a demonstrated relationship to organizational performance.

LEARNING OUTCOME 2 Piecework plans pay employees a given rate for each unit satisfactorily completed. Employers implement these plans when output is easily measured and when the production process is fairly standardized. Bonuses are incentive payments above base wages paid on either an individual or team basis. A bonus is offered to encourage employees to exert greater effort. Standard hour plans establish a standard time for job completion. An incentive is paid for finishing the job in less than the preestablished time. These plans are popular for jobs with a fixed time for completion.

LEARNING OUTCOME 3 Merit raises will not serve to motivate employees when they are seen as entitlements, which occurs when these raises are given yearly without regard to changes in employee performance. Merit raises are not motivational when they are given because of seniority or favoritism or when merit budgets are inadequate to sufficiently reward employee performance. To be motivational, merit raises must be such that employees see a clear relationship between pay and performance, and the salary increase must be large enough to exceed inflation and higher income taxes.

LEARNING OUTCOME 4 Salespeople may be compensated by a straight salary, a combination of salary and commission, salary plus bonus, or a commission only. Paying employees a straight salary allows them to focus on tasks other than sales, such as service and customer goodwill. A straight commission plan causes employees to emphasize sales goals. A combination of salary and commission or bonus provides the advantages of both the straight salary and the straight commission form of payments.

LEARNING OUTCOME 5 The Scanlon and Improshare gainsharing plans pay bonuses to employees unrelated to profit levels. Each of these plans encourages employees to maximize their performance and cooperation through suggestions offered to improve organizational performance. The Scanlon Plan pays an employee a bonus based on saved labor cost measured against the organization's sales value of production. The Improshare bonus is paid when employees increase production output above a given target level.

LEARNING OUTCOME 6 Profit sharing plans pay employees sums of money based on the organization's profits. Cash payments are made to eligible employees at specified times, normally yearly. The primary purpose of profit sharing is to provide employees with additional income through their participation in organizational achievement. Employee commitment to improved productivity, quality, and customer service will contribute to organizational success and, in turn, to their compensation. Profit sharing plans may not achieve their stated gains when employee performance is unrelated to organizational success or failure. This may occur because of economic conditions, other competition, or environmental conditions. Profit sharing plans can have a negative effect on employee morale when plans fail to consistently reward employees.

LEARNING OUTCOME 7 With an ESOP, each year the organization contributes stock or cash to buy stock that is then placed in an ESOP trust. The ESOP holds the stock for employees until they either retire or leave the company, at which time the stock is sold back to the company or through a brokerage firm. Employers receive tax benefits for qualified ESOPs; they also hope to receive their employees' commitment to organizational improvement. Employees, however, may lose their retirement income should the company fail or stock prices fall. Another drawback to ESOPs is that they are not guaranteed by any federal agency.

Key Terms

bonus
combined salary and commission
    plan
differential piece rate
employee stock ownership plans
    (ESOPs)
gainsharing plans

Improshare
merit guidelines
perquisites
profit sharing
salary plus bonus plan
Scanlon Plan
spot bonus

standard hour plan
straight commission plan
straight piecework
straight salary plan
team incentive plan
variable pay

Discussion Questions

LEARNING OUTCOME 1   Working individually or in groups, identify the factors for a successful incentive plan.

LEARNING OUTCOME 2   Contrast the differences between straight piecework, differential piece rate, and standard hour plans. Explain where each plan might best be used.

LEARNING OUTCOME 3   A frequently heard complaint about merit raises is that they do little to increase employee effort. What are the causes of this belief? Suggest ways in which the motivating value of merit raises may be increased.

LEARNING OUTCOME 4   What are the reasons behind the different payment methods for sales employees?

LEARNING OUTCOME 5   What are the reasons for the success of the Scanlon and Improshare plans?

LEARNING OUTCOME 6   Because of competitive forces within your industry, you have decided to implement a profit sharing plan for your employees. Discuss the advantages of profit sharing and identify specific characteristics that will ensure success for your plan.

LEARNING OUTCOME 7   What are some reasons for the implementation of ESOPs? Cite some of the potential problems concerning their use.

HRM EXPERIENCE
Awarding Salary Increases

Because pay-for-performance is an important factor governing salary increases, managers must be able to defend the compensation recommendations they make for their employees. Merit raises granted under a pay-for-performance policy must be based on objective appraisals if they are to achieve their intended purposes of rewarding outstanding employee performance. As managers know, however, they must deal with other factors that can affect salary recommendations. These may include the opinions of the employee's peers or extenuating circumstances such as illness or family responsibilities. The purpose of this exercise is to provide you with the experience of granting salary increases to employees based on their work performance and other information.

Assignment

Following are the work records of five employees. As their supervisor, you have just completed their annual appraisal reviews, and it is now time to make recommendations for their future salary. Your department budget has $5,780 allocated for salary increases. Distribute the $5,780 among your employees based on the descriptions for each subordinate.

a. Janet Jenkins currently earns $41,000. Her performance appraisal rating was very high. She is respected by her peers and is felt to be an asset to the work group. She is divorced and has three young children to support.

b. Russell Watts earns a salary of $36,000. His annual performance appraisal was average. Several members of the work group have spoken to you about the difficulty involved in Russell's job. They feel that it is a tough and demanding job and that he is doing his best.

c. Jack Perkins earns $31,250. His performance appraisal was below average, and he seems to have difficulty adjusting to his coworkers. Jack has had a difficult time this past year. His wife passed away early in the year, and his father has recently been diagnosed as terminally ill.

d. Rick Jacobson earns $28,000. His performance appraisal was above average. He is respected by his peers and is generally considered to be a "good guy."

e. Paula Merrill earns $28,850. Her performance appraisal was very high. Her peers are upset because they feel that she is working only to provide a second income. Moreover, her peers see her as trying to "show them up."

Share your results with other class members. Be prepared to explain your allocation of money.

On the Job: Video Cases

Bright Horizons: Incentive Plans & Executive Compensation

Bright Horizons was founded in 1986 by husband and wife team interested in improving early childhood education. Today, Bright Horizons Family Solutions is the world's leading provider of employer-sponsored child care, early education, and work/life solutions. Conducting business in the United States, Europe, and Canada, they have serviced more than 700 client companies, including more than 90 of the Fortune 500.

Known for excellence and innovation in child care and education, Bright Horizons is also a great place to work. They have consistently been the only child care organization named to the "100 Best Companies to Work for in America" list by *Fortune* magazine.

What to Watch for and Ask Yourself

- What motivates the president of Bright Horizons? In what way is compensation important for executives of Bright Horizons?

- Does Bright Horizons offer perks to its executive? Why?

- How do they reward teachers based on performance? Why is actual cash (direct compensation) not always the best way to reward and recognize performance?

- What does Bright Horizons do to make sure their rewards are perceived as fair?

Case Study 1

United States Auto Industry Back on Top ... of CEO Pay

During the financial crisis, many executives' pay was stifled, reduced, or even withheld. Among the hardest hit—the U.S. auto industry. Shareholder groups, union leaders, political officials, and the general public all demanded change in the way auto industry executives were getting rich while their cars were getting poor. For example, Ford made some major cuts for its executives and its employees.

This is why people were shocked to find out that for 2011 the CEO of Ford, Alan Mulally, was to receive $56.5 million in stock awards. It is one of the richest pay packages ever given to a top executive in the auto industry ... and it is even after all the clamor over sky-high executive paychecks. Is it too much?

That depends on who you ask. For most, it seems unreasonable that a boss would make more than 1,000 times the pay of their average worker. However, if you ask Ford workers who have seen Mulally steer Ford back from the edge of bankruptcy, they probably would not complain too much. If you asked Ford's shareholders, it would be hard for them to overlook the fact that Ford shares have gone from $1.56 when Mullaly first took over to $14 a share. If you ask Ford dealers, they may be too busy selling one of the strongest lineups of cars around to answer.

Of course, no one really knows if Ford would have been sitting in such a good position regardless of Mulally. On one hand, there are plenty of factors, such as a national economic recovery, that led to Ford's improvements that Mulally clearly could not have had a finger on. On the other hand, there are plenty of companies that would be willing to pay $50 million if they knew their company would rebound as Ford has under Mulally.

Questions

1. Are CEOs and key corporate executives worth the large pay packages they receive? Explain.
2. Do you agree with Peter Drucker that corporate executives should receive compensation packages no larger than a certain percentage of the pay of hourly workers? Explain.
3. Will the Dodd-Frank Wall Street Reform and Consumer Protection Act giving shareholders the right to vote on executive pay influence the size of these packages in the future? Explain.

Source: Adapted from Phil LeBeau, "Mulally and Bill Ford Collect $100 Million Pay Package," *CNBC*, (March 8, 2011).

Case Study 2

Done-Deal Paper, Inc. operates throughout central Pennsylvania with offices in Scranton, Harrisburg, and Altoona. Providing paper and paper needs to most of Central Pennsylvania, Done-Deal is one of the top two competitors in the area.

In January 2012, Michael Carell, office manager of one of the branch offices for Done-Deal somehow convinced company president and CEO Jerry Zucker that they needed to change the way their sales representatives were incentivized. He argued, "putting our sales reps into teams will not only increase cooperation, but it will increase sales ... right now there are too many sales being lost that could have been won through a team effort." Most of the time, sales made to clients required multiple interactions by multiple reps anyway. Zucker agreed with Carell and pointed out that teamwork can also improve morale and synergy. Based on these assessments, Carell organized his twenty sales reps into four teams of five reps. Sales teams would pool their commissions regardless of who initiated and worked on the sale. After the first year of this team-based incentive program, sales commissions across the four groups varied dramatically. For instance, the highest paid employees in a team made, on average, $50,000 more than the lowest paid team members.

During August 2012, Michael sent to all twenty sales reps a survey requesting feedback on the satisfaction with teams and, specifically, the team-based incentive rewards program. While survey results were generally positive, not everyone was happy in the office. Problems could be grouped into the following categories:

1. Some sales representatives believed that various team members did not "buy into" the team concept and were simply "free riding"—benefiting from the efforts of higher performing reps.
2. There was a general feeling that some teams were assigned difficult regions that prevented them from achieving higher sales.
3. Teams did not always display the motivation and synergy expected, since "bickering" was prevalent between stars and their lesser performing peers. Average performers complained that star reps made them look bad.
4. At least a third of the sales staff felt the incentive rewards program was unfair and asked for a return to individual sales incentives.[72]

Questions

1. Do results from the survey illustrate typical complaints about teams and specifically about team incentive rewards? Explain.
2. If appropriate, what changes would you recommend to improve the incentive reward program? Be specific.
3. Would management have benefited from employee involvement in the initial design and implementation of the program? Explain.

Notes and References

1. "Tech Industry Hiring on the Rise; CFO Compensation to Increase, but Tied More Closely to Performance." *World at Work* (March 2, 2011).

2. Frank Koller, "Spark: How Old-Fashioned Values Drive a Twenty-First Century Corporation: Lessons from Lincoln Electric's Unique Guaranteed Employment Program," (Perseus Books Group, 2010).

3. "2010–2011 Salary Budget Survey, 37th annual," (Scottsdale, AZ: WorldatWork Press, 2010).

4. Patricia K. Zingheim and Jay R. Schuster, "Designing Pay and Rewards in Professional Service Companies," *Compensation and Benefits Review*, 39, no. 1 (January/February 2007): 55.

5. Stephen Miller, "Companies Worldwide Rewarding Performance with Variable Pay," *Society for Human Resource Management* (March 1, 2010); "2010–2011 Salary Budget Survey, 37th annual," (Scottsdale, AZ: WorldatWork Press, 2010).

6. Kerry Chou, "Hedge Your Bets with Variable Pay." *WorldatWork* (2011).

7. Jean Martin and Conrad Schmidt, "How to Keep Your Top Talent," *Harvard Business Review*, (May 2010).

8. Jena McGregor, "How to keep your star employees," *Fortune*, (October 27, 2010).

9. Jean Martin and Conrad Schmidt, "How to Keep Your Top Talent," *Harvard Business Review* (May 2010).

10. Anthony Nyberg, "Retaining Your High Performers: Moderators of the Performance—Job Satisfaction—Voluntary Turnover Relationship," *Journal of Applied Psychology* 95(3): 440–453.

11. John A. Menefee and Ryan O. Murphy, "Rewarding and Retaining the Best," *Benefits Quarterly* 20, no. 3 (Third Quarter 2004): 13–21; Anthony Nyberg, "Retaining your High Performers: Moderators of the Performance-Job Satisfaction-Voluntary Turnover Relationship," *Journal of Applied Psychology* 95, no. 3 (2010): 440–453.

12. Enno Siemsen, Sridhar Balasubramanian, and Aleda V. Roth, "Incentives That Induce Task-Related Effort, Helping, and Knowledge Sharing in Workgroups," *Management Science* 53, no. 10 (October 2007): 1533.

13. Ann Bares, "Incentive Plan Design Begins with Good Questions," *Workforce Management* (October 2008); Fay Hansen, "Control and Customization," *Workforce Management* 86, no. 19 (November 5, 2007): 42; Luis R. Gomez-Mejia, Pascual Berrone, and Monica Franco-Santos, "Compensation and Organizational Performance: Theory, Research and Practice," (Armonk, NY: M. E. Sharpe Publishing, 2010).

14. Avery Comarow, "Best Hospitals 2010–2011: The Honor Roll," *US News and World* Report, (July 14, 2010); Corey Helm, Courtney L. Holladay, Frank R. Tortorella, and Christine Candio, "The Performance Management System: Applying and Evaluating a Pay-for-Performance Initiative," *Journal of Healthcare Management* 52, no. 1 (January/February 2007): 49.

15. Leo Jakobson, "All It's Quacked Up To Be," *Incentive* 181, no. 9 (September 2007): 24.

16. *Fortune* Magazine (2011). "100 Best Companies to Work For."

17. Franco-Santos, M. "Performance Measurement Issues, Incentive Application and Globalization," Chapter in Gomez-Mejia, L. R. and Werner, S. (eds.), *Global Compensation: Foundations and Perspectives* (London: Routledge, 2008).

18. Joanne Sammer, "Weighing Pay Incentives," *HR Magazine* 52, no. 6 (June 2007): 64.

19. Roisin Woolnough, "How to Set Up an Incentive Scheme," *Personnel Today* (February 14, 2005), 22.

20. M. Franco-Santos. "Performance measurement issues, incentive application and globalization," Chapter in Gomez-Mejia, L. R., and Werner, S. (eds.), *Global compensation: Foundations and Perspectives* (London: Routledge, 2008).

21. J. M Welbourne and L. R. Gomez-Mejia. (2008). "Team-based incentives," Chapter in L. A. Berger and D. R. Berger (eds.), *The Compensation Handbook: A State of the Art Guide to Compensation Strategy and Design* (New York: McGraw-Hill).

22. Jim McCoy, "How to Align Employee Performance with Business Strategy," *Workforce Management* 86, no. 12 (June 27, 2007): 55.

23. George T. Milkovich and Jerry M. Newman, *Compensation*, 10th ed. (Boston: McGraw Hill Irwin, 2010).

24. Patty Kujawa, "Private Firms Recognize Value of Cash Bonuses," *Workforce Management* 86, no. 21 (December 10, 2007): 11.

25. Beth J. Asch, Paul Heaton, James Hosek, Francisco Martorell, Curtis Simon, John T. Warner, *Cash Incentives and Military Enlistment, Attrition, and Reenlistment* (Rand Corporation, 2010).

26. Michael C. Sturman, "Using Your Pay System to Improve Employees' Performance: How You Pay Makes a Difference," Cornell Hospitality Report, 6 no. 13 (2006): 4–20.

27. Chris Taylor, "On-the-Spot Incentives," *HR Magazine* 49, no. 5 (May 2004): 80–84.

28. Don Hellriegel and John W. Slocum, Jr., *Organizational Behavior*, 12th ed. (Mason, OH: South-Western, 2009), Chapter 6.

29. Debra L. Nelson and James Campbell Quick, *Organizational Behavior: Science, The Real World, and You*, 6th ed. (Mason, OH: South-Western, 2009).

30. Employee perceptions of appropriate pay raises likely depend on the employer's ability to pay and the economics of the period. For example, when it is known that an employer's ability to pay is great and the economics of the industry are strong, then employees will expect larger percentage merit raises.

31. Susan J. Wells, "No Results, No Raise," *HR Magazine* 50, no. 5 (May 2005): 76.

32. David E. Terpstra and Andre L. Honoree, "Employees Responses to Merit Pay Inequity," *Compensation and Benefits Review* 37, no. 1 (January/February 2005): 51.

33. Donna M. Airoldi, "Two New Studies Show Significant Lack of Workplace Satisfaction and Employee Recognition," *Incentive* (March 9, 2011).

34. Leo Jakobson, "Where the Incentives Are," *Incentive* (March 2011).

35. Tyler Gentry, "Re-engineering Recognition," *Workspan* (February 2007): 47; see also Ann Norman, "Airs Budget Group: Using Recognition to Foster Engagement," *Workspan* (November 2007): 75.

36. Alison Avalos, "Recognition: A Critical Component of the Total Reward Mix," *Workspan*

(July 2007): 33; see also Scott Dow, Tom McMullen, Richard S. Sperling, and Bill Bowbin, "Reward Programs: What Works and What Needs to be Improved," *Worldat-Work* 16, no. 3 (Third Quarter 2007): 6.

37. Charlotte Garvey, "Meaningful Tokens of Appreciation," *HR Magazine* 49, no. 9 (August 2004): 102.

38. Amy Lyman, "Nordstrom—Great Service for Over 100 Years: Best Company for 25 Years," *2009 Great Place to Work Institute*, www.greatplacetowork-conference.com.

39. Michele Marchetti, "Rethinking Compensation Plans," *Sales and Marketing Management* 159, no. 7 (September 2007): 14.

40. Paul R. Dorf and Lisette F. Masur, "The Tough Economy Prompts Companies to Shift Their Approach to Sales Compensation," *Journal of Organizational Excellence* 23, no. 2 (Spring 2004): 35–42.

41. Joseph Dimisa, "How to Sell Your Sales Compensation Plan," *Workspan* (December 2007): 25.

42. Jim Stockmann, "Change on the Horizon: An Analysis of Sales Compensation Practices," *Workspan* (April 2007): 41.

43. George T. Milkovich and Jerry M. Newman, *Compensation*, 10th ed. (Boston: McGraw Hill Irwin, 2010).

44. Scott Dow, Paul Davis, and Chuck Cockburn, "Scanlon Principles and Processes: Building Excellence at Watermark Credit Union," *Worldat-Work* 16, no. 1 (First Quarter 2007): 29.

45. The Scanlon Leadership Network can be found at www.scanlonleader.org.

46. The standard of Improshare's measurement system is the base productivity factor (BPF), which is the ratio of standard direct labor hours produced to total actual hours worked in a base period. The productivity of subsequent periods is then measured by enlarging standard direct labor hours earned by the BPF ratio to establish Improshare hours (IH). The IH is then compared with actual hours worked in the same period. If earned hours exceed actual hours, 50 percent of the gain is divided by actual hours worked to establish a bonus percentage for all employees in the plan.

47. Benjamin B. Dunford, Deidra J. Schleicher, and Liang Zhu, "The Relative Importance of Psychological Versus Pecuniary Approaches to Establishing an Ownership Culture," *Advances in Industrial Relations* 16 (2007): 1–21.

48. Jason Kovac, "Stock Options," *Workspan* (August 2006): 23; see also Seymour

Burchman and Blair Jones, "The Future of Stock Options: From Starring Role to Ensemble Player," *WorldatWork* 13, no. 1 (First Quarter 2004): 29–38.

49. Mamdough Farid, Vincent Conte, and Harold Lazaus. (2011). "Toward a General Model for Executive Compensation," *Journal of Management Development*, 30 no. 1 (2011): 61–74; Ira T. Kay and Steve Seelig, "Revising the Use of a Management Stock Purchase Plan to Increase Management Ownership," *Journal of Deferred Compensation* 11, no. 3 (Spring 2006): 24.

50. Raquel Meyer Alexander, Mark Hirchey, and Susan Scholz, "Backdating Employee Stock Options: Tax Implications," *The CPA Journal* 77, no. 10 (October 2007): 24; see also T. Thomas Cottingham III, "The Stock Options Backdating Scandal: Critical First Response," *Risk Management* 54, no. 6 (June 2007): 12.

51. Based on research conducted by The National Center for Employee Ownership (NCEO) in 2010. The NCEO is a private, nonprofit membership and research organization that serves as the leading source of accurate, unbiased information on employee stock ownership plans (ESOPs), broadly granted employee stock options and related programs, and ownership culture. The NCEO can be reached at http://www.nceo.org or by phone at (510) 208-1300.

52. David H. Maister, *Managing the Professional Service Firm* (Simon & Schuster: New York, 1993).

53. Cappelli, P., "Talent management for the twenty-first century," *Harvard Bus. Rev.* 86 no. 3 (2008): 74–81.

54. C. Bell, "How to Create a High Performance Training Unit," *Training* (October 1980): 49–52.

55. Mark Reilly and Brian Enright, "A New Approach to Executive Compensation," *Workspan* (August 2007): 45.

56. Seymour Burchman and Blair Jones, "Executive Compensation as a Support for Growth Strategy," *WorldatWork* 15, no. 3 (Third Quarter 2006): 39.

57. Total annual compensation is the sum of an executive's annual and long-term compensation. Annual compensation consists of salary, bonus, and other yearly pay. Long-term compensation consists of stock awards, the value of any stock options exercised during the year,

and any other long-term compensation (such as payouts from long-term incentive plans, director's fees, and special bonuses).

58. Edward E. Lawler III and David Finegold, "CEO Compensation: What Board Members Think," *WorldatWork* 16, no. 3 (Third Quarter 2007): 38.

59. Brandon Cherry, "Executive Bonus Plans: Recent Trends in Equity Compensation," *Workspan* (January 2007): 22.

60. Darrell Rigby and Barbara Bilodeau, "Selecting Management Tools Wisely," *Harvard Business Review* 85, no. 12 (December 2007): 20.

61. Brad Hill and Christine Tande, "What's Next for Executive Incentives Now That Options Are Limited?" *Workspan* (September 2007): 47.

62. "CEO Compensation," *Forbes*, 179, no. 11 (May 21, 2007): 112.

63. Peter Burrows, "He's Making Hay as CEOs Squirm," *Business Week* (January 15, 2007): 64; see also Saado Abboud, "Best Buy Uses Flexibility and Choice to Improve Long-Term Incentive Design," *Workspan* (October 2007): 32.

64. Pam Delaney, "Filling the Executive Benefits Gap," *Workspan* (November 2007), 69.

65. "An Unfair Rap for CEO Perks?" *Business Week* (June 7, 2004): 32.

66. CEO Pay Database: 100 Highest-Paid CEOs, *AFL-CIO (2011)*.

67. John A. Byrne, "The Man Who Invented Management: Why Peter Drucker's Ideas Still Matter," *Business Week* (November 2004): 97.

68. Steven N. Kaplan, "Are CEOs Overpaid?" *WorldatWork* 16, no. 3 (Third Quarter 2007): 22; see also Ira Kay and Steve Van Putten, *Myths and Realities of Executive Pay* (Cambridge, MA: Cambridge University Press, 2007); Jessica Marquez, "5 Questions: in Defense of CEO Pay," *Workforce Management* 86, no. 16 (September 27, 2007): 8.

69. Louis Lavelle, "Everybody Should Be a Little Nervous," *Business Week* (December 22, 2003): 42.

70. Seymour Burchman and Blair Jones, "A New Day for Executive Compensation," *Workspan* (January 2007): 15; see also "Out at Home Depot," *Business Week* (January 15, 2007): 56.

71. Mark Gimein, "The Bottom Line on Options," *Business Week* (April 3, 2006): 32; see also Peter Burrows, "Is Steve's Job Untouchable?" *Business Week* (January 15, 2007): 28.

72. Fictional case adapted from the Network Cable, Inc. case

11

Employee Benefits

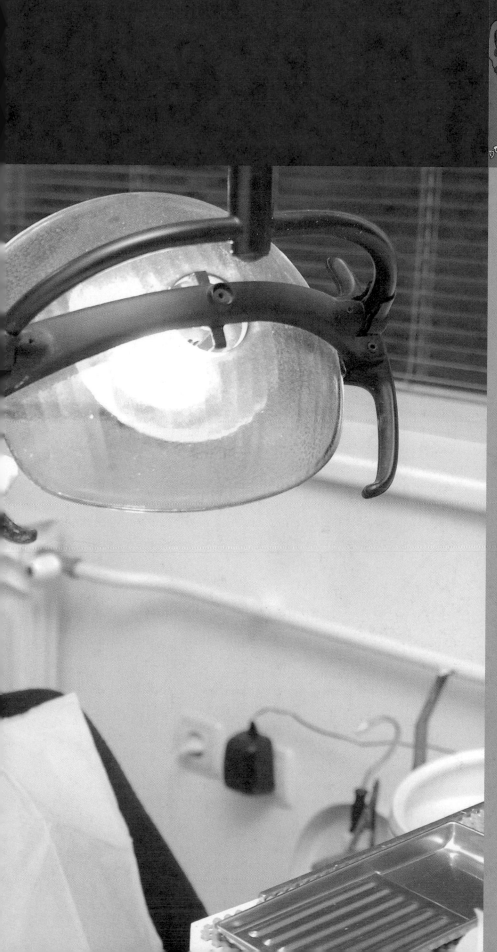

After studying this chapter, you should be able to

LEARNING OUTCOME 1 Explain why companies offer their employee's benefits and are concerned about their costs.

LEARNING OUTCOME 2 Describe the elements that have to be considered when developing a strategic benefits plan.

LEARNING OUTCOME 3 Identify and explain the employee benefits required by law.

LEARNING OUTCOME 4 Discuss the strategies companies utilize to control the costs of employee health care programs.

LEARNING OUTCOME 5 Describe benefits that involve payment for time not worked.

LEARNING OUTCOME 6 Discuss the recent trends in retirement policies and programs.

LEARNING OUTCOME 7 Describe the different types of pension plans employers offer and the regulations related to them.

LEARNING OUTCOME 8 Describe the types of work/life benefits that employers may provide.

Chapter 10 discussed wages and compensation. For most people, the wage, or salary, they are offered is the top factor they look at when they accept a job. But what about the benefits a job offers? How important they are? According to most studies, benefits are the second most important factor employees consider. But this was not always the case. For literally centuries, benefits were something only a firm's top ranking executives were given.[1]

Things changed for rank-and-file workers in the United States in 1935 when the government passed the Social Security Act. Via their employers, the act gave employees a safety net of benefits they had never before had. The proliferation of unions also resulted in an increase in benefits for workers, as did government price and wage controls during World War II. To attract employees during this time period, companies began offering employees nonmonetary benefits, such as pensions. In the 1950s, favorable tax treatment given employers who voluntarily offered workers benefits also fueled their growth.[2] Today most benefits (almost 80 percent) are provided voluntarily by employers.

However, the costs of the benefits provided by employers has been climbing sharply. As a percentage of payroll, since 1955 they have doubled.[3] In 1955, they were a little under 15 percent. Today, according to the Bureau of Labor Statistics, they constitute more than 30 percent, on average, of an employer's payroll costs. For many employers, benefits constitute more than 40 percent of payroll costs. Perhaps because of the rise in benefits costs and the news coverage associated with it, "employees are increasingly aware of the benefits they receive and how those benefits compare to what other companies are offering," the U.S. Chamber of Commerce reports.[4] For instance, many people have heard about the superior employee benefits Google offers. Clearly a well-thought-out benefits program can set a company apart from its competitors when it comes to attracting and retaining talent.

Strategic Benefits Planning

LEARNING OUTCOME 1

If your employer offered you money instead of benefits, would you take it? Do you see any drawbacks to doing so?

As we explained, benefits can represent more than 40 percent of the total payroll costs an employer pays, depending upon the types of benefits it offers. Some benefits are legally required, whereas others are voluntarily granted by employers. To put the cost of benefits in perspective, suppose you accept a job that pays a salary of $45,000 a year. What this means is that in addition to your $45,000 salary, your company could pay $18,000 or more for your benefits and their administration. Figure 11.1 shows the proportion of total pay U.S. organizations, on average, pay to their employees in the form of benefits, and a breakdown of how much goes to each.

Suffice it to say, benefits are expensive, which is why companies pay close attention to them. Health care costs, which have been growing at double and triple the rate of inflation, are of particular concern. Managers are also concerned about new health care reform laws that will require employers of a certain size to provide health care coverage to their employees and their dependents or pay fines to the federal government. We will discuss more about health care reform later in the chapter along with health care cost-containment measures firms are implementing.

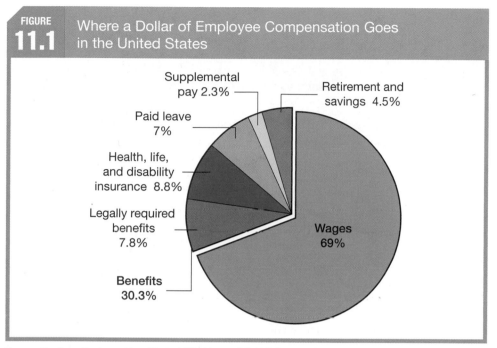

FIGURE 11.1 Where a Dollar of Employee Compensation Goes in the United States

Supplemental pay 2.3%

Retirement and savings 4.5%

Paid leave 7%

Health, life, and disability insurance 8.8%

Legally required benefits 7.8%

Benefits 30.3%

Wages 69%

Source: *Employer Costs per Hour Worked* (Washington DC: U.S. Bureau of Labor Statistics: 2011), http://www.bls.gov/news.release/ecec.t01.htm.

Elements of a Successful Benefits Program

Many forces must be weighed and kept in balance for a benefits program to succeed. For example, a firm's managers must consider how to fund its benefits program and sustain it, as well as the tax consequences related to it. The needs of a company's employees also must be considered because they can differ significantly from firm to firm. If the firm's industry is unionized, this will also affect the types of benefits the firm is likely to have to offer. So will the benefits its competitors are offering and the organization's strategic objectives. Microsoft, for example, picks up the full tab for medical care for all of its U.S. employees and their dependents, which is unusual. But the firm does so because one of its strategic objectives is to attract the top talent in the country. The benefits plan also needs to be compatible with the organization's strategic compensation plan (see Chapter 9), including its total rewards strategy.[5]

Competitive Benefits Information

The Chamber of Commerce, the Bureau of Labor Statistics (BLS), and the Society of Human Resources Management are good sources of competitive benefits information. Annually the BLS publishes a "National Compensation Survey—Benefits," a report that provides comprehensive data on the percentage of private and public workers with access to and participation in employer-provided benefit plans. The BLS's website also shows the average wages and benefits earned by people across industries, occupations, and companies of various sizes. Information firms can use to estimate the costs of various benefits can also be found on the BLS's site.

HR consulting firms, including Towers Watson, Mercer, and the Economic Research Institute, are other sources of information. These organizations have gathered

LEARNING OUTCOME 2

If you were a small business owner, how would you decide what benefits to offer your employees?

Salary Assessor is one of many software programs firms can buy to obtain competitive wage, salary, and benefits data.

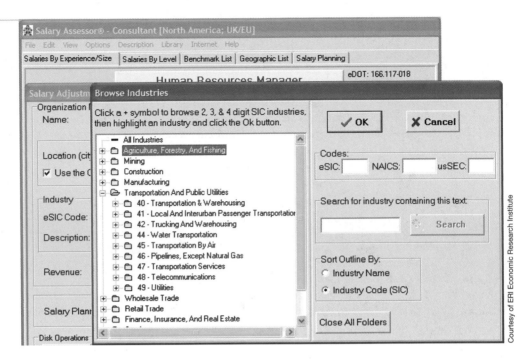

Courtesy of ERI Economic Research Institute

vast amounts of detailed compensation data a firm can purchase. Or the firm can hire them to help design a competitive benefits program. Smaller firms might prefer to collect as much information as they can on their own from the career portions of their competitors' websites, internal information they have collected from both current and former employees, and information from free sources such as the BLS.

Allowing for Employee Involvement

Before a new benefit is introduced, the need for it should first be determined through consultation with employees. This is important, because surveys show that employees who are satisfied with their benefits are more likely to be satisfied with their jobs. Many organizations establish committees composed of managers and employees to administer, interpret, and oversee their benefits policies. Opinion surveys can also be used to obtain employee input. Having employees participate in designing benefits programs helps ensure that management is moving in the direction of satisfying employee wants. The University of Virginia used focus groups to determine employee preferences before implementing a medical benefits plan. Employees indicated that they would rather make higher copayments when they pay for care in order to get lower premiums deducted from their paychecks on a regular basis. The focus groups also told management that employee meetings were the best way to communicate the program to workers.[6]

To make surveying large workforces less cumbersome, HR professionals can utilize a number of websites that enable employees to fill out the information online. EmployeeSurveys.com is one such site. HR managers simply e-mail employees a link to the survey and ask them to complete it. Of course, workers who lack computer access will need to be surveyed via another method.

Flexible Benefits for a Diverse Workforce

To serve their intended purpose, employee benefits programs must reflect the changes that are continually occurring within our society. As you have learned, three generations of employees now occupy the workplace, and each places a different priority on their benefits. Consequently, firms have to think about designing a benefits strategy that appeals to each group. For example, Generation Y employees are probably less likely to be concerned with having pensions than Baby Boomers. Likewise, Generation X employees who are raising their families are more likely to want family-friendly benefits and health care for their dependents than Baby Boomers and Generation Y employees. There are also more single-parent families and two-earner couples in the workplace than there have been in the decades past. As you can see, benefits programs need to take into account a highly diversified workforce to attract highly capable employees.

To make it easier to accommodate the individual needs of different employees, a wide range of organizations have begun offering **flexible benefits plans,** also known as **cafeteria plans.** Rather than one-size-fits-all plans, these plans allow individual employees to choose the benefits that are best suited to their particular needs. They also prevent certain benefits from being wasted on employees who have no need for them. Furthermore, companies realize they can get a better return on investment by tailoring benefits to an employee's stage of life or family status.[7]

Typically, employees are offered a basic or core benefits package of life and health insurance, sick leave, and vacation. Requiring a core set of benefits ensures that employees have a minimum level of coverage to protect against unforeseen financial hardships. Employees are then given a certain amount of funds to purchase whatever other benefits they need through the plan. Other benefit options might include prepaid legal services, financial planning, dental insurance, and long-term care insurance. Some of the less-routine options include elder care, public transportation vouchers, and even pet insurance. Not everyone is going to need or want services such as these, so they are optional. Compensation specialists often see flexible benefits plans as ideal. Employees select the benefits of greatest value to them, while employers manage benefits costs by limiting the dollars employees have to spend.

> **flexible benefits plans (cafeteria plans)**
> Benefit plans that enable individual employees to choose the benefits that are best suited to their particular needs

Administering Benefits

With the wide variety of benefits offered to employees today, administering an organization's benefits program can be both costly and time-consuming. Even for small employers with thirty to forty employees, keeping track of each employee's use of a benefit or request for a change of benefits can be cumbersome. Fortunately, online employee benefit systems have become mainstream for both large and small employers. Employees are provided with passwords that allow them to get information about their benefits plans, enroll in their plans of choice, change their coverage, or simply inquire about the status of their various benefit accounts without ever contacting a HR representative. Online benefits systems are often referred to as *employee self-service (ESS) systems* and can result in a significant cost savings in benefits administration.[8] As Mindy Kairey, e-business leader of the health care management practice for Hewitt Associates LLC, explains, "The Web puts benefits information right in the hands of the people who need it. Employees want to track their claims, review their current coverage levels, and compare their options. They want to take responsibility for their health plan."[9]

As with the benefits themselves, it can be helpful to obtain feedback on different online systems a firm is investigating adopting by asking employees to "test drive" them. Are employees able to find what they want on a site? If they cannot, or it is difficult to use, they will surely end up calling the human resources department for help, which could defeat the purpose of having the system.

Communicating Employee Benefits Information

Although employees are becoming more aware that benefits are costly, many of them still do not realize exactly how much their employers are paying or why they are trying so hard to keep benefits costs down. A Towers Watson study concluded that that problem is largely caused by poor benefits communication and lack of employee trust.[10] Interestingly, benefit specialists remark that the true measure of a successful benefits program is the degree of trust, understanding, and appreciation it earns from the employees.[11]

The communication of employee benefits information improved significantly with the passage of the Employee Retirement Income Security Act (ERISA) in 1974. The act requires that employees be informed about their pension and certain other benefits in a manner calculated to be understood by the average employee. Additionally, employees can sue their employers for misleading them about health and welfare benefits under ERISA. Problems can arise when managers discuss benefits with groups of employees or in one-on-one talks and employees receive inaccurate information. A manager could mislead an employee by stating that the organization's insurance policy does not cover a particular condition when, in fact, it does or that a maternity leave provision is 120 days when the plan is actually 60 days. These potential problems underscore the importance of communicating benefit information accurately and unambiguously.[12]

Employers use an array of methods to communicate benefits to employees, such as the following:

- In-house publications (employee handbooks, organizational newsletters, and postings on bulletin boards)

- Brochures and enrollment information mailed to employees

- Employee meetings and information sessions

- Employee meetings with benefits providers such as the representatives of health care companies, the investment company that manages a firm's pension, and so forth.

- E-mails with benefit information and enrollments reminders

- Blogs

- Social media

- Payroll inserts and pay stub messages

- Benefits hotlines

When communicating employee benefits, the best advice is to use multiple media techniques.[13] Different employee groups have different ways of learning and distinct preferences for how they receive information. Also, the level of complexity of the benefit information being communicated is likely to determine media selection.[14] Because about a third of IKEA's employees are members of Generation Y, the company was worried if it only mailed out benefit information to these employees, many of them would not bother to open the packages. So in addition to mailing information the company used Twitter to send a web link to its benefits site and remind employees about the firm's benefit enrollment deadline. "We wanted to talk to our co-workers in a way they are talking," says Beth Gleba, corporate information manager for IKEA North America.[15]

Intel and Sun Microsystems use blogs to communicate information about their benefits plans and engage employees in a conversation about them. Employees can post questions on the blogs and get answers, which can help other employees who might have the same questions. Sun used the virtual world of Second Life to hold a forum on benefits.[16]

Some general pointers for designing benefits information regardless of the medium include the following:

- Avoid complex language when describing benefits. Clear, concise, and understandable language is a must.

- Explain the purpose behind a benefit and the value it offers employees. Be up front about the pros and cons of different benefit plans.

- Use graphics whenever possible to make the information understandable at a glance.

- Provide numerous examples to illustrate how a benefit choice might affect different types of employees, depending upon their personal circumstances.

Even if employees can access their benefits information online, most firms periodically mail out printed benefit statements that detail the status of an employee's benefits. Highlights in HRM 1 shows an example of such a statement generated using a software product called CompPackage. Notice how the employee's total compensation is highlighted so that the full value of the benefits received is easier to see.

Employee Benefits Required by Law

Legally required employee benefits constitute nearly a quarter of the benefits package that employers provide. These benefits include employer contributions to Social Security, unemployment insurance, and workers' compensation insurance. We will discuss each of these benefits.

LEARNING OUTCOME 3

Some businesspeople and economists believe that U.S. companies are at a disadvantage because they pay for many worker benefits that in other countries are provided by the government. Do you think the U.S. is at a disadvantage because of this? What advantages does the U.S. system offer companies?

Social Security Insurance

The Social Security Act was designed to protect workers against the loss of earnings resulting from old age and unemployment. The act was later amended to include disability, or, in the case of dependents, the death of the worker supporting them. Together the programs have become referred to as Old Age, Survivors, and Disability Insurance (OASDI). According to the Social Security Administration, in 2011 about 50 million people received retirement survivors and disability benefits from Social Security.

To be eligible for OASDI, an individual must have been engaged in employment covered by the act. Most employment in private enterprise, most types of self-employment, active military service after 1956, and employment in certain nonprofit organizations and governmental agencies are subject to coverage under the act.[17] Railroad workers and civil service employees who are covered by their own systems and some occupational groups, under certain conditions, are exempted from the act.

The Social Security program is supported by means of a tax levied against an employee's earnings that must be matched by the employer in each pay period. In 2011, the tax was 6.2 percent. This percentage can vary, though. For example, to stimulate the economy during the last recession, the rate employees paid during 2011 was temporarily reduced to 4.2 percent. (The amount self-employed individuals paid was reduced from 12.4 to 10.4 percent.)[18] The tax revenues are used to pay three major types of benefits: (1) retirement benefits, (2) disability benefits, and (3) survivors' benefits. Because of

HIGHLIGHTS IN HRM

1 A Personalized Statement of Benefits Costs

 ABC Corporation

For Year Ending December 31, 2010
Your Total Compensation Report

Enclosed is a personalized Statement prepared specifically for you. This statement shows the contributions made by your company toward your total compensation package. As you review this statement, you will see that the value of your benefits, added to your annual pay, produce your total compensation. The statement is designed to show how much your service is valued by your company.

Chris Smith
123 Maple Street
Pittsburgh, PA 15212

Thank you for your service,

Jonathan Bigg, President

Department: Marketing

(Mid-Year Event Applies: Last Pay Raise: June 1, 2010)

Base Pay		Other Cash Benefits		Company Paid Benefits		Total Compensation
$40,000	+	$1,600	+	$19,579	=	$61,179

Pay		
Base Pay Total	**$**	**40,000**
Salary	$	40,000
Other Income Total	**$**	**1,600**
Holiday Bonus	$	200
Annual Bonus	$	500
Performance Bonus	$	900

Total Compensation Package
(Your Base Pay and Company-Paid Benefits)

$40,000	+	$21,179	=	$61,179
Your Base Pay		Company-Paid Benefits and Cash		Your Total Compensation

53% — **Your Company-Paid Benefits and Cash represent an additional 53% of Your Base Pay!**

Additional Company Perks
Free Coffee Service
Annual Holiday Gala
Annual Company Picnic

Benefits	Company Contribution			Your Contribution	
Insurance Benefits Total	**$**	**6,917**		**$**	**4,703**
Health Insurance	$	5,770		$	2,885
Dental Insurance	$	577		$	288
Vision Insurance	$	344		$	--
Short Term Disability	$	133		$	--
Long Term Disability	$	93		$	--
Aflac Short Term Disability	$	--		$	680
Aflac Personal Accident	$	--		$	522
Aflac Cancer	$	--		$	328
Retirement Benefits Total	**$**	**3,425**		**$**	**4,175**
Social Security	$	2,579		$	2,579
Medicare	$	596		$	596
401K	$	250		$	1,000
Time Off Benefits Total	**$**	**3,320**		**$**	**--**
PTO	$	3,320		$	--
Mandated Benefits Total	**$**	**1,747**		**$**	**--**
Federal Unemployment	$	56		$	--
State Unemployment	$	179		$	--
Worker's Compensation	$	1,512		$	--
Special Benefits Total	**$**	**4,170**		**$**	**--**
Free Parking	$	2,400		$	--
Fun Fridays Food Fests	$	250		$	--
Cell/PC/Technology	$	600		$	--
Education/Training	$	920		$	--
Benefits Total	**$**	**19,579**		**$**	**8,878**

69% — **Your Company-Paid Benefits represent 69% of your Total Benefits!**

the continual changes that result from legislation and administrative rulings, as well as the complexities of making determinations of an individual's rights under Social Security, we will describe these benefits only in general terms.

Retirement Benefits

To qualify for retirement benefits, a person must have reached retirement age and be fully insured. A *fully insured person* has earned forty credits—a maximum of four credits a year for ten years, based on annual earnings, a figure adjusted annually. The amount of monthly Social Security retirement benefits is based on earnings, adjusted for inflation, over the years an individual is covered by Social Security.[19] Under Social Security guidelines, an individual's *full retirement age* depends on the year of his or her birth.[20] Workers born before 1938 can collect full benefits at age sixty-five. Because of longer life expectancies, for those born after that date, the age to collect full benefits has been gradually raised to age sixty-seven.

Currently individuals can receive Social Security benefits as early as age sixty-two, but the amount they receive each month will be less than monthly benefits received at full retirement age. In addition, many people who are younger than full retirement age but are sixty-two or over work part-time as well as collect Social Security. However, they can only earn so much money before the government begins reducing their monthly Social Security checks. (In 2011 the earnings limit was $14,160). However, once workers reach their full retirement ages there is no limit on the amount they can earn; their Social Security checks will not be reduced. Human resources managers need to keep this in mind when they develop programs to retain and attract older workers.

Disability Benefits under Social Security

Social Security pays benefits to people who cannot work because they have a medical condition that is expected to last at least one year or result in death. Although some government programs provide money to people with partial disabilities or short-term disabilities, Social Security does not.[21] In addition to disability payments to the worker, certain members of an employee's family, such as spouses over sixty-two and dependent children, may qualify for benefits based on the person's work history. The Social Security Administration uses a five-step process to decide if a worker is disabled and eligible to collect benefits. Highlights in HRM 2 outlines this process.

Survivor's Benefits

Survivors' benefits represent a form of life insurance paid to members of a deceased person's family who meet the eligibility requirements.[22] Survivors' benefits can be paid only if the deceased worker had credit for a certain amount of time spent in work covered by Social Security. The exact amount of work credit needed depends on the worker's age at death. As with other benefits discussed earlier, the *amount* of benefit survivors receive is based on the worker's lifetime earnings doing work covered by Social Security.

Medicare

The Social Security Administration also administers the Medicare program, which is funded by a separate payroll tax. Retired people age sixty-five or older are eligible for Medicare, which includes both medical and hospital insurance and prescription drug coverage.[23] The program helps with the cost of health care, but it does not cover

Using the INTERNET

At the Social Security Administration website, you can download software that allows you to estimate your own personal Social Security benefit. Go to **www.cengagebrain.com**

HIGHLIGHTS IN **HRM**

2   Who Is Eligible to Collect Disability Payments under the Social Security Act?

If you experience a disability, the Social Security Administration in conjunction with a state agency will use the following five-step process to determine if you are eligible to collect benefits.

1.   **Are you working?** If you are working and your earnings average more than a certain amount each month, you will generally not be considered disabled. The amount changes each year. If you are not working, or your monthly earnings average this amount or less, a state agency will then look at your medical condition.

2.   **Is your medical condition "severe"?** For the state agency to decide that you are disabled, your medical condition must significantly limit your ability to do basic work activities—such as walking, sitting, and remembering—for at least one year. If your medical condition is not that severe, the state agency will not consider you disabled. If your condition is that severe, the state agency goes on to step three.

3.   **Is your medical condition on the List of Impairments?** The state agency has a list of impairments that describes medical conditions that are considered so severe that they automatically mean that you are disabled as defined by law. If your condition (or combination of medical conditions) is not on this list, the state agency looks to see if your condition is as severe as a condition that is on the list. If the severity of your medical condition meets or equals that of a listed impairment, the state agency will decide that you are disabled. If it does not, the state agency goes on to step four.

4.   **Can you do the work you did before?** At this step, the state agency decides if your medical condition prevents you from being able to do the work you did before. If it does not, the state agency will decide that you are not disabled. If it does, the state agency goes on to step five.

5.   **Can you do any other type of work?** If you cannot do the work you did in the past, the state agency looks to see if you would be able to do other work. It evaluates your medical condition, your age, education, past work experience, and any skills you may have that could be used to do other work. If you cannot do other work, the state agency will decide that you are disabled. If you can do other work, the state agency will decide that you are not disabled.

Source: *Disability Benefits, SSA Publication No. 05-10029* (Washington, DC: U.S. Social Security Administration, 2010), http://www.socialsecurity.gov.

all medical expenses or the cost of most long-term care.[24] A portion of the payroll taxes is paid by workers and matched by their employers. In 2011, workers and their employers each paid 1.45 percent on every dollar of salary or wages paid. Medicare is also financed in part by monthly medical premiums deducted from Social Security recipient's checks.

One of the concerns employers have about Medicare relates to the eligibility age. As we explained, it is currently sixty-five, but legislators are considering increasing the age to sixty-seven as they have done with Social Security. If this happens, employees ages sixty-five and older might continue to use their company-provided health care coverage rather than Medicare. This could more than double the cost employers pay for health care coverage for this group of employees and retirees whose union contracts require their former companies cover them until Medicare does. According to one survey, in 2010, the cost of employer-sponsored health care spent on Medicare-eligible retirees averaged just $4,654 per person compared to an average of $10,872 for pre-Medicare eligible retirees.[25]

Unemployment Insurance

Unemployment insurance is part of a national program administered by the U.S. Department of Labor under the Social Security Act and coordinated with the states. It protects workers who lose their jobs through no fault of their own. Employers entirely foot the bill for this benefit via a payroll tax, which can vary widely by the state. The rates firms pay also depend upon their layoff records, or what is referred to as their *experience ratings.* Generally speaking, a firm with a record of laying off large numbers of employees will have to pay a higher rate than those that do not. For example, in 2010, employers with the best experience ratings in South Dakota paid a 0 percent tax rate. Contrast this to Pennsylvania, where employers with the worst experience ratings paid a 13.6 percent unemployment tax rate. As you can see, unemployment taxes are something HR managers must consider when they make decisions about where to locate their operations and hire employees as well as lay them off.

Employees who are laid off are generally eligible for up to twenty-six weeks of unemployment insurance benefits during their unemployment. During periods of high unemployment, the federal government has sometimes passed legislation extending the amount of weeks employees can collect benefits. Extended-unemployment benefit programs in states with high unemployment rates have also been established. However, some states are backing away from twenty-six weeks. Despite its high unemployment rate, in 2011, Michigan became the first state to cut the number of weeks to twenty because its unemployment fund was so far in the red.[26] HR managers need to stay abreast of federal and state changes such as these so they communicate the right information to workers.

Workers eligible for unemployment benefits must submit an application for unemployment compensation with their state employment agencies, register for available work, and be willing to accept any suitable employment that may be offered to them. However, the term "suitable" gives individuals considerable discretion in accepting or rejecting job offers. The amount of compensation workers are eligible to receive, which also varies by the state, is determined by a worker's previous wage rate and length of employment.

Workers' Compensation Insurance

Workers' compensation insurance is a system whereby employers purchase private or state-funded insurance to cover employees injured at work. Workers' compensation law is governed by statutes in every state. Therefore, specific laws vary with each jurisdiction. For example, each state has different regulations governing the amount and duration of lost income benefits, including provisions for medical and rehabilitation services and how the state system is administered. Workers' compensation laws also provide death benefits to surviving spouses and dependent.

Workers' compensation insurance covers workers injured on the job, whether injured on the workplace premises, elsewhere, or in an auto accident while on business. It does not matter if the employee was at fault. In addition, workers that collect compensation cannot sue their employers for their injuries unless gross negligence by the employer led to the injury or the employer lacked the level of insurance required

workers' compensation insurance
State-mandated insurance provided to workers to defray the loss of income and cost of treatment due to work-related injuries or illness

by law. Workers' compensation insurance also covers certain work-related illnesses. Before any workers' compensation claim will be allowed, the work-relatedness of the disability must be established. Also, the evaluation of the claimant by a physician trained in occupational medicine is an essential part of the claim process.

While employers in all states pay "workers' comp" insurance, the amount they pay—through payroll taxes—varies. Like with unemployment insurance rates, the rate an employer pays depends upon its experience rating, which is based on various factors including the company's frequency and severity of employee injuries (referred to as the company's experience rating). Not surprisingly, organizations will strive to have good safety records (see Chapter 12 on creating a safe work environment) in order to pay a lower payroll tax rate.

COBRA Insurance

We first discussed COBRA in Chapter 3. Recall that the Consolidated Omnibus Budget Reconciliation Act mandates that employers make health care coverage—at the same rate the employer would pay—available to employees, their spouses, and their dependents on termination of employment, death, or divorce.[27] The coverage must be offered for eighteen to thirty-six months, depending on qualifying guidelines. Thus, former employees and their families benefit by paying a lower premium for health coverage than is available to individual policyholders. While the former employee pays the premiums, employers have to establish procedures to collect premiums and to keep track of former employees and their dependents.

Benefits Provided by the Patient Protection and Affordable Care Act (PPACA)

In 2010, the Patient Protection and Affordable Care Act (PPACA) became law. This act, along with the Health Care and Education Reconciliation Act of 2010, comprise the health care reform platform signed by President Obama. The Department of Labor and other agencies are responsible for rolling out the program gradually, so many of the provisions will not be implemented until they do. In addition, insurance policies issued before the law are exempt from many of the provisions.

The key provisions all employers need to be concerned about are the following:

- Beginning in 2014, firms that employ fifty or more people who work thirty or more hours per week but do not offer them health insurance will have to pay a penalty to the government. Also beginning in 2014, firms with 200 full-time employees will be required to automatically enroll new full-time employees in their health care plans.

- Employers must offer coverage for their employee's children until they turn twenty-six.

- No copays or deductibles can be charged to employees and their dependents for certain "essential" health care services, which are generally preventive care related.

- Lifetime dollar limits on key health care benefits are not allowed.

- Employees cannot lose their insurance coverage solely because of an honest mistake they or their employers made on their insurance applications.

Among the provisions employers seem most concerned about is having to provide health care coverage to the children of their employees up until they reach the age of twenty-six. Having to cover employees who work thirty hours a week is also a concern, as is a provision that reduced the value of federal subsidies paid to employers that provide prescription drug coverage to Medicare-eligible retirees.

There appears to be some good news for employers associated with health care reform, however. Small companies that pay relatively low salaries and provide their employees with health care are eligible for sizeable tax credits to offset their costs. Some businesspeople believe these credits could help level the playing field when it comes to small businesses competing with large ones on the basis of the benefits they offer. Other people believe that the coverage minimums provided by the law will help make employees aware of the standard benefits offered by firms. As a result, those firms that do offer superior benefits will be able to use them more effectively to gain a competitive advantage.

Benefits Provided under the Family and Medical Leave Act

The Family and Medical Leave Act (FMLA) was passed and became effective on August 5, 1993.[28] The FMLA applies to employers having fifty or more employees during twenty or more calendar workweeks in the current or preceding year. A covered employer must grant an eligible employee up to a total of twelve workweeks of unpaid leave in a twelve-month period for one or more of the following reasons:

- Birth of and care for a newborn child

- Adoption or foster care placement of a child

- Care for an immediate family member (spouse, child, or parent) with a serious medical condition

- Serious health condition of the employee[29]

Under the FMLA, employees are eligible to take leave if they have worked for their employers for at least twelve months, have at least 1,250 hours of service, and work in organizations that have fifty or more employees within a seventy-five-mile radius. An employer can require that the need for medical leave be supported by a certification issued by a health care provider. Highlights in HRM 3 shows the federally required poster for the FMLA. In studying the poster, note the other important stipulations, such as enforcement and unlawful acts, which are of direct concern to managers.

This law affects an organization's benefits program in several of its provisions: It mandates continuation of medical coverage, it prohibits loss of accrued benefits, it provides for restoration of benefits after leave, it permits substitution of paid leave and vacation during leave, it makes communication and notice compulsory, and it prohibits waiver of benefits. On return from FMLA leave, an employee must be restored to his or her original job or to an "equivalent" job. Equivalent jobs are those identical to the original job in terms of pay, benefits, and other employment terms and conditions.

Employers need to check their state employee-leave laws as well. Some states provide rights to employees that are greater than those provided by the FMLA. Wisconsin is an example. Two states—California and New Jersey—require employers to provide paid leave to parents following childbirth or adoption.[30]

In January 2008, Congress passed the National Defense Authorization Act which amended the FLMA to provide eligible employees working for covered employers

Parents of newborn children are guaranteed 12 weeks of unpaid leave under the provisions of the Family and Medical Leave Act.

OJO Images Ltd/Alamy

new leave rights related to military service. Specifically, an eligible employee who is the spouse, son, daughter, parent, or next of kin of a covered service member who is recovering from a serious illness or injury sustained in the line of duty on active duty is entitled to up to twenty-six weeks of leave in a single twelve-month period to care for the service member. Importantly, managers or supervisors with legal or administrative questions regarding the FMLA are advised to seek assistance from HR before proceeding with an employee's FLMA leave request.[31] Also, employers cannot penalize employees for requesting or taking FLMA leave in an employment action including hiring, promotion, transfer, training, disciplinary action, or awards for attendance (not missing work).

Major Discretionary Employee Benefits

The discretionary, or voluntarily provided, benefits employers offer range widely from firm to firm. Figure 11.1 showed some of the more common types of benefits employees receive. We will discuss these benefits and a number of others in this section. Later in the chapter, we will discuss discretionary benefits that are less common.

Health Care Benefits

Today, the majority of U.S. employees get health coverage through their employers. However, the exact amount of coverage they provide, if any at all, differs from firm to firm. The health care plans of medium- and large-sized firms often include medical, dental, surgical, hospital, and mental health care coverage, as well as coverage for prescription drugs and optical products and services. (See this chapter's Small Business feature for some of the health care products smaller businesses provide and how they finance them.)

Health care benefits are extremely important to employees. In a nationwide survey conducted by the National Business Group on Health, an organization whose

3 HIGHLIGHTS IN **HRM**
Your Rights under the Family and Medical Leave Act

Employers are required to provide employees with this general notice about FMLA, which must be posted at the worksite (or electronically) and published in an employee handbook or given to new employees upon hire.

EMPLOYEE RIGHTS AND RESPONSIBILITIES
UNDER THE FAMILY AND MEDICAL LEAVE ACT

Basic Leave Entitlement

FMLA requires covered employers to provide up to 12 weeks of unpaid, job-protected leave to eligible employees for the following reasons:

- For incapacity due to pregnancy, prenatal medical care or child birth;
- To care for the employee's child after birth, or placement for adoption or foster care;
- To care for the employee's spouse, son or daughter, or parent, who has a serious health condition; or
- For a serious health condition that makes the employee unable to perform the employee's job.

Military Family Leave Entitlements

Eligible employees with a spouse, son, daughter, or parent on active duty or call to active duty status in the National Guard or Reserves in support of a contingency operation may use their 12-week leave entitlement to address certain qualifying exigencies. Qualifying exigencies may include attending certain military events, arranging for alternative childcare, addressing certain financial and legal arrangements, attending certain counseling sessions, and attending post-deployment reintegration briefings.

FMLA also includes a special leave entitlement that permits eligible employees to take up to 26 weeks of leave to care for a covered servicemember during a single 12-month period. A covered servicemember is a current member of the Armed Forces, including a member of the National Guard or Reserves, who has a serious injury or illness incurred in the line of duty on active duty that may render the servicemember medically unfit to perform his or her duties for which the servicemember is undergoing medical treatment, recuperation, or therapy; or is in outpatient status; or is on the temporary disability retired list.

Benefits and Protections

During FMLA leave, the employer must maintain the employee's health coverage under any "group health plan" on the same terms as if the employee had continued to work. Upon return from FMLA leave, most employees must be restored to their original or equivalent positions with equivalent pay, benefits, and other employment terms.

Use of FMLA leave cannot result in the loss of any employment benefit that accrued prior to the start of an employee's leave.

Eligibility Requirements

Employees are eligible if they have worked for a covered employer for at least one year, for 1,250 hours over the previous 12 months, and if at least 50 employees are employed by the employer within 75 miles.

Definition of Serious Health Condition

A serious health condition is an illness, injury, impairment, or physical or mental condition that involves either an overnight stay in a medical care facility, or continuing treatment by a health care provider for a condition that either prevents the employee from performing the functions of the employee's job, or prevents the qualified family member from participating in school or other daily activities.

Subject to certain conditions, the continuing treatment requirement may be met by a period of incapacity of more than 3 consecutive calendar days combined with at least two visits to a health care provider or one visit and a regimen of continuing treatment, or incapacity due to pregnancy, or incapacity due to a chronic condition. Other conditions may meet the definition of continuing treatment.

Use of Leave

An employee does not need to use this leave entitlement in one block. Leave can be taken intermittently or on a reduced leave schedule when medically necessary. Employees must make reasonable efforts to schedule leave for planned medical treatment so as not to unduly disrupt the employer's operations. Leave due to qualifying exigencies may also be taken on an intermittent basis.

Substitution of Paid Leave for Unpaid Leave

Employees may choose or employers may require use of accrued paid leave while taking FMLA leave. In order to use paid leave for FMLA leave, employees must comply with the employer's normal paid leave policies.

Employee Responsibilities

Employees must provide 30 days advance notice of the need to take FMLA leave when the need is foreseeable. When 30 days notice is not possible, the employee must provide notice as soon as practicable and generally must comply with an employer's normal call in procedures.

Employees must provide sufficient information for the employer to determine if the leave may qualify for FMLA protection and the anticipated timing and duration of the leave. Sufficient information may include that the employee is unable to perform job functions, the family member is unable to perform daily activities, the need for hospitalization or continuing treatment by a health care provider, or circumstances supporting the need for military family leave. Employees also must inform the employer if the requested leave is for a reason for which FMLA leave was previously taken or certified. Employees also may be required to provide a certification and periodic recertification supporting the need for leave.

Employer Responsibilities

Covered employers must inform employees requesting leave whether they are eligible under FMLA. If they are, the notice must specify any additional information required as well as the employees' rights and responsibilities. If they are not eligible, the employer must provide a reason for the ineligibility.

Covered employers must inform employees if leave will be designated as FMLA-protected and the amount of leave counted against the employee's leave entitlement. If the employer determines that the leave is not FMLA-protected, the employer must notify the employee.

Unlawful Acts by Employers

FMLA makes it unlawful for any employer to:

- Interfere with, restrain, or deny the exercise of any right provided under FMLA;
- Discharge or discriminate against any person for opposing any practice made unlawful by FMLA or for involvement in any proceeding under or relating to FMLA.

Enforcement

An employee may file a complaint with the U.S. Department of Labor or may bring a private lawsuit against an employer.

FMLA does not affect any Federal or State law prohibiting discrimination, or supersede any State or local law or collective bargaining agreement which provides greater family or medical leave rights.

FMLA section 109 (29 U.S.C. § 2619) requires FMLA covered employers to post the text of this notice. Regulations 29 C.F.R. § 825.300(a) may require additional disclosures.

For additional information:
1-866-4US-WAGE (1-866-487-9243) TTY: 1-877-889-5627
WWW.WAGEHOUR.DOL.GOV

U.S. Wage and Hour Division

U.S. Department of Labor | Employment Standards Administration | Wage and Hour Division   WHD Publication 1420 Revised January 2009

Note: Other federally required posters are reproduced in Chapters 3, 9, and 12.

members include Fortune 500 companies, employees consider their health plans to be their most important benefit. Helen Darling, the president of the group, notes that employees would rather give up wage increases and other benefits to preserve health care coverage.[32] Most employees realize that if they have to purchase health care benefits on their own, they won't be able to get comparable rates to what their employers can procure for them because they have buying power. Employer-provided health care (and other) benefits also provide a convenient way for people to get their health care. "I would rather get coverage through my employer than having to shop around and compare all different kinds of policies," explains one employee. Moreover, without employer-provided coverage, some employees would have a difficult time getting health care coverage at all.

Unlike private plans, employer-provided plans frequently cover all employees and their dependents regardless of their current health conditions. In addition, the Health Insurance Portability and Accountability Act (HIPAA) of 1996 grants employees the right to switch their medical insurance between former and present employers. Once an employee earns twelve credits with his or her former employer (one credit per month of service), he or she can transfer into the new employer's health insurance plan without a gap in coverage. Coverage is guaranteed regardless of a preexisting health condition of the employee.

Medical Benefits

There are a number of different types of medical-care plans firms offer. Health maintenance organizations and preferred provider organizations have become popular elements of health care plans because they provide some cost savings. Health maintenance organizations (HMOs) are organizations of physicians and other health care professionals that provide a wide range of services to subscribers and their dependents on a prepaid basis. Employees pay a small fixed fee called a co-pay, often $25 or $30, whenever they get medical treatment. Employers pay a fixed annual fee to the HMO to cover the majority of their employees' medical costs. Because they must provide all covered services for a fixed dollar amount, HMOs generally emphasize preventive care and early intervention. Employees who sign up for the plan must choose a general-practice physician, called a *primary-care physician*, from the HMO's list of doctors. Their primary-care physicians provide them with their basic medical care. However, to see a specialist, employees need a referral from their primary-care physicians. This helps keep costs down as well because the fees specialists charge are generally higher than those charged by primary-care physicians. The copays employees pay to see specialists are also slightly higher, which gives employees an incentive to see their primary-care physicians first.

A preferred provider organization (PPO) is a group of physicians who establish an organization or a network of doctors that guarantees lower costs to the employer through lower service charges or agreed on utilization controls (such as a reduced number of diagnostic tests per employee). Unlike HMOs, where employees may have limited choices when it comes to the doctors they see, PPOs allow employees to select their doctor of choice from a wider list of physicians (participating doctors). Normally, a number of physicians are available to choose from for different medical needs, and employees do not need a referral to see a specialist. Small copays are a common feature of PPOs as well. Employees also have the option of using a doctor outside of the PPO, but it costs more.

health maintenance organizations (HMOs)

Organizations of physicians and health care professionals that provide a wide range of services to subscribers and dependents on a prepaid basis

preferred provider organization (PPO)

A network of physicians who establish an organization that guarantees lower health care costs to employers and their employees

Employers sometimes couple PPOs and HMOS with different types of tax-advantaged accounts employees can use to pay their out-of-pocket health care expenses such as their copays, the cost of prescription drugs, and so forth. A *health reimbursement account (HRA)* allows employees to be reimbursed by their companies for their out-of-pocket expenses. Employees do not have to pay taxes on the amounts they are reimbursed, which is what they would have to do if the reimbursements were made through their paychecks. A *flexible spending account (FSA)* is another type of account employees use to pay for their health-related expenses. Employees fund these accounts by having money deducted from their paychecks. The money deducted is not subject to taxes, so workers have more to spend on their health care than they would without the accounts. Companies can make contributions to FSAs as well. A disadvantage of FSAs is that funds not used by the end of the plan year revert back to one's employer.

A new trend are high-deductible health insurance plans (HDHPs). In conjunction with HDHPs, employees are provided with a *health care spending account (HSA)* they and their employees can contribute to on a pretax basis. In addition, employees can deduct the amounts they contribute from their earnings when they pay their income taxes. An advantage of HSAs is that the funds remaining in the account at the end of the year belong to the employee, even if he or she leaves the company. Employees often like HDHPs for this reason and because the regular premiums deducted from their paychecks for insurance are generally lower than they are with other types of health care plans such as HMOs and PPOs.

The downside is that with an HDHP, when employees receive treatment, they have to pay either a percentage of their care or all of it until they meet a high threshold called a deductible. These expenses are generally higher than the copays and deductibles associated with other types of plans. Because of this, employees are more conscious of medical costs. They have an incentive to spend their health care funds wisely, and over time to increase the value of their health savings accounts. For this reason, HDHPs are sometimes referred to as *consumer-driven plans*.

HDHPs do seem to help control costs. However, because they work differently and require higher-out-of-pocket costs for employees, HR managers need to carefully explain how they work and show employees how much long-term savings they can accumulate for their long-term medical care. Also, some studies have shown that employees with HSAs accounts tend to put off preventive care so as to grow their health savings accounts. This can be a mistake if an employee later develops a serious and costly disease that could have been prevented with early screening and treatment.

high-deductible health insurance plan (HDHP)

A medical insurance plan characterized by high deductibles but lower premiums for workers and a health spending account to which employers contribute funds employees can keep should they leave the organization

Dental, Optical, and Mental Health Benefits

Dental plans are designed to help pay for dental care costs and to encourage employees to receive regular dental attention. Like medical plans, dental care plans may be operated by insurance companies, dental service corporations, those administering Blue Cross/Blue Shield plans, HMOs, and groups of dental care providers. Typically, the insurance pays a portion of the charges, and the subscriber pays the remainder. Optical benefits work in a similar way. These benefits generally cover or offset the cost of seeing an optometrist once or twice a year as well as the cost of contacts lenses and glasses purchased periodically.

Almost all workers with health coverage receive mental health benefits as part of their plans. However, prior to 2009, most plans had limits on inpatient hospital stays and outpatient visits, and the copays were often higher than they were for medical-care copays. The Mental Health Parity and Addiction Equity Act of 2008 changed that. In terms of the costs and access to care, the law requires group health plans to treat mental health benefits the same way they do medical and surgical benefits.[33]

Cost Containment Strategies

Companies are pursuing all kinds of strategies to contain the costs of health care. Many firms have either begun requiring employees to pay part of the cost of their benefits, or, if they were already doing so, increasing the amounts they pay in the form of premiums, copays, and deductibles. In 2003, only 52 percent of employees had to pay a health insurance deductible. Today, more than three-quarters of employees have to, and the numbers are rising. During this same time period, employees already paying deductibles saw them climb by an average of 77 percent, according to a report by the Commonwealth Fund, a private foundation that is working to improve the nation's health care system.

In addition, it is not uncommon for larger companies to cut the health care plans they once provided their retirees. For years, GM, Ford, and Chrysler provided coverage for both their salaried and unionized retirees. All three organizations have since stopped covering retired salaried workers. These employees now have to use the Medicare system.[34] (The health care plans of unionized employees are protected by union contracts.)

What is causing the growth in health care costs? The rise has been attributed to many factors. One is the overuse of costly health care services by consumers. This is part of the reason why firms have turned to health savings accounts and HDHPs. Because HMOs and PPOs offer discounted rates, they have become another vehicle for reducing costs. In addition, many companies—even Fortune 500 companies— are limiting the plans employees can choose from to all but the least expensive ones and conducting audits to be sure noneligible dependents of employees are not being covered.

An aging U.S. population, high obesity rates, and the health problems associated with them are two other reasons cited for rising health care costs. To combat these problems, companies are offering employees lower health care premiums for adopting healthy habits and activities. Wellness programs (discussed shortly) are a part of this effort. Conversely, firms are also penalizing employees for unhealthy habits by charging them higher health care premiums for habits such as smoking. The state government of North Carolina is one of a growing number of organizations charging higher premiums to employees who are morbidly obese and will not lose weight.[35] To help cope with the rising costs of drugs, companies are encouraging their employees to use generic drugs and buy 90-day supplies through designated mail-order pharmacies that provide them at a discount.

One of the more dramatic moves companies are making is waiving the deductibles and copays employees must pay if they are willing to travel abroad for medical procedures where they often cost only a only a fraction of what they do in the United States. IDMI Systems, a Georgia company, is one such organization. Its employees and dependents covered by the company's self-funded health plan can visit any of twenty-nine hospitals and four dental clinics around the world—most with U.S. board-certified physicians on staff.[36] The practice of going abroad for medical procedures has become known as "medical tourism." Figure 11.2 shows the countries Americans most utilize for treatment abroad and the approximate cost of procedures as a percentage of U.S. costs.

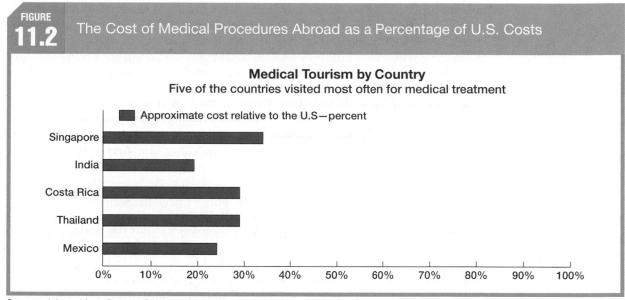

FIGURE 11.2   The Cost of Medical Procedures Abroad as a Percentage of U.S. Costs

Medical Tourism by Country
Five of the countries visited most often for medical treatment

Sources: Adapted from *Reuters,* Deloitte, and the research findings of Joseph Woodman, the author of *Patients without Borders.*

Value-Based Health Initiatives

A small but growing number of employers are turning to what is being called *value-based health initiatives.* Value-based initiatives focus on more than cost-cutting. Companies pursuing this strategy look at the medical care their employees most use and need, and target benefits and health programs toward them. For example, Cerner Corporation, a software company in Kansas City, found that six medical conditions made up nearly 30 percent of the company's total costs. Diabetes was one of them. After taking proactive steps to help employees with their diabetes, the average annual cost to treat employees with the disease declined by more than $2,500 per person.

Pitney Bowes is another company pursuing value-based health care initiatives. The company took a look at the chronic ailments its employees were most likely to suffer from, such as asthma, high blood pressure, and diabetes, and made the drugs to treat these diseases as inexpensive as possible or even free to employees. The idea is to encourage employees to seek treatment for and manage these conditions to avoid expensive complications later. "We see fewer emergency room visits, and we also see people being able to come to work and be more productive," says Andrew Gold, says the company's executive director of global benefits planning. "That creates an overall benefit to the company and to employees."[37]

Wellness Programs

Wellness programs are employer-sponsored programs designed to encourage employees to maintain and improve their health and well-being by getting regular checkups, eating properly, exercising, and managing their stress levels so as to prevent costly and protracted illnesses. Oftentimes the employee undergoes a basic health assessment to determine if he or she has any health problems a wellness program could improve. For example, an employee might take a quiz that asks how much he or she exercises, smokes, drinks alcohol, and so forth. Based on this

wellness programs
Employer-sponsored programs designed to encourage employees to maintain and improve their health and well-being by getting regular checkups, eating properly, exercising, and managing their stress levels so as to prevent costly and protracted illnesses

information a plan is developed to improve the health of the employee and lower his or her risk for disease. Some companies offer their employees incentives for taking a health-risk assessment. Franklin International, a Columbus, Ohio, manufacturer, provides its employees who do so $50 gift cards. Onsite fitness facilities or vouchers to offsite fitness facilities are also a common part of the wellness programs companies offer.

However, many firms are finding that they need to go further than just providing employees with health-assessment plans and telling them to hit the gym. Utilizing health coaches or personal trainers can help encourage employees to continue to participate in these programs. Clif Bar & Company, a California maker of natural and organic foods and drinks, has a free personal trainer at its onsite gym employees can utilize. The company also offers nutrition counseling and a $500 allowance toward the purchase of a commuter bicycle. This strategy fits well with the company's overall mission to provide consumers with healthy products. At the New York advertising agency J. Walter Thompson, the employee health management program includes both cardiovascular fitness and nutritional health. Bob Jeffrey, president of the agency's North American division, says, "Employees can work out and relax in a 'de-stress' room, get free massages and yoga or nutrition lessons, join a company sports team, and consult with a personal trainer."[38] Other wellness programs offer employees awards for achieving their health goals. The awards can consist of lower health care premiums, money, or prizes.

Disease Management Programs

disease management programs
Programs that provide patients and their caregivers with information on monitoring and treating medical conditions, while coordinating communication between them, their health care providers, employers, and insurers

Via medically trained personnel, **disease management programs** provide patients and their caregivers with information on monitoring and treating medical conditions, while coordinating communication between them, their health care providers, employers, and insurers. Bank One Corporation of Chicago developed such a program when managers noticed high absenteeism among employees with diabetes, asthma, and depression. Disease management programs can also be used in conjunction with the rehabilitation of employees who are injured on the job to help them recover more quickly and return safely to work.

employee assistance programs (EAPs)
Services provided by employers to help workers cope with a wide variety of problems that interfere with the way they perform their jobs

Walk while you work? To combat obesity and other health problems, GlaxoSmithKline, Humana, Mutual of Omaha, and Best Buy have begun utilizing treadmill desks like the one shown here. The treadmills move at a slow speed so employees do not get hot and sweaty and out of breath.

ANDA CHU/MCT/Landov

Employee Assistance Programs

To help workers cope with a wide variety of problems that interfere with the way they perform their jobs, all kinds of organizations, including the New York Mets, USAA, the Los Angeles Police Department, and Levi Strauss, have developed **employee assistance programs (EAPs).** An employee assistance program typically provides diagnosis, counseling, and referral for advice or treatment when necessary for problems related to alcohol or drug abuse, emotional difficulties, and financial or family difficulties.[39] The main intent is to help employees solve their personal problems or at least to prevent problems from turning into crises that affect their ability to work productively. To handle crises, many EAPs offer twenty-four-hour hotlines employees can call. After Cerner Corporation offered its employees an EAP program, the company's outpatient mental health care costs declined by nearly 41 percent.

Counseling Services

An important part of an EAP is the counseling services it provides to employees. While most organizations expect managers to counsel subordinates, some employees may have problems that require the services of professional counselors. Most organizations refer such individuals to outside counseling services such as family counseling services, marriage counselors, and mental health clinics. Some organizations have a clinical psychologist, counselor, or comparable specialist on staff to whom employees may be referred. Highlights in HRM 4 shows some additional ways firms are cutting their health-care related costs that we have not discussed here.

Payment for Time Not Worked

The "payment for time not worked" category of benefits includes paid vacations, bonuses given in lieu of paid vacations, payments for holidays not worked, paid sick leave, military and jury duty, and payments for absence due to a death in the family

LEARNING OUTCOME 5

In most countries around the world, employees get many more paid days off than they do in the United States. In your opinion, should employers have to offer U.S. workers more time off? Or would this be an additional burden that could hurt the competitiveness of these firms?

HIGHLIGHTS IN **HRM**

4 Other Methods for Containing Health Care Costs

- Pre-admission certification for surgical procedures
- Limits, or maximums, on benefits
- Financial incentives for outpatient surgery and testing
- Mandatory second opinions for surgical procedures
- Alternative approaches to health care treatment such as herbal therapy or homeopathy
- Educational programs encouraging health care consumers to assume more responsibility and accountability for the cost and quality of their health care
- Promoting websites or printed materials that list common conditions, treatment, drug prices, and effectiveness
- Implementation of step therapy programs, whereby the least invasive and expensive types of treatment are pursued before more costly treatments
- Multitier hospital coverage networks that allow employees to choose from a variety of hospitals with small, moderate, and steep copayments at the point of service
- Incentives for outpatient versus hospital treatment
- Use of variable copayments (for example, $30 for physician and $50 for specialists)
- Consolidation of health care plans offered by employers
- Requiring employees to pay an additional cost if a working spouse refuses coverage from his or her employer

Small Business Application

Creative Benefit Strategies Can Help Small Businesses Compete

For small business owners, controlling the cost of benefits is crucial. However, attracting and retaining employees is, too. Although competing with large companies on the basis of benefits might seem impossible, small business owners still have some other "cards" they can play that bigger companies might not offer. For example, if they cannot offer extensive benefits, it is not uncommon for small businesses to offer stock or shares in the company to their employees. If the company is successful this can pay off hugely. Flexible work hours and arrangements are also a low-cost strategic benefit small businesses can offer their employees without first having to cut through a lot of corporate red tape. In one survey, 87 percent of employees reported that flexibility in their jobs would be extremely or very important in deciding whether to take a new job.

As we mentioned earlier in the chapter, new health care reform provisions are helping to level the playing field, too. They allow small businesses with relatively low-average pay rates to receive tax credits for up to 50 percent of what they spend on health care for their employees. In addition, small businesses will be able to purchase health care insurance through state-based exchanges known as Small Business. Health Options Programs (SHOPs). These exchanges pool the risks of small employers together, making their insurance rates more affordable. The government is also offering $200 million in grants to businesses with fewer than 100 employees that launch new wellness programs. And via its "Small Business Wellness" website, the Department of Health and Human Services offers free downloads of workplace wellness plans. Simply sponsoring intramural sports teams can be a good way for a small business owner to motivate his or her employees to exercise as well as build camaraderie among them.

Firms that are finding their benefits hard to afford can start by talking to their employees about their benefits and looking at ones they are actually using and want, says Patrick Carragher, the director of benefits for CheckPoint HR, a New Jersey firm that provides human resources services to other companies. "Many companies purchase plans and stay with them for years, simply watering down the benefits to save money," explains Carragher. "Instead, they should be looking at which benefits are used and which aren't," "For example, if a hospital confinement benefit is only being used by 4 to 5 percent of the population, then eliminate it and offer it on a voluntary basis to employees for a very small premium." Also, check out what benefits the competition is providing, suggests Carragher.

Another way small businesses can augment their benefits programs is by partnering with companies that offer discount programs to employers' workers. Price Optical offers a discount program for employers who are not able to provide vision benefits for their employees. Discounts for homeowners, automobile and group life insurance, dental and chiropractic care, health club memberships, and weight-control programs are other benefits small businesses can procure on behalf of their employees as well as tickets to entertainment events and product discounts.

Finally, if a small business wants its employees to have benefits but does not want to either provide or administer them, it can contract with a Professional Employer Organization (PEO). Recall from Chapter 1 that a PEO is typically a larger company that for a fee takes over the management of a smaller company's HR tasks and can provide employees with benefits that small companies cannot afford.

Source: Gwen Moran, "The Business of Better Benefits," *Entrepreneur* (May 2011), http://www.workforce.com; Vicki Powers, "Green Benefits Helpful in a Down Economy," *Workforce Management* (May 2009), http://www.workforce.com; "Cost Shifting Initiatives," *Broad Reach Benefits* [blog] (February 15, 2011), http://broadreachbenefits.com/blog.

or other personal reasons. Figure 11.1 showed that these benefits constitute another large expenditure—7 percent—of an employer's total payroll costs, on average.

Paid time off is not mandatory in the United States, though. This contrasts sharply with the policies other countries around the world, including Austria, Peru, Spain, the United Arab Emirates, Finland, and Italy, where employees must be given thirty paid days off annually.[40] China is the only other country that does not mandate employees be given any paid time off.[41]

Vacations with Pay

Despite the fact that vacation pay is not required in the United States, most employers generally agree that vacations are essential to the well-being of an employee.[42] Research shows that workers who use their vacation time are more productive and less prone to job-related burnout.[43] Exactly how much paid vacation time firms provide their employees varies by a firm's industry, locale, size, and other factors. Employees in the United States who work for large companies often get ten paid days of vacation a year. To qualify for longer vacations of three, four, or five weeks, one may expect to work for seven, fifteen, and twenty years, respectively.

Most companies require their employees to take either take their vacation days by the end of the year or forfeit them ("use it or lose it"). An increasing number of employees say they are too busy at work to take all the vacation days they are allotted. According to an Expedia.com survey, Americans hand back more than $21 billion in unused vacation dollars to their employers each year.[44] Some companies, however, let their employees "roll over" at least some of their vacation days to the following year. Of those that do, the average they allow workers to roll over is twenty days, according to a survey by the Society for Human Resources Management.[45]

Paid Holidays

The federal government recognizes ten legal public holidays, which are shown in Figure 11.3. However, private employers are not required to offer employees these days off or pay them for them. Many companies do, though. Organizations that have to remain open during holidays (emergency services providers such as hospitals, transportation companies, and so forth) often pay employees who work on holidays extra pay for doing so. Many organizations also give workers an additional two or three personal days off to use at their discretion.

Of course, not all employees celebrate all the holidays their companies recognize, particularly Christian holidays. A variety of arrangements can be made for these employees. For example, they might be allowed to work the holidays and then take off other days as a substitute. Or they might be allowed to use personal days, vacation days, or, as a last resort, take the holidays they do not want to work off without pay. Another trend is to give all employees a certain number of paid days they can use as holidays whenever they want.

Sick Leave

There are several ways in which employees may be compensated during periods when they are unable to work because of illness or injury. Most public employees, as well as many in private firms, receive a set number of sick leave days each year to cover such absences. Where permitted, sick leave that employees do not use can be accumulated to cover prolonged absences. Accumulated vacation leave may sometimes be used as a source of income when sick leave benefits have been exhausted. Group insurance that

FIGURE 11.3   Federally Recognized Holidays in the United States

- New Year's Day, January 1
- Martin Luther King, Jr. Day, the third Monday in January
- President's Day, the third Monday in February
- Memorial Day, the last Monday in May
- Independence Day, July 4
- Labor Day, the first Monday in September
- Columbus Day, the second Monday in October
- Veterans Day, November 11
- Thanksgiving Day, the fourth Thursday in November
- Christmas Day, December 25

© Cengage Learning 2013

provides income protection during a long-term disability is also made available by some employers. As discussed earlier in the chapter, worker's compensation partially reimburses the income employees lose during absences resulting from job-related injuries.

Sabbaticals

sabbatical

Paid (or unpaid) time away from a job for four or more weeks employees take off to renew themselves before returning to work

A sabbatical is paid (or unpaid) time away from a job for four or more weeks employees take off to renew themselves before returning to work. Historically, sabbaticals have been associated with academia, but in the 1960s, companies including McDonald's began to adopt them. *Fortune* magazine has added sabbaticals to their criteria for naming the 100 Best Companies to Work For.[46] The AARP actually requires its employees to take one-month paid sabbaticals. At the foodmaker General Mills, employees can take either unpaid personal sabbaticals or paid "innovation" sabbaticals that restrict an employee's leave activities to those that can benefit the company.

Sabbaticals can also be used to develop talent as those that cover for the individual on sabbatical assume new responsibilities and get opportunities to prove themselves. For small businesses that need to temporarily cut their payroll costs, unpaid sabbaticals can be a short-term alternative to layoffs and a way to reward valuable employees who never previously imagined they would be able to take a significant amount of time off to pursue other activities.

Severance Pay

Severance pay

A one-time payment sometimes given to an employee who is being involuntarily terminated

Severance pay is a one-time payment sometimes given to an employee who is being involuntarily terminated. The severance pay may cover only a few days' wages or wages for several months. The pay received usually depends on the employee's years of service. However, severance pay can also be based on the reason for termination, the salary or grade level of the employee, the title or level in the organization, or a combination of factors. Employers that are downsizing often use severance pay as a means of lessening the negative effects of unexpected termination of employees. Other triggers for severance pay include job elimination, voluntary separation programs, or refusal of a reassignment or relocation. (Employees who quit do not ordinarily receive severance pay.) An employee who accepts severance pay is generally required to sign a release agreement waiving his or her right to take any kind of legal action against the company. To avoid legal action, companies sometimes offer severance pay to employees fired for cause.

Supplemental Unemployment Benefits

While not required by law, in cyclical industries, unemployment compensation is augmented by supplemental unemployment benefits (SUBs) paid for by employers. The mining industry is an example. If the price of a metal being mined falls sharply (which is not an uncommon occurrence), the firms mining the metal often slow down production until the price rises again. SUBs help attract employees to industries such as this. The amount of the benefits are generally determined by an employee's length of service and wage rate.

Life Insurance

One of the oldest and most popular employee benefits is group term life insurance, which provides death benefits to beneficiaries and may also provide accidental death and dismemberment benefits. The premium costs are normally paid by the employer, with the face value of the life insurance equal to two times the employee's yearly wages. These programs frequently allow employees to purchase additional amounts of insurance for nominal charges. In addition, many companies allow employees to purchase life insurance for their spouses and dependents via their company plans. This is an attractive benefit because the rates employees pay for the insurance is often lower when purchased through their company plans.

Long-Term Care Insurance

Long-term care insurance is designed to pay for nursing home and other medical-related costs during old age. Because the workforce is aging and people are living longer, a small but growing number of employers are finding that long-term care insurance can be a strategic benefit to attract and retain employees, particularly workers caring for older parents and relatives. Many of these employees have experienced firsthand the challenges of caring for aging loved ones who were unable to prepare properly for their long-term needs. An advantage of employer-sponsored long-term care insurance is that enrolled employees receive coverage automatically and often do not need to pass a physical examination. And like life insurance coverage, employer-provided long-term care insurance is usually cheaper to obtain because firms have buying power individuals lack.

Retirement Programs

Airline pilots are legally required to retire at age sixty-five. However, for most other professions in the United States there is no law mandating a retirement age. Therefore, whether an employee elects to retire depends on various factors such as personal/financial condition and health, other family obligations, the extent to which he or she receives satisfaction from work, and the ability to meet changing job demands.

Preretirement and Phased Retirement Programs

Although most people eagerly anticipate retirement, many of them find that it requires a major financial lifestyle adjustment. Employers sometimes offer preretirement planning seminars and workshops to help make employees aware of the kinds of adjustments they may need to make when they retire. The topics covered can include

supplemental unemployment benefits (SUBs)
A plan that enables an employee who is laid off to draw, in addition to state unemployment compensation, weekly benefits from the employer that are paid from a fund created for this purpose

LEARNING OUTCOME 6
Did you know there is a mandatory retirement age for airline pilots? Research some of the other jobs in the United States for which there are mandatory retirement ages.

phased retirement

A program that allows its employees to gradually cut their hours before retiring

---

LEARNING OUTCOME 7

The text mentions several kinds of pension plans. As an employee, which type would you prefer?

pension plans, health insurance coverage, Social Security and Medicare, personal financial planning, wellness and lifestyles, and the process of adjusting to being around one's spouse 24-7!

To help older workers get used to the idea of retirement, some organizations experiment with "retirement rehearsal." Polaroid, for example, offers employees an opportunity to try out retirement through an unpaid three-month leave program. Polaroid also allows its employees to gradually cut their hours before retirement. A program such as this is referred to as phased retirement. Formal phased-retirement programs are common in other countries but rarer in the United States because employees often need to get their health care coverage through their employers until they turn sixty-five. At this point they can go on Medicare. However, as more baby boomers want to continue to work and employers seek to retain them, the number of phased retirement programs is expected to grow. The programs also help organizations cope with the "brain drain" that occurs when people with vital knowledge, talent, and industrial memory retire suddenly.[47]

Pension Plans

Since the passage of the Social Security Act of 1935, pension plans have been used to supplement the floor of protection provided by Social Security. Pensions reward employees for their years of service with a company by providing them with income when they retire. However, like with other discretionary benefits, the decision whether to offer a pension plan is up to the employer.

Types of Pension Plans

There are two major ways to categorize pension plans: (1) according to contributions made by the employer and (2) according to the amount of pension benefits to

Many baby boomers in the U.S. are continuing to work long past the traditional retirement age of 65.

lightpoet/Shutterstock.com

be paid. In a contributory plan, contributions to a pension plan are made jointly by employees and employers. In a noncontributory plan, the contributions are made solely by the employer. When pension plans are classified by the amount of pension benefits to be paid, there are two basic types: defined benefit plan and defined contribution plan. Under a defined benefit plan,[48] the amount an employee is to receive on retirement is specifically set forth. The amount employees collect is usually based on their years of service, average earnings during a specific period of time, and age at time of retirement. While a variety of formulas exist for determining pension benefits, the one used most often is based on the employee's average earnings (usually over a three- to five-year period immediately preceding retirement), multiplied by the number of years of service with the organization. A deduction is then made for each year the retiree is under age sixty-five. For example, an employee with a four-year pre-retirement annual salary of $55,000 and thirty years of service may receive a yearly retirement payment of $23,000.

A defined-contribution plan establishes the basis on which an employer will contribute to the pension fund. The contributions may be made through profit sharing, thrift plans, matches of employee contributions, employer-sponsored individual retirement accounts (IRAs), and various other means. The amount of benefits employees receive on retirement is determined by the funds accumulated in their accounts and how well the investments purchased with the funds have grown over time. In other words, the amount employees get is not certain. As a result, these plans pose more financial risk for employees than defined benefit plans do. However, employers have come to prefer them because they do not have to shoulder all of the responsibility of funding them. In 1989, 39 percent of private sector employees were covered by defined benefit pension plans. Today, only 15 percent are.[49] Even Fortune 100 firms are scrapping their defined benefit plans. According to a survey by the HR consulting firm Watson Wyatt, today most Fortune 100 companies now offer their new salaried employees only a defined contribution plan.

401(k) Savings Plans

401(k) plans started to become extremely popular as an employee-savings vehicle beginning in the 1980s. This is a type of defined contribution plan named after section 401(k) of the Internal Revenue Code. The plan allows employees to save through payroll deductions that reduce their taxable income and have their contributions matched by the employer. Usually the employer matches the employee contributions at the rate of twenty-five to fifty cents for every worker dollar contributed. An organization's contribution can, however, run the gamut from doubling the worker's contribution to zero contribution.[50]

401(k) plans have been widely embraced by companies as a replacement for costly defined benefit pension funds. Today, about 60 percent of households nearing retirement have 401(k)-type of accounts.[51] However, unlike defined benefit pension plans, which guarantee payments based on years of service, the 401(k) plan guarantees nothing. The return depends entirely on how much money goes into the plan, the rate of return on the investments purchased with the funds contributed, and, with stock-funded plans, the price of the company's stock. As one benefit specialist noted, "Market risk is perhaps the most significant threat to an employee's retirement savings."[52] Indeed, in the last decade, economic downturns and stock market crashes have taken a heavy toll on 401(k) accounts.

contributory plan
A pension plan in which contributions are made jointly by employees and employers

noncontributory plan
A pension plan in which contributions are made solely by the employer

defined benefit plan
A pension plan in which the amount an employee is to receive on retirement is specifically set forth

defined contribution plan
A pension plan that establishes the basis on which an employer will contribute to the pension fund

Another problem is that employees do not have to participate in the plans, which can leave them short on retirement income aside from Social Security after they retire. Still another problem is that many employees lack investing experience and do not know the best way to invest the money in their 401(k)s. Consequently, a small but growing number of 401(k) plans let employees hand the management of their 401(k) to a professional financial planner. The new service, called *managed accounts*, seeks to help employees achieve higher returns with less risk.

In 2006, Congress passed the Pension Protection Act. Major provisions of the law include:

- Allowing employers to automatically enroll employees in defined contribution plans[53]

- Permitting higher contribution limits for 401(k) plans, enabling workers to build larger retirement holdings

- Giving workers greater control over how their accounts are invested. A current trend is for organizations to allow their employees considerable control over the investment of their 401(k) savings, including investing in the stock of other companies.[54]

Cash Balance Pension Plans

Along with 401(k) saving plans, a significant development in pension planning has been cash balance saving plans.[55] With cash balance plans, the employer makes a yearly contribution into an employee's retirement savings account.[56] The contributions are based on a percentage of the employee's pay—typically 4 percent. Additionally, the employee's account earns annual interest, often tied to the thirty-year Treasury rate. For example, an employee earning $35,000 a year would receive a yearly contribution of $1,400 to his or her account. After a year, the account would receive an interest credit of around 5 percent. Employees can normally roll their account balances into a personal Individual Retirement Account (IRA) should they change jobs.

Whether an individual employee benefits from a cash balance retirement plan depends on the employee's age and years of service with the company. Employees in their twenties or thirties with low years of service can build a substantial amount of retirement savings starting at an early age. However, if an employer switches from a defined benefit pension plan, employees in their forties, fifties, or sixties with lengthy years of service can lose from 20 to 50 percent under a cash balance program. To lessen the financial impact on older employees, some companies that change to cash balance plans increase the annual pay credit for older employees as compared with younger workers. Other employers allow older employees to remain in a defined benefit pension plan until retirement or grant them a "boost" by contributing a sizeable amount of money to their cash balance accounts when they are initially opened. Employers ranging from Federated Department Stores and Verizon to Colgate-Palmolive and Harvard University now cover their employees with cash balance plans.

Federal Regulation of Pension Plans

Private pension plans are subject to federal regulation, including vesting rules, under the Employee Retirement Income Security Act (ERISA).[57] **Vesting** is a process that guarantees pension-plan participants will receive their pensions when they reach

vesting
A guarantee of accrued pension benefits to participants at retirement age, regardless of their employment status at that time

retirement age, regardless of their employment status at that time. In other words, the benefits cannot be revoked, even if the employee no longer works for the company. Vesting prevents companies from laying off employees before they retire so they are unable to collect their pensions. Under ERISA, all pension plans must provide employees with vested rights to their accrued benefits after they meet a certain minimum years of service, say, five years. So, for example, an employee leaves the company prior to the minimum years of service, the person would lose any money the firm contributed to his or her pension. However, employers can pay out a departing employee's vested benefits if the present value of the benefit is small.

ERISA also requires minimum funding standards be followed to ensure pension benefits will be available to employees when they retire.[58] Currently the pensions of many older companies are underfunded, however. GM, Chrysler, U.S. Steel, and Delta Air Lines are among them. In addition, many state and local governments are facing billions in pension shortages due to the last recession. Equally worrisome are the number of pension plans in danger of failing altogether.

ERISA also created the Pension Benefit Guaranty Corporation (PBGC), a federal government agency. The PBGC ensures that if a plan is terminated, guaranteed minimum benefits are paid to participants. When companies go through bankruptcy proceedings, they often try to cancel their pension obligations, leaving employees to rely on the PBGC for retirement income. Unfortunately for retirees, the monthly pension payments from the PBGC are often significantly less than those promised under a company's original retirement plan. Another growing concern is that the PBGC—which has a $23 billion deficit of its own that has been growing annually—will be unable to meet its financial obligations. The PBGC is supported by premiums paid by employers. To improve its funding situation, the agency has asked Congress to allow it to increase the premiums it charges employers.

Domestic Partner Benefits

More employers are granting benefits to employees who establish *domestic partnerships*, which can consist of both same-sex and unmarried opposite-sex couples. Viacom, Gannett Company (publisher of *USA Today*), Levi Strauss, Silicon Graphics, Warner Bros., and Stanford University are among the many organizations that offer benefits to domestic partners of employees. Most Fortune 500 companies now provide benefits to same-sex partners.

The definition of a domestic partnership varies from company to company. However, Apple Computer's definition, which is as follows, is typical: A domestic partner, the company says, is "a person over age 18 who shares living quarters with another adult in an exclusive, committed relationship in which the partners are responsible for each other's common welfare." Employers that offer domestic partnership coverage typically require employees to sign an "Affidavit of Domestic Partnership" attesting that they meet certain conditions such as the following:

- A minimum age requirement

- A requirement that the couple live together

- A specification of financial interdependence

- A requirement that the relationship be a permanent one

- A requirement that each not be a blood relative[59]

Organizations that offer benefits to domestic partners are simply extending current benefits, normally full medical and dental plans, to all employees.[60] However, employer health benefits provided to unmarried partners, unlike health benefits for spouses, are taxable under federal law.[61] Furthermore, in 1996, Congress passed the Defense of Marriage Act, which provides that a same-sex domestic partner may not be treated as an employee's spouse for purposes of federal law.[62] Because domestic partners are at a disadvantage regarding taxes Google has decided to reimburse employees for the additional federal taxes they pay on their company-paid domestic partner benefits. A benefit such as this could be a good way for other companies to attract members of this demographic group while the courts decide on the constitutionality of the Defense of Marriage Act is repealed, should that come to pass. (Claiming that it violates equal protection under the Fifth Amendment, the Obama Administration has declined to defend the constitutionality of this law in court.)

Another implication of the DOMA is that a married same-sex partner is not eligible for his or her partners' Social Security survival benefits or employer-provided pension benefits if they are governed by ERISA, which most are. However, it may be possible to name a domestic partner as an heir by filling out extra forms. Employees are not protected by the FMLA when caring for domestic partners either, although a number of employers provide their workers with a similar amount of time off as the FMLA as a discretionary benefit. HR decisions about domestic partnership benefits also need to take into account local and state and how they are being implemented. For example, several California cities, including Berkeley, Los Angeles, Oakland, and San Francisco, have adopted an ordinance that requires all companies with city contracts to extend domestic partner benefits to their employees who reside in the city or who work on contracts for the city.[63]

Work-Life Balance and Other Benefits

What types of benefits that employers do not traditionally offer would most attract you as an employee? Discuss your preferences with classmates to see if their answers are similar or different than yours. Make a list of the benefits discussed and have everyone vote for the three benefits they would most want on the list.

Eddie Bauer, an outdoor clothing and equipment supplier, offers its employees takeout dinners and one paid "Balance Day" off a year. eBay sets aside spaces at its San Jose, California, campuses as prayer and meditation rooms where employees can "decompress" during the workday. Raytheon, Procter & Gamble, Unilever, Nortel Networks, Comcast, Yahoo, Google, and Apple offer classes on meditation to help their employees deal with stress and improve their ability to concentrate. Ben & Jerry's employees have access to a nap room. Lincoln National, a financial services company, offers a "homework assistance help line" staffed with teachers for children of its employees, and at Mitre, a nonprofit researcher, employees can take up to a week of paid time off to help with scouting trips or volunteer projects. These organizations, like many others, are seeking to create a work/life organizational climate that allows employees to balance their work with their personal needs.

A national survey conducted by Mellon Financial Human Resources and Investor Solutions found that 86 percent of surveyed employers used part-time employees, 88 percent offered work-related tuition reimbursement, 81 percent offered employee assistance programs, 71 percent offered flextime programs, 50 percent offered telecommuting and work-at-home arrangements, 44 percent offered compressed workweeks, 54 percent provided family sick days, and 47 percent offered unpaid family leave that goes beyond the requirements of the Family and Medical Leave Act. According to the study, employer reasons for offering work/life programs include raising morale

(74 percent of respondents), enhancing recruitment efforts (73 percent), and remaining competitive/industry image (72 percent).[64]

Companies are also adapting work-life programs to accommodate the entrance of Generation Y employees into the workplace.[65] This new group of workers has its own vision for the workplace and their careers, one that work-life programs can help fulfill.[66] Generation Y employees also have a reputation for being altruistic and wanting to work for socially responsible employees. To appeal to this demographic group and other employees concerned about the environment some companies have begun offering their employees "green" benefits. Clif Bar & Company, mentioned earlier in the chapter, gives employees $6,500 toward the purchase of a hybrid car. According to a study conducted by New York-based Buck Consultants, 47 percent of executives believe green programs help attract and retain top talent.[67]

Child and Elder Care

Consider these figures:

- Working parents take between five and twenty-nine days off work each year for sick children.

- Each day, more than 350,000 children younger than age 14 are too sick to attend school or day care.

- 21 percent of unscheduled absenteeism is family-related, costing employers billions in lost productivity and benefits costs.

These figures, combined with the increased employment of women with dependent children, illustrate the unprecedented demand for child care arrangements.[68] Some employers such as Fel-Pro, Merck, Syntex, Baptist Hospital of Miami, and Ben & Jerry's promote onsite or near-site child care centers. Employer-sponsored dependent care spending accounts allow employees to set aside a portion of their pay before taxes to care for a dependent child. New moms and dads at Google are able to expense up to $500 for take-out meals during the first three months that they are home with their new baby.

A growing benefit offered employees with children experiencing short illnesses is mildly ill child care. Medical supervision is the primary difference between mildly ill facilities and traditional day care arrangements. Mildly ill care facilities serve children recovering from colds, flu, ear infections, strep throat, chicken pox, or other mild illnesses that temporarily prevent them from attending regular school or day care. These facilities are either independently run, hospital-based, or affiliated with child care centers. Additionally, some employers offer emergency in-home child care benefits for sick children.[69]

According to a study of AARP and the National Alliance for Caregiving, today more than 44 million Americans are caring for an elderly parent. As noted in the study, "elder care is rapidly becoming the biggest family issue facing workers and their families."[70] The average caregiver costs an employer $2,110 per year. Forty percent of employed caregivers take seventeen days of unpaid leave per year to care for an aging family member.[71] The term elder care, as used in the context of employment, occurs when an employee provides care to an elderly relative while remaining actively at work. The majority of caregivers are women.

Beyond the loss of organizational productivity and higher employee costs, a growing concern of employers is the negative effects of caregiving on employee health.

elder care
Care provided to an elderly relative by an employee who remains actively at work

Not surprisingly, caregivers in the workforce suffer higher levels of stress since they find it difficult to respond to the demands of balancing work and family.[72] To help employees meet the challenges of caregiving, organizations may offer elder care counseling, educational fairs and seminars, printed resource materials, support groups, and special flexible schedules and leaves of absence.[73] Schering-Plough, a pharmaceuticals manufacturer, uses an 800 telephone line for elder care referrals, while IBM has a national telephone network of more than 200 community-based referral agencies. Employers may also band together for better elder care. The Partnership for Elder Care—a consortium of American Express, J. P. Morgan Chase, and Philip Morris and other companies—use the resources of the New York City Department of Aging, a public information and aging support agency. In addition, an increasing number of employers supply or subsidize temporary care for employee's elders and children when their regular arrangements fall through so these employees can come to work. A benefit such as this is referred to as a backup care program. Home Depot recently began offering a backup care program to its employees. The program provides a discount to employees who need spur-of-the-moment care so they can come to work.

backup care program
A benefit program whereby an employer provides or subsidizes temporary care for its employee's elders or children when their regular arrangements fall through

Other Benefits and Services

The variety of benefits and services that employers offer today is widespread. However, whether a company offers a particular service may depend on its size, ability to pay, industry pattern, or specific employee or organizational needs. Some benefits are fairly standard such as housing and moving expenses,[74] various food services (such as cafeteria or vending machines), and discounts on some merchandise. Other benefits are newer and reflect societal changes such as adoption expenses,[75] legal services, financial planning including tax and retirement planning, and identity theft protection.[76] Many organizations offer some type of sports program in which personnel may participate on a voluntary basis. Bowling, softball, golf, baseball, and tennis are often included in an intramural program. Two important benefits frequently offered employees are credit unions and educational assistance.

Credit Unions

Credit unions exist in many organizations to serve the financial needs of employees and attract potential employees. They offer a variety of deposits as well as other banking services and make loans to their members. Although the employer may provide office space and a payroll deduction service, credit unions are operated by the employees under federal and state legislation and supervision. Because credit unions are owned by their members, they often charge lower banking fees and offer loans at lower rates. Generally credit unions are located near an employer's facility, making it fast and convenient for employees to do their banking there. The service employees receive is also often more personal than the service they would get from bigger banks.

Educational Assistance

Proactive employers view educational assistance programs, also called tuition aid, as a strategic business tool that supports talent management as a critical human capital investment.[77] Educational reimbursement programs are also seen as encouraging employment retention and a hedge against the talent drain from increased retirements.[78] To be eligible for tuition aid, an employee may have to meet a length of service requirement and show that classes taken relate to job performance or organizational

FIGURE 11.4 Other Benefits Organizations Offer Employees

- Business travel insurance
- Time off for children's school activities
- Work-at-home arrangements/telecommuting
- Onsite cafeterias and take-home food
- Onsite laundry, dry cleaning, and hair-dressing services
- Employee referral bonuses
- Donation-gift matching
- Adoption assistance
- Onsite nurses and doctors
- Shuttle services for commuters
- Onsite massage services
- College scholarships

© Cengage Learning 2C13

career development. Employers may pay full or partial tuition costs plus related expenses such as books and supplies.

To help employees pay for the college expenses of their children and other family members, an increasing number of companies are offering employer-sponsored 529 college savings plans. Generally these savings plans are entirely funded by employees themselves with after-tax dollars. However, the plans accumulate money tax-free. Employees need not go through an employer to establish a 529 savings plan. They can do so on their own. The advantage of getting one through an employer is that a worker can have the deductions made automatically from their payroll checks, which can make saving for college easier. The investment fees an employer has to pay to administer the plan can also be lower than what an individual would pay.

Figure 11.4 shows some of the other benefits firms are offering employees that we have not already mentioned in this chapter. In summary, although benefits are expensive, they can be a good way for a company to differentiate itself, strengthen its employer "brand" to attract top talent, and retain that talent. However, both small and large employers need to implement their benefit plans strategically as well as continually monitor their effectiveness and costs.

Summary

LEARNING OUTCOME 1 Employee benefits were not always the norm in America. The situation changed in 1935 with the passage of the Social Security Act. However, benefits can add 30–40 percent or more to a company's payroll costs, and they continue to climb faster than the rate of inflation. As a result, firms look closely at their benefit costs.

LEARNING OUTCOME 2 A variety of factors need to be considered when designing a strategic benefits plan. Included among them are the relative preference shown for each benefit by managers and employees, the estimated cost of each benefit and the total amount of money available for the entire benefits package, and how it compares to the competition. Through committees and surveys, a benefits package can be developed to meet employees' needs. Through the use of flexible benefit, or cafeteria, plans, employees are able to choose the benefits that are best suited for their individual needs. An important factor in how employees view the program is the full communication of benefits information through various means and personalized benefits statements. Online systems have also helped with the communication process and made it easier for HR departments to administer employee benefits.

LEARNING OUTCOME 3 Nearly a quarter of the benefits package that employers provide is legally required. These benefits include employer contributions to Social Security, unemployment insurance, workers' compensation insurance, and state disability insurance. Social Security taxes collected from employers and employees are used to pay three major types of benefits: (1) retirement benefits, (2) disability benefits, and (3) survivors' benefits. Payroll deductions and taxes are also legally required to fund the government program, Medicare. Medicare provides medical and hospital insurance and prescription drug coverage for people over 65.

LEARNING OUTCOME 4 The cost of health care programs has become the major concern in the area of employee benefits. Organizations are taking a variety of approaches to contain health care costs. They include using health maintenance and preferred provider organizations and high-deductible health plans as well as reducing employees' coverage and increasing their deductibles or copayments. Employee assistance programs, disease management and wellness programs, and value-based initiatives that target the specific health needs of an employer's workers are other approaches.

LEARNING OUTCOME 5 Included in the category of benefits that involve payments for time not worked are vacations with pay, paid holidays, sick leave, and severance pay. Some companies offer their employees paid sabbaticals. A typical practice in the United States is to give employees ten days of vacation leave and ten holidays. In addition to vacation time, most employees, particularly in white-collar jobs, receive a set number of sick leave days. A one-time payment of severance pay may be given to employees who are being terminated.

LEARNING OUTCOME 6 For most professions in the United States, there is no mandatory retirement age. The topics covered can include pension plans, health insurance coverage, Social Security and Medicare, personal financial planning, wellness and lifestyles, and the general process of adjusting to retirement.

LEARNING OUTCOME 7 Whether to offer a pension plan is the employer's prerogative. However, once a plan is established, it is then subject to federal regulation under ERISA to ensure that benefits will be available when an employee retires. Two pension plans are available—defined benefit and defined contribution. With a defined benefit plan, the amount an employee receives on retirement is based on years of service, average earnings, and age at time of retirement. Two of the most significant trends are the growth of 401(k) plans and cash balance pension plans, both of which are defined contribution plans. A concern today is the underfunding of pension plans and the ability of the PGCA to meet its financial obligations.

LEARNING OUTCOME 8 The types of service benefits that employers typically provide include employee assistance programs, counseling services, educational assistance plans, child care, and elder care. Other benefits are food services, onsite health services, prepaid legal services, financial planning, housing and moving, transportation pooling, purchase assistance, credit unions, and social and recreational services.

Key Terms

backup care program
contributory plan
defined benefit plan
defined contribution plan
disease management programs
elder care
employee assistance program (EAP)
flexible benefits plans (cafeteria plans)

health maintenance organization (HMO)
high-deductible health insurance plan (HDHP)
noncontributory plan
phased retirement
preferred provider organization (PPO)
sabbatical

severance pay
supplemental unemployment benefits (SUBs)
vesting
wellness programs
workers' compensation insurance

HRM EXPERIENCE
Understanding Employer Benefit Programs

This exercise will help you more fully understand the benefits discussed in this chapter. Additionally, you will explore, in detail, the benefits and services offered by your employer and other employers in your area.

Assignment

Working in teams of four to six individuals, obtain information on the benefits package offered by your employer or other employers in your area. Once the information is gathered, be able to identify (1) each benefit offered, (2) what the benefit provides the employee, (3) employee eligibility (if required), and (4) how the benefit is paid for (employer, employee, or a combination of both). Compare benefit packages. Be prepared to discuss your findings with the class.

Discussion Questions

LEARNING OUTCOME 1 Many organizations are concerned about the rising cost of employee benefits and question their value to the organization and to the employees.

a. In your opinion, what benefits are of greatest value to employees? To the organization? Why?

b. What can management do to increase the value to the organization of the benefits provided to employees?

LEARNING OUTCOME 2 You are a small employer wishing to establish a benefits program for your

employees. What things should you consider to ensure that the program is a success for your employees?

LEARNING OUTCOME 3 Employers are required by law to provide specific benefits to employees. What laws mandate benefits to employees, and what are the provisions of those laws?

LEARNING OUTCOME 4 Identify and contrast the various ways employers can control the costs of health care.

LEARNING OUTCOME 5 Do you agree with the argument that benefits for time not worked are those most readily available to reduce employer costs? Explain.

LEARNING OUTCOME 6 Prior to 1979, all employers could prescribe a mandatory retirement age—usually 65 years. What would you think are the advantages and disadvantages of a mandatory retirement age? What factors might affect an individual's decision to retire at a particular time, and what factors might affect his or her ability to adjust to retirement?

LEARNING OUTCOME 7 Describe 401(k) pension plans, listing their advantages and disadvantages. As an employee, would you want control over the investment decisions of your 401(k) plan? Explain.

LEARNING OUTCOME 8 Working in teams of three or four, assume your team was hired as a benefits consultant to a small business having fifty to sixty employees. What benefits do you believe this employer should offer, given limited resources? Justify your reasons for offering these benefits.

On the Job: Video Cases

Benefits at Bright Horizons

Bright Horizons' chief operating officer, chief HR officer, and a teacher discuss the philosophy and specific benefits offered by the organization. The importance of investing in employees and being responsive to their needs is discussed. The problems in trying to balance the increasing costs of mandated benefits and the increasing expectations from employees are also presented.

What to Watch for and Ask Yourself

■ Describe how you think Bright Horizons' benefits create and maintain a competitive advantage for the firm. Bright Horizons also is a provider or vendor of benefits. How does this influence the company's decisions about its own benefit package?

■ Bright Horizons offers tuition reimbursement for education. What are two positive aspects and two concerns about tuition aid?

■ The video mentions that Bright Horizons offers some unique benefits such as pet care and tuition advising services. What are some other unique benefits that might be attractive to employees of Bright Horizons? How would you determine the return on investment for these benefits?

Case Study 1

Adobe's Family-Friendly Benefits: An Unexpected Backlash

Adobe Consulting Services (ACS), a provider of HR software application systems, prides itself on the variety of benefits it offers employees. In addition to health care, pension, and vacation benefits, the company also offers an attractive family-friendly benefits package including flexible schedules, child and elder care assistance, counseling services, adoption assistance, and extended parental leave. Unfortunately, in recent months, the company's progressive work/life policy has experienced a backlash from several employees, as the following case illustrates.

In March 20011, Teresa Wheatly was hired by Adobe as a software accounts manager. With excellent administrative and technical skills, plus four years of experience at Adaptable Software, Adobe's main competitor, Teresa became a valued addition to the company's marketing team. As a single mother with two grade-school children,

Teresa received permission to take Fridays off. She was also allowed to leave work early or come in late to meet the demands of her children. Teresa is one of eleven software account managers at Adobe.

The problem for Adobe, and particularly for Janis Blancero, director of marketing, began in the fall of 2011. On September 15, Dorothy McShee, citing "personal reasons"—which she refused to discuss—requested a four-day workweek for which she was willing to take a 20 percent cut in pay. When Dorothy asked for the reduced work schedule, she sarcastically quipped, "I hope I don't have to have kids to get this time off." On October 3, Juan Batista, a world-class marathon runner, requested a flexible work hours arrangement in order to accommodate his morning and afternoon training schedule. Juan is registered to run the London, England, marathon in May 2013. Just prior to Juan's request, Susan Woolf asked for and was granted an extended maternity leave to begin after the birth of her first child in December.

If these unexpected requests are not enough, Blancero has heard comments from senior account managers about how some employees seem to get "special privileges," while the managers work long hours that often require them to meet around-the-clock customer demands. Janis has adequate reason to believe that there is hidden tension over the company's flexible work hours program. Currently, Adobe has no formal policy on flexible schedules. Furthermore, with the company's growth in business combined with the increasing workload of software account managers and the constant service demands of some customers, Blancero realizes that she simply cannot grant all the time-off requests of her employees.

Questions

1. Do managers like Janis Blancero face a more complicated decision when evaluating the personal requests of employees versus evaluating employees' individual work performance? Explain.
2. a. Should Adobe establish a policy for granting flexible work schedules? Explain.
   b. If you answered yes, what might that policy contain?
3. If you were Janis Blancero, how would you resolve this dilemma? Explain.

Case Study 2

Evaluate the Work/Life Climate in Your Company

What is the quality of the work/life environment in your company? The following survey provided by the Work and Family Connection will help provide a "case analysis" of the climate in your organization. Answers to the twenty questions will provide clear insights about your company's position in the work/life area.

Agree or Disagree with the Following Statements:

1. My manager/supervisor treats my work/life needs with sensitivity.
2. It is usually easy for me to manage the demands of both work and home life.
3. My career path at this company is limited because of the pressure of home life demands.
4. My job at this company keeps me from maintaining the quality of life I want.

5. My manager/supervisor is supportive when home life issues interfere with work.
6. My manager/supervisor focuses on results, rather than the time I am at my desk.
7. My manager/supervisor has a good understanding of flexible work hour practices.
8. If I requested a flexible work arrangement, my manager/supervisor would support me.
9. My manager/supervisor is often inflexible or insensitive about my personal needs.
10. I believe my manager/supervisor treats me with respect.
11. My manager/supervisor allows me informal flexibility as long as I get the job done.
12. My manager/supervisor tends to treat us like children.
13. My manager/supervisor seldom gives me praise or recognition for the work I do.
14. My manager/supervisor seems to care about me as a person.
15. I would recommend this company to others.
16. The work I do is not all that important to this company's success.
17. If I could find another job with better pay, I would leave this organization.
18. If I could find another job where I would be treated with respect, I would take it.
19. If I could find another job where I could have more flexibility, I would take it.
20. I am totally committed to this company.

For a perfect score, you should answer **"Disagree"** to questions 3, 4, 9, 12, 13, 16, 17, 18, and 19 and **"Agree"** to all the rest, 1, 2, 5, 6, 7, 8, 10, 11, 14, 15, and 20.

To score, begin by giving yourself 20 points. Then deduct one point for every "wrong" response from the total score.

If your score is 18 to 20: Congratulations! Your organization is leading the nation in flexibility and supportiveness.

If your score is 14 to 17: Your organization is probably more supportive and flexible than most, but you have room to grow.

If your score is 11 to 13: You could be open to other job offers in the race for talent among employees.

If your score is 10 or less: Your managers will need help to manage the twenty-first-century workforce.

Source: Used with permission of the Work and Family Connection, 5195 Beachside Drive, Minnetonka, Minnesota 55343; 1-800-487-7898, or http://www.workfamily.com.

Notes and References

1. Keith Evans, "Pros and Cons of Employee Benefits, *eHow.com*, accessed May 5, 2011 at http://www.ehow.com.

2. Ibid.

3. *Employee Benefits Study, 2008* (Washington, DC: U.S. Chamber of Commerce, 2008); *Employer Costs per Hour Worked* (Washington DC: U.S. Bureau of Labor Statistics, 2011), http://www.bls.gov/news.release/ecec.t01.htm.

4. *Employee Benefits Study, 2008* (Washington, DC: U.S. Chamber of Commerce, 2008).

5. "Total Rewards" is all of the tools available to an employer that may be used to attract, motivate, and retain employees. Total rewards include everything the employee perceives to be of value resulting from the employment relationship.

6. Nina D. Cole and Douglas H. Flint, "Opportunity Knocks, Perceptions of Fairness in Employee Benefits," *Compensation and Benefits Review* 37, no. 2 (March/April 2005): 7.

7. Michelle Conlin and Jane Porter, "The Shape of Perks to Come," *Business Week* (August 20, 2007): 61.

8. Ashley Haynes, "Drowning in Paperwork: Self-Service Benefits System Provides Relief for Non-Profit Hospital," *Workspan* (January 2007): 43.

9. "Online Benefits Expected to Become Predominant," *Best Review* 105, no. 12 (April 2005): 106.

10. Stephen Miller, "Survey: Employees Undervalue Benefits," *HR Magazine* 52, no. 8 (August 2007): 30.

11. Lisa Patten, "Communicating the New Benefits Deals," *Benefits Quarterly* 23, no. 2 (Second Quarter 2007): 33.

12. Patricia Wiley, "What Keeps Human Resources Professionals Awake at Night?" *Benefits Quarterly* 23, no. 2 (Second Quarter 2007): 13.

13. Dennis Ackley, "Communication: The Key to Putting the 'Benefit' Back in Benefits," *Workspan* (February 2006): 32.

14. JoAnn Davis, "Communication: It Is More Than Distributing Information," *Employee Plan Benefits Review* 62, no. 1 (July 2007): 5.

15. Jeremy Smerd, "Tweeting Benefits in 140 Characters or Less," *Workforce Management* (August 2009), http://www.workforce.com.

16. Ibid.

17. Since the Social Security Act is continually subject to amendment, readers should refer to the literature provided by the nearest Social Security office for the most current details pertaining to the tax rates and benefit provisions of the act.

18. Jamie Dupree, "Summary of Tax Deal," *Atlanta-Journal Constitution* (December 10, 2010), http://www.ajc.com.

19. *How You Earn Credits*, Social Security Administration, SSA Publication No. 05-10072 (January 2007).

20. *How Work Affects Your Benefits*, Social Security Administration, SSA Publication No. 05-10069 (January 2007).

21. As an example, the Social Security Administration manages the Supplemental Security Income (SSI) program, which makes payments to people with low incomes who are age sixty-five or older or are blind or have disabilities. However, SSI is not paid for by Social Security taxes but by U.S. Treasury's general funds.

22. *Survivors Benefits*, Social Security Administration, SSA Publication No. 05-10084 (August 2007).

23. *Medicare*, Social Security Administration, SSA Publication No. 05-10043 (September 2007).

24. You may think that Medicaid and Medicare are the same. Actually, they are two different programs. Medicaid is a state-run program that provides hospital and medical coverage for people with low income and little or no resources. Each state has its own rules about who is eligible and what is covered under Medicaid. Some people quality for both Medicare and Medicaid. For more information about the Medicaid program, contact your local medical assistance agency, social services, or welfare office.

25. "Raising Medicare Age Could Cost Employers $4.5 Billion," *Workforce Management* (March 2011), http://www.workforce.com.

26. Annie Lowery, "Putting the Squeeze on Jobless Benefits," *Slate* (May 6, 2011), http://www.slate.com.

27. COBRA, P.L. 99-272, 100 Stat. 82 (1986).

28. FLMA, P.L. 103-3, 107 Stat. 6 (1993).

29. A "serious health condition" means an illness, injury, impairment, or physical or mental condition that involves any period of incapacity or treatment connected with patient care.

30. Janet Walsh, "Americans Value Moms, but Policies Don't," *Huffington Post* (May 5, 2011), http://www.huffingtonpost.com.

31. Daniel B. Ritter and Kari A. Legg, "Recent Developments under the Family and Medical Leave Act," *Compensation and Benefits Review* 39, no. 5 (September/October 2007): 32.

32. You Can Do Anything But Don't Mess with My Health Insurance,

33. Lydell C. Bridgeford, "Mental Health Parity and Addiction Equity Act Signed into Law," *Employee Benefit News* 22, no. 15 (December 2008): 44.

34. Nick Buckley, "Some GM Retirees Are in a Squeeze," *New York Times* (November 9, 2008), http://www.nytimes.com.

35. Susan J. Wells, "Getting Paid for Staying Well," *HRMagazine*, 55, no 2. (February 2010): 59–62.

36. Georgia Firm Adds 'Medical Tourism' to Benefits," *HR Specialist: Compensation & Benefits*, 5, no. 5 (May 2010): 7.

37. Joanne Sammer, "Big Picture on Drug Benefits," *HRMagazine* 55, no. 3 (March 2010): 32–38.

38. Christina Fuoco-Karasinski, "Building More Fit Employees: A Massachusetts General Hospital Case Study," *Workspan* (April 2007): 65.

39. Ira J. Morrow, "The Integration of Employee Assistance, Work/Life, and Wellness Services," *Personnel Psychology*, no. 4 (Winter 2006): 961.

40. "Mandatory Time Off around the Globe," *Open Forum* (May 2, 2011), http://www.openforum.com.

41. Ibid.

42. Michelle Conlin, "Do Us a Favor, Take a Vacation," *Business Week*, May 21, 2007: 88.

43. "HR and the Recession: 7 trends, 7 Solutions," *HR Specialist* 7, no. 7 (July 2009): 1–2.

44. Catherine A. Allen, "Burned Out?" *Life Science Leader* (May 3, 2011), http://www.lifescienceleader.com.

45. "No One in the Private Sector Gets Unlimited Vacation and Sick Leave," *Politifact* (January 28, 2011), http://www.politifact.com.

46. Catherine A. Allen, "Burned Out?" *Life Science Leader* (May 3, 2011), http://www.lifescienceleader.com.

47. Janet Kidd Stewart, "For Some, Retirement Just a Phase," *Chicago Tribune* (April 4, 2009), http://chicagotribune.com.

48. Hal Tepfer, "Step into the Freeze: A DB Pension Plan Primer," *Workspan* (July 2006): 51.

49. Dave Carpenter, "Boomers Facing Retirements in Jeopardy," *Associated Press* (December 27, 2010), http://www.ap.org.

50. Howard Gleckman, "A Nest Egg, That's a No-Brainer," *Business Week*, (April 25, 2005), 108.

51. E. S. Browning, "Boomers Find 401(k) Plans Fall Short," *Wall Street Journal* (February 19, 2009), http://online.wsj.com.

52. Joe Goldberg, "Educating Employees Can Increase 401(k) Participation," *Employee Plan Benefits Review* 62, no. 1 (July 2007): 18.

53. Patrick W. Spangler, "The Trend toward Automatic Enrollment in 401(k) Plans," *Employee Benefit Plan Review* 62, no. 5 (November 2007): 5.

54. Ibid.

55. Jessica Marquez, "Cash-Balance Plans Make a Comeback," http//www.workforce.com/section/02/feature/25/16/23/index.html.

56. Richard J. Bottelli, "Born Again: Cash Balance Plans Get New Lease on Life with Latest Rulings, Pension Reform 2006 Legislation," *Benefits Quarterly* 23, no. 1 (First Quarter 2007): 28.

57. ERISA, P.L. 93-406, 88 Stat. 829 (1974).

58. Carolyn Hirschman, "Overseeing Pension Management," *HR Magazine* 49, no. 7 (July 2004): 66.

59. "How HR Is Addressing Domestic Partner Benefits," *HR Focus* 81, no. 7 (July 2004): S-1.

60. Michael S. Travinski, "Employee Benefits for Domestic Partners and Same-Sex Spouses," *Journal of Pension Benefits* 13, no. 2 (Winter 2006): 29.

61. Debra A. Davis, "Employment Issues for Employee Benefit Plan: Designing Benefits for Domestic Partners," *Journal of Pension Benefits* 15, no. 1 (Autumn 2007): 56.

62. Public Law No. 104-199, 110 Stat. 2419 (September 21, 1996).

63. http://www.nmbar.org/AboutSBNM/sections/EmploymentLaborLaw/Enewsletters/Benefitsdomesticpartn.pdf.

64. Kathy Kacher and Rachel Hastings, "Training Managers to Meet Business Goals Using Work-Life Strategies," *WorldatWork* 16, no. 4 (Fourth Quarter 2007): 56.

65. Ira J. Morrow, "The Integration of Employee Assistance, Work/Life, and Wellness Services," *Personnel Psychology*, no. 4 (Winter 2006): 961.

66. Jessica Marquez, "5 Questions: The Balance-Workers Want," Workforce Management 86, no. 18 (October 22, 2007): 8.

67. Vicki Powers, "Green Benefits Helpful in a Down Economy," *Workforce Management* (May 2009), http://www.workforce.com.

68. Jessica Marquez, "5 Questions: The Balance Workers Want," Workforce Management 86, no. 18 (October 22, 2007): 8.

69. Ashley Johnson, "A Reliable Backup Plan," *Legal Assistant Today* 25, no. 3 (January/February 2007): 24.

70. Leah Dobkin, "How to Confront the Elder Care Challenge," *Workforce Management* at http://www.workforce.com/section/09/feature/24/85/10/index.html.

71. Scott Dingfied, "Senior Care Trends Expected to Mirror Child Care Industry," *Employee Benefit Plan Review* 62, no. 6 (December 2007): 20.

72. Bill Mulcany, "Why You Should Be Caring for Your Caregivers," *Workspan* (June 2007): 37.

73. Leah Dobkin, "10 Steps for Creating a Work Environment That Supports Caregivers," *Workforce Management* at http://www.workforce.com/section/09/feature/24/85/10/248514.html.

74. Lin Grensing-Pophal, "Partners on the Move," *HR Magazine* 52, no. 8 (August 2007): 87.

75. Candace E. Blair Cronin, "Adoption Policies That Work for Your, Company," *Workspan* (January 2008): 43. See also Carrie Boerio, "Adoption Benefits: Why They're Good for Business," *Workspan* (October 2007): 65.

76. Guillaume Deybach, "Identify Theft Protection as an Employee Benefit," *Employee Benefit Plan Review* 61, no. 7 (January 2007): 15.

77. Faith lvery, "Tuition-Aid Programs Are an Integral Part of Career Development," *Workspan* (January 2007): 29.

78. Erin White, "Theory and Practice: Corporate Tuition Aid Appears to Keep Workers Loyal; Studies Reinforce View of Improved Retention; UTC's Plan Stands Out," *The Wall Street Journal*, May 21, 2007, B-4.

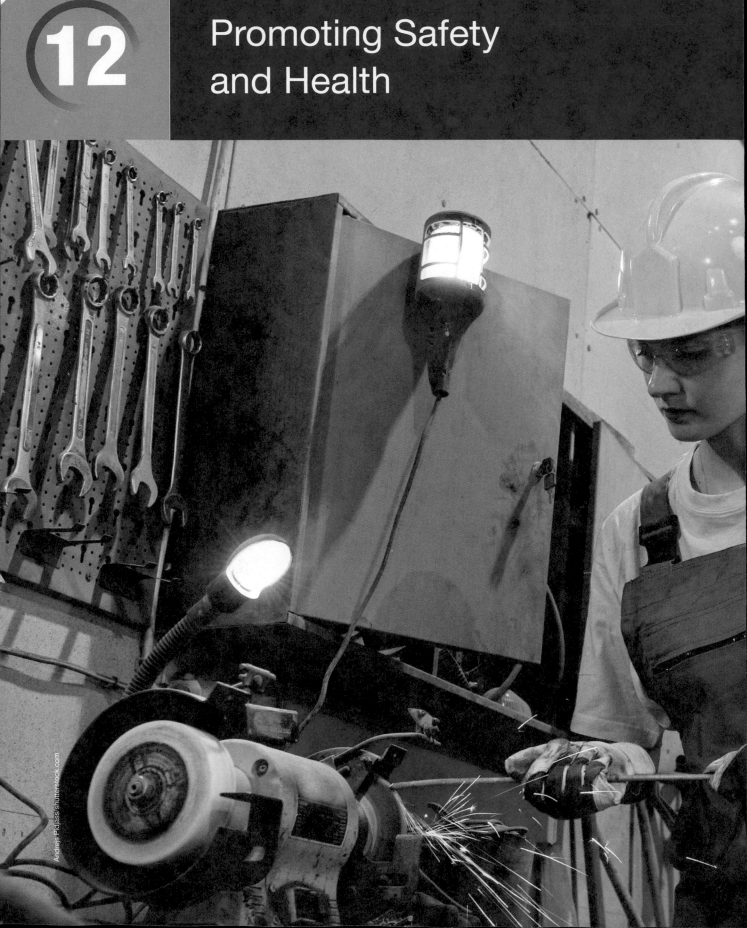

12 Promoting Safety and Health

After studying this chapter, you should be able to

LEARNING OUTCOME 1 Summarize the general provisions of the Occupational Safety and Health Act (OSHA).

LEARNING OUTCOME 2 Describe the measures managers and employees can take to create a safe work environment.

LEARNING OUTCOME 3 Identify ways to control and eliminate various on-the-job health hazards.

LEARNING OUTCOME 4 Describe the programs organizations utilize to build better health among their workforces.

LEARNING OUTCOME 5 Indicate the methods for coping with job stress.

G ood health and safety practices are indicative of top-notch organizations. Annually the Great Place to Work (GPTW) Institute surveys employees of organizations and compiles a list of the best places to work in the United States. In a recent survey, 96 percent of employees who work at the 100 best companies named by the institute answered "often true" or "almost always true" that their places of work are physically safe. Employers also recognize the importance of implementing safety and health programs because the benefits of doing so far exceed the costs associated with sick leave, workers' compensation, disability payments, and replacing employees who are injured or killed. A study conducted by the insurance company Liberty Mutual found that employers saved $3 for each $1 they invested in workplace safety.[1]

Employers are motivated by more than costs and their reputations to keep their workers safe and healthy, though. Most organizations provide their employees with good working conditions (1) because it is the right thing to do and (2) because firms realize people are the most strategic asset they have. Truly proactive companies can go further than this, though. Recall that in Chapter 1 we discussed total quality management (TQM). TQM is a set of principles and practices whose core ideas include understanding customer needs, doing things right the first time, and striving for continuous improvement. Interestingly, a study that looked at companies that had won awards for TQM concluded that these firms had not only maintained above-average earnings, productivity, and growth rates, but had improved worker safety by a remarkable amount. Perhaps part of the reason why this is so is that programs such as TQM result in greater employee engagement. We will talk more about employee engagement and safety later in the chapter.

Safety and Health: It's the Law

LEARNING OUTCOME 1

Most employers naturally hate to see their workers hurt or injured. Why then, do you think, so many safety and health laws have been enacted? Would individual employers or groups of employers be in a better position than the government to implement agreed-upon health and safety measures for their industries? Why or why not?

Consider these facts:

- In 2009, 3.6 million private-sectors workers suffered work-related injuries and illnesses.

- Back injuries, most of which occur because of improper lifting, are the nation's no. 1 workplace safety problem. More than 1 million workers suffer back injuries each year.

- Each year the cost of occupational injuries and illnesses totals more than $156 billion.

- In 2009, 4,340 employees died from work accidents.

- Ninety percent of fatal work injuries involve workers in private industry.[2]

Providing workers a safe and healthy environment is not just good for business and the right thing to do. It is the law. In 1970 Congress passed the Occupational Safety and Health Act (OSHA).[3] The mission of OSHA is to "assure the safety and health of America's workers by setting and enforcing standards; providing training, outreach, and education; establishing partnerships; and encouraging continual improvements in workplace safety and health." In spite of the figures previously cited, the act has

HIGHLIGHTS IN HRM
Test Your Safety Smarts

Take the following quiz to evaluate your knowledge and awareness of safety and health issues. The answers are found at the end of this chapter.

1. True or False? Employers have the right to be told by an Occupational Safety and Health Administration (OSHA) compliance officer the reason why it is undergoing a workplace inspection by the government agency.

2. True or False? Employers have the legal right to have a company representative accompany OSHA compliance officers on inspections.

3. True or False? OSHA requires employers to give its inspectors access to employees when inspecting medical and safety records of their firms.

4. What percentage of the U.S. population will be affected by back injuries?
   a. 23
   b. 47
   c. 60
   d. 80

5. True or False? In order to correct potential health and safety problems, employers have the right to know the name of an employee who files a complaint with OSHA.

6. Which causes more accidents: unsafe acts or unsafe conditions?

7. List five areas regarding safety that should be covered during a new employee orientation.

8. True or False? Employers are required to provide employee training on OSHA standards.

9. True or False? Employers are required to allow OSHA inspectors on premises for unannounced inspections.

10. True or False? Employers have twenty-four hours to report to OSHA accidents that result in a fatality.

been very effective in reducing the number of injuries resulting in lost work time, the incident rate of specific injuries such as back problems, and the number of job-related deaths. For example, even though there were twice as many workers in 2009 as in the 1960s, in 2009 worker fatalities were less than one-third of what they were in the late 1960s. Today, most employees report that the safety conditions in their organizations are very good. In a survey by the University of Chicago's National Opinion Research Center, 92 percent of employees "agree" or "strongly agree" that safety and health conditions where they work are good; 87 percent strongly agree that there are no significant compromises or shortcuts taken when worker safety is at stake.

OSHA's Coverage

OSHA covers all private sector employees and public employees in state and local governments. Self-employed workers are not covered by the law. Federal agencies are required to establish and maintain a safety and health program that is monitored by OSHA. Approximately half of the states currently have their own OSHA-approved

Because it slowed them down, the workers who built New York's skyline in the early 1900s were actually discouraged from using safety devices such as ropes to prevent falls. Not surprisingly, a disproportionate number of workers fell to their deaths.

SSPL/Getty Images

programs for private and public workers. Where state programs for the private sector have been approved by the federal government as meeting federal standards, the state carries out the enforcement functions that would otherwise be performed by the federal government.[4]

OSHA Standards

One of the responsibilities of the Occupational Safety and Health Administration is to develop and enforce mandatory job safety and health standards. These standards cover the workplace, machinery and equipment, materials, power sources, processing, protective clothing, first aid, and administrative requirements. To comply with OSHA, employers need to become familiar with those standards that are applicable to their establishments and to ensure that their employees use personal protective gear and equipment when required for safety. Employers can be cited and fined if they do not comply with OSHA standards.[5]

The Occupational Safety and Health Administration can begin standards-setting procedures on its own initiative or on petition from other parties, including the Secretary of Health and Human Services (HHS) and the National Institute for Occupational Safety and Health (NIOSH). Other bodies that may also initiate standards-setting procedures are state and local governments and any nationally recognized standards-producing organization, employer, or labor representative. NIOSH, however, is the major source of standards. As an agency of the Department of Health and Human Services, it is responsible for conducting research on various safety and health problems, including the psychological factors involved.[6]

Enforcing OSHA Standards

The Occupational Safety and Health Administration is authorized to conduct workplace inspections, issue citations, and impose penalties on employers. In recent years OSHA has stepped up its enforcement activities. In 201, OSHA workers conducted approximately 40,000 workplace inspections, and more than 96,000 workplace violations were found, a 15.3 percent increase since 2006.

Workplace Inspections

Under the act, "upon presenting appropriate credentials to the owner, operator, or agent in charge," an OSHA compliance officer is authorized to do the following:

- Enter without delay and at reasonable times any factory, plant, establishment, construction site or other areas, workplace, or environment where work is performed by an employee of an employer; and to

■ Inspect and investigate during regular working hours, and at other reasonable times, and within reasonable limits and in a reasonable manner, any such place of employment and all pertinent conditions, structures, machines, apparatus, devices, equipment and materials therein, and to question privately any such employer, owner, operator, agent, or employee.[7]

OSHA has further established a system of inspection priorities:[8]

First level: Inspection of imminent danger situations

Second level: Investigation of catastrophes, fatalities, and accidents that result in hospitalization of five or more employees

Third level: Investigation of valid employee complaints of alleged violations of standards or of unsafe or unhealthful working conditions

Fourth level: Special-emphasis inspections aimed at specific high-hazard industries, occupations, or substances that are injurious to health

Typically, OSHA inspectors arrive at a work site unannounced and ask for a meeting with a representative of the employer. At the meeting, the inspectors explain the purpose of the visit, describe the procedure for the inspection, and ask to review the employer's safety and health records. An employer may either agree voluntarily to the inspection or require the inspectors to obtain a search warrant.

The act gives both the employer and the employees the right to accompany inspectors on their tour of the work site. After the tour, the OSHA officials conduct a closing conference to inform the employer and employee representatives, if any, of the results of their inspection. They point out conditions or practices that appear to be hazardous and issue a written citation if warranted.[9]

Citations and Penalties

OSHA citations may be issued immediately following the inspection or later by mail. Citations tell the employer and employees which regulations and standards are alleged to have been violated and the amount of time allowed for their correction. The employer must post a copy of each citation at or near the place the violation occurred for three days or until the violation is abated, whichever is longer.

Under the act, OSHA may cite the following violations and propose the following penalties:

■ Other-Than-Serious: A violation that has a direct relationship to job safety and health, but one unlikely to cause death or serious physical harm. Such a penalty could be as low as $100. However, OSHA may propose a penalty of up to $7,000 for each violation depending upon the circumstances.

■ Serious: A violation for which there is substantial probability that death or serious physical harm could result *and* the employer knew, or should have known, of the hazard. The average penalty imposed by OSHA for serious violations is now $3,000–$4,000. The maximum penalty is $7,000 for each violation.

■ Willful: A violation that the employer intentionally and knowingly commits, or a violation that the employer commits with plain indifference to the law. OSHA may propose penalties of up to $70,000 for each violation or $75,000 per exposed employee for a willful penalty.

If a willful violation results in the death of an employee, OSHA can assess penalties up to $250,000 for an individual or $500,000 for a corporation, imprisonment of up to six months, or both. The largest ever fine by OSHA was an $87 million penalty levied in 2009 against the oil giant BP after a 2005 explosion killed 15 workers and injured 170 others at a BP refinery in Texas. (BP will likely face more fines as a result of the deadly explosion of its Deepwater Horizon platform in the Gulf of Mexico in 2010.) OSHA can adjust any penalty downward depending on the employer's good faith (such as demonstrating effort to comply with the act), history of previous violations, and size of business.[10] However, the agency can adjust penalties upward too. OSHA's Severe Violator Enforcement Program (SVEP) identifies employers with repeated, serious citations, and, among other things, subjects them to increased, multi-worksite inspections and higher penalties. The law provides for appeal by employers and employees under certain circumstances.

OSHA Consultation Assistance

Besides helping employers identify and correct specific hazards, OSHA can help employers develop and implement effective workplace safety and health programs that emphasize preventing worker injuries and illnesses.

Onsite Consultation

OSHA provides free onsite consultation services. Consultants from the state government or private contractors help employers identify hazardous conditions and determine corrective measures. Employers also may receive training and education services.[11] No citations are issued in connection with a consultation, and the consultant's files cannot be used to trigger an OSHA inspection. Additionally, the consultations may qualify employers for a one-year exemption from routine OSHA inspections.

Cooperative Programs

Voluntary, cooperative relationships among employers, employees, unions, and OSHA can be a useful alternative to traditional OSHA enforcement procedures, serving as an effective way to ensure worker safety and health. There are four specific cooperative programs—alliances, strategic partnerships, voluntary protection programs, and the Safety and Health Achievement Recognition Program:[12]

> ***Alliances.*** Alliances enable organizations to collaborate with OSHA to prevent injuries and illnesses in the workplace. OSHA and participating organizations define, implement, and meet a set of short- and long-term goals to improve workplace safety and health.
>
> ***Strategic Partnership Programs (SPPs).*** Strategic partnerships are long-term agreements between employers and OSHA aimed at reducing serious workplace hazards and achieving a high level of worker safety and health.
>
> ***Voluntary Protection Programs (VPPs).*** Voluntary protection programs represent OSHA's effort to extend worker protection beyond the minimum required OSHA standards. There are three VPPs—Star, Merit, and Demonstration—each designed to

recognize, motivate, or establish a cooperative relationship between employers and OSHA.[13]

Safety and Health Achievement Recognition Program (SHARP). SHARP is an OSHA certification program that recognizes small employers with exemplary achievements in workplace safety and health. Companies that receive SHARP recognition are exempted from OSHA's programmed, or regular, inspections as long as their certifications remain valid.

Responsibilities and Rights under OSHA

Both employers and employees have certain responsibilities and rights under OSHA. We will discuss only those that relate directly to the management of human resources.

Employers' Responsibilities and Rights

In addition to providing a hazard-free workplace and complying with the applicable standards, employers must inform all of their employees about the safety and health requirements of OSHA. Specific employer responsibilities are listed in OSHA's publication *All about OSHA* and illustrated in Highlights in HRM 2. Employers are also required to keep certain records and to compile and post an annual summary of work-related injuries and illnesses. From these records, organizations can compute their *incidence rate*, the number of injuries and illnesses per 100 full-time employees during a given year. The standard formula for computing the incidence rate is shown by the following equation, in which 200,000 equals the base for 100 full-time workers who work forty hours a week, fifty weeks a year:

$$\text{Incidence rate} = \frac{\text{Number of injuries and illnesses} \times 200,000}{\text{Total hours worked by all employees during period covered}}$$

It should be noted that the same formula can be used to compute incidence rates for (1) the number of workdays lost because of injuries and illnesses, (2) the number of nonfatal injuries and illnesses without lost workdays, and (3) cases involving only injuries or only illnesses.

Incidence rates are useful for comparing work groups, departments, and similar units within an organization. They also provide a basis for comparing multiple organizations doing similar work. The Bureau of Labor Statistics and other organizations, such as the National Safety Council, compile data that an employer can use as a basis for comparing its safety record with those of other organizations. These comparisons provide a starting point for analyzing problem areas, changing the working environment, and motivating personnel to promote safety and health.

It is the employer's responsibility to provide employees with protective equipment when necessary and ensure it is used. Employers must also provide their workers with safety training and be prepared to discipline employees for failing to comply with safety rules. In addition, employers must not discriminate against employees who exercise their rights under the act by filing complaints with OSHA. That said,

HIGHLIGHTS IN **HRM**

2 What Are My Responsibilities under the OSH Act?

If you are an **employer** the *OSH Act* covers, you must:

- Meet your general duty responsibility to provide a workplace free from recognized hazards that are causing or are likely to cause death or serious physical harm to employees, and comply with standards, rules, and regulations issued under the act.
- Be familiar with mandatory OSHA standards and make copies available to employees for review upon request.
- Inform all employees about OSHA.
- Examine workplace conditions to make sure they conform to applicable standards.
- Minimize or reduce hazards.
- Make sure employees have and use safe tools and equipment (including appropriate personal protective equipment), and that such equipment is properly maintained.
- Use color codes, posters, labels, or signs when needed to warn employees of potential hazards.
- Establish or update operating procedures and communicate them so that employees follow safety and health requirements.
- Provide training required by OSHA standards (e.g., hazard communication, lead, etc).
- Report to the nearest OSHA office within eight hours any fatal accident or one that results in the hospitalization of three or more employees.
- Keep OSHA-required records of work-related injuries and illnesses, and post a copy of the totals from the last page of OSHA No. 200 during the entire month of February each year. (This applies to employers with eleven or more employees.)
- Post, at a prominent location within the workplace, the OSHA poster (OSHA 2203) informing employees of their rights and responsibilities. (In states operating OSHA-'approved job safety and health programs, the state's equivalent poster and/or OSHA 2203 may be required.)
- Provide employees, former employees, and their representatives access to the Log and Summary of Occupational Injuries and Illnesses (OSHA 200) at a reasonable time and in a reasonable manner.
- Provide access to employee medical records and exposure records to employees or their authorized representatives.
- Cooperate with the OSHA compliance officer by furnishing names of authorized employee representatives who may be asked to accompany the compliance officer during an inspection. (If none, the compliance officer will consult with a reasonable number of employees concerning safety and health in the workplace.)
- Not discriminate against employees who properly exercise their rights under the act.
- Post OSHA citations at or near the worksite involved. Each citation, or copy thereof, must remain posted until the violation has been abated, or for three working days, whichever is longer.
- Abate cited violations within the prescribed period.

If you are an **employee** the *OSH Act* covers, you should:

- Read the OSHA poster at the job site.
- Comply with all applicable OSHA standards.
- Follow all employer safety and health rules and regulations, and wear or use prescribed protective equipment while engaged in work.

What Are My Responsibilities under the OSH Act? (continued)

- Report hazardous conditions to the supervisor.
- Cooperate with the OSHA compliance officer conducting an inspection if he or she inquires about safety and health conditions in your workplace.
- Exercise your rights under the act in a responsible manner.

Although OSHA does not cite employees for violations of their responsibilities, each employee must follow all applicable standards, rules, regulations, and orders issued under the *OSH Act*. OSHA, however, does not expect employees to pay for guardrails, floor cleaning, equipment maintenance, respirators, training, or other safety and health measures.

Source: *OSH Act, OSHA Standards, Inspections, Citations and Penalties OSH Act, OSHA Standards, Inspections, Citations and Penalties* (Washington, DC: Occupational Safety and Health Administration), accessed May 20, 2011, at http://www.osha.gov.

employers are afforded many rights under the act, most of which pertain to receiving information from OSHA, applying for variances in safety and health standards, and contesting the agency's penalties.[14]

Employees' Responsibilities and Rights

Employees are required to comply with all applicable OSHA standards, to report hazardous conditions, and to follow all employer safety and health rules and regulations, including those prescribing the use of protective equipment. Workers have a right to demand safe and healthy conditions on the job without fear of punishment. They also have many rights that pertain to requesting and receiving information about safety and health conditions.[15] For example, most states—and federal law—require that employers provide information to employees about the hazardous chemicals they handle. Commonly known as right-to-know laws, these statutes require employers and manufacturers to give employees information about the toxic and hazardous substances they could come into contact with on the job and what the health risks related to those substances are. Since state right-to-know laws can be more stringent than federal law, employers are encouraged to contact their state's health and safety agency for a copy of their appropriate hazard communication standards.[16]

right-to-know laws
Laws that require employers to advise employees about the hazardous chemicals they handle

OSHA's Enforcement Record

Perhaps no federal government agency has been more severely criticized than the Occupational Safety and Health Administration.[17] Unions and safety groups continue to worry that OSHA is lax in monitoring its agreements with organizations. These groups would prefer mandatory standards instead of voluntary guidelines for problems such as injuries related to jobs involving repetitive motion—a topic to be considered later in the chapter.[18]

OSHA regulations mandate the use of protective equipment in recognized hazardous conditions.

Meanwhile employers often say that OSHA's standards are unrealistic and inspectors are overzealous. "It seems OSHA administration conducts research and sets safety and health standards in an ivory tower, not knowing or caring if standards are valid for the real world," remarked one safety manager. Another criticism is that many of OSHA's standards are dangerously outdated.

However, the complaint most registered against OSHA is uneven enforcement efforts by the agency from one political administration to the next.[19] Under some administrations, the funding for the agency has been cut and enforcement efforts have been seen as virtually nonexistent (or at least very lax). Under other administrations, regulatory enforcement has seemed more proactive. In recent years, the funding for OSHA has increased, and it has stepped up its enforcement measures.

Promoting a Safe Work Environment

LEARNING OUTCOME 2

Discuss some of the safety programs at your college. In what ways do you think they might be similar to safety programs in the workplace? In what ways might they be different?

Typically, a firm's HR department or the industrial relations department is responsible for its safety program. Although the success of a safety program depends largely on managers and supervisors of operating departments, the HR department typically coordinates the safety communication and training programs, maintains safety records required by OSHA, and works closely with managers and supervisors in a cooperative effort to make the program a success.

Organizations with formal safety programs generally have employee-management safety committees that include representatives from management, each department or manufacturing/service unit, and employee representatives. Committees are typically involved in investigating accidents and helping to publicize the importance of safety rules and their enforcement.

Creating a Culture of Safety

Lower-level operational managers and supervisors have traditionally been the bedrock for encouraging health and safety in their organizations.[20] Indeed, one study by the American Institute of Plant Engineers showed that there was a direct correlation between an increase in the commitment to safety by managers and a decrease in accidents. However, firms today try to create a "culture" of safety within their organizations that goes beyond managing operational processes and reducing accidents.[21] A culture of safety exists when everyone within an organization consciously works to improve its safety and health conditions. HR managers play a key role in this effort. "HR executives should be the point persons on creating and making sure that a corporate safety culture exists," Carolyn Merritt, the late chairperson of the U.S. Chemical Safety Board (CSB) once noted. "These are the people who have their fingers on the culture pulses of the organization."[22]

Furthermore, the CSB advocates a culture of safety that focuses specifically on *process safety metrics*. For example, instead of counting injuries, managers should set goals on how many unit safety meetings should be held quarterly and measure goal attainment. Greg Andress, executive manager at Gallagher Bassett Services (safety consultants), states, "You want to measure the drivers within your organization that are going to create a change in the culture."[23]

Interviewing for Safety and Fitness-for-Duty Tests

One of the ways HR managers can help create a culture of safety within in an organization is to encourage supervisors to incorporate safety into their interviews with job candidates. Have you ever known someone who seemed accident prone? What about someone who rarely ever experienced a scratch? Several researchers have reported finding a correlation between different employees and their propensity for safety. Although asking job candidates about the injuries they have experienced is off limits, interviewers can ask candidates other behavioral-type questions designed to elicit their propensity for safety. For example, an interviewer might ask a candidate a question about an unsafe incident they witnessed and how they handled it.

Some companies periodically conduct fitness-for-duty evaluations on their current employees. Fitness-for-duty evaluations are similar to prehire physical exams but can be done any time during employment. They determine an employee's physical, mental, and emotional fitness and are most often used for in safety or security-sensitive positions. For example, federal rules require nuclear-plant workers to undergo random fitness-for-duty evaluations on the job to determine if they have been using alcohol or drugs.

fitness-for-duty evaluations
Evaluations randomly conducted to determine an employee's physical, mental, and emotional fitness for a job

The Key Role of the Supervisor

Supervisors can do much more than interview candidates for their safety tendencies, however. As we have explained, like HR managers, supervisors play a key role in their employer's safety programs. One of a supervisor's major responsibilities is to communicate to an employee the need to work safely.[24] Beginning with new employee orientation, safety should be emphasized continually. Proper work procedures, the use of protective clothing and devices, and potential hazards should be explained thoroughly.[25] Furthermore, employees' understanding of all these considerations should be verified during training sessions, and employees should be encouraged to be proactive when it comes to safety. In other words, they should be coached to look for safety problems before they occur. Moreover, supervisors must continually observe employees at work, reinforce safe practices, and immediately correct behaviors that are unsafe.[26]

Proactive Safety Training Programs

Safety training is not only good business; in certain occupational areas, safety and health training is legally required. For example, employers regulated by a federal agency called the Pipeline and Hazardous Materials Safety Administration are legally required to provide their employees with environmental-safety protection training. When training is mandated, employers must keep accurate records of all employee education. Violations can incur criminal penalties.

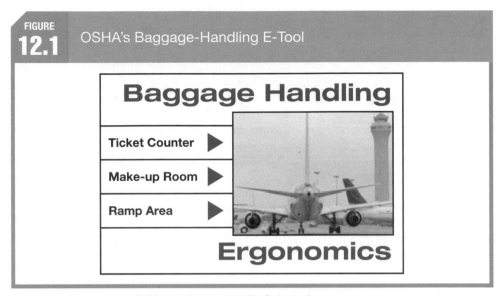

FIGURE 12.1   OSHA's Baggage-Handling E-Tool

Source: http://www.osha.gov/SLTC/etools/baggagehandling/index.html

Most organizations have a safety awareness program that entails the use of several different media. Safety lectures and courses, and printed and audiovisual material are common.[27] The use of games has also become an interactive way to provide employees with safety training. Costco and Amazon.com, for example, have successfully used a product called *Safety Bingo* to motivate employees on a daily basis to create a safety-conscious atmosphere and remind them of their safety goals.[28]

Of course, the Web has become a popular way to disseminate safety training materials as well. One safety manager went so far as to describe his company's intranet as the "the organization's SWAT team to develop and implement timely and efficient health and safety programs." In addition to distributing safety and compliance information via the Web, CDs, and PowerPoint presentations downloadable from its website, OSHA has developed online modules called "eTools" that deal with various safety and health topics and provide employers and employees information on how OSHA regulations apply to their work organizations.[29] Figure 12.1 shows OSHA's eTool designed to help workers who handle baggage do so safely.

HR professionals and safety directors in particular advocate employee involvement when designing and implementing safety programs.[30] Employees can offer valuable ideas regarding specific safety and health topics to cover, instructional methods, and proper teaching techniques. Furthermore, employees are more likely to embrace safety training when they feel a sense of ownership in the instructional program.[31]

Enforcing Safety Rules

Firms communicate specific safety rules and regulations in a variety of ways, including through supervisors, bulletin board notices, employee handbooks, and signs attached to equipment. To keep employees aware of hazards, some organizations provide their employees with small, laminated OSHA "Quick Cards." The cards contain brief, easy-to-follow safety and health information employees can keep on hand and refer to as necessary. Figure 12. 2 shows an example of a Quick Card. Safety rules are also

FIGURE
12.2 An Example of an OSHA Quick Card

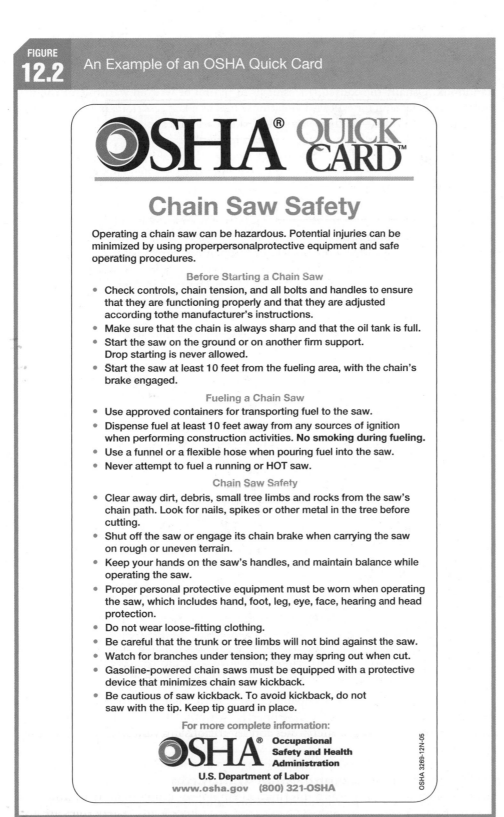

OSHA® QUICK CARD™

Chain Saw Safety

Operating a chain saw can be hazardous. Potential injuries can be minimized by using proper personal protective equipment and safe operating procedures.

Before Starting a Chain Saw

- Check controls, chain tension, and all bolts and handles to ensure that they are functioning properly and that they are adjusted according to the manufacturer's instructions.
- Make sure that the chain is always sharp and that the oil tank is full.
- Start the saw on the ground or on another firm support. Drop starting is never allowed.
- Start the saw at least 10 feet from the fueling area, with the chain's brake engaged.

Fueling a Chain Saw

- Use approved containers for transporting fuel to the saw.
- Dispense fuel at least 10 feet away from any sources of ignition when performing construction activities. **No smoking during fueling.**
- Use a funnel or a flexible hose when pouring fuel into the saw.
- Never attempt to fuel a running or **HOT** saw.

Chain Saw Safety

- Clear away dirt, debris, small tree limbs and rocks from the saw's chain path. Look for nails, spikes or other metal in the tree before cutting.
- Shut off the saw or engage its chain brake when carrying the saw on rough or uneven terrain.
- Keep your hands on the saw's handles, and maintain balance while operating the saw.
- Proper personal protective equipment must be worn when operating the saw, which includes hand, foot, leg, eye, face, hearing and head protection.
- Do not wear loose-fitting clothing.
- Be careful that the trunk or tree limbs will not bind against the saw.
- Watch for branches under tension; they may spring out when cut.
- Gasoline-powered chain saws must be equipped with a protective device that minimizes chain saw kickback.
- Be cautious of saw kickback. To avoid kickback, do not saw with the tip. Keep tip guard in place.

For more complete information:

OSHA® **Occupational Safety and Health Administration**
U.S. Department of Labor
www.osha.gov (800) 321-OSHA

OSHA 3269-12N-05

Source: http://www.osha.gov/OshDoc/data_Hurricane_Facts/chain_saw_safety.pdf

emphasized in regular safety meetings, at new employee orientations, and in an organization's manual of standard operating procedures.[32]

The consequences for violating safety rules are usually stated in a firm's employee handbook. Usually the consequences include an oral or written warning for the first violation, suspension for repeated violations, and, as a last resort, dismissal. However, for serious violations—such as smoking around volatile substances—even the first offense could be cause for an employee's termination.

While discipline may force employees to work safely, safety managers understand that the most effective enforcement of safety rules occurs when employees willingly adhere to and "champion" safety rules and procedures. This can be achieved when managers actively encourage employees to participate in all aspects of the organization's safety program. This is important because employees who are involved in their companies' safety programs are not only more engaged employees but safer employees. According to a study by the Society of Human Resources Management, engaged employees were five times less likely than nonengaged employees to have a safety incident and seven times less likely to have a lost-time safety incident. In addition, the average cost of a safety incident was $392 for nonengaged employees, but only $63 for engaged employees.

There are a number of ways to involve and engage employees in company safety programs. In addition to TQM programs, they include having employees (1) jointly set safety standards with managers, (2) participate in safety training, (3) help design and implement special safety training programs, (4) establish safety incentives and rewards, and (5) be involved in accident investigations. Other ways to engage employees is to solicit their ideas and opinions when assessing the risk of jobs during the job analysis process. The idea behind this is to help identify potential hazards and develop protective measures before accidents occur. Establishing an employee safety suggestion program and asking employees to formally participate in the process of observing the safety behavior of their coworkers are two other ways. So is soliciting employees' opinions about the safety of the tools a company is considering purchasing. At BNSF Railway, not only do employees offer suggestions on the tools the company is considering buying, it is not uncommon for the company's mechanical group to create new tools or retrofit them so they are safer for employees to use.

Safety rewards programs are another popular way to encourage workplace health and safety.[33] At Allied Waste Industries, a solid-waste management company, management offers a bilingual online/offline safety rewards program called the Dedicated to Safety Rewards Program.[34] The program encourages employees to accumulate safety vouchers that enable them to earn prizes they can purchase from a catalog on the company's website. A word of caution should be noted with regard to rewards programs, however: they can provide an incentive for employees not to report safety accidents.

Rather than awards, many companies prominently display in their workplaces the number of consecutive days they have operated without an injury. The idea is to motivate employees to keep the injury-free "streak" going and possibly set new records for injury-free performance.

Investigating and Recording Accidents

Every accident, even those considered minor, should be investigated by the supervisor and a member of the safety committee. Such an investigation may determine the factors contributing to the accident and reveal what corrections are needed to prevent it from happening again. Correction may require rearranging workstations, installing safety guards or controls, or, more often, giving employees additional safety training and reassessing their motivation for safety.

OSHA requirements mandate that employers with eleven or more employees maintain records of work-related occupational injuries and illnesses.[35] As stated in an earlier section, OSHA also requires a Log of Work-Related Injuries and Illnesses (OSHA Form 300) to be maintained by the organization. All recordable cases are to be entered in the log. A **recordable case** is any injury or illness that results in any of the following: death, days away from work, restricted work or transfer to another job, or medical treatment beyond first aid. Other problems employers must record as work-related include loss of consciousness or diagnosis of a significant injury or illness by a health care professional.[36] Figure 12.3 illustrates OSHA's diagram for classifying accidents under the law. For every recordable case written in the log, an Injury

recordable case

Any occupational death, illness, or injury to be recorded in the log (OSHA Form 300)

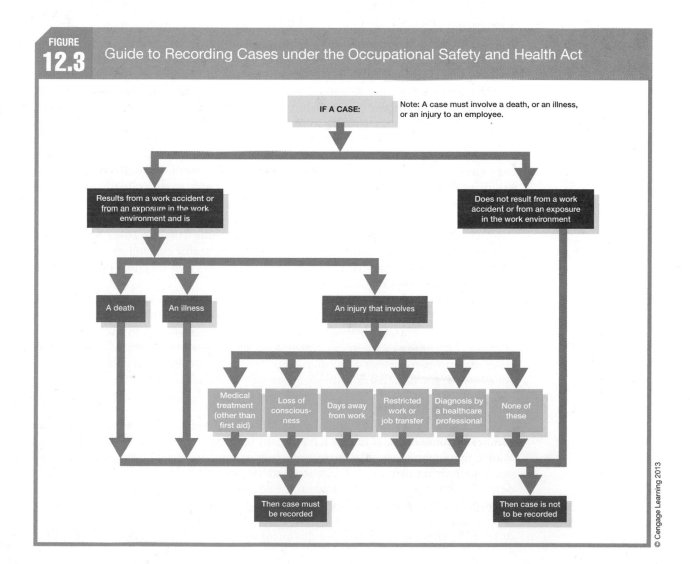

FIGURE 12.3   Guide to Recording Cases under the Occupational Safety and Health Act

© Cengage Learning 2013

and Illness Incident Report (OSHA Form 301) is to be completed. OSHA Form 301 requires answers to questions about the case. Each year OSHA Form 300A, Summary of Work-Related Injuries and Illnesses, must be completed and posted in a conspicuous place or places where notices to employees are customarily posted. Remember, when completing all OSHA forms, employers must not list the name of an injured or ill employee if the case has "privacy concerns," such as those involving sexual assault, HIV infection, and mental illness.[37]

We conclude our discussion of OSHA by showing the OSHA poster that employers are required to display at the workplace (see Highlights in HRM 5).

Safety Hazards and Issues

Workers face many different safety hazards on the job, which differ depending upon their occupations. It is impossible to discuss all of them in this chapter. However, we will discuss a number of hazards that have been getting a great deal of attention from HR managers and firms lately.

Fatigue

Few safety issues have been in the news more lately than employee fatigue. You have probably heard about air traffic controllers who have fallen asleep on the job and could not be awakened by pilots trying to contact them. Fatigue is more of a problem in organizations that operate around the clock or have night shifts. Studies show that 30 percent to 50 percent of night-shift workers report falling asleep at least once a week while on the job, according to Dr. Charles Czeisler, chief of sleep medicine at Brigham and Women's Hospital in Boston.[38]

Fatigue may not result in "life or death" consequences for most jobs. Nonetheless managers, employees, and the public are concerned about how it affects workplace safety and performance. The regulations in certain industries limit the number of hours employees can work per shift. The airline industry is one such industry. However, even with the limits, workers are finding themselves fatigued. Some experts say downsizing may be a factor as fewer workers are being asked to cover more shifts. Recently the U.S. government vowed it would give air traffic controllers an extra hour off between shifts to combat fatigue. Continental has given its pilots permission to call in and report they're too fatigued to fly.

Although OSHA currently has no fatigue standard, it is seeking to establish one, and unions are increasingly negotiating fatigue contracts. Employees at Dow Chemical's Freeport, Texas, facility have negotiated a fatigue standard in their new labor contract. Under the new agreement, employees who work three consecutive sixteen-hour days must receive a twenty-four-hour break. Employees on regular shifts must get a forty-eight-hour break if they work twenty-one days in a row.[39]

Distracted Driving

Do you know what the leading cause of worker fatalities each year is? Motor vehicle crashes. Moreover, according to a National Highway Traffic Safety Administration study, people who send text messages while driving are three times more likely to crash than other drivers, and distracted driving accounts for 80 percent of all accidents. When it comes to mass transit, the consequences of distracted driving can be catastrophic. For example, in 2008, a Los Angeles commuter train collided head on with another train. Twenty-five people died, including the operator of the train. Another 135 others were injured. A subsequent investigation of the accident found that operator had sent or received fifty-seven text messages while on the job that day, including one sent twenty-two seconds before the crash.

To help prevent distracted driving accidents, a growing number of employers are adopting mandatory cell-phone policies for their employees. A survey of more than 2,000 employers conducted by the National Safety Council found that 58 percent had some type of cell-phone usage policy in place, and roughly one-quarter of those surveyed prohibit both handheld and handsfree devices while driving for some or all employees.[40] Highlights in HRM 3 shows a template of such a policy developed by AT&T that companies can utilize. Other companies are doing more than establishing policies. They are outfitting their phones with apps like Phone Guard, which prevents drivers from texting, browsing the web, or checking e-mail when they are traveling ten miles per hour or faster.

OSHA does not have specific regulations on distracted driving. However, the agency has vowed that if an employer encourages or gives its workers an incentive to engage in distracted driving, it will penalize a company for creating an unsafe environment under OSHA's "general duty" clause. The general duty clause [Section 5(a)(1)] states that each employer "shall furnish . . . a place of employment which is free from recognized hazards that are causing or are likely to cause death or serious physical harm to his employees." The clause is used to enforce a wide range of safety and health violations for which specific regulations have not been implemented. In 2009 President Obama signed an Executive Order on distracted driving, which prohibits federal employees from texting behind the wheel while working or while using government vehicles and communications devices. More than thirty states also prohibit texting while driving.

Mobile phones are not the only electronic safety culprit, though. Workers who stop hearing the world around them because they are wired up to MP3 players also create risks. One aerospace manufacturer banned its 1,500 employees from using them at work. "Even though there have been no incidents, there are aircraft, forklifts, trucks, and so on moving around. We feel people should always be concentrating fully," said a spokesperson for the company.[41]

HIGHLIGHTS IN **HRM**
3 Texting While Driving: A Sample HR Policy

Employees are required to be familiar with and comply with local laws before using a wireless device while operating a motor vehicle for business purposes. Safe operation of any vehicle in the performance of company business is the responsibility of the driver and must be given appropriate attention at all times. In every situation, do not use a wireless device while the vehicle is in motion if doing so distracts attention from driving. Additionally, all employees are prohibited from using data services on their wireless devices, such as texting or accessing the mobile web or other distracting activities, while driving.

Source: "Texting While Driving Toolkit Sample Company Policy," AT&T, accessed May 20, 2011, http://www.att.com.

Workplace Violence

The National Institute for Occupational Safety and Health defines workplace violence as:

> Any physical assault, threatening behavior, or verbal abuse occurring in the work setting. It includes, but is not limited to, beatings, stabbings, suicides, shootings, rapes, near suicides, psychological traumas such as threats, obscene phone calls, an intimidating presence, and harassment of any nature such as being followed, sworn at, or shouted at.

According to OSHA, more than two million nonfatal workplace violence incidents are reported annually in the form of assaults, robberies, thefts, hostage takings, hijackings, rapes, and sexual attacks. Employees who have contact with the public; exchange money; deliver passengers, goods, or services; work in health care, social services, or criminal settings; or work alone or in small numbers are at a greater risk of encountering workplace assaults.

According to the Bureau of Labor Statistics, more women than men experience violence in the workplace. In fact, after traffic accidents, homicide is the second-leading cause of fatal occupational injuries for women.

Sexual harassment is often a precursor to the workplace violence women experience. Minority women, in particular, are vulnerable. The alleged sexual attacks of two maids at high-profile Manhattan hotels in 2011 cast a harsh light on the risks minority women face in the workplace. Anthony Roman, a hotel security consultant, says over the course of thirty years, he has seen dozens of such incidents involving maids. The assaults went from drunken propositions to rape. "They're not an infrequent occurrence," Roman says.[42]

The bullying of workers of both sexes is also a concern that is beginning to hit the radar of HR managers. Bullying is a form of violence; it is the repeated, health-harming mistreatment of one or more persons by one or more other people. It can consist of verbal abuse or offensive behaviors that are threatening, humiliating, intimidating, or interfere with someone's ability to work. In a Zogby poll, 37 percent of American adults said they had been bullied at work. Not only does bullying lead to lower morale, it can result in deadly suicides, violence, and homicides in the workplace.[43] A number of countries around the world, including France and Sweden, have enacted laws against bullying. About a quarter of U.S. states either have considered or are considering antibullying laws.

Using the INTERNET

OSHA creates and enforces workplace safety regulations. NIOSH researches ways to prevent workplace hazards. You can read the NIOSH study on workplace violence via the Student Resources at

www.cengagebrain.com

Reducing Workplace Violence. In addition to protecting workers at high risk of on-the-job assaults, OSHA recommends firms analyze their workplaces to uncover areas of potential violence and develop violence prevention programs and training for their employees. To begin, background checks on job applicants should be conducted to ensure they don't have histories showing a propensity toward aggression or violence.[44] Remember, employers can be sued for negligent hiring if they do not take this step and workplace injury occurs as a result. Managers, supervisors, and employees should also be trained to recognize violence indicators such as those listed in Figure 12.4.

Other measures to reduce workplace violence include having workers team up in pairs rather than working alone and making environmental adjustments, such as increasing lighting levels, locking down entries to prevent unauthorized people from

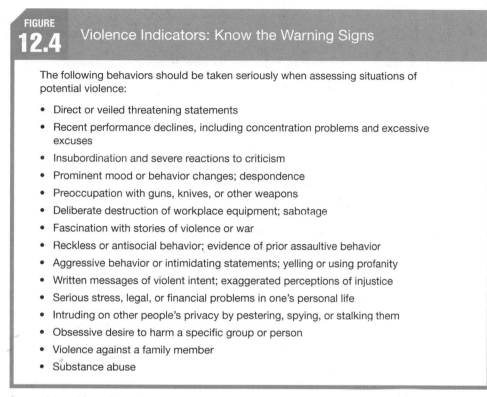

FIGURE 12.4 Violence Indicators: Know the Warning Signs

The following behaviors should be taken seriously when assessing situations of potential violence:

- Direct or veiled threatening statements
- Recent performance declines, including concentration problems and excessive excuses
- Insubordination and severe reactions to criticism
- Prominent mood or behavior changes; despondence
- Preoccupation with guns, knives, or other weapons
- Deliberate destruction of workplace equipment; sabotage
- Fascination with stories of violence or war
- Reckless or antisocial behavior; evidence of prior assaultive behavior
- Aggressive behavior or intimidating statements; yelling or using profanity
- Written messages of violent intent; exaggerated perceptions of injustice
- Serious stress, legal, or financial problems in one's personal life
- Intruding on other people's privacy by pestering, spying, or stalking them
- Obsessive desire to harm a specific group or person
- Violence against a family member
- Substance abuse

Source: Adapted from Violence in the Workplace: Risk Factors and Prevention Strategies, NIOSH Bulletin #59; David D. Van Fleet and Ella W. Van Fleet, "Preventing Workplace Violence: The Violence Volcano Metaphor," *Journal of Applied Management and Entrepreneurship* 12, no. 3 (July 2007): 17; Bella L. Galperin and Joanne D. Leck, "Understanding the Violent Offender in the Workplace," *Journal of American Academy of Business* 10, no. 2 (March 2007): 114,

gaining access to the firm's facilities, and providing personnel with mobile phones, walkie-talkies, and panic devices. Following the alleged attacks on the maids in Manhattan, the Pierre and Sofitel hotels decided to equip them with panic buttons. The Sofitel also changed its dress code to let maids wear pants.[45]

Last, but certainly not least, a firm's HR department must effectively communicate to a firm's employees that it has zero tolerance policy for violence.[46] Organizations such as Garden Fresh, a restaurant chain, Enterprise Rent-a-Car, JetBlue Airways, and the Ritz-Carlton have formalized workplace violence prevention policies informing employees that aggressive employee behavior will not be tolerated. Employees should encourage employees to report any possible or observed incidents to their firm's HR departments. Some firms have set up hotlines for employees to report incidents without having to fear repercussions for "getting involved."

Workplace Emergencies

Because an organization's HR department deals with every employee, it is in an ideal position to spearhead the effort to plan for emergencies, deal with them, and provide assistance to employees afterward. According to OSHA, a workplace emergency is an unforeseen situation that threatens employees, customers, or the public; disrupts or shuts down operations; or causes physical or environmental damage.

Emergencies can be natural or manmade. In addition to workplace violence, they can include the following.

- Floods
- Hurricanes
- Tornadoes
- Fires
- Toxic gas releases
- Chemical spills
- Radiological accidents
- Explosions
- Civil disturbances and terrorism

emergency action plan

A plan an organization develops that contains step-by-step procedures for dealing with various emergency situations

OSHA requires companies to have emergency action plans to deal with incidents such as these. An emergency action plan must include, among other things, procedures for reporting a fire or other emergency, evacuating a facility, and accounting for employees after an evacuation. The plan must also include procedures for employees who must remain in facilities to ensure critical plant operations continue, as well as procedures for workers performing rescue and medical duties. A copy of the emergency action plan should either be provided to employees or kept in a convenient location where employees can access it. Organizations with ten or fewer employees are allowed to communicate their emergency plans orally to employees.

Highlights in HRM 4 shows a readiness-assessment checklist organizations can complete to determine how prepared they are for an emergency. OSHA Publication 3088, *How to Plan for Workplace Emergencies and Evacuations* is also a helpful guideline for employers. To help small, low-hazard service or retail businesses implement an emergency action plan and comply with the agency's emergency standards, OSHA has an eTool.

Although it is not required, OSHA advises organizations to have alternative communication centers or backup computer servers they can use if their facilities are destroyed or inaccessible. The offsite physical or Web locations can be used to store originals or duplicate copies of accounting records, legal documents, emergency contact lists, and other essential records. Amazon.com, for example, has a computing service that allows companies to store data on its servers in addition to or in lieu of their own servers. HR managers should also make sure that employees know whom to contact and how during an emergency. Following a major earthquake in Seattle, Starbucks used a voicemail system to tell its employees to call or text message the company to make sure that everyone was accounted for. Prior to Hurricane Katrina, Marriott set up an 800 number employees and managers could call for status updates on the company's various facilities affected by the hurricane.[47] A firm's website can also be used to disseminate crisis information to employees, the press, and other entities that need information.

Crisis Management Teams

Organizations such as Motorola and Circle K Corporation have implemented formal crisis management teams. These teams, composed of hourly and managerial employees, work in conjunction with HR to conduct initial risk assessment surveys, develop emergency action plans, test them, and, perform crisis intervention during emergency

4 HIGHLIGHTS IN HRM
Emergency Readiness Checklist

Readiness Assessment

How Prepared Is Your Business for an Emergency?	Yes	No	Unsure
1. Does your business know what kinds of emergencies might affect it – both internally and externally?	☐	☐	☐
2. Does your business have a written, comprehensive emergency plan in place to help ensure your safety and take care of employees until help can arrive?	☐	☐	☐
3. Has your business created and practiced procedures to quickly evacuate and find shelter in case of an emergency?	☐	☐	☐
4. Has your business created a communication plan to communicate with employees in an emergency? (Examples include set up a telephone call tree, password-protected page on the company Web site, e-mail alert or call-in voice recording, and a contact list that includes employee emergency contact information.)	☐	☐	☐
5. Has your business talked with utility service providers about potential alternatives and identified back-up options?	☐	☐	☐
6. Has your business determined operations that need to be up and running first after an emergency and how to resume key operations?	☐	☐	☐
7. Has your business created a list of inventory and equipment, including computer hardware, software, and peripherals (such as backed up/protected records and critical data) for business continuity and insurance purposes?	☐	☐	☐
8. Has your business met with your insurance provider to review current coverage in case of an emergency?	☐	☐	☐
9. Does your business promote family and individual preparedness among co-workers (such as emergency preparedness information during staff meetings, newsletters, company intranet, periodic employee e-mails, and via other internal communication tools)?	☐	☐	☐
10. Have emergency shutdown procedures been developed for equipment such as boilers, automatic feeds or other operations that can not simply be left running in an emergency evacuation?	☐	☐	☐
11. Has your business worked with your community on emergency planning efforts and helped to plan for community recovery?	☐	☐	☐

Emergency Readiness Checklist (continued)

Readiness Results

Count your number of "Yes" responses to calculate a score. Your score is a **general reflection** of how much you know about emergency planning efforts at your business and/or how prepared your business may be for an emergency.

❑ If you have 8-11 "Yes" responses, you are well on your way to having a comprehensive and effective plan in place.

❑ If you have 4-7 "Yes" responses, while some aspects of your plan may be in place, you have some work to do to fill gaps.

❑ If you have 1-3 "Yes" responses, get started immediately on developing an emergency plan for your business. This training program is a great first step!

Planning for Emergencies
© 2007 National Safety Council

Source: National Safety Council.

events. For example, a crisis management team would investigate a threat reported by an employee. The team's mandate would be to gather facts about the threat, decide whether the organization should intervene, and, if so, determine the most appropriate method of doing so. Figure 12.5 shows what a crisis management team or other manager could do to calm an angry employee, for example.

Of course, it is impossible to prepare for every emergency or disaster that could affect a firm, so what crisis management teams typically do is learn from past incidents and formulate strategies for dealing with them should they occur in the future. The September 11, 2001, attacks on the World Trade Center and Pentagon are perfect examples. The attacks made U.S. companies, particularly those in high-profile industries such as the airline industry, sporting facilities, energy plants and dams, high-tech companies, financial institutions, and public and commercial buildings more cognizant of terrorism and how to prepare for it.[48] In unprecedented numbers, firms began looking at their operations for ways to improve their security. Among the measures organizations adopted following 9-11 were to lock all facilities and provide only employees with electronic cards for entry; check the IDs of visitors; install video monitors, alarms, and blast-resistant glass in buildings; tighten the entry and security of their garage and parking facilities; and protect their computer systems against unauthorized access and data theft.

Crisis management teams and HR managers also play a key role when it comes to getting employees back to work and paid on time following an emergency. For example, after Hurricane Katrina, the Ritz Carlton HR's department set up a central command

FIGURE 12.5 Calming an Angry Employee

If you try to defuse a tense situation, remember that anger frequently results from a person's feeling of being wronged, misunderstood, or unheard. Keep the following tips in mind to guide you.

- Strive to save the employee's dignity during an angry confrontation. Do not attack a person's rash statements or continue a muddled line of thinking.

- Hold all conversations in private. Do not allow the employee to create an embarrassing public situation for himself or herself, yourself, or other employees.

- Always remain calm. Anger or aggressiveness on your part will trigger a similar response in the employee.

- Listen to the employee with an open mind and nonjudgmental behavior. Give the employee the benefit of hearing him or her out.

- Recognize the employee's legitimate concerns or feelings. Agree that the employee has a valid point and that you will work to correct the problem.

- If the employee is very emotional or if the engagement seems out of control, schedule a delayed meeting so people can calm down.

- Keep the discussion as objective as possible. Focus on the problem at hand, not the personalities of individuals. A cornerstone of conflict resolution is to "attack the problem, not the personality."

- If the employee appears overly aggressive, withdraw immediately and seek professional help before any further discussion with the employee.

- If your efforts fail to calm the employee, report the incident to your manager, security, or human resource personnel.

Source: Adapted from professional literature on crisis management and seminars attended by the authors.

post. HR directors from all over the country helped employees affected by the storm quickly transfer to new locations.[49] Some workers may not want return to work due to the shock they experienced. Jim Martin, an employee assistance program professional with the Detroit Fire Department, notes that after an incident, employees can experience shock, guilt, grief, apathy, resentment, cynicism, and a host of other emotions.[50] Employee assistance programs (EAPs) can be utilized to help workers such as these, educate them about benefits available to them, and in some cases, even locate them. The U.S. Postal Service's EAP found families of 40 workers after Hurricane Katrina by sending a team wearing USPS EAP T-shirts and carrying signs to New Orleans' Astrodome where victims had taken shelter.[51] Crisis management teams are also responsible for disseminating public information and addressing the press.

Creating a Healthy Work Environment

As is apparent from its title, the Occupational Safety and Health Act was clearly designed to protect the health of employees as well as their safety. However, because of the dramatic impact workplace accidents have, managers and employees sometimes pay more attention to them than health hazards. Accidents happen quickly. The effect of health hazards show up only over time. When they do show up, though, they adversely affect workers, their families, and their companies.

LEARNING OUTCOME 3

How are health and safety related? If your workplace is safe, does that mean it is also healthy? Why or why not?

Job Safety and Health
It's the law!

OSHA
Occupational Safety
and Health Administration
U.S. Department of Labor

EMPLOYEES:
- You have the right to notify your employer or OSHA about workplace hazards. You may ask OSHA to keep your name confidential.

- You have the right to request an OSHA inspection if you believe that there are unsafe and unhealthful conditions in your workplace. You or your representative may participate in that inspection.

- You can file a complaint with OSHA within 30 days of retaliation or discrimination by your employer for making safety and health complaints or for exercising your rights under the *OSH Act*.

- You have the right to see OSHA citations issued to your employer. Your employer must post the citations at or near the place of the alleged violations.

- Your employer must correct workplace hazards by the date indicated on the citation and must certify that these hazards have been reduced or eliminated.

- You have the right to copies of your medical records and records of your exposures to toxic and harmful substances or conditions.

- Your employer must post this notice in your workplace.

- You must comply with all occupational safety and health standards issued under the *OSH Act* that apply to your own actions and conduct on the job.

EMPLOYERS:
- You must furnish your employees a place of employment free from recognized hazards.
-
  You must comply with the occupational safety and health standards issued under the *OSH Act*.

This free poster available from OSHA –
The Best Resource for Safety and Health

Free assistance in identifying and
correcting hazards or complying with
standards is available to employers,
without citation or penalty, through
OSHA-supported consultation
programs in each state.

1-800-321-OSHA
www.osha.gov

OSHA 3165-12-04R

Ergonomics

One way to help eliminate health hazards in the workplace is via ergonomics. Recall that we discussed ergonomics in Chapter 4 when we looked at job design. Ergonomics focuses on ensuring that jobs are designed for safe and efficient work while improving the safety, comfort, and performance of users. Ergonomics can be as simple as rearranging a work station so fewer steps are needed to gather items or organizing items so they are within easier reach.

An ergonomically designed computer workstation like this will reduce the strain on the worker's eyes, neck and shoulders, wrists, and back.

Jon Feingersh/Blend Images/Alamy

Part of ergonomics involves looking at the design of equipment and the physical abilities of the operators who use it. There is substantial variation in the way people move depending on their physical sizes, genders, ages, and other factors. Designing equipment controls to be compatible with both the physical characteristics and the reaction capabilities of the people who must operate them and the environment in which they work is critically important. Ergonomics also considers the requirements of a diverse workforce, accommodating, for example, women who may lack the strength to operate equipment requiring intense physical force or Asian Americans who may lack the stature to reach equipment controls.

Ergonomics has proven cost-effective at organizations such as Compaq Computer, 3M, Pratt and Whitney, and the U.S. Postal Service and eliminated, or at least reduced, many repetitive motion injuries, particularly those related to the back and wrist. At Cessna Aircraft, factory employees use specially designed hand tools to reduce hand and arm tension. Rockwell Automation reduced shoulder injuries to punch-press operators by purchasing hydraulic fork trucks to lift metal dies, a process formerly done manually, and Maple Landmark Woodcraft employed ergonomic education to reduce repetitive motion injuries caused by hammering. The key elements of successful ergonomic programs are shown in Figure 12.6.[52]

Health Hazards and Issues

At one time health hazards were associated primarily with jobs found in manufacturing operations. In recent years, however, hazards in jobs outside of plants, such as in offices, health care facilities, and airports, have been recognized, and methods to lessen these hazards have been adopted. Substituting materials, altering processes, enclosing or isolating a process, issuing protective equipment, and improving ventilation are some of the common preventions. This section will review several of the more important health concerns to employees and employers.

Cumulative Trauma Disorders

Meat cutters, fish filleters, cooks, dental hygienists, textile workers, violinists, flight attendants, office workers at computer terminals, and others whose jobs require repetitive motion of the fingers, hands, or arms are reporting injuries in growing

---

FIGURE 12.6 Key Elements for a Successful Ergonomics Program

Companies with award-winning ergonomics programs list the following as common elements of success:

- *Provide notice and training for employees.* Implement a well-publicized ergonomics policy or present ergonomic information in safety policies or training programs. Train employees, supervisors, and managers in basic workplace ergonomics.

- *Conduct preinjury hazard assessment.* Survey the workplace and work processes for potential hazards and adopt measures to lessen the exposure to ergonomic risk factors. Answer the question: "Are certain work areas more prone to ergonomic hazards than others?"

- *Involve employees.* Include employees in risk assessment, recognition of MSD symptoms, design of work-specific equipment or tools, and the setting of work performance rules and guidelines.

- *Plan and execute.* Integrate ergonomic responsibilities into the performance plans for all personnel. Demand accountability for program success.

- *File injury reports.* Encourage early reporting of MSD symptoms or injuries. Refer employees to the company's medical facilities or to the employee's personal physician for treatment.

- *Evaluate and assess the ergonomics program.* Periodically review the effectiveness of the ergonomics program. If the program appears to be ineffective, determine the underlying causes for failure and propose corrective changes.

---

cumulative trauma disorders

Injuries involving tendons of the fingers, hands, and arms that become inflamed from repeated stresses and strains

percentages.[53] Known as cumulative trauma disorders or repetitive motion injuries, these musculoskeletal disorders (MSDs) are injuries of the muscles, nerves, tendons, ligaments, joints, and spinal discs caused by repeated stresses and strains. One of the more common conditions is *carpal tunnel syndrome*, which is characterized by tingling or numbness in the fingers occurring when a tunnel of bones and ligaments in the wrist narrows and pinches nerves that reach the fingers and the base of the thumb. Without proper treatment, employees with carpal tunnel syndrome can lose complete feeling in their hands. Another cumulative trauma disorder prevalent among tennis players is tennis elbow.

Ergonomics techniques are also successfully used to improve or correct workplace conditions that cause or aggravate cumulative trauma disorders.[54] Continuous developments in office furniture, video display terminals, tool design, computer keyboards, and adjustable workstations are all attempts to make the work setting more comfortable—and, hopefully, more productive—but also to lessen musculoskeletal disorders. Minibreaks involving exercise and the changing of work positions have been found helpful. Importantly, these kinds of injuries often go away if they are caught early. If they are not, they may require months or years of treatment or even surgical correction. Also, when cumulative trauma disorders result from work activities, they serve to lower employee productivity, increase employer health costs, and incur workers' compensation payments.

Employees' musculoskeletal injuries are classified as recordable cases and must be reported on OSHA Form 300. OSHA enforces the removal of ergonomic hazards by issuing citations under the "general duty" clause of the Occupational Safety and Health Act. To help reduce musculoskeletal injuries, OSHA offers a series of eTools that address general ergonomic hazards and ergonomic hazards of specific occupations and industries. Baggage handling in the airline industry is an example. (See Figure 12.1.)

Computer Workstation Issues

Figure 12.7 provides a checklist of potential repetitive motion problem areas for employees using computers. Video display terminals (VDTs) are a particular concern. The problems that managers have to confront in this area fall into three major groups:

1. *Visual difficulties.* VDT operators frequently complain of blurred vision, sore eyes, burning and itching eyes, and glare.[55]

2. *Muscular aches and pains.* Pains in the back, neck, and shoulders are common complaints of VDT operators.

3. *Job stress.* Eye strain, postural problems, insufficient training, excessive workloads, and monotonous work are complaints reported by three-quarters of VDT users.

To capitalize on the benefits of VDTs while safeguarding employee health, Dr. James Sheedy, a VDT and vision expert, offers these tips on how to minimize the negative effects of computer use on the eyes and body:

- Place the computer screen four to nine inches below eye level.

- Keep the monitor directly in front of you.

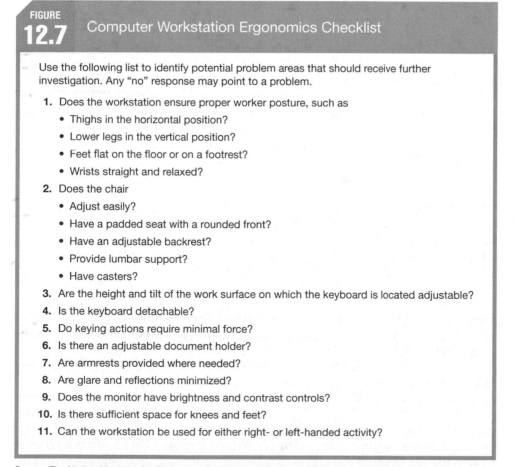

FIGURE 12.7 Computer Workstation Ergonomics Checklist

Use the following list to identify potential problem areas that should receive further investigation. Any "no" response may point to a problem.

1. Does the workstation ensure proper worker posture, such as
   - Thighs in the horizontal position?
   - Lower legs in the vertical position?
   - Feet flat on the floor or on a footrest?
   - Wrists straight and relaxed?
2. Does the chair
   - Adjust easily?
   - Have a padded seat with a rounded front?
   - Have an adjustable backrest?
   - Provide lumbar support?
   - Have casters?
3. Are the height and tilt of the work surface on which the keyboard is located adjustable?
4. Is the keyboard detachable?
5. Do keying actions require minimal force?
6. Is there an adjustable document holder?
7. Are armrests provided where needed?
8. Are glare and reflections minimized?
9. Does the monitor have brightness and contrast controls?
10. Is there sufficient space for knees and feet?
11. Can the workstation be used for either right- or left-handed activity?

Source: The National Institute for Occupational Safety and Health (NIOSH), *Elements of Ergonomics Programs: A Primer Based on Workplace Evaluations of Musculoskeletal Disorders* (Washington, DC: U.S. Government Printing Office, March 1997).

- Sit in an adjustable-height chair with lower back support and with feet flat on the floor.

- Use shades or blinds to reduce the computer screen glare created by window lighting.

- Elbows close to body and supported.

- Wrist and hands in-line with forearms.

Chemical Hazards

The Bureau of Labor Statistics estimates workers suffer more than 55,000 illnesses related to chemical exposures each year. It is not surprising, therefore, that the OSHA Hazard Communication Standard is the most frequently cited OSHA standard for general industry as well as for the construction industry. The purpose of the law is to ensure the testing and evaluation of chemicals by producers and the distribution of the chemical hazard information to users of the chemical.

All hazardous chemical containers must be labeled with the identity of the contents and must state any appropriate hazard warnings. OSHA-published hazardous chemical regulations known as the Hazard Communication Standard (HCS) prescribe a system for communicating these warnings. It includes a format for Material Safety Data Sheets (MSDSs). MSDSs must include the chemical name of a hazardous substance; all of the risks involved in using it, including any potential health risks; safe handling practices; personal protective equipment needed; first aid in the event of an accident; and information identifying the manufacturer. OSHA-required chemical training includes informing employees of the methods used to detect the presence or release of hazardous chemicals, the physical and health problems posed by hazardous chemicals, and the ways in which employees can protect themselves from chemical dangers.

Material Safety Data Sheets (MSDSs)
Documents that contain vital information about hazardous substances

Chemical hazards can affect the reproductive health of either women or men. In an important case concerning women, the U.S. Supreme Court ruled in *International Union v. Johnson Controls* (1991) that employers may not bar women of childbearing age from certain jobs because of potential risk to their fetuses.[56] The court said that such policies are a form of sex bias that is prohibited by federal civil rights law. The decision has made it important for employers to inform and warn female workers about fetal health risks on the job.

Smoking and Tobacco Smoke

Virtually all large organizations and even smaller ones have initiated smoking policies specifying when and where smoking will be allowed in their organizations, if at all. In developing smoking policies, it is advisable to have the involvement of both smokers and nonsmokers. Merck, Comerica, Hallmark, Southwest Airlines, and Marriot Hotels are among the companies that have involved both smokers and nonsmokers in the development of their smoking policies.

Bloodborne Pathogens

You have probably noticed that when technicians clean your teeth or draw your blood, they wear rubber gloves, eye protection, masks, and other protective devices. Exposures to blood and other body fluids occur across a wide variety of occupations and can result in employees contracting diseases. The pathogens of primary concern are the human immunodeficiency virus (HIV), hepatitis B virus (HBV), and hepatitis C virus (HCV). Workers can be exposed to blood through needlestick and other sharp-object injuries, mucous membranes, and skin exposures.

In industries where employees may come in contact with blood or other body fluids (such as medical response teams, hospitals, and nursing homes), employers are required to follow OSHA's numerous bloodborne pathogen standards. For example, employers must provide employees with protective equipment, train them to handle blood and body fluids, properly disinfect equipment, and dispose of waste materials.

Small Business Application

OSHA Resources for Small Businesses

Meeting all of OSHA's requirements can seem like a daunting task for small businesses, especially ones just setting up shop. Fortunately, for business owners and entrepreneurs, the Occupational Safety and Health Administration has a wealth of resources and programs designed to help small businesses keep their workers safe, lower employee injuries, illnesses, and absenteeism rates, decrease workers' compensation costs, and limit the damage to equipment and products as a result of accidents. The agency estimates that for every dollar a small business invests in safety in health measures, it can reap as much as $4–5 dollars in savings in terms of these costs.

We mentioned OSHA's eTools earlier in the chapter. In addition to numerous publications designed for small businesses, the agency also has online "Quick Start" modules for various industries located on its website. The modules, which are for businesses just being launched, contain step-by-step guidelines employers can use to generate an initial set of OSHA compliance materials tailored to their workplaces.

One of OSHA's most popular resources is its free and confidential Free Onsite Consultation Program, which helps small employers identify potential occupational hazards. In 2010, OSHA provided free onsite consultations to more than 30,000 small businesses that employ 1.5 million workers. To set up a consultation, an employer simply calls the nearest OSHA office in his or her area. On the day of the consultation, the employer, his or her employees, and an OSHA consultant do a walk-through to examine conditions in the workplace. The consultant will note both the safe and unsafe conditions and suggest approaches for solving the latter. Following the visit the consultant will provide the employer with a written report containing the information. The consultant can also provide training and education to the employees in the firm, and, if it meets the criteria for OSHA's SHARP program (see p. XXX), recommend the organization be given a one-year exclusion from OSHA's programmed, or regular, inspections.

Michael Foods, Inc., an Elizabeth, New Jersey, food company, scheduled an onsite consultation after receiving a letter from OSHA notifying the company that it was a likely candidate for inspection due to its workplace injury and illness rates. "When you want to know if your company is doing all the right things as it relates to health and safety, who better than OSHA to tell you," says Damir Tutundzic, the company's safety manager. Michael Foods went further than just getting a consultation. It followed OSHA's recommendations and now has the SHARP designation. Productivity is up, and at one point the distribution center had worked over 1,500 days without any lost time incidents and over 700 days without a reportable accident. "All of these efforts led to a reduction in workers' compensation costs of nearly $250,000 and 100 percent employee engagement," says Tutundzic.

Source: *Small Business Success Stories* (Washington, DC: Occupational Safety and Health Administration), accessed May 25, 2011 at http://www.osha.gov.

Employers must also make available to their employees any vaccines that could prevent a worker from becoming infected, such as the vaccine for hepatitis B. Additionally, OSHA requires specific record-keeping for "at-risk" employees who have been exposed to bloodborne pathogens.

Building Better Physical and Emotional Health among Employees

LEARNING OUTCOME 4

How would you describe the physical and emotional health of the people you work with or have worked with in the past? What role do employers play when it comes to the emotional health of their workers?

Along with improving working conditions that are hazardous to employee health, employers today are cognizant of the physical and emotional health of their employees and thus provide them with programs to maintain and improve both. Firms are doing so not only to lower their health costs but because they recognize that employees not distracted by health problems are able to operate more safely. Better health can also reduce absenteeism, increase efficiency and creativity on the part of employees, and lead to better morale and teamwork among them. An organization with a healthy, safe, resilient, and creative workforce is certainly in a better position to compete than an organization with unhealthy workers.

Recall that we discussed employee assistance programs (EAPs) in Chapter 11. As we have indicated, EAPs can help employees with a range of problems. We mentioned how the United States Postal Service utilized its EAP to locate workers after Hurricane Katrina. EAPs can also help workers with relationship, marital, and family problems; anger, depression, anxiety, and stress; and eldercare demands. Workplace issues, addiction, and self-improvement are other areas in which EAPs provide workers with help. If an employee's situation necessitates it, the EAP refers the worker to inhouse counselors or outside professionals. Next, we look at some of the issues employees face in terms of their physical and emotional health that EAPs and other workplace programs can address.

Wellness and Weight Issues

In Chapter 11 we mentioned wellness programs. Discovery Communication in Silver Spring, Maryland, provides a wellness center. The company employs a medical assistant, nurse practitioner, and physician who offer health services, including stress management, consultation and techniques, fitness programs, and podiatry care.[57] Appleton, a Wisconsin manufacturer of performance packaging products, promotes corporate fitness through its fitness facility, staffed with licensed trainers and YMCA physical fitness experts. The center offers four primary areas of programming: onsite physical rehabilitation, ergonomics/injury prevention, fitness, and education.[58] An organization might also distribute wellness literature to its employees obtained from the Association for Worksite Health Promotion or the National Wellness Institute.[59] Xerox gives its employees a publication titled *Fitbook* that includes chapters on the hazards of smoking and the effects of alcohol and drug abuse, facts on nutrition and weight control, and guidelines for managing stress and learning to relax. It is also not uncommon for wellness programs to utilize alternative medicine approaches such as relaxation techniques and hypnosis, chiropractic care, acupuncture, homeopathy, herbal therapy, special diets, and massage to help employees with a variety of health problems. For example, Paula Cates, a massage therapist in Denver, Colorado, uses massage to reduce the stress and tension employees experience and improve their circulation and range-of-motion activities.[60]

We also mentioned weight-related problems and obesity in Chapter 11. As you know, excess weight can affect the health of a worker and his or her productivity.

A study by Duke University researchers who examined the records of nearly 12,000 university employees found that obese employees experienced medical costs that were more than five times higher than those of nonobese workers. They also missed eight times the number of workdays, which by some estimates costs companies an estimated $5.5 billion a year in lost productivity.[61] The Duke study also found that morbidly obese workers file 45 percent more worker's compensation claims and take longer to recover from injuries.[62]

Not surprisingly, employers are launching or improving programs specifically designed to help employees maintain or lose weight by exercising and eating properly.[63] For example, a nutritional component is part of the wellness program of JWT, a New York advertising firm. Nutritional programs address two lifestyle changes: (1) increasing a person's physical exercise (via walking, jogging, bicycling, and so on) and (2) adopting nutritional dietary programs that emphasize eating lots of fruits and vegetables, fish, and low-fat dairy products.[64] Stephanie Pronk, the chief health officer at RedBrick Health, a Minneapolis health technology and services company, notes that employers today are trying to create a "culture of wellness" that makes thinking about maintaining a healthy weight second nature to employees.[65]

Case managers who manage the care of employees injured on the job are now taking people's weight into account when planning for their recovery, and if they are obese, getting them the resources they need to return to work more quickly than they otherwise would. For example, until they are fully recovered, they might be put on light duty, which is work that is less demanding.

Job Stress and Burnout

It is no secret that employees today are more stressed out than they have been in years past. A Gallup poll recently found that 30 percent of employees were dissatisfied with the amount of stress they experience in the workplace, a number that is up 10 percent since 2002. Stress is any demand on the individual that requires coping behavior. Stress comes from two basic sources: physical activity and mental or emotional activity. The physical reaction of the body to both types of stress is the same. Psychologists use two separate terms to distinguish between positive and negative forms of stress, even though reactions to the two forms are the same biochemically. Eustress is positive stress that accompanies achievement and exhilaration.[66] This type of stress is regarded as a beneficial force that helps us to forge ahead against obstacles. What is harmful is distress. Stress becomes distress when we begin to sense a loss of our feelings of security and adequacy. Helplessness, desperation, and disappointment turn stress into distress.

Burnout is a severe stage of distress. Career burnout generally occurs when a person begins questioning his or her own personal values. Quite simply, the person no longer feels that what he or she is doing is important. Depression, frustration, and a loss of productivity are all symptoms of burnout. Burnout is due primarily to a lack of personal fulfillment in the job or a lack of positive feedback about one's performance.[67] In organizations that have downsized, remaining employees can experience burnout because they must perform more work with fewer coworkers. Overachievers can experience burnout when unrealistic work goals are unattainable.[68]

The causes of workplace stress are many. However, according to a study by Lluminari, a national health care company, four factors have a major influence on employee stress:

- *High demand:* having too much to do in too short a time

- *High effort:* having to expend too much mental or physical energy over too long a period

stress

Any adjustive demand caused by physical, mental, or emotional factors that requires coping behavior

eustress

Positive stress that accompanies achievement and exhilaration

distress

Harmful stress characterized by a loss of feelings of security and adequacy

burnout

A severe stage of distress, manifesting itself in depression, frustration, and loss of productivity

■ *Low control:* having too little influence over the way a job is done on a day-to-day basis

■ *Low reward:* receiving inadequate feedback on performance and no recognition for a job well done.

Other job stressors include layoffs and organizational restructuring; disagreements with managers or fellow employees; prejudice because of age, gender, race, or religion; inability to voice complaints; and poor working conditions. Even minor irritations such as lack of privacy, unappealing music, and other conditions can be distressful to one person or another.

Job stress places both women and men at risk for fatigue, high blood pressure, cardiovascular problems, depression, and obesity and increases employee susceptibility to infectious diseases. Studies have shown that work-related stress contributes to injuries and illnesses. All of these contribute to higher health care costs and can lower productivity, job satisfaction, and retention.[69] Stress is also the most frequently cited reason employees give for why they would leave a company.[70]

HR professionals are well aware of the negative effects of workplace stress on employees' health and job performance.[71] In one study, 48 percent of employers said stress caused by working long hours affects business performance, and 29 percent said stress caused by widespread use of technology—such as cell phones and personal digital assistants—negatively affects business outcomes. Armed with this awareness, many employers have developed stress management programs to teach employees how to minimize the negative effects of job-related stress.[72] A typical program might include instruction in relaxation techniques, coping skills, listening skills, methods of dealing with difficult people, time management, and assertiveness.

All of these techniques are designed to break the pattern of tension that accompanies stressful situations and to help participants achieve greater control of their lives. Organizational techniques, such as clarifying the employee's work role, redesigning and enriching jobs, correcting physical factors in the environment, and effectively handling interpersonal factors should not be overlooked in the process of teaching employees how to handle stress. Stress management counselors recommend several ways to resolve job-related stress as described in Figure 12.8.

FIGURE 12.8   Tips for Reducing Job-Related Stress

- Build rewarding relationships with your coworkers.
- Talk openly with managers or employees about your job or personal concerns.
- Prepare for the future by keeping abreast of likely changes in your job's demands.
- Do not greatly exceed your skills and abilities.
- Set realistic deadlines; negotiate reasonable deadlines with managers.
- Act now on problems or concerns of importance.
- Designate dedicated work periods during which time interruptions are avoided.
- When feeling stressed, find time for detachment or relaxation.
- Do not let trivial items take on importance; handle them quickly or assign them to others.
- Take short breaks from your work area as a change of pace.

Depression

Emotional problems and personal crises become organizational problems when they affect people's behavior at work and interfere with their job performance.[73] The most prevalent problems among employees are personal crises involving marital, family, financial, or legal matters.[74] Most personal crises are resolved in a reasonable period of time. Unfortunately, when a personal crisis lingers, it can lead to depression. Depression is a decrease in functional activity accompanied by persistent symptoms of low spirits, gloominess, and sadness. The National Institute of Mental Health estimates that nearly 17 million Americans, or as much as 10 percent of the adult population, experience depression each year. A recent study by Harvard University School of Public Health and the World Health Organization found that by 2020, depression will be second only to heart disease as a cause of medical and physical disability.[75]

Fortunately, with available treatment, 70 percent of depressed individuals will significantly improve, usually within a matter of weeks. Managers are in a good position to identify the signs of depression on the job.[76] They include decreased energy on the part of an employee, concentration and memory problems, guilt feelings, irritability, and chronic aches and pains that do not respond to treatment. Managers and supervisors who suspect an employee is depressed are encouraged to express their concerns to the person, actively listen to him or her, and—should the depression persist—suggest professional help.[77] Under no circumstances should managers attempt to play amateur psychologist and try to diagnose an employee's condition.[78] Mood disorders such as depression are complex in nature and do not lend themselves to quick diagnoses. Furthermore, in reviewing such cases, the organization should pay particular attention to workplace safety factors because there is general agreement that emotional disturbances are primary or secondary factors in a large portion of industrial accidents and incidents of violence.

depression

A negative emotional state marked by feelings of low spirits, gloominess, sadness, and loss of pleasure in ordinary activities

Alcoholism

Nearly 6 million working Americans bring their alcohol problems to the workplace.[79] It has been estimated that business and industry lose more than $20 billion each year because of alcoholism. It is a disease that affects both the young and old, is prevalent across the sexes, and affects workers in every occupational category—blue-collar and white-collar.[80]

Alcoholism follows a rather predictable course. It typically begins with social drinking getting out of control. As the disease progresses, the alcoholic loses control over how much to drink and eventually cannot keep from drinking, even at inappropriate times. The person uses denial to avoid facing the problems created by the abuse of alcohol and often blames others for these problems.

The first step in helping the alcoholic is to awaken the person to the reality of his or her situation. A supervisor should carefully document the evidence of the person's declining performance on the job and then confront the employee with unequivocal proof to that effect. The employee should be assured that help will be made available without penalty. Because the evaluations are made solely in terms of poor on-the-job performance, a supervisor can avoid any mention of alcoholism and allow such employees to seek aid as they would for any other problem.

Employers must remember that alcoholism is classified as a disability under the Americans with Disabilities Act (ADA—see Chapter 3). Alcoholism is regarded as a disease, similar to a mental impairment. Therefore, a person disabled by alcoholism is entitled to the same protection from job discrimination as any other person with a disability. However, under the ADA, employers can discipline or discharge employees when job performance is so badly affected by alcohol usage that the employee is unable to perform the job.[81]

Drug Abuse

Like alcohol abuse, the abuse of illegal drugs by employees costs businesses billions annually in terms of safety risks, theft, reduced productivity, absenteeism, and accidents. A wide range of employers, including federal contractors and private and public transportation firms, are subject to regulations aimed at eliminating the use of illegal drugs on the job. The federal antidrug initiatives include the following:

1. The Drug-Free Workplace Act of 1988, which requires federal contractors and recipients of federal grants to take specific steps to ensure a drug-free work environment. One of the main provisions of the act is the preparation and distribution of an antidrug policy statement, a sample of which is shown in Highlights in HRM 6.

2. Department of Defense (DOD) contract rules, which specify that employers entering into contracts with the DOD must agree to a clause certifying their intention to maintain a drug-free workplace.

3. Department of Transportation (DOT) regulations, which require that employees whose jobs include safety- or security-related duties be tested for illegal drug use under DOT rules.

To help employers benefit from being drug-free and to further its mission to help companies maintain safe, healthy, and productive workplaces, the U.S. Department of Labor created the Working Partners for an Alcohol and Drug-Free Workplace. This goal of the agency is to raise awareness about the impact of substance abuse in the workplace and provide employers with substance abuse prevention information. Additionally, the Department's Drug-Free Workplace Advisor provides information to employers about how to establish and maintain an alcohol- and drug-free environment.[82]

The ADA considers an individual with a serious, life-affecting drug problem to be disabled, provided the person is enrolled in a drug treatment program and not currently using drugs. The person's employer therefore must make reasonable accommodations for his or her disability. Reasonable accommodations might include time off from work or a modified work schedule to obtain treatment. As we noted earlier, federal regulations require employers to test their workers for drug use under certain specified conditions.[83] The issues related to drug testing under state and local laws are discussed in Chapter 13 in the context of employee rights.

The abuse of legal drugs can also pose a problem for employees.[84] In fact, unlike marijuana, cocaine, and other illegal drugs, according to Quest Diagnostics, a blood-testing company, both employees' prescribed use and misuse of opiates such as Hydrocodone and Oxycodone have been rising sharply. Employees who abuse legal drugs—those prescribed by physicians—often do not realize they have become addicted or how their behavior has changed as a result of their addiction. Also, managers should be aware that some employees may be taking legal sedatives or stimulants as part of their medical treatment and that their behavior at work may be affected by their use of these drugs.

HIGHLIGHTS IN **HRM**
6 Substance Abuse Policy Statement for the "Red Lions"

The policy for the Marine Heavy Helicopter Squadron 363, or "Red Lions" reads: Substance abuse degrades the effective performance of Marines and Sailors, is a detriment to our combat readiness, and is contrary to our Core Values and, therefore, will not be tolerated. Additionally, substance abuse destroys the health of our Marines and Sailors, their careers, and eventually their families. As Red Lions, we are professionals and are responsible for our actions and will be held accountable. Those who tolerate substance abuse in others have let me and the squadron down as well. If you test positive for illegal drug use you will be charged under the UCMJ and processed for separation from the Corps.

Red Lions will not engage in, or tolerate in others, the possession, use, trafficking, or distribution of illegal drugs or drug paraphernalia—zero tolerance. Substance abuse is not just illegal drugs. Any drug not used for its intended purpose or used in excess constitutes substance abuse. Any substances used for the intent of getting high are included in substance abuse. We work daily in a hazardous environment. Drug and alcohol abuse reduces our ability to think clearly, assess risks, and react properly. This puts everyone in danger, which is why it is intolerable.

We will take care of our fellow Red Lions through prevention and timely identification. Anyone classified as having a drug or alcohol incident will be referred to the Substance Abuse Control Officer, screened, counseled, and, if needed, sent to the Substance Abuse Counseling Center for a medical evaluation. If diagnosed as drug or alcohol dependent, they will be assigned to the appropriate treatment program.

We must ensure that every member of HMH-363 is committed to eradicating substance abuse from our squadron. Leaders at all levels shall use available resources to eliminate substance abuse. We will take preemptive action through engaged leadership, training, counseling, and constant vigilance. Failure to do so unnecessarily exposes us to potential loss of life, damage to valuable equipment, degraded readiness, and the inability to complete our mission.

Summary

LEARNING OUTCOME 1 The Occupational Safety and Health Act was designed to assure, so far as possible, safe and healthful working conditions for every working person. In general, the act extends to all employers and employees. The Occupational Safety and Health Administration (OSHA) sets health and safety standards, ensures employers and employees comply with them, and provides safety and health consultation and training where needed. Both employers and employees have certain responsibilities and rights under OSHA. Employers not only are required to provide a hazard-free work environment, but also must keep employees informed about OSHA requirements and provide them with protective equipment when necessary and ensure they wear it. Under the "right to know" regulations, employers are required to keep employees informed of hazardous substances and instruct them in avoiding the dangers presented. Employees, in turn, are required to comply with OSHA standards, to report hazardous conditions, and to follow all employer safety and health regulations.

LEARNING OUTCOME 2 To provide safe working conditions for their employees, employers typically establish a formal safety program in liaison with their HR departments. The program may have many facets, including providing safety knowledge and motivating employees to use it, making employees aware of the need for safety, and rewarding them for safe behavior. Incentives such as praise, public recognition, and awards are used to involve employees in the safety program. Employers also engage their workers by asking them to join safety committees, help develop safety procedures, observe the safety practices of their coworkers, and investigate any accidents. The maintenance of required records from accident investigations provides a basis for information that can be used to create a safer work environment.

LEARNING OUTCOME 3 Job conditions that are dangerous to the health of employees are now receiving much greater attention than in the past. There is special concern for toxic chemicals that proliferate at a rapid rate and may lurk in the body for years without outward symptoms. Health hazards other than those found in manufacturing operations—such as video display terminals and cumulative trauma disorders—present special problems many firms are addressing with ergonomic solutions. Secondhand smoke and bloodborne pathogens are two other health hazards that have received greater attention in recent years.

LEARNING OUTCOME 4 Along with providing safer and healthier work environments, many employers establish programs that encourage employees to improve their health habits. Wellness programs that emphasize exercise, nutrition, weight control, and avoidance of harmful substances serve employees at all organizational levels. Alternative medicine approaches such as relaxation techniques and hypnosis, chiropractic care, acupuncture, homeopathy, herbal therapy, special diets, massage, and so forth are also used to help employees with a variety of health problems.

LEARNING OUTCOME 5 An important dimension to health and safety is stress that comes from physical activity and mental or emotional activity. Many sources of stress are job related. Employers can develop stress management programs to help employees learn techniques for coping with stress. In addition, organizations need to redesign and enrich jobs, clarify the employee's work role, correct physical factors in the environment, and take any other actions that will help reduce stress on the job. Unchecked, stress can lead to depression, alcoholism, and drug abuse, which if severe enough, can be regarded as disabilities under the Americans with Disabilities Act. Managers need to be aware of the signs of these diseases and be prepared to help employees via EAPs or counseling and by making reasonable accommodations for the employees' treatment.

Key Terms

burnout
cumulative trauma disorders
depression
distress
emergency action plan

eustress
fitness-for-duty evaluation
Material Safety Data Sheets
    (MSDSs)
recordable case

right-to-know laws
stress

Discussion Questions

LEARNING OUTCOME 1 When OSHA was enacted in 1970, it was heralded as the most important new source of protection for the U.S. worker in the second half of the twentieth century. From the information in this chapter, what is your opinion about the effectiveness or the ineffectiveness of the act? Should it be expanded, or it should businesses have more freedom to determine safety standards for their workers?

LEARNING OUTCOME 2 What steps should management take to increase the motivation of their employees to operate safely?

LEARNING OUTCOME 3 An unhealthy work environment can lower productivity, contribute to low morale, and increase medical and workers' compensation costs. Working individually or in teams, list specific ways managers can:
a. Reduce cumulative trauma injuries
b. Limit employees' exposure to chemicals
c. Address employee fears caused by bloodborne pathogens

LEARNING OUTCOME 4 To live a healthier life, medical professionals say we need to identify those things we currently do that either impair or contribute to our health. Prepare a list of those activities you do that are beneficial or harmful to your overall health. Discuss with others a way to develop a lifetime program for a healthy lifestyle.

LEARNING OUTCOME 5 Identify the sources of stress in an organization.
a. In what ways do they affect the individual employee? The organization?
b. What can managers and supervisors do to make the workplace less stressful?

HRM EXPERIENCE

Job stress and its negative effect on both employees and the organization are a growing concern for managers and supervisors. As the text discusses, employee distress costs employers staggering amounts of money in lost productivity, absenteeism, turnover, increased workers' compensation claims, and health care costs. The cost of distress on the personal lives of employees is immeasurable.

Stress management programs typically focus on three things to reduce workplace stress: (1) They identify factors in jobs that create stress, (2) they discuss specific techniques and managerial practices that help elevate workplace stress, and (3) they help individuals identify personal characteristics that serve to increase or decrease stress for them.

Assignment

1. Working in groups of four to six individuals, identify any personal experiences you or people you know have had with workplace stress. Explain exactly what conditions or incidents caused the stress. Suggest ways to reduce or eliminate these stressful conditions.

2. Stress management often begins by having individuals identify their skills and abilities and jobs that will help them succeed. Assessing our preferences and skills can help us understand why some tasks or roles are more stressful than others. Identify work-related stress by answering these questions:
   * What skills do I have that enjoy and am currently using in my job or would like to use in a job?
   * What skills do I enjoy that am I currently not using in any work-related capacity?
   * What specific things about my job or jobs that I have do I really like?
   * What are things about my job that I dislike?
   * Based on my personal skills and abilities, what would my perfect job be? What degree of stress might I experience? Does it depend entirely on my preferences, skills, or other factors?

On the Job: Video Cases

Employee Health and Safety at BuyCostumes.com

The COO of BuyCostomes.com discusses worker protection regarding the health, safety, and security of employees. The need for policies on safe equipment usage and the training and certification of employees is covered. Security issues are mentioned in the use of limited building access and video cameras in the parking lot. Health issues are addressed by noting the training of employees in CPR and the placement of medical kits in the workplace. The voice-over mentions other issues such as emergency planning, drugs, smoking, and wellness programs.

What to Watch for and Ask Yourself

■ What are the security issues that most concern to the company, What natural or manmade disasters would BuyCostumes.com be subject to for which it should be prepared? Note that BuyCostumes.com is located in New Berlin, Wisconsin, a suburb of Milwaukee.

- If BuyCostumes.com were concerned about whether forklift operators were impaired by drugs or alcohol, what could it do to prevent accidents due to impairment? If a qualified individual who had formerly been addicted to illegal drugs applied for a job as a forklift operator, would this count against him in hiring?

- Considering the intense workplace at BuyCostumes.com during the two months before Halloween, what would be the largest concern for the mental and emotional health of employees? How could the firm could the firm deal with this concern?

Case Study 1

Rambo Goes Violent

The facts of the case are straightforward. A shop floor dispute at an automobile parts manufacturing plant in Hamilton, Iowa, ended with one worker killing another. At about 2:00 p.m. on August 12, 2011, police responded to a report of a fight that erupted between two employees. When members of the Hamilton Police Department's Violent Crime Unit arrived, they found Mark Lomas seriously injured. Lomas, thirty, died three hours later at Good Samaritan Memorial Hospital. The other employee, Thomas Waycross, was charged with second-degree murder.

During the investigation of the incident, employees noted that Lomas and Waycross often "bickered" when working together. One employee remarked that Waycross liked to "act tough." Another employee claimed that Waycross had a "Rambo-type" personality. It was widely known that management had told both employees to "learn to get along" or quit.

When asked about the incident, police spokesperson Kathy Calder remarked, "Employers must be vigilant when monitoring for signs of potential workplace violence." Nancy Lomas, Mark's wife, has filed a negligence lawsuit against the company.

Questions

1. What are some violence indicators an employee might display?
2. What are some actions management can take to help prevent workplace violence?
3. How can employees protect themselves against workplace violence?

Source: Adapted from a case known to the authors. All names and locations are fictitious.

Case Study 2

Too Much Fatigue and Stress? You Decide

Job fatigue and stress are significant problems faced by employees and their managers. Unfortunately, when a case of depression arises as a result, trying to resolve the problem may be difficult—sometimes leading to conflict—as this case illustrates.

Donald Knolls was an air traffic control supervisor for International Gateway Airport (IGA), an airport serving a major metropolitan area. In 2011, Donald began to experience depression-related problems due largely to severe stress and fatigue on the job. A few months later, he requested and was granted a disability leave for treatment of his illness. After eight months, his personal physician, an expert in depression treatment and a licensed consulting psychologist, agreed that he was sufficiently improved to return to his former position.

IGA then sent Donald to the physician it had used when Donald first requested his disability leave. After an extensive evaluation, the doctor concluded that Donald, while he had made considerable strides in overcoming his depression, should not be immediately returned to his former supervisory position because the conditions of the job had not changed and Donald was apt to find the stress too great. Instead, he recommended that Donald be returned to a nonsupervisory position on a six-month trial basis, with the case to be reviewed at the end of that time. IGA followed the advice of its doctor and did not return Donald to a supervisory position. Donald, angered by management's decision, filed a grievance through IGA's alternative dispute resolution procedure, a procedure that could end in binding arbitration.

During several meetings between Donald and management, the employer maintained that it had the right to rely on the medical opinion of "a fair and impartial" doctor who had determined that Donald should not be returned to the position that was the cause of his original stress-related emotional problems. Additionally, management pointed out to Donald that IGA's disability leave provision states that it "may require appropriate medical documentation if it believes an employee is not fit to return to his or her former position."

Donald responded, through an attorney he hired to represent his position, that the disability leave provisions were clear but, nevertheless, biased against an employee because they completely disregarded the opinion of his physician and psychologist. According to Donald, "Why bother to get expert medical opinions if they are dismissed?" He further noted, "I have never felt better. I'm really ready to get back to my job." Finally, Donald's lawyer contended that Donald was the victim of discrimination based on his former state of depression: "What happened to Donald would not have happened if his illness had been a more conventional physical injury."

Questions

1. When conflicting medical opinions are presented, should the advice of a medical expert count more heavily than the opinion of a general physician? Explain your answer.
2. Is the charge of discrimination presented by Donald's lawyer relevant to this case? Explain your answer.
3. If you were presented with this case, what decision would you reach? Explain.

Source: Adapted from a case known to one of the authors. All names are fictitious.

ANSWERS TO HIGHLIGHTS IN HRM 1

1. True

2. True

3. True

4. d. 80

5. False

6. Unsafe acts (85 percent of all accidents)

7. The company position on safety and health

   The identity of the safety coordinator
   Rules and regulations

Hazard communication program elements
Safety programs in place
Employee and employer responsibilities
Safety communication in the workplace

8. True

9. False

10. False (eight hours)

Notes and References

1. Adrian Gostick, "Delivering Timely Safety Recognition," *Occupational Health and Safety* 73, no. 9 (September 2004): 94.

2. Compiled from Bureau of Labor statistics and Occupational Safety and Health Administration statistics.

3. P.L. 91-596, 91st Congress, S. 2193, December 29, 1970.

4. U.S. Department of Labor, Occupational Safety and Health Administration, *All about OSHA*, rev. ed. (Washington, DC: U.S. Government Printing Office, 2006), 4.

5. OSHA publishes many pamphlets pertaining to various aspects of the act, such as employee workplace rights and voluntary compliance programs. All OSHA publications can be downloaded at no cost from the agency website at http://www.osha.gov; you may also call (800) 321-OSHA or fax a request to (202) 693–2498.

6. *All about OSHA*, 14.

7. Ibid., 21.

8. Ibid., 22.

9. Ibid., 25.

10. Ibid., 27.

11. For a comprehensive list of compliance requirements of OSHA standards or regulations, refer to Title 29 of the Code of Federal Regulations at www.osha.gov or call (800) 321-OSHA.

12. *All about OSHA*, 31.

13. "C. Reiss Coal Co. Earns VPP Merit Status," *Professional Safety* 52, no. 1 (January 2007): 45.

14. *All about OSHA*, 13.

15. Ibid., 5.

16. Fred S. Steingold, *The Employer's Legal Handbook*, 9th ed. (Berkeley, CA: Nolo Press, 2009): 727.

17. Katherine Torres, "Draft Paper Criticizes OSHA's Approach to Safety," *Occupational Hazards* 69, no. 2 (February 2007): 8.

18. Jerry Laws, "75th Anniversary Issue: OSHA's Way Forward," *Occupational Health and Safety* 76, no. 1 (January 2007): 42.

19. Katherine Torres, "Congress Turns Up Heat on OSHA," *Occupational Hazards* 69, no. 4 (April 2007): 8.

20. Robert Pater, "Becoming a Safety Culture Kumu," *Occupational Health and Safety* 76, no. 2 (February 2007): 22.

21. Robert Pater, "Energizing Safety: Launching Performance and Culture," *Occupational Health and Safety* 76, no. 1 (January 2007): 24.

22. Jessica Marquez, "Creating a Culture of Safety," *Workforce Management* 86, no. 8 (April 23, 2007): 1.

23. David L. Goetsch, "Checking Your Culture," *Occupational Health and Safety* 76, no. 10 (October 2007): 22

24. Joe Tavenner, "Become a Safety Leader," *Occupational Hazards* 69, no. 12 (December 2007): 42.

25. Linda J. Sherrard, "Keys to Effective Programs," *Occupational Health and Safety* 76, no. 11 (November 2007): 60.

26. Donald R. Groover, "Attributes of an Injury-Free Culture, Part 4: Employee Engagement," *Occupational Health and Safety* 76, no. 11 (November 2007): 20.

27. Drue Townsend, "Increase Safety Awareness with Signs," *Occupational Health and Safety* 76, no. 12 (December 2007): 18.

28. Linda M. Tapp, "Better Safety Training with Fun and Games," *Professional Safety* 52, no. 2 (February 2007): 52.

29. http://ww.osha.gov; click on e-Tools.

30. Laura Walter, "Distributing Safety at W. W. Grainger Inc.," *Occupational Hazards* 69, no. 11 (November 2007): 42.

31. Donald R. Groover, "Attributes of an Injury-Free Culture: Ownership," *Occupational Health and Safety* 76, no. 8 (August 2008): 24.

32. M. Franz Schneider, "Driving Continuous Improvement in Plant Safety," *Occupational Hazards* 69, no. 8 (August 2007): 36.

33. Michelle M. Smith, "7 Steps to Safety Incentive Success," *Occupational Health and Safety* 76, no. 9 (September 2007): 52.

34. Brian Galonek, "No Waste of Effort," *Occupational Health and Safety* 77, no. 1 (January 2008): 45.

35. OSHA considers an injury or illness to be work-related if an event or exposure in the work environment either caused or contributed to the resulting condition or significantly aggravated a preexisting injury or illness. Work-relatedness is presumed for injuries and illnesses resulting from events or exposure occurring in the work environment. OSHA defines the work environment as "the establishment and other locations where one or more employees are working or are present as a condition of their employment. The work environment includes not only physical locations, but also the equipment or materials used by the employee during the course of his or her work."

36. For complete information on the recording and reporting of illnesses and injuries, see OSHA Publication 3169, *Recordkeeping*, particularly Sections 1904.5 (determination of work-relatedness) and 1904.7 (general recording criteria). See also the OSHA website at http://www.osha.gov.

37. If employers have a "privacy concern case," they may not enter the employee's name on the OSHA 300 log. Instead, they should enter "privacy case" in the space normally used for the employee's name. This will protect the privacy of the injured or ill employee when another employee, a former employee, or an authorized employee representative is provided access to the OSHA 300 log. Privacy cases must be recorded on a separate confidential list. Employers must consider the following injuries or illnesses privacy concern cases: (i) an injury or illness to an intimate body part of the reproductive system; (ii) an injury or illness resulting from a sexual assault; (iii) mental illnesses; (iv) HIV infection, hepatitis, or tuberculosis; (v) needlestick injuries and cuts from sharp objects that are contaminated with another person's blood or other potentially infectious material; and (vi) other illnesses, if the employee independently and voluntarily requests that his or her name not be entered on the log.

38. Randolph P. Schmid, "Odd Work Schedules Pose Health Risk," ABC News (April 16, 2011), http://abcnews.go.com.

39. L.M. Sixel, "Working: Beyond Exhausted, but Still on the Job," *Houston Chronicle* (May 5, 2011), http://www.chron.com.

40. Julie Ferguson, "Distracted Driving and Employer's Policies," *HR Web Café* (November 1, 2009), http://www.hrwebcafe.com.

41. Teresa Long, "Are Your Employees Dangerously 'Intexicated'?" *Workforce Management* (October 2009), http://www.workforce.com.

42. "Sofitel Maids Allowed to Wear Trousers," *Daily Mail* (May 26, 2011), http://www.dailymail.co.uk.

43. Diane Bandow, "The Rise of Workplace Incivilities: Has It Happened to You?" *The Business Review* 7, no. 1 (Summer 2007): 212.

44. Catherine Aldrich, "The Devil Inside: The Legal Liabilities of Background Screening," *Risk Management* 54, no. 2 (February 2007): 10.

45. Laura Walker, "Facing the Unthinkable: Fatality Prevention in the Workplace," *Occupational Hazards* 70, no. 1 (January 2008): 32. See also Jean Thilmany, "In Case of Emergency," *HR Magazine* 52, no. 11 (November 2007): 79; Lynn Lieber, "Workplace Violence—What Can Employers Do to Prevent It?" *Employees Relations Today* 34, no. 3 (Fall 2007): 91.

46. Marcia K. Korow, "How Reflective Is Our Policy?" *Nursing Management* 39, no. 1 (January 2008): 37; see also Scott R. Gane, "Avoiding Violent Outcomes," *Security Management* 51, no. 6 (June 2007): 140.

47. Sonya F. Premeaux and Denise Breaux, "Crisis Management of Human Resources: Lessons from Hurricanes Katrina and Rita," *Human Resources Planning* (September 2007), http://www.entrepreneur.com.

48. Rita Katz, "Web of Terror," *Forbes* 179, no. 10 (May 7, 2007): 184.

49. Sonya F. Premeaux & Denise Breaux, "Crisis Management of Human Resources: Lessons from Hurricanes Katrina and Rita," *Human Resources Planning* (September 2007), http://www.entrepreneur.com.

50. Nicola Guy and Keith Guy, "In Traumatic Times," *Occupational Health* 59, no. 8 (August 2007): 23.

51. Sonya F. Premeaux & Denise Breaux, "Crisis Management of Human Resources: Lessons from Hurricanes Katrina and Rita," *Human Resources Planning* (September 2007), http://www.entrepreneur.com.

52. John P. Baeseman and Douglas Newhand, "The Ergonomically Correct Workplace," *Document Processing Technology* 15, no. 7 (December 2007): 20.

53. Robert A. Wemer, "Evaluation of Work-Related Carpal Tunnel Syndrome," *Journal of Occupational Rehabilitation* 16, no. 2 (June 2006): 201; see also Fred Gerr, Carolyne P. Monteilh, and Michele Marcus, "Keyboard Use and Musculoskeletal Outcomes among Computer Users," *Journal of Occupational Rehabilitation* 16, no. 3 (September 2006): 259.

54. Michael S. Zedalis and Keitha Kessler, "Frequently Asked Questions: Ergonomics and Hand Protection," *Occupational Health and Safety* 76, no. 4 (April 2007): 64.

55. Reid Goldsborough, "Keeping Your Eyes Healthy in Front of a Computer Screen," *TECH Directions* 66, no. 10 (May 2007): 12.

56. The Supreme Court decision in *International Union v. Johnson Controls* may be found in 59 U.S. Law Week 4029.

57. Judy Ashley, "Building a Culture of Wellness the Discovery Way," *Workspan* (July 2007): 43.

58. Craig Halls and John Rhodes, "Employee Wellness and Beyond," *Occupational Health and Safety* 73, no. 9 (September 2004): 46. See also Julie L. Gerberding and James S. Marks, "Making America Fit and Trim—Steps Big and Small," *American Journal of Public Health* 94, no. 9 (September 2004): 1478.

59. Wellness Resources: Association for Worksite Health Promotion, 60 Revere Dr., Suite 500, Northbrook, IL 60062, (847) 637-9200; National Wellness Institute, 1045 Clark St. Suite 210, P.O. Box 827, Stevens Point, WI 54481-0828, (715) 342-2969.

60. Paula Cates, interview by author, Denver, Colorado, February 18, 2008.

61. Dale Kaplan and Park Dietz, "Use Employee Assistance to Manage Risk," *Occupational Health and Safety* 76, no. 7 (July 2007): 82.

62. Roberto Ceniceros, "Firms Weigh Impact of Obesity on Comp," *Workforce Management* (April 2009), http://www.workforce.com.

63. Josh Cable, "Shedding Pounds Good for Bottom Line," *Occupational Hazards* 69, no. 10 (October 2007): 18.

64. Jeremy Smerd, "Young and Unhealthy: Urgent Care Required," *Workforce Management* 86, no. 15 (September 10, 2007): 36.

65. "Obesity Programs Are Latest Wellness Focus," *HR Focus* 84, no. 7 (July 2007): 12.

66. Kerry Sulkowicz, "Stressed for Success," *Business Week* (May 21, 2007): 18.

67. "Many Workers Are Burning Out, and Here's Why," *HR Focus* 83, no. 7 (July 2006): 9.

68. "Beware the Dangers of Workaholism," *HR Focus* 85, no. 1 (January 2008): 9.

69. http://www.watsonsyatt.com/research/reports.asp.

70. Jenna Goudreau, Gail Edmondson, and Michelle Conlin, "Dispatches from the War on Stress: Business Begins to Recon with the Enormous Costs of Workplace Angst," *Business Week* (August 6, 2007): 74; see also Michael R. Frone, "Are Work Stressors Related to Employee Substance Use? The Importance of Temporal Context Assessments of Alcohol and Illicit Drug Use," *Journal of Applied Psychology* 93, no. 1 (January 2008): 199.

71. "Will Stress Be Your Next Wellness Target?" *HR Focus* 85, no. 1 (January 2008): 12.

72. Carole Spiers, "Providing Stress Counseling to Quest Internationals Employees," *Strategic HR Review* 5, no. 5 (July/August 2006): 10.

73. Dale Kaplan and Park Dietz, "Use Employee Assistance to Manage Risk," *Occupational Health and Safety* 76, no. 7 (July 2007): 82.

74. Gary M. Stem, "Not Tonight, Dear," *The Conference Room Review* 44, no. 2 (March/April 2007): 38.

75. Marianne Szegedy-Maszak, "Reason to be Happy," *U.S. News and World Report* (April 10, 2006): 41.

76. "Treating Depression Improves Productivity," *Industrial Engineer* 40, no. 1 (January 2008): 11.

77. "Depression Outreach Can Boost Productivity," *HR Focus* 84, no. 12 (December 2007): 12.

78. Rebecca R. Hastings, "Focus on Behavior, Not Psychiatric Conditions," *HR Magazine* 51, no. 11 (November 2006): 26.

79. Pearl Jacobs and Linda Scaain, "**Alcohol Abuse in the Workplace: Developing a Workable Plan of Action.**" *Research in Business & Economics Journal* (March 2010): 1.

80. Mindy Chapman, "Drugs and Alcohol Workplace Trends," *Occupational Health and Safety* 76, no. 8 (August 2007): 32.

81. *The Employer's Legal Handbook*, see section on preventing discrimination.

82. Information regarding the U.S. Department of Labors efforts to create a drug-free workplace can be found at http://www.dol.gov.

83. Kathy Gurchiek, "Employer Testing Credited for Lower Drug-Use Rates," *HR Magazine* 52, no. 6 (June 2007): 36.

84. Tracy S. Hunter, "Pharmacist Role in Prescription Drug Misuse, Abuse, and Addiction," *Drug Topics* 150, no. 18 (September 18, 2006): 42.

13

Employee Rights and Discipline

After studying this chapter, you should be able to

LEARNING OUTCOME 1 Explain the concepts of employee rights and employer responsibilities.

LEARNING OUTCOME 2 Explain the concepts of employment-at-will, wrongful discharge, implied contract, and constructive discharge.

LEARNING OUTCOME 3 Identify and explain what the privacy rights of employees are.

LEARNING OUTCOME 4 Discuss the meaning of discipline and why managers cannot ignore disciplinary problems.

LEARNING OUTCOME 5 Explain how to establish disciplinary policies and investigate disciplinary problems.

LEARNING OUTCOME 6 Differentiate between the two approaches to disciplinary action.

LEARNING OUTCOME 7 Identify the different types of alternative dispute resolution methods.

LEARNING OUTCOME 8 Discuss the role of ethics in the management of human resources.

In this chapter, we discuss the rights of employees, the privacy they can expect in the workplace, and employee discipline. According to Robert J. Deeny, an employment attorney, employee rights and workplace privacy continue to be the "hottest and expanding employment law topics into the twenty-first century."[1] Drug testing; the privacy of employees when they use the Internet, visit social networking sites, and send out Twitter messages; and camera surveillance in the workplace are among the topics routinely being debated today. Other employee-rights-related topics making their way into the debate are the use of radio frequency identification (RFID), global positioning systems, biometric technology, and company-provided cell phones to track and locate employees.

Without a doubt, the advance of technology and the tools it offers is blurring the lines between the personal freedom and privacy rights of workers and their employers to monitor and control their activities.[2] But despite the confusion, organizations and managers still need to have an idea of where the lines lay so they do not inadvertently cross them. This is where HR managers play a crucial role. To be effective they must stay abreast of current laws, agency regulations, and court rulings, establish written employment policies based on this information, and educate the staff members in their organizations about them. This is not that difficult, but it takes dedication. It also sets good HR managers apart from the pack.

Disciplining and discharging employees is another area in which HR managers need to help develop clear policies for their organizations. In one discharge case, General Electric was ordered to pay Hemant K. Mody, a long-time engineer, $11.1 million, including $10 million for punitive damages. The jury concluded that the discharge was improper since Mody had been fired in retaliation for complaining about bias.[3] Because disciplinary actions can be challenged and possibly reversed through government agencies or the courts, also included in this chapter is a discussion of alternative dispute resolution techniques as a way to settle differences between employees and their employers. Finally, because ethics is an important element of organizational justice, the chapter concludes with a discussion of organizational ethics in employee relations.

Employee Rights and Privacy

employee rights

Guarantees of fair treatment that become rights when they are granted to employees by the courts, legislatures, or employers

Employee rights can be defined as the guarantees of fair treatment that workers expect in return for their services to an employer. These expectations become rights when they are granted to employees by the courts, legislatures, or employers. Over the course of the last 50 or so years, various antidiscrimination laws, wage and hour statutes, and safety and health legislation have secured basic employee rights and brought numerous job improvements to the workers in the United States. Included among those rights are the rights of employees to protest unfair disciplinary actions, to question genetic testing, to have access to their personal files, to challenge employer searches and monitoring, and to be largely free from employer discipline for off-duty conduct.[4]

The evolution of employee rights is a natural result of the evolution of societal, business, and employee interests.[5] We have already explained that workplace-privacy issues have received a great deal of attention lately. For example, employees may feel they have an expectation of privacy regarding their personal phone calls made from work phones, their e-mail messages sent from computers in the workplace, or freedom from employers' random searches of their personal belongings. However, as one legal commentator notes, "When employers clearly state that there is no expectation of privacy, it's hard to argue that a reasonable person could have such an expectation." Legal scholars recognize that the protection of employee privacy rights extends only so far; federal and state courts generally view the privacy rights of employees as minimal.

For example, consider the issue of camera surveillance. Generally it is legal to install cameras in the workplace (except for installations in bathrooms and locker rooms), as long as employees are informed about them. However, after pornography was discovered on one of its computers, a California children's home for abused children installed hidden surveillance cameras in an office shared by two employees. The person who had accessed the pornography was never caught. However, the two employees who shared the office later discovered the camera and were upset they were being monitored. They claimed their privacy rights had been violated, but the Supreme Court of California ruled against them, saying that their employer had a legitimate business reason for conducting the surveillance.[6]

Employee Rights vs. Employer Responsibilities

LEARNING OUTCOME 1

Balanced against employee rights is the employer's responsibility to provide a safe workplace for employees while guaranteeing safe, quality goods and services to consumers.[7] An employee who uses drugs may exercise his or her privacy right and refuse to submit to a drug test. But should that employee produce a faulty product as a result of drug impairment, the employer can be held liable for any harm caused by that product. Employers must therefore exercise *reasonable care* in the hiring, training, and assignment of employees to jobs.[8]

Are the rights you have as a citizen of the United States the same as the rights you have as an employee? Why or why not?

It is here that employee rights and employer responsibilities often come into conflict. When employers fail to honor the rights of employees, it can result in costly lawsuits, damage the organization's reputation, and hurt employee morale. But the failure to protect the safety and welfare of employees or consumer interests can invite litigation from both groups. In one case, the retailer Dillard's was held accountable for the "hostile propensities" of one of its sales clerks toward an African American customer. The jury found that an employer can be held liable for the discriminatory conduct of its salesperson.[9]

Negligent Hiring

In Chapter 6 we discussed negligent hiring. In law, **negligence** is the failure to use a reasonable amount of care when such failure results in injury to another person. A general responsibility exists for employers to exercise *reasonable care* in preventing employees from intentionally harming other employees during the course of their work.[10]

negligence

The failure to provide reasonable care when such failure results in injury to consumers or other employees

Unfortunately, when one employee commits a violent act against another employee or an employee willfully defames another employee through e-mail messages communicated at work, the employer may face a negligent-hiring lawsuit claiming that the employer should have used more reasonable care in the hiring of its employees.[11] A negligent-hiring lawsuit can seem like a "Catch-22" for an employer. How is it possible for an employer to predict with certainty the future behavior of an individual employee? Nonetheless, negligent-hiring lawsuits have forced managers to take extra care in the employment and management of their workforces. In the remainder of this section, we will discuss various rights employees have come to expect from their employers.

Job Protection Rights

It is not surprising that employees should regard their jobs as a right that should not be taken away without "just cause" (a good reason) for doing so. Without the opportunity to hold a job, the well-being of a person suffers greatly. However, although employees might believe they have a right to their jobs, there are no laws in the United States guaranteeing them as much, as you will see shortly.

Nonetheless, workers have certain expectations about the employment relationships they have with their employers.[12] This expectation is referred to as the **psychological contract**. It consists of an employer and an employee's beliefs about the mutual obligations they have towards one another.[13] For example, in exchange for their talents, energies, and technical skills, workers expect employers to provide fair compensation, steady work, job training, and promotions. Employees also expect to be treated with dignity and their firms to adhere to sound business practices.[14] Although the psychological contract is not a legal mandate, it has led to the development of certain legal principles about the security of one's job, which we will discuss next.

Employment-at-Will

The employment relationship has traditionally followed the common-law doctrine of employment-at-will. An **employment-at-will relationship** is created when an employee agrees to work for an employer for an unspecified period of time. Because the duration of the employment is indefinite, it can, in general, be terminated at the whim of either party. The employee has a right to sever the employment relationship at any time for a better job opportunity or for other personal reasons. Employers, likewise, are free to terminate the employment relationship at any time—and without notice—for any reason, no reason, or even a bad reason. In essence, employees are said to work "at the will" of the employer.[15] In 1908 the Supreme Court upheld the employment-at-will doctrine in *Adair v. United States*, and this principle continues to be the basic rule dominating the private-sector employment relationship.[16]

Employees are often surprised when they learn about the employment-at-will doctrine. To make them aware of it, most employers are careful to point out, in their written policies, in handbooks, and on job applications that their relationship with their employees is an at-will relationship. Does the employment-at-will doctrine give managers and supervisors the unrestricted right of termination? No.[17] First, as we have emphasized throughout this text, federal and state laws, court decisions, and administrative rulings restrict termination decisions. For example, as you learned in Chapter 3, people cannot be fired because of certain characteristics such as their race, gender, and so forth. Second, in unionized organizations, union collective bargaining agreements limit automatic discharges. These agreements specify the kinds of infractions that can lead to termination.

Not all employers operate on the at-will principle, however. Some have written policies that require good cause to terminate an employee. In any case, despite the at-will doctrine, in today's litigious environment, most employers are very cautious about terminating employees. Barry Roseman, employment attorney, notes, "Employers

---

psychological contract

Expectations of a fair exchange of employment obligations between an employee and employer

---

LEARNING OUTCOME 2

Think about the jobs you may have held or hold now. Were you (or are you) employed "at will"? How would you know?

---

employment-at-will principle

The right of an employer to fire an employee without giving a reason and the right of an employee to quit when he or she chooses

increasingly need to operate under the premise that they have to 'prove' that an employee's conduct or action warrants termination, if they hope to prevail in court."

Wrongful Discharge

Approximately two million workers are discharged each year. A substantial number of these employees sue their former employers for wrongful discharge. A wrongful discharge is one that is illegal. Wrongful discharge suits challenge an employer's right under the employment-at-will concept to unilaterally terminate employees.[18] Various state courts now recognize the following three important exceptions to the employment-at-will doctrine:

wrongful discharge
A discharge, or termination, of an employee that is illegal

1. *Violation of public policy.* This exception occurs when an employee is terminated for refusing to commit a crime; for reporting criminal activity to government authorities; for disclosing illegal, unethical, or unsafe practices of the employer; or for exercising employment rights. See Figure 13.1 for examples of public policy violations.

2. *Implied contract. This exception* occurs when employees are discharged despite the employer's promise (expressed or implied) of job security or contrary to established termination procedures. An employer's oral or written statements may constitute a contractual obligation if they are communicated to employees and employees rely on them as *conditions of employment.*[19]

3. *Implied covenant.* This exception occurs when an employer has acted with a lack of good faith and fair dealing. For example, an employer would be doing so if it were to terminate a salesperson simply to avoid having to pay him or her a commission. By inflicting harm without justification, the employer violated the implied covenant between the two parties.

The confusion and conflict between the traditional rights of employers to terminate at will and the rights of employees to be protected from unjust discharge are far from resolved. Therefore, to protect themselves from wrongful discharge terminations and from large jury awards—sometimes exceeding $1 million—HR specialists recommend firms follow the suggestions given in Figure 13.2.[20] Next, let's look at some situations that can result in wrongful discharge suits.

FIGURE 13.1   Discharges That Violate Public Policy

An employer may not terminate an employee for:

- Refusing to commit perjury in court on the employer's behalf
- Cooperating with a government agency in the investigation of a charge or giving testimony
- Refusing to violate a professional code of conduct
- Reporting Occupational Safety and Health Administration (OSHA) infractions
- Refusing to support a law or a political candidate favored by the employer
- Whistle-blowing, or reporting illegal conduct by the employer
- Informing a customer that the employer has stolen property from the customer
- Complying with summons to jury duty

© Cengage Learning 2013

© Cengage Learning 2013

FIGURE 13.2   Tips to Avoid Wrongful Employment Termination Lawsuits

- *Terminate an employee only if there is an articulated reason.* An employer should have clearly articulated, easily understandable reasons for discharging an employee. The reasons should be stated as objectively as possible and should reflect company rules, policies, and practices.

- *Set and follow termination rules and schedules.* Make sure every termination follows a documented set of procedures. Procedures can be from an employee handbook, a supervisory manual, or even an intraoffice memorandum. Before terminating, give employees notices of unsatisfactory performance and improvement opportunities through a system of warnings and suspensions.

- *Document all performance problems.* A lack of documented problems in an employee's personnel record may be used as circumstantial evidence of pretextual discharge if the employee is "suddenly" discharged.

- *Be consistent with employees in similar situations.* Document reasons given for all disciplinary actions, even if they do not lead to termination. Terminated employees may claim that exception-to-the-rule cases are discriminatory. Detailed documentation will help employers explain why these "exceptions" did not warrant termination.

Whistle-blowing

whistle-blowing

Complaints to governmental agencies by employees about their employers' illegal or immoral acts or practices

Employees engage in whistle-blowing when they report an employer's illegal actions, immoral conduct, or illegal practices to governmental agencies charged with upholding the law. A number of federal and state laws protect whistle-blowers from retaliation from their employers. Some provide whistle-blowers with financial incentives to expose wrongdoings.[21] In response to corporate scandals, the Sarbanes-Oxley (SOX) Act was passed in 2002 to protect whistle-blowers employed in publicly traded companies.[22] The law encourages whistle-blowing by motivating publicly held companies to promote a more open culture that is sympathetic to employees who have a "reasonable belief" that a law has been violated. Federal employees are covered by the federal Whistleblower Protection Act (WPA).[23] The Notification and Federal Employee Antidiscrimination and Retaliation Act (No Fear Act), also passed in 2002, requires federal agencies to be more accountable for violations of antidiscrimination and whistle-blower protection laws. The False Claims Act (FCA) and Dodd-Frank Wall Street Reform and Consumer Protection Act protect and financially reward whistle-blowers who expose fraud related to governmental programs and wrongdoing related to consumer financial products or services, respectively. OSHA administers the whistle-blowing provisions in fifteen federal statutes protecting whistle-blowers in such industries as airline, nuclear power, and public transportation.

Not only is whistle-blowing a protected right of employees, these cases result in embarrassment for employers, harassment for employees, and large fines for employers that are found guilty.[24] In one whistle-blowing case, federal prosecutors fined Saint Barnabas Health Care Systems $265 million for inflating hospital charges. The hospital charged Medicare patients more than non-Medicare patients to exploit Medicare reimbursement regulations.[25] In another case, Medical World Communications paid the government $3.7 million to settle charges of mail fraud.

To prevent cases such as these, HR professionals recommend companies implement a whistle-blowing policy that encourages employees to report illegal or immoral conduct internally rather than externally. The policy should provide for the safeguard of employee rights, a complete and unbiased investigation of the incident, a speedy report of findings, and an appeals procedure for employees who are dissatisfied with company findings.[26]

Implied Contract

Although it is estimated that 80 percent of employees in the United States work without benefit of an employment contract, under certain conditions these employees may be granted contractual employment rights. This can occur when an implied promise by the employer suggests some form of job security to the employee. These implied contractual rights can be based on either oral or written statements made during the preemployment process or subsequent to hiring. Often these promises are contained in employee handbooks, HR manuals, or employment applications, or they are made during the selection interview. For example, in *Toussaint v. Blue Cross and Blue Shield of Michigan*, a court found that a provision in an employee handbook constituted a unilateral enforceable contract with employees.[27] Once these explicit or implicit promises of job security have been made, courts have generally prohibited the employer from terminating the employee without first exhausting the conditions of the contract. The following are some examples of how an implied contract may become binding:

■ Telling employees their jobs are secure as long as they perform satisfactorily and are loyal to the organization

■ Stating in the employee handbook that employees will not be terminated without the right of defense or access to an appeal procedure

■ Urging an employee to leave another organization by promising higher wages and benefits, then reneging on those promises after the person has been hired

Employers can lessen their vulnerability to implied contract lawsuits by prudent managerial practices, training, and HR policies. HR experts recommend the following approaches:

1. Training supervisors and managers not to imply contract benefits in conversations with new or present employees.

2. Including in employment offers a statement that an employee may voluntarily terminate his or her employment with proper notice and may be dismissed by the employer at any time and for a justified reason. The language in this statement must be appropriate, clear, and easily understood.

3. Including employment-at-will statements in all employment documents—for example, employee handbooks, employment applications, and letters of employment.[28] (See Highlights in HRM 1.)

4. Having written proof that employees have read and understood the employment-at-will disclaimers provided to them.

Explicit Contracts

Explicit employment contracts are formal written (signed) agreements that grant to employees and employers agreed-upon employment benefits and privileges. The contracts normally state the period of employment, terms and conditions of employment (for example, salary and benefits), and severance provisions. Explicit contracts are popular with executives, senior managers, and people with highly technical or professional skills and abilities. When an employee has an explicit contract, he or she cannot be dismissed at-will.

In today's highly competitive environment, before hiring employees, employers sometimes impose certain restrictions, or provisions, in explicit contracts. The most widely used restrictions are:

- *Nondisclosure of information agreement.* This provision forbids employees from revealing proprietary information outside the company, either during or following their employment. Courts widely enforce these agreements.

- *Intellectual property agreement.* This provision grants to an employer the ownership of an idea, invention or process, or work of authorship developed by the employee during the time of employment. Such an agreement expressly states that the employer retains all rights, titles, and interests in ideas that are subject to patent laws and developed during the employee's period of hire.

- *Noncompete agreement.* This provision prevents ex-employees from either becoming a competitor or working for a competitor for a designated period of time, for example, one or two years.[29] Noncompete agreements are designed to protect confidential information, customer relations, and other valuable assets.[30] However, they are often challenged in courts. Some states, including California, Oklahoma, Montana, and North Dakota, prohibit them. Other states, including Colorado, only allow them for high-level employees such as executives and managers.[31]

- *Nonpiracy agreements.* These agreements prohibit ex-employees from soliciting clients or customers of former employers for a specific period of time *and* from disclosing or making use of confidential employer information. Because these agreements restrict workers and competition to a lesser degree, courts have been more willing to uphold them than noncompete agreements. Today, most legal experts suggest employers use antipiracy agreements rather than noncompete agreements.

The Bratz-vs.-Barbie doll war isn't child's play. What's the fight about? Mattel says the toy's inventor, Carter Bryant, designed the doll when he was working for Mattel, so it should be a Mattel product. Bryant says he invented the toy on his own time, and when Mattel showed no interest in the product, he sold the idea to rival toymaker MGA.

PRNewsFoto/MGA Entertainment

HIGHLIGHTS IN **HRM**
Examples of Employment-at-Will Statements

1

Employment handbooks frequently include an opening statement that employees are employed at will, that is, there are no duration guarantees. They also typically state that no supervisors or managers, except specified individuals (that is, the HR director or company president), have the authority to promise any employment benefit—including salaries, job positions, and the like. All handbooks should include a disclaimer that expressly provides that all employment policies and benefits contained in the handbook are subject to change or removal at the sole and exclusive discretion of the employer.

Two examples of at-will statements are as follows:

I acknowledge that if hired, I will be an at-will employee. I will be subject to dismissal or discipline without notice or cause, at the discretion of the employer. I understand that no representative of the company, other than the president, has authority to change the terms of an at-will employment and that any such change can occur only in a written employment contract.

I understand that my employment is not governed by any written or oral contract and is considered an at-will arrangement. This means that I am free, as is the company, to terminate the employment relationship at any time for any reason, so long as there is no violation of applicable federal or state law. In the event of employment, I understand that my employment is not for any definite period or succession of periods and is considered an at-will arrangement. That means I am free to terminate my employment at any time for any reason, as is the company, so long as there is no violation of applicable federal or state law.

Note of caution: Because at-will employment is governed by state laws, in order for an employer to preserve its at-will status, it must follow the regulations of its jurisdiction. This includes the writing of employment-at-will statements.

Explicit contracts are enforceable in court when either the employee or employer violates any provisions of the agreement.

Constructive Discharge

It is increasingly common for employees to quit or resign from their jobs because the intolerable acts of their employers left them no choice. This situation is referred to as a **constructive discharge.** That is, the employees were "forced" to resign because of intolerable working conditions purposefully placed upon them by the employer.[32] In a leading constructive discharge case, *Young v. Southwestern Savings and Loan Association*, the court noted:

> The general rule is that if the employer deliberately makes an employee's working conditions so intolerable that the employee is forced into involuntary resignation, then the employer has encompassed a constructive discharge and is as liable for any illegal conduct involved therein as if he had formally discharged the aggrieved employee.

The courts, by formulating the constructive discharge doctrine, attempt to prevent employers from accomplishing covertly what they are prohibited by law from achieving

constructive discharge

An employee's voluntary termination of his or her employment because of harsh, unreasonable employment conditions placed on the individual by the employer

overtly. For example, instead of simply terminating an employee, an employer might deliberately impose upon the person working conditions that are so intolerable he or she quits.[33] By getting the employee to quit, the employer avoids having to pay the person unemployment benefits or other compensation such as severance pay. But if an employee can prove a constructive discharge occurred, he or she might be able to remedy this situation. However, to prove a constructive discharge, the employee generally has to show that she gave the employer written notice that the conditions were intolerable and that it did nothing to correct the conditions.

Discharge as a Result of Retaliation

Title VII of the Civil Rights Act, the Age Discrimination in Employment Act, the Americans with Disabilities Act, and other employment laws prohibit employers from retaliating against employees when they exercise their rights under these statutes (see Chapter 3). Employees may believe retaliation occurs when managers transfer them to lower-rated jobs, deny them salary increases or promotions, impose on them unrealistic job assignments, or become belligerent or uncommunicative with them after they file discrimination complaints or receive a favorable settlement.[34] As we explained in Chapter 3, retaliation has become the most frequent EEO complaint. As one attorney put it, many minor complaints raised by employees blow up into costly lawsuits after firms make the mistake of retaliating against these workers.

To prevent retaliation charges, William Kandel, employer defense attorney, encourages employers to implement a separate antiretaliation policy and to train managers and supervisors in acceptable and unacceptable methods to resolve employee complaints.[35] A key component to any antiretaliation policy is to treat employees with dignity and respect. Other suggestions to reduce retaliation discharges include the following:

- Take no adverse employment action against employees when they file complaints. Let them know you take their complaints seriously and are looking into them.

- Keep complaints confidential.

- Be consistent and objective in your treatment of employees. Evaluate employees on how well they perform, not on their personalities.

- Harbor no animosity toward employees when they file discrimination lawsuits. Treat every employee the way you would want to be treated—fairly.

Discharges and the WARN Act

The federal government, several states, and local jurisdictions have passed legislation restricting the unilateral right of employers to close or relocate their facilities. In 1989, Congress passed the Workers' Adjustment Retraining and Notification Act (WARN), which requires organizations with more than 100 employees to give employees and their communities sixty days notice of any closure or layoff affecting fifty or more full-time employees.[36] Notice must be given to collective bargaining representatives, unrepresented employees, the appropriate state dislocated worker agency, and the highest elected local official. Terminated employees must be notified individually in writing. The act allows for several exemptions, including "unforeseeable circumstances" and "faltering businesses."

Privacy Rights

According to Janis Procter-Murphy, employment attorney, "employee privacy is recognized as one of the most significant workplace issues facing companies today."[37] The

LEARNING OUTCOME 3

What are the privacy settings on your Facebook page? Do you think your employer, or prospective employer, should be allowed to look at it?

right of privacy is the freedom from unwarranted government or business intrusion into one's personal affairs. It involves the individual's right to be given personal autonomy and left alone.[38] Not surprisingly, employees strongly defend their right to workplace privacy. Meanwhile, employers defend their right to monitor employees' activities when they directly affect a business, its productivity, workplace safety, and/or morale.[39] So who is right? Employers or employees? Laws and court cases related to workplace privacy generally attempt to balance an employee's legitimate expectation of privacy against the employer's need to supervise and control the efficient operation of the organization. In this section, we will discuss some of the most pressing privacy issues being debated by employees and employers today and how they are being resolved.

Substance Abuse and Drug Testing

As you learned, in the United States companies can legally test workers for drugs. But can they do so under any and all circumstances? The answer is no. Certain restrictions apply. In the private sector, drug testing is largely regulated by individual states. Pro-drug testing states generally permit testing, provided that strict testing procedures are followed. States such as these sometimes offer employers a discount on their workers' compensation insurance premiums if they take certain steps to maintain a drug-free workplace, which may include testing job applicants.[40] By contrast, states with restrictive drug testing laws generally prohibit testing for drugs except in very specific circumstances and for drugs listed in state regulations.[41]

Federal regulations and laws restrict drug testing as well. Recall from Chapter 3 that the EEOC does not allow job applicants to be tested before they are extended offers. The Americans with Disabilities Act protects employees who have been addicted to drugs and are recovering from them. And some drugs that would otherwise be illegal, such as opiates and medical marijuana, are legitimately prescribed for certain conditions.[42]

Safety Sensitive Positions. Drug testing is most prevalent among employees in sensitive positions within the public sector, in organizations doing business with the federal government, and in public and private transportation companies. Since the passage of the Drug-Free Workplace Act of 1988, applicants and employees of federal contractors have become subject to testing for illegal drug use. Barring state and federal laws that restrict or prohibit drug testing, however, private employers generally have a right to require employees to submit to the tests. The exception is unionized workforces. Drug-testing programs for these employees must be negotiated by their unions.

Criticisms of Drug Testing. In Chapter 6, we explained that some recent studies have failed to show that drug testing makes the workplace safer and that alcohol appears to create more problems than drugs.[43] Another criticism of drug tests, including urinalysis and hair tests, is that they do not reveal if a person is currently under the influence of a drug. Illegal substances remain in urine for various periods of time: cocaine for approximately 72 hours, marijuana for three weeks or longer.[44] Therefore, an employee can test positive for a drug days or weeks after using it but not be impaired on the job. Alcohol will not show up in a urinalysis or hair test. For that, a breathalyzer, blood, or saliva test must be used. The question becomes, which test should an employer use?

Organizations also have to ensure that any samples taken from employees are properly handled and that accredited labs are used to test them. The results of the tests must be kept confidential and provided only to those who need to know—for example, supervisors or HR staff members—and not to other coworkers or disinterested managers. Boeing, 3M, United Airlines, and Motorola use an independent medical review officer (MRO) to ensure the integrity of their drug testing programs. MROs are required in certain states for tests mandated by the federal government.

For reasons such as these, companies have become less aggressive about drug testing than they were in decades past when the tests first found their way into the workplace. Today, most companies only test when reasonable suspicion or probable cause exists. According to the Society of Human Resources Management, drug testing is now by far the least popular way for employers to deal with substance abuse. Drug-free workplace policies or employee assistance services are far more common. A drug-free policy should state under what conditions employees may be subject to a drug test, the testing procedures used, and the consequences of a positive report. Figure 13.3 shows an example of a drug-free work policy.

Impairment Testing

impairment testing

Also called fitness-for-duty or performance-based testing, it measures whether an employee is alert enough to work

An alternative to drug testing is to evaluate an employee's suitability for work through impairment testing. Also called fitness-for-duty or performance-based testing, impairment testing measures whether an employee is alert enough to work. One impairment test requires an employee to keep a cursor on track during a video game–like simulation. Another testing technique evaluates an employee's eye movements. The employee looks into a dark viewport and follows a light with his or her eyes. Test results, when compared against baseline data gathered earlier on the employee, mimic those of a sobriety test. One advantage of impairment testing is that it focuses on workplace conduct rather than off-duty behavior. Furthermore, it identifies employees who are impaired because of problems that a drug test cannot spot: fatigue, stress, and alcohol use.

FIGURE 13.3   Recommendations for a Drug-Free Workplace Policy

1. Adopt a written zero tolerance drug-free workplace policy and provide a copy to all employees. A signed copy should be placed in the employee's personnel file.

2. Post "We Are a Drug-Free Workplace" signs where employees will widely observe them.

3. Provide employees with substance abuse prevention educational materials. Arrange substance abuse awareness training for employees and managers.

4. Consider performing preemployment drug testing on all new hires.

5. Advise employees that they are subject to drug testing when "reasonable suspicion" exists.

6. Provide for follow-up testing to ensure that an employee remains drug-free after return from a substance abuse treatment program.

7. Provide for "postaccident" drug testing when justified by property loss or damage, serious injury, or death.

8. Use only federally or state-approved certified labs for analysis.

9. Utilize the services of a medical review officer for all positive drug test results.

10. Maintain strict confidentiality of all test results. Provide information only on a "need-to-know" basis.

11. Apply terms of a written policy strictly, fairly, and equally among employees and managers.

Electronic Surveillance

Why do companies use surveillance and other technology to watch what their employees do? One reason is employee theft, such as the stealing of merchandise, supplies, or equipment, the selling of information such as customer lists and trade secrets, embezzlement, and so on.[45] Monitoring quality control, ensuring the safety of employees, and eliminating the amount of time they spend surfing the Web and doing personal business on company time are other reasons.[46] Next, let us look at some of the most common methods of surveillance, and the employer-employee rights associated with them.

Camera Surveillance

DuPont uses long-distance cameras to watch employees on its loading docks. The Cheesecake Factory, a restaurant chain, uses video surveillance of kitchens, dining rooms, and hostess stations to monitor how workers treat customers and each other. Most high-end hotels have cameras in their facilities to protect both workers and guests. Employers also install cameras in their parking lots and remote workplace areas to help improve safety. Few federal laws protect workers from being watched. As we explained earlier in the chapter, in general, employers can train video cameras on their employees without significant legal concerns as long as they have a legitimate business reason for doing so and inform employees they are doing as much. States, however, set their own regulations.

Employers are not the only ones with cameras, though. You might be surprised to know that employees' cameras have become a new issue firms are dealing with. In just a few seconds, a coworker with a camera phone can take offensive pictures of his or her coworkers in private or embarrassing situations and disseminate them around the world via the Web.[47] A few years ago, Domino's Pizza workers posted a YouTube video of themselves doing vulgar things to customers' pizzas in one of the restaurant's kitchens. The workers were later fired, but Domino's suffered a serious PR disaster that took a toll on its reputation and revenues.

Small cameras and camera phones can also be used to quickly and efficiently conduct industrial espionage and steal a company's patents and trade secrets. As a result, some employers ban the use of these devices in the workplace unless employees are given special permission to use them. Workers in Apple's testing rooms are required to cover up devices with black cloaks when they are working on them so the company can be assured no "rogue" cameras are being used to take pictures of the products.[48]

Phone Conversations and Text Communications

In general, employers have the right to monitor calls and text messages sent from their telecommunications devices, provided they do so for compelling business reasons and employees have been informed that their communications will be monitored. However, a federal law, the Electronic Communications Privacy Act (ECPA), places some limitations on that right.[49] The ECPA restricts employers from intercepting wire, oral, or electronic communications. For example, under the law, if an employee receives a personal call, the employer must hang up as soon as he or she realizes the call is personal. However, if employees are told *not* to make personal calls or send text messages from their business phones, the ECPA no longer applies, and their communications may be monitored.

E-Mail, Internet, and Computer Use

Many employees are unaware that their employers can monitor what they do online and fire or discipline them based on that information.[50] According to a recent report by the American Management Association, more than a quarter of employers have fired workers for misusing e-mail, and about a third have fired workers for misusing the Internet.[51] Until recently employers were allowed to monitor any and all e-mail communications their employees sent from work computers. However, recent court rulings have limited employer's rights somewhat. For example, some courts have ruled that employers can monitor incoming and outgoing data on their *own* e-mail systems, but not e-mail sent via outside e-mail systems such as Yahoo, Google, or AOL's systems. One firm discovered this the hard way after monitoring an employee who was planning to go to work for a competitor. She believed her e-mails sent on her employer's computer, but via a nonwork e-mail system, were private. A New Jersey court agreed with her.[52]

Other privacy issues relate to Internet sites employees are allowed to access. A Gallup poll found that the average employee with Internet access spends more than an hour per day surfing websites that have nothing to do with their jobs. Companies can legally create electronic communication policies like the one in Highlights in HRM 2 that limit employees' Internet use. Blocking employees from accessing sites such as Facebook, eBay, gambling, and pornographic websites has also become a common tactic for firms.

The measures employees need to take to protect their laptops and what to do if they are stolen or should also be part of an electronic policy.[53] If they go missing, a mountain of valuable corporate data can fall into the wrong hands. Likewise, policies surrounding electronic storage devices such as USB drives are also being adopted by organizations. Studies have shown that people own a lot of USB drives and often don't keep good track of them and what they contain. USB drives can also infect a company's computers and servers with viruses.

HIGHLIGHTS IN **HRM**

2 A Sample Electronic Communications Policy

Policy Statement

The use of the firm's automation systems, including computers, fax machines, and all forms of Internet/intranet access, is for company business and for authorized purposes only. Brief and occasional personal use of the electronic mail system or the Internet is acceptable as long as it is not excessive or inappropriate, occurs during personal time (lunch or other breaks), and does not result in expense or harm to the company or otherwise violate this policy.

The use of the company's computers, networks, and Internet access is a privilege granted by management and may be revoked at any time for inappropriate conduct carried out on such systems, including, but not limited to:

- Sending chain letters or participating in any way in the creation or transmission of unsolicited commercial e-mail ("spam") that is unrelated to legitimate company purposes;
- Engaging in private or personal business activities, including excessive use of instant messaging and chat rooms (see below);
- Accessing networks, servers, drives, folders, or files to which the employee has not been granted access or authorization from someone with the right to make such a grant;
- Making unauthorized copies of company files or other company data;

A Sample Electronic Communications Policy (continued)

- Destroying, deleting, erasing, or concealing company files or other company data, or otherwise making such files or data unavailable or inaccessible to the company or to other authorized users of company systems;
- Misrepresenting oneself or the company;
- Engaging in unlawful or malicious activities;
- Deliberately propagating any virus, worm, Trojan horse, trap-door program code, or other code or file designed to disrupt, disable, impair, or otherwise harm either the company's networks or systems or those of any other individual or entity;
- Using abusive, profane, threatening, racist, sexist, or otherwise objectionable language in either public or private messages;
- Sending, receiving, or accessing pornographic materials;
- Becoming involved in partisan politics;
- Causing congestion, disruption, disablement, alteration, or impairment of company networks or systems;
- Using recreational games

Policy Statement for Internet/Intranet Browser(s)

The Internet is to be used to further the company's mission, to provide effective service of the highest quality to the company's customers and staff, and to support other direct job-related purposes. Supervisors should work with employees to determine the appropriateness of using the Internet for professional activities and career development. The various modes of Internet/Intranet access are company resources and are provided as business tools to employees who may use them for research, professional development, and work-related communications. Limited personal use of Internet resources is a special exception to the general prohibition against the personal use of computer equipment and software. Employees are individually liable for any and all damages incurred as a result of violating company security policy, copyright, and licensing agreements.

Personal Electronic Equipment

The company prohibits the use or possession in the workplace of any type of camera phone, cell phone camera, digital camera, video camera, or other form of image- or voice-recording device without the express permission of the company and of each person whose image and/or voice is/are recorded. Employees with such devices should leave them at home unless expressly permitted by the company to do otherwise. This provision does not apply to designated company personnel who must use such devices in connection with their positions of employment.

Employees should not bring personal computers or data storage devices (such as floppy disks, CDs/DVDs, external hard drives, flash drives, iPods, or other data storage media) to the workplace or connect them to company electronic systems unless expressly permitted to do so by the company. Any employee bringing a personal computing device, data storage device, or image-recording device onto company premises thereby gives permission to the company to inspect the personal computer, data storage device, or image-recording device at any time with personnel of the company's choosing and to analyze any files, other data, or data storage devices or media that may be within or connectable to the personal computer or image-recording device in question. Employees who do not wish such inspections to be done on their personal computers, data storage devices, or imaging devices should not bring such items to work at all.

Source: Excerpted from "Employee Rights and Identity Theft," *Texas Workforce Commission*, accessed June 2, 2011, http://www.twc.state.tx.us.

Searches

Can employers search employees' work lockers, desks, suitcases, toolboxes, and general work areas without their knowledge? Generally speaking, yes. However, random searches of employees' personal belongings without probable cause should be avoided. Even if a firm has probably cause, legal experts advise that a company should first look at the information it has from available from sources such as security cameras, timecards, and so forth to see whether the search is truly warranted. Body searches should be done only under emergency situations. If conducted, the searches should be made by a security officer and a person of the same sex.

A firm that reserves the right to search employees under warranted circumstances should have a written plan as to the privacy employees can expect.

1. The search policy should be clearly outlined in a firm's employee handbook. The handbook should explain that searches will not be conducted without a compelling reason.

2. When possible, searches should be conducted in private.

3. The employer should attempt to obtain the employee's consent prior to the search.

4. The search should be conducted in a humane and discreet manner to avoid infliction of emotional distress.

5. The penalty for refusing to consent to a search should be specified.

Small Business Application

SBA Offers Small Businesses Handbook Help

Throughout this chapter, we have emphasized how extremely important it is for an employer to have a handbook. The question is, how do you begin to put one together, and what information should it contain? To help entrepreneurs and small business owners avoid having to create handbooks from scratch, the U.S. Small Business Administration has developed a free template downloadable from its site. The basic *Employee Handbook Template* covers the topics listed below and can be customized using a company's specific policies.

Table of Contents

SECTION 1 - INTRODUCTION

1.1 Changes in Policy   1.3 Employment Relationship
1.2 Employment Applications

SECTION 2 - DEFINITIONS OF EMPLOYEE STATUS

"Employees" Defined

SECTION 3 - EMPLOYMENT POLICIES

3.1 Non-Discrimination   3.4 Probationary Period for New Employees
3.2 Non-Disclosure/Confidentiality   3.5 Office Hours
3.3 New Employee Orientation   3.6 Lunch Periods

Small Business Application

SBA Offers Small Businesses Handbook Help (continued)

3.7 Break Periods
3.8 Personnel Files
3.9 Personnel Data Changes
3.10 Inclement Weather/Emergency Closings
3.11 Performance Review and Planning Sessions
3.12 Outside Employment
3.13 Corrective Action
3.14 Employment Termination
3.15 Safety

3.16 Health Related Issues
3.17 Employee Requiring Medical Attention
3.18 Building Security
3.19 Insurance on Personal Effects
3.20 Supplies; Expenditures; Obligating the Company
3.21 Expense Reimbursement
3.22 Parking
3.23 Visitors in the Workplace
3.24 Immigration Law Compliance

SECTION 4 - STANDARDS OF CONDUCT

4.1 Attendance/Punctuality
4.2 Absence Without Notice
4.3 Harassment, including Sexual Harassment
4.4 Telephone Use

4.5 Public Image
4.6 Substance Abuse
4.7 Tobacco Products
4.8 Internet Use

SECTION 5 - WAGE AND SALARY POLICIES

5.1 Wage or Salary Increases
5.2 Timekeeping

5.3 Overtime
5.4 Paydays

SECTION 6 - BENEFITS AND SERVICES

6.1 Insurance
6.2 Cobra Benefits
6.3 Social Security/Medicare
6.4 Simple IRA
6.5 Vacation

6.6 Record Keeping
6.7 Holidays
6.8 Jury Duty/Military Leave
6.9 Educational Assistance
6.10 Training and Professional Development

SECTION 7 - EMPLOYEE COMMUNICATIONS

7.1 Staff Meetings
7.3 Suggestion Box

7.2 Bulletin Boards
7.4 Procedure for Handling Complaints

Access to Personnel Files

Employees entrust their employers with a wealth of personal information for various purposes, including their social security numbers, home addresses, family information, bank account numbers so they can have their paychecks deposited directly, and so forth. Personnel files also generally contain performance appraisal and salary information, background and credit reports, criminal records, and test scores.

HR's Responsibility to Safeguard Personnel Information. A firm's HR department is almost always responsible for maintaining this information and safeguarding its flow to prevent, among other things, identity theft, which as you are probably aware is a growing problem. One computer that is not properly protected or one hard drive that is not adequately erased can provide thieves with access to thousands of employee records—which they can use to apply for credit cards, spend money that is not their own, and wreak havoc on the lives of people whose only crime was trusting their employer.[54] ePrivacy Rights Clearinghouse, a nonprofit privacy advocate organization, estimates that over 50 million people have been put at risk as a result of these breaches. In one of the largest breaches, the personal records for more than a half-million employees of Time Warner were lost.

HR managers need to take the lead when it comes to safeguarding employee information. Not only do workers expect their information to be safeguarded, many states, including New York, California, and Texas, have passed laws requiring employers to protect this information. Under the Privacy Act of 1974, federal agencies must safeguard the personal information of their employees. Figure 13.4 shows the steps employers can take to safeguard employees' personal information. Also, as you learned in Chapter 3, employees' medical and genetic information must be kept confidential in a separate file from any employee's other personnel information.

Employee Access to Personnel Files. Legislation at the federal level (see Figure 13.5) and various states laws permit employees to inspect their own personnel files. How

FIGURE 13.4   Guidelines for Safeguarding Personnel Files

- Define exactly what information is to be kept in employee files. Do not collect information from employees or applicants you do not need or use. Do not collect information that could be viewed as discriminatory or could form the basis for an invasion-of-privacy suit.

- Identify the individuals allowed to view personnel files and when and why they should be allowed to do so. Keep employee records in a locked and secured area that only qualified personnel can access on a need-to-know basis. Maintain a log that shows who accessed what records and when.

- Specify where, when, how, and under what circumstances employees may review or copy their files.

- Do not use social security numbers as employee identifiers. Rather, use random identifiers and keep the social security numbers as narrowly distributed as possible. Do not print social security numbers on people's paychecks or send documents to employees via mail or e-mail that contain their social security numbers. The exception are IRS documents mailed at year-end for tax purposes.

- Use encryption software that translates personnel data into a code that can only be accessed using a key or password.

- Do not give out information about employees over the phone. The person might claim they are a prospective employer or banker looking to help process a loan for an employee but in reality could be a debt collector, stalker, or person engaging in identity theft. Instead tell the person to send you a written authorization form signed by the employee that allows you to disclose the information. When you receive the form, verify it with the employee.

- Audit employment records on a regular basis to remove irrelevant, outdated, or inaccurate information.

- Use up-to-date digital and/or hardware-based methods, thoroughly wipe all data from the hard drive and removable magnetic media of any obsolete computers discarded or sold by the company, and physically destroy any data CDs or DVDs containing company and employee information.

- Shred and securely dispose of any paper records containing sensitive company and employee information.

Source: Adapted from "Employee Rights and Identity Theft," *Texas Workforce Commission*, accessed June 2, 2011, http://www.twc.state.tx.us.

much access is allowed varies from state to state.[55] The states that grant employees the privilege to see their personnel files generally provide:

- The right to know of the existence of one's personnel file

- The right to inspect one's own personnel file

- The right to correct inaccurate data in the file

Typically, if a state law allows employees to examine their files, employers can insist that someone from HR, or a supervisor, be present to ensure that nothing is taken, added, or changed. Even in the absence of specific legislation, most employers give their employees access to their personnel files. Employment professionals recommend that organizations develop a policy on employee files that includes, as a minimum, the points noted in Figure 13.5.

Off-Duty Employee Conduct

Consider the following case. On Monday morning the owner of ABC Corporation reads in the newspaper that a company employee has been charged with robbery and assault on a local convenience store owner. The employee has been released pending trial. A phone call to the employee's supervisor reveals that the employee has reported to work. What should the owner do?

A number of states have passed laws that prohibit employers from disciplining or firing employees for activities they pursue offsite on their own time as long as they are legal.[56] However, even when the activities are illegal, court rulings have suggested that the conduct may not, in some circumstances, be a lawful justification for employee discipline. Organizations that want to discipline employees for off-duty misconduct must establish a clear relationship between the misconduct and its negative effect on other employees or the organization.[57] This might be established, for example, in

FIGURE 13.5   Right-to-Privacy Laws

LAW	EFFECT
Electronic Communications Privacy Act (1986)	Prohibits the interception, recording, or disclosure of wire, electronic, and aural communications through any electronic, mechanical, or other device. An interception takes place when an employer monitors a telephone call while it is occurring. Permits employer monitoring for legitimate business reasons.
Privacy Act (1974)	Applies to federal agencies and to organizations supplying goods or services to the federal government; gives individuals the right to examine references regarding employment decisions; allows employees to review their personnel records for accuracy. Employers who willfully violate the act are subject to civil suits.
Family Education Rights and Privacy Act—The Buckley Amendment (1974)	Prohibits educational institutions from supplying information about students without prior consent. Students have the right to inspect their educational records.
Fair Credit Reporting Act (1970)	Permits job applicants and employees to know of the existence and context of any credit files maintained on them. Employees have the right to know of the existence and nature of an investigative consumer report compiled by the employer.

cases in which off-duty criminal misconduct (such as child molestation) creates a disruptive impact on the workplace. Another example might be when the public nature of the employee's job (such as police or fire department personnel) creates an image problem for the organization. However, before banning specific off-duty behavioral conduct, employers are advised to obtain legal advice.

Off-Duty Employee Speech

Some organizations have social networking and blogging policies that restrict employees from making disparaging remarks about their firms or its supervisors, or otherwise casting their organizations in a bad light. You might wonder how this is legal in light of the free speech rights granted by the First Amendment. What you may not be aware of is that the First Amendment prohibits the government—not private employers—from telling us what we can and cannot say.

However, like off-duty conduct, state laws and courts have tried to balance the rights of employees with those of their employers in this regard. For example, if an employee-blogger lives in a state in which off-duty conduct is protected, he or she might be protected by the law. If his or her comments relate to illegal labor practices and work conditions, the comments would probably be protected under whistle-blower provisions. [58] In addition, the National Labor Relations Act, which allows workers to form unions, protects the rights of employees to talk to one another about their working conditions. In a landmark case, the National Labor Relations Board filed a complaint against an ambulance company for firing a Connecticut woman who posted on her Facebook page a negative remark about her supervisor. The company later settled the case and agreed to revise its policies so they do not restrict employees from discussing their employment outside of work.[59]

As you can tell from this discussion, employers who are thinking about disciplining or firing an employee for off-the-job speech should seek legal advice before doing so. Meanwhile, employees need to realize that what they say online can put their employers in an awkward situation to which they are going to feel compelled to respond. Moreover, online posts that are racist, sexist, demean or harass one's coworkers, and reveal confidential company information are not likely to be legally protected. They can also be career enders for employees.

Workplace Romances

Workplace romances create a dilemma for organizations. Acceptable behavior in a consensual relationship between employees can become harassing behavior if one party to the relationship no longer welcomes the conduct, and it may result in violence should a scorned lover seek violent revenge at the work site. Of particular concern is an employer's liability if a coworker, supervisor-subordinate, or other power-differentiated romance goes sour and leads to charges of sexual harassment.[60] A supervisor in a romantic relationship with a subordinate becomes immediately vulnerable to a sexual harassment claim, as does his or her employer. Furthermore, workplace romances can lead to employee charges of favoritism against a coworker involved in a supervisor-subordinate romance. These "reverse harassment" claims are based on preferential treatment given an employee engaged in a romantic affair. Workplace romances can also create morale problems when other employees feel unfairly treated; such situations can lead to jealousy, resentment, and hard feelings.[61]

As we mentioned in Chapter 3, although some companies have strict antifraternization policies, such a policy can lead to lawsuits. However, recall that the rights of companies to control the legal, off-duty conduct of their employees are limited. Sexual harassment policies have become the preferred way to deal with the issue. To minimize the negative effects of a romantic relationship between supervisor-subordinate, most attorneys advise HR managers to talk to the two people in an effort to get one of them to agree to move to another department. However, this can be a problem if a firm is a small one and there is no other department to transfer to. One person may have to be asked to resign. As an alternative, some employers have dating parties sign *consensual relationship agreements* stating that they will not let their relationship affect the work environment or sue their employer should the relationship go sour.[62]

Body Art, Grooming, and Attire

Tattoos and body piercing are increasingly popular, particularly among Generation X and Y workers. Employers have the right to establish reasonable standards for grooming, attire, and tattoos and facial piercings, and to require employees to abide by those standards.[63] An at-will employee who does not do so can be let go. However, policies on appearance should reflect the nature of the organization and its industry, the types of safety concerns it faces, and not impinge on an employee's religious rights.[64] For example, after UPS fired a worker of the Rastafarian faith for not cutting his dreadlocks, the company was sued by the EEOC. Dreadlocks and beards are protected religious observance rights under Title VII of the Civil Rights Act.[65]

Lisa Nowak made headlines in 2007. A relationship with a fellow astronaut fizzled, and Nowak was later arrested for attempting to kidnap her former lover's new girlfriend. The girlfriend was able to escape unharmed from Nowak, who was later discovered and arrested. NASA didn't institute a nonfraternization policy following the incident, but it did, beef up its screening policies to help screen out candidates with psychological issues.

Disciplinary Policies and Procedures

When managers are asked to define the word *discipline*, their most frequent response is that discipline means punishment. That definition isn't necessarily wrong. However, in the context of management, discipline does not mean punishment. Rather, discipline is a tool used to correct the practices of employees to help them perform better so they conform to acceptable standards. Many organizations, such as Goodyear Aerospace and Arizona State University, define *discipline* in their policy manuals as training that "corrects, molds, or perfects knowledge, attitudes, behavior, or conduct." To view discipline in any other way—as punishment or as a way of getting even with employees—can only invite problems for management, including possible lawsuits. Figure 13.6 lists the more common disciplinary problems identified by managers.

It goes without saying that disciplinary actions should be taken only for justifiable reasons, and that employees should be treated fairly and consistently. This is important because employees and their coworkers are highly sensitive to disciplinary procedures. They pay close attention to how they are implemented and make judgments

LEARNING OUTCOME 4

Have you ever worked with someone who broke the rules repeatedly but was never disciplined for it? How did it affect your morale and willingness to follow the rules?

discipline

A tool, used to correct and mold the practices of employees to help them perform better so they conform to acceptable standards

FIGURE 13.6 Common Disciplinary Problems

ATTENDANCE PROBLEMS

- Unexcused absence
- Chronic absenteeism
- Unexcused/excessive tardiness
- Leaving without permission

DISHONESTY AND RELATED PROBLEMS

- Theft
- Falsifying employment application
- Willfully damaging organizational property
- Punching another employee's time card
- Falsifying work records

WORK PERFORMANCE PROBLEMS

- Failing to complete work assignments
- Producing substandard products or services
- Failing to meet established production requirements

ON-THE-JOB BEHAVIOR PROBLEMS

- Bullying
- Intoxication at work
- Insubordination
- Horseplay
- Smoking in unauthorized places
- Fighting
- Gambling
- Failing to use safety devices
- Failing to report injuries
- Carelessness
- Sleeping on the job
- using abusive or threatening language with supervisors
- Possessing illegal narcotics or alcohol
- Possessing of firearms or other weapons
- Sexual harassment

© Cengage Learning 2013

about their fairness. Good guidelines will help a firm not only avoid lawsuits but prevent creating a poisonous atmosphere at work that can lead to low morale among employees and high turnover, which, as you have learned, is very costly.

The Result of Inaction

Even when it's justified, managers don't generally enjoy disciplining their employees. However, failing to do so generally aggravates a problem that eventually must be resolved. As Grant Freeland, an HR consultant puts it, "Few things de-motivate an organization faster than tolerating and retaining low performers."[66] Moreover, if and when disciplinary action is taken, the delay will make it more difficult to justify if the employee contests the action. Why wasn't the employee previously disciplined?[67] Why did he or she receive satisfactory performance ratings and perhaps even merit raises? Contradictions such as these will make it more difficult for the employer to make its case.

Figure 13.7 presents a disciplinary model that illustrates the areas where provisions should be established. The model also shows the logical sequence in which disciplinary steps must be carried out to ensure enforceable decisions. A major responsibility of the HR department is to develop and to have top management approve an organization's disciplinary policies and procedures. The HR department is also responsible for ensuring that disciplinary policies, as well as the disciplinary action taken against employees, are consistent with any labor agreements and conform to current laws. However, the primary responsibility for preventing or correcting disciplinary problems rests with an employee's immediate supervisor. This person is best able to observe evidence of unsatisfactory behavior or performance and to discuss the matter with the employee. Should discipline become necessary, the employee's immediate supervisor is the logical person to apply the company's disciplinary procedures and monitor the employee's improvement.

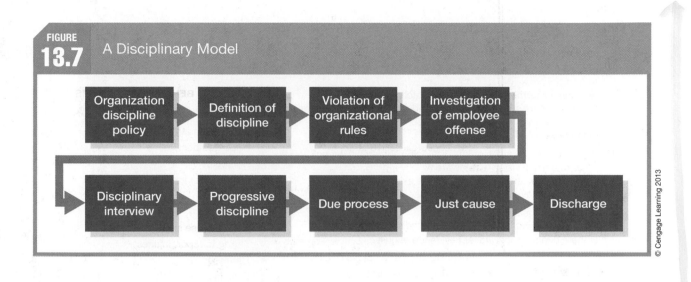

FIGURE 13.7   A Disciplinary Model

Organization discipline policy → Definition of discipline → Violation of organizational rules → Investigation of employee offense → Disciplinary interview → Progressive discipline → Due process → Just cause → Discharge

© Cengage Learning 2013

Setting Organizational Rules

Setting an organization's rules is the foundation for an effective disciplinary system. These rules govern the type of behavior expected of employees. Organizations as diverse as Gerber Products, Walmart, JetBlue, and Staples have written policies explaining the type of conduct required of employees. The following suggestions can help HR managers and their firms when they are considering the rules the organization should adopt and how they should be implemented:

1. The rules must be reasonable and relate to the safe and efficient operation of the organization.

2. The rules as well as the consequences for breaking them should be written down and widely disseminated to all employees. Neglecting to communicate the rules is a major reason disciplinary actions taken against employees are reversed.[68]

3. The rules should be clearly explained. Employees are more likely to accept a rule if they understand the reason behind it.

4. Employees should sign a document stating that they have read and understand the organizational rules.

5. The rules should be reviewed periodically—perhaps annually—especially those rules critical to work success.

Investigating a Disciplinary Problem

It is a rare manager who has a good, intuitive sense of how to investigate employee misconduct. Perhaps because managers are reluctant to discipline employees, too frequently investigations are conducted in a haphazard manner; worse, they overlook one or more investigative concerns.[69] Figure 13.8 lists seven questions to consider when investigating an employee offense. Attending to each question will help ensure a full and fair investigation while providing reliable information free from personal prejudice.

Documenting Misconduct

When a manager fails to record the misconduct of employees, it can undermine a firm's efforts to deal with the behavior. A manager's records of employee misconduct

LEARNING OUTCOME 5

What are the disciplinary policies and procedures at your school? In what ways do you think they might be similar to those implemented in the workplace? In what ways do you think they might be different?

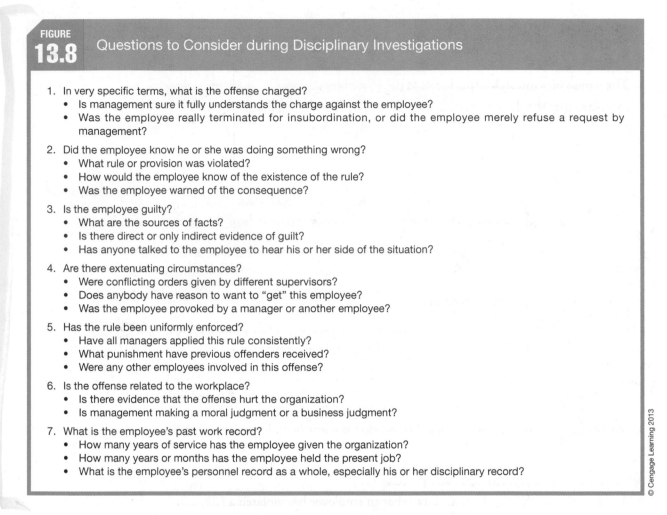

FIGURE 13.8   Questions to Consider during Disciplinary Investigations

1. In very specific terms, what is the offense charged?
   - Is management sure it fully understands the charge against the employee?
   - Was the employee really terminated for insubordination, or did the employee merely refuse a request by management?

2. Did the employee know he or she was doing something wrong?
   - What rule or provision was violated?
   - How would the employee know of the existence of the rule?
   - Was the employee warned of the consequence?

3. Is the employee guilty?
   - What are the sources of facts?
   - Is there direct or only indirect evidence of guilt?
   - Has anyone talked to the employee to hear his or her side of the situation?

4. Are there extenuating circumstances?
   - Were conflicting orders given by different supervisors?
   - Does anybody have reason to want to "get" this employee?
   - Was the employee provoked by a manager or another employee?

5. Has the rule been uniformly enforced?
   - Have all managers applied this rule consistently?
   - What punishment have previous offenders received?
   - Were any other employees involved in this offense?

6. Is the offense related to the workplace?
   - Is there evidence that the offense hurt the organization?
   - Is management making a moral judgment or a business judgment?

7. What is the employee's past work record?
   - How many years of service has the employee given the organization?
   - How many years or months has the employee held the present job?
   - What is the employee's personnel record as a whole, especially his or her disciplinary record?

© Cengage Learning 2013

are considered business documents, and as such they are admissible evidence in arbitration hearings, administrative proceedings, and courts of law. "It's too complicated," "I just didn't take time to do it," "I have more important things to do" are some of the reasons managers give for failing to do so.

The most significant cause of inadequate documentation, however, is that managers often do not know what constitutes good documentation. This is another area where HR managers can help supervisors. The documentation need not be lengthy, but to be complete it should include the following eight items:

1. The date, time, and location of the incident(s)

2. The behavior exhibited by the employee (the problem)

3. The consequences of that action or behavior on the employee's overall work performance and/or the operation of the employee's work unit

4. Prior discussion(s) with the employee about the problem

5. The disciplinary action to be taken and the improvements expected should be documented

6. The consequences of failing to make the improvements by a certain follow-up date

7. The employee's reaction to the supervisor's attempt to change his or her behavior

8. The names of witnesses to the incident (if applicable)

To ensure that the documentation is as accurate as possible, a manager should record the previous eight items immediately after an incident takes place while it is still fresh in his or her mind.

The Investigative Interview

Before any disciplinary action is initiated, an investigative interview should be conducted to make sure the employee is fully aware of the organization's rules and that he or she has not followed them.[70] The interview should concentrate on how the offense violated the performance and behavior standards expected. Most important, the employee must be given a full opportunity to explain his or her side of the issue so that any deficiencies for which the organization may be responsible are revealed. Giving the employee an opportunity to explain his or her side is also necessary because the supervisor's perceptions of the employee's behavior may not be entirely accurate.[71]

Employees do not have the right to have an attorney present during an investigative interview. However, in *NLRB v. Weingarten, Inc.*, the Supreme Court upheld a National Labor Relations Board ruling in favor of a unionized employee's right to have a union representative with him or her during an investigative interview—if the employee reasonably believes that discipline could result from the interview.[72] Within the past twenty-five years, the National Labor Relations Board has flip-flopped four times on whether nonunion employees enjoy *Weingarten* rights. Currently, nonunion employees do not have the right to have a coworker present in an investigatory interview that may lead to disciplinary action.

Approaches to Disciplinary Action

Assuming a thorough investigation shows that an employee has violated a rule, a firm can take one of two approaches to disciplinary action: progressive discipline and positive discipline.

Progressive Discipline

Progressive discipline is the application of corrective measures by increasing degrees. Progressive discipline is designed to motivate an employee to correct his or her misconduct voluntarily. The technique is aimed at nipping the problem in the bud, using only enough corrective action to remedy the shortcoming. Because each situation is unique, a number of factors must be considered in determining how severe a disciplinary action should be. Some of the factors to consider were listed in Figure 13.8.

The typical progressive discipline procedure includes four steps. From an oral warning (or counseling), the action may progress to a written warning, to a suspension without pay, and ultimately to discharge only as a last resort. When progressive discipline is applied properly:

1. Employees always know where they stand regarding offenses.

2. Employees know what improvement is expected of them.

3. Employees understand what will happen next if improvement is not made.

LEARNING OUTCOME 6
Why do you think supervisors often verbally warn employees first before disciplining them? Do they need to? Are there any professions in which verbal warnings are skipped?

progressive discipline
The application of corrective measures by increasing degrees

Positive Discipline

Some HR professionals believe that the intimidating and adversarial nature of progressive discipline keeps it from achieving the intended purpose. For these reasons, organizations such as Saint Alphonsus Regional Medical Center, Ocean Spray, Banner Health, Pennzoil, and Bay Area Rapid Transit have instead used an approach called positive, or nonpunitive, discipline. Positive discipline is based on the concept that employees must assume responsibility for their personal conduct, job performance, and careers.[73]

Positive discipline requires a cooperative environment in which the employee and the supervisor engage in a joint discussion to agree on a way to resolve the performance issue. The employee then bears the sole responsibility of implementing the solution. Rather than reprimands, the supervisor provides the employee with reminders to improve his or her performance. HR managers often describe positive discipline as "nonpunitive discipline that replaces threats and punishment with encouragement."

Positive discipline is implemented in three steps. The first is the conference between the employee and the supervisor to find a solution to the problem. Stephen Meyer, the CEO and director of learning and development at the Rapid Learning Institute, a business training company, suggests supervisors position themselves as "career advocates." They should frame the conversation in terms of the person's career with the company and explain that they want to help the employee change the short-term behavior that could jeopardize his or her career. Supervisors can document this conference, but a written record of this meeting is not placed in the employee's file unless the misconduct occurs again.

If improvement does not occur after the first step, the supervisor holds a second conference with the employee to determine why the solution agreed to in the first conference did not work. At this stage, however, a written reminder is given to the employee. This document states the new or repeated solution to the problem, with an affirmation that the improvement is the responsibility of the employee and a condition of his or her continued employment.

When both conferences fail to produce the desired results, the third step is to give the employee a one-day *decision-making leave* (a paid leave). The purpose of this paid leave is for the employee to decide whether he or she wishes to continue working for the organization. The organization pays for the leave to demonstrate its desire to retain the person. Also, paying for the leave eliminates the negative financial effects and emotions the employee experiences when losing a day's pay. Employees given a decision-making leave are instructed to return the following day with a decision either to make a total commitment to improve their performance or to quit the organization. If a commitment is not made, the employee is dismissed with the assumption that he or she lacked responsibility toward the organization.

Discharging Employees

Because discharging a worker poses serious consequences for the employee—and possibly for the organization—it should be undertaken only after a deliberate and thoughtful review of the situation.[74] If an employee is fired, he or she may file a wrongful discharge suit claiming the termination was "without just or sufficient cause," implying a lack of fair treatment by management.

How does an employer know if it has just cause to terminate an employee? This question is not easily answered, but standards governing discharges do exist in the

---

positive, or nonpunitive, discipline

A system of discipline that focuses on early correction of employee misconduct, with the employee taking total responsibility for correcting the problem

form of rules developed in the field of labor arbitration.[75] These rules consist of a set of guidelines that are applied by arbitrators to determine if a firm had just cause for a termination. These guidelines are normally set forth in the form of questions, provided in Figure 13.9. For example, before discharging an employee, did the manager forewarn the person of possible disciplinary action? A no answer to any of the seven questions in the figure generally means that just cause was not established and that the decision to terminate was arbitrary, capricious, or discriminatory. The significance of these guidelines is that they are being applied not only by arbitrators, but also by judges in wrongful discharge suits. It is critical that managers at all levels understand the just cause guidelines, including their proper application.

Informing the Employee

Regardless of the reasons for a discharge, it should be done with personal consideration for the employee affected. Every effort should be made to ease the trauma a discharge creates.[76] The employee must be informed honestly, yet tactfully, of the exact reasons for the action. Doing so can help the employee face the problem and adjust to the termination in a constructive way.

To gain confidence, a supervisor might want to discuss, and even rehearse, with his or peers and an HR manager the upcoming termination meeting to ensure that all important points are covered and presented in the best way possible. Although managers agree that there is no single right way to conduct the discharge meeting, the following guidelines will help make the discussion more effective:

1. Come to the point within the first two or three minutes, and list in a logical order all reasons for the termination.[77]

2. Be straightforward and firm, yet tactful, and remain resolute in your decision.

3. Make the discussion private, businesslike, and fairly brief.

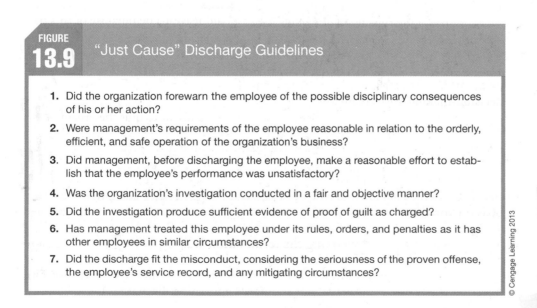

FIGURE 13.9 "Just Cause" Discharge Guidelines

1. Did the organization forewarn the employee of the possible disciplinary consequences of his or her action?

2. Were management's requirements of the employee reasonable in relation to the orderly, efficient, and safe operation of the organization's business?

3. Did management, before discharging the employee, make a reasonable effort to establish that the employee's performance was unsatisfactory?

4. Was the organization's investigation conducted in a fair and objective manner?

5. Did the investigation produce sufficient evidence of proof of guilt as charged?

6. Has management treated this employee under its rules, orders, and penalties as it has other employees in similar circumstances?

7. Did the discharge fit the misconduct, considering the seriousness of the proven offense, the employee's service record, and any mitigating circumstances?

© Cengage Learning 2013

4. Do not mix the good with the bad. Trying to sugarcoat the problem sends a mixed message to the employee.

5. Avoid making accusations against the employee and injecting your personal feelings into the discussion.

6. Avoid bringing up any personality differences between you and the employee.

7. Provide the employee with any severance pay information, and let the person know about the status of his or benefits and coverage.

8. Explain how you will handle employment inquiries from future employers looking to hire the person.[78]

Termination meetings should be held in a neutral location, such as a conference room, to prevent the employee from feeling unfairly treated. The manager should never provoke the employee. Should the employee become belligerent, agitated, or show signs of hostility, the meeting should be stopped immediately and the firm's HR department and security notified.

It is common for managers or security officers to accompany employees back to their work areas to collect their belongings and then escort them off the premises. However, this should be done as discreetly as possible to lessen any embarrassment the employee may experience.

A manager who terminates an employee should keep the details of the termination private and not disparage the person when to talking to other people, including other managers, customers, and the person's former coworkers. Doing so might make a manager feel better, but for the people who have to hear it, it is a morale killer. Even worse, it gives the terminated employee grounds to sue the manager and firm for defamation.

due process

Procedures that constitute fair treatment, such as allowing an employee to tell his or her story about an alleged infraction and defend against it

alternative dispute resolution (ADR)

A term applied to different employee complaint or dispute resolution methods that do not involve going to court

Due Process

Despite the at-will employment doctrine, most people believe that employees should not be disciplined without the protection of due process. HR managers normally define **due process** as the employee's right to be heard—the right of the employee to tell his or her side of the story regarding the alleged infraction of organizational rules. Due process serves to ensure that a full and fair investigation of employee misconduct occurs. Normally, due process is provided employees through the employer's appeals procedure. Employers risk having their terminations overturned— even when they are justified—when employees are denied due process.

Alternative Dispute Resolution Procedures

LEARNING OUTCOME 7

What pros and cons do you think employees who agree to settle their grievances via alternative dispute resolution methods face?

In unionized workplaces, grievance procedures are stated in virtually all labor agreements. In nonunion organizations, however, **alternative dispute resolution (ADR)** methods are often used.[79] Alternative dispute resolution methods address employee discharges and complaints outside of court, which is generally faster and cheaper for both parties. Employers often ask workers to sign ADR agreements when they receive their offer letters or sign their employee handbooks.

Although the right to require employees to sign ADR agreements is supported by court decisions, to be enforceable—they must be fair and equitable to both employees and employers.[80] Employers can't "stack the deck" against employees by imposing rules on employees that clearly favor the employer. As one legal expert has noted, "As much as possible, the agreement should provide employees with the same rights and remedies that they would have enjoyed had their day in court been available to them."[81] Next we will look at some of the different types of alternative dispute resolution methods organizations use.

Step-Review Systems

As Figure 13.10 illustrates, a step-review system is based on a preestablished set of steps—normally four—for the review of an employee's complaint by successively higher levels of management. These procedures are patterned after the union grievance systems we will discuss in Chapter 14. For example, they normally require that the employee's complaint be formalized as a written statement. Managers at each step are required to provide a full response to the complaint within a specified time period, perhaps three to five working days.

An employee is sometimes allowed to bypass meeting with his or her immediate supervisor if the employee fears reprisal from this person. Unlike appeal systems in unionized organizations, however, nonunion appeal procedures ordinarily do not provide for a neutral third party—such as an arbitrator—to serve as the judge of last resort. In most step-review systems, the president, chief executive officer, vice president, or HR director acts as the final authority, and this person's decision is not appealable. Some organizations give employees assistance in preparing their complaint cases. For example, an employee who desires it may be able to get advice and counsel from a designated person in the HR department before discussing the issue with management.

step-review system
A system for reviewing employee complaints and disputes by successively higher levels of management

Peer-Review Systems

A peer-review system, also called a complaint committee, is composed of equal numbers of employee and management representatives. The employees on the committee are normally elected by secret ballot by their coworkers for a rotating term, whereas the managers are assigned, also on a rotating basis. A peer-review system functions as a jury because its members weigh evidence, consider arguments, and, after deliberation, vote independently to render a final decision.

The peer-review system can be used as the sole method for resolving employee complaints, or it can be used in conjunction with a step-review system. For example, if an employee is not satisfied with management's action at step 1 or 2 in the step-review system, the employee can submit the complaint to the peer-review committee

peer-review system
A system for reviewing employee complaints that utilizes a group composed of equal numbers of employee representatives and management appointees. The group weighs evidence, considers arguments, and, after deliberation, votes to render a final decision

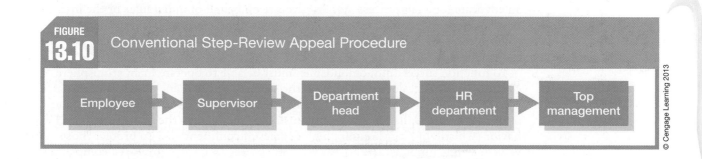

FIGURE 13.10   Conventional Step-Review Appeal Procedure

Employee → Supervisor → Department head → HR department → Top management

© Cengage Learning 2013

for final resolution. Organizations such as Northrop Grumman, Polaroid, Citicorp, and Turner Brothers Trucking consider one of the benefits of the peer-review system to be the sense of justice that it creates among employees.

Open-Door Policy

open-door policy

A policy of settling grievances that identifies various levels of management above the immediate supervisor for employee contact

The idea behind an open-door policy is that to facilitate communication and the free exchange of ideas, every manager's office door should be open to every employee. The policy is also an old standby method for settling employee complaints. In an organization that has such a policy, an employee is allowed to contact various managers above his or her immediate supervisor for various reasons, including grievances; the levels may extend as high as a vice president, president, or chief executive officer. The person who acts as "the court of last resort" is the HR director or a senior staff official.

There are some problems associated with open-door policies, however. One is that some managers do not like to listen honestly to employee complaints. As an employee once told the authors of this text, "My manager has an open-door policy, but the door is only open one inch." Because of this, employees are often reluctant to approach managers with their problems. In addition, an open-door policy generally fails to guarantee consistent decision making because what is fair to one manager may seem unfair to another. Higher-level managers tend to support supervisors for fear of undermining their authority, and as a system of justice, open-door policies may lack credibility with employees. Still, the open-door policy is often successful when it is supported by all levels of management and when management works to maintain a reputation for being fair and open-minded. One way to make an open-door policy work better is to ensure employees with grievances first try to work out their problems with their immediate supervisors before contacting higher-up managers. This way, the chain of command isn't violated, and the supervisor of the employee who aired the grievance does not feel as if he or she was not given a chance to resolve the issue.

Ombudsman System

ombudsman

A designated individual from whom employees may seek counsel for resolution of their complaints

Rockwell, Johnson & Johnson, Herman Miller, Eastman Kodak, and Pace University are just a few organizations that employ ombudsmen. An ombudsman is a designated individual from whom employees may seek counsel for the resolution of their complaints. The ombudsman listens to an employee's complaint and attempts to resolve it by seeking an equitable solution between the employee and the supervisor. This individual works cooperatively with both sides to reach a settlement, often employing a problem-solving approach to the issue. As Gordon Halfacre, the ombudsman for faculty and graduate students at Clemson University, notes, "The ombuds is an advocate for a fair process, not an advocate on behalf of individuals or the institution." Because the ombudsman has no authority to finalize a solution to the problem, compromises are highly possible, and all parties concerned tend to feel satisfied with the outcome.

To function successfully, ombudsmen must be able to operate in an atmosphere of confidentiality that does not threaten the security of the managers or subordinates who are involved in a complaint. For example, complaints of sexual harassment, abuse of power, or issues that deal with circumstances that violate the law or unethical behavior (whistle-blowing) require high degrees of confidentiality to protect those involved. While ombudsmen do not have the power to decide employee complaints, it is recommended that they have access to high levels of management to ensure that employee complaints receive fair treatment.

Mediation

Along with arbitration, mediation is fast becoming a popular way to resolve employee complaints. During mediation, which also discussed in Chapter 14 in conjuction with labor agreements, a neutral person (mediator) helps employees and managers negotiate and reach a voluntary agreement acceptable to both parties. The essence of mediation is compromise. The mediator holds a meeting with the employee and management, listens to the position of each side, gathers facts, and then through discussion, suggestions, and persuasion obtains an agreement that satisfies the needs and requirements of both sides.

A mediator serves primarily as a fact finder and as an open channel of communication between the parties. Unlike arbitrators, mediators have no power or authority to force either side toward an agreement. They must use their communication skills and the power of persuasion to help the parties resolve their differences. A cornerstone of mediation is that the parties maintain control over the settlement outcome.[82]

Mediation is a flexible process that can be shaped to meet the demands of the parties. Also, it can be used to resolve a wide range of employee complaints, including discrimination claims or traditional workplace disputes.[83] Employees like the process because of its informality. According to one authority, "Mediation might be described as a private discussion assisted by an impartial third party."[84] Settlements fashioned through mediation are generally readily acceptable by the parties, thus promoting a favorable working relationship.

mediation

The use of an impartial neutral to reach a compromise decision in employment disputes

mediator

A third party in an employment dispute who meets with one party and then the other in order to suggest compromise solutions or to recommend concessions from each side that will lead to an agreement

Discussion and compromise are cornerstones of employment mediation, which is a highly effective method of resolving disputes.

Blend Images/Alamy

Arbitration

Private employers may require that employees settle their disputes through arbitration.[85] Arbitration, which is fully explained in Chapter 14, works like this: The employee and employer present their cases, or arguments, to an arbiter, who is typically a retired judge. He or she then makes a decision that the parties have agreed to be bound by. Arbitration is used primarily to resolve discrimination suits related to age, gender, sexual harassment, and race.[86] Other workplace issues such as promotions, compensation, discipline, and application of company policies can be arbitrated if an employer's arbitration program allows it.

While arbitration agreements normally mandate that employees arbitrate their discrimination claims and may prevent workers from suing their employers in court, they cannot prohibit employees from filing discrimination charges with the EEOC and other government agencies in an effort to pursue their statutory rights. In *EEOC v. Waffle House Inc.*,[87] the U.S. Supreme Court ruled that even when an employee has signed a mandatory arbitration agreement, if it chooses to, the EEOC can file a suit in its own name and recover monetary damages for the individual. Writing for the court, Justice John Paul Stevens noted, "The EEOC has the authority to pursue victim-specific relief regardless of the forum that the employer and the employee have chosen to resolve their dispute."[88]

Managerial Ethics in Employee Relations

Throughout this textbook, we have emphasized the legal requirements of HRM. Laws, agency rulings, and court decisions affect all aspects of the employment process—recruitment, selection, performance appraisal, safety and health, labor relations, and testing—and how managers must heed these legal constraints to avoid litigation.

However, beyond what is required by the law is the question of organizational ethics and the ethical—or unethical—behavior engaged in by managers. Ethics can be defined as a set of standards of acceptable conduct and moral judgment. Ethics provides cultural guidelines—organizational or societal—that help us decide between proper or improper conduct.[89] How a firm treats its employees largely distinguishes an ethical organization from an unethical one. In an ethical organization, managers are honest in their dealings with employees, and each group has mutual respect for the other. Interestingly, a research study, *Employee Trust and Organizational Loyalty*, sponsored by the Society for Human Resource Management, showed that employees' perceptions of ethical behavior on the part of their managers may be the most important driver of the trust and loyalty their subordinates have for them and the organization as a whole. According to the study, of critical interest to employees is the consistent and credible communication of information about the organization's ethical standards and its values, the organization's mission, and its workplace policies.[90]

As you learned earlier in the book, many organizations have their own codes of ethics that govern how they deal with their employees and the public. These written codes focus attention on an organization's ethical values and provide a basis for its managers to evaluate their plans and actions. HR departments have been given a greater role in communicating an organization's values and standards, monitoring compliance with its code of ethics, and enforcing the standards throughout the

LEARNING OUTCOME 8

Name some companies you believe treat their employees ethically and some that do not. Why do you think the two groups differ in this regard? Does it depend upon the type of industry the company competes in?

ethics

A set of standards of conduct and moral judgments that help to determine right and wrong behavior

organization. Organizations now have ethics committees and ethics ombudsmen to provide training in ethics to employees. The ultimate goal of ethics training is to avoid unethical behavior and adverse publicity; to gain a strategic advantage; and most of all, to treat employees in a fair and equitable manner, recognizing them as productive members of the organization.

Summary

LEARNING OUTCOME 1 Workers have certain expectations about the employment relationship they have with their employers, including the mutual obligations they have to one another. Included among those expectations are a certain degree of privacy and fair and equitable treatment while on the job. Employers, however, have the responsibility to monitor the activities of their workers in order to provide a safe and secure workplace free from harmful employee acts. When the perceived rights of employees differ from the reasonable responsibilities of management, conflict can result.

LEARNING OUTCOME 2 The employment-at-will doctrine gives employees and employers the right to terminate their employment relationship with one another at any time; the implied contract concept is an exception to the employment-at-will doctrine. Under this concept, an employer's oral or written statements may constitute a contractual obligation in which case the at-will doctrine does not apply. Constructive discharge occurs when an employee voluntarily terminates employment but subsequently alleges that he or she was forced to quit because of intolerable working conditions imposed by the employer. Employees may claim they are retaliated against when employers punish them for exercising their rights under law or for receiving favorable EEOC or court awards.

LEARNING OUTCOME 3 Once employed, employees expect certain privacy rights, such as the freedom from unwarranted intrusion into their personal affairs. Laws and court cases related to workplace privacy generally attempt to balance employees' legitimate expectation of privacy against the need of employers to supervise and control the efficient operations of the organizations. Testing for substance abuse and searching and monitoring employees while on the job and off are among the many privacy-rights issues employers and their workers face.

LEARNING OUTCOME 4 In the context of management, discipline does not mean punishment. Rather, discipline is a tool used to correct the practices of employees to help them perform better so they conform to acceptable standards. Even when it is justified, managers do not generally enjoy disciplining their employees. However, failing to do so generally aggravates a problem that eventually must be resolved.

LEARNING OUTCOME 5 A firm's HR professionals, in combination with other managers, should establish disciplinary policies, or rules, that relate to the safe and efficient operation of the organization. The rules should be written down, explained, widely communicated within the organization, and consistently applied. They should also be revised regularly as laws, regulations, and court rulings change. An investigation of an infraction begins with properly documenting it. To determine the severity of the disciplinary measure, managers need to know whether the employee knew of the rule that was violated, any extenuating circumstances that might justify the employee's conduct, the employee's past work record, and various other factors.

LEARNING OUTCOME 6 The two approaches to discipline are progressive discipline and positive discipline. Progressive discipline follows a series of steps based on increasing the degrees of corrective action. Positive discipline, based on reminders, is a cooperative discipline approach in which employees accept responsibility for the desired employee improvement. The corrective action taken should match the severity of the misconduct.

LEARNING OUTCOME 7 Alternative dispute resolution procedures are ways to resolve disputes out of court while ensuring employees receive fair treatment. The most common forms of ADRs are step-review systems, peer-review systems, the open-door system, the ombudsman system, mediation, and arbitration.

LEARNING OUTCOME 8 Ethics in HRM extends beyond the legal requirements of managing employees. Managers engage in ethical behavior when employees are treated in an objective and fair way and when an employee's personal and work-related rights are respected and valued.

Key Terms

alternative dispute resolution (ADR)
constructive discharge
discipline
due process
employee rights
employment-at-will principle

ethics
impairment testing
mediation
negligence
ombudsman
open-door policy
peer-review system

positive, or nonpunitive, discipline
progressive discipline
psychological contract
step-review system
whistle-blowing
wrongful discharge

Discussion Questions

LEARNING OUTCOME 1 Explain three areas in which employee rights and employer responsibilities could result in conflict. How might this conflict arise?

LEARNING OUTCOME 2 Define the employment-at-will doctrine. What are the three major court exceptions to the doctrine?

LEARNING OUTCOME 3 What are the legislative and court restrictions on employer drug testing in both the private and the public sector?

LEARNING OUTCOME 4 If you were asked to develop a policy on discipline, what topics would you cover in the policy?

LEARNING OUTCOME 5 What should be the purpose of an investigative interview, and what approach should be taken in conducting it?

LEARNING OUTCOME 5 Discuss why documentation is so important to the disciplinary process. What constitutes correct documentation?

LEARNING OUTCOME 6 Describe progressive and positive discipline, noting the differences between these two approaches.

LEARNING OUTCOME 7 What do you think would constitute an effective alternative dispute resolution system? What benefits would you expect from such a system? If you were asked to rule on a discharge case, what facts would you analyze in deciding whether to uphold or reverse the employer's action?

LEARNING OUTCOME 8 Working by yourself, or in a team, identify ethical dilemmas that could arise

in the HR areas of selection, performance appraisal, safety and health, privacy rights, and compensation.

On the Job: Video Cases

UNITE HERE Local 1 Chicago

The staff of the UNITE HERE international union and Local 1 Chicago discuss various issues related to employee rights, including drug testing, free speech, and wrongful discharge. The video also discusses the importance of employee handbooks.

What to Watch for and Ask Yourself

- Both the president of the local union and one of the shop stewards in the video talk about the problems with drug testing. From a policy standpoint, what are the conditions when it is most appropriate to test for drugs? Do you think

that preemployment drug testing is appropriate? Why or why not?

- The video starts off with UNITE staff members discussing a case of alleged wrongful discharge when an employer fired or eliminated a department where employees were strong union supporters. Henry Tamarin (the president of UNITE HERE Local 1 Chicago) states in the video: "Under the law, you can get fired for any reason at any time as long as it's not discriminatory and that's very hard to prove." What concept is he referring to?

HRM EXPERIENCE
Learning about Employee Rights

In the constantly changing field of human resources, it is imperative that both HR managers and supervisors be aware of changes that affect the organization and the process of managing employees. Nowhere is this more true than in the growing field of employee rights. As employees demand more job and employment rights regarding drug testing, monitoring, unjust dismissals, off-duty conduct, and genetic testing, employers must be knowledgeable about new laws, court rulings, and the policies of other organizations that influence each area. This knowledge will enable managers to respond to these employee concerns in a positive and proactive manner. The failure to provide employees their rights could lead to costly and embarrassing lawsuits, resulting in diminished employee loyalty or morale. The purpose of this exercise, therefore, is to enable you to familiarize yourself with issues of employee rights.

Assignment

Working individually or in teams, for each of the following employee rights topics, identify and discuss the privacy concerns for both employees and employers. You may wish to review articles in HR journals such as *Labor Law Journal*,

(continued)

Learning about Employee Rights (continued)

HRMagazine, Workforce Management, Employee Relations Law Journal, and *Employee Responsibility and Rights Journal* as you complete this assignment. Answer the questions below pertaining to each of the following topics.

- Employment-at-will and wrongful discharge suits
- Substance abuse and drug testing
- Searches and monitoring
- Employee conduct away from the workplace
- Genetic testing
- E-mail, Internet

1. What is the issue concerned with?
2. Why is this issue of current interest to employees and managers?
3. What rights are employees demanding?
4. What, if any, laws or court cases affect this right?
5. Generally, how are employers responding to this employee right?

Case Study 1

Discharged for Off-Duty Behavior

The following case illustrates the off-duty privacy claim of an employee and management's right to uphold the reputation of the company.

Before his termination on Monday, May 6, 2011, John Hilliard worked as a senior sales representative for Advanced Educational Materials (AEM), a provider of high-quality educational books and supplies to junior and senior high schools. During his twelve years of employment, John was recognized as an outstanding employee with close working relationships with the schools he served. His sales record was excellent. John's discharge resulted from what AEM claimed was a serious breach of its code of conduct for employees.

On Saturday, May 4, 2011, due to a chance meeting between John and his manager, Jean Ellison, John was observed leaving an adult video store carrying what his manager described as pornographic magazines and an X-rated video. The following Monday, Jean discussed the incident with AEM's vice-president for sales and a representative from HR. All agreed that John's off-duty behavior constituted a serious violation of the company's code of conduct for employees, which read, in part, "Employee off-duty behavior in no way should reflect unfavorably upon the company, its employees, or sales of any educational materials." AEM has traditionally held its sales representatives to high moral standards because the company sells extensively to public school administrators and teachers.

At his discharge meeting, John vigorously opposed his firing. While he acknowledged making the purchases, he argued strongly that what he did on his personal time was "no business of the company's" and his behavior in no way reflected unfavorably upon AEM or the sales of its products. Besides, he said, "The purchases were made as jokes for a stag party."

Questions

1. Given the facts of this case, should John have been discharged? Why or why not?
2. Should the sales representatives of AEM be held to a higher standard of personal conduct than sales representatives for other types of organizations? Explain.
3. Should management have considered John's past work record before deciding on discharge? Explain.

Source: This case is based on an actual termination for off-duty misconduct. All names are fictitious.

Case Study 2

You Can't Fire Me! Check Your Policy

Supervisors report that discharging an employee is one of the toughest tasks they perform as managers. Furthermore, termination for absenteeism can be particularly difficult due to the causes of absenteeism and, in some cases, the past work record of the employee. This case illustrates a typical absentee problem faced by management.

Mary Schwartz was employed by Beach Electrical Systems for nine years. For the first six years of her employment, she was considered a model employee. Mary's annual performance reviews were always above average or exceptional, and she was described by her managers as a loyal and dedicated employee. However, things changed rapidly in 2004 when Mary became, as her current manager stated, "an absentee problem."

According to HR department records, in 2008 and 2009 Mary was absent 12 percent and 19 percent of the time, respectively. Her worst year was 2010, when she was absent 27.2 percent of the time. However, unlike other absent employees, Mary was always absent because of genuine and verifiable illnesses or work-related accidents. Mary's supervisor had talked to her periodically about her attendance problem, but she was never given an official warning notice—oral or written—that she would be fired if her attendance record did not improve.

The incident that caused her termination occurred on Thursday, May 20, 2011. On that day her manager notified all department employees (eight in total) that they would need to work overtime on Saturday, May 22, 2011, to complete a critical order for a highly valued and important customer. All employees agreed to work Saturday, except Mary, who cited "personal reasons," which she refused to disclose, for her refusal to work.

On Monday, May 24, 20011, her supervisor, with concurrence from the department manager, terminated her employment for "unsatisfactory attendance." Mary did not dispute the attendance record; however, she filed a grievance through the company's alternative dispute resolution procedure alleging that management did not discharge her according to the organization's published disciplinary policy. She pointed to the section in the policy manual that states, "Employees will be warned for absenteeism before they are terminated." Mary maintained that she was never officially warned as required. Management replied that Mary was well aware of her absentee problem but that warning her would have served no purpose since she was unable to prevent her continued illnesses from occurring. Additionally, her refusal to work overtime on Saturday was a further indication of her lack of concern for her job or the welfare of the company.

Questions

1. What role, if any, should Mary's past work record play in this case? Explain your answer.
2. Does management have a right to know why employees refuse to work overtime? Why or why not.
3. Evaluate the arguments of Mary Schwartz and management in this case.
4. If you were a member of the company's peer-review complaint committee, how would you vote in this case? What facts would cause you to vote this way?

Source: Based on an arbitration case heard by George W. Bohlander. Names have been changed.

Notes and References

1. Robert J. Denny, interview by author, March 6, 2008, Phoenix, Arizona.
2. "How to Get More Control Over 'Virtual' Workplace Devices," *HR Focus* 84, no. 6 (June 2007): 9. See also John D. Canoni, "Location Awareness Technology and Employee Privacy Rights," *Employee Relations Law Journal* 30, no. 1 (Summer 2004): 26.
3. Michael Orey, "Fear of Firing," *Business Week* (April 23, 2007), 52.
4. David J. Walsh, *Employment Law for Human Resource Practice* (Mason, OH: South-Western, 2007): Chapter 17.
5. Jeffery A. Mello, "Introduction: The Evolving Nature of the Employment Relationship: Reconsidering Employee Responsibilities and Rights," *Employee Responsibility and Rights Journal* 15, no. 3 (September 2003): 99.
6. Mike McKee, "California Supreme Court Narrows Workplace Privacy," *Law.com* (August 5, 2009), http://www.law.com.
7. John L. Henshaw, Shannon H. Gaffney, Amy K. Madl, and Dennis J. Paustenbach, "The Employer's Responsibility to Maintain a Safe and Healthful Work Environment: An Historical Review of Societal Expectations and Industrial Practice," *Employee Responsibility and Rights Journal* 19, no. 3 (September 2007): 173.
8. "Background Checks Are on the Rise," *HR Focus* 84, no. 7 (July 2007): 51.

9. Maria Greco Danahar, "Retailer Sued over Clerk's Conduct" *HR Magazine* 52, no. 6 (June 2007): 141.
10. Donna Scimia, "A Common Sense Approach to Reducing Liability in Today's Workplace," *Employee Relations Law Journal* 33, no. 2 (Autumn 2007): 23.
11. Rita Zeidner, "How Deep Can You Probe?" *HR Magazine* 52, no. 10 (October 2007): 57. See also Jena McGregor, "Background Checks That Never End," *Business Week* (March 20, 2006), 40.
12. In some fields, such as academia, after someone has worked for several years there are expectations of continuing employment.
13. Bonnie S. O'Neill, Jonathon R. B. Halbesleben, and John C. Edwards, "Integrating Employment Contracts and Comparisons: What One Can Teach Us about the Other," *Journal of Managerial Issues* 19, no. 2 (Summer 2007): 161.
14. Robert Del Campo, "Psychological Contract Violation: An Individual Difference Perspective," *International Journal of Management* 24, no. 1 (March 2007): 43.
15. Ellen Dannin, "Why At-Will Employment Is Bad for Employers and Just Cause Is Good for Them," *Labor Law Journal* 58, no. 1 (Spring 2007): 5.
16. *Adair v. United States*, 2078 U.S. 161 (1908).

17. "How At-Will Employment Is Changing," *HR Focus* 84, no. 10 (October 2007): 1
18. Patric J. Cihon and James Ottavio Castagnera, *Employment and Labor Law*, 6th ed. (Mason, OH: South-Western, 2008): 3–4.
19. Lawrence Peikes, "Employer Pays for Reneging on a Promise," *HR Magazine* 49, no. 3 (March 2004): 109.
20. Quiang Lin and Brian H. Kleiner, "New Developments Concerning Termination in Violation of Public Policy," *Management Research Review Feature Edition*, no. 4 (2010): 111; Susan H. Roos, "Fired Fendi Manager Bags Over $1 Million," *HR Magazine* 52, no. 6 (June 2007): 141.
21. David C. Lindsay and Sabrina Rockoff, "State Regulations Update: Beyond Sarbanes-Oxley: State Law Protection in the Era of the Whistleblower," *Employment Relations Today* 34, no. 1 (Spring 2007): 69. See also Paul D. Scott, "Whistleblowers Wanted," *Journal of Accountancy* 203, no. 5 (May 2007): 86.
22. 18 U.S.C.S. § 1514A (a) (2002). See D. Bruce Shine, "Pity the Sox Whistleblower: Pity the Sox Lawyer Whistleblower!" *Labor Law Journal* 58, no. 4 (Winter 2007): 228.
23. 21.5 U.S.C.S. § 2302 (2002).
24. Ben Levisohn, "Getting More Workers to Whistle," *Business Week* (January 28, 2008), 18.

25. Mark Taylor, "N. J. System Settles Lawsuit" *Modern Health Care* 36, no. 25 (June 19, 2006): 4.

26. Benisa Berry, "Organizational Culture: A Framework and Strategies for Facilitating Employee Whistleblowing," *Employee Responsibilities and Rights Journal* 16, no. 1 (March 2004): 1.

27. "*Toussaint v. Blue Cross and Blue Shield of Michigan:* Employee Rights and Wrongful Discharge, 408 Mich. 579, 292 N.W.2d 880 (1980)," *Michigan Bar Journal* (March 2009): 15.

28. "Employee Handbooks: Have You Updated Yours Lately?" *HR Focus* 83, no. 7 (July 2006): 5.

29. Lawrence P. Postol, "Drafting Non-compete Agreements for All 50 States," *Employee Relations Law Journal* 33, no. 1 (Summer 2007): 65.

30. Howard J. Rubin and Gregg A. Gilman, "Will Garden Leaves Blossom in the States," *Employee Relations Law Journal* 33, no. 2 (Autumn 2007): 3. See also Brian L. Lemer and Jeffrey K. Geldens, "Ensuring Fair Play: Using Common Law to Protect against Unfair Competition from Former Employees," *Employee Relations Law Journal* 32, no. 3 (Winter 2006): 41.

31. Steven M. Gutierrez, Joseph D. Neguse, and Steven Collis, "The Human Limits of Human Capital: An Overview of Noncompete Agreements and Best Practices for Protecting Trade Secrets from Unlawful Misappropriation," *Employee Relations Law Journal* (Summer 2010): 64.

32. Jonathan A. Segal, "I Quit! Now Pay Me," *HR Magazine* 49, no. 10 (October 2004): 129.

33. Martha Crumpacker, "The U.S. Supreme Court Clarifies Constructive Discharge under Title VII: Responsibilities and Opportunities for Human Resources Practitioners," *Public Personnel Management* 36, no. 1 (Spring 2007): 1.

34. Rebecca M. Archer and Stephen T. Lanctot, "Are Your Hands Tied? A Practical Look at Employee Claims for Retaliation," *Employee Relations Law Journal* 33, no. 1 (Summer 2007): 53.

35. Mary Price Birk, "Walking on Eggshells—Avoiding Retaliation Claims When an Employee Who Files a Discrimination Claim Does Not Leave," *Employee Relations Law Journal* 32, no. 2 (Winter 2006): 10.

36. 29 U.S.C.A. §§ 2101–2109 (2001).

37. Janis Procter-Murphy, employment attorney, interview by author, December 9, 2007.

38. "Balancing HR Systems with Employee Privacy," *HR Focus* 83, no. 11 (November 2006): 11.

39. Diana Cadrain, "Are Your Employee Drug Tests Accurate?" *HR Magazine* 48, no. 1 (January 2003): 41.

40. "If You're Asked to Take a Drug Test," *Nolo,* accessed June 1, 2011, http://www.nolo.com.

41. "New Year, New Scams, New Risks—What to Watch for Now," *Security Director's Report* 11, no. 2 (February 2011): 1.

42. "If You're Asked to Take a Drug Test," *Nolo,* accessed June 1, 2011, http://www.nolo.com.

43. "Constitution Limits Pre-employment Drug Testing by Public Employers," *Venulex Legal Summaries* (2008 Q1): 1; "Drug Testing Is Common and Codified at Many Workplaces," *HRFocus* 83, no. 6 (June 2006): 9; "New Developments Question the Use of Drug Tests in the Workplace," *Safety Director's Report* 4, no. 9 (September 2004): 3–6; Sandy Smith, "What Every Employer Should Know about Drug Testing in the Workplace," *Occupational Hazards* 66, no. 8 (August 2004): 45–48.

44. T. L. Stanly, "Workplace Drug Testing and the Growing Problem of Methampheta-mines," *Supervision* 68, no. 8 (August 2007): 3.

45. William I. Sauser, Jr., "Employee Theft: Who, How, Why, and What Can Be Done," *S.A.M. Advanced Management Journal* 72, no. 3 (Summer 2007): 13.

46. Adrienne Fox, "Caught in the Web," *HR Magazine* 52, no. 12 (December 2007): 35.

47. "Employee Rights and Identity Theft," *Texas Workforce Commission,* accessed June 2, 2011, http://www.twc.state.tx.us.

48. Brad Stone and Ashlee Vance, "Apple's Obsession with Secrecy Grows," *New York Times* (June 22, 2009), http://www.nytimes.com.

49. Electronic Communications Privacy Act, 18 U.S.C. § 2510–2720.

50. Rita Zeidner, "Keeping E-mail in Check," *HR Magazine* 52, no. 6 (June 2007): 70.

51. Mark Szakonyi, "Big Brother at Work," *Portfolio* (February 8, 2010), http://www.portfolio.com.

52. Paul E. Paray, "N.J. Supreme Court Sides with Employee on Email Privacy Case," *Digital Risk Strategies* [blog] (April 5, 2010), http://blog.digitalriskstrategies.com.

53. "Why It's Time to Update Your Privacy Policies," *HR Focus* 84, no. 4 (April 2007): 3.

54. Dan Caterinicchia, "Safeguarding HR Information," *HR Magazine* (November 1, 2005).

55. Diane Cadrain, "Setting the Records Straight," *HR Magazine* 52, no. 6 (June 2007): 82.

56. "Fired for Blogging," accessed June 3, 2011, http://www.nolo.com.

57. Cynthia F. Cohen and Murray E. Cohen, "On-Duty and Off-Duty: Employee Rights to Privacy and Employers Right to Control in the Private Sector," *Employee Responsibilities and Rights Journal* 19, no. 4 (December 2007): 235.

58. "Fired for Blogging," accessed June 3, 2011, http://www.nolo.com.

59. Julianne Pepitone, "Facebook Firing Settled out of Court" *CNNMoney* (February 8, 2011), http://money.cnn.com.

60. Charles A. Pierce, Brandee J. Broberg, Jamie R. McClure, and Herman Aquinis, "Responding to Sexual Harassment Complaints: Effects of a Dissolved Workplace Romance on Decision Making Standards," *Organizational Behavior and Human Decision Processes* 95, no. 1 (September 2004): 83.

61. Judy Greenwald, "Employers Are the Losers in the Dating Game," at http://www.workforce.com/section/09/feature/24/93/98/index. html.

62. Kathryn Tyler, "Sign in the Name of Love," *HR Magazine* 53, no. 2 (February 2008): 41.

63. "How Companies Are Dealing with Workplace Body Art Issues," *HR Focus* 81, no. 4 (April 2004).

64. Carolyn Sayre, "Tattoo Bans," *Time* (November 5, 2007), 55.

65. "UPS Driver Sues over Dreads," *Business Management Daily* (February 5, 2009), http://www.businessmanagementdaily.com.

66. Orey, "Fear of Firing," 54.

67. A more recent workplace problem faced by employers is employee bullying behavior. See Mark Larson, "Stamping out

Workplace Bullies," *Workforce Magazine* at http://www.workforce.com/section/09/feature/25/00/29/index.html, and John Hollon, "Zero Tolerance for Jerks," *Workforce Magazine* at http://www.workforce.com/section/01/feature/24/74/76/index.html.

68. George W. Bohlander and Donna Blancero, "A Study of Reversal Determinants in Discipline and Discharge Arbitration Awards: The Impact of Just Cause Standards, *Labor Studies Journal* 21, no. 3 (Fall 1996): 3–18.

69. "Steps to Take before Recommending Disciplinary Action," *PM Public Management* 86, no. 6 (July 2004): 43.

70. Jathan W. Janove, "Private Eye 101," *HR Magazine* 49, no. 7 (July 2004): 127.

71. Mollica Kelly, "Perceptions of Fairness," *HR Magazine* 49, no. 6 (June 2004): 169.

72. *NLRB v. Weingarten Inc.*, 95 S.Ct. 959 (1975), 402 U.S. 251, 43 L.Ed.2d. 171.

73. Readers interested in the pioneering work on positive discipline should see James R. Redeker, "Discipline, Part 1: Progressive Systems Work Only by Accident," *Personnel* 62, no. 10 (October 1985): 8–12, and James R. Redeker, "Discipline, Part 2: The Nonpunitive Approach Works by Design," *Personnel* 62, no. 11 (November 1985): 7–14.

74. Stephen P. Postalakis, "Avoiding a Sticky Situation: A Guide to Firing an Employee," *Catalyst 2002* (March/April 2007): 22.

75. For an excellent explanation of just cause discharge guidelines, see Frank Elkouri and Edna Asper Elkouri, *How Arbitration Works*, 5th ed. (Washington, DC: Bureau of National Affairs, 1997).

76. Jack and Suzy Welch, 'The Right Way to Say Goodbye," *Business Week* (March 25, 2007), 144.

77. Elizabeth Agnvall, "Case Closed. Now What?" *HR Magazine* 53, no. 2 (February 2008): 69.

78. Nancy Hatch Woodward, "Smoother Separations," *HR Magazine* 52, no. 6 (June 2007): 94.

79. Michael Orey, "The Vanishing Trial: As Court Battles Become More Rare, Some Experts Fear the Effects on the Law," *Business Week* (April 30, 2007), 38.

80. Louise Lamothe, "Avoiding Potholes in Mandatory Arbitration: A Look at Recent California Decisions," *Dispute Resolution Journal* 58, no. 2 (May–June 2003): 18. See also D. Diane Hatch, James T. Hall, Mark T. Kobata, and Marty Denis, "Law Firm's Arbitration Procedures Rules Unfair," *Workforce Management* 86, no. 13 (July 23, 2007): 10.

81. Walsh, *Employment Law for Human Resource Practice*, 19.

82. Ruth D. Raisfeld, "How Mediation Works: A Guide to Effective Use of ADR," *Employee Relations Law Journal* 33, no. 2 (Autumn 2007): 30.

83. Joseph Camarra and James Foster, "Benefits of Mediation," *Risk Management* 54, no. 4 (April 2007): 12.

84. Kathryn Tyler, "Mediating a Better Outcome," *HR Magazine* 52, no. 11 (November 2007): 63.

85. Jennifer J. Froehlich, "The New Company Unions: Mandatory Individual Employment Arbitration Agreements and Section 8 (a) (2) of the National Labor Relations Act," *Labor Law Journal* 58, no. 3 (Fall 2007): 195.

86. Elizabeth F. R. Gingerich, "Enforcing Arbitration Agreements in Discrimination Claims: Judicial Reconsideration," *Employee Relations Law Journal* 33, no. 4 (Spring 2008): 61.

87. *EEOC v. Waffle House Inc.*, 534 U.S. 279 (2002).

88. "EEOC May Sue Even If Arbitration Agreement Exists," *HR Focus* 79, no. 3 (March 2002): 2.

89. Betsy Stevens, "Corporate Ethical Codes: Effective Instruments for Influencing Behavior," *Journal of Business Ethics* 78, no. 4 (April 2008): 601.

90. Jennifer Schramm, "Perception on Ethics," *HR Magazine* 49, no. 11 (November 2004): 176.

AP Photo/Ed Andrieski

After studying this chapter, you should be able to

LEARNING OUTCOME 1 Identify and explain the main federal laws that provide the framework for labor relations.

LEARNING OUTCOME 2 Explain the reasons employees join unions.

LEARNING OUTCOME 3 Describe the process by which unions organize employees and gain recognition as their bargaining agent.

LEARNING OUTCOME 4 Discuss the bargaining process and the bargaining goals and strategies of a union and an employer.

LEARNING OUTCOME 5 Differentiate the forms of bargaining power that a union and an employer may utilize to enforce their bargaining demands.

LEARNING OUTCOME 6 Describe a typical union grievance procedure and explain the basis for arbitration awards.

LEARNING OUTCOME 7 Discuss some of the contemporary challenges to labor organizations.

Have you ever been frustrated with your employer? Well you are not alone. Most everyone, at some point in their lives, will work for someone else. And most everyone will become frustrated with policies, practices, or proclamations made by their employers. Your frustration may stem from a wage level that does not allow you to pay your bills—or textbook costs. It may stem from a manager who will not let you take off for spring break. Or it may stem from your employer's refusal to provide health insurance. Whatever the reason, employee/employer relations are not getting any better.

Americans are less satisfied with their employers than they were at any point in the last twenty years. The trend is strongest among people who have recently entered the job market. According to a study by the American Federation of Labor and Congress of Industrial Organizations (AFL-CIO), employees between the age of eighteen and thirty-four are less satisfied with their work situation than employees of the same age group were ten years ago. Only 31 percent make enough money to pay their bills and put some money aside for savings—22 percent fewer than ten years ago. Thirty-one percent are without health insurance, up from 24 percent ten years ago. Finally, only 47 percent have retirement plans from their employers, down six percent from ten years ago. Moreover, more than half of eighteen- to thirty-four-year-old workers in the United States fall into the low-income bracket, making less than $30,000 per year. These people report that they are the least satisfied with their employers.[1]

But satisfaction with your employer is not just about making enough money to pay the bills. National Football League (NFL) players, who almost entirely fall within the eighteen- to thirty-four-year-old worker age, make an average of $770,000 per year.[2] In 2011, NFL players were embroiled in a labor dispute to increase their salaries. They wanted a larger share of the $9 billion annual revenue generated by the NFL. Owners of NFL teams such as the Pittsburg Steelers and San Francisco 49ers said they needed the money to reinvest into the league. Roger Goodell, the NFL commissioner, said the hesitation on management's part was justified to "make the kinds of investments that grow this game."[3] The players, however, were skeptical of management. They wanted the owners to show them where all the money was being spent. The owners refused. The players turned to their union.

Mention the word *union* and most people will have some opinion, positive or negative, regarding U.S. labor organizations. To some, the word evokes images of labor-management unrest—grievances, strikes, picketing, and boycotts. To others, the word represents industrial democracy, fairness, opportunity, and equal representation.[4] Many think of unions as simply creating an adversarial relationship between employees and managers.

Regardless of attitudes toward them, since the mid-1800s, unions have been an important force shaping organizational practices, legislation, and political thought in the United States. Today unions remain of interest because of their influence on organizational productivity, U.S. competitiveness, the development of labor law, and HR policies and practices. Despite the strong influence of unions, many individuals are unfamiliar with the intricacies of labor relations.

This chapter describes government regulation of labor relations, the labor relations process, reasons why workers join labor organizations, and the structure and leadership of labor unions. Importantly, according to labor law, once the union is certified to negotiate for bargaining unit members, it must represent everyone in the unit equally, regardless of whether employees subsequently join the union or elect to remain nonmembers. Therefore, in the latter sections of the chapter, we discuss the important topics of contract administration, particularly the handling of employee grievances and arbitration. The chapter concludes with a discussion of contemporary challenges to labor organizations.

Unions and other labor organizations can affect significantly the ability of managers to direct and control the various functions of HRM. For example, union seniority provisions in the labor contract may influence who is selected for job promotions or training programs. Pay rates may be determined through union negotiations, or unions may impose restrictions on management's employee appraisal methods. Therefore, it is essential that managers in both the union and nonunion environment understand how unions operate and be thoroughly familiar with the important body of law governing labor relations. Remember, ignorance of labor legislation is no defense when managers and supervisors violate labor law. Before reading further, test your knowledge of labor relations law by answering the questions in Highlights in HRM 1.

HIGHLIGHTS IN **HRM**
Test Your Labor Relations Know-How

1. An auto mechanic applied for a job with an automotive dealership. He was denied employment because of his union membership. Was the employer's action lawful?

    _____ Yes _____ No

2. During a labor organizing drive, supervisors questioned individual employees about their union beliefs. Was this questioning permissible?

    _____ Yes _____ No

3. When members of a union began wearing union buttons at work, management ordered the buttons to be removed. Was management within its rights?

    _____ Yes _____ No

4. While an organizing drive was under way, an employer agreed—as a social gesture—to furnish refreshments at a holiday party. Was the employer acting within the law?

    _____ Yes _____ No

5. A company distributed to other antiunion employers in the area a list of job applicants known to be union supporters. Was the distribution unlawful?

    _____ Yes _____ No

(Continued)

1 Test Your Labor Relations Know-How (continued)

6. During a union organizing drive, the owner of Servo Pipe promised her employees a wage increase if they would vote against the union. Can the owner legally make this promise to her employees?

_____ Yes _____ No

7. Employees have the right to file unfair labor practice charges against their employer even when the organization is nonunion.

_____ Yes _____ No

8. The union wishes to arbitrate a member's grievance, which management has demonstrated is completely groundless. Must management arbitrate the grievance?

_____ Yes _____ No

9. John Green, a maintenance engineer, has a poor work record. Management wishes to terminate his employment. However, Green is a union steward, and he is highly critical of the company. Can management legally discharge this employee?

_____ Yes _____ No

10. During an organizing drive, an office manager expressed strong antiunion beliefs and called union officials "racketeers," "big stinkers," and a "bunch of radicals." He told employees who joined the union that they "ought to have their heads examined." Were the manager's comments legal?

_____ Yes _____ No

Answers are found at the end of this chapter.

 # Government Regulation of Labor Relations

LEARNING OUTCOME 1

What role did the government play in the dispute between NFL owners and players? Which law protects both the NFL owners and players' union?

The development of U.S. labor legislation has its foundation in the social, economic, and political climate of America. Generally, we can say that the growth of the labor movement has paralleled the passage of prolabor legislation and the ability of workers to impose their economic demands on management. Clearly labor laws passed in the 1920s and 1930s favored the growth and stability of labor organizations.[5] As unions became stronger under federal laws, legislation was passed to curb union abuses of power and to protect the rights of union members from unethical union activities. Today the laws governing labor relations seek to create an environment in which both unions and employers can discharge their respective rights and responsibilities. Knowledge of labor relations laws will assist the understanding of how union-management relations operate in the United States. The first federal law pertaining to labor relations was the Railway Labor Act of 1926. Other major laws that affect labor relations in the private sector are the Norris-LaGuardia Act, Wagner Act, Taft-Hartley Act, and Landrum-Griffin Act. (See HRM 2 for key dates regarding government involvement in labor relations.)

Railway Labor Act

The primary purpose of the Railway Labor Act (RLA), enacted in 1926, is to avoid service interruptions resulting from disputes between railroads and their operating unions. To achieve this end, the RLA contains two extensive procedures to handle these labor-management disputes. First, a National Mediation Board exists to resolve conflicts by using mediation and/or arbitration. The board is additionally charged with holding secret ballot elections to determine whether employees desire unionization. Second, the National Railway Adjustment Board handles grievance and arbitration disputes arising during the life of an agreement. In 1936, the RLA was amended to extend coverage to the airline industry.

Norris-LaGuardia Act

The Norris-LaGuardia Act, or Anti-Injunction Act, of 1932 severely restricts the ability of employers to obtain an injunction (i.e., equitable remedy through a court order) forbidding a union from engaging in peaceful picketing, boycotts, or various striking activities. Previously, federal court injunctions had been an effective anti-union weapon because they forced unions to either cease such activities or suffer the penalty of being held in contempt of court. Injunctions may still be granted in labor disputes. Before an injunction may be issued, however, employers must show that lack of an injunction will cause greater harm to the employer than to the union. Like the RLA, this Act promotes the existence, formation, and effective operation of labor organizations. It also allows for negotiations between employers and their respective labor organizations.

Wagner Act

The Wagner Act of 1935 (or National Labor Relations Act) has had by far the most significant impact on union-management relations. It placed the protective power of the federal government firmly behind employee efforts to organize and bargain collectively through representatives of their choice.

The Wagner Act created the National Labor Relations Board (NLRB) to govern labor relations in the United States. Although this Act was amended by the Taft-Hartley Act, most of its major provisions that protected employee bargaining rights were retained. Section 7 of the law guarantees these rights as follows:

> Employees shall have the right to self-organization, to form, join, or assist labor organizations, to bargain collectively through representatives of their own choosing, and to engage in concerted activities, for the purpose of collective bargaining or other mutual aid or protection, and shall also have the right to refrain from any or all of such activities except to the extent that such right may be affected by an agreement requiring membership in a labor organization as a condition of employment.[6]

To guarantee employees their Section 7 rights, Congress outlawed specific employer practices that deny employees the benefits of the law. Section 8 of the Act lists five unfair labor practices (ULPs) of employers:

1. Interfering with, restraining, or coercing employees in the exercise of their rights guaranteed in Section 7

2. Dominating or interfering with the formation or administration of any labor organization, or contributing financial or other support to it

unfair labor practices (ULPs)
Specific employer and union illegal practices that deny employees their rights and benefits under federal labor law

3. Discriminating in regard to hiring or tenure of employment or any term or condition of employment so as to encourage or discourage membership in any labor organization

4. Discharging or otherwise discriminating against employees because they file charges or give testimony under this act

5. Refusing to bargain collectively with the duly chosen representatives of employees

Many ULPs are either knowingly or unknowingly committed each year by employers. In fiscal year 2010, for example, 23,381 unfair labor practices were filed with the NLRB. When a charge against an employer is filed, it is assigned to an investigator, and if the charges show merit, they try to settle the case between the individual and employer out of court. Around 36 percent of the cases filed prove that labor rights have been violated. In 2010, only 4 percent of unfair labor practices filed actually went to court. The rest (96 percent) were settled out of court.

If the case does not settle out of court, it will be assigned to an NLRB lawyer—at no cost to the individual who filed the complaint. On average, the NLRB wins more than 90 percent of these cases. The average time it takes for these cases to be heard is 87 days. Of all the cases settled in and out of court in 2010, the NLRB recovered $86.6 million for employees, and 2,250 employees were reinstated to their old jobs.[7]

National Labor Relations Board

The agency responsible for administering and enforcing the Wagner Act is the National Labor Relations Board (NLRB). It serves the public interest by reducing interruptions in production or service caused by labor-management strife. To accomplish this goal, the NLRB is given two primary charges: (1) to hold secret ballot elections to determine whether employees wish to be represented by a union and (2) to prevent and remedy unfair labor practices. The NLRB does not act on its own initiative in either function. It processes only those charges of unfair labor practices and petitions for employee elections that may be filed at one of its thirty-two regional offices or other smaller field offices.

> **Using the INTERNET**
>
> The U.S. National Labor Relations Board has its own Web site. There you can find details of its organization, current cases, and decisions. Go to
>
> **www.cengagebrain.com**

The NLRB operates in a dynamic field in which information about the operation of the agency and answers to legal questions can be critical to both employees and managers. The NLRB maintains a toll-free telephone number designed to provide cost-free and easy access about the agency to the public.[8] Additionally, each regional office has an "information officer" available to answer specific legal questions about the law and the NLRB.

Taft-Hartley Act

Passage of the Wagner Act spurred the huge growth of unionization during the 1930s and 1940s. Union membership in the United States reached 9 million in 1940, and with membership gains, labor's increased use of the strike became problematic to employers. With the bargaining power of unions now significantly increased, coupled with reports of union abuses of employee rights, certain restraints on unions were considered necessary. The Taft-Hartley Act of 1947 (also known as the Labor-Management Relations Act) met these objectives by defining unfair labor practices of unions and curbing various strike activities of labor organizations. The unfair labor practices of unions are as follows:

1. Restraint or coercion of employees in the exercise of their rights

2. Restraint or coercion of employers in the selection of the parties to bargain on their behalf

3. Persuasion of employers to discriminate against any of their employees

4. Refusal to bargain collectively with an employer

5. Participation in secondary boycotts and jurisdictional disputes

6. Attempt to force recognition from an employer when another union is already the certified representative

7. Charge of excessive initiation fees and dues

8. "Featherbedding" practices that require payment of wages for services not performed

In short, by passing the Taft-Hartley Act, Congress balanced the rights and duties of labor and management in the collective bargaining arena. No longer could the law be criticized as favoring unions.

Federal Mediation and Conciliation Service

Because of the high incidence of strikes after World War II, the Taft-Hartley Act also created the Federal Mediation and Conciliation Service (FMCS) to help resolve negotiating disputes. The function of this independent agency is to help labor and management reach collective bargaining agreements through the processes of mediation and conciliation. These functions use a neutral party who maintains communications between bargainers in an attempt to gain agreement. Unlike the NLRB, the FMCS has no enforcement powers, nor can it prosecute anyone. Rather, the parties in a negotiating impasse must voluntarily elect to use the service. Once the FMCS is asked to mediate a dispute, however, its involvement in the process can greatly improve labor-management relations while providing a vehicle for the exchange of collective bargaining proposals.[9] In recent years, the FMCS has been highly visible in resolving deadlocks involving the communications, sports, education, and transportation industries.

For example, in 2011 the FMCS mediated the negotiations between the National Football League (NFL) and the National Football League Players Association (NFLPA). The role of the FMCS was to get the parties together on a regular basis, establish an atmosphere conducive to meaningful negotiation, and to help with the negotiation process. Director George H. Cohen of the FMCS reported that the atmosphere during the discussions reflected a noteworthy level of mutual respect, despite their strongly competing positions.[10]

Landrum-Griffin Act

In 1959, Congress passed the Landrum-Griffin Act (also known as the Labor-Management Reporting and Disclosure Act) to safeguard union member rights and prevent racketeering and other unscrupulous practices by employers and union officers. One of the most important provisions of the Landrum-Griffin Act is the Bill of Rights of Union Members, which requires that every union member must be given the right to (1) nominate candidates for union office, (2) vote in union elections or referendums, (3) attend union meetings, and (4) participate in union meetings and vote on union business. Union members are also granted the right to examine union accounts and records to verify information contained in union reports and to bring suit against union officers as necessary to protect union funds. Moreover, under the act, unions are required to submit a financial report annually to the Secretary of Labor, and employers must report any expenditures that are made in attempting to exercise their bargaining rights.

HIGHLIGHTS IN **HRM**

2 A Timeline of Government Involvement in American Labor Relations

The following timeline covers the period from the first government-mediated settlement in 1838, to the creation of FMCS in 1947, to the West Coast port Mediation of 2002, to today.[11]

1838–1900

1838   President Martin Van Buren facilitates a settlement of a strike by shipyard workers, the first government mediated labor settlement in America.

1840   President Martin Van Buren signs an Executive Order providing a 10-hour workday for employees on federal public works projects.

1900–1946

1902   In a message to Congress following a strike in the anthracite coal fields in Pennsylvania, President Theodore Roosevelt recognizes the public interest in labor-management relations.

1918   The federal mediation function is born. The U.S. Conciliation Service is created at the Department of Labor.

1926   After major rail strikes of the early 1920s, Congress enacts the Railway Labor Act, establishing the National Mediation Board with jurisdiction in the railroad industry, and with the power to prevent interruptions in commerce in the railroad industry. The law allows railroad unions to organize and bargain collectively.

1932   Norris/La Guardia (Anti-Injunction Act) enacted to limit the power of federal courts to issue injunctions in labor disputes which would deny workers full freedom of association, self-organization, designation of bargaining representatives of their own choosing, or negotiation of terms and conditions of employment.

1934   The Railway Labor Act is amended to include airlines.

1935   The National Labor Relations Act (Wagner Act) becomes law, guaranteeing employees the right to organize and, if necessary, government-supervised representation elections. The act includes the right to bargain collectively and sets forth prohibitions against employer interference or unfair labor practices.

1944   The duty of fair representation is first announced in a 1944 Supreme Court case decided under the Railway Labor Act, Steele v. Louisville & Nashville R.R.

1947–1969

1947   Congress enacts the Labor-Management Relations Act of 1947 (Taft-Hartley Act). The Federal Mediation and Conciliation Service is created as an independent agency of the U. S. government. The agency is given the mission of preventing or minimizing the impact of labor-management disputes on the free flow of commerce by providing mediation, conciliation, and voluntary arbitration.

1959   Congress enacts the Landrum-Griffin Act (Labor Management Reporting and Disclosure Act) which establishes a bill of rights for union members—a right to sue their union, have a voice in union affairs and control of dues increases, among others.

A Timeline of Government Involvement in American Labor Relations (continued)

1960 "The Steelworker's Trilogy" —The Supreme Court hands down three decisions that give full support to the arbitration process.

1970–1990

1970 The first mass work stoppage in the history of the U.S. Post Office occurs. Postal workers in New York walk out. President Nixon declares a national emergency and assigns military units to New York City post offices.

1971 The Collyer Doctrine defines the NLRB's policy on deferring decisions in unfair labor practice cases until after parties have been through the grievance arbitration procedure. Under Collyer deferral, a union is expected to use its grievance procedure to resolve certain unfair labor practice issues.

1973 A Relationship-by-Objectives (RBO) program is developed for use in extreme cases of poor labor-management relations, when continued deterioration of the relationship could have a drastic economic effect. The first RBO program is delivered in Maine on behalf of the Georgia-Pacific Company and Paperworkers Local 27.

1975 FMCS officially enters a new arena: Alternative Dispute Resolution (ADR). Congress passes Public Law 93-531, directing the service to mediate a 100-year old land dispute between the Hopi and Navajo Indian Tribes in Arizona. The rights of unionized employees to have a union representative present during investigatory interviews are secured by a 1975 U.S. Supreme Court ruling (*NLRB v. Weingarten, Inc. 420 U.S. 251, 88 LRRM 2689*). These become known as the Weingarten rights.

1981 President Reagan fires striking Professional Air Traffic Controllers (PATCO) and uses replacement workers. The Major League Baseball Players Association strikes.

1982 FMCS plays a major part in the creation of the Independent Mediation Service in South Africa.

1983 FMCS convenes one of the first regulatory negotiations, mediating between the Federal Aviation Administration and domestic airlines over flight and rest time requirements.

1990–2008

1990 Congress enacts the Administrative Dispute Resolution Act and the Negotiated Rulemaking Act. Both are aimed at increasing the use of ADR to reduce the cost of litigation in government and improve government decision-making.

1993 President Clinton issues Executive Order 12871 which creates the National Partnership Council and directs each executive agency to form a partnership with its employees and their representatives to create a government that "works better and costs less."

2002 Peter J. Hurtgen, former chairman of the National Labor Relations Board, is appointed by President Bush as FMCS's fifteenth director and successfully mediates a number of national labor conflicts, including the 10-day West Coast Ports closing in 2002 that cost the national economy an estimated $1 billion a day.

2004 Director Hurtgen mediates an end to the 141-day southern California grocery strike, the longest in the industry's history.

2008 Director Rosenfeld oversees five days of mediation in Washington, DC to end a 52-day national strike by members of the International Association of Machinists and Aerospace Workers against the Boeing Company with a tentative agreement announced on October 27, 2008.

2011 FMCS mediates the disputes between NFL owners and players over health-care provisions, rookie salary cap, and whether to extend the season to 18 games from 16.

The Labor Relations Process

LEARNING OUTCOME 2

While unionization in the private sector is declining, certain industries, such as the hospitality industry, are gaining ground in unionization. If you were a service worker in a hotel, what factors would make you want to join a union?

Individually, employees may be able to exercise relatively little power in their relationship with employers. Of course, if they believe they are not being treated fairly, then Section 7 of the National Labor Relations Act grants them the legal right to organize and bargain with the employer collectively. When employees pursue this direction, the labor relations process begins. As Figure 14.1 illustrates, the labor relations process consists of a logical sequence of five events: (1) workers desire collective representation, (2) the union begins its organizing campaign, (3) the NLRB representation procedure begins, (4) collective negotiations lead to a contract, and (5) the contract is administered. Laws and administrative rulings influence each of the separate events by granting special privileges to or imposing defined constraints on workers, managers, and union officials.[12]

Why Employees Unionize

The majority of research on why employees unionize comes from the study of blue-collar employees in the private sector. These studies generally conclude that employees unionize as a result of economic need, because of a general dissatisfaction with managerial practices, and/or as a way to fulfill social and status needs. In short, employees see unionism as a way to achieve results they cannot achieve acting individually.

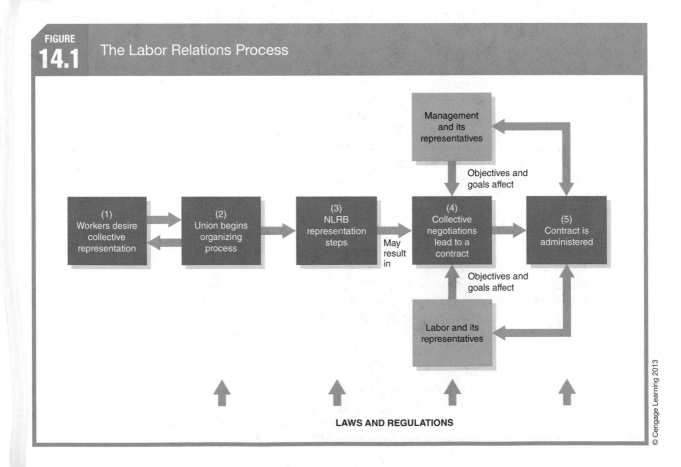

FIGURE 14.1   The Labor Relations Process

© Cengage Learning 2013

It should be pointed out that some employees join unions because of the union shop provisions of the labor agreement. In states where it is permitted, a union shop is a provision of the labor agreement that requires employees to join as a condition of employment. Even when compelled to join, however, many employees accept the concept of unionism once they become involved in the union as a member. The three primary reasons unorganized workers elect to unionize are:

- **Economic needs.** Dissatisfaction with wages, benefits, and working conditions appears to provide the strongest reason to join a union. This point is continually supported by research studies that find that both union members and nonmembers have their highest expectations of union performance regarding the "bread and butter" issues of collective bargaining.[13] It is these traditional issues of wages, benefits, and working conditions on which unions are built.

- **Dissatisfaction with management.** Employees may seek unionization when they perceive that managerial practices regarding promotion, transfer, shift assignment, or other job-related policies are administered in an unfair or biased manner. Employees cite favoritism shown by managers as a major reason for joining unions. This is particularly true when the favoritism concerns the HR areas of discipline, promotion, job assignments, and training opportunities. Furthermore, the failure of employers to give employees an opportunity to participate in decisions affecting their welfare may encourage union membership. It is widely believed that one reason managers begin employee involvement programs and seek to empower their employees is to avoid collective action by employees. For example, one reason employers in the auto, semiconductor, and financial industries involve employees in collaborative programs is to stifle unionization.

- **Social and leadership concerns.** Employees whose needs for recognition and social affiliation are being frustrated may join unions as a means of satisfying these needs. Through their union, they have an opportunity to fraternize with other employees who have similar desires, interests, problems, and gripes. Such concerns often revolve around job insecurity, broken promises, lack of autonomy, double standards, hopelessness, humiliation, and lack of recognition. Employees may join unions to benefit in the dignity and fairness that organization membership may provide. Additionally, the union enables them to put leadership talents to use as officers of the union and representatives of fellow employees. One study found that employees became union stewards so that they could be seen as "a fellow your buddies look to" and as a person who "stands up to the boss."

Of the factors mentioned above, organizing campaigns based on social concerns (e.g., justice, fairness, and dignity) are more successful than campaigns based on dissatisfaction with management or even economic issues.[14] In other words, it is not the fact that employees in a particular organization have to pay 20 percent of their health care premiums but that management has to pay only 10 percent of theirs.

Union Avoidance Practices

Philip Murray, the first president of the United Steel Workers of America and the longest-serving president of the Congress of Industrial Organizations (1940–1952) once stated that "employers generally get the kind of labor relations they ask for."[15] In other words, there are things companies can do from an HRM perspective to decrease

labor relations process

A logical sequence of five events: (1) workers desire collective representation, (2) the union begins its organizing campaign, (3) the NLRB representation process begins, (4) collective negotiations lead to a contract, and (5) the contract is administered

union shop

A provision of the labor agreement that requires employees to join the union as a requirement for their employment

the chances that their employees will want to form a union in the first place, thus avoiding the union organizing campaign altogether. Specifically, there are six practices or principles companies can adopt to decrease the chances of employees wanting to unionize.[16]

The first practice has to do with pay. As discussed in Chapter 9, not only do above market wages and benefits potentially increase performance and decrease turnover, they also decrease the likelihood that employees will want to unionize. For example, very few companies that have above market wage and benefits policies have unions.

The second practice is to promote more employees from within and to do it often. People like to feel that they are progressing and that there is a chance for growth and advancement. Opportunities for career advancement help to bolster hope and a sense of equity in work environments where employees who do a good job are recognized and given chances to better their positions in the organization.

Third, conduct cultural audits. As discussed in Chapter 2, cultural audits provide managers with a picture of what the company needs. It tells management how employees feel about what is going on in the organization and the quality of the working environment. Organizations can then take this information and facilitate developmental programs for employees, focus more on employee needs, and correct problems before they become too large. Attitude surveys also provide a way for employees to feel they are being listened to. Management must take care with these surveys, however. Organizations that do not respond to or act upon this valuable feedback risk developing even more discontent in their workforce, as employees feel that their suggestions are not valued.

The fourth practice is to offer job rotations and training programs. In Chapter 7 we talk about effective ways to manage training programs and job rotation assignments. Specifically, job rotations help reduce burnout, which can lead to people either leaving their jobs or feeling trapped and hopeless. Job rotations also lead to increased employee satisfaction. If variety is the spice of life, then job rotation is the spice of work. This leads to increased commitment to the organization.

These teachers are exercising their legal rights to protest perceived unfair management actions. Perhaps their school system's administrators could have prevented this demonstration by conducting a cultural audit.

Fifth, share information with employees about the state of the organization. Companies that practice open book management are more likely to earn the trust and commitment of their employees. When difficult times arise, they may be more willing to take cuts if they can see that everyone is equally suffering. One of the primary complaints NFL players had against the owners was that they would not open their books to the players so they could see how much money the owners were actually making and how much they had to allocate to the players.

Finally, organizations should make sure they have desirable working conditions. While it is not feasible to make the working environment pleasant in all industries, an organization should make sure its work environment for its employees is equally desirable as other firms in the same industry. This means having appropriate and sufficient lighting, ergonomic work spaces, and a nonhostile environment. The computer software programming company, SAS, has shown that a desirable workplace not only helps to avoid unions, it improves the productivity of the employees and decreases turnover. Some things SAS has done to make the work environment nice are providing a piano player during the lunch hour, hiring two full-time artists to decorate the building and make it a beautiful place to work, and offering a 50,000-square-foot, state-of-the-art fitness center with exercise classes free to all employees.[17] With such desirable work conditions, even Philip Murray might have said that SAS does not need a union.

In sum, employers are providing wages, benefits, and services designed to make unionism unattractive to employees. In addition, a participative management style, profit sharing plans, and alternative dispute resolution procedures (see Chapter 13) are offered to counteract the long-established union goals of improved wages and working conditions. It is important to recognize that these strategies react to the conditions cited at the beginning of the chapter as the main reasons why workers unionize. Because these conditions are under the direct control of management, they can be changed to help discourage or prevent unionism.

Small Business Application

Unions and Small Business—Like Water and Oil

While most small businesses are not unionized and prefer it that way, it is not uncommon for employees to unionize even when they are small in number. This is especially the case as unions are losing ground with large companies. For example, building and electrical contractors will often hire people who are members of a union, such as the International Brotherhood of Electrical Workers. The need for small business owners to work with unions not only makes the relationship between employee and employer more formal, it also complicates the matter.

So why, then, might employees of small businesses want to unionize? Usually when businesses are small they are much less formal and more personal. This informality presents advantages in being able to adapt to the environment and devote needed resources to building the business. However, as small businesses grow, the benefits of informality decrease and the costs of having informal relationships increase. Some employees may begin to feel singled out . . . or worse yet, left out. Such situations sow seeds of discontent. Employees may feel that they are not being treated

(Continued)

Small Business Application

Unions and Small Business—Like Water and Oil (Continued)

fairly. If this happens to enough employees, then the small business is in threat of becoming unionized. To reduce the threat of unionization among small businesses, employers must consider "how" and "when" to formalize the employer-employee relationship to ensure equity and fairness. One way to formalize your employee-employer relationship is to prepare a personnel policy manual or employee handbook. This can help employees know the basic ground rules, what is and is not acceptable, and what they can expect from the company. This handbook provides a basis for equity and fairness in management decisions that may affect the employees. The handbook can include such things as the company philosophy (an overall view of what is considered important), criteria for being hired and fired, training and growth opportunities that are available to everyone, vacation and sick day policies, and grievance procedures and discipline. Be careful what you say, however. Some states consider an employee handbook a binding contract, and if you veer from the handbook you can potentially be taken to court.

To know when to implement these policies is also important. A firm with only a few employees cannot afford a full-time specialist to deal with employer-employee problems. However, as a small firm grows it should start implementing some of these policies. Below are a few conditions to help understand when you should appoint a human resource manager to deal with these issues:

- You have over 100 employees
- Labor turnover rate is high or dramatically increasing
- You have a difficult time in recruitment and selection of new employees
- Supervisors or key employees need substantial training
- Employee morale is low
- You operate in a competitive industry for labor[18]

Organizing Campaigns

LEARNING OUTCOME 3

Despite union avoidance efforts, some employees may still want to unionize. What steps can they take in unionizing? What steps can employers take in trying to stop the union from organizing?

Once employees desire to unionize, a formal organizing campaign may be started either by a union organizer or by employees acting on their own behalf.[19] Contrary to popular belief, most organizing campaigns are begun by employees rather than by union organizers. Large national unions such as the United Auto Workers, the United Brotherhood of Carpenters, the United Steelworkers, and the Teamsters, however, have formal organizing departments whose purpose is to identify organizing opportunities and launch organizing campaigns.

Organizing Steps

Terry Moser, former president of Teamster Local 104, once told the authors that the typical organizing campaign follows a series of progressive steps that can lead to employee representation. The organizing process as described by Moser normally includes the following steps:

1. Employee/union contact

2. Initial organizational meeting

3. Formation of in-house organizing committee

4. Election petition and voting preparation

5. Contract negotiations

Step 1. The first step begins when employees and union officials meet up to explore the possibility of unionization. During these discussions, employees investigate the advantages of labor representation, and union officials begin to gather information on employee needs, problems, and grievances. Labor organizers also seek specific information about the employer's financial health, supervisory styles, and organizational policies and practices. To win employee support, labor organizers must build a case *against* the employer and *for* the union.

Step 2. As an organizing campaign gathers momentum, the organizer schedules an initial union meeting to attract more supporters. The organizer uses the information gathered in Step 1 to address employee needs and explain how the union can secure these goals. Two additional purposes of organizational meetings are (1) to identify employees who can help the organizer direct the campaign and (2) to establish communication chains that reach all employees.

Step 3. The third important step in the organizing drive is to form an in-house organizing committee composed of employees willing to provide leadership to the campaign. The committee's role is to interest other employees in joining the union and in supporting its campaign. An important task of the committee is to have employees sign an authorization card (see Highlights in HRM 2) indicating their willingness to be represented by a labor union in collective bargaining with their employer. The number of signed authorization cards demonstrates the potential strength of the labor union.[20] At least 30 percent of the employees must sign authorization cards before the National Labor Relations Board will hold a representation election.

authorization card
A statement signed by an employee authorizing a union to act as a representative of the employee for purposes of collective bargaining

Step 4. If a sufficient number of employees support the union drive, the organizer seeks a government-sponsored election. A representation petition is filed with the NLRB, asking that a secret ballot election be held to determine whether employees actually desire unionization. Before the election, a large publicity campaign is directed toward employees, seeking their support and election votes. This is a period of intense emotions for the employees, the labor organization, and the employer.

Step 5. Union organizing is concluded when the union wins the election. The NLRB "certifies" the union as the legal bargaining representative of the employees. Contract negotiations now begin; these negotiations represent another struggle between the union and employer. During negotiations each side seeks employment conditions favorable to its position. Members of the in-plant organizing committee and the union organizer attempt to negotiate the employees' first contract. In about one out of four union campaigns, unions are unable to secure a first contract after winning a representation election.[21] Should the union fail to obtain an agreement within one year from winning the election, the Taft-Hartley Act allows the employees to vote the union out through a NLRB "decertification" election.

Aggressive Organizing Tactics

Without question, a strategic objective of the labor movement is to become more aggressive and creative in its organizing tactics. Unions have been shocked into developing these "revolutionary" organizing strategies to compensate for a decline in membership and to counteract employer antiunion campaigns. (Both topics will be discussed later.) To accomplish their agenda of "vitalizing" the labor movement, unions employ the following organizing weapons—in varying degrees—to achieve their goals:

1. *Political involvement.* Unions have become more selective in their support of public officials, giving union funds to candidates who specifically pledge support for pro-labor legislation. During the 2008 national and local elections, the AFL-CIO and other large unions spent a total of about $300 million to help elect Democratic candidates to the White House and Congress.[22] Specific efforts focused on identifying and registering Democrats to vote. In 2011, as states scrambled to tackle large budget deficits, unions found themselves embroiled in a fight with both Republican and Democrat governors over who should shoulder the burdens of budget cuts.[23]

2. *Neutrality agreements.* Neutrality agreements secure a binding commitment from the employer to remain neutral during the organizing drive. The employer agrees that managers will not campaign against or disparage the union and managers will only provide facts about the union when questioned by employees. Furthermore, the employer agrees to accept a card check to recognize the union if the union produces sufficient employee signed authorization cards.[24]

3. *Organizer training.* Traditionally, organizing has been part-time work. Today, the AFL-CIO's Organizing Institute is actively training a new generation of professional, highly skilled, full-time organizers. Organizers who successfully complete the training program are usually hired by local and national unions. They work to assist workers to gain representation. They do this by educating workers about their rights, identify and develop leadership skills, and run campaigns for union recognition. Starting salaries range from $30,000 to $40,000 with great benefits.[25]

4. *Corporate campaigns.* Unions may enlist political or community groups to boycott the product(s) of a targeted company. Other tactics include writing newspaper editorials chastising specific company decisions; filing charges with administrative agencies such as OSHA, the Department of Labor, and the NLRB; and pressuring an organization's financial institution to withhold loans or demand payments. According to the U.S. Chamber of Commerce, "the role of the corporate campaign is to force management to accede to union demands for the card check and neutrality agreements."[26]

5. *Information technology.* E-mail and the web are fast becoming effective union organizing tools. Websites exist that link employees to union literature, union membership applications, and individual union web pages. "Cyberunions" seek to apply computer technology to all aspects of organizing activity.[27]

Employer Tactics Opposing Unionization

Employers use a two-pronged campaign to fight unionization. First, when possible, employers stress the favorable employer-employee relationship they have experienced in the past without a union. Employers may emphasize any advantages in wages, benefits, or working conditions the employees may enjoy in comparison with those provided by organizations that are already unionized. "While you have a right to join a union," the employers may remind their employees, "you also have a right not to join one and to deal directly with the organization free from outside interference."

Second, employers emphasize any unfavorable aspects of unionism including strikes, the payment of union dues and special assessments, and published abuses of members' legal rights, along with any false promises made by the union in the course

HIGHLIGHTS IN HRM

3

United Food and Commercial Workers International Union Authorization Card

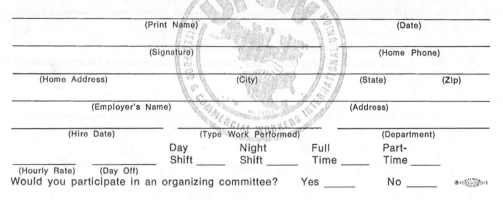

United Food & Commercial Workers International Union

Affiliated with AFL-CIO-CLC

AUTHORIZATION FOR REPRESENTATION

I hereby authorize the United Food & Commercial Workers International Union, AFL-CIO-CLC, or its chartered Local Union(s) to represent me for the purpose of collective bargaining.

_____ (Print Name)   _____ (Date)

_____ (Signature)   _____ (Home Phone)

_____ (Home Address)   _____ (City)   _____ (State)   _____ (Zip)

_____ (Employer's Name)   _____ (Address)

_____ (Hire Date)   _____ (Type Work Performed)   _____ (Department)

                      Day   Night   Full   Part-
                      Shift _____ Shift _____   Time _____   Time _____
_____ _____
(Hourly Rate) (Day Off)
Would you participate in an organizing committee?   Yes _____   No _____

of its campaign. Union rules on member conduct, such as being fined for crossing a picket line, are emphasized to employees. Employers may also use government statistics to show that unions commit large numbers of unfair labor practices. For example, 6,386 unfair labor practices were charged against unions in 2009; the majority (5,017) alleged illegal restraint and coercion of employees.[28] Employers may initiate legal action should union members and/or their leaders engage in any unfair labor practices during the organizing effort.

Within the limits permitted by the Taft-Hartley Act, employers can express their views about the disadvantages of being represented by a union. However, when counteracting a union campaign, managers must not threaten employees with loss of jobs or loss or reduction of other employment benefits if they vote to unionize. Nor may employers offer new or improved employee benefits or higher wages as a means of getting employees to vote "no union." Highlights in HRM 4 lists some of the activities in which managers or supervisors should not engage.[29]

How Employees Become Unionized

The employees to be organized constitute the bargaining unit to be covered by the labor agreement. The NLRB defines a bargaining unit as a group of two or more employees who have common employment interests and conditions and may reasonably be grouped together for purposes of collective bargaining. If an employer and a union cannot agree on who should be in the bargaining unit, an appropriate bargaining unit will be determined by the NLRB on the basis of a similarity of interests (such as wages, job duties, or training) among employees within the unit. For example, in hospitals,

bargaining unit

A group of two or more employees who share common employment interests and conditions and may reasonably be grouped together for purposes of collective bargaining

HIGHLIGHTS IN HRM

4 Employer "Don'ts" during Union Organizing Campaigns

Union organizing drives are emotionally charged events. Furthermore, labor law, NLRB rulings, and court decisions greatly affect the behavior and actions of management and union representatives. During the drive, managers and supervisors should avoid the following:

- Attending union meetings, spying on employee-union gatherings, or questioning employees about the content of union meetings
- Questioning present or current employees about their union sentiments, particularly about how they might vote in a union election
- Threatening or terminating employees for their union support or beliefs
- Changing the working conditions of employees because they actively work for the union or simply support its ideals
- Supplying the names, addresses, and phone numbers of employees to union representatives or other employees sympathetic to the union
- Promising employees improvements in working conditions (wage increases, benefit improvements, and so on) if they vote against the union
- Accepting or reviewing union authorization cards or prounion petitions because employees' names are listed on these documents

the NLRB has designated separate units for nurses, technicians, doctors, maintenance employees, office clerical personnel, all other nonprofessionals, and guards.

NLRB Representation Election

If it succeeds in signing up 30 percent of employees within the bargaining unit, the union petitions for a NLRB-conducted election. The petition to hold representation elections usually is initiated by the union, although employers, under certain circumstances, have the right to petition for one (see Highlights in HRM 5). Prior to the election, the NLRB holds a *preelection hearing* with the employer and union, or unions, seeking to represent the employees. At this meeting several important issues are determined, including verification of the authorization cards, the NLRB's jurisdiction to hold the election, determination of the bargaining unit (if contested by the parties), the date of the election, and the voting choice(s) to appear on the ballot. The ballot lists the names of the unions that are seeking recognition and also provides a choice of "no union."

After the election is held, the winning party is determined on the basis of the number of actual votes, not on the number of members of the bargaining unit. For example, suppose the bargaining unit at XYZ Corporation has 100 employees, but only 27 employees voted in the election. A union receiving 14 yes votes among the 27 voting (a majority) would be declared the winner, and the union would bargain for all 100 employees. By law the union would be granted **exclusive representation** over all

exclusive representation
The legal right and responsibility of the union to represent all bargaining unit members equally, regardless of whether employees join the union or not

bargaining unit employees.[30] The union is *certified* by the NLRB as the bargaining agent for at least a year or for the duration of the labor agreement. Once the union is certified, the employer is obligated to begin negotiations leading toward a labor agreement.

An important statistic in labor relations is the win/loss record of unions in certification elections. In 1950, the union win rate in elections held by the NLRB was 74.50 percent. This percentage dropped dramatically to 60.2 percent in 1965 and to 48.20 percent in 1995. In 2009, the NLRB held 1,619 conclusive representation elections, of which 1,033 resulted in union wins—a 63.8 percent win rate.[31] Employees can unionize without a NLRB election. This NLRB procedure is referred to as "certification on a card check." If the union succeeds in signing up at least 50 percent of employees within the bargaining unit, the union may request recognition by the employer. Typically, evidence is produced in the form of authorization cards signed by employees. However, if the employer believes that a majority of its employees do not want to belong to the union or if the employer questions the authenticity of the cards, the employer can insist that a representation election be held. In recent years, a growing number of unions, including the Communications Workers of America (CWA), United Auto Workers, Service Employees International Union, and the Teamsters have employed card checks as an expedient way to organize employees.[32]

Impact of Unionization on Managers

Why do employers aggressively oppose the unionization of their employees? First, studies from the field of labor economics routinely show that wages and benefits are higher in union organizations compared to similar nonunion organizations. Second, unions can have a significant effect on the prerogatives exercised by management in making decisions about employees. Third, unionization restricts the freedom of management to formulate HR policy unilaterally and can challenge the authority of supervisors.

Challenges to Management Prerogatives

Unions typically attempt to achieve greater participation in management decisions that affect their members. Specifically, these decisions may involve such issues as the subcontracting of work, productivity standards, and job content. Employers quite naturally seek to claim many of these decisions as their exclusive *management prerogatives*—decisions over which management claims exclusive rights. However, these prerogatives are subject to challenge and erosion by the union. They may be challenged at the bargaining table, through the grievance procedure, and through strikes.

Loss of Supervisory Authority

At a recent labor-management conference, a union official commented, "Contract terms covering wages, benefits, job security, and working hours are of major importance to our membership." However, for managers and supervisors, the focal point of the union's impact is at the operating level (the shop floor or office facility), where the terms of the labor agreement are implemented on a daily basis. For example, these terms can determine what corrective action is to be taken in directing and in disciplining employees. When disciplining employees, supervisors must be certain they can demonstrate *just cause* (see Chapter 13) for their actions. Additionally, specific contract language can also reduce the supervisor's ability to manage in such areas as scheduling, training, transfers, performance evaluation, and promotions. Under provisions of the labor agreement, supervisors may have to promote employees by seniority rather than by individual merit.

5 HIGHLIGHTS IN **HRM**
NLRB Election Poster

NOTICE TO EMPLOYEES

FROM THE
National Labor Relations Board

A PETITION has been filed with this Federal agency seeking an election to determine whether certain employees want to be represented by a union.

The case is being investigated and NO DETERMINATION HAS BEEN MADE AT THIS TIME by the National Labor Relations Board. IF an election is held Notices of Election will be posted giving complete details for voting.

It was suggested that your employer post this notice so the National Labor Relations Board could inform you of your basic rights under the National Labor Relations Act.

YOU HAVE
THE RIGHT
under
Federal Law

- **To self-organization**
- **To form, join, or assist labor organizations**
- **To bargain collectively through representatives of your own choosing**
- **To act together for the purposes of collective bargaining or other mutual aid or protection**
- **To refuse to do any or all of these things unless the union and employer, in a state where such agreements are permitted, enter into a lawful union-security agreement requiring employees to pay periodic dues and initiation fees. Nonmembers who inform the union that they object to the use of their payments for nonrepresentational purposes may be required to pay only their share of the union's costs of representational activities (*such as collective bargaining, contract administration, and grievance adjustments*).**

It is possible that some of you will be voting in an employee representation election as a result of the request for an election having been filed. While NO DETERMINATION HAS BEEN MADE AT THIS TIME, in the event an election is held, the NATIONAL LABOR RELATIONS BOARD wants all eligible voters to be familiar with their rights under the law IF it holds an election.

The Board applies rules that are intended to keep its elections fair and honest and that result in a free choice. If agents of either unions or employers act in such a way as to interfere with your right to a free election, the election can be set aside by the Board. Where appropriate the Board provides other remedies, such as reinstatement for employees fired for exercising their rights, including backpay from the party responsible for their discharge.

NOTE:

The following are
examples of conduct
that interfere with
the rights of
employees and may
result in the setting
aside of the election.

- **Threatening loss of jobs or benefits by an employer or a union**
- **Promising or granting promotions, pay raises, or other benefits to influence an employee's vote by a party capable of carrying out such promises**
- **An employer firing employees to discourage or encourage union activity or a union causing them to be fired to encourage union activity**
- **Making campaign speeches to assembled groups of employees on company time within the 24-hour period before the election**
- **Incitement by either an employer or a union of racial or religious prejudice by inflammatory appeals**
- **Threatening physical force or violence to employees by a union or an employer to influence their votes**

Please be assured that IF AN ELECTION IS HELD every effort will be made to protect your right to a free choice under the law. Improper conduct will not be permitted. All parties are expected to cooperate fully with this Agency in maintaining basic principles of a fair election as required by law. The National Labor Relations Board, as an agency of the United States Government, does not endorse any choice in the election.

NATIONAL LABOR RELATIONS BOARD
an agency of the
UNITED STATES GOVERNMENT

THIS IS AN OFFICIAL GOVERNMENT NOTICE AND MUST NOT BE DEFACED BY ANYONE

FORM NLRB-666 (5-90)   ☆ U.S. Government Printing Office: 1990-270-493/10127

Structures, Functions, and Leadership of Labor Unions

Unions that represent skilled craft workers, such as carpenters or masons, are called craft unions. Craft unions include the International Association of Machinists, United Brotherhood of Carpenters, and United Association of Plumbers and Pipefitters. Unions that represent unskilled and semiskilled workers employed along industry lines are known as industrial unions. The American Union of Postal Workers is an industrial union, as are the United Auto Workers; United Steelworkers; American Federation of State, County, and Municipal Employees; and Office and Professional Employees International Union. While this distinction still exists, technological changes, union mergers, and competition among unions for members have helped reduce it. Today skilled and unskilled workers, white-collar and blue-collar workers, and professional groups are being represented by both types of union. For example, the UAW represents workers in diverse industries from auto manufacturing to agriculture to health care to higher education.[33]

Besides unions, employee associations represent various groups of professional and white-collar employees. Examples of employee associations include the National Education Association, Michigan State Employees Association, American Nurses' Association, and Air Line Pilots Association. In competing with unions, these associations, for all purposes, may function as unions and become just as aggressive as unions in representing members.

Regardless of their type, labor organizations are diverse organizations, each with its own method of governance and objectives. Furthermore, they have their own structures that serve to bind them together. For example, when describing labor organizations, most researchers divide them into three levels: (1) American Federation of Labor–Congress of Industrial Organizations (AFL-CIO), (2) national unions, and (3) local unions belonging to a parent national union. Each level has its own purpose for existence as well as its own operating policies and procedures.

craft unions
Unions that represent skilled craft workers

industrial unions
Unions that represent all workers—skilled, semiskilled, unskilled—employed along industry lines

employee associations
Labor organizations that represent various groups of professional and white-collar employees in labor-management relations

Structure and Functions of the AFL-CIO

In 1955, the American Federation of Labor—composed largely of craft unions—and the Congress of Industrial Organizations—made up mainly of industrial unions—merged to form the AFL-CIO. The AFL-CIO is a federation of fifty-six autonomous national and international unions.[34]

In effect, the AFL-CIO is the "House of Labor" that serves to present a united front on behalf of organized labor. It disseminates labor policy developed by leaders of its affiliated unions, assists in coordinating organizing activities among its affiliated unions, and provides research and other assistance through its various departments. Most major unions belong to this federation.[35] The affiliated unions pay per capita dues (currently 50 cents per member per month) to support federation activities. Specifically, the AFL-CIO serves its members by:

1. Lobbying before legislative bodies on subjects of interest to labor

2. Coordinating organizing efforts among its affiliated unions

3. Publicizing the concerns and benefits of unionization to the public

4. Resolving disputes between different unions as they occur

Besides offering these services, the AFL-CIO maintains an interest in international trade and domestic economic issues, foreign policy matters, social issues, and national and regional politics.

A goal of the AFL-CIO is to build solidarity among its members. However, the interests and organizing activities of AFL-CIO unions do not always coincide. In 2005, six unions representing 5.4 million workers split from the AFL-CIO to form Change to Win (CTW), a rival national federation.[36] The new alliance seeks to rededicate union resources and energies toward organizing the unorganized while also revitalizing the entire labor movement.[37] CTW leaders argue that the AFL-CIO places too much emphasis on political action and too little action on organizing new members.[38] Organizing will be directed at semiskilled and low-skilled workers in industries such as hotels, health care, and retail.

Structure and Functions of National Unions

The center of power in the labor movement resides with national and international unions. These organizations set the broad guidelines for governing union members and for formulating collective bargaining goals in dealing with management. National unions hold conventions to pass resolutions, amend their constitutions, and elect officers. The president of the national union is responsible for the overall administration of the unions, and he or she exerts a large influence—if not control—over the union's policies and direction.[39]

A national union, through its constitution, establishes the rules and conditions under which the local unions may be chartered. Most national unions have regulations governing dues, initiation fees, and the internal administration of the locals. National unions also may require that certain standard provisions be included in labor agreements with employers. Standard contract terms covering safety or grievance procedures and seniority rights are examples. In return for these controls, they provide professional and financial assistance during organizing drives and strikes and help in the negotiation and administration of labor agreements. Other services provided by national unions include (1) training of union leaders, (2) legal assistance, (3) leadership in political activity, (4) educational and public relations programs, and (5) discipline of union members.

Structure and Functions of Local Unions

To the "rank-and-file" union member, the importance of unionism resides in the activities of the local union and its leaders. The officers of a local union are usually responsible for negotiating the local labor agreement and for investigating and processing member grievances. Most important, they assist in preventing the members of the local union from being treated by their employers in ways that run counter to management-established HR policies.

The officers of a local union typically include a president, vice president, secretary-treasurer, and various committee chairpeople. Depending on the size of the union, one or more of these officers may be paid by the union to serve on a full-time basis. The remaining officers are members who have regular jobs and who serve the union without pay except perhaps for token gratuities and expense allowances. Paid officers from the national union—called CWA representatives by the Communication Workers of America—will assist the local union with functions such as organizing, negotiating the labor agreement, arbitration of member grievances, and legal matters.

An extremely important position in the local union is the union steward. The **union steward** represents the interests of union members in their relations with their immediate supervisors and other members of management. Stewards are normally elected by union members within their department and serve without union pay. Because stewards are full-time employees of the organization, they often spend considerable time after working hours investigating and handling member problems. When stewards represent members during grievance meetings on organizational time, their lost earnings are paid by the local union.

A union steward can be viewed as a "person in the middle," caught between conflicting interests and groups. It cannot be assumed that stewards will always champion union members and routinely oppose managerial objectives. Union stewards are often insightful individuals working for the betterment of employees and the organization. Therefore, it is *highly* encouraged that supervisors and managers at all levels develop a professional working relationship with stewards and all union officials. This relationship can have an important bearing on union-management cooperation and on the efficiency and morale of the workforce.

One of the functions of a union steward is to discuss issues with management as they arise. Here, a steward is discussing a safety issue with the site manager.

union steward
An employee who as a non-paid union official represents the interests of members in their relations with management

Union Leadership Commitment and Philosophies

To evaluate the role of union leaders accurately, one must understand the nature of their backgrounds and ambitions and recognize the political nature of the offices they occupy. Union leaders—at all levels—often possess enthusiasm and a commitment to the ideals of unionism and employee welfare that is difficult for managers to understand and accept. To some managers, union officials have a "religious" zeal toward the labor movement and the advancement of member bargaining rights. Additionally, it is important for managers to understand that union officials are elected to office and, like any political officials, must be responsive to the views of their constituency. The union leader who ignores the demands of union members may risk being voted out of office or having members vote the union out as their bargaining agent.

To be effective leaders, labor officials must also pay constant attention to the general goals and philosophies of the labor movement.[40] **Business unionism** is the general label given to the goals of U.S. labor organizations: increased pay and benefits, job security, and improved working conditions. Furthermore, union leaders also know that unions must address the broader social, economic, and legislative issues of concern to members. For example, the United Auto Workers continually lobbies Congress for protective legislation affecting the auto industry. The American Federation of State, County, and Municipal Employees; The Union of Needletrades, Industrial

business unionism
A term applied to the goals of U.S. labor organizations, which collectively bargain for improvements in wages, hours, job security, and working conditions

and Textile Employees; and The Association of Flight Attendants, representing flight attendants at United Airlines and US Airways, have been active supporters of women's issues at both the state and national levels.

Labor Relations in the Public Sector

Collective bargaining among federal, state, and local government employees has been an area of important activity for the union movement since the early 1960s. Today unions represent more than 36 percent of all government workers in the United States (compared with just 11 percent in 1960).[41] The latest union membership figures show that some of the nation's largest labor organizations represent employees in the public sector—the National Education Association (3.2 million members), American Federation of Teachers (1.5 million members), and State, County, and Municipal Employees (1.6 million members), for instance.[42] As unions and employee associations of teachers, police, firefighters, and state employees have grown in size and political power, they have demanded the same rights to bargain and strike that private-sector employees have.

While public sector and private sector collective bargaining have many features in common, a number of factors differentiate the two sectors. First, there are no national laws, like the National Labor Relations Act in the private sector, governing public sector labor relations. Public sector collective bargaining falls within the separate jurisdiction of each state, and great diversity exists among the various state laws. For example, some states, such as Arizona, Utah, and Mississippi, have no collective bargaining laws; other states, such as Florida, Hawaii, and New York, have comprehensive laws granting collective bargaining rights to all public employees. Between these extremes are state laws granting collective bargaining rights only to specific employee groups such as teachers and the uniformed services (police and fire). For federal employees, collective bargaining is governed by executive orders (regulations issued by the U.S. president) and the Civil Service Reform Act of 1978.[43]

In 2011, Governor Scott Walker of Wisconsin stripped public employees of their rights to collective bargaining. A battle ensued between public sector labor unions and the state of Wisconsin. In an attempt to cut state budgets, other states considered following suit by removing collective bargaining rights from public employees. The International Labor Organization called this move an attack on a fundamental human right: "the right to associate freely and have an independent voice at work."[44] Overall, this has become one of the "hot button" issues for unions as they strive to maintain their strength in the public sector.

Second, public jurisdictions often establish the wages, employee benefits, and organizational rules under which their employees work. Public *civil service systems* exist to address employee complaints or grievances. With wages and working conditions set by law, unions are largely denied the opportunity to negotiate for the traditional bread-and-butter issues of collective bargaining.[45] Unions see this arrangement as a loss of opportunity to "champion" their cause to employees.

Lastly, striking in the public sector is largely prohibited. Because the services that government employees provide are often considered essential to the well-being of the public, public policy is opposed to such strikes. Thus most state legislatures have not granted public employees the right to strike. In those states where striking is permitted, the right is limited to specific groups of employees—normally nonuniformed employees—and the strikes cannot endanger the public's health, safety, or welfare. Public employee unions contend, however, that denying them the same right to strike as employees in the private sector means that their power during collective bargaining is greatly reduced. Union officials often describe negotiating with public officials as a process of "meet and beg."

To provide some equity in bargaining power, various arbitration methods are used for resolving collective bargaining deadlocks in the public sector. One is *compulsory binding arbitration* for employees such as police officers, firefighters, and others in jobs for which strikes cannot be tolerated. Another method is *final offer arbitration*, under which the arbitrator must select one or the other of the final offers submitted by the disputing parties. With this method, the arbitrator's award is more likely to go to the party whose final bargaining offer has moved the closest toward a reasonable settlement.

The Bargaining Process

Those unfamiliar with contract negotiations often view the process as an emotional conflict between labor and management, complete with marathon sessions, fist pounding, and smoke-filled rooms. In reality, negotiating a labor agreement entails long hours of extensive preparation combined with diplomatic maneuvering and the development of bargaining strategies. Furthermore, negotiation is only one part of the collective bargaining process. (See Figure 14.2.) Collective bargaining also may

LEARNING OUTCOME 4

If you were a manager in charge of bargaining with the union, what would be the first steps you would take in the collective bargaining process? How would you ensure that the bargaining does not become highly adversarial?

collective bargaining process

The process of negotiating a labor agreement, including the use of economic pressures by both parties

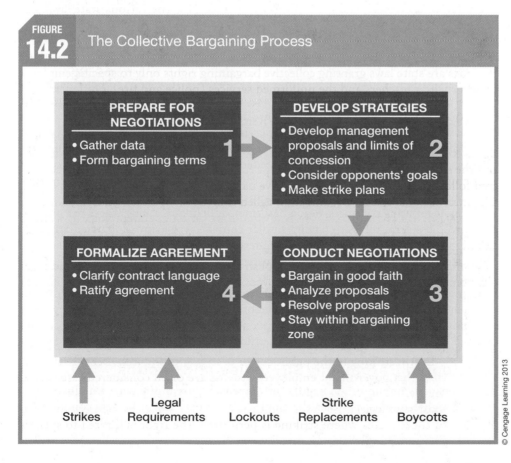

FIGURE 14.2 The Collective Bargaining Process

PREPARE FOR NEGOTIATIONS
- Gather data
- Form bargaining terms

1

DEVELOP STRATEGIES
- Develop management proposals and limits of concession
- Consider opponents' goals
- Make strike plans

2

FORMALIZE AGREEMENT
- Clarify contract language
- Ratify agreement

4

CONDUCT NEGOTIATIONS
- Bargain in good faith
- Analyze proposals
- Resolve proposals
- Stay within bargaining zone

3

Strikes   Legal Requirements   Lockouts   Strike Replacements   Boycotts

© Cengage Learning 2013

include the use of economic pressures in the form of strikes and boycotts by a union. Lockouts, plant closures, and the replacement of strikers are similar pressures used by an employer. In addition, either or both parties may seek support from the general public or from the courts as a means of pressuring the opposing side.

Preparing for Negotiations

Preparing for negotiations includes assembling data to support bargaining proposals and forming the bargaining team. This permits collective bargaining to be conducted on an orderly, factual, and positive basis with a greater likelihood of achieving desired goals. Assuming that the labor agreement is not the first to be negotiated by the parties, preparation for negotiations ideally start soon after the current agreement has been signed. This practice allows negotiators to review and diagnose weaknesses and mistakes made during the previous negotiations while the experience is still current in their minds.

Normally, each side has four to six representatives at the negotiating table. The chief negotiator for management is the vice president or manager for labor relations; the chief negotiator for the union is the local union president or national union representative. Others making up management's team may include representatives from accounting or finance, operations, employment, legal, or training. The local union president is likely to be supported by the chief steward, various local union vice presidents, and a representative from the national union. Importantly, it is widely accepted that the conduct of the negotiators strongly influences individual bargaining sessions and the outcomes reached. According to one experienced negotiator, "The conduct of negotiations largely depends on the relationship and attitude of negotiators toward one another. If you want conflict in your bargaining sessions just start off attacking the other side."[46]

Gathering Bargaining Data

Employers gather economic data primarily in the areas of wages and benefits. However, internal data relating to grievances, disciplinary actions, transfers, promotions, overtime, and former arbitration awards are useful in formulating and supporting the employer's bargaining position. The supervisors and managers who must live with and administer the labor agreement can be very important sources of ideas and suggestions concerning changes that are needed in the *next* agreement. Their contact with union members and representatives provides them with firsthand knowledge of the changes that union negotiators are likely to propose.

When negotiating contracts, union bargainers talk about "taking wages out of competition." This term refers to having similar contract provisions—particularly concerning wages and benefits—between different companies in order to prevent one employer from having a favorable labor cost advantage over another. For example, the United Auto Workers representing workers at both General Motors and Ford will seek similar contract provisions. Furthermore, this allows unions to show their members that they are receiving wages and benefits comparable to those of other employees doing like work. Other negotiated labor agreements, particularly at the local and regional levels, play a significant part in settling the terms of the labor agreement.

Developing Bargaining Strategies and Tactics

Both management and union negotiators approach bargaining with a defined strategy. In tough economic periods, the employer's strategy might be cost containment or specific reductions in wages or benefits such as health care or pension costs. Conversely, in times of economic growth—when a union strike would harm sales—the employer will be more willing to meet union demands. The employer's strategy should also consider proposals the union is likely to submit, goals the union is striving to achieve, and extent to which it may be willing to make concessions or to resort to strike action in order to achieve these goals.

At a minimum, the employer's bargaining strategy must address these points:

- Likely union proposals and management responses to them

- A listing of management demands, limits of concessions, and anticipated union responses

- Development of a database to support management bargaining proposals and to counteract union demands

- A contingency operating plan should employees strike

Certain elements of strategy are common to both the employer and the union. Generally, the initial demands presented by each side are greater than those it actually may hope to achieve.[47] This is done to provide room for concessions. Moreover, each party usually avoids giving up the maximum it is capable of conceding to allow for further concessions that may be needed to break a bargaining deadlock.

The negotiation of a labor agreement can have some of the characteristics of a poker game, with each side attempting to determine its opponent's position while not revealing its own.[48] Each party normally tries to avoid disclosing the relative importance that it attaches to a proposal so that it will not be forced to pay a higher price than is necessary to have the proposal accepted. As in buying a new car, the buyer and seller employ a lot of strategy to obtain the best outcome possible.

Negotiating the Labor Agreement

While there is no "exact" way to negotiate a labor agreement, typically each side focuses on one issue or several related issues until agreement is reached.[49] For each bargaining issue to be resolved satisfactorily, the point at which agreement is reached must be within limits that the union and the employer are willing to accept. In a frequently cited bargaining model, Ross Stagner and Hjalmar Rosen call the area within these two limits the bargaining zone. In some bargaining situations, such as the one illustrated in Figure 14.3, the solution desired by one party may exceed the limits of the other party. Thus that solution is outside the bargaining zone. If that party refuses to modify its demands sufficiently to bring them within the bargaining zone or if the opposing party refuses to extend its limit to accommodate the demands of the other party, a bargaining deadlock results.[50] For example, when bargaining a wage increase for employees, if the union's lowest limit is a 4 percent increase and management's top limit is 6 percent, an acceptable range—the bargaining zone—is available to both parties. If management's top limit is only 3 percent, however, a bargaining zone is not available to either side, and a deadlock is likely to occur. Figure 14.3, which is based on the original model by Stagner and Rosen, shows that as bargaining takes place, several important variables influence the negotiators and their ability to reach agreement within the bargaining zone.

bargaining zone

An area in which the union and the employer are willing to concede when bargaining

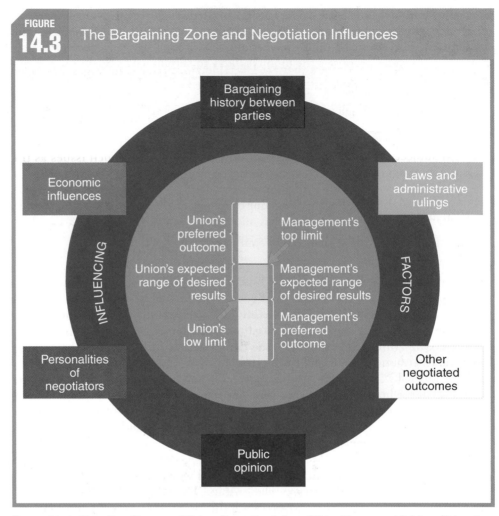

FIGURE **14.3**   The Bargaining Zone and Negotiation Influences

Source: Adapted from Ross Stagner and Hjalmar Rosen, *Psychology of Union-Management Relations* (Belmont, CA: Wadsworth Publishing Company, 1965), 96. Adapted with permission from Brooks/Cole Publishing Co.

Good Faith Bargaining

The Taft-Hartley Act requires an employer to negotiate in good faith with the union's representatives over conditions of employment (the same obligation applies to the union representatives).[51] Good faith requires meetings to be held at reasonable times and places to discuss employment conditions. It requires also that the proposals submitted by each party be realistic. In discussing the other party's proposals, each side must offer reasonable counterproposals for those it is unwilling to accept. Finally, both parties must sign the written document containing the agreement reached through negotiations.

Additionally, to help the parties bargain in good faith, the National Labor Relations Board has divided the subjects of bargaining into three distinct categories. Each category confers specific rights and responsibilities on labor and management negotiators. The three categories of bargaining are:

1. Mandatory subject. All matters concerning rates of pay, hours of employment, and other conditions of employment. Both the employer and the union must bargain

in good faith over the issues. The law, however, does not require either party to agree to a proposal or to make concessions while negotiating these subjects. The parties may bargain to an impass over these topics.

2. **Permissive subjects.** Matters that are lawful but not related to wages, hours, or other conditions of employment—the parties are free to bargain, but neither side can force the other side to bargain over these topics. Permissive subjects might include a union demand to ratify supervisory promotions or consultation on setting the price of the organization's product or service.

3. **Illegal subjects.** These subjects of bargaining would include such issues as the closed shop or compulsory dues checkoff. If a demand is made concerning an illegal item, the NLRB finds a violation of good-faith bargaining under section 8(a)(5) of the Taft-Hartley Act. When labor or management negotiators cannot agree on whether a bargaining proposal is a mandatory or a permissive issue—such as drug testing or employee surveillance—the NLRB decides the dispute.

Interest-Based Bargaining

U.S. labor-management negotiations are characterized as adversarial. With adversarial bargaining, negotiators start with defined positions, and through deferral, persuasion, trade, or power, the parties work toward the resolution of individual bargaining demands. Unfortunately, as noted by one labor negotiator, "adversarial bargaining does little to establish a long-term positive relationship based on open communications and trust. By its nature, it leads to suspicion and compromise."[52] To overcome these negative feelings, labor and management practitioners may use a nonadversarial approach to negotiating.

Interest-based bargaining is based on the identification and resolution of mutual interests rather than the resolve of specific bargaining demands.[53] As defined by the Federal Mediation and Conciliation Service, interest-based bargaining is "a problem-solving process conducted in a principled way that creates effective solutions while improving the bargaining relationship." The focus of bargaining strategy is to discover mutual bargaining interests with the intent of formulating options and solutions for mutual gain.[54] Rather than using proposals and counterproposals as a means of reaching agreement (as with adversarial negotiations), participants use brainstorming, consensus decision-making, active listening, process checking, and matrix building to facilitate the settlement of issues. An underlying goal of interest-based bargaining is to create a relationship for the future based on trust, understanding, and mutual respect.

interest-based bargaining
Problem-solving bargaining based on a win-win philosophy and the development of a positive long-term relationship

Management and Union Power in Collective Bargaining

Fortunately, the great majority of labor-management negotiations are settled peacefully. However, should negotiations become deadlocked, bargaining can become highly adversarial as each side will now employ its bargaining power to achieve its desired ends. The party's bargaining power consists of its economic, political, and social influence to achieve its demands at the expense of the other side.

bargaining power
The power of labor and management to achieve their goals through economic, social, or political influence

LEARNING OUTCOME 5

When the NFL and the NFL Players Association came to a deadlock, what forms of bargaining power did each side possess? Who do you think had more power?

Union Bargaining Power

The bargaining power of the union may be exercised by striking, picketing, or boycotting the employer's products or services. A strike is the refusal of a group of employees to perform their jobs. Unions usually seek strike authorization from their members

A strike is one way union members can exercise their bargaining power.

AP Photo/John Bazemore

to use as a bargaining ploy to gain concessions that will make a strike unnecessary. A strike vote by the members does not mean they actually want or expect to go out on strike. Rather, it is intended as a vote of confidence to strengthen the position of their leaders at the bargaining table.

Of critical importance to the union is the extent, if any, to which the employer will be able to continue operating through the use of supervisory and nonstriking personnel and employees hired to replace the strikers. In organizations with high levels of technology and automation, and consequently fewer employees, continuing service with supervisors and managers is more likely. Among the highly automated telephone companies, most services can be maintained by supervisors during a strike. According to one authority, "Because of technological change, striking in many industries no longer has the effect of curtailing the employer's operations significantly."[55] Consequently, the greater the ability of the employer to continue operating, the less the union's chances of gaining its demands through a strike.

When a union goes on strike, it pickets the employer by placing people at business entrances to advertise the dispute and to discourage others from entering the premises. Because unions often refuse to cross another union's picket line, the pickets may serve to prevent the delivery and pickup of goods or performance of other services. For example, a Teamster truck driver may refuse to deliver produce to a food store whose employees are out on strike with the United Food and Commercial Workers Union.

Another economic weapon of the union is the *boycott*, which is a refusal to patronize the employer. For example, production employees on strike against a hand tool manufacturer might picket a retail store that sells the tools made by the struck employer. Unions will also use handbills, radio announcements, e-mail campaigns, and newspaper ads to discourage the purchase of the employer's product or service.

Management Bargaining Power

When negotiations become deadlocked, the employer's bargaining power largely rests on being able to continue operations in the face of a strike *or* to shut down operations entirely.

Should employees strike the organization (referred to as an economic strike), employers have the legal right to hire replacement workers. With this right, employers acquire a bargaining weapon equal in force to the union's right to strike. As one observer noted, "The availability of a worker replacement strategy improves management's ability to battle a union head-on in the way that unions have battled employers for decades."

Another prevalent bargaining strategy is for the employer to continue operations by using managers and supervisors to staff employee jobs. In one case, nearly 30,000 managers left their offices to serve as operators, technicians, and customer service representatives during a strike between Verizon and the Communications Workers of America. As noted previously, technological advances enhance the employer's ability to operate during a strike.

In extreme situations, the employer may elect to lock out its employees. The lockout is a bargaining strategy by which the employer denies employees the opportunity to work by closing its operations. Besides being used in bargaining impasses, lockouts may be used by employers to combat union slowdowns, damage to their property, or violence within the organization that may occur in connection with a labor dispute. Employers may still be reluctant to resort to a lockout, however, because of their concern that denying work to regular employees might hurt the organization's image.

Resolving Bargaining Deadlocks

Unions and employers in all types of industries—sports, transportation, entertainment, manufacturing, communication, and health care—have used mediation and arbitration to help resolve their bargaining deadlocks.[56] As discussed in Chapter 13, mediation is a voluntary process that relies on the communication and persuasive skills of a mediator to help the parties resolve their differences. The federal government is likely to become involved in labor disputes through the services of the FMCS.

Unlike a mediator, an **arbitrator** assumes the role of a decision maker and determines what the settlement between the two parties should be. In other words, arbitrators write a final contract that the parties *must* accept. Compared with mediation, arbitration is not often used to settle private sector bargaining disputes. In the public sector, where strikes are largely prohibited, the use of *interest arbitration* is a common method to resolve bargaining deadlocks. Generally, one or both parties are reluctant to give a third party the power to make the settlement for them. Consequently, a mediator typically is used to break a deadlock and assist the parties in reaching an agreement. An arbitrator generally is called on to resolve disputes arising in connection with the administration of the agreement, called *rights arbitration* or *grievance arbitration*, which will be discussed shortly.

arbitrator

A third-party neutral who resolves a labor dispute by issuing a final decision in the disagreement

The Labor Agreement

When negotiations are concluded, the labor agreement becomes a formal *binding* document listing the terms, conditions, and rules under which employees and managers agree to operate. Highlights in HRM 6 shows some of the major articles in a labor agreement and also provides examples of some new and progressive contract clauses. Two important items in any labor agreement pertain to the issue of management rights and the forms of security afforded the union.

The Issue of Management Rights

Management rights have to do with the conditions of employment over which management is able to exercise exclusive control. Almost without exception, the labor agreement contains a *management rights* clause. This clause states that "management's authority is supreme in all matters except those it has expressly conceded in the collective agreement, or in those areas where its authority is restricted by law." Management rights might include the right of management to determine the products to produce, to determine the location of production or service facilities, or to

HIGHLIGHTS IN **HRM**

Items in a Labor Agreement

Typical clauses will cover:
- Wages
- Vacations
- Holidays
- Work schedules
- Management rights
- Union security
- Transfers
- Discipline
- Training
- Grievance procedures
- No strike/no lockout clause
- Overtime
- Safety procedures
- Severance pay
- Seniority

- Pensions and benefits
- Outsourcing
- Work rules

Progressive clauses will cover:
- Employee access to records
- Limitations on use of performance evaluation
- Elder care leave
- Flexible medical spending accounts
- Protection against hazards of technology equipment (VDTs)
- Limitations against electronic monitoring
- Procedures governing drug testing
- Bilingual stipends
- Domestic partnership benefits
- Employee involvement programs

select production equipment and procedures. The following is an example of a clause defining management rights in one labor agreement:

> It is agreed that the company possesses all of the rights, powers, privileges, and authority it had prior to the execution of this agreement; and nothing in this agreement shall be construed to limit the company in any way in the exercise of the regular and customary functions of management and the operation of its business, except as it may be specifically relinquished or modified herein by an express provision of this agreement.[57]

Union Security Agreements

As we noted at the beginning of this chapter, unions must represent all bargaining unit members equally regardless of whether employees join the union or not. In exchange for this obligation, union officials will seek to negotiate some form of compulsory membership as a condition of employment. This form of agreement where an employer and the union agree on the extent to which the union may compel employees to join the union and how the dues will be collected is known as the **union security agreement**. Union officials argue that compulsory membership precludes the possibility that some employees will receive the benefits of unionization without paying their fair share of the costs. A standard union security provision is

union security agreement

Where an employer and the union agree on the extent to which the union may compel employees to join the union and how the dues will be collected

dues checkoff, which gives the employer the responsibility of withholding union dues from the paychecks of union members who agree to such a deduction.

Other common forms of union security found in labor contracts are different types of "shop" agreements.[58] These agreements—in varying degrees—attempt to require employees to join the union. For example, the *union shop* provides that any employee who is not a union member upon employment must join the union within thirty days or be terminated. Another, the *agency shop*, provides for voluntary membership. However, nonunion employees are still required to pay an "agency fee" to cover collective bargaining costs. For example, according to the NFL Collective Bargaining Agreement of 2006–2012, "every NFL player has the option of joining or not joining the NFLPA...." This agency agreement was contingent upon the player being in good standing with the NFLPA. If the player was not in good standing he would be required to pay "an annual service fee in the same amount as any initiation fee and annual dues required of members of the NFLPA."[59]

Few issues in collective bargaining are more controversial than the negotiation of these agreements.[60] The most popular union security clause, the union shop, is illegal in twenty-two states having right-to-work laws.[61] Right-to-work laws ban any form of compulsory union membership. Section 14(b) of the Taft-Hartley Act permits individual states to enact legislation prohibiting compulsory union membership as a condition of employment.

Administration of the Labor Agreement

Negotiation of the labor agreement, as mentioned earlier, is usually the most publicized and critical aspect of labor relations. Strike deadlines, press conferences, and employee picketing help create this image. Nevertheless, as managers in unionized organizations know, the bulk of labor relations activity comes from the day-to-day administration of the agreement because no agreement could possibly anticipate all the forms that disputes may take. In addition, once the agreement is signed, each side will naturally interpret ambiguous clauses to its own advantage.[62] These differences are traditionally resolved through the grievance procedure.

LEARNING OUTCOME 6

How would you resolve a complaint about your boss making you do work that is not in your contract? Would you need an arbitrator?

Negotiated Grievance Procedures

The grievance procedure typically provides for the union to represent the interests of its members (and nonmembers as well) in processing a grievance. It is considered by some authorities to be the heart of the bargaining agreement, or the safety valve that gives flexibility to the whole system of collective bargaining.[63]

The grievance procedure is normally initiated by the union—or an individual employee—when it feels management has violated some article of the labor agreement. In one case, the union filed a grievance against a supervisor when it believed the supervisor promoted an employee out of seniority order—called a bypass grievance. A significant benefit of the grievance procedure is that it provides a formal and orderly procedure for the union to challenge the actions of management without resort to force. One authority has noted, "The grievance procedure fosters cooperation, not conflict, between the employer and the union."[64]

The operation of a grievance procedure is unique to each individual collective bargaining relationship, although there are common elements among systems. For example, grievance procedures normally specify how the grievance is to be initiated, the

grievance procedure

A formal procedure that provides for the union to represent members and nonmembers in processing a grievance

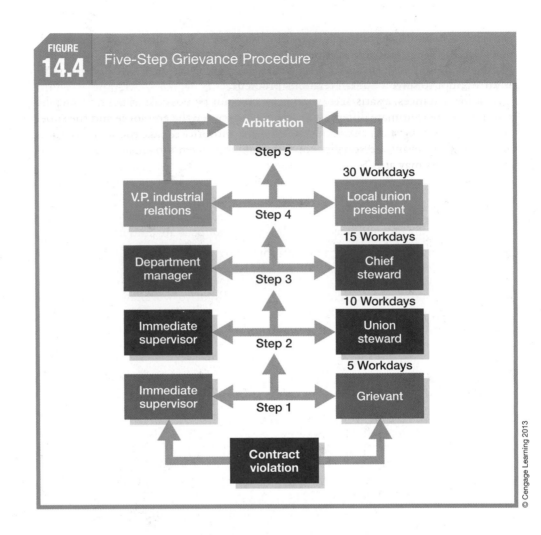

FIGURE 14.4   Five-Step Grievance Procedure

Arbitration
Step 5

30 Workdays

V.P. industrial relations — Step 4 — Local union president

15 Workdays

Department manager — Step 3 — Chief steward

10 Workdays

Immediate supervisor — Step 2 — Union steward

5 Workdays

Immediate supervisor — Step 1 — Grievant

Contract violation

© Cengage Learning 2013

number and timing of steps that are to compose the procedure, and the identity of representatives from each side who are to be involved in the hearings at each step. (See Figure 14.4.) When a grievance cannot be resolved at one of the specified steps, most agreements provide for the grievance to be submitted to a third party—usually an arbitrator—whose decision is final. Some labor agreements provide for mediation as a way to resolve employee grievances. When used, *grievance mediation* will be listed as a formal step in the grievance procedure preceding arbitration.

The Grievance Procedure in Action

For an employee's grievance to be considered formally, it must be expressed orally and/or in writing, ideally to the employee's immediate supervisor. Because grievances are often the result of an oversight or a misunderstanding, many of them can be resolved at this point. Whether it is possible to resolve a grievance at the initial step will depend on the supervisor's ability and willingness to discuss the problem with the employee and the steward. Additionally, HR professionals acknowledge that grievance handling is more successful when supervisors are trained formally in resolving grievances, including familiarization with the terms of the labor agreement and the discussion of the problem in a rational and objective manner. A grievance should not be viewed as something to be won or lost. Rather, both sides must view the situation as an attempt to solve a human relations problem.

In some instances, a satisfactory solution may not be possible at the first step because there are legitimate differences of opinion between the employee and the supervisor or because the supervisor does not have the authority to take the action required to satisfy the grievant. Personality conflicts, prejudices, emotionalism, stubbornness, or other factors may also be barriers to a satisfactory solution at this step.

Grievance Arbitration

The function of rights arbitration is to provide the solution to a grievance that a union and an employer have been unable to resolve by themselves. As mentioned earlier, arbitration is performed by a neutral third party (an arbitrator or impartial umpire). This third party's decision dictates how the grievance is to be settled.[65] Both parties are obligated to comply with the decision.

rights arbitration
Arbitration over interpretation of the meaning of contract terms or employee work grievances

Decision to Arbitrate

In deciding whether to use arbitration, each party must weigh the costs involved against the importance of the case and the prospects of gaining a favorable award. It would seem logical that neither party would allow a weak case to go to arbitration if there were little possibility of gaining a favorable award. Logic, however, does not always prevail. For example, it is not unusual for a union to take a weak case to arbitration in order to demonstrate to the members that the union is willing to exhaust every remedy in looking out for their interests. Union officers also are not likely to refuse to take to arbitration the grievances of members who are popular or politically powerful in the union, even though their cases are weak. Moreover, under the fair representation doctrine, unions have a legal obligation to provide assistance to members who are pursuing grievances. Because members can bring suit against their unions for failing to process their grievances adequately, many union officers are reluctant to refuse taking even weak grievances to arbitration.

fair representation doctrine
A doctrine under which unions have a legal obligation to assist both members and nonmembers in labor relations matters

Management, on the other hand, may allow a weak case to go to arbitration to demonstrate to the union officers that management "cannot be pushed around." Also, managers at lower levels may be reluctant to risk the displeasure of top management by stating that a certain HR policy is unworkable or unsound. Stubbornness and mutual antagonism also may force many grievances into arbitration because neither party is willing to make concessions to reach an agreement, even when it may recognize that it is in the wrong.

Arbitration Hearing

In our experience, employees unfamiliar with arbitration find the process confusing and often stressful. This is true for employees in the nonunion, as well as the union, setting. Arbitration hearings have the appearance of a court hearing but without many of the formalities of a court proceeding. The process begins with the swearing-in of witnesses and the introduction of the *submission agreement*. The submission agreement is a statement of the problem to be resolved. Such a statement might read: "Was the three-day suspension of Alex Hayden for just cause? If not, what is the appropriate remedy?" The parties will then make opening statements, followed by the presentation of facts and evidence, and the oral presentation of witnesses. The hearing will conclude with each side making summary statements that are arguments in support of its position.

In arbitrating a dispute, it is the responsibility of the arbitrator to ensure that each side receives a fair hearing during which it may present all of the facts it considers pertinent to the case. The primary purpose of the hearing is to assist the arbitrator in obtaining the facts necessary to resolve a human relations problem rather than a legal one. The arbitrator, therefore, has a right to question witnesses or to request additional facts from either party. After conducting the hearing and receiving post-hearing briefs (should the parties choose to submit them), the arbitrator customarily has thirty days in which to consider the evidence and render an award. In most labor contracts, the costs of arbitration are shared equally by the parties.

Arbitration Award

The arbitration award is a formal written document given to both sides. As in grievance procedures, there is no specific format to an arbitration award, but typically the award contains five parts: (1) submission agreement, (2) facts of the case, (3) positions of the parties, (4) opinion of the arbitrator, and (5) decision rendered. As might be expected, the decision of the arbitrator is of major importance to the parties. However, the reasoning behind the decision—the opinion—is equally important since it can provide guidance concerning the interpretation of the labor agreement and the resolution of future disputes arising from its administration. In pointing out the merits of each party's position, the reasoning that underlies the award can help lessen the disappointment and protect the self-esteem of those representing the unsuccessful party. The opinion will also evaluate the evidence presented by each side in support of its position and, in discipline cases, whether management had just cause for the action taken against an employee. (See Chapter 13 for a discussion of just cause in arbitration.) Importantly, in deciding a case, the arbitrator has the power to modify the outcome requested by both sides. It is not uncommon, for example, for an arbitrator to reduce a discharge to a suspension without pay for a specific time period.

Because of the importance and magnitude of arbitration in both the union and nonunion setting, the process by which arbitrators make decisions and the factors that influence those decisions are of continuing interest to managers. Typically, arbitrators use four factors when deciding cases:

1. The wording of the labor agreement (or employment policy in nonunion organizations)

2. The submission agreement as presented to the arbitrator

3. Testimony and evidence offered during the hearing

4. Arbitration criteria or standards (similar to standards of common law) against which cases are judged

When deciding the case of an employee discharged for absenteeism, for example, the arbitrator would consider these factors separately and/or jointly. Arbitrators are essentially constrained to decide cases on the basis of the wording of the labor agreement, or employment policy, and the facts, testimony, and evidence presented at the hearing.

In practice, arbitration decision-making is not an exact science. In fact, the decisions of arbitrators can be rather subjective. Arbitrators can, and do, interpret contract language differently (for example, what does "just cause discharge" actually mean), they assign varying degrees of importance to testimony and evidence, they judge the truthfulness of witnesses differently, and they give arbitration standards greater or lesser weight as they apply to facts of the case. Each of these influences introduces subjectivity into the decision-making process.[66]

Contemporary Challenges to Labor Organizations

We conclude our discussion of labor relations by highlighting two important issues facing unions today: decrease of union membership and foreign competition and technological advances.

Decrease in Union Membership

A major challenge confronting organized labor is to halt the decline in union membership. The magnitude of the problem is illustrated by statistics that show how union membership has declined in total numbers and as a percentage of the total civilian labor force. In 1970, union membership totaled approximately 21 million, or 25 percent of the civilian labor force. In 1990, those figures dropped to 16.7 million union members, or slightly more than 16 percent of the civilian workforce. Twenty years later, in 2010, union membership was approximately 14.7 million, or 11.9 percent of employed wage and salary workers.[67] In the private sector, union membership accounted for approximately 6.9 percent of all those employed, or about 7.1 million workers. The loss of union jobs reflects, in part, the decline in U.S. manufacturing jobs, coupled with the failure of unions to draw membership from among the white-collar and service ranks, where the labor force is growing more rapidly.[68] Other reasons for the decline in union membership include the following:

- A shift from traditional unionized industries (manufacturing, mining) to high-technology industries (computers, pharmaceuticals).[69]

- Growth in the employment of part-time and temporary workers.

- Growth in small businesses, in which unionization is more costly and difficult to perform.

- Globalization of the workforce particularly among low wage employers.[70]

What are labor organizations doing to stem the decline in union membership? The answer, according to one union official, is "energized organizing." First, unions are targeting workers they have long ignored: low-wage service workers on the bottom tier of the U.S. economy—for example, janitors, maids, and service workers; food service employees; and retail clerks. Furthermore, unions see recent immigrants, the fastest-growing segment of working people, as potent prospects for union growth. Haitian cab drivers, Latino airport workers, Vietnamese warehouse distribution workers, Russian truck drivers, and Asian American service workers are targeted for union representation.[71]

Second, the AFL-CIO has embraced an aggressive unionization strategy. Richard Trumka, president of the AFL-CIO, argued that "the labor movement has a rich and vibrant future." In a speech regarding the disputes over collective bargaining in

Wisconsin in 2011, Trumka argued that the backlash by politicians against unions has provided an opening for them to show that unions are still a vital component of giving workers a voice in their organizations—from a local high school math teacher to an NFL football player.[72] Finally, national unions are restructuring in order to increase their ability to effectively organize. Two examples are noteworthy. The Union of Needletrades, Industrial and Textile Employees (UNITE), and the Hotel Employees and Restaurant Employees (HERE) merged to become UNITE HERE. According to Chris Chafe, spokesperson for the union, "We all benefit from working more closely together on solidarity issues, organizing campaigns, and contract battles."

As previously discussed, the new national labor federation Change to Win has as its primary goal the unionization of low skill, low wage employees. Will labor's efforts reverse the decline in membership? Bureau of Labor Statistics figures for 2010 show that the number of workers belonging to unions dropped from 15.7 million in 2008 to 14.7 million in 2010.[73]

Globalization and Technological Change

LEARNING OUTCOME 7

Do technology changes and globalization improve the situation of unions in America?

The importation of steel, consumer electronics, automobiles, clothing, textiles, and shoes from foreign countries creates a loss of jobs in the United States for workers who produce these products. Furthermore, foreign subsidiaries of American corporations such as Nike, Westinghouse, and Xerox have been accused by labor unions of exporting the jobs of U.S. workers. As a result, unions are demanding more government protection against imports, seeking to protect U.S. jobs from low-cost overseas producers. Furthermore, in recent years, the service sector of the U.S. economy has witnessed the outsourcing of white-collar jobs to foreign employers in locations such as India and Indonesia.

offshoring

work that was previously carried out in one country is moved to another country

As a result, more and more Americans are worried about their jobs being filled by people in other countries. Offshoring, defined as work that was previously carried out in one country to another, has been examined with great fear and trepidation in the last 20 years. The U.S. is now at a critical crossroads in how we deal with offshoring of American jobs. There is no question that most of the recent growth in U.S. companies comes from outside of the country. Companies argue that to remain competitive against foreign companies they must take advantage of lower cost labor in countries like India and China—perpetuating the continual loss of union jobs in the United States. Statistics show that approximately 38 million jobs in the United States can be offshored, while 55 million can not.[74] Surprisingly, the least offshorable jobs are correlated with low salary and educational levels. So what does this mean for unions and employers?

Employers need to pay more attention to the relevant stakeholders such as unions, employees and communities in which they operate. Not only will unions fight offshoring but employees can lose morale and loyalty when they experience insensitive approaches to jobs being offshored. To avoid this, employers can take a more open book management approach to show unions and employees the financial challenges that come from not offshoring.[75] Not doing so leads to push back from unions and consumers alike. For example, in 2011 Delta Airlines brought back call center jobs to the United States from Jamaica. CEO Richard Anderson said that "one of the ways to mitigate the impact of the recession is to insource work." In 2009 Delta also closed a call center in India, sparking a trend among airlines and U.S. companies in general to bring back jobs.[76] Yet most job loss in America is not due to offshoring, but rather to technological changes.[77]

Improvements in computer technology and highly automated operating systems have lowered the demand for certain types of employees. Decline in membership in the auto, steel, rubber, and transportation unions illustrates this fact. As previously discussed, technological advances have also diminished the effectiveness of strikes because highly automated organizations are capable of maintaining satisfactory levels of operation with minimum staffing levels during work stoppages.

Summary

LEARNING OUTCOME 1 The Railway Labor Act (1926) affords collective bargaining rights to workers employed in the railway and airline industries. The Norris-LaGuardia Act (1932) imposes limitations on the granting of injunctions in labor-management disputes. Most private employees are granted representation rights through the Wagner Act (1935), which has helped protect and encourage union organizing and bargaining activities. The passage of the Taft-Hartley Act (1947) and the Landrum-Griffin Act (1959) has served to establish certain controls over the internal affairs of unions and their relations with employers.

LEARNING OUTCOME 2 Studies show that workers unionize for different economic, psychological, and social reasons. While some employees may join unions because they are required to do so, most belong to unions because they are convinced that unions help them improve their wages, benefits, and most importantly, equality. Employee unionization is largely caused by dissatisfaction with managerial practices and procedures.

LEARNING OUTCOME 3 A formal union organizing campaign is used to solicit employee support for the union. Once employees demonstrate their desire to unionize through signing authorization cards, the union petitions the NLRB for a secret ballot election. If 51 percent of those voting in the election vote for the union, the NLRB certifies the union as the bargaining representative for all employees in the bargaining unit.

LEARNING OUTCOME 4 Negotiating a labor agreement is a detailed process. Each side prepares a list of proposals it wishes to achieve while additionally trying to anticipate proposals desired by the other side. Bargaining teams must be selected and all proposals must be analyzed to determine their impact on and cost to the organization. Both employer and union negotiators are sensitive to current bargaining patterns within the industry, general cost-of-living trends, and geographical wage differentials. Managers establish goals that seek to retain control over operations and to minimize costs. Union negotiators focus their demands around improved wages, hours, and working conditions. An agreement is reached when both sides compromise their original positions and final terms fall within the limits of the parties' bargaining zone.

Traditionally, collective bargaining between labor and management has been adversarial. Presently, there is an increased interest in nonadversarial negotiations—negotiations based on mutual gains and a heightened respect between the parties. What the FMCS calls interest-based bargaining is one form of nonadversarial negotiations.

LEARNING OUTCOME 5 The collective bargaining process includes not only the actual negotiations, but also the power tactics used to support negotiating demands. When negotiations become deadlocked, bargaining becomes a power struggle to force from either side the concessions needed to break the deadlock. The union's power in collective bargaining comes from its ability to picket, strike, or boycott the employer. The employer's power during negotiations comes from its ability to lock out employees or to operate during a strike by using managerial or replacement employees.

LEARNING OUTCOME 6 When differences arise between labor and management, they are normally resolved through the grievance procedure. Grievance procedures are negotiated and thus reflect the needs and desires of the parties. The typical grievance procedure consists of three, four, or five steps—each step having specific filing and reply times. Higher-level managers and union officials become involved in disputes at the higher steps of the grievance procedure. The final step of the grievance procedure may be arbitration. Arbitrators render a final decision to problems not resolved at lower grievance steps.

The submission agreement is a statement of the issue to be solved through arbitration. It is simply the problem the parties wish to have settled. The arbitrator must answer the issue by basing the arbitration award on four factors: contents of the labor agreement (or employment policy), submission agreement as written, testimony and evidence obtained at the hearing, and various arbitration standards developed over time to assist in the resolution of different types of labor-management disputes. Arbitration is not an exact science because arbitrators give varying degrees of importance to the evidence and criteria by which disputes are resolved.

LEARNING OUTCOME 7 Challenges facing union leaders today include declining membership caused by technological advancements and increased domestic and global competition. Offshoring is when jobs done in one country are lost to another country. Companies argue that to remain competitive they must offshore more and more jobs to lower wage economies. While technological change has much more to do with job loss in America, employers need to be more open in their decisions to move jobs offshore or to replace them with technology.

Key Terms

arbitrator
authorization card
bargaining power
bargaining unit
bargaining zone
business unionism
collective bargaining process

craft unions
employee associations
exclusive representation
fair representation doctrine
grievance procedure
industrial unions
interest-based bargaining

labor relations process
rights arbitration
unfair labor practices (ULPs)
union shop
union steward
offshoring

Discussion Questions

LEARNING OUTCOME 1 Under the provisions of the Taft-Hartley Act, which unfair labor practices apply to both unions and employers?

LEARNING OUTCOME 2 Contrast the arguments concerning union membership that are likely to be presented by a union with those likely to be presented by an employer.

LEARNING OUTCOME 3 Describe the steps in the traditional organizing drive. What "nontraditional" organizing tactics are unions using to increase their membership ranks?

LEARNING OUTCOME 4 Of what significance is the bargaining zone in the conduct of negotiations? What are some influences affecting negotiated outcomes?

LEARNING OUTCOME 5 The negotiations between Data Services International and its union have become deadlocked. What form of bargaining power does each side possess to enforce its bargaining demands? What are the advantages and disadvantages of each form of bargaining power for both the employer and union?

LEARNING OUTCOME 6 Nancy Buffett has decided to file a grievance with her union steward. The grievance alleges that she was "bypassed" by a junior employee for a promotion to senior technician.

a. Explain the steps her grievance will follow in a formal union-management grievance procedure.
b. Should her grievance go to arbitration, explain the process of an arbitration hearing and identify the criteria used by the arbitrator to resolve her claim.

LEARNING OUTCOME 7 **a.** What are some of the actions being taken by unions to cope with the contemporary challenges they face?
b. How can companies respond to the labor changes that result from increased technology and globalization?

HRM EXPERIENCE
Learn about Unions

Unions, like business organizations, are dynamic and varied organizations. Some unions are very large, such as the United Auto Workers (UAW) and the American Federation of State, County and Municipal Employees (AFSCME), and represent workers nationally or even internationally. Others are smaller in size—for example, the Writers Guild of America (WGA) or the Air Traffic Controllers Association (ATCA)—and represent only specific groups of employees or organize only in a designated geographic area. This exercise will help you learn more about unions.

Assignment

Working individually or in teams, select four or five different unions or employee associations and report on the following. Vary your selections (large/small, public/private, and so on) to widen your understanding of labor organizations.

- History of the union
- Membership size and type of employees represented
- Mission of the union
- Structure of the union, including its major departments
- National officers
- Names of employers with whom they have an agreement
- Special benefits they offer members
- Other interesting or pertinent information

The AFL-CIO website (http://www.afl-cio.org) provides a list of all unions—and their websites—affiliated with the federation. National unions and their locals along with library research can also provide information. Be prepared to present your findings during a class discussion.

On the Job: Video Cases

UNITE HERE: Local 1 Chicago

Watch the video clip on UNITE HERE as they describe disagreements between employees and management about wages and work standards. Relationships between organizations and unions and the challenges in organizing nonunion workers to increase the number of unionized workers are also discussed.

Questions and Exercises

1. a) The video talks about UNITE HERE, an international union, and Local 1 Chicago, a local. Describe the relationship between an international and a local union. Is UNITE HERE an industrial or craft union?

   b) Two union stewards are included in the video. What is the role of a union steward?

2. a) Patrick Mooney is an organizer for UNITE HERE Local 1 Chicago. He talks in the video about working with casino employees that are willing to serve as shop stewards and each shop steward works with an organizing committee of employees that they train how to organize. What are some other methods unions use to persuade employees to sign authorization cards?

   b) What are three union prevention efforts that management might do to prevent employees from signing authorization cards?

3. In the video, one of the union stewards mentions that the union is negotiating with the employer but the union has taken a strike vote. Why would a union take a strike vote if it is still negotiating with management? What is the difference between a strike and a lockout? Why would management prevent union members from working?

   If the union and management reach an impasse, what are three possible processes to deal with a bargaining impasse other than a strike or lockout?

4. At the end of the video, the president of the UNITE HERE Local 1 Chicago talks about the challenges of organizing non-union workers. One of the controversial issues surrounding unionization is about "right-to-work" laws. These laws prohibit requiring employees to join unions as a condition of obtaining or continuing employment. In other words, in states with right-to-work laws, employers may have an open shop, which indicates workers cannot be required to join or pay dues to a union. Do you think "right-to-work" laws are a good idea? Why or why not?

Case Study   1

The New Union Battles: Public Unions vs. Rich World Governments

While private sector unions may be rapidly declining in the United States, public sector unions are still strong . . . or at least were. In 2011, public sector unions representing teachers, prison guards, police officers, railworkers, and civil servants were dealt a blow by their employers—the government. At the forefront of the battle was the issue of collective bargaining. And it began in Wisconsin.

But this is not the first time Wisconsin has been at the forefront of collective bargaining. The Wagner Act of 1934 (discussed in this chapter) did not grant public employees the right to collective bargaining. In the 1950s and 1960s public sector employees pushed for collective bargaining rights. Finally, in 1959 Wisconsin became the first state to grant this right to public employees. In a dramatic turn of events,

Wisconsin is now the first to repeal collective bargaining rights for its public sector employees.

After a standoff with state Democrats and prounion demonstrators, Wisconsin Governor Scott Walker and the state legislature decided that public employees did not have the right to collective bargaining. This set off a chain reaction in eighteen other states where they had also proposed legislation that would remove all or some collective bargaining powers from unions (e.g., Maine, Arizona, Indiana, Alaska, Michigan, and Ohio). This could potentially increase the number of states that do not allow collective bargaining to go from five (see map below) to nearly half of the states.

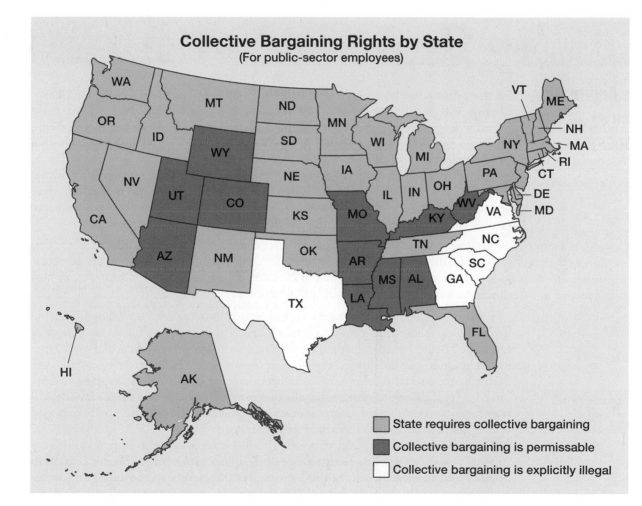

Collective Bargaining Rights by State
(For public-sector employees)

State requires collective bargaining

Collective bargaining is permissable

Collective bargaining is explicitly illegal

Questions

1. Why were politicians in 2011 so interested in trying to repeal collective bargaining rights for public sector employees?
2. What risks does losing their collective bargaining rights hold for public employees?

3. As an elected politician charged with major cuts in your state budget, how would you negotiate with the public sector unions? As a public sector union leader, how would you negotiate with the state legislature?

Source: Thomas Kochan, "Protective bargaining: How to prevent the labor wars," *Boston Review* (March 23, 2011), http://www.bostonreview.net/BR36.2/thomas_kochan_wisconsin_labor_wars.php; "The battle ahead: The struggle with public-sector unions should be about productivity and parity, not just spending cuts," *The Economist* (January 6, 2011), http://www.economist.com/node/17851305; David Morris, "When unions are strong, Americans enjoy the fruits of their labor," *Huffington Post* (April 8, 2011), http://www.huffingtonpost.com/david-morris/when-unions-are-strong-am_b_846802.html.

Case Study 2

The Arbitration Case of Jesse Stansky

At the arbitration hearing, both parties were adamant in their positions. Nancy Huang, HR manager of Phoenix Semiconductor, argued that the grievant, Jesse Stansky, was justly terminated for arguing and hitting a coworker—a direct violation of company policy and the employee handbook. Stansky argued that he had been a good employee during his ten years of employment.

The submission agreement governing the case read, "It is the employer's position that just cause existed for the discharge of Mr. Jesse Stansky and the penalty was appropriate for the offense committed." Additionally, the employer introduced into evidence the labor agreement, which defined just cause termination as follows:

> Just cause shall serve as the basis for disciplinary action and includes, but is not limited to: dishonesty, inefficiency, unprofessional conduct, failure to report absences, falsification of records, violation of company policy, destruction of property, or possession or being under the influence of alcohol or narcotics.

Stansky was hired as a systems technician on November 20, 1998, a position he held until his termination on October 25, 2011. According to the testimony of Huang, Phoenix Semiconductor strived to maintain a positive and cordial work environment among its employees. Fighting on the job was strictly prohibited. Stansky's performance evaluation showed him to be an average employee, although he had received several disciplinary warnings for poor attendance and one three-day suspension for a "systems control error." Stansky was generally liked by his coworkers, and several testified on his behalf at the arbitration hearing.

The termination of Stansky concerned an altercation between himself and Gary Lindekin, another systems technician. According to witnesses to the incident, both Stansky and Lindekin became visibly upset over the correct way to calibrate a sensitive piece of production equipment. The argument—one witness called it no more than a heated disagreement—lasted approximately three minutes and concluded when Stansky was seen forcefully placing his hand on Lindekin's shoulder. Lindekin took extreme exception to Stansky's behavior and immediately reported the incident to management. After interviews with both Stansky and Lindekin and those who observed the incident, Huang; Samantha Lowry, the employee's immediate supervisor; and Grant Ginn, department manager, decided that Stansky should be terminated for unprofessional conduct and violation of company policy.

Questions

1. Which arguments should be given more weight: those based on company policy, the employee handbook, and the labor agreement or mitigating factors given by the grievant and his witnesses? Explain.
2. How might unprofessional conduct be defined? Explain.
3. If you were the arbitrator, how would you rule in this case? Explain fully the reasons for your decision.

Source: Adapted from an arbitration heard by George W. Bohlander. All names are fictitious.

ANSWERS TO HIGHLIGHTS IN HRM 1

1. No. Applicants are considered as employees and, as such, are protected under the law.

2. No. Individual questioning of employees about their union membership or activities in unlawful.

3. No. Except in specific situations (for example, to promote safety), employees have the right to wear union insignia.

4. Yes.

5. Yes. Blacklisting of job applicants or employees is against labor law.

6. No. During an organizing drive, an employer cannot promise improvements in wages or benefits as a means of defeating the union.

7. Yes. Both nonunion and union employers are subject to unfair labor practice charges.

8. Yes. When a grievance arbitration clause exists in a labor agreement, management must arbitrate cases that seem baseless.

9. Yes. Employees can be disciplined or discharged for work-related misconduct but not solely because of their union affiliations or union sentiments.

10. Yes. Antiunion remarks are not unlawful, provided they are not coercive.

Notes and References

1. Elizabeth Shuler, "Next up for labor: America's young workers," *Perspectives on Work* (Spring 2010): 11; LERA, *Young workers: A lost Decade*, AFL-CIO report, 2009; John Gibbons, "I can't get no ... job satisfaction, that is," The Conference Board Report: R-1459-09-RR, (January, 2010).

2. USA Today Salaries Databases., http://content.usatoday.com/sports/football/nfl/salaries/mediansalaries.aspx?year=2009.

3. "The owners take a punt," *Economist* (March 10, 2011).

4. Robert Bussel, "Why Unions Matter: An Orientation for Oregon Legislators,

Candidates, and Their Staffs," *Labor Studies Journal* 32, no. 2 (June 2007): 210.

5. Cindy Fazzi, "All You Need to Know about the History of Labor Union Law," *Dispute Resolution Journal* 59, no. 2 (May–June 2004): 87.

6. Labor-Management Relations Act, Public Law 101, 80th Congress (1947).

7. Ellen Dannin, "Enforcing labor rights," *Employment Policy Research Network* (January 23, 2011); Office of the NLRB General Counsel, *Summary of Operations—2010.*, Memorandum GC 11-03 (January 10, 2011).

8. The NLRB toll-free telephone number is (866) 667-NLRB.

9. Douglas E. Noll, "A Theory of Mediation," *Dispute Resolution Journal* 56, no. 2 (May–June 2001): 78–84.

10. "Statements by FMCS Director George H. Cohen on NFL-NFLPA Talks," News Release from FMCS (February 24, 2011).

11. Adapted from the FMCS "A Timeline of Events in Modern American Labor Relations," http://www.fmcs.gov/internet/itemDetail.asp?categoryID=21&itemID=15810.

12. For an expanded model of the labor relations process, see John Dunlop, *Industrial Relations*

Systems (New York: Henry Holt, 1958), Chapter 1. This book is a classic in the labor relations field. Also, those interested in labor relations may wish to explore in greater detail the historical developments of the U.S. labor movement. Much can be learned about the current operations of labor organizations and the philosophies of labor officials from labor's historical context. A brief but comprehensive history of labor unions can be found in undergraduate labor management textbooks such as those listed among these references.

13. Christopher Palmeri, "Workers Say: We Want an Upgrade," *Business Week* (April 16, 2007): 11.

14. Kate Bronfenbrenner, "The role of union strategies in NLRB certification elections," *Industrial and Labor Relations Revie* 50, no. 2 (1997): 195–212.

15. Pat Angelo, Philip Murray, *Union Man. A Life Story* (Philadelphia, Pa.: Xlibris Corporation, 2003).

16. Jeffrey Pfeffer, "The Human Equation: Building Profits by Putting People First," (Cambridge, MA: Harvard Business School Press, 1998); William Holley, Jr., Kenneth Jennings, and Roger Wolters, "The Labor Relations Process," (Mason, OH: South-Western Cengage Learning: 2009).

17. Rebecca Leung, "Working the good life: SAS provides employees with generous work incentives," 60 Minutes Transcript, (April 20, 2003), http://www.cbsnews.com/stories/2003/04/18/60minutes/main550102.shtml.

18. Justin Longenecker, Carlos Moore, J. William Petty, Leslie Palich, "Small Business Management: Launching and Growing Entrepreneurial Ventures, 15th ed. (Mason, OH: Cengage Learning, 2010).

19. Kate Bronfenbrenner and Robert Hickey, "Successful Union Organizing in the United States—Clear Lessons, Too Few Examples," *Multinational Monitor* 24, no. 6 (June 2003): 9.

20. William H. Holley, Kenneth M. Jennings, and Roger S. Wolters, *The Labor Relations Process*, 9th ed. (Mason, OH: South-Western, 2009).

21. While most employers will readily negotiate with the union once it is certified as the bargaining representative of employees, other employers will continue to vigorously oppose unionization. This may be accomplished by taking a very aggressive bargaining posture against union demands. NLRB statistics show that unions file a large number of unfair labor practice charges [8(a)(5) violations] when they believe employers illegally hinder the bargaining process.

22. Brody Mulling, "Campaign 08: Groups Unveil Plans to Bankroll Democrats," *Wall Street Journal* (March 19, 2008): A-18.

23. Neil King Jr., Thomas M. Burton, and Kris Maher, "Political fight over unions escalate," *Wall Street Journal* (February 22, 2011).

24. Richard W. Hurd, "Neutrality Agreements: Innovative, Controversial, and Labor's Hope for the Future," *New Labor Forum* 17, no. 1 (Spring 2008): 34.

25. "Organizing institute: Three-day training," AFL-CIO, http://www.aflcio.org/aboutus/oi/3daytraining.cfm

26. Jarol B. Manheim, *Trends in Union Corporate Campaigns* (New York U.S. Chamber of Commerce, 2005).

27. Arthur B Shostak, (ed.), *The CyberUnion Handbook* (Armonk, NY: M. E. Sharpe, 2002).

28. *Annual Report of the National Labor Relations Board—2009*, 5.

29. Jonathan A. Segal, "Labor Pains for Union-Free Employers," *HR Magazine* 49, no. 3 (March 2004): 113.

30. Raymond Hogler, "Exclusive Representation and the Wagner Act: The Structure of Federal Collective Bargaining Law," *Labor Law-Journal* 58, no. 3 (Fall 2007): 157.

31. *Annual Report of the National Labor Relations Board—2007*, 16.

32. Jeffrey S. Bosley, "NLRB Modifies Recognition and Contract Bar Doctrines to Provide 45-Day Window to Challenge Voluntary Recognition," *Employee Relations Law Journal* 33, no. 4 (Spring 2008): 89.

33. See UAW website at www.uaw.org.

34. The number of unions associated with the AFL-CIO has steadily declined during the past twenty years. The decline has largely been caused by the mergers of unions through absorptions, amalgamations, or affiliations. Several prominent mergers include the merger of the International Ladies Garment Workers Union and the Amalgamated Clothing and Textile Workers Union into the Union of Needletrades, Industrial and Textile Employees; the merger of the Packinghouse and Industrial Workers with the United Food and Commercial Workers; and the merger of the Woodworkers with the Machinists.

35. Statistical information on the AFL-CIO can be obtained at http://www.aflcio.org.

36. Robert J. Grossman, "Reorganized Labor," *HR Magazine* 53, no. 1 (January 2008): 37; see also Samuel Estreicher, "Disunity within the House of Labor: Change to Win or Stay the Course," *Journal of Labor Research* 27, no. 4 (Fall 2006): 505.

37. Tracy Roof, "CTW vs. AFL-CIO: The Potential Impact of the Split on Labor's Political Action," *International Journal of Organizational Theory and Behavior* 10, no. 2 (Summer 2007): 245.

38. Gary Chaison, "The AFL-CIO Split: Does It Really Matter?" *Journal of Labor Research* 28, no. 2 (Spring 2007): 301.

39. Paul F. Clark and Lois S. Gray, "Administrative Practices in American Unions," *Journal of Labor Research* 29, no. 1 (March 2008): 42.

40. Dean Foust, "Sending the Teamsters a Message," *Business Week* (July 17, 2006), 9.

41. "The battle ahead: The struggle with public-sector unions should be about productivity and party, not just spending cuts," *The Economist* (January 6, 2011).

42. Data obtained from union web pages, (March 26, 2008).

43. The two executive orders pertaining to public sector collective bargaining are EO 10988, signed by President Kennedy in 1962, and EO 11491, issued in 1971 by President Nixon.

44. Thomas Kochan, "Protective bargaining: How to prevent labor wars," *Boston Review* (March 23, 2011).

45. Jeffery K. Guiler and Jay M. Shatritz, "Dual Personnel System—Organized Labor and Civil Service: Side-by-Side in the Public Sector," *Journal of Labor Research* 25, no. 2 (Spring 2004): 199.

46. William A Donohue and Paul J. Taylor, "Role Effects in Negotiation: The One-Down Phenomenon," *Negotiation Journal* 23, no. 3 (July 2007): 307.

47. Leigh Thompson, *The Mind and Heart of the Negotiator*, 3rd ed. (Upper Saddle River, NJ: Prentice Hall, 2004).

48. Thomas R. Colosi, "The Principles of Negotiation," *Dispute Resolution Journal* 57, no. 1 (February–April 2002): 28–31.

49. Joel Cutcher-Gershenfeld, Thomas Kochan, John-Paul Ferguson, and Betty Barrett,

"Collective Bargaining in the Twenty-First Century: A Negotiations Institution at Risk," *Negotiation Journal* 23, no. 3 (July 2007): 249.

50. Ross Stagner and Hjalmar Rosen, *Psychology of Union-Management Relations* (Belmont, CA: Wadsworth, 1965), 95–97. This is another classic in the field of labor-management relations.

51. The National Labor Relations Board offers an excellent book on the National Labor Relations Act. This book discusses good faith bargaining as well as other important legal issues—for example, employers covered by the law, unfair labor practices, and election procedures. See *Basic Guide to the National Labor Relations Act* (Washington, DC: U.S. Government Printing Office, 1997).

52. Joe Stanley, interview by author, Phoenix, AZ, January 5, 2008.

53. The FMCS has a complete and comprehensive program to train labor and management negotiators in the art and techniques of interest-based bargaining (IBB). Information on the IBB program can be obtained from the FMCS national headquarters at 2100 K Street, N.W., Washington, DC 20427 or from FMCS district offices.

54. Robert B. McKersie, Teresa Sharpe, Thomas A. Kochan, and Adrienne E. Eaton, "Bargaining Theory Meets Interest-Based Negotiations: A Case Study," *Industrial Relations* 47, no. 1 (January 2008): 66.

55. Bill McDonough, president of United Food and Commercial Workers Union Local 99, interview by author, January 12, 2008, Phoenix, AZ.

56. Roger J. Peters and Deborah Bavarnick Mastin, "To Mediate or Not to Mediate: That is the Question," *Dispute Resolution Journal* 62 no. 2 (May–July 2007): 14.

57. Labor agreement, Wabash Fibre Box Company and Paperworkers.

58. Helen Lam and Mark Harcourt, "A New Approach to Resolving the Right-to-Work Ethical Dilemma," *Journal of Business Ethics* 73, no. 3 (July 2007): 231.

59. "NFL Collective Bargaining Agreement, 2006–2012," NFL Players Association.

60. Judith L. King and Laurel C. Catlett-King, "Cowboy Campaigning: Patriotism, Freedom, and Right-to-Work in Oklahoma," *Labor Studies Journal* 32, no. 1 (March 2007): 5; see also Raymond L Hogler, "Right-to-Work and the Colorado Labor Peace Act: How Politics Trumped Policy," *Labor Law Journal* 58, no. 2 (Summer 2007): 85.

61. Right-to-work states are Idaho, Nevada, Wyoming, Utah, Arizona, North Dakota, South Dakota, Nebraska, Kansas, Oklahoma, Texas, Iowa, Arkansas, Louisiana, Mississippi, Tennessee, Alabama, Georgia, Virginia, North Carolina, South Carolina, and Florida.

62. John B. Larocco, "Ambiguities in Labor Union Contracts: Where Do They Come From?" *Dispute Resolution Journal* 59, no. 1 (February–April 2004): 38.

63. *Grievance Guide*, 12th ed. (Washington, DC: BNA Books, 2007).

64. Vera Riggs, Labor-Management Relations Conference, August 11, 2007, Phoenix, AZ.

65. Arbitration awards are not final in all cases. Arbitration awards may be overturned through the judicial process if it can be shown that the arbitrator was prejudiced or failed to render an award based on the essence of the agreement.

66. Nels E. Nelson and Sung Min Kim, "A Model of Arbitral Decision Making: Facts, Weights, and Decision Elements," *Industrial Relations* 47, no. 2 (April 2008): 266.

67. Statistics are from the U.S. Department of Labor, Bureau of Labor Statistics website at http://www.bls.gov.

68. Arthur Shostak, "Trends in U.S. Trade Unionism," *Employment Relations Today* 34, no. 2 (Summer 2007): 2.

69. David Welch, "Twilight of the UAW," *Business Week* (April 10, 2006), 62.

70. Matthew J. Slaughter, "Globalization and Declining Unionization in the United States." *Industrial Relations* 46, no. 2 (April 2007): 329.

71. Kent Wong and Victor Narro, "Educating Immigrant Workers for Action," *Labor Studies Journal* 32, no. 1 (March 2007): 113; Chris Tilly, "An opportunity not taken ... Yet: U.S. labor and the current economic crisis," *The Journal of Labor and Society* 14, no. 1: 73–85.

72. Richard Trumka, "The Future of Unions," remarks by AFL-CIO President Richard L. Trumka, Wayne State University, Detroit, Michigan, (April 7, 2011), press release by AFL-CIO, http://www.aflcio.org/mediacenter/prsptm/sp04072011.cfm.

73. Statistics are from the U.S. Department of Labor, Bureau of Labor Statistics website, http://www.bls.gov.

74. Jagdish Bhagwati and Alan S. Blinder, "Offshoring of American jobs: What response from U.S. economy policy?" (Cambridge, MA: MIT Press).

75. Shad S. Morris, "Book Review of Offshoring of American Jobs," *Human Resource Management* 50, no. 2: 303–306.

76. Tracey E. Schelmetic, "Delta to shut down contact center in Jamaica; Bring jobs to U.S.," TMCnet, (January 14, 2011).

77. Jagdish Bhagwati and Alan S. Blinder. "Offshoring of American jobs: What response from U.S. economy policy?" (Cambridge, MA: MIT Press).

Pankaj & Insy Shah/Getty Images

When you pick up a newspaper or turn on the TV, you will notice that stories are constantly being told about companies competing globally. These stories might include the joint ventures and mergers of U.S. and international companies, such as Walmart's bid to take over the South African retail store, Massmart, in 2011. Or they might highlight companies expanding into other markets, such as the U.S.-based deli Quiznos' expansion into Kuwait. Or the stories might focus on international companies such as Hyundai rapidly outpacing its Japanese competitors to gain dominance here in the United States. "No matter what kind of business you run, no matter what size you are, you are suddenly competing against companies you have never heard of all around the world that make a very similar widget or provide a very similar service," as one global manager put it. Some companies are handling the challenge well. Others are failing miserably as they try to manage across borders. More often than not, the difference boils down to how people are managed: the ability of HR managers to adapt practices to local cultures while at the same time developing some level of global standardization.

Up until this point in the book, we have paid primary attention to HRM practices and systems in the United States. Nonetheless, the topic of international HRM is so important that we dedicate an entire chapter to its discussion. The first part of this chapter describes some of the environmental factors that affect the work of managers in a global setting. Just as with domestic operations, the dimensions of the environment form a context in which HRM decisions in foreign countries are made. Next, we present a brief introduction to international business firms. In many important respects, the way a company organizes its international operations influences the type of managerial and human resources issues it faces. A major portion of this chapter deals with the various HR activities involved in the recruitment, selection, development, and compensation of employees working abroad. However, as we explain later in this chapter, workers stationed all over the United States are increasingly finding themselves working virtually with people from other cultures who speak different languages. This creates challenges not only for them, but for firms' HR managers.

Using the INTERNET

The Society for Human Resource Management Global Forum provides current news updates on issues concerning HRM from around the world. Go to **www.cengagebrain.com**

The Global Environment

LEARNING OUTCOME 1

What environmental factors should Quiznos consider in its move to Kuwait? How do economics, politics, and culture impact the way Quiznos manages its employees in Kuwait?

In Chapter 1, we highlighted some of the global trends affecting human resource management. The global environment of today is much different than it was 10 years ago. Because technological, political, cultural, and economic conditions are constantly shifting across the world, how people are managed in those changing environments will shift as well. On one hand, free trade agreements between countries, technological advances that increase individual productivity, and the development of common platforms for moving knowledge and information will draw more tightly the bonds that connect us, increasing global similarities and the need for HRM to integrate practices. On the other hand, political and cultural differences create global environments that present needs for HRM to adapt practices to the local countries in which they are operating.

Global Similarities

Some key factors that have influenced human resource management include increased (1) free trade, (2) service-based business, and (3) integrated technology platforms. Because these factors have increased the economic integration across countries, they have emphasized the need for HRM practices and systems to be more globally integrated and consistent across countries.

Free Trade. In 1995, the World Trade Organization (WTO) was formalized as a cooperative forum for countries' leaders to come together and increase free trade across the world. Today, the WTO member countries represent over 155 member nations and cover 97 percent of all international trade.[1] In addition, countries are continually negotiating free trade agreements with each other in hopes of increasing their economic activity and power. Twenty-seven member countries now comprise the European Union (EU), whose goal is to facilitate the flow of goods, services, capital, and human resources across national borders in Europe in a manner similar to the way they cross state lines in the United States.[2] A similar transition occurred within North America with the passage of the North American Free Trade Agreement (NAFTA) in 1994. NAFTA created the world's largest free market. Since its passage, commerce between the United States, Canada, and Mexico has more than tripled, growing from $290 billion in 1994 to nearly $1 trillion in 2010. There has been a great deal of criticism about NAFTA and its effect on the U.S. job market. Among the most vocal criticisms of NAFTA are (1) the loss of jobs to Mexico, (2) the loss of foreign companies coming into the United States, (3) lower salaries for American manufacturing jobs, and (4) increased illegal migration from Mexico. However, other than increased illegal migration from Mexico, these criticisms are not supported by the data.[3] As discussed in Chapter 14, technological changes have created more disruptions to the American job market than free trade. In fact, the free trade agreement has resulted in lower product prices for Americans overall, giving them more money to spend, thereby stimulating other parts of the U.S. economy.[4] In 2011 the U.S. entered a free trade agreement with the country of Colombia. The agreement decreased tariffs and taxes on goods and services traded between the two countries. While certain jobs may go to Colombia as a result of the free trade agreement, the net result in jobs for the United States was predicted to be positive. According to the U.S. Commerce Department, the agreement would increase exports by $1.1 billion per year, increasing the number of jobs created in the United States.[5]

Like NAFTA and the U.S.-Colombia Free Trade Agreement, numerous trade agreements, including the Association of Southeast Asian Nations (ASEAN), East Asia Economic Group, Asia-Pacific Economic Cooperation (APEC), and South Asian Association for Regional Cooperation (SAARC), have significantly facilitated trade among Asian countries, making Asia the fastest-growing region in the world. China—its fastest-growing country—has emerged as a dominant trade leader since instituting trade reforms in the late 1970s. Since joining the WTO in 2001, China's economy has grown dramatically, drastically altering political and trading relations among nations. China's 1.3 billion people represent a massive, largely untapped consumer market for global companies. Today more cars are sold in China than in Europe, for example. Driving this trend are big multinational corporations, which are expanding into the country. But many smaller firms are heading to China as well. "It's not so much that [companies] want to go East: They feel that they have no choice," said one international HR staffing consultant. "They must be in China. It's not a question of if, but a question of how." In addition to China, India's economy is also growing very quickly, as is Brazil's.[6]

Business Services vs. Manufacturing. Through technological advances, the number of manufacturing jobs is decreasing in proportion to the number of service-based jobs. Companies are increasingly turning to sophisticated machinery that requires fewer workers to produce the same amount of product, such as cars, clothes, and computers. For example, increased automation of manufacturing processes in the auto industry has eliminated the number of workers needed on the shop floor. Even in less-developed countries where manufacturing is typically stronger due to low cost of labor and high cost of capital intensive equipment, labor saving technology is becoming more affordable and accessible. Take, for instance, a textile factory in Vietnam. It is more cost effective for the factory to purchase high-tech threading equipment to spin the cotton into thread than to hire hundreds of people to thread the cotton by hand, even when the average wage for such employees is less than $100 a month.

On the other hand, service-based jobs are much harder to replace with technology than manufacturing jobs. Most people would prefer to talk with a real person instead of a computer-generated program regarding wireless Internet connection problems with their computer. While technology can provide you with the classes you need to graduate, talking with a career counselor can help you choose the right classes to get a job after graduating.

Services will always be in demand, regardless of whether you are in a developed country such as the United States or a less-developed country such as Haiti. Service-based jobs that can be traded across borders span from highly complex to simple, including research and development, consulting, finance and accounting, human resource management, tech support, customer service, and basic data entry jobs. Traditionally, during trade negotiations less-developed countries have expressed concern over the advantages that developed countries have over them in the service sectors. While this is still true in certain areas today, many less-developed countries have developed strong capabilities in different service sectors. For example, with companies such as Infosys and thousands of small- and medium-sized IT companies, India is often seen as a hub for information technology services that can be sold anywhere in the world.

Integrated Technology Platforms. While increases in technology have pushed for more service-based jobs, technology has also increased the rate at which these services

Multinational and global companies have the challenge of managing operations and people in many different countries and cultures.

Greg Balfour Evans/Alamy

can be traded across countries. Along with the creation of the World Trade Organization, 1995 also signifies the beginning of the Internet era. America Online (AOL) went public in 1995 to mark the beginning of integrated technology platforms that could be shared instantaneously across the world. In the words of Thomas Friedman, these events "flattened the world," making many service-based jobs able to be done anywhere in the world. *Integrated technology platforms* represent common operating systems such as Microsoft Windows 7 that can be used across multiple computers connected through the Internet. Through these common platforms, work becomes less specific to particular companies and countries.

In this era, employees become empowered to compete without the need of a large company. For example, many websites such as guru.com have developed an online marketplace where individuals can offer various services and compete for business throughout the world. Imagine you are interested in developing a new website for your company. By going to the Internet you can select various individuals offering these specific services. They may be from Manila, Philippines; Mumbai, India; Manhattan, New York; or Munich, Germany.

In sum, these three factors of increased trade, service-based business, and integrated technology platforms have shifted the way companies are managing their human resources. HR units can no longer operate as separate groups attached only by a common brand and finances. HR managers must integrate their operations to capture the benefits that come from having people all on the same page.

Global Differences

While free trade agreements and technological factors may call for a more unified HR system in your company, other global factors can act as major obstacles. These factors consist of political and cultural differences. First, political differences are found in a country's labor laws, property rights, and patents. For example, when the Ohio-based welding company Lincoln Electric started operations in Brazil, they were not able to offer their yearly bonus program based on performance because any bonuses paid for two consecutive years become a legal entitlement.[7]

In many countries, particularly those in Africa, property rights are poorly protected by governments. Whoever has the political power or authority can seize others' property with few or no repercussions. Civil unrest can also lead to the poor enforcement of property rights. Companies have less incentive to locate factories or invest in countries experiencing strife. Another issue relates to intellectual property rights: rights related to patents, trademarks, and so forth. Despite the fact that private property rights are now generally enforced in China, intellectual property rights have seen little protection. For example, when General Motors formed a joint venture with a Chinese company to produce and sell a new automobile in the country, a knockoff version of the car could be seen on China's streets even before GM and its partner were able to manufacture their first car. Environmental restrictions also make some countries more attractive to do business in than others.

Beyond the political issues just mentioned, a country's cultural environment (communications, religion, values and ideologies, education, and social structure) also has important implications when it comes to a company's decision about when and how to do business there. Because of low labor costs and language similarities, many U.S. companies are finding India an attractive place to locate their facilities, particularly call centers. Eastern Europe has also begun to attract interest because citizens there are well educated and largely possess English-speaking skills. Similarly, the U.S. military's departure from Panama in recent years left that country with a bilingual workforce that is very attuned to the American work culture.[8]

Figure 15.1 summarizes the complexity of the cultural environment in which HR must be managed. Culture is an integrated phenomenon. By recognizing and

cultural environment

The communications, religion, values and ideologies, education, and social structure of a country

host country

A country in which an international corporation operates

accommodating taboos, rituals, attitudes toward time, social stratification, kinship systems, and the many other components listed in Figure 15.1, managers stand a better chance of understanding the culture of a host country—a country in which an international business operates. Different cultural environments require different approaches to human resources management. Strategies, structures, and management styles that are appropriate in one cultural setting may lead to failure in another.

Even in countries that have close language or cultural links, HR practices can be dramatically different. In some countries, night shifts are taboo. In other countries, employers are expected to provide employees with meals and transportation between home and work. In India, workers generally receive cash bonuses on their wedding anniversaries to use to purchase gifts for their spouses, and dating allowances are provided to unmarried employees. These are practices that would never occur to American managers and HR practitioners.[9] Throughout this chapter we will discuss several issues related to managing people across borders.

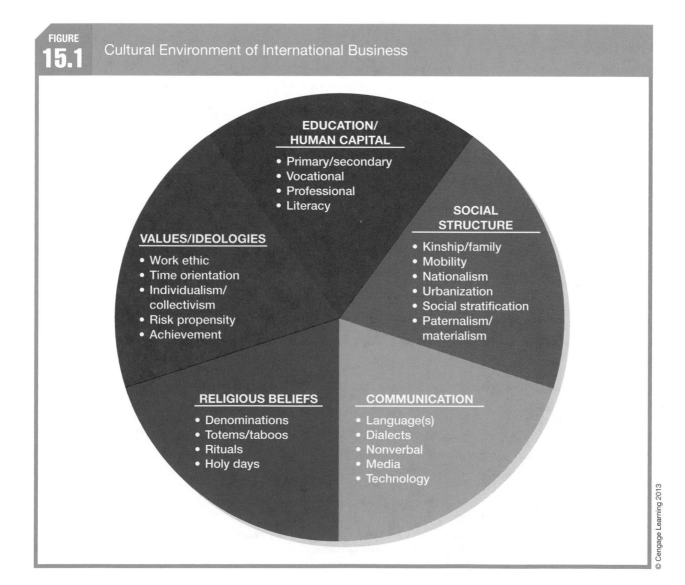

FIGURE 15.1   Cultural Environment of International Business

EDUCATION/ HUMAN CAPITAL
- Primary/secondary
- Vocational
- Professional
- Literacy

SOCIAL STRUCTURE
- Kinship/family
- Mobility
- Nationalism
- Urbanization
- Social stratification
- Paternalism/ materialism

VALUES/IDEOLOGIES
- Work ethic
- Time orientation
- Individualism/ collectivism
- Risk propensity
- Achievement

RELIGIOUS BELIEFS
- Denominations
- Totems/taboos
- Rituals
- Holy days

COMMUNICATION
- Language(s)
- Dialects
- Nonverbal
- Media
- Technology

Managing across Borders

International business operations can take several different forms. A large percentage carry on their international business with only limited facilities in foreign countries. Others, particularly Fortune 500 corporations, have extensive facilities and personnel in various countries of the world. Dell, for example, actually employs more people outside the United States than within it. Managing these resources effectively and integrating their activities to achieve global advantage is a challenge to the leadership of these companies.

Figure 15.2 shows four basic types of organizations and how they differ in the degree to which international activities are separated to respond to the local regions and integrated to achieve global efficiencies. The international corporation is essentially a domestic firm that builds on its existing capabilities to penetrate overseas markets. Companies such as Honda, General Electric, and Procter & Gamble used this approach to gain access to Europe—they essentially adapted existing products for overseas markets without changing much else about their normal operations. (One such adaptation, for example, was P&G's extremely successful introduction of a detergent brick used on washboards in India.)

A multinational corporation (MNC) is a more complex form that usually has fully autonomous units operating in multiple countries. Shell, Philips, and ITT are three typical MNCs. These companies have traditionally given their foreign subsidiaries a great deal of latitude to address local issues such as consumer preferences, political pressures, and economic trends in different regions of the world. Frequently these subsidiaries are run as independent companies without much integration. The global corporation, on the other hand, can be viewed as a multinational firm that maintains control of its operations worldwide from the country in which it is

LEARNING OUTCOME 2

If you were a global HR manager, you would want to make sure your HR practices match the structure of the organization. What is the ideal organizational structure in a global environment?

international corporation
A domestic firm that uses its existing capabilities to move into overseas markets

multinational corporation (MNC)
A firm with independent business units operating in multiple countries

global corporation
A firm that has integrated worldwide operations through a centralized home office

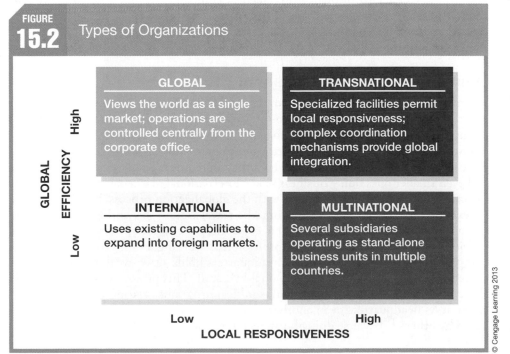

FIGURE 15.2   Types of Organizations

GLOBAL EFFICIENCY — High / Low

GLOBAL
Views the world as a single market; operations are controlled centrally from the corporate office.

TRANSNATIONAL
Specialized facilities permit local responsiveness; complex coordination mechanisms provide global integration.

INTERNATIONAL
Uses existing capabilities to expand into foreign markets.

MULTINATIONAL
Several subsidiaries operating as stand-alone business units in multiple countries.

LOCAL RESPONSIVENESS — Low / High

© Cengage Learning 2013

headquartered. Japanese companies, such as Matsushita and NEC, tend to treat the world market as a unified whole and try to combine their activities in each country to maximize their efficiencies on a global scale. These companies operate much like a domestic firm, except that they view the whole world as their marketplace.

Finally, a transnational corporation attempts to achieve the local responsiveness of an MNC while also achieving the efficiencies of a global firm. To balance this "global/ local" dilemma, a transnational corporation uses a network structure that coordinates specialized facilities positioned around the world. By using this flexible structure, a transnational corporation provides autonomy to its operations in foreign countries but brings these separate activities together into an integrated whole. For most companies, the transnational form represents an ideal, rather than a reality. However, companies such as IBM, Ford, Unilever, and Shell have made good progress in restructuring their operations to function more transnationally.[10]

Although various forms of organization exist, in this chapter we will generally refer to any company that conducts business outside its home country as an international business. The United States, of course, has no monopoly on international business. International enterprises are found throughout the world. A number of European and Pacific Rim companies have been conducting business on an international basis for much longer than their U.S. counterparts. The close proximity of European countries, for example, has facilitated international trade among them for centuries. More recently, companies from Japan and China have proven to be some of the most powerful companies in the world. A Global Fortune 500 list from the year 2000 would have revealed that the top 10 companies were all located in the United States. In 2010, only two of the top ten companies came from the United States. The others are based out of Europe and Asia. Many of these companies generate more revenue annually than do entire small nations. Consequently, they are corporations that have a significant impact on the world economy.

With the global environment being filled by companies originating from different countries and operating in multiple cultures, increased pressure is being placed on the HRM function. International HRM is being seen more and more as a key source of competitive advantage for international businesses.

Domestic versus International HRM

LEARNING OUTCOME 3

What is the best way to make HR practices transnational?

transnational corporation

A firm that attempts to balance local responsiveness and global scale via a network of specialized operating units

International HRM differs from domestic HRM in several ways. In the first place, it necessarily places a greater emphasis on functions and activities such as relocation, orientation, and translation services to help employees adapt to new and different environments outside their own countries and to help local employees adapt and integrate into the foreign companies in which they were hired. Many larger corporations and even smaller ones doing business in key international markets have full-time HR managers devoted solely to assisting with the globalization process. British Airways, for example, has a team of HR directors who travel around the world to help country managers stay updated on international concerns, policies, and programs. Coca-Cola provides support to its army of HR professionals working around the world. A core HR group in the company's Atlanta headquarters holds a two-week HR orientation twice a year for Coca-Cola's international HR staff. This program helps Coca-Cola share information about its HR philosophies, programs, and policies established either at its headquarters or in another part of the world that can be successfully adopted by others.[11] Because doing business internationally can be extremely complex, many companies also hire international staffing firms such as Boston Global Consulting and Cendant Mobility, a Connecticut-based company. These firms have expertise when it comes to relocating employees, establishing operations abroad, and helping with import/export and foreign tax issues.

HR information systems have also come a long way in terms of helping firms improve their international coordination. A good HR information system can facilitate communication, recordkeeping, and a host of other activities worldwide. Some HRISs are designed to track the whereabouts of employees traveling or on assignment. This can be important in the event of a transportation accident, a natural disaster such as a tsunami, a terrorist attack, or civil strife if evacuation plans must be implemented. Occasionally, however, even what seems to be the simplest of cultural differences can be difficult to overcome when a company attempts to set up a global HRIS. For example, when Lucent first rolled out a PeopleSoft system to more than ninety countries, the company's managers found that the order of employees' names was so important—and so varied—that it took two months to settle on a name format allowing employees to be entered into the system. As you can see, even seemingly small cultural differences can create major challenges for the international HR manager. As a result, many companies rely on outsourcing firms such as Mercer Consulting and Korn/Ferry International to help them better manage the challenges, risks, and regulations associated with their HRM activities abroad.[12]

Staffing Internationally

When a company expands globally, HR managers are generally responsible for ensuring that operations are staffed. There are three main ways a company can staff a new international operation. First, the company can send people from its home country. These employees are often referred to as expatriates, or home-country nationals. Second, it can hire host-country nationals, natives of the host country, to do the managing. Third, it can hire third-country nationals, natives of a country other than the home country or the host country. Each of these three sources provides certain advantages and certain disadvantages. Most corporations use all three for staffing their multinational operations, although some companies exhibit a distinct bias for one or another.[13] It is important to note, however, that host countries sometimes restrict their choices by passing laws and regulations designed to employ host-country individuals. Tax incentives, tariffs, and quotas are frequently implemented by the host country to encourage local hiring.

As shown in Figure 15.3, at early stages of international expansion, organizations often send home-country nationals to establish activities (particularly in less-developed countries) and to work with local governments. This is generally very costly. Traditionally, expatriates have received generous salaries, automobiles, full relocation services, private schooling for their children, trips home, and other perks. These services frequently end up costing more than $300,000 yearly, on average, making the cost of a typical three-year expatriate assignment more than $1 million. Some companies find it more cost-effective to hire young, single management trainees who are interested in career growth. Companies are also taking greater pains to more clearly outline the overall goal of the foreign assignment and its timetable for completion. Ingersoll-Rand, an international equipment manufacturer, now carefully documents in detail what should be accomplished during an assignment abroad—whether the assignment is designed to enhance an assignee's leadership skills, improve productivity

LEARNING OUTCOME 4

Why would PepsiCo want to send as few U.S.-based managers as possible to run operations in Peru?

expatriates, or home-country nationals
Employees from the home country who are on international assignment

host-country nationals
Employees who are natives of the host country

third-country nationals
Employees who are natives of a country other than the home country or the host country

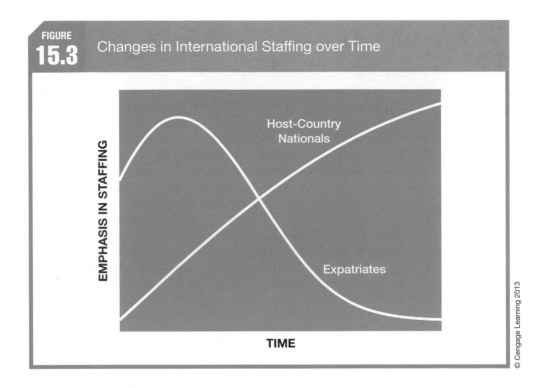

FIGURE 15.3   Changes in International Staffing over Time

© Cengage Learning 2013

and sales targets abroad, transfer specific technology to a foreign operation, or staff it with local, expatriate, or third-country nationals.

In recent years, there has also been a trend to send expatriates on shorter, project-based assignments (two to twelve months versus one to three years) and to shift more quickly toward hiring host-country nationals. This has three main advantages:

1. Hiring local citizens is generally less costly than relocating expatriates. Local citizens also know the cultural and political landscape of the country and are often more likely to be able to gain the support of local staff members.

2. Since local governments usually want good jobs for their citizens, foreign employers may be required to hire locally.

3. Most customers want to do business with companies (and people) they perceive to be local versus foreign.

Because U.S. companies want to be viewed as true international citizens, there has also been a trend away from hiring expatriates to head up operations in foreign countries, especially European countries. ABB, Eli Lilly, and PepsiCo, which have strong regional organizations, have tended to replace their U.S. expatriate managers with local managers as quickly as possible. In addition to hiring local managers to head their foreign divisions and plants, more companies are using third-country nationals. Third-country nationals are often multilingual and already acclimated to the host country's culture—perhaps because they live in a nearby region. Thus, they are also less costly to relocate and sometimes better able to cope culturally with foreign environments.

Companies tend to continue to use expatriates only when a specific set of skills is needed or when individuals in the host country require development. For example, after embarking on a joint venture in China with a formerly state-owned enterprise, Ingersoll-Rand discovered that it had to educate its Chinese employees not only on the company's practices and culture, but on free-market, Western business practices. This required the company's expatriates to stay in China longer than planned.[14] In fact, many expatriates find that in Asia, it takes more time to adapt to the culture and win over employees so as to impart a company's work values. Personal relationships are everything in Asia, and business there can only be conducted after relationships have been established. To help their expatriates adapt in Asia and elsewhere, firms are finding it helpful to pair them with local "buddies," or host-country mentors. At SAS Institute's regional headquarters in Heidelberg, Germany, mentors such as these are assigned to expatriate newcomers to help answer any questions they might have about the firm or culture. The practice seems to be improving the odds of an expatriate succeeding.[15]

Recruiting Internationally

Improved telecommunications and travel have made it easier to match up employers and employees of all kinds worldwide. As we mentioned earlier in the chapter, most of Dell's employees work outside the United States. Rolls-Royce, headquartered in the United Kingdom, hires over 25 percent of its 38,900 employees abroad. Because its customers come from around the globe, Rolls-Royce figures its workforce should as well. The German company Siemens would like to hire more employees from abroad. "Our top managers are predominantly white German males," said its chief executive Peter Loscher, adding, "If you are not representing your global customer base, then you won't tap your full potential." Airbus, the European commercial jet manufacturer, recruits engineers from universities and colleges all over Europe. American-based Boeing's need for engineers is so great that it also recruits internationally and has even opened a design center in Moscow. In 2010 Intel set up the largest computer equipment and manufacturing plant in Vietnam. They initially needed 300 highly qualified engineers. However, they struggled to find this many qualified employees and had to start by bringing in foreign nationals until they could hire enough local employees. The HR manager for Vietnam noted, "We had everything set up for the new factory. The only thing we were missing was the qualified engineers."

HR departments must be particularly responsive to the cultural, political, and legal environments both domestically and abroad when recruiting internationally. Companies such as Starbucks, Lockheed Martin, and Honeywell have made a special effort to create codes of conduct for employees throughout the world to ensure that standards of ethical and legal behavior are known and understood. PepsiCo has taken a similar approach to ensuring that company values are reinforced (even while recognizing the need for adapting to local cultures). The company has four core criteria that are viewed as essential in worldwide recruiting efforts: (1) personal integrity, (2) a drive for results, (3) respect for others, and (4) capability. Zurich, a Swiss financial and insurance company with operations throughout the world, makes sure its employees assigned to the United States take diversity and sexual harassment courses.

Lockheed Martin has also developed a strong international ethics program to ensure all decisions throughout the company are made with integrity. For example, their vision statement stresses the following factors: (a) doing what is right, (b) respecting others, and (c) performing with excellence. All employees are required to undergo business conduct and compliance training. This training helps employees deal with difficult issues related to export control, insider trading, international business practices, kickbacks and gratuities, and the Truth in Negotiations Act. The programs are offered in over twenty-one languages. Furthermore, Lockheed Martin provides integrity video scenarios on issues such as export control, currency exchange, and respect, available to everyone on their website for practice. Are there things you can learn in terms of developing your own cultural sensitivity?[16]

The regulatory environment outside the United States often differs substantially. The regulations range from those that cover procedures for recruiting and screening to their working conditions, pay and incentives, and retirement provisions. In Japan, for example, criminal background checks on candidates are not allowed. In France, employees can only work thirty-five hours per week. Similarly, many Central American countries have stringent regulations about the number of foreigners that can be employed as a percentage of the total workforce. Virtually all countries have work permit or visa restrictions that apply to foreigners.

work permit, or visa

A government document granting a foreign individual the right to seek employment

A work permit or visa is a document issued by a government granting authority to a foreign individual to seek employment in that government's country. Since 9/11, there has been a backlash against immigration and a backup in the number of visas granted to foreign workers and students entering the United States. U.S. managers complain that this is making it harder for them to hire top talent. Firms lament that they are experiencing a "reverse brain drain" as skilled foreign workers leave the United States or seek work in other countries. It is a more serious problem than you might think. The fact is that the United States has traditionally benefited from its ability to attract the world's best talent. Did you know that annually foreigners residing in the United States file about 25 percent of international patent applications? The financial crisis of 2008–2010 only made matters worse, as companies were even less likely to offer jobs to foreigners who might be seen as taking jobs from national citizens. As a result, many Indian and Chinese living in the United States are being heavily recruited by companies and governments to work back in their home countries. Making matters worse, other countries have become less restrictive than the United States in terms of granting foreign residents citizenship and work permits. The United Kingdom, for example, gives graduates of the world's top fifty business schools an automatic right to work in the United Kingdom for a year. In addition, the European Union is contemplating introducing a "blue card" system designed to expedite the EU citizenship of talented employees.[17] Whatever the employee's destination, HR managers need to ensure that work permits and visas are applied for early in the relocation process.

In terms of recruiting at the executive level, companies use executive recruiting firms such as Heidrick & Struggles in the United States or Spencer Stuart in the United Kingdom. At lower levels, as Chapter 7 explained, companies recruiting abroad often need to advertise their firms and employment "brand" to recruits who are not familiar with it. In countries such as India and China, an employer's reputation is extremely important to candidates' families—sometimes more important than pay.

Many employers have learned that the best way to find workers in these less well-developed countries is through referrals and radio announcements because many people lack sufficient reading or writing skills. Other firms use international recruiting firms to find skilled labor abroad. As we have explained, some countries, in fact, require the employment of locals if adequate numbers of skilled people are available. Specific exceptions are sometimes granted (officially or unofficially) for contrary cases, as for Mexican farm workers in the United States and for Italian, Spanish, Greek, and Turkish workers in Germany and the Benelux countries (Belgium, the Netherlands, and Luxembourg). Foreign workers invited to perform needed labor are usually referred to as guest workers. Foreign workers with H2B visas can come to the United States for a maximum of nine months to perform temporary, nonagricultural seasonal work that is one-time-only. These types of visas are often used in conjunction with recruiting workers for entry-level positions in hotels and restaurants during peak travel seasons.

A worker who moves to another country to perform his or her job may be required to get a work permit or visa in order to lawfully stay in that country.

Tim Hall/Digital Vision/Getty Images

Although hiring nonnationals can result in lower direct labor costs for a company, the indirect costs—those related to housing, language training, health services, recruitment, transportation, and so on—can be substantial. Some companies competing in industries with acute talent shortages are nonetheless finding the expenditures worthwhile. Nursing is one such industry. (See the Case Study at the end of the chapter.)[18]

guest workers
Foreign workers invited to perform needed labor

Apprenticeships

A major source of trained labor in European nations is apprenticeship training programs (described in Chapter 7). On the whole, apprenticeship training in Europe is superior to that in the United States. In Europe, a dual-track system of education directs a large number of youths into vocational training. The German system of apprenticeship training, one of the best in Europe, provides training for office and shop jobs under a three-way responsibility contract between the apprentice, his or her parents, and the organization. At the conclusion of their training, apprentices can work for any employer but generally receive seniority credit with the training firm if they remain in it. France has been able to draw on its "Grandes Ecoles" for centuries. Created during the Renaissance to fulfill a need that universities were not meeting at the time, the Grandes Ecoles educate prospective engineers up to the equivalent level of master of engineering. Snecma, an international equipment supplier headquartered in Paris, hires about 80 percent of its employees from the Grandes Ecoles.[19]

Staffing Transnational Teams

In addition to focusing on individuals, it is also important to note that companies are increasingly using transnational teams to conduct international business. Transnational teams are composed of members of multiple nationalities working virtually on projects that span multiple countries. General Electric's LightSpeed VCT, a state-of-the-art medical scanner, was designed with input from cardiologists around the world. The machine's innards were designed by GE engineers in four different countries, and the software to run it was written by multiple teams working together from India, Israel, France, and Wisconsin.[20] Aware that many products developed in developed economies will have a limited market in developing economies, companies such as P&G, GE, and Tata Motors have turned to transnational teams

transnational teams
Teams composed of members of multiple nationalities working on projects that span multiple countries

to help develop low cost but high quality products for the poor. For example, Tata Motors developed the "Tata Nano," a car for nearly $2,000. As the cheapest car in the world, the Tata Nano was developed by a large transnational team, with suppliers in different countries designing specific parts to meet a price-sensitive threshold.

Teams such as these are especially useful for performing tasks that the firm as a whole is not yet structured to accomplish. For example, they may be used to transcend the existing organizational structure to customize a strategy for different geographic regions, transfer technology from one part of the world to another, and communicate between headquarters and subsidiaries in different countries. In GE's case, the company realized its competitors were developing their own medical scanning technology more quickly. GE decided it could no longer afford to duplicate its efforts in different divisions around the world—that these groups would have to work together as a team.

Sometimes companies send employees on temporary assignments abroad as part of transnational teams lasting perhaps a few months. This might be done to break down cultural barriers between international divisions or disseminate new ideas and technologies to other regions. In other instances, employees are transferred for extended periods of time. Years ago, Fuji sent fifteen of its most experienced engineers from Tokyo to a Xerox facility in Webster, New York. Over a five-year period, the engineers worked with a team of U.S. engineers to develop the "world" copier. The effort led to a joint venture that has lasted for decades. Fuji-Xerox now employs approximately 40,000 people globally at thirteen companies around the world.[21]

The fundamental task in forming a transnational team is assembling the right group of people who can work together effectively to accomplish the goals of the team. For GE's LightSpeed team, this frequently meant holding eight-hour global conference calls encompassing numerous time zones. (The call times were rotated so that no single team had to stay up all night for every call.) Many companies try to build variety into their teams in order to maximize responsiveness to the special needs of different countries. For example, when Heineken formed a transnational team to consolidate its production facilities, it ensured that team members were drawn from each major region within Europe. Team members tended to have specialized skills, and members were added only if they offered some unique skill that added value to the team. Cross-cultural training can benefit transnational teams by helping them overcome language and cultural barriers they face.

Selecting Employees Internationally

Selecting employees in a foreign country environment can be difficult. When embarking on hiring employees in a new country, a firm's international HR managers should get to know the local market and customs in hiring. This will help the firm understand what to look for in an employee. When GE first entered India it did not realize that much of the effective hiring was done through family ties and friendship networks. Not wanting to appear biased, GE at first did not allow such practices. However, after struggling to select good recruits GE finally incorporated peer and family referral systems into their selection practices. This led to selection of employees that stayed within the organization much longer.

To better understand the local market there are a few things firms can do. First, international HR managers should get to know the universities, technical schools, and primary schools in the area. More than ensuring qualifications, schools provide extensive networks to future employees and provide insight on the type of hires managers would want to select. This means taking time to understand how the local schools operate. In many developing countries, higher education systems are underdeveloped and either do not provide enough future employees or employees with suitable skills. For example, Rolls-Royce and Intel have both become involved in the development of school curriculum for both managerial and engineering skill development. By partnering with local universities, Rolls-Royce and Intel offer funding and curriculum design to better prepare students for the work environment. At their own expense, these companies see such costs as investments in future employees as well as a chance to shape the skills they need to run their companies in those countries.

Second, international HR managers should develop networks in the business and government communities. Because many companies' reputations may not precede them, they must use personal networks to develop trust in the company. An international HR manager's job will not be just to select the right people that come to the office but to go out and select the right people within the community. For instance, when Unilever, a large British-Dutch consumer products company, opens up operations in a foreign environment it often becomes heavily involved in the local community by conducting community feedback meetings, local education programs, and environmental studies. The company's heavy involvement in the local environment helps to rapidly build its local reputation, which increases its knowledge of potential new hires.

Finally, to effectively select employees in a local environment, international HR managers must understand the employees of the firm's competitors. As they map out and get to know key employees in competing organizations, they develop a better understanding of what to look for in other employees while building up a new pool of applicants to recruit in the future. For example, companies such as Exxon and GE, as well as smaller companies, will turn to employees of competing companies because they already know that these employees have the necessary skills and abilities to survive in their company. This is especially important to note, as more and more domestic companies are hiring away foreign international firms' employees, with the lure of patriotism and staying power of a local company.

Selecting Global Managers

What if an organization cannot find the appropriate talent in the local country? What if a firm is opening up operations in a foreign country but needs managers who know the ins and outs of the company or who have company specific expertise? In this case, organizations need to select managers from one country and move them to another. Unfortunately, many of these decisions are based primarily upon company specific expertise and not on country or culture specific expertise. In other words, little attention is paid to how likely the person will be able to complete the task in a very specific environment.

The demand for expatriate employees is growing rapidly. In fact, companies repeatedly report that one of their top strategies is to "deploy more staff on international assignments."[22] Selecting someone for an international assignment depends on a variety of different employment factors, including the extent of contact the employee will have with local citizens and the government and the degree to which the foreign environment differs from the home environment. For example, if the job involves extensive contacts with the community, as with a chief executive officer, this factor should be given appropriate weight. The magnitude of differences between the political, legal, socioeconomic, and cultural systems of the host country and those of the home country should also be assessed.[23]

global manager
A manager equipped to run an international business

Levi Strauss has identified the following six skill categories for the global manager, or manager equipped to run an international business:

- The ability to seize strategic opportunities

- The ability to manage highly decentralized organizations

- An awareness of global issues

- Sensitivity to diversity issues

- Competence in interpersonal relations

- Community-building skills[24]

If a candidate for expatriation is willing to live and work in a foreign environment, an indication of his or her tolerance of cultural differences should be obtained. This can often be done by testing, which we will discuss shortly. On the other hand, if local nationals have the technical competence to carry out the job successfully, they should be carefully considered for the job before the firm hires a domestic candidate and sends the person abroad. As we explained, most corporations realize the advantages to be gained by staffing international operations with host-country nationals wherever possible.

Selecting home-country and third-country nationals requires that more factors be considered than in selecting host-country nationals. While the latter must of course possess managerial abilities and the necessary technical skills, they have the advantage of familiarity with the physical and cultural environment and the language of the host country. Figure 15.4 compares the advantages and disadvantages of hiring global managers from these three different groups. The discussion that follows, however, will focus on the selection of expatriate managers from the home country, along with their compensation and performance appraisals.

core skills
Skills considered critical to an employee's success abroad

augmented skills
Skills helpful in facilitating the efforts of expatriate managers

Colgate-Palmolive, Whirlpool, and Dow Chemical have further identified a set of core skills that they view as critical for success abroad and a set of augmented skills that help facilitate the efforts of expatriate managers. These two types of skills are shown in Highlights in HRM 1. Many of these skills are not significantly different from the skills managers need to succeed domestically. Although in years past the average U.S. expatriate manager was an American-born Caucasian, more companies today are seeing the advantages of assigning expatriates depending on their ethnicity. But such a decision needs to be considered carefully. For example, an Indian candidate applying for a position in India may never have actually visited the country or may not relate well to the culture. Ultimately, the candidate best qualified for the job should be sent. In the past, women were overlooked for global managerial positions—perhaps because companies believed they would fare poorly in foreign, male-dominated societies or because they believed women have less desire to go abroad. Today women comprise around 20 percent of expatriates. Moreover, multiple studies show that women expatriates perform just as well as men.[25] In some countries, women expatriates are novel (particularly in managerial positions). They are very visible and distinctive and may even receive special treatment not given their male colleagues.

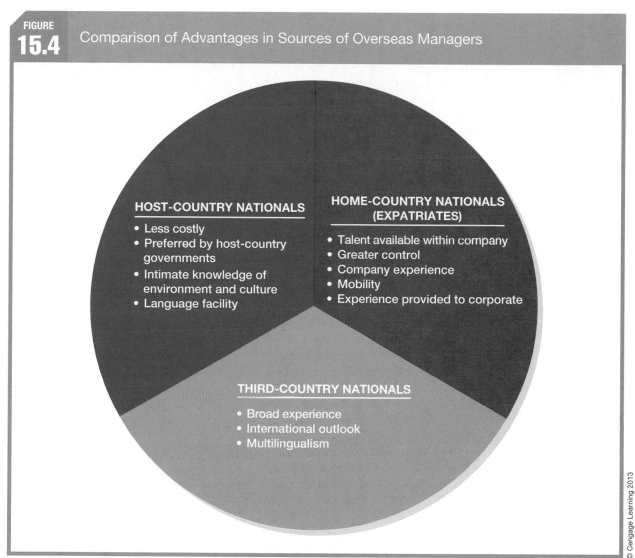

FIGURE 15.4 Comparison of Advantages in Sources of Overseas Managers

HOST-COUNTRY NATIONALS

- Less costly
- Preferred by host-country governments
- Intimate knowledge of environment and culture
- Language facility

HOME-COUNTRY NATIONALS (EXPATRIATES)

- Talent available within company
- Greater control
- Company experience
- Mobility
- Experience provided to corporate

THIRD-COUNTRY NATIONALS

- Broad experience
- International outlook
- Multilingualism

Several steps are involved in selecting individuals for an international assignment, and the sequencing of these activities can make a big difference:

Step 1: Begin with self-selection. Employees should begin the process years in advance by thinking about their career goals and how interested they are in working abroad. By beginning with self-selection, companies can more easily avoid the problems of forcing otherwise promising employees into international assignments that are a bad fit for them. For individuals with families, relocating decisions are more complicated. Employees should seek information to help them predict their chances of success living abroad. Companies such as EDS and Deloitte & Touche give their employees self-selection instruments to help them consider the pros and cons of international assignments. Performance Program Inc.'s Overseas Assignment Inventory and the International Mobility Assessment test, developed by Tucker International, are two

1 HIGHLIGHTS IN **HRM**
Skills of Expatriate Managers

CORE SKILLS

Experience

Decision making

Resourcefulness

Adaptability

Cultural sensitivity

Team building

Maturity

AUGMENTED SKILLS

Technical Skills

Negotiation Skills

Strategic thinking

Delegation Skills

Change management

such tests. Other companies assess candidates' spouses as well. At Solar Turbines, a San Diego–based manufacturer of industrial gas turbines, a candidate's spouse and sometimes his or her children undergo a day of assessment to see how well they are likely to respond to an international assignment.[26]

Step 2: Create a candidate pool. After employees have self-selected, organizations can build a database of candidates for international assignments. Information in the database might include availability, languages, country preferences, and skills.

Step 3: Assess candidates' core skills. From the short list of potential candidates, managers can assess each candidate in terms of their technical and managerial readiness relative to the needs of the assignment.

Step 4: Assess candidates' augmented skills and attributes. As Figure 15.5 shows, expatriate selection decisions are typically made based upon the technical competence of candidates as well as their professional and international experience. In addition, organizations are beginning to pay more attention to an individual's ability to adapt to different environments. How well a person adjusts depends on his or her flexibility, emotional maturity and stability, empathy for the culture, language and communication skills, resourcefulness and initiative, prior international experience, exposure to different cultures, and diplomatic skills. If these skills are lacking, no amount of technical competency is likely to result in a successful assignment.[27]

Even companies that believe they have selected the best candidates frequently experience high expatriate **failure rates**. Figure 15.6 shows the major causes of assignment failure. Poor cultural fit is a major reason why assignments fail. For example, although China is among the easiest countries to which to attract Western expatriates, it is also one of the hardest places for them to succeed because the country's culture is so different. A lack of expatriate support from headquarters is another major cause. Expatriates often describe themselves as "out of sight and out of mind." This highlights the importance of headquarters maintaining close contact with them to see how they are faring. Yet another big factor is a spouse's inability to adjust to his or her new surroundings. Today, more companies are preparing families by offering them cultural and language training. ARAMCO, a Saudi Arabian corporation, has such a program. The program includes practical information such as how to deal with

failure rate

The percentage of expatriates who do not perform satisfactorily

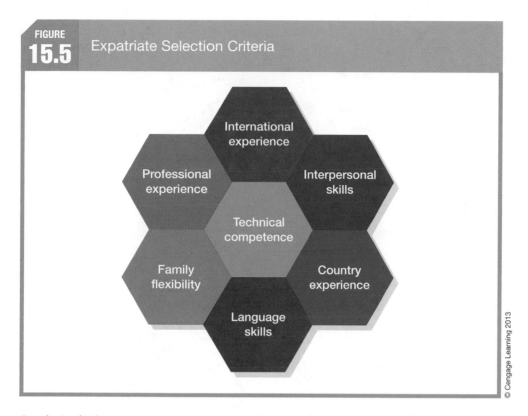

FIGURE 15.5   Expatriate Selection Criteria

© Cengage Learning 2013

Saudi Arabia's transportation systems, where to shop, day-to-day finances, and an explanation of the differences between the beliefs and customs of Saudis and people from other cultures.[28]

There are number of ways to improve the success of expatriate assignments. Ultimately the expatriate must find a way to adjust to the demands of their company, the country environment, and their family needs. Employees who share a common vision with the company are willing to undergo difficulties for the organization. Employees who take time to understand the culture and market in which they are operating will be better able to cope with unexpected changes and demands. Finally, employees who have family members that are supportive and interested in an overseas assignment are much more successful in their international assignments. As a result, expatriates stand a greater chance of being able to successfully adjust to their international positions. See Figure 15.7 to examine how these three factors must be aligned to ensure expatriate adjustment. In addition, training and development for both expatriates and their spouses can have a big impact.

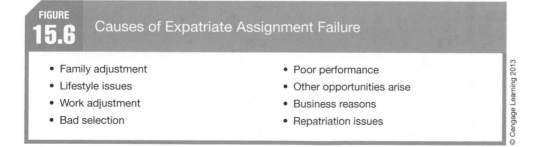

FIGURE 15.6   Causes of Expatriate Assignment Failure

- Family adjustment
- Lifestyle issues
- Work adjustment
- Bad selection

- Poor performance
- Other opportunities arise
- Business reasons
- Repatriation issues

© Cengage Learning 2013

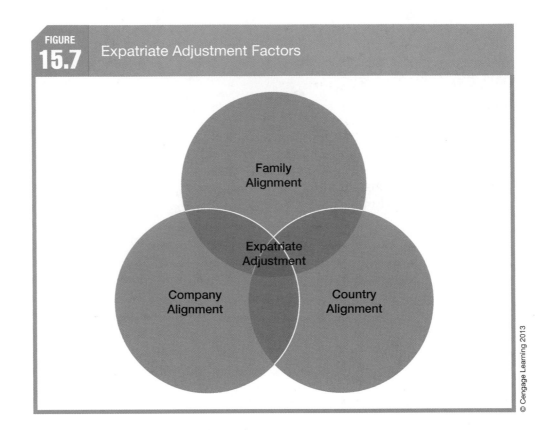

FIGURE 15.7   Expatriate Adjustment Factors

Family Alignment

Expatriate Adjustment

Company Alignment

Country Alignment

© Cengage Learning 2013

 # Training and Development

LEARNING OUTCOME 5

If you were going to send a new manager to South Korea, what specific types of training would you provide her before she left?

Although companies try to recruit and select the very best people to send abroad, once they are selected, it is critical to their success to provide them with training. Not only is this type of training important for expatriate managers, it is also important for the foreign employees they will ultimately supervise. For example, to know and understand how the Japanese or Chinese negotiate contracts or how businesspeople from Latin America view the enforcement of meeting times can help expatriate managers and their employees deal with each other more successfully. The biggest mistake managers can make is to assume that people are the same everywhere. Corporations that are serious about succeeding in global business are tackling these problems head-on by providing intensive training. At Motorola this type of training is conducted at divisions worldwide by Motorola University, the company's educational arm. All employees worldwide, including division heads, receive forty hours of training each year to learn, in part, how to work together as "Motorola People."[29]

Apart from developing talent for overseas assignments, most companies have found that good training programs also help them attract the employees they need from host countries. In less-developed countries especially, individuals are quite eager to receive the training they need to improve their work skills. One of the greatest contributions that the United States has made to work organizations is in improving the competence of managers. Americans have a facility for analytical reasoning that is part of their lives. They tend to make decisions on a rational basis, giving them a better background for decision making. Foreign nationals have generally welcomed the type of training they have received through management development programs offered by U.S. organizations. It should be noted that host-country nationals also provide a great deal of business-specific and cultural know-how to expatriates. Learning is clearly a two-way street for companies doing business abroad.

Content of Training Programs

Lack of training is one of the principal causes of failure among employees working internationally. Those working internationally need to know as much as possible about (1) the country where they are going, (2) that country's culture, and (3) the history, values, and dynamics of their own organizations. Figure 15.8 gives an overview of what one needs to study for an international assignment. In many cases, the employee and his or her family can obtain a great deal of general information about the host country, including its culture, geography, social and political history, climate, food, and so on, via the Internet, books, lectures, videotapes, and DVDs. The knowledge gained will at least help the participants have a better understanding of their assignments. Sensitivity training can also help expatriates overcome ethnic prejudices they might harbor. The Peace Corps uses sensitivity training supplemented by field experiences. Expatriates can simulate a field experience in sensitivity training by visiting a nearby subculture in their native countries or by actually visiting a foreign country prior to relocating there.

However, at least five essential elements of training and development programs prepare employees for working internationally: (1) language training, (2) cultural training, (3) assessing and tracking career development, (4) managing personal and family life, and (5) repatriation—a final, but critical, step.[30]

Language Training

Communication with individuals who have a different language and a different cultural orientation is extremely difficult. Most executives agree that it is among the biggest problems for the foreign business traveler. Unfortunately, only a small percentage of Americans are skilled in a language other than English. But this is changing. Students who plan careers in international business should start instruction in one or

FIGURE 15.8   Preparing for an International Assignment

To prepare for an international assignment, one should become acquainted with the following aspects of the host country:

1. Social and business etiquette
2. History and folklore
3. Current affairs, including relations between the host country and the United States
4. Cultural values and priorities
5. Geography, especially its major cities
6. Sources of pride and great achievements of the culture
7. Religion and the role of religion in daily life
8. Political structure and current players
9. Practical matters such as currency, transportation, time zones, and hours of business
10. The language

© Cengage Learning 2013

Using the INTERNET

Thunderbird at the American Graduate School of International Management is devoted solely to the education of college graduates for international careers. Native speakers of English receive thorough training in nine languages. Go to

www.cengagebrain.com

more foreign languages as early as possible. Penn State University requires all students in business management to take four college semesters of a foreign language. Other programs designed to train participants for international business, such as those offered at the American Graduate School of International Management in Glendale, Arizona, and the Global Management Program at the University of South Carolina, provide intensive training in foreign languages. The top-ranked China Europe International Business School (CEIBS), jointly founded by the Chinese government and the European Union in 1994, also offers language training. Some companies do their own language training. When ARCO Products, a U.S. firm, began exploring potential business opportunities in China, its HR department set up a language training class (with the help of Berlitz International) in conversational Mandarin Chinese. Multinational companies as well as businesses that outsource work abroad stand to benefit from this type of training.

Fortunately for most Americans, English is almost universally accepted as the primary language for international business. Particularly when many people from different countries are working together, English is usually the designated language for meetings and formal discourse. Many companies provide instruction in English for those who are required to use English in their jobs. Dow Chemical requires that all employees across the globe be fluent in English so that they can communicate more easily with one another. At Volkswagen's Shanghai operation, only after workers pass German language examinations do they become eligible for further training in Germany. Learning the language is only part of communicating in another culture. Even with an interpreter, much is missed. The following list illustrates the complexities of the communication process in international business.

1. In England, to "table" a subject means to put it on the table for present discussion. In the United States, it means to postpone discussion of a subject, perhaps indefinitely.

2. In the United States, information flows to a manager. In cultures in which authority is centralized (such as Europe and South America), the manager must take the initiative to seek out the information.

3. Getting straight to the point is uniquely American. Many Europeans, Arabs, Asians, and others resent the directness of American-style communication.

4. In Japan, there are sixteen ways to avoid saying "no."

5. When something is "inconvenient" to the Chinese, it is most likely downright impossible.

6. In most foreign countries, expressions of anger are unacceptable; in some places, public display of anger is taboo.

7. The typical American must learn to treat silences as "communication spaces" and not interrupt them.

8. In general, Americans must learn to avoid gesturing with the hand. A couple of cases in point: when former President Richard Nixon traveled to Brazil in the 1950s, he waved and gave the "A-OK" sign to the country's citizens. But in Brazil, the gesture is considered obscene and insulting. Similarly, a college sports–related hand signal made by former President George W. Bush and his family members

during his second inauguration shocked Norwegians around the world; in Norway, the gesture is a satanic symbol. Nonverbal communication training can help businesspeople avoid some of these communication pitfalls. Highlights in HRM 2 illustrates that some of our everyday gestures have very different meanings in other cultures.[31]

HIGHLIGHTS IN **HRM**
2 Nonverbal Communications in Different Cultures

Calling a Waiter

In the United States, a common way to call a waiter is to point upward with the forefinger. In Asia, a raised forefinger is used to call a dog or other animal. To get the attention of a Japanese waiter, extend the arm upward, palm down, and flutter the fingers. In Africa, knock on the table. In the Middle East, clap your hands.

Insults

In Arab countries, showing the soles of your shoes is an insult. Also, an Arab may insult a person by holding a hand in front of the person's face.

A-Okay Gesture

In the United States, using the index finger and the thumb to form an "o" while extending the rest of the fingers is a gesture meaning okay or fine. In Japan, however, the same gesture means money. Nodding your head in agreement if a Japanese uses this sign during your discussion could mean you are expected to give him some cash. In Brazil the same gesture is considered a seductive sign to a woman and an insult to a man.

Eye Contact

In Western and Arab cultures, prolonged eye contact with a person is acceptable. In Japan, on the other hand, holding the gaze of another is considered rude. The Japanese generally focus on a person's neck or tie knot.

Handshake and Touching

In most countries, the handshake is an acceptable form of greeting. In the Middle East and other Islamic countries, however, the left hand is considered the toilet hand and is thought to be unclean. Only the right hand should be used for touching.

Scratching the Head

In most Western countries, scratching the head is interpreted as lack of understanding or noncomprehension. To the Japanese, it indicates anger.

Indicating "No"

In most parts of the world, shaking the head left and right is the most common way to say no. But among the Arabs, in parts of Greece, Yugoslavia, Bulgaria, and Turkey, a person says no by tossing the head to the side, sometimes clicking the tongue at the same time. In Japan, no can also be said by moving the right hand back and forth.

Agreement

In addition to saying yes, Africans will hold an open palm perpendicular to the ground and pound it with the other fist to emphasize "agreed." Arabs will clasp their hands together, forefingers pointed outward, to indicate agreement.

Source: S. Hawkins, *International Management* 38, no. 9 (September 1983): 49. Copyright 1983 by Reed Business Information Ltd. Reprinted with permission.

Cultural Training

Cross-cultural differences represent one of the most elusive aspects of international business, but successfully done, it tends to improve the satisfaction and success of expatriates and their employers.[32] Brazilians tend to perceive Americans as always in a hurry, serious, reserved, and methodical, whereas the Japanese view Americans as relaxed, friendly, and impulsive. Why do these different perceptions exist, and how do they affect the way we do business across borders? People's attitudes and behaviors are influenced, in large part, by the culture and society in which they have been educated and trained. Each culture has its expectations for the roles of managers and employees. On her first day on the job abroad, one expatriate manager recalls her boss ordering a bottle of wine to split between the two of them at lunch. Although this is a common practice in Britain, the expatriate manager was initially taken aback. Likewise, an American manager in Asia once complained that meetings held in his foreign place of employment accomplished nothing. He was used to arriving at a final decision during meetings. But to his Asian coworkers, meetings were solely a place in which to share ideas. Decisions were to be made only later. Being successful abroad depends on a person's ability to understand the way things are normally done and to recognize that changes cannot be made abruptly without considerable resistance, and possibly antagonism, on the part of local nationals.

A wealth of data from cross-cultural studies reveals that nations tend to cluster along certain cultural dimensions such as their work goals, values, needs, and attitudes toward work. Using data from eight comprehensive studies of cultural differences, Simcha Ronen and Oded Shenkar have grouped countries into the clusters shown in Figure 15.9. Ronen and Shenkar point out that while evidence for the grouping of countries into Anglo, Germanic, Nordic, Latin European, and Latin American clusters appears to be quite strong, clusters encompassing the Far Eastern and Arab countries are ill-defined and require further research, as do clusters of countries classified as independent. Many areas, such as Africa, have not been studied much at all. It should also be noted that the clusters presented in Figure 15.8 do not include Russia and the former satellites of the Soviet Union. Those countries, if added to the figure, would likely fall between the Near Eastern and Nordic categories.

Studying cultural differences can help managers identify and understand work attitudes and motivation in other cultures. When compared with the Japanese, for example, Americans may feel little loyalty to their organizations. In Japan, employees are more likely to feel a strong loyalty to their company, although this has been changing. Japanese companies no longer universally guarantee an employee a job for life, and layoff decisions are increasingly being made based on merit, not seniority—a practice unthinkable in the country in the past. Latin Americans tend to view themselves as working not only for a particular company, but also for an individual manager. Thus managers in Latin American countries can encourage performance only by using personal influence and working through individual members of a group. In the United States, competition has been the name of the game; in Japan, Taiwan, and other Asian countries, cooperation is more the underlying philosophy.[33]

One of the important dimensions of leadership, whether in international or domestic situations, is the degree to which managers invite employee participation in decision making. While it is difficult to find hard data on employee participation across different countries, careful observers report that American managers are

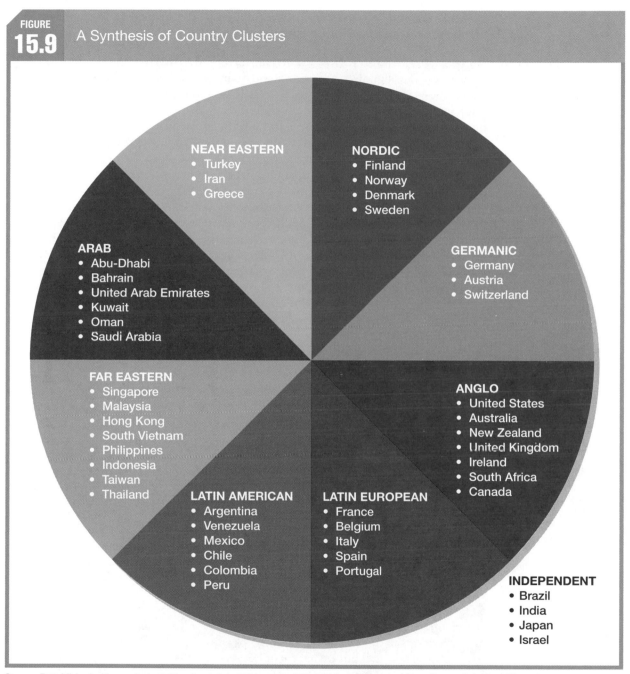

FIGURE 15.9   A Synthesis of Country Clusters

NEAR EASTERN
- Turkey
- Iran
- Greece

NORDIC
- Finland
- Norway
- Denmark
- Sweden

ARAB
- Abu-Dhabi
- Bahrain
- United Arab Emirates
- Kuwait
- Oman
- Saudi Arabia

GERMANIC
- Germany
- Austria
- Switzerland

FAR EASTERN
- Singapore
- Malaysia
- Hong Kong
- South Vietnam
- Philippines
- Indonesia
- Taiwan
- Thailand

ANGLO
- United States
- Australia
- New Zealand
- United Kingdom
- Ireland
- South Africa
- Canada

LATIN AMERICAN
- Argentina
- Venezuela
- Mexico
- Chile
- Colombia
- Peru

LATIN EUROPEAN
- France
- Belgium
- Italy
- Spain
- Portugal

INDEPENDENT
- Brazil
- India
- Japan
- Israel

Source: Republished with permission of the Academy of Management Review, from "Clustering Countries on Attitudinal Dimensions: A Review and Synthesis," by Simcha Ronen and Oded Shenkar, vol 10, no. 3 (July 1985), 435–54. Copyright © 1985 by Academy of Management Review; permission conveyed through Copyright Clearance Center.

about in the middle on a continuum of autocratic to democratic decision-making styles. Scandinavian and Australian managers also appear to be in the middle. South American and European managers, especially those from France, Germany, and Italy, are toward the autocratic end of the continuum. Japanese managers are at the most participatory end. Because Far Eastern cultures and religions tend to emphasize harmony, group decision making predominates there.[34]

Assessing and Tracking Career Development

International assignments provide some definite developmental and career advantages. For example, working abroad tends to increase a person's responsibilities and influence within the corporation. In addition, it provides a person with a set of experiences that are uniquely beneficial to both the individual and the firm. In this way, international assignments enhance a person's understanding of the global marketplace and offer the opportunity to work on a project important to the organization.[35] Furthermore, research shows that international assignments increase a person's creative problem-solving skills and receptivity to new ideas.[36]

In recent years, U.S. companies have become a melting pot of CEOs. Increasingly, foreign-born CEOs are making up the Fortune 500 top slots. Figure 15.10 presents a number of foreign-born CEOs. Executive recruiters say corporate boards are asking for leaders with experience outside of the United States. As one foreign CEO of a U.S.-based firm put it, "Having a foreign perspective gives you an advantage not only for doing business outside the United States, but also domestically, where we have the most diverse society in the world." Some companies such as Coca-Cola have traditionally appointed chief executives with foreign roots, perhaps because the growth of the firm's markets lies abroad.[37]

To maximize the career benefits of a managerial assignment, a candidate should ask two key questions before accepting a foreign post.

1. Do the organization's senior executives view the firm's international business as a critical part of their operation? Research shows that expatriates with clear goals

A foreign assignment can be an excellent step in a person's career. But to be successful, expatriates often need extensive training on their host countries' languages, cultural differences, business practices, and other related issues.

Matthew Antrobus/The Image Bank/Getty Images

FIGURE 15.10 Selected Foreign-Born Executives

COMPANY, NAME, AND COUNTRY OF ORIGIN

Chevron, David O'Reilly (Ireland)

Citigroup, Vikram Pandit (India)

Dow Chemical, Andrew Liveris (Australia)

PepsiCo, Indra Nooyi (India)

Coca-Cola, Muhtar Kent (Turkey)

Alcoa, Alain J. P. Belda (Morocco)

Eli Lily, Sydney Taurel (Morocco)

3M, George W. Buckley (Great Britain)

Eastman Kodak, Antonio Perez (Spain)

Nissan Motor Manufacturing, Carlos Ghosn (Brazil)

Sony, Howard Stringer (Wales)

© Cengage Learning 2013

that truly need to be accomplished are likely to find their assignments more rewarding. Realizing this, fewer companies are sending expatriates abroad for career development purposes only.

2. Within top management, how many executives have a foreign-service assignment in their background, and do they feel it important for one to have overseas experience? Colgate-Palmolive sees a foreign assignment as part of an extended career track rather than as a one-off assignment. A successful foreign assignment tends to lead to another and another. "Our top priority is to identify, develop, and retain the next two to three generations of leaders," said one Colgate-Palmolive manager. Part of that strategy includes directly using the knowledge of the company's current and former expatriates.

Managing Personal and Family Life

As noted previously, one of the most frequent causes of an employee's failure to complete an international assignment is personal and family stress. Culture shock—a disorientation that causes perpetual stress—is experienced by people who settle overseas for extended periods. The stress is caused by hundreds of jarring and disorienting incidents such as being unable to communicate, having trouble getting the telephone to work, being unable to read the street signs, and a myriad of other everyday matters that are no problem at home. Soon minor frustrations become catastrophic events, and one feels helpless and drained, emotionally and physically.

In Chapter 5, we explained that more and more employers are assisting two-career couples in terms of finding suitable employment in the same location. To accommodate dual-career partnerships, some employers offer spouses career and life planning counseling, continuing education, intercompany networks to identify job openings in other companies, job-hunting/fact-finding trips, and help securing work permits

culture shock
Perpetual stress experienced by people who settle overseas

abroad. In some cases, a company may even create a job for the spouse, though this is not widely practiced.[38]

Repatriation

An increasing number of companies such as Monsanto, 3M, EDS, and Verizon are developing programs specifically designed to facilitate repatriation—that is, helping employees make the transition back home. Repatriation programs are designed to prepare employees for adjusting to life at home (which at times can be more difficult than adjusting to a foreign assignment). ExxonMobil employees are given a general idea of what they can expect following a foreign assignment even before they leave home.

Unfortunately, not all companies have career development programs designed for repatriating employees or do not do an effective job of it. Employees often lament that their organizations are vague about repatriation, their new roles within the company, and their career progression. In many cases, employees abroad have learned how to run an entire international operation—or at least significant parts of it. When they return home however, their responsibilities are often significantly diminished. Some surveys have found that up to 60 percent of expatriates believed their careers had not advanced after returning home.[39] It is also not at all uncommon for employees to return home after a few years to find that there is *no* position for them in the firm and that they no longer know anyone who can help them—their longtime colleagues have moved to different departments or even different companies. This frequently leaves the repatriated employee feeling alienated. Wondering about their future also creates stress for them and their families while they are abroad.

Even when employees are successfully repatriated, their companies often do not fully utilize the knowledge, understanding, and skills developed on their assignments. This hurts the employee, of course, but it also hurts the firm's chances of utilizing the employee's expertise to gain a competitive advantage. Not surprisingly, expatriates frequently leave their companies within a year or two of coming home. Some studies say the number of expatriates who do so is as high as 50 percent.

At companies with good repatriation processes, employees are given guidance about how much the expatriate experience may have changed them and their families. Some firms introduce former expatriates and their spouses to other former expatriates at special social events, and more companies are making an effort to keep in touch with expatriates while they are abroad, which has been made easier by e-mail, instant messaging, voice over Internet protocol, and videoconferencing. Colgate's division executives and other corporate staff members frequently visit international transferees. Dow appoints a high-level manager to serve as a stateside contact for information about organizational changes, job opportunities, and anything related to salary and compensation. Monsanto's repatriation program is designed not only to smooth the employee's return to the home organization, but to ensure that the expatriate's knowledge and experience are fully used. To do so, returning expatriates get the chance to showcase their new knowledge in debriefing sessions. Some companies also create databases of expatriates to help other employees who go abroad later.[40] Of course, if a firm is able to retain its current repatriates, it will have better success recruiting future expatriates. A repatriation checklist is shown in Highlights in HRM 3.

3 HIGHLIGHTS IN **HRM**
Repatriation Checklist

Before they go:

- Make sure there is a clear need for the international assignment. Do not send someone abroad unnecessarily. Develop a clear set of objectives and expectations and time frames in which they should be met.
- Make sure that your selection procedures are valid. Select the employee and also look at and involve the employee's family.
- Provide (or fund) language and cultural training for the employee and the employee's family.
- Offer counseling and career assistance for the spouse.
- Establish career planning systems that reward international assignments and lead to promotion and knowledge sharing.

While they are away:

- Jointly establish a developmental plan that focuses on the goal to be achieved.
- Tie performance objectives to the achievement of the goal.
- Identify mentors who can be a liaison and support person from home.
- Keep communications open so that the expatriate is aware of job openings and opportunities.
- Arrange for frequent visits back home (for the employee and the family). Make certain they do not lose touch with friends and relatives.

When they come back home:

- Throw a "welcome home" party and arrange for a meeting with other former expatriates.
- Offer counseling to ease the transition.
- Arrange conferences and presentations to make certain that knowledge and skills acquired away from home are identified and disseminated.
- Set up an expatriate database to help other employees who go abroad later.
- Get feedback from the employee and the family about how well the organization handled the repatriation process.

Sources: Adapted from Bennet & Associates, Price Waterhouse, and Charlene Marmer Solomon, "Repatriation Planning Checklist," *Personnel Journal* 14, no. 1 (January 1995): 32; Charlene Marmer Solomon, "Global HR: Repatriation Planning," *Workforce* 2001, special supplement: 22–23.

Compensation

LEARNING OUTCOME 6

One of the most complex areas of international HRM is compensation. Different countries have different norms for employee compensation. For Americans, while nonfinancial incentives such as prestige, independence, and influence may be motivators, money is likely to be the driving force. Other cultures are more likely to emphasize respect, family, job security, a satisfying personal life, social acceptance, advancement, or power. Since there are many alternatives to money, the rule is to

Should compensation packages be equal across the world, or should they be adapted to the local cultures and economies?

match the reward with the values of the culture. In individualistic cultures, such as the United States, pay plans often focus on individual performance and achievement. However, in collectively oriented cultures such as Japan and Taiwan, pay plans focus more on internal equity and personal needs.[41]

In general, a guiding philosophy for designing pay systems might be "think globally and act locally." That is, executives should normally try to create a pay plan that supports the overall strategic intent of the organization but provides enough flexibility to customize particular policies and programs to meet the needs of employees in specific locations. After a brief discussion of compensation practices for host-country employees and managers, we will focus on the problems of compensating expatriates.

Compensation of Host-Country Employees

As shown in Figure 15.11, hourly wages vary dramatically from country to country. Production workers in manufacturing positions in Norway make more than $53 per hour. By contrast, in many developing countries, production workers earn less than a dollar an hour, on average. Host-country employees are generally paid on the basis of productivity, time spent on the job, or a combination of these factors. In industrialized countries, pay is generally by the hour; in developing countries, pay is generally by the day. The piece-rate method is quite common. In some countries, including Japan, seniority is an important element in determining employees' pay rates. In Italy, Japan, and some other countries, it is customary to add semiannual or annual lump sum payments equal to one or two months' pay. These payments are not considered profit sharing but an integral part of the basic pay package. Profit sharing is legally required for certain industry categories in Mexico, Peru, Pakistan, India, and Egypt among the developing countries and in France among the industrialized countries.

Employee benefits can range dramatically from country to country as well. In France, for example, benefits comprise a much higher proportion of people's pay than they do in the United States. In contrast to ten vacation days in the United States, workers in the United Kingdom, France, and the Netherlands receive about twenty-five days of paid vacation. Workers in Sweden and Austria receive thirty. Whereas in the United States most benefits are awarded to employees by employers, in other industrialized countries most of them are legislated or ordered by governments.[42]

Because the largest cost for most companies is labor, it plays a prime role in international HR decision making. However, some people believe that companies are overcapitalizing on worldwide compensation differences. Many firms (Nike included) have generated bad press for charging hundreds of dollars for their individual products while the people who make them earned only a few cents on the dollar. This has led to international political protests, as was mentioned in Chapter 1, and pressure on firms to exercise greater global social responsibility.

As Nike discovered, this is pressure they cannot afford *not* to take seriously. The bad press finally took a toll on Nike's bottom line. As a result, Nike now monitors all its partner factories to ensure that workers are not underage, that pay is competitive, and that working conditions are compliant with international standards. Over 100 full-time staff are dedicated to monitoring these partner factories. While this cost Nike around $11 million per year, they have unexpectedly realized additional cost savings as their monitoring staff are also able to help the factories with streamlining the work processes, training managers, and decreasing corrupt practices by the factories.[43]

**FIGURE
15.11** Hourly Wages in Different Countries

Country or Area	Hourly Compensation Costs* in U.S. dollars	
	1997	**2009**
Norway	26.97	53.89
Denmark	24.64	49.56
Belgium	28.23	49.40
Austria	27.38	48.04
Germany	29.26	46.52
Switzerland	28.33	44.29
Finland	22.17	43.77
Netherlands	23.44	43.50
France	24.99	40.08
Sweden	25.11	39.87
Ireland	17.15	39.02
Italy	19.67	34.97
Australia	19.12	34.62
United States	22.67	33.53
United Kingdom	18.24	30.78
Japan	22.28	30.36
Canada	18.89	29.60
Spain	13.91	27.74
Greece	NA	19.23
Israel	12.32	18.39
Singapore	12.15	17.50
New Zealand	12.37	17.44
Korea, Republic of	9.42	14.20
Portugal	6.38	11.95
Slovakia	2.86	11.24
Czech Republic	3.24	11.21
Argentina	7.43	10.14
Estonia	NA	9.83
Hungary	3.05	8.62
Brazil	7.11	8.32
Taiwan	7.04	7.76
Poland	3.13	7.50
Mexico	3.30	5.38
Philippines	1.14	1.50

NA = data not available.
*Hourly compensation costs in U.S. dollars for production workers in manufacturing.

Source: U.S. Department of Labor, Bureau of Labor Statistics, May 2011.

Starbucks is another company that takes good corporate citizenship seriously. Among Starbucks' many initiatives is its association with Fair Trade and Conservation International to help farmers in third-world countries get a premium for the coffee they grow. We will discuss more on the fair treatment of workers in third-world countries toward the end of the chapter.

Compensation of Host-Country Managers

In the past, the compensation of host-country managers has been based on local salary levels. Today, however, more companies are offering their host-country employees a full range of training programs, benefits, and pay comparable with their domestic employees back in the country of origin but adjusted for local differences. These programs are known as global compensation systems. Among other benefits, the agricultural processing firm Archer Daniels Midland offers its employees abroad an employee assistance program. At first many employees were suspicious about the program, believing that it was designed to collect private information about them. However, after employees became confident that their information was confidential, the program sent a message that the company is interested in their well-being and values them.

According to a survey by the HR consulting firm Watson Wyatt, companies are split evenly as to whether they have central (global) compensation systems or decentralized (local) systems. Companies with centralized systems report having higher effectiveness and satisfaction levels with their compensation systems, and more companies are saying they are moving toward centralized systems. Unilever, for example, used to leave the compensation arrangements largely to the boss of a region or a big country. Now brand managers in different countries increasingly compare notes so they see potential discrepancies based on market differences and expatriate assignments. So the company moved from a narrow grading structure to five global work levels.[44]

The benefits of a global compensation system are realized more and more as people are becoming mobile across borders. For example, multinational companies hiring Chinese and Indian nationals from U.S. universities to go back to India and China are finding that they must offer similar compensation packages to those they offer employees in the United States. In fact, for some who have been working in the United States, they argue for expatriate compensation plans in order to return to their home countries.

Compensation of Expatriate Managers

If the assignment is going to be successful, the expatriate's compensation plan must be competitive, cost-effective, motivating, fair, easy to understand, consistent with international financial management, relatively easy to administer, and simple to communicate. To be effective, an international compensation program must:

1. Provide an incentive to leave the United States

2. Allow for maintaining an American standard of living

3. Provide for security in countries that are politically unstable or present personal dangers

4. Include provisions for good health care

global compensation system

A centralized pay system whereby host-country employees are offered a full range of training programs, benefits, and pay comparable with a firm's domestic employees but adjusted for local differences

5. Reimburse the foreign taxes the employee is likely to have to pay (in addition to having to pay domestic taxes) and help him or her with tax forms and filing

6. Provide for the education of the employee's children abroad, if necessary

7. Allow for maintaining relationships with family, friends, and business associates via trips home and other communication technologies

8. Facilitate the expatriate's reentry home

9. Be in writing[45]

For short-term assignments, usually those that are project-based, expatriates are frequently given per diem (per day) compensation. These managers might reside in hotels and service apartments instead of leasing houses. They are also less likely to bring their family members with them. The assignment becomes more like a commuting assignment in which the expatriate spends the week in the host country and returns home on the weekend.

For longer-term assignments, there are two basic types of compensation systems. The first is home-based pay, based on the balance sheet approach, a system designed to equalize the purchasing power of employees at comparable positions living overseas and in the home country and to provide incentives to offset qualitative differences between assignment locations.[46] The balance sheet approach generally comprises the following steps:

Step 1: Calculate base pay. Begin with the home-based gross income, including bonuses. Deduct taxes, Social Security, and pension contributions.

Step 2: Figure cost-of-living adjustment (COLA). Add a cost-of-living adjustment to the base pay. Typically, companies do not subtract when the international assignment has a lower cost of living. Instead, they allow the expatriate to benefit from the negative differential. Often a housing allowance is added in here as well.

Step 3: Add incentive premiums. General mobility premiums and hardship premiums compensate expatriates for separation from family, friends, and domestic support systems; usually 15 percent of base salary, although in recent years, some companies have reduced this amount. Oftentimes incentive premiums are paid for hazardous duty or harsh conditions the expatriate might experience while abroad. Expatriates who locate to war zones, for example, can sometimes earn three times their base salary.

Step 4: Add assistance programs. These additions are often used to cover added costs such as moving and storage, automobile, and education expenses.

The differentials element is intended to correct for the higher costs of overseas goods and services so that in relation to their domestic peers expatriates neither gain purchasing power nor lose it. It involves a myriad of calculations to arrive at a total differential figure, but in general, as we have said, the cost typically runs between three and five times the home-country salary. Fortunately, employers do not have to do extensive research to find comparative data. They typically rely on data published quarterly by the U.S. State Department for use in establishing allowances to compensate U.S. civilian employees for costs and hardships related to assignments abroad. Alternately, they consult international relocation experts to make sure all of the relocation bases are covered. For example, in some countries expatriates are mandated by local law to participate in host-country programs—whether or not their pay packages are home- or host-based. Other countries have negotiated bilateral agreements that allow expatriates to opt out of state-sponsored benefit programs such as Social

home-based pay
Pay based on an expatriate's home country's compensation practices

balance sheet approach
A compensation system designed to match the purchasing power in a person's home country

split pay

A system whereby expatriates are given a portion of their pay in the local currency to cover their day-to-day expenses and a portion of their pay in their home currency to safeguard their earnings from changes in inflation or foreign exchange rates

host-based pay

Expatriate pay comparable to that earned by employees in a host country

localization

Adapting pay and other compensation benefits to match that of a particular country

Security, as long as the expatriates are covered by similar programs in their home countries. The United States currently has bilateral agreements of this type with a number of countries.[47] Recently, splitpay plans have become popular among companies. Under a split pay system, expatriates are given a portion of their pay in the local currency to cover their day-to-day expenses. The rest of their pay is distributed in their home currency to safeguard their earnings should changes in foreign exchange rates or inflation adversely affect their pay.

Another type of compensation system is host-based pay. Companies are under pressure to move expatriates to host-based pay because it is generally less costly. Host-based pay is compensation that is equivalent to that earned by employees in the country where the expatriate is assigned. This process is called localization. When an employee is localized, his or her compensation is set on par with local standards and practices. Incentive premiums are generally phased out, and the employee pays only local taxes and falls under the social benefit programs established by the government of the host country. Some companies localize only certain aspects of the pay package or do so gradually over a course of three to five years.

Usually the decision to localize an employee depends on whether he or she will ultimately remain abroad or return home. In many companies, the decision depends on whether the employee or the employer is the driving force behind the localization. An expatriate employee with a strong desire to remain in the host country beyond the planned length of assignment (perhaps because he or she married a local or has simply fallen in love with the country) is likely to be more amenable to localization. Localization should not be viewed as a cost-saving panacea, however. There are many countries in which expatriates would refuse to "go local." Forcing an employee to do so can ultimately result in a failed assignment, costing the company much more money than it would have saved by localizing him or her.

One of the disadvantages of not localizing an employee's pay, however, is that in low-cost countries, this can breed resentment among local staff members if they are earning significantly less. This can affect the amount of cooperation they are likely to give an expatriate and adversely affect the success of an assignment. Whether they are intentional or not, any HR practice that results in more favorable treatment for an expatriate versus local employees sends a message that locals are less valued by the firm. This is another reason why firms are moving to global compensation systems.[48]

Another serious issue related to expatriate compensation is medical care. Employees are unlikely to consent to going abroad if they cannot get health care comparable to what is available in their home countries. Often U.S.-based plans cannot cover expatriate employees or efficiently deal with claims that need to be reimbursed in foreign currency. Drugs prescribed abroad that are not FDA approved can also cause reimbursement problems for U.S. expatriates. One solution is to provide the expatriate with a global health benefits plan such as Cigna International Expatriate Benefit. The Cigna plan covers 200,000 expatriates and their dependents for 700 different international client companies. Another alternative is to transfer the employee to a global employment company that can provide these types of benefits. A global employment company is similar to a PEO (professional employer organization), discussed in Chapter 5. Basically, the employee is transferred to the global employment company, which administers all of his or her benefits as well as those of numerous employees working for other companies. These are not options in all countries. In some countries, such as Saudi Arabia, for example, expatriates must be covered by a local insurer.

Still another issue is the need to provide expatriates and employees who travel abroad with security. Citigroup hires private drivers for employees doing business in countries such as Mexico—even for employees on extended stays. Archer Daniels Midland uses a travel management company that provides travel security climate information to employees as soon as they book their trips. Companies can also purchase travel-related insurance covering a range of services such as evacuation and disability or travel-related injuries. HR managers are generally responsible for evaluating and implementing these different types of programs. Oftentimes this involves hiring a local security firm when an expatriate is sent abroad.

Lastly, what your competitors are paying should also factor into the compensation mix. In the United Kingdom, firms typically provide their expatriates with cars as part of their compensation. So to be competitive, any company operating in that marketplace has to do the same, explains Steve Rimmer from the consulting firm Price Waterhouse Coopers International Ltd.

Performance Appraisal

As we noted earlier, individuals frequently accept international assignments because they know that they can acquire skills and experiences that will make them more valuable to their companies. Frequently, however, it can be difficult for the home office to evaluate the performance of employees working abroad. Even the notion of performance evaluation is indicative of a U.S. management style that focuses on the individual, which can cause problems in Asian countries such as China, Japan, and Korea and Eastern European countries such as Hungary and the Czech Republic. Performance appraisal problems can contribute to failure rates among expatriates and actually derail an individual's career rather than enhance it.[49]

LEARNING OUTCOME 7
Assume you are working for GE in Afghanistan. The power often goes out in your building, business deals take longer than in the United States, and you experience a great amount of stress due to the unstable political environment. Would you want your performance to be assessed in relation to the difficulty of doing business in Afghanistan?

Who Should Appraise Performance?

In many cases, an individual working internationally has at least two allegiances: one to his or her home country (the office that made the assignment) and the other to the host country in which the employee is currently working. Superiors in each location frequently have different information about the employee's performance and may also have very different expectations about what constitutes good performance. For these reasons, the multirater (360-degree) appraisal discussed in Chapter 8 is gaining favor among global firms. There are exceptions, however. For example, Thai workers do not see it as their business to evaluate their bosses, and Thai managers do not think subordinates are in any way qualified to assess them. Before implementing a different appraisal process, HR managers need to understand how the process is likely to be received in the host country.[50]

Home versus Host-Country Evaluations

Domestic managers who have not worked abroad are frequently unable to understand an expatriate's or host-country manager's experiences, value these employees, or accurately measure their contribution to the organization. Geographical distances create communication problems for expatriates and home-country managers, although e-mail, instant messaging, and other HR information systems technologies have begun to close the gap.[51] Still, local managers with daily contact with the person are more likely to have an accurate picture of his or her performance. Host-country evaluations can sometimes be problematic. First, local cultures can influence a person's perception of how well an individual is performing. As we noted earlier in the chapter, participative decision making may be viewed either positively or negatively, depending on the culture. Such cultural biases may not have any bearing on an individual's true level of effectiveness. In addition, local managers sometimes do not have enough of a perspective on the entire organization to know how well an individual is truly contributing to the firm as a whole.

Even if the formal appraisal is conducted in the home office and promotion, and pay and other administrative decisions are made there, most HR experts agree that performance evaluations should try to balance the two sources of appraisal information. As we discussed in Chapter 8, multiple sources of appraisal information can be extremely valuable for providing independent points of view—especially if someone is working as part of a team. If there is much concern about cultural bias, it may be possible to have people of the same nationality as the expatriate conduct the appraisal.

Performance Criteria

Because expatriate assignments are so costly, many HR managers are increasingly under pressure to calculate the return on investment of these assignments. What did the firm get for the million dollars it spent to send an expatriate abroad? Has the expatriate achieved the goals set forth in the assignment in the appropriate time frame? Obviously, the goals and responsibilities inherent in the job assignment are among the most important criteria used to evaluate an individual's performance, and different goals necessitate measuring different criteria. The criteria are tied to the various reasons employees were sent abroad in the first place—whether it was part of a goal to transfer technical skills or best practices, as a result of a merger or new division, to improve a division's financial performance, or to develop managerial talent.

There are five steps related to calculating the ROI of an assignment:

1. Defining the assignment's objectives.

2. Agreeing on the quantifiable measurements for the assignment.

3. Developing an equation that converts qualitative behavior into quantifiable measurements.

4. Evaluating the expatriate's performance against these measurements.

5. Calculating the ROI. This can be a complex cost accounting or a simple calculation to see if the expatriate covered the cost of keeping them on assignment.

Companies also look at how well the total cost of the assignment was managed, taking into account any tax efficiencies and whether the right mix of expatriates, third-country nationals, and locals were used to minimize the assignment's costs.[52]

The danger with ROI calculations, however, is that there is a temptation to resort to using "easy" criteria such as productivity, profits, and market share to measure an expatriate's performance. These criteria may be valid, but they are still deficient if they do not capture the full range of an expatriate's responsibility. Other, more subtle factors should be considered as well. Leadership development, for example, involves a much longer-term value proposition. In many cases, an expatriate is an ambassador for the company, and a significant part of the job is cultivating relationships with citizens of the host country.

As we discussed at the beginning of this chapter, an individual's success or failure is affected by a host of technical and personal factors, as well as the acceptance and help they get from their staff members abroad. For example, as one might guess, it is much easier to adjust to similar cultures than to dissimilar ones. An American can usually travel to the United Kingdom or Australia and work with locals almost immediately. Send that same individual to Hungary or Malaysia, and the learning curve is steeper. The expatriate's adjustment period may be even longer if the company has not yet established a good base of operations in the region. The first individuals transferred to a country have no one to show them the ropes or to explain local customs. Even relatively simple activities such as navigating the rapid transit system can prove to be problematic. The U.S. State Department and defense forces have developed rating systems that attempt to distinguish the different degrees of difficulty associated with different regional assignments. These difficulty factors need to be considered and built into the appraisal system. For example, if living in Afghanistan, the rate of difficulty is expected to be 35 percent greater than in the United States. As a result, salary should reflect this hardship.[53]

Providing Feedback

Performance feedback in an international setting is clearly a two-way street. Although the home-country and host-country superiors may tell an expatriate how well he or she is doing, it is also important for expatriates to provide feedback regarding the support they are receiving, the obstacles they face, and the suggestions they have about the assignment. More than in almost any other job situation, expatriates are in the very best position to evaluate their own performance.

In addition to ongoing feedback, an expatriate should have a debriefing interview immediately on returning home from an international assignment. These repatriation interviews serve several purposes.

1. They help expatriates reestablish old ties with the home organization and may prove to be important for setting new career paths.

2. The interview can address technical issues related to the job assignment itself.

3. The interview can address general issues regarding the company's overseas commitments, such as how relationships between the home and host countries should be handled.

4. The interview can be very useful for documenting insights an individual has about the region. These insights can then be incorporated into training programs for future expatriates. However, if the learning is not shared, then each new expatriate to a region may have to go through the same cycle of adjustment.[54]

The Labor Environment Worldwide

A country's labor environment plays a large role in international business and HR decisions. As we have said, wages and benefits vary dramatically across the world as do safety, child, and other legal regulations. In many countries, the regulation of labor contracts is profound and extensive. Labor unions around the world differ significantly as well. Differences exist not only in the collective bargaining process, but also in the political-legal conditions. For example, the EU prohibits discrimination against workers in unions, but in many other countries, including countries in Central America and Asia, labor unions are illegal. China has only one union, the All-China Federation of Trade Unions, an eighty-year-old Communist Party institution that for

LEARNING OUTCOME 8

Do you think there should be some international standard for labor rights? If so, what should that standard be and how should it be enforced?

decades has aligned itself more closely with management than workers. As Walmart discovered, Western firms that want to do business in China have to reach collective bargaining agreements with the ACFTU. In some countries, only workers at larger firms are allowed to organize.[55]

Union strength depends on many factors, such as the level of employee participation, per capita labor income, mobility between management and labor, homogeneity of labor (racial, religious, social class), and unemployment levels. Nearly all of Sweden's workers are organized, giving the unions in this country considerable strength and autonomy. By contrast, in countries with relatively high unemployment, low pay levels, and no union funds with which to support social welfare systems, unions are driven into alliance with other organizations: political parties, churches, or governments. This is in marked contrast to the United States, where the union selected by the majority of employees bargains only with the employer, not with other institutions. By contrast, the unions in many European countries (such as Sweden) have a great deal of political power and are often allied with a particular political party. When employers in these countries deal with unions, they are, in effect, dealing indirectly with governments.

In a number of countries, however, including Japan, Germany, New Zealand, and the United Kingdom, unions have been losing some of their power. Ironically, the power of the unions to gain high wages and enforce rigid labor rules has been blamed for hurting competitiveness, particularly in European countries. Laws make it difficult to fire European employees, so workers are hired only sparingly. Unemployment benefits are very generous, so people tend to remain unemployed for longer rather than seek work. But because companies are increasingly tempted to offshore jobs to countries where labor costs are lower, unionized workers have been forced to make more concessions. For example, at Bosch in France, union bosses opposed management's plan to lengthen the workweek. But fearful workers overruled the union bosses, voting instead for the longer workweek.[56] As the power of unions declines a bit, the trend has been to demand compensation in other ways—through benefits

Around the world, collective bargaining processes vary widely. The ILO and other international labor organizations promote the rights of workers to organize.

or through greater participation in company decision making. Various approaches to participation will be discussed later.

Collective Bargaining in Other Countries

We saw in Chapter 14 how the collective bargaining process is typically carried out in companies operating in the United States. When we look at other countries, we find that the process can vary widely, especially with regard to the role of government. Collective bargaining can take place at the firm, local, or national levels. In Australia and New Zealand for most of the twentieth century, labor courts had the authority to impose wages and other employment conditions on a broad range of firms (many of which were not even privy to the suits brought before the courts). In the United Kingdom and France, the government intervenes in all aspects of collective bargaining. Government involvement is only natural where parts of industry are nationalized. In developing countries, the governments commonly have representatives present during bargaining sessions to ensure that unions with relatively uneducated leaders are not disadvantaged in bargaining with skilled management representatives. Still, in these countries a union may do little more than attempt to increase wages and leave the rest of the employment contract unchanged. In more-developed countries, goals related to other aspects of the employment relationship, such as workweek lengths, safety requirements, and grievance procedures, are more likely to be pursued.

International Labor Organizations

The most active of the international union organizations has been the International Trade Union Confederation (ITUC), which has its headquarters in Brussels. The ITUC is a confederation of 311 national trade union centers, representing 175 million trade union members in 155 countries and territories. The ITUC's mission is to promote worker rights and interests through international cooperation between trade unions, campaigning, and advocacy with governments and global institutions. The ITUC also cooperates with the European Trade Union Confederation (ETUC), the most prominent European trade worker federation. The ETUC represents trade workers in eighty-three trade unions in thirty-six western, central, and eastern European countries.

Another active and influential organization is the International Labour Organization (ILO), a specialized agency of the United Nations created in 1919. The ILO perhaps has had the greatest impact on the rights of workers throughout the world. It promotes the rights of workers to organize, the eradication of forced and child labor, and the elimination of discrimination. The organization has been effective because it involves nation-states as well as workers and their employers. In recent years, the ILO has redefined its mission based on the "Decent Work Agenda." The Decent Work Agenda promotes the idea that there is an ethical dimension of work. This ethical dimension includes decent homes, food, education, the right to organize, and social programs to protect workers when they are elderly, disabled, or unemployed. Moreover, the agenda pertains to workers worldwide, including the self-employed—a situation common in agricultural-based, developing countries. Given the fact that half of the world's population lives on $2 a day or less, 250 million children around the world are forced to work, and only 20 percent of people globally are covered by any sort of social insurance programs, these are worthy goals. Some companies, however, oppose the decent pay initiative, believing it promotes unionization. A new initiative of the ILO is to support fairness in economies that are globalizing. To some extent, the effort is working. For example, in 2007, the World Bank started including the ILO's core labor standards requirement as part of its lending and procurement practices.[57]

Labor Participation in Management

In many European countries, provisions for employee representation are established by law. An employer may be legally required to provide for employee representation on safety and hygiene committees, worker councils, or even boards of directors. While their responsibilities vary from country to country, worker councils basically provide a communication channel between employers and workers. The legal codes that set forth the functions of worker councils in France are very detailed. Councils are generally concerned with grievances, problems of individual employees, internal regulations, and matters affecting employee welfare.

codetermination

Representation of labor on the board of directors of a company

A higher form of worker participation in management is found in Germany, where representation of labor on the board of directors of a company is required by law. This arrangement is known as codetermination and often referred to by its German word, *Mitbestimmung*. While sometimes puzzling to outsiders, the system is fairly simple. Company shareholders and employees are required to be represented in equal numbers on the supervisory boards of large corporations. Power is generally left with the shareholders, and shareholders are generally assured the chairmanship. Other European countries and Japan either have or are considering minority board participation.[58]

Each of these differences makes managing human resources in an international context more challenging. But the crux of the issue in designing HR systems is not choosing one approach that will meet all the demands of international business. Instead, organizations facing global competition must balance multiple approaches and make their policies flexible enough to accommodate differences across national borders. Throughout this book we have noted that different situations call for different approaches to managing people, and nowhere is this point more clearly evident than in international HRM.

Summary

LEARNING OUTCOME 1 Economic, political-legal and cultural factors in different parts of the world influence the need for global integration of HR practices as well as the need for local adaptation. These competing forces create a tension for HR managers. The tension is found in how to manage people in a way that is compliant to cultural and political-legal norms while at the same time taking advantage of globally standardized practices.

LEARNING OUTCOME 2 There are four basic ways to organize for global competition: (1) the international corporation is essentially a domestic firm that has leveraged its existing capabilities to penetrate overseas markets; (2) the multinational corporation has fully autonomous units operating in multiple countries in order to address local issues; (3) the global corporation has a worldview but controls all international operations from its home office; and (4) the transnational corporation uses a network structure to balance global and local concerns.

LEARNING OUTCOME 3 International HRM places greater emphasis on a number of responsibilities and functions such as relocation, orientation, and translation services to help employees adapt to a new and different environment outside their own country.

LEARNING OUTCOME 4 Many factors must be considered in the selection and development of employees for international assignments. Hiring host-country nationals or third-country nationals versus sending expatriates is generally less costly. When expatriates are hired, most companies try to minimize their stays. Operations are handed off to host-country nationals as soon as possible.

LEARNING OUTCOME 5 Once an expatriate is selected, an intensive training and development program is essential to qualify that person and his or her spouse and family for the assignment. Wherever possible, development should extend beyond information and orientation training to include sensitivity training and field experiences which will enable the manager to understand cultural differences better. Those in charge of international programs should provide the help managers need with the career development risks they face, reentry problems, and culture shock. E-mail, instant messaging, and videoconferencing are making it easier for companies to stay in touch with their expatriates.

LEARNING OUTCOME 6 Compensation systems should support the overall strategic intent of the organization but be customized for local conditions. Compensation plans must give expatriates an incentive to leave the United States; meet their standards of living, health care, and safety needs; provide for the education of their children, if necessary; and facilitate their repatriation.

LEARNING OUTCOME 7 Although home-country managers frequently have formal responsibility for appraising individuals on foreign assignments, they may not be able to fully understand an expatriate's experiences because geographical distances pose communication problems. Host-country managers may be in the best position to observe day-to-day performance but may be biased by cultural factors and may not have a view of the organization as a whole. To balance the pros and cons of home-country and host-country evaluations, performance evaluation that combines the two sources of appraisal information is one option.

LEARNING OUTCOME 8 In many European countries—Germany, for one—employee representation is established by law. Organizations typically negotiate the agreement with the union at a national level, frequently with government intervention. In other countries, union activity is prohibited or limited to only large companies. European unions have much more political power than many other unions around the world, although their power has declined somewhat due to globalization forces. The International Confederation of Free Trade Unions (ICFTU), European Trade Union Confederation (ETUC), and International Labour Organization (ILO) are among the major worldwide organizations endeavoring to improve the conditions of workers.

Key Terms

augmented skills
balance sheet approach
codetermination
core skills
cultural environment
culture shock
expatriates, or home-country nationals
failure rate

global compensation system
global corporation
global manager
guest workers
home-based pay
host-based pay
host country
host-country nationals
international corporation

localization
multinational corporation (MNC)
repatriation
split pay
third-country nationals
transnational corporation
transnational teams
work permit, or visa

Discussion Questions

LEARNING OUTCOME 1 In recent years, we have observed an increase in foreign investment throughout the world. What effect are international ventures, such as the acquisition of Massmart by Walmart, having on HRM?

LEARNING OUTCOME 2 What major HR issues must be addressed as an organization moves from an international form to a multinational, to a global, and to a transnational form?

LEARNING OUTCOME 3
1. If you were starting now to plan for a career in international HRM, what steps would you take to prepare yourself?
2. Describe the effects that different components of the cultural environment can have on HRM in an international firm.

LEARNING OUTCOME 4
1. Starbucks is opening new stores abroad every day, it seems. If you were in charge, would you use expatriate managers or host-country nationals to staff the new facilities? Explain your thinking.
2. In what ways are U.S. managers likely to experience difficulties in their relationships with employees in foreign operations? How can these difficulties be minimized?

LEARNING OUTCOME 5
1. This chapter places considerable emphasis on the role spouses play in terms of the success of an overseas manager. What other steps should companies take to increase the likelihood of a successful experience for all parties involved?
2. Talk with a foreign student on your campus; ask about his or her experience with culture shock on first arriving in the United States. What did you learn from your discussion?

LEARNING OUTCOME 6 If the cost of living is lower in a foreign country than in the United States, should expatriates be paid less than they would be at home? Explain your position. Who should ultimately decide whether an employee should be localized or not?

LEARNING OUTCOME 7 If grooming a talented individual for a leadership role is an important outcome of a foreign assignment, how can this be worked into a performance appraisal system? How would a manager assess leadership accomplishments?

LEARNING OUTCOME 8
1. What are the major differences between labor-management relations in Europe and those in the United States?
2. Do you believe that codetermination will ever become popular in the United States? Explain your position.

HRM EXPERIENCE
An American (Expatriate) in Paris

There is often a great deal of work involved in setting up expatriate assignments. The administrative requirements can be far ranging and extend beyond the employee to also include family issues. Suppose you were faced with the following scenario. What would be the most pressing considerations that you would need to address?

The Scenario
You are the head of HR for Sarip International, a consulting firm specializing in hotel and restaurant management. Your firm is opening an office in Paris, France, and Jim Verioti, director of sales and marketing, has been asked to assume responsibilities for the expansion. Jim understands that the expatriate assignment will last two to three years, and although he has traveled to Europe for work on several occasions, this is his first long-term assignment overseas. He has a lot of questions about what he can expect and also some personal constraints.

HRM EXPERIENCE
An American (Expatriate) in Paris (continued)

Jim and his wife Betty have just moved into their new home (their mortgage is around $1,750 per month). In addition, Betty is an elementary school teacher and doesn't really know how the move will affect her job security. Their three children, Veronica (14), Reggie (12), and Archie (10), are of an age at which school considerations are very important. A friend told them about the American School in Paris, and this is a consideration. None of the Veriotis speak French.

Assignment

Working in teams of four to six individuals, put together the package that would allow Jim to move his family to Paris while still maintaining his present lifestyle (his current annual salary is $160,000 plus incentives). Address at least the following issues:

1. Visas and permits
2. Relocation allowance and housing
3. Language and culture training
4. Spousal employment concerns
5. Health/medical/insurance issues
6. Compensation and incentives
7. Education for the children

The following websites may be helpful to you, but other resources may prove valuable as well:

- U.S. embassy in Paris (http://france.usembassy.gov)
- French consulates in the United States (http://france.visahq.com/embassy/United-States)
- Expatica.com (http://www.expatica.com/fr/main.html)
- Americans in Paris (http://www.americansinfrance.net)
- The Paris France Guide (http://www.parisfranceguide.com)
- Easy Expat (http://www.easyexpat.com/paris_en.htm)
- Centers for Disease Control and Prevention (http://wwwn.cdc.gov/travel/default.aspx)
- American School in Paris (http://www.asparis.org/about)
- Medibroker (insurance) (http://www.medibroker.com)
- Access USA (mail) (http://myus2.myus.com/)
- Travlang (currency calculator) (http://www.travlang.com/money)

On the Job: Video Cases

Texas Instruments: Recruiting in the International Labor Market

Texas Instruments, also known as TI, is a Fortune 500 company based in Dallas, Texas. TI is the third largest manufacturer of semiconductors worldwide, the second largest supplier of chips for cellular handsets, and the largest producer of digital signal processors (DSPs) and analog semiconductors. The company is most widely known, however, for the TI handheld calculator that you may have owned in grade school.

Texas Instruments' success depends largely upon its people for continual innovations in the electronics industry as well as exceptional service to its customers. Because they are a globally operating company, they hire people from all over the world. This means that TI must consider the specific labor markets in which they are operating. Doing so requires knowledge of the local labor market and being able to find people who fit the core values of TI.

What to Watch for and Ask Yourself

1. How do they find the people they need all over the world?

2. Should TI's recruiting methods differ across countries?

3. What recruiting principles used by TI should be standardized across the world?

4. What factors do companies need to consider when they measure their costs per hire?

Case Study 1

How about a 900 Percent Raise?

Registered nurse Carmen Lopez wants a raise—so she's leaving Mexico and moving to California to take a job at Desert Valley Medical, a hospital near Los Angeles, where her income will increase tenfold. "I was making US$500 a month in Mexico, and in the U.S. I will be making between $25 to $28 an hour," Lopez says. Lopez, upon finishing her U.S. nursing exam, will be joining nine other Mexican nurses at Desert Valley Medical.

As U.S. baby boomers—now in their early sixties—age, the number of registered nurses in the United States is not keeping up. The U.S. government forecasts that by 2020 the demand for registered nurses will have increased by 40 percent while the number of nurses will have risen by just 6 percent. There are currently 2.2 million working nurses.

Lopez and her colleagues were recruited by MDS Global Medical Staffing in Los Angeles. Roger Viera, cofounder of MDS Global Staffing, says he and his business partner have invested $1 million, and the Mexican government added another $1 million, to open a nurse residency program in Mexico that trains and certifies nurses to work in the United States. "We only recruit qualified nurses. They must have a four-year bachelor of science degree and four years of work experience," Viera says. MDS expects to recruit from Mexico's twelve nursing schools and from Costa Rica in the near future.

MDS has also recruited Maria de la Cruz Gonzalez, who says she's excited about this opportunity to emigrate with her husband and work as a nurse in the United States. "The hospitals offer us a two-year contract where our nuclear family can come along to live with us in the U.S.," she says. MDS gives the nurses three months of paid rent and transportation, provides placement with client hospitals, and provides training in technology and language. They will be able to work in U.S. hospitals for two years under a North American Free Trade Agreement visa.

Donna Smith, chief nursing officer at Desert Valley Medical, says she is happy to have the Mexican nurses join her staff and believes that they are as qualified as U.S. nurses. But, she says, they will need more technical experience before they can go to work, since technology is different in the hospitals of Mexico. "We will provide them with extra training once they get here," she says.

Questions

1. Is recruiting nurses abroad a good idea for U.S. hospitals facing worker shortages?
2. Can you think of any cultural problems U.S. hospitals might encounter as a result?
3. What long-term recruiting measures should U.S. hospitals strive for?

Source: Condensed from Aisha Belone, "How about a 900 Percent Raise? Mexican Nurses Head North to Cure the Ballooning U.S. Health Care Labor Shortage," *Latin Trade* 12 no. 7 (July 2004): 30.

Case Study 2

In an unusual move, a seriously ailing Dallas software company, i2 Technologies, resettled 209 Indian engineers, programmers, and managers in their South Asian homeland on a voluntary basis to help stem losses as it laid off thousands of other employees. A series of corporate crises led to the mass repatriation back to India beginning in 2001.

Many returnees had worked in Texas, Massachusetts, and California for five to seven years on H-1B visas designed for temporary, highly skilled workers, although about 10 percent had acquired permanent residency green cards or U.S. citizenship. They found the company's Move to India Program too good to turn down—even if it meant a pay cut of 50 percent or more. None was pressured by management to return, said Gunaranjan "Guna" Pemmaraju, a 30-year-old engineer, who returned home. The returnees, many graduates of India's top technical universities, were confident of finding other U.S. jobs if i2 laid them off and were prepared to "change industries if need be," he asserted.

"When I left America, I actually kissed the ground," Pemmaraju said. "It helped me grow as an individual, and it enriched my thought process." Significantly, though, Pemmaraju says the quality of life in his middle-class Bangalore neighborhood is comparable—with a few minor downsides that he and his wife are willing to accept. Although their pay shrank in dollar terms, the repatriates are relatively better off in India.

"If we were in the top 25 percent in the United States, we're in the top 5 percent here," said one repatriate.

"We may not have 54-inch TV sets, but we have more of a sense of community and belonging here," another added.

Pemmaraju relies on DSL Internet access, fields morning calls from Dallas colleagues on a cell phone, and watches satellite TV while pedaling his new exercise bike. Instead of a Honda Accord, he drives a much smaller Suzuki Zen sedan.

For i2, the wage and benefit savings are helping it edge toward profitability. The company says the savings have been substantial. At its peak, i2 employed 6,349 people, with about 800 in India. It has since scaled down to 2,500 workers, 1,100 of whom are based in Bangalore.

Pemmaraju's family expresses no regrets about returning, yet they retain fond memories of the United States, a country of "milk and honey"—not to mention seven-layer Taco Bell burritos and Krispy Kreme doughnuts. Pemmaraju was tickled by a recent call to a fast-food restaurant in Bangalore. "A guy answered the phone saying, 'Thank you for calling Pizza Hut. Would that be for delivery or carry out?' he said. It's just what they said in Arlington [Texas]!"

A "TurnAround" Repatriate Plan: U.S. Company Moves Indian Workers Back Home

Questions

1. Does repatriation represent a good financial strategy for firms with international employees?
2. Besides cost savings, does i2 have anything to gain by repatriating its Indian employees?
3. What type of repatriation preparation training do you think i2's repatriates should receive before going home?

Source: Condensed from Barry Shlachter, "Software Firm Resettles Indian Workers in Turnaround Plan," *Fort Worth* (Texas) *Star-Telegram* (via Knight-Ridder/Tribune Business News), June 24, 2004.

Notes and References

1. See www.wto.org for more information on the World Trade Organization.

2. M. F. Wolff, "Innovation and Competitiveness among EU Goals for Knowledge Economy," *Research Technology Management* 44, no. 6 (November/December 2001): 2–6; Tony Emerson, "The Great Walls: The United States and Europe Are Leading the Race to Carve Up the Trading World," *Newsweek* (April 23, 2001), 40. For more information about the European Union online, see the Europa website at http://europa.eu.

3. Steven W. Hartman, "NAFTA, the controversy," *The International Trade Journal.* Vol. 25, Issue 1, (2011): 5–34.

4. Kris Axtman, "NAFTA's Shop-Floor Impact; Ten Years Later, The Trade Deal Costs Some U.S. Jobs but Buoys Trade and Efficiency," *Christian Science Monitor*, (November 4, 2003): 1; Sarah Schweitzer, "As Jobs Fall, Maine Blames Free Trade; Anti-NAFTA Rhetoric Echoes U.S. Anxiety," *The Boston Globe* (via Knight-Ridder/Tribune Business News), (March 28, 2004); John D. McKinnon, "Nafta, Under Attack, Gets Bush's Backing. Preview" *Wall Street Journal* 251, no. 94 (April 22, 2008): A3. See www.ustr.gov for up to date information on the U.S. trade balance with NAFTA countries.

5. Mark Drajem, "The benefits of a U.S.-Columbia free-trade deal," *Bloomberg Businessweek* (April 14, 2011).

6. Sadanand Dhume, "Just Quit It," *Far Eastern Economic Review* 165, no. 36 (September 12, 2002): 46–50; George Koo, "Fast Lane to China: Companies That Never Thought of Doing Business Overseas Are Now Looking to the Thriving Chinese Economy," *Computer Technology Review* 24, no. 4 (April 2004): 42.

7. Jordan Siegel and Barbara Zepp Larson, "Labor market institutions and global strategic adaptation: Evidence from Lincoln Electric," *Management Science* 55, no. 9 (2009): 1527–1546.

8. Julia Christensen Hughes, "HRM and Universalism: Is There One Best Way?" *International Journal of Contemporary Hospitality Management* 14, no. 5 (2002): 221–28;

"What's Keeping HR from Going Global?" *HRFocus* 77, no. 8 (August 2000): 8; "Culture: A Key Ingredient for International HR Success," *HRFocus* 78, no. 7 (July 2001): 1–3.

9. Beth McConnell, "Global Forum Speakers to Share Insights on International HR," *HRMagazine* 48, no. 3 (March 2003): 115–17.

10. Abagail McWilliams, David Van Fleet, and Patrick Wright, "Strategic Management of Human Resources for Global Competitive Advantage," *Journal of Business Strategies* 18, no. 1 (Spring 2001): 1–24. Shad Morris and Robert Calamai, "Dynamic HR: Global Applications from IBM," *Human Resource Management*, 18, no. 4 (July–August 2009). Shad Morris and Scott Snell, "Intellectual Capital Configurations and Organizational Capability: An Empirical Examination of Human Resource Subunits in the Multinational Enterprise," *Journal of International Business Studies* (April 2011).

11. DeeDee Doke, "Perfect Strangers: Cultural and Linguistic Differences between U.S. and U.K. Workers Necessitate Training for Expatriates," *HRMagazine* 49, no. 12 (December 2004): 62.

12. Readers interested in codes of conduct and other ethical issues pertaining to international business might read the following: Bill Roberts, "Going Global," *HRMagazine* 45, no. 8 (August 2000): 123–28.

13. Carla Joinson, "No Returns," *HRMagazine* 47, no. 11 (November 2002): 70–77; Frank Jossi, "Successful Handoff," *HRMagazine* 47, no. 10 (October 2002): 48–52; Steve Bates, "Study Discovers Patterns in Global Executive Mobility," *HRMagazine* 47, no 10 (October 2002): 14; Morgan McCall and George Hollenbeck, "Global Fatalities: When International Executives Derail," *Ivey Business Journal* 66, no. 5 (May/June 2002): 74–78; Leslie Gross Klass, "Fed Up with High Costs, Companies Thin the Ranks of Career Expats," *Workforce Management* 83, no. 10 (October 1, 2004): 84.

14. David Lipschultz, "Bosses from Abroad," *Chief Executive* 174 (January 2002): 18–21; Siew Seem Sing, "Many Challenges Await

Those Who Expatriate," *Plastics News* 20, no. 13 (June 2, 2008): 8–19.

15. Soo Min Toh and Angelo S. DeNisi, "A Local Perspective to Expatriate Success," *Academy of Management Executive* 19, no. 1 (February 2005): 132–146.

16. Readers interested in codes of conduct and other ethical issues pertaining to international business might read Nadar Asgary and Mark Mitschow, "Toward a Model for International Business Ethics," *Journal of Business Ethics* 36, no. 3 (March 2002): 238–46; Diana Winstanley and Jean Woodall, "The Adolescence of Ethics in Human Resource Management," *Human Resource Management Journal* 10, no. 4 (2000): 45; J. Brooke Hamilton and Stephen Knouse, "Multinational Enterprise Decision Principles for Dealing with Cross-Cultural Ethical Conflicts," *Journal of Business Ethics* 31, no. 1 (May 2001): 77–94; Michael Maynard, "Policing Transnational Commerce: Global Awareness in the Margins of Morality," *Journal of Business Ethics* 30, no. 1 (March 2001): 17–27.

17. Ben Wildavsky, "Reverse Brain Drain: How Much Should the U.S. Worry?" *The Chronicle of Higher Education*, March 28, 2011. "Keeping Out the Wrong People: Tightened Visa Rules Are Slowing the Vital Flow of Professionals into the U.S.," *Business Week* no. 3902 (October 4, 2004): 90; "Security Delays Hurt U.S. Business," *Legal Times*, (August 23, 2004); "Skilled Workers Leave in Reverse Brain Drain," *Fort Worth Star Telegram* (August 25, 2007): 9A.

18. "Society: Affirmative Action? Oui! At Long Last, France Takes a Page from America in Order to Manage Diversity—and Bring Minorities into Elite Schools," *Newsweek International*, (April 12, 2004): 30; Leo D'Angelo Fisher, "The Hunt for a New Work Order," *BRW* 30, no. 9 (May 15, 2008): 46–52.

19. Snell et al., "Designing and Supporting Transnational Teams," 147–58; Debra Shapiro, Stacie Furst, Gretchen Spreitzer, and Mary Ann Von Glinow, "Transnational Teams in the Electronic Age: Are Team Identity and High Performance at Risk?" *Journal of Organizational Behavior* 23 (June

2002): 455–67; Claude Philipps, Harold Sirkin, Duane Filtz, and Scott Kirsner, "Time [Zone] Travelers: They Bounce from Beijing to Bangalore at a Moment's Notice," *Fast Company*, no. 85 (August 2004): 60–67; Marie Adenfelt, and Katarina Lagerström, "Knowledge Development and Sharing in Multinational Corporations: The Case of a Centre of Excellence and a Transnational Team," *International Business Review* 15, no. 4 (August 2006): 381–400.

20. Snell et al., "Designing and Supporting Transnational Teams," 147–58; Leslie Gross Klass, "Fed Up with High Costs, Companies Thin the Ranks of Career Expats," *Workforce Management* 83, no. 10 (October 1, 2004): 84.

21. See Fuji Xerox website for detailed information about the company, http://www .fujixerox.com/eng/. Andrea Poe, "Selection Savvy," *HRMagazine* 47, no. 4 (April 2002): 77–83; "Exploiting Opportunity: Executives Trade Stories on Challenges of Doing Business in Global Economy," *Business Mexico* 15, no. 2 (February 2005): 54–58.

22. Dennis Nally, "14th Annual Global CEO Survey: Main Report," PricewaterhouseCoopers, (2011), http://www.pwc.com/gx/en/ceo-survey/download.jhtml.

23. Yehuda Baruch, "No Such Thing as a Global Manager," *Business Horizons* 45, no. 1 (January/February 2002): 36–42.

24. Sheree R. Curry, "Offshoring Swells Ranks of 'Returnees' Working Back in Their Native Countries," *Workforce Management* 84, no. 2 (February 1, 2005): 59; Yochanan Altman and Susan Shortland, "Women and International Assignments: Taking Stock— a 25-Year Review," *Human Resource Management* 47, no. 2 (Summer 2008): 199–216; Handan Kepir Sinangil and Deniz S. Ones, "Gender Differences in Expatriate Job Performance," *Applied Psychology: An International Review* 52, no. 3 (July 2003): 461–475; "More Women Sent on International Assignment," *Compensation & Benefits* 39, no. 2 (March– April 2007): 14–15.

25. Nina Cole and Yvonne McNulty, "Why do female expatriates "fit-in" better than males?," *Cross Cultural Management*, Vol. 18, No. 2, 2011. Robert O'Connor, "Plug the Expat Knowledge Drain," *HRMagazine* 47, no. 10 (October 2002): 101–107; Andrea Graf

and Lynn K. Harland, "Expatriate Selection: Evaluating the Discriminant, Convergent, and Predictive Validity of Five Measures of Interpersonal and Intercultural Competence," *Journal of Leadership & Organizational Studies* 11, no. 2 (Winter 2005): 46–63.

26. McCall and Hollenbeck, "Global Fatalities: When International Executives Derail," 74–78; Poe, "Selection Savvy," 77–83; Juan Sanchez, Paul Spector, and Cary Cooper, "Adapting to a Boundaryless World: A Developmental Expatriate Model," *Academy of Management Executive* 14, no. 2 (May 2000): 96–106; Eric Krell, "Evaluating Returns on Expatriates: Though Difficult to Ascertain, Measuring the Return on the Cost of Expatriate Assignments Is Necessary to Justify the Expensive Investment," *HRMagazine* (March 2005): 12.

27. Paula Caligiuri, Ibraiz Tarique and Rick Jacobs, "Selection for International Assignments," *Human Resource Management Review*, vol. 19, no. 3 (2009). Riki Takeuchi, "A Critical Review of Expatriate Adjustment Research through a Multiple Stakeholder View: Progress, Emerging Trends, and Prospects," *Journal of Management*, vol. 36, no. 4 (2010). Riki Takeuchi, Seokhwa Yun, and Paul Tesluk, "An Examination of Crossover and Spillover Effects of Spousal and Expatriate Cross-Cultural Adjustment on Expatriate Outcomes," *Journal of Applied Psychology* 87, no. 4 (August 2002): 655–66; Riki Takeuchi, Seokhwa Yun, and Paul Tesluk, "An Examination of Crossover and Spillover Effects of Spousal and Expatriate Cross-Cultural Adjustment on Expatriate Outcomes," *Journal of Applied Psychology* 87, no. 4 (August 2002): 655–66; Andrea Poe, Iris I. Varner, and Teresa M. Palmer, "Role of Cultural Self-Knowledge in Successful Expatriation," *Singapore Management Review* 27, no. 1 (January–June 2005): 1–25; Semere Haile, Marcus D. Jones, and Tsegai Emmanuel, "Challenges Facing Expatriate Performance Abroad," *International Journal of Business Research* 7, no. 5 (2007): 100–105; Margery Weinsten, "China a Double-Edged Sword for Ex-Pats," *Training* 43, no. 11 (November 2006): 12.

28. "Motorola to Increase Operations in China," *The New York Times* (November 8, 2001), C4; Peter J. Buckley, Jeremy Clegg, and Hui

Tan, "Knowledge Transfer to China: Policy Lessons from Foreign Affiliates," *Transnational Corporations* 13, no. 1 (April 2004): 31–73.

29. Lionel Laroche, John Bing, and Catherine Mercer Bing, "Beyond Translation," *Training & Development* 54, no. 12 (December 2000): 72–73; Sabrina Hicks, "Successful Global Training," *Training & Development* 54, no. 5 (May 2000): 95; Vesa Peltokorpi, "Intercultural Communication Patterns and Tactics: Nordic Expatriates in Japan," *International Business Review* 16, no. 1 (February 2007): 68–82.

30. Managers who are interested in setting up a language training program or who wish to evaluate commercially available language training programs should consult the "Standard Guide for Use-Oriented Foreign Language Instruction." The seven-page guide is put out by the American Society for Testing and Materials (ASTM), (610) 832-9585, http://www.astm.org. See also "Why Top Executives Are Participating in CEIBS and IESE's Joint Global Management Programme," *PR Newswire* (July 19, 2004). John Okpara and Jean Kabongo, "Cross-Cultural Training and Expatriate Adjustment: A Study of Western Expatriates in Nigeria," *Journal of World Busines*, 46, no. 1 (2011).

31. Jared Wade, "The Pitfalls of Cross-Cultural Business," *Risk Management* 51, no. 3 (March 2004): 38–43; Semere Haile, Marcus D. Jones, and Tsegai Emmanuel, "Challenges Facing Expatriate Performance Abroad," *International Journal of Business Research* 7, no. 5 (2007): 100–105.

32. Vipin Gupta, Paul Hanges, and Peter Dorman, "Cultural Clusters: Methodology and Findings," *Journal of World Business* 37, no. 1 (Spring 2002): 11–15; Jane Terpstra-Yong and David Ralston, "Moving toward a Global Understanding of Upward Influence Strategies: An Asian Perspective with Directions for Cross-Cultural Research," *Asia Pacific Journal of Management* 19, no. 2 (August 2002): 373–404.

33. Ping Ping Fu et al., "The Impact of Societal Cultural Values and Individual Social Beliefs on the Perceived Effectiveness of Managerial Influence Strategies: A Meso Approach," *Journal of International Business Studies* 35, no. 4 (July 2004): 33; Geert Hofstede,

Culture's Consequences: Comparing Values, Behaviors, Institutions, and Organizations across Nations (Thousand Oaks, CA: Sage, 2001).

34. Justin Martin, "The Global CEO: Overseas Experience Is Becoming a Must on Top Executives' Resumes, According to This Year's Route to the Top," *Chief Executive* no. 195 (January–February 2004): 24–31; Alizee B. Avril and Vincent P. Magnini, "A Holistic Approach to Expatriate Success," *International Journal of Contemporary Hospitality Management* 19, no. 1 (2007): 53–64.

35. David Lipschultz, "Bosses from Abroad," *Chief Executive* 174 (January 2002): 18–21; Denis Lyons and Spencer Stuart, "International CEOs on the Rise," *Chief Executive* 152 (February 2000): 51–53; U.S. Companies with Foreign-Born Executives," *Workforce Management* 83, no. 7 (July 1, 2004): 23.

36. Leung, A. & Chiu, C. (2010). Multicultural Experience, Idea Receptiveness, and Creativity, *Journal of Cross-Cultural Psychology*, 41(5–6): 723 –741. Maddux, W., & Galinsky, A. (2009). Cultural Borders and Mental Barriers: The Relationship Between Living Abroad and Creativity, Journal of Personality and Social Psychology, 96, No. 5: 1047–1061.

37. "Prudential Relocation Survey Finds Spouses' Experiences a Key Factor in the Success of International Work Assignments," *Canadian Corporate News* (December 7, 2004).

38. Avan Jassawalla, Traci Connolly, and Lindsay Slojkowski, "Issues of Effective Repatriation: A Model and Managerial Implications," *SAM Advanced Management Journal* 69, no. 2 (Spring 2004): 38–47; Mila B Lazarova and Jean-Luc Cerdin, "Revisiting Repatriation Concerns: Organizational Support versus Career and Contextual Influences," *Journal of International Business Studies* 38, no. 3 (May 2007): 404–429; "Life Not So Sweet for Repatriates," *In the Black* 78, no. 1 (February 2008): 13–14.

39. Phyllis Tharenou and Natasha Caulfield, "Will I Stay or Will I Go? Explaining Repatriation by Self-Initiated Expatriates," *Academy of Management Journal*, 53, No. 5 (2010). "Expatriate Administration: New Realities and HR Challenges," *Employee Benefit News* (March 1, 2005): 11; "For Those Working Abroad, Moving Home Can Be

Jarring," *The Kansas City (Missouri) Star* (via Knight-Ridder/Tribune Business News), (February 22, 2005); Mark C. Bolino, "Expatriate Assignments and Intra-Organizational Career Success: Implications for Individuals and Organizations," *Journal of International Business Studies* 38, no. 5 (September 2007): 819–835.

40. Lynette Clemetson, "Special Report on Globalization: The Globe Trotters," *Workforce Management* (December 2010). Calvin Reynolds, *Guide to Global Compensation and Benefits* (New York: Harcourt, 2001); Gary Parker, "Establishing Remuneration Practices across Culturally Diverse Environments," *Compensation & Benefits Management* 17, no. 2 (Spring 2001): 23–27; Timothy Dwyer, "Localization's Hidden Costs," *HRMagazine* 49, no. 6 (June 2004): 135–141.

41. Caroline Fisher, "Reward Strategy Linked to Financial Success: Europe," *Benefits & Compensation International* 32, no. 2 (September 2002): 34–35; "Comparative Analysis of Remuneration: Europe," *Benefits & Compensation International* 31, no. 10 (June 2002): 27–28; Fay Hansen, "Currents in Compensation and Benefits: International Trends," *Compensation and Benefits Review* 34, no. 2 (March/April 2002): 20–21.

42. Chao Chen, Jaepil Choi, and Shu-Cheng Chi, "Making Justice Sense of Local-Expatriate Compensation Disparity: Mitigation by Local Referents, Ideological Explanations, and Interpersonal Sensitivity in China-Foreign Joint Ventures," *Academy of Management Journal* 45, no. 4 (August 2002): 807–17.

43. Richard Locke, "Does Monitoring Improve Labor Standards? Lessons from Nike," *Industrial and Labor Relations Review* 61, no. 1 (2007).

44. Patricia Zingheim and Jay Schuster, "How You Pay Is What You Get," *Across the Board* 38, no. 5 (September/October 2001): 41–44; "Benefits for Expatriate Employees: International," *Benefits & Compensation International* 31, no. 10 (June 2002): 26–27; Steven P. Nurney, "The Long and Short of It: When Transitioning from a Short-Term to a Long-Term Expatriate Assignment, Consider the Financial Implications," *HRMagazine* 50, no. 3 (March 2005): 91–95.

45. Stephan Kolbe, "Putting Together an Expat Package: As More and More Companies

Adopt an International Outlook, They Are Increasingly Sending Staff on Overseas Assignments—Usually Involving a Complex Relocation Package," *International Money Marketing* (September 2004): 33.

46. The U.S. State Department Index of Living Costs Abroad can be found on the Web at http://www.state.gov/travel.

47. Barbara Hanrehan and Donald R. Bentivoglio, "Safe Haven: Accommodating the Needs of Employees and Families in Hostile Environments Can Increase Expenses and Alter Tax Liability," *HRMagazine* 47, no. 2 (February 2002): 52–54; Soo Min Toh and Angelo S. DeNisi, "A Local Perspective to Expatriate Success," *Academy of Management Executive* 19, no. 1 (February 2005): 132–146.

48. Xavier Baeten, "Global Compensation and Benefits Management: The Need for Communication and Coordination," *Compensation and Benefits Review* 42, no. 5 (2010). Paul Hempel, "Differences between Chinese and Western Managerial Views of Performance," *Personnel Review* 30, no. 2 (2001): 203–15; Hsi-An Shih, Yun-Hwa Chiang, and In-Sook Kim, "Expatriate Performance Management Form MNEs of Different National Origins," *International Journal of Manpower* 26, no. 2 (2005): 157–176.

49. "Cross-Cultural Lessons in Leadership: Data from a Decade-Long Research Project Puts Advice to Managers in Context, Country by Country," *MIT Sloan Management Review* 45, no. 1 (Fall 2003): 5–7.

50. Paula Caligiuri, "The Big Five Personality Characteristics as Predictors of Expatriate's Desire to Terminate the Assignment and Supervisor-Rated Performance," *Personnel Psychology* 53, no. 1 (Spring 2000): 67–88; Calvin Reynolds, "Global Compensation and Benefits in Transition," *Compensation and Benefits Review* 32, no. 1 (January/ February 2000): 28–38; Charlene Marmer Solomon, "The World Stops Shrinking," *Workforce* 79, no. 1 (January 2000): 48–51; Stephenie Overman, "Mentors without Borders: Global Mentors Can Give Employees a Different Perspective on Business Matters," *HRMagazine* 49, no. 3 (March 2004): 83–87.

51. Frank Jossi, "Successful Handoff," *HRMagazine* 47, no. 10 (October 2002): 48–52; Paula Caligiuri, David Day, and Shirley

Puccino, "Worldwide Practices and Trends in Expatriate Compensation and Benefits," *Benefits & Compensation Digest* 44, no. 1 (January 2007): 34–38; Eric Krell, "Evaluating Returns on Expatriates," *HRMagazine* 50, no. 3 (March 2005): 60–65.

52. M. Mendenhall and G. Oddou, *International Human Resources Management: Readings and Cases*, 2nd ed. (Boston, Mass.: P.W.S. Kent Publishing Co., 1995).

53. U.S. Department of Sate Indexes of Living Costs Abroad, Quarters Allowances, and Hardship Differentials—Januay 2011. Ariane Berthoin, "Expatriates' Contributions to Organizational Learning," *Journal of General Management* 26, no. 4 (Summer 2001): 62–84; Peter J. Buckley, Jeremy Clegg, and Hui Tan, "Knowledge Transfer to China: Policy Lessons from Foreign Affiliates," *Transnational Corporations* 13, no. 1 (April 2004): 31–73.

54. Bernhard Ebbinghaus and Jelle Visser, *The Societies of Europe: Trade Unions in Western Europe since 1945* (London, England: Palgrave Macmillan, 2000); John Pencavel, "Unionism Viewed Internationally," *Journal of Labor Research* 26, no. 1 (Winter 2005): 65–98; "Membership Required," *Economist* 87, no. 8591 (August 2, 2008): 66; Jeremy Smerd, "Unions Reverse Decline," *Workforce Management* 87, no. 2 (February 4, 2008): 1–3.

55. Christopher Rhoads, "Germany Faces Storm over Tech Staffing—Labor Groups Are Enraged by Proposal to Import Badly Needed Workers," *The Wall Street Journal* (March 7, 2000): A23; "European Workplaces Tighten Policies as Countries Struggle to Compete Worldwide," *Pittsburgh (Pennsylvania) Post-Gazette* (via Knight-Ridder/Tribune Business News), (November 28, 2004).

56. Dharam Gahi, "Decent Work: Universality and Diversity" (discussion paper, International Institute for Labour Studies 2005), 1–22; "Philosophical and Spiritual Perspectives on Decent Work," *International Labour Review* 143, no. 3 (Autumn 2004): 290–292.

Interested readers can find more information about international trade unions by checking out the websites of the ICFTU (http://www.icftu.org) and the ILO (http://www.ilo.org); "Communication on Decent Work," *European Industrial Relations Review* 389 (June 2006).

57. Dirk Kolvenbach and Ute Spiegel, "The Reform of the Works Council Constitution Act in Germany and Its Effects on the Co-Determination Rights of the Works Council," *International Financial Law Review* (2001): 59–65; Pencavel, "Unionism Viewed Internationally," 65–98; Simon Renaud, "Dynamic Efficiency of Supervisory Board Codetermination in Germany," *Review of Labour Economics & Industrial Relations* 21, no. 4/5 (December 2007): 689–712.

58. Herbert Spiro, "Co-Determination in Germany," *The American Political Science Review*, 48, no. 4 (December 1954): 1114–1127.

16 Creating High-Performance Work Systems

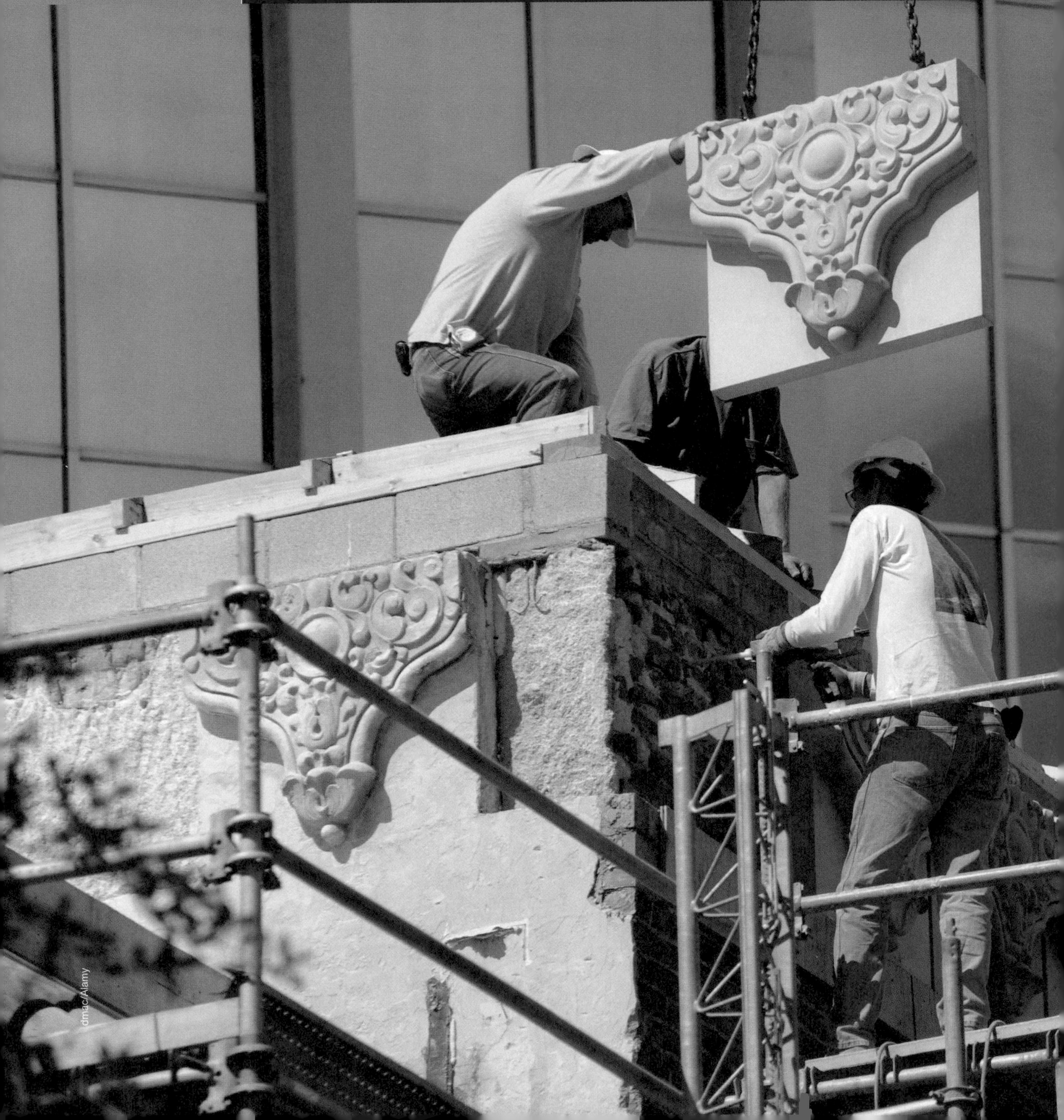

dmac/Alamy

After studying this chapter, you should be able to

LEARNING OUTCOME 1 Discuss the underlying principles of high-performance work systems.

LEARNING OUTCOME 2 Identify the components that make up a high-performance work system.

LEARNING OUTCOME 3 Describe how the components fit together and support strategy.

LEARNING OUTCOME 4 Recommend processes for implementing high-performance work systems.

LEARNING OUTCOME 5 Discuss the outcomes for both employees and the organization.

So you have finished reading fifteen chapters on HRM. Congratulations—textbooks do not always make for the most gripping reading. But before you close this book, think about the following question: What is more difficult—designing effective HR practices or managing them all together as one system?

In the past, HR textbooks simply ended after each individual aspect of HRM was introduced and explained. But in today's competitive environment, many organizations are discovering that it is how the pieces are combined that makes all the difference. After all, managers typically do not focus on staffing, training, and compensation practices in isolation from one another. These HR practices are combined into an overall system to enhance employee involvement and performance. So now that we have talked about the individual pieces, we thought it might be useful to spend some time talking about how they fit together into *high-performance work systems*.

A high-performance work system (HPWS) can be defined as a specific combination of HR practices, work structures, and processes that maximizes the knowledge, skills, commitment, flexibility, and resilience of employees. The key concept is based on the system. High-performance work systems are composed of many interrelated parts that complement one another to reach the goals of an organization, large or small.

We will start by discussing the underlying principles that guide the development of high-performance work systems and the potential benefits that can occur as a result. Then we will outline the various components of the system, the work-flow design, HR practices, management processes, and supporting technologies. (See Figure 16.1.) We will also describe the ways in which organizations try to tie all the pieces of the system together and link them with strategy. We end the chapter with a discussion of the processes organizations use to implement high-performance work systems as well as the outcomes that benefit both the employee and the organization as a whole.

high-performance work system (HPWS)

A specific combination of HR practices, work structures, and processes that maximizes employee knowledge, skill, commitment, and flexibility

Fundamental Principles

LEARNING OUTCOME 1

This textbook has emphasized the goals of competing through people, getting the best from employees, treating them fairly, and building an excellent organization. What key points have you learned in this regard, and how do they tie together in your mind when it comes to managing human resources?

In Chapter 1, we noted that organizations face a number of important competitive challenges such as adapting to greater global competition, harnessing technology, managing change, responding to customers, developing intellectual capital, and containing costs. We also noted some very important employee concerns that must be addressed, such as managing a diverse workforce, recognizing employee rights, adjusting to the new work attitudes of employees, and the need to balance work and family demands. We now know that the best organizations go beyond simply balancing these sometimes competing demands; they create work environments that blend these concerns to simultaneously get the most from their employees and meet their needs while reaching the short-term and long-term goals of the organization.

The notion of high-performance work systems was originally developed by David Nadler to capture an organization's "architecture" that integrates the technical and social aspects of work. Edward Lawler and his associates at the Center for Effective Organization at the University of Southern California have worked with Fortune 1000 corporations to identify the primary principles that support

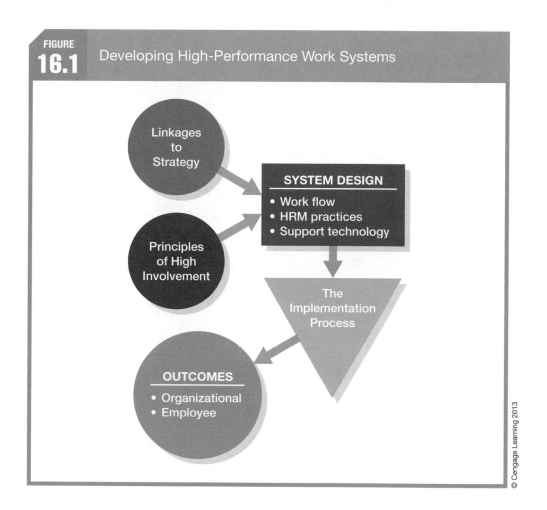

FIGURE 16.1   Developing High-Performance Work Systems

Linkages to Strategy

Principles of High Involvement

SYSTEM DESIGN
- Work flow
- HRM practices
- Support technology

The Implementation Process

OUTCOMES
- Organizational
- Employee

© Cengage Learning 2013

high-performance work systems. There are four simple but powerful principles, as shown in Figure 16.2:

- Egalitarianism and engagement

- Shared information

- Knowledge development

- Performance-reward linkage[1]

In many ways, these principles have become the building blocks for managers who want to create high-performance work systems. We will use them as a framework for the rest of the chapter. In addition, it should be noted that in a 2006 review and statistical analysis of ninety-two studies involving more than 19,000 organizations, researchers James Combs, Yongmei Liu, Angela Hall, and David Ketchen identified a number of major findings related to high-performance work systems. First, the systems have a larger influence on the performance of organizations than other highly visible governance practices, such as the independence of a firm's board of directors. Second, because of their synergistic effects, the elements of the systems have a larger impact when they are implemented as a bundle. Third, the systems have a significant

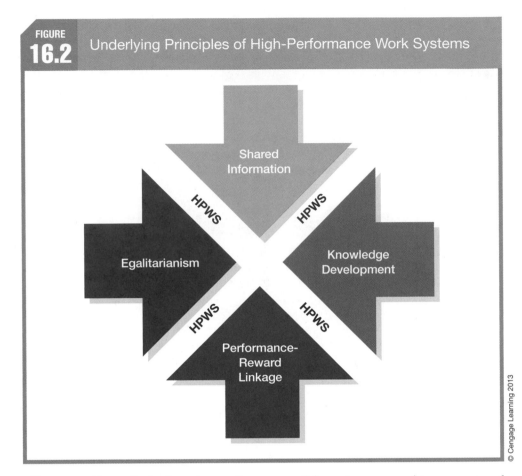

FIGURE 16.2 Underlying Principles of High-Performance Work Systems

Shared Information

HPWS   HPWS

Egalitarianism

Knowledge Development

HPWS   HPWS

Performance-Reward Linkage

© Cengage Learning 2013

effect regardless of whether the performance of firms is measured in operational terms or financial terms. Finally, high-performance work systems can be successfully implemented in all types of organizations, including both manufacturing and service organizations and organizations of different sizes.

Egalitarianism and Engagement

People want a sense that they are members, not just workers, in an organization. Status and power differences tend to separate people and magnify whatever disparities exist between them. The "us versus them" battles that have traditionally raged between managers, employees, and labor unions are increasingly being replaced by more cooperative approaches to managing work. More egalitarian work environments lessen status and power differences and, in the process, increase collaboration and teamwork. When this happens, productivity can improve if people who once worked in isolation from (or in opposition to) one another begin to work together.

Nucor Steel has an enviable reputation not only for establishing an egalitarian work environment, but for the employee loyalty and productivity that stem from that environment. Upper-level managers do not enjoy better insurance programs, vacation schedules, or holidays. In fact, certain benefits such as Nucor's profit sharing plan, scholarship program, employee stock purchase plan, extraordinary bonus plan, and service awards program are not available to Nucor's officers at all. Senior executives do not enjoy traditional perquisites such as company cars, corporate jets, executive dining rooms, or executive parking places. On the other hand, every Nucor employee is eligible for incentive pay and is listed alphabetically on the company's annual report.

Moving power downward in organizations—that is, empowering employees—frequently requires structural changes. Managers often use employee surveys, suggestion systems, quality-assurance teams, employee involvement groups, and/or union-management committees that work in parallel with existing organizational structures. In addition, work flows can be redesigned to give employees more control and influence over decision making. At Old Home Foods in St. Paul, Minnesota, one of the few independent, exclusively cultured dairy product manufacturers in the country, all employees are involved in the decision-making process of the business. "It's part of the Old Home Foods culture," says owner Peter Arthur "P. A." Hanson. "To be a successful independent, you need to empower your employees and let them know they are critical to success."[2] Job enlargement, enrichment, and self-managing work teams are typical methods for increasing the power of employees to influence decisions, suggest changes, or act on their own.

Involving employees in decision making and giving them the power to act also tends to increase employee engagement. Recall that engaged employees are employees who consistently perform at high levels, are enthusiastic about what they do, and look for better, more efficient ways of doing things. Surveys on engagement statistics vary. However, according to the research organization Gallup, only 29 percent of U.S. employees are actively engaged on the job, 15 percent are actively disengaged, and 54 percent are somewhere in the middle—not disengaged, but not engaged either.

Disengaged employees and employees who are only semiengaged can cost a company dearly, as the French bank Société Générale learned after a junior-level trader lost billions of the company's money making illicit trades. Some experts believe that a number of Société Générale employees were perhaps aware that there was a problem but did not report it, possibly because of poor employee engagement. "There's plenty of evidence that suggests that strategic human resources management and high-performance work systems are foundational in driving employee engagement," says Ellie Maggio, the managing director of Emend Management Consultants in Toronto, Canada. "If an organization is strategic about human resources, they're going to have higher engagement."[3]

Shared Information

The principle of shared information is critical to the success of employee empowerment and involvement initiatives in organizations. In the past, employees traditionally were not given—and did not ask for—information about the organization. People were hired to perform narrowly defined jobs with clearly specified duties, and not much else was asked of them. One of the underlying ideas of high-performance work systems is that workers are intimately acquainted with the nature of their own work and are therefore in the best position to recognize problems and devise solutions to them. Today organizations are relying on the expertise and initiative of employees to react quickly to incipient problems and opportunities. Without timely and accurate information about the business, employees can do little more than simply carry out orders and perform their roles in a relatively perfunctory way. They are unlikely to understand the overall direction of the business or contribute to organizational success.

On the other hand, when employees are given timely information about business performance, plans, and strategies, they are more likely to make good suggestions for improving the business and to cooperate in major organizational changes. They are also likely to feel more committed to new courses of action if they take part in the decision making, and happier, which seems to be at least one key to high-performance work systems, new research shows.[4] The principle of shared information typifies a shift in organizations away from the mentality of command and control toward one more focused on employee commitment. It represents a fundamental shift in the relationship between employer and employee. If executives do a good job of communicating with employees and create a culture of information sharing, employees are perhaps more likely to be willing (and able) to work toward the goals for the organization. They will "know more, do more, and contribute more."[5] Moreover, as we have suggested, the communication should not be one-way. Managers need to listen to employees' ideas and suggestions and act upon them.

Knowledge Development

Knowledge development is the twin sister of information sharing. As Richard Teerlink, former CEO of Harley-Davidson, noted, "The only thing you get when you empower dummies is bad decisions faster." Throughout this text, we have noted that the number of jobs requiring little knowledge and skill is declining, while the number of jobs requiring greater knowledge and skill is growing rapidly. As organizations attempt to compete through people, they must invest in employee development. This includes both selecting the best and the brightest candidates available in the labor market and providing all employees opportunities to continually hone their talents.

High-performance work systems depend on the shift from touch labor to knowledge work. Employees today need a broad range of technical, problem-solving, and interpersonal skills to work either individually or in teams on cutting-edge projects. Because of the speed of change, knowledge and skill requirements must also change rapidly. In today's work environment, employees must learn continuously. Stopgap training programs may not be enough. Companies have found that employees in high-performance work systems need to learn in "real time," on the job, using innovative new approaches to solve novel problems. At Ocean Spray's Henderson, Nevada, plant, making employees aware of the plant's progress has been a major focus. A real-time scoreboard on the Henderson plant floor provides workers with streaming updates of the plant's vital stats, including average cost per case, case volumes filled, filling speeds, and injuries to date. When people are better informed, they do better work. "We operate in real time, and we need real-time information to be able to know what we have achieved and what we are working towards," says an Ocean Spray manager.

Performance-Reward Linkage

It is not uncommon for employees to intentionally or unintentionally pursue outcomes that are beneficial to them but not necessarily to the organization as a whole. A corollary of this idea, however, is that things tend to go more smoothly when there is some way to align the interests of an organization and its employees. When companies reward their employees based on their performance, workers naturally pursue outcomes that are mutually beneficial to themselves and the organization. When this happens, some amazing things can result. For example, supervisors do not have to constantly watch to make sure that employees do the right thing. Instead, employees are more likely to go out of their way—above and beyond the call of duty—to make certain that their coworkers are getting the help they need, systems and processes are functioning efficiently, and the firms' customers are happy.

As Case Study 2 at the end of the chapter explains, every four weeks, the natural foods grocery Whole Foods calculates the profit per labor hour for every team in every store. Teams that exceed a certain threshold get a bonus in their next paycheck. Performance-based rewards such as these ensure that employees share in the gains that result from any performance improvement. This also ensures fairness and tends to focus employees on the organization. In fact, at Whole Foods, each employee has access to what other employees make in terms of their compensation.

Anatomy of High-Performance Work Systems

We said at the beginning of this chapter that high-performance work systems combine various work structures, HR practices, and management processes to maximize employee performance and well-being. Although we outlined the principles underlying such systems, their specific characteristics have not as yet been described in detail.

Although it may be premature to claim that there is a foolproof list of "best practices" that can be implemented by every organization for every work situation, some clear trends in work design, HR practices, leadership roles, and information technologies tell us what high-performance work systems look like.[6] Some of these are summarized in Figure 16.3.

LEARNING OUTCOME 2

Consider the chapters in this book. How do you think the topics of each one tie in with high-performance work systems? Are there any chapters that do not?

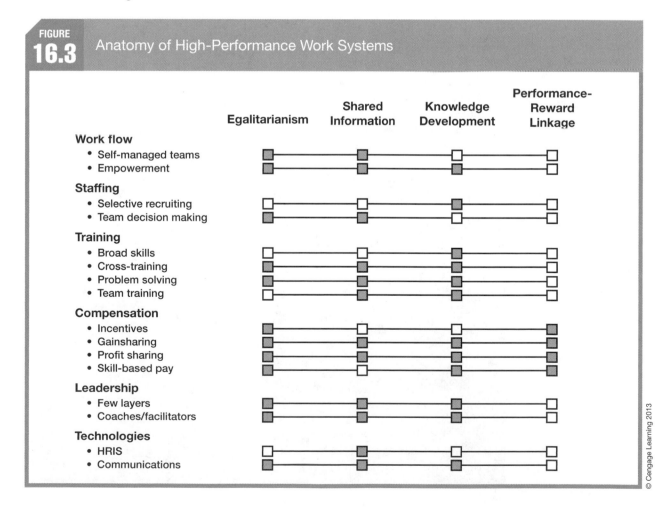

FIGURE 16.3   Anatomy of High-Performance Work Systems

© Cengage Learning 2013

Work-Flow Design and Teamwork

High-performance work systems frequently begin with the way work is designed. Total quality management (TQM), reengineering, six sigma, and the like have driven many organizations to redesign their work flows. Instead of separating jobs into discrete units, most experts now advise managers to focus on the key business processes that drive customer value—and then create teams that are responsible for those processes. Recall that this is the idea behind self-directed work teams. Federal Express redesigned its delivery process to give truck drivers responsibility for scheduling their own routes and for making necessary changes quickly. Because the drivers have detailed knowledge of customers and routes, Federal Express managers empowered them to inform existing customers of new products and services. In so doing, drivers now fill a type of sales representative role for the company. In addition, FedEx drivers also work together as a team to identify bottlenecks and solve problems that slow delivery. To facilitate this, advanced communications equipment was installed in the delivery trucks to help teams of drivers balance routes among those with larger or lighter loads.[7] By redesigning the work flow around key business processes, companies such as Federal Express have been able to establish a work environment that facilitates teamwork, takes advantage of its employees' skills and knowledge, empowers employees to make decisions, and provides them with more meaningful work.[8]

Complementary Human Resources Policies and Practices

Work redesign, in and of itself, does not constitute a high-performance work system. Neither does total quality management or reengineering. Other supporting elements of HRM are necessary. Several recent studies suggest that both the performance of employees as well as their satisfaction are much higher when organizations combine their changes in work-flow design with HR practices that encourage skill development and employee involvement.[9]

High-performance work systems have helped many auto manufacturers improve production and quality.

Fabrizio Costantini/Stringer/Getty Images

Staffing Practices

Many high-performance work systems begin with highly directive recruitment and selection practices. The recruitment tends to be both broad and intensive in order to get the best pool of candidates from which to choose. Human resources information systems have made it easier for firms to compile an inventory of their talent and search for employees with the specific skills they need. Talented employees "come up to speed" more quickly and take less time to develop. At Whole Foods Market, Macy's, and W.L. Gore, team members select their teammates. This practice gives employees more control over decisions about who their coworkers will be and forges relationships more quickly than if new members were simply assigned to a team.[10]

Too often, however, organizations try to save money by doing a superficial job of hiring. As a consequence, they run the risk of hiring the wrong people and spending more on training and/or outplacement, severance, and recruitment of replacements. Other hiring pitfalls include simply looking for skills and experience in candidates and not looking for cues to see if they are truly engaged employees capable of contributing adequately to a high-performance work system. Kris Dunn, a human resources executive and writer, suggests asking candidates behavioral questions such as the following: "Tell me about a time in a past job that you got really excited about something you were working on. Now tell me about a situation at work in which you got bored." If a candidate struggles to come up with relevant examples, there is no reason to think the person will be a fully engaged employee in your company.[11]

Training and Development

Like recruitment and selection, training focuses on ensuring that employees have the skills they need to assume greater responsibility in a high-performance work environment. For example, Schindler Elevator Corporation, the world's second-largest manufacturer of elevators, provides a sixty-hour prehire training program of instruction and testing in such subjects as orientation/company history, safety, plant policies and procedures, just-in-time (JIT) techniques, and basic shop math. The company also has an apprenticeship program that focuses on key areas based on its specific business needs. Apprentices are hired as machinists, tool and die makers, welders, electricians, mechanics, and so forth. In addition, Schindler gives each of its employees at least five days of classroom training every year. Typically, the training focuses on technical, problem-solving, and interpersonal skills. Emphasis on teamwork, engagement, and continuous improvement requires that employees develop a broader understanding of work processes performed by others around them rather than rely on just knowing their own jobs. To accomplish this, organizations increasingly use cross-training, discussed earlier in the book. Recall that this involves training employees in jobs in areas closely related to their own. For example, nurses in the perinatal unit of Cincinnati-based TriHealth System implemented cross-training to facilitate teamwork and cooperation across units; even more, it helps nurses identify trouble spots that cut across several jobs and allows them to suggest areas for improvement.

Beyond individual training, Eastman Chemical Company has established a training certification process that helps ensure its teams progress through a series of maturity phases. The teams certify their abilities to function effectively by demonstrating knowledge and skills in such areas as customer expectations, business conditions, and safety. Because these skills must be continually updated, Eastman Chemical requires that even certified teams periodically review their competencies.[12]

Compensation

Another important piece of a high-performance work system is the compensation package. Because high-performance work systems ask many different things from employees, it is difficult to isolate one single approach to pay that works for everyone. As a consequence, many companies are experimenting with alternative compensation plans. In order to link pay and performance, high-performance work systems often include some type of employee incentives. At Henry Ford Health System, a Detroit-area hospital network, employees' monetary performance incentives are tied to the system's strategic plan. If the system exceeds its financial targets, and if a business unit also achieves its targets and budget, then employees are awarded commensurately.[13] Other organizational incentives such as gain sharing, profit sharing, and employee stock ownership plans focus employee efforts on outcomes that benefit both themselves and the organization as a whole. The Scanlon Plan, Rucker Plan, and Improshare, three systems discussed in Chapter 10, have been used by companies such as TRW, Weyerhaeuser, and Whole Foods to elicit employee suggestions and reward them for contributions to productivity.

High-performance work systems can also incorporate skill-based pay plans. By paying employees based on the number of different job skills they have, organizations such as Shell Canada, Nortel Networks, and Honeywell hope to create both a broader skill base among employees and a more flexible pool of people to rotate among interrelated jobs. Both of these qualities are beneficial in a high-performance work environment and may justify the added expense in compensation. Honeywell has even experimented with what it calls "intracapital"—a pool of money employees can spend on capital improvements if the company meets its profitability goals.[14] Lastly, more companies are connecting their firm's corporate responsibility goals with their compensation systems. Whole Foods Market, the retailer Marks & Spencer, and Tesco, a global grocer and merchandiser, are among the companies that incorporate climate change targets into their performance goals. Whole Foods and Tesco's goals include community-involvement initiatives as well.[15]

Recall that in addition to linking pay and performance, high-performance work systems are also based on the principle of egalitarianism. To reinforce this principle in plants utilizing high-performance work systems, Monsanto, AES, and Honeywell recently implemented an all-salaried workforce. The open pay plan, in which everyone knows what everyone else makes, is yet another feature of compensation systems used to create a more egalitarian environment that encourages employee involvement and commitment.[16] At Henry Ford Health System each staff member within a business unit—including physicians—get the same incentive reward if the unit's goals are met, which in a recent year averaged about $800.[17] Likewise, not only are staff members' and executive bonuses tied to Tesco's corporate social responsibility goals, so is the pay for the members of the firm's board of directors.[18]

Management Processes and Leadership

Organizations such as Motorola, Doubletree Hotels, American Express, and Reebok International found that the success of any high-performance work system depends on first changing the roles of managers and team leaders. With fewer layers of management and a focus on team-based organization, the role of managers and supervisors is substantially different in an environment of high-performance work systems. Managers and supervisors are seen more as coaches, facilitators, and integrators of team efforts.[19] Rather than autocratically imposing their demands on employees and closely watching to make certain the workers comply, managers in high-performance work systems share responsibility for decision making with employees. Typically, the term *manager* is replaced by the term *team leader*. In a growing number of cases, leadership is shared among team members. Kodak, for example, rotates team leaders at various stages in team development. Alternatively, different individuals can assume functional leadership roles when their particular expertise is needed most.

Supportive Information Technologies

Communication and information technologies are yet one more piece that has to be added to the framework of high-performance work systems. Technologies of various kinds create an infrastructure for communicating and sharing information vital to business performance. Federal Express, for example, is known for its use of information technology to route packages. Its tracking system helps employees monitor each package, communicate with customers, and identify and solve problems quickly. Sally Corporation in Jacksonville, Florida, uses information technology to assign employees to various project teams. The company specializes in animatronics, the combination of wires and latex that is used to make humanoid creatures like those found in Disney's Hall of Presidents. Artisans employed by Sally Corporation work on several project teams at once. A computerized system developed by the company helps budget and track the employee time spent on different projects.

But information technologies need not be so high-tech. The richest communication occurs face to face. The important point is that high-performance work systems cannot succeed without timely and accurate communications. (Recall the principle of shared information.) Typically the information needs to be about business plans and goals, unit and corporate operating results, incipient problems and opportunities, and competitive threats.[20]

LEARNING OUTCOME 3

Fitting It All Together

Each of these practices highlights the individual pieces of a high-performance work system. You have learned that certain HR practices are better than others. However, recall that in high-performance work systems the pieces are particularly valuable in terms of how they help the entire system function as a whole. As we discussed in Chapter 2, careful planning helps ensure that the pieces fit together and are linked with the overall strategic goals of the organization. This philosophy is reflected at Whole Foods Market. The company's "Whole food, whole people, whole planet" is the framework for its high-performance work system, which you will learn about in Case Study 2 at the end of this chapter. Figure 16.4 summarizes the internal and external linkages needed to fit high-performance work systems together.

Ensuring Internal Fit

Recall from Chapter 2 that internal fit occurs when all the internal elements of the work system complement and reinforce one another. For example, a first-rate selection system may be of no use if it is not working in conjunction with a firm's training and development activities. If a new compensation program elicits and reinforces behaviors that are directly opposed to the goals laid out in the firm's performance plan, the two components would be working at cross purposes.

Have you ever moved a piece of furniture in your house or dorm room and noticed that once you did, everything else needed to be moved, too? How do you think this same principle might work when it comes to high-performance work systems?

internal fit
The situation in which all the internal elements of the work system complement and reinforce one another

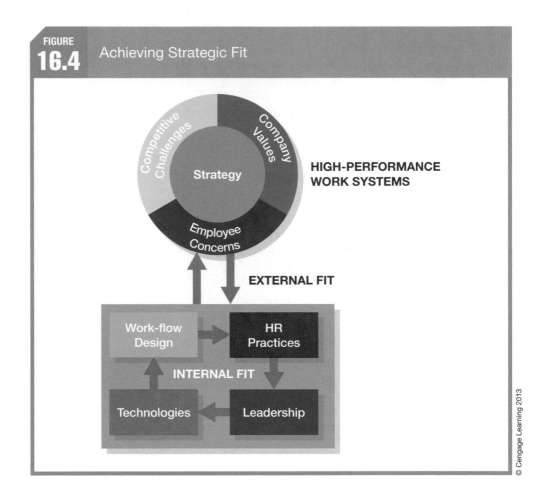

FIGURE 16.4 Achieving Strategic Fit

© Cengage Learning 2013

This is the true nature of systems. Changes in one component affect all of the other components. Because the pieces are interdependent, a new compensation system could have no effect on an organization's performance if it is implemented on its own. Achieving horizontal fit means testing to make certain that all of the HR practices, work designs, management processes, and technologies complement one another. The synergy achieved through overlapping work and human resources practices is at the heart of what makes a high-performance system effective.

Establishing External Fit

external fit

The situation in which the work system supports the organization's goals and strategies

To achieve **external fit**, high-performance work systems must support the organization's goals and strategies. This begins with an analysis and discussion of competitive challenges, organizational values, and the concerns of employees and results in a statement of the strategies being pursued by the organization.[21]

Xerox, for example, uses a planning process known as "Managing for Results," which begins with a statement of corporate values and priorities. These values and priorities are the foundation for establishing three-to-five-year goals for the organization. Each business unit establishes annual objectives based on these goals, and the process cascades down through every level of management. Ultimately, each employee within Xerox has a clear "line of sight" to the values and goals of the organization so he or she can see how individual effort makes a difference.[22]

Efforts such as this to achieve vertical fit help focus the design of high-performance work systems on a firm's strategic priorities. Objectives such as cost containment, quality enhancement, customer service, and speed to market directly influence what is expected of employees and the skills they need to be successful. Terms such as

1A HIGHLIGHTS IN **HRM**
Diagnosing Internal Fit

In the following chart, please estimate the degree to which the various HR management subsystems work together harmoniously or "fit" together. Think of the degree of fit and internal consistency as a continuum from −100 to +100, and assign a value in that range to each relationship. Examples of the extremes and midpoints on that continuum are as follows:

−100: The two subsystems work at cross purposes.

0: The two subsystems have little or no effect on one another.

+100: Each subsystem is mutually reinforcing and internally consistent.

DNK: Don't know or have no opinion.

	HR Planning	Recruiting and Selection	Training and Development	Performance Management and Appraisal	Compensation and Benefits	Work Organization (e.g., Teams)	Communication Systems	HR Performance Measurement	
								Cost	Value Creation
HR planning	—	−30	0	−20	0	0	0	0	0
Recruiting and selection		—	0	−10	−20	−30	0	+30	−40
Training and development			—	0	0	0	0	+30	−10
Performance management and appraisal				—	0	−30	+20	0	−20
Compensation and benefits					—	−50	0	+40	0
Work organization (e.g., teams)						—	0	0	0
Communication systems							—	0	0
HR performance measurement								—	

Source: Brian Becker, Mark Huselid, and Dave Ulrich, *The HR Scorecard* (Cambridge, MA: Harvard University Press, 2001).

HIGHLIGHTS IN **HRM**

1B Testing the Alignment of the HR System with HR Deliverables

Please indicate the degree to which the following elements of the HR system facilitate the HR deliverables shown, on a scale of −100 to + 100. Examples of the extremes and midpoints on that continuum are as follows:

−100: This dimension is counterproductive for enabling this deliverable.

0: This dimension has little or no effect on this deliverable.

+100: This dimension significantly enables this deliverable.

DNK: Don't know or have no opinion.

	HR Planning	Recruiting and Selection	Training and Development	Management and Appraisal	Compensation and Benefits	Work Organization (e.g., Teams)	Communi-cation Systems
Employment stability	0	0	0	0	−50	−20	0
Team-based behaviors	0	0	−30	−20	−40	0	0
Strategy-focused behaviors	0	0	0	0	+40	0	0
High-talent staffing level	0	−50	0	−50	0	0	0

involvement, flexibility, efficiency, problem solving, and *teamwork* are not just buzzwords. They are translated directly from the strategic requirements of today's organizations. High-performance work systems are designed to link employee initiatives to those strategies.

Assessing Strategic Alignment: The HR Scorecard

In Chapter 2, we introduced the balanced scorecard as a tool that helps managers evaluate the link between strategic goals and operational activities. Professors Brian Becker, Mark Huselid, and Dave Ulrich have adapted that model to create a *HR Scorecard* that helps managers assess the strategic alignment of their work systems.[23]

The HR Scorecard can be used to diagnose internal fit and external fit in a relatively straightforward way. First, managers diagnose internal fit by assessing whether particular HR practices reinforce one another or work at cross purposes (see Highlights in HRM 1A). Second, managers assess whether the HR practices significantly enable key workforce deliverables such as employment stability and teamwork (see Highlights in HRM 1B). Third, the degree of external fit is evaluated by assessing the degree to which the workforce deliverables are connected with key strategic performance drivers (see Highlights in HRM 1C). These three assessments are extremely useful not just for deriving measures of internal and external fit of high-performance work systems, but for engaging a broader set of managers and employees in the discussion of how to best implement the system.

In addition to making sure their HR practices are aligned, companies with disparate operations often align the HR scorecards of their various divisions. That is

HIGHLIGHTS IN **HRM**
1C Testing the Alignment of HR Deliverables

Please indicate the degree to which each HR deliverable in the following chart would *currently* enable each strategic driver, on a scale of - 100 to + 100. Empty cells indicate this is not a key deliverable for a particular driver. Examples of the extremes and midpoints on that continuum are as follows:

   −100:   This deliverable is counterproductive for enabling this driver.

       0:   This deliverable has little or no effect on this driver.

 +100:   This deliverable significantly enables this driver.

    DNK: Don't know or have no opinion.

| | HR Deliverable | | | |
Strategic Performance Drivers	Employment Stability among Senior R&D Staff	Team-Based Behaviors	Strategy-Focused Performance	High-Talent Staffing Level
1. Shorten product development times	−80	−30	+30	
2. Enhance customer focus and responsiveness	−20		−20	
3. Enhance productivity		−10	−50	−40
4. Develop and successfully manage joint ventures	−10	−50		

what Borealis, a manufacturer of polyolefin plastics, has done. In addition to an overall corporate HR scorecard that supports the company's corporate strategy, Borealis's foreign HR divisions have created their own scorecards that support both the firm's corporate-level HR scorecard and the company's local business unit scorecards.

Implementing the System

So far we have talked about the principles, practices, and goals of high-performance work systems. Unfortunately, these design issues compose probably less than half of the challenges that must be met in ensuring the success of a system. Much of what looks good on paper gets messy during implementation. The American Society for Training and Development (ASTD) asked managers and consultants to identify the critical factors that can make or break a high-performance work system. The respondents identified the following actions as necessary for success (see Figure 16.5):

LEARNING OUTCOME 4

What obstacles do you think managers might face when implementing a high-performance work system?

■ Make a compelling case for change linked to the company's business strategy.

■ Ensure that change is "owned" by senior and line managers.

■ Allocate sufficient resources and support for the change effort.

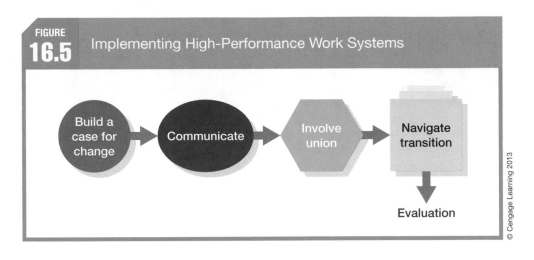

FIGURE 16.5   Implementing High-Performance Work Systems

Build a case for change → Communicate → Involve union → Navigate transition → Evaluation

© Cengage Learning 2013

- Ensure early and broad communication of the effort.

- Ensure that teams are implemented in a systemic way.

- Establish methods for measuring the results of the change.

- Ensure continuity of leadership and appoint "champions" of the initiative.[24]

Many of these recommendations are applicable to almost any change initiative, but they are especially important for broad-based change efforts that characterize high-performance work systems. Some of the most critical issues are discussed next.

Building a Business Case for Change

Change can be threatening because it asks people to abandon the old ways of doing things and accept new approaches that, to them at least, are untested. Managers have to build a case that the changes are needed for the success of the organization. This can be more readily accomplished if a member of top management plays the role of sponsor, or champion, and spends a substantial portion of his or her time in that role communicating with employees about the reasons and approaches to change.

The champion and top managers then need to work closely with middle managers to make the change happen. According to research by Dr. Ethan Mollick at the Wharton School at the University of Pennsylvania, because middle managers operate in the trenches of an organization amid both its people and processes, they can have a big impact on a firm's performance and how fast changes take place.[25]

Nonetheless, major transformations should not be shouldered by middle managers alone. Rather, the CEO and the senior management team need to establish the context for change and communicate the vision more broadly to the entire organization. For example, executives at Harley-Davidson tried to institute employee involvement groups without first demonstrating their own personal commitment to the program. Not surprisingly, employees were apathetic and in some cases referred to the proposed changes as just "another fine program" put in place by the personnel department. Harley-Davidson executives learned the hard way that commitment from the top is essential in order to establish mutual trust between employees and managers.

Similarly, the CEO of a business consulting company was adamant that his twenty-four vice presidents understand a new initiative and give a short speech at an introductory session. On the day of the program's launch, however, the CEO himself did not show up. The message to the vice presidents was clear. The CEO did not think the change was important enough to become an active participant. Not surprisingly, the change was never implemented.[26]

One of the best ways to communicate business needs is to show employees where the business is today—its current performance and capabilities. Then show them where the organization needs to be in the future. The gap between today and the future represents a starting point for discussion. When executives at TRW wanted to make a case for change to high-performance work systems, they used employee attitude surveys and data on turnover costs. The data provided enough ammunition to get conversation going about needed changes and sparked some suggestions about how they could be implemented.

Establishing a Communications Plan

While we have emphasized the importance of executive commitment, top-down communication is not enough. Two-way communication not only can result in better decisions, it may help to diminish the fears and concerns of employees when facing changes. For example, prior to being purchased by a competitor, Solectron Corporation, a winner of the Baldrige National Quality Award, tried to implement high-performance work systems to capitalize on the knowledge and experience of its employees. A pilot program showed immediate gains in productivity of almost 20 percent after the switch to self-managed teams and team-based compensation. Although Solectron's rapid growth of more than 50 percent per year made it unlikely that middle managers would be laid off, the loss of control to empowered teams made many of them reluctant to implement a high-performance work system.

Sharing information, at all levels, during implementation and after a high-performance system is in place is the key to its success.

Dennis MacDonald/Alamy

Using the **INTERNET**

You can find more information about the Baldrige Award, including a list of the most recent winners, at the National Institute of Standards and Technology website. Go to

www.cengagebrain.com

If the managers had participated in discussions about operational and financial aspects of the business, they might not have felt so threatened by the change. Open exchange and communication at an early stage pay off later as the system unfolds. Ongoing dialogue at all levels helps reaffirm commitment, answer questions that come up, and identify areas for improvement throughout implementation. Recall that one of the principles of high-performance work systems is sharing information. This principle is instrumental to success both during implementation and once the system is in place.

Involving Unions

Some research studies have found that unions can be a barrier to high-performance work systems, perhaps because unions are concerned that the efficiencies achieved might be so great that workers can be eliminated.[27] However, as we mentioned in Chapter 14, autocratic styles of management and confrontational approaches to labor negotiations are giving way to more enlightened approaches that promote cooperation and collaboration. This is especially true given globalization and other economic pressures. Unless better, more competitive ways can be found to operate, not only are union and non-union jobs at risk, so are the survival of the firms that employ them. Thus, it makes good sense to involve union members early and to keep them as close partners in the design and implementation process. Figure 16.6 shows how to "build a bridge" toward a cooperative relationship with unions in implementing high-performance work systems.[28]

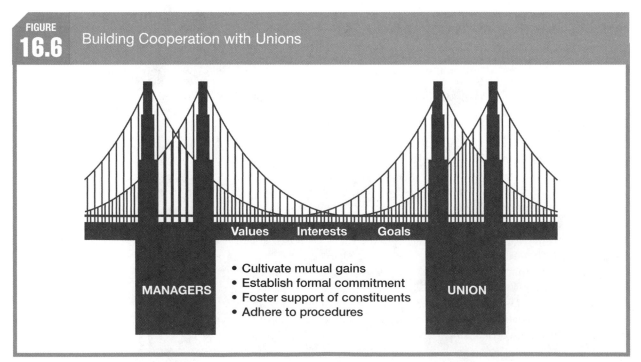

FIGURE 16.6   Building Cooperation with Unions

Values   Interests   Goals

MANAGERS

- Cultivate mutual gains
- Establish formal commitment
- Foster support of constituents
- Adhere to procedures

UNION

Source: The Conference Board of Canada.

Cultivating Mutual Gains

To establish an alliance, managers and labor representatives should try to create "win-win" situations, in which all parties gain from the implementation of high-performance work systems and openly communicate what the changes entail for each group and the firm as a whole. Organizations such as Shell and Novartis have found that "interest-based" (win-win) negotiation rather than positional bargaining leads to better relationships and outcomes with union representatives. Trust is a fragile component of an alliance and is reflected in the degree to which parties are comfortable sharing information and decision-making responsibilities. MTS, a telecommunications company based in the Canadian province of Manitoba, has involved union members in decisions about work practices, and because of this, company managers have been able to build mutual trust and respect with the union. This relationship has matured to a point at which union and company managers now design, select, and implement new technologies together. By working hard to develop trust up front, in either a union or a nonunion setting, it is more likely that each group will understand how high-performance work systems will benefit everyone. The organization will be more competitive, employees will have a higher quality of work life, and unions will have a stronger role in terms of representing employees.[29]

Formalizing the Commitment

Most labor-management alliances are made legitimate through some tangible symbol of commitment. This might include a policy document that spells out the union's involvement, letters of understanding, clauses in a collective bargaining agreement, or the establishment of joint forums with explicit mandates. MacMillan Bloedel, a Canadian wood products company now owned by Weyerhaeuser, formed a joint operations committee of senior management and labor representatives to routinely discuss a wide range of operational issues related to high-performance work systems. These types of formal commitments, with investments of tangible resources, serve two purposes: (1) They are an outward sign of the commitment of managers and (2) they institutionalize the initiative so that it keeps going even if key project champions leave.[30]

Gaining the Support of Other Key Groups

In addition to union leaders, it is critical for the firm to gain the support of other key groups. Leaders must ensure that understanding and support are solid at all levels, not just among those in the executive suite. To achieve this commitment, some organizations have decentralized the labor relations function, giving responsibility to local line managers and human resources generalists, to make certain that they are accountable and are committed to nurturing a high-performance work environment. Nortel Networks, for example, formally transferred accountability for labor relations to its plant managers through its collective bargaining agreement. Giving line managers responsibility for employee relations helps them establish a direct working relationship with the union.

Similarly, multinational firms need to gain the support of their key groups abroad. For example, Celestica, Inc., a Canadian-based provider of electronics manufacturing services and products started out as a single, wholly owned subsidiary of IBM. Today, however, the spin-off company has dozens of electronics manufacturing and design centers around the world. Being sensitive to different cultures and their ways of doing business as well as building relationships with them has been critical to the success of Celestica's high-performance work system.

Adhering to Procedures

Once processes, agreements, and ground rules are established, they are vital to the integrity of the relationship. As Ruth Wright, manager of the Council for Senior Human Resource Executives, puts it, "Procedure is the 'rug' on which alliances stand. Pull it out by making a unilateral management determination or otherwise changing the rules of the game, and the initiative will falter. Procedure keeps the parties focused, and it is an effective means of ensuring that democracy and fairness prevail."[31]

In most cases, a "homegrown" process developed by a firm's managers and employees works better than one that is adopted from elsewhere. Each organization has unique circumstances, and parties are more likely to commit to procedures they create and own. But this can give a firm a competitive advantage because homegrown, or unique, processes are harder for competitors to imitate.

Navigating the Transition to High-Performance Work Systems

Building and fostering high-performance work systems is an ongoing activity. Perhaps the job is never fully completed. As with any change activity, there will be missteps during the system's implementation for any number of reasons. For example, in already existing organizations, the pieces of the system often have to be changed incrementally rather than as a total program. Xerox Corporation found that when it implemented teams without also changing the compensation system to support teamwork, it got caught in a bad transition. The teams actually showed poorer performance than did employees working in settings that supported their individual contributions. Xerox's executives concluded that they needed to change the entire system at once because piecemeal changes were actually detrimental.

The other mistake organizations often make is to focus on either top-down changes driven by executives or bottom-up changes cultivated by the employees. In reality, firms such as Champion International, now a part of International Paper, and ASDA, a low-cost British retailer, are among the many companies that have found that the best results occur when managers and employees work together. The top-down approach communicates manager support and clarity, while the bottom-up approach ensures employees accept and are committed to the approach.[32]

Building a Transition Structure

Different organizations implement high-performance work systems in different ways. In start-up firms, managers have the advantage of being able to put everything in place at once. However, when organizations have to be retrofitted, the process can be a bit more cumbersome. For example, when Honeywell switched to high-performance work systems in its plant in Chandler, Arizona, employees attended training programs and participated in the redesign of their jobs while the plant was shut down to be reequipped with new technology. When the new plant was reopened, self-managing teams were put in place, and a new pay system was implemented for the high-performance workforce.[33]

Not every organization has the luxury of suspending operations while changes are put in place. Nevertheless, establishing an implementation plan that provides a timetable and process for mapping key business processes, redesigning the work flow, and training employees can keep the effort from bogging down.

Incorporating the HR Function as a Valuable Partner

Although line managers typically own the responsibility for implementing high-performing work systems, a firm's HR department can be an invaluable partner because the group is the key enabler of a company's human capital. As we explained in Chapter 2, global competition in many industries has led to the commoditization of products based on price, making talent the "great differentiator" among firms. Thus, the recruiting, evaluation, and reward systems devised by HR groups can have a huge impact on how well high-performance work systems are implemented. In addition, when high-performance work systems are used in their firms, managers perceive their HR departments as having more strategic value.[34]

Because change is difficult, HR managers are in a good position to help employees in transition handle what they are going through. When the "old ways" of doing things are abandoned, many experienced employees begin to feel like "beginners" again on the job. This can be stressful and sometimes polarizes employees. As a coping mechanism, many are likely to fall back on older routines. Texas Instruments created its High Performance Organization Development unit to facilitate the transition to a high-performance work system. Other organizations such as Merck, Ford, and Deutsche Bank have also developed special HR units to manage organizational change. Unilever created a transition team of senior line and HR managers to oversee the implementation of high-performance teams and develop an implementation road map.[35]

Evaluating and Sustaining the Success of the System

Once high-performance work systems are in place, they need to be monitored and evaluated over time. Several aspects of the review process should be addressed. First, there should be a process audit to determine whether the system has been implemented as it was designed and whether the principles of high-performance work systems are being reinforced. Questions such as the following might be included in the audit:

process audit
Determining whether the high-performance work system has been implemented as designed

- Are employees actually working together, or is the term "team" just a label?

- Are employees getting the information they need to make empowered decisions, and are they engaged?

- Are training programs developing the knowledge and skills employees need?

- Are employees being rewarded for good performance and useful suggestions?

- Are employees treated fairly so that power differences are minimal?

Second, the evaluation process should focus on the goals of high-performance work systems. To determine whether the program is succeeding, managers should look at issues such as the following:

- Are the behaviors the organization desires being exhibited on the job?

- Are quality, productivity, flexibility, and customer service objectives being met?

- Are quality-of-life goals being achieved for employees?

- Is the organization more competitive than in the past?

Implementing an HPWS is one thing. Sustaining it is another. Even though an HPWS can increase employee satisfaction and engagement, because the work teams in such a system are performing at their peak, burnout can be an issue. For example, employees of Facebook are the youngest and most satisfied of workers in big U.S. tech firms, but a recent survey found they are also the most stressed out.[36] (Will the social media behemoth eventually crash and burn as a result?) If there are not enough staff members to manage the volume of work, stress is almost guaranteed.

Employee poaching by competitors can be an issue, too. Motorola's Indian division discovered this firsthand. The division strategically recruited its employees and put together a high-performance work system, thereby capturing a significant amount of India's mobile device business. Later the division discovered that its employees were being hotly sought after by other companies such as Nokia. Consequently, Motorola had to look for new ways to retain and motivate the division's workforce.

Finally, high-performance work systems should be periodically evaluated in terms of new organizational priorities and initiatives. Because high-performance work systems are built on key business processes that deliver value to customers, as these processes and customer relationships change, so too should the work system. The advantage of high-performance work systems is that they are flexible and, therefore, more easily adapted. When change occurs, it should be guided by a clear understanding of the business needs and exhibit a close alignment with strategy.

Small Business Application

Are Your Employees Engaged, or Do You Need an HPWS?

Companies with disengaged workforces suffer from problems that do not seem to get better, including excessive employee turnover, lower productivity, and profits. When employees are engaged, however, the results can be much different. A recent Gallup study reported that firms with top engagement scores had 18 percent higher productivity and 16 percent higher profitability. According to a study by the Corporate Executive Board, engaged employees outperform average employees by 20 percent, and are 87 percent less likely to leave their organizations than highly disengaged employees. In a small business, because there simply is not enough margin for error when it comes to performance in today's highly competitive environment, engagement can have an even bigger impact.

As a small business owner how do you know if your employees are engaged or not? One way would be to survey them. Gallup has come up with a 12-question survey designed to gauge employee engagement that includes:

- Do you have the materials and equipment you need to do your work right?
- At work, do you have the opportunity to do what you do best every day?
- In the last seven days, have you received recognition or praise for doing good work?
- Does your supervisor, or someone at work, seem to care about you as a person?
- Is there someone at work who encourages your development?
- At work, do your opinions seem to count?

Barb Taylor Krantz, the author of *HR Professionals, Leadership, Personal Growth* has a better idea about how to measure engagement: Why not just talk to your employees? There is no way a CEO of a large company could talk to all

Small Business Application

Are Your Employees Engaged, or Do You Need an HPWS? (Continued)

of a firm's employees. Small businesspeople have that luxury. Do not do it during a performance evaluation, but during a relaxed and casual conversation, Clough suggests. Ask employees to talk about why they work for your organization, what motivates them to achieve, and what success on the job looks like. Which aspects of their jobs are most satisfying, and how could they contribute more in those areas? What challenging goals can they set for their own development? If they cannot answer these questions, chances are good that they are not engaged.

So how can you increase the engagement of employees other than by asking them to work harder than they already are? Simply looking for a quick-fix to engagement is not likely to be a solution because engagement is a measurement. "People who think their holy grail is increasing their employee engagement score are sorely mistaken," says HR blogger Gautam Ghosh. "For world-class companies like Southwest Airlines, employee engagement is a way of life that's taken them years to build into their cultures. It's not a strategy or program to them. It's just part of their corporate DNA."

Thus, what you may need to do as a small business owner is look at the culture of your firm, rethink how you operate, and implement the concepts in this chapter. In addition to the suggestions in this chapter, two good publications that can help a small business person implement an HPWS are *The HR Scorecard: Linking People, Strategy, and Performance* by Dave Ulrich, Mark A Huselid, and Brian E. Becker, and *The Power of Full Engagement: Managing Energy, Not Time, Is the Key to High Performance and Personal Renewal* by Jim Loehr and Tony Schwartz. Research has shown that high-performance work systems can successfully be used by small- and medium-sized organizations as well large ones.

Sources: Barb Krantz Taylor, "Are Employees Going Above and Beyond?" *The Bailey Group* (July 10, 2009) http://www.thebaileygroup.com; "The Backlash against Employee Engagement," Rise Smart (April 2, 2010); http://www.risesmart.com.

Outcomes of High-Performance Work Systems

Organizations achieve a wide variety of outcomes from high-performance work systems and effective human resources management. We have categorized these outcomes in terms of either *employee concerns* such as quality-of-work-life issues and job security or *competitive challenges* such as the firm's performance, productivity, and profitability. Throughout the text, we have emphasized that the best organizations find ways to achieve a balance between these two sets of outcomes and pursue activities that improve both.

LEARNING OUTCOME 5

As an employee, how do you think a high-performance work system might benefit you personally? What drawbacks might you experience because of such a system?

Employee Outcomes and Quality of Work Life

Properly implemented, managed, and monitored, high-performance work systems offer employees a myriad of potential benefits. In high-performing workplaces, employees have greater latitude to decide how to achieve their goals. Because the systems emphasize learning, people can take more risks, generate new ideas, and make mistakes, which in turn can actually lead to new products, services, and markets. As Richard Carlton, a former executive of 3M, put it, "You can't stumble if you're not in motion."[37] Because employees are more informed and empowered, they are likely to feel that they have a fuller role to play in the organization and that their opinions and expertise are valued more. As a result, they are likely to be more satisfied and find that their needs for career growth are being met. With higher skills and greater potential for contribution, they are likely to have more job security as well as be more marketable to other organizations, as employees in Motorola's Indian division discovered.

Conversely, when employees are underutilized, the performance of an organization suffers, and employees develop poor work attitudes and habits. Some years ago, the British Land Rover Company, a manufacturer of four-wheel-drive vehicles, found itself saddled with a notorious reputation for poor quality and productivity. Then it underwent a fundamental transformation. The company instituted extensive training (including giving every employee a personal training fund to be used on any subject), implemented more team-based production methods, reduced the number of separate job classifications, developed more cooperative relations with organized labor, and began a total quality program. As a result of these changes, productivity, quality, and the company's sales soared. However, despite massive evidence documenting the effectiveness of the new system, BMW, which later bought the company, began to dictate changes after taking over Land Rover—changes that ultimately undid its transformation.[38]

Organizational Outcomes and Competitive Advantage

Several organizational outcomes also result from using high-performance work systems. These include higher productivity, lower costs, better responsiveness to customers, greater flexibility, and higher profitability. Highlights in HRM 2 provides a sample of the success stories that companies have shared about their use of high-performance work systems. Benchmarks such as these are not enough. Recall that in Chapter 2 we said that organizations can create a sustainable competitive advantage through people if they focus on four criteria. They must develop competencies in their employees that have the following qualities:

- *Valuable:* High-performance work systems increase value by establishing ways to increase efficiency, decrease costs, improve processes, and provide something unique to customers.

- *Rare:* High-performance work systems help organizations develop and harness skills, knowledge, and abilities that are not equally available to all organizations.

- *Difficult to imitate:* High-performance work systems are designed around team processes and capabilities that cannot be transported, duplicated, or copied by rival firms.

- *Organized:* High-performance work systems combine the talents of employees and rapidly deploy them in new assignments with maximum flexibility.[39]

These criteria clearly show how high-performance work systems, in particular, and human resources management, in general, are instrumental in achieving competitive advantage through people.

High-performance work systems benefit employees by keeping them involved and informed, while giving organizations a competitive edge.

HIGHLIGHTS IN **HRM**

2 The Impact of High-Performance Work Systems

- Amcs Corporation, a New Jersey–based manufacturer of rubber products and office machine components, experienced a 48 percent increase in productivity and five straight years of revenue growth.
- Sales at Connor Manufacturing Services, a San Francisco firm, grew by 21 percent, while new orders rose 34 percent and the company's profit on operations increased 21 percent to a record level.
- Over a seven-year period, Graniterock, a construction material and mining company in Watsonville, California, experienced an 88 percent increase in market share, its standard for on-time delivery grew from 68 to 95 percent, and revenue per employee was 30 percent above the national average.
- At One Valley Bank of Clarksburg, West Virginia, employee turnover dropped by 48 percent, productivity increased by 24 percent, return on equity grew 72 percent, and profits jumped by 109 percent in three years.
- The Tennessee Eastman Division of the Eastman Chemical Company experienced an increase in productivity of nearly 70 percent, and 75 percent of its customers ranked it as the top chemical company in customer satisfaction.
- A study by John Paul MacDuffie of sixty-two automobile plants showed that those implementing high-performance work systems had 47 percent better quality and 43 percent better productivity.
- A study by Jeff Arthur of thirty steel minimills showed a 34 percent increase in productivity, 63 percent less scrap, and 57 percent less turnover.
- A study by Mark Huselid of 962 firms in multiple industries showed that high-performance work systems resulted in an annual increase in profits of more than $3,800 per employee.

Source: Martha A. Gephart and Mark E. Van Buren, "The Power of High Performance Work Systems," *Training & Development* 50, no. 10 (October 1996): 21–36.

However, for all their potential, implementing high-performance work systems is not an easy task. The systems are complex and require a good deal of close partnering among executives, line managers, HR professionals, union representatives, and employees. Ironically, this very complexity can lead to a competitive advantage. Because high-performance work systems are difficult to implement, successful organizations are difficult to copy. The ability to integrate business and employee concerns is indeed rare, and doing it in a way that adds value to customers is especially noteworthy. Organizations such as Google and Southwest Airlines have been able to do it, and as a result they enjoy a competitive advantage.

Summary

LEARNING OUTCOME 1 High-performance work systems are specific combinations of HR practices, work structures, and processes that maximize the knowledge, skills, commitment, and flexibility of employees. The systems are TQM oriented and based on the principles of shared information, knowledge development, performance-reward linkages, and egalitarianism and employee engagement.

LEARNING OUTCOME 2 High-performance work systems are composed of several interrelated components. Team members are carefully selected and undergo extensive training, including cross training, and often share leadership duties. Typically, the system begins with designing empowered work teams to carry out key business processes. Integrated information technology systems can help ensure that employees have the information they need to make timely and productive decisions. To align the interests of employees with those of the organization, the reward systems associated with high-performance work systems are performance-based, and often include group and organizational incentive pay and sometimes skill-based pay.

LEARNING OUTCOME 3 The pieces of the system are important only in terms of how they help the entire system function. When all the pieces support and complement one another, high-performance work systems achieve internal fit. When the system is aligned with the competitive priorities of the organization as a whole, it achieves external fit as well.

LEARNING OUTCOME 4 Implementing high-performance work systems within existing organizations often has to be done in stages. The implementation is much more likely to go smoothly if a business case is first made for the HPWS and fully communicated to employees. The support of the firm's top and middle managers is critical, and so too is the support of union representatives and the company's other key groups and divisions. Because firms today gain a competitive advantage primarily from the capabilities of their talent, a company's HR department can be an invaluable partner when it comes to implementing a HPWS. HR personnel can also help establish a transition structure to shepherd the implementation through its various stages and reassure employees they will be successful working in the new system. Once the system is in place, it should be evaluated in terms of its processes, outcomes, sustainability, and ongoing fit with strategic objectives of the organization.

LEARNING OUTCOME 5 Progressive organizations of all sizes have successfully implemented high-performance work systems. When implemented effectively, high-performance work systems benefit both employees and their organizations. Employees become more engaged and empowered to make decisions, experience greater career growth and satisfaction, and become more valuable contributors to their firms. Organizations benefit from higher productivity, quality, flexibility, and customer satisfaction. These features together can provide a company with a sustainable competitive advantage.

Key Terms

high-performance work system   internal fit   process audit
  (HPWS)   external fit

Discussion Questions 💬

LEARNING OUTCOME 1 Do you think the four principles of high involvement provide an adequate context for designing high-performance work systems? What other concerns or guidelines for developing high-performance work systems would you suggest?

LEARNING OUTCOME 2 In many cases, organizations use teams as a part of their high-performance work systems. Could a high performance work system be useful in an organization that does not use teams? What special concerns might have to be addressed?

LEARNING OUTCOME 3 Although achieving both internal and external fit are important with regard to

high-performance work systems, which do you consider more critical and why?

LEARNING OUTCOME 4 This chapter emphasizes the processes required to implement high-performance work systems. What are the most critical steps to successful implementation?

LEARNING OUTCOME 5 How do you think employee-related outcomes and organizational outcomes are related to one another? Is it possible to achieve one set of outcomes without the other? Why or why not?

On the Job: Video Cases 🎬

Fruit Guys: A Sweet Way to Deal with Stakeholders

Fruit Guys' chief executive officer (CEO) and founder, an operational manager, and a supplier (organic farm owner) discuss the philosophy and specific practices and models that Fruit Guys use in their dealings with employees, customers, and suppliers. The company is concerned about being compassionate and thoughtful more than just ways to increase sales. The importance of not only having healthy and quality products but also using a new business model that treats customers, employees, and suppliers with respect is emphasized.

What to Watch for and Ask Yourself

- The CEO states that HR is more than staffing; it is about creating cultures. How does the integration of HR with the organizational culture contribute to the success of Fruit Guys? Describe the social responsibility dimensions of Fruit Guys that are discussed in the video. What are the implications for HR?

- What do you think will be the most important challenges for HR at Fruit Guys in the next five years?

- Fruit Guys has a very small HR staff. What are some special issues of HR in smaller organizations?

HRM EXPERIENCE
Assessing the Strategic Fit of High-Performance Work Systems

High-performance work systems (HPWSs) are potentially powerful tools. However, ensuring that all of the HR practices support one another—and the principles underlying the HPWS—is not always easy. At times, certain HR practices might support the HPWS while others actually may work against the system's principles. This can result in failure. It takes only one misaligned practice to crash the whole system. Recall that the HPWS principles include the following:

- Egalitarianism and engagement
- Shared information
- Knowledge development
- Performance-reward linkage

Assignment

The following figure lists the main HR practices used at Egan Clothiers, Ltd. Working in teams of four to six, assess the extent to which you believe each HR practice supports (or works against) each of the HPWS principles.

1. For each cell in the matrix, insert a number indicating the extent to which you believe the HR practice supports the principle or is counterproductive. The scale runs from −5 (strongly counterproductive) to 5 (very supportive). Zero indicates neither support nor detriment.

2. When you are done filling in each cell, add the numbers across each row to determine how supportive each HR practice is of all of the principles. Which HR practice is most supportive of the HPWS principles? Which HR practice is of most concern?

3. Add each column to see how the overall set of HR practices supports each principle. Which principle is most strongly supported? Which principle is the biggest concern?

4. Add the rows and/or columns to see how well the HPWS is supported overall. What changes would you recommend to improve the system?

Note: This figure corresponds to the integrative case on Egan Clothiers, Ltd., in the back of the text. The exercise can be used in conjunction with the case, or you may simply refer to the case as background reading.

EGAN CLOTHIERS, LTD.

HPWS PRINCIPLES

HR PRACTICES	Egalitarianism	Shared Information	Knowledge Development	Performance-Reward Linkage	TOTAL
STRUCTURE					
• Cross-functional team					Row 1
• Department rotation					Row 2
STAFFING					
• Select for experience					
• Promote from within					
TRAINING					
• Retail selling skills					
• Customer service					
REWARDS					
• Results appraisal					
• Forced distribution					
• Individual incentives					
TECHNOLOGY					
• HR Info System					
• Post performance					
	Column 1	Column 2	Column 3	Column 4	TOTAL

SCORING KEY

5 = strongly supports the principle
0 = neutral

Case Study 1

High turnover and so-so customer service characterizes much of the hospitality industry, but not at Las Vegas' MGM Grand Hotel. The property has one of the lowest turnover rates in Las Vegas and has outperformed nearly all of its competitors. In the course of three years, profits at the hotel doubled and revenues increased from $700 million to $1.2 billion.

It doesn't hurt that the MGM Grand underwent a massive renovation a few years ago and brought in top acts such as Cirque du Soleil. But if you ask the hotel's CEO Gamal Aziz why MGM is different, he will tell you it is because of the company's 10,000 employees and how engaged they are. "Employees are willing to give their all when they are well-treated and appreciated. Imagine taking 10,000 employees, and each and every one of them wanting to give more. That's really the difference between [us and] a company that has its employees just punching the clock and trying to get through the day," says Aziz.

But this scenario wasn't always the case. When Aziz took the helm of the MGM Grand in 2001, its customer service numbers were not good. The lights were on at the strip, but at MGM, employees were in the dark: An employee survey showed that workers received very little communication from their managers. If important guests were staying at the hotel, workers had no clue. Many times, they did not know what conventions were being held at the hotel and how or what to offer these guests. Not surprisingly, it was hard to provide customers a high level of service and earn their loyalty.

Aziz changed that. At the start of every shift, he instituted short meetings to let the staff know what's happening in the hotel each day. He also expanded MGM Grand University, the company's managerial training program, and involved employees in decisions about its offerings. Another thing that has changed is that the company now goes out of its way to recognize employees who do a great job. The hotel's award-winning recognition programs include employee-of-the month luncheons, recognition posters, a "star of the month" board, coffee chats with employees, mandatory employee recognition training, appreciation dinners for top performers hosted by Aziz, and plain old pats on the back. Before new recognition programs are instituted, the company seeks feedback from previous employee recognition "champions" and focus groups to ensure that they are aligned with the company's core business goals.

Today, more than 90 percent of MGM Grand employees say they are satisfied with their jobs, and 89 percent say their work has special meaning. "Having happy, motivated employees is one of the great differentiators that makes us great in our industry," says John Shigley, who was recently named the company's chief operating officer. Translation: Happy employees = happy customers.

Of course, the most recent recession followed by high unemployment made everyone on the strip a little *less* happy as hotel bookings in Las Vegas dropped across the board. As a result, Aziz has had to cut spending on some of the hotel's recognition programs. But he did not do so before sharing with employees the challenges the hotel faces and vowing not move away from commitment to employees. "Employee engagement in times of difficulties and severe economic climate is far more profoundly important," he says.

Jim Harter, the chief scientist for Gallup's workplace management practice arm, agrees with Aziz. Harter argues that employee engagement is actually important in a bad economy because it makes employees resilient, which helps them get through tough times. Resilient employees have the flexibility to bounce back from bad news and immediately focus on ways to improve the business.

Despite the challenges, MGM employees are willing to give their all and then some, says Aziz. "We will survive. Once we get through this, the employees will be the ones who have gotten us through."

Questions

1. Identify the ways in which the MGM Grand Hotel engages its employees.
2. What HR aspects of the hotel resemble high-performance work systems?
3. What role does information sharing plays in supporting its efforts?

Sources: Nannette Byrnes, "The Issue: Maintaining Employee Engagement," *Business Week* (January 16, 2009), http://www.businessweek.com; Denise L. White, "Employee Recognition in Hospitality Industry: A Fresh Look," *Diversity in Hospitality.com* (January 2008), http://www.diversityinHospitality.com; Michael Bungay, "Gamal Aziz President and CEO of MGM Mirage Hospitality," *Great Work Interviews* (September 10, 2010); http://www.greatworkinterviews.com; Stephen J. Gill, "Employee Engagement in a Recession," *The Performance Improvement Blog* (January 21, 2009), http://stephenjgill.typepad.com.

Case Study 2

Whole Foods Market

In this chapter we talked about how hierarchical, command-and-control type of organizational structures are giving way to high performing work systems—systems characterized by egalitarianism, knowledge and information sharing, employee empowerment, and reward and performance linkages. Such a system pretty well sums up Whole Foods Market, the world's leading natural and organic foods grocer. Whole Foods started out in 1980 with one small store in Austin, Texas. Today it employs 54,000 employees in more than 300 stores in North America and the United Kingdom. And despite having higher product prices than most of its competitors, during the recession, following a downward dip, the company managed to emerge with higher sales and strong profits. How has Whole Foods done it?

For one, as the company expanded, Whole Foods adopted many of the successful practices of the companies it bought—especially those of Boston-based Bread & Circus, renowned for its fresh produce, meat, and seafood. "Whole Foods has been very smart about their expansion program, taking time to digest acquisitions before moving on to the next one," says Darrell Rigby, a retail consultant. Second, the company has stayed true to its vision. It works to ensure that all of its efforts and practices are externally and internally aligned with the following three principles: Whole Foods, Whole People, and Whole Planet.

The "Whole Foods" principles relates to the company's mission to provide customers the highest quality, least processed, most flavorful and natural foods possible. "Whole planet" relates to the company's endeavors to protect the environment and nurture the communities in which it operates. For example, in addition to participating in a multitude of green initiatives, at least 5 percent of annual profits go to local charities.

The company's "whole people" principle is arguably a huge part of its success. Whole Foods' website points out that the grocer's employees *are* the company:

> Our success is dependent upon the collective energy and intelligence of all our Team Members. In addition to receiving fair wages and benefits, belief in the value of our work and finding fulfillment from our jobs is a key reason we are part of Whole Foods Market.

The key word? *Team.* Whole Food isn't "run" by executives and store managers but by in-store teams. Each team is responsible for one area of the store, such as baked goods, meat, poultry, and so forth, and is empowered to make product, pricing, and staffing decisions. This high degree of decentralization allows the stores to better tailor their offerings and services to meet the needs of the communities, which helps them be more competitive.

The decentralized approach begins on the front end with hiring. As Whole Foods grew, it found that centralized, online recruiting left local stores awash with resumes but not much knowledge of applicants. Applicants can still submit resumes online, but now each store has its own human resources department that aids in hiring and recruiting and in-store kiosks where applicants can apply.

Many interviews at Whole Foods Market are conducted by teams of employees who look for applicants who share the "whole food, whole people, whole planet" vision. Once an applicant is hired, he or she is assigned to one of the store's teams for a trial period, after which the team members vote to determine if the person deserves a full-time spot on the team. Think of it in terms of the TV show *Survivor*, but in reverse in that newcomers have to be voted *onto* the island, or team. The same process is used at the corporate level for employees who want to join the firm's marketing, human resources, finance, and IT departments.

The voting is not done for entertainment or team-building purposes, though. It's crucial because it affects workers' paychecks. The teams are treated as separate profit centers and rewarded with monthly bonuses if their profits exceed a certain level. Consequently, nobody wants to vote in a slacker. (Talk about peer pressure.) Not surprisingly, the company does not have to do a lot of monitoring of its employees. They do it themselves. "We don't have lots of rules handed down from headquarters in Austin," John Mackey, the founder of the company and its CEO, has said. "Peer pressure enlists loyalty in ways that bureaucracy doesn't."

Speaking of bureaucracy, Mackey has also been quoted as saying that Whole Foods is a "social system" and not a "hierarchy." He wasn't kidding. In many companies CEOs earn literally hundreds of times what the average worker does. Not at Whole Foods. Mackey's salary and those of other executives are capped at 14 times the average annual salary of a full-time employee. If he and other executives want a raise, they have to increase what employees are paid. Employees also vote on all company-wide initiatives, and full-timers get 100 percent of their health care costs paid for—under plans the employees have selected. And unlike most firms, employees own about 95 percent of the company's stock options.

Invariably, Whole Foods lands on *Fortune's* 100 Best Companies to Work For list each year. "I love working at Whole Foods, and I hope to grow with this company for years and years to come," says Simon William Griffith, one of its employees. "This company empowers me and makes me feel valued and valuable."

Questions

1. Why don't all companies treat their employees like Whole Foods does? Do you think they will in the future?
2. Mackey is one of the firm's founders. But is the company at a disadvantage once he retires, given Whole Foods' salary cap? And will the new CEO have to be voted "in"?
3. Can "eco-consciousness" effectively be incorporated into high-performance work systems?

Sources: Gary Hael and Bill Breen, "Creating a Community of Purpose: Management Innovation in Action," *Harvard Business School Press*, 2007; "Whole Foods Market's Unique Work Culture and Practices," *ICMR* (2006), http://www.icmrindia.org;

Frank Roche, "HR Lessons from Whole Foods," *KnowHR*, http://www.knowhr.com.

Notes and References

1. D. A. Nadler and M. S. Gerstein, "Designing High-Performance Work Systems: Organizing People, Work, Technology, and Information," *Organizational Architecture* (San Francisco: Jossey-Bass, 1992), 195–208; E. Lawler III, Susan Albers Mohrman, and Gerald E. Ledford, *Creating High Performance Organizations: Practices and Results of Employee Involvement and Total Quality Management in Fortune 1000 Companies* (San Francisco: Jossey-Bass, 1995); Edward Lawler III, Susan Albers Mohrman, and George Benson, *Organizing for High Performance: Employee Involvement, TQM, Reengineering, and Knowledge Management in the Fortune 1000: The CEO Report* (San Francisco: Jossey-Bass, 2001). See also David Nadler, Michael Tushman, and Mark Nadler, *Competing by Design: The Power of Organizational Architecture* (New York: Oxford University Press, 1997); Jody Gitell Hoffer, "Relationships and Resilience," *Journal of Applied Behavioral Science* 44, no. 1 (March 2008): 25–47.

2. J. B. Arthur, "Effects of Human Resource Systems on Manufacturing Performance and Turnover," *Academy of Management Journal* 37 (1994): 670–87; M. Huselid, "The Impact of Human Resource Management Practices on Turnover, Productivity, and Corporate Financial Performance," *Academy of Management Journal* 38 (1995): 635–72; Mark A. Youndt, Scott A. Snell, James W.

Dean, Jr., and David P. Lepak, "Human Resource Management, Manufacturing Strategy, and Firm Performance," *Academy of Management Journal* 39, no. 4 (August 1996): 836–66; John F. Tomer, "Understanding High-Performance Work Systems: The Joint Contribution of Economics and Human Resource Management," *The Journal of Socio-Economics* 30, no. 1 (January 2001): 63; Kris Dunn, "Rules of Engagement," *Workforce Management Online* (July 2008).

3. Rasha Mourtada, "Bosses Fan the Flames of Burnout," *Globe and Mail* (June 8, 2011), http://www.theglobeandmail.com.

4. Linda Anderson, "A Little Something for the Weekend," *Financial Times* (June 3, 2011), http://www.ft.com.

5. Carlton P. McNamara, "Making Human Capital Productive," *Business and Economic Review* 46, no. 1 (October–December 1999): 10–13; Meagan Stovel and Nick Bontis, "Voluntary Turnover: Knowledge Management—Friend or Foe?" *Journal of Intellectual Capital* 3, no. 3 (2002): 303–22.

6. Martin Eppler and Oliver Sukowski, "Managing Team Knowledge: Core Processes, Tools and Enabling Factors," *European Management Journal* 18, no. 3 (June 2000): 334–41; Andrea Foote, "One in a Million: Ocean Spray Henderson Has Parlayed Hard Work and Dedication into a Remarkable Operations Milestone," *Beverage World* 122, no. 8 (August 15, 2003): 22–29; Rick

Frattali, "The Company That Teaches Together Performs Together," *T+D* 61, no. 7 (July 2007).

7. Jeffrey Kling, "High Performance Work Systems and Firm Performance," *Monthly Labor Review*, May 1995, 29–36; Chad Kaydo, "Top of the Charts: FedEx," *Sales and Marketing Management* 150, no. 7 (July 1998): 46, 48; Michael Trachtman, "Roving Internet Appliances," *Web Techniques* 6, no. 10 (October 2001): 55–57; Richard Shulman, "Just Say the Word," *Supermarket Business* 56, no. 6 (June 15, 2001): 19–20; "Customer Service Excellence: Continuously Delighting Your Customers," *PR Newswire* (February 24, 2005).

8. For more information about designing teams around critical work processes, see Mark Chen, "Applying the High Performance Work Team to EPC," *AACE International Transactions* (2002): PM61–PM67; Valerie Sessa, "Supporting Work Team Effectiveness: Best Management Practices for Fostering High Performance," *Personnel Psychology* 53, no. 2 (Summer 2000): 457–60.

9. See Lawler, Mohrman, and Ledford, *Creating High Performance Organizations*; Eileen Appelbaum, Thomas Bailey, Peter Berg, and Narne Kalleberg, *Manufacturing Advantage: Why High-Performance Work Systems Pay Off* (Ithaca, NY: Cornell University Press, 2000); Gil Preuss and Brenda Lautsch, "The Effect of Formal versus Informal Job Security

on Employee Involvement Programs," *Relations Industrielles* 57, no. 3 (Summer 2002): 517–39; Wendy S. Becker, "Manufacturing Advantage: Why High-Performance Work Systems Pay Off," *Personnel Psychology* 56, no. 2 (Summer 2003): 549–53; "Nike Factories to Get Help from MIT's Sloan School," *Information Week* (April 13, 2005).

10. Laurie J. Bassi and Mark E. Van Buren, "Sustaining High Performance in Bad Times," *Training & Development* 51, no. 6 (June 1997): 32–42; Michael J. Stevens and Michael A. Campion, "Staffing Work Teams: Development and Validation of a Selection Test for Teamwork Settings," *Journal of Management* 25, no. 2 (1999): 207–28; Richard Camp, Eric Schulz, Mary Vielhaber, and Fraya Wagner-Marsh, "Human Resource Professionals' Perceptions of Team Interviews," *Camp Journal of Managerial Psychology* 19, no. 5 (2004).

11. Carolee Coleter, "To Build a Productive Team, Interview Effectively," *Natural Foods Merchandiser* 25, no. 12 (December 2004); Kris Dunn, "Rules of Engagement," *Workforce Management Online* (July 2008).

12. Mark E. Van Buren and Jon M. Werner, "High Performance Work Systems," *B&E Review* (October–December 1996): 15–23; "Schindler Elevator Announces Center for Service Excellence, Holland, OH Facility to Serve as National Support Center," *PR Newswire* (July 21, 2004); "Large Organizations That Focus on Excellence in Human Capital Management May Be More Likely to Outperform the Market, According to Taleo Customer Study," *PR Newswire* (March 30, 2005).

13. Douglas McCarthy, Kimberly Mueller, and Jennifer Wrenn, "Henry Ford Health System: A Framework for System Integration, Coordination, Collaboration, and Innovation," *Commonwealth Fund* (August 2009), http://www.commonwealthfund.org.

14. Rosemary Batt and Lisa Moynihan, "The Viability of Alternative Call Centre Production Models," *Human Resource Management Journal* 12, no. 4 (2002): 14. For more information on the potential application of "intracapital," see Gifford Pinchot, "Free Intraprise," *Executive Excellence* 18, no. 1 (January 2001): 10; Frank Giancola, "Skill-Based Pay—Issues for Consideration," *Benefits &*

Compensation Digest 44, no. 5 (May 2007): 1–15.

15. Rod Newing, "Targets are Linked to Pay by Early Adopters," *Financial Times* (June 7, 2011), http://www.ft.com.

16. David Paper, James Rodger, and Parag Pendharker, "A BPR Case Study at Honeywell," *Business Process Management Journal* 7, no. 2 (2001): 85–93. See also Robert McNabb and Keith Whitfield, "Job Evaluation and High Performance Work Practices: Compatible or Conflictual?" *Journal of Management Studies* 38, no. 2 (March 2001): 293–312; Leslie A. Weatherly, "Performance Management: Getting It Right from the Start," *HRMagazine* 49, no. 3 (March 2004): S1–S11.

17. Douglas McCarthy, Kimberly Mueller, and Jennifer Wrenn, "Henry Ford Health System: A Framework for System Integration, Coordination, Collaboration, and Innovation," *Commonwealth Fund* (August 2009), http://www.commonwealthfund.org.

18. Rod Newing, "Targets Are Linked to Pay by Early Adopters," *Financial Times* (June 7, 2011), http://www.ft.com.

19. Warren Bennis, "The Future Has No Shelf Life," *Executive Excellence* 17, no. 8 (August 2000): 5–6; Peggy Holman, "Culture Change," *Executive Excellence* 17, no. 7 (July 2000): 16; Clinton Longenecker, "Building High Performance Management Teams," *Industrial Management* 43, no. 6 (November/December 2001): 21–26; Wendy S. Becker, "Manufacturing Advantage: Why High-Performance Work Systems Pay Off," *Personnel Psychology* 56, no. 2 (Summer 2003): 549; Srivastava Pallavi and Jyotsna Bhatnagar, "Turnaround at Motorola India—Mobile Devices Business through the HR Lever," *The Journal for Decision Makers* 33, no. 1 (January–March 2008): 119–129.

20. Keith Newton, "The High Performance Workplace: HR-Based Management Innovations in Canada," *International Journal of Technology Management* 16, no. 1–3 (1998): 177–92; Georg Von Krogh, Kazuo Ichijo, and Ikujiro Nonaka, *Enabling Knowledge Creation: How to Unlock the Mystery of Tacit Knowledge and Release the Power of Innovation* (New York: Oxford University Press, 2000); Lawler, Mohrman, and Benson, *Organizing for High Performance.*

21. Patrick M. Wright and Scott A. Snell, "Toward a Unifying Framework for Exploring Fit and Flexibility in Strategic Human Resource Management," *Academy of Management Review* 23, no. 4 (October 1998): 756–72; Clair Brown and Michael Reich, "Micro-Macro Linkages in High-Performance Employment Systems," *Organization Studies* 18, no. 5 (1997): 765–81; S. A. Snell, M. Shadur, and P. M. Wright, "Human Resources Strategy: The Era of Our Ways," in M. A. Hitt, R. E. Freeman, and J. S. Harrison (eds.), *Handbook of Strategic Management* (London: Blackwell, 2002): 627–49.

22. Van Buren and Werner, "High Performance Work Systems," 15–23; Gilbert Probst, Steffen Raub, and Kai Romhardt, *Managing Knowledge—Building Blocks for Success* (New York: Wiley, 2000). For a similar example of vertical fit within European firms, see Sue Hutchinson, John Purcell, and Nick Kinnie, "Evolving High Commitment Management and the Experience of the RAC Call Center," *Human Resource Management Journal* 10, no. 1 (2000): 63–78.

23. Brian Becker, Mark Huselid, and Dave Ulrich, *The HR Scorecard: Linking People, Strategy, and Performance* (Cambridge, MA: Harvard Business School Press, 2001).

24. Arup Varma, Richard W. Beatty, Craig Eric Schneier, and David O. Ulrich, "High Performance Work Systems: Exciting Discovery or Passing Fad?" *Human Resource Planning* 22, no. 1 (1999): 26–37; Martha Gephart and Mark Van Buren, "Power of High Performance Work Systems," *Training & Development* 50, no. 10 (October 1996): 21–36; Foote, "One in a Million: Ocean Spray Henderson," 22–29.

25. Ethan R. Mollick, "People and Process, Suits and Innovators: The Role of Individuals in Firm Performance" *Social Science Research Network* (June 27, 2010), http://papers.ssrn.com.

26. Varma, Beatty, Schneier, and Ulrich, "High Performance Work Systems," 26–37; Gephart and Van Buren, "Power of High Performance Work Systems"; "Making Change Work—for Real," *HRFocus* 80, no. 1 (January 2003): S1.

27. Wenchuan Liu,; James P. Guthrie, Patrick C. Flood, Sarah Maccurtain, "**Unions and the Adoption of High Performance Work**

Systems: Does Employment Security Play a Role?" *Industrial & Labor Relations Review*, 63, no. 1 (October 2009): 109.

28. Louise Clarke and Larry Haiven, "Workplace Change and Continuous Bargaining," *Relations Industrielles* 54, no. 1 (Winter 1999): 168–91; Ruth Wright, "Forging Sustainable Alliances in a New Economy," *Canadian Business Review* (Summer 1995): 20–24; Sukanya Sengupta, "The Impact of Employee-Share-Ownership Schemes on Performance in Unionised and non-Unionised Workplaces," *Industrial Relations Journal* 39, no. 3 (May 2008): 170–190.

29. Clarke and Haiven, "Workplace Change," 168–91; Wright, "Forging Sustainable Alliances," 20–24; Joel Cuthcer-Gershenfeld, Thomas Kochan, and John Calhoun Wells, "In Whose Interest? A First Look at National Survey Data on Interest-Based Bargaining in Labor Relations," *Industrial Relations* 40, no. 1 (January 2001): 1–21; Michael White "Cooperative Unionism and Employee Welfare," *Industrial Relations Journal* 36, no. 5 (September 2005): 348–366.

30. Wright, "Forging Sustainable Alliances," 20–24; Hannele Rubin, "How CEOs Get Results," *Chief Executive* (February 2001): 8.

31. Wright, "Forging Sustainable Alliances," 20–24.

32. Gephart and Van Buren, "Power of High Performance Work Systems"; Michael Beer, "How to Develop an Organization Capable of Sustained High Performance: Embrace the Drive for Results-Capability Development Paradox," *Organizational Dynamics* 29, no. 4 (Spring 2001): 233–47.

33. Judith A. Neal, Cheryl L. Tromley, Ernie Lopez, and Jeanne Russell. "From Incremental Change to Retrofit," *The Academy of Management Executive* 9, no. 1 (February 1995): 42–54.

34. Wenchuan Liu, James P. Guthrie, Patrick C. Flood, Sarah Maccurtain, and Claire Armstrong, "Big Hat, No Cattle? The Relationship between the Use of High-Performance Work Systems and Managerial Perceptions of HR Departments,".International Journal of Human Resource Management, 22, no. 8 (April 2011): 1672.

35. Randa A. Wilbur, "Making Changes the Right Way," *Workforce*, Supplement (March 1999): 12–13; Gephart and Van Buren, "Power of High Performance Work Systems"; Irena St. John-Brooks, "CEOs SeeHR as Helping to Lead Organizational Efforts: USA," *Benefits & Compensation International* 32, no. 1 (July/August 2002): 73–74; "Human Resources Role Transformed at Deutsche Bank," *Human Resource Management International Digest* 10, no. 5 (2002): 12–14; Michael Svoboda and Silke Schroder, "Transforming Human Resources in the New Economy: Developing the Next Generation of Global HR Managers at Deutsche Bank AG," *Human Resource Management* 40, no. 3 (Fall 2001): 261–73; "HR Advice: Manage Transition—Not Just Change," *HR Briefing* (November 15, 2002): 1–2; "HR Must Seize Major Role over Change Management," *Personnel Today* (May 20, 2003): 8.

36. "Facebook Employees Most Stressed," Marketing-interactive.com (June 13, 2011), http://marketing-interactive.com.

37. "How to Take the 'Non' out of Your Non-Performers,'" *Human Resource Department Management Report* (February 2005): 1–5; Paul Lukas and Maggie Overfelt, "3M, a Mining Company Built on a Mistake, Stuck It Out Until a Young Man Came Along with Ideas about How to Tape those Blunders Together As Innovations—Leading to Decades of Growth," *Fortune* (April 1, 2003); http://money.cnn.com/smallbusiness.

38. Jeffrey Pfeffer, "When It Comes to 'Best Practices'—Why Do Smart Organizations Occasionally Do Dumb Things?" reprinted from *Organizational Dynamics*, Summer 1996 with permission from Elsevier; Cordelia Brabbs, "Rover's White Knight," *Marketing*, May 18, 2000, 28; Georg Auer, "Burela to Insti ll Quality Culture at Land Rover," *Automotive News* 75, no. 5902 (November 6, 2000): 32x–32z; Ronald W. Pant, "Land Rover History Lesson," *Truck Trend* 8, no. 3 (May–June 2005): 12; Bradford Wernle, "Solihull Must Do 'a Halewood' to Survive; Jaguar Plant Is the Example Land Rover Factory Must Follow," *Automotive News Europe* 9, no. 19 (September 20, 2004): 39.

39. John Purcell, "Best Practice and Best Fit: Chimera or Cul-de-Sac?" *Human Resource Management Journal* 9, no. 3 (1999): 26–41; Snell, Shadur, and Wright, "Human Resources Strategy: The Era of Our Ways," 627–649; Patrick M. Wright, Benjamin Dunford, and Scott A. Snell, "Human Resources and the Resource-Based View of the Firm," *Journal of Management* 27, no. 6 (2001): 701–21.

Microsoft's MACH Program Designed to Help Millennial Grads Make a Difference—Fast

Case 1

In 2005, Microsoft executives were faced with the challenge of finding ways to accelerate the careers of new hires. Like many companies, Microsoft found that its fast-track program was not especially helpful when it came to onboarding millennial employees. As Leigh Cresswell, a millennial corporate sales account manager for Microsoft, put it, too often millennials aren't given challenging work when they are first hired, which can be frustrating for them and lead to turnover. That is what happened to Cresswell at her previous employer, a multinational maker of office equipment. Their onboarding program was "just training; they didn't understand what we wanted, which was to have an impact and a voice straight away."

Microsoft did not want to make the same mistake. To deal with this issue, attract top graduates, and begin utilizing their skills quickly, the company launched the "Microsoft Academy for College Hires" or MACH for short. The two-year program has been designed to provide top new university graduates hired into the company's sales, marketing, and services divisions with onboarding courses, hands-on training, coaching, and networking opportunities. The main objective of MACH is not only to onboard new graduates so they can start adding value to their teams quickly, but to help them more efficiently navigate the corporate culture and politics. Approximately 2,000 new grads have gone through MACH since its inception. One of those individuals, Francesco Esposito, noted that because new grads have small or nonexistent professional networks and are typically entering a large corporation for the first time, they can have a hard time launching their careers.

Graduates of the MACH noted that the program not only helped them network with senior employees, it helped them connect with other Microsoft employees around the world. MACH has expanded to include participants in 50 countries who attend global and regional conferences with each other. This has given participants a worldwide group of peers who can provide them with support as they transition from school to the working environment. The global aspect also had the added benefit of exposing them to vastly different parts of the company and the opportunities offered there.

According to Maryann Baumgarten, Microsoft's curriculum manager of MACH, they have learned that the program needs to follow several key steps to have maximum impact. In the first year, MACH students focus on moving from the academic world to Microsoft's corporate environment. "It's a critical first step in employee retention as we help them to understand our culture, strategy, and customers," Baumgarten explains. In the second year, the participants go through career coaching and peer reviews to help them determine which career paths in the company will best suit their needs. Once a path is determined, they can choose mentors whom they can job shadow to learn more about the job's duties and responsibilities.

To facilitate the job-shadowing process, senior employees fill out an online form to make themselves available for the MACH program, but they can opt out as needed for specific time periods. The form identifies the mentor's top three skill sets, languages, and geographical location. This makes it easier for a junior employee to find a suitable match. The form also allows junior employees to search for available mentors and request career-shadowing time. To help senior employees become good mentors who can help develop and retain young workers, Microsoft offers them classes on generational milestones and characteristics as well as scenario training.

At this point in time, Microsoft is trying to decide if MACH is effective—is it worth the time and expense? Is it speeding up the contributions of millennials and improving their job satisfaction at Microsoft? The evidence is starting to show. Joseph Ibarra, a MACH 2008 grad, is a supporter of the program. "I've seen alumni at the MACH events, people who have accelerated quickly throughout the company and won some of Microsoft's most prestigious awards. It's really inspirational to see people come to the company and have a huge influence. It shows it can be done, even at a company with so many people."

Questions

1. How does orientation differ from onboarding?
2. Why do you think Microsoft implemented the MACH program? Can you see any drawbacks of doing so?
3. How might the program improve Microsoft's employer brand and help it attract talent?

Sources: Jennifer J. Salopek, "Onboarding Program Indoctrinates New Workers at MACH Speed," *Workforce Management* (June 2011) http://www.workforce.com; Randy Woods, "Grooming New Hires with Microsoft's MACH program," *NWjobs* (March 13, 2010), http://blog.nwjobs.com; "Case Study: A Customized Office and SharePoint Solution for Microsoft's Internal Career Shadowing Program," *3sharp.com*, accessed July 7, 2011 at http://www.3sharp.com.

BNSF Railway: Training New Hires for Safety

In 2011, BNSF rolled out a plan to hire more than 4,000 new employees—one of the most ambitious hiring plans ever for the company. Of the new hires, the majority of them (about 2,400) are being hired into the company's Transportation Group as conductors. The hiring is essential to fill vacancies due to retirements and to respond to the increasing business volumes BNSF is shipping. While these new people will help BNSF continue providing the level of service that meets customer expectations, they must also be equipped with the knowledge, tools, focus, and skills to work safely. According to a Training Services department spokesperson, "Safety permeates all of our training programs, and with the influx of new employees, we want to be sure the concepts are clear and effective."

Multiple Training Methods

As new hires come on board, BNSF provides training through multiple methods, including on-the-job training in the field with input from experienced employee mentors and safety assistants or safety coordinators. Formal training is provided for many positions at the company's Technical Training Center (TTC) in Overland Park, Kansas, as well as in the field. New hires at BNSF have an interim period before they officially become conductors. During this period, candidates must successfully respond to an interview panel, pass safety and rules exams, and complete either a 13- or 15-week intensive training program (depending on the location) that includes classroom and on-the-job training. The program culminates in a final exam which, when passed, qualifies students as conductors.

United Transportation Union (UTU) training coordinators help with the first week of training and pair students with experienced conductors who mentor students during the on-the-job training segment. One of UTU's training coordinators explains that he sets the tone on his territory by focusing most of his instruction on safe work practices: "I particularly focus on the Deadly Decisions—and consequences of at-risk behaviors." Once the new hires are paired, the experienced conductors play a significant role in conductor training, teaching 9 to 10 weeks of the 13- to 15-week program.

Cross-Training the Trainers

Because so many new employees are joining BNSF as conductors, 42 Transportation trainers deliver training at 71 locations across BNSF's system. To meet the increased volume of training needed for Transportation, BNSF implemented cross-training for all Transportation trainers. The trainers became qualified to train locomotive engineers and conductors, as well as to provide training on simulators and rules and remote train-control operations. In other words, the Transportation trainers are now cross-functional, which has effectively increased training capacity while also expanding individual trainers' areas of specialty. The cross-functional approach allows BNSF to efficiently meet the needs of the company, while still maintaining the integrity of the core program with safety at the center.

Additionally, the Transportation team places significant energy into helping transition new conductors. "Involvement begins during the initial interview sessions when a supervisor communicates our safety vision along with safety expectations," says one of BNSF's managers. The team also provides an overview of local terrain and environmental extremes that a potential employee is likely to encounter. Montana is a good example, where hiring is especially active. Trainers help employees understand the challenges of operating through the mountains and in winter conditions.

Supervisors interact with trainees throughout the program, both in group settings and one-on-one. To further integrate a new conductor, the division's UTU training coordinators established a day of enhanced safety training specific to location, with plans to expand that training to a broader overview. Graduates of BNSF's conductor training say the training program is vital, and that they appreciate the high priority placed on safety.

Managing Safety through Best Practices

The BNSF management team members who are responsible for the locomotive engineer training program have identified numerous best practices for the trainers to incorporate into their training. BNSF feels these best practices help the organization meet its hiring goals while maintaining its focus on a safe, efficient, and accident-free workplace.

Questions

1. What methods does BNSF use as part of its comprehensive training system for new hires?
2. Explain the company's team approach to training. How does cross-training the company's trainers benefit BNSF?
3. What is the purpose of explaining during interviews BNSF's safety practices and on-the-job working challenges?

Source: Excerpted/adapted from "Trainers Carry Forward BNSF's Safety Vision to New Hires," *Railway* (Spring 2011): 16–17. [Note: Permission is needed for this article. Contact: Susan Green, BNSF, phone: 817-867-6344, e-mail: susan.green@bnsf.com.]

Job Analysis and Hiring Decisions at Ovania Chemical

Company Background

Ovania Chemical Corporation is a specialty chemicals producer of polyethylene terephthalate (PET) thermoplastic resins primarily used to make containers for soft drinks and bottled water, as well as packaging for food and pharmaceutical products. Though smaller than other chemical producers that produce globally, Ovania has competed successfully in the specialty chemical business. Its main plant is located in Steubenville, Ohio, positioned along the Ohio River midway between Pittsburgh, Pennsylvania, and Wheeling, West Virginia. In recent years, advances in technology have altered the nature of chemical production, and like other firms in the industry, Ovania Chemical is taking steps to modernize its facilities. Not surprisingly, these technological changes have been accompanied by redesign in employee jobs. In fact, over the last three years, there have been drastic changes in both the number and the kinds of jobs being performed by employees. The latest change at the Steubenville plant involves the job transformation of the system analyzer position.

The System Analyzer

Because chemical production involves highly integrated process technologies, someone is needed who can monitor all of the individual components simultaneously. The system analyzer is primarily responsible for this monitoring function. It is one of the most prestigious nonmanagerial jobs in the entire plant, and its importance is likely to grow.

Formerly, the position was classified as that of a semiskilled maintenance technician, but as the plant has become more automated, the requirements for the system analyzer job have become much more extensive. Knowledge of pneumatics, hydraulics, information technology, programming, and electrical wiring are all increasingly critical aspects of this job. The three men who currently hold the position admit that they will be incapable of performing adequately in the future. It is estimated that within two years, the tasks, duties, and responsibilities of the system analyzer will have changed by more than 70 percent. For these reasons, the decision was made to recruit and select three new people for the rapidly transforming position.

Job Analysis and New Position Analysis

Ovania's Steubenville plant manager, Jack Sarabe; the HR manager, Emily Claire; and two senior engineers, Dave Packley and Mark Young, formed a selection committee. With the help of two consultants, they first conducted a job analysis for the new position of system analyzer. Although they had to project into the future regarding the specific nature of the job, they collectively felt they had created an accurate depiction of the requirements for someone who would occupy the position. Figure 3.1 shows a list of the major performance dimensions of the job and a subsample of specific tasks characteristic of each dimension.

From this list of tasks, the selection committee then delineated a set of personal qualities required for anyone who would hold the system analyzer position. These

FIGURE
3.1
Performance Dimensions (Duties and Tasks).

MAINTAINING SPARES AND SUPPLIES

1. Anticipates future need for parts and supplies and orders them.
2. Stocks parts and supplies in an orderly fashion.
3. Maintains and calibrates test equipment.

TROUBLESHOOTING

4. Applies calibration standards to verify operation by subjecting the system to known standards.
5. Decides whether the problem is in the sensor, in the processor, in the process stream, and/or in the sample system.
6. Uses troubleshooting guides in system manuals to determine the problem area.
7. Uses test equipment to diagnose the problem.
8. Makes a general visual inspection of the analyzer system as a first troubleshooting step.
9. Replaces components such as printed circuit boards and sensors to see if the problem can be alleviated.

HANDLING REVISIONS AND NEW INSTALLATIONS

10. Makes minor piping changes such as size, routing, and additional filers.
11. Makes minor electrical changes such as installing switches and wires and making terminal changes.
12. Uses common pipefitting tools.
13. Uses common electrical tools.
14. Reads installation drawings.

RECORD-KEEPING

15. Maintains system files showing historical record of work on each system.
16. Maintains loop files that show the application of the system.
17. Updates piping and instrument drawings if any changes are made.
18. Maintains Environmental Protection Agency records and logbooks.
19. Disassembles analyzers to perform repairs onsite or back in the shop.
20. Replaces damaged parts such as filters, electronic components, light source, lenses, sensors, and values.
21. Uses diagnostic equipment such as oscilloscopes, ohmmeters, and decade boxes.
22. Tests and calibrates repaired equipment to ensure that it works properly.
23. Reads and follows written procedures from manuals.

ROUTINE MAINTENANCE

24. Observes indicators on systems to ensure that there is proper operation.
25. Adds reagents to systems.
26. Decides whether the lab results or the system is correct regarding results (i.e., resolves discrepancies between lab and analyzer results).
27. Performs calibrations.

> **FIGURE 3.2** Abilities and Tasks
>
> Numbers represent tasks cited in Figure 3.1. Asterisks indicate abilities considered critical by the committee.
>
> | SKILLS | TASK NUMBERS |
> |---|---|
> | *Finger dexterity | 3, 4, 7, 9, 10, 11, 12, 13, 19, 20, 21, 22, 25, 27 |
> | *Mechanical comprehension | 3, 5, 6, 8, 9, 10, 12, 13, 7, 14, 19, 20, 22, 23, 24, 27, 11, 17 |
> | *Numerical ability | 11, 3, 4, 24, 10, 21, 12, 13, 14, 27 |
> | *Spatial ability | 2, 4, 5, 9, 10, 11, 14, 19, 20 |
> | *Visual pursuit | 3, 4, 5, 6, 7, 8, 9, 10, 11, 14, 16, 17, 19, 20, 21, 22, 27 |
> | *Detection | 2, 3, 5, 6, 8, 9, 10, 14, 19, 20, 23, 7 |
> | Oral comprehension | 1, 2, 5, 6, 26, 7, 8, 9, 19, 21, 25 |
> | Written comprehension | 1, 15, 16, 17, 18 |
> | Deductive reasoning | 1, 5, 3, 6, 7, 8, 9, 10, 11, 19, 21, 20, 22, 2, 26, 27 |
> | Inductive reasoning | 1, 3, 5, 6, 7, 8, 9, 10, 11, 19, 21, 20, 22, 2, 26, 27 |
> | Reading comprehension | 3, 6, 14, 7, 22, 23, 21, 9, 27 |
> | Reading scales and tables | 3, 4, 7, 8, 9, 21, 23, 24, 27, 2, 6, 14 |
>
> © Cengage Learning 2013

qualities included the twelve abilities shown in Figure 3.2. The numbers beside each ability indicate the tasks (see Figure 3.1) to which it is related. The abilities marked with an asterisk (*) were considered by the committee to be "critical." Any applicant not scoring well on each of the critical dimensions would be considered unqualified for the job.

Anticipated Selection Process

The committee hoped to gain "new blood" for the redesigned system analyzer job and therefore wanted to recruit externally for the best available talent they could find. However, as a matter of policy, management was also deeply committed to the idea of promoting from within. After deliberation, the committee decided to recruit both internally and externally for the new position. It was also decided to especially encourage current system analyzers to "reapply" for the job.

Because there was a two-year lead time before the newly transformed position would be put in place, the committee was very careful not to include in the selection battery any skills or knowledge that could reasonably be trained within that two-year period. Only aptitude or ability factors were incorporated into the selection process, rather than achievement tests.

The three present system analyzers were white males. However, since Ovania Chemical had a rather unenviable history of employment discrimination charges, the decision was made to have applicants undergo a battery of tests but not look at their previous experience. This strategy was thought to encourage minorities and women to apply for the new position regardless of their prior experience in the field, which in the case of these two groups of applicants might be somewhat sparse.

It should be noted, however, that there was some concern about prejudice if a woman or minority member were to get the job. Several people at the company had commented that a woman would not get down into the treatment tanks to check gauge readings. All of these factors, taken together, made for a very sensitive selection process. Ovania's managers, however, were dedicated to making the procedures and decisions fair and objective.

Fifty-six employees applied for the new position of system analyzer. Twenty-one were female; fifteen were African American. Only two of the three current system analyzers reapplied for the new position. The company decided that an overall total score of 800 on the twelve tests would be the cutoff score in order for an applicant to be seriously considered for the system analyzer position. This criterion resulted in the primary pool of twenty candidates shown in Figure 3.3 It should be noted

FIGURE 3.3 Primary Pool of Candidates

NAME	RACE	SEX	EXTERNAL/ INTERNAL	FINGER DEXTERITY	MECHANICAL COMPREHENSION	NUMERICAL ABILITY	SPATIAL ABILITY	VISUAL PURSUIT	DETECTION	ORAL COMPREHENSION	WRITTEN COMPREHENSION	DEDUCTIVE REASONING	INDUCTIVE REASONING	READING COMPREHENSION	READING SCALES AND TABLES		
Baldwin, T.	W	M	I	83	76	78	76	69	71	90	70	74	72	88	92	=	941
Bittner, D.	W	M	E	92	62	88	89	96	85	90	94	93	89	97	87	=	1062
Bohlander, G.	W	M	E	67	78	74	70	76	62	80	69	71	76	78	82	=	883
Buffett, J.	B	M	E	87	97	89	61	94	93	75	90	85	96	85	80	=	1032
Denny, A.	B	F	I	92	88	72	72	78	79	69	76	81	83	81	78	=	949
Egan, M.	W	F	E	93	80	76	98	76	88	93	92	93	78	81	92	=	884
Granger, D.	W	F	I	82	82	79	75	77	73	72	80	81	77	70	80	=	856
Haney, H.	W	M	E	82	76	76	71	69	80	62	76	75	74	78	67	=	810
Kight, G.	W	F	E	65	75	72	67	80	74	62	47	66	67	60	80	=	815
Kovach, S.	W	M	E	82	87	85	85	83	88	81	80	80	83	84	80	=	998
Laukitis, T.	B	F	E	87	97	63	89	93	90	91	85	86	96	88	89	=	1054
Lesko, B.J.	B	F	I	83	84	89	91	80	82	86	88	85	84	90	89	=	1031
Rom, D.	B	M	I	80	60	67	66	67	62	74	80	67	72	75	66	=	835
Sara, E.	W	F	I	89	91	77	93	90	91	88	78	98	80	80	76	=	1021
Sauder, C.	W	F	E	76	72	78	81	80	72	73	77	75	79	82	82	=	927
Sherman, A.	W	F	I	91	82	78	93	92	94	89	77	95	77	81	92	=	1041
Snell, J.	W	M	E	80	85	84	81	81	80	89	88	84	86	81	82	=	1001
Timothy, S.	W	F	E	82	78	76	71	69	80	62	76	76	70	71	67	=	878
Whitney, J.	W	M	I	67	71	70	76	76	62	81	69	71	76	78	82	=	815
Wright, P.	W	M	I	80	60	57	56	57	62	74	80	69	72	75	65	=	887

that although each of the aptitude tests has been published, standardized (100 points possible for each test), and validated for other jobs, the same is not true of the system analyzer job because it's a new position. Therefore, whether the tests are predictive depends upon content validity judgments made by the managers of the company. The final cutoff scores and methods for combining the multiple predictors are problematic for the selection committee as well.

Questions

1. How would you go about conducting a job analysis for a job that does not yet exist?
2. What reasons did the selection committee have for selecting only those factors that could not be acquired in a two-year training program?
3. Should the concern for women getting down into the dirty treatment tanks have been a selection issue?
4. Would this test battery and selection procedure be defensible in court?

Case 4) Ill-Fated Love at Centrex Electronics

Nancy Miller-Canton never imagined she would lose her job at Centrex Electronics Corporation (CEC), and certainly not under such unpleasant circumstances. Unfortunately, after eleven years of employment, the last two as a senior product engineer in the firm's military/space division in Atlanta, she made a mistake; she fell in love.

CEC is highly regarded as a quality employer in the electronics industry. It is a multinational corporation with engineering services and production facilities in Spain, Canada, Hong Kong, Mexico, and Germany. With more than 12,000 employees in the United States, the firm has been named as one of the country's top 100 organizations to work for by several studies. The firm is known as a top-paying corporation with proactive employee relations policies.

Kathryn Garner, the vice president of human resources for CEC, is credited with establishing many positive employee rights policies, including those covering electronic communications, drug testing, search and surveillance, access to employee files, and off-duty conduct. The corporation permits marriage between employees except in cases where one employee is in a direct reporting relationship with the other.

Miller-Canton joined Centrex Electronics shortly after graduating from Georgia State University in 2006. At that time she was married to Tom Canton, her college sweetheart. In 2009, Canton died suddenly. As a single parent, his widow then became dependent upon her job for the majority of her family's support.

Miller-Canton enjoyed rapid promotions through various engineering positions until reaching her present job as senior product engineer. In 2010, the year before her dismissal, she had been awarded the firm's Engineering Distinction Award for her research and development work in metallography. But in January 2011, one week after receiving a significant raise, she was called into the firm's human resources department. The question from the military/space division manager was clear and direct: "Are you dating Mike Domzalski?" Domzalski was a former CEC senior engineer who had changed employment in 2009 to work for International Technologies, a direct competitor of CEC. There was no denying the romance. The two had dated while Domzalski was with CEC, and he still remained friends with other Centrex Electronics Engineers. It was widely known among Miller-Canton's friends that she was "extremely fond" of Domzalski.

Now, chastised for her involvement, Miller-Canton was ordered to forget about Domzalski or be demoted. After the meeting she told a friend, "I was so socialized in CEC culture and so devoted to my job that I thought seriously about breaking up with Mike." As she later testified in court, however, she never got the chance because she was dismissed the day after the meeting with her manager.

At the root of Miller-Canton's dismissal was a corporate policy regarding the leakage of confidential product information. The policy seeks to avoid situations where an employee of CEC might be compromised into providing sensitive or confidential information to an employee of a competing organization. Miller-Canton's work in research and development made her subject to the following CEC policy:

Employees performing jobs where they have access to sensitive or confidential information which could benefit competitors are prohibited from being married to or from having a romantic relationship with individuals employed by competing organizations.

Since Mike Domzalski's work at International Technologies was similar to Miller-Canton's at CEC, the corporation felt their "romantic relationship" made her discharge appropriate. Feeling aggrieved, Miller-Canton engaged the services of an attorney specializing in employee rights claims. In preparing her wrongful discharge suit, the attorney told her that given the nature of her case and the continuous erosion of the employment-at-will doctrine, he believed she could win the lawsuit. Furthermore, while gathering background information for the trial, the attorney discovered something that her former division manager did not know. Shortly before her discharge, no less an authority than former CEC chairman Joseph M. Torell had declared that "CEC employees are responsible for their own off-the-job behavior. We are concerned with an employee's off-the-job conduct only when it reduces the employee's ability to perform normal job assignments."

A jury trial in state court upheld the wrongful discharge suit and awarded Miller-Canton $425,000 in back pay and punitive damages. Like other trials, however, this one took its toll on the parties involved. "I couldn't function for four or five months after the trial, I was so emotionally upset and drained," Miller-Canton said. She is now employed as an engineer for a computer company; she and Domzalski are no longer dating. "It was a bad experience all around," she says. "There was a real sense of belonging and a feeling of personal job worth at CEC. If I had my way, I'd take my old job back today."

Questions

1. What exceptions to the employment-at-will doctrine would the attorney have used to file the lawsuit?
2. Comment on the confidential information policy adopted by Centrex Electronics. Do you agree with the way it is used? Explain.
3. Is dating a "romantic relationship"? Explain.

Source: This case is adapted from an actual situation known to the authors. All names are fictitious.

Case 5 — Pepper Construction Group: Change in Safety Leads to Decline in Injuries and Illnesses

In 2004, Dave Pepper, the third-generation owner of Pepper Construction, met with his insurance group to review the group's annual summary of safety performance. To his surprise, Pepper Construction's experience modification rate (EMR) placed them in the bottom third of the group. The EMR compares the frequency and severity of workers' compensation claims between companies of similar size operating in the same type of business and reflects the degree to which a particular company's experience is better or worse than the industry as a whole. At the time, Pepper Construction Group's EMR was 0.71, nearly 30 percent better than the national average for general contractors, but two-thirds of the insurance group members were even better. Safety performance was good, but not good enough.

The Solution

Pepper Construction had begun to develop a long-range strategic planning initiative. The initial goals set by the company's leaders were related to business growth—profit, efficiency, information technology, and production—but not one mentioned safety. Pepper reminded his team members that the company's most valuable asset has always been its people, and he encouraged them to shift their focus. It was as if a light went on within his management group. They fully embraced the commitment to safety and saw that it would protect the company's greatest asset—their people. The strategic plan shifted, and safety became the first priority. Their initial goals remained, but safety was now the foundation on which profit, growth, and productivity would be built.

Senior management, along with a newly formed safety committee, developed the following TEAM safety mission statement to communicate the company's commitment to an accident free workplace:

- **T**raining for all employees

- **E**mpowerment where everyone has the authority to say "no" to unsafe conditions

- **A**ction—the commitment to taking the steps necessary to protect employees and continuously strive to improve the safety program

- **M**otivation—making sure the safety of the company's people is the top priority, above all else

The challenge was to communicate the safety mission through the entire company, from the hourly craftsmen through the executive level. Previous annual safety seminars included every craftsman in the company, often more than 600 people in the same lecture hall listening to lectures and generic training topics. To emphasize their commitment to safety, Pepper and Ken Egidi, the president of Pepper Construction Company, held much smaller meetings limited to no more than 40 people. They took the time to shake every employee's hand and made it very clear that everyone had the right, and responsibility, to work safely.

Pepper and his team worked hard to ensure all employees knew the company was serious about safety. They put in place additional resources to support this goal. For example, the company hired a new corporate safety director, increased training opportunities, and formed trades safety committees.

Pepper Construction now offers safety training in Spanish, including an OSHA-developed training program that consists of a 10-hour course and first-aid training. The company also provides comprehensive safety orientations on every job site. In addition, the company provides safety seminars for the trades. These seminars include up to four hours of training specific to the skills needed by the craftspeople, such as powered lift training, fall protection, and emergency response. Almost 90 percent of the company's current craftspeople have completed OSHA's 30-hour construction safety course.

Pepper Construction has also worked through OSHA's cooperative programs to improve its safety performance. The company is a gold level participant in OSHA Region V's Strategic Partnership with the Builders Association. OSHA and the Builders Association signed their second Strategic Partnership on December 18, 2009. The goals of this strategic partnership include reducing injuries, illnesses, and fatalities in construction by addressing key industry hazards, promoting recognition for construction safety excellence, and sharing best practices. Gold level participants must meet a number of requirements, including the implementation of a comprehensive safety and health management program and maintaining an injury/illness rate at least 10 percent lower than the Bureau of Labor Statistics (BLS) rate for their industries. Pepper Construction is also a participant in the OSHA Challenge Program, a three-stage process to implement an effective system to prevent fatalities, injuries, and illnesses. An electronic tool that breaks down the actions, documentation, and results desired is provided by OSHA to participating companies as well . Pepper Construction is also applying for recognition under OSHA's Voluntary Protection Programs (see Chapter 12).

The Impact

Since the strategic planning initiative and subsequent restructuring of the safety and health program, Pepper Construction Company has seen a dramatic decrease in OSHA recordable injury and illness rates.

	TCIR*	BLS National Average (TCIR)	DART**	BLS National Average (DART)
2004	5.64	6.1	1.40	3.0
2006	4.64	5.4	1.36	2.7
2008	2.96	4.5	0.7	2.1
2009	2.01	not available	0.5	not available

*TCIR is the Total Case Incident Rate.
**DART is the Days Away, Restricted and/or Transferred Case Incidence Rate.

Based on available data through 2009, Pepper Construction Company is well below the national average for TCIR and DART incidence rate in the construction industry. In addition, Pepper Construction Group's EMR has continued to drop from 0.71 in 2004 to 0.64 in 2009.

When asked about the return on investment, Pepper has said the biggest benefit he has seen is the improved company culture: "Our workers are looking after each other, watching out for hazards and eliminating them—and really caring for their fellow employees." Pepper Construction is committed to building on this success and continuing to improve its safety performance. Management commitment, employee engagement and providing every employee the tools they need to work safely will continue to be the keys to Pepper Construction's workplace safety and health program.

Pepper's improved safety culture has also spread to its subcontractors. When Pepper Construction bids out jobs, it reviews each subcontractor's safety and health records. This includes EMR and OSHA 300A data, job safety performance, and the historical safety performance of individual foremen on Pepper projects. All subcontractors are prequalified, and no bids are awarded to subcontractors that do not meet the company's safety performance standards.

As a result of Pepper Construction's increased scrutiny of its subcontractors' safety records, it has removed contractors from its list of prequalified contractors because of poor safety performance. For example, several years ago an iron worker was observed standing on the rail of an aerial lift without proper fall protection. Because the steel erecting company officials did not consider this a serious safety problem, they were removed from the job site and did not work on another Pepper Construction site for four years. After this contractor initiated an intensive safety management program, their performance improved; they are currently applying for reinstatement to Pepper Construction's prequalified contractors list.

Questions

1. How does the Pepper Construction's "TEAM" mission help keep the company on track toward better safety.
2. Why should Pepper Construction be concerned about the safety of its subcontractors?

Source: Paul Flentge, "Change in Safety Culture at Pepper Construction Group Leads to Dramatic Decline in Injuries and Illnesses," *Success Stories and Case Studies* (Washington, D.C.: Occupational Safety and Health Administration), July 2010, http://www.osha.gov/.

Realigning HR Practices at Egan's Clothiers

Case 6

At the end of fiscal year 2011, revenues at Egan's Clothiers, Inc., had increased 12 percent over 2010 and had increased at a compounded rate of 14 percent over the past five years. That is the good news. The bad news is that costs have risen at an even more rapid rate, thereby shrinking the company's gross margins. As a consequence, Egan's profitability (measured as return on sales and return on net assets) has actually fallen by 6 percent over the past three years.

The drop in profitability at Egan's is particularly worrisome. In fact, according to Egan's chief financial officer, Richard Coyle, if something is not done immediately to control material and labor costs, as well as administrative expenses, the company may need to restructure its operations. In the short run, Coyle, company president Karen Egan, and vice president of HR Pam McCaskey have put an indefinite freeze on all hiring. Further, they are contemplating layoffs of nearly one-quarter of Egan's sales staff and are weighing the benefits of cutting back on HR-related expenses such as training. Compared to others in the industry, the firm's labor costs are very high.

Company Background

Gene Egan and Pat Pollock opened their first store in Baldwin, New York, in 1958. The company grew rapidly during the 1980s and now operates a chain of thirty-four medium-sized stores located throughout Connecticut, New York, Pennsylvania, and New Jersey. Since the beginning, Egan's customers have been primarily middle-class and upper middle-class families purchasing sportswear, dresswear, and fashion accessories. The company has established a longstanding tradition of quality and cus-tomer service. In addition to its thirty-four stores, the company also maintains two distribution centers and its administrative offices in Stamford, Connecticut. The total employment currently stands at approximately 2,400 people: 15 executives, 40 staff specialists, 40 store managers, 215 sales managers, 250 administrative per-sonnel, 1,600 salespeople, and 240 distribution workers. Except for the employees at the distribution centers, the company is not presently unionized. However, it is no secret that Egan's management has been trying very hard recently to keep cur-rent labor organizing activities to a minimum, viewing it as a threat to the company's success. Egan's HR department has been called upon to conduct a program audit of various personnel practices utilized at Egan's. The purpose of this audit is to assess the impact of Egan's HR policies and practices on employee outcomes (for example, performance, employee satisfaction, absenteeism, and turnover). The objective of the audit is to identify specific problem areas where policy adjustments may be necessary. The final report to the executive staff will include the HR department's evaluation of current problems and the changes it recommends.

Human Resources Management History

Over the past five years, Egan's has made several changes in order to implement the best HR practices possible. Partially, this has been to circumvent unionization efforts, but primarily it is indicative of Egan's longstanding belief that success in retailing depends on the competencies and efforts of its employees.

The commitment to HR is demonstrated by the fact that in 2011 the company spent $1.3 million on an intranet-based human resources information system (HRIS). The HRIS has successfully automated the company's employment records and connects each of the retail stores, distribution centers, and executive offices. Also, Egan's has maintained an ongoing training program for the past five years to help salespeople improve their retail selling skills (RSS) and customer service. The annual cost of this program has been roughly $750,000. To further ensure high ability levels in its workforce, the company sets selection standards substantially higher than its competitors. Whereas other retail companies typically hire inexperienced high school students, Egan's generally requires some retailing or sales experience before considering an applicant for employment. Although this policy increases Egan's overall labor costs, management has been confident that the added expense is well justified over the long run. However, recently even the strongest proponents of HR have been wondering if it might be a good idea to cut back on training, given the company's current financial picture.

By far the most problematic and volatile HR issues at Egan's have revolved around promotions and salary increases. Because the company promotes from within and distributes raises on a companywide basis, comparisons generally have to be made across employees in different jobs and departments. To combat arguments of subjectivity and bias pertaining to these decisions, Egan's links these rewards to objective measures of performance. Specifically, rather than utilizing subjective managerial evaluations of employee performance, ongoing accounts of sales results are maintained for each employee through use of the HRIS. On the basis of this information, each department manager assigns each employee to one of five categories:

Superior—top 10 percent

Very good—next 20 percent

Good—middle 40 percent

Fair—lower 20 percent

Poor—lowest 10 percent

Administrative decisions are then made across departments utilizing these standardized distributions. Additionally, to provide constant feedback to each employee about his or her relative performance, data are updated and posted daily. It is hoped that this feedback is motivating to employees. In this way, there are no surprises when the time comes for semiannual performance appraisal interviews. It is interesting to note that since these changes have been made in the performance appraisal system, there has not been one formal complaint registered regarding salary or promotion decisions. However, sales managers themselves have mentioned occasionally that they do not feel as comfortable now that they are required to assign employees to the "fair" and "poor" categories.

HR Outcomes

Despite the concerted efforts of Egan's management to create a first-rate system of human resources management, there are several troubling issues facing the company.

The HR practices are not having their desired effects. For example, there have been recent complaints that employees have not been as patient or courteous with customers as they should be. This was best summarized by Paul Kelly, a store manager in White Plains, New York, who noted, "My people are beating up the clientele in order to make a sale—the very opposite of what the RSS program trains them to do." This lapse in customer service is frustrating to management since the RSS training has proven effective in the past. Additionally, there seems to be a great deal of competition *within* departments that is hurting a team effort. Although intergroup rivalries *between* departments have always been viewed as normal and healthy, the lack of intragroup cohesiveness is seen as a problem.

Additionally, Egan's has been plagued with increases in lost and damaged merchandise. Management attributes this to the fact that storage rooms are disorganized and unkempt. This is in sharp contrast to the selling floors, which have remained fairly well ordered and uncluttered. Nevertheless, inventory costs have been increasing at an alarming rate.

Everyone notices that something is wrong. But the behavior patterns are perplexing. Absenteeism has decreased by 23 percent, but employee turnover has actually increased from 13 percent to over 29 percent, thereby increasing labor costs overall. Unfortunately, many of those who left the company (43 percent) were rated as very good to superior employees.

As executives in the company look at these trends, they are understandably concerned. The success of the company and its reputation for quality and service depend on solid investments in HR to ensure the best possible workforce. However, the expenses are eroding the company's profits, and worse, it now looks like these investments are not paying off.

Questions

1. What overall changes could you recommend to the executive team at Egan's about its HR practices?
2. What are the pros and cons of Egan's performance appraisal system? Do you think it identifies the best employees? Do you think it helps develop employees to perform the best they can?
3. Can increased sales be linked directly and/or indirectly to the appraisal system? How about some of the other performance effects? How would you change the system?
4. How do you account for the fact that absenteeism has decreased at Egan's while turnover has increased?

Case 7

A Performance Appraisal Snafu

Research has shown that the performance appraisal process, particularly the interaction between employees and managers, is a key determinant affecting employee motivation and productivity. Understandably, managers can view the appraisal of employee performance as a "catch-22" in which the slightest mistake can cause employee resentment, as this case illustrates.

Marcus Singh, a naturalized U.S. citizen from India, is a research economist in the Office of Research and Evaluation in the city of Newport, Oregon. He is forty years old and has worked for the city of Newport for the past ten years. During that time, Singh has been perceived by his supervisors as an above-average performer. However, due to the small size of the department and the close working relationship between employees and management, a formal evaluation of employees was considered unnecessary. About ten months ago, Singh was transferred from the department's Industrial Development unit to the newly formed Office of Research and Evaluation. Other employees were also transferred as part of an overall reorganization.

Out of concern for equal employment opportunity, plus the realization that employee performance should be evaluated formally and objectively, Victoria Popelmill, department director, issued a directive to all unit heads to formally evaluate the performance of their subordinates. Attached to her memorandum was a copy of a new performance appraisal form to be used in conducting the evaluations. Garth Fryer, head of the Office of Research and Evaluation, decided to allow his subordinates to have some input in the appraisal process. (In addition to Garth Fryer, the Office of Research and Evaluation comprised Marcus Singh, five other research economists—Jason Taft, Susan Mussman, Richard Gels, Marsha Fetzer, and Juan Ortiz—and one administrative assistant, Connie Millar.) Fryer told each of the researchers to complete both a self-appraisal and a peer appraisal. After reviewing these appraisals, Fryer completed the final and official appraisal of each researcher. Before sending the forms to Popelmill's office, Fryer met with each researcher individually to review and explain his ratings. Each researcher signed the appraisal and indicated agreement with the ratings.

About one week after submitting the appraisals to the director, Fryer received a memorandum from Popelmill stating that his evaluations were unacceptable. Fryer was not the only unit head to receive this memorandum; in fact, they all received the same note. On examination of the completed appraisal forms from the various departments, the director had noticed that not one employee was appraised in either the "fair" or "satisfactory" category. In fact, most employees were rated as "outstanding" in every category. Popelmill felt that the unit heads were too lenient and asked them to redo the evaluations in a more objective and critical manner. Furthermore, because the department's compensation budget for salary increases was largely based on a distribution of employee ratings, evaluating all employees as outstanding would result in raises that exceeded the company's budget limits.

Garth Fryer explained the director's request to his subordinates and asked them to redo their appraisals with the idea of being more objective this time. To Fryer's astonishment, the new appraisals were not much different from the first ones. Believing he had no choice in the matter, Fryer unilaterally formulated his own ratings and discussed them with each employee.

Marcus Singh was not pleased when he found out that his supervisor had rated him one level lower on each category. (Compare Figures 7.1 and 7.2.) Although he signed the second appraisal form, he indicated on the form that he did not agree with the evaluation. Jason Taft, another researcher in the Office of Research and Evaluation, continued to receive all "outstanding" ratings on his second evaluation.

FIGURE 7.1 Employee Appraisal Form

Employee Name: Marcus Singh   Date: October 4, 2011

Job Title: Economist/Researcher

Please indicate your evaluation of the employee in each category by placing a check mark (✓) in the appropriate block.

	Outstanding	Good	Satisfactory	Fair	Unsatisfactory
KNOWLEDGE OF JOB Assess overall knowledge of duties and responsibilities of current job.	✓	☐	☐	☐	☐
QUANTITY OF WORK Assess the volume of work under normal conditions.	☐	✓	☐	☐	☐
QUALITY OF WORK Assess the neatness, accuracy, and effectiveness of work.	☐	✓	☐	☐	☐
COOPERATION Assess ability and willingness to work with peers, superiors, and subordinates.	☐	✓	☐	☐	☐
INITIATIVE Assess willingness to seek greater responsibilities and knowledge. Self-starting.	☐	✓	☐	☐	☐
ATTENDANCE Assess reliability with respect to attendance habits.	✓	☐	☐	☐	☐
ATTITUDE Assess disposition and level of enthusiasm. Desire to excel.	✓	☐	☐	☐	☐
JUDGMENT Assess ability to make logical decisions.	☐	✓	☐	☐	☐

Comments on ratings: Valuable employee!

Supervisor's signature: Garth Fryer

Department: Office of Research and Evaluation   Date: October 4, 2011

Employee's signature: Marcus Singh

Does the employee agree with this evaluation? __X__ Yes _____ No

FIGURE 7.2 Employee Appraisal Form

Employee Name: Marcus Singh   Date: October 18, 2008

Job Title: Economist/Researcher

Please indicate your evaluation of the employee in each category by placing a check mark (✓) in the appropriate block.

	Outstanding	Good	Satisfactory	Fair	Unsatisfactory
KNOWLEDGE OF JOB Assess overall knowledge of duties and responsibilities of current job.	☐	☑	☐	☐	☐
QUANTITY OF WORK Assess the volume of work under normal conditions.	☐	☐	☑	☐	☐
QUALITY OF WORK Assess the neatness, accuracy, and effectiveness of work.	☐	☐	☑	☐	☐
COOPERATION Assess ability and willingness to work with peers, superiors, and subordinates.	☐	☐	☑	☐	☐
INITIATIVE Assess willingness to seek greater responsibilities and knowledge. Self-starting.	☐	☐	☑	☐	☐
ATTENDANCE Assess reliability with respect to attendance habits.	☐	☑	☐	☐	☐
ATTITUDE Assess disposition and level of enthusiasm. Desire to excel.	☐	☑	☐	☐	☐
JUDGMENT Assess ability to make logical decisions.	☐	☐	☑	☐	☐

Comments on ratings: Marcus needs to increase the quantity of his work to receive higher ratings. Also, he should take a greater initiative in his job.

Supervisor's signature: Garth Fryer

Department: Office of Research and Evaluation   Date: Oct. 18, 2011

Employee's signature: Marcus Singh

Does the employee agree with this evaluation? _____ Yes ___X___ No

Like Singh, Taft has a master's degree in economics, but he has been working for the city of Newport for less than two years and is only twenty-four years old. Taft had also worked closely with Garth Fryer before being transferred to his new assignment ten months ago. Recently, the mayor of the city had received a letter from the regional director of a major government agency praising Jason Taft's and Garth Fryer's outstanding research. Marcus Singh's working relationship with Garth Fryer and Jason Taft and with others in the department has been good. On some occasions, though, he has found himself in awkward disagreements with his coworkers in areas where he holds strong opinions.

After Singh and Taft had signed the appraisals, Garth Fryer forwarded them to Popelmill's office, where they were eventually added to the employees' permanent files. When pay raises were awarded in the department three weeks later, Marcus Singh did not receive a merit raise. He was told that it was due to his less-than-outstanding appraisal. He did, however, receive the general increase of $1,200 given to all employees regardless of their performance appraisals. This increase matched the increase in the CPI for the Newport, Oregon, area.

Singh has refused to speak one word to Garth Fryer since they discussed the appraisal, communicating only through Connie Millar or in writing. Singh has lost all motivation and complains bitterly to his colleagues about his unfair ratings. While he reports to work at 8 A.M. sharp and does not leave until 5 P.M. each day, he has been observed to spend a lot of time reading newspapers and surfing the Internet while at work.

Questions

1. What do you see as the problems in this case? Explain.
2. Could these problems have been avoided? How?
3. Comment on the advantages and disadvantages of using peer evaluations in the appraisal process.
4. What can be done to resolve the problem with Marcus Singh?

Source: This case was adapted from a case prepared by James G. Pesek and Joseph P. Gronenwald of Clarion University in Pennsylvania.

Case 8 The Last Straw for Aero Engine

The meeting lasted only ten minutes, since all those present quickly agreed that Tom Kinder should be fired. According to management, Kinder had caused the company numerous problems over the last eighteen months, and the incident that Saturday had been "the straw that broke the camel's back." Plant management believed it had rid itself of a poor employee, one the company had offered numerous opportunities for improvement. It seemed like an airtight case and one the union could not win if taken to arbitration.

Tom Kinder had worked for the Aero Engine Company for fourteen years prior to being terminated. He was initially employed as an engine mechanic servicing heavy-duty diesel engines. For his first nine years with Aero Engine, he was considered a model employee by his supervisors and plant management. Kinder was also well liked by his fellow employees. His performance appraisals were always marked "exceptional," and his personnel folder contained many commendation letters from customers and supervisors alike. Supervisor Mary Lee described Kinder as "devoted to his job of building and repairing engines." Through company-sponsored training classes and courses taken at a local trade school, Kinder had acquired the knowledge and experience to build and repair specialty engines used in arctic oil exploration.

The Aero Engine Company, with headquarters in the Midwest, was engaged primarily in the production and maintenance of specialty engines used in drilling, heavy manufacturing, and diesel transportation. The company had experienced very rapid growth in sales volume, number of products produced, and the size of its workforce since 2005. (At the time of Tom Kinder's termination, the company employed about 1,700 employees.) Aero Engine avoided hiring new personnel and then laying them off when they were no longer needed. Company policy stated that layoffs were to be avoided except in extreme circumstances. When heavy workloads arose, the natural solution to the problem was to schedule large amounts of overtime and to hire temporary employees through one of the local temporary help services.

Tom Kinder's work problems had begun approximately five years prior to his discharge when he went through a very emotional and difficult divorce. He was a devoted family man, and the divorce was a shock to his values and his way of life. The loss of custody of his children was particularly devastating to his mental well-being. He became sullen, withdrawn, and argumentative with his supervisors. Several of Tom's close friends described him as having a "depressed attitude" at work. Aero Engine has a comprehensive employee assistance program (EAP) for employees experiencing personal and family problems. Tom's supervisor, Gordon Thompson, had recommended the services of the EAP to Kinder, but it was unknown if he had used counseling since the EAP program is voluntary and confidential. Management professes that it took a very proactive and humanistic approach toward Kinder, an employee the company valued and respected. However, regardless of the company's concern for Tom, his work performance had become problematic.

An absenteeism problem developed and continued until his discharge. Over the eighteen months prior to this termination, Tom was absent twenty-seven complete days and nine partial days and was tardy nineteen times. Twelve months before termination, he had been given a written warning that his attendance must improve or he would face further disciplinary action, including possible discharge. Unfortunately, his attendance did not improve; however, he received no further disciplinary action until his discharge on Monday, June 9, 2011.

Management had experienced problems other than absenteeism with Tom Kinder. The quantity and quality of his work had decreased to only an acceptable level of performance. His supervisor had discussed this with him on two occasions, but no disciplinary action was ever instituted. Furthermore, during heavy production periods Kinder would either refuse to work overtime assignments or, once assigned, would often fail to report for work. It was an incident that occurred during a Saturday overtime shift that caused his discharge.

On Saturday, June 7, Kinder was assigned to a high-priority project that required him to build a specialty engine for a large and loyal customer. The big new engine was needed to replace a smaller engine that had exploded on an Alaskan drilling rig. The engine was being built in a newly constructed plant building located one-half mile from the company's main production facilities. At approximately 9:15 A.M. on that Saturday, Gordon Thompson had walked over to the new building to check on the progress of the engine. As Thompson passed by a window, he noticed Kinder sitting at a desk with his feet up, reading a magazine. The supervisor decided to observe him from outside the building. After about twenty-five minutes, Kinder had not moved, and Thompson returned to the plant to report the incident to Glenn Navarro, the plant production manager. Neither the supervisor nor the production manager confronted Kinder about the incident.

At 8:15 the next Monday morning, supervisor Thompson and production manager Navarro met with the director of human resources to review the total work performance of Tom Kinder. After this short meeting, all those present decided that Tom Kinder should be fired. Tom's discharge notice read, "Terminated for poor work performance, excessive absenteeism, and loafing." At 10:15 that morning Kinder was called into Navarro's office and told of his discharge. Navarro then handed him his final paycheck, which included eight hours of work for Monday.

Questions

1. Comment on the handling of this case by the supervisor, production manager, and director of human resources.
2. How much concern should organizations show employees before taking disciplinary action for personal family problems? Explain.
3. To what extent were consistent discipline and due process applied prior to the discharge?
4. If Tom Kinder's discharge went to arbitration, how would you decide the case? Why? What arguments would labor and management present to support their respective positions?

Source: This case is based on an actual arbitration heard by George W. Bohlander. All names are fictitious.

Case 9

Employee Selection and Training at Meadowbrook Golf and Golf Ventures West

Meadowbrook Golf, headquartered in Championsgate, Florida, is a leader in golf course management, maintenance, and supplies in the United States. Today the organization is comprised of four companies that meet the demands of the market: Meadowbrook Golf provides the management, International Golf Maintenance provides the maintenance, and Golf Ventures East and West are the golf supply arms of the business.

Ron Jackson is the CEO of Meadowbrook. The turf business is a highly specialized, tight-knit industry. The company's strong reputation was built on its expertise in providing superior products and services to golf courses and municipalities. Ron knew the only way he could take the company to the next level was to not only find the right people with the specific experience they needed but to find a way to keep them happy and motivated so they would stay.

Jackson learned of a behavioral assessment tool called Predictive Index, produced by the Wellesley, Massachusetts-based management consulting company PI Worldwide, and brought it into Meadowbrook as a way to help the managers understand what motivated their employees to come to work every day. By obtaining this insight, Jackson says Meadowbrook was able to keep its talent by "managing them for their individual success." Meadowbrook also realized that their top performers possessed very similar behavioral characteristics. Using this information, Meadowbrook was able to incorporate this information into its hiring process.

Golf Ventures West (GVW), the supply division of Meadowbrook in the western United States, offers equipment that ranges from a string trimmer to a $70,000 rotary motor, along with fertilizer, seed, and specialty products. Mike Eastwood, the president of GVW, had the best talent in the industry, long-time clients, and very low turnover. While it all seemed idealistic, Eastwood had a problem. He needed his team to sell more. The challenge was how to identify what they needed in sales training to help them grow their sales.

In sharing his concerns with Jackson, Eastwood learned that the publishers of the Predictive Index also offered a selling training tool that identified the strengths of salespeople and areas for their development as well as offered customer-focused sales (CFS) training. To explore the tool further, he and his senior management team took the assessment themselves. The results accurately identified Eastwood's selling style. His general managers, most with over 30 years in the industry, scored in the mid to high range.

Next, Eastwood gave his sales team members the assessment. However, their overall scores were in the mid-to-low range. Eastwood quickly realized that despite the talent of his sales team, 80 percent of them did not know how to sell. The results of the assessment showed most of them were not asking enough investigative questions when speaking with their clients. This was a huge breakthrough. Eastwood's team members then took the CFS workshop to learn how to think like customers do and investigate and uncover their needs.

The results? "My most senior and successful salesperson followed the CFS process and closed a $40,000 deal with a customer that had only purchased from our competitor for the last ten years," says Eastwood. In another instance, Eastwood had a salesperson who was underperforming but knew he had the potential to be successful. This salesperson went through the sales training and was moved to a new territory. "In four months he has sold more in his new territory than he had in a year in his original territory," says Eastwood. Apparently, the training is paying off. Even though golf courses, in general, have been struggling in recent years, Golf Ventures West has expanded its operations to a number of new locations across the country.

Questions

1. Why did Eastwood and his general managers take PI's competency assessment prior to administering it to the company's other salespeople?
2. How did the assessment help uncover the skills gap handicapping Golf Ventures West's salespeople?
3. What does the case indicate about the training "readiness" of the company's salespeople?

Source: Adapted from "Hire Smart, Develop Selling Skills and Manage for Individual and Team Success" *PI Worldwide*, accessed June 21, 2011 at http://www.piworldwide.com. (This case is based on press release-type information on the company's website. Phone: 800-832-8884 or info@piworldwide.com.)

Case 10 — Newell's Decision to Downsize: An Ethical Dilemma

A particular issue in business ethics is: "What exactly does the term ethics mean?" Various writers have described ethics as rules that govern behavior, desired societal values such as respect for justice, or accepted principles of right or wrong. One author noted, "While laws concern what we must do, ethics concerns what we should do."*

In the practice of HR, managers and supervisors are continually faced with ethical dilemmas regarding the fair and equitable treatment of employees. Ethical choices abound in areas such as recruitment and selection, employee privacy, whistle-blowing, sexual harassment, and diversity or affirmative action. An important ethical dilemma faced by managers today is the fair and correct way to downsize organizations. The decisions involved in downsizing a workforce are complex and, as one manager stated, "gut-wrenching."

The Need to Downsize

Newell Corporation is a medium-sized manufacturer of navigational systems for commuter and larger airplanes. The company operates two plants—one in Atlanta, Georgia, and the other in Norwood, California. In 2011, the Norwood plant employed 273 employees, most of them engaged in the manufacture and technical support of company products.

Newell is regarded as an excellent place to work by its employees and within the surrounding communities. Employee morale and loyalty have always been high, and job satisfaction studies conducted by the company consistently rate the organization as a fair and equitable place to work. The company's HR policies can be described as proactive and progressive. With its positive reputation, Newell has been able to select new employees from a large pool of job applicants.

One cornerstone of HR policy has been to use the principle of seniority when training, assigning, transferring, and promoting employees. Additionally, with Newell's emphasis on employee retention, employees have experienced and come to expect long and steady employment. Prior to 2011, Newell has never downsized its workforce. Employment growth at the Norwood facility can be described as moderate and steady.

The racial composition of the company has been predominately Caucasian, for two reasons. First, the racial composition of the company's local labor market has historically been Caucasian. Second, the skill levels needed for the company's technical jobs have come primarily from a trained Caucasian labor force. A review of the company's federally required EEO-1 report for 2010 showed that Newell had few employees in each of the minority categories listed. This is true for both hourly and managerial positions. However, since approximately 2005, the demographic characteristics of the local labor market have changed dramatically to include more Hispanics, African Americans, and Asian Americans. Minority job applicants have generally not possessed the skills needed for entry-level manufacturing and technical support jobs.

In 2007, Newell experienced a large increase in the demand for its products. To meet customer orders, the Norwood plant hired twenty-seven new manufacturing assemblers and fourteen new technical support technicians. With the increased diversity of the external labor force, plus the desire to increase the minority composition of its internal workforce, thirty-four of the forty-one new hires were minorities. It is noteworthy that Newell welcomed the opportunity to rapidly increase the diversity of its workforce for both business and ethical reasons. The following is an excerpt from Newell's statement of vision and values published in July 2008:

> Newell Corporation believes that a work environment that reflects a diverse workforce, values diversity, and honors the worth of its employees benefits the company, its customers, and its employees. Employment decisions will be made on these principles while also considering the efficient and effective operation of the organization.

Because new minority employees generally did not possess the skills needed for its manufacturing and technical jobs, the company spent approximately $1.7 million on entry-level skills training. The integration of minorities into the Norwood facility was seamless and without racial tension.

In 2008, sales for Newell's products once again followed historical patterns. Unfortunately, sales then unexpectedly took a sharp downturn: a 12 percent decline in 2009 and a 23 percent decline in 2010. Causes for the decline in sales were attributed to two new low-wage foreign competitors that had entered the market, a decline in the market demand for the products made by Newell and its competitors, and higher-than-average production costs due to Newell's older, less efficient manufacturing equipment. Future demand for company products was projected to be moderate for 20011, 2012, and 2013.

In February 2011, Tom Malcom, Norwood's director of HR; Steven L. Davis, corporate vice president for manufacturing; and Mary Umali, Norwood's plant manager, decided to downsize the workforce at the Norwood facility. Specifically, they decided to lay off thirty-seven manufacturing employees and eleven technical support personnel. The difficult question faced by senior management was how to lay off employees in a manner that would be fair and equitable to individuals and legally defensible, while maintaining the integrity of Newell's HR policies and the productivity of the Norwood plant.

Questions

1. What is the ethical dilemma faced by management in this case? Explain.
2. What specific problems might Newell face in its downsizing decision?
3. What options might Newell employ in its downsizing decision? Explain.
4. How would you downsize the Norwood facility? Explain.

Source: This case was adapted from an actual case known to the authors. All names are fictitious.

*Terry Halbert and Elaine Ingulli, *Law and Ethics in the Business Environment*, 7th ed. (Mason, OH: Cengage Learning, 2011).

Case 11   Someone Has to Go: A Tough Layoff Decision

Located in the Los Angeles area, Aero Performance, with twenty-seven employees, is a sales and maintenance company that provides equipment upgrades and general aircraft maintenance to regional airlines, corporate aircraft, and small international carriers. When Aero Performance was created twelve years ago, the company faced little competition, and a robust airline market seemed to present an unlimited potential for growth. Unfortunately, industry economics coupled with cost-cutting measures by airlines and new competition from similar airline service companies means that Aero's business performance has stabilized, and the company has actually experienced losses in certain specialized areas. One of these areas is the sales of the company's technologically advanced equipment. Airline companies as well as the owners of corporate jets have delayed the purchase and installation of Aero's advanced electronic equipment.

Mike Martinez, manager of the technology upgrade unit, faces a tough decision. With a significant downturn in his unit's work, he must lay off one employee. The decision is made particularly difficult because all employees of the unit are qualified employees with average or better work records. Additionally, each employee has a unique personal background directly affecting his or her work life. A summary of the background and work record of each of the four employees follows. No question, Martinez faces a difficult decision.

Gary Meadors is married and has two children in high school. He lives modestly in order to send his kids to college. His wife works evenings at a convenience store to assist with family expenses. Meadors has worked nine years with Aero Performance, six years in airline maintenance and three years in the technology upgrade unit. He has learned airline technology largely through technical articles, trade journals, and on-the-job experience. His performance evaluations are average, and he is considered a consistent and reliable employee. His attendance and company loyalty are exceptional.

Brenda Baldwin is the only woman in the technology upgrade unit. She is a single mother with a child in elementary school. Brenda has three years of service with Aero Performance, all in Martinez's unit. She joined the company after obtaining an airline technology degree from a well-respected four-year university. Brenda continues to take evening classes in her field and seems to have, according to Martinez, "the most potential for growth in the company." However, her performance has slipped the past year, and she has been counseled for an attendance problem. She has felt somewhat resented as a female in a traditionally male-dominated industry.

Udit Chopra is a dedicated employee. In fact, everyone says he is "married to his job." He will work long hours to complete technical installations and is regarded as a perfectionist. Udit has a college degree in marketing but has found his home in airline technology. He possesses an excellent ability to persuade Aero Performance customers to upgrade their technology systems. Udit drives a new BMW and is believed to come from a wealthy family.

Craig Cottrell joined Aero Performance three years ago, having been hired away from a competitor. He has a total of twelve years of experience in the airline service industry. Craig has a complete understanding of airline technology. Cottrell's work performance the first two years with Aero Performance was barely average; however, his work record the past year was evaluated as very high. Currently, he is the top performer in the unit. There has been work friction between him, Baldwin, and Chopra over the selection and installation of cockpit instruments.

	SENIORITY (Years)	Salary	Performance			
			2004	2005	2006	2007
Gary Meadors	9	$74,250	Avg	Good	Avg	Avg
Brenda Baldwin	3	$81,190		High	Good	Avg
Udit Chopra	5	$78,500	Avg	Good	Good	Good
Craig Cottrell	3	$75,960		Avg	Avg	High

Mike Martinez must make his decision by this Friday. Aero Performance will grant the laid-off employee a severance package to assist transition to other employment. Martinez is committed to aiding his employee in finding another job in the airline service industry.

Questions

1. What criteria should be used to determine potential layoff candidates? What emphasis, if any, should be given to non-job-related factors such as personal problems or a spouse's need to work? Explain your answer.
2. What should be included in a severance package for laid-off employees? How long should the severance package last?
3. Are there any potential legal implications in Martinez's decision?
4. How would you handle the termination interview?

Glossary

A

Adverse impact

A concept that refers to the rejection of a significantly higher percentage of a protected class for employment, placement, or promotion when compared with the successful, nonprotected class

Affirmative action

A policy that goes beyond equal employment opportunity by requiring organizations to comply with the law and correct any past discriminatory practices by increasing the numbers of minorities and women in specific positions

Alternative dispute resolution (ADR)

A term applied to different employee complaint or dispute resolution methods that do not involve going to court

Applicant tracking system

A software application recruiters use to post job openings, screen résumés, and contact via e-mail potential candidates for interviews, and track the time and costs related to hiring people

Apprenticeship training

A system of training in which a worker entering the skilled trades is given thorough instruction and experience, both on and off the job, in the practical and theoretical aspects of the work

Arbitrator

A third-party neutral who resolves a labor dispute by issuing a final decision in the disagreement

Assessment center

Places in which job candidates undergo performance simulation tests that evaluate managerial potential

Augmented skills

Skills helpful in facilitating the efforts of expatriate managers

Authorization card

A statement signed by an employee authorizing a union to act as a representative of the employee for purposes of collective bargaining

B

Backup care program

A benefit program whereby an employer provides or subsidizes temporary care for its employee's elders or children when their regular arrangements fall through

Balance sheet approach

A compensation system designed to match the purchasing power in a person's home country

Balanced scorecard (BSC)

A measurement framework that helps managers translate strategic goals into operational objectives

Bargaining power

The power of labor and management to achieve their goals through economic, social, or political influence

Bargaining unit

A group of two or more employees who share common employment interests and conditions and may reasonably be grouped together for purposes of collective bargaining

Behavior modeling

An approach that demonstrates desired behavior and gives trainees the chance to practice and role-play those behaviors and receive feedback

Behavior modification

A technique that operates on the principle that behavior that is rewarded, or positively reinforced, will be exhibited more frequently in the future, whereas behavior that is penalized or unrewarded will decrease in frequency

Behavior observation scale (BOS)

A behavioral approach to performance appraisal that measures the frequency of observed behavior

Behavioral description interview (BDI)

An interview in which an applicant is asked questions about what he or she actually did in a given situation

Behaviorally anchored rating scale (BARS)

A behavioral approach to performance appraisal that consists of a series of vertical scales, one for each important dimension of job performance

Benchmarking

The process of measuring one's own services and practices against the recognized leaders in order to identify areas for improvement

Blended learning

The use of multiple training methods to achieve optimal learning on the part of trainees

Bonus

An incentive payment that is supplemental to the base wage

Branding

A company's efforts to help existing and prospective workers understand why it is a desirable place work

Broadbanding

Practice in which the number of grades in a payscale structure is reduced, and the differential between one grade and the next is increased

Burnout

A severe stage of distress, manifesting itself in depression, frustration, and loss of productivity

Business necessity

A work-related practice that is necessary to the safe and efficient operation of an organization

Business unionism

A term applied to the goals of U.S. labor organizations, which collectively bargain for improvements in wages, hours, job security, and working conditions

C

Calibration

A process whereby managers meet to discuss the performance of individual employees to ensure their employee appraisals are in line with one another

Career counseling

The process of discussing with employees their current job activities and performance, personal and career interests and goals, personal skills, and suitable career development objectives

Career networking

The process of establishing mutually beneficial relationships with other businesspeople, including potential clients and customers

Career paths

Lines of advancement in an occupational field within an organization

Career plateau

A situation in which for either organizational or personal reasons the probability of moving up the career ladder is low

Change management

Change management is a systematic way of bringing about and managing both organizational changes and changes on the individual level

Charge form

A discrimination complaint filed with the EEOC by employees or job applicants

Chief diversity officer

A top executives responsible for implementing a firm's diversity efforts

Chief ethics officer

A high-ranking manager directly responsible for fostering the ethical climate within the firm

Chief learning officer

A high-ranking manager directly responsible for fostering employee learning and development within the firm

Codetermination

Representation of labor on the board of directors of a company

Collaborative software

Software that allows workers to interface and share information with one another electronically

Collective bargaining process

The process of negotiating a labor agreement, including the use of economic pressures by both parties

Combined salary and commission plan

A compensation plan that includes a straight salary and a commission

Compensatory model

A selection decision model in which a high score in one area can make up for a low score in another area

Competence-based pay

Pay based on an employee's skill level, variety of skills possessed, or increased job knowledge

Competency assessment

Analysis of the sets of skills and knowledge needed for decision-oriented and knowledge-intensive jobs

Concurrent validity

Validity is demonstrated where a test correlates well with a measure that has previously been validated

Construct validity

The extent to which a selection tool measures a theoretical construct or trait

Constructive discharge

An employee's voluntary termination of his or her employment because of harsh, unreasonable employment conditions placed on the individual by the employer

Consumer price index (CPI)

A measure of the average change in prices over time in a fixed "market basket" of goods and services

Content validity

The extent to which a selection instrument, such as a test, adequately samples the knowledge and skills needed to perform a particular job

Contrast error

A performance rating error in which an employee's evaluation is biased either upward or downward because of comparison with another employee just previously evaluated

Contributory plan

A pension plan in which contributions are made jointly by employees and employers

Cooperative training

A training program that combines practical on-the-job experience with formal educational classes

Core capabilities

Integrated knowledge sets within an organization that distinguish it from its competitors and deliver value to customers

Core skills

Skills considered critical to an employee's success abroad

Core values

The strong and enduring beliefs and principles that the company uses as a foundation for its decisions

Corporate social responsibility

The responsibility of the firm to act in the best interests of the people and communities affected by its activities

Craft unions

Unions that represent skilled craft workers

Criterion-related validity

The extent to which a selection tool predicts, or significantly correlates with, important elements of work behavior

Critical incident

An unusual event that denotes superior or inferior employee performance in some part of the job

Critical incident method

A job analysis method by which important job tasks are identified for job success

Cross-training

The process of training employees to do multiple jobs within an organization

Cross-validation

Verifying the results obtained from a validation study by administering a test or test battery to a different sample (drawn from the same population)

Cultural audits

Audits of the culture and quality of work life in an organization

Cultural environment

The communications, religion, values and ideologies, education, and social structure of a country

Culture shock

Perpetual stress experienced by people who settle overseas

Cumulative trauma disorders

Injuries involving tendons of the fingers, hands, and arms that become inflamed from repeated stresses and strains

Customer appraisal

A performance appraisal that, like team appraisal, is based on TQM concepts and includes evaluation from both a firm's external and internal customers

D

Defined benefit plan

A pension plan in which the amount an employee is to receive on retirement is specifically set forth

Defined contribution plan

A pension plan that establishes the basis on which an employer will contribute to the pension fund

Dejobbing

refers to a process of structuring organizations not around jobs but around projects that are constantly changing

Depression

A negative emotional state marked by feelings of low spirits, gloominess, sadness, and loss of pleasure in ordinary activities

Differential piece rate

A compensation rate under which employees whose production exceeds the standard amount of output receive a higher rate for all of their work than the rate paid to those who do not exceed the standard amount

Disabled individual

Any person who (1) has a physical or mental impairment that substantially limits one or more of the person's major life activities, (2) has a record of such impairment, or (3) is regarded as having such an impairment

Discipline

A tool, used to correct and mold the practices of employees to help them perform better so they conform to acceptable standards

Disease management programs

Programs that provide patients and their caregivers with information on monitoring and treating medical conditions, while coordinating communication between them, their health care providers, employers, and insurers

Disparate treatment

A situation in which protected class members receive unequal treatment or are evaluated by different standards

Distress

Harmful stress characterized by a loss of feelings of security and adequacy

Downsizing

Planned elimination of jobs

Dual career partnerships

Couples in which both members follow their own careers and actively support each other's career development

Due process

Procedures that constitute fair treatment, such as allowing an employee to tell his or her story about an alleged infraction and defend against it

E

EEO-1 report

An employer information report that must be filed annually by employers of 100 or more employees (except state and local government employers) and government contractors and subcontractors to determine an employer's workforce composition

Elder care

Care provided to an elderly relative by an employee who remains actively at work

E-learning

Learning that takes place via electronic media

Emergency action plan

A plan an organization develops that contains step-by-step procedures for dealing with various emergency situations

Employee assistance program (EAP)

Services provided by employers to help workers cope with a wide variety of problems that interfere with the way they perform their jobs

Employee associations

Labor organizations that represent various groups of professional and white collar employees in labor management relations

Employee empowerment

Granting employees power to initiate change, thereby encouraging them to take charge of what they do

Employee engagement

A situation in which workers are enthusiastic and immersed in their work to the degree that it improves the performance of their companies

Employee leasing

The process of dismissing employees who are then hired by a leasing company (which handles all HR-related activities) and contracting with that company to lease back the employees

Employee profile

A profile of a worker developed by studying an organization's top performers in order to recruit similar types of people

Employee rights

Guarantees of fair treatment that become rights when they are granted to employees by the courts, legislatures, or employers

Employee stock ownership plans (ESOPS)

Stock plans in which an organization contributes shares of its stock to an established trust for the purpose of stock purchases by its employees

Employee teams

An employee contributions technique whereby work functions are structured for groups rather than for individuals and team members are given discretion in matters traditionally considered management prerogatives, such as process improvements, product or service development, and individual work assignments

Employment-at-will principle

The right of an employer to fire an employee without giving a reason and the right of an employee to quit when he or she chooses

Environmental scanning

Systematic monitoring of the major external forces influencing the organization

Equal employment opportunity (EEO)

The treatment of individuals in all aspects of employment—hiring, promotion, training, etc.—in a fair and nonbiased manner

Ergonomics

The process of studying and designing equipment and systems that are easy and efficient for people to use and that ensure their physical well-being

Error of central tendency

A performance rating error in which all employees are rated about average

Escalator clauses

Clauses in labor agreements that provide for quarterly cost-of-living adjustments in wages, basing the adjustments on changes in the consumer price index

Essay method

A trait approach to performance appraisal that requires the rater to compose a statement describing employee behavior

Ethics

A set of standards of conduct and moral judgments that help to determine right and wrong behavior

Exclusive representation

The legal right and responsibility of the union to represent all bargaining unit members equally, regardless of whether employees join the union or not

Exempt employees

Employees not covered by the overtime provisions of the Fair Labor Standards Act

Expatriates, or home-country nationals

Employees from the home country who are on international assignment

External fit

The situation in which the work system supports the organization's goals and strategies

Eustress

Positive stress that accompanies achievement and exhilaration

F

Failure rate

The percentage of expatriates who do not perform satisfactorily

Fair employment practices (FEPS)

State and local laws governing equal employment opportunity that are often more comprehensive than federal laws and apply to small employers

Fair representation doctrine

A doctrine under which unions have a legal obligation to assist both members and nonmembers in labor relations matters

Fast-track program

Accelerated development or promotion of individuals to positions with more responsibility

Fitness-for-duty evaluation

Evaluations randomly conducted to determine an employee's physical, mental, and emotional fitness for a job

Flexible benefits plans (cafeteria plans)

Benefit plans that enable individual employees to choose the benefits that are best suited to their particular needs

Flextime

Flexible working hours that permit employees the option of choosing daily starting and quitting times, provided that they work a set number of hours per day or week

Focal performance appraisal

An appraisal system in which all of an organization's employees are reviewed at the same time of year rather on the anniversaries of their individual hire dates

Forced-choice method

A trait approach to performance appraisal that requires the rater to choose from statements designed to distinguish between successful and unsuccessful performance

Forced distribution

A performance appraisal ranking system whereby raters are required to place a certain percentage of employees into various performance categories

Four-fifths rule

A rule of thumb followed by the EEOC in determining adverse impact for use in enforcement proceedings

Functional job analysis (FJA)

A job-analysis approach that utilizes an inventory of the various types of work activities that can constitute any job

Furloughing

A situation in which an organization asks or requires employees to take time off for either no pay or reduced pay

G

Gainsharing plans

Programs under which both employees and the organization share financial gains according to a predetermined formula that reflects improved productivity and profitability

Global compensation system

A centralized pay system whereby host-country employees are offered a full range of training programs, benefits, and pay comparable with a firm's domestic employees but adjusted for local differences

Global corporation

A firm that has integrated worldwide operations through a centralized home office

Global manager

A manager equipped to run an international business

Global sourcing

The business practice of searching for and utilizing goods sources from around the world

Globalization

The trend toward opening up foreign markets to international trade and investment

Graphic rating scale method

A trait approach to performance appraisal whereby each employee is rated according to a scale of characteristics

Grievance procedure

A formal procedure that provides for the union to represent members and nonmembers in processing a grievance

Guest workers

Foreign workers invited to perform needed labor

H

Hay profile method

A job evaluation technique using three factors—knowledge, mental activity, and accountability—to evaluate executive and managerial positions

Health maintenance organization (HMO)

Organizations of physicians and health care professionals that provide a wide range of services to subscribers and dependents on a prepaid basis

High-deductible health plans (HDHP)

A medical insurance plan characterized by high deductibles but lower premiums for workers and a health spending account to which employers contribute funds employees can keep should they leave the organization

High-performance work system (HPWS)

A specific combination of HR practices, work structures, and processes that maximizes employee knowledge, skill, commitment, and flexibility

Home-based pay

Pay based on an expatriate's home country's compensation practices

Host-based pay

Expatriate pay comparable to that earned by employees in a host country

Host country

A country in which an international corporation operates

Host-country nationals

Employees who are natives of the host country

Hourly work

Work paid on an hourly basis

Human capital

The knowledge, skills, and capabilities of individuals that have economic value to an organization

Human capital readiness

The process of evaluating the availability of critical talent in a company and comparing it to the firm's supply

Human resources information system (HRIS)

A computerized system that provides current and accurate data for purposes of control and decision-making

Human resources management (HRM)

The process of managing human talent to achieve an organization's objectives

Human resources planning (HRP)

The process of anticipating and providing for the movement of people into, within, and out of an organization

I

Impairment testing

Also called fitness-for-duty or performance-based testing, it measures whether an employee is alert enough to work

Improshare

A gain sharing program under which bonuses are based on the overall productivity of the work team

Industrial engineering

A field of study concerned with analyzing work methods and establishing time standards

Industrial unions
Unions that represent all workers—skilled, semiskilled, unskilled—employed along industry lines

Instructional objectives
Desired outcomes of a training program

Interest-based bargaining
Problem-solving bargaining based on a win-win philosophy and the development of a positive long-term relationship

Internal fit
The situation in which all the internal elements of the work system complement and reinforce one another

Internal labor market
Labor markets in which workers are hired into entry level jobs and higher levels are filled from within

International corporation
A domestic firm that uses its existing capabilities to move into overseas markets

Internship programs
Programs jointly sponsored by colleges, universities, and other organizations that offer students the opportunity to gain real-life experience while allowing them to find out how they will perform in work organizations

J

Job
A task or group of tasks performed as a routine part of one's occupation usually in exchange for money

Job analysis
The process of obtaining information about jobs by determining their duties, tasks, or activities

Job characteristics model
A job design theory that purports that three psychological states (experiencing meaningfulness of the work performed, responsibility for work outcomes, and knowledge of the results of the work performed) of a jobholder result in improved work performance, internal motivation, and lower absenteeism and turnover

Job classification system
A system of job evaluation in which jobs are classified and grouped according to a series of predetermined wage grades

Job crafting
A naturally occurring phenomenon whereby employees mold their tasks to fit their individual strengths, passions, and motives better

Job description
A statement of the tasks, duties, and responsibilities of a job to be performed

Job design
An outgrowth of job analysis that improves jobs through technological and human considerations in order to enhance organization efficiency and employee job satisfaction

Job enlargement
The process of adding a greater variety of tasks to a job

Job enrichment
Enhancing a job by adding more meaningful tasks and duties to make the work more rewarding or satisfying

Job evaluation
A systematic process of determining the relative worth of jobs in order to establish which jobs should be paid more than others within an organization

Job progressions
The hierarchy of jobs a new employee might experience, ranging from a starting job to jobs that successively require more knowledge and/or skill

Job ranking system
The simplest and oldest system of job evaluation by which jobs are arrayed on the basis of their relative worth

Job rotation
An approach to management development where an individual is moved through a schedule of assignments designed to give him or her a breadth of exposure to the entire operation

Job specification
A statement of the specific knowledge, skills, and abilities of a person who is to perform a job needs

Just-in-time training
Training delivered to trainees when and where they need it to do their jobs, usually via computer or the Internet

K

Knowledge workers
Workers whose responsibilities extend beyond the physical execution of work to include planning, decision-making, and problem-solving

L

Labor relations process
A logical sequence of five events: (1) workers desire collective representation, (2) the union begins its organizing campaign, (3) the NLRB representation process begins, (4) collective negotiations lead to a contract, and (5) the contract is administered

Learning management system (LMS)
Online system that provides a variety of assessment, communication, teaching, and learning opportunities

Leniency or strictness error
A performance rating error in which the appraiser tends to give employees either unusually high or unusually low ratings

Line managers
Non-HR managers who are responsible for overseeing the work of other employees

Localization

Adapting pay and other compensation benefits to match that of a particular country

Lump sum merit program

A lump sum merit is a one-time award, not added to base pay, that can be awarded to an individual for meritorious job performance.

M

Management by objectives (MBO)

A philosophy of management that rates performance on the basis of employee achievement of goals set by mutual agreement of employee and manager

Management forecasts

The opinions (judgments) of supervisors, department managers, experts, or others knowledgeable about the organization's future employment needs

Manager and/or supervisor appraisal

A performance appraisal done by an employee's manager and often reviewed by a manager one level higher

Managing diversity

Leveraging differences among employees to improve products and services delivered to customers

Markov analysis

A method for tracking the pattern of employee movements through various jobs

Material safety data sheets (MSDSs)

Documents that contain vital information about hazardous substances

Mediation

The use of an impartial neutral to reach a compromise decision in employment disputes

Mediator

A third party in an employment dispute who meets with one party and then the other in order to suggest compromise solutions or to recommend concessions from each side that will lead to an agreement

Mentors

Individuals who coach, advise, and encourage individuals of lesser rank

Merit guidelines

Guidelines for awarding merit raises that are tied to performance objectives

Mission

The basic purpose of the organization as well as its scope of operations

Mixed-standard scale method

A trait approach to performance appraisal similar to other scale methods but based on comparison with (better than, equal to, or worse than) a standard

Multinational corporation (MNC)

A firm with independent business units operating in multiple countries

Multiple cutoff model

A selection decision model that requires an applicant to achieve some minimum level of proficiency on all selection dimensions

Multiple hurdle model

A sequential strategy in which only the applicants with the highest scores at an initial test stage go on to subsequent stages

N

Negligence

The failure to provide reasonable care when such failure results in injury to consumers or other employees

Negligent hiring

The failure of an organization to discover, via due diligence, that an employee it hired had the propensity to do harm to others

Nepotism

A preference for hiring relatives of current employees

Noncontributory plan

A pension plan in which contributions are made solely by the employer

Nondirective interview

An interview in which the applicant is allowed the maximum amount of freedom in determining the course of the discussion, while the interviewer carefully refrains from influencing the applicant's remarks

Nonexempt employees

Employees covered by the overtime provisions of the Fair Labor Standards Act

O

Offshoring

The business practice of sending jobs to other countries

Ombudsman

A designated individual from whom employees may seek counsel for resolution of their complaints

Onboarding

The process of systematically socializing new employees to help them get "on board" with an organization

On-the-job training (OJT)

A method by which employees are given hands-on experience with instructions from their supervisor or other trainer

Open-door policy

A policy of settling grievances that identifies various levels of management above the immediate supervisor for employee contact

Organization analysis

Examination of the environment, strategies, and resources of the organization to determine where training emphasis should be placed

Organizational capability

The capacity of the organization to act and change in pursuit of sustainable competitive advantage

Orientation

The formal process of familiarizing new employees with the organization, their jobs, and their work units

Outplacement services

Services provided by organizations to help terminated employees find a new job

Outsourcing

Contracting outside the organization to have work done that formerly was done by internal employees

P

Panel interview

An interview in which a board of interviewers questions and observes a single candidate

Passive job seekers

People who are not looking for jobs but could be persuaded to take new ones given the right opportunity

Pay equity

An employee's perception that compensation received is equal to the value of the work performed

Pay-for-performance standard

A standard by which managers tie compensation to employee effort and performance

Pay grades

Groups of jobs within a particular class that are paid the same rate

Pay rate compression

Compression of pay between new and experienced employees caused by the higher starting salaries of new employees; also the differential between hourly workers and their managers

Peer appraisal

A performance appraisal done by one's fellow employees, generally on forms that are compiled into a single profile for use in the performance interview conducted by the employee's manager

Peer-review system

A system for reviewing employee complaints that utilizes a group composed of equal numbers of employee representatives and management appointees. The group weighs evidence, considers arguments, and, after deliberation, votes to render a final decision

Performance appraisal

The result of an annual or biannual process in which a manager evaluates an employee's performance relative to the requirements of his or her job and uses the information to show the person where improvements are needed and why

Performance management

The process of creating a work environment in which people can perform to the best of their abilities

Perquisites

Special nonmonetary benefits given to executives; often referred to as *perks*

Person analysis

Determination of the specific individuals who need training

Phased retirement

A program that allows its employees to gradually cut their hours before retiring

Piecework

Work paid according to the number of units produced

Point system

A quantitative job evaluation procedure that determines the relative value of a job by the total points assigned to it

Position analysis questionnaire (PAQ)

A questionnaire identifying approximately 200 different tasks that, by means of a five-point scale, seeks to determine the degree to which different tasks are involved in performing a job

Positive, or nonpunitive, discipline

A system of discipline that focuses on early correction of employee misconduct, with the employee taking total responsibility for correcting the problem

Predictive validity

The extent to which applicants' test scores match criterion data obtained from those applicants/employees after they have been on the job for some indefinite period

Preemployment test

An objective and standardized measure of a sample of behavior that is used to gauge a person's knowledge, skills, abilities, and other characteristics (KSAOs) relative to other individuals

Preferred provider organization (PPO)

A network of physicians who establish an organization that guarantees lower health care costs to employers and their employees

Proactive change

Change initiated to take advantage of targeted opportunities

Process audit

Determining whether the high-performance work system has been implemented as designed

Profit sharing

Any procedure by which an employer pays, or makes available to all regular employees, in addition to base pay, special current or deferred sums based on the profits of the enterprise

Progressive discipline

The application of corrective measures by increasing degrees

Promotion

A change of assignment to a job at a higher level in the organization

Protected classes
Individuals of a minority race, women, older people, and those with disabilities who are covered by federal laws on equal employment opportunity

Psychological contract
Expectations of a fair exchange of employment obligations between an employee and employer

Q

Quality of fill
A metric designed to measure how well new hires that fill positions are performing on the job

R

Reactive change
Change that occurs after external forces have already affected performance

Real wages
Wage increases larger than rises in the consumer price index, that is, the real earning power of wages

Realistic job preview (RJP)
Informing applicants about all aspects of the job, including both its desirable and undesirable facets

Reasonable accommodation
An attempt by employers to adjust, without undue hardship, the working conditions or schedules of employees with disabilities or religious preferences

Recency error
A performance rating error in which the appraisal is based largely on the employee's most recent behavior rather than on behavior throughout the appraisal period

Recordable case
Any occupational death, illness, or injury to be recorded in the log (OSHA Form 300)

Recruiting process outsourcing (RPO)
The practice of outsourcing an organization's recruiting function to an outside firm

Red circle rates
Payment rates above the maximum of the pay range

Reengineering
Fundamental rethinking and radical redesign of business processes to achieve dramatic improvements in cost, quality, service, and speed

Reliability
The degree to which interviews, tests, and other selection procedures yield comparable data over time and alternative measures

Relocation services
Services provided to an employee who is transferred to a new location, which might include help in moving, selling a home, orienting to a new culture, and/or learning a new language

Repatriation
The process of transition for an employee home from an international assignment

Replacement charts
Listings of current jobholders and people who are potential replacements if an opening occurs

Rerecruiting
The process of keeping track of and maintaining relationships with former employees to see if they would be willing to return to the firm

Reverse discrimination
The act of giving preference to members of protected classes to the extent that unprotected individuals believe they are suffering discrimination

Right-to-know laws
Laws that require employers to advise employees about the hazardous chemicals they handle

Rights arbitration
Arbitration over interpretation of the meaning of contract terms or employee work grievances

S

Sabbatical
An extended period of time in which an employee leaves an organization to pursue other activities and later returns to his or her job

Sabbatical
Paid (or unpaid) time away from a job for four or more weeks employees take off to renew themselves before returning to work

Salary plus bonus plan
A compensation plan that pays a salary plus a bonus achieved by reaching targeted sales goals

Scanlon plan
A bonus incentive plan using employee and management committees to gain cost reduction improvements

Selection
The process of choosing individuals who have relevant qualifications to fill existing or projected job openings

Selection ratio
The number of applicants compared with the number of people to be hired

Self-appraisal
A performance appraisal done by the employee being evaluated, generally on an appraisal form completed by the employee prior to the performance interview

Sequential interview
A format in which a candidate is interviewed by multiple people, one right after another

Severance pay
A one-time payment sometimes given to an employee who is being involuntarily terminated

Sexual harassment

Unwelcome advances, requests for sexual favors, and other verbal or physical conduct of a sexual nature in the working environment

Similar-to-me error

A performance rating error in which an appraiser inflates the evaluation of an employee because of a mutual personal connection

Situational interview

An interview in which an applicant is given a hypothetical incident and asked how he or she would respond to it

Six sigma

A process used to translate customer needs into a set of optimal tasks that are performed in concert with one another

Skill inventories

Files of personnel education, experience, interests, skills, and so on that allow managers to quickly match job openings with employee backgrounds

Split pay

A system whereby expatriates are given a portion of their pay in the local currency to cover their day-today expenses and a portion of their pay in their home currency to safeguard their earnings from changes in inflation or foreign exchange rates

Spot bonus

An unplanned bonus given for employee effort unrelated to an established performance measure

Spot rewards

Programs that award employees "on the spot" when they do something particularly well during training or on the job

Staffing tables

Graphic representations of all organizational jobs, along with the numbers of employees currently occupying those jobs and future (monthly or yearly) employment requirements

Standard hour plan

An incentive plan that sets rates based on the completion of a job in a predetermined standard time

Step-review system

A system for reviewing employee complaints and disputes by successively higher levels of management

Straight commission plan

A compensation plan based on a percentage of sales

Straight piecework

An incentive plan under which employees receive a certain rate for each unit produced

Straight salary plan

A compensation plan that permits salespeople to be paid for performing various duties that are not reflected immediately in their sales volume

Strategic human resources management (SHRM)

The pattern of human resources deployments and activities that enable an organization to achieve its strategic goals

Strategic planning

Procedures for making decisions about the organization's long-term goals and strategies

Strategic vision

A statement about where the company is going and what it can become in the future; clarifies the long-term direction of the company and its strategic intent

Stress

Any adjustive demand caused by physical, mental, or emotional factors that requires coping behavior

Structured interview

An interview in which a set of standardized questions having an established set of answers is used

Subordinate appraisal

A performance appraisal of a superior by an employee, which is more appropriate for developmental than for administrative purposes

Succession planning

The process of identifying, developing, and tracking key individuals for executive positions

Supplemental unemployment benefits (SUBs)

A plan that enables an employee who is laid off to draw, in addition to state unemployment compensation, weekly benefits from the employer that are paid from a fund created for this purpose

SWOT analysis

A comparison of strengths, weaknesses, opportunities, and threats for strategy formulation purposes

T

Task analysis

The process of determining what the content of a training program should be on the basis of a study of the tasks and duties involved in the job

Task inventory analysis

An organization-specific list of tasks and their descriptions used as a basis to identify components of jobs

Team appraisal

A performance appraisal, based on TQM concepts, that recognizes team accomplishment rather than individual performance

Team incentive plan

A compensation plan in which all team members receive an incentive bonus payment when production or service standards are met or exceeded

Telecommuting

Use of personal computers, networks, and other communications technology such as fax machines to do work in the home that is traditionally done in the workplace

Third-country nationals
Employees who are natives of a country other than the home country or the host country

Total quality management (TQM)
A set of principles and practices whose core ideas include understanding customer needs, doing things right the first time, and striving for continuous improvement

Transfer
Placement of an individual in another job for which the duties, responsibilities, status, and remuneration are approximately equal to those of the previous job

Transfer of training
Effective application of principles learned to what is required on the job

Transnational corporation
A firm that attempts to balance local responsiveness and global scale via a network of specialized operating units

Transnational teams
Teams composed of members of multiple nationalities working on projects that span multiple countries

Trend analysis
A quantitative approach to forecasting labor demand based on an organizational index such as sales

U

Unfair labor practices (ULPS)
Specific employer and union illegal practices that deny employees their rights and benefits under federal labor law

Uniform Guidelines on Employee Selection Procedures
A procedural document published in the Federal Register to help employers comply with federal regulations against discriminatory actions

Union security agreement
Where an employer and the union agree on the extent to which the union may compel employees to join the union and how the dues will be collected

Union shop
A provision of the labor agreement that requires employees to join the union as a requirement for their employment

Union steward
An employee who as a nonpaid union official represents the interests of members in their relations with management

V

Value creation
What the firm adds to a product or service by virtue of making it; the amount of benefits provided by the product or service once the costs of making it are subtracted

Values-based hiring
The process of outlining the behaviors that exemplify a firm's corporate culture and then hiring people who are a fit for them

Virtual team
A team that utilizes telecommunications technology to link team members who are geographically dispersed—often worldwide across cultures and across time zones

Validity
The degree to which a test or selection procedure measures a person's attributes

Validity generalization
The extent to which validity coefficients can be generalized across situations

Virtual interviews
Interviews conducted via videoconferencing or over the web

Video résumés
Short video clips that highlight applicants' qualifications beyond what they can communicate on their résumés

Variable pay
Tying pay to some measure of individual, group, or organizational performance

Vesting
A guarantee of accrued pension benefits to participants at retirement age, regardless of their employment status at that time

W

Wage and salary survey
A survey of the wages paid to employees of other employers in the surveying organization's relevant labor market

Wage curve
A curve in a scattergram representing the relationship between relative worth of jobs and pay rates

Workforce utilization analysis
A process of classifying protected-class members by number and by the type of job they hold within the organization

Y

Yield ratio
The percentage of applicants from a recruitment source that make it to the next stage of the selection process

Name Index

Organization Index

Subject Index